Lecture Notes in Computer Science　　　10601

Commenced Publication in 1973
Founding and Former Series Editors:
Gerhard Goos, Juris Hartmanis, and Jan van Leeuwen

Editorial Board

Michael Maximilien · Antonio Vallecillo
Jianmin Wang · Marc Oriol (Eds.)

Service-Oriented Computing

15th International Conference, ICSOC 2017
Malaga, Spain, November 13–16, 2017
Proceedings

 Springer

Editors
Michael Maximilien
IBM Clouds Lab
San Francisco, CA
USA

Antonio Vallecillo (iD)
ETSI Informatica
Universidad Malaga
Malaga
Spain

Jianmin Wang
Tsinghua University
Tsinghua
China

Marc Oriol
Polytechnic University of Catalonia
Barcelona
Spain

ISSN 0302-9743   ISSN 1611-3349 (electronic)
Lecture Notes in Computer Science
ISBN 978-3-319-69034-6   ISBN 978-3-319-69035-3   (eBook)
https://doi.org/10.1007/978-3-319-69035-3

Library of Congress Control Number: 2017956085

LNCS Sublibrary: SL2 – Programming and Software Engineering

Printed on acid-free paper

This Springer imprint is published by Springer Nature
The registered company is Springer International Publishing AG
The registered company address is: Gewerbestrasse 11, 6330 Cham, Switzerland

Preface

Welcome to the Proceedings of ICSOC 2017, the 15th International Conference on Service-Oriented Computing. ICSOC is the premier international forum for academics, industry researchers, developers, and practitioners to report and share ground-breaking work on all topics related to services and service-oriented computing. ICSOC fosters cross-community scientific innovation and excellence by gathering experts from various disciplines, such as business process management, distributed systems, computer networks, wireless and mobile computing, cloud computing, cyber-physical systems, networking, scientific workflows, services science, data science, management science, and software engineering.

ICSOC 2017, the 15th event in this series, took place in Málaga, Spain, during November 13–16, 2017. Following on the ICSOC tradition, it featured three keynote presentations, a research and industry presentations track, as well as workshops, tool demonstrations, tutorials, and a PhD track.

Since its beginnings, services have become a core principle in software development. They provide perfect mechanisms for modularization, encapsulation, and for designing, analyzing, and deploying the architecture of large software systems, at the right level of abstraction, and in terms of loosely coupled, independent, and reusable parts with well-defined interfaces. Recently, services have gained rapid popularity across most software disciplines, showing all their benefits for building complex and critical applications in domains such as cloud computing, the Internet of Things (IoT), cyber-physical systems, mobile computing, and so on. This pervasive use of services has become industrially accepted best practice in all these application areas.

The increased success of using services in software and systems engineering has also raised new challenges, requiring collaborative research across multiple disciplines, groups, companies, and centers. As with previous editions, this year's call for papers generated substantial interest from the community. A total of 179 full research and industry submissions were received from 23 countries across six continents. Each paper submission was carefully reviewed by at least three members of the Program Committee (PC), followed by discussions moderated by a senior PC member who made a recommendation in the form of a meta-review. The PC consisted of 172 world-class experts in service-oriented computing and related areas (153 PC members and 19 senior PC members) from 28 different countries. The ICSOC 2017 program featured 33 full papers (acceptance rate of 18%) and 20 short papers. The selected papers cover a wide variety of important topics in the area of service-oriented computing, including foundational issues on service discovery and service-systems design, business process modelling and management, economics of service-systems engineering, as well as services on the cloud, social networks, IoT, and data analytics.

We would like to express our gratitude to all individuals, institutions, and sponsors that supported ICSOC 2017. This high-quality program would not have been possible without the expertise and dedication of our PC members and in particular our senior PC members. We are also grateful for the guidance of the General Chair, Carlos Canal, the untiring efforts of external reviewers, and the complete ICSOC Steering Committee. All of them helped make ICSOC 2017 a great success. Finally, we would like to thank all the authors who submitted papers to the conference, and we congratulate those authors whose papers appear in these proceedings. These papers reflect the quality of the current state of the art in service oriented computing research and practice. We hope that you find these papers interesting and stimulating.

August 2017   Michael Maximilien
                                                                 Antonio Vallecillo
                                                                 Jianmin Wang

Organization

General Chair

Carlos Canal   University of Málaga, Spain

Program Chairs

Michael Maximilian   IBM Cloud Labs, USA
Antonio Vallecillo   University of Málaga, Spain
Jianmin Wang   Tsinghua University, China

Steering Committee Liaison

Jian Yang   Macquarie University, Australia

Steering Committee

Boualem Benatallah   UNSW, Australia
Fabio Casati   University of Trento, Italy
Bernd J. Krämer   FernUniversität in Hagen, Germany
Winfried Lamersdorf   University of Hamburg, Germany
Heiko Ludwig   IBM, USA
Mike Papazoglou   Tilburg University, The Netherlands
Jian Yang   Macquarie University, Australia
Liang Zhang   Fudan University, China

Workshop Chairs

Lars Braubach   Hochschule Bremen, Germany
Juan M. Murillo   University of Extremadura, Spain

Demonstration Chairs

Nima Kaviani   IBM and Curatio.me, USA
Manuel Lama   University of Santiago de Compostela, Spain

Industry Chairs

Flavio de Paoli   University of Milano-Bicocca, Italy
Antonio Ruiz   University of Seville, Spain

Panel Chairs

Schahram Dustdar   Technical University, Vienna, Austria
Michael Sheng   University of Adelaide, Australia

PhD Symposium Chairs

Loli Burgeño   University of Málaga, Spain
Naouel Moha   Université du Qüebec à Montréal, Canada

Finance Chair

Bernd J. Krämer   FernUniversität in Hagen, Germany

Local Organization Chair

Ernesto Pimentel   University of Málaga, Spain

Local Organization

Jose M. Álvarez Palomo   University of Málaga, Spain
Francisco Durán   University of Málaga, Spain
Nathalie Moreno   University of Málaga, Spain
Alejandro Pérez Vereda   University of Málaga, Spain
Mónica Trella   University of Málaga, Spain

Publication Chair

Marc Oriol   Universitat Politècnica de Catalunya

Publicity Chairs

Guadalupe Ortiz   University of Cádiz, Spain
Juan Manuel Vara   Rey Juan Carlos University, Spain
Genoveva Vargas-Solar   CNRS, France

Web Chairs

Javier Berrocal   University of Extremadura, Spain
J. Manuel García-Alonso   University of Extremadura, Spain

Senior Program Committee

Boualem Benatallah   UNSW, Australia
Athman Bouguettaya   University of Sydney, Australia
Fabio Casati   University of Trento, Italy

Flavio De Paoli	Università di Milano Bicocca, Italy
Schahram Dustdar	TU Wien, Austria
Xavier Franch	Universitat Politècnica de Catalunya, Spain
Aditya Ghose	University of Wollongong, Australia
Mohand Said Hacid	University of Lyon, France
Grace Lewis	Carmegie Mellon Software Engineering Institute, USA
Cesare Pautasso	University of Lugano, Switzerland
Barbara Pernici	Politecnico di Milano, Italy
Gustavo Rossi	UNLP, Argentina
Antonio Ruiz-Cortés	University of Seville, Spain
Michael Sheng	University of Adelaide, Australia
Stefan Tai	TU Berlin, Germany
Zahir Tari	RMIT University, Australia
Samir Tata	IBM Research – Almaden, USA
Mathias Weske	HPI/University of Potsdam, Germany
Jian Yang	Macquarie University, Australia
Liang Zhang	Fudan University, China

Program Committee

Rama Akkiraju	IBM, USA
Pedro Álvarez	Universidad de Zaragoza, Spain
Vasilios Andrikopoulos	University of Groningen, The Netherlands
Alvaro Arenas	Instituto de Empresa Business School, Spain
Ebrahim Bagheri	Ryerson University, Canada
Luciano Baresi	Politecnico di Milano, Italy
Nejib Ben Hadj-Alouane	National School of Engineers of Tunis (ENIT), Tunisia
Moez Ben Haj Hmida	National Engineering School of Tunis (ENIT), Tunisia
Salima Benbernou	Université Paris Descartes, France
Djamal Benslimane	University of Lyon, France
Sami Bhiri	Telecom SudParis, France
Domenico Bianculli	University of Luxembourg, Luxembourg
Walter Binder	University of Lugano, Switzerland
Omar Boucelma	Aix-Marseille University, France
Lars Braubach	Hochschule Bremen, Germany
Christoph Bussler	Oracle Corporation, USA
Cristina Cabanillas	Vienna University of Economics and Business, Austria
Manuel Carro	UPM and IMDEA Software Institute, Spain
Wing-Kwong Chan	City University of Hong Kong, SAR China
Francois Charoy	University of Lorraine, France
Faouzi Ben Charrada	University of Tunis El Manar, Tunisia
Sanjay Chaudhary	Ahmedabad University, India
Liang Chen	RMIT, Australia
Shiping Chen	CSIRO, Australia
Lawrence Chung	The University of Texas at Dallas, USA
Edward Curry	Insight Centre, Ireland

Hoa Khanh Dam	University of Wollongong, Australia
Florian Daniel	University of Trento, Italy
Bruno Defude	Telecom Sud Paris, France
Shuiguang Deng	Zhejiang University, China
Nirmit Desai	IBM T.J. Watson Research Center, USA
Hai Dong	RMIT, Australia
Khalil Drira	LAAS Toulouse, France
Yucong Duan	Hainan University, China
Joyce El Haddad	University of Paris Dauphine, France
Rik Eshuis	Eindhoven University of Technology, The Netherlands
Onyeka Ezenwoye	Georgia Regents University, USA
Noura Faci	Université Lyon 1, CNRS, France
Marcelo Fantinato	University of São Paulo, Brazil
Pablo Fernández	Universidad de Sevilla, Spain
Joao E. Ferreira	University of Sao Paulo, Brazil
Marios-Eleftherios Fokaefs	York University, Canada
Xiang Fu	Hofstra, USA
Walid Gaaloul	Telecom SudParis, France
N.D. Gangadhar	MS Ramaiah University of Applied Sciences, India
G.R. Gangadharan	IDRBT, Hyderabad, India
Felix Garcia	Universidad Castilla-La mancha, Spain
Paolo Giorgini	University of Trento, Italy
Claude Godart	University of Lorraine, France
Mohamed Graiet	ISIMM, Tunisia
Sven Graupner	HP Labs, Palo Alto, USA
Daniela Grigori	University of Paris Dauphine, France
Georg Grossmann	University of South Australia, Australia
Armin Haller	Australian National University, Australia
Jun Han	Swinburne University of Technology, Australia
Chihab Hanachi	IRIT Laboratory, Toulouse University, France
Qiang He	Swinburne University of Technology, Australia
Bernhard Holtkamp	Fraunhofer ISST, Germany
Richard Hull	IBM Research, USA
Patrick Hung	University of Ontario, Canada
Fuyuki Ishikawa	National Institute of Informatics, Japan
Hai Jin	HUST, China
Nima Kaviani	IBM and Curatio.me, USA
Ejub Kajan	State University of Novi Pazar, Serbia
Anup Kalia	IBM Research NY, USA
Dimka Karastoyanova	Kühne Logistics University, Germany
Raman Kazhamiakin	Fondazione Bruno Kessler, Italy
Marouane Kessentini	University of Michigan–Dearborn, USA
Kais Klai	University of Paris 13, France
Ryan Ko	University of Waikato, New Zealand
Gerald Kotonya	Lancaster University, UK
Peep Kungas	University of Tartu, Estonia

Philippe Lalanda	Joseph Fourier University, France
Manuel Lama	University of Santiago de Compostela, Spain
Philipp Leitner	University of Zurich, Switzerland
Henrik Leopold	VU University Amsterdam, The Netherlands
Frank Leymann	University of Stuttgart, Germany
Ying Li	Zhejiang University, China
Marin Litoiu	York University, Canada
Xuanzhe Liu	Peking University, China
Xumin Liu	Rochester Institute of Technology, USA
Alessio Lomuscio	Imperial College London, UK
Jiangang Ma	Victoria University, Australia
Zakaria Maamar	Zayed University, United Arab Emirates
Javam Machado	UFC, Brazil
Zaki Malik	Wayne State University, USA
Maude Manouvrier	University of Paris Dauphine, France
Jordi Marco	Universitat Politècnica de Catalunya, Spain
Massimo Mecella	Sapienza Università di Roma, Italy
Brahim Medjahed	University of Michigan – Dearborn, USA
Tommi Mikkonen	Mozilla and Tampere University of Technology, Finland
Lars Moench	University of Hagen, Germany
Mohamed Mohamed	IBM Almaden Research Center, USA
Hamid Reza Motahari-Nezhad	IBM Research, USA
Juan M. Murillo	Universidad Extremadura, Spain
Michael Mrissa	University of Lyon, France
Nanjangud C. Narendra	Ericsson Research, Bangalore, India
Surya Nepal	CSIRO, Australia
Anne Ngu	Texas State University, USA
Talal H. Noor	Taibah University, Saudi Arabia
Alex Norta	Tallinn University of Technology, Estonia
Helen Paik	UNSW, Australia
Olivier Perrin	Lorraine University, France
Pierluigi Plebani	Politecnico di Milano, Italy
Pascal Poizat	Université Paris Ouest and LIP6, France
Artem Polyvyanyy	Queensland University of Technology, Australia
Karthikeyan Ponnalagu	IBM Research, India
Mu Qiao	IBM Almaden Research Center, USA
Mohamed Quafafou	Aix-Marseille University, France
Manfred Reichert	University of Ulm, Germany
Wolfgang Reisig	Humboldt-Universität zu Berlin, Germany
Stefanie Rinderle-Ma	University of Vienna, Austria
Colette Roland	Universite Paris1 Panthéon Sorbonne, France
Mohammad Sadoghi	IBM T.J. Watson Research Center, USA
Diptikalyan Saha	IBM Research, India
Iman Saleh	University of Miami, USA

Aviv Segev	KAIST, South Korea
Lionel Seinturier	University of Lille, France
Mohamed Sellami	ISEP, France
Jun Shen	University of Wollongong, Australia
Ignacio Silva-Lepe	IBM, USA
Sergey Smirnov	SAP, Germany
George Spanoudakis	City University London, UK
Eleni Stroulia	University of Alberta, Canada
Yehia Taher	University of Versailles-St-Quentin-en-Yvelines, France
Guiling Wang	North China University of Technology, China
Jianwu Wang	University of Maryland, Baltimore County, USA
Xianzhi Wang	The University of Adelaide, Australia
Yan Wang	Macquarie University, Australia
Zhongjie Wang	Harbin Institute of Technology, China
Ingo Weber	NICTA, Australia
Lijie Wen	Tsinghua University, China
Matthias Weidlich	Imperial College London, UK
Hanchuan Xu	Harbin Institute of Technology, China
Hamdi Yahyaoui	Kuwait University, Kuwait
Sami Yangui	Concordia University, Canada
Lina Yao	UNSW, Australia
Jianwei Yin	Zhejiang University, China
Sira Yongchareon	Unitec Institute of Technology, New Zealand
Jian Yu	Auckland University of Technology, New Zealand
Qi Yu	Rochester Institute of Technology, USA
Uwe Zdun	University of Vienna, Austria
Weiliang Zhao	Macquarie University, Australia
Yan Zheng	Aalto University/Xidian University, Finland
Zibin Zheng	Sun Yat-sen University, China
Zhangbing Zhou	China University of Geosciences (Beijing), China
Floriano Zini	University of Bologna, Italy
Andrea Zisman	City University London, UK
Ying Zou	Queens University, Canada

Additional Reviewers

Hiba Alili	Paris-Dauphine University, France
Moayad Alshangiti	Rochester Institute of Technology, USA
Mohammad-Javad Amiri	University of California at Santa Barbara, USA
Kahina Bessai	Lorraine University, France
Walid Fdhila	University of Vienna, Austria
Manuel Gall	University of Vienna, Austria
Conrad Indiono	University of Vienna, Austria
Diana Jlailaty	Paris-Dauphine University, France
Georg Kaes	University of Vienna, Austria

Keynote Papers

A Research Agenda for the Programmable World: Software Challenges for IoT Era

Tommi Mikkonen

University of Helsinki, Gustav Hällströmin katu 2b, Helsinki, Finland
tommi.mikkonen@helsinki.fi

Abstract. The Internet of Things (IoT) represents the next significant step in the evolution of the connectivity and programmability. While the majority of research work in the IoT area today is about data acquisition, real-time and offline analytics, machine learning, data visualization and other fashionable big data topics, in this keynote we argue that there is in fact even more profound change that we are facing – the programmability aspect that is intimately associated with all IoT systems. Advances in computing hardware development are making it feasible to introduce full-fledged operating systems in even smallest devices; advances in radio and battery technologies are enabling constant connectivity in the Global scale. This new world that is populated by programs of various degree of complexity requires programming skills in various fields that we now typically consider distinct, including in particular web and mobile development on the surface, and embedded and distributed software development at the core. Combining the characteristics of these fields will also force us to reconsider some of the fundamentals of software engineering in the process.

Keywords: Internet of Things · Programmable world · Software engineering · Embedded software · Web programming

Semantic Search

Ricardo Baeza-Yates

NTENT, USA & Spain
ricardo.baeza@upf.edu

Abstract. Semantic search lies in the cross roads of information retrieval and natural language processing and is the current frontier of search technology. The first part consist in building a semantically annotated index with the help of a knowledge base. For this we first need to predict the language of each document and parse it accordingly to that language. Second, we need to extract all entities and concepts mentioned in the document with the help of the knowledge base. All the knowledge base infrastructure needs to be independent of the language and we instantiate each language in the lexicon of the knowledge base.

The second part is predicting the intention behind the query, which implies doing semantic query understanding. This process implies the same semantic processing as document. After, based on all this information, we have to predict one or more possible intentions with a certain probability, which is particularly important for ambiguous queries. These scores will be one of the inputs for the final semantic ranking. For example, given the query "bond", possible results for query understanding are a financial instrument, the movie character, a chemical reaction, or a term for endearment.

Semantic ranking refers to ranking search results using semantic information. In a standard search engine, a rank is computed by using signals or features coming from the search query, from the documents in the collection being searched and from the search context, such as the language and device being used. In our case we add semantic relations between the entities and concepts found in the query was the same objects in the documents, that will come from different data sources. For this we use machine learning in several stages. The first stage selects the data sources that we should use to answer the query. In the second stage, each data source generates a set of answers using "earning to rank." The third and final stage ranks these data sources, selecting and ordering the intentions as well as the answers inside each intention (e.g., news) that will appear in the final composite answer. All these stages are language independent, but may use language dependent features.

We will cover the process above having in mind a services-based approach, including the data science needed to use as relevance feedback the usage log stream of the semantic search engine.

"Uber Scale". Stories and Lessons from the History of Scaling Uber SOA

Chritopher Adams

UBER
cadams@uber.com

Abstract. In this talk, Chris will discuss how Uber scaled several key components of its SOA infrastructure, and extrapolate some lessons and useful strategies that other companies can apply as they scale.

Contents

Service Recommendation

Services in Organizations, Business and Society

Services in the Cloud

Applications

Similarity Computation Exploiting the Semantic and Syntactic Inherent Structure Among Job Titles

Sarthak Ahuja[1]([✉]), Joydeep Mondal[1], Sudhanshu Shekhar Singh[1],
and David Glenn George[2]

[1] IBM Research Lab, New Delhi, India
sarahuja@in.ibm.com
[2] IBM Talent Management Solutions, Portsmouth, UK

Abstract. Solutions providing hiring analytics involve mapping company provided job descriptions to a standard job framework, thereby requiring computation of a similarity score between two jobs. Most systems doing so apply document similarity computation methods to all pairs of provided job descriptions. This approach can be computationally expensive and adversely impacted by the quality of the job descriptions which often include information not relevant to the job or candidate qualifications. We propose a method to narrow down pairs of job descriptions to be compared by comparing job titles first. The observation that each job title can be decomposed into three components, domain, function and attribute, forms the basis of our method. Our proposal focuses on training the machine learning models to identify these three components of any given job title. Next we do a semantic match between the three identified components, and use those match scores to create a composite similarity score between any two pair of job titles. The elegance of this solution lies in the fact that job titles are the most concise definition of the job and the resulting matches can easily be verified by human experts. Our results show that the approach provides extremely reliable results.

1 Introduction

The problem of finding similarity between a pair of documents lays groundwork for the problem of clustering similar documents together. Most of the initial research in this domain was based on standard document similarity computing methods such as tf- IDF, LSA, LDA etc. In certain specific scenarios, such as job descriptions in recruitment domain, the documents have very precise titles as well. Doing a preliminary match between pairs of titles can greatly reduce the effort required to eventually compare documents for similarity.

In our work for the recruitment analytics domain, and the recent developments therein, one problem that we have faced time and again is that of identifying which job requisitions are similar. This problem arises in two contexts:

© Springer International Publishing AG 2017
M. Maximilien et al. (Eds.): ICSOC 2017, LNCS 10601, pp. 3–18, 2017.
https://doi.org/10.1007/978-3-319-69035-3_1

1. Machine Learning models to identify good candidates: A typical application of machine learning in hiring is to learn success models for various jobs. To be meaningful, the models need to be learnt at a job group level instead of job level, so that sufficient data can be obtained for training the models.
2. Candidates' previous jobs need to be matched with the opening they apply to (or to the openings that can be recommended to them). This requires comparing an applicant's job previous jobs to the job openings available in the applicant tracking system.

Job requisitions typically consist of several well-defined components: required skills, years of experience, job title, job location and a job description. Since required skills, years of experience and job location are well-defined structured fields, the complexity comes in matching job title and job descriptions across jobs. In this paper, we present a Parts Of Title (POT) tagging and wordnet based matching technique to create a match score for two job titles.

Our work here is based on the basic premise that any given job title can be broken into three components Attribute, Function and Domain. Attribute typically denotes some sense of hierarchy (Senior, Junior, lead etc.), function denotes functionality (Manager, supervisor, director etc.), while domain is about the core job area. For example, a senior software engineer is a software (domain) engineer (function) at senior level. A senior electrical engineer is an electrical (domain) engineer at senior level. Although the two job titles have two out of three common words, they are obviously not the same jobs. A software engineer or even a junior software developer is a much closer job to senior software engineer than senior electrical engineer.

These three components might contains multiple words, or can also be null depending upon the context. Our work here describes a method that utilizes semantic match scoring between the three components, and combining those scores using logical domain insights to create a match score between a pair of job titles.

This paper is organized as follows. The next section describes some literature on title or phrase similarity/clustering. Section 3 describes the complete pipeline and methodology. Section 4 explains the methodology, Sect. 5 presents our evaluation and results. Section 6 concludes and discusses some future work.

2   Literature Survey

In typical text document classification and clustering tasks, the definition of a distance or similarity measure is essential. The most common methods employ keyword matching techniques. Methods such TFIDF [2] leverage the frequency of words occurring in a document to infer on similarity. The assumption is that if two documents have a similar distribution of words or have common keywords, then they are similar. Researchers have also extended this to N-gram based models, where group of consecutive words are taken together to capture the context. With large N gram models, typically large corpus of documents are required to obtain sufficient statistical information. As could be seen from the senior software engineer versus senior electrical engineer example in the previous section, these traditional document similarity methods do not work so well when matching short snippets of text, such as job titles. There are methods involving web based kernel function [10], wherein results of web search query are used to provide context to the short terms being compared. This paper defines a semantic similarity kernel function based on query search results, mathematically analyze some of its properties (similarity score going to 1 for similar queries as the query results sets cover all the relevant documents; the kernel measuring mean topical distance between the queries), and provide examples of its efficacy.

An alternative classification system [3] employs lazy learning from labeled phrases, and present a strong argument in favor of their method when the property of near sufficiency (most of information on document labels is captured in phrases) holds. They also reveal that in all practical cases from small-scale to very large-scale manual labeling of phrases is feasible as natural language constrains the number of common phrases composed of a vocabulary to grow linearly with the size of the vocabulary. Variants of phrase based classification have been studied in Information retrieval [9] and it has the advantage of ease of explainability.

Rich document representations and similarity measures are also an option for job title classification [11]. Semantic enrichment strategies replace the bag of words (BOW) representation that is more popular text classification as it is less adept at handling synonyms, polysemous words and multi word expressions. A machine learning- based semi-supervised job title classification system [4], leveraging a varied collection of classification and clustering tools and techniques, can be used to tackle the challenges of designing a scalable classification system for a large taxonomy of job categories.

A technical report [8] on learning compound noun semantics discusses an annotation scheme for compound nouns to derive compound relations (BE, HAVE, IN, ABOUT, ACTOR, (INST(rument))), and uses this annotation scheme to meaningfully compare compound nouns. This report inspired us to create learners to tag the three components of a job descriptions for a meaningful comparison between them. The final paper [7] combines pattern-based extraction and bootstrapping for noun compounds interpretation. They use a two-step algorithm to jointly harvest NCs and patterns (verbs and prepositions) that interpret them for a given abstract relation.

3   Methodology

Our proposed approach to generate a similarity score between two titles T and T' is illustrated in Figs. 1 and 2. In the former we illustrate the steps for setting up the system and in the latter we depict the steps that take place in the deployed system.

We start with a labeled dataset of titles, where each constituent keyword has been labeled with a particular context in which it occurs. For our training phase as described in Fig. 1 we use 90% of this data, while the remaining 10%

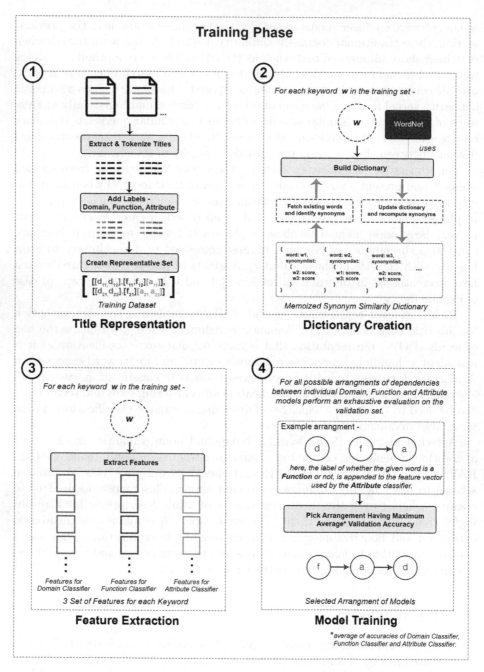

Fig. 1. Training Phase. In (1) titles for all documents available in the training set are extracted and their keywords are labeled with the ground truth context. Next in (2) for each of these keywords a dictionary is built using WordNet to maintain top synonyms and corresponding similarity scores on a cloud database for faster computation. Later in (3) feature vectors for each keyword are extracted and passed onto the Model Training phase. Finally, all permutations of arrangement of models are trained on the dataset and the arrangement with the highest validation accuracy is stored for deployment and evaluation on the testing dataset.

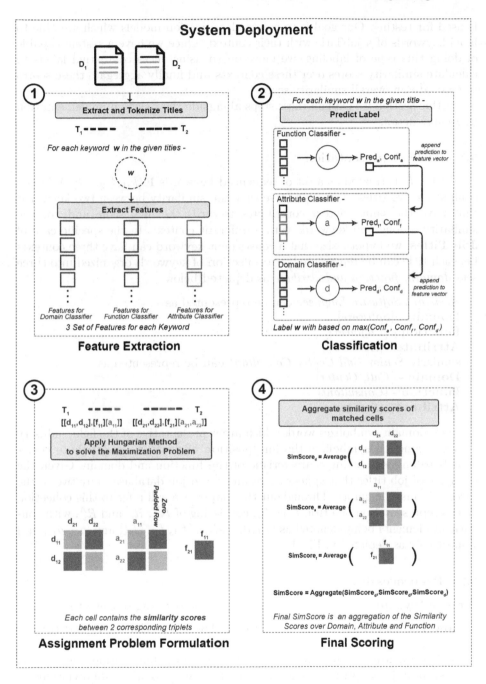

Fig. 2. System Deployment. In (1) incoming documents have their titles extracted and feature vectors for their constituent keywords created. Moving to (2), based on the arrangement of the models, the keywords are labeled with their context. Next in (3), for each context the assignment problem is formulated and solved to identify one-to-one matches for keywords within a particular context. Here, these matches are depicted in green. Finally in (4) the similarity scores over each context are computed using the dictionary created over the training phase and later aggregated to generate an overall similarity score.

is used for testing. Our goal is to create classification models which are able to label keywords of a jobTitle with their context. Once we have a system capable of doing this type of labeling, we move on to using these contextual labels to calculate similarity scores over these contexts and finally aggregate these scores to generate an overall similarity score.

In this section we explain these steps alongside their system implementation in greater detail.

3.1   Title Representation

Each title T_i is treated as a set of sequenced keywords $\mathbf{K}(k_{i1}, k_{i2}, ...k_{in})$. When comparing two titles, it is imperative that the similarity between two keywords that have the same context contributes towards the final score and not the similarity among two keywords with a different context. In the specific case of **Job Titles**, we hypothesize that a constituent keyword can have three contexts i.e. each title can be represented as a collection of keywords organized into three sets *domain, function and attribute* as depicted below

> *Assistant Software Engineer* can be represented as -
> **Domain** - [*Software*]
> **Function** - [*Engineer*]
> **Attribute** - [*Assistant*]
> similarly *Senior Call Center Consultant* can be represented as -
> **Domain** - [*Call, Center*]
> **Function** - [*Consultant*]
> **Attribute** - [*Senior*]

Here domain symbolizes words which are representative of the field/industry of work, function symbolizes the line/position of work, while attribute corresponds to any supporting characteristic of the function and domain. Given the diversity of job titles that appear on resumes and job databases, any two of the three sets may be empty. Throughout this paper, we will refer to this collection of sets representation of a title T_i as R_i, consisting of R_i^D, R_i^F and R_i^A, with constituent elements being denoted as $[d_{i1}, d_{i2}...d_{ij}]$, $[f_{i1}, f_{i2}...f_{ik}]$ and $[a_{i1}, a_{i2}...a_{il}]$ respectively as depicted in Fig. 1.

3.2   Preprocessing

For each keyword in a title we perform basic preprocessing to clean the data:

1. **Lower Case:** All titles are converted to lower case characters and trailing spaces are trimmed off.
2. **Abbreviation Expansion:** We expand common abbreviations such as **sr.** to **senior**, **jr.** to **junior** using a hard coded list of common abbreviations.
3. **Punctuation and Number Pruning:** Punctuation marks like '_', '-', etc. are removed by pruning all non-alphabet characters.

Once the data is cleaned, we move on to constructing the feature vectors on which the classification models will be trained.

3.3 Feature Extraction

In our approach we create 3 separate binary classification models for each of the aforementioned contexts - *domain, function* and *attribute*. For each title T_i, the three classifiers label each constituent keyword K_i. The label with the highest confidence for the positive class is taken as the label for the keyword. This section elaborates on the features extracted features and the intuition behind choosing them.

Position. The position of a keyword comes out to be an important parameter in determining it's context. For example, in the job titles - ***Assistant*** *Software Engineer* and ***Assistant*** *Manager*, the word ***Assistant*** acts as an *attribute* when it appears in the beginning of the word, while in the job title *Lab **Assistant***, it acts as a *function*.

It is important to understand at this juncture, that the same word can appear in different contexts depending on it's position, hence making **position** an important feature. In our approach we define 3 boolean features - *position_begin* which denotes whether the keyword appears at the beginning of the title, *position_end* which denotes whether the keyword appears at the end of the title and *position_between* which denotes whether the keyword appears in the middle of the title.

Suffix. We listed a set of common keywords found in Domains, Functions and Attributes and noticed some patterns with the suffixes. For example:

Words labeled as Domain: Ophthalmologist, Dentist, Psychiatrist, etc.
Words labeled as Function: Engineer, Doctor, Manager, etc.
Words labeled as Attribute: Junior, Senior, etc.

Our first observation was the pattern of **-ist** suffix for the *Domain* words. This observation is consistent with the definition of **-ist** being forming nouns denoting a member of a profession or business activity [1]. However for the *Functions* and *Attributes* the suffix usage is tightly correlated with its context. As example, **-or** can be used to denote a person or thing performing the action of a verb [1]. It also can be used to form comparative adjectives.

Based on these observations, in our approach we define two suffix lists for the three contexts and for each define the feature as a boolean on whether the suffix of the keyword is present in the concerned list. For example, the suffix list defined for the *function* and *attribute* classifier was defined as ['or', 'er', 'ors', 'ers', 'ar', 'ars'] and hence, the feature vector for the keyword ***Manager*** marks the **suffix** feature as 1 for the *function* classifier. Similar list is created for the *domain* classifier as ['ist', 'ists'].

It should be noted that we limit the size of these lists, to only include the most common observations using basic knowledge of English grammar and vocabulary, and do not mine for any suffix patterns explicitly.

Keyword POS Tag. Next we append to the feature vector a Part-Of-Speech Tag for the corresponding keyword using the Stanford POS Tagger. The tagger can tag the keyword with 1 of the 36 labels.

An important fact we note is that the POS Tag of the keyword is at times different from the POS Tag of other versions of the same keyword. For example, **manager** is tagged as **noun** while **manage** is tagged as **verb**. Considering that ideally both should be labeled with the same context, besides the original POS Tag, we reduce the keyword to it's root and add the POS Tag of the root word as well. Hence, for this feature we append two values to the feature vector, POS Tag of the keyword and POS Tag of the root of the keyword.

In our implementation, we refer to vocabulary.com to extract the root of a keyword.

3.4   Feature Vector Construction

The features explained in the previous subsection are combined to form a feature vector. If we assume that all three classification models are independent of each other we get each keyword being depicted in the form of 3 feature vectors each of length 7. But we observe that as humans we do not label all the keywords independently. Once we have obtained the prediction for one or two of the context labels for a keyword in the title, we get contextual information that increases our confidence to label it for a different context. For example, for **Assistant Software Developer**, once we identify that **Software** is not the *function* word, we get more confident about labeling it as *domain*. Given our problem, we assert that this *ruling out* step will play a crucial role in improving the classifier accuracies. Keeping this in mind, based on the dependencies amongst classifiers, the feature vector for a classifier may also have the predicted label of a previously checked classifier. In the previously mentioned example, if we identify that the *domain* classifier is dependent on the *function* classifier, we will see the feature vector being fed into the former be of length $(7 + 1)$, after appending the prediction of the *function* classifier to the feature vector. In the training stage, instead of actual model predictions we use the ground truth value, while in the testing (system deployment) stage, we use the actual prediction of the trained models. Figure 3 displays the possible arrangements of the models.

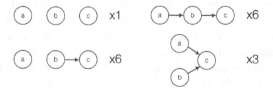

Fig. 3. All possible dependency relationships that can exist between three models. Here *a*, *b* and *c* can represent any of *Domain*, *Function* and *Attribute*, hence generating a total of 16 possible arrangements.

In our case we perform an evaluation on all 16 possible arrangements, explained in Sect. 5 and choose the best arrangement based on validation accuracy. This selected arrangement of models represents the identified dependencies among the context classifiers, and is deployed in the system and used on the testing dataset for our final evaluation.

The next section explains the training procedure for each individual model.

3.5   Model Creation

For each context, we train models using SPSS's autoclassifier module which trains a bunch of classifiers on the data - neural net, C5, Logistic Regression, CHAID, Quest, C&R, Bayesian Network, Decision List. We use 90% of our labeled dataset for this model creation. We apply a 10-fold validation on this dataset and select the model with the highest average validation accuracy as depicted in Table 1. Our selected arrangement of models is depicted in Figs. 1 and 2. The best classifier for *Domain* and *Function* context comes out to be C5, while for *Attribute* it comes out to be a neural net.

3.6   Assignment Problem Formulation

As depicted in Fig. 2, the two documents, D_1 and D_2, are represented by their tokenized titles T_1 and T_2. After our selected arrangement of the three context classifiers labels these keywords as either *Domain,Function* or *Attribute* they are then represented as two sets of triplets, $S_1([R_1^D, R_1^F, R_1^A])$ and $S_2([R_2^D, R_2^F, R_2^A])$, each with elements $[[d_{11}, d_{12}...d_{1j}], [f_{11}, f_{12}...f_{1k}], [a_{11}, a_{12}...a_{1l}]]$ and $[[d_{21}, d_{22}...d_{2j}], [f_{21}, f_{22}...f_{2k}], [a_{21}, a_{22}...a_{2l}]]$ respectively. Similarity score between these two documents can be interpreted as the similarity score between these two sets of triplets. The similarity function is explained in detail in the next subsection, and is denoted by **F** for now. As mentioned earlier, when comparing two titles, it is imperative that the similarity between two keywords that have the same context contributes towards the final score. There is no relevance in the similarity among two keywords with a different context. To calculate the similarity score between two sets, we calculate the similarity score independently amongst the three contexts and aggregate them to get a final similarity score. This aggregator function is explained in detail in the next subsection, and is denoted by **A** for now. To find the similarity between two sets of the same context, a naive approach would be to calculate the similarity score between each pair of elements from two sets (example, R_1^D and R_2^D), greedily pick the pair with the highest similarity score and repeat the process till either one of the sets has no element left. This greedy approach, although simple, does not provide an optimal match between the sets being compared. We assume that there are no repeating keywords in the Job Title, hence, the representative set for a document too will not have synonymous elements. This assumption motivates a one-to-one mapping among the two sets being compared for similarity.

To find this mapping among the aforementioned two sets, we formulate the problem as an assignment problem. In a generic assignment problem, given the cost of assignment among each pair of elements in two sets, the task is to find an optimal one-to-one assignment among the elements that maximizes/minimizes the total cost of assignment. Our problem of finding such a one-to-one mapping among one of the context sets of the S_1 and S_2 can be formulated in a similar way - given $\mathbf{F}$ as the cost of assignment function among each pair of elements in the two sets, the task is to find an optimal one-to-one assignment among the elements that maximizes the aggregate similarity score.

Next, we use the *Hungarian Method* to extract out the matches. This method takes as input a *nxn* square cost matrix and post applying a set of matrix operations, outputs an optimal set of n assignments, one per row and column, which offer a maximum cumulative assignment score. Given ours is an imbalanced assignment problem, the 2 sets with m and n keywords each, we start with a *mxn* cost matrix, where each cell contains the similarity score between the corresponding row and column elements of the matrix. Without loss of generality, we assume $n > m$, and add zero padding to extend the *mxn* matrix to a *nxn* one. Rest of the steps for applying the *Hungarian Method* remain the same, as for a typical score maximization assignment problem.

This assignment task is done independently for each of the three contexts. Post this assignment, the following subsection defines the similarity and aggregation functions.

3.7 Final Score Computation

In this subsection we define the previously mention similarity($\mathbf{F}$) and aggregator($\mathbf{A}$) functions.

Similarity Function. We use WordNet as the basis of our similarity function to compute a semantic similarity score between two keywords. Any other methods such as Word2Vec, etc. which provide a semantic similarity score between two words could be possible alternatives to WordNet. WordNet is a large lexical database of English language. Nouns, verbs, adjectives and adverbs are grouped into sets of cognitive synonyms which is called *synsets*. Each *synsets* expresses a distinct concept which interlinked by means of conceptual-semantic and lexical relations. Wordnet provides synsets for a given English word [6]. To calculate sim_{sem} between w_1 and w_2 we calculate *wup similarity* score between two synsets corresponding to w_1 and w_2. *Wu Palmer Similarity* or *wup similarity* provides a score denoting how similar two word senses are, based on the depth of the two senses in the taxonomy and that of their Least Common Subsumer (most specific ancestor node). After getting the scores between each sysnset we took an average of the scores to get the semantic similarity score between w_1 and w_2 and denoted it as $sim_{sem_{w_1,w_2}}$. Algorithm to find sim_{sem} is described in Algorithm 1. On obtaining the sim_{sem} score between matches provided by the solution of the assignment problem, the final Similarity Score for a context is taken to be the average of all the sim_{sem} scores. We denote the Similarity Score for each context - *Domain, Function* and *Attribute* as $SimScore_d$, $SimScore_f$ and $SimScore_a$ respectively.

To make the computation of this Similarity Score faster we employed some optimizations in the scoring process. After obtaining the tokenized keywords from a Job Title we used *memoization* and *precomputation* techniques to build a dictionary *Dict* of keywords. The structure of the dictionary is depicted as in Fig. 4. In the dictionary, every word w has been stored with its synonym list syn_w. We used Wordnet dictionary from NLTK [5] to get syn_w for a given w. We used cloudant Database to store this dictionary as JSONs. The structure of the JSON is in Fig. 4. syn_w for a w consists of only the words which exist in *Dict* and cross a threshold of semantic similarity score (sim_{sem}).

When *Dict* is empty and the algorithm encounters a new word it creates *Dict* and stores an entry corresponding to the word. When *Dict* exists in the cloudant database and algorithm encounters a w then it first checks whether it is present in *Dict* or not. If w is not present in *Dict* then it will create an entry for w and will generate a corresponding syn_w by calculating sim_{sem} with every other words in *Dict*. The sim_{sem} of every other words of *Dict* will also be updated accordingly. While processing each keyword, we precompute the semantic similarity scores among the words and store them in a database.

Algorithm 1. SimSem Function

1: **procedure** SimSemFunction
2:     **Input:** w_1, w_2
3:     **Output:** $sim_{sem_{w_1,w_2}}$
4:     $sim_{sem_{w_1,w_2}} \leftarrow 0$
5:     $synSets_{w_1} \leftarrow null$
6:     $synSets_{w_2} \leftarrow null$
7:     $synSets_{w_1} \leftarrow synsets\ from\ Wordnet\ for\ w_1$
8:     $synSets_{w_2} \leftarrow synsets\ from\ Wordnet\ for\ w_2$
9:     $div \leftarrow 0$
10:     **for** *each* $synSet_{w_1}$ *of* $synSets_{w_1}$ **do**
11:         **for** *each* $synSet_{w_2}$ *of* $synSets_{w_2}$ **do**
12:             $wup_{score} \leftarrow wup\ similarity\ between\ synSet_{w_1}\ \&\ synSet_{w_2}$
13:             **if** wup_{score} is not *null* **then**
14:                 $sim_{sem_{w_1,w_2}} \leftarrow sim_{sem_{w_1,w_2}} + wup_{score}$
15:                 $div \leftarrow div + 1$
16:             **end if**
17:         **end for**
18:     **end for**
19:     $sim_{sem_{w_1,w_2}} \leftarrow \dfrac{sim_{sem_{w_1,w_2}}}{div}$
20: **end procedure**

Aggregator Function. The aggregator function is meant to collate the similarity scores generated among matches provided by the solution of the assignment problem. The definition of this function is described in Algorithm 2. The equation is basically a weighted average of the three context similarity scores where more weight is given to the *Domain* similarity, *Function* similarity and

$$[\\ w_1: syn_{w1}:\{w_2:sim_{sem\ w1,w2}, w_3:sim_{sem\ w1,w3}\}, \\ w_2: syn_{w2}:\{w_1:sim_{sem\ w1,w2}\}, \\ w_3: syn_{w3}:\{w_1:sim_{sem\ w1,w3}\} \\ ]$$

```
{
  "title": "academic",
  "synonymlist":{
    "coach": 0.319
    "managed": 0.316
  }
}
```

(a) Dictionary Structure for Keyword   (b) JSON Structure for saving on Cloudant

Fig. 4. (a) Dictionary Structure for Keyword (b) JSON Structure for saving on Cloudant

then *Attribute* similarity, in that order. Special care is taken in the averaging process so that if both sets of a particular context turn out to be empty, they are not included in the normalizing denominator.

Algorithm 2. Aggregator Function

1: **procedure** AGGREGATORFUNCTION
2:      **Input:** $SimScore_d, SimScore_f, SimScore_a$
3:      **Output:** $SimScore$
4:      $SimScore = \dfrac{1}{(\mathbf{1}_{SimScore_a \neq 0} + \mathbf{1}_{SimScore_f \neq 0} + \mathbf{1}_{SimScore_d \neq 0})} * (SimScore_d *$
        $(1 + SimScore_f * (1 + SimScore_a)))$
5: **end procedure**

---

4   Experimental Setup and Dataset

We used a Spark cluster with 6 executors each having 8GB of RAM for running our experiments. Apache Spark framework has been used to incorporate parallelization to carry out the experiments. All the codes have been written in python. We used PySpark library to include Apache Spark environment into our system. Cloudant services have been incorporated as database resource. We also used Standford Core NLP Parser and Wordnet from NLTK library.

Job description documents from IBM Talent Framework Data sets have been used to carry out all the experiments. Our training and validation set consists of 4471 job titles, leading up to 16180 keywords. For our test set, we have 421 job titles corresponding to 71 different job families. Other details of the dataset can't be revealed here due to confidentiality issues.

5   Evaluation

As part of our evaluation we first present the results of the training phase in Table 1. Here for all 16 possible arrangements of model dependencies we calculate the training and validation accuracy. We observe that the maximum validation accuracy of

Table 1. Selecting best arrangement of models

Arrangement	Domain		Function		Attribute		Average	
	Training Accuracy	Validation Accuracy	Training Accuracy	Validation Accuracy	Training Accuracy	Validation Accuracy	Training Accuracy	Validation Accuracy
(d) (f) (a)	80.48	80.507	88.54	88.77	92.25	92.257	87.093	87.178
(d) (f→a)	80.48	80.507	88.54	88.77	92.77	**92.91**	87.26	87.39
(f) (d→a)	80.48	80.507	88.54	88.77	**92.80**	92.62	87.27	87.30
(a) (d→f)	80.48	80.507	90.96	91.94	92.25	92.257	87.9	87.96
(a) (f→d)	86.62	86.36	88.54	88.77	92.25	92.257	89.14	89.12
(d) (a→f)	80.48	80.507	89.18	89.227	92.25	92.257	87.30	87.33
(f) (a→d)	83.81	83.75	88.54	88.77	92.25	92.257	88.20	88.26
(f→d→a)	86.62	86.36	88.54	88.77	92.78	92.76	89.31	89.29
(f→a→d)	**90.71**	**90.59**	88.54	88.77	92.77	**92.91**	90.67	**90.76**
(a→f→d)	**90.71**	**90.59**	89.18	89.227	92.25	92.257	**90.71**	90.69
(a→d→f)	83.81	83.75	**92.89**	**92.79**	90.25	90.257	89.65	89.60
(d→a→f)	80.48	80.507	**92.89**	**92.79**	**92.80**	92.62	88.72	88.64
(d→f→a)	80.48	80.507	90.96	91.94	92.78	92.76	88.07	88.13
tree [a, d]→f	80.48	80.507	**92.89**	**92.79**	92.25	92.257	88.54	88.51
tree [f, d]→a	80.48	80.507	88.54	88.77	92.78	92.76	87.27	87.34
tree [f, a]→d	**90.71**	**90.59**	88.54	88.77	92.25	92.257	90.50	90.54

90.76% is obtained for a linear relationship among the context classifiers ($f \rightarrow a \rightarrow d$). This arrangement is hence chosen for deployment and testing.

For our chosen model, in the testing phase we observe

1. an accuracy of **78.04%** for the domain classifier
2. an accuracy of **87.01%** for the function classifier.
3. an accuracy of **93.43%** for the attribute classifier.

We did a job family based evaluation to test our method. Since we are using IBM Kenexa talent frameworks, we can utilize its default clustering of jobs into job families. We would expect jobs within a family (intra) to have higher title similarity scores than those outside the job family (inter). The scores for intra vs inter job family titles' similarity were calculated, and averaged for reporting. The comparison of scores for some of the biggest job families can be seen in Fig. 5.

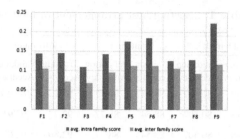

Fig. 5. Inter versus intra job family title comparison scores.

As expected, the scores for inter job family title distances are higher than those for intra job family distances. They are not very high, as there are many different roles and functions even within the same job family. For example, both "talent analyst senior" and "international human resources manager" in the job family "HR", but they are very different from each other.

In some of the smaller job families, the intra scores average was lower (or equal) than the inter scores average. On investigation we found out that those job families had only 2–3 jobs, and they all seemed very different. Where as those jobs seem to have several common domain synonyms with job titles in other families.

We compare our method to another approach of directly using WordNet semantic similarity. For this comparison, we use the ratio of the average inter and intra cluster similarity as our evaluation metric. The lower this ratio is, the better is the cluster quality. For WordNet based semantic similarity we take the average of all WordNet generated similarity scores for all possible pairs of keywords between two given titles. We show the results for the biggest job families in Fig. 6. We observe that our method leads to a consistently better cluster quality compared to the method of simply using WordNet based average score as the similarity metric.

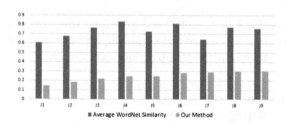

Fig. 6. Comparison based on inter/intra cluster similarity ratio

6   Conclusion and Future Work

In this paper, we described an approach to find similarity between job titles based on the observation that each job title consist of three components - domain, function and attribute. We used classifier models to identify the tokens in a job description as one of the three components. Then we used a hierarchical approach with domain, function and attribute as the levels of hierarchy to find the similarity score between any two jobs.

As we observed via the intra vs inter job title similarity scores, the approach gives fairly accurate results. In some of the smaller job families, the intra scores average were not higher than the inter scores average. The accuracy of overall matching scores depends on the accuracy of classifiers and the engine used to match the three components with each other.

We believe that another way of identifying the three components of a job description could be based on approaches used for finding similarities between compound nouns. That exact approach will not suffice since job titles do not just consist of nouns. Other semantic approaches to identify the three components, or compound noun based approach to find similarity between domain words can improve our results.

References

1. English   Dictionary.   https://en.oxforddictionaries.com/spelling/nouns-ending-in-er-or-and-ar
2. Aizawa, A.: An information-theoretic perspective of Tf-idf measures. Inf. Process. Manag. **39**, 45–65 (2003)
3. Bekkerman, R., Gavish, M.: High-precision phrase-based document classification on a modern scale. In: Proceedings of the 17th ACM SIGKDD International Conference on Knowledge Discovery and Data Mining. ACM (2011)
4. Javed, F., Luo, Q., McNair, M., Jacob, F., Zhao, M., Kang, T.S.: Carotene: a job title classification system for the online recruitment domain. In: 2015 IEEE First International Conference on Big Data Computing Service and Applications (BigDataService), pp. 286–293. IEEE (2015)
5. Loper, E., Bird, S.: NLTK: the natural language toolkit. In: Proceedings of the ACL-02 Workshop on Effective Tools and Methodologies for Teaching Natural Language Processing and Computational Linguistics, ETMTNLP 2002, Association for Computational Linguistics, Stroudsburg, PA, USA, vol. 1, pp. 63–70 (2002). http://dx.doi.org/10.3115/1118108.1118117
6. Miller, G.A.: WordNet: a lexical database for english. Commun. ACM **38**(11), 39–41 (1995)
7. Nakov, P.I., Hearst, M.A.: Semantic interpretation of noun compounds using verbal and other paraphrases. ACM Trans. Speech Lang. Process. (TSLP) **10**(3), 13 (2013)
8. Ó Séaghdha, D.: Learning compound noun semantics. Technical report, University of Cambridge, Computer Laboratory (2008)
9. Riloff, E., Lehnert, W.: Information extraction as a basis for high-precision text classification. ACM Trans. Inf. Syst. (TOIS) **12**(3), 296–333 (1994)

10. Sahami, M., Heilman, T.D.: A web-based kernel function for measuring the similarity of short text snippets. In: Proceedings of the 15th International Conference on World Wide Web, pp. 377–386. ACM (2006)
11. Zhu, Y., Javed, F., Ozturk, O.: Semantic similarity strategies for job title classification. arXiv preprint arXiv:1609.06268 (2016)

RISE: Resolution of Identity Through Similarity Establishment on Unstructured Job Descriptions

Rakesh Rameshrao Pimplikar[1]([✉]), Kalapriya Kannan[2], Abhik Mondal[3],
Joydeep Mondal[1], Sushant Saxena[4], Gyana Parija[1], and Chandra Devulapalli[5]

[1] IBM Research, Bangalore, India
rakesh.pimplikar@gmail.com, {jomondal,gyana.parija}@in.ibm.com
[2] Hewlett Packard Enterprise, Bangalore, India
kalapriya@gmail.com
[3] Department of Computer Science, IIT Madras, Chennai, India
abhik.mondal1992@gmail.com
[4] Department of Computer Science, IIT Delhi, New Delhi, India
sushant3012@gmail.com
[5] IBM Software Lab, Bangalore, India
cdevulap@in.ibm.com

Abstract. Identity resolution of job description involving cross organizational data would go a long way in addressing several high valued business problems. Job data normalization/sanitation, automated creation of better job descriptions with context preference, description reuse and validation across different sources, semantic classification of jobs, routing of candidates to suitable jobs across different organization etc. are some of the business centric functionalities that can be efficiently built by resolving job description identities. Job descriptions are highly unstructured with free flow textual data consisting of lines describing important attributes of job requirements, like education, skills, experience, role, responsibility etc. Much of the problem is due to the highly unstructured nature of job descriptions. Further, the attributes that are representative of the information in a job description are not readily available from the description. Thus, the process of resolution involves deep data cleansing, classification, attributes identification, and building highly scalable similarity detection algorithms. In this paper, we propose RISE - that uses values of attributes in the underlying job description data and similarity observed in the attributes to resolve identities across organizations. It proposes classification followed by similarity establishment processes that eventually provides high quality of resolution. Through extensive experiments performed on corpus of job descriptions from several real world recruitment systems, we demonstrate that RISE can resolve the identities with high precision and recall.

K. Kannan—A part of the work was done when the author was an employee at IBM Research - India.

A. Mondal and S. Saxena—A part of the work was done when the authors were interns at IBM Research - India.

M. Maximilien et al. (Eds.): ICSOC 2017, LNCS 10601, pp. 19–36, 2017.
https://doi.org/10.1007/978-3-319-69035-3_2

1   Introduction

Identifying right job positions is a key to right opportunity. Job descriptions (JDs) expose job positions by providing information about the positions. To-date job descriptions are prescriptive and dependent solely on expression of job details from employers or recruiting systems. As a result job descriptions differ significantly from one employer to another even for the same role or responsibility, making it difficult for job seekers to identify the right set of jobs. Thus, Job Data Normalization would go a long way assisting the community of job seekers to identify the right set of opportunities for their profiles through standardization of job requirements.

Functional commonalities observed in recruiting systems such as hiring, selection etc., among organizations result in data (JDs, candidate CVs, processes for hiring etc.) that exhibit high commonalities. Such data is often non-standard and each organization chooses its own identifier to refer to each of the records. Our own analysis of about 27000 JDs across 28 different organizations has revealed that terms used to refer to roles vary significantly by name. Thus identifying similar JDs by role names becomes difficult if not impossible. Often times, manual inspection of data is employed to assess contents of JDs and establish similarity and thus identities.

In this paper, we address one such critical problem of resolving identities of JDs and normalizing them across organizations. We present RISE, an identity resolution engine that uses underlying similarity in the nature of the data, representing attributes as a fundamental concept to resolve identities. It establishes novel methods to process unstructured JDs, identify attributes and convert unstructured textual descriptions into structured information. Similarity is established against the first class attributes identified to represent the data. Identities (Job Titles/Department) pertaining to JDs, which are established as similar, are used to build rules to construct equivalence. We enumerate each of the steps in the process in detail and show that our approach identifies similarity across JDs with high accuracy.

Our contributions in this paper can be summarized as follows:

1. Identity resolution of JDs
   (a) Identification of important attributes that are descriptive of the information in JDs.
   (b) Build highly accurate classifier that labels the unstructured text into one or more of the attributes.
   (c) Identify and extract keywords for each of the attributes from unstructured text.
   (d) Establish similarity among JDs based on extracted keywords.
   (e) Establish equivalence among identity titles/roles of JDs.
2. Experiments on real world data sets
   (a) We performed each of above 5 steps on real world data sets collected across 28 different organizations.
   (b) We extensively validated results at each step to ensure that the overall process derives similarity with high accuracy.

Rest of the paper is organized as follows. The system and steps are presented in detail in Sect. 2. Section 3 is used to present the algorithms that we have used. We review some of the existing literature as applicable for our work in Sect. 5. Section 4 presents the details of the experiments and the results. We conclude with directions to future work in Sect. 6.

2   System Overview and Approach

Before providing system details, we present a list of terms along with their definitions in Table 1. We use these terms throughout our paper. It will help readers not to get confused with terms having literally similar meaning.

Table 1. Important terms and definitions

Terms	Definitions
Job Description (JD)	It is an unstructured textual information describing job requirements that a candidate profile should satisfy in order to be considered for the job
Keywords	We use this term to refer to a set of words from an unstructured line of a JD. In general, keywords provide some specific information
Category	It represents a concept/topic for a combination of certain keywords/single key word. We are going to use categories as a feature set as described in Sect. 3.2
Attributes	It is a set of independent identifiable variables that can be used to tag the information provided by every line in a JD. It is also used as a set of labels as described in Sect. 3.2

Our system RISE comprises six different phases. Figure 1 shows all the phases and respective steps involved in extracting the relevant information from highly unstructured text describing a job requirement. Details of every phase are as follows.

1. Attribute Identification Phase (AIP). It uses Principal Component Analysis (PCA) to identify attributes that are representatives of the information in JDs (Step 1 in Fig. 1). This is done with the help of the domain and subject matter experts. Algorithm for identification of these attributes is presented in detail in Sect. 3.1. The five attributes those were determined through this analysis are {*Education, Skills, Experience, Roles, Responsibilities*}.

2. Classifier Training Phase (CTP). It is responsible for training a multi-label ensemble classifier to assign one or more attributes to each line in a JD. The input to this step is training data where every line of historical JDs is already labeled. Output is a classifier model. Ground truth, collected through manual labeling (as described in Sect. 4.1), is used to train the classifier.

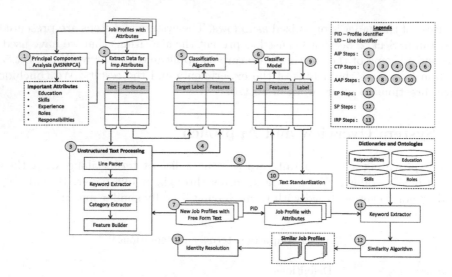

Fig. 1. Phases and steps involved in processing unstructured job descriptions

In step 2 (refer to Fig. 1), we extract unstructured text information from the JDs only for attributes identified in *AIP*. Step 3 involves unstructured text processing, where text is parsed to be broken into a set of lines. Delimiters that have been used to break the unstructured text into lines are {, . ; newline}. Based on the keywords present in a line, a set of categories are extracted for that line. These categories can be in hierarchical order. Eventually a binary feature set is built for every line where every entry in a feature set indicates whether the corresponding category is present or absent. In step 4, this feature set is used to create training data for a classification algorithm. In step 5, a classifier is trained to output a classifier model as shown in step 6. Details of the algorithms that are involved in category extraction, feature set generation, and classifier training are presented in Sect. 3.2.

3. Attribute Association Phase (*AAP*). It uses the classifier model built in step 5 of *CTP* for the classification. Every new JD is passed through unstructured text processing (step 7), which extracts the features against each line (step 8). The extracted features are passed through the classifier which associates each line with one or more attributes (step 9). The output of classifier passes through text standardization (step 10). The main functionality of this component is to convert the keywords available in each labeled line into standard recognizable forms. Trivial differences such as multiple spaces between keywords, presence of delimiters are also cleaned by the text standardization process. Algorithmic details of the text standardization process is presented in Sect. 3.3.

4. Extraction Phase (*EP*). The text is still in the form of unstructured lines after *AAP*. This textual lines now with labels are passed into the Extraction Phase (step 11). In this phase, keywords referring to each of the attributes are identified and extracted from the text. This step converts the unstructured text into a structured JD. The keywords for each of the attributes are stored in the form of comma separated values. Section 3.4 presents the complete set of algorithms for extracting keywords related to each of the attributes from the lines.

5. Similarity Phase (*SP*). Step 12 of Fig. 1 represents a similarity algorithm to find similarity between any two JDs. We have used *Jaccard* similarity measure to determine the similarity of two JDs based on the attributes education, skills, roles, and responsibilities. For similarity measures on the experience, we have provided our own approach of computing similarity based on the number of years of experience. Algorithmic details are provided in Sect. 3.6.

6. Identity Resolution Phase (*IRP*). In this phase, we establish and build a set of rules that can be used to easily identify two equivalent JDs (Step 13 in Fig. 1). Each job description is identified by its job title (a role oriented descriptor) and department. For every pair of similar JDs identified in previous phase, their job titles and departments are stored as a rule in the rules repository. We don't have to analyze any two JDs for similarity in future, if their jobs titles and departments are already present among rules.

3 Algorithms

In this section, we primarily describe 4 algorithms, (1) for identifying important attributes for JDs, (2) for tagging unstructured lines of JDs as one of 5 attributes {*Education, Skills, Experience, Roles, Responsibilities*}, (3) for creating structured job descriptions, and (4) for finding similarity between two job descriptions.

3.1 Identifying Important Attributes for Job Descriptions

This algorithm is used in the *AIP* described in Sect. 2. Our aim is to identify a set of important attributes that are representatives of the information in JDs. *Principal Component Analysis* (PCA) is used in dimensionality reduction. We use a hybrid feature reduction method MSNRPCA based on the combination of feature ranking with PCA. This method was proposed by Yang et al. [20].

We use labeled data set of JDs, as described in Sect. 4.1 to run MSNRPCA on it. Labeled data has values of every attribute for all JDs. An exhaustive list of different attributes derived by qualitative analysis on these JDs is as shown below.

Depth of knowledge, Process, Tools and Technologies, Skills, Domain knowledge, Experience, Business knowledge, Efficiency of communication, Roles expected to perform, Performance expected, Project Management, Schedule Management, Training undergone, Education level, Education streams, Responsibilities

---

MSNRPCA assigns a score to each of these attributes, based on the importance of every attribute. Higher the score, higher is the importance. For robustness, we create 5 sets of labeled JDs, by randomly sampling 80% of total JDs every time. MSNRPCA is used to assign an importance score to every attribute for every sampled instance of labeled JDs. To simplify the analysis, we map all scores on a rating of 10. Table 2 captures all such scores. You can think of these scores as ratings given to every attribute by 5 different domain experts. Co-related variables are removed from this list thus reducing the set of variables to a minimum number of independent attributes. We perform factor analysis on these scores to eventually identify 5 important attributes. Those are {*Education, Skills, Experience, Roles, Responsibilities*}. Skills attribute can further be classified into "Technical Skills" and "Soft Skills". All skills that involve a known technology, tools, product or methodology are categorized under technical skills. Soft skills include those which do not involve a known tool, but are gained through experience and personal affiliation. Examples of such skills include management skill, communication skill, etc. In this paper we do not discuss this classification of skills and consider only 5 important attributes. We refer these attributes using the notations y_{edu}, y_{skill}, y_{exp}, y_{role} and y_{resp} respectively.

3.2   Unstructured Text Classification

The bunch of algorithms presented here are used in the *CTP* and *AAP* phases explained in Sect. 2. A job description generally contains unstructured text describing the requirements of an open job position in terms of important attributes {*Education, Skills, Experience, Roles, Responsibilities*}. It is observed that every line of such a job description describes one or more attributes. So in order to create a structured description out of an unstructured one, we first identify which line describes what attributes. This leads to a multi-label classification problem where we need to assign one or more labels to every line L of a job description. In our case, a set of possible labels is $\mathcal{Y} = \{y_{edu}, y_{skill}, y_{exp}, y_{role}, y_{resp}\}$. As described in [19], there are two main methods for tackling multi-label classification problem, (1) problem transformation methods that transform the multi-label problem into a set of binary classification problems and (2) algorithm adaptation methods that adapt the algorithms to directly perform multi-label classification. We use the problem transformation method, where we create 5 binary classifiers one for each label in $\mathcal{Y}$. All the steps involved in multi-label classification are explained in detail below.

Feature Extraction. This section provides an approach to unstructured text processing as mentioned in Sect. 2. A set of features is required for a line L to use any standard classification algorithm. So feature extraction is an important step in our approach. In a way, our labels $\mathcal{Y}$ are the categories which we have to identify for every line. Such a category identification needs a mapping between categories and keywords as an input. It looks for keywords in text and based on mapping it figures out most appropriate category. We use Naive Bayes classifier

Table 2. Importance scoring of all attributes

Depth of knowledge	Process	Tools and technologies	Skills	Domain knowledge	Experience	Business knowledge	Efficiency of communication	Roles	Performance expected	Project management	Schedule management	Training undergone	Education level	Education streams	Responsibilities
2	2	5	8	2	8	4	2	8	4	5	2	3	8	7	7
4	3	5	8	4	6	5	3	6	3	4	2	1	7	7	8
5	4	6	6	3	7	6	2	8	3	6	3	4	8	9	8
2	3	6	8	4	7	2	2	6	2	6	2	2	7	8	9
5	3	6	8	4	7	3	3	7	2	5	1	2	7	7	7

to classify text into one of the categories [9]. There are mainly two problems with this approach, (1) one keyword may be mapped to multiple categories, resulting in more than one possible categories for L, and (2) it is very difficult to come up with an exhaustive list of keywords for every category. Thus, using category identification approach for our problem leads to poor results.

Instead we can have a taxonomy for several different categories (including $\mathcal{Y}$), such as *academics, products, work, business*, etc. An example of such a taxonomy is shown in Fig. 2. Similar taxonomy can easily be found in public domain. Every parent node in a taxonomy can be considered as a category and children can be considered as relevant keywords. Using this taxonomy, we can find a set of most suitable categories for a line L. Resultant categories may or may not have categories from $\mathcal{Y}$, but we can deduce categories from $\mathcal{Y}$ provided we have some knowledge about which combination of categories result in which categories from $\mathcal{Y}$.

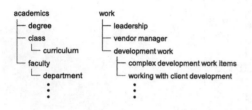

Fig. 2. Taxonomy of categories

Being a good indicator of information present in L, we can use extracted categories as features f^L for L. If given taxonomy has m categories, then there will be m binary features for every L. For all $i \in \{1, ..., m\}$, feature $f_i = 1$ if category c_i is extracted for L, otherwise $f_i = 0$. It creates a feature vector $f^L = \{f_1, f_2, ..., f_m\}$.

Classifier Training. We provide a multi-label classifier training algorithm in this section, which is used by step 5 of *CTP* phase as described in Sect. 2. As mentioned in the previous section, if we know the rules that map combinations of categories into one of the categories from $\mathcal{Y}$, we can easily assign a label from $\mathcal{Y}$ to L. Decision Tree is a good choice to learn such a set of rules from the given data. It also generates a classification tree, which can be used to classify L into one of the labels from $\mathcal{Y}$. Decision tree assigns only one label to L, while we need multiple labels. So we create a decision tree for every label in $\mathcal{Y}$. Though there are several flavors of Decision Tree available in literature, we have used its generic form for simplicity of explanations. However we have presented results for C5.0 [1], CHAID [12] and C&RT [5] in Sect. 4.

Decision Tree requires labeled data for training. So we parse several job descriptions to get a set of lines. During a ground truth collection phase, we receive a multi-label set $y^L \subseteq \mathcal{Y}$ for every line L. Thus we get pairs $\{L, y^L\}$ in training dataset $\mathcal{D}_{\text{train}}$. To train a particular classifier for $y_i \in \mathcal{Y}$, we replace y^L from every $\{L, y^L\}$ pair with a binary value b_i^L where $b_i^L = 1$ if $y_i \in y^L$, otherwise $b_i^L = 0$. This gives us pairs $\{L, b_i^L\}$ in training dataset $\mathcal{D}_{\text{train}}^i$ for label y_i.

Having all labeled data with us and features vectors for every line as described in Sect. 3.2, we build a decision tree T_i for every label y_i.

Multi-label Classification. Given a new unseen line L, we classify it using each of the decision trees built in training phase. Decision Tree T_i classifies a line L and provides label b_i^L. For example, consider a decision tree T_{edu} for y_{edu}. For any L, decision tree returns $b_{edu}^L = 1$ indicating that L describes education requirements and it returns $b_{edu}^L = 0$ when L is not about education. We combine all such labels for L from all decision trees and generate a multi-label set y^L where y^L contains a label y_i if $b_i^L = 1$. This approach can be used in step 9 of AAP phase as mentioned in Sect. 2.

3.3 Text Standardization

To address the problem of standardizing text in step 10 of AAP phase as mentioned in Sect. 2, we use ontologies like WordNet[1] and Yago[2]. For example, some recruiters may write "MS Office" and others may write "Microsoft Office". If we don't standardize words like 'MS' into 'Microsoft', it would be difficult to find similarity between two job descriptions, which is our final goal. Ontologies are useful, because they usually contain common entities and their abbreviations. WordNet can be used to find even synonyms which can replace certain keywords in a line. We also use Jaro-Winkler distance [6] on keywords to group similar keywords together. Input to this distance estimator are keywords from lines and dictionary of keywords collected through large databases from organizations. For instance, names of all skills relevant to an organization can be made available in the form of a dictionary. Each of the keywords of the lines are compared with the keywords in the dictionary using the Jaro-Winkler distance estimator to determine the closeness. If two keywords are identified as similar by the algorithm with high confidence level, the keyword in the line is replaced with the keyword from the dictionary. This ensures uniform representation of keywords across text.

3.4 Building Structured JDs Using Keywords Extraction

Once we have every line L of every job description classified as one or more labels from $\mathcal{Y}$, our next task is to extract certain keywords from L, which precisely tells about the job requirements. This set of algorithms relate to the EP phase in Sect. 2. For example, consider following line of a job description.

... **Masters in statistics** or quant-heavy social science program, **bachelor grad** must have extensive research assistant experience; experience of programming in **SPSS** or **SAS**, **C**, **C++** or **Visual BASIC** required...

This line should ideally receive labels y_{edu}, y_{skill} and y_{exp}, as it is talking about education, skills and experience requirements. After labeling, we should extract bold keywords from this line so as to organize it as follows. Observe that though the line is labeled as y_{exp}, we do not extract any keywords for experience. It is because we extract only numeric information for experience attribute,

---

[1] http://wordnet.princeton.edu.
[2] www.mpi-inf.mpg.de/yago.

for example, number of years of experience. Line given in this example doesn't contain any such information.

Education: **Masters in statistics, bachelor grad**
Skills: **SPSS, SAS, C, C++, Visual BASIC**
Experience:

We get a set of keywords S_i^L for each attribute y_i from $\mathcal{Y}$ for every line L. Eventually we take union of all sets S_i^* over all lines to get a final set of keywords S_i for attribute y_i. Such sets for all y_i together forms a structured job description. Next we describe how we can extract important keywords from a line L after it has been classified into a set of attributes y^L.

Keywords Extraction for Education. It is observed that education is usually specified in following format.

$$\texttt{<Degree>} \ \{\texttt{of,in,} \dots\} \ \texttt{<Field>}$$

For example, "Bachelor of Engineering". It is easier to get an exhaustive list of possible values of degree, while set of possible values of field/stream/department can be huge and we may not be able to create an exhaustive list. But we can utilize the correlation among keywords of education phrase. It is very clear from the above format that parts of speech of an education phrase are Noun-Preposition-Noun. We use NLP (Natural Language Processing) based part of speech (POS) tagging [3] to tag every phrase of a line, which is labeled as y_{edu}. We use OpenNLP[3] tool, which can tag every keyword from a set of 36 different POS tags. We pick all the Noun-Preposition-Noun phrases and lookup for degree related keywords in Noun phrases. For this purpose, we maintain a dictionary of keywords for degree. This dictionary is used for lookup. Once we find a degree keyword that must have been tagged as Noun in a phrase, we can tag other Noun of the phrase as field of the degree. Finally we extract all such phrases, where we can find degree and field combination.

Another possible format for education phrase can be only `<Degree>`. It is applicable for education level lower than graduation where they don't have any specialization. This case is easier to handle by having only dictionary lookup for degree.

Keywords Extraction for Experience. We extract years or months of experience required for a job position if a line is labeled as y_{exp}. To find experience phrases in a line, we can use an approach similar to what we do for extracting education phrases. Formats of experience phrases are observed to be as follows.

$$\texttt{<Number>} \ \{\texttt{years, months}\}$$
$$\texttt{<Number> - <Number>} \ \{\texttt{years, months}\}$$
$$\texttt{<Number>} \ \{\texttt{to}\} \ \texttt{<Number>} \ \{\texttt{years, months}\}$$

---

[3] http://opennlp.apache.org.

For example, "... **5 years** of experience in Java...", "... 2–3 years of experience in Databases...", etc. A number can be written either in digits or in words. So we again use NLP based POS tagging to find phrases those are tagged as numbers. If a number phrase is found along with 'year' or 'months' keywords then we extract such number as experience. This can be ambiguous sometime when a time duration is not associated with experience, for example, "... candidate should be at least **25 years** old...". To resolve such ambiguities and boost our confidence, we also look for skills or work related keywords in the vicinity of experience number. Skills and work related keywords can be found using taxonomy of categories mentioned in Sect. 3.2. If we find two numbers separated by '-' or keywords like 'to' as shown in possible formats above, we extract the average of both numbers as experience. For example, we extract keywords "2.5 years" from a line "... 2–3 years of experience in Databases".

Keywords Extraction for Skills and Roles. Skills required for a job position and roles in an organization can be very specific and recruiters use them again and again while writing job descriptions for several job positions. Hence, it is easier to maintain dictionaries of exhaustive keywords for skills and roles. If a line in a job description is labeled as y_{skill}, we lookup into skills dictionary to check if any keywords from dictionary are present in the line. We extract all such matching keywords to tag them as skills. We follow the same procedure for the lines which are labeled as y_{role}.

Responsibilities of a job position are well understood from entire line instead of few keywords. Hence we don't extract any specific keywords for responsibilities attribute. We consider entire line among responsibilities if the line is labeled as y_{resp}. We use Jaro-Winkler distance [6] based string similarity for all dictionary lookups, because it takes into consideration minor spelling mistakes and white spacing between keywords.

3.5 Enriching Dictionaries

The present dictionaries of exhaustive keywords for skills, roles and education may not be exhaustive tomorrow due to ever evolving needs of new skills, roles and education. We propose a way to keep enriching these dictionaries with new keywords by analyzing the frequent occurrences of nouns in lines labeled as one or more of y_{skill}, y_{role} and y_{edu}. As described in algorithm 1, if a noun is not in any of the dictionaries, we count its frequency in the context of different labels. For every such noun, we find a label where the noun has maximum frequency and insert it into the dictionary corresponding to that label, if maximum frequency is above certain threshold. Frequency based analysis is important, because every line can be assigned multiple labels and it can be confusing do decide which dictionary a noun should be inserted into. For simplicity and accuracy, we assume that a noun belongs to only one dictionary.

Algorithm 1. Enrich Dictionaries

Input   : Dictionaries Dict^i $\forall y_i \in \{y_{\text{skill}}, y_{\text{role}}, y_{\text{edu}}\}$, set of lines $\mathcal{L}$, label vector y^L $\forall L \in \mathcal{L}$

Output : Updated dictionaries

Counts of keywords for different labels, $C \leftarrow 0$

forall $L \in \mathcal{L}$ **do**
    $L_{\text{tagged}} \leftarrow$ Tag all keywords in L with part of speech [3]
    $N \leftarrow$ All nouns from L_{tagged}
    forall $n \in N$ **do**
        if $n \notin \text{Dict}^i$ $\forall y_i \in \{y_{skill}, y_{role}, y_{edu}\}$ **then**
            forall $y_j \in y^L$ **do**
                | $C_{n,j} \leftarrow C_{n,j} + 1$
            end
        end
    end
end
forall $C_n \neq 0$ **do**
    $i \leftarrow \text{argmax}_j C_{n,j}$
    if $C_{n,i} \geq threshold$ **then**
        | $\text{Dict}^i \leftarrow \text{Dict}^i \cup n$
    end
end

Following the keywords extraction methods for skill, roles and education, as described in Sect. 3.4, we run the process of enriching dictionaries and then again try to extract keywords. It helps in extracting those keywords, which we could not extract in previous iteration due to lack of their presence in relevant dictionaries.

3.6   Similarity of Job Descriptions

Given two job descriptions J_1 and J_2, our aim is to find how similar they are in terms of attributes y_{edu}, y_{skill}, y_{exp}, y_{role} and y_{resp}. We have provided a detailed procedure in Sects. 3.2 and 3.4 about how to arrive at a structured job description which has sets of keywords S_{edu}, S_{skill}, S_{exp}, S_{role} and S_{resp} for respective attributes. Having these keyword sets where text has been standardized using ontologies as mentioned in Sect. 3.3, we just have to find keywords based overlap between respective sets of job descriptions. $S_i^{J_k}$ represents a set of keywords for job description J_k and attribute y_i. We compute *Jaccard* similarity score between two respective sets $S_i^{J_k}$ and $S_i^{J_l}$ of job descriptions J_k and J_l to get a score $\text{sim}_i^{k,l}$ as follows. *Cosine* similarity [2] can also be used instead of *Jaccard*. For the ease of explanation we mention only *Jaccard* similarity here.

$$\mathrm{sim}_i^{k,l} = \frac{|S_i^{J_k} \bigcap S_i^{J_l}|}{|S_i^{J_k} \bigcup S_i^{J_l}|} \tag{1}$$

This is repeated for all y_i except y_{exp}, because we extract only numbers for experience attribute and not keywords. So *Jaccard* does not work for y_{exp}. Instead we propose a novel similarity measure for finding similarity based on the numeric values.

Similarity for Experience. Given two numeric values e_k and e_l of experience attributes for job descriptions J_k and J_l, dissimilarity of experience is equivalent to normalized gap between two values. As both are non-negative numbers, maximum gap is equal to $\max\{e_k, e_l\}$, which is used for normalization. Thus similarity of experience values can be formulated as follows.

$$\mathrm{sim}_{\mathrm{exp}}^{k,l} = 1 - \frac{|e_k - e_l|}{\max\{e_k, e_l\}} \tag{2}$$

We also define a weight vector $w = \{w_{\mathrm{edu}}, w_{\mathrm{skill}}, w_{\mathrm{exp}}, w_{\mathrm{role}}, w_{\mathrm{resp}}\}$ to specify importance of every attribute for all job descriptions. A weight can be any non-negative number. All similarity scores sim_i are scaled by weights w_i, added up and then normalized to get the final similarity score between two job descriptions. It can be summarized with following equation.

$$\mathrm{JobSim}(J_k, J_l) = \frac{\sum_{i \in \{\mathrm{edu,skill,exp,role,resp}\}} \left(w_i \times \mathrm{sim}_i^{k,l} \right)}{\sum_{i \in \{\mathrm{edu,skill,exp,role,resp}\}} w_i} \tag{3}$$

4   Experiments

We evaluated the performance of every phase of our system by running a set of experiments over a data set as described below. We categorize our experiments mainly into three sets. First set of experiments were conducted to assess the accuracy of classification algorithm (*CTP* and *AAP* phases). Second set of experiments were conducted to assess the accuracy of keyword extraction from labeled text for creating structured JDs (*EP* phase), and third set of experiments were conducted to assess the accuracy of similarity algorithm (*SP* phase). All of these experiments are described in following subsections.

4.1   Data Set

We collected approximately 27000 JDs from 28 organizations including IBM and its clients. Client names are not mentioned in this paper to preserve confidentiality. These JDs were picked from actual jobs posted by organizations for hiring candidates. Distribution of number of JDs picked from 28 organizations is 8000, 4000, 2500 and 500 each from remaining organizations. The organizations are in the area of Information Technology. Thus diverse set of JDs for a single domain were considered. It was observed that these JDs were highly unstructured with free flow text expressing requirements of the job. There was no explicit or consistent expression of lines as skills, experience, roles, etc. These JDs produced about 0.18 million lines which were used as data.

Approximately 5000 lines, chosen randomly, were manually tagged for collecting the ground truth. Human labelers assigned one or more of the labels $\{y_{edu}, y_{skill}, y_{exp}, y_{role}, y_{resp}\}$ to every line, depending on what a line was describing. Along with labels, human labelers also annotated the phrases that actually described the labels assigned. Total 6367 phrases were annotated. 10 people contributed in this ground truth collection activity. Every line is labeled and annotated by 2 labelers. Overall agreement on labels and annotations was 86%. We carefully resolved the conflicts while finalizing the ground truth.

4.2   Classifier Evaluation

We compare the performance of our classification algorithm as described in Sect. 3.2 with a baseline approach. Our algorithm uses decision tree classifier, that automatically generates a set of rules for assigning an attribute as a label to every line. On the contrary, baseline approach relies on a set of rules manually provided by domain experts for every attribute. Given a set of categories extracted for a line, baseline approach scans through rules for an attribute and if any rule is satisfied, that particular attribute is assigned to the line. This process is repeated for every attribute.

We conducted experiments of baseline and our algorithm over a ground truth of 5000 lines labeled manually. As rules are readily available, baseline approach doesn't require any training phase. Baseline predicted attributes for every line and later we compared them against the ground truth. Whereas a 5 fold cross validation was used to report precision and recall for our algorithm.

While comparing with baseline, we computed three different set of results for our classification algorithm by selecting a different decision tree algorithm every time. Namely we used C5.0 [1], CHAID [12] and C&RT [5] decision tree algorithms.

As this is multi-label classification problem, we report F1 score for every attribute as shown in Fig. 3. It is clear that F1 score of our algorithm beats baseline F1 score or at least at par with baseline F1 score in all three settings for all attributes except for experience. Improvement ranges from 0 for skills using C&RT to 0.23 for roles using CHAID. For experience, drop in F1 score ranges from 0.04 using CHAID to 0.15 using CR&T. Thus, our algorithm works better than baseline in most of the cases. In remaining cases, our algorithm is not far behind the baseline in terms of F1 score. Additionally, our algorithm can be used with larger data sets. Manual rules in baseline approach may not be exhaustive in case of larger data sets.

Comparing among three different settings for our algorithm, we can infer from above analysis that CHAID is the best suited for our algorithm and C&RT is the worst among three.

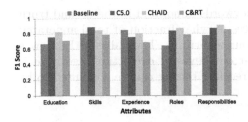

Fig. 3. F1 score based comparison

We plot ROC curves for decision tree classifiers for every attribute with CHAID technique. Classification scores obtained for every attribute and for every line are used for this purpose. These ROC curves are shown in Fig. 4. It is observed that area under ROC curve (AU-ROC) is high for all attributes, that establishes the quality of our algorithm for classification.

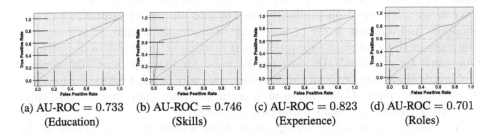

(a) AU-ROC = 0.733   (b) AU-ROC = 0.746   (c) AU-ROC = 0.823   (d) AU-ROC = 0.701
   (Education)   (Skills)   (Experience)   (Roles)

Fig. 4. ROC curve along with AU-ROC value of a classifier for every attribute

4.3 Keyword Extractor Evaluation

We used 5000 lines from ground truth having attributes assigned to them. For each of these lines, we extracted keywords based on the attributes of lines. We compare the extracted keywords for every line with the annotated keywords for that line in the ground truth. We adopt the standard definition of precision to find the precision of our keyword extraction algorithm in terms of following formula.

$$\text{Precision} = \frac{\sum_{L \in \{\text{all lines}\}} \sum_{i \in \{\text{edu,skill,exp,role,resp}\}} N_{\text{anno, ext}}^{i,L}}{\sum_{L \in \{\text{all lines}\}} \sum_{i \in \{\text{edu,skill,exp,role,resp}\}} N_{\text{ext}}^{i,L}} \quad (4)$$

where $N_{\text{anno, ext}}^{i,L}$ is the total number of keywords those were annotated in the ground truth as well as extracted by our algorithm for a line L and for attribute i. $N_{\text{ext}}^{i,L}$ is the total number of keywords extracted by our algorithm for a line L and for attribute i. We calculated the value of above formula to find what fraction of total extracted keywords were actually describing the attributes of the lines. The value of Eq. 4 was computed to be as high as 0.954.

We also adopt the standard definition of recall to find the recall of our keyword extraction algorithm as follows.

$$\text{Recall} = \frac{\sum_{L \in \{\text{all lines}\}} \sum_{i \in \{\text{edu,skill,exp,role,resp}\}} N_{\text{anno, ext}}^{i,L}}{\sum_{L \in \{\text{all lines}\}} \sum_{i \in \{\text{edu,skill,exp,role,resp}\}} N_{\text{anno}}^{i,L}} \quad (5)$$

where $N_{anno}^{i,L}$ is the total number of keywords annotated in the ground truth for a line L and for attribute i. This gives us what fraction of total annotated keywords were actually recognized by our algorithm. The value of Eq. 5 was computed to be 0.842. This implies that our keyword extraction algorithm is highly effective with high precision and recall. F1 score can be computed to be 0.896.

4.4 Similarity Algorithm Evaluation

Similarity algorithm provides a score between 0 to 1 for a pair of JDs. Similarity is high, if the score high. One way to evaluate similarity algorithm is to find similarity scores of a JD with every other JD from our data set of 27000 JDs. We can set a threshold on similarity score to find all pair of similar JDs. Then manually find out how many of those pair are actually similar. There are two problems in this evaluation approach. First, setting a threshold value is tricky. One value for a pair of JDs may not be valid for other pair of JDs. Second problem is that inspecting all similar pairs manually is not feasible for possible 27000×27000 pairs. Collecting ground truth for those many pairs is also time consuming and need a lot many human resources.

We decided to go with ranking approach to address these two problems in evaluation. We randomly selected 50 JDs out of a data set of 27000 JDs. For every JD in this set of 50 JDs, we computed similarity scores with every other JD in 27000 set. For a selected JD, we ranked all JDs in decreasing of their similarity scores. We picked top 10 and manually observed how many of them were actually similar. We repeated this for each of the 50 selected JDs. Thus ground truth collection efforts was brought down to 50×10 from previous value 27000×27000. Setting a threshold value is also not required for this evaluation. Just that instead of computing precision and recall, we computed area under ROC curve (AU-ROC) in this setting for each of these 50 ranked lists with 10 JDs each.

We observed that minimum AU-ROC was 0.642, maximum AU-ROC was 0.9 and mean AU-ROC was 0.779. This highlights the effectiveness of similarity algorithm in ranking similar JDs at the top. Ranked list certainly does not provide exact list of similar job descriptions, but it provides an ordered list of JDs, which user can follow to find similar job descriptions. It reduces tremendous efforts of user of scanning all JDs in random order. Based on the application, a threshold value for similarity scores can as well be used or top k JDs can be picked. It will further reduces the screening efforts of user.

We also report precision of similarity algorithm for the sake of completeness, by setting up following experiment. Given above mentioned 50 ranked lists, we set a high threshold of 0.7 for two JDs to be similar. It gave us a set of pairs of JDs, that we predicted as similar. It shortlisted on an average top 15 JDs from every ranked list which increases manual labeling effort from 50×10 to 50×15 pairs. Based on manual labeling, we observed that 88% of predicted similar JDs were truly similar. This sets a high precision value for our similarity algorithm.

5 Related Work

Importance of entity and identity resolution have been established earlier in several research works [4,13,17]. Our work is along the lines of recent approaches which are variants of Fellegi-Sunter Model [8]. In [8] identity resolution is solved as a classification problem - given a set of similarity scores for different attributes of two candidates, classify it as a match or a non-match. Several bodies of research work have advised, compared and learned similarity measures for use in entity resolution (example, [7,18]). Typically in such work, matching is performed individually on each of the attributes and then a transitive closure is used to eliminate inconsistencies. In our work, we establish these attributes through MSNRPCA [20], a hybrid approach for feature reduction based on the combination of feature ranking with PCA, and utilize the similarity to resolve identity. We train classification models for attributes using well established decision tree algorithms such as C5.0 [1], CHAID [12] and C&RT [5].

Entity resolution has been solved in several domains by various research works (example, [15,16]) and to different types of data, including text (example, [14]) and images (example, [11]). RISE targets resolution of entities in the domain of Job Descriptions in a recruiting system. We have highlighted the importance of the problem earlier and the goals of our work have been motivated by real world requirements of recruiting systems. There has been a pressing demand for identity resolution systems where identifying right candidates through one channel for specific organization can be routed to other job descriptions if not found suitable. Furthermore, there has been demands for creation of context sensitive job descriptions based on the existing job descriptions that had the best convergence. For all these purposes, one requires that similarities are established and identities are resolved. A big distinguishing factor is that our data source have been cross organizational. Thus we expect the identities of these job descriptions to be completely different from one organization to another. The problem is more challenging also due to the nature of the attributes. For instance, the numeric values for *experience* attribute requires different measures for obtaining similarity.

A group of researchers have focused on large databases and resolving identities in them. Methods were provided to avoid the quadratic number of comparisons between all pairs of entities (example, [10]). Such methods can be leveraged to reduce number of comparisons while finding similarities between every pair of JDs.

6 Conclusion and Future Work

We have built a system called **RISE** that addresses one of the key issues of identity resolution among job descriptions in recruitment systems. Recruitment systems typically employ technologies that allow centralized storage of data across different organizations. Although, centralized yet underlying unstructured data and lack of resolution techniques have rendered the data less usable for several valuable applications. RISEprovides an end-to-end system for establishing equivalence among identities and resolving them with high precision and recall.

Our future work includes enabling several key capabilities on top of this system such as automated creation of job description based on the context, routing of profiles across different jobs etc.

References

1. C5.0 Decision Tree Algorithm. http://www.rulequest.com/see5-info.html
2. Cosine Similarity Algorithm. http://en.wikipedia.org/wiki/Cosine_similarity
3. Stanford Log-linear Part-Of-Speech Tagger. http://nlp.stanford.edu/software/tagger.shtml
4. Benjelloun, O., Garcia-Molina, H., Menestrina, D., Su, Q., Whang, S.E., Widom, J.: Swoosh: a generic approach to entity resolution. VLDB J. **18**, 255–276 (2009)
5. Breiman, L., Friedman, J.H., Olshen, R.A., Stone, C.J.: Classification and Regression Trees. Statistics/Probability Series. Wadsworth Publishing Company, Belmont (1984)
6. Cohen, W.W., Ravikumar, P., Fienberg, S.E.: A comparison of string distance metrics for name-matching tasks. In: IJCAI 2003 Workshop on Information Integration, pp. 73–78 (2003)
7. Cohen, W.W., Ravikumar, P., Fienberg, S.E.: A comparison of string metrics for matching names and records. In: Proceedings of the KDD 2003 Workshop on Data, pp. 13–18 (2003)
8. Fellegi, I.P., Sunter, A.B.: A theory for record linkage. J. Am. Stat. Assoc. **64**(328), 1183–1210 (1969)
9. Frank, E., Bouckaert, R.R.: Naive Bayes for text classification with unbalanced classes. In: Fürnkranz, J., Scheffer, T., Spiliopoulou, M. (eds.) PKDD 2006. LNCS (LNAI), vol. 4213, pp. 503–510. Springer, Heidelberg (2006). doi:10.1007/11871637_49
10. Hernández, M.A., Stolfo, S.J.: The merge/purge problem for large databases. SIGMOD Rec. **24**(2), 127–138 (1995). http://doi.acm.org/10.1145/568271.223807
11. Huang, T., Russell, S.: Object identification: a Bayesian analysis with application to traffic surveillance. Artif. Intell. **103**(1–2), 77–93 (1998)
12. Kass, G.V.: An exploratory technique for investigating large quantities of categorical data. J. R. Stat. Soc. Ser. C **29**(2), 119–127 (1980)
13. Li, J., Wang, G.A., Chen, H.: Identity matching using personal and social identity features. Inf. Syst. Front. **13**(1), 101–113 (2011)
14. Li, X., Morie, P., Roth, D.: Semantic integration in text: from ambiguous names to identifiable entities. AI Mag. **26**(1), 45–58 (2005)
15. Norén, G.N., Orre, R., Bate, A.: A hit-miss model for duplicate detection in the who drug safety database. In: KDD 2005, pp. 459–468 (2005)
16. Ong, I.M., Page, D., Dutra, I., Costa, V.S.: Hyperpaths: extending pathfinding to moded languages. In: Proceedings of MRDM 2005, p. 57. ACM (2005)
17. Singla, P., Domingos, P.: Entity resolution with Markov logic. In: Proceedings of ICDM 2006, pp. 572–582. IEEE Computer Society (2006)
18. Tejada, S., Knoblock, C.A., Minton, S.: Learning domain-independent string transformation weights for high accuracy object identification. In: Proceedings of KDD 2002, pp. 350–359 (2002)
19. Tsoumakas, G., Katakis, I.: Multi label classification: an overview. Int. J. Data Warehouse Min. **3**(3), 1–13 (2007)
20. Yang, M.J., Zheng, H.R., Wang, H.Y., McClean, S., Harris, N.: Combining feature ranking with PCA: an application to gait analysis. In: ICMLC 2010, vol. 1, pp. 494–499 (2010)

Social-Sensor Cloud Service for Scene Reconstruction

Tooba Aamir[1]([✉]), Athman Bouguettaya[2], Hai Dong[1], Sajib Mistry[2], and Abdelkarim Erradi[3]

[1] School of Science, RMIT University, Melbourne, Australia
{tooba.aamir,hai.dong}@rmit.edu.au
[2] School of Information Technologies, The University of Sydney, Sydney, Australia
{athman.bouguettaya,sajib.mistry}@sydney.edu.au
[3] College of Engineering, Qatar University, Doha, Qatar
erradi@qu.edu.qa

Abstract. We propose a new social-sensor cloud services selection framework for scene reconstruction. The proposed research represents social media data streams, i.e., images' metadata and related posted information, as social sensor cloud services. The functional and non-functional aspects of social sensor cloud services are abstracted from images' metadata and related posted information. The proposed framework is a 4-stage algorithm, to select social-sensor cloud services based on the user queries. The selection algorithm is based on spatio-temporal indexing, spatio-temporal and textual correlations, and quality of services. Analytical results are presented to prove the efficiency of the proposed approach in comparison to a traditional approach of image processing.

1 Introduction

The user-base of multiple social networks is getting wider and more active in producing content about real world events almost in real time [1]. *Social sensors*, i.e., users contributing their individual 'data' [3], publish a large amount of data streams (images, videos and texts) over the social networks (also called social clouds [2]). Social-sensor data streams related to public events, especially multimedia content, may contain critical information that describes a situation from various aspects, e.g., what is happening, where it is happening, who are involved and what the effects on surrounding are. Monitoring the events or scenarios over social-sensor data streams assists concerned officials to analyse an unfolding situation, such as in crisis management, urban management and scene analysis. Hence, utilising these social-sensor data streams can significantly facilitate the task of scene reconstruction and aid in comprehending evolving situations [3].

Scene reconstruction is generating a 3D model of a scene given multiple 2D photographs of the scene [19]. The extensive availability of social sensors (e.g. twitter feeds) helps in gathering indirect pictorial view of the event. Various studies focus on visual and spatio-temporal scene reconstruction in social media [3,5].

M. Maximilien et al. (Eds.): ICSOC 2017, LNCS 10601, pp. 37–52, 2017.
https://doi.org/10.1007/978-3-319-69035-3_3

One of the major challenges in current scene reconstruction process is the efficient and real time delivery of sensors' (e.g., cctv, accelerometer, etc.) data to the end users, e.g., urban management, that meet their requirements (time, location, content relatedness, quality, price, coverage, etc.) [5]. Most of current work focuses on utilising image processing. However, the traditional approach of image processing relies on performance of hardware and software which is both costly and time consuming [20]. To overcome this challenge, this research *employs the theory of Service Oriented Architecture (SOA) instead of image processing, by defining a social sensor cloud service model based on metadata of social media images and related posted information.*

Social-sensor data streams are generated from multiple sources and in multiple formats. SOA abstracts social-sensor data streams into small independent function(s), namely services. This results in uniform and ubiquitous delivery of social-sensor data as a service, making it easy to access and reuse in multiple applications over different platforms. This reduces the complexity of social-sensor data collection. The functionality of social-sensor data (e.g., spatio-temporal, textual and context information of an image) is abstracted as a service and the qualitative features (e.g., price, coverage) are abstracted as non-functional properties of the service. Access to social sensor data streams and implementation for scene reconstruction will be simplified based on the service model. Other benefits include higher availability, better scalability, dynamic deployment and greater testability.

Usually a single service may not satisfy users' requirements. The challenge is to design an efficient method for selecting the social-sensor cloud services that are in the same information context, i.e., covering same event or segment of an area at any given time required by the user and also meet user's quality demand. Most of the existing techniques developed for standard Web service discovery cannot be directly applicable to sensor services [4]. Due to the large number of images over the Web and its time-location dependency, sensor services need to be organised in a way to allow efficient search based on their spatio-temporal properties, e.g., time or location.

This paper focuses on proposing a novel *social-sensor cloud service model* and *a social-sensor service selection algorithm for collecting images for scene reconstruction based on spatio-temporal, textual and QoS parameters of the service.* To the best of our knowledge, existing approaches to use social media data are mainly data centric. Current approaches are built upon data mining and information retrieval techniques without concerning qualitative aspects of images. The proposed approach conceptualize the spatio-temporal and textual aspects of social-sensor data streams as *social-sensor cloud services'* functional attributes, and the qualitative aspects as their non-functional attributes. The proposed framework is a 4-stage algorithm capable of context-aware selection of social-sensor cloud services by using their functional and non-functional properties. Functional properties includes spatio-temporal parameters, spatio-textual context, etc., and non-functional requirements includes image quality, price, resolution, etc. The 4-stages of algorithm are (1) service indexing, (2) selection w.r.t spatio-temporal features, (3) filtering w.r.t textual-correlation and (4) coverage assessment and QoS-aware selection.

The novelty of this research lies on (1) abstracting social media image metadata and related posted data, i.e., social-sensor data streams, as *social-sensor cloud services*, (2) supporting efficient and real time access to high-quality and related images for scene reconstruction without image processing. The rest of the paper is structured as follows: Sect. 2 reviews the related background work. Section 3 describes the motivating scenario. Section 4 formally defines the model for a social-sensor cloud service along with functional and quality attributes. Section 5 details the proposed selection approach. Section 6 describes the experiments and evaluation of the approach. Section 7 concludes the work.

2   Related Work

Our social-sensor cloud service selection approach draws background work from two main areas: sensing-as-a-service and service selection [1–9].

Social Sensing and Sensing-as-a-Service. is a large-scale sensing paradigm based on the power of IoT devices, including smart phones, smart vehicles and wearable devices, etc. [3,5]. This allows the increasing number of mobile phone users to share local knowledge (e.g., local information, event coverage, and traffic conditions) acquired by their sensor-enhanced devices and the information can be further aggregated in the cloud for large-scale sensing [10]. A broad range of applications are thus enabled, including traffic planning [3], environment monitoring [13], mobile social recommendation [17], public safety [18], and so on. Spatio-temporal social media analysis for abnormal event detection is discussed in [6]. Another research proposes an approach towards multi-scale event detection using social media data, which takes into account different temporal and spatial scales of events in the data [7]. However, most of these approaches are data centric, built upon data mining and analysis techniques. This require considerable amount of expertise and time. Moreover, transition from a traditional cloud systems to the SOA-based sensor-cloud raises the need to consider spatio-temporal aspects of sensor data with better performance and faster access to new services. Thus, using SOA and social sensors for scene analysis is far better than using image processing over the batch of images or traditional cloud computing to build the scene.

Service Selection. is one of the major research problems in service-oriented computing [4,9,11,12]. The service selection and composition have been applied in a number of domains including scene analysis and visual surveillance [12]. The service composition problem can be categorized into two areas. The first area focuses on the functional composability among component services. The second area aims to do optimal service composition based on non-functional properties (QoS). In [11], service composition from media service perspective has been discussed. [4] and [9] propose a composition approach for Sensor-Cloud and crowd sourced services based on dynamic features such as spatio-temporal aspects.

Algorithms are presented in both papers to support the proposed approaches. Analytical and simulation results of the proposed approaches are presented to validate their feasibility. However, social-sensor cloud service selection using functional/non-functional attributes through social-sensor is yet to be explored.

3   Motivating Scenario

A typical scenario of scene reconstruction for car accidents is used to illustrate the challenges in scene analysis. Given a segment A on the road, suppose an accident happens at time t_0, as shown in Fig. 1a, b and c, depicts the scenario before the accident happens. The fan shapes are 2D representation of the *social-sensor cloud services'* coverage.

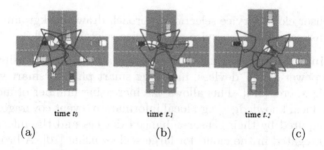

        time t_0 time t_{-1} time t_{-2}

        (a)   (b)   (c)

Fig. 1. Accident timeline

It is assumed that scene reconstruction of the accident is required by urban management to determine the cause(s) or aftermath(s) of the accident to prevent further incidents of a similar kind. The wide deployment and availability of smart-phones users and their connectivity with social networks and services, i.e., the commuters using social media/networks, might provide extra visual coverage by either sharing images or posts. For instance, in the South Melbourne Bus Accident[1], multiple posts with hundreds of images on this event were reported on various social networks. In such cases, the commuters can be regarded as social sensors sharing their image data over *social sensor clouds*, i.e., social networks. Using social media images' metadata and related posted data as services, i.e., *social-sensor cloud services*, can help to fulfil the user's need of maximum coverage. The idea is to leverage freely available information over social network clouds to help investigators to analyse the accidents scene.

The aim is to develop a new framework for social-sensor cloud services selection. The algorithm will be based on spatio-temporal information, textual features, spatio-textual correlation and quality of service parameters. As

---

[1] Bus Crash in South Melbourne - http://www.theage.com.au/victoria/bus-crashes-in-south-melbourne-trapping-commuters-20160221-gmzyko.html.

shown in Fig. 4, the proposed solution would be a multi-stage selection algorithm, to select social-sensor cloud services based on a user's query. Let us assume that the user's query q is defined as (R, d, t_s, t_e, Q_U). R is represented as a tuple $(P < x, y >, l, w)$ that indicates the region of interest, where $P < x, y >$ is a geospatial co-ordinate set, i.e., decimal longitude-latitude position (e.g., -37.8089435,144.9651172) and l (e.g., 5 m) and w (e.g., 2m) are length and width distances from P to the edge of region of interest. t_s (e.g., 2:29:23 pm AEST, Wednesday, 14 June 2017) and t_e (e.g., 2:59:23 pm AEST, Wednesday, 14 June 2017) give start and end time of scene. d is a phrase describing the event (e.g., 'Melbourne Central, Accident'). Q_U is a set of non-functional attributes (e.g., P, i.e., price of the service is not more than \$0.5). Therefore, given the services, the proposed framework will select the services that, in the given time frame, are spatially located in the user defined region and textually related to the user's description, and meet the user's QoS requirements.

The functional attributes of a social-sensor cloud service $Serv$ include:

- Time T of the service at which the image is taken
- Set of special mentions and keywords M providing additional information regarding an image or a service
- Service location $L(x, y)$, i.e., longitude and latitude position of the service

The non-functional attributes of a social-sensor cloud service $Serv$ include:

- Textual correlation $TxtCo$, the textual similarity between the tags/keywords, i.e., $Serv.M$, of an atomic service $Serv$ and the query q's description $q.d$.
- Coverage Cov of the total area covered in the user required region R

First, for any location of the query q, all indexed services available in the area of interest defined by the region R, across time t_s to t_e are selected. However, the region R is expanded if the selection does not meet query demands. It is assumed that the R encloses S, a set of services, relevant to query q. Textual correlation is considered next, i.e., similarity between d and M, between the query and services in the region R. For example for every special mention M (e.g., Melbourne Central station) of the service $Serv$ and description d (e.g., Melbourne center) of the query q, their textual correlation $relation_t$ is calculated as the similarity ratio between a service $Serv_i$ and a query q. The similarity is measured between 0.0 (the lowest) and 1.0 (the highest) and denoted as θ. This gives a subset of services that are spatio-temporally and textually correlated to the query. Next, the coverage of all selected services is assessed. The best available services are selected that are both spatially located in the user defined region and textually related to the user's description. The selection is finalized until all selected services achieve the maximum coverage. The selected services can assist in reconstruction for the required scene.

4   Model for Social Sensor Cloud Service

In this section, we define several concepts to locate a social-sensor cloud service. The aim is to locate and select the social-sensor cloud services which are in the same spatial and visual context based on the functional properties of the service. The selected services can assist in building a *visual summary* of a required *scene* in given space and time.

4.1 Model for an Atomic Social Sensor Cloud Service

Here we discuss the key concepts to model an atomic social-sensor cloud. We define the model of a crowd-sourced social sensor cloud service, in terms of spatio-temporal features of crowd-sourced social sensor.

Definition 1: Scene S is defined as an observation on a real world happening. This observation is a collection of connected images in same spatial and temporal dimension.

Definition 2: Visual summary *VisSum* is defined by a set of 2D images that are highly relevant to the scene S. *VisSum* gives viewer an accurate impression of what a particular scene S looks like. Any two images are considered highly relevant if at least one feature of the images is common.

Next we define the model of social-sensor cloud service, in terms of spatio-temporal features of social-sensor.

Definition 3: Crowd-sourced Social Sensor *SocSen* is the user of a social media. A sensor posts content on social media, i.e., Social Sensor Cloud. It is assumed that the data shared by a social sensor contains visual information, textual reference, time and location.

Definition 4: Social Sensor Cloud *SocSenCl* is a social media hosting data from the social sensors. It is defined by

- Social Sensor Cloud ID *SocSenCl_id*, i.e., a unique sensor id
- Sensor Set *SenSet* = {SocSen_id$_i$, $1 \leq i \leq m$} represents a finite set of sensors *SocSen* that collect and host sensor data in the respective cloud. It is assumed that each cloud hosts data from at least one sensor.

Definition 5: Atomic Social Sensor-Cloud service *Serv* is defined by

- *Serv_id* is a unique service id of the service provider *SocSen*.
- *SocSenCl_id* is an ID of the cloud where the service is available.
- F is a set of functional properties of the service *Serv*. For each *Serv*, $F = \{T, M, L, dir, VisD, \alpha\}$.
- nF is a set of non-functional properties of the service *Serv*. For each *Serv*, $nF = \{TxtCo\}$.

4.2 Functional Model of an Atomic Social Sensor Cloud Service

Functional requirements capture the intended behaviour of the service and forms the baseline functionality necessary from an *Atomic Service*. The following propose the minimal functional requirements associated with an atomic service:

- T is time of the service at which the image is taken
- M is special mentions and keywords, providing additional information regarding image.
- $L \langle x,y \rangle$ is the service location where $\langle x,y \rangle$ is longitude and latitude position of the service
- $VisD$ is the visible distance i.e., the maximum distance, covered by the service.
- dir is the orientation angle of the service.
- α is the angular extent of the *scene* covered by the service.

Thus, the functional model of each service is represented by the service coverage model $Serv_c$, as shown in Fig. 2.

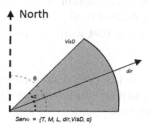

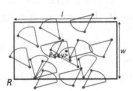

Fig. 2. $Serv_c$ model   **Fig. 3.** Query region and coverage model $q.R$

4.3 Quality Model of an Atomic Social Sensor Cloud Service

Discovering and selecting the *best available* services satisfying the user's requirements is an important challenge. The first step is to define a QoS model, i.e., a set of QoS aggregation rules. However, the user's QoS demands can be different from the system's QoS matrix for optimal and effective selection. For this purpose the QoS model for both User and Social Sensor Cloud services are introduced. The proposed system-defined QoS criteria of an atomic services include:

- Q_{serv} is a tuple $\langle Q_1, Q_2... Q_n \rangle$, where each Q_i denotes a *Quality of service (QoS)* of *Serv*. The QoS criteria include:
  - *TxtCo* is the textual similarity between the tags/keywords, i.e., *Serv.M*, of an atomic service *Serv* and the query q's description $q.d$. WordNet-based approach LIN [15] is used to calculate the textual similarity between textual description $q.d$ and *Serv.M* of the service *Serv*. It measures semantic relatedness of concepts based on the ratio of the amount of information needed to state the commonality of the information content of the d, i.e., $IC(q.d)$, along with the information content of *Serv*, i.e., $IC(Serv.M)$, to the amount of information needed to describe them. The measure is determined by [15]:

$$related_{LIN}(q.d, Serv.M) = \frac{2IC(lcs(q.d, Serv.M))}{IC(q.d) + IC(Serv.M)} \tag{1}$$

where, $IC(description) = -log(Probability(description))$, and, $lcs(q.d, Serv.M)$, i.e., *least common subsumer* is the quantity of information common to two descriptions. It is determined by the information content of the lowest concept in the hierarchy that subsumes both $q.d$ and $Serv.M$ [15].

- *Cov* is the total area of patches covered in the user required region R (Fig. 3). Coverage can be illustrated by:

$$Cov \longleftarrow \{\sum_{i=1}^{n} Serv_i \in S' \mid \sum_{i=1}^{n} Serv_i < \cdot R, t_0 \leq t \leq t_1\} \qquad (2)$$

where, $Serv_i < \cdot \ R$ means $Serv_i$ covers some of the region R. S' is the set of services spatio-temporally and textually related to the query. Since it is uncertain that the user desired time gives the best available results, we limit the temporal range between t_0 and t_1.

Moreover, for the effective and efficient selection as per user demands, user defined QoS parameters are also required. For this purpose some baseline QoS attributes for Social Sensor Cloud services are introduced:

- Q_U is a tuple $\langle$ Q_{U1}, Q_{U2}... Q_{Un} $\rangle$, where each Q_{Ui} denotes a *Quality of service (QoS)* requirement of user. The QoS criteria include:
  - *P* is the price of the service, i.e., does the service need any sort of financial incentive for service providers or not.
  - *Res* is the minimum requirement of image resolution to be provided by services.
  - *ColQ* is images' definition, i.e., grey scale or high definition.

5   QoS-Aware Social Sensor Cloud Service Indexing and Selecting Approach

We propose a framework to index, filter and select the best available Social Sensor Cloud Service according to a user's query. The query q can be defined as $q = (R, d, t_s, t_e Q_U)$, giving the region of interest, description and quality parameters of the required service(s). The entry:

- $R = \{P < x, y >, l, w\}$ (Fig. 3), where P is a geospatial co-ordinate set, i.e., decimal longitude-latitude position and l and w are length and width distance from P to the edge of region of interest.
- t_s is the start time of the query
- t_e is the end time of query.
- d is a phrase describing the query e.g., Melbourne Central.
- Q_U is a set of non-functional attributes, e.g., Coverage, Resolution, Pricing etc.

Figure 4 shows the proposed selection framework for social-sensor cloud services. The aim of our approach is to efficiently locate the available services that match with the users' requirements by constructing and indexing the information and location context of the service with the functional and non-functional properties. To manage and enable fast discovery of the social sensor cloud services:

- First we index all the available services. Considering the spatio-temporal nature of the services, we index both location and time of service using R-tree.
- Then the search space is reduced by selecting a set of all the spatio-temporally close services S from the BR. BR is the user-defined region of interest defined in a spatio-temporal cube.
- Further, we calculate $txtCo$ of each service in S with $q.d$. Considering $txtCo$, we select set S' of services textually related to the query.
- Next, we assess the coverage, i.e., $Serv_C$ of all the services in S' and compute the spatial coverage of region.
- Finally, Q_U is used to select the best available service(s).

If the desired coverage is not achieved the search space BR is increased dynamically until the maximum coverage and QoS parameters are achieved. The system defined QoS attributes are determined in two ways:

- Before selection, the values are given based on previous executions of services or user's feedback.
- During selection, the values are given by monitoring services and query QoS attributes and dynamically evaluating the attributes.

The implementation process of the selection approach is:

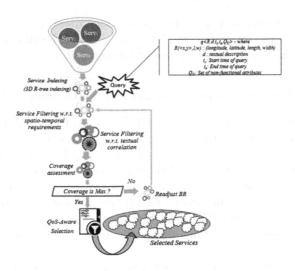

Fig. 4. Social-sensor cloud service selection framework

5.1   Service Indexing and Spatio-Temporal Filtering

Indexing and spatio-temporal filtering of services enable the fast discovery of services (Algorithm 1). We index services considering their spatio-temporal features using a 3D R-tree [4]. 3D R-tree [21] is a tree data structure which is used as a spatio-temporal index to handle time and location based queries. Time is considered as the third dimension in the 3D-R Tree. The leaf nodes of the 3D R-tree represent services which are organized using minimum bounded region (MBR) [21] that encloses the service spatio-temporal region. It is assumed that all available services are associated to a two-dimensional geo-tagged location and time. For the effective area of query q, we define a cube shape region BR using user-defined rectangular event area R and start and end time of the service, i.e., t_s and t_e. Region BR encloses a set of services relevant to q. The services outside this region are assumed to have little probability of being relevant to the query. Figure 5 illustrates the query region R and the bounded region BR across time t_s to t_e.

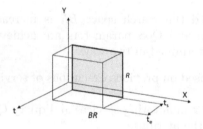   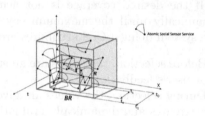

Fig. 5. Illustration of $q.R$ and BR **Fig. 6.** Illustration of coverage

The 3D R-tree efficiently answers typical range queries, e.g., "select all services bounded by the rectangle R in time t_s to t_e". This results in filtering of all the services outside the bounded region of interest BR.

5.2   Textual Co-relation Between Service and Query

To improve the efficiency of the proposed approach, the textual correlation is considered. It might happen that the service does lie spatially in the query area *Region*, but has no textual relation with the query q. In such cases the textual correlation in terms of spatio-textual similarity is used for service filtration.

Equation (1) measures the relatedness of the two descriptions. The relatedness score is between 0.0 (the lowest) to 1.0 (the highest). For implementation a Java based library, WS4J (WordNet Similarity for Java) is used. The use of this library is defined in an on-line documentation[2]. We have used θ' to define

---

[2] "JWNL - JavaWordNet Library - Dev Guide", http://jwordnet.sourceforge.net/handbook.html.

Algorithm 1. Service indexing and spatio-temporal filtering

Input: S is the collection of services - each service is associated with its geo-tagged location $< x, y >$; a query q with location $l < x, y >$; a query region's length l and width w, start and end time of service, i.e., t_s and t_e.

Output: The set S' of all services which lie in region BR

1: BR = Cube Region based on $R = \{P < x, y >, l, w\}$, t_s and t_e
2: **for** Each i **do**
3:      **Insert** $Serv_i$ in 3D R-Tree
4:      **for** Each indexed $Serv$ in S **do**
5:          **if** $Serv \cap BR$ **then**
6:              $Serv \in S'$

Algorithm 2. Textual Correlation Filtering

Input: S' is the collection of services - each service is associated with its geo-tagged location $< x, y >$ and mention M; a query q with location $l < x, y >$ and textual description d; a query region's length l and width w, start and end time of the service, i.e., t_s and t_e; textual similarity threshold θ

Output: The set of all spatio-textually correlated services S'' which lie in the region BR such that d is similar to M

1: **for** Each $Serv$ in S' **do**
2:      Calculate θ' between $Serv.M$ and $q.d$ using **LIN**
3:      **if** $\theta' \geq \theta$ **then**
4:          $Serv \in S''$

$related_{lin}(q.d, Serv.M)$. The higher value of θ' shows higher textual correlation. On the basis of $TxtCo$, the set of services S' is selected. Algorithm 2 shows the textual correlation filtering.

5.3 Coverage Assessment Using Serv$_C$

Serv$_C$ is a 2D representation of the service coverage, illustrated as the grey region in Fig. 3. If the user requires the coverage of R between time t_s to t_e, all the $Serv$ in S' overlapping the bounded region BR are selected. The relationship between Serv$_C$ and R can be illustrated as:

$$Coverage \longleftarrow \{Serv_i \in S' \mid Serv_i \cap BR, t_0 \leq t \leq t_1\}$$

Thus all the services with Serv$_C$ which overlap with the region BR are selected (Algorithm 3). Since it is uncertain that the user desired time gives the best available results, we limit the temporal range between t_0 and t_1. Pictorial illustration of coverage is shown in Fig. 6.

Coverage can be calculated by:

$$Cov = \int_{t=s}^{e} AREA(R)dt - (\int_{t=s}^{e} Area(\cup_{i=1}^{n} Serv_i)dt - \int_{t=s}^{e} Area(\cap_{i=1}^{n} Serv_i)dt)\}$$
(3)

Algorithm 3. Coverage Computation and re-adjusting R

Input: S' is the collection of services - each service is associated with its geo-tagged location $< x, y >$; a query q with location $l < x, y >$; a query region's length l and width w, start and end time of service, i.e., t_s and t_e

Output: The set of all spatio-textually correlated services S'' which lie in the region BR and meet the coverage requirements

1: **for** Each *Serv* in S' **do**
2:     Calculate *Cov* using Eq. (3)
3:     **if** $CoV = max$ **then**
4:         $EXIT$
5:     else$R \longleftarrow R'(P < x, y >, l + 7, w + 7)$

where:

$$AREA(R) = l * w \qquad (4)$$

$$Area(\cup_{i=1}^{n} Serv_i) = \sum_{i=1}^{n} (\cup_{i=1}^{n} (0.5 * Serv_i.VisD * Serv_i.\alpha) \qquad (5)$$

$$Area(\cap_{i=1}^{n} Serv_i)) = \sum_{i=1}^{n} (\cap_{i=1}^{n} (0.5)(Serv_i.VisD)((Serv_i.\alpha)) \qquad (6)$$

If selection does not meet the maximum achievable coverage, i.e., *Cov* is not met, the R is adjusted and increased to R'. Further, spatio-temporal selection and filtering w.r.t textual correlation is repeated until the maximum coverage is achieved. R' is achieved by increasing the length l and width w of the region R. The minimum unit of increase is 7 m, i.e., average lease measurable increment in decimal latitude and longitude values. If required l and w are further incremented in multiples of 7 m.

5.4 QoS-Aware Service Selection

In the final stage of service selection (Algorithm 4), the user defined quality parameters are considered in selection of the best suited services. The threshold values of these parameters are adjusted by the user of the service at time of query generation.

6 Experiments and Results

A set of experiments is conducted to evaluate, analyse and investigate the contribution of our proposed framework in comparison to image processing.

Algorithm 4. QoS-Aware Service Selection

Input: Q_U, i.e., quality requirements of the user and S' is the set of filtered services related to query
Output: The set of selected services $SelServ$, related to query.

1: **for** Each $Serv$ in S' **do**   ▷ System defined QoS
2:      **for** Each Q_i in Q_{Serv} **do**
3:          **if** $Serv.Q \geq Q_i$ **then**   ▷ TxtCo and CovR are separately
4:              $Serv \in S''$ ▷ compared. If all true then condition satisfies
5: **for** Each $Serv$ in S'' **do**   ▷ User defined QoS
6:      **for** Each Q_i in Q_i **do**
7:          **if** $Serv.Q \geq Q_i$ **then**   ▷ Res, ColQ are separately
8:              $Serv \in SelServ$ ▷ compared. If all true then condition satisfies

---

6.1 Experimental Setup

To the best of our knowledge, there is no real spatio-temporal service test case to evaluate our approach. Therefore, we focus on evaluating the proposed approach using the real dataset. The set is a collection of 10000 user uploaded images downloaded from social networks (flicker, twitter, google images, etc.). To create the services based on images, we have extracted its geo-tagged location, special mentions and tags as its textual description. Time when an image was captured, camera direction, maximum visible distance of a camera and camera viewable angle are abstracted as the functional property values dir, $VisD$ and α respectively. Quality features, i.e., colour quality and resolution, are abstracted as QoS property values. In addition, QoS parameters of price are manually assigned to all services. The threshold values of these parameters {$textual\ correlation$} are adjusted by the user of the service. For textual correlation, using previous research as reference we have set the value of threshold $\theta = 0.5$ [16]. For coverage, we have arbitrarily used above 80% for experimental purpose.

We generated 10 different queries based on the locations in our dataset. In these experiments we evaluate service selection based spatio-textual features. For our proposed approach, we have conducted the experiments with 10 different queries, e.g.,

   $q < R, d, ts, te, Q_i >$ - where

 - $R(< x, y >, l, w) = (-37.8101008, 144.9634339,\ 5\,m,\ 2\,m)$
 - $d = (Melbourne\ Central,\ Melbourne\ CBD)$
 - $t_s = 2{:}39{:}20\ pm\ AEST,\ Wednesday,\ 14\ June\ 2017$
 - $t_e = 2{:}59{:}23\ pm\ AEST,\ Wednesday,\ 14\ June\ 2017$
 - $Q_U = (\$0.0,\ 1600x1200,\ any)$

The results of these experiments are evaluated against the traditional image processing technique using SIFT (Scale-Invariant Feature Transform) [14]. In the second part of the experiment we have set a baseline for comparison. All the images are manually analysed by human to form a baseline for this experiment. We have used a $360°$ structured image dataset I of the area of interest R.

The image set is extracted from Google Map Street View. The selection is achieved by similarity analysis between the SIFT features of the image set I and our experiment dataset. This is achieved by individually comparing the key point feature vector of the images in I and the experiment dataset, and finding the images' matching features based on Euclidean distance of their feature vectors. To transform the matching keypoints into a scalar quantity, the percentage of keypoints that match the reference map is calculated [14], i.e., the number of matching keypoints (Number of mKP) divided by the total number of keypoints (Total number of KP) for each image [14]. Further, images are selected if the percentage of similarity is above 80% for the experiment purpose.

All the experiments are implemented in Java and Matlab. All the experiments are conducted on a Windows 7 desktop with a 2.40 GHZ Intel Core i5 processor and 8 GB RAM.

6.2   Evaluation

We have aimed to evaluate the proposed approach on the basis of (1) effectiveness in selecting related services (precision), (2) accurate and required coverage of the user required region (recall) and (3) time taken to select related services (execution time). Precision and recall matrices are used for evaluating the proposed framework against the image processing approach. All the images and selected services are manually analysed by human to form a baseline for this experiment. We have investigated that how precision and recall of the query result vary by applying the proposed approach in comparison to SIFT image processing. The experiments show that in terms of precision and recall the proposed approach shows slightly better performance than the image processing. The reason being that the proposed approach focuses on event based selection where as the image processing approach is location oriented. Our proposed approach helps in better selection of images for scene reconstruction because it considers the related textual data that describes a situation from various aspects, e.g., what is happening, where it is happening, who are involved and what are the effects on surrounding. Whereas, the image processing approach is more location oriented because it selects the images based on the similarity of surrounding landmarks rather than the insight of event being covered. Moreover, in terms of execution time efficiency, the experiments' results show that the time ratio between the

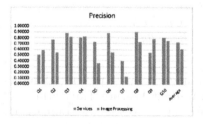

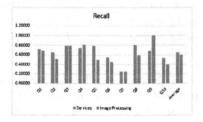

Fig. 7. Precision   Fig. 8. Recall

Table 1. Execution time

Queries	Q1	Q2	Q3	Q4	Q5	Q6	Q7	Q8	Q9	Q10	Average
Services	50.73273	33.42438	58.31660	59.96793	37.88908	61.06881	33.54670	61.43578	69.57009	33.48554	**49.94376**
Image Processing	4757.41782	2735.87241	5643.18330	5836.05159	3257.33112	5964.63045	2750.15895	6007.49007	6957.54498	2743.01568	**4665.26964**

proposed approach and image processing is 1:100. The results are depicted in Figs. 7 and 8 and Table 1.

7 Conclusion

In conclusion, this paper proposes a social-sensor cloud service selection framework based on spatio-temporal and textual correlation, and QoS parameters. We conducted the experiments to evaluate the proposed framework in comparison to a traditional image processing approach. Experimental results show that our approach is better than the traditional image processing approach. In future, we plan to focus on social-sensor clouds services composition for fast visual summary of the scene for scene building and event analysis.

Acknowledgement. This research was made possible by DP160103595 grant from Australian Research Council and NPRP 9-224-1-049 grant from the Qatar National Research Fund (a member of The Qatar Foundation). The statements made herein are solely the responsibility of the authors.

References

1. Rosi, A., Mamei, M., Zambonelli, F., Dobson, S., Stevenson, G., Ye, J.: Social sensors and pervasive services: approaches and perspectives. In: PERCOM 2011 (2011)
2. Chard, K., Caton, S., Rana, O., Bubendorfer, K.: Social cloud: cloud computing in social networks. In: IEEE 3rd ICCC 2010, pp. 99–106 (2010)
3. Aggarwal, C., Abdelzaher, T.: Social sensing. In: Aggarwal, C. (ed.) Managing and Mining Sensor Data, pp. 237–297. Springer, Boston (2013)
4. Neiat, A.G., Bouguettaya, A., Sellis, T., Ye, Z.: Spatio-temporal composition of sensor cloud services. In: ICWS 2014 (2014)
5. Elers, S.: Online investigation: using the internet for investigative policing practice. Australasian Policing **6**(1), 7–9 (2014)
6. Socialsensors.com.sg, Social Sensors - Sensing real-world activities from Social Media. http://socialsensors.com.sg/. Accessed 10 Dec 2015
7. Chae, J., Thom, D., Bosch, H., Jang, Y., Maciejewski, R., Ebert, D.S., Ertl, T.: Spatiotemporal social media analytics for abnormal event detection and examination using seasonal-trend decomposition. In: VAST 2012 (2012)
8. Dong, X., Mavroeidis, D., Calabrese, F., Frossard, P.: Multiscale event detection in social media. In: DMKD 2014 (2014)
9. Ghari Neiat, A., Bouguettaya, A., Sellis, T.: Spatio-temporal composition of crowd-sourced services. In: Barros, A., Grigori, D., Narendra, N.C., Dam, H.K. (eds.) ICSOC 2015. LNCS, vol. 9435, pp. 373–382. Springer, Heidelberg (2015). doi:10.1007/978-3-662-48616-0_26

10. Guo, B., et al.: From participatory sensing to mobile crowd sensing. In: PERCOM Workshops. IEEE (2014)
11. Fernndez, J., et al.: An intelligent surveillance platform for large metropolitan areas with dense sensor deployment. Sensors **13**(6), 7414–7442 (2013)
12. Balke, W.-T., Diederich, J.: A quality-and cost-based selection model for multimedia service composition in mobile environments. In: ICWS 2006 (2006)
13. Perera, C., Arkady, Z., Peter, C., Dimitrios, G.: Sensing as a service model for smart cities supported by internet of things. Trans. ETT **25**(1), 81–93 (2014)
14. Lowe, D.G.: Distinctive image features from scale-invariant key points. Int. J. Comp. Vis. **60**(2), 91–110 (2004)
15. Patwardhan, S., Banerjee, S., Pedersen, T.: Using measures of semantic relatedness for word sense disambiguation. In: Gelbukh, A. (ed.) CICLing 2003. LNCS, vol. 2588, pp. 241–257. Springer, Heidelberg (2003). doi:10.1007/3-540-36456-0_24
16. Mihalcea, R., Corley, C., Strapparava, C.: Corpus-based and knowledge-based measures of text semantic similarity. In: AAAI 2006, vol. 6 (2006)
17. Gretzel, U., Marianna, S., Zheng, X., Chulmo, K.: Smart tourism: foundations and developments. Electron. Mark. **25**(3), 179–188 (2015)
18. Kantarci, B., Hussein, M.: Trustworthy crowdsourcing via mobile social networks. In: GLOBECOM 2014, pp. 2905–2910. IEEE (2014)
19. Slabaugh, G., et al.: A survey of methods for volumetric scene reconstruction from photographs. In: Mueller, K., Kaufman, A.E. (eds.) Volume Graphics 2001. Eurographics. Springer, Vienna (2001)
20. Limna, T., Tandayya, P.: A flexible and scalable component-based system architecture for video surveillance as a service, running on infrastructure as a service. Multimed. Tools Appl. **75**(4), 1765–1791 (2016)
21. Theodoridis, Y., Vazirgiannis, M., Sellis, T.: Spatio-temporal indexing for large multimedia applications. In: Proceedings of the 3rd IEEE International Conference on Multimedia Computing and Systems, pp. 441–448 (1996)

Quark: A Methodology to Transform People-Driven Processes to Chatbot Services

Anup K. Kalia[1]([✉]), Pankaj R. Telang[2], Jin Xiao[1], and Maja Vukovic[1]

[1] IBM T.J. Watson, Yorktown Heights, NY, USA
anup.kalia@ibm.com, {jinoaix,maja}@us.ibm.com
[2] SAS Institute Inc., Cary, NC, USA
ptelang@gmail.com

Abstract. Human is a key cost factor in today's service- and business-oriented processes. To reduce labor, we propose an approach to convert people driven processes to a chatbot service. Current approaches to create a chatbot service are based on formal representations or dialog based methodologies. Formal representations provide techniques for soundness verification and exception handling, however, do not provide a software methodology that capture steps for developers to build a chatbot service. Dialog based methodologies provide different step-wise approaches to create a chatbot service, however, ignore the formal aspects. To bridge the gap, we propose a novel methodology, Quark, that guides developers in producing a model that is complete and sound. Specifically, Quark takes a business process flow as input and produces a Watson Conversation model. Quark employs the notions of goals and commitments which provide a formal means for completeness and soundness. We present Quark using a change management process scenario.

1 Introduction

Traditional business processes involve multiple process steps that humans execute. Such processes suffer from unpredictable delays and errors caused by the humans. The human errors may arise due to inadequate skill level or other cognitive state such as disinterest, distraction, and tiredness. The delays and errors can be reduced by employing automated agents for a subset of business tasks that do not need human oversight. An automated agent that provides an effective natural language interface for a human to interact is a chatbot.

To ensure a desired business outcome, the human-chatbot interactions need to be designed in a principled manner. Researchers have proposed various approaches for designing human-chatbot interactions. These approaches are either too formal for practitioners' effective use, or too informal leading to specifications that cannot be effectively verified. We propose a novel methodology, Quark, to bridge the gap between the formal and informal approaches.

Quark employs well studied abstractions of goals and commitments [11,13] for designing the human-chatbot interactions. A goal models a condition that a human or an (automated) agent desires to bring about. In a commitment,

M. Maximilien et al. (Eds.): ICSOC 2017, LNCS 10601, pp. 53–61, 2017.
https://doi.org/10.1007/978-3-319-69035-3_4

a debtor agent commits to a creditor agent to bring about a consequent condition if an antecedent condition holds.

Quark considers a business process model as its input and produces a dialog model. Specifically, we adopt BPMN [10] for the process model, and Watson Conversation [7] for the dialog model. From the process model, Quark identify roles that can be automated by a chatbot. For each role, Quark identifies goals and commitments. From the goals and commitments, Quark produces a set of interactions that are complete and sound. Finally, it generates a set of intents and a dialog model for the Watson conversation to build a chatbot service.

Contributions. This paper proposes a novel methodology, Quark, for developing a Watson Conversation model starting from a business process model. We demonstrate the methodology on a change management process.

2 Related Work

Researchers have extensively studied the topic of developing conversation models. For example, in services, Ardissono et al. [2] propose a conversation model that enables a conversation flow between the web-service consumers and the web-service providers. Bentahar et al. [3] provide a formal model of conversations based on the concepts of commitments and arguments. Cost et al. [5] propose Colored Petri Nets (CPN) for modeling conversations. Nezhad et al. [9] propose eAssistant that identifies actions in terms of request and promises to auto-triage the user conversations.

In the area of dialog-based approaches Traum [6] provides a methodology to create a computational model for a virtual human meant to operate in a specific domain. In terms of robustness checking, Traum do not clearly emphasize that his model will be robust on all interaction paths. Alès et al. [1] provide a methodology to extract a dialog model from a corpus by extracting several aspects from human dialogs, such as speech acts, social aspects, and gazes.

In multiagent systems, Bresciani et al. [4] propose the Tropos methodology that allows developers to design softwares in terms of goals. The methodology Gaia [14] assists developers to design organizations using responsibilities, permission, activities, and protocols. The methodology Comma [12] helps developers to capture business scenarios using commitments and creates a process that is sound with respect to commitments. The methodology Muon [8] helps developers to capture commitments semantics from interaction scenarios, handle exceptions, and then use the semantics to create sound processes. These methodologies unlike dialog based methodologies are formal, however, do not provide an approach to create a chatbot service.

From the related work, we infer the following requirements for a chatbot service: (1) ascribe meanings to messages or requests, (2) provide a meaningful response at each conversational turn that ensures reliability and flexibility provided by the chatbot, (3) ensure soundness of a conversation. To meet the requirements, we use the notion of goals and commitments to model a chatbot service. Goals capture the agent intentions, and commitments capture the meanings of messages exchanged between the participants in a service. The meanings provide a basis for verifying the soundness of conversations.

3 Quark Methodology

To describe our methodology, we consider the change management business process. In the process, a user interacts with a help desk to provide its request. The help desk validates the request of the user and sends it to a dispatcher. The dispatcher comprehends the intent of the request (e.g., a database change request or a memory change request) and sends it to the appropriate subject matter expert (SME). The SME extracts the parameters in the request. If the SME finds a parameter missing in the request, the SME requests the parameter from the user. Once the user provides the missing parameter, the SME sends the complete parameters to the change owner for a technical risk assessment. Then, the change owner sends them to the account owner for a business risk assessment. The account owner after its assessment, sends the request to the approver. Once the approver approves the request, it sends the request to the change owner. The change owner sends the request to the executor. The executor executes the request and sends the report to the user.

Quark takes a business process model as its input and produces an IBM Watson model of human-chatbot interactions that are necessary to realize the business process. We now describe the steps of the Quark methodology.

3.1 M₁: Identify Roles Served by Humans That Can Be Automated

This step identifies roles served by humans that can be automated by a service. The step requires organizational knowledge and domain expertise. A human is necessary for a role in a process if that role's business tasks are not clearly defined, or if the business tasks inherently require human insight. Generally, a role whose business tasks are formally defined is a good candidate for automation. After identifying the roles for automation, this step combines those roles in a single role. For convenience, we call this role BOT. Next, the step reduces the business process by removing the roles identified for automation, and adds the single role BOT. All the tasks under the roles identified for automation are transferred over to the role BOT.

For the change management process, we identify HELP DESK, DISPATCHER, SME, ACCOUNT OWNER, CHANGE OWNER, APPROVER, and EXECUTOR as roles that can be automated.

3.2 M₂: Identify Goals of Each Role

This step identifies the goals of each role. For each role, the tasks from the business process map into the (success conditions of) goals of that role. Specifically, for a task a in the process model, we specify a goal $G(x, p, a, f)$ in which x

is the role, p is the preceding task that is a necessary precondition for task a, the success condition is the task a, and the failure condition is f. If the failure condition is not explicitly modeled in the business process, then process domain expertise is necessary to identify it. For example, USER wants to execute its change request. Thus, *execute change* is as a goal of USER. Similarly, given a change request, BOT needs to identify the correct parameters for the change. Thus, *correct params* is a goal of BOT with the precondition that the change request has been provided.

Table 1 shows the goals of the roles: USER and BOT. In the table, t is a timeout that represents the failure condition, and the operator $\wedge$ represents logical conjunction.

Table 1. Roles and their goals for the change management process.

Actors	Goals
USER	$G_1 = \mathsf{G}(\text{USER},\ T,\ execute\ change,\ t)$
BOT	$G_2 = \mathsf{G}(\text{BOT},\ provide\ request,\ validate\ request,\ t)$
	$G_3 = \mathsf{G}(\text{BOT},\ validate\ request,\ identify\ intent,\ t)$
	$G_4 = \mathsf{G}(\text{BOT},\ identify\ intent,\ correct\ params,\ t)$
	$G_5 = \mathsf{G}(\text{BOT},\ correct\ params,\ perform\ tech\ risk\ assessments,\ t)$
	$G_6 = \mathsf{G}(\text{BOT},\ correct\ params,\ perform\ biz\ risk\ assessments,\ t)$
	$G_7 = \mathsf{G}(Bot,\ perform\ tech\ risk\ assessments \wedge perform\ biz\ risk\ assessments,\ approve,\ t)$
	$G_8 = \mathsf{G}(\text{BOT},\ approve,\ execute\ change,\ t)$
	$G_9 = \mathsf{G}(\text{BOT},\ execute\ change,\ send\ report\ to\ user,\ t)$

3.3   M₃: Identify Commitments Between Roles

This step identifies the commitments by analyzing goals of each role. For each goal, the step first asks the question: can the role satisfy the goal on its own, that is, can the role bring about the success condition of the goal on its own? If yes, then a commitment is not necessary. If no, then the step adds a commitment. The different elements of the commitment are identified as below.

- Debtor: is the role that can be bring about the goals's success condition.
- Creditor: is the role that has the given goal.
- Antecedent: is a form of a precondition that the creditor brings about in exchange of bringing about the goal's success condition. The precondition might be a form of a payment, or some other action. In some cases, the precondition might be already met. In those cases, it is set to true ($\top$).
- Consequent: is the success condition of the goal.

In the change management scenario from user has the goal of *execute change*. The user cannot satisfy this goal on her own. BOT can bring about *execute change*. So the step identifies a commitment: C(BOT, USER, provide request, send report to user). Observe that provide request is a necessary precondition for BOT to execute the change and to send a report. Similarly, BOT has a goal to identify correct parameters for the change. BOT cannot achieve this goal on her own. So, the step identifies a commitment: C(USER, BOT, modification request, correct params). Here, USER commits to BOT to provide the correct parameters when BOT makes a modification request.

Table 2 shows the commitments from the change management process.

Table 2. Commitments for the change management process.

Roles	Commitments
USER	C_1 = C(USER, BOT, *modification request, correct params*)
BOT	C_2 = C(BOT, USER, *provide request, send report*)

3.4 M_4: Produce a Set of Interactions

The fourth step in our methodology is to identify a set of interactions based on the roles, goals, and commitments identified from Steps M_1, M_2, and M_3. Kalia et al. [8] provides several guidelines for developers to create such interactions. They are as follows.

- *Interactions should represent the core positive outcomes.* For example the scenario where USER provides a request and it's executed by BOT provides desirable enactments. However, a scenario where USER refusing to provide appropriate request when asked for is not useful.
- *Interactions should reflect social or organizational relationships.* For example, the interactions between BOT and USER should lead to creation of commitments.
- *Interactions should ignore irrelevant messages.* For example, greeting message exchanged between USER and BOT can be ignored.
- *Interactions should avoid irrelevant roles and role instances.* For example, we cannot add additional roles that are not part of desirable enactments.

Based on the guidelines, we create a set of interactions that activate and satisfy the goals and commitments for USER and BOT. Table 3 describes a set of interactions that captures the modeled goals and commitments.

Table 3. A set of interactions between USER(S) and BOT(R), act represents active, and sat represents satisfied.

S	R	Message	Goals	Commitments
USER	BOT	*Hi*		
BOT	USER	*provide your request*		$act(C_2)$
USER	BOT	*add 2GB of memory to my server*	$act(G_1) \wedge act(G_2) \wedge$ $act(G_3) \wedge act(G_4)$	$det(C_2)$
BOT	USER	*provide the server details*	$sat(G_2, G_3)$	$act(C_1) \wedge det(C_1)$
USER	BOT	*server info is cobalt.ibm.com*	$sat(G_4) \wedge act(G_4) \wedge$ $act(G_5) \wedge act(G_6) \wedge$ $act(G_7) \wedge act(G_8) \wedge$ $act(G_9)$	$sat(C_1)$
BOT	USER	*here is the report*	$sat(G_4) \wedge sat(G_5) \wedge$ $sat(G_6) \wedge sat(G_7)$ $\wedge sat(G_8) \wedge sat(G_9)$	$sat(C_2)$

3.5 M_5: Repeat Steps M_2 and M_3 to Produce Additional Goals and Commitments

The fifth step of our methodology is to repeat steps M_2 and M_3 to identify additional goals and commitments required to provide robustness to the chatbot service. In this step, developers can consider scenarios that are not present in the current change management process. For example, developers can think of possible deviations such as *what happens if* BOT *could not identify the intent of* USER*'s request?* or *what happens if* BOT *does not approve* USER*'s request?*. To address such scenarios, we can first create goals and commitments required to address the scenarios and then we can add additional set of interactions to satisfy the goals and commitments.

For addressing *what happens if* BOT *could not identify the intent of* USER*'s request?*, we look for the goals and commitments. Since, the goal of BOT to identify the intent is present in Table 1, we do not add any new goal. To achieve the goal, BOT needs a new request from USER. Thus, it requests a commitment from USER to provide a correct change request. If USER agrees, the new commitment is created. Similarly, for the second scenario, the goal of BOT to approve is present in Table 1. However, if BOT cannot achieve its goal, it can request USER to create a commitment to provide a correct change request. In both the cases, USER has the autonomy to create new commitments or terminate the existing commitments. Based on new commitments identified we generate a new set of interactions that create and satisfy the commitments. We show the interactions in the next step of our methodology (Table 4).

Table 4. Additional commitments for the change management process.

Roles	Commitments
USER	$C_3 = C($USER, BOT, *intents not identifiable, provide new request*$)$
USER	$C_4 = C($USER, BOT, *cannot be approved, provide new request*$)$

3.6 M_6: Translate the Interactions to IBM Watson Model

In this step, we accomplish two things. First, we add the natural language interface to the current methodology. Then, we build a chatbot service. In IBM Watson's model [7], the first step is create intents and entities.

An intent captures the purpose of USER'S request. BOT, identifies the intent and then make an appropriate response. The guidelines to construct an intent is as follows.

- *Collect as many as* USER*'s request and categorize them.* For example, for the change management process, we can gather USER'S request for different kinds of change requests such as hardware, database, os management, and so on.
- *If intents are too similar cluster them together or else keep them separate.* For example, we can keep hardware related change requests such as cpu and memory specific changes together. Similarly, we can keep database run operations and management together.
- *Keep refining the intents.* With more data, intents can be refined further.

Based on specific entities, BOT chooses specific actions to perform. For example, consider two change requests. One, where USER requests to add memory to its VM and another where USER requests to add cpu to its VM. Both the change request gets identified with #hardware intent. Then, based on the entities such as *cpu* and *memory*, appropriate action is taken by BOT.

A child node is same as a node, however, it matches a user requests with an entity as its condition. Recall, that the output from the previous step M_4 was a set of additional commitments. Using the additional commitments, we refine the interactions in Table 5. We considered the interactions that is verified with respect to goals and commitments for creating a dialog model. Based on user's request, we identify intents and entities.

Based on intents and entities identified, we construct a dialog model as shown in Fig. 1. Consider an example, if USER provides a hardware request *add 2cpu to server cobalt.ibm.com*. The dialog model in can identify cpu as one of the entity, however, it cannot identify the server information, if it's not explicitly provided. Thus, goals and commitments to validate cpu request could have been used to refine the dialog model.

Table 5. A set of interactions between USER and BOT that captures the intents I and the entities E.

S	R	Message	Intents	Entities
USER	BOT	*Hi*	$I_1 = \#conv\_start$	
BOT	USER	*provide your request*	$resp(I_1)$	
USER	BOT	*add 2 to my server*	$I_2 = \#none$	
BOT	USER	*provide a valid request*	$resp(I_2)$	
USER	BOT	*add 2GB memory to my server*	$I_3 = \#hardware$	$E_1 = memory$
BOT	USER	*provide server details*	$resp(I_3)$	
USER	BOT	*server info is cobalt.ibm.com*		$E_2 = server$
BOT	USER	*here is the report*	$resp(E_2)$	

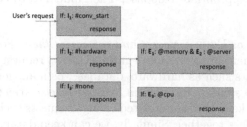

Fig. 1. *Output*: the dialog model created from intents and entities.

4   Conclusion and Future Work

This paper describes a novel methodology for developing human-chatbot interactions. We develop Quark using a typical change management process. We formally define the concepts that Quark employs. We evaluate Quark on a loan processing scenario. Quark produces human-chatbot interactions that are complete and sound.

In the future, we plan to develop tooling for Quark that will guide developers through the methodology steps. We will also conduct developer studies to evaluate Quark's effectiveness.

References

1. Alès, Z., Duplessis, G.D., Şerban, O., Pauchet, A.: A methodology to design human-like embodied conversational agents. In: International Workshop on Human-Agent Interaction Design and Models, Valencia, Spain, pp. 1–16 (2012)
2. Ardissono, L., Cardinio, D., Petrone, G., Segnan, M.: A framework for the server-side management of conversations with web services. In: Proceedings of the 13th International World Wide Web Conference on Alternate Track Papers and Posters, pp. 124–133. ACM, New York (2004)

3. Bentahar, J., Moulin, B., Chaib-draa, B.: Towards a formal framework for conversational agents. In: Proceedings of Agent Communication Languages and Conversation Policies Workshop, Melbourne, Australia, pp. 1–11 (2003)
4. Bresciani, P., Perini, A., Giorgini, P., Giunchiglia, F., Mylopoulos, J.: Tropos: an agent-oriented software development methodology. J. Auton. Agents Multi Agent Syst. **8**(3), 203–236 (2004)
5. Cost, R.S., Chen, Y., Finin, T., Labrou, Y., Peng, Y.: Using colored petri nets for conversation modeling. In: Dignum, F., Greaves, M. (eds.) Issues in Agent Communication. LNCS, vol. 1916, pp. 178–192. Springer, Heidelberg (2000). doi:10.1007/10722777_12
6. Traum, D.: Talking to virtual humans: dialogue models and methodologies for embodied conversational agents. In: Wachsmuth, I., Knoblich, G. (eds.) Modeling Communication with Robots and Virtual Humans. LNCS, vol. 4930, pp. 296–309. Springer, Heidelberg (2008). doi:10.1007/978-3-540-79037-2_16
7. IBM. Conversation. IBM (2016). https://www.ibm.com/watson/developercloud/conversation.html
8. Kalia, A.K., Singh, M.P.: Muon: designing multiagent communication protocols from interaction scenarios. JAAMAS **29**(4), 621–657 (2015)
9. Nezhad, H.R.M., Gunaratna, K., Cappi, J.: eAssistant: cognitive assistance for identification and auto-triage of actionable conversations. In: Proceedings of the 26th International Conference on World Wide Web Companion, WWW, Perth, Australia, pp. 89–98 (2017)
10. OMG. Business process model and notation (BPMN), version 2.0 beta. Object Management Group (2010). http://bpmn.org/
11. Singh, M.P.: An ontology for commitments in multiagent systems: toward a unification of normative concepts. Artif. Intell. Law **7**(1), 97–113 (1999)
12. Telang, P.R., Kalia, A.K., Singh, M.P.: Engineering service engagements via commitments. IEEE Internet Comput. **18**(3), 46–54 (2014)
13. Telang, P.R., Meneguzzi, F., Singh, M.P.: Hierarchical planning about goals and commitments. In: Proceedings of the 2013 International Conference on Autonomous Agents and Multi-Agent Systems, St. Paul, MN, USA, pp. 877–884 (2013). IFAAMS
14. Woolridge, M., Jennings, N., Kinny, D.: The gaia methodology for agent-oriented analysis and design. J. Auton. Agents Multi Agent Syst. **3**(3), 285–312 (2000)

Foundations

Cloud Certification Process Validation Using Formal Methods

Maria Krotsiani[✉], Christos Kloukinas, and George Spanoudakis

City, University of London, London, UK
{Maria.Krotsiani,C.Kloukinas,G.E.Spanoudakis}@city.ac.uk

Abstract. The importance of cloud-based systems is increasing constantly as they become crucial for completing tasks in an effective and affordable manner. Yet, their use is affected by concerns about the security of the data and applications provisioned through them. Security certification provides a means of increasing confidence in such systems, by establishing that they fulfil certain security properties of interest. Certification processes involve security property assessments against specific threat models. These processes may be based on self-assessment, testing, inspection or runtime monitoring of security properties, and/or combinations of such methods (hybrid certification). One important question for all such processes is whether they actually deliver what they promise. This question is open at the moment and is the focus of our work. To address it, we have developed an approach that formalises certification processes, by translating them in the language of the Prism model-checker and uses Prism to verify properties of interest on the model of the certification process, under specific environmental assumptions.

Keywords: Cloud certification · Validation · Probabilistic model checking

1 Introduction

Certification of cloud systems security is important for increasing confidence in cloud service provision. Security certification has traditionally been based on standards and certification schemes (*e.g.*, ISO27001 [22], ISO27002 [22], Common Criteria [9]), which define the security controls that a system should implement to be secured under specific threat models. Certification processes tend to be lengthy and costly, reducing their use [14]. A number of certification schemes focusing on cloud systems and services has also emerged. Some of these schemes are based on self-assessment [12,15,16]. Other certification processes use testing [13] or a combination of formal analysis and testing [8]. Most current certification schemes do not involve a continuous assessment of security, leading to proposals incorporating continuous monitoring of cloud systems and services security, as for example in the CUMULUS project [19,20]. In CUMULUS, security properties are expressed in Event Calculus [27] and are continuously monitored using the EVEREST [28] monitoring platform.

© Springer International Publishing AG 2017
M. Maximilien et al. (Eds.): ICSOC 2017, LNCS 10601, pp. 65–79, 2017.
https://doi.org/10.1007/978-3-319-69035-3_5

In this paper, we present an approach that enables the analysis and validation of cloud certification processes themselves – a necessity for both certifiers
and those seeking certification, so that they can better understand what they
are committing to when agreeing to a particular certification process. It is based
on formalising the process, in order to enable the formal analysis of its consequences under different environment assumptions, *i.e.*, different probabilities for
the occurrence of specific environment events (*e.g.*, monitoring results and/or
outcomes of the testing process).

Our approach allows a Certification Authority (CA), *i.e.*, the stakeholder,
who establishes and oversees the operation of a certification scheme, to define a
Certification Model (CM) as an input for the certification process. These CMs are
specified in an XML-based language and then translated into probabilistic timed
automata, in the language of the probabilistic model-checker PRISM [4,21].
Thus, one can verify different properties, *e.g.*, find the probability of issuing
a certificate after monitoring a cloud system for a given period of time, or the
probability of revoking a certificate within a given period time after it was issued.

In the following, Sect. 2 presents the overall framework and Sect. 3 gives a
running example of a CM. Section 4 presents the certification process and how
this is mapped at a high-level into a PRISM model. In Sect. 5 we present the
translation from our CM language to PRISM. Section 6 presents the outcomes
of experiments that we have conducted, while Sect. 7 reviews related work and,
finally, Sect. 8 provides concluding remarks and future directions.

2   Framework Overview

A certification process starts when a *Certification Authority (CA)* submits a
Certification Model (CM) to the CUMULUS Certification Platform. The Certification Platform in Fig. 1 has three main components. The *CM2Monitor Translator* component translates the CM into an executable format for the platform.
It also extracts the operational monitoring specification (*i.e.*, monitoring rules)
for the *Monitor* to check against the systems events. The *Certification Manager*
component manages the overall certification process. It receives the translated
CM and it communicates with the monitor (sending rules and receiving monitoring results). Finally, the *Anomaly Manager* component detects *anomalies* by
using the monitoring results. Monitoring rules in CUMULUS are divided into
anomaly and assertion rules, *i.e.*, soft constraints requiring further inspection
(anomalies) and hard constraints that must be met always (assertions).

The Deployment Infrastructure builds on a general-purpose monitoring architecture [17], and it consists of *event sensors*, a *monitor*, and a *CM2Monitor
Translator*. This infrastructure automates the certification process at run-time,
but since CMs and system behaviours can be complex, CMs themselves must be
validated. For this purpose, we have extended the framework with a tool-chain
for formal validation of CMs. We have also re-implemented the Certification
Manager execution engine to follow the formal semantics. Validation is based on
translating CMs to the Prism model-checker's language [4,21]. In order to explore

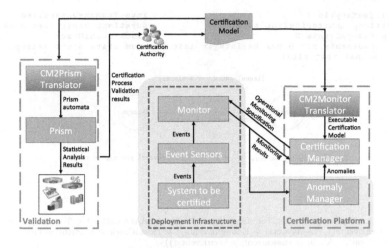

Fig. 1. Overall Architecture (Color figure online)

the CM consequences for specific systems, it also produces a formal model of its environment. This environment is inside the light blue shaded area in Fig. 1, comprising the Anomaly Manager, the system itself, and the system's monitor. Since the environment is too complex to be described formally in details, it is abstracted away and represented as a source of stochastic monitoring results. By using Prism, involved parties can check for properties such as:

- Is the CM respecting the high-level certificate life cycle?
- What is the probability of having to revoke an issued certificate?
- How is this probability affected by other parameters through time?

The outcomes of this validation are passed back to the responsible CA to adapt the CM accordingly, *e.g.*, adjust terms to reduce the possibility of a revocation.

3   Running Example

Figure 2 presents an example to demonstrate the different aspects of our approach. In this example, a certificate starts in the sInit state. The transition issue to the state sAccept occurs when guard$_I$ is satisfied. This guard states that: *(i)* violated assertion rules should not be excessive (Violated-Assertions() < TooManyVio); *(ii)* unresolved anomalies should be below their threshold; *(iii)* accumulated evidence should be at least EnoughEvents; and *(iv)* the cloud service should be monitored for at least the defined monitoringTime.

The satisfaction of the guard$_{Rf}$ in the state sInit fires the refuse transition that leads to the final state sFinal. The satisfaction of the guard$_{Rv}$ in the sAccept state fires the revoke transition, which also leads to the sFinal state. Finally, the satisfaction of the guard$_E$ in the sAccept state fires the expire transition that leads back to the sInit state, where the whole process starts again.

```
1   intp TooManyVio 1                        intp TooManyUnresolved 1
2   durationp monitoringTime secs(20)        durationp expiryTime secs(10)
3   intp EnoughEvents 2                       clock localClock
4   int usedevents min 0 max MaxInteger init 0  enum state sInit sAccept
        sFinal init sInit
```

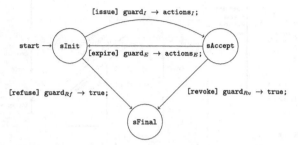

where:

guard$_I$: (ViolatedAssertions() < TooManyVio) & (UnresolvedAnomalies() < TooManyUnresolved)
    & ((SeenEvents() - usedevents) ≥ EnoughEvents)) & (localClock ≥ monitoringTime)
actions$_I$: (localClock'=0) & (usedevents'=SeenEvents())
guard$_E$: (ViolatedAssertions() < TooManyVio) & (UnresolvedAnomalies() < TooManyUnresolved)
    & (localClock ≥ expiryTime)
actions$_E$: (localClock'=0)
guard$_{Rf}$: ((ViolatedAssertions() ≥ TooManyVio) | (UnresolvedAnomalies() ≥ TooManyUnre-
    solved))
guard$_{Rv}$: ((ViolatedAssertions() ≥ TooManyVio) | (UnresolvedAnomalies() ≥ TooManyUnre-
    solved))

Fig. 2. Example Certification

4 Certification Process and Prism Model

4.1 Certification Model

Schema. The certification model is specified in XML, with its BNF equivalent as produced by the 𝕂 Framework [26] shown in Fig. 3. The top element of the model of interest to this paper is the `LifeCycle`. `LifeCycle` declares the unit of time that is assumed for the certification process and a list of typed parameters (*i.e.*, constants) of interest to the specifier *"Ps"*, such as the `TooManyVio` in Fig. 2. Parameters can be of four different types: *boolp, intp, floatp,* and *durationp* (*i.e.*, integers associated with a time unit). `LifeCycle` also declares typed variables *"Vs"*. These can be of one of the following five types: *bool, int, duration, enumeration,* and *clock.* Variables cannot be of type float as Prism does not support such a type [4]. Parameters and variables have a name and an initial value. In addition, *int* and *duration* variables have min and max values, *e.g.,*usedevents in Fig. 2. Finally, `LifeCycle` declares a list *"Ts"* of model transitions Each transition has a type, a guard, and a sequence of variable assignments. Type can be a user-defined one (`other`) or a fixed one (`issue`, `expire`, `refuse`, and `revoke`). The guard is a predicate (*Pred* in Fig. 3) over variables and parameters and the predefined Certification Manager functions (`SeenEvents`, *etc.– cf.* next section).

A certification model also contains other XML elements of use to the framework that we omit here as they are of no relevance to this paper (*e.g.*, the Target of Certification defining the service to be certified, *etc.*).

MODULE CERT-LIFECYCLE-SYNTAX

SYNTAX   *CLifeCycle* ::= **LifeCycle** {*TimeUnit Ps Vs Ts*}

SYNTAX   *TimeUnit* ::= **TimeUnit** *NExp*

SYNTAX   *Param* ::= **boolp** *Id Pred* | **intp** *Id NExp*
                    | **durationp** *Id NExp* | **floatp** *Id NExp*

SYNTAX   *Var* ::= **bool** *Id Pred* | **int** *Id* **min** *NExp* **max** *NExp* **init** *NExp*
                  | **duration** *Id* **min** *NExp* **max** *NExp* **init** *NExp*
                  | **clock** *Id* | **enum** *Id IdList* **init** *Id*

SYNTAX   *Transition* ::= **issue** *Pred Actions* | **expire** *Pred Actions*
                         | **refuse** *Pred Actions* | **revoke** *Pred Actions*
                         | **other** *Id Pred Actions*

SYNTAX   *Action* ::= *Id* = *Pred* | *Id* = *NExp* | *Id* **reset**

SYNTAX   *Function* ::= **secs** | · · · | **weeks** | **SeenEvents** | **DetectedAnomalies**
                       | **ViolatedAssertions** | **SatisfiedAssertions**
                       | **ResolvedAnomalies** | **UnresolvedAnomalies**

END MODULE

Fig. 3. BNF representation of the Certification Model XML Schema (fragment)

Semantics. The overall model comprises the certification process manager that receives events from its environment, which is represented by five parameters:

AnomalyP : Probability of an event to be an anomaly and not an assertion rule;
ViolationP : The (conditional) probability of an assertion rule to be violated;
UnresolvedP : The (conditional) probability of an anomaly to not be resolved;
minRuleTime : Minimum time it takes for a new rule event; and
maxRuleTime : Maximum time it takes for a new rule event.

Using these parameters, the environment produces anomaly and assertion events with a temporal distance in [minRuleTime, maxRuleTime]. Moreover, it updates a set of model variables representing the Certification Manager counter functions:

SeenEvents : Events produced since the beginning of time, $t = 0$;
DetectedAnomalies : Anomaly events produced since $t = 0$;
ResolvedAnomalies : Anomaly events resolved since $t = 0$;
UnresolvedAnomalies : Anomaly events not resolved since $t = 0$;
SatisfiedAssertions : Satisfied assertion events since $t = 0$;
ViolatedAssertions : Violated assertion events since $t = 0$;

Formal Modelling Framework. As we require probabilities and time to represent the environment and express the properties of interest for validating a certification process, our model uses Probabilistic Timed-Automata (PTA) [25], as supported by the Prism model checker [21]. A PTA is a tuple $P = (Locs, l_0, Clocks, Act, Inv, EnabConds, ProbTrans, Lab)$, where [25]:

- *Locs* is a finite set of locations, and $l_0 \in Locs$;
- *Clocks* is a finite set of clocks, and *Act* a finite set of action names;
- *Inv* is an invariant on *Locs* and clock constraints – $Inv : Locs \rightarrow CC(Clocks)$;

Listing 1.1. Environment in Prism

```
1   formula SeenEvents =
2       min(MaxInteger,  SatisfiedAssertions + ViolatedAssertions + ResolvedAnomalies +
            UnresolvedAnomalies);
3   formula DetectedAnomalies = min(MaxInteger,  ResolvedAnomalies + UnresolvedAnomalies);
4   timeToNextRuleResult : clock; // Clock used for the environment events.
5   // Functions.
6   ViolatedAssertions : [0 .. MaxInteger] init 0;  UnresolvedAnomalies: [0 .. MaxInteger
            ] init 0;
7   SatisfiedAssertions: [0 .. MaxInteger] init 0;  ResolvedAnomalies : [0 .. MaxInteger]
            init 0;
8   invariant (timeToNextRuleResult<=maxRuleTime) endinvariant
9   // The stochastic behaviour of the environment:
10  [event] (timeToNextRuleResult>=minRuleTime)
11      ->     AnomalyP *(1-UnresolvedP): (timeToNextRuleResult'=0)
12      & (ResolvedAnomalies'   = min(MaxInteger,ResolvedAnomalies+1))
13      +     AnomalyP *   UnresolvedP : (timeToNextRuleResult'=0)
14      & (UnresolvedAnomalies' = min(MaxInteger,UnresolvedAnomalies+1))
15      + (1-AnomalyP)*(1-ViolationP) : (timeToNextRuleResult'=0)
16      & (SatisfiedAssertions' = min(MaxInteger,SatisfiedAssertions+1))
17      + (1-AnomalyP)* (ViolationP)   : (timeToNextRuleResult'=0)
18      & (ViolatedAssertions'  = min(MaxInteger,ViolatedAssertions+1));
```

- $EnabConds$ are clock conditions – $EnabConds : Locs \times Act \rightarrow CC(Clocks)$;
- $ProbTrans$ is a partial probabilistic transition function, which given a location and an action name, gives a probability distribution over the next states (defined by a subset of clocks that are reset to zero by the transition named with action that leads to a new location, and that location) – $ProbTrans : Locs \times Act \rightarrow Dist(2^{Clocks} \times Locs)$; and
- Lab labels each location with a set of atomic propositions – $Lab : Locs \rightarrow 2^{AP}$

Clock constraints over a set of $Clocks$, $CC(Clocks)$, are defined by the syntax $\chi ::= true|x \leq d|c \leq x|x + c \leq y + d|\neg\chi|\chi \wedge \chi$, where $x, y \in Clocks$ and $c, d \in \mathbb{N}$ [25]. A PTA is *well-formed* when all enabled transitions take the automaton to states satisfying the clock invariant – see [25].

Environment Model. Listing 1.1 shows the environment part of the Prism model. It uses the clock variable `timeToNextRuleResult` (in line 4) to produce events between minRuleTime and maxRuleTime time units. The clock invariant (line 8) imposes the upper bound, while the clock guard (line 10) imposes the lower bound. Each time an event is produced we have a probabilistic choice between four possible alternative new states – two relating to anomalies (so conditioned on AnomalyP) and two to assertions (conditioned on (1−AnomalyP)). In each case the event is marked as negative (with probability UnresolvedP or ViolationP) or positive (with their complements), and we update the respective counter function.

Environment transitions are followed by transitions encoding the CM process. Process transitions in the Prism model correspond one-to-one to the actions in the process definition. Thus, for each action in the definition, there is a new transition with the same guard as the action and the same assignments. The transition name is the same as the name of the action. An action can be one of the standard ones: `issue`, `refuse`, `expire`, and `revoke`. For non-standard actions, the transition name is prefixed with "u_", to highlight it as non-standard.

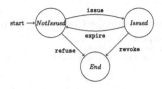

Fig. 4. High-level Certificate Life Cycle

Similarly, all user variables have the same prefix to avoid clashes with the constants, variables, and formulæ that we use for book-keeping, *e.g.*, `MaxInteger`, `SatisfiedAssertions`, `SeenEvents`. In this way, non-standard actions, *e.g.*, "`notify`", and user-specified variable assignments cannot alter the model semantics.

Listing 1.2. Lifecycle Observer Module

```
1    module HighLevelLifecycle
2      error : bool init false;
3      active: bool init true;
4      issued: bool init false;
5      [issue]    active & !issued & !error
6              -> (issued'=true);
7      [issue]  !(active & !issued & !error)
8              -> (error'=true);
9      [refuse]   active & !issued & !error
10              -> (issued'=false) & (active'=false);
11     [refuse] !(active & !issued & !error)
12              -> (error'=true);
13     [expire]   active & issued & !error
14              -> (issued'=false);
15     [expire] !(active & issued & !error)
16              -> (error'=true);
17     [revoke]   active & issued & !error
18              -> (issued'=false) & (active'=false);
19     [revoke] !(active & issued & !error)
20              -> (error'=true);
21   endmodule//
```

Semantics of the High-Level Certificate Life Cycle. The semantics also include the definition of the high-level certificate life cycle as shown in Fig. 4. A certificate starts at the state *NotIssued*, where it can be either refused or issued. If it is issued (*Issued*), then it can be either expired or revoked. Actions refuse and revoke end the certificate life cycle, while action expire changes the abstract certificate state back to the *NotIssued* state. The high-level certificate life cycle does not consider any user-defined actions. The `HighLevelLifecycle` module in Listing 1.2 observes whether one of the standard actions is taken in a state where it is not applicable. In this case it sets the variable `error` to true and refuses to take any more standard actions (all guarded by `!error`). The Prism property "`Pmax=? [F (error)]|`" verifies that this life cycle is respected, by asking for the maximum probability of eventually (F) reaching a state where `error` is true – this should be zero.

5 Code and Prism Model Generator

As shown in Fig. 1, there are two components that translate the Certification Model (CM) – the CM2Prism Translator and the CM2Monitor Translator.

Listing 1.3. Pseudo-code for Combining Types (fragment)

```
1    conv combineAdd(type tpA, type tpB) {
2      bool swapd=false; type tp1=tpA, tp2=tpB;
3      if (tpA > tpB) {tp1=tpB; tp2=tpA; swapd=true;}
4      switch (tp1) {
5          case INT:
6              switch (tp2) {
7              case INT:   return INT;
8              case FLOAT: return FLOAT;
9              }
10         case SECONDS:
11             switch (tp2) {
12             case SECONDS: return SECONDS;
13             case MINUTES:
14             return conv(SECONDS,
15               swapd ? 60 :  1, swapd ?  1 : 60);
16             default: // ask MINUTES
17             conv r=combineAdd(MINUTES, tp2);
18             return conv(SECONDS,
19               (swapd? 60*r.scale1 :r.scale0),
20               (swapd? r.scale0 :60*r.scale1));
21             }
22         // ... other types
23     }
24     return NONE;
25   }
```

The former component is responsible for producing a formal Prism model for analysing the CM and deciding whether it is fit for purpose. The latter component produces a set of monitoring rules that are passed to the runtime monitor (work described in [17]) and at the same time produces an executable version of the CM for the Certification Manager. As the translation happens at runtime, we translate to Lisp, as it can execute code produced dynamically.

The translations to the Prism model and Lisp code are done by the same piece of code – a decision taken to make it easier to track both artefacts and increase our confidence that they follow the same logic. The translator traverses the XML structure of the CM using a reflective Java visitor and applies a method visitX to each element X. Each method visitX updates certain global information (*e.g.*, names and types of variables), calls the appropriate visitors for the sub-elements of the element X and produces one string for the Prism model and another one for the Lisp code. We keep a (hash) Map of IDs to type information (a name and a type pair). Thus, a variable definition "bool foo false" will insert into the symbol map the mapping "foo" → ("u_foo", BOOL). The abstract syntax tree node for each XML element X contains the type of X, its representation in Prism, and its representation in Lisp. So for a declaration like "int bar min (3 * 6) max (100 - 7) init (40 + 2)", which declares an integer variable with min/max values and an initial value, we create a node of type INT with the following two strings: (i) "u_bar : [(3 + 6)..(100 - 7)] init (40 + 2);" for Prism, and (ii) "(defparameter u_bar (+ 40 2))" for the Lisp interpreter (which does not need any type information, nor min/max values for the variable).

Type Conversions. The translation is mostly straightforward – what makes it more interesting is the type-checking and type promotion that is performed, *e.g.*, when we add a float to an integer the result is a float, in particular for

Listing 1.4. Life-cycle Execution Loop Body

```
1  (defun lifecycle-loop ()
2   (progn
3    (update-time) ;; used by guard and actions
4    (let ((tr (find-if (lambda (x)
5                        (funcall (transition-guard x)))
6                     ***transitions***)))
7     (when tr
8      (funcall (transition-action tr))))))
```

duration expressions. Expressions involving durations are being transformed into the lowest unit used, *e.g.*,adding seconds to minutes results in seconds. Listing 1.3 shows the pseudo-code for type conversion when we have an *additive* expression. We see that INT+INT produces an INT, INT+FLOAT a FLOAT, and SECONDS+MINUTES produces SECONDS with scaling factors of 1 for the first expression and 60 for the second one. When the first type is SECONDS and the other is not MINUTES, we call the same function recursively pretending that the first type was MINUTES, so as to see if we can convert to MINUTES first and then to SECONDS. The recursion terminates at type WEEKS, the last duration type, that knows only how to add itself to another type WEEKS – it is always the smaller type that knows how to convert the type that is one level up. Similar functions exist for multiplication and division, as one can multiply two INTs to get an INT, an INT and a DURATION to get a DURATION but cannot multiply two DURATIONs, and can divide two DURATIONs but not an INT and a DURATION. Type translation is needed for both the Prism formal model and the Lisp code we generate, as otherwise we would not be able to have duration expressions where units are mixed. For the Lisp code all durations are eventually converted to nano-seconds, as that is the smallest unit supported by its system clock.

Lisp Interpreter. The Lisp code that is called continuously at run-time is shown in Listing 1.4. It first updates the time of the clocks by storing the current time in global variable ***now***. It then selects the first transition (based on the order defined in the CM), whose guard is true. If there is such a transition, it executes its actions. Listing 1.5 shows the code corresponding to the issue transition of the example in Fig. 2. We use ABCL, a Java-based Common Lisp, to execute the CM, as this allows smooth interfacing with the rest of the framework.

Language Constraints. As aforementioned in Sect. 4, our XML schema permits FLOAT parameters but not FLOAT variables, as the Prism modelling language does not support the latter – see the on-line Prism Manual [4]. Another inherited constraint has to do with the treatment of clock variables. While PTAs allow comparisons between clocks and both strict (*e.g.*, $<$) and non-strict (*e.g.*, $\leq$) comparisons, currently Prism only supports non-strict ones in all the analysis engines it has. For this reason we decided to also include this constraint, which may make it somewhat harder to express some guards, as now one needs to be careful to not introduce strict comparisons, *e.g.*, through negation.

Listing 1.5. Transition Definition in Lisp

```
1   (make-transition :name "issue"
2    :guard (lambda ()
3    (and (= u_state u_sInit)
4        (< (***ViolatedAssertions***) u_TooManyVio)
5        (< (***UnresolvedAnomalies***)
6            u_TooManyUnresolved)
7        (>= (- (***SeenEvents***) u_usedevents)
8            u_EnoughEvents)
9        (>= (- ***now*** u_localClock)
10           (* 1000000000 u_monitoringTime))))
11   :action (lambda ()
12   (progn
13    (assert (= *lstate* *slPreIssued*) ()
14      "*lstate*␣is␣~S" *lstate*)
15    (setq *lstate* *slIssued*)
16    (setq u_state u_sAccept)
17    (setq u_localClock ***now***)
18    (setq u_usedevents (***SeenEvents***)))))
```

5.1   Differences Between Prism Model and Code

Variable types & limits. We have already seen that variable names in Lisp do not have types, as they do in the Prism model, and integers do not have min/max values either, as they are actually bignums, *i.e.*, arbitrary length integers. But these are not the only differences between the two artefacts we produce.

Clock resets. By comparing the issue transition in Fig. 2 and in Listing 1.5, we can see that instead of resetting the clock variable localClock to zero, as it is done in the Prism model, we assign to it the current time of the global clock ***now***. A similar change is also in the guard – instead of comparing the clock against the duration monitoringTime directly, we compare its distance from ***now*** (after converting the duration to nano-seconds).

Time granularity. In the implementation, all clocks and durations are expressed in nano-seconds. In the Prism model, clocks do not have a unit, so all durations are transformed to the same unit (that needs to be provided in the CM as Time-Unit). Dividing a duration expression by TimeUnit should produce a natural number, since clocks in PTAs can be compared against natural numbers only.

Tracking of the high-level life cycle state. The model and the implementation track the high-level life cycle state differently. In the Prism model we use an additional module called HighLevelLifecycle (see Listing 1.2), which synchronises with the main model module and checks if there are erroneous transitions. Instead, in the Lisp code each transition assigns an internal variable *llstate* to keep track of the current high-level life cycle state of the certificate – see line 15 in Listing 1.5. It uses this variable to assert the correct state of the certificate, before performing any of the transition assignments – see line 13 in Listing 1.5.

Continuous vs discrete execution points. In the Prism model, a transition like the issue one (Listing 1.2) can fire at any time point that satisfies its guard. In the Lisp code, the respective transition (Listing 1.5) will only be considered every d seconds, where d depends on implementation issues, *e.g.*, the delay we have introduced in the main evaluation loop to avoid constant re-evaluation of transitions.

Non-deterministic vs deterministic behaviour and eager execution. The most important difference is that the Prism model has a non-deterministic behaviour – whenever multiple transitions are enabled it can execute any of them. It can actually elect to not execute any transition at all and instead simply let the time pass – Prism does not support *urgent* transitions [25] that must be taken immediately when they are enabled without allowing time to advance. The code we produce on the other hand, will always choose the first enabled transition and will execute it in an eager manner, without allowing time to pass.

Due to the last difference (and the one before it), the Lisp code that we produce *simulates* the behaviour of the Prism model, *i.e.*, exhibits only one possible behaviour among the behaviours that it can have. This is the usual case with all implementations of some formal model – the model is by definition more general, both because it has abstracted a number of implementation details away (*e.g.*, the execution speed of the system), and because it needs to describe a *family* of implementations and not a single one. For example, another reasonable implementation may choose to execute the last enabled transition. Yet another may choose a transition "non-deterministically", by evaluating the guards of the transitions in parallel and choosing the one whose guard evaluates to true first. This is something that will depend heavily not only on the expression each guard has to evaluate, but also on the current system state when evaluating these expressions, such as the current memory usage, the CPU load, *etc.*

6   Experimental Results

We have performed a number of experiments with the CM example of Sect. 3.

Experiment 1 – Respecting the high-level certificate life-cycle. Prism establishes that there is no error in the defined life-cycle of the CM, by calculating that the maximum probability of "Pmax=? [F (error)]" is zero (in 197.063 s). In a previous version of the CM, the result of this probability was non-zero, as we had mistakenly guarded the refuse action, with the certificate being at the sAccept instead of the sInit state.

Experiment 2 – Establish the maximum probability of revoking an issued certificate. Given the "Pmax=? [F (revokeGuard)]", Prism reports that Pmax is 0.262144 (in 209.7 s), which is too high – revoking a certificate is undesirable, since we have certified something as trustworthy, when in fact it is not.

Experiment 3 – Explore the system behaviour. We need to explore the system behaviour to understand why revocations can occur with such a high probability. One can analyse the probability of having an assertion or an anomaly

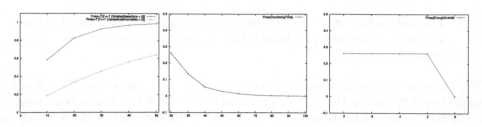

Fig. 5. Violations of assertions vs anomalies

Fig. 6. [F (revokeGuard)] vs monitoringTime

Fig. 7. [F (revokeGuard)] vs EnoughEvents

rule violation within T time units, as in Fig. 5. Anomaly rule violations start with a probability of 0.19 at time point 10 and reach a probability of 0.64 at time point 50. Assertion violations are more probable – they start with 0.58 and reach 0.99, so it is almost certain to have observed an assertion violation by time point 50.

Experiment 4 – Identify parameters that should be modified. We need to identify parameters that are too lax and discover better values for them to exclude this undesirable behaviour. A primary target is monitoringTime – maybe increasing it will render revocations improbable. Figure 6 shows the results (maximum probability for revocation) when monitoringTime ranges in $[20, 100]$ with a step of 10 (each point calculated in between 241.859 s and 694.947 s). The maximum probability drops constantly as the minimum monitoring time is increased. For a duration of 90 it drops to 0.00154 and for 100 to practically zero ($6.33 * 10^{-4}$).

Another interesting parameter is EnoughEvents – the minimum number of monitoring results we wish to observe before issuing a certificate. Exploring the behaviour of the system for values of this variable in the range $[2, 6]$ with a step of 1, produces the results in Fig. 7 (calculated in between 6.928 s and 237.929 s). The maximum probability for revoking the certificate stays constant at 0.262144 until we ask to observe at least 6 monitoring results, in which case it drops to exactly zero. So the parameter EnoughEvents offers better control. It also leads to models that can be analysed much faster than those that depend on the monitoringTime – this is because temporal constraints are far more expensive to analyse in PTAs than constraints involving discrete variables.

Experiment 5 – Re-validating chosen parameter values. The maximum probability of revoking a certificate when the probability of violation ranges in $[0.01, 0.35]$ (with a step of 0.02) validates setting EnoughEvents to 6 as a good choice. All cases report a zero probability, in between 6.372 and 8.201 s for each case.

7   Related Work

There is substantial work in validating and verifying cloud service providers or cloud services. Extensive work concerns the way evidence is collected to verify security properties of cloud services. Evidence collection can be based on *(i)* assessments regarding specific standards or regulations, performed by either the cloud providers or third party authorities, known as self-assessment; *(ii)* trusted platform modules (TPM); *(iii)* performing tests; or *(iv)* continuous monitoring.

In self-assessment one either completes a specific questionnaire, as in the case of CSA STAR Level 1 and Level 2 [12], or completes reports regarding specific national or international standards, such as the CIF Guidance [10], COBIT [2], the compliance framework FISMA [16], or TRUSTe [6].

Trusted computing targets the integrity of software, processes, or data by collecting evidence through TPMs and related hardware. Muñoz and Maña [24] combine software and hardware-based cloud certification, aiming to bridge the gap between cloud certification and trusted computing. Another approach is MyCloud by Li *et al.* [23]. MyCloud is an architecture used for privacy protection based on traditional encryption mechanisms. It aims to allow clients to configure their own privacy protection, by decreasing as much as possible the trusted computing base and the cloud providers' ability to modify privacy settings.

With test-based evidence collection, research has mostly focused on the problem of testing web services. Damiani *et al.* [13] use security certificates based on signed test cases for assessing and certifying web services. A first step in the area of web service certification was done by SEI in 2008, which defined a web service certification and accreditation process for the US Army CIO/G-6 [5]. Anisetti *et al.* [7] provided a test-based security certification solution for services and a first approach to its integration within the SOA environment. The ASSERT-4SOA EU project also focused on formal and test-based service certification [8].

Finally, monitoring and dynamic collection of evidence for cloud services is a more recent development, due to its additional complexity. It requires uninterrupted monitoring services, even though the monitoring capabilities available in a service-based system change due to the dynamic nature of cloud services. To address these needs the SLA@SOI EU project has developed a dynamically configurable monitoring infrastructure for dynamically checking SLA monitorability, which runs on cloud systems and adapts automatically to changes in the available monitoring capabilities in service based systems [17,18]. Monitoring has also been used at the hypervisor layer to provide incident detection even when the guest OS experiences critical conditions and monitoring agents are unable to communicate with monitoring systems. Amazon's CloudWatch is a system of this category [1]. Moreover, Cloud Security Alliance's Cloud Trust Protocol [11] provides interfaces for extracting monitoring data from cloud systems.

Thus, most of the work in cloud certification focuses so far mainly on verifying and validating security properties of cloud providers and cloud services. To the best of our knowledge, our approach is the first one focusing on the exploration and validation of the certification process itself, prior to employing it.

8 Conclusion and Future Work

In this paper, we have presented an approach for analysing and validating cloud certification processes based on formal method techniques. This approach translates a certification model (CM) into a model for the Prism model checker and into an executable version of it, in Lisp code.

For the Prism model, the environment of the certification process is modelled with probabilistic timed automata. The actions of the environment are abstracted by the probability of their occurrence. This probability is either estimated, obtained from historical data, or obtained by observing the system at run-time. This formal model enables analysing the process for different properties, from adherence to the expected high-level certificate life cycle, to min/max probabilities of revoking an issued certificate, *etc.* This allows one to explore whether the CM behaves as desired and can be used to certify cloud services.

At the same time, we translate the CM to code to be executed at run-time for certifying the cloud service in question. This code is produced alongside the Prism model and follows its behaviour, so that the analysis results remain valid.

In the future we plan to extend our framework so that it can also consider additional constraints on the expected behaviour of a cloud service and sufficiency conditions on this behaviour that must be met in order to issue a certificate. Currently our approach considers only the monitoring results for the properties we check on the cloud service, while the extended version would also observe the primitive execution events of the service. This capability would allow to observe a particular set of primitive event patterns for issuing a certificate.

Acknowledgments. This work was partly supported by the EU-funded project CyberSure [3] (grant no 734815).

References

1. Amazon CloudWatch, http://aws.amazon.com/cloudwatch/
2. COBIT, http://www.isaca.org
3. CyberSure (CYBER Security inSURancE), http://cybersure.eu/
4. Prism Model Checker, http://www.prismmodelchecker.org/
5. Securing Web services for army SOA, www.sei.cmu.edu/solutions/softwaredev/securing-web-services.cfm
6. TRUSTe, http://www.truste.com/
7. Anisetti, M., Ardagna, C.A., Damiani, E.: Defining and matching test-based certificates in open SOA. In: 2011 IEEE Fourth International Conference on Software Testing, Verification and Validation Workshops (ICSTW), pp. 520–522. IEEE (2011)
8. Anisetti, M., Ardagna, C.A., Guida, F., Gürgens, S., Lotz, V., Maña, A., Pandolfo, C., Pazzaglia, J.-C., Pujol, G., Spanoudakis, G.: ASSERT4SOA: toward security certification of service-oriented applications. In: Meersman, R., Dillon, T., Herrero, P. (eds.) OTM 2010. LNCS, vol. 6428, pp. 38–40. Springer, Heidelberg (2010). doi:10.1007/978-3-642-16961-8_11
9. Ccdb, USB Working Group: Common Criteria (CC) for Information Technology Security Evaluation (2012), http://www.commoncriteriaportal.org
10. Cloud Industry Forum: CIF Guidance, www.cloudindustryforum.org/about-us
11. CSA: Cloud Trusted Protocol, https://cloudsecurityalliance.org/research/ctp/
12. CSA: CSA Security, Trust and Assurance Resigtry (STAR), https://cloudsecurityalliance.org/star/

13. Damiani, E., Ardagna, C.A., El Ioini, N.: Open Source Systems Security Certification. Springer, US (2008)
14. ENISA: Security Certification Practice in the EU: Information Security Management Systems - A Case Study (2013), https://www.enisa.europa.eu/
15. FedRAMP Office: Guide to Understanding FedRAMP (2013), www.gsa.gov/portal/mediaId/170599/fileName/Guide_to_Understanding_FedRAMP_042213
16. FISMA: Federal Information Security Management, https://www.dhs.gov/federal-information-security-management-act-fisma
17. Foster, H., Spanoudakis, G.: Advanced service monitoring configurations with SLA decomposition and selection. In: Proceedings of ACM Symposium on Applied Computing, pp. 1582–1589. ACM (2011)
18. Foster, H., Spanoudakis, G.: Smart: A workbench for reporting the monitorability of services from SLAs. In: Proceedings of 3rd International Workshop on Principles of Engineering Service-Oriented Systems, pp. 36–42. ACM (2011)
19. Katopodis, S., Spanoudakis, G., Mahbub, K.: Towards hybrid cloud service certification models. In: IEEE International Conference on Services Computing, SCC, pp. 394–399. IEEE Computer Society (2014), http://dx.doi.org/10.1109/SCC.2014.59
20. Krotsiani, M., Spanoudakis, G., Mahbub, K.: Incremental certification of cloud services. In: SECURWARE 2013–7th International Conference on Emerging Security Information, Systems and Technologies, pp. 72–80 (2013)
21. Kwiatkowska, M., Norman, G., Parker, D.: PRISM 4.0: verification of probabilistic real-time systems. In: Gopalakrishnan, G., Qadeer, S. (eds.) CAV 2011. LNCS, vol. 6806, pp. 585–591. Springer, Heidelberg (2011). doi:10.1007/978-3-642-22110-1_47
22. Lagazio, M., Barnard-Wills, D., Rodrigues, R., Wright, D.: Certification schemes for cloud computing. EU Commission Report, http://dx.doi.org/10.2759/64404
23. Li, M., Zang, W., Bai, K., Yu, M., Liu, P.: MyCloud: Supporting user-configured privacy protection in cloud computing. In: Proceedings of 29th Annual Computer Security Applications Conference, pp. 59–68. ACM (2013)
24. Muñoz, A., Maña, A.: Bridging the gap between software certification and trusted computing for securing cloud computing. In: Ninth World Congress on Services, pp. 103–110. IEEE (2013)
25. Norman, G., Parker, D., Sproston, J.: Model checking for probabilistic timed automata. Formal Methods Syst. Des. **43**(2), 164–190 (2013), http://dx.doi.org/10.1007/s10703-012-0177-x
26. Rosu, G., Serbanuta, T.: An overview of the K semantic framework. J. Log. Algebr. Program. **79**(6), 397–434 (2010), http://dx.doi.org/10.1016/j.jlap.2010.03.012
27. Shanahan, M.: The event calculus explained. In: Wooldridge, M.J., Veloso, M. (eds.) Artificial Intelligence Today. LNCS, vol. 1600, pp. 409–430. Springer, Heidelberg (1999). doi:10.1007/3-540-48317-9_17
28. Spanoudakis, G., Kloukinas, C., Mahbub, K.: The SERENITY runtime monitoring framework. In: Kokolakis, S., Gómez, A.M., Spanoudakis, G. (eds.) Security and Dependability for Ambient Intelligence. AIDS, vol. 45, pp. 213–237. Springer, Boston (2009), http://dx.doi.org/10.1007/978-0-387-88775-3_13

Validation of Service Blueprint Models by Means of Formal Simulation Techniques

Montserrat Estañol[2], Esperanza Marcos[1], Xavier Oriol[2], Francisco J. Pérez[1], Ernest Teniente[2], and Juan M. Vara[1(✉)]

[1] Kybele Research Group, University Rey Juan Carlos, Madrid, Spain
{esperanza.marcos,francisco.perez,juanmanuel.vara}@urjc.es
[2] Universitat Politàcnica de Catalunya, Barcelona, Spain
{estanyol,oriol,teniente}@essi.upc.edu

Abstract. As service design has gained interest in the last years, so has gained one of its primary tools: the Service Blueprint. In essence, a service blueprint is a graphical tool for the design of business models, specifically for the design of business service operations. Despite its level of adoption, tool support for service design tasks is still on its early days and available tools for service blueprint modeling are mainly focused on enhancing usability and enabling collaborative edition, disregarding the formal aspects of modeling. In this paper we present a way to support the validation of service blueprint models by simulation. This approach is based on annotating the models with formal semantics, so that each task can be translated into formal logics, and from them, to executable SQL statements. This works opens a new direction in the way to bridge formal techniques and creative service design processes.

Keywords: Service blueprint · Validation · Simulation

1 Introduction

Beyond the computational point of view, services have been a matter of interest for the academia since the appearance of the first studies on services marketing in the early 50's [1] to the advent of Service Science from IBM [2]. More recently, the fact that approximately 60% of the world's workforce is currently employed by either public or private branches of the Service Sector and this value rises to 80% in developed countries has significantly contributed to renew the interest in services and related disciplines.

One of those disciplines is Service Design, which aims at helping in the development or improvement of services in order to deliver user-centered services by focusing on the interactions (or touchpoints) between the provider and the consumer [3]. Its main principles are: human-orientation, value co-creation, process-based nature, tangible evidences and holistic view. Born also in the context of research on services marketing, service design evolved and gained impact through

© Springer International Publishing AG 2017
M. Maximilien et al. (Eds.): ICSOC 2017, LNCS 10601, pp. 80–95, 2017.
https://doi.org/10.1007/978-3-319-69035-3_6

the impulse of $IDEO^1$ and has finally been established as the entry point to service development for any organization seriously concerned about user experience, digital transformation and the like (see for instance the efforts on this issue of the British government around the *Government Digital Service*[2]).

The most popular service design technique is service blueprinting [4]. In essence, a (service) blueprint is a graphical tool to visualize the different parts of a given service and the interactions between the stakeholders of such service. In contrast with BPMN, an organization-focused notation for business process modeling, service blueprinting is a user-centered approach to business process modeling. This has turned to be key for service designers in the digital age, where most of the innovation has to happen at the touch points between provider and consumer.

Despite the fact that service blueprinting was originally intended to enable a more rigorous control and analysis of service delivery, it has partially failed since despite its widespread adoption, it is most commonly used as an sketching tool to provide first-draft solutions but they are rarely used to support any kind of formal reasoning.

By contrast, bringing some degree of formability to service blueprinting has proven to contribute to ensure the success of the process and in turn increases the effectiveness of the blueprint, improving the rationality of the decisions within the company [5]. As a matter of fact, even though there exists a number of proposals to bring formalization to other existing techniques for business process modeling exist (see [6,7] for instance), to the best of our knowledge there exists no similar proposal for service blueprinting.

The main goal of this paper is to introduce a framework that permits formally defining service blueprints, and validating them. To do so, we propose to, during the definition of the service blueprint, annotate its tasks with some formal semantics. Thus, each task unambiguously specify its behavior. As a result, we can validate the service blueprint by interpreting such semantics, simulating its execution, and checking that no undesirable situation occurs during the simulation.

In order to support the full process of this framework, we extend the *INNo-VaServ*[3] modeling tool, and propose its integration with the *OpExec* simulating library[4]. The former is an EMF-based toolkit [8] with a visual DSL for service blueprint modeling, thus, offering very good capabilities for easily defining service blueprints. The latter is a Java library that permits simulating processes described in formal logics, while checking validation conditions (aka integrity constraints). Thus, the integration of both tools covers our framework entirely, permitting the definition and formal validation of service blueprints.

---

2   Context

This section presents the research context of this work. To that end, we first summarize service blueprinting notions, to later introduce *INNoVaServ*, the toolkit in which to integrate the process simulation capabilities.

2.1   Service Blueprinting

The service blueprint is a graphical tool for the design of business models, specifically for the design of business service operations, which is focused on detailing the interaction between the customer and the service provider in the provision of a given service [9]. Being a tool for service design and giving the process nature of services, service blueprinting is actually another technique for process modeling. The notably difference being in this case the focus on the customer experience, which is clearly illustrated by making explicit the touchpoints, the *physical* evidences related with the provision of the service and the limits between frontstage and backstage.

For instance, Fig. 1 shows an excerpt[5] of the renting process of *car2go* service blueprint: the user needs to rent a car and therefore he turns to the *car2go* app (online/physical evidence); a couple of consumer-provider interactions take then place along the *line of interaction*. Data provided by the user is then checked in the *backstage* whereas external entities are contacted to order vehicle maintenance and process payments.

As can be shown, a service blueprint is composed by five lanes or regions of activity that help to distinguish those actions that are specific to the service provider from those performed by the customer/consumer. Such lanes are listed below from top to bottom:

- *Physical Evidence.* This region represents the evidences, facts or global actions that give rise to the interaction between the customer and the service provider. A user who has the need of renting a car for private transportation to go somewhere is something that gives rise to the interaction between the customer and *car2go.*
- *Attendee Action.* It is devoted to describing the actions that a client performs while interacting with the *front-end* of the service, like selecting the car to rent or notifying *car2go* when he has arrived to the destination. Lower bound of this region is called *Line of Interaction* and it detaches the actions performed by the customer from those performed by the service provider.
- *Frontstage Interactions.* The activities performed by the service provider which entail some type of interaction with the customer are represented here. Asking the user to select a car or to check his *car2go* account are examples of this kind of activities.

---

[5] Full version can be found at http://www.kybele.es/publications/-car2go_renting Process_extended.png.

– *Back of Stage Interactions.* The activities performed in the shadow by the provider to operate the service, like updating the vehicle status when a car is rented, are represented in this region. These are actions needed to deliver the service but which the customer cannot see or interact with.
– *Support Processes.* Actions supporting the service, sometimes performed by third parties, are represented here. The interaction between the maintenance company and *car2go* to order vehicles maintenance is one of those actions that remain hidden for the customer.

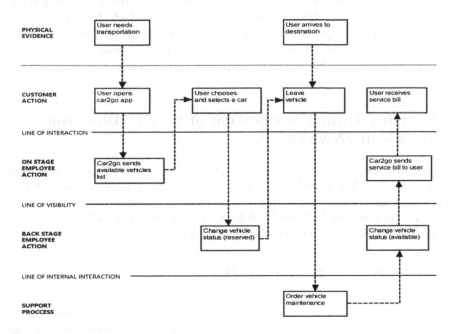

Fig. 1. Excerpt of a service blueprint made with INNoVaServ - *car2Go* renting process

As the next section will show, service blueprint diagrams can be faithfully represented with the modeling environment provided by *INNoVaServ*.

2.2   Introducing INNoVaServ

INNoVaServ[6] is a modeling environment for the design of business models and service process operations which, to date, supports 4 different notations: Canvas [10], e3Value [11], Process Chain Network (PCN) [12] and the Service Blueprint.

It is a first step towards solving the lack of proper tool support for bridging existing business modeling notations. To that end, *INNoVaServ* integrates different tools to register and manage the relationships between models defined with

---

[6] http://www.kybele.etsii.urjc.es/innovaserv.

the different techniques for business (process) modeling. In the medium term, the aim is at automating the identification of such relationships and enlarge the number of notations supported.

Basically, the toolkit can be thought of as a set of four integrated visual DSLs, one for each modeling notation supported by the tool. Each of such DSLs was developed atop EMF and GMF [8] following the guidelines sketched in [13] for the development of model-based tools that take the shape of DSL toolkits.

It is worth noting that due to the fact that it has been entirely developed atop of EMF/GMF, it is immediately interoperable with any other EMF/GMF based tool. Since EMF/GMF has converted in the de-facto standard for the development of model-based tooling, the scope of tools with which *INNoVaServ* can then interoperate is huge. The different tools supporting BPMN, like the Eclipse BPMN Modeler[7] or the Obeo BPMN Designer[8] (there is indeed many others BPMN editors based on EMF/GMF), Papyrus UML and any other EMG/GMF-based editor, etc.

3 Enabling Formal Verification of Service Blueprint Models in *INNoVaServ*

This section describes our approach for enabling formal verification of service blueprint models. We start by showing the architecture for integrating INNo-VaServ with the OpExec tool, which will be the basis for this verification. Then, we explain our proposal for formally defining service blueprint tasks and we show how to achieve the intended formal semantics for validation.

3.1 Functional Architecture and Design

In Fig. 2 we summarize the architecture of *INNoVaServ* (according to the convention widely adopted by Eclipse developers to represent the architecture of their proposals), together with our proposed integration with the OpExec simulation tool.

The technological basis of *INNoVaServ* is Eclipse. DSLs are mainly developed atop of EMF/GMF while some minor refinements coded with the aid of JFace and SWT to obtain the desired functionality from diagrammers. *INNoVaServ* can validate its defined processes by means of bringing them to the OpExec tool, and simulating the execution of its tasks. In its turn, OpExec works by storing in memory a logic representation of the process to simulate, and persisting the data of the process in a relational database.

3.2 Formally Defining Service Blueprint Tasks

Service blueprints, as they are, provide an intuitive and understandable overview of the different tasks and activities required to provide a service or achieve a

---

[7] http://www.eclipse.org/bpmn2-modeler/.
[8] http://marketplace.obeonetwork.com/module/bpmn.

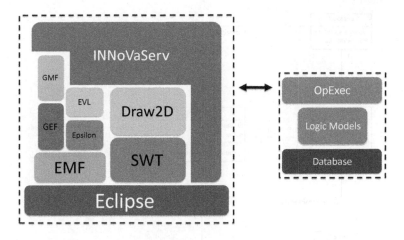

Fig. 2. Overview of technological dependencies of INNoVaServ and OpExec

certain goal. However, there is no formal meaning attached to each of the tasks. From their names, we may have an intuitive idea of what they imply, but we do not know exactly what it is they do. Therefore, if we wish to validate the model considering what the tasks do, it is necessary to enrich the initial service blueprint as explained below.

In order to provide the tasks with meaning, it is necessary to have an underlying data model, to represent the relevant information that will be manipulated by them. We propose using a UML class diagram for this purpose. Figure 3 shows the class diagram for the service blueprint in Fig. 1.

This class diagram keeps information about the company's *Vehicles* (id, status, battery level, etc.) together with their *Location* and the *ServiceBills* which have resulted from the use of the *Vehicle*. The system also stores information about which *User* is currently using or has booked a *Vehicle* (if any) and the *ServiceBills* of a certain *User*. Apart from the *User* basic information, such as id, name or accountStatus, the system also keeps track of the *BankAccounts* of *User* and their funds.

The data represented in the class diagram should satisfy some additional conditions (aka integrity constraints), in order to ensure the correct behavior of the service. For instance, each UML class could have an identifier (i.e. "primary key"). In our example, *Vehicle*, *User*, *ServiceBill* and *BankAccount* are identified by their *id*. *Location*, on the other hand, is identified by its *coordinates*. More complex conditions might be observed. For example, *damaged Vehicles cannot be booked by a User*.

Then, given the data model, it is possible to specify unambiguously what each of the tasks is doing. Our approach will use structured natural language for this purpose.

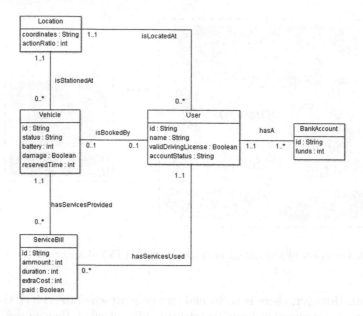

Fig. 3. Class diagram representing the underlying data model for *car2go*.

Structured Natural Language. In order to formalize the meaning of the tasks in the service blueprint we propose using structured natural language. This language is based on using a few keywords and following certain patterns, which result in sentences which can be easily understood. By using these it is possible to state selection and basic changes over data (creation, updates, deletions). Hence, we strike a balance between understandability, simplicity and expressibility.

The grammar defining this structured language is the following:

select *ClassName* [**with** Attributes]
delete_c *ClassName*
ClassAction *ClassName* Attributes

AssociationAction *AssociationName* (*ClassName*, Classes)

ClassAction → **check** | **change** | **create**
AssociationAction → **associate** | **delete_a**

Attributes → *attributeName(value)* | *attributeName(value)*, Attributes
Classes → *ClassName* | *ClassName*, Classes

Keywords are in bold. Class and attribute names are in italics, and should be replaced by any class or attribute name in the model, respectively. Square brackets represent optional parameters. *value* should be replaced by either a value (e.g. string, integer) or an input parameter, the latter representing an input value provided by the user.

select and **check** both refer to conditions that must be true of the particular object they are applied to. **check** refers to an object that has been obtained previously and which must fulfill a certain condition. **select**, on the other hand, obtains a new object which had not been obtained previously; **select...with...** obtains a new object which fulfills the conditions stated in the **with** (which will refer to its attributes).

The remaining keywords correspond to changes made to the underlying data. **create** will create a new instance of a class with the given attribute values. **delete_c** will delete the given instance of a class. **change** will update an attribute (or several) of a class to the given values or input parameters.

Similarly, **associate** will create an instance of the named association with the indicated classes. **delete_a** will delete the instance of the association with the given name and the participating classes.

This results in statements such as the following, where the first corresponds to task *User chooses and selects a car* and the second to *Change Vehicle Status (reserved)*:

select *Vehicle* **with** *status('available')*
change *Vehicle status('reserved')*

We assume that references to a class point to an instance or object of the class in question which has obtained previously. Therefore, in the previous example statements refer to the same vehicle.

3.3 Executing the Formal Semantics for Validation

Once the service blueprint is annotated with the formal semantics, it is unambiguous enough to validate its execution. In particular, we aim at ensuring that, when executing the process, its data state never becomes inconsistent (i.e., never stores a state that cannot occur in the real world). For doing so, we need to define some *integrity constraints*, that is, some conditions that *consistent data states* always satisfy, thus, any violation of a constraint points an inconsistency.

Hence, our validation approach consists in (1) translating such annotations into an executable language, (2) run the process, and (3) check that such execution satisfies our defined set of integrity constraints.

For our purposes, we use as executable language (a subset of) the executable logic rules stated in [14]. Such rules can be executed by means of a prototype tool we call OpExec, which essentially persists the data of the process into a relational database, and checks that such data satisfy a set of user-defined integrity constraints. In this manner, if the OpExec tool detects a violation of some of these constraints, we can realise that the service is ill-defined.

In the following, we first present the executable logic rules we use. Then, we show how to translate the previous patterns annotated in the service blueprint into such logics. Finally, we show how to validate the service blueprint by running these rules over the OpExec tool.

Executable Logic Rules. In our particular case, the executable logic rules are some rules following one of these forms:

$$ins\_C(\overline{x}) : -taskName(), arg_0(x_0), ..., arg_n(x_n)$$
$$ins\_Select\_C(x) : -taskName(), arg_0(x_0), ..., arg_n(x_n), C(\overline{x})$$
$$del\_C(\overline{x}) : -taskName(), Select\_C(x)$$
$$del\_Select\_C(x) : -taskName(), Select\_C(x)$$
$$ins\_R(\overline{x}) : -taskName(), Select\_C_0(x), ..., Select\_C_n(x)$$
$$del\_R(\overline{x}) : -taskName(), Select\_C_0(x), ..., Select\_C_n(x)$$
$$query(\overline{x}) : -taskName(), arg_0(x_0), ..., arg_n(x_n), C(\overline{x})$$

Intuitively, the first two rules state that an insertion/selection of an instance of class C should be realized if the task called *taskName* is invoked with arguments $x_0, ..., x_n$, where such arguments are used to specify the values of attributes of the object being created/selected. In addition, the second rule forces the instance of C to exists in order to be selected. Similarly, the third and forth rule states a deletion/deselection of an instance of C that was previously selected. Then, the fifth and sixth rules state that a creation/deletion of an association R with the selected objects should be performed. The last rule is only a query to check the existence/inexistence of some instance of C.

Translating Natural Language Patterns into Executable Logic Rules. Now, we show how to translate the natural language patterns used to annotate the service blueprint into such executable logic rules.

Intuitively, each natural pattern presented is mapped to one or more executable rules. This is because, for instance, the creation/deletion of an object in some class C might encompass the creation/deletion of the same object in its sub/superclasses C'/C'', and each creation requires its own executable logic rule.

Table 1 summarizes these mappings. For each task in the service blueprint with its corresponding annotation in natural language, we generate the executable logic rules stated in the right column. In particular, the task name of the pattern brings the name to the *taskName()* atom of the rule, and each user given value v_i in the pattern originates a $arg_i(v_i)$ atom. As expected, the atoms using classes/associations C/R take its name from the classes/associations C/R used in the pattern, and user-defined constants from the pattern are propagated to the rule.

For instance, in our example, the annotation of the tasks *User chooses vehicle* and *Change vehicle status* would be translated into:

$ins\_Select\_Vehicle(v) :- UserChoosesVehicle(), Vehicle(v, \text{`available'}, b, d, rt)$

$del\_Select\_Vehicle(v) :- UserChoosesVehicle(), Select\_Vehicle(v)$

$ins\_Vehicle(v, \text{`reserved'}, b, d, rt):-ChangeVehicleStatus(), Select\_Vehicle(v), Vehicle(v, s, b, d, rt)$

$del\_Vehicle(v, s, b, d, rt) :- ChangeVehicleStatus(), Select\_Vehicle(v), Vehicle(v, s, b, d, rt)$

Table 1. Natural language patterns to executable logic rules

N.L. Pattern	Derivation rules to create
create C	ins_C(c, v_0, ..., v_n) :- taskName(), arg$_0$(v_0), ..., arg$_n$(v_n)
at$_0$(v_0), ..., at$_n$(v_n)	ins_C'(c, v_0, ..., v_0) :- taskName(), arg$_0$(v_0), ..., arg$_n$(v_n); for each $C \sqsubseteq C'$
delete_c C	del_C(c) :- taskName(), Select_C(c)
	del_C'(c) :- taskName(), Select_C(c), C'(c); for each $C' \sqsubseteq C$
	del_C''(c) :- taskName(), Select_C(c); for each $C \sqsubseteq C''$
associate R(C$_0$,...,C$_n$)	ins_R(c$_0$,...,c$_n$) :- taskName(), Select_C_0(c$_0$), ..., Select_C_n(c$_n$)
delete_a R(C$_0$,...,C$_n$)	del_R(c$_0$,...,c$_n$) :- taskName(), Select_C_0(c$_0$), ..., Select_C_n(c$_n$)
change C at(v_i)	ins_C(c, ..., v_i, ...) :- taskName(), arg$_0$(v_i), Select_C(c), C(c, v_0, ..., v_n)
	del_C(c) :- taskName(), Select_C(c)
select C with	ins_Select_C(c) :- taskName(), arg$_0$(v_0), ..., arg$_0$(v_n), C(c, v_0, ..., v_n)
at$_0$(v_0), ..., at$_n$(v_n)	del_Select_C(c) :- taskName(), Select_C(c)
check C	query(v_0, ..., v_n) :- taskName(), arg$_0$(v_0), ..., arg$_n$(v_n), C(c, v_0, ..., v_n)
at$_0$(v_0), ..., at$_n$(v_n)	

The first rule selects a vehicle that is available when the user executes the task *UserChoosesVehicle*. The second rule is used to deselect any other previously selected vehicle. The third and forth rule are in charge of updating the state status of the selected vehicle to "reserved" when the user executes the *ChangeVehicleStatus* task.

Validation Through Executing the Logic Rules. The idea now is to use the OpExec tool to (1) load the executable logic rules representing the business process tasks, (2) load some integrity constraints to check while executing the process, and (3) execute the process to validate the satisfaction of the constraints.

In order to load the executable logic rules, OpExec only needs the rules themselves, and some relational database connection containing one table for each class/association, and one *Select_C* table for each class C in order to store the current instances selected for each class.

OpExec can then load integrity constraints written in the of form *denial constraints*, that is, logic formulas stating the condition that should never occur in the database. For instance, the condition *damaged Vehicles cannot be booked by a User* can be written as

$$\bot :\text{-} \; Vehicle(v, s, b, d, rt), s = \text{'reserved'}, d = \text{'true'}$$

Then, at runtime, OpExec is in charge of executing the logic rules according to the client invocations (*INNoVaServ*, in this case). Such invocations cause the insertion/deletion of objects in the database, or their selection (which is stored in the corresponding *Select_C* table), according to the translation of the natural language patterns. The *check* pattern requires special attention since it is translated as a new query that checks the condition. In this case, OpExec executes the query and returns the result to the client, so, the client can take the decision of what to do next (such as repeating the last task if the checking did not succeed).

The important feature of OpExec w.r.t. validating the process is its ability to validate user-defined integrity constraints over its execution. That is, whenever a new object/relation is created/deleted, OpExec ensures that no defined constraint is being violated, otherwise, the data update is rejected and a warning is returned to the client. For instance, when executing the *Change Vehicle Status* task, we might violate the condition that *damaged Vehicles cannot be booked by a User*. If this is the case, *OpExec* notifies the client about this problem and rejects the execution of the task. Thus, the user might notice that the *User chooses and selects a car* task, requires selecting a car which is not only available, but also not damaged. Note that data inconsistencies might arise independently of the Service Blueprint lane in which the data update is performed, thus, they are not taken into account in our validation approach.

In order to ensure the efficiency of these checking, OpExec integrates an incremental checking approach [15], that is, it only checks those constraints that might be violated according to the data update, and only for the relevant values. It is worth mentioning that OpExec is implemented as a Java library that can be invoked from any other tool.

We plan then to integrate both OpExec and INNoVaServ as follows: model validation will rely on EVL scripts bundled in INNoVaServ, so that when such validation is run, the EVL rules invoke internally OpExec functions, which will then return the results that will be graphically displayed by INNoVaServ. Even though this process is slightly less efficient than simple EVL or OCL-based validation, it ensures not only syntactic but also semantic correctness.

4   Related Works

This section reviews existing works in the are of service blueprinting and process executability.

Even though service blueprinting emerged in the 80's [4], it has not attracted too much attention from academics until recently and most of the existing literature is focused on the application of the technique to different contexts. Regarding the combination with formal techniques, in [16] Berkley uses phase distributions to control service operations whereas fuzzy graph is used in [17] to modularize product extension service blueprints. There are also some works on the combination of service blueprinting with the Theory of Inventive Problem Solving (TRIZ), like the one from Lee et al. [18]. As well, there are different works on the revision or extension of service blueprinting for specific purposes. For instance, Flieb and Kleinatelkamp presented a revised version of service blueprints in [19] based on the production-theoretic approach to identify starting points for improving process efficiency.

Regarding tool-support for service blueprinting, as the rise of product-service-systems [20] has contributed to increase the interest in this user-centered technique for business process modeling, most of existing works have emerged recently from the industry. This way, tools like Canvanaizer[9] and Real Time Board[10] to name a few are web-based applications that support collaborative edition of (canvas and) service blueprints. They bundle a simple and intuitive graphical interface (specially the latter) but, in contrast with *INNoVaServ* they were not devised to work with models, so they are limited to offer graphical representations of the blueprint, which can not be processed later.

From a more academic point of view, some remarkable works are those from Liang et al. [21], who use a CAD-based system for service blueprinting and the one from Lao [22] who developed a collaborative tabletop tool for service design based on some of the principles of service blueprinting. All in all, these are tools focused on usability and collaborative properties which have dismissed the utility of model-based tool support as a way to enable the systematic processing of the information collected in the blueprint. Thus they are very far from being ready to incorporate any kind of formal reasoning.

On the other hand, a quick look at the plenty of systematic literature reviews on business process modeling and the topics covered by them shows that this is somehow a most mature field. Recent reviews are indeed not focused on characterizing existing proposals, since that has been largely done in the past, but on available mechanisms to assess their quality [23] or complexity [24].

Regarding process executability, the approach in [14] uses a UML class diagram, a BPMN diagram and a set of OCL operation contracts to achieve process executability. Some of the advantages of [14] in contrast to our work are that it uses the *de-facto* standard modeling languages for data and processes, together with the fact that the OCL language has a more expressive power than structured natural language. Thus, it requires that the modeler and business people know BPMN and OCL, whereas service blueprints and structured natural language are simpler and more intuitive.

BPEL (or WS-BPEL) allows to specify executable business processes using an XML format which makes it difficult to read. Although there is a mapping between BPMN 2.0 and BPEL it is incomplete and suffers from several issues [25]. The approach in [26] uses XML nets, a Petri-net-based process modelling approach which is meant to be executable. It uses a graphical language, which maps to a DTD (XML Document Type Definition) to represent the data required by the process, and the data manipulations are graphically

---

[9] https://canvanizer.com/.
[10] https://realtimeboard.com/.

shown in the XML net. In contrast to our approach, this solution is technology-based, as the specification of the models is based on XML, and details of how to achieve executability are not explained.

YAWL [27] is a workflow graphical language whose semantics are formally defined and based on Petri nets, with its corresponding execution engine. Intuitively, the tasks are annotated with their inputs and outputs, without defining what changes are made by each of them. Thus, the execution engine only detects missing information and it is not able to fully execute the operation.

In [28] it is possible to obtain automatically an imperative model that is executable in a standard Business Process Management System. However, data is defined as a set of unstructured variables and the pre and postconditions merely state conditions over the data, instead of indicating exactly what is done by the different tasks.

Earlier attempts are [29,30]. Both approaches focus on defining a conceptual model which can then be automatically translated to achieve execution. However, the purpose of [29] is different to ours: their main goal is to be able to validate the model through execution, while ours is to achieve executability by using a combination of UML class diagram and service blueprint enriched with structured natural language. Similarly, the approach in [30] - which translates the models into Pascal - is outdated by object-oriented programming languages.

Finally, there are many different works that deal with verification and validation in business process models, such as [31,32]. However, these techniques do not execute the model as we do and, to the best of our knowledge, none of them use service blueprints.

To sum up, none of the analysed works rely on service blueprints as a way of modeling the business process. Moreover, not all of them provide the ability of executing the model automatically using a structured data model. Finally, none use structured natural language to specify the meaning of each of the tasks, thus requiring concrete knowledge of the language used to do so.

5   Conclusion and Further Work

This work has presented a framework for defining service blueprints that can be validated using simulation techniques. Moreover, we have proposed the implementation of the framework integrating two tools: *INNoVaServ*, which is model-based tool for service blueprinting, and *OpExec* which is a model simulator. The linkage is done by attaching semantic annotations to service blueprint tasks, and translating them into executable logic rules.

To the best of our knowledge, this is the first work that relies on service blueprinting as an executable business process modeling technique. Moreover, it does so in the context of a toolkit for business modeling that enables the development of bridges with other notations for business (process) like Canvas [33], e3Value [11], Process Chain Networks [12] or BPMN.

This paper addresses consequently one of those which has been acknowledged to be the main problems of service design: the lack of proper technical support [20]. The constant and rapid development of new services, products or product-service offerings to address new needs as soon as they appear is indeed a must for any organization, giving rise to an increasing interest in the discipline of service design. However, being an emerging field, this is one of those areas in which industry is ahead of academia, giving rise to the advent of solutions which does not always meet the desirable criteria in terms of quality.

The development of this type of proposals will help as well to mitigate the differences and challenges that emerge between different worlds that speak different languages, as it is the case with the variety of stakeholders typically involved in the development of digital products or services nowadays [34].

Acknowledgments. This research has been funded by the Ministry of Science and Innovation under the ELASTIC project (TIN2014-52938-C2-1-R), the Government of Madrid under the SICOMORo-CM project (S2013/ICE- 3006) and by the SSME Research Excellence Group (Ref. 30VCPIGI05) co-funded by URJC and Banco Santander.

References

1. Fisk, R.P., Brown, S.W., Bitner, M.J.: Tracking the evolution of the services marketing literature. J. Retail. **69**(1), 61–103 (1993)
2. Spohrer, J., Maglio, P.P., Bailey, J., Gruhl, D.: Steps toward a science of service systems. Computer **40**(1), 71–77 (2007)
3. Cook, L.S., Bowen, D.E., Chase, R.B., Dasu, S., Stewart, D.M., Tansik, D.A.: Human issues in service design. J. Oper. Manage. **20**(2), 159–174 (2002)
4. Shostack, G.L.: Designing services that deliver. Harvard Bus. Rev. **62**(1), 133–139 (1984)
5. Gounaris, S., Tanyeri, M., Kostopoulos, G., Gounaris, S., Boukis, A.: Service blueprinting effectiveness: drivers of success. Int. J. Manag. Serv. Qual. **22**(6), 580–591 (2012)
6. Van Gorp, P., Dijkman, R.: A visual token-based formalization of BPMN 2.0 based on in-place transformations. Inf. Softw. Technol. **55**(2), 365–394 (2013)
7. Noguera, M., Hurtado, M.V., Rodríguez, M.L., Chung, L., Garrido, J.L.: Ontology-driven analysis of UML-based collaborative processes using OWL-DL and CPN. Sci. Comput. Program. **75**(8), 726–760 (2010)
8. Gronback, R.C.: Eclipse Modeling Project: A Domain-specific Language (DSL) Toolkit. Pearson Education, London (2009)
9. Bitner, M.J., Ostrom, A.L., Morgan, F.N.: Service blueprinting: a practical technique for service innovation. Calif. Manag. Rev. **50**(3), 66–94 (2008)
10. Osterwalder, A., Pigneur, Y.: Business Model Generation: A Handbook for Visionaries, Game Changers, and Challengers. Wiley, Hoboken (2010)
11. Gordijn, J., Akkermans, H., Van Vliet, J.: Designing and evaluating e-business models. IEEE Intell. Syst. **16**(4), 11–17 (2001)
12. Sampson, S.E.: Visualizing service operations. J. Serv. Res. **15**(2), 182–198 (2012)

13. Vara, J.M., Marcos, E.: A framework for model-driven development of information systems: technical decisions and lessons learned. J. Syst. Softw. **85**(10), 2368–2384 (2012)
14. De Giacomo, G., Oriol, X., Estañol, M., Teniente, E.: Linking data and BPMN processes to achieve executable models. In: Dubois, E., Pohl, K. (eds.) CAiSE 2017. LNCS, vol. 10253, pp. 612–628. Springer, Cham (2017). doi:10.1007/978-3-319-59536-8_38
15. Oriol, X., Teniente, E., Rull, G.: TINTIN: a tool for incremental integrity checking of assertions in SQL server. In: Proceedings of the 19th International Conference on Extending Database Technology, EDBT 2016, Bordeaux, France, 15–16 March 2016, pp. 632–635 (2016)
16. Berkley, B.J.: Analyzing service blueprints using phase distributions. Eur. J. Oper. Res. **88**(1), 152–164 (1996)
17. Song, W., Wu, Z., Li, X., Xu, Z.: Modularizing product extension services: an approach based on modified service blueprint and fuzzy graph. Comput. Indust. Eng. **85**, 186–195 (2015)
18. Lee, C.H., Wang, Y.H., Trappey, A.J.: Service design for intelligent parking based on theory of inventive problem solving and service blueprint. Adv. Eng. Inform. **29**(3), 295–306 (2015)
19. FlieB, S., Kleinaltenkamp, M.: Blueprinting the service company. J. Bus. Res. **57**(4), 392–404 (2004). European Research in Service Marketing
20. Cavalieri, S., Pezzotta, G.: Product - service systems engineering: state of the art and research challenges. Comput. Ind. **63**(4), 278–288 (2012)
21. Liang, T.P., Wang, Y.W., Wu, P.J.: A system for service blueprint design. In: 2013 Fifth International Conference on Service Science and Innovation (ICSSI), pp. 252–253. IEEE (2013)
22. Lau, N.: ServiceSketch: a collaborative tabletop tool for service design (2011)
23. de Oca, I.M.M., Snoeck, M., Reijers, H.A., Rodriguez-Morffi, A.: A systematic literature review of studies on business process modeling quality. Inf. Softw. Technol. **58**, 187–205 (2015)
24. Polančič, G., Cegnar, B.: Complexity metrics for process models - a systematic literature review. Comput. Stand. Interfaces **51**, 104–117 (2017)
25. Fabra, J., de Castro, V., Álvarez, P., Marcos, E.: Automatic execution of business process models: exploiting the benefits of model-driven engineering approaches. J. Syst. Softw. **85**(3), 607–625 (2012)
26. Lenz, K., Oberweis, A.: Modeling interorganizational workflows with XML nets. In: HICSS-34. IEEE Computer Society (2001)
27. Foundation, T.Y.: YAWL - User Manual. Version 4.1. (2016). http://www.yawlfoundation.org/pages/support/manuals.html
28. Parody, L., López, M.T.G., Gasca, R.M.: Hybrid business process modeling for the optimization of outcome data. Inf. Softw. Technol. **70**, 140–154 (2016)
29. Lindland, O.I., Krogstie, J.: Validating conceptual models by transformational prototyping. In: Rolland, C., Bodart, F., Cauvet, C. (eds.) CAiSE 1993. LNCS, vol. 685, pp. 165–183. Springer, Heidelberg (1993). doi:10.1007/3-540-56777-1_9
30. Mylopoulos, J., Borgida, A., Greenspan, S.J., Wong, H.K.T.: Information system design at the conceptual level - the taxis project. IEEE Database Eng. Bull. **7**(4), 4–9 (1984)

31. Gonzalez, P., Griesmayer, A., Lomuscio, A.: Verification of GSM-based artifact-centric systems by predicate abstraction. In: Barros, A., Grigori, D., Narendra, N.C., Dam, H.K. (eds.) ICSOC 2015. LNCS, vol. 9435, pp. 253–268. Springer, Heidelberg (2015). doi:10.1007/978-3-662-48616-0_16
32. Deutsch, A., Hull, R., Vianu, V.: Automatic verification of database-centric systems. SIGMOD Rec. **43**(3), 5–17 (2014)
33. Ovans, A.: What is a business model. Harvard Bus. Rev. **23** (2015)
34. Gray, J., Rumpe, B.: Models for the digital transformation. Softw. Syst. Model. **16**(2), 1–2 (2017)

Deadlock-Freeness Verification of Business Process Configuration Using SOG

Souha Boubaker[1,2], Kais Klai[3(✉)], Katia Schmitz[3], Mohamed Graiet[4],
and Walid Gaaloul[1]

[1] Telecom SudParis, UMR 5157 Samovar, Universite Paris-Saclay, Paris, France
souha.boubaker@telecom-sudparis.eu
[2] ENIT, UR-OASIS, University of Tunis El Manar, Tunis, Tunisia
[3] LIPN, CNRS UMR 7030, University of Paris 13, Villetaneuse, France
kais.klai@lipn.univ-paris13.fr
[4] ISIMM, Monastir University, Monastir, Tunisia

Abstract. Configurable process models are increasingly used in many industries as reference processes shared between different process tenants. These processes are configured and adapted according to their specific needs through *configurable elements* (i.e. the variation points). Since configuration decisions are taken prior to execution, incorrect ones may lead to critical behavioral issues such as deadlocks. In this work, we propose a formal behavioral model based on the Symbolic Observation Graph (SOG) allowing to find the set of correct configuration choices while avoiding the state-space explosion problem. This set of configuration choices, jointly provided with the configurable process, will support and help business analysts in deriving deadlock-free variants.

Keywords: Business process management · Configurable process model · Process variants · Formal verification

1 Introduction

A configurable business process model [11,17] represents a family of a large number of related process models. Such a process model is reused and configured according to a given application context by selecting one design option for each configurable element (i.e. a *variation point*). The non-configurable elements represent the commonalities in the configurable model. The configuration decisions of a configurable element are made at design-time [17] leading to configured processes called *variants*. For instance, In Fig. 1, a simplified example of a configurable process model designed by a process provider for a hotel booking agency is presented. The process is modeled using the Configurable Business Process Model and Notation (C-BPMN) [5,14], a configurable extension to BPMN. The travel agency has a number of branches in different countries. Depending on specific needs of a country, each branch performs a different variant of this process model in terms of structure and behavior. For instance, a process tenant may

© Springer International Publishing AG 2017
M. Maximilien et al. (Eds.): ICSOC 2017, LNCS 10601, pp. 96–112, 2017.
https://doi.org/10.1007/978-3-319-69035-3_7

need an exclusive execution of the connector *S1*'s outputs (configurable connectors are modeled with a thicker border). This refers to configuring *S1* to an *XOR-split*. Another tenant may choose to execute them concurrently by configuring *S1* to an *AND-split*.

As the configuration decisions of the configurable elements are applied at design-time [17], any design mistake (e.g. configuring *S1* to *OR-split* and *j3* to *AND-join* leads to a deadlock) should be avoided in order to avert execution errors in the derived variants. Furthermore, configurable processes may be large with complex inter-dependencies between the different possible configurations. Consequently, the configuration can not be done manually and a correctness verification phase is essential. So far, a number of approaches have addressed the verification of the process configuration correctness. Some of them have only discussed the syntactical correctness (e.g. [11,17]), others have attempted to verify behavioral correctness but have faced the exponential number of state-space problems (e.g. [13]). Very few have addressed the configuration behavior verification while trying to reduce state explosion problem (e.g. [1,4]) but still suffer from the exponential complexity of generating their reachability graph.

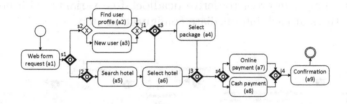

Fig. 1. A configurable hotel booking process model

The aim of this paper is to address this state space problem while verifying one of the most important behavioral correctness properties a process execution should hold, the deadlock-freeness. We propose an abstraction of a configurable process model using the Symbolic Observation Graph (SOG for short) [12,15] based on its configurable elements. This abstraction offers a two-fold advantage: (1) the analysis and the verification of the corresponding configurable process can be reduced to the analysis of its abstraction, and (2) the set of possible combinations of elements configurations that result in deadlock-free variants are obtained prior to configuration time. Once found, these combinations are used to assist the business analyst in deriving deadlock-free variants.

The SOG is a versatile symbolic representation formalism that allows to build an abstraction of the reachability state graph of a formally modeled system (e.g. using Petri net). In our case, this abstraction is achieved by observing the configurable elements of the process (that label the SOG arcs) and by hiding non configurable elements inside the aggregates (the SOG nodes). Moreover, without limiting the generality of our approach, we propose to use C-BPMN as input notation. BPMN is highly adopted by stakeholders of different roles (e.g. IT architects, business analysts, etc.) since it is considered as the internationally recognized industry standard notation for business process description. Also, since the large majority of modeling languages can be mapped into it, we use Petri-net as a pivot formalism to represent C-BPMN process model and its corresponding semantics. This semantics depicts the generic behavior of configurable connectors and thus all possible behavior.

Figure 2 depicts the milestones followed in order to obtain deadlock-free process variants using our SOG-based approach. First of all, as depicted on the left-hand side of the figure, C-BPMN is used as input process. Then, we map this process to a Petri net-based model; and we define new semantics to take into account configurable connectors (step 1, see Sect. 3). Afterward, we extend the algorithm of SOG graph construction by three main points (step 2): (i) by observing and highlighting configurable connectors in the graph arcs; (ii) by hiding non-configurable elements' states in aggregates (see Sect. 4.1); and (iii) by restricting the graph nodes to the ones leading to deadlock-free configurations (see Sect. 4.2). As a result, we obtain a reduced SOG graph that groups the behavior of all correct configurations. The set of correct configurations combinations is then extracted (step 3). The last three steps are performed on-the-fly during the SOG construction. The correct configurations are finally supplied to the business analyst in order to derive deadlock-free variants, with no need to verify correctness at each intermediate configuration step.

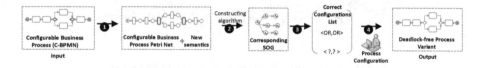

Fig. 2. Our approach overview

The remainder of the paper is organized as follows. In Sect. 2, some preliminary concepts on Petri nets are described. New Petri net-based models for business process and then for configurable process models as well as their semantics are defined in Sect. 3. Then, in Sect. 4.1, we define a new Symbolic Observation Graph associated with the configurable Petri net-based model and we explain our approach based on the SOG construction algorithm. Our approach is evaluated in Sect. 5. We present the related work in Section 6. Finally, we conclude and provide insights for future work.

2   Preliminaries and Notations

In this work, we use Petri nets, which offer a formal model for concurrent systems. Note that our approach does not rely on specific Petri net properties but can be applied to any formal model as soon as states and transition relation are well defined.

Definition 1 (Petri Nets). *A Petri net is a tuple $N = \langle P, T, F, W \rangle$ s.t.:*

- *P is a finite set of places and T a finite set of transitions with $(P \cup T) \neq \emptyset$ and $P \cap T = \emptyset$,*
- *A flow relation $F \subseteq (P \times T) \cup (T \times P)$,*
- *$W : F \rightarrow \mathbb{N}^+$ is a mapping assigning a positive weight to arcs.*

Each node $x \in P \cup T$ of the net has a pre-set and a post-set defined respectively as follows: $^{\bullet}x = \{y \in P \cup T \mid (y, x) \in F\}$, and $x^{\bullet} = \{y \in P \cup T \mid (x, y) \in F\}$. For a transition t, $W^-(t) \in \mathbb{N}^{|P|}$ (resp. $W^+(t) \in \mathbb{N}^{|P|}$) denotes the vector where, $\forall p \in P$, $W^-(t)(p) = W(p, t)$ (resp. $W^+(t)(p) = W(t, p)$). A marking of a Petri net N is a function $m : P \rightarrow \mathbb{N}$.

Semantics: Let m be a marking of $t \in T$, a transition t is said to be enabled by m, denoted by $m \xrightarrow{t}$, iff $W^-(t) \leq m$. When t is enabled by m, its firing leads to a new marking m', denoted by $m \xrightarrow{t} m'$, s.t. $m' = m - W^-(t) + W^+(t)$.

For a finite sequence $\sigma = t_1 \ldots t_n$, $m_i \xrightarrow{\sigma} m_n$ denotes the fact that σ is enabled by m_i, and that its firing leads to m_n. Given a set of markings S, we denote by $Enable(S)$ the set of transitions enabled by elements of S. The set of markings reachable from a marking m in N is denoted by $R(N, m)$. The reachability graph of a Petri net N, denoted by $G(N, m_i)$ (m_i is the initial marking), is the graph where nodes are elements of $R(N, m_i)$ and an arc from m to m', labeled with t, exists iff $m \xrightarrow{t} m'$. The set of markings reachable from a marking m, by firing the transitions of a subset T' only is denoted by $Sat(m, T')$. By extension, given a set of markings S and a set of transitions T', $Sat(S, T') = \bigcup_{m \in S} Sat(m, T')$. For a marking m, $m \nrightarrow$ denotes that m is a dead marking (i.e., there is no transition s.t. $m \xrightarrow{t}$ which means $Enable(\{m\}) = \emptyset$).

Definition 2 (WF-Nets). *Let $N = \langle P, T, F, W \rangle$ be a Petri net and F^* is the reflexive transitive closure of F. N is a Workflow net (WF-net) iff:*

- *there exists exactly one input place $i \in P$, s.t. $|^{\bullet}i| = 0$,*
- *there exists exactly one output place $o \in P$, s.t. $|o^{\bullet}| = 0$,*
- *each node is on a directed path from the input place to the output place, i.e. $\forall n \in P \cup T, (i, n) \in F^* and (n, o) \in F^*$.*

Definition 3 (Deadlock-free WF-Net). *Let $N = \langle P, T, F, W \rangle$ be a WF-net and m_i, m_f be the initial (i.e. only i is marked) and final (i.e. only o is marked) markings respectively. N is said to be deadlock-free iff $\nexists m \in (R(N, m_i) \setminus \{m_f\})$ s.t. $m \nrightarrow$.*

3 Formal Model for Configurable Business Processes

In order to obtain an abstract formal definition of a business process model, we formally map a process in BPMN notation to *Petri nets*, specifically into a new model called Business Process Petri Nets (*BP2PN*). Then, we extend the

BP2PN to take into account configurable connectors, leading to a new model, namely the Configurable Business Process Petri Nets (*CBP2PN*). Authors in [10] have established a mapping from well-formed BPMN models to Petri nets. In this work, we extend this mapping by preserving blocks as transitions allowing to define configurable transitions.

3.1 Business Process Petri Nets (BP2PN)

Definition 4 (BP2PN). *A BP2PN is a tuple* $B = \langle P, T \cup OP, F, W, O \rangle$ *where:*

- $\langle P, T \cup OP, F, W \rangle$ *is a WF-Net,*
- $F \subseteq (P \times T \cup OP) \cup (T \cup OP \times P)$ *is the flow relation,*
- $O : OP \rightarrow \{OR^-, OR^+, XOR^-, XOR^+, AND^-, AND^+\}$ *is a mapping that assigns a type to each operator,*

BP2PN is a *Workflow net* such that, the set of places P corresponds to the set of conditions determining the enabling of a task or a connector; and the set of transitions $T \cup OP$ corresponds to the set of tasks and connectors. These nodes are interconnected through a set of arcs (using F). Each connector must either be a join (the $-$ right exponent) or a split (the $+$ exponent) while having a type: OR, XOR or AND.

Semantics: In the previous notation, we retain the connectors blocks and we define new execution semantics inspired from the original semantics of Petri nets.

Given a marking m of a *BP2PN* B, the fireability and the firing of any transition in $T \cup \{t \in OP \mid O(t) \in \{AND^-, AND^+\}\}$ follows the original semantics of Petri nets. However, transition t s.t. $O(t) \in \{OR^-, OR^+, XOR^-, XOR^+\}$ follows a new semantics:

Let m be a marking and t be a transition of OP, the fact that t is enabled by m is denoted by $m \xrightarrow{t}$, and $m \xrightarrow{t} m'$ denotes that m' is reached by firing t from m:

- $O(t) = OR^-$
  - m enables t iff $\exists S \subseteq {}^{\bullet}t$ s.t. $m_{|S} \geq W^-(t)_{|S}$
  - when m enables t, the firing of t from m leads to a marking m' iff $m' = m - W^-(t)_{|S} + W^+(t)$ where S is the biggest subset of ${}^{\bullet}t$ satisfying $m_{|S} \geq W^-(t)_{|S}$.
- $O(t) = XOR^-$
  - m enables t iff $\exists p \in {}^{\bullet}t$ s.t. $m(p) \geq W^-(t)(p) \wedge \forall q \in {}^{\bullet}t, m(q) < W^-(t)(q)$
  - when m enables t, the firing of t from m leads to a marking m' iff $m' = m - W^-(t))_{|\{p\}} + W^+(t)$ where p is the sole place satisfying the firability condition.
- $O(t) = OR^+$ (**resp.** $O(t) = XOR^+$)
  - when m enables t, the firing of t from m leads to a marking m' iff $\exists S \subseteq t^{\bullet}$ (**resp.** $\exists p \in t^{\bullet}$) s.t. $m' = m - W^-(t) + W^+(t)_{|S}$ (**resp.** $m' = m - W^-(t) + W^+(t)_{|\{p\}}$).

Note that only the firing of transitions t s.t. $O(t) \in \{OR^+, XOR^+\}$ is defined because the fireability follows original semantics. It is worth mentioning that the previous semantics of OR^+ and XOR^+ leads to non-deterministic firing. For instance, having a split transition OR^+ with 2 output places p_1 and p_2, its firing leads to 3 possible reachable markings m_1 (only p_1 is marked), m_2 (only p_2 is marked), and m_{1_2} (both places are marked). Also, we emphasize that the semantics of a join transition OR^- is inline with the well defined pattern 8 in [3] (*Multi merge*), that expressly allows the firing of the join as soon as it condition is satisfied (without synchronizing the different flows).

3.2 Configurable Business Process Petri Nets (CBP2PN)

Definition 5 (CBP2PN). *A CBP2PN is a tuple $CB = \langle P, T \cup OP, F, W, O, C \rangle$ where:*

- $\langle P, T \cup OP, F, W, O \rangle$ *is a BP2PN;*
- $C : OP \rightarrow \{true, false\}$ *is a function determining the configurable operators (i.e. any $t \in OP$ s.t. $C(t) = true$).*

Back to our example, our *C-BPMN* process is mapped onto *CBP2PN* in Fig. 3. In this notation, according to Definition 5, activities and connectors are modeled by transitions and their ordering is modeled by places connecting the different transitions. Configurable transitions are also highlighted with a thick border. This example includes 6 configurable transitions: s_1, s_3, s_4, j_2, j_3 and j_4. We denote by OP^c the set of configurable operators s.t. $OP^c = \{o \in OP \mid C(o) = true\}$. A configurable operator $c^c \in OP^c$ includes a generic behavior which is restricted using the configuration phase. It is configured by changing its type (e.g. from OR to AND) w.r.t. the set of configuration constraints [17] defined in Table 1. Each row corresponds to a configurable connector that can be configured to one or more of the connectors in columns. Thus, these constraints allow to specify which regular connector's type may be used in the derived process variant. For example, a configurable OR can be configured to any connector's type while a configurable AND can only be configured to an AND. In the following, we define a configuration of a connector $t^c \in OP^c$ by $Conf(t^c) \in \{OR^-, OR^+, XOR^-, XOR^+, AND^-, AND^+\}$ and the set of all possible configurations of t^c by $AllConf(t^c)$.

Note that, when configuring all configurable connectors of a *CBP2PN*, we obtain a *BP2PN*, as a configurable connector is changed into regular connector after configuration. One possible configuration of the process net of Fig. 3 can be done by selecting the following configuration choices: (i) s_1, s_3 and s_4 are configured to regular XOR^+, (ii) j_2 is configured to a regular AND^-; and (iii) j_3 and j_4 are configured to regular XOR^-.

Table 1. Constraints for the configuration of connectors [17], $x \in \{+, -\}$.

	OR^x	XOR^x	AND^x
OR^x	✓	✓	✓
XOR^x		✓	
AND^x			✓

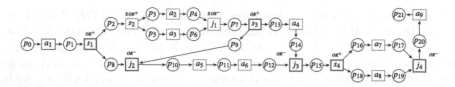

Fig. 3. The CBP2PN of the configurable process in Fig. 1

Semantics: The semantics of *CBP2PN* is described in the following, on the one hand, by inheriting the dynamics of *BP2PN* for non configurable connectors, on the other hand, by adding new semantics for configurable ones. This semantics is defined such that any reachable marking by any possible instance of a configuration is represented. In the following, we consider a configurable transition as the union of all possible configurations. That way, we can define its enabling and firing rules as if it is the union of all executable configured transitions. Since a configuration of AND^-, AND^+, XOR^- and XOR^+ do not change type, its semantics remains the same as previously defined. Regarding configurable OR^- and OR^+ transitions, the fireability and the firing rules follow the new semantics as follows. Let m be a marking and t^c be a transition of OP^c, s.t. $O(t^c) \in \{OR^-, OR^+\}$:

- m enables t^c, denoted by $m \xrightarrow{t^c}$ iff $\exists x \in AllConf(t^c)$ s.t. $m \xrightarrow{x}$
- when m enables t^c, for some configuration x of t^c, the firing of t^c from m, under configuration x, leads to a marking m', denoted by $m \xrightarrow{t^c,x} m'$ iff $m \xrightarrow{x} m'$

Using this semantics, the reachability marking graph associated with a *CBP2PN* covers the behavior of all the possible configurations. For instance, having the *CBP2PN* of Fig. 3, the configurable transition $s1$ could be configured either to: (i) AND^+, with all of its output places marked, (ii) XOR^+, with only one of the output places marked, or (iii) OR^+ with one or more output places marked.

Definition 6 (Deadlock-free CBP2PN). *Let $\underline{CB}$ be a CBP2PN. CB is said to be deadlock-free if at least one deadlock-free BP2PN could be configured from CB.*

Our *CBP2PN* of Fig. 3 is considered correct since one can configure at least one correct variant by choosing XOR type as configuration choice for all its configurable connectors (the correctness of such a variant is proven in Sect. 4.2). However, incorrect variants could be derived from this process as well. For instance, one can choose the alternatives presented earlier that leads to a deadlock caused by an exclusive choice XOR^+ (i.e. s_1) followed by a synchronizing join AND^- (i.e. j_2). In this situation, in order to be enabled, the transition AND^- will be waiting for both places p_8 and p_9 to be marked, however only one could be marked. So, the resulting variant could never terminate properly and the corresponding reachability graph contains a dead marking. In the following, we propose to use the SOG in order to abstract the reachability graph of a *CBP2PN*, and to extract the correct configurations (leading to deadlock-free *BP2PN*).

4 Symbolic Observation Graph for Process Configuration

In this paper, we check the behavior correctness of all possible configurations of a configurable model. This refers to verifying the reachability graph that covers them all. In order to reduce the underlying state space explosion problem, we propose to use the Symbolic Observation Graph (SOG). The SOG-based abstraction technique was introduced for model checking of concurrent systems [12] and then applied on the verification of inter-enterprise business processes [15].

4.1 Symbolic Observation Graph

Given a *CBP2PN*, the set of observed transitions, denoted by *Obs* is the set of configurable connectors i.e. $Obs = OP^c$, while any other transition belongs to the set of unobserved transitions, denoted by *UnObs*, i.e., $UnObs = (T \cup OP) \setminus Obs$. In such a way, we construct the Symbolic Observation Graph (SOG) as a graph where each node is a set of states linked by unobserved transitions and each arc is labeled by an observed transition. Nodes of the SOG are called aggregates and are represented and managed efficiently using Binary Decision Diagrams (BDDs). As a result, by highlighting observable transitions, the SOG represents the global behavior of a process configuration in only one reduced graph. In the following, we first formally define *an aggregate*, and then the SOG associated with a *CBP2PN*.

Definition 7 (Aggregate). *Let $N = \langle P, T \cup OP, F, W, O, C \rangle$ be a CBP2PN having m_i and m_f as initial and final markings respectively. An aggregate of N is a triplet $\langle S, d, f \rangle$ s.t.:*

- $S \subseteq R(N, m_i)$ *is a set of reachable markings, where $\forall s \in S$:*
  - $(\exists (s', u) \in R(N, m_i) \times UnObs \mid s \xrightarrow{u} s') \Leftrightarrow s' \in S;$
  - $(\exists (s', o) \in R(N, m_i) \times Obs \mid s \xrightarrow{o} s') \wedge (\nexists (s'', u) \in S \times UnObs) \mid s'' \xrightarrow{u} s') \Leftrightarrow s' \notin S.$
- $d \in \{true, false\}; d = true$ *iff S contains a dead state.*
- $f \in \{true, false\}; f = true$ *iff S contains a final state.*

In addition to the d and f attributes of an aggregate, the above definition specifies the states that must belong to an aggregate (the aggregation criterium) and those that must be excluded: For any state s in the aggregate, any state s' being reachable from s by the occurrence of an unobserved transition, belongs necessarily to the same aggregate. (2) For any state s in the aggregate, any state s' which is reachable from s by the occurrence of an observed transition is necessarily outside the aggregate, unless s' is reachable from a state s' in the aggregate by an unobserved transition.

Before defining the SOG, let us introduce the following operation: $Out(a, t)$: returns, for an aggregate a and an observed transition t, the set of states outside a that are reachable from some state in a by firing t, i.e., $Out(a, t) = \{s' \in R(N, m_i) \mid \exists s \in a.S, s \xrightarrow{t} s'\}$

Definition 8 (Deterministic SOG). *Let $N = \langle P, T \cup OP, F, W, O, C \rangle$ be a CBP2PN having m_i and m_f as initial and final markings respectively. The Deterministic Symbolic Observation Graph (SOG) associated with N is a graph $\mathscr{G} = \langle A, Obs, \rightarrow, A_0, \Omega \rangle$ where:*

(1) A is a non empty finite set of aggregates satisfying :
   - *$\forall a \in A, \forall t \in Obs, Out(a, t) \neq \emptyset \implies \exists a' \in A$ s.t. $a' = Sat(Out(a, t), UnObs)$*
(2) $\rightarrow \subseteq A \times Act \times A$ is the transition relation where:
   - *$((a, t, a') \in \rightarrow') \Leftrightarrow ((t \in Obs) \wedge Out(a, t) \neq \emptyset \wedge a' = Sat(Out(a, t), UnObs))$*
(3) A_0 is the initial aggregate s.t. $A_0.S = Sat(m_i, UnObs)$.
(4) $\Omega = \{a \in \mathscr{A} \mid m_f \in a.S\}$.

The nodes of the symbolic observation graph are aggregates (1). The finite set of aggregates A of a SOG is defined in a complete manner so that the necessary aggregates are represented. Point (2) defines the transitions relation: there exists an arc, labeled with an observed transition t, from a to a' iff a' is obtained by saturation on the set of reached states ($Out(a, t)$) by the firing of t from $a.S$. The last two points of Definition 8 characterize the initial aggregate and the set of final aggregates respectively. Starting from the initial marking, the original SOG construction algorithm introduced in [12] follows a classical depth first search based traversal of the built aggregates. Each aggregate is built by a transitive closure application on unobserved transitions. The successor a' of an aggregate a is built by, first, firing an observed transition from states of a, then by adding all the reachable states by unobserved transition.

At this stage, the correctness of the *SOG* can be characterized as follows.

Definition 9 (Correct SOG). *Let $N = \langle P, T \cup OP, F, W, O, C \rangle$ be a CBP2PN. Let $\mathscr{G} = \langle A, Obs, \rightarrow, A_0, \Omega \rangle$ the SOG associated with N.*

*$\mathscr{G}$ is correct **iff** there exists a configuration c of N ($c = \{\langle t, Conf(t) \rangle : t \in OP^c\}$) s.t. for every path $\pi = A_0 \xrightarrow{t_1, conf(t_1)} A_1 \ldots A_{n-1} \xrightarrow{t_n, conf(t_n)} A_n$, with $A_n \in \Omega$; if $\{\langle t_i, Conf(t_i) \rangle : 0 \leq i \leq n\} = c$ then $\forall 0 \leq i \leq n, A_i.d = false$.*

Based on Definition 6, characterizing a deadlock-free *CBP2PN*, and Definition 9, characterizing a correct *SOG* associated with a *CBP2PN*, the following result naturally links these two characterizations.

Proposition 1. *Let $N = \langle P, T \cup OP, F, W, O, C \rangle$ be a CBP2PN. Let $\mathscr{G} = \langle A, Obs, \rightarrow, A_0, \Omega \rangle$ the SOG associated with N. Then, N is deadlock-free **iff** $\mathscr{G}$ is correct.*

Proof. Let N be a *CBP2PN* and $\mathcal{G}$ its corresponding *SOG*. First, according to Definition 9, if $\mathcal{G}$ is correct then there exists a configuration c s.t. for every path π in the *SOG* having $\pi = A_0 \xrightarrow{t_1, conf(t_1)} A_1 \dots A_{n-1} \xrightarrow{t_n, conf(t_n)} A_n$, with $A_n \in \Omega$; if it's configurations set $\{\langle t_i, Conf(t_i) \rangle : 0 \le i \le n\}$ is equal to c, then all aggregates are deadlock-free, i.e. $A_i.d = false, 0 \le i \le n$. Since the *SOG* preserves by construction all possible configurations of N, then each path from the initial to the final aggregate represents one configuration allowing to derive one variant. Hence, there exist at least a deadlock-free variant of N. Consequently, according to Definition 6, N is correct.

In the following, we propose to adapt the original SOG construction algorithm [12], associated with a *CBP2PN*, in three ways. First, by adopting the new semantics. Second, the deadlock-freeness property is checked on the fly, such that any aggregate containing a deadlock state is not inserted in the graph and so are all the underlying paths. Finally, the set of correct configurations is extracted on-the-fly.

4.2   Extracting Correct Configurations Using the SOG

In this section, we present the core contribution of this paper: A construction algorithm of the SOG associated with a *CBP2PN*. Regarding to the original SOG construction algorithm [12], Algorithm 1 allows to reduce the SOG, by removing, on-the-fly, the paths involved in incorrect configurations, and by saving, within the initial aggregate the correct configurations. To reach this goal, two new attributes are added to an aggregate: (1) c, which is the set of correct (possibly partial) configurations, starting from this aggregate (and leading to a final aggregate). (2) nc, which is the set of incorrect (possibly partial) configurations, starting from this aggregate (leading to a dead one). Once the *SOG* is built, the set of correct configurations will be saved within the initial aggregate.

In the following, we go through Algorithm 1 to explain the main steps while using our running example, and the corresponding (reduced) SOG, in Fig. 4a for illustration. Note that the main novelties of this algorithm w.r.t. the algorithm of [12], are underlined.

Two main data are used: The SOG graph $\mathcal{G}$, containing aggregates and edges, and a stack containing the to-be-treated aggregates associated with the set of fireable observed transitions F_{obs}.

The first step of Algorithm 1 (lines 5–10) allows to build the initial aggregate and to push it onto the stack. Then, the main loop (lines 11–49) processes the set of to-be-treated aggregates as follows: a stack item (line 12) and the corresponding current observed transition in F_{obs} (line 14) are picked, and the successor of the current aggregate by that transition, if any, is calculated using the semantics of Subsect. 3.2 (line 15–20). This includes the computation of the dead (line 19) and final (line 20) attributes of the obtained successor aggregate. If the latter is deadlock-free aggregate, and if it has not already been explored, then it is pushed onto the stack with its set if fireable observed transitions (lines 21–24). For instance, following the path at the top of Fig. 4a, new aggregates A_0 until the final one A_6 are consecutively pushed onto the stack. Since A_6 is a final aggregate (does not enable any observable transition), it will be popped from the stack (line 38), and we start the loop again by picking A_5 to consider its remaining observed transitions (in this case the transition $\langle j4, OR \rangle$ leads again to A_6), and so on.

If the newly built successor aggregate a' has already been treated (lines 25–30), then the current aggregate a inherits from a' its correct and incorrect configuration (to which the transition linking a to a' is added). This is ensured by functions $UpdateC$ and $UpdateNC$ (lines 26–29). The function $UpdateC$ also verifies that, starting from the same aggregate a, a correct configuration do not include an existing (or to-be-treated) incorrect one, as in this case it leads to a deadlock in a different transitions' firing order. This way, correct and incorrect configurations are computed backwards starting from the final aggregate to the initial one. For instance, in Fig. 4a, consider the aggregate A_{10} obtained through A_8 and A_9, the firing of $\langle j3, AND \rangle$ leads to the existing aggregate A_4. As A_4 was already dealt with earlier through the path on top of the graph, this means that 3 correct *partial* configurations are added to this aggregate, namely $\{\langle s4, XOR \rangle, \langle j4, XOR \rangle\}$, $\{\langle s4, XOR \rangle, \langle j4, OR \rangle\}$ and $\{\langle s4, AND \rangle, \langle j4, AND \rangle\}$. Hence, A_{10} inherits these configurations while being concatenated to the current fired transition $\langle j3, AND \rangle$. Similarly, going backwards to A_0 after entirely processing A_8 and A_9, we obtain the complete correct configurations $13 - 15$ depicted in Fig. 3(b).

Regarding an aggregate a' holding a dead state, firstly, the corresponding fired observed transition is concatenated to the incorrect configurations of its predecessor a (line 33). Obviously, a' is not pushed onto the stack and no edge is created. Then, we recursively verify its predecessors starting from a using the function $recRemoveAggregate(a, t)$ (line 34). Using this function, each predecessor aggregate is removed only if the states enabling the current one becomes dead (i.e. there is no other enabled transition from that state). In this case, its successors are also recursively eliminated in case they do not have other predecessors. As an example, the red path in Fig. 4(a) refers to firing $\langle s_1, AND \rangle$, $\langle s_3, XOR \rangle$ then $\langle j_2, OR \rangle$. According to our semantics, $\langle j_3, OR \rangle$ may be fired by 4 possible markings in the aggregate A_{12}, namely m_{12}, m_{10_14}, m_{11_14} and m_{12_14}. However, in case of firing by either m_{10_14} or m_{11_14}, the obtained aggregate will allow a second firing of the same transition (i.e. using the remaining token in p_{10} or p_{11}). This leads to a final state holding two tokens, which is a dead state in our approach. Hence, according to Algorithm 1 the obtained aggregate is eliminated as well as its predecessors A_{12} and A_{11} (following the blue dashed line). And yet, since it enables $\langle S_3, AND \rangle$, A_{10} is not deleted.

It is worth noting that before popping an aggregate from the stack and storing it in the graph (lines 38–39), a final check is carried out on its correct configurations by the function $CompareCorrect$ (line 37). Actually, many observed transitions may be fired from the same aggregate, so some of the corresponding correct configurations may refer to the same one. Hence, a correct sequence is preserved if, for every first fired observed transition op, (i) it is fireable by

nofillcomment 1. Deadlock-free Symbolic Observation Graph

Require: $N\langle P, T \cup OP, F, W, O, C\rangle$, Obs, m_i, m_f
Ensure: $\mathscr{G}\langle A, Obs, \rightarrow, A_0, \Omega\rangle$, C

```
 1: Vertices A=∅; vertex a, a';                          # Aggregates
 2: Vertices C=∅;                                        # Correct configurations
 3: set S, S', UnObs = (T ∪ OP) \ Obs, F_obs, F'_obs;
 4: stack st; Edges E= ∅;
 5: S = Sat({m_i}, UnObs);                               # first Aggregate
 6: a.S = S;
 7: a.d = DetectDead(a.S);
 8: a.f = IsFinal(a);
 9: F_obs = fireableObs(a);                              # fireable observed transitions of a
10: st.Push(⟨a, F_obs⟩);
11: while st == ∅ do
12:    ⟨a, F_obs⟩ = st.Top();
13:    if (F_obs ≠ ∅) then
14:       t = F_obs.next();
15:       S' = Out(a.S, t)
16:       if (S' ≠ ∅) then
17:          S' = Sat(S', UnObs);
18:          a'.S = S';
19:          a'.d = DetectDead(a'.S);
20:          a'.f = IsFinal(a');
21:          if (¬a'.d) then                             # there is no dead state in a'
22:             if (∄x ∈ A s.t. x == a') then            # a' found for the first time
23:                F'_obs = fireableObs(a');
24:                st.Push(⟨a', F'_obs⟩);
25:             else                                     # a' is an existing aggregate
26:                free a';
27:                Let a' be the already existing aggregate;
28:                UpdateC(a, a', t);
29:                UpdateNC(a, a', t);
30:             end if
31:             E = E ∪{a, ⟨t, Conf(t)⟩, a'};
32:          else                                        # there is a dead state in a'
33:             a.nc = a.nc ∪ {⟨t, Conf(t)⟩};
34:             recRemoveAggregate(a, t)
35:          end if
36:       end if
37:       CompareCorrect(a);
38:       st.Pop();
39:       A = A ∪ {a} ;
40:       if (m_i ∈ a.S) then
41:          C = a.c;
42:       end if
43:    end if
44: end while
```

the states that have fired another sequence starting by op (i.e. different configurations), or (ii) if their common operators have the same configured type (i.e. the same configurations but in a different order). Otherwise, the sequence is considered as incorrect and is eliminated.

Finally, the set of correct configurations is obtained from the initial aggregate, the last one popped from the stack. As a result, each path of the obtained SOG starting from the initial aggregate and leading to a final aggregate, represents one possible configuration and belongs to the set of configurations C. In this case, this configuration leads to a deadlock-free $BP2PN$. Note that, different paths could represent a configuration (e.g. two concurrent configurable connectors).

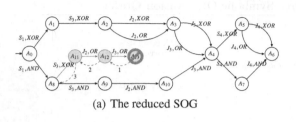

(a) The reduced SOG

	S1	S2	J2	J3	S4	J3
1	XOR+	XOR+	XOR-	XOR-	XOR+	XOR+
2	XOR+	XOR+	XOR-	XOR-	XOR+	OR+
3	XOR+	XOR+	XOR-	XOR-	AND+	AND+
4	XOR+	XOR+	XOR-	OR-	XOR+	XOR+
5	XOR+	XOR+	XOR-	OR-	XOR+	OR+
6	XOR+	XOR+	XOR-	OR-	AND+	AND+
7	XOR+	XOR+	OR-	XOR-	XOR+	XOR+
8	XOR+	XOR+	OR-	XOR-	XOR+	OR+
9	XOR+	XOR+	OR-	XOR-	AND+	AND+
10	XOR+	XOR+	OR-	OR-	XOR+	XOR+
11	XOR+	XOR+	OR-	OR-	XOR+	OR+
12	XOR+	XOR+	OR-	OR-	AND+	AND+
13	AND+	AND+	AND-	AND-	XOR+	XOR+
14	AND+	AND+	AND-	AND-	XOR+	OR+
15	AND+	AND+	AND-	AND-	AND-	AND-

(b) Deadlock-free configurations

Fig. 4. Reduced SOG and extracted configurations for the CBP2PN in Fig. 3

The reduced SOG of our example contains 8 nodes and 10 arcs, and all correct configurations are summarized in Fig. 3(b). Hence, the analyst may be helped on-the-fly during the configuration process by confronting his/her configurations with the correct configurations in this table.

For instance, we can evaluate the correctness of the *BP2PN* variant discussed in Sect. 3.2. After applying $\langle s_1, XOR \rangle$, the control-flow is either propagated through the place p_2 or p_8. In this case, it is clear that the connector j_2 (i.e. after applying $\langle j_2, AND \rangle$) could never be enabled, which causes a deadlock. Relying on Fig. 3(b), we can notice that there is no configuration starting with $\{\langle s_1, XOR \rangle, \langle j_2, AND \rangle\}$.

Using the SOG, the state space is greatly reduced in three fashions: (i) only configurable transitions are observed, and the remaining transitions are hided in aggregates; (ii) the graph is deterministic since it groups, for each configuration, all reachable markings in one aggregate; and (iii) the different process variants share common markings in one common SOG graph, instead of constructing graphs as much as the number of possible configurations. In the following section, we conduct experiments to demonstrate such mitigation of the state explosion problem as well as the feasibility of our approach.

5   Experiments and Evaluation

To prove its feasibility, we have implemented and deployed our approach as an extension of an existing tool that initially computes the SOG of a petri-net model w.r.t. a set of observed transitions. As explained previously, this extension takes into account the new semantics presented in this paper for *CBP2PN* models. It also allows to symbolically detect on-the-fly deadlocks within aggregates and to reduce the SOG accordingly. The developed tool takes as input a GrML (Graph Markup Language) file [8] describing the *CBP2PN* model (i.e. transitions, operators annotated as configurable, and arcs) and returns the reduced SOG and the correct configurations.

In order to evaluate its performances and to demonstrate the opportunities offered by our approach, we performed experiments to show (i) the reduction

of the space explosion problem and (ii) the impact of the input model structure on the size of the obtained SOG. Firstly, we propose to explore the size of the constructed SOG using our tool against a naive approach, where each variant of a *CBP2PN* is built and analyzed separately. Secondly, we propose to analyse the impact of the variation of the structure complexity and the number of observed transitions of a *CBP2PN*, on the size of the corresponding SOG. Taking our running example model (Fig. 3), this variation leads to 86 different process models. We basically evaluate the structure complexity using the well known metric CFC (Control Flow Complexity)[9] which is defined as:
$\sum_{c \in AND+} 1 + \sum_{c \in XOR+} |c^{\bullet}| + \sum_{c \in OR+} (2^{|^{\bullet}c|} - 1)$.

Table 2 contains three multi-columns. The first one varies the considered parameters of the *CBP2PN* model (i.e. CFC and observed transitions (Obs)) and gives the number of possible configurations for each variation. Then, the size of the obtained SOG is evaluated in terms of number of correct configurations (Nb correct confs), aggregates (A), edges (E) and execution time. This graph is finally compared against the naive approach. However, since the naive approach is very fastidious, we built only the reachability graphs corresponding to the correct configurations. The three first columns give the average number if states, arcs and execution time over these correct configurations. The last column, gives the worst execution time in case all the configuration have been analyzed to extract correct ones. The construction of the reachability graph has been performed with our SOG-based tool as well, by observing all the transitions of the model (in this case, the SOG coincides with the reachability graph).

In this evaluation, as we can observe from the Table 2, we took into account three levels of complexity (depending on the number of OR+). The higher the value of CFC, the more complex is a process's configuration, since the number of

Table 2. Checking deadlock-freeness on SOG vs RG

CBP2PN			SOG				Naive approach (RG)			
CFC (avg)	Obs	Nb possible confs(avg)	Nb correct confs(avg)	A(avg)	E(avg)	Exec time (sec)	Sates (sum)	Arcs (sum)	Exec time correct (sec)	Overall Exec time(sec)
21	6	729	15	13	26	1.580	283.50	331.95	0.051	2.478
	5	243	5.66	8.66	16	0.693	104.14	133.57	0.017	0.729
3OR+	4	81	2.33	5.66	8.66	0.353	42.17	49.62	0.007	0.243
	3	27	1	4	4	0.044	18	21	0.003	0.070
15.5	6	243	11.33	11	21	0.093	208.47	243.25	0.037	0.802
	5	81	5	7.77	13.77	0.051	93	106.30	0.017	0.267
2OR+	4	57.85	3.66	6.09	10.33	0.030	66.72	77.81	0.012	0.191
	3	22.50	2	4.33	5.83	0.018	36.20	42.20	0.006	0.068
10	6	81	8	9.50	17.50	0.015	144	168	0.024	0.243
	5	54	4	7	11.83	0.010	72	84	0.014	0.184
1OR+	4	18	4.25	5.75	9.87	0.008	76.71	89.46	0.014	0.058
	3	13.24	2.58	4.23	6.29	0.006	46.44	54.18	0.008	0.040

possible configurations increases with the number of configurable OR connectors. For example, the CFC value 21 regards the process with only OR connectors, we can observe that the number of possible configurations as well as the extracted correct ones are relatively high compared to those having CFC 10. Moreover, the more transitions are observed, the less reduced is the SOG comparing to the reachability graph.

Comparing to the naive approach, the obtained results in Table 2 show that the SOG is always significantly smaller in terms of number of states and arcs. For example, in case of a model having 6 configurable operators with OR type (i.e. the first row), we can observe that the obtained SOG includes only 13 aggregates and 26 arcs which is very reduced comparing to the size of the original graph of 729 possible configurations. Indeed, after applying a naive approach on only correct configurations (i.e. extracted from the SOG), the obtained graph has almost 283 states and 331 arcs resulting from the sum of 15 reachability graphs. Consequently, our work not only helps finding correct configurations but also further minimize the memory usage and the computing time, since only one reduced graph is constructed. To ensure the reproducibility of our experiments, please refer to our web page[1].

6   Related Work

In order to facilitate the design of configurable process models, a range of process modeling languages have been recently extended with variable elements such as Event-driven Process Chain (EPC) (e.g. [17,18]), Business Process Model Notation (BPMN) (e.g. [5,14]) and Yet Another Workflow Language (YAWL) (e.g. [11]). Based on some of them, a number of approaches have attempted to reach correct process configuration either syntactically [11,17] or behaviorally. Traditionally, behavioral correctness related to process configuration can be handled by verifying every single possible configuration using existing work on verification of business processes and workflows [2] and some existing tools such as Woflan [19]. However, these methods are too time-consuming and lead to the state space explosion problem. Authors in [13] discuss the Provop approach [14] for ensuring soundness of process variants derived by options. However, this approach is not feasible in large processes and runs into the state space problem. In [1], Petri net was used to formalize and verify correctness and soundness properties of Configurable EPC (C-EPC) processes. They derive propositional logic constraints that guarantee the behavioral correctness of the configured model. However, in these approaches authors achieve correctness by checking constraints at each configuration step. Also, authors impose that the C-EPC process model should be syntactically correct. In our work, we propose a model that finds all possible correct configurations at design time instead of configuration time without any restriction on the input C-BPMN process. This allows the process analyst to derive correct processes without intermediate computing. In [4], based on partner synthesis, the approach characterize all weakly terminating configurations

---

[1] http://www-inf.it-sudparis.eu/SIMBAD/tools/SOGImplementation.

using configuration guidelines. This technique was applied on C-YAWL and the configuration is built by hiding and blocking transitions while our approach configures C-BPMN process by changing configurable connectors behavior.

[16], which is applied on C-EPC using questionnaire models, and [6], which is applied on C-BPMN using configuration guidelines, have attempted to provide guidance to analysts for process configuration, however, these approaches especially ensure domain compliant variant and they do not consider any correctness criterion.

In our previous work [7], a formal approach for deriving correct process variants from a C-BPMN was proposed. It models the process using Event-B language and verifies the different constraints and properties using predicates. These predicates must be satisfied by each configuration step. This work contributes essentially to prevent structural correctness issues in process models configuration using a systematic design. However, structural correctness may not be sufficient. To the best of our knowledge, our previous work is the first one attempting to achieve correctness for specifically C-BPMN configurations. In the current work, we aim to especially achieve the behavioral correctness capturing the dynamics of the executable configured process model. Thus, for all possible instances of an executable configured process model, deadlocks should never occur. Our approach can be easily adapted to obtain *sound* [2] process variants, due to the lack of space, we focus in this work on the deadlock-freeness property.

7   Conclusion and Further Work

In this work, we propose an approach to assist business analyst to configure configurable processes correctly. In this paper, the correction criterion is characterized by the deadlock freeness of the obtained variant. We use a SOG-based abstraction model to find all correct configurations, i.e. leading to deadlock-free process variants. Such anomalies are excluded on-the-fly during the construction of the SOG. As a result, we obtain a reduced graph as well as a set of correct configurations. Then, this set will serve to support analysts during configuration. Our approach was implemented as an extension to an existing tool. And preliminary experiments show that our approach outperform naive approaches in terms of size of the explored configurable model.

As future work, we plan to first take into account other types of process configurations such as, activity and resource configuration as well as other patterns of OR-join, i.e. *Synchronizing merge* and *Discriminator* [3]. Then, we aim to entirely automate our approach procedure (depicted by Fig. 2). Finally, we aim to adapt the SOG construction algorithm in order to integrate other correctness constraints: generic properties, e.g. *soundness*, and specific properties, e.g. domain constraints.

References

1. Aalst, W.V.D., et al.: Preserving correctness during business process model configuration. Formal Asp. Comput. **22**(3–4), 459–482 (2008)
2. Aalst, W.V.D., et al.: Soundness of workflow nets: classification, decidability, and analysis. Formal Asp. Comput. **23**(3), 333–363 (2011)
3. Aalst, W.V.D., ter Hofstede, A.H.M., Kiepuszewski, B., Barros, A.P.: Workflow patterns. Distrib. Parallel Databases **14**(1), 5–51 (2003)
4. Aalst, W.V.D., Lohmann, N., Rosa, M.L.: Ensuring correctness during process configuration via partner synthesis. Inf. Syst. **37**(6), 574–592 (2012)
5. Assy, N.: Automated support of the variability in configurable process models. Ph.D. thesis, University of Paris-Saclay, France (2015)
6. Assy, N., Gaaloul, W.: Extracting Configuration Guidance Models from Business Process Repositories. In: Motahari-Nezhad, H.R., Recker, J., Weidlich, M. (eds.) BPM 2015. LNCS, vol. 9253, pp. 198–206. Springer, Cham (2015). doi:10.1007/978-3-319-23063-4_14
7. Boubaker, S., et al.: A formal guidance approach for correct process configuration. In: Service-Oriented Computing - 14th International Conference, pp. 483–498 (2016)
8. Brandes, U., et al.: GraphML Progress Report Structural Layer Proposal, pp. 501–512 (2002)
9. Cardoso, J.S.: Business process control-flow complexity: Metric, evaluation, and validation. Int. J. Web Serv. Res. **5**(2), 49–76 (2008)
10. Dijkman, R., Dumas, M., Ouyang, C.: Semantics and analysis of business process models in BPMN. Inf. Softw. Technol. **50**(12), 1281–1294 (2008)
11. Gottschalk, F., et al.: Configurable workflow models. Int. J. Coop. Inf. Syst. **17**(02), 177–221 (2008)
12. Haddad, S., Ilié, J.-M., Klai, K.: Design and evaluation of a symbolic and abstraction-based model checker. In: Wang, F. (ed.) ATVA 2004. LNCS, vol. 3299, pp. 196–210. Springer, Heidelberg (2004). doi:10.1007/978-3-540-30476-0_19
13. Hallerbach, A., et al.: Guaranteeing soundness of configurable process variants in provop. In: IEEE Conference on Commerce and Enterprise Computing, CEC, pp. 98–105 (2009)
14. Hallerbach, A., et al.: Capturing variability in business process models: the provop approach. J. Softw. Maintenance **22**(6–7), 519–546 (2010)
15. Klai, K., Tata, S., Desel, J.: Symbolic abstraction and deadlock-freeness verification of inter-enterprise processes. Data Knowl. Eng. **70**(5), 467–482 (2011)
16. La Rosa, M., et al.: Questionnaire-based variability modeling for system configuration. Softw. Syst. Model. **8**(2), 251–274 (2008)
17. Rosemann, M., Aalst, W.V.D.: A configurable reference modelling language. Inf. Syst. **32**(1), 1–23 (2007)
18. Van Der Aalst, W., et al.: Configurable Process Models as a Basis for Reference Modeling, pp. 512–518. Springer, Berlin (2006)
19. Verbeek, H., Basten, T., Aalst, W.V.D.: Diagnosing workflow processes using woflan. Comput. J. **44**(4), 246–279 (2001)

Formally Modeling, Executing, and Testing Service-Oriented Systems with UML and OCL

Loli Burgueño[1,2]([✉]) and Martin Gogolla[3]

[1] Universidad de Málaga, Málaga, Spain
loli@lcc.uma.es
[2] Marbella International University Centre, Marbella, Spain
loli@miuc.org
[3] University of Bremen, Bremen, Germany
gogolla@informatik.uni-bremen.de

Abstract. One of the issues that developers of service-oriented systems currently discuss is the lack of practical, but formal modeling notations and tools that can address the many different, important aspects. This paper presents an approach to model structural and behavioral properties of service-oriented systems with UML and OCL models. Essential service-oriented concepts as service request, service provision or orchestration are formally represented by UML concepts. The models can be executed, tested and analyzed. Feedback is given to the developer in terms of the UML and OCL model.

1 Introduction

In recent years, service-oriented systems have become increasingly complex. There has been an explosion on the number of services available—either produced within the companies internal development process or provided by third parties—that are integrated into service-oriented applications. Although following the principles of the Service-Oriented Architecture (SOA), this fact of encompassing such a high number of software components makes the task of reasoning about the systems as a whole difficult. Another reality that has a strong impact on the complexity of these applications is that SOA systems are generally distributed and weakly-coupled among themselves.

As for any software to be developed, it has been proved over the years [1,3,4] that the modeling of SOA applications is an essential task. This is the reason why there exists a wide range of tools and frameworks. In our view, there is a lack of practical tools for reasoning about the compositions of the services that service developers, integrators and choreographers build. To the best of our knowledge, current "formal" models for service composition or choreography rely on formalisms such as process algebras, temporal logic or petri nets. These models are useful to analyze some properties, but not so easy to be practically applied from a development perspective. In this sense, a lightweight approach with strong formal foundations could provide easy and cheap formalization of

© Springer International Publishing AG 2017
M. Maximilien et al. (Eds.): ICSOC 2017, LNCS 10601, pp. 113–122, 2017.
https://doi.org/10.1007/978-3-319-69035-3_8

systems. Specially if its models are not only useful from a theoretical perspective but also from a practical point of view.

In this contribution we have decided to make use of the tool USE (UML-based Specification Environment)[1]. Instead of using proprietary modeling techniques, USE is based on the Unified Modeling Language (UML) [5] extended with OCL constraints. The main motivation for our decision is the fact that, UML/OCL models can be formal and at the same time they are very useful from a practical point of view, because they can be applied to develop systems in an automated (or semi-automated) way using MDE (Model-Driven Engineering) principles, techniques and tools.

In this paper we present an approach to model structural and behavioral properties of service-oriented systems with UML and OCL models. Essential SOA concepts as service request, service provision or orchestration are formally represented by UML concepts. Behavioral properties are formally described with UML protocol state machines and operation contracts. OCL is applied for making the structure and behavior precise. Our models can be executed and analyzed for consistency, among other properties. Feedback is given to the developer solely in terms of the UML model. There is no need to work with a second verification language. Our approach supports the automatic generation of test scenarios in which, for example, the availability of services or requests can be checked. The consistency of the service model can be proved by constructing test scenarios.

The rest of the paper is organized as follows. Section 2 introduces the proposed approach and Sect. 3 concludes and outlines future research lines. Due to space limitations both the background to our work and related work are not discussed in this contribution, but in a full version of this work available in [2].

2   Service Modeling, Execution and Testing

This section explains our approach to model service-oriented systems with a case study, a *process* for an Online Test for students: A teacher designs an online test and then requests from a *service provider* to make the test online available; students as *service requester* conduct the test online; the results are recorded and are passed to the teacher for evaluation and result declaration as another service; a second service provider is the examination administration that offers a service to check for the legitimation of the students to participate in the test and record their results.

2.1   Case Study: Online Test

Figure 1 illustrates the basic artifacts for our case study. The left upper part displays a question sheet stating several questions and possible answers for an online multiple choice test that is designed by a teacher and is to be conducted by students. From the sheet, an online form (in the right part of the figure) will

---

[1] http://useocl.sourceforge.net/w/index.php/Main_Page.

be generated where students enter their email address and their answers to the questions. Each student reply will be recorded in an answer sheet (in the left bottom part of the figure) with a line for each student holding the student's email and her answers as well as two evaluation columns indicating the number of achieved points and a list of incorrectly answered questions.

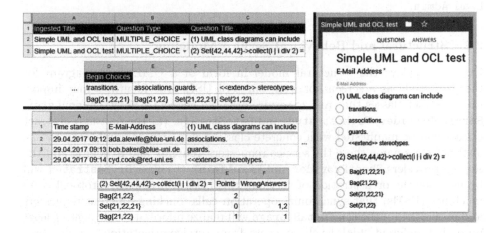

Fig. 1. Artifacts for the case study Online Test.

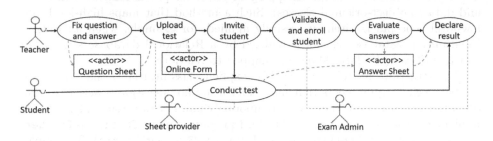

Fig. 2. Use case flow diagram for the Online Test.

The use case diagram-like representation in Fig. 2 gives an overview on the case study and shows the involved actors and use cases as well as the flow between the use cases. In the following text, actors and use cases are indicated using the codetypewriter font. We call this representation a use case flow diagram. We identify two service requesters (Student, Teacher) and two service providers (Sheet Provider, Exam Admin as a shortcut for Examination Administration). The process is initiated by the actor Teacher through fixing the Question Sheet by stating questions and answers. We represent data storages like the Question Sheet as (passive) actors. The use case fix question and answer may be repeated several times. The Teacher then uploads the online test. In this use case also the Sheet Provider is involved and responsible for transforming the Question Sheet into an Online Form. The Teacher then invites some Students to participate in the online test. The email addresses of the Students have to be validated by the Exam Admin before they get enrolled for the test. Every Student can then conduct the test through which the Sheet Provider fills the Answer Sheet. After closing the test, the Teacher can evaluate the answers and declares the result to the Students and to the Exam Admin.

2.2 Structural and Behavioral Service Modeling

Figure 3 displays the structural model in form of a UML class diagram for the case study as a screenshot from our tool USE. One identifies four important abstract classes that realize service-oriented concepts: ServiceRequester, ServiceProvider, Orchestrated, and DataStorage: (a) the first two abstract classes will be manifested with concrete classes taking the role indicated by the abstract class name (here the service requesters Teacher and Student, and the service providers SheetProvider and ExamAdmin); (b) class Orchestrated will be used for the orchestration of services; this class will embody protocol state machines (PSMs) that synchronize operation calls touching different requesters and providers; (c) the class DataStorage will realize information storages. Please note that different 'high-level' concepts from service-orientation (service provision, service request, orchestration, data) are formally realized by the same 'low-level', modeling concept (mapping of requests, provisions, orchestrations and data to object-oriented classes). Such a method that maps high-level into low-level concepts is often successfully applied, for example, when an Entity-Relationship database schema is realized by a Relational database schema, in which entities and relationships are mapped to relations.

The structural model is enriched by explicit class invariants that formulate model-specific requirements that must hold when no operation is active; during operation execution invariants may temporarily fail. For the case study, we have implemented some typical invariants (uniqueName, uniqueEMail, oneTeacher, oneExamAdmin, oneSheetProvider and Points_VS_WrongAnswers). The implementation of some is shown in the following listing.

```
context Teacher inv uniqueName: Teacher.allInstances->isUnique(name)
context Teacher inv oneTeacher: Teacher.allInstances->size=1
context AnswerSheet inv Points_VS_WrongAnswers:
  Rows->forAll(r|r.Points+r.WrongAnswers->size=r.answers->size)
```

The class diagram in Fig. 3 also shows operation signatures and thus determines part of the behavioral model. In order to distribute the functionality required by the use case flow diagram in Fig. 2 to the individual classes, we have applied the following method: If a class Cls participates in a use case u, that class will embody an operation uC (use case name u and C being the first letter of the class name) that is responsible for performing the respective actions of the use case on Cls objects. For example, the use

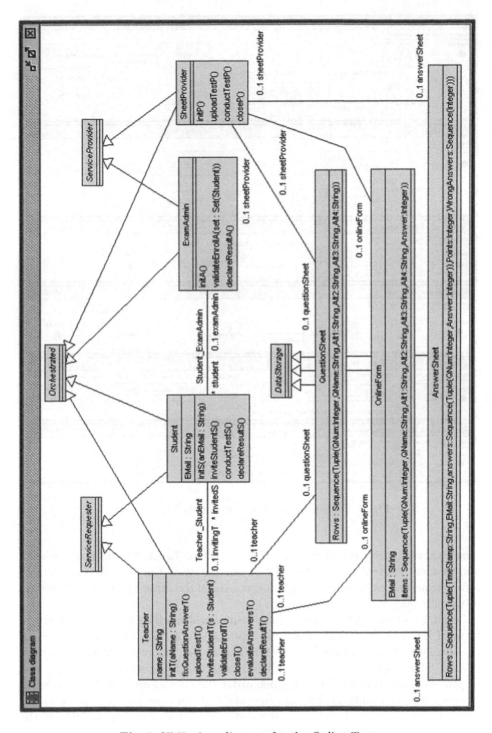

Fig. 3. UML class diagram for the Online Test.

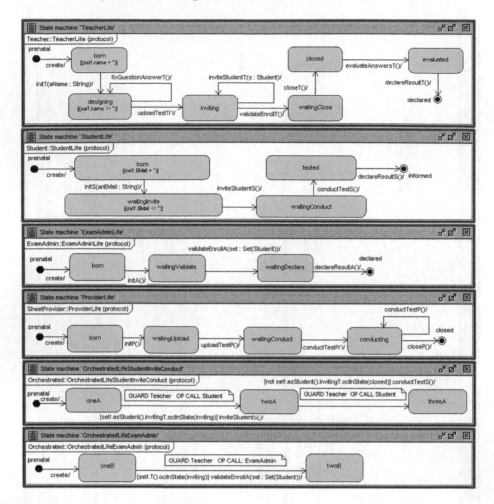

Fig. 4. UML protocol machines for the Online Test.

case `inviteStudent` is realized with the operations `Teacher::inviteStudentT` and `Student::inviteStudentS`. The object initiating the use case performs its own actions and calls the respective operations on the other objects participating in the use case.

Figure 4 shows central parts of the behavioral model for the case study in form of UML protocol state machines from our tool USE. One can identify in the top four protocol machines, one for each of the four provider and requester classes. These machines determine the order in which the services are requested or provided, i.e., it is specified in which order the operations from the respective classes are called; only guards and operations from a single class are handled here. The two protocol state machines at the bottom are responsible for the essential orchestration task. These two machines are attached to the abstract class Orchestrated, and the behavior restrictions are inherited to the specialized requester and provider classes. *Orchestration* in this context means that conditions (in form of guards) and events (in form of operation calls) from *different* classes are considered. The class referred to in the guard and the class belonging to the operation are different. For example, the next-to-last machine restricts a sequence of Student::inviteStudentS() and Student::conductTestS() operation calls by guards that refer to the inviting Teacher and require that this inviting teacher is in a particular protocol state.

In addition to the protocol state machine, the behavioral model is determined by giving an operation an imperative implementation, which is formulated on the modeling level without going into programming language details and is written in the language SOIL (Simple OCL-like Imperative Language). The behavioral model can be further sharpened by stating the operation effects in a declarative way with operation contracts in form of OCL pre- and postconditions. The operation implementation in terms of SOIL is guided and must respect the operation contracts. Correctness of the operation implementation relative to the operation contracts is checked in USE when test cases are run. As an example we show the implementation and the contract for one operation.

```
Teacher::inviteStudentT(s:Student)
  begin
  insert (self,s) into Teacher_Student;
  s.inviteStudentS()
  end
  pre   studentHasEMail: s.EMail<>null and s.EMail<>''
  pre   notInvited: self.invitedS->excludes(s)
  post invited: self.invitedS->includes(s)
```

2.3 Service Model Execution

Figure 5 shows an example execution run of the complete model. The twelve executed operations are stated as a listing in the lower right corner. The execution run involves exactly one object from every class, and each operation from every class is called once. Therefore, this run demonstrates that the behavioral service model can be instantiated and that the model is consistent and free from contradictions: All protocol state machines work properly together, and the reached final system state as well as the intermediate system states satisfy the model-inherent constraints (wrt multiplicity) and all explicit invariants from the class diagram; all operation contracts are satisfied. The sequence diagram shows lifelines for the single objects. The operation calls are indicated as message arrows from one lifeline to another lifeline. On the lifelines, the reached protocol states of the respective object are indicated. Thus the development of the objects from one protocol state to the next protocol state can easily be traced.

Due to space limitations, our testing approach to service-oriented systems is not presented in this paper. It is available in our technical report in [2].

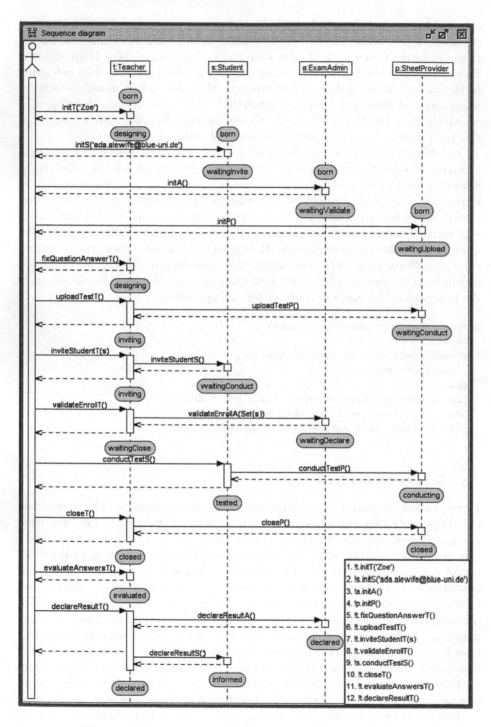

Fig. 5. UML sequence diagram for an example execution run.

3   Conclusions and Future Work

This paper presents an approach in which service-oriented systems are modeled using UML in combination with OCL. These models do not only focus on one aspect in service-orientation, but consider requests, provisions, orchestrations and data in a coherent manner. Based on the models of a system, properties such as the consistency and instantiability of service request, service provision and service orchestration can be verified by automatically building test scenarios where both processes and data are considered. The application of our approach to practical cases requires developer expertise in UML and OCL. The static system properties must be formulated with UML class diagrams and OCL invariants, and the dynamic properties with UML protocol machines and OCL contracts. The developer is supported in the process by USE in semi-automatically constructing test scenarios.

Currently, the test cases generated by our approach are system states that embody (a) structural aspects in form of object attributes and links between objects and (b) behavioral aspects in form of object states referring to the dynamic behavior and the orchestration in form of protocol state machines. We can check for the applicability of services, i.e. operations. In the future, we will consider system state sequences with service request and service provisions as transitions in between and properties of such system state sequences. Our plans also include the extension of our approach in order to allow the definition of initial states and support for checking whether a particular generated system state can be reached via service requests/provisions from the initial states. This implies an extension of the model validator in order to handle protocol states. Direct support for concepts like requester, provider, or data will be provided as well. To do so, we will equip such classes with predefined PSMs that can be extended according to the application needs. Furthermore, we will ease the definition of PSMs by allowing the definition of regular expressions over operations and derive PSMs from them. We also plan to provide predefined interfaces among requesters and providers supporting a direct and better communication between them. In order to check the applicability of our approach, firstly, we will work on larger and existing case studies based on real data and; finally, on the integration of our approach with existing SOA systems that needs to be modernized or integrated with others.

Acknowledgments. This work has been partially funded by Spanish Research Project TIN2014-52034-R.

References

1. Barjis, J.: The importance of business process modeling in software systems design. Sci. Comput. Program. **71**(1), 73–87 (2008)
2. Burgueño, L., Gogolla, M.: Formally modeling, executing, and testing service-oriented systems with UML and OCL. Technical report (2017). http://www.db.informatik.uni-bremen.de/publications/intern/BG2017.pdf

3. France, R., Rumpe, B.: Model-driven development of complex software: a research roadmap. In: Proceedings of the FOSE 2007, pp. 37–54. IEEE Computer Society (2007)
4. Mohammadi, M., Mukhtar, M.: A review of SOA modeling approaches for enterprise information systems. Procedia Technol. **11**, 794–800 (2013)
5. Rumbaugh, J., Jacobson, I., Booch, G.: The Unified Modeling Language Reference Manual. Pearson Higher Education, London (2004)

Mining and Analytics

App Update Patterns: How Developers Act on User Reviews in Mobile App Stores

Shance Wang[1], Zhongjie Wang[1($\boxtimes$)], Xiaofei Xu[1], and Quan Z. Sheng[2]

[1] Harbin Institute of Technology, Harbin 150001, Heilongjiang, China
{shance.wang,rainy,xiaofei}@hit.edu.cn
[2] Macquarie University, Sydney, NSW 2109, Australia
michael.sheng@mq.edu.au

Abstract. Mobile app stores receive numerous reviews that contain valuable feedbacks raised by users. Incorporating user reviews into iterative delivery of new App versions would improve the quality and ratings of Apps. To date, there is no explicit answer on whether and to what degree App developers make use of user reviews sufficiently and timely. In this paper, we extract requested features in user reviews and updated features in new versions, identify the latent relation between them, and discover 7 types of Update Patterns (UPs) by grouping similar Atomic Update Units (AUs). UPs delineate common behavioral characteristics of acting on user reviews from perspectives of feature intensity trend, sufficiency and responsiveness. Statistics are conducted to explore the similarity/difference between exhibited update patterns w.r.t. Apps, features, and time. Results would help developers get a clear understanding on their own habits on how to act on user reviews, and thus offer suggestions on utilizing user reviews more efficiently in App development.

Keywords: Mobile App · App store · User review · Atomic Update Unit (AU) · Update Pattern (UP) · Empirical study

1 Introduction

With the flourish of mobile Internet and service-dominant industries, the number of available mobile Apps grows drastically with the rate 4–7% per month. Mobile Apps dominate people's daily lives and have been a major channel through which people access cloud services anytime and anywhere to fulfill personal demands [2].

App store is a centralized platform for users to acquire Apps. In an App store, each App has a homepage showing its descriptions along with its developer, size, versions, etc. Users can submit reviews through its homepage. There are valuable information lurking in enormous amount of user reviews, such as bug reports, feature requests, complaints or appraisal, and the rating [10]. Potential App users could gain a first impression on an App from reviews of its previous users.

User reviews are important to App developers, too. As today's Internet-based services usually adopt agile development approaches such as rapid iterations and

© Springer International Publishing AG 2017
M. Maximilien et al. (Eds.): ICSOC 2017, LNCS 10601, pp. 125–141, 2017.
https://doi.org/10.1007/978-3-319-69035-3_9

continuous delivery, App developers would like to acquire feature requests from reviews, and then to consider fulfilling them in subsequent releases [17]. There has reached a consensus that user reviews bring positive effects to every phase of App development, especially requirement engineering and testing [14].

Because the number of user reviews is enormous and high-quality reviews are often intermingled with much more low-quality ones, App developers have to filter out those informative reviews [3], read them, extract useful requested features and perceive customer preferences [23], and fulfill these feature in next iteration. These actions are regarded as "response to customer voices". However, it is not sure whether all developers follow the same behavior pattern, i.e., do they have the same opinion on the value of user reviews and therefore utilize them timely and sufficiently? As far as we know, until now there are not enough research investigating this issue, which is still a great challenge.

The first work of this paper is to reveal the potential correlation between the features requested in user reviews and the behaviors performed by App developers on updating App into a new version. Since most of Apps are proprietary but open source Apps are in the minority, it is difficult to obtain fined-grained update descriptions by tracking changes of source code or documents. To achieve this goal, we can make use of update logs (i.e., "What's New") written by developers and publicized on the App homepage. An update log of a specific version is a text list describing what features have been added or updated in this version (compared with the previous version) [8]. As there have been many approaches for extracting *requested features* from review texts [5,7], it is possible to apply similar methods to extract *updated features* mentioned in "What's New", too. If a frequently-requested feature in a specific period appears strikingly in the update log of a subsequent version, it is indicated that there is latent correlation between user reviews and update behaviors during this period, thus we may think developers do elaborately consider user reviews when the App is updated. Detailed analysis is conducted from the following four perspectives:

- Changing trend of the intensity of a feature requested in user reviews, i.e., how does the intensity of a feature mentioned in users reviews fluctuate in the time interval between two neighboring versions of an App?
- Intensity of a feature updated in a new version, i.e., to what extent is a feature mentioned in "What's New" of the version?
- Update sufficiency for a specific feature, i.e., to what extent do App developers act on specific user expectations sufficiently in a new version?
- Update responsiveness for a specific feature, i.e., how long does it take for App developers to update an App in terms of the requested feature, or, to what degree do App developers respond to user requests timely?

Next task is to identify common behavior patterns of how App developers act on requested features. They are denoted as *Update Pattern* (UP). The second work is to present an update pattern mining method by splitting App update history into a set of Atomic Update Units (AU) and clustering them into groups. Obtaining UPs would further help us identify their pros and cons, respectively, so as to utilize user reviews more effectively.

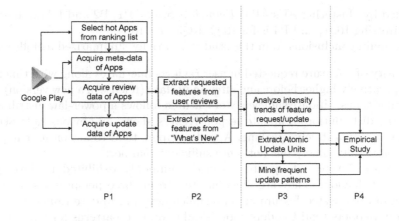

Fig. 1. Overall research framework with four phases

As Apps belong to different categories, offering diversified functionality to diversified target users, and developed by different developers having different working habits, we conjecture that update patterns in different Apps might not be the same. Even in one App, as it contains multiple features such as UI aesthetics, security, performance, we guess that the update patterns for different features might be different. Furthermore, as each feature is updated multiple times in multiple versions, the update patterns exhibited in different time might also be different.

The third work is to conduct an empirical study to observe the similarity/ difference among update patterns exhibited in different Apps, on different/ similar features, and at different times, respectively.

To sum up, we address the following research questions (RQs) in this study:

– RQ1: Does the correlation between user reviews and App updates really exist? If yes, are there common update patterns? And how to identify them?
– RQ2: In terms of different features of the same App, are there significant difference/similarity between their update patterns?
– RQ3: In terms of similar features of different Apps, are there significant similarity between their update patterns?
– RQ4: For a single feature of an App, are there significant changes of its update patterns exhibited in different time?

Figure 1 demonstrates our research approach consisting of four phases: (P1) *Data Collection*: user reviews and update logs (between March 2016 and March 2017) of 120 representative Apps are collected from Google Play; (P2) *Feature Extraction*: topic-based features are extracted from collected texts by NLP approaches so that raw corpus are transformed into numerical vectors; (P3) *Update Pattern Mining*: intensity trend of each feature along with time is calculated and decomposed into "Atomic Update Units (AUs)", along with the measurement of sufficiency and responsiveness of each AU, and update patterns are identified by clustering AUs; (P4) *Empirical Study*. P1, P2 and P3 are together for addressing RQ1, and P4 is for RQ2, RQ3 and RQ4.

The main conclusions from this study are briefly summarized as follows:

- Intensity of a feature requested in user reviews fluctuates along with time: it is comparatively higher before and after an update (release of a new version) than at other times. Update sufficiency of features follows a power-law distribution, but the distribution of update responsiveness shows an obvious right-skewed shape. Comparatively speaking, App developers tend to act on user requests in a preferably timely but not quite sufficient manner;
- There are 7 types of update patterns commonly exhibited in developers' update behaviors. They are differentiated from three perspectives: intensity trend of a requested feature, update sufficiency, and update responsiveness.
- App developers tend to adopt more similar update patterns for different features in their own App. Similar features across multiple Apps more tend to exhibit diversified update patterns. Therefore the adoption of update patterns depends largely on "App developers" rather than on "features". However, developers' behaviors lack enough coherence/continuity when they update the same feature at different times.

The remainder of the paper is organized as follows. Section 2 introduces the related work. Section 3 describes data collection and processing. Section 4 presents the methods on feature extraction and update pattern mining. Finally, Sect. 5 reports experimental results and Sect. 6 offers some concluding remarks.

2   Related Work

Extracting Features from Reviews and Update Logs. Feature extraction from "big data" in App stores is a fundamental problem in the App Store Analysis [14]. Various NLP techniques have been developed for this purpose. Finkelstein et al. [5] defined a feature as "a claimed functionality offered by an App, captured by a set of collocated words in App description and shared by a set of Apps in the same category"; a tool N-gramCollocationFinder in NLTK was used to extract *featurelets* from reviews. Guzman et al. [7] also used collocation finding approach, but added sentiment analysis for extracting sentiments and opinions associated to features, and topic modeling for grouping related features. Differently, Iacob et al. [9] used syntax templates (keywords + syntax rules) to identify features automatically from reviews. The third dominant approach is statistics-based models such as Latent Dirichlet Allocation (LDA), e.g., [1,6,21]. Since user reviews are numerous, informative reviews should be selected and recommended to App developers for elaborate considerations. Chen et al. [3] used a machine learning approach, EMNB, to classify reviews into "informative" and "non-informative" ones, then used LDA/ASUM to group reviews into clusters and prioritize them. Vu et al. [22] analyzed user reviews for keywords of potential interest which developers can use to search for useful opinions, including keyword extracting, keyword grouping, and keyword ranking.

Feature Classification. It is necessary to classify extracted features into categories so that they are handled by different strategies. Khalid et al. [11] presented a 12-category classification, e.g., `App Crashing`, `Compatibility`, `Feature Removal`, `Hidden Cost`, `Functional Error`, etc. Pagano and Maalej [18] presented a classification with four coarse-grained categories and 17 fine-grained ones, and they used manual annotation and frequent item mining approaches to identify the frequent co-occurrence of features in reviews. Maalej and Nabil [12] utilized several probabilistic techniques to automatically classify reviews into `bug reports`, `feature requests`, `user experiences`, and `ratings`. McIlroy et al. [16] distinguished 14 types of features and introduced a supervised multilabel classification method. In terms of features in "What's New", McIlroy et al. [15] introduced a classification with 5 types, i.e., `new content`, `new features`, `improvement`, `bug fix`, `permission`, and the frequency of their co-occurrence is analyzed to empirically study frequently-updated mobile Apps.

Incorporating User Reviews in App Development. Apps as typical Internet-based services, evolve fast in both external interfaces and internal functionalities [8]. To cope with unpredictable changes and failures, Apps need to be adaptive, too [4]. Syer et al. [20] found that the evolution of Apps are quite different from the evolution of traditional software, and direct feedback contained in user reviews facilitates design and testing respectively [10,14]. Nayebi et al. [17] studied how developers organize release strategy of Apps, and found that the majority of developers are willing to bend their time-based strategies to accommodate users' feedback, and believe that the rationale for release decisions affects user feedback. Martin et al. [13] studied App update logs and analyzed the causality between continuous updates of an App and its influence/rating, i.e., what types of updates would upgrade Apps' rating more easily. Palomba et al. [19] analyzed how developers utilize user reviews to improve App rating: they traced user reviews onto source code changes for monitoring the extent to which developers accommodate crowd requests and follow-up user reactions as reflected in their ratings, and results indicate that developers implementing user reviews are rewarded in terms of ratings.

3   Data Collection and Preprocessing

3.1   App Selection

We choose Google Play as the source to collect mobile Apps and their update logs and user reviews. Firstly, Android dominates mobile OS marketplace with the market share above 74%. Secondly, the amount of Apps and users in Google Play are both the biggest among Android App stores in the world, and the amount and quality of user reviews are the highest, too. Thirdly, its users are distributed across the world, thus the user reviews are extensively representative. To specify the candidate Apps in our study, we choose the top-100 free Apps and top-20 paid Apps from the hot ranking list of Google Play (date: March 1, 2016). User reviews and update logs of the 120 Apps between March 31, 2016 and March

30, 2017 are collected. In terms of user reviews, we collect nickname of users, review text, review date, and ratings. In terms of update logs, we collect App descriptions, distribution of user ratings, and the text of "What's new".

3.2 Dataset Preparation

User reviews and update logs of Apps are both dynamically updated, and Google Play only shows the latest version in the homepage of an App (previous versions cannot be seen), and shows only a set of latest user reviews (i.e., not complete historical reviews). Therefore, it is impossible to crawl required data all at once. What we adopt is to constantly monitor the homepage of each App and identify changes of update logs and reviews and record them instantly. We develop our own Google Play crawler which regularly crawls updated information from Apps' homepages and store them in an incremental manner. The tool constructs a virtual HTTP request and sends it to Google Play, then collects the returned review data (in JSON format), compares with local files, extracts updated reviews and saves to local files. Similarly, after an App update log is crawled, the tool compares it with previous update logs and check if it has been changed or not; if yes, a new version has been released and "What's New" is stored in local files.

As update frequency of user reviews is higher, we use five servers for the crawling task. Tasks for collecting reviews of 120 Apps are allocated onto these servers (each is responsible for 15–25 Apps). The sixth server is responsible for collecting update logs of 120 Apps one time per day (because the update frequency of Apps is comparatively lower). All the six servers are virtual machines on Aliyun (the biggest PaaS cloud service provider in China), with the configuration as: 1 GHz CPU, 1 GB memory, 2 Mpbs bandwidth, 40 GB harddisk, OS Windows Server 2008 R2. The servers are physically located in Silicon Valley, USA.

After 12-month collection, 17,557,170 reviews are collected, with 1,296 times of App updates. There are totally 5,923,379 distinct users each having contributed at least one review. Majority of the Apps have less than 500 daily reviews in most of days, while a few Apps have above 4,000 reviews in one day.

Preprocessing of the crawled data includes two main steps as the following:

(1) *Remove non-English texts.* Although our crawler access Apps only from English zone of Google Play, there are still some non-English review texts. We use *table lookup* to filter them out. English vocabulary table is offered by aspell[1]. If a word belongs to this table, it is considered as an English word. If the ratio of non-English words in a review is higher than a threshold (we use 0.3), this review is considered as a non-English one and is to be discarded. Finally, 51.16% reviews are discarded and 8,575,276 reviews remain in the dataset.

---

[1] http://wordlist.aspell.net/dicts.

(2) *Remove stopwords and stemming.* This is a common step in natural language processing. Besides the `Lextek`'s stopword list[2], when the reviews of a specific App are handled, the full and abbreviated names of this App and the names of its common operations are added to the stopword list.

4 Mining App Update Patterns

4.1 Extracting Features from User Reviews and "What's New"

BTM (Biterm Topic Model) is employed to extract features from texts of user reviews and "What's New". BTM is an optimized unsupervised LDA model especially for short texts (e.g., tweets, short reviews) by explicitly modeling the word co-occurrence patterns to enhance the topic learning and using aggregated patterns in the whole corpus for learning topics to solve the problem of sparse word co-occurrence patterns at document-level [24].

Reviews and "What's New" of each App are the input of BTM and a topic distribution matrix A is generated. If the total number of reviews is m, total number of update logs is l, and the number of topics generated by BTM is n, then A is $(m+l) \times n$ dimensions, and the value A_{ij} is the probability with which the i-th review or update log covers the j-th topic. Each topic is represented by a set of keywords and is used as a feature covered by the App.

4.2 Intensity Trend Chart of Feature Request/Update

Next step is to measure the daily intensity of each feature requested in reviews and updated in new versions, and to get intensity trend of each feature. In terms of one App, suppose $Day(i)$ is the day when the i-th review is published to App store, then the daily intensity of the j-th feature f_j in the k-th day is $I^R(f_j, k) = \sum_{Day(i)=k} A_{ij}$ (abbr. I^R_{jk}). Intensity of feature update in the update log of a new version $I^U(f_j, k)$ (abbr. I^U_{jk}) is measured similarly.

Changing trend of feature intensity along with time (*intensity trend* in short) is obtained based on a feature's daily intensity. Taking the data of `Instagram` App as an example, the intensity trend of a feature f related to *feed* with keywords `feed`, `chronological`, `posts`, etc., is shown in Fig. 2. X-axis is timeline, y-axis is the intensity of feature request/update, the curve is the intensity trend of the feature requested in reviews, and the vertical lines represent the intensity of the feature updated in new versions. This chart is described by $TC(f, t_s, t_e) = \{(k_1, I^R_{f,k_1}, I^U_{f,k_1}), ..., (k_N, I^R_{f,k_N}, I^U_{f,k_N})\}$ where N is the total number of days between date t_s and t_e, and $k_1, ..., k_N$ are N consecutive days. Such chart combines intensity trends of a specific feature in both user reviews and update logs, thus is helpful to observe the global correlation between them.

---

[2] http://www.lextek.com/manuals/onix/stopwords1.html.

Fig. 2. Feature trend of a feature of Instagram App (Color figure online)

4.3   Atomic Update Units (AU)

The intensity trend for one feature is to be decomposed into a set of "Atomic Update Units (AU)" in terms of a set of App updates which are considered as the actions developers take to respond to user requests in reviews. $TC(f, t_s, t_e) \rightarrow \{AU(f, T_1), AU(f, T_2), ...\}$, and $\forall i$, $AU(f, T_i) =< \{(k_{i1}, I_{f,k_{i1}}^R), (k_{i2}, I_{f,k_{i2}}^R), ...\}, I_{f,T_i}^U >$, where $k_{i1}, k_{i2}, ...$ are consecutive days during the time interval T_i, and I_{f,T_i}^U is the intensity of f updated in the last day of T_i. $AU(f, T_i)$ represents an interval T_i in which users make continuous requests on f in their reviews, and what the developers act on these requests is to make an update on f in the last day of T_i but there are no other updates during T_i.

Easily to imagine, lengths of different AUs are different. To help identify update patterns from AUs, we make normalization on the length of AUs by transforming *absolute dates* into *relative dates* and consequently all AUs are with the same length (e.g., 20 relative time points). A piecewise fitting method is adopted for this transformation. Detailed steps for decomposing intensity trend chart into normalized AUs are listed in Algorithm 1.

For each AU, we calculate the sufficiency and responsiveness to measure the speed and degree describing how developers act on a requested feature in user reviews after the last update (version) on this feature.

Update sufficiency for a feature, i.e., ratio of the update intensity w.r.t. aggregated request intensity in user views, measures to what degree App developers could consider the expectation of users. The higher the value is, the more sufficient the update is. It is measured by $Suf(f, AU_i) = Norm(\frac{I_{f,T_i}^U}{\sum_{k=t_i^s}^{t_i^e} I_{f,k}^R})$ where $Norm(\cdot)$ is a normalization function to make $Suf(f, AU_i) \in (0, 1]$.

Update responsiveness for a feature, i.e., how long it takes for a developer to decide whether to update a requested feature into a new version, is measured by the ratio of the interval in which the features are significantly mentioned w.r.t. the interval between two neighboring versions that both update this feature. It demonstrates to what degree developers act on user expectations timely. To measure responsiveness, in an AU_i, we first calculate a specific time d_i to which

Algorithm 1. Decomposing intensity trend chart into normalized AUs
***
Input: Intensity trend $TC(f, t_s, t_e)$ of a specific feature f in a time interval (t_s, t_e),
   Number of relative time points in one normalized AU: N
Output: A set of normalized atomic update patterns AU_Set
 1: $size \leftarrow$ number of updates during $(t_s, t_e) - 1$, $AU\_Set \leftarrow \emptyset$
 2: **for** each $i \in [1, size]$ **do**
 3:     $NIS \leftarrow \emptyset$, $T_i = (t_i^s, t_i^e)$ is the time interval of the i-th AU, $N_i = t_i^e - t_i^s + 1$
 4:     $OIS = getFeatureIntensityByDay(TC(f, t_s, t_e), T_i)$
 5:     $max\_int = getMaxIntensity(OIS)$
 6:     **for** each $k \in [t_i^s, t_i^e]$ **do**
 7:         $OIS[k] \leftarrow \frac{OIS[k]}{max\_int}$
 8:     **end for**
 9:     $NIS[1] \leftarrow OIS[t_i^s]$, $NIS[N] \leftarrow OIS[t_i^e]$
10:     **for** each $k \in [2, N-1]$ **do**
11:         $index \leftarrow \frac{k}{(N-1) \times (t_i^e - t_i^s)}$
12:         **if** $index$ is an Integer **then**
13:             $NIS[k] \leftarrow OIS[index]$
14:         **else**
15:             $NIS[k] \leftarrow \frac{1}{2}(OIS[\lfloor index \rfloor] + OIS[\lceil index \rceil])$
16:         **end if**
17:     **end for**
18:     $AU(f, T_i) \leftarrow < NIS, I_{f,T_i}^U >$ and add $AU(f, T_i)$ into AU_Set
19: **end for**
20: **return** AU_Set
***

the interval from the last update is (t_i^s, d_i); in this interval, aggregated intensity of the requested feature is high enough (above a threshold τ), i.e., $\sum_{k=t_i^s}^{d_i} I_{f,k}^R \geq \tau$, thus $Resp(f, AU_i) = \frac{d_i - t_i^s}{t_i^e - t_i^s}$. A special case is $\sum_{k=t_i^s}^{t_i^e} I_{f,k}^R \leq \tau$, indicating that before the aggregated intensity of f in reviews has not yet reached the threshold, the developers make update on it, thus $Resp(f, AU_i) = 1$. This is the best case indicating developers always take actions on feature requests as quickly as possible. In the study we set $\tau = 4$. It should be noted that we have checked that choosing different *threshold* results in similar CDF of the responsiveness of all AUs.

Sufficiency and responsiveness are both relative measures, i.e., we can compare $Suf(f, AU_i)$ and $Suf(f, AU_j)$ to infer in which AU the feature f is updated more sufficiently, and compare $Resp(f, AU_i)$ and $Resp(f, AU_j)$ to infer in which AU the feature f is updated more timely. Solely observing the values of $Suf(f, AU)$ or $Resp(f, AU)$ does not help to draw meaningful conclusions.

Figure 3(a) shows an example AU extracted from the history of Instagram, for a feature Feed, between May 21, 2016 and August 3, 2016 (i.e., the part between the first and second red lines in Fig. 2). It is normalized by Algorithm 1 and the result is shown in Fig. 3(b). The responsiveness is 1 and the sufficiency is 0.0249, indicating that this update is comparatively timely, but the developers did not address the requested feature adequately.

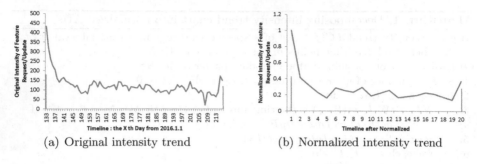

(a) Original intensity trend   (b) Normalized intensity trend

Fig. 3. An example Atomic Update Unit for a feature in *Instagram*

Figure 4(a) and (b) give the distribution of responsiveness and sufficiency of all 2,429 AUs of 120 Apps, respectively. Sufficiency follows power-law distribution, while responsiveness is a right-skewed distribution. To note that, we have checked and found that changing the threshold in the two measurement does not drastically change the shape of their distribution.

4.4 Mining Frequent Update Patterns

Now the "intensity trend" for each feature is decomposed into a set of AUs, and one $AU(f, T_i)$ is with four parts: normalized requested intensity in each day $\{(k_{i1}, I^R_{f,k_{i1}}), ...\}$, normalized update intensity in the last day of this AU (I^U_{f,T_i}), and sufficiency (Suf) and responsiveness ($Resp$) of this update.

We try to find out the common patterns among all AUs of all Apps in their history. A clustering approach is employed to partition AUs into groups: AUs in the same group share comparatively more similar characteristics (requested feature intensity trend, update intensity, sufficiency and responsiveness), while distances between AUs in different groups are larger. We take the centroid of each group to be a representative "Update Pattern". k-Means algorithm is employed for clustering and Euclidean distance is used for similarity measurement.

A key issue is to specify the number of clusters (k) in k-Means algorithm. We assign different values (2 to 18) to k and make experiments and calculate

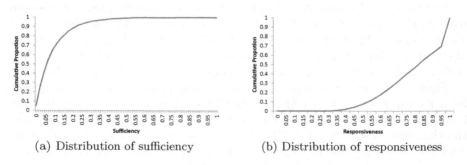

(a) Distribution of sufficiency   (b) Distribution of responsiveness

Fig. 4. Distribution of Sufficiency and Responsiveness of AUs of 120 Apps in one year

the average distance between `centroids` of clustering results; along with the increase of k, the average distance gradually decreases, and when $k = 7$, the decreasing speed becomes significantly slow. Thus we choose $k = 7$.

Table 1 gives an overview of the 7 update patterns. It is easy to see that these patterns show significant diversity on intensity trend of features in user reviews (column 5), update sufficiency (column 2), and update responsiveness (column 3), implying they have the ability of differentiating how developers take update behaviors on user reviews. Take Pattern 2 and Pattern 4 as examples, Pattern 2's responsiveness and sufficiency are comparatively lower than the ones

Table 1. Overview of the identified 7 Update Patterns

No.	Sufficiency (ranking)	Responsiveness (ranking)	Ratio	Intensity trend
Pattern 1	0.195(2)	0.803(4)	6.67%	
Pattern 2	0.050(6)	0.455(7)	7.70%	
Pattern 3	0.058(4)	0.606(6)	16.43%	
Pattern 4	0.349(1)	0.996(1)	8.53%	
Pattern 5	0.049(7)	0.745(5)	18.66%	
Pattern 6	0.102(3)	0.995(2)	24.84%	
Pattern 7	0.054(5)	0.891(3)	17.17%	

of Pattern 4, and the decreasing trend of the requested intensity in Pattern 2 is more gentle than the one in Pattern 4. Ratios of these UPs (column 4) vary from 6.67% to 24.84%, indicating that they are widespread in real world.

5   Empirical Study

Since we have got 7 diversified UPs, now we focus on how UPs are adopted on different/similar features in the same or different Apps, and at different times.

5.1   Update Patterns w.r.t. Different Features in One App

In terms of one App, there are multiple features requested in reviews and updated in new versions that are conducted by the same developers. We check whether different update patterns are adopted for different features in the same App.

For each feature in an App, we construct a vector containing the ratios of 7 Update Patterns adopted in all AUs of this App, i.e., $v(App, f) = (r_1, r_2, ..., r_7)$, and r_i is ratio of the i-th UP. If $v(App, f_j)$ and $v(App, f_k)$ are similar, we can infer that f_j and f_k exhibit similar update pattern distributions in this App. Cosine similarity is used to measure the similarity of two vectors.

For all Apps, the distribution of the similarity of arbitrary feature pairs in the same App is shown in Fig. 5(a), where each column is an App. Most Apps show quite scattered distributions in $[0, 1]$, and there are 73.2% Apps having the variance of feature pair similarity being above 0.2.

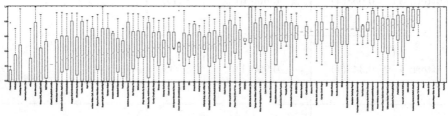

(a) w.r.t. different features in one App

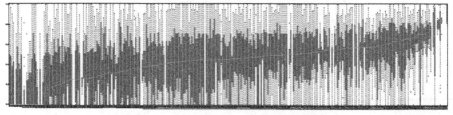

(b) w.r.t. similar features in one group

Fig. 5. Distribution of update patterns similarity

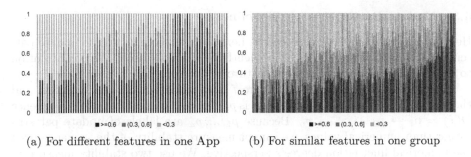

(a) For different features in one App   (b) For similar features in one group

Fig. 6. Classification of update pattern similarity (high, medium, low)

We calculate the ratios of feature pairs in the same App with high (≥ 0.7), medium $[0.3, 0.7)$ and low (< 0.3) similarity, respectively. Result is shown in Fig. 6(a) where each column is an App. Different Apps show quite different observations: a small proportion of Apps on the left side tend to adopt different update patterns for different feature pairs, while a larger proportion on the right side tend to adopt similar update patterns. Holistically, developers tend to adopt more similar update patterns for different features in their own Apps.

5.2   Update Patterns w.r.t. Similar Features Across Multiple Apps

Considering multiple Apps together, there are common features across them. We care about whether similar features in different Apps follow similar update patterns. First we identify similar features among feature sets of different Apps. Keyword matching is used for this purpose, i.e., if two features are described by two similar sets of keywords, there is high probability with which the two features represent the same one. 17,906 pairs of similar features across Apps are identified, and they are grouped into 328 clusters in terms of feature similarity.

Similar as in Sect. 5.1, we construct a vector $v(App, f) = (r_1, r_2, ..., r_7)$ for each f in each *App*, and then calculate the Cosine similarity between two vectors $v(App_i, f_k)$ and $v(App_j, f_l)$ where $i \neq j$ and f_k, f_l belong to the same feature group. For feature groups, the distribution of similarity of feature pairs in the same group is shown in Fig. 5(b) where each column is a feature group. We can see the degree of dispersion is higher than the one in Fig. 5(a).

Figure 6(b) shows the ratios of feature pairs in the same group with high (≥ 0.7), medium ($[0.3, 0.7)$) and low (< 0.3) similarity, respectively. Compared with Fig. 6(a), a larger proportion of groups tend to adopt different update behaviors. Statistics show that there are 83.5% groups having the variance of feature pair similarity above 0.2. This implies that similar features across multiple Apps more tend to adopt diversified update patterns compared with different features in the same App, and the adoption of update patterns on App features depends more largely on "App developers" themselves rather than on "features".

5.3   Update Patterns w.r.t. Timeline

Here we consider the time perspective, i.e., along with time, do the update patterns of a specific feature change frequently or remain stable? We pay attention to the "update history" of a single feature in an App.

Suppose in a time interval, a feature f is updated n times in n versions, and the update pattern for the i-th updates is p_i. There is an update pattern sequence $Q(f) = p_1 \rightarrow p_2 \rightarrow ... \rightarrow p_n$. Because $p_1, ..., p_n$ are labels of update patterns rather than numerical values, we cannot measure stability of the sequence from the numerical fluctuation degree's perspective. We use two stability measures:

(1) *local stability*: what proportion of two neighboring updates follow the same update patterns, i.e., $Stab^l(f) = \frac{1}{n-1} \times |\{(p_i, p_{i+1})|p_i = p_{i+1}, i = 1, 2, ..., n-1\}|$;
(2) *global stability*: how many different update patterns appear in the sequence and what the degree of their dispersion is, measured by `negative entropy`, i.e., $Stab^g(f) = \sum_i N(p_i) \log N(p_i)$ where $N(p_i)$ is the times of p_i appearing in $Q(f)$. Then $Stab^l(f)$ and $Stab^g(f)$ are combined with an average to get $Stab(f)$.

Figure 7 shows the distribution of update pattern stability of multiple features in the history of each App. We found that the dispersity of such stability are smaller compared with Fig. 5(a) and (b), with only about 36.0% having the invariance larger than 0.2. The median of most Apps is less than 0.4, indicating that most of them are not stable, i.e., developers tend to lack enough coherence/continuity

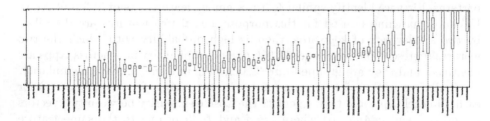

Fig. 7. Distribution of update pattern stability of features w.r.t. Apps

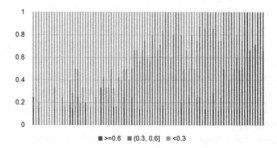

■ >=0.6 ■ (0.3, 0.6] ■ <0.3

Fig. 8. Classification of update pattern stability w.r.t. Apps (Color figure online)

when they consider to update the same feature at different time. This can be also proved by Fig. 8 where the green (very unstable) and red (medium stable) are dominating, and the blue (very stable) are the minority.

6 Conclusions

In this paper, we identified 7 types of common Update Patterns which generally appear in App developers' behaviors that they perform to act on the requests raised by App users in their reviews. Update patterns are characterized by the feature intensity trend between two neighboring updates, the update sufficiency, and the update responsiveness. Statistics are made to validate a set of hypothesis. This would help developers get a clear understanding on the common habits of how they act on user reviews during delivery and evolution of their Apps.

Future work is to empirically validate whether there is latent causality between update patterns and the popularity/rating of an App, i.e., would some update patterns significantly boost the recognition of Apps, while others not? This helps recognize App developers' bad habits on incorporating user reviews in App updates and give suggestions on adopting more appropriate update patterns in future's App updates. Another work is to exploit a machine learning based predication method which gives App developers advices to update specific features based on user reviews published from the last update to the current date, so that "voices" of App users are to be addressed more timely and adequately.

Acknowledgments. Work in this paper is supported by the Natural Science Foundation of China (No. 61772155, 61472106).

References

1. Carreño, L.V.G., Winbladh, K.: Analysis of user comments: an approach for software requirements evolution. In: International Conference on Software Engineering, pp. 582–591. IEEE (2013)
2. Cerf, V.G.: Apps and the web. Commun. ACM **59**(2), 7–7 (2016)
3. Chen, N., Lin, J., Hoi, S.C., Xiao, X., Zhang, B.: Ar-miner: mining informative reviews for developers from mobile app. marketplace. In: International Conference on Software Engineering, pp. 767–778. ACM (2014)
4. Cugola, G., Ghezzi, C., Pinto, L.S., Tamburrelli, G.: Adaptive service-oriented mobile applications: A declarative approach. In: International Conference on Service-Oriented Computing, pp. 607–614. Springer (2012)
5. Finkelstein, A., Harman, M., Jia, Y., Martin, W., Sarro, F., Zhang, Y.: App. store analysis: Mining app. stores for relationships between customer, business and technical characteristics. Research Note of UCL Department of Computer Science 14, 10 (2014)
6. Gorla, A., Tavecchia, I., Gross, F., Zeller, A.: Checking app. behavior against app. descriptions. In: International Conference on Software Engineering, pp. 1025–1035. ACM (2014)

7. Guzman, E., Maalej, W.: How do users like this feature? a fine grained sentiment analysis of app. reviews. In: International Conference on Requirements Engineering, pp. 153–162. IEEE (2014)

8. Hao, Y., Wang, Z., Xu, X.: Empirical study on the interface and feature evolutions of mobile apps. In: International Conference on Service-Oriented Computing, pp. 657–665. Springer (2016)

9. Iacob, C., Harrison, R.: Retrieving and analyzing mobile apps feature requests from online reviews. In: IEEE Working Conference on Mining Software Repositories, pp. 41–44. IEEE (2013)

10. Iacob, C., Harrison, R., Faily, S.: Online reviews as first class artifacts in mobile app. development. In: International Conference on Mobile Computing, Applications, and Services, pp. 47–53. Springer (2013)

11. Khalid, H., Shihab, E., Nagappan, M., Hassan, A.E.: What do mobile app users complain about? IEEE Softw. **32**(3), 70–77 (2015)

12. Maalej, W., Nabil, H.: Bug report, feature request, or simply praise? on automatically classifying app. reviews. In: IEEE International Conference on Requirements Engineering, pp. 116–125. IEEE (2015)

13. Martin, W., Sarro, F., Harman, M.: Causal impact analysis applied to app. releases in google play and windows phone store. Research Note of UCL Department of Computer Science 15, 07 (2015)

14. Martin, W., Sarro, F., Jia, Y., Zhang, Y., Harman, M.: A survey of app. store analysis for software engineering. IEEE Transactions on Software Engineering, PP(99), 1–32 (2016)

15. McIlroy, S., Ali, N., Hassan, A.E.: Fresh apps: an empirical study of frequently-updated mobile apps in the google play store. Emp. Softw. Eng. **21**(3), 1346–1370 (2016)

16. McIlroy, S., Ali, N., Khalid, H., Hassan, A.E.: Analyzing and automatically labelling the types of user issues that are raised in mobile app reviews. Emp. Softw. Eng. **21**(3), 1067–1106 (2016)

17. Nayebi, M., Adams, B., Ruhe, G.: Release practices for mobile apps-what do users and developers think?. In: IEEE International Conference on Software Analysis, Evolution, and Reengineering, vol. 1, pp. 552–562. IEEE (2016)

18. Pagano, D., Maalej, W.: User feedback in the appstore: An empirical study. In: IEEE International Conference on Requirements Engineering, pp. 125–134. IEEE (2013)

19. Palomba, F., Linares-Vásquez, M., Bavota, G., Oliveto, R., Di Penta, M., Poshyvanyk, D., De Lucia, A.: User reviews matter! tracking crowdsourced reviews to support evolution of successful apps. In: IEEE International Conference on Software Maintenance and Evolution, pp. 291–300. IEEE (2015)

20. Syer, M.D., Nagappan, M., Hassan, A.E., Adams, B.: Revisiting prior empirical findings for mobile apps: An empirical case study on the 15 most popular open-source android apps. In: Conference of the Center for Advanced Studies on Collaborative Research, pp. 283–297. IBM Corp. (2013)

21. Takahashi, H., Nakagawa, H., Tsuchiya, T.: Towards automatic requirements elicitation from feedback comments: Extracting requirements topics using lda. In: International Conference on Software Engineering and Knowledge Engineering, pp. 489–494 (2015)

22. Vu, P.M., Nguyen, T.T., Pham, H.V., Nguyen, T.T.: Mining user opinions in mobile app. reviews: A keyword-based approach. In: International Conference on Automated Software Engineering, pp. 749–759. IEEE (2015)

23. Wang, H., Wang, Z., Xu, X.: Time-aware customer preference sensing and satisfaction prediction in a dynamic service market. In: International Conference on Service-Oriented Computing, pp. 236–251. Springer (2016)
24. Yan, X., Guo, J., Lan, Y., Cheng, X.: A biterm topic model for short texts. In: International World Wide Web Conference, pp. 1445–1456. ACM (2013)

Predicting the Evolution of Service Value Features from User Reviews for Continuous Service Improvement

Xu Chi[1], Haifang Wang[1], Zhongjie Wang[1(✉)], Shiping Chen[2], and Xiaofei Xu[1]

[1] Harbin Institute of Technology, Harbin 150001, Heilongjiang, China
{chixujohnny,wanghaifang,rainy,xiaofei}@hit.edu.cn
[2] CSIRO DATA61, Eveleigh, NSW 2109, Australia
shiping.chen@data61.csiro.au

Abstract. Facing with a highly competitive service market where customers have more choices on services to fulfill their demands, service providers have to improve their services continuously to make them adapt to constantly-changing value expectations of customers. An enormous quantity of reviews published by customers who have experienced services is an essential basis for service providers to understand which fine-grained features are cared more by customers and what others are less. In this paper, we present a method (`VFAMine`) for extracting Service Value Features (VF) from review texts by text mining and measuring customers' attention degrees on VFs by sentiment analysis. As a result, a Time-series Service Value Feature Distribution model (TSVFD) is constructed to delineate the evolution history of attention degrees on various VFs. To help providers identify VFs which are to be extensively concerned by customers and improve them in advance, we give a convolutional sliding window and random forest based algorithm (`CSRF`) for predicting the future trend of the attention degree on one VF, either for a single service or for services belonging to the same region/domain. In terms of Maximum Information Coefficient (MIC) based correlation analysis, we find that there are latent correlations between the evolution history of different VFs, and such correlation would help service providers improve multiple correlated VFs together. Experiments are conducted on a Yelp dataset and the results demonstrate the effectiveness of our approach.

Keywords: Service Value Feature (VF) · Service improvement · User reviews · Attention degree · Evolution trend · Prediction

1 Introduction

More and more services have been deployed on Internet and thus offer a wider range of choices to customers for fulfilling their demands [18]. On the condition that there are abundant mutually-substitutable competitive services for customers to choose, services providers are faced with a great pressure on improving their services to cater to the common value expectations of a larger scale

© Springer International Publishing AG 2017
M. Maximilien et al. (Eds.): ICSOC 2017, LNCS 10601, pp. 142–157, 2017.
https://doi.org/10.1007/978-3-319-69035-3_10

of customers. Besides, customers' demands and preferences evolve as time goes by [16], which requires service providers to continuously improve their services accordingly. User reviews, which are direct feedback submitted by users after they use a service, contain valuable information that have been considered as an important basis for service improvement.

Take a service named `Liholiho Yacht Club` in San Francisco as an example. It joined Yelp in February 2015. Because it is very popular in the local region, in most cases customers have to wait in line in order to enjoy the service; thus it is as expected that most user reviews on Yelp are mainly focused on "wait time". In July 2017, this club improved its service by adding an *online reservation* feature; from then on, its ratings on Yelp increased significantly.

However, as user reviews are numerous and the amount increases drastically along with time, service providers cannot go through all the reviews piece by piece [4]. It is needful to extract high-level valuable information from reviews and offer them to service providers for references. A customer tends to focus on one or several specific features in each of his review. For example, a customer has a review on a restaurant: *The staff was super friendly and most importantly the food was tasty and fresh*, and we see that he cares about `staff` and `food`. We call them Service Value Features (VF). Compared with the numeric ratings (e.g., scores between 1 and 5), VFs delineate more specific facets that customers care about and are considered as "focus of attentions" or "preferences" of customers [15], hence they are useful for service providers to have a deeper understanding on their customers and could be used as important evidences for further improvement on their services. There are diversified VFs in each service, but common VFs across different services in the same domain do widely exist.

Due to constant changes of the service market, changes of user identities and social positions, etc., the scope of VFs that customers are concerned and their attention degrees on each specific VF at different times change frequently, too. In order for service providers to improve their services in advance as far as possible, it is useful to predict the future changing trend of massive customers' attention degrees on VFs and find out those VFs that would have growth spurts in the recent future. In RQ1 of this paper, we focus on such prediction for one service provider with the objective of providing service improvement suggestions to it. In RQ2, we focus on the prediction for a group of services that belong to the same "region" (such as the Bay Area in California) or the same "service domain" (such as `food` and `nightlife`), with the objective of analyzing and predicting the holistic evolution trend of one region or service domain, so that new service providers who would like to enter this region or service domain may have a deeper acquaintance on how to set up their new services to better cater to the future's customer expectations.

Besides, as there are many VFs hidden in user reviews, we wonder if there are latent correlations between the attention degrees of different VFs. For instance, for three VFs $\{f_1, f_2, f_3\}$, when the attention degree on f_1 increases along with time, the one of f_2 increases synchronously, while the one on f_3 decreases synchronously. If such correlations really exist, VFs are to be grouped and VFs in each group should be simultaneously considered when service providers improve their services. If they do like this, the difficulty of service improvement would be significantly decreased. RQ3 of this paper is to present a method of validating the existence of the correlation among the changing trends of attention degrees on different VFs and measure the correlation degrees.

To mine VFs from massive user reviews, we propose a mining algorithm VFAMine based on text mining and sentiment analysis. It looks for VFs by analyzing grammatical structures of review texts by applying a set of heuristic rules and represents a VF as one or several keywords, and sentiment analysis is employed to measure the attention degree by emotional factors such as dissatisfaction, criticism, complains or praise exposed in review texts.

For RQ1, we use a machine learning approach and propose a convolutional sliding window method (CSRF) to build a model that depict the underlying characteristics of the evolution of the attention degree on one VF in a certain period, then use this model to predict the attention degree on the same VF in the recent future. RQ2 adopts a quite similar approach but the prediction is for a group of services in the same region or service domain. In both RQ1 and RQ2, a time-series prediction accuracy index (*loss*) is used to assess the prediction accuracy. For RQ3, we adopt Maximum Information Coefficient (MIC) to measure the correlation between the evolution history of attention degrees on multiple VFs. Experiments are conducted on a dataset released by Yelp Dataset Challenge[1] (including 800,000 services, 680,000 users, and 2.68 million user reviews published between Jan. 2010 and Jun. 2016), and the results validate the effectiveness of the proposed methods.

In summary, this paper makes the following contributions:

- We define a Time-series Service Value Distribution model (TSVFD) to quantitatively delineate the evolution history of users' attention degrees on VFs. It is a useful tool for the prediction and correlation analysis of VFs.
- Based on the experiments conducted on Yelp dataset, the text mining and sentiment analysis based VF mining method VFAMine is effective for identifying VFs from review texts, with the accuracy being more than 86%.
- The prediction model for the future evolution of attention degrees of VFs can reach good performance for both one service provider and multiple providers in one region/domain, and the average loss value is limited within 0.15.
- Certain correlations do really exist between the evolution of different VFs' attention degrees, but the density of highly correlated VF pairs is rather low. The adopted correlation measurement (i.e., MIC) can reach at an accuracy rate above 0.85.

The remainder is organized as follows. Section 2 presents the VF mining algorithm VFAMine. Section 3 presents the TSVFD model and gives the method CSRF for predicting the evolution trend of one VF. Section 4 gives the correlation

---

[1] https://www.yelp.com/dataset_challenge

analysis method for the co-evolution of multiple VFs' attention degrees. Section 5 is related work, and Sect. 6 is conclusions and future work.

2   Service Value Feature and the Mining Algorithm

2.1   Service Value Feature (VF)

User reviews contain latent information on how a user looks upon a service, i.e., what features he prefers more when he chooses candidate services to fulfill his demand [16]. If he does not mention a feature in his review at all, there are two possibilities: (1) the performance that the service exhibits on this feature is equal to or beyond his expectation on this feature; (2) he does not care about the performance on this feature. To sum up, user reviews reveal what a user minds and indirectly, what he does not mind; or to say, his value preferences. We define it by "Service Value Features (VF)".

Definition 1. A review is denoted by $r = (s, u, d, text)$, representing that a user u publishes a review r with $text$ in natural language on a service s on the date d.

Definition 2. Service Value Feature (VF). A VF is a noun or a noun phrase describing a specific feature that a service could deliver to its customers, and there is a numeric value associated with the VF to quantitatively measure the degree with which it is concerned by one or a group of customers (namely, attention degree).

Since service are significantly "personalized", different users have quite diversified value propositions and value expectations, thus the VFs hidden in the reviews of different users might be quite diversified. Still, there are some common VFs that multiple users together care about.

2.2   VFAMine: Mining Service Value Features from User Reviews

It is difficult to get value propositions/expectations directly from users, i.e., most users cannot express their preferences explicitly before he uses a service. Only after he uses a service and has got rich experiences on it, does he find out what he cares and what does not. As text mining has been proved to be an effective way of extracting structural information from texts, here we use a heuristic text mining approach to identify VFs from user reviews.

The heuristic rules are straightforward:

- Rule 1: If a noun is modified by one or multiple qualifiers (e.g., adjectives) which appear in a limited range before or after this noun, then there is a significant probability that it represent a VF;
- Rule 2: If two candidate VFs identified by Rule 1 are neighbors in review texts or they are connected by conjunctions such as `of` and `for`, and they are modified by the same qualifiers, then they are combined into one VF.

Although these heuristic rules cannot cover all possible circumstances (especially on the condition that users seldom follow strict grammar rules when they write review texts), our approach tries to reach at a tradeoff between the mining precision and the computation time by avoiding complicated semantics analysis. The mining process includes three steps:

- Review texts are separated into words and part-of-speech (POS) tagging is conducted to give each word a tag such as NN (Noun), NNS (Noun, plural), J (Adjective), JJR (Adjective, comparative), and JJS (Adjective, superlative). This is implemented based on NLTK APIs[2];
- Irrelevant words such as articles (a, an, the) and verbs are removed;
- For each sentence in review texts, above-mentioned heuristic rules are applied and a set of candidate VFs are identified.

Here is an example review on a restaurant service: *The environment of the restaurant is nice, but size of food is too big.* There are four nouns: environment, restaurant, size, and food. The nouns environment and restaurant are both modified by the qualifier nice and they are connected by of, so they are combined into one VF: environment of restaurant. Similarly there is another VF size of food modified by the adjective big. Here the range where qualifiers are detected is 3–5 words before and after a noun.

After VFs are identified, the next step is to measure the attention degree on each VF. In natural languages, different adverbs or adjectives exhibit different degrees of emotions (e.g., excellent food and good food), or called emotional factors. For each VF which has been represented by a noun phase, we first extract all the emotional words that appear in a specific range before and after the noun phase, and then look up the emotional factors (ranging from 1 to 5) of these words from the publicly-available emotional term dictionary[3]. The aggregated value of these emotional factors are used to measure the user's attention degree on this VF. If there are no emotional words found around the VF, the value is set to 2.5 (indicating it is a VF with neutral attention degree).

The mining process is conducted on each review r_i correspondingly, and one or several VFs are identified. After all reviews are dealt with (no matter which services they belong to), synonym dictionary based similarity analysis is conducted to merge similar candidate VFs. The final identified VFs are $VF = \{f_1, f_2, ..., f_n\}$. $\forall f_j \in VF$ and a review r_i, v_{ij} is the emotional factor of f_j in r_i, i.e., the attention degree of the user $u(r_i)$ on f_j in r_i. If r_i does not cover f_j, then $v_{ij} = 0$, indicating that $u(r_i)$ does not care about f_j in this review.

To sum up, we identify VFs from review texts and merge similar VFs, and approximately measure the attention degrees of each VF in each review. Due to limited space, we do not show the detailed algorithm for this process.

---

[2] http://www.nltk.org/api/nltk.tag.html.
[3] http://www.keenage.com/download/sentiment.rar.

We conduct an experiment on Yelp dataset to validate the accuracy of VFAMine. We select top-5 hottest service domains in terms of the amount of reviews: Food, Nightlife, Shopping Medical, and Home-Service. From each domain we use a random sampling approach to choose 230 reviews, respectively, and manually annotate VFs covered by these reviews. The annotation results are used as the test set. Then, VFAMine is applied to automatically identify VFs from the same reviews, and the results are compared with manually-annotated results.

Experiment result: for the five domains, the precisions are 91.3%, 92.1%, 88.6%, 85.4%, and 89.7%, respectively. All precisions keep above 85%, indicating that the mining accuracy is relatively high. The *nightlife* domain receives the highest precision, while the *medical* domain has the lowest precision. As for the reasons, we guess that customers of *nightlife* services are mostly young guys who would like to carefully write reviews on the services they have experienced, while customers of *medical* services tend to be older and they are apt to write shorter reviews which are more unlikely to follow strict grammar rules, and consequently, the accuracy of VF mining is deteriorated.

2.3   Time-Series Service Value Feature Distribution (TSVFD)

To facilitate predicting the changing trend of VFs in the future, for each service s, we construct a matrix $M(s)$ to represent the distribution of aggregated attention degrees by all users on each VF over a long period. It is called Time-Series Service Value Feature Distribution matrix (TSVFD). Table 1 shows the visual form of TSVFD.

Table 1. Time-series service value feature distribution (TSVFD) matrix

	t_1	t_2	$\ldots$	t_m
f_1	$v_{1,1}^{\Diamond}$	$v_{1,2}^{\Diamond}$	$\ldots$	$v_{1,m}^{\Diamond}$
f_2	$v_{2,1}^{\Diamond}$	$v_{2,2}^{\Diamond}$	$\ldots$	$v_{2,m}^{\Diamond}$
$\ldots$	$\ldots$	$\ldots$	$\ldots$	$\ldots$
f_n	$v_{n,1}^{\Diamond}$	$v_{n,2}^{\Diamond}$	$\ldots$	$v_{n,m}^{\Diamond}$

Rows of the matrix are n VFs (i.e., $f_1, f_2, ..., f_n$) identified from reviews of all services, and columns are m consecutive but non-overlapping time intervals with equal lengths (i.e., $t_1, t_2, ..., t_m$), e.g., each t_j is a calendar month. $v_{k,j}^{\Diamond}$ is the aggregated attention degree on f_k in the reviews that are published for the service s during the period t_j and is calculated by:

$$v_{k,j}^{\Diamond} = \sum_{\forall r_i, s(r_i)=s, d(r_i) \in t_j} v_{ik} \tag{1}$$

where v_{ik} is the attention degree of f_k in the review r_i.

Similarly, we can construct the TSVFD for a group of services belonging to the same region R or domain D, denoted by $M(R)$ and $M(D)$. The only difference is that when calculating $v_{k,j}^{\diamond}$, we replace the condition $s(r_i) = s$ by $s(r_i) \in R$ or $s(r_i) \in D$, i.e., to group reviews by regions or domains instead of just for one service.

$$v_{k,j}^{\diamond} = \sum_{\forall r_i, s(r_i) \in R, d(r_i) \in t_j} v_{ik} \tag{2}$$

TSVFD of a service/region/domain demonstrates the global view of how massive users care about various VFs at different times, i.e., the changing history of "user concerns". It is used for VF's evolution analysis and prediction in subsequent sections.

Figure 1 shows the evolution of four VFs (abbr. `service`, `location`, `coffee` and `customer`) in the TSVFD of the *nightlife* service domain. The history of how attention degree changes from Jan. 2010 to Jun. 2016 is visualized by line charts. We can see that different VFs shows quite diversified changing trends: the first and the second VFs show an increasing trend, the third VF shows a decreasing trend, while the fourth VF fluctuates with a smaller scale compared with the other three.

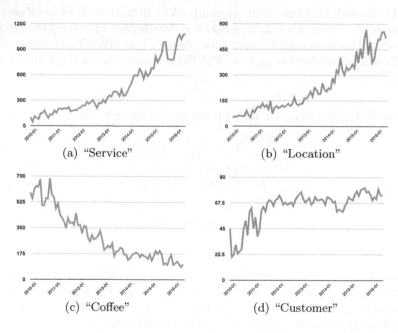

(a) "Service"   (b) "Location"

(c) "Coffee"   (d) "Customer"

Fig. 1. Evolution history of attention degrees of 4 VFs in *Nightlife* domain

3   Evolution Analysis and Trend Prediction of an VF

In this section we focus mainly on one VF and study how to predict the future changing trend of users' attention degree on this VF. In Sect. 4 the focus is switched to the correlation between the evolution history of multiple VFs.

3.1   CSRF: A ML-based Model for VF Evolution and Prediction

In the matrix of TSVFD, the changing history of the attention degree of a VF f_k in m consecutive time intervals is represented by the row vector $V(f_k) = (v_{k,1}^{\diamond}, ..., v_{k,m}^{\diamond})$. Our goal is to predict the values of $(v_{k,m+1}^{\diamond}, v_{k,m+2}^{\diamond}, ..., v_{k,m+\rho}^{\diamond})$, where ρ is the prediction horizon, i.e., the number of future time intervals in which the attention degrees on f_k are to be predicted.

Since $V(f_k)$ is time-series data, this is a typical time series prediction problem. There are many time series prediction models such as ARIMA (Auto Regressive Integrated Moving Average) which has been proved to have good prediction accuracy. Nevertheless, before prediction by ARIMA, manual interventions have to be conducted for stationary handling in case that original data is non-stationary. This is a time-consuming task, especially when there are hundreds of VFs each of which requires prediction. To deal with this issue, we propose a machine learning based method (CSRF) which learns the fluctuation characteristics of the time series data, so that the pre-processing and prediction process becomes more efficient.

Specifically, CSRF has two phases: a convolutional sliding window model (CS) is firstly used to split the time-series data into multiple time-series samples in terms of specific size and step value of sliding windows, and then a random forest regression model (RF) is applied on these samples to learn the latent fluctuation patterns and to predict the changing trend of $V(f_k)$ in the recent future. Detailed steps are shown in Algorithm 1.

CSRF algorithm has four inputs: V is the row vector for a specific VF whose changing trend is to be predicted; ws_{min} and ws_{max} are the minimal and maximal sizes of sliding windows, respectively; ρ is the prediction horizon (the number of time intervals during which the values of attention degree on the VF is to be predicted); and δ is the step value when V is split into samples by the convolutional sliding window approach.

The outer loop (Steps 3–19) is to predict the attention degree of the VF in the next period, i.e., $v_{k,m+1}^{\diamond}$ where m is the length of current V; in the next loop for predicting $v_{k,m+2}^{\diamond}$, the predicted value in the first loop is added into V (Step 18) and thus its length becomes $m + 1$; the loop continues until all the expected values within the time intervals in the prediction horizon ρ are obtained and recorded in V_{pred} as the output.

The inner loop (Steps 4–17) is to look for a best size of sliding windows that could result in minimal *loss* (measuring the error between the real value and the predicted value) and get the best prediction value *bestPrediction* by looking for the minimal *loss* (see Steps 14–15). In terms of the selected size

---

Algorithm 1. The CSRF Algorithm

Require: $V, ws_{min}, ws_{max}, \rho, \delta$
Ensure: V_{pred}
1: $V_{pred} \leftarrow \emptyset, bestLoss \leftarrow 1, bestPrediction \leftarrow 0$
2: $train \leftarrow V[:-\rho], test \leftarrow V[-\rho:]$
3: **for** $\forall round \in [1, \rho]$ **do**
4:     **for** $\forall w \in [ws_{min}, ws_{max}]$ **do**
5:         $Samples \leftarrow \emptyset, y \leftarrow \emptyset, i \leftarrow 0$
6:         **while** $i \leq length(train - w - 1)$ **do**
7:             $Samples.add(train[i, i + w])$
8:             $y.add(train[i + w + 1])$
9:             $i \leftarrow i + \delta$
10:         **end while**
11:         $Regression\_model \leftarrow sklearn.\text{RandomForestRegressor}(Samples, y)$
12:         $prediction \leftarrow \text{Predict}(Regression\_model, train[-w,])$
13:         $loss \leftarrow \text{Loss}(test, prediction)$
14:         **if** $loss < bestLoss$ **then**
15:             $bestLoss \leftarrow L, bestPrediction \leftarrow prediction$
16:         **end if**
17:     **end for**
18:     $train.add(bestPrediction), V_{pred}.add(bestPrediction)$
19: **end for**
20: **return** V_{pred}

---

of sliding windows (w in Step 4), Steps 6–10 are to use convolutional sliding window modeling to split V into a set of samples. Each sample is composed of w time-series features (denoted by w columns in Table 2, i.e., $t'_1, t'_2, ..., t'_w$) and a target value (i.e., the last column y in Table 2). All obtained samples (denoted by *Samples* in the algorithm) are used as the train set for training the regression model between the first w attention degrees and the $(w + 1)$-th one. We will discuss the regression process later.

Here we take f_i as an example to demonstrate the process of constructing samples from $V(f_i)$. The first sample starts from the first time interval and ends with the w-th time interval, and the attention degrees are $<v^{\diamond}_{i,1}, v^{\diamond}_{i,2}, ..., v^{\diamond}_{i,w}>$ (see the second row of Table 2), and the value $v^{\diamond}_{i,w+1}$ in the $(w+1)$-th time interval is used as the target value y. Hence, the first sample has been constructed. For the second sample, in terms of the step value δ, it should start from the $(\delta + 1)$-th time interval and ends with $(\delta + w)$-th time interval with the corresponding attention degrees, namely $<v^{\diamond}_{i,\delta+1}, v^{\diamond}_{i,\delta+2}, ..., v^{\diamond}_{i,\delta+w}>$, and $v^{\diamond}_{i,\delta+w+1}$ is used as the target value y. Repeatedly, total $k = m - w - 1$ samples are to be constructed (where m is the length of vectors in the train set of the current loop) and they are shown in Table 2.

Based on the constructed training set (*Samples*), Step 11 is to use random forest as the regression model for training. Here we use `RandomForestRegressor`

Table 2. Constructing samples by convolutional sliding window approach

	t_1'	t_2'	$\cdots$	t_w'	y
$Sample_1$	$v_{i,1}^{\diamond}$	$v_{i,2}^{\diamond}$	$\cdots$	$v_{i,w}^{\diamond}$	$v_{i,w+1}^{\diamond}$
$Sample_2$	$v_{i,\delta+1}^{\diamond}$	$v_{i,\delta+2}^{\diamond}$	$\cdots$	$v_{i,\delta+w}^{\diamond}$	$v_{i,\delta+w+1}^{\diamond}$
$\cdots$	$\cdots$	$\cdots$	$\cdots$	$\cdots$	$\cdots$
$Sample_k$	$v_{i,(k-1)\times\delta+1}^{\diamond}$	$v_{i,(k-1)\times\delta+2}^{\diamond}$	$\cdots$	$v_{i,(k-1)\times\delta+w}^{\diamond}$	$v_{i,(k-1)\times\delta+w+1}^{\diamond}$

provided by *sklean* ML library[4]) to fulfill this task. Afterwards, Step 12 makes the prediction, and the *loss* is measured by comparing the prediction value and the test set in Step 13.

3.2 Predicting a VF's Future Trend for One Service and for One Region or Service Domain

We first apply the CSRF algorithm on the reviews of one single service and predict the changing trend of a VF's attention degree in the future ρ times intervals. The result would be a valuable reference for the service provider to know which perspectives should be improved with higher priority in the future.

The prediction horizon (the parameter ρ in Algorithm 1) could be of any length, but along with the increasing ρ, the prediction accuracy would decrease drastically. In our experiments, we set $\rho = 6$, i.e., we predict the attention degrees of a VF in the subsequent $1^{st}, 2^{nd}, ...,$ and 6th months, respectively.

The CSRF algorithm could also be applied on the reviews of services belonging to the same region or the same service domain to predict the changing trend of a VF's attention degree, so that new service providers who would like to join this region or domain may have a clear acquaintance on how to set up their new services to better cater to user expectations. Compared with the prediction for a service provider, this prediction involves a broader range of services.

Figure 2(a) and (b) shows the prediction results of two VFs of a restaurant service, and Fig. 2(c) and (d) is the results of two VFs from the food domain. Blue lines are the evolution history of VFs' attention degrees, and red lines are the prediction results.

To evaluate the prediction accuracy, we use the *loss* metrics which measures the aggregated errors between the prediction and the real values of all the features in one service or in all services belonging to the same region/domain:

$$loss = \frac{1}{n \times m} \sum_{i=1}^{n} \sum_{t=1}^{m} |\frac{v_{i,t}^{\diamond} - v_{i,t}^{P}}{v_{i,t}^{\diamond} + v_{i,t}^{P}}| \tag{3}$$

where $v_{i,t}^{\diamond}$ is the real value of the attention degree of the i-th VF in the t-th month, and $v_{i,t}^{P}$ is the corresponding prediction value.

---

[4] http://scikit-learn.org.

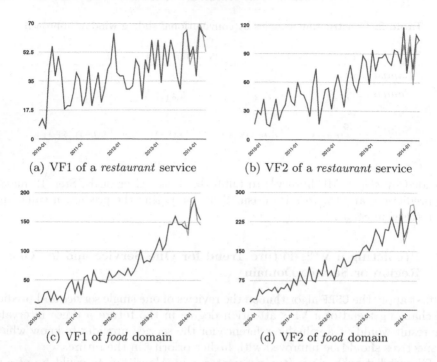

(a) VF1 of a *restaurant* service   (b) VF2 of a *restaurant* service

(c) VF1 of *food* domain   (d) VF2 of *food* domain

Fig. 2. Comparison between the actual evolution history and the prediction

Figure 3 shows the distribution of *loss* values for multiple services in each service domain. In the five domains, the values are mostly distributed in the range $[0.08, 0.15]$ with the medium in the range $[0.11, 0.13]$. This indicates that the prediction results are accurate and acceptable. For comparison, the Food domain has more amount of reviews and thus has higher prediction accuracy than other domains, and we do find that CSRF performs better on the services that have more reviews than on the services having fewer reviews.

4   Correlation Analysis for the Evolution of Multiple Service Value Features

4.1   MIC-based Correlation Analysis on Multiple VFs

We conjecture that the evolution of multiple VFs might not be absolutely independent but sometimes they are correlated, i.e., there is a phenomenon called "co-evolution of VFs". In this section we validate whether this hypothesis is true. If it is valid, it is possible to group highly-correlated VFs together so that service providers would improve them holistically and consequently, more efficiently.

The first step is to determine which correlation measure is suitable for this goal. Pearson correlation coefficient[5], Kenall's rank coefficient[6], and Spearman's

---

[5] https://en.wikipedia.org/wiki/Pearson_product-moment_correlation_coefficient.
[6] https://en.wikipedia.org/wiki/Kendall_rank_correlation_coefficient.

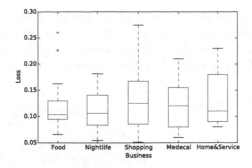

Fig. 3. Distribution of *loss* values for VFs in 5 service domains

rank correlation coefficient[7] are all widely-adopted correlation measures. However, because a VF's attention degree usually evolves periodically, there would be nonlinear correlations between the evolution history of different VFs, and unfortunately, above three correlation measures are all weak in handling such nonlinear correlation. If they are applied in this scenario, some closely-related VFs might be considered as weakly- or non-correlated ones.

Here we use MIC (Maximal Information Coefficient)[8] to measure the correlation between non-linearly correlated VFs. In statistics, MIC is a measure of the strength of the linear or non-linear association between two random continuous variables X and Y. It uses binning as a means to apply mutual information on X and Y, i.e., $I[X;Y] = \int_Y \int_X p(x,y) \log \frac{p(x,y)}{p(x)p(y)}$, and the rationale is that the bins for both variables should be chosen in such a way that the mutual information between the variables be maximal.

MIC coefficient falls in the range $[-1, 1]$, and the sign of MIC (i.e., <0 or >0) indicates whether it is negative or positive correlation. If the correlation between the evolution history of attention degrees of two VFs falls in the range $[0.8, 1]$ or $[-1, -0.8]$, the two VFs are closely correlated.

In terms of one service or one region/domain, for arbitrary two VFs f_i and f_j and their corresponding attention degrees' time-series evolution vectors $V(f_i)$ and $V(f_j)$, we calculate their MIC correlation coefficient $MIC(f_i, f_j)$ using the MIC API provided by `minepy` library[9]. In order to evaluate the effectiveness, similar as the approach in Algorithm 1, we split each $V(f_i)$ into train set and test set, measure $MIC(f_i, f_j)$ on the two sets separately, and then compare their results to measure *precision*, *recall* and F1-score, respectively.

4.2   Experiments

We select top-100 popular services from five domains and conduct MIC-based correlation analysis on their VFs. We manually identify and label some corre-

---

[7] https://en.wikipedia.org/wiki/Spearman%27s_rank_correlation_coefficient.

[8] https://en.wikipedia.org/wiki/Maximal_information_coefficient.

[9] https://pypi.python.org/pypi/minepy.

lations, then compare them with the analysis results of the proposed approach to measure the performance. It is shown in Fig. 4(a). The *precision* is above 85% in average, the *recall* is above 65% in average, and F1-Score is above 0.75, indicating that MIC has good performance for correlation analysis.

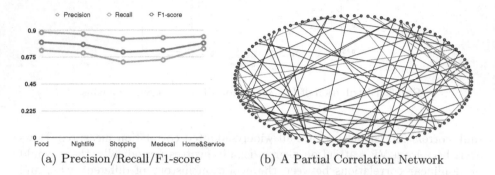

(a) Precision/Recall/F1-score   (b) A Partial Correlation Network

Fig. 4. Experiment results of VF correlation analysis

Experiment result shows that there are 73.86% VF pairs that have no correlation or are weakly correlated ($|MIC| \in [0, 0.2)$), 23.59% VF pairs being slightly correlated ($|MIC| \in [0.2, 0.4)$), 1.62% VF pairs being moderately correlated ($|MIC| \in [0.4, 0.6)$), 0.72% VF pairs being relatively correlated ($|MIC| \in [0.6, 0.8)$), and only 0.21% VF pairs being closely correlated ($|MIC| \geq 0.8$). This shows that such time-series correlation between the attention degrees' evolution of different VFs does really exist but the density of highly or moderately correlated VF pairs is fairly low, and most of VF pairs keep relatively independent. Because of this, it is of great significance to identify those highly correlated VF pairs from a mass of VFs and recommend them to service providers, so that these VF pairs are to be considered simultaneously when services are improved.

Specifically, Table 3 demonstrates detailed distribution of various correlation levels in five popular domains in Yelp. Chi-square test shows there is no significant difference among the MIC distribution in different domains, indicating that different domains exhibit similar correlation characteristics among their VFs.

Table 3. Distribution of MIC correlation coefficient between VFs in 5 domains

$|MIC|$	Food	Nightlife	Shopping	Medical	Home & Service
[0.8, 1]	0.21%	0.20%	0.12%	0.18%	0.15%
[0.6, 0.8)	0.72%	0.83%	0.64%	0.92%	0.79%
[0.4, 0.6)	1.62%	2.06%	1.98%	2.59%	2.28%
[0.2, 0.4)	23.59%	26.09%	24.32%	30.33%	20.01%
[0, 0.2)	73.86%	70.55%	72.94%	64.98%	76.77%

Here are two examples of highly related VF pairs: a VF `flavor` is positively correlated with another VF `size of food`, while `size of food` is negatively correlated with the VF `price`, and the correlation degree between `flavor` and `ize of food` (0.893) is higher than the one between `size` and `price` (−0.831).

Another interesting phenomenon is that, in terms of those closely correlated VF pairs, there are about 77.9% correlations being positive ones, and only 22.1% correlations being negative ones; for those relatively correlated VF pairs, the two numbers are 71% and 29%, respectively. This can be observed from Fig. 4(b) which is partial correlation network among VFs in the `food` domain. Closely correlated VF pairs with $|MIC| \geq 0.8$ are connected by lines, red lines are for negative correlated VFs, and black lines are for positive correlated VFs. The ratio of positive ones is much higher than the ratio of negative ones.

5 Related Work

Values are the ultimate goal that providers and customers expect to get from delivering and using a service. Provider value is often exhibited by the earning from the economics perspective, while customer value concerns mainly with experiences and satisfactions, i.e., whether and to what degree a service could meet a customer's demand. Zeithaml [19] defined customer value as "customers overall assessments on products". Gale [7] defined customer value as the relative price in market and product quality adjustment. Patricio et al. [13] proposed a multilevel service design method which takes customer value into full consideration. On the other hand, research on how to improve provider value seems inadequate. Wang et al. [17] suggested that dynamic service selection and composition should consider costs and earning of service providers. Wancheng et al. [14] put forward a competitive mechanism in commodity market to maintain balance in service selection by pricing based on member services. Chawathe et al. [3] proposed a method of distributing combined service earnings.

Mining user reviews has attracted wide attentions in previous research. Using available training corpus from open websites where each review has been appointed a class (e.g., thumbs-up and thumbs-downs, or some other quantitative or binary ratings), Hu et al. [9] designed and experimented a number of methods for building sentiment classifiers of reviews. Eirinaki et al. [6] presented a method to mine users' opinions from blogs and social network. Zhang et al. [20] gave a method to extract entity from users' opinions. To analyze the sentimental opinion expressed in a review, sentiment analysis techniques are typically conducted at two levels: (1) in the document level: to distinguish positive reviews from negative ones [2]; (2) in the sentiment level or phrase level: to perform tasks such as multi-perspective question answering and summarization, and opinion-oriented information extraction [11]. However, these methods are of limited usefulness for deriving useful information to represent the value features of services that are cared by customers.

Time-series correlation analysis is an important issue in data mining [1,5] and is applied in various domains, e.g., Kumar et al. [10] adopted the ARIMA algorithm to forecast the ambient air pollutants and achieves good performance; Gao et al. [8] used the random forest regression model to predict the volume of railway freight. CNN for extracting and modeling samples is also used in time-series data mining to create convolution sliding window modeling method [12].

6   Conclusions and Future Work

Numerous user reviews on third-party service platforms such as Yelp are a great treasure for service providers to collect valuable feedbacks from customers so as to improve their services. We propose two methods (VFAMine and CSRF) to help service providers extract Service Value Features (VFs) from review texts, quantify the evolution history of the attention degrees on these VFs (e.g., TSVFD), and predict the future trends of their attention degrees. They are not only useful for a single service provider to improve his service in advance in terms of user concerns (e.g., the VFs with increasing attention degrees in the future), but also for providers who plan to enter a new region or a new service domain to be full aware of the trend of massive users' attention degrees on specific VFs. Based on MIC-based correlation analysis, we also find that the evolution of different VFs are sometimes closely correlated.

Future work include: (1) Deep semantics analysis techniques are required to further improve the precision and recall of VFAMine (currently only some simplified heuristic rules are used); (2) After the prediction of a VF's attention degree in the future time intervals is obtained, how are service providers to be given more specific suggestions for improving the VF? (3) A method for grouping VFs in terms of the MIC correlation degree between them is required, and operational suggestions on how to take highly-correlated VFs into consideration at the same time during service improvement is of significance to service providers, too.

Acknowledgments. This work is supported by Natural Science Foundation of China (No. 61772155, 61472106)

References

1. Bankó, Z., Abonyi, J.: Correlation based dynamic time warping of multivariate time series. Expert Syst. Appl. **39**(17), 12814–12823 (2012)
2. Cambria, E., Schuller, B., Xia, Y., Havasi, C.: New avenues in opinion mining and sentiment analysis. IEEE Intell. Syst. **28**(2), 15–21 (2013)
3. Chawathe, S.S.: Strategic web-service agreements. In: International Conference on Web Services, pp. 119–126. IEEE (2006)
4. Chen, N., Lin, J., Hoi, S.C., Xiao, X., Zhang, B.: AR-Miner: mining informative reviews for developers from mobile app marketplace. In: International Conference on Software Engineering, pp. 767–778. ACM (2014)
5. Dorr, D.H., Denton, A.M.: Establishing relationships among patterns in stock market data. Data Knowl. Eng. **68**(3), 318–337 (2009)
6. Eirinaki, M., Pisal, S., Singh, J.: Feature-based opinion mining and ranking. J. Comput. Syst. Sci. **78**(4), 1175–1184 (2012)

7. Gale, B., Wood, R.C.: Managing Customer Value: Creating Quality and Service that Customers can See. Simon and Schuster, New York (1994)

8. Gao, J., Lu, X.: Forecast of china railway freight volume by random forest regression model. In: International Conference on Logistics, Informatics and Service Sciences, pp. 1–6. IEEE (2015)

9. Hu, M., Liu, B.: Mining and summarizing customer reviews. In: ACM SIGKDD International Conference on Knowledge Discovery and Data Mining, pp. 168–177. ACM (2004)

10. Kumar, U., Jain, V.: ARIMA forecasting of ambient air pollutants (O_3, NO, NO_2 and CO). Stoch. Env. Res. Risk Assess. **24**(5), 751–760 (2010)

11. Liu, B., Hu, M., Cheng, J.: Opinion observer: analyzing and comparing opinions on the web. In: International World Wide Web Conference, pp. 342–351. ACM (2005)

12. Papandreou, G., Kokkinos, I., Savalle, P.A.: Modeling local and global deformations in deep learning: epitomic convolution, multiple instance learning, and sliding window detection. In: IEEE Conference on Computer Vision and Pattern Recognition, pp. 390–399 (2015)

13. Patricio, L., Fisk, R.P., Cunha, J.F., Constantine, L.: Multilevel service design: from customer value constellation to service experience blueprinting. J. Serv. Res. **14**(2), 180–200 (2011)

14. Wancheng, N., Lingjuan, H., Lianchen, L., Cheng, W.: Commodity-market based services selection in dynamic web service composition. In: IEEE Asia-Pacific Service Computing Conference, pp. 218–223. IEEE (2007)

15. Wang, H., Chi, X., Wang, Z., Xu, X., Chen, S.: Extracting fine-grained service value features and distributions for accurate service recommendation. In: International Conference on Web Services. IEEE (2017)

16. Wang, H., Wang, Z., Xu, X.: Time-aware customer preference sensing and satisfaction prediction in a dynamic service market. In: Sheng, Q.Z., Stroulia, E., Tata, S., Bhiri, S. (eds.) ICSOC 2016. LNCS, vol. 9936, pp. 236–251. Springer, Cham (2016). doi:10.1007/978-3-319-46295-0_15

17. Wang, X.Z., Xu, X.F., Wang, Z.J.: A profit optimization oriented service selection method for dynamic service composition. Chin. J. Comput. **33**(11), 2104–2115 (2010)

18. Yao, L., Sheng, Q.Z., Segev, A., Yu, J.: Recommending web services via combining collaborative filtering with content-based features. In: IEEE International Conference on Web Services, pp. 42–49. IEEE (2013)

19. Zeithaml, V.A.: Consumer perceptions of price, quality, and value: a means-end model and synthesis of evidence. J. Mark. **52**, 2–22 (1988)

20. Zhang, L., Liu, B.: Aspect and entity extraction for opinion mining. In: Chu, W. (ed.) Data Mining and Knowledge Discovery for Big Data. Studies in Big Data, vol. 1, pp. 1–40. Springer, Heidelberg (2014). doi:10.1007/978-3-642-40837-3_1

Confidence-Aware Reputation Bootstrapping in Composite Service Environments

Lie Qu[✉], Athman Bouguettaya, and Azadeh Ghari Neiat

University of Sydney, Sydney, Australia
{lie.qu,athman.bouguettaya,azadeh.gharineiat}@sydney.edu.au

Abstract. We propose a novel reputation bootstrapping approach for both composite and atomic services in service-oriented environments. We consider multiple factors which may implicitly represent reputations of new services. Our approach does not rely on empirical assumptions. In contrast, we propose a data-driven method to determine how much a factor can represent service reputation. The reputation-related factors are modelled in a layer-based framework. This aims to quantitatively describe the importance of factors in reputation bootstrapping. Furthermore, we define *confidence* to represent how reliable the bootstrapped reputation of a new service is. We evaluate our approach based on a real-world dataset. The experimental results demonstrate the feasibility and outperformance of our approach.

1 Introduction

Reputation is an effective way to determine the performance quality of a service based on prior performance experiences (or records). However, performance experiences may not be always available when a new service emerges. Consequently, its reputation cannot be assessed, and thus trust establishment between consumers and the new service becomes challenging. Reputation bootstrapping is a key enabler to assign appropriate initial reputations for new services.

Reputation bootstrapping has been extensively studied in the literature [1,6,8,10,14,15]. These studies are typically based on particular empirical assumptions in which the reputation of a new service can be extracted from its inherent characteristics. For example, the approach proposed in [11] presents that a new service provided by a reputable provider tends to offer good performance. The approach proposed in [14] assumes that the reputation of a new service may approach to those of its similar services. However, such an assumption may not always hold under various circumstances. Moreover, because a new service usually has multiple characteristics, each of which can relatively reflect its future performance to some extent. How effectively each characteristic can represent the new service's reputation is usually unclear in real-world situations. Therefore, we investigate that reputation bootstrapping should only depend on the assumptions that can be practically validated in particular cases. Otherwise, the validity of the assumptions should be studied, i.e., determining which characteristic can more effectively reflect new services' future reputations.

© Springer International Publishing AG 2017
M. Maximilien et al. (Eds.): ICSOC 2017, LNCS 10601, pp. 158–174, 2017.
https://doi.org/10.1007/978-3-319-69035-3_11

Service composition provides an elegant means to aggregate services to provide a value-added service that meets consumers' complex requirements. Reputation bootstrapping for composite services is a key challenge because the correlation between the performance of a composite service and that of its corresponding component services is unclear and may vary case by case. Whether the reputation of a composite service can be represented by those of its component services may usually be unknown in practice. Therefore, such a correlation should be studied in a particular case, and cannot be taken as a common assumption for reputation bootstrapping. Furthermore, although the reputations of a composite service and its component services are quite correlated, the reputation bootstrapping for composite services is more challenging than that for atomic services. It needs to be addressed in the following three cases: (1) reputations of component services are available; (2) reputations of component services are partially available. (3) reputations of component services are totally unavailable. In the first case, an effective reputation bootstrapping approach should first determine the effectiveness of reputation correlation between a composite service and its component services, and then identify the specific correlation between each other. For the other cases, reputation bootstrapping for atomic services should be performed first to predict the unavailable reputations of component services. The first-case approach is then applied for further bootstrapping. In this paper, we focus on the first case. The other cases will be discussed in our future work.

In this paper, we study reputation bootstrapping in composite service environments. Our main contributions are summarised as follows:

1. We propose a novel service reputation bootstrapping approach by considering multiple characteristic factors[1] which may implicitly represent new services' future reputations. Our approach does not rely on particular empirical assumptions. Instead, a data-driven method is proposed to explore the importance of reputation-related factors in terms of particular cases.
2. A layer-based bootstrapping framework is proposed, which aims to quantitatively model the importance of reputation-related factors. The proposed framework can easily be extended to a general case. That makes the framework compatible with diverse situations in service-oriented environments.
3. We define *confidence* which describes the reliability of new services' bootstrapped reputations. The notion *confidence* would help consumers make a more comprehensive evaluation on reputation bootstrapping.
4. We conduct experiments based on a real-world dataset from GitHub to evaluate the proposed approach. The experimental results demonstrate the feasibility and outperformance of our work.

Motivating Scenario: the problem of reputation bootstrapping is illustrated using a real-world scenario of a mobile application company which provides a location-based review service through an app (e.g., Foursquare App[2]).

---

[1] To avoid ambiguity, we use the term "factor" to represent "inherit characteristic" in the rest of this paper.
[2] foursquare.com.

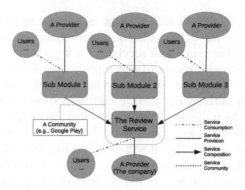

Fig. 1. The Motivating Scenario

The company outsources the sub-functional modules from an open-source software platform (e.g., GitHub) to reduce development cost. By composing these sub modules, the company can offer its own review service to a market. Although the newly developed service has no past performance records, it has multiple characteristic factors to represent its future reputation. The factors include the reputation of its provider (the company), the reputation of the community (e.g., Google Play) it belongs to, the reputations of similar review services, the past performance records of its sub modules, etc. In this scenario, we consider the review service as a composite service whose component services are the sub modules. Figure 1 illustrates the scenario. The review service is composed of three sub modules. In practice, the sub modules of a repository at GitHub are specified in a .gitmodules file. The review service and its sub modules have their distinct providers. On the other hand, there are a number of users for each service. They consume the services and provide feedback (e.g., the star reputation system at GitHub[3]) for service performance assessment. In addition, a service may belong to a community which may be a reputable commercial company or a certified organisation. For example, some open-source repositories at GitHub belong to Google. In this scenario, although the review service has no historical performance records, its reputation can be predicted according to multiple factors, e.g., provider reputation, community reputation and component service reputation. However, which factor is dominant in reputation representing is still unclear. Our proposed approach focuses on determining the importance of factors in reputation bootstrapping, and presents the confidence of every bootstrapped reputation. As the data at GitHub contain all the features which can appear in service-oriented environments, we employ a GitHub dataset to evaluate our proposed approach.

---

[3] help.github.com/articles/about-stars

2   The Layer-Based Framework

In this section, we propose a layer-based framework to model the importance of reputation-related factors of a service. Considering our motivating scenario, the boostrapped reputation of the new review service can be computed based on some implicit factors. Specifically, the factors are summarised as follows: a reputable provider has a high probability of providing good services; a service belonging to a reputable community may have good quality; a service composed of good-performance component services tends to perform well since the quality of its sub modules is satisfactory. Moreover, similar services may have similar reputations in some cases. In this regard, service similarity can also be used to predict new services' reputations [14]. However, the importance degree of each factor in representing service reputation is still unknown. In practice, the factor importance may change in terms of different circumstances.

We propose a layer-based framework to quantitatively model the importance of these reputation-related factors. Figure 2 describes the proposed framework of reputation transfer among the factors. Each factor is modelled in a layer of the framework. The main reason that we model the reputation-related factors in a layer-based structure is to intuitively illustrate the importance of these factors. According to our motivating scenario, the framework consists of *user layer*, *provider layer*, *community layer*, *similar service layer* and *component service layer*, where the user layer outputs the direct reputation of a service, and all the other layers reflect its indirect reputation. In this paper, we consider that consumers' feedback is the most reliable information to assess service reputation. That is because feedback is generated based on the actual experiences of service performance. Although there may exist biased or malicious feedback, user feedback is still the most direct way to evaluate service reputation. Furthermore, some studies [7,13] focus on credibility evaluation of user feedback to improve its

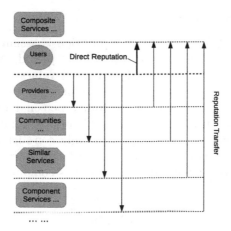

Fig. 2. The Layer-based Framework

reliability. Consequently, the feedback from the user layer is employed to evaluate the direct reputation of a service. The reputations computed from other layers are taken as the indirect reputations of the service. Except for the user layer, each of the other layers contains a reputation transfer process. The reputation transfer processes are shown via arrow lines in Fig. 2. In a reputation transfer process, the direct reputation of a new service is estimated through the indirect reputations from other layers.

In particular cases, some reputation-related factors may be unavailable. For example, if a service does not belong to any community, then community information cannot be used to estimate its reputation. On the other hand, there may also exist new factors, which are not included in Fig. 2. A new factor can be modelled in a new layer of the framework. This guarantees the generality of our reputation bootstrapping approach. The proposed framework can also be applied for reputation bootstrapping of atomic services. This is equivalent to the case of removing the component service layer from the framework.

The reputation-related factors may have different degrees of importance in representing a service's reputation. We model these factors in the framework by following this rule: "the more important a factor is in reputation representing, the higher layer it stays in". Therefore, as aforementioned, we put the user layer in the first place as it represents the direct reputation. The order of other layers is not fixed, and depends on particular cases. The layer order is determined by our data-driven bootstrapping approach introduced in the next section.

3   The Reputation Bootstrapping Approach

In this section, we first introduce the details of the proposed reputation bootstrapping approach in Sects. 3.1 and 3.2, and then introduce *confidence* in Sect. 3.3.

3.1   Reputation Evaluation

In this paper, the evaluation of service reputation is assumed to be performed by aggregating users' feedback during a particular period. We assume that user feedback is converted into normalised numerical values in this paper. In [7], Malik and Bouguettaya propose that service reputation evaluation should consider multiple metrics, including rater credibility, personal preferences, temporal sensitivity, majority ratings and past rating history. As reputation evaluation is not the main contribution of this paper, we only consider users' credibility of giving feedback since it is the most influential factor in reputation evaluation. In this regard, the direct reputation of a service is computed as follows:

$$r_j = \frac{\sum_u (f_j^u \times c_u)}{\sum_u c_u},\tag{1}$$

where r_j denotes the direct reputation of service j, f_j^u denotes the feedback given by user u to service j, and c_u is the credibility of u.

User credibility is usually computed in different ways under various circumstances. As we apply a GitHub dataset to evaluate our work (see Sect. 4), we consider how to compute the credibility of GitHub users and reputations of repositories. At GitHub, a user gives stars to other users to express his/her appreciation on their work. Through this starring system, all users are connected as a directed graph. Figure 3 illustrates an example of the star network. In this network, if a user obtains more stars from others, he/she is considered more capable of giving fair feedback since many other users recognise his/her expertise. In addition, a star given by a user who has more stars should be considered more important than a star given by a user who has fewer stars. Given a star network, we compute user credibility of giving feedback using PageRank [12], which is a well-known approach to identify the importance of Web pages. In PageRank, a Web page has a high rank if the sum of the ranks of the pages which cite it is high. As a result, it is a recursive process to compute the importance of all pages. Due to the space limitation, we omit the detailed process of applying PageRank to compute the user credibility c_u at GitHub. Furthermore, the GitHub users also give stars to repositories. The direct reputation of a repository is computed based on the number of stars it obtains. Every star is weighted by the credibility of the user who gives the star.

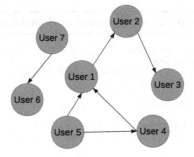

Fig. 3. User Starring Network

3.2 Reputation Bootstrapping

Suppose a complete framework denoted as $\mathbb{L}$ contains all possible reputation-related factors. $L \subseteq \mathbb{L}$ is a subset of $\mathbb{L}$. L describes the situation where some of the reputation-related factors for services may be unavailable. Let r denote the direct reputation of a service. Our reputation bootstrapping approach aims to identify a function $R(L) = \hat{r}$ to make $\hat{r} \approx r$, where $\hat{r}$ is the bootstrapped reputation of a new service, and is computed based on the reputation-related factors modelled in L. Furthermore, our approach quantitatively determines the importance of factors in reputation bootstrapping. Given the complete framework $\mathbb{L}$, a function $I(\mathbb{L}) = \vec{i}$ outputs a vector $\vec{i}$ which contains the importance value of every factor in $\mathbb{L}$. The functions R and I are learned based on the historical records of existing services. A set of features are extracted based on the factor modelled in each layer of $\mathbb{L}$. For example, the factor "provider" is modelled in the provider layer of $\mathbb{L}$, in which several features related to service providers are extracted. These features may include the reputation of a provider, the reputations of the provider's past services, the number of its services, etc. The features in every layer of $\mathbb{L}$ are then collected and trained through a learning method to compute functions R and I.

Function Learning: we apply Random Decision Forest [2], which is an ensemble learning algorithm based on Decision Tree, to determine the functions R and I. The standard Random Forest algorithm is modified to apply to our work. The reason to adopt Random Forest is: (1) in comparison with the complete framework $\mathbb{L}$, some reputation-related factors may be unavailable in a particular case L, i.e., $L \subseteq \mathbb{L}$. Random Forest can naturally handle various cases of incomplete factors through a feature bagging process [2]; (2) Random Forest can easily compute feature importance in a learning process. As a result, the importance of each reputation-related factor can be computed by summing up the importance value of every feature in each layer of $\mathbb{L}$; and (3) the efficiency of Random Forest is very high in training and prediction processes, compared to most of other learning algorithms.

Algorithm 1. Forest Building for Reputation Bootstrapping

Input:
   the training set N containing n samples;
   the complete layer-based framework $\mathbb{L}$;
   the set $\{L_i\}$ containing all possible subsets of $\mathbb{L}$, where $L_i \subset \mathbb{L}$;
   the feature set F containing all features in $\mathbb{L}$;
   the feature set F_i for L_i, where $F_i \subset F$.
Output: the structure of a decision forest.
1: **for** each $L_i \in \{L_i\}$ **do**
2:    **for** $t = 1 \ldots T$ (T is the number of times of bagging.) **do**
3:       *Sample Bagging*: randomly select samples from N with replacement for n times to form a new sample set N_i^t;
4:       *Feature Bagging*: randomly select features from F_i to form a sub feature set f_i^t;
5:       *Tree Building*: build an unpruned decision tree tr_i^t based on N_i^t and f_i^t.
6:    **end for**
7: **end for**
8: Build a standard random forest $\{tr^{t'}\}$ containing trees denoted as $tr^{t'}$ based on N and F;
9: **return** a decision forest FR based on the combination of $\{tr_i^t\}$ and $\{tr^{t'}\}$.

In the standard tree bagging process [2] of Random Forest, data samples and data features are randomly selected with replacement from the original dataset. The random selection process is repeated several times to form a number of subsets of data. A decision tree is built based on each subset. All of these trees form a forest. The result of a prediction is the aggregation of the results obtained from all the trees in the forest. The randomness and aggregation in Random Forest improve prediction accuracy and effectively control overfitting. In our work, we modify the standard bagging process in order to deal with various cases of L. For every possible L, a corresponding sub forest is built only based on the reputation-related factors modelled in L before the standard bagging process. If a service can only be modelled in a particular L according to its factors, its future reputation is predicted only through the sub forest that is built on L. For example, a new composite service only has the information of its provider and component services. It is reasonable to bootstrap its reputation only based on a particular L consisting of a provider layer and a component service layer. On the other hand, the importance of all possible reputation-related factors is learned based on the complete framework $\mathbb{L}$.

Compared to standard Random Forest, the bagging process of our modified forest consists of two steps:

1. Build a sub forest for every possible $L \subset \mathbb{L}$, where each sub forest is a standard random forest which is built on L only.
2. Build a standard random forest based on $\mathbb{L}$.

The whole forest for reputation bootstrapping is the combination of the decision trees built in Steps 1&2. Algorithm 1 presents the details of the forest building process. Lines 1–7 describe the sub forest building process in Step 1, where Lines 2–7 is a standard bagging process in Random Forest. Lines 8 and 9 describe the process in Step 2. In the end, a forest-based reputation prediction model is built by training actual data. The sub forest building in Step 1 effectively addresses the real-world situations where only partial reputation-related factors are available for service reputation bootstrapping.

Note that we apply classification trees in our proposed approach rather than regression trees. The reason is that a reputation value of a service usually needs to be mapped into a *trust* degree to describe how possible the service performs satisfactorily. A trust degree is typically represented by a probabilistic tuple (*belief, uncertainty, disbelief*) [5]. In this regard, classification trees are more suitable and easier to map reputation values into a trust degree.

Factor Importance: Random Forest has the ability to rank feature importance in a training process. Given a decision forest FR, the importance of every reputation-related factor is determined by aggregating the importance values of all the features belonging to the factor. In a ready-trained decision tree, every node of the tree contains a part of samples. Except for leaf nodes, every node is split into two child nodes in order to make similar samples stay in the same node. Every split is performed according to a condition on a single feature. The optimal condition is determined by sample "*impurity*", which describes the confusion degree of samples in a node. The training process of a decision tree is to determine how quickly each feature can reduce sample impurity until similar samples stay in the same node. Therefore, in a single decision tree, the unnormalized importance of a feature can be defined as follows:

$$importance = im_n \times s_n - im_l \times s_l - im_r \times s_r, \tag{2}$$

where im denotes impurity values, s denotes the number of samples in a node. n, l and r respectively denote the current node, its left child node and right child node. The impurity values are typically computed through Gini impurity or information gain [2]. The unnormalised importance values are then normalised, i.e., make the sum of the importance of all features equal to 1. The global importance of features in a decision forest is the average of the importance of features computed in every single tree. Let $importance_f$ denote the importance of a factor f in FR built on $\mathbb{L}$; $importance_f^i$ denotes the importance of a feature i belonging to f. The importance of f in reputation bootstrapping is the sum of the importance of all the features belonging to it:

$$importance_f = \sum_i importance_f^i. \tag{3}$$

Through factor importance, the order of layers in $\mathbb{L}$ can be determined. Consequently, the bootstrapped reputations computed based on more important factors are considered more reliable.

3.3 Confidence of Bootstrapped Reputations

We propose $confidence$ to describe how much a bootstrapped reputation is reliable. The confidence of a bootstrapped reputation is denoted as a tuple (a, e), where a represents the overall accuracy of reputation bootstrapping in a particular case (i.e., for a particular L), and e describes the uncertainty of the bootstrapped reputation of a particular service. For example, suppose a new service s only has its provider information and community information. Its reputation-related factors are modelled in a framework L_{pc} which is composed of a provider layer and a community layer. After training a decision forest FR through Algorithm 1, a is the prediction accuracy computed from the sub forest which is built on L_{pc}. The accuracy a describes the general accuracy of reputation bootstrapping in the case of L_{pc}. a is computed as follows:

$$a = \frac{The\ number\ of\ correctly\ predicted\ samples}{The\ total\ number\ of\ samples}. \tag{4}$$

On the other hand, e is computed based on the probability estimate of the bootstrapped reputation of s. In a decision tree, given a particular sample, the probability of every class to which the sample belongs can be estimated. Suppose there exist c classes. After the tree training, a sample s (i.e., service s) is finally classified into a leaf node l. The probability of s belonging to a particular class C is computed using Laplace estimate [9] as follows:

$$Probability\ Estimate = \frac{The\ number\ of\ samples\ belonging\ to\ C\ in\ l + 1}{The\ total\ number\ of\ samples\ in\ l + c}. \tag{5}$$

This probability estimate is suitable for balanced datasets, i.e., the number of samples belonging to each class is approximately equal. In this paper, we use a balanced dataset to evaluate the proposed approach.

In a random forest, the overall probability estimate of every class to which s belongs is the mean probability estimate of all the trees. e describes how

Table 1. Dataset Statistics

Data Type	Statistic
The number of repositories	4715
The number of repositories with sub modules	417
The average number of sub modules per repository	1.28
The minimum number of stars a repository obtains	1
The maximum number of stars a repository obtains	9992

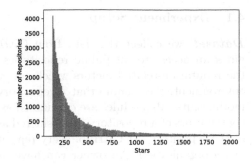

Fig. 4. The Distribution of Stars

certainly the bootstrapped reputation of s belongs to a particular reputation class, and is a necessary amendment for a. For example, suppose there are three reputation classes for services, which are represented by "*bad*", "*fair*" and "*good*". The probability estimate for s is $(0.2, 0.6, 0.2)$. Another new service s' is bootstrapped under the same circumstance. The probability estimate of s' is $(0.1, 0.9, 0)$. Although the predicted reputation class of s and s' is the same (i.e., "*fair*"), the uncertainty of their predictions is not equal. The prediction of s is less reliable than that of s' since the probability of s belonging to "*fair*" is smaller than that of s'. To this end, we use the entropy of a probability estimate to quantitatively describe the uncertainty e:

$$e = - \sum_j p(C_j) \log p(C_j), \tag{6}$$

where $p(C_j)$ denotes the probability estimate of a new service's bootstrapped reputation belonging to a particular reputation class C_j. The higher e is, the more unreliable the bootstrapped reputation is. It should be noted that, the effectiveness of e representing uncertainty of reputation bootstrapping is influenced by the bootstrapping accuracy a. If a is quite low, the effectiveness of e is low as the bootstrapping model learned via Algorithm 1 cannot output correct probability estimates. Even if such a situation occurs, a is still an effective metric to evaluate the confidence of reputation bootstrapping.

4   Experimental Results

We conduct a set of experiments to evaluate the proposed reputation bootstrapping approach. These experiments show: (1) the importance levels of reputation-related factors; (2) reputation bootstrapping accuracy; and (3) the effectiveness of reputation bootstrapping uncertainty e.

4.1 Experiment Setup

Dataset: we collect the data from GitHub via its RESTful API[4] that provides an access to all public repositories. The collected information contains the reputation-related factors which can appear in a general composite service environment. We assume that a repository is a service. If a repository has sub modules, its sub modules are considered as its component services. The multiple contributors of a repository is considered as a whole entity, which is the provider of the repository. At GitHub, every repository has an owner that can be a user or an organisation. An owner can have multiple repositories. We assume that the owner of a repository is a community. In addition, similar repositories with the same keywords can be identified through the semantic search function provided by the API. The keywords are extracted from repository descriptions by removing stop words and duplicated words.

After analysing the GitHub data, we discover that the number of stars of a repository follows a Pareto (long tail) distribution that is illustrated in Fig. 4. As can be seen, most of repositories have been given quite few stars. The number of repositories having a particular number of stars is quite imbalanced. An imbalanced dataset would bring bias in prediction accuracy evaluation. To avoid such bias, we collect the approximately same number of repositories from five different reputation intervals. Every reputation interval represents a reputation class to which a repository can belong. The dataset contains 4715 repositories, in which 417 repositories have sub modules. At GitHub, most of repositories with sub modules have zero star. The repositories with zero star cannot provide effective information. Therefore, we only keep the repositories having at least one star in the dataset. This also indicates the small proportion of repositories with sub modules in the dataset (i.e., only 417 from 4715 repositories). In addition, we find that most of the repositories with sub modules have only one sub module. Table 1 reports the statistics of the GitHub dataset.

We apply the reputation evaluation approach introduced in Sect. 4.1 to compute the reputations of either repositories or users. The actual reputations of repositories are taken as a ground truth to evaluate whether the proposed approach can accurately bootstrap service reputation.

Model Learning: we build a framework based on Fig. 2. The features are extracted from each layer of the framework:

- There is one feature in the provider layer: the average reputation of top-10 contributors of a repository. The reputations of these contributors are weighted by the numbers of their commits.
- There are three features in the community layer: the reputation of the owner of a repository, the average reputation of the owner's other repositories, and whether the owner is a user or an organisation.
- There are two features in the similar service layer: the average reputation of Top-5 similar repositories, and the average reputation of the owners of similar

---

[4] developer.github.com/v3.

repositories. The reputations of the similar repositories and their owners are weighted by the similarity scores computed by the search API.
– There are two features in the component service layer: the average reputation of sub module repositories, and the average reputation of the owners of sub module repositories.

80% of the dataset forms a training set. The rest forms a test set. We apply Algorithm 1 to build a decision forest. We evaluate the proposed approach by comparing the predicted reputations of repositories and their corresponding actual reputations.

Table 2. The Importance Level of Factors

Features	Normalised Importance
Provider Layer:	**0.238**
Average reputation of contributors	0.238
Community Layer:	**0.722**
Reputation of the owner	0.127
Average reputation of the other repositories of the owner	0.532
User or organisation	0.063
Similar Service Layer:	**0.024**
Average reputation of similar repositories	0.013
Average reputation of the owners of similar repositories	0.011
Component Service Layer	**0.016**
Average reputation of sub modules	0.010
Average reputation of the owners of sub modules	0.006

4.2 Results

Factor Importance: in the first experiment, we explore which factor plays an important role. Table 2 reports the normalised importance of the factors on the GitHub dataset through model learning. The results demonstrate that the factor *community* is the dominant factor to predict service reputation. Consequently, it is more reliable for reputation bootstrapping of new services. In contrast, the other factors are insignificant. An interesting finding is that, in the provider layer, the reputations of the contributors of a repository do not directly influence the reputation of the repository. The importance of the factor *provider* is only 0.238. In addition, the reputation of the owner of a repository also has low importance (0.127). On the contrary, the reputations of the other repositories of the owner has very high importance (0.532). This phenomenon may be caused by the starring system at GitHub. The stars given to a user may more greatly reflect his/her social relations (following or followed at GitHub) rather than his/her reputation on project development. Instead, his/her past experiences more effectively reflect his/her ability on providing valuable repositories.

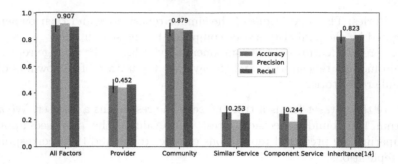

Fig. 5. User Starring Network

The experimental results also show that the factors *similar service* and *component service* have quite low importance in reputation prediction. The possible reasons may include: (1) semantic similarity cannot be applied to group repositories with similar reputations; and (2) the reputation of a composite repository is more influenced by its own developers rather than its sub module repositories.

Bootstrapping Accuracy: In the second experiment, we evaluate the reputation bootstrapping accuracy of our approach. We apply the proposed approach in five cases, i.e., consider all the reputation-related factors and consider every single factor (*provider, community, similar service* and *component service*). In addition, we compare our approach to a baseline approach that applies the *inheritance mechanism* proposed in [11]. The baseline approach uses the past reputations of the existing services of a provider to bootstrap the reputation of the provider's new service.

We use the metrics *accuracy, precision* and *recall* to illustrate the comparison results. Figure 5 demonstrates that the accuracy of our approach is quite low in terms of the factors *similar service* and *component service*. The accuracy is slightly higher than that of random guessing (approximate 0.2 due to five classes with approximately equal size). The accuracy in terms of the factor *provider* is higher, but only 0.452. As the dominant factor, the accuracy in terms of *community* is much higher and reaches approximate 0.88. In addition, the baseline approach is equivalent to reputation bootstrapping based on the feature *average reputation of the other repositories of the owner*. This feature is in the community layer, and its importance is very high (0.532). Therefore, the bootstrapping accuracy of the baseline approach reaches approximate 0.82. However, it is still 8% lower than the accuracy of our approach in terms of all the factors (0.907). The comparison results demonstrate that the more important a reputation-related factor is, the more accurate the reputation bootstrapping in terms of the factor is. Compared to the baseline approach which only takes a single factor into account, our reputation bootstrapping approach considers multiple factors and is able to identify the most important factor. Therefore, our approach is more adaptable under diverse circumstances.

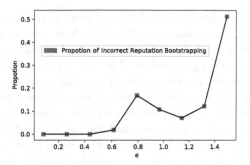

Fig. 6. Evaluation of e

Evaluation of e: In the last experiment, we evaluate the effectiveness of the proposed bootstrapping uncertainty e. For every sample in the dataset, we conduct reputation bootstrapping and compute its e using Eq. (6). All the e values are sorted in a descending order. The maximum and minimum values of e are used to build an uncertainty interval $[Min(e), Max(e)]$. The interval is equally divided into several sub intervals. We collect all the samples whose reputations are not correctly bootstrapped. The number of incorrectly reputation bootstrapping in every uncertainty sub interval is counted. We compute the proportion of incorrectly reputation bootstrapping in each sub interval over the total number of incorrectly bootstrapping. The proportions are shown in Fig. 6. The results demonstrate that most of incorrectly bootstrapping has a high value of e. Over 99% of incorrectly bootstrapping has an e over 0.5. The overall trend indicates that the higher an uncertainty e is, the more unreliable a bootstrapped reputation is. Although the trend fluctuates in particular cases due to reputation prediction errors, the overall trend remains stable.

5   Related Work

The approaches of reputation or trust bootstrapping are typically classified into three categories: *characteristic*-based, *guarantee*-based and *trial*-based approaches. We briefly overview the principal related work in these three areas.

Characteristic-based Approaches: this category of approaches focuses on predicting a new service's future reputation via its reputation-related characteristics. In [11], a reputation bootstrapping model is proposed through three mechanisms: *inheritance, referral* and *guarantee*. The inheritance mechanism uses provider reputation to predict service reputation; the referral mechanism uses community reputation to estimate service reputation; the guarantee mechanism is a guarantee-based approach which allows a new service to provide a commitment for its future performance. In [1], a trust bootstrapping approach is proposed in a multi-agent environment based on the notion *stereotype*. A stereotype is learned from past experiences to describe the correlation between an agent's characteristics and its expected probability of good performance. This approach does not consider concrete characteristics and their corresponding importance in trust bootstrapping. In [14], a trust bootstrapping approach is proposed for Web services based on a tagging system. The system allows users to tag different services which they are interested in. Therefore, similar services can be identified through the tagging system. The trustworthiness of a new service is predicted according to the similarity of other services with common tags. In addition, some approaches assign a single population statistic as the bootstrapped reputation or trust for every new entity. In [3] and [16], the mean trust value and the minimum trust value of the whole system is assigned to every newcomer respectively. None of the above studies take factor/characteristic importance and bootstrapping confidence into account.

Guarantee-based Approaches: this category of approaches allows a newcomer to provide evidence to guarantee that it will offer good performance. The guarantee can be the referral from other trustworthy parties [4,8,10]. The referral also requires past transactions between newcomers and the trustworthy parties. However, this requirement can be hardly meet in practice as newcomers may be quite new without any historical transaction records. Another way to obtain a guarantee is to ask a newcomer to offer a monetary commitment before transactions [6,11]. In such a case, if the newcomer performs unsatisfactorily, it will lose money. This also requires a centralised authority to manage monetary commitments.

Trial-based Approaches: this category of approaches gives a newcomer a trial period to build its reputation. In this period, newcomers are allowed to make transactions with other parties under some restrictions. In [8], a newcomer can only make transactions with the selected parties that have high credibility. In addition, the full transaction payment can be obtained only when the trial period finishes. The newcomer's reputation is then computed based on its performance during the trial period. In [15], the trust patterns of service performance are first modelled through Hidden Markov Model (HMM) based on the prior observations of the entire service population. The performance of a new service is then evaluated during a trial period to obtain its specific trust pattern.

Our proposed approach is classified into the characteristic-based category. Compared to the other two categories, it requires no extra process (e.g., commitment management or a trial period). As a result, it is more practical and easier to achieve in real-world situations.

6   Conclusion

This paper proposed a novel reputation bootstrapping approach in composite service environments. The proposed approach is based on a number of factors which may implicitly reflect new services' future reputations. We introduced a layer-based framework where the importance of these factors are modelled. A data-driven approach based on a modified version of Random Forest was proposed to quantitatively determine the importance of the factors and predict new services' reputations. The proposed framework can also be extended to a general case, and thus can effectively deal with diverse reputation-related factors in real-world situations. In addition, the notion *confidence* was proposed to describe the reliability of bootstrapped reputations. In our experiments, we demonstrated the effectiveness of our approach using a GitHub dataset.

Acknowledgement. This research was made possible by DP150100149 grant from Australian Research Council. The statements made herein are solely the responsibility of the authors.

References

1. Burnett, C., Norman, T.J., Sycara, K.P.: Bootstrapping trust evaluations through stereotypes. In: 9th International Conference on Autonomous Agents and Multiagent Systems (AAMAS), pp. 241–248 (2010)
2. Ho, T.K.: Random decision forests. In: 3rd International Conference on Document Analysis and Recognition (ICDAR), pp. 278–282 (1995)
3. Huang, K., Liu, Y., Nepal, S., Fan, Y., Chen, S., Tan, W.: A novel equitable trustworthy mechanism for service recommendation in the evolving service ecosystem. In: Franch, X., Ghose, A.K., Lewis, G.A., Bhiri, S. (eds.) ICSOC 2014. LNCS, vol. 8831, pp. 510–517. Springer, Heidelberg (2014). doi:10.1007/978-3-662-45391-9_43
4. Huynh, T.D., Jennings, N.R., Shadbolt, N.R.: Certified reputation: how an agent can trust a stranger. In: 5th International Joint Conference on Autonomous Agents and Multiagent Systems (AAMAS), pp. 1217–1224 (2006)
5. Ismail, R., Jøsang, A.: The beta reputation system. In: 15th Bled eConference: eReality: Constructing the eEconomy, pp. 324–337 (2002)
6. Jiao, H., Liu, J., Li, J., Liu, C.: A framework for reputation bootstrapping based on reputation utility and game theories. In: IEEE 10th International Conference on Trust, Security and Privacy in Computing and Communications (TrustCom), pp. 344–351 (2011)
7. Malik, Z., Bouguettaya, A.: Rateweb: reputation assessment for trust establishment among web services. VLDB J. **18**(4), 885–911 (2009)
8. Malik, Z., Bouguettaya, A.: Reputation bootstrapping for trust establishment among web services. IEEE Internet Comput. **13**(1), 40–47 (2009)
9. Margineantu, D.D., Dietterich, T.G.: Improved class probability estimates from decision tree models. Nonlinear Estimation Classif. **171**, 173–188 (2003)
10. Maximilien, E.M., Singh, M.P.: Reputation and endorsement for web services. SIGecom Exchanges **3**(1), 24–31 (2002)
11. Nguyen, H.T., Yang, J., Zhao, W.: Bootstrapping trust and reputation for web services. In: 14th IEEE International Conference on Commerce and Enterprise Computing (CEC), pp. 41–48 (2012)
12. Page, L., Brin, S., Motwani, R., Winograd, T.: The pagerank citation ranking: bringing order to the web. In: 7th International World Wide Web Conference, pp. 161–172 (1998)
13. Qu, L., Wang, Y., Orgun, M.A., Liu, L., Liu, H., Bouguettaya, A.: CCCloud: Context-aware and credible cloud service selection based on subjective assessment and objective assessment. IEEE Trans. Serv. Comput. **8**(3), 369–383 (2015)

14. Skopik, F., Schall, D., Dustdar, S.: Start trusting strangers? bootstrapping and prediction of trust. In: Vossen, G., Long, D.D.E., Yu, J.X. (eds.) WISE 2009. LNCS, vol. 5802, pp. 275–289. Springer, Heidelberg (2009). doi:10.1007/978-3-642-04409-0_30
15. Yahyaoui, H., Zhioua, S.: Bootstrapping trust of web services through behavior observation. In: Auer, S., Díaz, O., Papadopoulos, G.A. (eds.) ICWE 2011. LNCS, vol. 6757, pp. 319–330. Springer, Heidelberg (2011). doi:10.1007/978-3-642-22233-7_22
16. Zacharia, G., Moukas, A., Maes, P.: Collaborative reputation mechanisms for electronic marketplaces. Decis. Support Syst. 29(4), 371–388 (2000)

Compound Trace Clustering to Generate Accurate and Simple Sub-Process Models

Yaguang Sun[1]($\boxtimes$), Bernhard Bauer[1], and Matthias Weidlich[2]

[1] Software Methodologies for Distributed Systems, University of Augsburg,
Augsburg, Germany
{yaguang.sun,bernhard.bauer}@informatik.uni-augsburg.de
[2] Humboldt-Universität zu Berlin, Berlin, Germany
matthias.weidlich@hu-berlin.de

Abstract. Business process model discovery targets the construction of conceptual models from event data that has been recorded during the execution of a business process. While a plethora of discovery techniques have been proposed in the literature, most existing techniques fail to cope with complex control-flow patterns as they are observed in event logs of highly flexible processes. In this paper, we follow the idea of splitting-up an event log into sub-logs, before applying process model discovery. This yields a set of sub-process models, one per sub-log, each describing a major variant of the business process. Unlike existing techniques, our clustering approach is guided by the result of model discovery: It first optimises the average complexity of the resulting models, before improving the accuracy of each model in isolation. Our experimental evaluation highlights that our approach yields more accurate sub-process models (that are of comparatively low complexity) than state-of-the-art trace clustering techniques.

Keywords: Business process mining · Process model discovery · Trace clustering · Model fitness improvement · Model complexity reduction

1 Introduction

Manual elicitation of business process models is regarded a complex, time consuming, and error-prone task. In recent years, therefore, techniques for automated business process model discovery (BPMD) have been developed, which aim at the construction of conceptual models from event data that has been recorded during the execution of a business process [1]. The starting point for BPMD is an event log that is generated by information systems and contains information on *traces*. A trace is a sequence of events that denote activity executions for a particular instance of a business process.

While a large number of BPMD techniques have been described in the literature, see [7,11,18], most existing approaches fail to cope with complex control-flow patterns in real-life event logs, which usually stem from business processes

M. Maximilien et al. (Eds.): ICSOC 2017, LNCS 10601, pp. 175–190, 2017.
https://doi.org/10.1007/978-3-319-69035-3_12

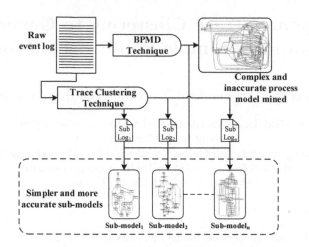

Fig. 1. The basic setting of using trace clustering in business process model discovery.

implemented in highly flexible environments, e.g., healthcare, customer relationship management (CRM), and product development [6]. For such processes, the phenomenon of *'spaghetti-like'* process models has been described in multiple case studies. Such models are often inaccurate and too complex to be interpreted by domain experts [4], and thus of limited use. This problem is largely due to the presence of diverse variants of a business process within a single event log [3].

Against this background, it has been argued that *trace clustering* [2–6, 8–10] shall be applied before BPMD. As outlined in Fig. 1, an event log is first split into sub-logs, each containing traces of similar structure. Afterwards, BPMD techniques are applied to each of the generated sub-logs to obtain a set of sub-process models that provide a more accurate and comprehensible view on the business process. However, existing trace clustering techniques are largely decoupled from process model discovery. They are primarily guided by the similarity of traces in an event log, but are agnostic to the impact of clustering decisions on the quality of the discovered models. Consequently, applying traditional trace clustering in BPMD may yield inaccurate sub-process models.

In this paper, we therefore put forward a new trace clustering technique named *Compound Trace Clustering* (CTC). It considers the accuracy and complexity of the resulting sub-process models during the clustering procedure. More specifically, it first optimises the average complexity of the sub-process models, before the accuracy of each model is improved separately.

In the remainder of this paper, we first exemplify the issues of applying traditional trace clustering in BPMD with experimental results (Sect. 2) and introduce basic formal notions and notations (Sect. 3). We then elaborate on the details of the proposed CTC technique (Sect. 4). To test the efficiency of our method, we carried out a comprehensive evaluation with four real-world event logs (Sect. 5). As part of that, we also compared CTC with six traditional trace clustering techniques. Finally, we review related work (Sect. 6) and conclude (Sect. 7).

2 Issues of Traditional Trace Clustering in BPMD

Existing trace clustering techniques are decoupled from business process model discovery and focus on the detection of similarity between traces in a given event log. As such, they largely neglect the implications of certain clustering decisions on the accuracy of the sub-process models derived per sub-log [6]. Some of the resulting sub-process models are therefore likely to be of low quality.

We illustrate this issue with experimental insights obtained for the event log of the loan and overdraft approval process [12] that has been published as part of the Business Process Intelligence Challenge (BPIC) in 2012. Using two traditional trace clustering techniques, namely GED [4] and sequence clustering (SCT) [5], and setting the number of generated sub-logs to five, yields the results shown in Table 1. For each method, the table lists the number of traces in the respective sub-logs as well as the quality of the sub-process model discovered from it. Models have been constructed with the Flexible Heuristics Miner (FHM) [11] and accuracy is measured in terms of fitness [13], i.e., the amount of behaviour present in the log that is covered by the discovered model.

Table 1. The information about the sub-process models mined from the sub-logs of LOA generated by two traditional trace clustering techniques.

Method	Metrics	Model of sub-log 1	Model of sub-log 2	Model of sub-log 3	Model of sub-log 4	Model of sub-log 5
GED	Fitness	0.9718	0.9959	0.8049	0.5193	0.6197
	#Traces	1509	1607	8073	784	1114
SCT	Fitness	0.9095	0.8436	0.9636	0.932	0.7828
	#Traces	2091	1839	1740	2765	4652

The results illustrate that both trace clustering techniques will generate one or more sub-logs, for which the discovered sub-process models have low fitness. For example, the fitness of the model discovered from sub-log 4 as constructed by GED is only 0.5193, meaning that a large part of the behaviour of the sub-log cannot be replayed in the model. For the case of SCT, we observe that the model generated for sub-log 5 has a comparatively low fitness value of 0.7828.

The above results exemplify that conducting trace clustering independent of business process model discovery may yield sub-process models of low quality. In the remainder, we will therefore present a new clustering mechanism that helps to generate accurate and simple sub-process models.

3   Preliminaries

In this section, we introduce fundamental concepts and notations needed to define our approach to compound trace clustering.

Let I be a set of items (we will later consider activities as items), $\mathcal{S}(I)$ be the set of all finite sequences over I. A sequence $s \in \mathcal{S}(I)$ of length m is denoted $\langle it_1, it_2, \ldots, it_m \rangle$, where each element it_k is an item from I. For two sequences $X = \langle x_1, x_2, \ldots, x_l \rangle$ and $Y = \langle y_1, y_2, \ldots, y_q \rangle$ from $\mathcal{S}(I)$, of length l and q, respectively, X is a sub-sequence of Y, denoted as $X \sqsubseteq Y$, if $1 \leq p_1 < p_2 < \cdots < p_l \leq q$ such that $x_1 = y_{p_1}, x_2 = y_{p_2}, \ldots, x_l = y_{p_l}$.

We also need notions related to frequent sequences. Let DS be a set (or database) of sequences. By $support(seq)$, we denote the number of sequences in DS that contain the sequence seq as a sub-sequence. Given a minimum support value min_sup, with $0 < min\_sup < 1$, a sequence seq is called a *sequential pattern* (or a frequent sequence), if $support(seq) \geq min\_sup \times |DS|$. The set of sequential patterns, SP, consists of all sub-sequences of DS, for which the support values are no less than $min\_sup \times |DS|$. Acknowledging that SP contains partly redundant information in terms of sequential patterns that are contained in other patterns, we also define the set of *closed sequential patterns* as $CSP = \{\alpha \in SP \mid \nexists \beta \in SP : \alpha \sqsubseteq \beta \wedge support(\alpha) = support(\beta)\}$. Many algorithms for the detection of sequential patterns have been proposed in the literature, see [15, 16]. For our purposes, it suffices to abstract from a specific algorithm for closed sequential pattern mining, which we assume to be given as $\Gamma : DS^+ \xrightarrow{min\_sup} CSP^+$, where DS^+ is the universe of sequence databases, CSP^+ is the universe of sets of closed sequential patterns, and min_sup is a minimum support value.

Next, we turn to the notion of an event log, as recorded by information systems during the execution of a business process. Let A be the universe of activities of a business process. Then, an event e denotes the execution of an instance of a particular activity $a \in A$. With E as the universe of such events, we define an event log as follows.

Definition 1 *(Trace, Event Log). A trace $t \in \mathcal{S}(E)$ is a sequence of events. An event log L is a non-empty multiset of traces.*

For instance, $L = \{\langle a, b, c, d \rangle^{23}, \langle a, c, b, d \rangle^{16}\}$ denotes an event log built of 156 events that refer to four activities (a, b, c and d). The events are part of 39 traces, with the variant $\langle a, b, c, d \rangle$ appearing 23 times, while the variant $\langle a, c, b, d \rangle$ appears 16 times in L.

With L^+ as the universe of event logs and M^+ as the universe of process models, $\Lambda : L^+ \to M^+$ is a BPMD algorithm. To evaluate the result quality of BPMD, we further consider a process model complexity measure, $\Sigma : M^+ \to \mathbb{R}$.

4   Compound Trace Clustering for Process Discovery

This section presents a novel trace clustering technique named *Compound Trace Clustering* (CTC) for process discovery. An overview of our approach is given in

Fig. 2. In essence, we proceed in two stages. In the first stage, the given event log is split into sub-logs, so that the sub-process models derived from these logs with some business process model discovery technique have an optimal average complexity. In a second stage, the accuracy of these sub-models created in stage 1 is assessed and, if needed, improved by employing an algorithm proposed in our earlier work [17]. Below, we first present details of our novel trace clustering technique for stage 1 (Sect. 4.1), before providing a short summary of the algorithm for improving model accuracy in stage 2 (Sect. 4.2). Finally, we integrate these building blocks and define the complete algorithm for compound trace clustering for process discovery (Sect. 4.3).

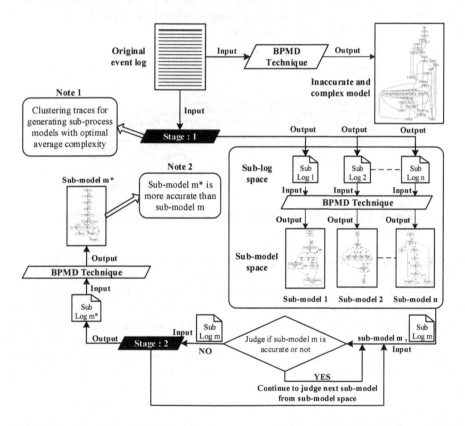

Fig. 2. Outline of the basic idea for the proposed trace clustering technique CTC.

4.1   Stage 1: Trace Clustering

For the first stage of our approach, we developed a new trace clustering method, referred to as *top-down trace clustering* (TDTC). The main idea of our method is to convert the traditional trace clustering problem that is based on a notion of similarity of traces, into a clustering problem that is guided by the complexity of the sub-process models derived for the sub-logs.

Let $\Phi = \{\phi_1, \phi_2, \ldots, \phi_n\}$ be a solution space, where each solution $\phi_m \in \Phi$ stands for a unique way to divide the original event log into a fixed number of sub-logs. TDTC employs a greedy strategy to search for the optimal solution ϕ_{op} of Φ, which is characterised by an optimal weighted average complexity of the sub-process models constructed for the generated sub-logs. As shown in Fig. 3, for a log L and a target number (three in this example) of sub-logs, TDTC first searches for the optimal way to divide L into two sub-logs L_1 and L_2. Then, TDTC continues to detect the optimal way to split L_2 (which is assumed to lead to a sub-model with the highest complexity) into L_3 and L_4. This basic idea is instantiated based on the following concepts related to sequential patterns in traces, henceforth called trace behaviours.

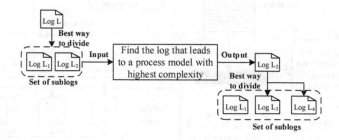

Fig. 3. Illustration of the basic idea for top-down trace clustering.

Significant Trace Behaviours. A complex business process can often be divided into several simpler sub-processes, where each sub-process is characterised by specific behavioural patterns [6]. We refer to the representation of these behavioural patterns in the event log as *trace behaviours*. When conducting trace clustering, we are particularly interested in trace behaviours that adhere to a sub-process model that is simpler than the one that would be discovered for the whole event log. We call these trace behaviours *complexity-related significant behaviours* (CRSB) and detecting them enables us to split up an event log, such that the discovered sub-process models are of low complexity.

We first define trace behaviours in a formal way, based on the notion of sequential patterns as introduced in Sect. 3. That is, a trace behaviour is a sequential pattern mined from a given event log, as the latter can be seen as a database of sequences.

Definition 2 *(Trace Behaviours). Let Γ be a closed sequential pattern mining algorithm and min_sup be a minimum support value. Then, the set of trace behaviours Θ of an event log L is defined as $\Theta = \{\theta \mid \theta \in \Gamma(L, min\_sup)\}$.*

The idea behind grounding trace behaviours in sequential patterns is that certain frequent sub-sequences among the traces of an event log are able to reveal some significant criteria about the behavioural patterns in business processes. They may therefore help to distinguish sub-process models that represent different variations of a business process. Moreover, we note that relying on sequential patterns is also in line with the idea of most advanced BPMD algorithms, which cope with noise in the event data by taking the frequency of behavioural patterns into account in the construction of a process model.

As a next step, we classify trace behaviours of an event log into complexity-related significant behaviours (CRSB) and complexity-related insignificant behaviours (CRIB). Let L be an event log; θ be a trace behaviour of L; $L_1 \subseteq L$ be a sub-log of L which contains all the traces with sub-sequence θ from L; $L_2 \subseteq L$ be a sub-log of L which consists of all the traces from L without sub-sequence θ; and $m_1 = |L_1|$ and $m_2 = |L_2|$ be the total numbers of traces in sub-logs L_1 and L_2 respectively. Furthermore, let $v_L = \Sigma(\Lambda(L))$, $v_{L_1} = \Sigma(\Lambda(L_1))$ and $v_{L_2} = \Sigma(\Lambda(L_2))$ be three assessed values generated by implementing the process model complexity evaluation mechanism Σ on the process models for L, L_1 and L_2. Based thereon, we define *sub-model improvement on complexity* $SMI_C(L_1, L_2, L)$ as a measure to quantify the impact of a particular trace behaviour to split the log L into sub-logs L_1 and L_2:

$$SMI_C(L_1, L_2, L) = \frac{(v_L - (m_1 \cdot v_{L_1} + m_2 \cdot v_{L_2})/(m_1 + m_2))}{v_L}. \tag{1}$$

Using this measure, we characterise complexity-related significant behaviours (CRSB) and complexity-related insignificant behaviours (CRIB). That is, a trace behaviour θ is judged to be a CRSB, if it is able to divide the original event log L into two sub-logs, such that the weighted average complexity of the sub-models discovered from the sub-logs can be decreased by at least η, in comparison to the complexity of the model discovered for the original event log.

Definition 3 *(CRSB and CRIB). Given a minimum threshold η, a trace behaviour $\theta \in \Theta_L$ is a complexity-related significant behaviour, if $SMI_C(L_1, L_2, L) \geq \eta$, otherwise θ is a complexity-related insignificant behaviour.*

Top-Down Trace Clustering (TDTC). Using the above notions, Algorithm 1 describes our top-down trace clustering method. TDTC applies a greedy strategy, which detects the best CRSB for iteratively splitting the event log. According to Algorithm 1, for an input event log L, TDTC first acquires the set of trace behaviours TB for L and initialises the set of logs SL (line 1). Afterwards, TDTC iteratively divides the log L into several sub-logs until the total number of generated sub-logs reaches μ or no log in SL can be further divided (lines 2–9). As shown in line 6, if the found trace behaviour tb_m is not a CRSB, then it will not be utilised for dividing the log. This means that, if the average complexity of the sub-process models discovered from the generated sub-logs (i.e., L_{n1} and L_{n2}) cannot be decreased to a certain extent compared to the quality of the model discovered from the original event log (i.e., L_n), then it is not worth splitting the log. Intuitively, this requirement is derived from the goal to achieve a balance between the integrity and the quality of the resulting models. Additionally, if the number of traces in the generated sub-logs (i.e., L_{n1} and L_{n2}) is less than threshold κ, then the found trace behaviour tb_m will also not be used for splitting. Here, threshold κ is used to prevent TDTC from generating sub-logs with too few traces. Finally, an array of sub-logs SL is returned by TDTC.

Algorithm 1.   Top-down trace clustering (TDTC)

Input: an event log L, a minimum support min_sup for mining closed sequential patterns, a minimum threshold η for detecting CRSB, the minimum size κ for each generated sub-log, the target number of generated sub-logs μ.

    Let TB be a set of trace behaviours.
    Let SL be a set of event log.
1: $TB \leftarrow \Gamma(L, min\_sup)$, $SL \leftarrow SL \cup L$
2: **repeat**
3:     find the log $L_n \in SL$ which leads to a model with the highest complexity
4:     find the trace behaviour $tb_m \in TB$ to generate the highest SMI_C for log L_n
5:     split log L_n into L_{n1} and L_{n2} by employing trace behaviour tb_m
6:     **if** $SMI_C(L_{n1}, L_{n2}, L_n) \geq \eta$ and $|L_{n1}| \geq \kappa$ and $|L_{n2}| \geq \kappa$ **then**
7:         remove L_n from SL and put L_{n1} and L_{n2} in SL
8:     **end if**
9: **until** (no log in SL can be further divided or the cluster number μ is reached)
Output: a set of event logs SL.

4.2   Stage 2: Process Model Fitness Improvement

As part of our compound trace clustering technique, the accuracy of the sub-process models stemming from stage 1 is improved in a second stage (see Fig. 2). In particular, we consider fitness [13] as a well-established measure for the accuracy in process model discovery. Specifically, we employ a fitness improvement algorithm named HIF [17] and apply it to each of the sub-process models. In essence, HIF locates behavioural patterns recorded in the event log, which cannot be expressed by the utilised BPMD algorithm. It then converts these patterns into behavioural structures that can be expressed by the discovery algorithm, so that a more fitting process model will be obtained.

4.3   The Compound Trace Clustering (CTC) Algorithm

Putting the above techniques together, the complete approach of compound trace clustering for process discovery is formalised in Algorithm 2. In addition to the above notions, this algorithm relies on a process model fitness evaluation measure $\Delta : (M^+, L^+) \rightarrow \mathbb{R}$, where M^+ is the universe of process models and L^+ is the universe of event logs.

    As described above before, CTC contains two stages. In stage 1, TDTC (introduced in Algorithm 1) is employed to divide the original event log L into a fixed number (indicated by parameter μ) of sub-logs, which are then stored in set SL (line 2 of Algorithm 2). In stage 2, if a sub-log sl from SL leads to a sub-process model with a fitness value less than a given target value ϵ (line 4), then HIF is used to transform the respective sub-log until the discovered sub-process model has a fitness value of no less than ϵ (line 5). Finally, the sub-process models with improved fitness are stored in MO (lines 6 and 8), which forms the output of CTC. Note that the time complexity of CTC depends on the chosen algorithms for closed sequential pattern mining (Γ) and BPMD (Λ).

Algorithm 2.   The compound trace clustering technique: CTC

Input: an event log L, a minimum support min_sup for mining closed sequential
    patterns, a minimum threshold η for detecting CRSB, the minimum size κ for each
    generated sub-log, the target number of generated sub-logs μ, a target fitness value
    ϵ for the sub-process model.
    Let SL be an array of event log.
    Let MO be a set of sub-process models.
1: $SL \leftarrow null$, $MO \leftarrow null$
    ***Stage 1:** cluster traces for generating sub-process models with optimal complexity*
2: $SL \leftarrow TDTC(L, min\_sup, \eta, \kappa, \mu)$
    ***Stage 2:** generate high-fitness sub-process models*
3: **for** each sub-log $sl \in SL$ **do**
4:      **if** $\Delta(\Lambda(sl), sl) < \epsilon$ **then**
5:          $sl \leftarrow HIF(sl, \epsilon)$
6:          $MO \leftarrow MO \cup \Lambda(sl)$
7:      **else**
8:          $MO \leftarrow MO \cup \Lambda(sl)$
9:      **end if**
10: **end for**
Output: a set of sub-process models MO, an array of event log SL.

---

5   Evaluation

This section presents an experimental evaluation of the proposed method of compound trace clustering for process discovery. We first review the used datasets and experimental setup, before turning to a discussion of the obtained results.

Datasets. We tested the effectiveness of CTC on four real-life event logs: an event log of a Volvo IT incident and problem management process (VIPM) published as part of the Business Process Intelligence Challenge (BPIC) 2013; a log of a loan and overdraft approvals process (LOA) of BPIC 2012; a log of an ICT service process (KIM); and a log of a CRM process (MCRM) from [6]. Descriptive statistics of these event logs are given in Table 2.

Experimental setup. To evaluate the quality of the discovered models, a process model complexity measure is used. To this end, we exploit the insights reported in [14], which highlight that the density, the number of control-flows arcs, and the number of model elements are the main factors that influence the

Table 2. Basic information of the evaluated logs.

Log	Traces	Events	Event types
VIPM	7554	65533	13
LOA	13087	262200	36
KIM	24770	124217	18
MCRM	956	11218	22

comprehensibility of a process model that is expressed as a Petri-net [1]. More specifically, we rely on the Place/Transition Connection Degree (PT-CD) metric for quantifying complexity of a Petri-net, see [6]. With $|ar|$ as the total number of arcs in the model, $|P|$ as the number of places, and $|T|$ as the number of transitions, the PT-CD is defined as:

$$PT - CD = \frac{1}{2}\frac{|ar|}{|P|} + \frac{1}{2}\frac{|ar|}{|T|} \tag{2}$$

Here, large values of the PT-CD metric indicate a high complexity of the model. As an alternative measure for model complexity, we further consider the Extended Cardoso metric (E-Cardoso) [19]. It quantifies the control flow complexity of process models. A higher E-Cardoso value indicates a more complex model.

In our experiments, we further use the Flexible Heuristics Miner (FHM) [11], as implemented in ProM 6[1] as the business process model discovery algorithm. This choice is motivated by the algorithm's robustness against noise and its computational efficiency. Since FHM constructs a process model that is given as a Heuristics Net, we rely on the *Heuristics Net to Petri Net* plugin in ProM 6 to convert the result of FHM into a Petri-net. The complexity of this Petri-net is then assessed based on the aforementioned measures.

To assess the accuracy of the discovered models, we rely on the ICS fitness measure [13], which falls into rage $(-\infty, 1]$ and can be computed efficiently. In addition, we consider the *F-score*, which is defined as the harmonic mean of recall (fitness) and precision (appropriateness) [18]. To quantify precision of the discovered sub-process models, we utilise the ETConformance Checker as it is implemented in ProM 6.

When running CTC, the minimum support value min_sup for closed sequential pattern mining is set to 0.1 for the logs VIPM, KIM, and MCRM; and to 0.25 for log LOA. The reason being that the first three logs contain less process variants compared to LOA. The minimum threshold η for detecting CRSB is set to 0 (i.e., condition $SMI_C > 0$ should be fulfilled), while the minimum size κ for each sub-log is set to 50. The target number of generated sub-logs μ is varied in the experiments up to a value of 6. The target fitness value ϵ for each sub-process model is set to 1.

---

[1] http://www.promtools.org.

Results. A first overview of our evaluation results (when μ is set to 5) is shown in Table 3. For each measure and log, Table 3 first gives the obtained value for the sub-process models obtained by CTC (averaged over all sub-process models), before also listing the value for the model discovered from the original event log. For instance, the weighted average ICS fitness of the sub-process models obtained with CTC on the log VIPM is 0.9159 while the ICS fitness of the model discovered from the original event log is 0.3594.

The evaluation results shown in Table 3 highlight that the weighted average fitness of the generated sub-models for each event log is much higher than the fitness of the model discovered from the original log, whereas the average complexity of these sub-models is relatively low. As such, the results demonstrate the effectiveness of our approach to compound trace clustering for process discovery.

Table 3. Evaluation results for the sub-models generated by CTC. First values are the average over all sub-process models, whereas the second values are those obtained for the model discovered from the original event log.

Event log	Weighted average ICS fitness	Weighted average PT-CD	Weighted average E-Cardoso
VIPM	0.9159/0.3594	2.3577/2.8848	47.3313/54
LOA	0.9909/0.7878	2.4845/3.1478	110.7463/148
KIM	0.9461/0.7904	2.8626/3.4797	63.2614/79
MCRM	0.9512/−0.1379	2.2818/2.4545	51.7364/64

We also compared CTC to six traditional trace clustering techniques, specifically 3-gram [2], ATC [6], MR and MRA [3], GED [4] and sequence clustering (SCT) [5]. For each log, we evaluate the trace clustering technique with different numbers of clusters (from 3, 4, 5 and 6). Figure 4 shows the comparison results from the perspective of fitness. The results illustrate that CTC performs much better on event logs LOA, VIPM and MCRM than the other six trace clustering methods. For the log KIM, ATC has better overall performance than CTC because ATC also has a fitness improvement mechanism that is applied to the sub-process models. However, the mechanism provided by CTC seems more stable on the four real-world event logs.

Figure 5 shows the comparison results on F-score. It can be seen that CTC also performs better than the traditional trace clustering techniques on most of the tested logs. Figure 6 highlights the comparison results from the angle of PT-CD. Here, CTC and SCT outperform the other techniques. Figure 7 depicts the comparison results on E-Cardoso, hinting at an average performance of CTC in comparison to the other methods. The main reason is that the fitness improvement method HIF utilised by CTC may decrease the performance of CTC on optimising the complexity (evaluated by E-Cardoso) of the potential sub-models. Nevertheless, we conclude that under a comprehensive assessment, CTC improves beyond the state-of-the-art in trace clustering in the context of process model discovery.

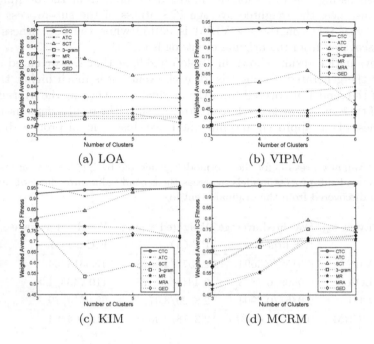

Fig. 4. Comparison of weighed average fitness of the sub-models output by the seven trace clustering techniques.

6   Related Work

In the literature, many trace clustering techniques have been put forward to overcome the negative impact of a large variety of complex control-flow patterns recorded in event logs. We classify these proposed techniques into *passive trace clustering methods* and *active trace clustering methods*.

Passive trace clustering methods such as [2–5] try to detect the similarity of traces recorded in event logs and then group the traces with similar structures into the same sub-log. For example, in [2], traces are expressed by profiles. Every profile is a set of items that characterise a trace in terms of a particular aspect. Five profiles, such like the case attributes profile and the event attributes profile, are introduced in [2]. The distance between any two traces is then measured by transforming the defined profiles into an aggregate vector. In [3], the authors pointed out that the feature sets based on repeated sub-sequences of traces are context-aware and able to exhibit some common functionality. The traces that have a lot of common features should be placed in the same cluster. In [4], an

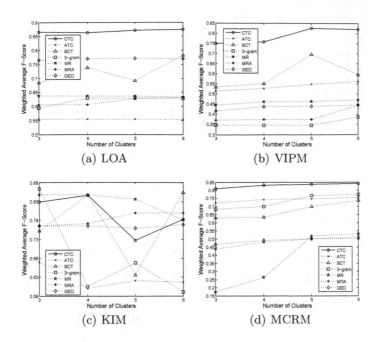

Fig. 5. Comparison of weighted average F-score of the sub-models output by the seven trace clustering techniques.

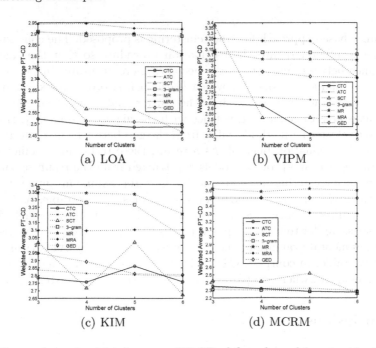

Fig. 6. Comparison of weighted average PT-CD of the sub-models output by the seven trace clustering techniques.

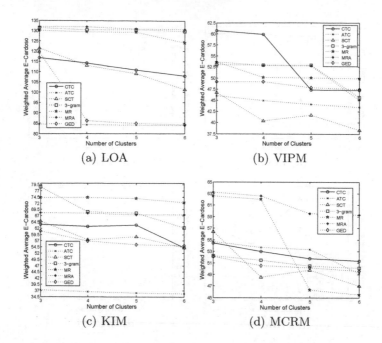

Fig. 7. Comparison of weighted average E-Cardoso of the sub-models output by the seven trace clustering techniques.

edit distance-based approach for trace clustering is proposed. The context-aware knowledge is integrated into the calculation procedure so that the calculated edit distance between any two traces becomes more accurate. In [5], sequence clustering technique is proposed, which learns a first-order Markov model for each cluster. A trace will be put into the cluster that is assigned the Markov model that is able to generate this trace with the highest probability. However, passive trace clustering methods suffer from the gap between the clustering bias and the model evaluation bias [6]. As a result, these techniques cannot ensure the accuracy of the sub-process models constructed from the resulting sub-logs.

Active trace clustering methods such as [6,8–10] assume an integrated view on the clustering bias and the model evaluation bias. For example, ATC as presented in [6], directly optimises the accuracy of the sub-process models derived from sub-logs, similar to CTC proposed in this paper. However, as demonstrated in our experimental evaluation, the mechanism provided by ATC turns out to be not very stable. In contrast, CTC achieves the best results under a comprehensive assessment, when compared to existing active trace clustering methods.

7   Conclusions

In this paper, we proposed a new trace clustering technique named CTC to generate accurate and simple sub-process models. Our technique consists of two stages. In a first stage, it generates sub-process models while striving for an optimal average complexity of the resulting models. In a second stage, the accuracy of the resulting models is improved. Our experimental results demonstrated the effectiveness of our technique, also in comparison to six traditional trace clustering techniques.

In future work, we will focus on improving the performance of CTC by developing new methods to filter trivial trace behaviours found by CTC from real-life event logs. Also, techniques that help to explore the parameter spaces in the configuration of our technique (such as the minimum threshold to detect complexity-related significant behaviours or the minimum size per sub-log) will be explored. Furthermore, we plan to conduct further evaluation studies, validating our methods in additional application domains.

References

1. van der Aalst, W.M.P.: Process Mining: Data Science in Action. Springer, Berlin (2016)
2. Song, M., Günther, C.W., van der Aalst, W.M.P.: Trace clustering in process mining. In: Ardagna, D., Mecella, M., Yang, J. (eds.) BPM 2008. LNBIP, vol. 17, pp. 109–120. Springer, Heidelberg (2009). doi:10.1007/978-3-642-00328-8_11
3. Bose, R.P.J.C., van der Aalst, W.M.P.: Trace clustering based on conserved patterns: towards achieving better process models. In: Rinderle-Ma, S., Sadiq, S., Leymann, F. (eds.) BPM 2009. LNBIP, vol. 43, pp. 170–181. Springer, Heidelberg (2010). doi:10.1007/978-3-642-12186-9_16
4. Bose, R., van der Aalst, W.M.P.: Context aware trace clustering: towards improving process mining results. In: SIAM International Conference on Data Mining, pp. 401–402 (2009)
5. Ferreira, D., Zacarias, M., Malheiros, M., Ferreira, P.: Approaching process mining with sequence clustering: experiments and findings. In: Alonso, G., Dadam, P., Rosemann, M. (eds.) BPM 2007. LNCS, vol. 4714, pp. 360–374. Springer, Heidelberg (2007). doi:10.1007/978-3-540-75183-0_26
6. Weerdt, J.D., vanden Broucke, S., Vanthienen, J., Baesens, B.: Active trace clustering for improved process discovery. IEEE Trans. Knowl. Data Eng. 25(12), 2708–2720 (2013)
7. Leemans, S.J.J., Fahland, D., van der Aalst, W.M.P.: Discovering block-structured process models from event logs - a constructive approach. In: Colom, J.-M., Desel, J. (eds.) PETRI NETS 2013. LNCS, vol. 7927, pp. 311–329. Springer, Heidelberg (2013). doi:10.1007/978-3-642-38697-8_17
8. Ekanayake, C.C., Dumas, M., García-Bañuelos, L., La Rosa, M.: Slice, mine and dice: complexity-aware automated discovery of business process models. In: Daniel, F., Wang, J., Weber, B. (eds.) BPM 2013. LNCS, vol. 8094, pp. 49–64. Springer, Heidelberg (2013). doi:10.1007/978-3-642-40176-3_6
9. Garcia, L., Dumas, M., Rosa, M.L., Weerdt, J.D., Ekanayake, C.C.: Controlled automated discovery of collections of business process models. Inf. Syst. 46, 85–101 (2014)
10. Greco, G., Guzzo, A., Pontieri, L.: Discovering expressive process models by clustering log traces. IEEE Trans. Knowl. Data Eng. 18(8), 1010–1027 (2006)

11. Weijters, A.J.M.M., Ribeiro, J.T.S.: Flexible Heuristics Miner (FHM). BETA Working Paper Series, WP 334. Eindhoven University of Technology, Eindhoven (2010)
12. Adriansyah, A., Buijs, J.C.A.M.: Mining process performance from event logs. In: La Rosa, M., Soffer, P. (eds.) BPM 2012. LNBIP, vol. 132, pp. 217–218. Springer, Heidelberg (2013). doi:10.1007/978-3-642-36285-9_23
13. de Medeiros, A.A.: Genetic process mining. Ph.D. thesis, Eindhoven University of Technology (2006)
14. Mendling, J., Strembeck, M.: Influence factors of understanding business process models. In: Abramowicz, W., Fensel, D. (eds.) BIS 2008. LNBIP, vol. 7, pp. 142–153. Springer, Heidelberg (2008). doi:10.1007/978-3-540-79396-0_13
15. Han, J., Kamber, M.: Data Mining: Concepts and Techniques. Morgan Kaufmann, San Francisco (2000)
16. Shengnan, C., Han, J., David, P.: Parallel mining of closed sequential patterns. In: Proceedings of the Eleventh ACM SIGKDD International Conference on Knowledge Discovery in Data Mining, KDD 2005, pp. 562–567. ACM, New York (2005)
17. Sun, Y., Bauer, B.: A novel heuristic method for improving the fitness of mined business process models. In: Sheng, Q.Z., Stroulia, E., Tata, S., Bhiri, S. (eds.) ICSOC 2016. LNCS, vol. 9936, pp. 537–546. Springer, Cham (2016). doi:10.1007/978-3-319-46295-0_33
18. Conforti, R., Dumas, M., García-Bañuelos, L., La Rosa, M.: Beyond tasks and gateways: discovering BPMN models with subprocesses, boundary events and activity markers. In: Sadiq, S., Soffer, P., Völzer, H. (eds.) BPM 2014. LNCS, vol. 8659, pp. 101–117. Springer, Cham (2014). doi:10.1007/978-3-319-10172-9_7
19. Lassen, K.B., van der Aalst, W.M.P.: Complexity metrics for workflow nets. Inf. Softw. Technol. 51(3), 610–626 (2009)

An Approach to Modeling and Discovering Event Correlation for Service Collaboration

Meiling Zhu[1,2,3(✉)], Chen Liu[2,3], Jianwu Wang[4],
Shen Su[2,3], and Yanbo Han[2,3]

[1] School of Computer Science and Technology,
Tianjin University, Tianjin 300350, China
meilingzhu2006@126.com
[2] Beijing Key Laboratory on Integration and Analysis of Large-Scale Stream
Data, North China University of Technology, Beijing 100144, China
{liuchen, sushen, hanyanbo}@ncut.edu.cn
[3] Cloud Computing Research Center, North China University of Technology,
Beijing 100144, China
[4] Department of Information Systems, University of Maryland,
Baltimore County, Baltimore, MD 21250, USA
jianwu@umbc.edu

Abstract. In an IoT (Internet of Things) environment, event correlation becomes more complex as events usually span over many interrelated sensors. This paper refines event correlations in an IoT environment. We extend our previous service hyperlink model to encapsulate such event correlations. To effectively discover service hyperlinks, we transform the event correlation discovery problem into a frequent sequence mining problem and propose *CorFinder* algorithm. Moreover, we apply our approach to improve anomaly warning in a power plant instead of simulation. Besides the application, we have made extensive experiments to verify the effectiveness of our approach.

Keywords: IoT service · Service hyperlink · Sensor event · Event stream · Event correlation

1 Introduction

Nowadays, sensors are widely deployed in industrial environments to monitor devices' status in real-time. A sensor continuously generates sensor events and a series of sensor events are correlated with each other. Such event correlations are modeled to enable application-level sensor collaboration. We designed an event log based on a stream data processing infrastructure [1, 2]. However, the correlations can be dynamically interwoven, and data-driven analysis would be of help.

Event correlation discovery problem is concerned about how to identify relationships among sensor events. Similar research has also received notable attention for the discovery, monitoring and analysis of processes. In those studies, relationships among sensor events refer to semantic relationship herein [3–7].

© Springer International Publishing AG 2017
M. Maximilien et al. (Eds.): ICSOC 2017, LNCS 10601, pp. 191–205, 2017.
https://doi.org/10.1007/978-3-319-69035-3_13

In our previous work [1, 2], we studied a new kind of relationship among sensor events, called statistical correlation. We used Pearson coefficient to measure such relationship. Specifically, we tried to map physical sensors into a software-defined abstraction, called proactive data service. A proactive data service takes event streams derived from physical sensors or other services as inputs and transforms them into new streams based on user-defined operations. In [2], we also proposed a new abstraction, called *service hyperlink*, to encapsulate correlations between streams received and outputted by two data services. With service hyperlinks, a service can dynamically route an event to other services at runtime. In this way, the knowledge segment about how these sensors collaborate with each other can be depicted at the software layer.

In this paper, we further refine event correlation on when and how a type of event causes another type. Such event correlation can be easily transformed into a relationship between two IoT services. The main contributions include: (1) We propose an algorithm, called *CorFinder*, to discover such event correlations in a log of sensor events. To reach this goal, we update classic frequent sequence mining algorithm. (2) In a real application, we apply our approach to make anomaly warnings in a power plant based on discovered event correlations. We elaborate on how our approach works and what the differences with the traditional approaches are. (3) Furthermore, a lot of experiments are done to show the effectiveness of our approach based on a dataset from a power plant.

2   Problem Analysis

Figure 1 shows a real case of anomaly detection in a power plant. Fan stall is a major failure for the important equipment – primary air fan (PAF) in a power plant. It will cause severe damages to the whole air and flue system. Currently, detecting such equipment failures in a power plant mainly depends on the observation and judgment of envelope range. They detect anomalies through various phenomena, like the sharp descending of exit air pressure, electricity, and air volume in a PAF. However, when such phenomena are observed, an anomaly has already occurred and the loss is inevitable.

From a systematic view, a severe failure is often caused by some trivial anomalies step by step. The paths of anomaly propagation are usually hidden behind the correlations of sensor events in an IoT system. Figure 1 shows several possible event propagation paths lead to the fan stall failure. We can observe that each propagation path is formed of several correlated sensors.

For example, a decrease of valve degree (Valve Degree Descending Event) will reduce the inlet air header pressure (Inlet Air Header Pressure Descending Event). To maintain the output of the boiler, valve degree (Valve Degree Ascending Event) is automatically increased to prevent inlet air header pressure event from decreasing in this case. Following its rise, air pressure (Air Degree Ascending Event) increases and will lead to the growth of electricity and exit air pressure. Unfortunately, excess air pressure will cause a fan stall, which manifests as a sharp drop of electricity (Electricity Descending Event) and exit air pressure (Exit Air Pressure Descending Event).

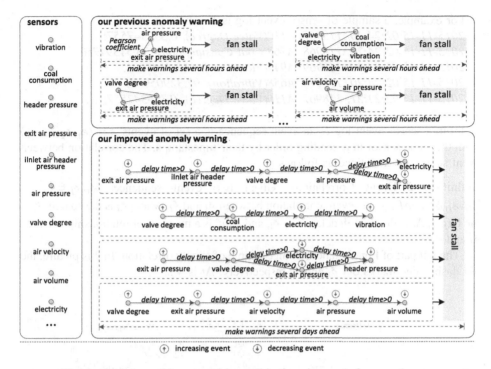

Fig. 1. Partial possible cases of fan stall in the primary air fan: a real case.

However, we find such correlations are not always available. For example, considering *exit air pressure* sensor and *inlet air header pressure* sensor, their correlations only exist when the value of *exit air pressure* sensor exceeds 5. In this situation, the value of *inlet air header pressure* sensor usually will keep the accordance with *exit air pressure* sensor after about 3 min. Lots of similar cases can be found.

The above case shows, to make warnings in advance, we need to clearly under-stand the way how an event transforms itself and propagates among different devices. An effective way is to mine the event correlations. If we find such correlations, we can merge these correlations to form an event propagation path as Fig. 1 shows.

3 Definitions

A sensor event e consists of four elements: *a generation timestamp, a unique identifier, a sensor id* and *a value*. A sensor event log records events from all sensors in an IoT system. We formulate a sensor event log as follows.

Definition 1 (Sensor Event log): given a set of sensors $S = \{s_1, s_2, \ldots, s_m\}$, a sensor event log is a set of sensor events $L = \{e_1, e_2, \ldots, e_n\}$, where $e_i (i = 1, .., n)$ is a sensor event generated from a sensor $s_j \in S$.

For example, a sample of sensor event log is L = {

2015-11-15 02:24:20, 118967, A110(Valve Degree), 0.359347557;
2015-11-15 02:24:20, 118968, A763(Coal Consumption), 36.54394756;
2015-11-15 02:24:20, 118969, A945(Electricity), 123.4148096;
2015-11-15 02:24:20, 118970, A658(Vibration), 97.32905983;
2015-11-15 02:24:21, 118967, A110(Valve Degree), 0.359347557; ...

}.

From a sensor event log L, an event sequence is a set of events $s = \langle e_1, e_2, ..., e_k \rangle$ from the same sensor in ascending order by their timestamps. The correlation between event sequences is defined as follows.

Definition 2 (Event Correlation): Given two event sequences $s_i, s_j \in L$, let $(s_i, s_j, \Delta t, conf)$ be the event correlation between s_i and s_j, where s_i is the source, s_j is the target, Δt is the time s_j delayed to s_i, and $conf$ is a measure of relationship between s_i and s_j.

The left part of Fig. 2 elaborates an example of event correlation. In this picture, the red dashes line marks out s_i and s_j respectively. Δt is 4 s.

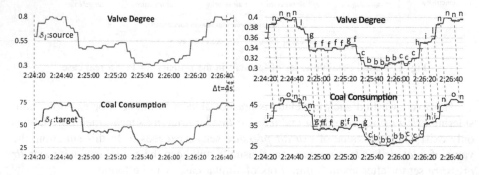

Fig. 2. An example of event correlation.

4   Discovery of Event Correlation

4.1   The Rationales

The main idea is to transform the event correlation discovery into a frequent sequence mining problem. To do this, as the right part of Fig. 2 shows, a numerical event sequence from a sensor is firstly transformed into a symbol sequence [8]. Essentially, symbolization is a coarse-grained description since each symbol corresponds to a segment of the original sequence. In this manner, if a sequence correlates with another one, there probably exists a frequent sequence between their symbolized sequences [8]. It inspires us to use the frequent sequence to measure event correlation. In another word, if two symbolized sequences s_i and s_j have a long enough frequent sequence, there is a correlation between them.

One challenge is how to identify the time delay between two correlated event sequences shown in Fig. 2. It actually reflects how long that a sensor will be affected by the value changes of its correlated sensor. However, traditional frequency sequence mining algorithm cannot directly solve such problem. Traditional algorithms only focused on the occurrence frequency of a sequence in a sequence set [9, 10]. Hence, we try to design an algorithm which can discover a frequent sequence, each element of which occurs in a sequence set within a short time period, i.e., time delay Δt in Definition 2. Another challenge is how to determine the target and source by a frequent sequence. If each element of a frequent sequence occurs in same order in the sequence set, such frequent sequence can identify the target and source. Taking the right picture in Fig. 2 as an example, each element occurs a little earlier (no more than 4 s) in valve degree sequence than in coal consumption sequence. It indicates that valve degree sequence is the source, and coal consumption sequence is the target. In a word, if two symbol sequences s_i and s_j have a long-enough frequent sequence, each element of which occurs in s_i and s_j in same order within the time period Δt, the original sequences of s_i and s_j have an event correlation $(s_i, s_j, \Delta t, conf)$. In this way, $conf$ can be computed as the ratio of the frequent sequence length to the length of s_i.

Based on the above discussion, we propose an algorithm called *CorFinder* to discover event correlations. Firstly, it uses a classic algorithm, called *SAX* [8], to symbolize each event sequence in a sensor event log. Secondly, it mines the above frequent sequences. Notably, we take gap constraint [9] into consideration. A gap constraint γ means any two adjacent elements in a frequent sequence skip no more than the predefined consecutive elements in any sequence containing the frequent sequence. A gap constraint can identify uncorrelated segments from correlated sequences.

Symbolization. In this paper, the classic symbolic representation algorithm Symbolic Aggregate approXimation (*SAX*) [8] is used to preprocess our input numerical event sequences. *SAX* algorithm allows an event sequence of length n to be reduced to a symbol sequence of length m ($m \ll n$) composed of k different symbols. We will attach a timestamp to each symbol. The sequences in Table 1 are the symbolization of four event sequences from a sensor event log in a power plant via *SAX* algorithm with $k = 15$. The first two event sequences are shown in Fig. 2.

Table 1. A sample of a symbolized event sequence set (running example).

SID	t_1	t_2	t_3	t_4	t_5	t_6	t_7	t_8	t_9	t_{10}	t_{11}	t_{12}	t_{13}	t_{14}	t_{15}	t_{16}	t_{17}	t_{18}	t_{19}	t_{20}	t_{21}	t_{22}	t_{23}	t_{24}	t_{25}	t_{26}	t_{27}	t_{28}	t_{29}	t_{30}
VD	l	n	n	n	n	l	g	f	f	f	f	f	g	f	c	b	b	b	b	b	c	c	c	h	i	l	n	n	n	n
CC	i	l	n	o	n	n	m	g	f	f	f	g	f	h	g	c	b	b	b	b	b	c	c	c	h	i	l	n	o	n
E	i	k	m	n	o	n	n	l	e	e	e	e	e	c	e	c	b	b	b	b	b	c	e	f	g	i	k	m	n	o
V	i	j	n	o	o	n	n	k	e	f	f	f	f	f	g	d	b	b	b	b	b	c	c	d	f	i	j	n	o	o

VD: Valve Degree, CC: Coal Consumption, E: Electricity, V: Vibration; t_1 = 02:24:24, t_2 = 02:24:29, t_3 = 02:24:34, ..., t_{30} = 02:26:49.

Frequent Sequence Mining. Before introducing our algorithm, we list some related concepts about frequent sequence mining. A sequence in a sequence set D is associated with an identifier, called a *SID*. A support of a sequence is the number contained in *D*. A sequence becomes frequent if its support exceeds a pre-specified minimum support threshold in *D*. A frequent sequence with length *l* is called *l*-frequent sequence. It becomes closed if there is no super-sequence of it with the same support in *D*. A projection database of sequence s in *L* is defined as $D_s = \{\alpha | \eta \in D, \eta = \beta \circ \alpha\}$ (β is the minimum prefix of η containing s).

Projection-based algorithms are a classic category of traditional algorithms in frequent sequence mining [10]. They adopt a divide-and-conquer strategy to discover frequent sequences by building projection database. These algorithms firstly generate 1-frequent sequences F_1, where $F_1 = \{s_1 : sup_1, s_2 : sup_2, \ldots, s_n : sup_n\}$, s_i is a 1-frequent sequence and sup_i is its support. This step is followed by the construction of projection database for each 1-frequent sequence. In each projection database above, they generate 1-frequent sequences F_2 and projection database of each element in F_2. The process is repeated until there is no 1-frequent sequence. We propose two data structures as follows to update the classic algorithms.

Loose $(\lambda, \Delta t, l)$-frequent sequence and λ-projection database. We propose several concepts in this section. Traditionally, a frequent sequence with length 1 is called 1-frequent sequence. In this paper, a 1-frequent sequence occurring in time period Δt is called $(\Delta t, 1)$-frequent sequence. The concept is extended as loose $(\Delta t, 1)$-frequent sequence $s' : \langle (SID_1, t_1), (SID_2, t_2), \ldots, (SID_m, t_m) \rangle$, where s' occurs in SID_i at t_i and $t_{i+1} - t_i \leq \Delta t$. Generalize loose $(\Delta t, 1)$-frequent sequence into length l as follows. Given a set of $(\Delta t, 1)$-frequent sequences $s_1', s_2', \ldots, s_l'$ for id-list $\langle SID_1, SID_2, \ldots, SID_m \rangle$, if $s_1', s_2', \ldots, s_l'$ orderly occurs in $SID_j (j = 1, 2, \ldots, m)$, $s' = \langle s_1', s_2', \ldots, s_l' \rangle$ is a loose $(\Delta t, l)$-frequent sequence for the id-list. A loose $(\Delta t, l)$-frequent sequence s' becomes a loose $(\lambda, \Delta t, l)$-frequent sequence if it satisfies gap constraint λ, i.e., s_i' and s_{i+1}' $(i = 1, 2, \ldots, l-1)$ skips no more than λ consecutive elements in $SID_j (j = 1, 2, \ldots, m)$.

According to previous analysis, loose $(\lambda, \Delta t, l)$-frequent sequences is the formulation of the frequent sequences our algorithm focuses on. It can identify our event correlations. To discover loose $(\lambda, \Delta t, l)$-frequent sequences, we propose γ-projection database. γ-projection database of sequence s is denoted as $\gamma D_s = \{\alpha | \eta \in D, \eta = \beta \circ \theta, \theta = \alpha \circ \mu\}$ (β is the minimum prefix of η containing, α is the prefix of θ with length $\gamma + 1$).

Some examples of the above concepts are shown in Table 1. Let $\Delta t = 5$ s and $\gamma = 2$. *l*: $\langle (VD, t_1), (CC, t_2) \rangle$ is a $(\Delta t, 1)$-frequent sequence (grey squares in Table 1); *c*: $\langle (E, t_{14}), (VD, t_{15}), (CC, t_{16}) \rangle$ is a loose $(\Delta t, 1)$-frequent sequence (blue squares in Table 1), and $\{(VD, \langle (b, t_{16}), (b, t_{17}) \rangle), (CC, \langle (b, t_{17}), (b, t_{18}) \rangle), (E, \langle (e, t_{15}), (c, t_{16}) \rangle)\}$ is its γ-projection database (red squares in Table 1); $\langle c, h \rangle$: $\langle (VD, \langle t_{23}, t_{24} \rangle), (CC, \langle t_{24}, t_{25} \rangle) \rangle$ is a loose $(\gamma, \Delta t, 2)$-frequent sequence (green squares in Table 1); $\langle c, i \rangle$: $\langle (E, \langle t_{22}, t_{26} \rangle), (V, \langle t_{22}, t_{26} \rangle) \rangle$ is a loose $(\Delta t, 2)$-frequent sequence but not $(\gamma, \Delta t, 2)$ one (purple squares in Table 1).

4.2 The *CorFinder* Algorithm

In this paper, we improve the classic projection-based algorithms and propose the *CorFinder* algorithm to solve our problem. Traditional 1-frequent sequence $s{:}sup$ does not consider occurrence time of s. Consequently, we propose the concept of $(\Delta t, 1)$-frequent sequence. However, any adjacent $(\Delta t, 1)$-frequent sequences for same sequence s are overlapped. It will increase storage cost and lead to repeated counting. For instance, adjacent $(\Delta t, 1)$-frequent sequences for c, $c{:}\langle(E, t_{14}), (VD, t_{15})\rangle$ and $c{:}\langle(VD, t_{15}), (CC, t_{16})\rangle$, are overlapped in (VD, t_{15}). Therefore we extend $(\Delta t, 1)$-frequent sequence into loose $(\Delta t, 1)$-frequent sequence. The following Theorem 1 lays the foundation of the completeness of our algorithm.

Theorem 1. Each $(\Delta t, 1)$-frequent sequence in a given sequence set D is contained by a loose $(\Delta t, 1)$-frequent sequence in D. Versa, any element of each loose $(\Delta t, 1)$-frequent sequence in D is contained by a $(\Delta t, 1)$-frequent sequence.

Proof. We prove the theorem by reduction to absurdity. Let D be a sequence set, and there is a $(\Delta t, 1)$-frequent sequence $s: \langle(SID_1, t_1), (SID_2, t_2), \ldots, (SID_k, t_k)\rangle$ in D. Assume that there is no loose $(\Delta t, 1)$-frequent sequence containing s. Thus, any $SID_i \in s(i<k)$, $t_{i+1} - t_i > \Delta t$. Obviously, $t_k - t_1 > (k-1) * \Delta t$. Therefore $s: \langle(SID_1, t_1), (SID_2, t_2), \ldots, (SID_k, t_k)\rangle$ is not a $(\Delta t, 1)$-frequent sequence. It is a contradiction in the assumption.

On the other hand, assume that there is an element (SID_i, t_i) of a loose $(\Delta t, 1)$-frequent sequence $s': \langle(SID_1, t_1), (SID_2, t_2), \ldots, (SID_m, t_m)\rangle$, and (SID_i, t_i) is contained by none of $(\Delta t, 1)$-frequent sequences in D. Let SID_j be the nearest element to SID_i under $SID_i \neq SID_j$. Since (SID_i, t_i) is not contained by any $(\Delta t, 1)$-frequent sequence, $|t_i - t_j| > \Delta t$. It is in contradiction with the assumption that s' is a loose $(\Delta t, 1)$-frequent sequence. So far, Theorem 1 is proved.

Loose $(\Delta t, l)$-frequent sequence can tell the target and source in an event correlation while considering time delay Δt between the target and source. It is a measure of our event correlation. Our *CorFinder* algorithm aims at discovering loose $(\lambda, \Delta t, l)$-frequent sequences for finding event correlations. The Theorem 2 inspires us to discover a loose $(\lambda, \Delta t, l)$-frequent sequence in γ-projection database of its l-1 prefix.

Theorem 2. Any loose $(\lambda, \Delta t, l)$-frequent sequence $s' = s'_{l-1} \diamond s'_l$ can be discovered in the id-lists of s'_{l-1} and s'_l, where s'_{l-1} is the prefix of s' with length l-1 and s'_l is a loose $(\Delta t, 1)$-frequent sequence in γ-projection database of s'_{l-1}.

Proof. Obviously, s'_{l-1} is a loose $(\lambda, \Delta t, l-1)$-frequent sequence. Let $\gamma D_{s'_{l-1}}$ be the γ-projection database of s'_{l-1}. Because s' is a loose $(\lambda, \Delta t, l)$-frequent sequence, assume its id-list is $\langle SID_1, SID_2, \ldots, SID_m \rangle$, we get $\{SID_1, SID_2, \ldots, SID_m\} \in \gamma D_{s'_{l-1}}$ and s'_l must be a loose $(\Delta t, 1)$-frequent sequence for the id-list. Therefore, s'_l is a loose $(\Delta t, 1)$-frequent sequence in $\gamma D_{s'_{l-1}}$. Theorem 2 is proved.

Theorem 2 indicates that we can discover a loose $(\lambda, \Delta t, l)$-frequent sequence s' with l-1 prefix s'_{l-1} by the following steps. (1) Generate $\gamma D_{s'_{l-1}}$ and all loose $(\Delta t, 1)$-frequent sequence in $\gamma D_{s'_{l-1}}$. (2) For each loose $(\Delta t, 1)$-frequent sequence s'_l, discover frequent sequences in id-lists of $\mathcal{S}'_{l-1}$ and s'_l. (3) Generate loose $(\lambda, \Delta t, l)$-frequent sequences in the frequent sequences.

Consequently, the recursion of generating γ-projection databases and loose $(\Delta t, 1)$-frequent sequences can discover all loose $(\lambda, \Delta t, l)$-frequent sequences. Finally, *CorFinder* algorithm can discover event correlations by these loose $(\lambda, \Delta t, l)$-frequent sequences.

5   Application of Event Correlation for Anomaly Warning

5.1   The Service Collaboration Framework

Our previous work proposed an IoT service model to encapsulate sensor events into a service [1, 2]. It can serve as the fundamental unit to form an IoT application. When building a service, a user customizes its functionality by customizing the input event sensors as well as operations. Each service processes its input sensor events by pre-defined operations and generates higher-level events in form of stream. A created service can be encapsulated into a Restful-like API so that other services or applications can use it conveniently and simply. Moreover, our service has an important component, which is called service hyperlink. Hyperlink is responsible for indicating target services for an outputted event. In this way, our services can run proactively to

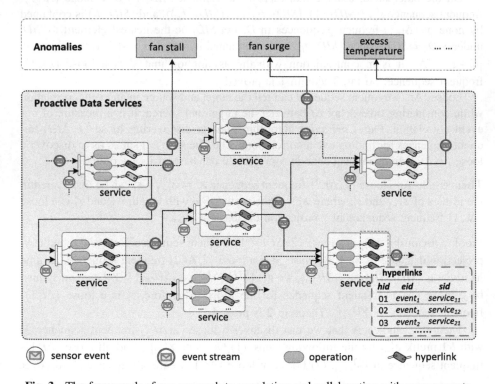

Fig. 3. The framework of our approach to correlating and collaborating with sensor events.

correlate and collaborate with sensor events to serve IoT applications. Figure 3 presents the framework of our approach.

Different from traditional service models and frameworks with the "request-and-response" model, ours works in a more automatic and real-time way with the 'stimuli-and-response' pattern while maintaining the common data service capabilities. To reach this goal, service hyperlink is the key point. A service hyperlink enables higher-level events outputted from a service (source service) to be routed to another one (target service). After a higher-level event is routed to a target service, the target service will be stimulated and autonomously respond to the event.

Our previous work encapsulated correlations among input sensor events as service hyperlinks and used Pearson coefficient to weigh the correlation degree. However, it is hard to tell the source and the target between two correlated services. To consummate the previous work, we encapsulate event correlation in this paper as service hyperlinks. With hyperlinks, a service can route an event to another service involving the target sequence of encapsulated event correlation.

5.2 The Process to Make Anomaly Warnings in a Power Plant

Service Customization. Making early warnings in a power plant is a typical case for our framework. As the beginning of the paper elaborates, we make early warnings by event propagation paths, e.g., a valve degree ascending event propagates along the way as valve degree → coal consumption → electricity → vibration and finally leads to a fan stall in Fig. 1. To reach this goal, we create services inputting sensor events from different sensors. Each service will detect and output trivial anomaly events, such as a valve degree ascending event. How to define and detect the trivial anomaly events precisely is the first problem in this case. It can be solved in two ways. On the one hand, such events can be defined based on business knowledge. On the other hand, those events can be identified by clustering techniques [11]. According to the defined events, we customize operations in each service so that a service can detect these trivial anomaly events autonomously.

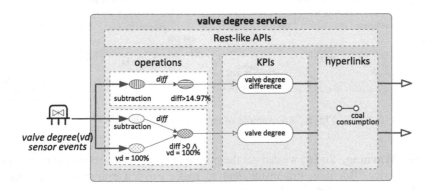

Fig. 4. The example of valve degree service.

For example, we build a valve degree data service as Fig. 4 presents. In this service, we select valve degree sensor events as its inputs. To detect a valve degree ascending event, we customize subtraction as one of its operations. The subtracting operation will subtract the value of a sensor event from that of the previous one. We perform K-means algorithm on a real data set within 6 months in a power plant and conclude that valve degree difference (short for *diff*) exceeding 14.97% is a trivial anomaly event. Thus, a filtering operation *diff* > 14.97% is selected to detect valve degree ascending events. Besides, inspection man concludes that the valve degree suddenly opening to all is a trivial anomaly event. According to the business knowledge, we select another filtering operation: *diff* > 0 ∧ valve degree = 100%. Valve degree and valve degree difference is the key attributes (KPIs) to be exposed with REST-like APIs. Based on the Fig. 2, the hyperlink of this service indicates that coal consumption service is its target service.

Event Propagation. A service hyperlink encapsulates an event correlation $(\mathcal{S}_i, \mathcal{S}_j, \Delta t, conf)$. An outputted event e related to sensor of $\mathcal{S}_i$ will be routed along the hyperlink to its target service. The target service keeps detecting trivial anomaly events. If it detects e' with respect to sensor of $\mathcal{S}_j$ in time period Δt after e arrives, the target service will record a composite event by appending e to trivial anomaly event e'. Instead of e', the composite event will be routed along the hyperlink related to e'. A composite event records the event propagation path. Figure 5 presents four correlated services. The composite event in vibration service indicates an event propagation path as valve degree ascending event → coal consumption ascending event → electricity ascending event → vibration ascending event.

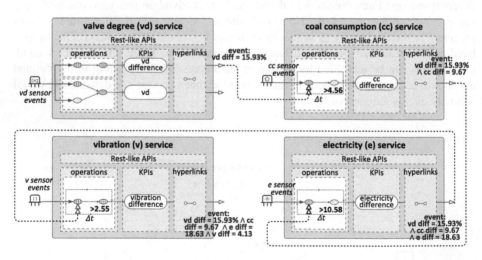

Fig. 5. An example of event propagation path.

Anomaly Warning. So far, we can get the propagation paths of trivial anomaly events in each service. But it is still insufficient to make early warnings since the trivial anomaly events are not equal to equipment anomalies. Practically, an inspector performs scheduled maintenances and records equipment anomalies in maintenance records. A maintenance record $r = \langle rid, anomaly\_desc, rec\_time, anomaly\_obj \rangle$ consists of record id, anomaly description, recorded time, and anomaly object. For example, there is a maintenance record $r = \langle 118977, vibration\ increases - fan\ stall, 2015/10/12\ 05:12:00, vibration\ in\ \#2\ primary\ air\ fan\ in\ \#3\ boiler \rangle$. According to recorded time and anomaly description in a maintenance record, we can infer causality between event propagation paths and anomalies. For instance, an event propagation path in Fig. 5 often occurred before a fan stall anomaly. Thus we can infer causality as valve degree ascending event $\rightarrow$ coal consumption ascending event $\rightarrow$ electricity ascending event $\rightarrow$ vibration ascending event $\Rightarrow$ fan stall. Once such a propagation path occurs in the runtime, a warning of a fan stall can be made. Consequently, each service is initialized with an operation for comparing runtime event propagation paths with historical ones. This operation takes composite events as input, and outputs warnings to users or other applications. The process to make anomaly warnings in a service after receiving a sensor event is shown in Fig. 6.

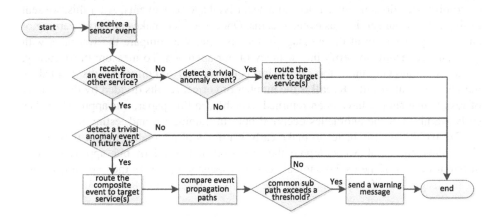

Fig. 6. Process of responding stimuli autonomously and proactively in a service.

6 Experiments

6.1 Experiment Setup

Datasets: The following experiments use a sensor event log from a power plant. The log contains sensor events from 2015-07-26 23:58:30 to 2016-08-17 07:55:00. Totally 480 sensors are involved and each sensor generates one event per second. The log is divided into two sets. The training set is from 2015-07-26 23:58:30 to 2016-01-31 23:59:55. This set is responsible for discovering event correlations. The testing set is from 2016-02-01 00:00:00 to 2016-08-17 07:55:00. It is used for making early warnings by our approach. In this set, events from same source are sent to our services as a stream. The time interval between two adjacent events is in accordance with real intervals when they were generated. Besides, we use maintenance records of this plant power from 2015-07-26 23:58:30 to 2016-01-31 23:59:55 to verify the accuracy of our approach.

Environments: The experiments are done on a PC with four Intel Core i5-2400 CPUs 3.10 GHz and 4.00 GB RAM. The operating system is Windows 7 Ultimate. All the algorithms are implemented in Java with JDK 1.8.0.

6.2   Experiment Results

To verify the effectiveness of our approach, firstly, we create services according to physical sensors. We learn business knowledge from a power plant during the creation. Besides, sensors related to one attribute of devices' status are inputted into one service, such as events from *bearing temperature 1*, *2*, *3* and *4* sensor in primary air fan are the inputs of bearing temperature service. We created 108 services from all 440 sensors. Secondly, we input the training set into *CorFinder* algorithm to discover service hyperlinks. Next, on top of business knowledge and K-means clustering algorithm, we customize operations in our services to detect trivial anomaly events. After this, we sent testing set into our services as event streams. Once a service makes an early warning of an anomaly, it will print the message in the console. We compare the warnings with maintenance records to verify the accuracy of our approach. To measure the accuracy, we use the following indicators. **Precision** is the number of correct results divided by the number of all results. **Recall** is the number of correct results divided by the number of results that should have been returned. Notably, in this paper, our approach makes early warnings of the anomalies occurred both in training set and testing set.

To avoid loss, it is better to make early warnings of anomalies before they occur. To achieve this goal, we compute the precision and recall of our approach under different lengths of the trivial anomaly event propagation path. In the experiments, we set the length from 5 to 20 and draw the results as Figs. 7 and 8.

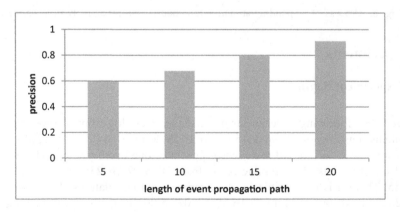

Fig. 7. The precision of our approach.

As Fig. 7 shows, the precision of our approach increases with the growth of propagation path's length. The reason is that longer propagation path can specify an anomaly more clearly. When the length is short, the event has multiple possible propagation paths so that it may evolve into different anomalies. Consequently, the shorter the length of event propagation path is, the lower the precision of our approach is. Meanwhile, shorter path needs less time to make a warning. It indicates that higher precision needs more time. In this experiment, our approach makes warnings of anomalies before the complete event propagation path is formed. It is the main reason that the precision keeps below 100%.

On the other hand, as the Fig. 8 shows, our approach's recall decreases with the rise of propagation path's length. Different from precision, our recall can reach 91.67% when the length is 5. It is because shorter event propagation path can specify more possibilities of anomalies, including those should have been made warnings. Besides, we analyze the details of the results and find that, regardless of the path's length, there are several anomalies our approach cannot discover. The reason is their propagation path is not completely covered by the paths in training set. Our approach cannot search the corresponding anomaly in training set. Fortunately, the anomaly occurs frequently in testing set, and we find that paths of the undiscovered anomalies can be covered by testing set. It inspires us to solve this problem by updating training set periodically.

Our experiment results show that we can make warnings of anomalies before they happen for 5 days ahead at most and 39.8 h ahead averagely, while the precision and recall exceeding 80%.

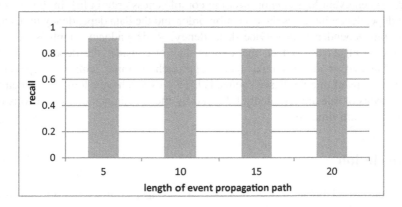

Fig. 8. The recall of our approach.

7 Related Works

Service correlation has attracted much attention in the field of service computing. Dong et al. tried to capture the temporal dependencies based on the amounts of calls to different services [12]. Hashmi et al. proposed a framework for web service negotiation management based on dependency modeling for different QoS parameters among multiple services [13]. Wang et al. considered that a dependency is a relation between services wherein a change to one of the services implies a potential change to the others [14]. They utilized a service dependency matrix to solve the service replacement problem.

However, most of the existing work only considers input/output dependency, pre/post condition dependency, correlations among services and so on. Neither of them takes the dependency of the involved data, which can be regarded as events. Hence, existing studies of event correlation is also the foundation of our work.

Reguieg et al. regarded event correlation as correlation condition, which is a predicate over the attributes of events that can verify which sets of events belong to the same instance of a process [3]. It presented a framework and techniques with multi-pass algorithms to discover correlation conditions in process discovery and analysis tasks over big event datasets using MapReduce framework. It guarantees the efficiency and scalability by partitioning, replication and optimizing the I/O cost. Motahari-Nezhad et al. focused on event correlations in service-based processes [4]. It proposed the notion of correlation condition mentioned above. It developed an algorithm to discover event correlation (semi-) automatically from service interaction logs. Liu et al. presented an event correlation service for distributed middleware-based applications [5]. It enables complex event properties and dependencies to be explicitly expressed in correlation rules. Remarkably, these correlation rules can be accessed and updated at runtime. These event correlation studies provide foundations for our study. However, they do not consider the event correlation in an IoT environment.

Recently, some researchers focus on event dependencies. Song et al. mined activity dependencies (i.e., control dependency and data dependency) to discover process instances when event logs cannot meet the completeness criteria [6]. In this paper, the control dependency indicates the execution order and the data dependency indicates the input/output dependency in service dependency. A dependency graph is utilized to mine process instances. In fact, the authors do not consider the dependency among events. Plantevit et al. presented a new approach to mine temporal dependencies between streams of interval-based events. [7]. Two events have a temporal dependency if the intervals of one are repeatedly followed by the appearance of the intervals of the other, in a certain time delay.

8 Conclusion

In this paper, we elaborate service hyperlink by encapsulating event correlations in an IoT environment to consummate our previous work. We transform service hyperlink discovery into frequent sequence mining problem and propose the *CorFinder* algorithm. Moreover, we apply our approach to make anomaly warnings in a power plant. Experiments show that, our approach can make warning of anomalies before they happen for 5 days ahead at most, and 39.8 h ahead in average while the precision and recall exceed 80%.

Acknowledgement. Funding: This work was supported by National Natural Science Foundation of China (No. 61672042), Models and Methodology of Data Services Facilitating Dynamic Correlation of Big Stream Data; Beijing Natural Science Foundation (No. 4172018), Building Stream Data Services for Spatio-Temporal Pattern Discovery in Cloud Computing Environment; The Program for Youth Backbone Individual, supported by Beijing Municipal Party Committee Organization Department, Research of Instant Fusion of Multi-Source and Large-scale Sensor Data.

References

1. Han, Y., Wang, G., Yu, J., Liu, C., Zhang, Z., Zhu, M.: A service-based approach to traffic sensor data integration and analysis to support community-wide green commute in china. IEEE Trans. Intell. Transp. Syst. **17**(9), 2648–2657 (2016)
2. Han, Y., Liu, C., Su, S., Zhu, M., Zhang, Z.: A proactive service model facilitating stream data fusion and correlation. Int. J. Web Serv. Res. **14**(3), 1–16 (2017)
3. Reguieg, H., Benatallah, B., Nezhad, H.R.M., Toumani, F.: Event correlation analytics: scaling process mining using mapreduce-aware event correlation discovery techniques. IEEE Trans. Serv. Comput. **8**(6), 847–860 (2015)
4. Motahari-Nezhad, H.R., Saint-Paul, R., Casati, F., Benatallah, B.: Event correlation for process discovery from web service interaction logs. VLDB J. **20**(3), 417–444 (2011)
5. Liu, Y., Gorton, I., Lee, V.: The architecture of an event correlation service for adaptive middleware-based applications. J. Syst. Softw. **81**(12), 2134–2145 (2008)
6. Song, W., Jacobsen, H.A., Ye, C., Ma, X.: Process discovery from dependence-complete event logs. IEEE Trans. Serv. Comput. **9**(5), 714–727 (2016)
7. Plantevit, M., Robardet, C., Scuturici, V.M.: Graph dependency construction based on interval-event dependencies detection in data streams. Intell. Data Anal. **20**(2), 223–256 (2016)
8. Lin, J., Keogh, E., Lonardi, S., Chiu, B.: A symbolic representation of time series, with implications for streaming algorithms. In: Proceedings of the 8th ACM SIGMOD Workshop on Research Issues in Data Mining and Knowledge Discovery, pp. 2–11. Association for Computing Machinery, San Diego, CA, United States (2003)
9. Pei, J., Han, J., Wang, W.: Constraint-based sequential pattern mining: the pattern-growth methods. J. Intell. Inf. Syst. **28**(2), 133–160 (2007)
10. Mooney, C.H., Roddick, J.F.: Sequential pattern mining - approaches and algorithms. ACM Comput. Surv. **45**(2), 1–39 (2013)
11. Ahmed, M., Mahmood, A.N., Islam, M.R.: A survey of anomaly detection techniques in financial domain. Future Gener. Comput. Syst. **55**(6), 278–288 (2016)
12. Dong, F., Wu, K., Srinivasan, V., Wang, J.: Copula analysis of latent dependency structure for collaborative auto-scaling of cloud services. In: Proceedings of the 25th International Conference on Computer Communication and Networks, pp. 1–8. Institute of Electrical and Electronics Engineers Inc., Waikoloa, HI, United States (2016)
13. Hashmi, K., Malik, Z., Najmi, E., Alhosban, A., Medjahed, B.: A web service negotiation management and QoS dependency modeling framework. ACM Trans. Manag. Inf. Syst. **7**(2), 1–33 (2016)
14. Wang, R., Peng, Q., Hu, X.: Software architecture construction and collaboration based on service dependency. In: Proceedings of 2015 IEEE 19th International Conference on Computer Supported Cooperative Work in Design, pp. 91–96. Institute of Electrical and Electronics Engineers Inc., Calabria, Italy (2015)

Energy Efficient Scheduling of Application Components via Brownout and Approximate Markov Decision Process

Minxian Xu[✉] and Rajkumar Buyya

Cloud Computing and Distributed Systems (CLOUDS) Laboratory,
School of Computing and Information Systems,
The University of Melbourne, Melbourne, Australia
minxianx@student.unimelb.edu.au, rbuyya@unimelb.edu.au

Abstract. Unexpected loads in Cloud data centers may trigger over-loaded situation and performance degradation. To guarantee system performance, cloud computing environment is required to have the ability to handle overloads. The existing approaches, like Dynamic Voltage Frequency Scaling and VM consolidation, are effective in handling partial overloads, however, they cannot function when the whole data center is overloaded. Brownout has been proved to be a promising approach to relieve the overloads through deactivating application non-mandatory components or microservices temporarily. Moreover, brownout has been applied to reduce data center energy consumption. It shows that there are trade-offs between energy saving and discount offered to users (revenue loss) when one or more services are not provided temporarily. In this paper, we propose a brownout-based approximate Markov Decision Process approach to improve the aforementioned trade-offs. The results based on real trace demonstrate that our approach saves 20% energy consumption than VM consolidation approach. Compared with existing energy-efficient brownout approach, our approach reduces the discount amount given to users while saving similar energy consumption.

Keywords: Cloud energy efficiency · Application component · Microservices · Brownout · Markov decision process

1 Introduction

Given the scenario that budget and resource are limited, overloaded situation may lead to performance degradation and resource saturation, in which some requests cannot be allocated by providers. Thus, some users may experience high latencies, and others may even not receive services at all [14], which directly affects the requests that have Quality of Service (QoS) constraints. Unfortunately, current resource management approaches, like Dynamic Voltage Frequency Scaling (DVFS) [13] and VM consolidation [18], cannot function when the **holistic** data center is overloaded. The saturated resource not only brings over-utilized situation to hosts, but also causes high energy consumption.

M. Maximilien et al. (Eds.): ICSOC 2017, LNCS 10601, pp. 206–220, 2017.
https://doi.org/10.1007/978-3-319-69035-3_14

Energy consumed by the cloud data centers has currently become one of the major concerns of the computing industry. It is reported that U.S. data centers will consume 140 billion kWh of electricity annually by 2020, which equals to the annual output of about 50 brown power plants [9]. Analysts also forecast that data centers will roughly triple the amount of electricity consumed in the next decade [2]. The servers hosted in data centers dissipate heat and need to be maintained in a fully air-conditioned and engineered environment. Though the cooling system is already efficient, servers remain one of the major energy consumers. One of the main reasons of high energy consumption lies in that computing resource are not efficiently utilized by server applications. Currently, building applications with microservices provides a more efficient approach to utilize infrastructure resource.

Applications can be constructed via set of self-contained components which are also called microservices. The components encapsulate its logic and expose its functionality through interfaces, which makes them flexible to be deployed and replaced. With components or microservices, developers and users can benefit from their technological heterogeneity, resilience, scalability, ease of deployment, organizational alignment, composability and optimization for replaceability [16]. This also brings the advantage of more fine-grained control over the application resource consumption.

Therefore, we take advantage of a paradigm called **brownout** [14] to handle with overloaded situation and save energy. It is inspired by the concept of brownout in electric grids and originates from the voltage shutdown that copes with emergency cases, in which light bulbs emit fewer lights and consume less power [10]. In Cloud scenario, brownout can be applied to applications components or microservices that are allowed to be disabled temporarily.

It is common that application components or microservices have this brownout feature. A brownout example for online shopping system is introduced in [14], in which the online shopping application provides a recommendation engine to recommend products that users may be interested in. The recommendation engine component helps service provider to increase profits, but it is not required to be running all the time. Recommendation engine also requires more resource in comparison with other components. Accordingly, with brownout, under overloaded situation, the recommendation engine could be deactivated to serve more clients who require essential services and have QoS constraints. Another example is the online document process application that contains the components for spell checking and report generation. These components are not essential to run all the time and can be deactivated for a while to reduce resource utilization. Apart from these two examples, brownout is available for other application components or microservices that are not required to be available all the time.

In this paper, we consider component-level control in our system model. The model could also be applied to container or microservices architecture. We model the application components as either mandatory or optional, and if required, optional components can be deactivated. By deactivating the optional components selectively and dynamically, the application utilization is reduced to save total energy consumption. While under market scenario, service provider may provide discount for users as one or more services are deactivated.

In our scenario, the meaning of discount is not limited to the discount offered to users. Additionally, it can also be modelled as the revenue loss of service providers (i.e. SaaS service providers) that they charge lower price for services under brownout. For example, in an online shopping system, the recommendation engine helps the service provider to improve their revenue by recommending similar products. If the recommendation engine is deactivated, the service provider is unable to obtain the revenue from recommendation engine.

The key **contributions** of this paper are: our approach considers the trade-offs between saved energy and the discount that is given to a user if components or microservices are deactivated; we propose an efficient algorithm based on brownout and approximate Markov Decision Process that considers the afore-mentioned trade-offs and achieves better trade-offs than baselines.

The remainder of this paper is organized as follows: after discussing the related work in Sect. 2, we present the brownout system model and problem statement in Sect. 3. Section 4 introduces our proposed brownout-based Markov Decision Process approach, and Sect. 5 demonstrates the experimental results of our proposed approach. The summary along with the future work are concluded in Sect. 6.

2   Related Work

A large body of literature has focused on reducing energy consumption in cloud data centers, and the dominant categories for solving this problem are VM consolidation and Dynamic Voltage Frequency Scaling (DVFS).

VM consolidation is viewed as an act of combining into an integral whole, which saves energy by allocating work among fewer machines and turning off unused machines [18]. Using this approach, VMs allocated to underutilized hosts are consolidated to other servers and the remaining hosts are transformed into low power mode. Mastroianni et al. [15] presented a self-organizing and adaptive approach for consolidation of VMs CPU and RAM resource, which is driven by probabilistic processes and local information. Corradi et al. [8] considered VM consolidation in a more practical viewpoint related to power, CPU and networking resource sharing and tested VM consolidation in OpenStack, which shows VM consolidation is a feasible solution to lessen energy consumption.

The DVFS technique introduces a trade-off between computing performance and energy consumed by the server. The DVFS technique lowers the frequency and voltage when the processor is lightly loaded, and utilizes maximum frequency and voltage when the processor is heavily loaded. Kim et al. [13] proposed several power-aware VM schemes based on DVFS for real-time services. Hanumaiah et al. [12] introduced a solution that considers DVFS, thread migration and active cooling to control the cores to maximize overall energy efficiency.

Most of the proposed brownout approaches in Cloud scenarios focused on handling overloads or overbooking rather than energy efficiency perspective. Klein et al. [14] firstly borrowed the approach of brownout and applied it to cloud applications, aiming to design more robust applications under unpredictable loads. Tomas et al. [19] used brownout along with overbooking to ensure graceful degradation during load spikes and avoid overload. In a brownout-compliant application or service, the optional parts are identified by developers, and a control knob called **dimmer** that controls these optional parts is also introduced. The dimmer value represents a certain probability given by a control variable and shows how often these optional parts are executed. Moreover, a brownout controller is also required to adjust the dimmer value.

Markov Decision Process (MDP) is a discrete time stochastic optimization approach and provides a way to solve the multiple state probabilistic decision-making problem, which has been adopted to solve resource management problems in Cloud scenarios. Toosi et al. [20] used finite MDP for requests admission control in Clouds, while their objective is maximizing revenues rather than reducing power consumption. Han et al. [11] applied MDP to determine VM migration for minimizing energy consumption, while our work is adopting MDP to determine the deactivation of application components.

In our previous work [21], several heuristic policies were proposed to find the components that should be deactivated and investigated the trade-offs between energy and discount. In this paper, we adopt approximate MDP to improve the aforementioned trade-offs.

3   System Model and Problem Definition

3.1   System Model

Our system model is presented in Fig. 1 and it consists of the following entities:

Users: Users submit service requests to cloud data centers. The users entity contains user information and requested applications (services).

Applications: The applications provide different services for users and are consisted of a set of components, which are identified as mandatory or optional.

Mandatory component: The mandatory component keeps running all the time when the application is launched.

Optional component: The optional component can be set as activated or deactivated according to the system status. These components have parameters like utilization $u(App_c)$ and discount $d(App_c)$. Utilization indicates the amount of utilization, and discount represents the amount of discount that is offered to the users (or revenue loss of service provider). The operations of optional components are controlled by the **brownout controller**, which makes decisions based on the system overloaded status and brownout algorithm.

To adapt the dimmer to our model, different from the dimmer in [14] that requires a dimmer per application, our dimmer is only applied to the applications with optional components. Rather than response time, another adaptation is that our dimmer value is computed based on the number of overloaded hosts and adapts to the severity of overloaded events (more details are presented in Sect. 4.1).

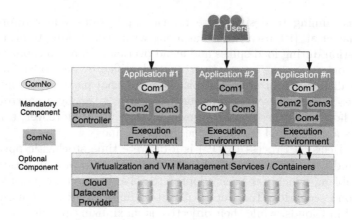

Fig. 1. System model with brownout

Cloud Providers: Cloud providers offer physical resources to meet service demands, which host a set of VMs or containers to run applications.

3.2 Power Model

We adopt the servers power model derived from [22]. The power of server i is $P_i(t)$ that is dominated by the CPU utilization:

$$P_i(t) = \begin{cases} P_i^{idle} + \sum_{j=1}^{N_i} u(VM_{i,j}(t)) \times P_i^{dynamic} & , N_i > 0 \\ 0 & , N_i = 0 \end{cases} \quad (1)$$

$P_i(t)$ is composed of idle power and dynamic power. The idle power is regarded as constant and the dynamic power is linear to the total CPU utilization of all the VMs on the server [22]. If no VM is hosted on a server, the server is turned off to save power. $VM_{i,j}$ refers to the jth VM on server i, N_i means the number of VMs assigned to server i. And $u(VM_{i,j}(t))$ refers to the VM utilization at time interval t, which is represented as:

$$u(VM_{i,j}(t)) = \sum_{c=1}^{C_j} u(App_c) \quad (2)$$

where C_j is the number of application components on VM, and $u(App_c)$ is the utilization of application component c when it is activated.

Then the total energy consumption during time interval t, with M servers is:

$$E(t) = \sum_{i=1}^{M} \int_{t-1}^{t} P_i(t)dt \quad (3)$$

Notes: In our power model, we assume that the time required to turn on/off hosts (including the time to deactivate and activate components) is lees than a scheduling time interval (like 5 min). When the host is turned off/on, the host is assumed to be consuming the idle power.

3.3 Discount Amount

As introduced in Sect. 1, the meaning of discount could be either the discount offered to users or the revenue loss of service providers that they charge lower price for services under brownout. In this paper, we note them as discount.

The total discount amount at time interval t is modeled as the sum of discount of all deactivated application components at t:

$$D(t) = \sum_{i=1}^{M} \sum_{j=1}^{N_i} d(VM_{i,j}(t)) \tag{4}$$

where $D(t)$ is the total discount amount at t that obtained from all VMs on hosts, N_i is the number of VMs assigned to server i, M is the number of servers. The individual discount $d(VM_{i,j}(t))$ is the sum of discount amount of deactivated application components $d(App_c)$ of $VM_{i,j}$, which is shown in Eq. (5):

$$d(VM_{i,j}) = \sum_{c=1}^{C_j} d(App_c) \tag{5}$$

where C_j is the number of application components hosted on VM_j, and only the deactivated components are counted.

3.4 Problem Definition

Let $Q(t) \in \mathbb{Q}$, where $\mathbb{Q} = \eta_1, \dots, \eta_{|\mathbb{Q}|}$, $\eta_i \in \mathbb{Q}$. The $Q(t)$ is a combination of two vectors: energy consumption vector $E(t)$ and discount amount vector $D(t)$, representing the possible energy consumption and discount amount at different system states. Let $C(t)$ to be all the application component states at t, we have

Definition 1. *The system state at time interval t can be specified as:*

$$S(t) \triangleq [Q(t), C(t)] \tag{6}$$

The system state $S(t)$ contains the energy consumption and discount amount as well as their corresponding application components states.

At each time interval, we calculate the state information as:

$$g(t) = E(t) + \lambda D(t) \tag{7}$$

where λ is the weight of discount. The higher λ implicates that more weights are given to the discount amount. In the whole scheduling period T under policy π, our optimization objective is:

$$\min_{\pi} \quad g(\pi) = \sum_{t=0}^{T} [E(t) + \lambda D(t)] \tag{8}$$

4   Proposed Approach

4.1   Approximate Markov Decision Process Model

To adopt the Markov model, we assume that the workload satisfies the Markov property, which means the state transitions caused by workloads are memory-less. Our experiments are conducted with Planetlab workload, which has been validated to satisfy Markov chain property [4]. In our model, we assume that the probability of application components to transfer their states at the next time period only depends on the workloads of the current time period and independent on earlier states. We formulate our problem as finite horizon MDP that we investigate a fixed length of time.

Then we can solve our objective function by using Bellman equation [3]:

$$V^*(S_i) = \arg\min_{\gamma \in \mathbb{R}}[g(S_i) + \sum_{S_j \in S} Pr[S_j|S_i, \gamma]V^*(S_j)] \tag{9}$$

$g(S_i)$ is the instant cost under system state S_i, and $V^*(S_i)$ is the expected energy consumption and discount obtained from S_j to S_i. We also denote $\gamma(t) \triangleq [\gamma_1(t), \ldots, \gamma_n(t)] \in \mathbb{R}$ as the operations (activation or deactivation actions) for application components. $V^*(S_i)$ can be found by iteratively obtaining minimum energy consumption and discount until convergence.

Let $\hat{p_{i,j}}$ denote the estimated transition probability that the application component changes its state. The transition probability is computed as:

$$\hat{p}_{i,j} = \sqrt{\frac{\hat{M}}{M}} \times Pr(\frac{u(App_c)}{d(App_c)} = z_C) \tag{10}$$

$Pr(\frac{u(App_c)}{d(App_c)} = z_C)$ is the probability that the ratio of component utilization and discount $\frac{u(App_c)}{d(App_c)}$ falls into category z_C. We divide the probability into C (the maximum number of components on a VM) categories. For all the components with the probability falls into the same category, we apply the same operation. To avoid the curse of dimension, noted by [11], we adopt key states to reduce state space. With key states, the component states on a VM is reduced to the maximum number of components on a VM as $|C|$. $\hat{M}$ is the estimated number of overloaded hosts, which is calculated based on a sliding window [5]. The advantage of sliding window is to give more weights to the values of recent time intervals. Let L_w to be the window size, and $N(t)$ to be the number of overloaded hosts at t, we estimate $\hat{M}$ as:

$$\hat{M}(L_w) = \frac{1}{L_w} \sum_{t=0}^{L_w-1} N(t) \tag{11}$$

We denote the states as key states S_k as described above. With proof in [11], $\forall S_i \in S_k$ for all the VMs, the equivalent Bellman's equation in Eq. (9) can be approximately formulated as:

$$V^*(S_i) \approx \sum_{m=1}^{M} \sum_{n=1}^{N_m} (g(S_i) + \arg\min_{\gamma_n \in \mathbb{R}_n} \{ \sum_{S_j \in S_k} Pr[S_j|S_i, \gamma_n] \widetilde{V_n^*}(S_j) \}) \qquad (12)$$

The state spaces thus are reduced to polynomial with linear approximation. The M is the number of hosts and N_m is the number of VM assigned to server m.

4.2 Brownout Algorithm Based on Markov Decision Process (BMDP)

Our novel brownout algorithm is embedded within a VM placement and consolidation algorithm. We adopt the VM placement and consolidation algorithm (PCO) proposed in [4], which is also one of our baselines in Sect. 5.

The PCO algorithm is a heuristic to reduce energy consumption through VM consolidation. In the initial VM placement phase, PCO sorts all the VMs in decreasing order by their current CPU utilization and allocates each VM to the host that increases the least power consumption due to this allocation. In the VM consolidation phase, PCO optimizes VM placement by separately picking VMs from over-utilized and under-utilized hosts to migrate, and finding new placements for them. After migration, the over-utilized hosts are not overloaded any more and the under-utilized hosts are switched to sleep mode.

Our brownout algorithm based on approximate Markov Decision Process is shown in Algorithm 1 and includes 6 steps:

(1) **System initialization (lines 1–2):** Initializing the system configurations, including overloaded threshold TP, dimmer value θ_t, vector $\mathbb{Q}$ that contains the $D(t)$ and $E(t)$ information, as well as objective states $\mathbb{S}_d$, and applying VM placement algorithm in PCO to initialize VM placement.

(2) **Estimating transition probability of each application component (lines 3–14):** At each time interval, the algorithm firstly estimates the number of overloaded hosts. The dimmer value is computed as $\sqrt{\frac{\widetilde{M}}{M}}$, which is adaptive to the number of overloaded hosts. If no host is overloaded, the value is 0 and no component is deactivated. If there are overloaded hosts, the transition probabilities of application components are computed using Eq. (10).

(3) **Finding the states that minimize the objective function (lines 15–17):** Traversing all the key states by value iteration according to Eq. (12), where $D'(t)$ and $E'(t)$ are the temporary values at the current state.

(4) **Updating system information (lines 18–20):** The algorithm updates the obtained energy consumption and discount values if $g(t)$ in Eq. (7) is reduced, and records the optimized states. The current states are substituted by the state with lower $g(t)$.

(5) **Deactivating the selected components (line 22):** The brownout controller deactivates the selected components to achieve objective states.

(6) **Optimize VMs placement (line 24):** The algorithm uses the VM consolidation approach in PCO to optimize VM placement via VM consolidations.

Algorithm 1 Brownout based Markov Decision Process Algorithm (BMDP)

Input: host list hl with size M, VM list, application components information, overloaded power threshold TP, dimmer value θ_t at time t, destination states $S_d(t)$, energy consumption $E(t)$ and discount amount $D(t)$ in $\mathbb{Q}$

Output: total energy consumption, discount amount

1: $TP \leftarrow 0.8$; $\theta_t \leftarrow 0$; $\forall E(t), \forall D(t) \in \mathbb{Q} \leftarrow max$; $S_d(t) \in \mathbb{S}_d \leftarrow NULL$
2: use PCO algorithm to initialize VMs placement
3: **while** true **do**
4:    **for** $t \leftarrow 0$ to T **do**
5:       $\theta_t \leftarrow = \sqrt{\frac{\bar{M}_t}{M}}$
6:       **for all** h_i in hl **do**
7:          **if** h_i is overloaded **then**
8:             **for all** $VM_{i,j}$ on h_i **do**
9:                **for all** App_c on $VM_{i,j}$ **do**
10:                   $Pr(App_c) \leftarrow \theta_t \times Pr(\frac{u(App_c)}{d(App_c)} = z_C)$
11:                **end for**
12:             **end for**
13:          **end if**
14:       **end for**
15:       **for all** $S_j(t) \in S_k(t)$ **do**
16:          $V^*(S_i) = \sum_{m=1}^{m=M} \sum_{n=1}^{n=N_m} (g(S_i) + \min_{\gamma_n \in \mathbb{R}_n} \{\sum_{S_j \in S_k} Pr[S_j|S_i, \gamma_n] \widetilde{V}_n^*(S_j)\})$
17:          $g(t) = E^{'}(t) + \lambda D^{'}(t)$
18:          **if** $g(t) < E(t) + \lambda D(t)$ **then**
19:             $E(t) \leftarrow E^{'}(t)$; $D(t) \leftarrow D^{'}(t)$; $S_d(t) \leftarrow S_j(t)$
20:          **end if**
21:       **end for**
22:       deactivate the selected components to achieve state $S_d(t)$
23:    **end for**
24:    use VM consolidation in PCO algorithm to optimize VM placement
25: **end while**

The complexity of the BMDP algorithm at each time interval is consisted of the brownout part and VM consolidation part. The complexity of the transition probability computation is $O(C \cdot N \cdot M)$, where C is the maximum number of components in all applications, N is the maximum number of VMs on all the hosts and M is the number of hosts. With the key states, the space state of the MDP in brownout part is $O(C \cdot N \cdot M)$. According to Eq. (12), the actions are reduced to $O(C \cdot N \cdot M)$, so the overall MDP complexity is $O(C^2 \cdot N^2 \cdot M^2)$. The complexity of the PCO part is $O(2M)$ as analyzed in [4]. Therefore, the overall complexity is $O(C \cdot M \cdot N + C^2 \cdot N^2 \cdot M^2 + 2M)$ or equally $O(C^2 \cdot N^2 \cdot M^2)$.

5 Performance Evaluation

5.1 Methodology

We use the CloudSim framework [6] to simulate a cloud data center. The data center contains two types of hosts and four types of VMs that are modeled based on current offerings in EC2 as shown in Table 1. The power models of the adopted hosts are derived from IBM System x3550 M3 with CPU Intel Xeon X5670 and X5675 [1]. We set the time required to turn on/off hosts as 0.5 min.

We implemented application with optional components, and each component has its corresponding CPU utilization and discount amount. The components are uniformly distributed on VMs.

We adopt the realistic workload trace from more than 1000 PlanetLab VMs [17] to create an overloaded environment [5]. Our experiments are simulated under one-day scheduling period and repeated for 10 different days. The brownout is invoked every 5 min (one time interval) if hosts are overloaded. The sliding window size L_w in Eq. (11) to estimate the number of overloaded hosts is set as 12 windows (one hour).

The CPU resource is measured with capacity of running instructions. Assuming that the application workload occupies 85% resource on a VM and the VM has 1000 million instructions per second (MIPS) computation capacity, then it represents the application constantly requires $0.85 \times 1000 = 850$ MI per second in the 5 min time interval.

Table 1. Host/VM types and capacity

Name	CPU	Cores	Memory	Bandwidth	Storage
Host Type 1	1.86 GHz	2	4 GB	1 Gbit/s	100 GB
Host Type 2	2.66 GHz	2	4 GB	1 Gbit/s	100 GB
VM Type 1	2.5 GHz	1	870 MB	100 Mbit/s	1 GB
VMType 2	2.0 GHz	1	1740 MB	100 Mbit/s	1 GB
VM Type 3	1.0 GHz	1	1740 MB	100 Mbit/s	1 GB
VM Type 4	0.5 GHz	1	613 MB	100 Mbit/s	1 GB

We use three baseline algorithms for comparison as below:

(1) **VM Placement and Consolidation algorithm (PCO)** [4]: the algorithm has been described at the beginning of Sect. 4.2.

(2) **Utilization-based Probabilistic VM consolidation algorithm (UBP)** [7]: for VM initial placement, UBP adopts the same approach as PCO. For VM consolidation, UBP applies a probabilistic method [15] to select VMs from overloaded host. The probabilistic method calculates the migration probability $f_m(u)$ based on host utilization u as: $f_m(u) = (1 - \frac{u-1}{1-T_h})^\alpha$, where T_h is the upper threshold for detecting overloads and α is a constant to adjust probability.

(3) **Brownout algorithm with Highest Utilization and Price Ratio First Component Selection Algorithm (HUPRFCS)** [21]: it is a brownout-based heuristic algorithm. This algorithm deactivates the application components from the one with the highest $\frac{u(App_c)}{d(App_c)}$ to the others with lower $\frac{u(App_c)}{d(App_c)}$ until the deactivated components obtain the expected utilization reduction, which is a deterministic algorithm. HUPRFCS is an efficient approach to reduce energy consumption under discount amount constraints.

To evaluate algorithms' performance, we mainly explore two parameters:

(1) **Overloaded threshold:** it identifies the CPU utilization threshold that determines the overloaded hosts, and it is varied from 80% to 95% in increments of 5%. We adopt this parameter since both [4] and [15] have shown that it influences energy consumption.

(2) **Percentage of optional utilization in an application:** it shows how much utilization in application is optional and can be deactivated. It is varied from 25% to 100% in increments of 25%. An application with 100% optional utilization represents that the application components or microservices are self-contained and each of them is allowed to be disabled temporarily (not disabling all the components at the same time), such as a stateless online document processing application. We assume the application maximum discount is identical to the percentage of optional utilization, for example, 50% optional utilization in an application comes along with 50% discount amount.

We assume that the optional components utilization $u(App_c)$ and discount $d(App_c)$ conform normal distribution $u(App_c) \sim N(\mu, \sigma^2)$, $d(App_c) \sim N(\mu, \sigma^2)$, the μ is the mean utilization of component utilization or discount, which is computed as the percentage of optional utilization (or discount amount) divided by the number of optional components. The σ^2 is the standard deviation of optional components utilization or discount. In our experiments, we consider both optional component utilization standard deviation and discount standard deviation are less than 0.1, which represents that the optional components are designed to have balanced utilization and discount.

5.2   Results

5.2.1   Comparison with Different λ

To investigate the impacts of different discount weights in Eq. (7), we conduct a series of experiments with different λ. In these evaluations, the hosts number and VMs number are set to 200 and 400 respectively, the overloaded threshold is set to 85% and the percentage of optional utilization is set to 50%. Figure 2 indicates that energy consumption increases and discount amount decreases when λ increases. The reason lies in that larger λ will guide our algorithm to find the states that offer less discount. From the results, we notice that when λ value is less than 4500, BMDP saves more energy than UBP and PCO, and in comparison to HUPRFCS, BMDP has similar energy consumption and reduces significant discount amount.

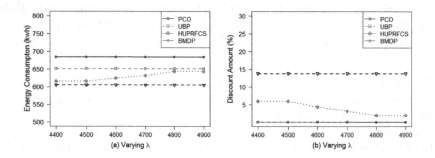

Fig. 2. Comparison with different λ. The parameter λ is the weight of discount.

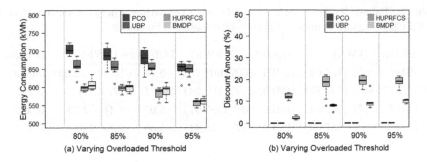

Fig. 3. Varying overloaded threshold

In the following evaluations, we set λ to a small value (i.e. $\lambda = 100$) so that the energy consumption of BMDP is below two baselines (PCO and UBP) and close to HUPRFCS. Additionally, with this λ value, the discount of BMDP is less than the discount produced by HUPRFCS.

5.2.2 Comparison Under Varied Overloaded Thresholds

The performance evaluated under different overloaded thresholds is shown in Fig. 3. Other parameters are configured as same as in Sect. 5.2.1. In Fig. 3(a), we observe that the energy consumption of all the algorithms are reduced when the overloaded threshold increases, for example, PCO-80% has 699.6 kWh with 95% Confidence Interval (CI) (682.6, 716.6) and reduces it to 649.9 kWh with 95% CI: (635.8, 664.1) in PCO-95%; BMDP-80% has 607.8 kWh with 95% CI: (598.1, 617.4) and saves it as 558.4 kWh with 95% CI: (549.6, 567.2) in BMDP-95%. The reason lies in that higher overloaded thresholds allow more VMs to be packed on the same host, so that more hosts are shutdown. When overloaded thresholds are between 80% to 90%, UBP reduces around 5% energy consumption compared to PCO, while HUPRFCS and BMDP save about 14–16% more energy consumption than PCO. When the overloaded threshold is 95%, PCO and UBP achieve close energy consumption, while HUPRFCS and BMDP still reduce around 16% energy compared with them.

As the energy consumption of HUPRFCS and BMDP are quite close, we conduct paired t-tests for HUPRFCS and BMDP as shown in Table 2. We notice that the differences between them are less than 2%, and when the overloaded thresholds are 85% and 95%, the *p-values* are 0.09 and 0.45 respectively, which indicates weak evidence to prove that they are different.

Comparing the discount amount, Fig. 3(b) shows that there is no discount offered in PCO and UBP, but HUPRFCS offers 11% to 20% discount and BMDP reduces it to 3% to 11% as the trade-off due to components deactivation. This is because, based on heuristics, HUPRFCS quickly finds the components with higher utilization and discount ratio, while BMDP steps further based on MDP to optimize the component selection.

Table 2. Paired T-Tests with 95% CIs for Comparing Energy Consumption by HUPRFCS and BMDP under Different Overloaded Thresholds

Algorithm 1 (kWh)	Algorithm 2 (kWh)	Difference (kWh)	*p-value*
HUPRFCS-80% (598.01)	BMDP-80% (607.78)	−9.77 (−15.14, −4.39)	0.0026
HUPRFCS-85% (595.87)	BMDP-85% (599.24)	3.37 (−0.77, 7.52)	0.099
HUPRFCS-90% (581.91)	BMDP-90% (587.97)	−6.05 (−9.41 −2.69)	0.0027
HUPRFCS-95% (557.03)	BMDP-95% (558.41)	−1.38 (−5.36, 2.6)	0.45

5.2.3   Comparison Under Varied Percentage of Optional Utilization

In Fig. 4, we compare the algorithms with different percentages of optional utilization. Other parameters are set the same as those in Sect. 5.2.1. As shown in Fig. 4(a), for PCO and UBP, their energy consumption are not influenced by different percentage of optional utilization. PCO has 684 kWh with 95% CI: (667.4, 700.6), and UBP has reduced 4.7% to 651.9 with 95% CI: (637.3, 666.5). Compared with PCO, HUPRFCS-25% reduces 11% energy to 605kWh with 95% CI: (596.6, 613.4), and BMDP-25% reduces 9% energy to 615.9 kWh with 95% CI: (605.9, 625.8). When the percentage of optional utilization increases, the more energy consumption is saved by HUPRFCS and BMDP. For instance, HUPRFCS-100% and BMDP-100% achieve around 20% energy saving as 556.9kWh with 95% CI: (550.9, 562.3) and 551.6kWh with 95% CI: (545.8, 557.4) respectively. The reason is that higher percentage of optional percentage allows more utilization to be reduced. For the discount amount comparison in Fig. 4(b), it shows that HUPRFCS offers 10% to 25% discount amount as trade-offs, while BMDP only offers 3% to 10% discount amount.

Because the energy consumption of HUPRFCS and BMDP are quite close, we conduct the paired t-test for HUPRFCS and BMDP as illustrated in Table 3. When the percentage of optional utilization are 75% and 100%, the *p-values* are 0.099 and 0.057, which indicates weak evidence to prove that they are different. And with other percentage of optional utilization, the energy consumption differences are less than 2%.

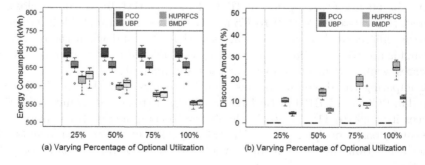

Fig. 4. Varying percentage of optional utilization

Table 3. Paired T-Tests with 95% CIs for Comparing Energy Consumption by HUPRFCS and BMDP under Different Percentage of Optional Utilization

Algorithm 1 (kWh)	Algorithm 2 (kWh)	Difference (kWh)	*p-value*
HUPRFCS-25% (617.57)	BMDP-25% (628.10)	-10.52 $(-12.52, -8.52)$	0.00082
HUPRFCS-50% (595.0)	BMDP-50% (605.88)	-10.88 $(-15.26, -6.5)$	0.00032
HUPRFCS-75% (575.87)	BMDP-75% (579.24)	-3.37 $(-7.52\ -0.78)$	0.099
HUPRFCS-100% (551.56)	BMDP-100% (556.59)	-3.12 $(-5.08, -1.16)$	0.0057

6   Conclusions and Future Work

Brownout has been proven to be effective to solve the overloaded situation in cloud data centers. Additionally, brownout can also be applied to reduce energy consumption. In this paper, we introduced the brownout system model by deactivating optional components in applications or microservices temporarily. In the model, the brownout controller can deactivate the optional components or microservices to deal with overloads and reduce data center energy consumption while offering discount to users. We also propose an algorithm based on brownout and approximate Markov Decision Process namely BMDP, to find the components should be deactivated. The simulations based on real trace showed that BMDP reduces 20% energy consumption than non-brownout baselines and saves discount amount than brownout baseline. As future work, we plan to implement a brownout prototype based on Docker Swarm.

Acknowledgments. This work is supported by China Scholarship Council, Australia Research Council Future Fellowship and Discovery Project Grants. We thank Chenhao Qu, Adel Nadjaran Toosi and Satish Narayana Srirama for their valuable suggestions.

References

1. Standard performance evaluation corporation. http://www.spec.org/power-ssj2008/results/res2010q2/
2. Bawden, T.: Global warming: Data centres to consume three times as much energy in next decade, experts warn (2016). http://www.independent.co.uk/environment/global-warming-data-centres-to-consume-three-times-as-much-energy-in-next-decade-experts-warn-a6830086.html
3. Bellman, R.: Dynamic programming and lagrange multipliers. Proc. Nat. Acad. Sci. **42**(10), 767–769 (1956)
4. Beloglazov, A., Abawajy, J., Buyya, R.: Energy-aware resource allocation heuristics for efficient management of data centers for cloud computing. Future Gener. Comput. Syst. **28**(5), 755–768 (2012)
5. Beloglazov, A., Buyya, R.: Managing overloaded hosts for dynamic consolidation of virtual machines in cloud data centers under quality of service constraints. IEEE Trans. Parallel Distrib. Syst. **24**(7), 1366–1379 (2013)

6. Calheiros, R.N., Ranjan, R., Beloglazov, A., De Rose, C.A., Buyya, R.: CloudSim: a toolkit for modeling and simulation of cloud computing environments and evaluation of resource provisioning algorithms. Softw. Pract. Experience **41**(1), 23–50 (2011)
7. Chen, Q., Chen, J., Zheng, B., Cui, J., Qian, Y.: Utilization-based VM consolidation scheme for power efficiency in cloud data centers. In: 2015 IEEE International Conference on Communication Workshop (ICCW), pp. 1928–1933. IEEE (2015)
8. Corradi, A., Fanelli, M., Foschini, L.: VM consolidation: a real case based on openstack cloud. Future Gener. Comput. Syst. **32**, 118–127 (2014)
9. Delforge, P.: Data center efficiency assessment - scaling up energy efficiency across the data center industry: evaluating key drivers and barriers (2014). https://www.nrdc.org/sites/default/files/data-center-efficiency-assessment-IP.pdf
10. Dürango, J., Dellkrantz, M., Maggio, M., et al.: Control-theoretical load-balancing for cloud applications with brownout. In: 53rd IEEE Conference on Decision and Control, pp. 5320–5327 (2014)
11. Han, Z., Tan, H., Chen, G., Wang, R., Chen, Y., Lau, F.C.M.: Dynamic virtual machine management via approximate markov decision process. In: IEEE INFOCOM 2016 - The 35th Annual IEEE International Conference on Computer Communications, pp. 1–9, April 2016
12. Hanumaiah, V., Vrudhula, S.: Energy-efficient operation of multicore processors by DVFs, task migration, and active cooling. IEEE Trans. Comput. **63**(2), 349–360 (2014)
13. Kim, K.H., Beloglazov, A., Buyya, R.: Power-aware provisioning of virtual machines for real-time cloud services. Concurrency Comput. Pract. Experience **23**(13), 1491–1505 (2011)
14. Klein, C., Maggio, M., Årzén, K.E., Hernández-Rodriguez, F.: Brownout: building more robust cloud applications. In: Proceedings of the 36th International Conference on Software Engineering, pp. 700–711 (2014)
15. Mastroianni, C., Meo, M., Papuzzo, G.: Probabilistic consolidation of virtual machines in self-organizing cloud data centers. IEEE Trans. Cloud Comput. **1**(2), 215–228 (2013)
16. Newman, S.: Building Microservices. O'Reilly Media Inc., Sebastopol (2015)
17. Park, K., Pai, V.S.: CoMon: a mostly-scalable monitoring system for planetlab. ACM SIGOPS Operating Syst. Rev. **40**(1), 65–74 (2006)
18. Pecero, J.E., Huacuja, H.J.F., Bouvry, P., Pineda, A.A.S., Locés, M.C.L., Barbosa, J.J.G.: On the energy optimization for precedence constrained applications using local search algorithms. In: International Conference on High Performance Computing and Simulation (HPCS), pp. 133–139 (2012)
19. Tomás, L., Klein, C., Tordsson, J., Hernández-Rodríguez, F.: The straw that broke the camel's back: safe cloud overbooking with application brownout. In: International Conference on Cloud and Autonomic Computing, pp. 151–160 (2014)
20. Toosi, A.N., Vanmechelen, K., Ramamohanarao, K., Buyya, R.: Revenue maximization with optimal capacity control in infrastructure as a service cloud markets. IEEE Trans. Cloud Comput. **3**(3), 261–274 (2015)
21. Xu, M., Dastjerdi, A.V., Buyya, R.: Energy efficient scheduling of cloud application components with brownout. IEEE Trans. Sustain. Comput. **1**(2), 40–53 (2016)
22. Zheng, K., Wang, X., Li, L., Wang, X.: Joint power optimization of data center network and servers with correlation analysis. In: IEEE INFOCOM 2014-IEEE Conference on Computer Communications, pp. 2598–2606 (2014)

Predicting the Available Bandwidth on Intra Cloud Network Links for Deadline Constrained Workflow Scheduling in Public Clouds

Rachael Shaw$^{(\boxtimes)}$, Enda Howley, and Enda Barrett

College of Engineering and Informatics,
National University of Ireland, Galway, Ireland
{r.shaw4,ehowley,enda.barrett}@nuigalway.ie

Abstract. Cloud computing infrastructure has in recent times gained significant popularity for addressing the ever growing processing, storage and network requirements of scientific applications. In public cloud infrastructure predicting bandwidth availability on intra cloud network links play a pivotal role in efficiently scheduling and executing large scale data intensive workflows requiring vast amounts of network bandwidth. However, the majority of existing research focuses solely on scheduling approaches which reduce cost and makespan without considering the impact of bandwidth variability and network delays on execution performance. This work presents a time series network-aware scheduling approach to predict network conditions over time in order to improve performance by avoiding data transfers at network congested times for a more efficient execution.

Keywords: Cloud computing · Workflow scheduling · Public cloud · ARIMA modelling

1 Introduction

Data-intensive applications often modelled as workflows are routinely used throughout many fields of scientific research. Workflows play a key role in assisting scientists to orchestrate complex multi-step computational analysis on extensively large data sets. Modern day scientific workflows have advanced considerably and are becoming increasingly large, generating terabytes of data which is expected to soar over the next decade [1]. As a result, workflows require vast amounts of rich and diverse resources accessible across distributed platforms in order to address their ever growing processing, storage and network requirements.

Recently, cloud computing has emerged as a new service provisioning model which offers an alternative and more scailable solution to traditional infrastructure such as computational grids and clusters. Cloud computing services deliver

R. Shaw—This work is supported by the Irish Research Council through the Government of Ireland Postgraduate Scholarship Scheme.

© Springer International Publishing AG 2017
M. Maximilien et al. (Eds.): ICSOC 2017, LNCS 10601, pp. 221–228, 2017.
https://doi.org/10.1007/978-3-319-69035-3_15

on demand access to vast amounts of compute resources charged on a pay per use basis. The use of virtualisation technology enables users to dynamically procure virtual machines and release resources on demand with varying combinations of CPU, memory and storage available to meet both performance requirements and budget constraints. Through the advancement of cloud based services and in particular High Performance Computing (HPC) platforms scientists have immediate access to large scale distributed infrastructure and customized execution environments to meet their growing needs. As a result, cloud computing infrastructure is fast evolving as the target platform for executing large scale scientific applications requiring high throughput and data analysis [2].

Despite the recent introduction of HPC resources such as Amazons Cluster Compute (CC) platform which offers improved networking capabilities research has shown that the overall performance of HPC applications in public clouds remains limited by poor network throughput [3]. Large data transfers across distributed cloud resources often hinge on unstable bandwidth availability on network links due to the shared nature of the resource. Consequently, a decrease in bandwidth causes an increase in data transfer times, thus increasing total execution time and associated rental costs of cloud resources. This highlights a fundamental workflow scheduling issue which is the impact of bandwidth variability and network congestion on data transfer times between workflow tasks.

As the adoption of cloud computing services continues to grow to facilitate a new generation of scientific users with high computational and data transfer requirements, estimating network resources gains significant importance in the development of efficient and reliable schedulers capable of anticipating dynamically changing network conditions in order to generate more efficient scheduling decisions. To address this issue we propose a network-aware scheduling approach which employs a time series Autoregressive Integrated Moving Average (ARIMA) forecasting algorithm. Our approach promotes efficient utilization of limited network resources by scheduling workflow tasks agnostic to underlying network conditions in order to avoid peak hours of network congestion while also meeting a hard deadline constraint and reducing overall costs.

The remainder of the paper is structured as follows. In Sect. 2 related work in the field is discussed. Section 3 formulates the problem. Section 4 introduces time series ARIMA modelling. Section 5 presents our preliminary results. Lastly, Sect. 6 concludes the paper and discusses future work.

2   Related Research

Much of the existing work in this area has focused on scheduling algorithms which aim to satisfy user Quality of Service (QoS) requirements, namely execution time and cost [4–6]. However, these works naively assume access to unlimited network bandwidth at run time and fail to consider the implications of network constraints on the execution performance of scientific workflows. However, research has also been proposed to target issues concerning the availability of resources on workflow schedules primarily in the form of reactive techniques [7–9].

While these approaches consider changes in resource availability at run time the available bandwidth is assumed to be entirely certain. However network resources are volatile and a function of system load at discrete time intervals [10]. Additionally, some of the suggested approaches involve task rescheduling, this additional overhead may not be a feasible solution in public clouds due to the associated rental costs of computational resources.

We propose an alternative approach which we expect to impact the state-of-the-art in two regards. Firstly, we address a key limitation of current approaches by considering the implications of dynamically changing network behaviour on execution time and associated costs of leasing resources from public clouds. More concretely, we develop a network-aware scheduling algorithm capable of predicting bandwidth availability in public cloud infrastructure where the competition for network resources is far greater. Secondly, we demonstrate the use of a statistical time series ARIMA modelling approach to the workflow scheduling problem for learning and predicting bandwidth availability. In particular, we demonstrate how our approach has the capacity to better align workflow scheduling requirements with the dynamic nature of network resources in order to generate a more reliable schedule and improve execution efficiency.

3 Problem Formulation

A scientific application (workflow) is often modelled as a Directed Acyclic Graph (DAG) denoted as $W = \{ V, E \}$ where $V = \{ T_1, T_2, ..., T_n \}$ is a set of tasks in the workflow which are assigned to a specific resource and E is the set of directed edges representing the data dependencies between tasks. A directed edge $E_{i,j}$ signifies that task T_i is the parent task of task T_j. Child tasks can only execute once all parent tasks have been processed and the data has been transferred, while nodes on the same level can be executed in parallel using multiple resources in order to speed up execution time. In addition, each workflow W has an assigned deadline constraint. Figure 1(a) illustrates a workflow example consisting of 7 nodes in which the edges between tasks denote the file inputs and outputs. Figure 1(b) depicts a valid schedule for the adjacent workflow. The objective of our scheduler is to find a mapping of tasks to resources at more optimal times for large data transfers that meet the specified deadline and reduces the overall execution cost.

The cloud infrastructure network model used in this work was generated based on measurements of Amazons EC2 network performance [11]. This benchmark study provides a model of the bandwidth within Amazons EU region. In order to keep the focus of the performance around the network we consider a finite set of homogeneous resources $R = \{ r_1, r_2 ... r_n \}$ which we assume have sufficient CPU, memory and disk to execute each task T_i which has a fixed processing time of 1 h. We consider file sizes that are fixed but vary across individual tasks in the workflow. The execution of task T_i on resource r_j incurs an execution cost. Generally, there is no charge for the transfer of data between tasks in the same region. Total cost is calculated as a function of processing and

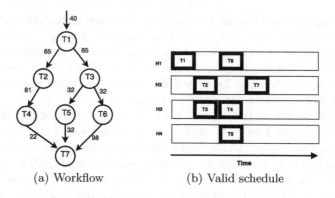

(a) Workflow   (b) Valid schedule

Fig. 1. Sample workflow application with valid schedule

data transfer time. In addition, total execution time can be defined as the latest completion time of all tasks executed on all cloud resources.

4 Time Series Forecasting: ARIMA Modelling

ARIMA models have become a widely popular methodology for time series forecasting [12]. An ARIMA model consists of three fundamental components denoted as (p, d, q). Identifying a valid model is the process of finding suitable values for (p, d, q) which capture the systematic patterns in the data. The autoregressive (AR) component (p) represents the influence of past values on current values in the series. For example An $AR(1)$ model predicts future values based on the value of the preceding observation defined as:

$$y_t = \phi(y_{t-1}) + \varepsilon_t .\tag{1}$$

Where ϕ is a parameter of the model and ε_t is random variation at time t. The moving average (MA) term (q) models the random variation of the model as a combination of previous error terms. For example An $MA(1)$ model forecasts future values based on a combination of the current random variation and previous error as defined in Eq. 2:

$$y_t = \theta(\varepsilon_{t-1}) + \varepsilon_t .\tag{2}$$

Where ε_{t-1} is the value of the previous random shock and θ is a parameter of the model. The integrated component of the model (d) is the order of differencing applied to the series in order to render the series stationary. A stationary series is one whose statistical properties such as mean and variance are constant over time. A non-stationary time series is often unreliable and can result in false autocorrelations in the series. The combined model assuming differenced data is defined in Eq. 3:

$$y_t = c + \phi_1(y_{t-1}) + ... + \phi_p(y_{p-1}) + \theta_1(\varepsilon_{t-1}) + ... + \theta_q(\varepsilon_{t-q}) + \varepsilon_t .\tag{3}$$

In addition, Seasonal ARIMA models can be used to model highly seasonal data formed by including additional ARIMA terms $(P, D, Q)_m$, where m signifies the number of periods per season. To generate the proposed model the Box-Jenkins methodology was employed which is composed of several steps outlined below [13].

4.1 Model Identification

The bandwidth data used in this work showed a significant seasonal periodic component which occurs within each 24 h period. The Autocorrelation Function (ACF) plot also revealed strong periodic oscillations indicating the implementation of a seasonal ARIMA model as defined in Eq. 4 to capture the strong seasonality present. It also confirmed the series was non stationary.

$$\phi_p(B)\Phi_P(B^s)W_t = \theta_q(B)\Theta_Q(B^s)Z_t . \tag{4}$$

Where B denotes the lag operator, ϕ_p, Φ_P, θ_q, Θ_Q are parameters of the seasonal and non-seasonal model components $(p, q)(P, Q)$ respectively and Z_t represents the error. In addition, a first order seasonal difference was applied to the data which proved sufficient in transforming the non stationary series into a stationary series.

To select the appropriate orders of both the non-seasonal components p, q and seasonal components P, Q of the model the ACF and Partial Autocorrelation Function (PACF) plots of the differenced data W_t were examined which identified several alternative values to select from.

4.2 Model Estimation and Diagnostics

To estimate the model parameters $\phi'_p s$, $\Phi'_P s$, $\theta'_q s$, $\Theta'_Q s$ in the forecast equation above the Maximum Likelihood Estimation (MLE) was adopted using R software. In order to select the best model to fit the data a common criterion known as Akaike Information Criterion (AIC) was used. This statistic as defined in Eq. 5 is a fundamental measurement of the quality of a statistical model for a series. ARIMA$(0, 0, 0)(0, 1, 1)[144]$ was deemed the best model as it produced the lowest AIC value.

$$AIC = -2log(L) + 2(p + q + k + 1) . \tag{5}$$

Where L is the maximum likelihood of the data, $k = 1$ if $c \neq 0$ while $k = 0$ if $c = 0$ and the final term represents the number of parameters in the model. A formal Ljung-Box test was also conducted on the residuals which generated a p-value of 0.735, which concluded that the residuals are independent.

4.3 Forecasting and Validation

To assess the accuracy of the forecasts a test set which equated to 1 week of bandwidth values over 10 min intervals was used as a comparison measure. The results

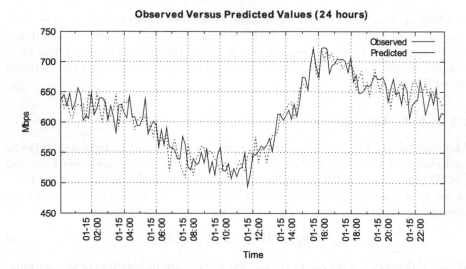

Fig. 2. Predicted and observed values for the subsequent day based on the previous weeks bandwidth values used to fit the model

showed that the forecasts generated were all within the 95% confidence limit. Additionally the Mean Absolute Percentage Error (MAPE) as given by Eq. 6 was calculated where O_t and P_t are the observed and predicted values of the time series. The MAPE from the resulting forecasts was 2.81% which is deemed highly accurate [14].

$$MAPE = \frac{100}{n} \sum_{t=1}^{n} \left| \frac{O_t - P_t}{O_t} \right| . \tag{6}$$

5   Preliminary Results

A cloud simulator was developed to evaluate the proposed network-aware scheduling procedure. As an initial benchmark we compare our approach to a non network-aware heuristic called *Execute-First*. To evaluate the proposed procedure using reasonable deadline constraints the *Execute-First* heuristic was run over 30 iterations calculating the makespan of each 10 min interval in a single day. The average earliest and latest finish times were computed in order to define deadline D denoted in Eq. 7, where parameter m is defined as 1, 30 and 60 to evaluate the performance of the algorithms over low, medium and high deadline constraints.

$$D = EFT_{average} + m \times \left(LFT_{average} - EFT_{average} \right) . \tag{7}$$

Figure 3(a) shows the total execution time in hours for all 3 deadline categories. These results show the advantage of using the predictive capabilities of

ARIMA modelling to inform our scheduling decision, our approach selects the most opportunistic time frame within the deadline to transfer data resulting in shorter execution times. Evidently, the performance of our approach continues to increase when deadlines span over a greater number of hours. This is largely due to the visibility our ARIMA driven algorithm has over dynamically changing bandwidth availability. Figure 3(b) also shows a significant reduction in cost as our network-aware scheduler postpones execution until network conditions are more optimum. Conversely, the *Execute-First* algorithm incurs larger costs due to poor scheduling decisions resulting in longer transfer times when the network is saturated.

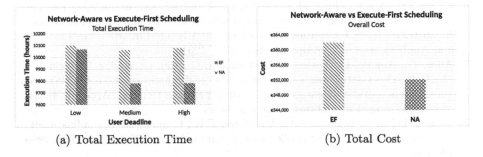

(a) Total Execution Time   (b) Total Cost

Fig. 3. Total execution time over low, medium and high deadline constraints and overall cost generated by both approaches

6   Conclusion

This work presented an efficient network-aware workflow scheduler based on time series ARIMA modelling designed to minimize total execution time and costs. Our empirical results have shown that by adopting a scheduling procedure which has the capacity to reason over the impact of dynamically changing bandwidth availability we can achieve significant cost reductions and reduce execution time. In future work we intend on extending our solution to consider heterogeneous workflow tasks and cloud resources to further optimize resource availability, while also considering the impact of additional factors such as queuing and propagation delays in order to deliver a more complete solution. Eventually, we hope to evaluate our approach using a live virtualised test bed.

Acknowledgments. The primary author would like to acknowledge the ongoing financial support provided to her by the Irish Research Council.

References

1. Yang, X., Wallom, D., Waddington, S., Wang, J., Shaon, A., Matthews, B., Wilson, M., Guo, Y., Guo, L., Blower, J.: Cloud computing in e-Science: research challenges and opportunities. J. Supercomput. **70**(1), 408–464 (2014). Springer

2. Lifka, D., Foster, I., Mehringer, S., Parashar, M., Redfern, P., Stewart, C., Tuecke, S.: XSEDE cloud survey report. Technical report, National Science Foundation (2013)
3. Expósito, R.R., Taboada, G.L., Ramos, S., González-Domínguez, J., Touriño, J., Doallo, R.: Analysis of I/O performance on an Amazon EC2 cluster compute and high I/O platform. J. Grid Comput. 4(11), 613–631 (2013). Springer
4. Abrishami, S., Naghibzadeh, M., Epema, D.: Deadline-constrained workflow scheduling algorithms for infrastructure as a service clouds. Future Gener. Comput. Syst. 29(1), 158–169 (2013). Elsevier
5. Barrett, E., Howley, E., Duggan, J.: A learning architecture for scheduling workflow applications in the cloud. In: 2011 Ninth IEEE European Conference on Web Services (ECOWS), pp. 83–90. IEEE (2011)
6. Pandey, S., Wu, L., Guru, M.S., Buyya, R.: A particle swarm optimization-based heuristic for scheduling workflow applications in cloud computing environments. In: 2010 24th IEEE International Conference on Advanced Information Networking and Applications (AINA), pp. 400–407. IEEE (2010)
7. Allen, G., Angulo, D., Foster, I., Lanfermann, G., Liu, C., Radke, T., Seidel, E., Shalf, J.: The Cactus worm: experiments with dynamic resource discovery and allocation in a grid environment. Int. J. High Perform. Comput. Appl. 15(4), 345–358 (2001). Sage Publications, Thousand Oaks
8. Batista, D.M., da Fonseca, N.L., Miyazawa, F.K., Granelli, F.: Self-adjustment of resource allocation for grid applications. Comput. Netw. 52(9), 1762–1781 (2008). Elsevier
9. Tang, W., Jenkins, J., Meyer, F., Ross, R., Kettimuthu, R., Winkler, L., Yang, X., Lehman, T., Desai, N.: Data-aware resource scheduling for multicloud workflows: a fine-grained simulation approach. In: 2014 IEEE 6th International Conference on Cloud Computing Technology and Science (CloudCom), pp. 887–892. IEEE (2014)
10. Duggan, M., Duggan, J., Howley, E., Barrett, E.: A network aware approach for the scheduling of virtual machine migration during peak loads. Cluster Comput. 20(2083), 1–12 (2017)
11. Sanghrajka, S., Mahajan, N., Sion, R.: Cloud performance benchmark series: Network performance-Amazon EC2. Technical report, Stony Brook University (2011)
12. Hyndman, R.J., Athanasopoulos, G.: Forecasting: Principles and Practice. OTexts, Melbourne (2013)
13. Box, G.E., Jenkins, G.M.: Time Series Analysis, Control, and Forecasting, vol. 3226(3228), p. 10. Holden Day, San Francisco (1976)
14. Kenneth, D.L., Ronald, K.K.: Advances in Business and Management Forecasting. Emerald Books, UK (1982)

Inferring Calling Relationship Based on External Observation for Microservice Architecture

Shinya Kitajima[✉] and Naoki Matsuoka

Software Laboratory, Fujitsu Laboratories Limited, 4-1-1 Kamikodanaka,
Nakahara, Kawasaki, Kanagawa 211-8588, Japan
{kitajima.shinya,matsuoka.naoki}@jp.fujitsu.com

Abstract. In recent years, a web service architecture namely microservices has attracted attention. Although the microservice architecture provides various advantages, it also has the disadvantage of making the root cause analysis of the complicated system. For root cause analysis, it is important to know the calling relationships between services since the service may call the other service and the latency of the called service may be wrong. Therefore, in this paper, we propose a method to infer the calling relationship between the services from communication logs observed from outside of the services.

Keywords: Microservice architecture · Distributed tracing system · Visualization · PaaS

1 Introduction

In recent years, a web service architecture namely microservices has attracted attention. In the microservice architecture, a web system is structured as a collection of loosely coupled services, and the services in the microservice architecture communicate via web APIs [5]. Microservice architecture was originally a spontaneously generated technique from companies with huge web system, such as Amazon and Netflix. Lewis *et al.* named the technique microservices [4].

There are various advantages of microservice architecture, including diversity of technologies, resilience, scalability, reliability, reusability and agility [2]. There are disadvantages, however, to constructing a web system as a distributed system [3], one of which is the complexity of root cause analysis. For root cause analysis, it is important to know the calling relationships between services since the service may call the other service and the latency of the called service may be wrong. It is thus difficult to discover the cause of a processing delay or error from the services since there are dozens or hundreds of services in a microservice architecture.

In the microservice architecture, a distributed tracing system, such as OpenZipkin[1] and OpenTracing[2], are the most famous methods for solving this problem. However, in order to use OpenZipkin and OpneTracing, it is necessary to

---

[1] http://zipkin.io/.
[2] http://opentracing.io/.

© Springer International Publishing AG 2017
M. Maximilien et al. (Eds.): ICSOC 2017, LNCS 10601, pp. 229–237, 2017.
https://doi.org/10.1007/978-3-319-69035-3_16

modify the source code of each service. This forms large barriers toward the use of these methods since developers must add codes and libraries that are specific to the distributed tracing system. In addition, Aguilera *et al.* [1] proposed methods that can trace the system without modifications to the source code of the services, their methods do not consider reusability, scalability and agility of the microservice architecture.

Therefore, in this paper, we propose a method for inferring the calling relationship between the services from communication logs observed from outside of the services. We call the trigger message as the *parent message*, and the triggered message by the parent message as the *child message*.

The remainder of this paper is organized as follows. We describe our assumptions in Sect. 2. We explain our method for inferring the parents from communication logs in Sect. 3. We then evaluate the accuracy of our method in Sect. 4. Finally, we provide our conclusions in Sect. 5.

2 Assumptions

The typical examples of systems based on microservice architecture are A huge EC site and online movie site. Figure 1 shows our assumed environment. Each service is developed and operated by the independent team. In addition, each service is constantly updated and new services are added to the system at any time. Each service runs in cooperation with loosely coupled with other services.

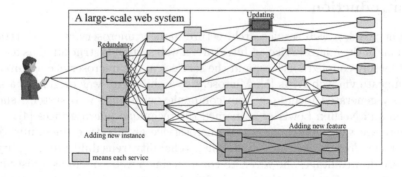

Fig. 1. The assumed environment.

Each service is often executed as a container application, since the characteristics of the container, such as portability and agility, match well for the microservice architecture. A container management infrastructure, such as Kubernetes[3] and Cloud Foundry[4], is often used to manage the container.

---

[3] https://kubernetes.io/.
[4] https://www.cloudfoundry.org/.

The advantages of the microservice architecture are various, including diversity of technologies, resilience, scalability, reliability, reusability and agility. However, in the microservice architecture, it is very difficult to find out the cause when a processing delay or an error occurs, since the configuration of the system changes from time to time. Therefore, it is important to know the calling relationships between services in the microservice architecture. We call the visualized calling relationships between the services *flow*.

3   Method for Inferring the Parents

In this section, we propose a method for inferring the calling relationship between the services in the microservice architecture using communication logs (sender, receiver, and timestamp) that can be acquired on each server. Our method assumes that each message was triggered by another message, and collects communication logs of messages received within a given threshold from the sent time of the child message as the *parent candidate messages*. After our method has performed this process for a certain number of messages and obtained a set of parent candidate messages, it infers the parent messages heuristically.

3.1   Enumeration of the Parent Candidate Messages

Our method infers the calling relationship by assuming that there is another message that triggered the message of interest. In general, web applications are listening for connections from clients on specific ports with specific IP addresses. Here, we define an IP address as IP and the pair of listening IP address and port of a service as S. In addition, we define a mapping function $getip : S \rightarrow IP$.

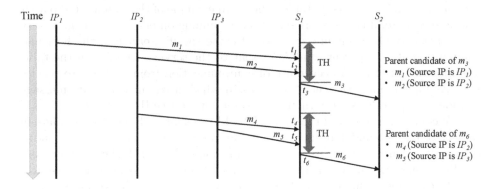

Fig. 2. Overview of proposed method for inferring the method.

Figure 2 shows that our method focuses on S_1 and enumerates all of the messages of which the source IP address is $getip(S_1)$ (m_3 and m_6 in the figure) and that are received within the threshold TH from the sent time of m_3 and m_6

(t_3 and t_6 in the figure) as the parent candidate messages (m_1 and m_2 for m_3, and m_4 and m_5 for m_6 in the figure). We cannot determine which message is the parent message if the service receives messages from multiple IP addresses within the threshold TH. We suppose that the optimal TH is different for each service. In this paper, for simplicity, we use the same TH for all services.

The amount of communication logs that our method uses for the inferring varies depending on the purpose. For example, we acquire the communication logs at all times, and when a failure occurs, our method uses the communication logs of the past hour to infer the flow to identify the cause.

We define the number of hosts as p and the set of communication logs acquired on a host $H_k(1 \leq k \leq p)$ as $M_k = \{m_{k,1}, m_{k,2}, \ldots, m_{k,n_k}\}$. Moreover, we define the source IP address of a communication $m_{k,i}$ as $IPs_{k,i}$, the destination IP address as $IPr_{k,i}$, the destination port number as $Pr_{k,i}$, and the occurrence time as $t_{k,i}$. $t_{k,i}$ is the sent time if H_k sent $m_{k,i}$, and $t_{k,i}$ is the received time if H_k received $m_{k,i}$. We define the set $CM_{k,i}$ of the parent candidate messages for $m_{k,i}$. $CM_{k,i}$ is the set of all communications for which the source IP address is the same as the source IP address $IPs_{k,i}$ of $m_{k,i}$, and for which the occurrence time $t_{k,j}$ is before $t_{k,i}$ and after $t_{k,i} - TH$. So, $CM_{k,i}$ can be represented as,

$$CM_{k,i} = \{m_{k,j} \mid IPr_{k,j} = IPs_{k,i}, t_{k,i} - TH < t_{k,j} < t_{k,i}\}(1 \leq j \leq n_k). \quad (1)$$

3.2   Aggregation of the Parent Candidate Messages

In this section, we aggregate the enumerated set of parent candidate messages and calculate how often the parent candidates appear, among those appearing in message from a certain host to a certain service. First, among the communication logs acquired by a certain host H_k, we enumerate the parent candidates sent to the service $s_{k,i}(1 \leq i \leq ns_k)$. Table 1 shows an example of the enumerated parent candidates. Here, if two or more services are running on one host, it is necessary to extract only the communication logs by the specific service in the host and enumerate only the parent candidates sent to the service. The IDs in the table are allocated in order of occurrence of communication from host H_x to service $s_{x,y}$. As for ID3 and ID5, there are cases in which a parent candidate message includes an IP address more than once among its source IP addresses.

We count the number of the source IP addresses for each parent candidate in the set of parent candidate messages enumerated in the above. Table 2a shows the result of counting these using the information in Table 1. If there is no parent candidate message, we count the number as "*None*." Moreover, when a source IP address appears more than once for a given parent candidate message, we only count it once. This is because several communications that have the same source IP address are included in a set of parent candidate messages when the access frequency from the client is high.

Table 1. From the communication logs acquired on the host H_x, the set of the parent candidate messages for communication sent to the service $s_{x,y}$

	Source IP addresses of parent candidate messages
ID1	IP_1
ID2	IP_1, IP_3
ID3	IP_1, IP_2, IP_4, IP_1
ID4	IP_2, IP_5
ID5	IP_1, IP_1, IP_4, IP_1
ID6	IP_2, IP_3
ID7	$None$

Table 2. Number of source IP addresses appearing as parent candidate messages.

(a) The communication logs acquired by host H_x.

	IP_1	IP_2	IP_3	IP_4	IP_5	$None$
ID1	1	0	0	0	0	0
ID2	1	0	1	0	0	0
ID3	1	1	0	1	0	0
ID4	0	1	0	0	1	0
ID5	1	0	0	1	0	0
ID6	0	1	1	0	0	0
ID7	0	0	0	0	0	1
Total	4	3	2	2	1	1

(b) The result excluding candidates having IP_1.

	IP_2	IP_3	IP_4	IP_5	$None$
ID4	1	0	0	1	0
ID6	1	1	0	0	0
ID7	0	0	0	0	1
Total	2	1	0	1	1

3.3 Inferring the Parent Message

In this section, we guess the parent based on the result of Sect. 3.2 with the following steps.

1. We select the parent candidate massage for which the source IP address appears most frequently as the parent message.
2. We check whether the parent message is included in each set of parent candidate messages, and exclude those set of parent candidate messages that include the parent message.
3. We go back to the Step 1 while a set of parent candidate messages exists.

As an example, we apply these steps to Table 2a. In Step 1, IP_1 is selected as the parent message since it has the highest total number of appearances. Next by applying Step 2, we get Table 2b by excluding the sets of the parent candidate messages that include IP_1. After that, we apply Step 3, which takes us back to Step 1 by which we select IP_2 as the parent message, since it has the most appearances at this point. In this way, we apply these steps until we finally select "None" as the parent message and conclude the process. As a result, we select the communication from IP_1 to H_1, IP_2 to H_1, and "None" as the parent message of the communication from H_x to $s_{x,y}$.

4   Evaluation

In this section, we evaluate our method according to the following three criteria. We define the set of parent messages in the inferred result as C_{result}, the set of correct parent messages, which we defined in advance, as $C_{correct}$, and the intersection of these sets as $C_{TP} = C_{result} \cap C_{correct}$.

- **Precision:** The ratio of the number of messages included in the set the correct parent messages divided by the number of parent messages included in the inferred result $(Precision = |C_{TP}|/|C_{result}|)$.
- **Recall:** The ratio of the number of messages included in the set of parent messages in the inferred result divided by the number of correct parent messages $(Recall = |C_{TP}|/|C_{correct}|)$.
- **F-measure:** Defined as follows using Precision and Recall:

$$F = \frac{2 \times Precision \times Recall}{Precision + Recall}. \tag{2}$$

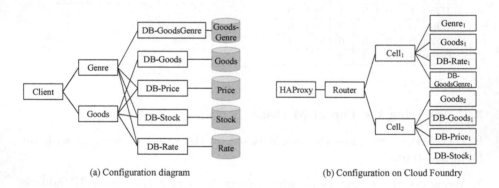

(a) Configuration diagram   (b) Configuration on Cloud Foundry

Fig. 3. Configurations.

4.1   Evaluation Environment

For the evaluation, we used a system based on microservice architecture that we implemented by imitating an EC site. Figure 3a shows the configuration of this system. This system consists of seven services, five of which are services connected to the database and the other two of which are services accessing multiple services. The Genre service and the Goods service each call four services that connect to the database at the same time. After all results are returned to them, they return results to the user. The implementation languages of the services and the databases are Go and MySQL, respectively.

Each service is running as an application on Cloud Foundry. A unique URL is allocated to each application, and we can access each application using that URL. Figure 3b shows the communication path to the applications inside Cloud Foundry. The access from the client to the application is sent to the Router via HAProxy, and the Router allocates access to instances of each application. When there are multiple instances of an application, access is sequentially allocated in a round-robin manner. Each application instance is running as an application container on the Cell, and each application listens for access at a specific port on the Cell.

If we applied the method as it is to the Cloud Foundry environment, the parent message of all messages would be message from the HAProxy to the Router. Therefore, we added a process to check which message calls the message from the HAProxy to the Router and to rewrite the sender of the message. That is, the source of the message from the HAProxy to the Router is replaced by client or one of the services.

We define the message from component A to component B as $[A, B]$. In addition, we call the Goods service and the Genre service *Front* because client accesses them first, and we call the other services, which access the database, *Backend*.

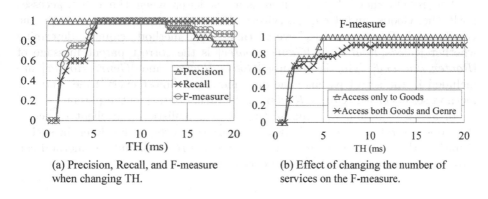

(a) Precision, Recall, and F-measure when changing TH.

(b) Effect of changing the number of services on the F-measure.

Fig. 4. Evaluation results.

4.2   Evaluation Result

Impact of TH. Figure 4a shows the evaluation result of Precision, Recall and F-measure of our method while changing TH from 0.5 to 20 ms. In this evaluation, clients only access the Goods service, and a client's access pattern is equal access once every 5 s for 5 min. We set the number of each service to 1.

The results show that Recall is low when TH is low, and Precision is low when TH is high. As a result, the F-measure is highest when $5.5 \leq TH \leq 12.5$. When TH is low, there are few messages included in the set of parent candidate messages, and the correct parent message is not included in the result.

On the other hand, when the TH is high, the set of parent candidate messages includes message that is not correct parent message, and the result also includes message that is not correct.

The breakdown of the incorrect answers shows that $[Client, Router]$ is selected as the parent message of $[Router, Backend]$ in addition to $[Goods, Router]$, which is the correct answer, resulting in low Precision. In the system that we used for the evaluation, first the client accesses the Goods service, and then the Goods service calls the Backend. Therefore, when TH is high, $[Client, Router]$ is included as parent candidate message of $[Router, Backend]$, resulting in low Precision.

Impact of the Number of Services. Figure 4b shows the F-measure when the client accesses only the Goods service and when the client accesses both the Goods and the Genre services. We set the number of instances of each service to 1, and we vary TH from 0.5 to 20 ms. In this evaluation, the client's access pattern is equal access once every 5 s. When the client accesses both the Goods and Genre services, the client's access pattern is equal access once every 5 s for both the Goods and Genre services, and the Goods and Genre services are accessed at almost the same time every time.

The results show that the F-measure is lower when the client accesses both the Goods and Genre services. When the client accesses both the Goods and Genre services every time, our method cannot determine whether $[Goods, Router]$ or $[Genre, Router]$ is the correct parent message of $[Router, Backend]$. This is because $[Goods, Router]$ and $[Genre, Router]$ are included in the set of parent candidate messages almost every time, and our method selects either $[Goods, Router]$ or $[Genre, Router]$ as the parent.

In a real situation, we suppose that it is unrealistic for a client to access the same several services at almost the same time every time. Even in such a situation, the F-measure is more than 0.9 when $TH > 10$, and our method can mostly infer the calling relationship correctly.

5   Conclusion

In this paper, we proposed a method to infer the calling relationship between the services from the communication logs observed outside the services, such as sender, receiver, and timestamp. Our method assumes that each message is triggered by another message, and infers the trigger message considering scalability and agility of the microservice architecture. The evaluation results show that our method can infer the calling relationships with high accuracy.

In the future, we will propose a method that automatically defines the optimal TH. In addition, we will confirm and improve the performance of our method in real systems based on microservice architecture.

References

1. Aguilera, M.K., Mogul, J.C., Wiener, J.L., Reynolds, P., Muthitacharoen, A.: Performance debugging for distributed systems of black boxes. In: 9th ACM Symposium on Operating Systems Principles (SOSP), pp. 74–89 (2003)
2. Balalaie, A., Heydarnoori, A., Jamshidi, P.: Microservices architecture enables DevOps: migration to a cloud-native architecture. IEEE Softw. **33**(3), 42–52 (2016)
3. Ciuffoletti, A.: Automated deployment of a microservice-based monitoring infrastructure. Procedia Comput. Sci. **68**, 163–172 (2015)
4. Lewis, J., Fowler, M.: Microservices (2014). http://martinfowler.com/articles/microservices.html
5. Newman, S.: Building Microservices, Designing Fine-Grained Systems. O'Reilly Media, Sebastopol (2015)

Quality of Service

A QoS-Aware Resource Allocation Controller for Function as a Service (FaaS) Platform

MohammadReza HoseinyFarahabady[1](✉), Young Choon Lee[2],
Albert Y. Zomaya[1], and Zahir Tari[3]

[1] Centre for Distributed and High Performance Computing,
The University of Sydney, Sydney, NSW, Australia
{reza.hoseiny,albert.zomaya}@sydney.edu.au
[2] Department of Computing, Macquarie University, Sydney, NSW, Australia
young.lee@mq.edu.au
[3] School of Computer Science and IT, RMIT University, Melbourne, VIC, Australia
zahir.tari@rmit.edu.au

Abstract. Function as a Service (FaaS) is a recent event-driven server-less paradigm that allows enterprises to build their applications in a fault tolerant distributed manner. Having been considered as an attractive replacement of traditional Service Oriented Architecture (SOA), the FaaS platform leverages the management of massive data sets or the handling of event streams. However, the realization of such leverage is largely dependent on the effective exploitation of FaaS elasticity/scalability.

In this paper, we present a closed-loop resource allocation controller to dynamically scale resources by predicting the future rate of incoming events and by considering the Quality of Service (QoS) enforcements requested by end-users. The performance evaluation is carried out by comparing the proposed controller with some well-known heuristics such as round robin and best-effort strategies. Experimental results confirm that the proposed controller increases the overall resource utilization by 21% on average, while reducing QoS violations by a factor of almost 3.

Keywords: Function as a Service (FaaS) · Microservices · Serverless
Lambda Platform · Dynamic resource allocation

1 Introduction

Function as a Service (FaaS) provides enterprises with a cloud-native serverless solution to build robust, scalable, and loosely-coupled distributed applications with a low operational cost. Clients can use such a platform to encapsulate the complex business logic into independent micro-services that communicate with each other via provided application programming interfaces (API). The FaaS platform is responsible for responding properly to outside events by triggering calls to such APIs in a loosely-coupled manner [16]. Amazon Web Services (AWS) and Google provide an enterprise-scale realization of such a paradigm as the *AWS*

© Springer International Publishing AG 2017
M. Maximilien et al. (Eds.): ICSOC 2017, LNCS 10601, pp. 241–255, 2017.
https://doi.org/10.1007/978-3-319-69035-3_17

Lambda [1] and *Google Cloud Functions* [12] services, respectively. Due to the intrinsic ability of FaaS to be hosted as a platform for concrete implementation of applications that follow decoupled architecture principles, it is believed to play the major role of future SOA [1,14,18]. In this paper, we use FaaS and Lambda platform interchangeably.

By using a combination of in-house and cloud-based FaaS servers, developers can put their attentions fully to the design and implementation of business logic without concerning about activities related to servers' maintenance issues (such as server provisioning, capacity planning, configuration setup, deploying the micro-services, and so on). The main idea behind using a FaaS platform is to remove the need for the traditional "always on" servers running behind the users' scripts [26]. FaaS can remarkably bring down the operational cost at least in a twofold aspect. In particular, its adoption helps in realizing "pay-per-use" pricing at finer granularity than current hourly base cloud pricing. In addition, it enables users to create applications much faster by developing fine-grained actions (e.g., micro-services) rather than handling coarse-grained components (e.g., monolithic applications); this in turn contributes to cost reduction.

To enable better scaling, a service provider of FaaS platform may decide to host thousands of function services (or Lambda functions in AWS Lambda) on the available resources to achieve both clients and operator goals with low cost. In many situations, however, these goals are conflicting with each other, e.g. the fast execution time demanded by the end-users versus the high resource utilization targeted by the service providers. Scheduling and resource allocation plays a crucial role in reconciling these conflicting objectives. Current resource allocation strategies for distributed systems and virtualized platforms are often QoS-oblivious. In other words, resource allocation is carried out irrespective of the QoS requirement of each application or the ever-changing resource utilization level of each host [29,32]. While each application has its own utilization characteristics (e.g. CPU/memory requirements) and different incoming traffic rate of each event source, none of them is known to the scheduler in advance [28,30,33].

In this paper, we present a closed-loop (feedback) resource controller, which increases the overall utilization of the resources while achieving QoS levels enforced by the end-users. The proposed controller makes its decisions based on the following parameters in each time epoch: (1) an estimation of the generation rate of events associated with each FaaS function that is taking place in the near future time periods, (2) the amount of QoS violation incidents occurred in the past epochs as the feedback loop, and (3) the reconfiguration cost (similar to the migration cost in a hypervisor-based system). We have conducted our evaluation study with two existing heuristics (round-robin and best-effort) with respect to three different metrics of resource utilization, QoS violation and scalability. Our solution outperforms both the round-robin and best-effort strategies by an average improvement of 21% in the overall resource utilization, while it reduces the QoS violation incidents by a factor of 3 on average.

The rest of the article is organized as follows. In Sect. 2, we give the background knowledge and related work associated with the FaaS platform. In Sect. 3, we define a metric for measuring QoS violation incidents. Section 4 formally presents the design principle of our resource allocation controller. In Sect. 5, we evaluate the performance of our solution through experiments on real systems. We then draw our conclusion in Sect. 6.

2   Background and Related Work

To build an application using a FaaS (Lambda) platform, the software development team needs to represent the whole business logic as the two core components of *actions* and *event sources*. An event is simply the detection of an internal or external condition which triggers a signal to be sent to a set of proper actions [6]. Examples include a change in database records, reading data by an Internet of things (IoT) sensor, posting a new tweet, an HTTP request, and a file uploading notice. Each event normally invokes a corresponding action by triggering a specific set of rules that is defined by the application owner.

Nevertheless, a FaaS action (also called *Lambda function* in platforms like AWS Lambda) is a piece of code which must be instantaneously executed whenever a corresponding event trigger fires. In some platforms, a chain of actions can be defined such that each action is executed one after another once the associated event occurs [17]. Each action needs to be designed as a *stateless* (or idempotent) component; hence, all the required data must be given as the input parameters [16]. This allows the platform to execute multiple instantiations of an action at the same time, while each instantiation keeps its own state. Typical examples of use-cases that can be adapted seemly to this paradigm include decomposition of traditional applications into micro-services, mobile server-side applications, file processing, big data analytic, and web servers [1,17,18].

The kernel of FaaS/Lambda platform is responsible for determining the amount of CPU, RAM, and other resources that must be devoted to the run-time in order to execute instantiations of every action. We assume that every action in the system is accompanied by a QoS enforcement level which is stated in the service level agreement (SLA). This value defines the minimum service level (expressed as a set of performance metrics) to be guaranteed by the platform for actions.

QoS enforcements and the concept of fairness can significantly affect the way that a resource allocation strategy works. Many studies in the context of the distributed platforms tend to focus on devising a "fair" resource allocation strategy, e.g. [5,9,10,23]. Some suggested that simply minimizing the total number of QoS violations is sufficient for satisfying SLA, e.g., [3]. In contrast, Gabor *et al.* [9] justified that employing a *fair* schema (as suggested by [5,10,23]) cannot always provide a proper satisfaction level in such systems as promised. Gabor *et al.* in [9] also showed that in a fair resource allocation strategy a situation can be considered good as long as almost every action running in the system experiences a similar performance degradation level (even a severe one).

Obviously such a constraint is not permissible in practice; hence, *fair policy* cannot lead a desirable output for all cases. Yet the strategy suggested by [3] which minimizes the number of QoS violations could cause some adverse consequence, too. Let us consider a moment when the rate of multiple events abruptly increases at once. So, applying the avoidance strategy proposed in [3] might end up revoking resources from important actions, as such a strategy only concerns with reducing the total number of QoS violations of all hosts. As a result, our aim is to find a sensible objective function to minimize explicitly the number of QoS violations of *important* actions/clients in case of *resource scarcity*. It seems that a similar metric first proposed by [15,16] can be adjusted to the new platform.

The goal of an elastic solution is to devise some mechanisms to scale up or down the assigned resources when the rate of requests fluctuates. Authors in [8,31] introduced several techniques that use threshold-based rules on the actual CPU and I/O capacities for deciding when to add/remove resources. In [11] a new metric called *congestion* index was introduced to decide the number of replica in an SPE platform. However, almost all techniques ignore different level of QoS constraints that can be enforced by different applications. Our approach is different from the mentioned projects as we propose a well-defined controlling mechanism to be replaced with a heuristic-based algorithm. To this end, we introduce a set of metrics to address the resource utilization, QoS constraints, and the cost of changing re-configuration.

3   QoS Detriment Metric

We define a metric to distinguish a situation where any QoS violation happens during the execution time (the original idea is borrowed from [15]). Apparently different applications tolerate the performance degradation occurrence in different manners (e.g., delay in average response time). For example, the QoS level of actions tied with the applications in the high-frequency trading domain can be easily affected by any delay in response time, while an action in the domain of environmental monitoring is less sensitive to such an issue. This confirms that the service provider has to devise a mechanism to categorize and charge applications' owners independently based on their QoS levels. In this section, we explain why both solutions might lead to some adverse outcomes in a Lambda platform. We then fill this gap by introducing a new metric, called *QoS detriment*, to quantify the QoS violation incidents.

We assume that there are exactly Q different classes, each represents a QoS contract that users can ask. We also assume that the desirable performance metric from user's perspective is the average end-to-end delay of running the corresponding actions during a given interval $T = (t, t + \Delta T)$. Thus, a value of ω_q^* is assigned to each class $1 \leq q \leq Q$ (q is the quantifier of each QoS class) that represents an upper-bound of the absolute delay that is acceptable and must be guaranteed by the Lambda kernel for all actions that belong to class q. To decide if an action experiences a QoS *violation* within a given interval, we need to compare the value of the measured target performance (i.e., end-to-end delay) with the value of ω_q^*.

However, avoiding QoS violation incidents is almost impossible when actions are executed. To relax this limit, we allow the resource allocation controller to violate QoS constraints for some actions in a managed way. Thus, we define a new function for each class of QoS contract, denoted by $\mathcal{V}_q(\Delta T)$, that accepts class q as its input, and its output regulates the percentage of QoS violation incidents that is allowed to happen during any interval of size ΔT for all actions belong to such a class.

Based on this new concept, we can express the definition of a QoS violation incident as follows. A sensible choice for $\mathcal{V}$ is a simple linear rule like $\mathcal{V} = 1 - \frac{q}{Q+C}$, where C is a constant and Q denotes the total number of QoS contract classes. Thus, for any arbitrary action a_i that belongs to class q, we say it is experiencing a QoS violation incident during any arbitrary interval T if the delay of processing is higher than ω_q^* for a fraction of time more than $\left(1 - \frac{q}{Q+C}\right)\%$ of any arbitrary interval.

We can define *QoS detriment*, denoted by $\mathcal{D}_{m,T}$, as a metric to quantify the total amount of QoS violations happening in any host m as follows.

$$\mathcal{D}_{m,T} = \sum_{a_i \in \mathcal{V}_{m,T}} \mathcal{I}(a_i), \tag{1}$$

where $\mathcal{V}_{m,T}$ denotes the set of Lambda functions experiencing a QoS violation during interval T. Symbol $\mathcal{I}(a_i)$ is the *importance* coefficient of each action a_i. This term expresses the amount of contribution of action a_i to the total amount of QoS detriment factor in case of a_i experiences any QoS violation. One good candidate for such an importance function can be regarded as $\mathcal{I}(a_i) = q_{a_i}$. This means the higher the QoS enforcement level is, the more it is counted in Eq. 1. One of the main goals of our work is to cut (or reduce) the total amount of QoS enforcement over all running hosts, i.e., to decrease $\sum_{m,T} \mathcal{D}_{m,T}$.

4   Closed-Loop Resource Allocation Controller

The proposed strategy is essentially a closed-loop (feedback) model predictive controller (MPC) that seeks a model to predict the dynamic behavior of the underlying platform in the near future, and then makes the (near-) optimal decision based on the value of input vectors as the feedback loop. The resource allocation controller employs an action that forces the output of the system to follow a *"reference trajectory"*. Such a method has been widely accepted in multiple domains of computing systems, such as energy-aware capacity provisioning in Cloud platforms [15,21], as well as elastic scaling of stream data processing [3,4]. Interested readers are referred to [25] for a thorough review in the theory and design of MPC.

There are three main components of the proposed controller: the *model*, the *predictor*, and the *optimizer*. The model provides the controller with an abstraction layer of the run-time behavior of the Lambda platform. The predictor can be used by the controller to give a rough estimation of future input values such as incoming traffic rates. The optimizer is responsible for finding the best possible values for controllable variables, which are denoted by $\mathbf{u}_\tau$, such that the output of the system, shown by $\mathbf{z}_\tau$, converges to an ideal set-point trajectory, denoted as $\mathbf{r}_\tau$, at any time τ.

An important property of the proposed controller is that we gradually (i.e., in more than one step) apply the supposedly optimum input vector, i.e., $\tilde{\mathbf{u}}_{\tau+1}$, into the system. More formally, let us suppose that $\mathcal{T}_{ref} > 1$ represent a response speed. Also, let us assume that $\zeta_\tau = |\mathbf{z}_\tau - \mathbf{r}_\tau|$ represent the deviation of the current output from the ideal set-point trajectory, at time τ. In our controller, we expect that such a deviation converges to zero with an exponential rate in the next f steps, i.e., $\zeta_{\tau+f} = e^{-f\Delta/\mathcal{T}_{ref}}\zeta_\tau$, where Δ is the sampling interval. For example, choosing the ratio of $\Delta/\mathcal{T}_{ref} = 1/3$ is a sensible choice in practical situations that not only imposes a low computational overhead, but also provides an effective mechanism to reduce the adverse impact of errors in the prediction tool or the system model.

Response Time Model. We use a Kalman filter as a light optimal estimator tool to effectively infer input parameters from uncertain past observations by taking advantage of correlations between the values of the system state and the input vector. By propagating the current state of the system, including the statistical influence of dynamic perturbations and the outcomes of all previous measurements, the Kalman filter can minimize the mean square error of the estimated input parameters if the system noise is Gaussian [13].

Let $\bar{\mathcal{N}}(e_j, \tau)$ and $\bar{T}(a_i, \tau)$ denote the average number of events emitted by the event source e_j and the average computation time of the associated action a_i at any arbitrary interval τ, respectively. Hence, the average response time of the event e_j associated with each instance of the action a_i at machine p_k, shown by $RT^\tau_{a_i|p_k}$, can be estimated by employing a proper Kalman filter over the past record of resource usage measurements allocated in each machine to run the action at any arbitrary interval τ. For the sake of this project, we focus our attention on CPU and RAM as the two main resources in each server, but an extension of this work can be employed to include other I/O or network resources similarly. The values of dependency of response time parameter to the resource utilization need to be continuously updated whenever a new measurement data is collected by the controller.

Prediction Model. To predict the future values of non-controllable input parameters (i.e., $\bar{\mathcal{N}}(e_j, \tau)$, as an indicator for the future rate of incoming events, and $\bar{T}(a_i, \tau)$ as an indicator for the total computational requests), we employ the well-known auto regressive integrated moving average (ARIMA). Using such a model, the future values of a random variable, such as $\hat{u}$, can be prognosticated by applying a linear model over a series of past observations as: $\hat{u}_\tau = c + \epsilon_t + \sum_{\ell=1}^h \beta_\ell u_{\tau-\ell} + \theta_\ell \epsilon_{\tau-\ell}$, where c is a constant and ϵ's are *independent* and *identically distributed* errors from a normal distribution with mean zero and a finite variance, e.g., a *white noise function*. β_ℓ's and θ_ℓ's are coefficients to be updated using least-squares regression method right after a new observation becomes known.

Optimization Process. The controller continuously solves an optimization problem with an objective function that is the sum of three cost functions as given below.

- *Resource utilization residue* ($\mathcal{C}_{(U)}$). The study in [27] discussed the need to keep CPU utilization constantly between 60%–80% in order to reach the best balance between the performance of each host and its energy consumption (the exact value depends on the CPU architecture). We use the residue function to penalize any derivation from the ideal utilization level for CPU. We propose a cost function that penalizes more any derivation from the upper bound comparing to the derivation from the lower threshold, employing such a cost function enables us to avoid the exploitation of full CPU capacity, known as "meltdown point" problem, that has the over-utilized CPU become a bottleneck of the system.

$$\mathcal{C}_{(U)} = \begin{cases} |\frac{U - \mathcal{U}_{CPU}^{*,upper}}{1 - \mathcal{U}_{CPU}^{*,upper}}|^2 & \text{if } U \geq \mathcal{U}_{CPU}^{*,upper} \\ 0 & \text{if } \mathcal{U}_{CPU}^{*,lower} \leq U \leq \mathcal{U}_{CPU}^{*,upper} \\ |1 - \frac{U}{\mathcal{U}_{CPU}^{*,lower}}|^2 & \text{if } U \leq \mathcal{U}_{CPU}^{*,lower} \end{cases}, \tag{2}$$

where U is the measured value of average CPU utilization of the host at any given interval.
- *Total QoS detriment* ($\sum_{p_k} \mathcal{D}_{p_k}$). To favor a resource allocation decision that results in fewer QoS violations, we propose a cost function that explicitly evaluates the sum of QoS detriment over all machines (Sect. 3).
- *Total switching cost* ($\sum \mathcal{SW}$). Changing the current configuration is costly. The switching cost evaluates the difference (e.g. the Euclidean norm) between the decision vectors applied at two successive steps to avoid exceeding changes in the configuration states. This enables the controller to be more conservative in adopting abrupt changes in the reconfiguration decisions.

The proposed objective function to be minimized is expressed as the sum of three above-mentioned costs as Eq. 3.

$$\min \mathcal{J}_\tau = \sum_{t=\tau+1}^{\tau+f} \sum_{p_k} \left(\gamma_1 \mathcal{C}_{(U)} + \gamma_2 \mathcal{D}_{p_k,t} + \gamma_3 \mathcal{SW}_t \right), \tag{3}$$

where f is the prediction horizon length, and γ_i coefficients are the weight for each cost function to be set separately. We compute the norm of a normalized vector of all terms in Eq. 3 whose components are the original values of the measured/estimated values of the corresponding metrics, each divided by its maximum expected value. For simplicity, we use equal weights for γ_i's in this paper. While the optimizer module solves the above problem for the future $f > 1$

steps, the controller only applies the solution for the *first* step as the system's input vector. Then, the whole cycle of prediction and optimization process is repeated in the next step (as the *feedback* loop).

To solve the optimization problem, we use a technique based on particle swarm optimization (PSO) heuristic. PSO is a population based stochastic optimization technique developed by Eberhart and Kennedy in 1995 as an advanced fast evolutionary computational technique [20] for solving continuous and discrete optimization problems with multiple local extrema. PSO can converge to the (near-) optimal results in a faster, cheaper way comparing with other optimization methods [24].

We adopt two additional techniques to reduce the potentially large computational overhead due the exponential size of the feasible state space. Firstly, we allow the optimization module to run only for a fix fraction (e.g. 1%) of the control step interval. For example, if ΔT is selected to be one minute, then the maximum time that the solver is allowed to find a solution is limited to 600 ms. Within such a period, the best solution obtained by the PSO solver, is considered as the input vector of the controller in the next step. Secondly, we allow the PSO solver to continue searching for a better solution until the data of the next step comes out. While such a solution cannot be used for the system input at the current step, it is greatly beneficial as the starting point for the next round of the PSO solver.

5   Experimental Evaluation

In this section, we present our evaluation results in terms of primarily (1) response time (latency), (2) resource utilization and (3) QoS violations. We also present the sensitivity analysis and the scalability of our resource controller.

5.1   Experimental Setup

System Environment. We evaluated our approach by conducting an extensive set of experiments on our local cluster to measure the effectiveness of our approach with respect to the three parameters of resource utilization, QoS violation incidents, and scalability. We used a local cluster consisting of two machines with a total of 16 cores, and 32 GB of main memory. Each machine equipped with a 3.40 GHz i7 CPU, 16 GB of RAM, and 8 MB LLC and Ubuntu 14.04. To imitate a heterogeneous environment, we use Xen hypervisor 4.4.2 to create 8 virtual machines each with one dedicated core and 2 GB of main memory (one VM shared with Dom-0), and another 4 virtual machines (VM), each with two dedicated cores and 4 GB of RAM. All Dom-0 and guest VMs run the same Linux kernel version 4.2.0.

The proposed solution as a feedback controller for the above-mentioned platform is implemented in Python 2.7 and runs in a dedicated machine equipped with Intel i7-4712HQ 2.3 GHz with 16 GB of RAM, and 512 Samsung PM851 SSD disk. We installed *Dask* framework [22] on all guest VMs to implement a Lambda platform as a distributed cluster. Being equipped with a versatile library for distributed computing over a cluster of hundreds of machines, Dask provides a library for running a set of pre-defined functions in parallel and/or out-of-core computational fashion [19]. The Dask model allows us to build a complex network of actions that might depend on each other to be run once after an associated event occur. It has dynamic asynchronous primitives that provide a very low-latency mechanism among working threads. Due to its asynchronous nature, the task scheduler of Dask framework can flexibly handle a variety of functions simultaneously [22].

Workload Attributes. We created a synthetic event/action data-set by analyzing on a subset of real twitter data gathered by [2]. For the scope of this paper, our comprehensive analysis relies on a synthetic workload that runs in our own test-bed, we left exploration of such an analysis in the real implementation with alternatives found in the industry as a subject for future investigation.

We created $|\mathcal{A}| = \{10, 20, 30, 40, 50, 60\}$ functions each running either a web-service script, representing *latency-sensitive* workloads, or a data-analytic script, representing *data-intensive* workloads. Both workloads are taken from Cloud-Suite benchmark [7]. Each action $a_i \in \mathcal{A}$ is associated with only one event source e_i. The rate of event generation of each event source is taken from a Poisson distribution with parameter of $\lambda \in \{1, 3, 6\}$. The λ parameter indicates the average number of events generated per millisecond. The execution time required to process each event ranges from 40 ms up to 21 s, with an average of 1078 ms. The number of generated events per action in each scenario varies from 5000 to 10000 depending on the scenario parameters, with an average of 7000 events per action. We allow each scenario to run for the period of one hour. There are two different QoS enforcement classes, i.e. $|Q| = 2$ in our setting. The associated upper bounds of QoS classes are $\mathcal{V}_{q=1..2} \in \{0.99, .090\}$. In this way, we assign each stream to one of the QoS classes randomly. We choose the sampling interval epoch and the maximum number of CPU cores to be used in each scenario to be one second and $M = 16$, respectively.

Compared Heuristics. The proposed solution is compared against two other heuristics, namely *round robin* and *best-effort*. The former uses a round robin policy to balance the associated events amongst the associated threads with the main aim of distributing evenly the incoming events among each Lambda functions. This is the policy which is mainly implemented in major Lambda engines, including IBM OpenWhisk. Based on our implementation, we fixed the number of threads associated with each action based on the QoS class that it belongs to (i.e. 9 and 7 for two different QoS classes, respectively).

The best-effort approach uses first fit decreasing (FFD) algorithm to determine the number of appropriate worker threads per Lambda function in order to achieve a compromise between resources' usages and QoS violation incidents. Best-effort adds an additional worker thread only if the amount of QoS violation experienced by the corresponding function exceeds a certain threshold (i.e. 2 min in our experiments). Further, if a physical host becomes fully utilized, then best-effort looks for the next machine to execute a thread.

5.2 Results

All reported analytical results reflect the behavior of the system when the performance of the system remains stable right after passing a short transient state. During such a transient period, the latency of serving events might be noticeably higher than its average in the steady states. We left the study of the transient period behavior of a Lambda platform as a future work.

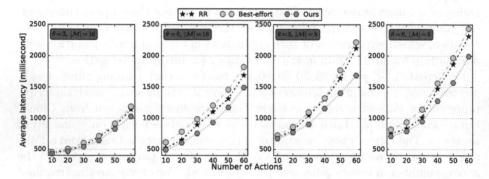

Fig. 1. Average latency achieved by the proposed algorithm against round robin and best-effort as the number of actions varies from 10 to 60. Scenarios are distinguished by different values of $\theta \in \{3, 6\}$, and number of cores $|\mathcal{M}| \in \{8, 16\}$.

Response Time. Figure 1 demonstrates the average response time (latency) achieved by our approach as it is compared with the other two heuristics in four different scenarios. The x axis in all figures represents the number of Lambda functions that is increasing gradually from 10 to 60. Each scenario differs with another one with respect to either the event generation rate, θ, or the maximum number of cores that can be employed in that scenario, denoted by $|\mathcal{M}|$. The result achieved by the proposed approach when $\theta = 1$ is similar to the ones shown here and we do not repeat them.

The trend confirms that the response time monotonically increases when the number of actions increases (from 10 to 60) or when the rate of event generation increases (from 1 to 6) irrespective of resource allocation strategies. Further, no anomalies can be seen in any scenario. This result is expected because the workload of each working thread monotonically increases in both cases. However, the effectiveness of both the round-robin and best-effort schema is less than the proposed algorithm mainly because ours can dynamically adapt to the spike in the event generation rates by assigning more computing resources to those actions which are suffering from obtaining enough resources to process the corresponding events (as reflected via the first term of the objective function). Particularly, the improvement in average processing time per Lambda function achieved by the proposed controller is more significant when $\theta = 6$ (high incoming traffic rate) and less resources are available. Overall, the proposed controller enhances the average processing time by 19.9% on average compared with the best outcome of other two heuristics.

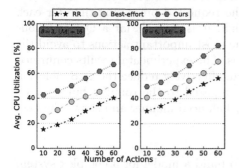

Fig. 2. Steady state core utilization for active CPUs which are appointed by different resource allocation policies to run some Lambda functions. Two Scenarios are selected based on different values of θ as the event generation rate, and the total number of available cores, $|\mathcal{M}|$, to be employed by each policy.

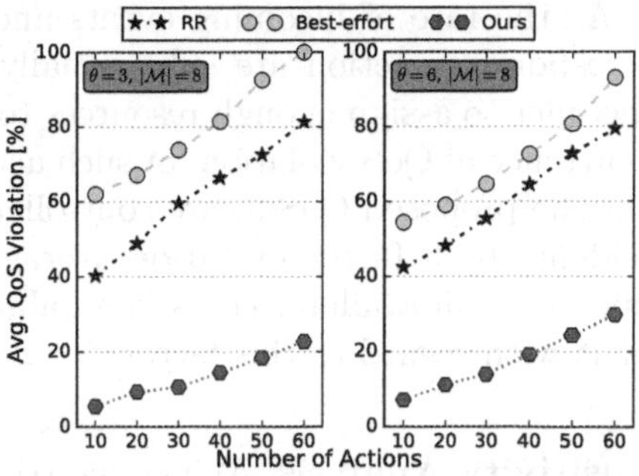

Fig. 3. Normalized percentage of QoS violation incidents achieved by each resource allocation heuristic as the number of Lambda functions varies from 10 to 60 for the two extreme scenarios when $|\mathcal{M}| = 8$. The improvement of the proposed solution is 301% in average (max 358%) comparing to round-robin policy.

Resource Utilization. Figure 2 depicts a summary of the average core utilization gathered in all machines achieved by three resource allocation strategies under the two synthetic scenarios distinguished by different values of θ as the event generation rate, and the total number of accessible cores by each policy, $|\mathcal{M}|$. A significant achievement by applying the proposed controller is its ability to keep the utilization of all the employed CPU cores around the ideal utilization level in most scenarios (which is set to between [60%–80%] throughout the experiments). Such an achievement can be leveraged by putting other non-working cores into the deep sleep mode to save energy usage.

In contrary, both the round robin and best-effort policies are oblivious of such ideal level. By employing almost all available cores blindly, these policies keep the CPU utilization of some cores higher than the ideal level, i.e., more than 80%, while allowing the rest of cores run at a level much below the ideal value. It is worth noting that because the core utilization has a direct impact on the total energy consumption of each host, it is desirable to force each core to work either on 0% or close to the ideal level. Altogether, the results obtained from all experiments scenarios (including those who are not depicted here) revealed that the proposed controller enhances the utilization of working CPUs by 21% on average compared with the best outcome of the other heuristics which is achieved by employing best-effort policy.

QoS Violation. Figure 3 depicts the percentage of QoS violation incidents, according to the definition of QoS detriment metric in Sect. 3. The results compared the amount of QoS violation achieved by the proposed controller versus those achieved by the other two strategies. We only depict the results in scenarios that the event generation rate is deliberately high, i.e., the value of θ is 6, while the number of CPU cores to be used in each scenario is low (=8).

As the rate of incoming events and the requested processing time for each corresponding action are substantially high, it is difficult for a QoS-oblivious scheduler to assign enough resources to the most important actions to avoid the occurrence of QoS violation for such actions. The experimental results confirmed that the proposed QoS-aware controller can effectively reduce the QoS violation incidents by a factor of 3.0 on average compared to the round-robin strategy which uses all available cores in an almost balanced manner and shows the best result with regard to this factor.

Sensitivity Analysis. When one tries to build a model for a complex system (such as a Lamdba platform), it is almost impossible to prevent the occurrence of errors in prediction phase. A promising controller must be tolerant to the negative consequences of such errors in the decision making phase. To help reduce the risk of such errors, we incorporate two methods in the proposed controller as follows.

– Using ϵ_t in prediction model to explicitly introduce randomness
– Choose the value of response speed rate, $\mathcal{T}_{ref}$, strictly greater than one (in our case 3). Such a selection allows the system to gradually adapt to the input changes in more than one step (see Sect. 4).

To perform the sensitivity analysis, we first start with a prediction model with zero error. Progressively, we inject errors ranging from 10% to 90% to the prediction of input variables, and then measure the influence of such errors on the system outputs. We define a parameter called *sensitivity coefficient*, denoted by κ, for each performance metrics, such as Z, as follows.

$$\kappa_{\epsilon,Z} = \frac{\|Z(x) - Z(x \pm \epsilon)\|}{\|Z(x)\|} \tag{4}$$

κ reflects how much the target output is sensitive when the input parameter x is estimated with an error of ϵ_x.

Figure 4 shows a summary of average sensitivity coefficients for both response time and CPU utilization with respect to the errors in the prediction model. The trend confirms that even an error of 90% puts a little negative stress on the target performance metrics (below 34% in the worst case scenario).

Scalability. As we force the optimizer module to return the best achievable solution found within the 1% of the time-frame, the computational time of the proposed controller is limited to a fixed amount (e.g., 600 ms in our experiments).

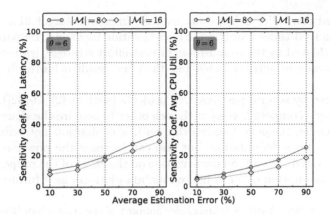

Fig. 4. The sensitivity coefficient curve for two parameters of average latency (left) and average CPU utilization (right) as the prediction error varies from 10% to 90% (x-axis).

We performed a set of experiments (by increasing the number of active cores and Lambda actions) to examine the scalability of the proposed controller. So, we allow the optimizer module to find an approximate solution within 10% of the optimal solution and collect the running time of such an optimizer. Table 1 presents the computational time that the optimizer module needs to find such a solution. The results confirmed that the technique can find a reasonable effective solution in less than 2.15 s when the number of machines and Lambda actions increase to 100 and 800, respectively.

Table 1. Average Running time of the optimizer module to find an 1.1 approximation solution when the number of cores and FaaS actions varies.

$|\mathcal{M}|$	$|\mathcal{A}|$	Running time
30	100	0.7 s
50	250	1.05 s
100	800	2.15 s

6 Conclusion

Understanding the run-time behavior of FaaS/Lambda functions can be of great practical importance for designing efficient resource allocation strategies for a FaaS/Lambda platform. We have presented a solution based on the famous model predictive controller (MPC) for achieving a dynamic QoS-aware resource allocation in such a platform. Our solution makes appropriate resource allocation decisions by predicting the future rate of events coming to the system as well as considering the QoS enforcements requested by each function.

The proposed controller achieves an average improvement of 21% in resource utilization and a 3-times reduction of QoS-violation incidents compared with the best result achieved by the round-robin or best-effort strategy, while maintaining the mean latency of actions 19.9% less than the result achieved by best-effort strategy.

As reported by several past research projects (such as [27, 29, 32]), collocated applications can compete fiercely with each other to acquire the shared resources (e.g., CPU cache, memory bandwidth). Such a contention not only causes an overall performance degradation, but also can increase the power consumption of the whole system. We left an investigation on the effect of the proposed method on energy consumption of an in-house Lambda platform as a future work.

Acknowledgments. Authors acknowledge support of the Australian Research Council Linkage-Industry Grant (LP160100406). Authors are also thankful to the anonymous reviewers whose constructive suggestions helped improve and clarify this manuscript.

References

1. Amazon Inc.: AWS Lambda: How It Works (2016). http://docs.aws.amazon.com/lambda/
2. Cheng, Z., Caverlee, J., Lee, K., Sui, D.: Exploring millions of footprints in location sharing services. In: International Conference on Weblogs & Social, pp. 81–88. AAAI (2011)
3. De Matteis, T., Mencagli, G.: Proactive elasticity and energy awareness in data stream processing. J. Syst. Softw. **127**(C), 302–319 (2017)
4. De Matteis, T., Mencagli, G.: Keep calm & react with foresight: strategies for low-latency & energy-efficient elastic data stream processing. In: SIGPLAN Principles & Practice of Parallel Programming, pp. 13:1–13:12. ACM (2016)
5. Ebrahimi, E., Lee, C.J., Mutlu, O., Patt, Y.N.: Prefetch-aware shared resource management for multi-core systems. In: International Symposium on Computer Architecture, ISCA 2011, vol. 39, pp. 141–152. ACM (2011)
6. Faison, T.: Event-Based Programming: Taking Events to the Limit. Apress, Berkely (2006)
7. Ferdman, M., Adileh, A., Kocberber, O., Volos, S., Alisafaee, M., Jevdjic, D., Kaynak, C., et al.: Clearing the clouds: a study of emerging scale-out workloads on modern hardware. SIGPLAN Not. **47**(4), 37–48 (2012)
8. Fernandez, R.C., Migliavacca, M., Kalyvianaki, E., Pietzuch, P.: Integrating scale out & fault tolerance in stream proc. using operator state management. In: SIGMOD Management of Data, pp. 725–736. ACM (2013)
9. Gabor, R., Mendelson, A., Weiss, S.: Service level agreement for multithreaded processors. ACM Trans. Archit. Code Optim. **6**(2), 1–33 (2009)
10. Gabor, R., Weiss, S., Mendelson, A.: Fairness enforcement in switch on event multithreading. ACM Trans. Archit. Code Optim. **4**(3), 34 (2007)
11. Gedik, B., Schneider, S., Hirzel, M., Wu, K.L.: Elastic scaling for data stream processing. IEEE Trans. Parallel Distrib. Syst. **25**(6), 1447–1463 (2014)
12. Google Inc.: Google Cloud Functions (2016). http://cloud.google.com/functions/docs/

13. Grewal, M.S., Andrews, A.P.: Kalman Filtering: Theory and Practice with MAT-LAB, 4th edn. Wiley-IEEE Press (2014)
14. Heck, D.: Lambda architecture with SAP HANA platform (2016). www.linkedin.com/pulse/ep-7-lambda-architecture-sap-hana-platform-didier-heck
15. Hoseinyfarahabady, M., Lee, Y.C., Zomaya, A., Tari, Z., Song, A.: A model predictive controller for contention-aware resource allocation in virtualized data centers. In: Symposium on Modeling, Analysis & Simulation of Computer & Telecommunication Systems (MASCOTS 2016), pp. 277–282. IEEE, London (2016)
16. Hoseinyfarahabady, M., Taheri, J., Tari, Z., Zomaya, A.: A dynamic resource controller for a lambda architecture. In: 46th International Conference on Parallel Processing (ICPP). IEEE, Bristol (2017)
17. IBM Corp.: High Level Architecture (2016). http://developer.ibm.com/openwhisk/
18. IBM Corp.: IBM Bluemix OpenWhisk (2016). www.ibm.com/cloud-computing/bluemix/openwhisk/
19. VanderPlas, J.: Out-of-Core Dataframes in Python (2015). http://jakevdp.github.io/blog/2015/08/14/out-of-core-dataframes-in-python/
20. Kennedy, J., Eberhart, R.: Particle swarm optimization. In: Neural Networks, vol. 4, pp. 1942–1948. IEEE, November 1995
21. Kusic, D., Kephart, J.O., Hanson, J.E., Kandasamy, N., Jiang, G.: Power & performance management of virtualized computing environments via lookahead control. Cluster Comput. **12**(1), 1–15 (2009)
22. Rocklin, M.: Dask (2017). http://dask.pydata.org
23. Mutlu, O., Moscibroda, T.: Stall-time fair memory access scheduling for chip multi-processors. In: Symposium on Microarchitecture, pp. 146–160. IEEE/ACM (2007)
24. Poli, R., Kennedy, J., Blackwell, T.: Particle swarm optimization. Swarm Intell. **1**(1), 33–57 (2007)
25. Rawlings, J.B., Mayne, D.Q.: Model Predictive Control: Theory and Design. Nob Hill, Madison (2009)
26. Sbarski, P.: Serverless Architectures on AWS: With examples using AWS Lambda. Manning Publications, Shelter Island (2017)
27. Srikantaiah, S., Kansal, A., Zhao, F.: Energy aware consolidation for cloud computing. In: Power Aware Computing and Systems, HotPower 2008, p. 10. USENIX Association (2008)
28. Subramanian, L., Seshadri, V., Ghosh, A., Khan, S., Mutlu, O.: The application slowdown model: Quantifying and controlling the impact of inter-application interference at shared caches and main memory. In: International Symposium on Microarchitecture, pp. 62–75. MICRO-48. ACM (2015)
29. Tembey, P., Gavrilovska, A., Schwan, K.: Merlin: application & platform-aware resource allocation in consol. servers. In: SOCC 2014, pp. 1–14 (2014)
30. Usui, H., Subramanian, L., Chang, K.K.W., Mutlu, O.: Dash: deadline-aware high-performance memory scheduler for heterogeneous systems with hardware accelerators. ACM Trans. Archit. Code Optim. **12**(4), 1–28 (2016)
31. Valduriez, P., Soriente, C., Jim, R.: Streamcloud: elastic & scalable data streaming. IEEE Trans. Parallel Distrib. Syst. **23**(12), 2351–2365 (2012)
32. Yang, H., Breslow, A., Mars, J., Tang, L.: Bubble-flux: precise online QOS management for increased utilization in warehouse scale computers. SIGARCH Comput. Archit. News **41**(3), 607–618 (2013)
33. Ye, K., Wu, Z., Wang, C., Zhou, B.B., Si, W., Jiang, X., Zomaya, A.Y.: Profiling-based workload consolidation and migration in virtualized data centers. IEEE Trans. Parallel Distrib. Syst. **26**(3), 878–890 (2015)

Probabilistic Qualitative Preference Matching in Long-Term IaaS Composition

Sajib Mistry[1](✉), Athman Bouguettaya[1], Hai Dong[2], and Abdelkarim Erradi[3]

[1] School of Information Technologies, University of Sydney, Sydney, Australia
{sajib.mistry,athman.bouguettaya}@sydney.edu.au
[2] School of Science, RMIT University, Melbourne, Australia
hai.dong@rmit.edu.au
[3] Department of Computer Science and Engineering, Qatar University, Doha, Qatar
erradi@qu.edu.qa

Abstract. We propose a qualitative similarity measure approach to select an optimal set of probabilistic Infrastructure-as-a-Service (IaaS) requests according to the provider's probabilistic preferences over a long-term period. The long-term qualitative preferences are represented in probabilistic temporal CP-Nets. The preferences are indexed in a k-d tree to enable the multidimensional similarity measure using tree matching approaches. A probabilistic range sampling approach is proposed to reduce the large multidimensional search space in temporal CP-Nets. A probability distribution matching approach is proposed to reduce the approximation error in the similarity measure. Experimental results prove the feasibility of the proposed approach.

1 Introduction

IaaS providers (e.g., Amazon and Windows Azure) offer Virtual Machines (VMs) as services in a cloud market [1]. IaaS services (i.e., configurations of VMs) are usually customized to fit the requirements of consumers. Consumers (e.g., universities, governments, and Software-as-a-Service (SaaS) providers) are more likely to require long-term IaaS services according to their business goals and budget constraints. A typical IaaS request includes functional attributes, such as CPU, memory, and network units, and Quality of Services (QoSs) attributes, such as availability, throughput, response time and price [1]. *The IaaS composition is defined as to select an optimal set of custom consumer requests that maximizes the revenue and profit of the provider* [8,16].

The provider's long-term business strategies are typically qualitative in nature. For example, the provider may have a promotional strategy (discounted prices for services) in the first year. In the following years, it may have profit-maximization strategies considering the market completion. Similarly, long-term consumer requests are usually variable over a time period and qualitative in nature. For example, a consumer may prefer an IaaS service that has higher throughput in the first year. While in the second year, the consumer may find throughput is less important and may require price-sensitive services.

M. Maximilien et al. (Eds.): ICSOC 2017, LNCS 10601, pp. 256–271, 2017.
https://doi.org/10.1007/978-3-319-69035-3_18

In the *qualitative IaaS composition*, the acceptance or rejection of an incoming request should follow the business strategies of the provider as accepted requests are committed for the whole period [9]. A key limitation of exiting approaches is that the business strategies need to be deterministic, i.e., the provider should have 100% confidence to determine future changes in advance. Another limitation is that consumers are not allowed to represent their preferences in a qualitative manner.

We consider probabilistic qualitative IaaS requests from the consumers and probabilistic qualitative business strategies of the providers in the long-term composition. Here, consumers provide their probabilistic IaaS service requests based on their predicted business needs. For example, a university may calculate the required IaaS services based on the number of students and staffs for the first year. However, there is a 40% chance that the number of students and staffs will increase in two folds in the second year. Hence, there is 60% probability that the consumer's preference will remain similar and 40% probability to be changed in the second year. Similarly, providers' business strategies are constructed based on different environment variables such as available resources and number of consumers. For example, business strategies are constructed assuming a fixed size of resources for a long-term period in [9]. However, such an assumption is hardly applicable in the real world as available resources tend to be probabilistic rather than deterministic. For example, the provider may invest in increasing new resources or sell a part of existing resources to other providers in the following years [5]. Similarly, the future demand for IaaS services is probabilistic in nature and hard to predict with 100% confidence.

We assume that an IaaS provider has already developed its long-term probabilistic qualitative service delivery preferences. It receives different long-term probabilistic qualitative service requirements from different consumers. Note that, how the probabilities are determined is out of the scope of this paper. *Our target is to find the optimal set of requests where their probable preferences are best matched with the provider's uncertain preferences.* We have identified the following research challenges in the probabilistic long-term IaaS composition:

- **Probabilistic temporal preference representation:** We require not only an intuitive tool for structuring the provider's qualitative preferences but also a support for assigning temporal transition probabilities. For example, a provider may prefer providing CPU based services over Network based services in the first year. In the second year, there is 80% probability that provider will stick to its existing preference order, but there is 20% probability to deliver services with a different preference order. The semantics of preferences may not be static during the whole period of composition. For example, 10ms response time is treated as a high QoS in this year, but it may become a moderate QoS in the next year due to an upgrade of the hardware in the market.
- **Probabilistic qualitative similarity measure:** Upon receiving probabilistic qualitative temporal preferences from the consumers, we have to quantify their similarity measure with the provider's temporal qualitative preferences.

However, as we are considering long-term composition, each time segments should have several probable temporal preferences and each of them may have several probable temporal preferences in the next temporal segments. Hence, the number of temporal sequences or orders of preferences might be large for the whole composition period. It is computationally inefficient to compare every pair of sequences for the similarity measure. We require a probabilistic similarity matching approach that can approximate to the optimal result using fewer number of comparisons.

We represent preferences in probabilistic Temporal CP-Nets (PrTempCP-Net), where dynamic TempCP-Nets have a transition probability matrix among composition intervals. The dynamic semantics of the preferences are indicated using a Conditional Preference Table (CPT) [3] of the PrTempCP-Net. We assume that the dynamic semantics of preferences are global across the consumers for simplicity. However, we transform semantics of consumers' preferences to match the dynamic semantics of the provider's preferences and apply composition aggregation rules [16] for the similarity measure. Moreover, the induced preference graph [13] from TempCP-Net is indexed in a multidimensional k-d tree [2] to effectively match with the attributes of the consumer preferences.

Although long-term IaaS composition is a preference maximization combinatorial optimization problem [8], *we only focus on probabilistic similarity matching approach in the composition.* We apply a brute force approach to generate all possible combinations of IaaS requests. Instead of comparing all preference sequences in the PrTempCP-Net (a computationally inefficient matching process), we propose a novel probabilistic range sampling approach. The ranges are selected in a way so that they approximate to an optimal spectrum of similarity deviations from any random preference sequences matching. We use the Kolmogorov-Smirnov test (K-S test) [4] as a statistical distribution matching algorithm to determine the weight of a given preference range in the similarity measure. The weighted similarity measures of all the preference range samples are aggregated to determine the highest matched, i.e., the optimal set of requests.

2   Related Work

Graphical models are proposed to represent user-preferences where relative ordering among preference attributes are determined by economic variables such as cost and profit [14]. A Conditional Preference Network (CP-Net) [3] is a dependency graph that represents consumers' preferences qualitatively. A CP-Net based graphical model is proposed for the service composition from the consumers' perspective [12]. The composition approach from incomplete consumer preferences [13] performs preference amendment, i.e., the similar consumer detection and historical preference voting. Graph based similarity measure are applied to find the optimal composition in web service compositions [7]. A deterministic temporal CP-Net is proposed to represent the provider's long-term qualitative preferences [9]. *To the best of our knowledge, exiting research does not consider probabilistic qualitative preferences in the long-term IaaS composition.*

Cluster sampling and multistage sampling are applied to generalize the results to the target population [10]. Convenience sampling and probabilistic range sampling are nonprobability sampling techniques which approximate a sample of subjects/units from a population [15]. It is useful especially when randomization is impossible like when the population is very large [15]. Kolmogorov-Smirnov (K-S) test is efficient to measure the similarity between the probability distributions of two samples [4]. *To the best of our knowledge, statistical analysis is yet to be applied to reduce the large search space and to perform similarity measure in the probabilistic qualitative IaaS composition.*

3   Motivation: Probabilistic Qualitative IaaS Composition

Let us assume, a new IaaS provider starts offering virtual CPU services associated with QoS of availability for simplicity. Consumer A and B are interested in using services from the provider. We assume that both the provider and consumers have same semantic interpretation of the qualitative preferences on CPU, availability, and price for simplicity. We represent the semantic levels as high, moderate, and low, as shown in Fig. 1(a).

The CP-Net can elegantly represent these qualitative preferences. For example, an arc from "CPU" to "availability" means the preference of "availability" depends on the preference of "CPU" units. The provider may have different business strategies represented in CP-Nets. For example, the provider prefers to provide high-quality services with relatively lower prices, to build its reputation in the market. Hence, the provider decides that "availability" of a service is the most important attribute, followed by "CPU" and "price". $CP1$ is the corresponding CP-Net for reputation building (Fig. 1(b)). In $CP1$, the "high" availability has a higher priority than the "moderate" availability, i.e., $A1 \succ A2$. Note that, the "low" availability ($A3$) is not in the provider's preference in $CP1$. The choice of availability dictates the choice of CPU units. Finally, the price of the service is chosen based on the selection of the levels of availability and CPU units. As this is a reputation building phase, the provider will not charge "high" price ($P1$) while providing "moderate" CPU units ($C2 : P2 \succ P3$). In $CP1$, the most preferred service provision is ($A1, C1, P1$) and the least preferred choice is ($A2, C1, P3$). Similarly, $CP2$ and $CP3$ capture the profit maximization and risk management strategies respectively (Fig. 1(b)). In $CP2$, the most preferred service provision is ($P1, C3, A3$) and the least preferred service is ($P2, C2, A2$) expressing the preference on the higher price. In $CP3$, the most preferred service provision is ($C3, P1, A3$) and the least preferred service provision is ($C2, P3, A3$).

Consumers may have different qualitative preferences represented in CP-Nets based on their requirements. In Fig. 1(c), $CP4$ captures the "availability sensitive" preferences. Here, consumers do not prefer "low" availability and are able to pay "high" price for "high" availability and CPU units. $CP5$ captures the "price sensitive" preferences where consumers do not prefer "high"-priced services and are satisfied with "low" CPU and availability if the service price is "low". $CP6$ captures the "CPU sensitive" preferences. Here, consumers do not prefer "low" CPU and are able to pay "high" price for "high" CPU units and availability. $CP7$ also captures the "availability sensitive" preferences. It decides CPU and price values based on "low to moderate" availability preferences. In $CP7$, the highest preferred service is $(A2, C1, P2)$ and the least preferred service is $(A3, C1, P3)$.

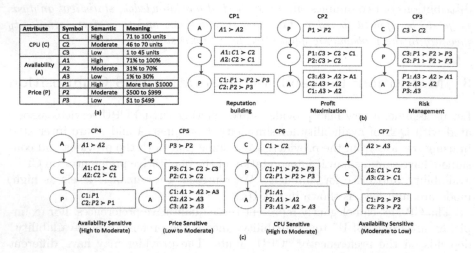

Fig. 1. (a) Semantic representation of preferred service attributes, (b) A provider's qualitative preferences, (c) Consumers' qualitative preferences

The provider's business strategies probably change in the long-term period (Fig. 2(a)). For example, the provider is determined to apply the reputation building strategy ($CP1$) in the first year. In the second year, the profit maximization strategy ($CP2$) has a 60% chance to be applied, because the number of consumers may turn out lower than expected. Hence, there is 40% probability to continue the reputation building strategy ($CP1$) from the first year. Similarly, the risk management strategy ($CP3$) has a 10% chance to be applied in the third year due to possible hardware failures in the aging infrastructure. Uncertainties around consumers' qualitative preferences are also a natural phenomena in a long-term period (Fig. 2(a)). For example, consumer A may forecast a 60% chance of using "availability-sensitive" services ($CP4$) only for the three year period. It also predicts that there is a 40% chance to use "price-sensitive" services ($CP4$) due to a possible economic recession in business. The temporal changes in qualitative preferences and their transition probabilities from one CP-Net to another CP-Net are captured in a probabilistic temporal CP-Net model denoted as PrTempCP-Net. In Fig. 2(a), the provider uses $\{CP1, CP2 \text{ and } CP3\}$, the Consumer A uses $\{CP4, CP5 \text{ and } CP6\}$, and Consumer B uses $\{CP6, CP7 \text{ and } CP4\}$ to build their PrTempCP-Nets.

Here, all possible compositions in a brute force manner are $\{A\}$, $\{B\}$ and $\{A, B\}$. The aggregated CPU and availability requirements of Consumer A and

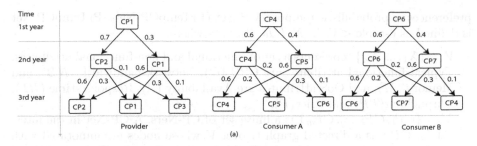

Fig. 2. (a) Probabilistic Temporal CP-Nets (b) Runtime similarity index

B are greater than the provider's maximum resource limit, we select either $\{A\}$ or $\{B\}$ as the best composition. Each PrTempCP-Net in Fig. 2(a) has 6 sequences of CP-Nets with different probabilities. First, we apply a greedy approach and match the highest probable sequences (Provider: $(CP1, CP2, CP2)$, Consumer A: $(CP4, CP4, CP4)$, Consumer B: $(CP6, CP6, CP6)$) in Fig. 2(b). Here, $CP2$ is highly matched with $CP4$ and $CP6$ as consumers are able to pay "high" prices for "high" availability and CPU units. However, $CP1$ is better matched with $CP4$ (higher availability in both preferences) than $CP6$ (CPU-sensitive preferences). Hence, A is better matched (high) than B (almost high) for highest probable CP-Net sequences. Next, we compare the provider's highest sequences $(CP1, CP2, CP2)$ with second highest sequences of Consumer A $(CP4, CP4, CP5)$ and Consumer B $(CP6, CP6, CP7)$. As $CP5$ does not prefer higher priced services, but $CP2$ does prefer the opposite, the similarity measure between the provider and Consumer A is lower than the similarity measure between the provider and Consumer B. The similarity measure of the first two probable sequences are described in Fig. 2(b). Although $\{A\}$ is best matched with the highest probable sequences, B has the best averaged similarity in all the sequences (it never goes low in similarity measure). Hence, the greedy approach may not be applicable in runtime. If there are m CP-Nets and t time segments in a PrTempCP-Net, $O(m^{t^2})$ are required to find the optimal composition. It may not be feasible to compare all the sequences for large m and t values. *Hence, we apply probabilistic statistical sampling and matching techniques to reduce the search space in runtime.*

4   Probabilistic Temporal CP-Net

We require not only an intuitive tool for structuring the probabilistic qualitative preferences, but also a support for a matching process. We model the long-term preferences as probabilistic temporal CP-Net (PrTempCP-Net). PrTempCP-Net is defined as 6-tuple $< V, M, N, I, I_0, P(.,.) >$ where:

- $V = \{X_1, ..., X_n\}$ represents a set of functional and non-functional attributes. Typical functional attributes are CPU (C), Network bandwidth (NB), and Memory (M), and QoS attributes are Availability (A), Response time (RT), Throughput(TP) and Price(P).
- $M = \{CP_1, CP_2, ..., CP_m\}$ is a finite set of CP-Nets. A CP-Net in the interval I_k, CP^{I_k} is a directed graph G over V whose nodes are annotated with conditional preference tables $CPT(X_i)$ for each $X_i \in V$. Each conditional preference table $CPT(X_i)$ describes the qualitative preferences over the values of the variable X_i given every combination of parent values. For example, in $CP1$, the $CPT(C)$ contains $\{A1, A2\}$ while preferences are made over $\{C1, C2\}$ (Fig. 1(b)). A CP-Net generates a total ordered $(\succeq)$ preference ranking over the set of service configurations: $o_1 \succeq o_2$ means that a configuration o_1 is equally or more preferred than o_2. We use $o_1 \succ o_2$ to denote the fact that provisioning or consuming service o_1 is more preferred than o_2 (i.e., $o_1 \succeq o_2$ and $o_2 \nsucceq o_1$), while $o_1 \sim o_2$ denotes that the provider's or consumers' preference is indifferent between the configurations o_1 and o_2 (i.e., $o_1 \nsucceq o_2$ and $o_2 \nsucceq o_1$).
- $N = \{Sem\_Table_1, Sem\_Table_2, ..., Sem\_Table_n\}$ is a finite set of semantic tables. Sem_Table_k represents the kth semantic interpretations over ranges of the variable X_i. Figure 1(a) is such a semantic table that maps 70–100 units of CPU as a "high" CPU value.
- $I = \{I_1, I_2, ..., I_t\}$ is the finite set of intervals. Here, the total composition time, T is divided into t intervals where, $T = \sum_{i=1}^{t} I_i$.
- I_0 represents the starting interval in the matching process of a composition which is defined by the provider or consumer.
- $P(CP_s, Sem\_Table_s, I_s | C\acute{P}_s, Sem\_\acute{T}able_s, \acute{I}_s)$ is the probability to choose a particular service preference CP_s in interval I_s with the corresponding semantic table (Sem_Table_s) from service preference $C\acute{P}_s$ which is applied in interval $\acute{I}_s$ with the semantic table $Sem\_\acute{T}able_s$. We assume that all probabilities are generated before the composition. In Fig. 2(a), the probability to transit from $(CP1$, first year$)$ to $(CP2$, second year$)$ is 0.7.

A probabilistic TempCP-Net produces different deterministic TempCP-Nets based on I_0. A deterministic TempCP-Net is generated by applying transition probabilities to a CP-Net in an interval. Usually, the matching process is performed from left to right, i.e., first interval to second interval and so on. Here, the first interval is set as I_0. For example, $\{(CP1$, 1st Year$), (CP2$, 2nd year$), (CP2$, 3rd year$)\}$ is the highest probable deterministic TempCP-Net as the transition probabilities are 0.7 and 0.7 respectively. The set of consequences $o \succ \acute{o}$ of an acyclic TempCP-Net constitutes a partial order over the service configuration. This partial order can be represented by an acyclic directed graph, referred to as the *induced preference graph*. The nodes of the induced preference graph correspond to the complete assignments to the variables of the network. There is an edge from node $\acute{o}$ to node o iff the assignments at $\acute{o}$ and o differ only in the

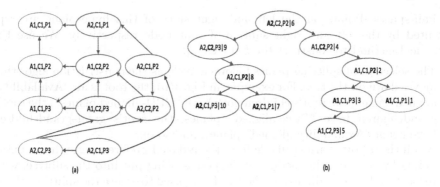

Fig. 3. (a) Induced preference model, (b) k-d tree indexing

value of a single variable X. Given the values assigned by $ó$ and o to $Pa(X)$, the value assigned by o to X is preferred to the value assigned by $ó$ to X. Figure 3(a) depicts the induced preference graph of $CP1$. There is no outgoing edge from $(A1, C1, P1)$ as it is the most preferred request configuration. Similarly, there is no incoming edge to $(A2, C1, P3)$ as it is the least preferred configuration. If n is the number of attributes in the TempCP-net and q is the number of output configurations in an interval, the time complexity for ordering queries in an interval is $O(nq^2)$.

5   TempCP-Net Matching Using k-d Tree Indexing

First, we perform similarity measure between two deterministic TempCP-Nets, $A = \{(CP_A^1, Sem\_Table_A^1, I_1), ..., (CP_A^m, Sem\_Table_A^m, I_m)\}$ and $B = \{(CP_B^1, Sem\_Table_B^1, I_1), ..., (CP_B^m, Sem\_Table_B^m, I_m)\}$. We consider it as a base to match probabilistic TempCP-Nets. We assume that the temporal lengths of the CP-Nets are same in each TempCP-Nets. CP-Nets within the same interval are matched and the similarity measure is averaged over the number of intervals (m) as follows:

$$Sim(A, B) = \frac{\sum_{i=1}^{m} Sim_{A,B}(CP_A^i, Sem\_Table_A^i, CP_B^i, Sem\_Table_B^i)}{m} \quad (1)$$

The induced preference graph enables similarity measure between two CP-Nets constructed with the same semantic table (i.e., $Sim_{A,B}$). Each tuple $(s_1, ..., s_n)$ in the induced preference graph of CP_A^i is linearly traversed over the induced preference graph of CP_B^i. The similarity measure is then defined as the averaged number of traversals required to search all tuples (time complexity $O(n^2)$) [12]. Here, a lower value indicates a higher similarity index. Considering the tuple $(s_1, ..., s_n)$ as a multidimensional vector, we improve the matching process using the k-d tree [2]. The k-d tree is a binary tree in which every node is a k-dimensional point (Fig. 3(b)). Every non-leaf node can be thought of as implicitly generating a splitting hyperplane that divides the space into two parts, known as half-spaces. Points on the left and right sides of this hyperplane are represented by the left and right subtree of that node respectively. We use the canonical method to construct the k-d tree [2]:

- The selection of splitting planes follows a cycle as the construction algorithm moves down on the tree. For example, in Fig. 3(b), the root is an "Availability-aligned" plane, the root's children both have "CPU-aligned planes", the root's grandchildren have "Price-aligned" planes, the root's great-grandchildren have again "Availability-aligned" planes, and so on.
- As all the n points are available from the induced preference graph, we insert points by selecting the median of the points being put into the subtree, with respect to their coordinates in the axis being used to create the splitting plane. This would result in a balanced k-d tree construction in $O(n \ log(n))$ times [2]. Each node in the k-d tree is annotated with its respective preference order from the induced graph. For example, the root node $(A2, C2, P2)$ is annotated with the preference ranking 6 in Fig. 3(b).

At first, CP_A^i and CP_B^i are indexed in corresponding k-d trees. We apply semantic transformation to one of the k-d trees as follows:

- **Semantic Transformation:** if $Sem\_Table_A^i \neq Sem\_Table_B^i$ and the average value of "high" semantics in $Sem\_Table_A^i$ is greater than the average value of "high" semantics in $Sem\_Table_B^i$, semantic transformation is applied to CP_B^i. The average value of a semantic "X" in range $[a, b]$ is calculated as $Avg(X) = \frac{(a+b)}{2}$. For all "X" in CP_B^i, if $Avg(X)$ is within the range $[\acute{a}, \acute{b}]$ of a semantic "Y" in $Sem\_Table_A^i$, "X" is replaced with "Y" in CP_B^i. If $Avg(X)$ is below the "low" semantic in $Sem\_Table_A^i$ (i.e., no range found), "X" is replaced with "low" in CP_B^i. For example, if "high" availability ($A1$) of CP_A^i is ranged in [80,100] (avg. 90) and "high" availability ($A1$) of CP_B^i is ranged in [60,90] (avg. 75), $A1$ of CP_B^i is semantically transformed to "moderate" $A2$ as it is ranged in [60,80] in $Sem\_Table_A^i$.

We start the matching process $Sim_{AB}(CP_A^i, CP_B^i)$ using the indexed k-d trees after the semantic transformation. We consider each tuple $(s_1, ..., s_n)$ of CP_B^i as search points. Starting with the root node of CP_A^i, a search point (ranking r_b) moves down on the tree recursively, in the same way that it would if the search point was being inserted. If the search point is matched with a node, it returns the annotated ranking value, r_a. For example, the search point $(A2, C1, P3)$ of rank 1 in CP_B^i returns rank 10 in CP_A^i using only 4 comparisons. A non-matched search point returns L which is a large number indicating the lowest ranking. The normalized difference between r_a and r_b indicates a similarity measure (Eq. 2). In the previous example, it indicates a dissimilarity as the non-negative normalized difference between r_a and r_b is 0.9. $Sim_{AB} = 0$ indicates the highest match and $Sim_{AB} = 1$ indicates the lowest match, i.e., dissimilarity. The time complexity of the k-d tree based similarity measure in an interval is $O(n \ log(n))$.

$$Sim_{AB}(CP_A^i, CP_B^i) = \frac{abs|r_a, r_b|}{max(r_a, r_b)} \mid \forall \ r_a \in CP_A^i \ and \ r_b \in CP_B^i \qquad (2)$$

6   Similarity Measure Between PrTempCP-Nets

The similarity measure between probabilistic temporal CP-Nets should be reflective of a matching between runtime temporal CP-Nets. Let us assume there
are two probabilistic temporal CP-Nets (PA and PB) and two random deterministic or runtime tempCP-Nets, A and B are generated from PA and PB
respectively. If $Sim(A, B) = \alpha$, then the similarity measure between PrCP-Nets,
$Sim(PA, PB) = \beta$ indicates that the difference $|\alpha - \beta|$ has a higher probability
to be less than the standard deviation. Based on the prediction of the possible
runtime CP-Nets, two approaches could be applied for the similarity measure
between PrTempCP-Nets:

- *Greedy approach:* The most runtime likelihood sequences of CP-Nets are gen-
  erated from PA and PB and are matched using Eqs. 1 and 2 in this approach.
  We define the following recursive procedure:
    1. Base case: $O(0) = \{\phi\}$ denotes the empty sequence at no interval and the
       total probability $TP(0) = 1$.
    2. Recursion: $O(n) = \{CP^n, O(n - 1)\}$ denotes the maximum likelihood
       sequence where, $TP(n) = P(X, CP^{n-1}) \times TP(n)$ is maximum for $X =$
       CP^n.
- *Brute force approach:* It is not guaranteed that the similarity measure with
  the greedy approach has a higher probability to be less than the standard
  deviation from all possible sequences in PrTempCP-Nets. Hence, the brute
  force approach generates all possible sequences of deterministic TempCP-Nets
  from PA and PB and perform pair-wise similarity measure using Eqs. 1 and
  2. If q is the total number of comparisons, the probabilistic similarity measure
  is calculated as the averaged mean value:

$$Sim(PA, PB) = \frac{\sum_{i=1}^{q} Sim_i(A, B)}{q} \mid \forall\, A \in PA,\, B \in PB \qquad (3)$$

We apply statistical analysis and sampling techniques to reduce the large
number of comparisons in the brute force approach and to approximate the
similarity measure within the standard deviation. The approach consists of two
steps: (a) *probabilistic range sampling* to compress CP-Nets into fewer numbers,
(b) *reducing approximation error* by applying deviations in probability distributions using the K-S test.

6.1   Probabilistic Range Sampling of PrTempCP-Net

Stratified sampling is an effective technique where the solution space embraces
a number of distinct categories, the whole solution space can be organized into
separate "strata" [15]. Each stratum is then sampled as an independent sub-
space, out of which individual elements can be randomly selected [15]. Due to
different probability distributions in a PrTempCP-Net, we can apply stratified
sampling to compress CP-Nets into fewer numbers, where each "starta" is a

probability range. We create the set of m probability ranges, denoted as RG, where each interval in a range is $\frac{1}{m}$. If $m = 5$, the set of probability ranges are $\{[0, 0.2), [0.2, 0.4), [0.4, 0.6), [0.6, 0.8), [0.8, 1.0)\}$. For each probability range in RG, we compress CP-Nets with the same probability interval. Total $|RG|$ numbers of deterministic TempCP-nets are created from a PrTempCP-Net. Given a probability range $[x, y]$, we apply weighted aggregation to compress the CP-Nets. For each interval I in a PrTempCP-Net, we filter CP-Nets where their probabilities are within the range $[x, y]$. For example, if the probability range is $[0,0.4]$, the filtered provider's PrTempCP-Net is $\{(CP1, I_1), (CP1, I_2), (CP1, CP3, I_3)\}$ in Fig. 2. Note that, $CP2$ is excluded because its probabilities is out of the range $[0,0.4]$.

We aggregate CP-Nets as a compression mechanism in each interval to create the deterministic TempCP-Nets. Pairwise aggregation order is applied for multiple CP-Nets. For example, CP^a, CP^b, and CP^c are aggregated as $((CP^a + CP^b) + CP^c)$. The aggregation procedure of CP^a and CP^b along with associated probabilities P^a and P^b uses tuple aggregation rules [9] as follows:

1. CP^a and CP^b are transformed into their corresponding k-d trees where each node is a tuple $(x_1, x_2, ..., x_n)$.
2. Select tuples from the same level of the k-d trees. For example, both roots of k-d trees are selected in the first level. If N tuples are selected, we apply the following weighted summation rule for resource attributes (x) and weighted maximization rule for QoS attributes (y):

$$\text{Summation: } \bar{x}_i = \sum_{i=1}^{N} P^i \times x_i, \text{where } x_i \in \{C, M, NB, RT, P, Rank\} \quad (4)$$

$$\text{Maximization: } \bar{y}_i = max(P^i \times y_i), \forall\, i \in [1, N] \text{ where } y_i \in \{A, TP\}$$

3. Starting from the first level, the aggregation is performed in every level and the corresponding ranking in attached with each tuple.

The m probability ranges are applied in both PA and PB. If P^i_{mean} is the mean probability of the ith probability range, the similarity measure is calculated as follows:

$$Sim(PA, PB) = \frac{\sum_{i=1}^{m^2}(P^i_{mean} \times Sim_i(A, B))}{m^2} \,|\, \forall\, A \in PA,\ B \in PB \quad (5)$$

6.2   Reducing Approximation Error in Sim(PA, PB) Using K-S Test

The similarity measure between TempCP-Nets with higher probability ranges is given higher weight in the computation of total similarity measure between PrTempCP-Nets in Eq. 5. It is based on the heuristic that the probability distribution of attributes in a higher probability range TempCP-Net is significantly greater than the probability distribution of attributes in a lower probability range TempCP-Net. Hence, a change in the probability distribution may not change the similarity measure in the runtime. For example, the similarity measure with the probability range [80,100] is not expected to change to a similarity measure with the probability range [0,20] in runtime. However, such heuristic may not be applicable when probability distributions of TempCP-Nets are close to each other.

We apply Kolmogorov-Smirnov test (K-S test) [4] to find the closeness of probability distribution of TempCP-Nets which are filtered with probabilistic range sampling. Given two TempCP-Nets A and B and an attribute x, we first derive the cumulative probability distribution $F_A(x)$ and $F_B(x)$. *The null hypothesis is that both the preferences are generated by the same distribution.* The null hypothesis is tested in the K-S test with two values $L_{m,n}$ and $L_{m,n,\alpha}$ defined in Eq. 6. Here $L_{m,n}$ is the maximum difference in the cumulative distribution functions and $L_{m,n,\alpha}$ is the critical value from Kolmorogov distribution functions [4]. α is the confidence level to reject the null hypothesis. According to the recommendation in [4], we reject the null hypothesis (at significance level α) if $L_{m,n} > L_{m,n,\alpha}$. For example, $\alpha = 0.05$ gives 95% confidence to reject the null hypothesis.

$$L_{m,n} = max_x|F(x) - G(x)| \qquad (6)$$

$$L_{m,n,\alpha} = c(\alpha)\sqrt{\frac{m+n}{mn}}$$

$c(\alpha) =$ the inverse of the Kolmorogov distribution at α

Let us assume, $Avg_A(\alpha)$ is the averaged similarity measure in the pairwise probability distributions between A and rest of the TempCP-Nets. A higher $Avg_A(\alpha)$ indicates that A is highly similar with other distributions and it has higher chance to change in runtime. Hence, the initial probability which is attached to A should consider such changing probability to reduce the approximation error. Hence, we update the Eq. 5 using (α) as follows:

$$Sim(PA, PB) = \frac{\sum_{i=1}^{m^2} \frac{P_{mean}^i \times Sim_i(A,B)}{max(Avg_A(\alpha),Avg_B(\alpha))}}{m^2} \mid \forall\, A \in PA,\ B \in PB \qquad (7)$$

7   Experiments and Results

As our focus is not on the optimization of IaaS composition, the optimal composition is selected by the brute-force combinatorial optimization. It generates all combinations of consumers' PrTempCP-Nets along with the brute-force similarity measure. The brute-force similarity measure compares all possible TempCP-Nets with the provider's PrTempCP-Net. We compare the efficiency of the proposed similarity measure with the greedy approach to find the optimal composition in a fewer number of comparisons between TempCP-Nets. All the experiments are conducted on computers with Intel Core i7 CPU (2.13 GHz and 4GB RAM). Java is used to implement the algorithms.

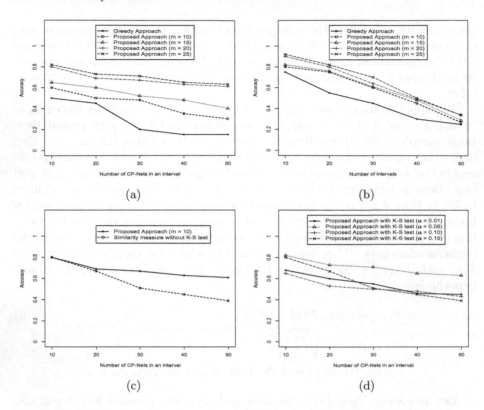

Fig. 4. (a) Accuracy in different m values, (b) Accuracy in scalable intervals, (c) Importance of K-S tests, (d) Accuracy in different α values

7.1 Data Description

We create the PrTempCP-Nets using Google Cluster resource utilization [11], real world cloud QoS performance [6], and synthetic price. Google Cluster data include CPU and Memory utilization and allocation time series of 70 jobs over a 1-month period. The real world QoS data [6] include two time series (i.e., response time and throughput) for 100 cloud services over a 6-month period. We randomly pick 70 Google Cluster jobs and make one-to-one mapping with the 100 sets of QoS data. A 6-month request is extended to a 12-month request using ARIMA model [17] with a confidence score. We create 50 such long-term requests from one Google Cluster job with random confidence scores in the range (0, 100]. Each TempCP-Net has 12 monthly intervals and each interval contains different CP-Nets where dependencies among the attributes are randomly generated from the same segment of 50 long-term requests. The probabilities in the transition matrix are mapped with the confidence scores which are used to generate the long-term preferences. The generated PrTempCP-Nets are separated into 10 groups (G_1 to G_{10}). In a group, a random PrTempCP-Net is considered as the provider's business strategy and the rest 6 PrTempCP-Nets are considered as consumers' preferences. For the K-S test, we set $\alpha = 0.05$.

7.2 Efficiency of the Proposed Probabilistic Range Sampling

We consider the brute force similarity measure as our baseline. Let us assume, s optimal compositions are returned from m groups by the brute force approach. However, r compositions are optimal from the m returned compositions using greedy or the proposed approach. Hence, we compute the accuracy of a similarity measure as $\frac{r}{s}$ in the range $[0,1]$. Here, 1 means the perfect accuracy. Figure 4(a) depicts the accuracy of the proposed probabilistic sampling with different numbers of probability ranges (m). We find that the proposed approach is more accurate when higher numbers of probability ranges are used to sample. There are no significant improvement in accuracy after $m = 20$. The greedy approach performs similar to the proposed approach when the number of CP-Nets is lower in the PrTempCP-Net. We find that the proposed approach is significantly accurate than the greedy approach for higher numbers of CP-Nets in Fig. 4(a). Figure 4(b) depicts the scalablity of the proposed approach in long-term compositions. We find that the accuracy is relatively lower when the number of intervals is increased. The proposed approach does not perform better than the greedy approach when the number of intervals are set to 50. If each interval represents a month, the proposed approach is applicable in a 4-year long composition which is acceptable in the real world. Figure 4(c) depicts the importance of reducing approximation error using K-S tests. We find that K-S tests are unnecessary when the number of CP-Nets is lower in an interval. However, it improves the accuracy significantly for a higher number of CP-Nets. Figure 4(d) depicts the importance of appropriate significance level (α) in K-S tests in the proposed similarity measure. We find that $\alpha = 0.5$, i.e., 95% confidence interval is appropriate as it maximizes the similarity measures than other values.

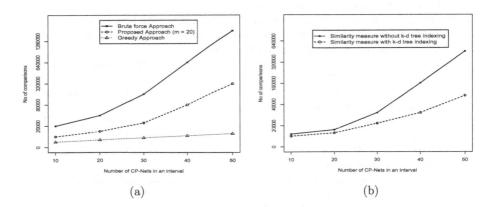

(a)   (b)

Fig. 5. (a) Time complexity, (b) Significance of k-d tree indexing

7.3   Time Complexity Analysis

Although the brute force approach is more accurate, it is not appreciable in runtime due to its exponential nature (Fig. 5(a)). We find that the greedy approach is the most time efficient which is linearly correlated with the number of CP-Nets in an interval. However, the time complexity of proposed approach is quadratic and related to the value of m. For $m = 20$, the proposed similarity measure takes around 75% less time than the brute force approach. Figure 5(b) depicts the importance of k-d tree indexing. For a large number of CP-Nets in TempCP-nets, k-d tree reduces the number of comparisons by the factor $\frac{log(n)}{n}$.

8   Conclusion

We represent the long-term qualitative preferences using a novel probabilistic temporal CP-Nets in the IaaS composition. We propose sampling and probabilistic distribution matching in the similarity measure between PrTempCP-Nets. Although the greedy approach is the most time-efficient, the proposed approach is significantly accurate than the greedy approach and has an acceptable runtime efficiency. In the future work, we explore an efficient optimization process in relation with PrTempCP-Nets.

Acknowledgements. This research was made possible by NPRP 7-481-1-088 grant from the Qatar National Research Fund (a member of The Qatar Foundation). The statements made herein are solely the responsibility of the authors.

References

1. Armbrust, M., Fox, A., Griffith, R.: Above the clouds: a berkeley view of cloud computing. Technical Report. University of California, Berkeley (2009)
2. Bentley, J.L.: Multidimensional binary search trees used for associative searching. Commun. ACM **18**(9), 509–517 (1975)
3. Boutilier, C., Brafman, R.I., Domshlak, C., Hoos, H.H., Poole, D.: Cp-nets: A tool for representing and reasoning with conditional ceteris paribus preference statements. J. Artif. Intell. Res. **21**, 135–191 (2004)
4. Fasano, G., Franceschini, A.: A multidimensional version of the kolmogorov-smirnov test. Roy. Astron. Soc. **225**(1), 155–170 (1987)
5. Goiri, Í., Guitart, J., Torres, J.: Economic model of a cloud provider operating in a federated cloud. Inf. Syst. Front. **14**, 827–843 (2012)
6. Jiang, W., Lee, D., Hu, S.: Large-scale longitudinal analysis of soap-based and restful web services. In: Proceedings of ICWS, pp. 218–225 (2012)
7. Limthanmaphon, B., Zhang, Y.: Web service composition with case-based reasoning. In: Proceedings of ADC, pp. 201–208. ACS (2003)
8. Mistry, S., Bouguettaya, A., Dong, H., Qin, A.K.: Metaheuristic optimization for long-term IaaS service composition. IEEE TSC **PP**(99), 1 (2016)
9. Mistry, S., Bouguettaya, A., Dong, H., Erradi, A.: Qualitative economic model for long-term IaaS composition. In: Sheng, Q.Z., Stroulia, E., Tata, S., Bhiri, S. (eds.) ICSOC 2016. LNCS, vol. 9936, pp. 317–332. Springer, Cham (2016). doi:10.1007/978-3-319-46295-0_20

10. Puzicha, J., Hofmann, T., Buhmann, J.M.: A theory of proximity based clustering: Structure detection by optimization. Pattern Recogn. **33**(4), 617–634 (2000)
11. Reiss, C., Wilkes, J., Hellerstein, J.L.: Google cluster-usage traces: format + schema, Technical report. Google Inc., Mountain View, CA, USA (2011)
12. Santhanam, G.R., Basu, S., Honavar, V.: Web service substitution based on preferences over non-functional attributes. In: Proceedings of SCC, pp. 210–217 (2009)
13. Wang, H., Shao, S., Zhou, X., Wan, C., Bouguettaya, A.: Preference recommendation for personalized search. Knowl.-Based Syst. **100**, 124–136 (2016)
14. Wang, H., Zhang, J., Sun, W., Song, H., Guo, G., Zhou, X.: WCP-nets: a weighted extension to CP-nets for web service selection. In: Liu, C., Ludwig, H., Toumani, F., Yu, Q. (eds.) ICSOC 2012. LNCS, vol. 7636, pp. 298–312. Springer, Heidelberg (2012). doi:10.1007/978-3-642-34321-6_20
15. Wang, J.F., Stein, A., Gao, B.B., Ge, Y.: A review of spatial sampling. Spat. Stat. **2**, 1–14 (2012)
16. Ye, Z., Bouguettaya, A., Zhou, X.: QoS-aware cloud service composition based on economic models. In: Liu, C., Ludwig, H., Toumani, F., Yu, Q. (eds.) ICSOC 2012. LNCS, vol. 7636, pp. 111–126. Springer, Heidelberg (2012). doi:10.1007/978-3-642-34321-6_8
17. Zhang, G.P.: Time series forecasting using a hybrid arima and neural network model. Neurocomputing **50**, 159–175 (2003)

An Embedding Based Factorization Machine Approach for Web Service QoS Prediction

Yaoming Wu[1,2], Fenfang Xie[1,2], Liang Chen[1,2], Chuan Chen[1,2], and Zibin Zheng[1,2(✉)]

[1] School of Data and Computer Science, Sun Yat-sen University, Guangzhou, China
{wuym25,xieff5}@mail2.sysu.edu.cn,
{chenliang6,chenchuan,zhzibin}@mail.sysu.edu.cn
[2] Key Laboratory of Machine Intelligence and Advanced Computing, Ministry of Education, Sun Yat-sen University, Guangzhou, China

Abstract. As an important property of Web services, Quality of Service (QoS) is usually engaged for describing the non-functional characteristics of Web services. However, QoS value is considerable sparse since users only invoke a limited number of services in the real-world applications. In this way, predicting QoS value is a good choice to solve such 'sparsity' problem. Although several methods have been proposed to predict QoS value for users, most of them are always time-consuming and expensive to implement.

To solve the drawbacks of high dimensionality and huge sparse, we introduce embedding technique to map data from resource space to target space in injective and structural-preserving way. To efficiently express pairwise interactions in sparse datasets, we further introduce factorization machine, which is an impactful algorithm to deal with sparse data prediction in the world of machine learning and can be computed in linear time.

Based on the above characteristics of our scenario and the advantages of factorization machine and embedding, this paper proposes an embedding based factorization machine approach to predict missing QoS values for Web services. First of all, user id and service id are encoded by one-hot encoding. And then, the one-hot encoding of user id and service id are mapped to different embedding vectors. Finally, the embedding vectors are regarded as implicit vectors and the idea of factorization machine is exploited to make missing QoS value prediction. Experiments on real-world dataset validate the effectiveness of our approach, which outperforms the other state-of-the-art methods in terms of QoS prediction accuracy.

Keywords: Web service · QoS prediction · Embedding · Factorization machine

1 Introduction

Web services are self-described software applications designed to support interoperable machine-to-machine interaction over a network via standard interfaces

M. Maximilien et al. (Eds.): ICSOC 2017, LNCS 10601, pp. 272–286, 2017.
https://doi.org/10.1007/978-3-319-69035-3_19

and communication protocols [17]. With the increasing adoption of Service Oriented Architecture (SOA), the number of Web services are increasing rapidly on the Internet. Among the massive Web services, lots of them provide similar functions. However, the quality of these similar Web services is different. Quality of Service (QoS) is usually used to describe the nonfunctional characteristics of Web services [16]. In general, the QoS of Web services has some properties, including price, response time, throughput, reliability, availability, etc. In the scenario of service selection, QoS is an important factor to impact users' decision. How to choose the services that satisfy users is an urgent problem. On the basis of functional matching, considering the QoS of Web services is an effective solution. Therefore, investigating Web services QoS is becoming more and more important.

Previous QoS-based studies have been applied for Web service recommendation, Web service composition, Web service selection, and so on. It's essential to provide accurate QoS value of Web services to make these QoS-based approaches work well. In general, the QoS value of Web services can be measured on the server-side or client-side. As for measured by server-side (e.g., price, popularity, etc.), QoS value is usually declared by service providers or the third party (e.g., UDDI), and it is identical for different users. The QoS value measured by client-side (e.g., response-time, throughput, availability, etc.) is closely related to network status, geographical location, service runtime environment, etc. Therefore, the QoS experience of different users is quite different. In reality, a service user usually only invokes a limited number of Web services in the past and thus only observes QoS values of these invoked Web services. For the sake of obtaining accurate and personalized QoS value of users, Web service QoS evaluation is indispensable for enhancing the service users' experience.

However, in practice, invoking Web service for evaluation purpose at the client-side is quite difficult and has the following critical drawbacks:

1. Web service invocations may be charged because the Web services are usually provided and hosted by other organizations. Even if the Web services are free, executing real-world Web service invocations for evaluation purposes consumes resources of service providers and imposes costs of service users.
2. It is time-consuming and impractical for service users to evaluate all the Web service candidates, since there are massive Web services in the Internet.
3. Service users are usually not experts on Web service evaluation and the common time-to-market constraints make in-depth evaluations of the target Web services difficult.

Based on the above analysis, it is an urgent task to accurately predict the missing QoS value of the candidate services for different service users, so that it can provide support for Web service recommendation, Web service composition, Web service selection, and so on. Although several methods [9, 18, 19] have been proposed to predict QoS value for users, most of them are always time-consuming and expensive to implement. In neural network, embedding maps the data from resource space to target space injective and structural-preserving. Further, the processing of embedding can solve the drawbacks of high dimensionality and huge sparse. In the world of machine learning, factorization machine can estimate interactions even in problems with huge sparsity. It is a remarkably smart way to express pairwise interactions in sparse datasets. Moreover, it can be computed in linear time and it depends only on a linear number of parameters [5].

Due to the above characteristics of our scenario and the advantages of factorization machine and embedding, we propose an **E**mbedding based **F**actorization **M**achine approach, called EFMPred, to **Pred**ict missing QoS values for Web services. User id and service id are firstly encoded by one-hot encoding. And then, the one-hot encoding of user id and service id are mapped to embedding vectors. Specifically, the embedding vectors are regarded as implicit vectors to model the pairwise interaction between users and services. Finally, we exploit EFMPred model to make missing QoS value prediction. Extensive experiments on real-world dataset demonstrate that our EFMPred model can improve the QoS value prediction accuracy effectively.

In summary, the main contributions of this paper are as follows:

1. To the best of our knowledge, this is the first work applying embedding technique to traditional factorization machine for QoS prediction.
2. EFMPred can capture the implicit relationship between users and services by performing user id and service id embedding. In addition, EFMPred can predict missing QoS information for every user-service pair.
3. Extensive experiments on real-world dataset are conducted to evaluate the effectiveness of our approach. The experimental results demonstrate that our approach outperforms the other state-of-the-art baseline methods in terms of prediction accuracy.

The remainder of this paper is organized as follows. Section 2 presents our missing QoS prediction problem and gives an overview of our framework. Section 3 introduces our EFMPred model for personalized QoS value prediction. Section 4 discusses and analyses the experimental results. Related works are presented in Sect. 5 and a conclusion of this paper is drawn in Sect. 6.

2   Preliminaries

In this section, we firstly describe the QoS property prediction problem in Sect. 2.1. Then we introduce the framework of our embedding based factorization machine model in Sect. 2.2.

2.1   Problem Description

In this paper, the problem we investigate is how to accurately predict missing QoS information for service users based on the historical QoS usage experience. Given a list of users and services, users invoke services to mark the property of QoS. The detailed description is as follows.

Let $U = \{u_1, u_2, ..., u_m\}$ be the set of m users and $S = \{s_1, s_2, ..., s_n\}$ be the set of n Web services. The QoS value q_{ij} of service s_j which is observed by user

u_i is presented as a triple (i, j, q_{ij}). As mentioned before, the QoS property of Web services includes price, response time, throughput, reliability, availability, etc. Herein, q_{ij} denotes a k dimension vector representing the QoS values of $k - th$ criteria. Let Ω be the set of all QoS values, Δ be the set of all existing known QoS values, $\Lambda = \Omega - \Delta$ is the set of missing QoS values. The missing QoS values y_{ij} will be predicted by the existing QoS values in Δ.

A toy example is shown in Fig. 1 to better comprehend the idea of unknown QoS prediction. The interaction between users and services is illustrated by a user-service matrix as shown in Fig. 1(a), each element in the user-service matrix denotes a QoS value observed by a user on a certain service. The problem we study in this paper is then transferred to how to precisely predict the missing entries in the user-service matrix based on the existing entries. We can provide users with personalized QoS information once the missing entries are accurately predicted. We observe that although a part of the entries are already known in Fig. 1(a), every pair of users still have very few commonly invoked services. Based on the idea of collaborative filtering and our embedding based factorization machine model, we can complete the missing entries in the matrix for service users as shown in Fig. 1(b).

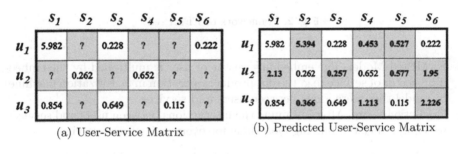

(a) User-Service Matrix   (b) Predicted User-Service Matrix

Fig. 1. A toy example for missing QoS prediction

2.2 Prediction Framework of EFMPred

In this section, we present our missing QoS value prediction framework of EFMPred. As shown in Fig. 2, our QoS prediction framework mainly includes four components: Input Feature Vector, Embedding Vectors, EFMPred Model and Prediction Score. The detailed functionality of each component is as follows:

1. Input Feature Vector. Based on the historical Web service QoS data that a service user observes on a certain service, the user id and service id are encoded with one-hot encoding respectively.
2. Embedding Vectors. After being encoded, the one-hot encoding of user id and service id are mapped into different embedding vectors via back propagation algorithm [11].

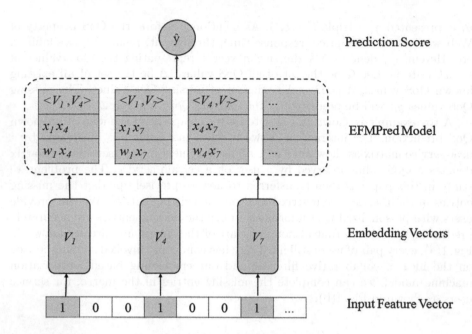

Fig. 2. Framework of EFMPred

3. EFMPred Model. The embedding vector of user is multiplied by the embedding vector of service (e.g. the dot product operation in factorization machine) to model the interactions between users and services.
4. Prediction Score. After obtaining the interactions between users and services, we can predict the missing QoS value for every pair of user-service.

Unlike the traditional factorization machine, our EFMPred model apply embedding technique to represent feature vectors. The detailed description about how to map the user id and service id to embedding vectors is shown in Fig. 3. We present the user id and service id (e.g., ID = 3) to the corresponding one-hot encoding (e.g., '001000'), and then, the one-hot encoding of user id and service id are mapped to the corresponding embedding vector (e.g., V_3) via a fully connected mapping. As can be seen in Fig. 3, the weight of red line directly corresponds to the output node value (e.g., v_{31}, v_{32}, v_{33}). That is the value of each dimension of the embedding vector.

3 Approach

In this section, we introduce our embedding based factorization machine approach for the missing QoS value prediction. Our EFMPred model mainly include two phases, we will describe them in detail in the following subsections.

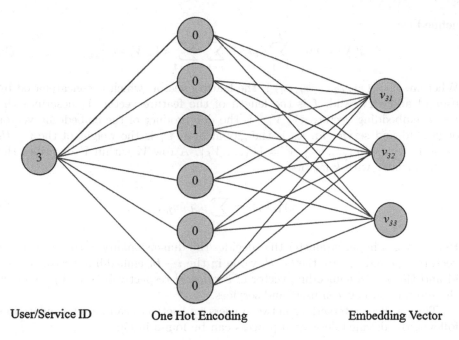

Fig. 3. Toy example of id embedding

3.1 Extracting Embedding Features from User ID and Service ID

The method of one-hot encoding is using n bit status register to encode the n states, each state has an independent register bit. For example, if we want to use one-hot coding to express four seasons in a whole year, we need four binary features, each of them representing one season. That is, '1000' indicates spring, '0100' indicates summer, '0010' indicates autumn, '0001' indicates winter.

In order to obtain the embedding vectors, we firstly exploit one-hot encoding to represent user id and service id. And then, we regard the one-hot encoding vectors as input of the full connection layer. Next, we apply back propagation algorithm [11] to calculate the weight of every edge in the full connection layer. The output layer of the full connection layer is embedding layer (e.g., embedding vectors of user id and service id).

Embedding maps the data from resource space to target space injective and structural-preserving. The processing of embedding can solve the drawbacks of one-hot encoding, e.g. high dimensionality and huge sparse.

3.2 Embedding Based Factorization Machine Model

After obtaining the embedding vectors of user id and service id, we exploit the idea of factorization machine to predict the missing QoS value for Web services. Given a $m * n$ user-service matrix, the factorization machine model equation is defined as:

$$\hat{y}(X) = w_0 + \sum_{i=1}^{f} w_i x_i + \sum_{i=1}^{f} \sum_{j=i+1}^{f} <V_i, V_j> x_i x_j, \tag{1}$$

Wherein, $X = (x_1, x_2, ..., x_{m+n})$ is the feature vector, which is concatenated by user id and service id. f is the length of the feature vector. V_i describes the $i - th$ embedding vector. $<V_i, V_j>$ is the dot product of the embedding vector of user id and service id. w_0 is the global bias, w_i is the weight of the $i - th$ variable. $W = \{w_1, ..., w_f\}$, $V = \{V_1, ..., V_f\}$. A row V_i within V describes the $i - th$ variable with k factors.

$$<V_i, V_j> = \sum_{l=1}^{k} v_{i,l} \cdot v_{j,l}, \tag{2}$$

Herein, k is a hyperparameter that decides the dimensionality of the embedding vectors. $v_{i,l}$ and $v_{j,l}$ are the $l - th$ value in the $i - th$ embedding vector of user id and the $j - th$ embedding vector of service id respectively. $<V_i, V_j>$ models the interaction between users and services.

The pairwise interactions between users and services can be reformulated as follows, the detailed derivation process can be found in [5]:

$$\sum_{i=1}^{f} \sum_{j=i+1}^{f} <V_i, V_j> x_i x_j = \frac{1}{2} \sum_{l=1}^{k} ((\sum_{i=1}^{f} v_{il} x_i)^2 - \sum_{i=1}^{n} v_{il}^2 x_i^2), \tag{3}$$

In order to estimate the quality of EFMPred model, a loss function should be conducted for evaluating the error between the estimated value and the original value. The square of the errors between the estimated value and the original value is usually applied to define the loss function. Therefore, the loss function of our EFMPred model is as follows:

$$\min_{\theta} L(y, \hat{y}) = \frac{1}{2} \sum_{i=1}^{m} \sum_{j=1}^{n} I_{ij} (y_{ij} - \hat{y}_{ij})^2, \tag{4}$$

where, $\theta = \{w_0, W, V\}$ is the model parameters, I_{ij} is the indicator function that is equal to 1 if user u_i invoked Web service v_j and is equal to 0 otherwise. The optimization problem of the loss function is to minimize the sum-of-squared-errors objective function.

A local minimum of the objective function given by (4) can be solved by performing stochastic gradient descent in θ:

$$\frac{\partial L(y, \hat{y})}{\partial \theta} = (\hat{y} - y) \frac{\partial \hat{y}}{\partial \theta}, \tag{5}$$

$$\frac{\partial \hat{y}}{\partial \theta} = \begin{cases} 1, & if \ \theta = w_0 \\ x_i, & if \ \theta = w_i \\ x_i \sum_{j=1}^{f} v_{jl} x_j - v_{il} x_i^2, & if \ \theta = v_{il} \end{cases} \tag{6}$$

3.3   Complexity Analysis

The main computation of our embedding based factorization machine model is to evaluate the object function L and its gradients against the variables. Since $x_i \sum_{j=1}^{f} v_{jl}x_j - v_{il}x_i^2$ is extensively related to l, in the process of parameters iteration, we only need to compute all of the l in the formulation $\sum_{j=1}^{f} u_{jl}x_j$ in the first time. And then, it is convenient to obtain all of the gradient of v_{jl}. Obviously, the complexity of computing all l in the formulation $\sum_{j=1}^{f} u_{jl}x_j$ is $O(kf)$. When $\sum_{j=1}^{f} u_{jl}x_j$ is known, the complexity to compute every gradient of parameter is $O(f)$. After obtaining the gradient of parameters, the complexity of updating parameters is $O(1)$. In the EFMPred model, the number of parameters is $kf + f + 1$. Therefore, the computation complexity of our EFMPred model is $O(kf)$. In summary, our EFMPred algorithm can complete the training model in linear time. This complexity analysis demonstrates that our EFMPred model is very efficient and can be scaled to large datasets.

4   Experiment

In this section, we conduct a series of extensive experiments on a real-world dataset to validate our EFMPred model by comparing our approach with several state-of-the-art approaches and analyzing the experimental results.

In the following subsections, we describe the statistics of our dataset in Sect. 4.1. The evaluation metrics are presented in Sect. 4.2. The performance comparison between our EFMPred model and other state-of-the-art approaches is introduced in Sect. 4.3. And the impact of parameters and the analysis of experimental results are presented in Sects. 4.4 and 4.5 respectively.

4.1   Dataset Description

We conduct experiments on a publicly accessible dataset: WSDream[1]. Which includes 339 service users and 5825 Web services. Moreover, it collects 1,974,675 records that service users invoke Web services, namely, the QoS properties values are observed by service users on real-world Web services. The WSDream dataset we use mainly collects the response time and throughput values. Therefore, we can obtain two $339 * 5825$ user-service matrices. The entries on the two user-service matrices are response time values and throughput values respectively. The ranges of response time and throughput are in the interval $[0, 20]$ and $[0, 1000]$ respectively (Table 1).

Although we mainly focus on two QoS properties (e.g. response time and throughput) in this paper, Our EFMPred model can be easily scaled to the prediction of other QoS properties without any modification. When conducting experiments to predict the other QoS properties, the entries on user-service matrix are just need to be set to the corresponding QoS property value that observed by a user on a certain Web service.

---

[1] http://inpluslab.sysu.edu.cn/wsdream/.

Table 1. Statistics of web service QoS dataset

Statistics	Values
Number of service users	339
Number of web services	5825
Number of web services invocations	1,974,675
Range of response time	0–20 s
Range of throughput	0–1000 kbps

4.2 Metrics

In statistics, Mean Absolute Error (MAE) and Root Mean Squared Error (RMSE) are evaluation metrics used to measure how close the prediction results are to the reality outcomes [12]. In the experiment, we use MAE and RMSE to evaluate the errors between our prediction results and the real QoS properties values. MAE is given by:

$$MAE = \frac{\sum_{ij} |\hat{r}_{ij} - r_{ij}|}{N}, \tag{7}$$

and RMSE is defined as follows:

$$RMSE = \sqrt{\frac{\sum_{ij} (\hat{r}_{ij} - r_{ij})^2}{N}}. \tag{8}$$

where, N represents the number of predicted QoS values, $\hat{r}_{ij}$ represents the predicted QoS value of service s_j observed by user u_i, while r_{ij} is the real QoS value of service s_j would be observed by user u_i in the dataset. Smaller MAE and RMSE values indicate better performance.

4.3 Performance Comparison

In this section, in order to verify the effectiveness of our EFMPred model, we compare our approach with the following approaches:

1. UMEAN (user mean). This approach employs a service user's average QoS value on the used Web services to predict the QoS values of the unused Web services.
2. IMEAN (item mean). This approach employs the average QoS value of the Web services observed by other service users to predict the QoS value for a service user who never invoke this Web service previously.
3. UPCC (user-based collaborative filtering method using PCC) [8]. This approach is a very classical approach. In this paper, it employs similar users for the QoS value prediction.
4. IPCC (item-based collaborative filtering method using PCC) [6]. This approach is widely used in industry company. In this paper, it employs similar Web services for the QoS value prediction.

5. UIPCC [18]. This approach employs both of the user-based and item-based collaborative filtering approaches to make QoS prediction. It utilizes the historical QoS usage experience from similar users and similar services to predict missing QoS values.
6. PMF (probabilistic matrix factorization) [7]. This approach is proposed by Salakhutdinov and Minh, and it employs user-item matrix to predict the missing QoS value.
7. NMF (nonnegative matrix factorization) [2]. This approach is proposed by Lee and Seung. Compared to traditional matrix factorization approach, it mainly add an extra constraint to the model. That is the values in the factorized latent factors must be nonnegative.
8. NIMF (neighborhood-integrated matrix factorization) [19]. This approach employs the concept of user-collaboration for Web service QoS prediction. It finds out a list of similar users for the current user and integrate the information of similar users and all available QoS values to predict missing QoS values for service users.

In practice, service users only invoke a limited number of Web services. Therefore, the user-service matrix is very sparse. In this paper, we conduct the experiments by randomly remove a part of entries on the user-service matrix to make the matrix with different sparsity (i.e., 10% to 90%). For example, 10% denotes that we remove 90% entries on the user-service matrix. And then we set the 90% entries as testing set, the remaining 10% entries as training set. The QoS prediction accuracy results are shown in Table 2. As can be seen that our EFMPred model outperforms other state-of-the-art approaches in both of the response time and throughput. The table only presents the results of matrix density that is 10% and 90%, all results and impact of matrix density will be presented and discussed in Sect. 4.4.

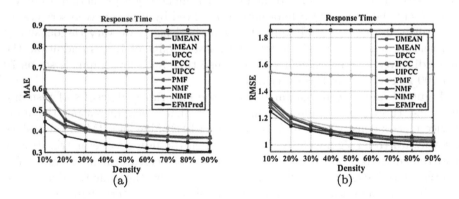

Fig. 4. Impact of matrix density (QoS property is response time)

Table 2. QoS prediction accuracy comparison

QoS properties	Methods	Matrix density = 10%		Matrix density = 90%	
		MAE	RMSE	MAE	RMSE
Response time	UMEAN	0.8767	1.8540	0.8738	1.8527
	IMEAN	0.6894	1.5416	0.6790	1.5267
	UPCC	0.5561	1.3092	0.3999	1.0857
	IPCC	0.5962	1.3433	0.3464	1.0280
	UIPCC	0.5836	1.3298	0.3447	1.0175
	PMF	0.4865	1.3134	0.3733	1.0505
	NMF	0.4785	1.2813	0.3700	1.0524
	NIMF	0.4792	1.2912	0.3677	1.0399
	EFMPred	**0.4446**	**1.2475**	**0.3048**	**0.9914**
Throughput	UMEAN	53.8912	110.3553	53.6560	109.7997
	IMEAN	26.8734	64.8046	26.4225	63.3956
	UPCC	22.6047	54.5224	13.5505	39.6461
	IPCC	26.1821	60.3531	16.9515	42.9243
	UIPCC	22.3635	54.4206	13.1886	38.4147
	PMF	15.9794	48.1784	11.9442	35.5825
	NMF	15.5678	47.9248	11.7964	35.9721
	NIMF	15.1393	47.0530	11.7977	35.6185
	EFMPred	**15.0268**	**44.0291**	**9.8157**	**30.5278**

4.4 Impact of Matrix Density

The matrix density is an important factor to impact QoS prediction accuracy. It represents how much QoS information observed by users on Web services we can utilize. In order to study impact of matrix density, we vary the density of user-service matrix from 10% to 90% with a step value of 10%. In addition, the embedding vector dimensionality of response time and throughput is set as 70 and 400 respectively in this experiment.

Figures 4 and 5 correspondingly show the experimental results of response time and throughput. Figure 4 demonstrates that when increasing the user-service matrix density from 10% to 50%, the MAE value and RMSE value show a downward trend significantly. However, when the user-service matrix density is increased from 50% to 90%, the magnitude of decrease in MAE value and RMSE value changes to relatively slow. Figure 5 shows the same trend as Fig. 4. This observation indicates that when the matrix density is very sparse, collecting more QoS information can do great favor to QoS prediction accuracy. However, when the matrix density is come to some extent (e.g. 50%), the effect of collecting more QoS information is not quite so obvious.

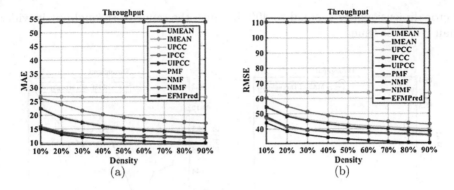

Fig. 5. Impact of matrix density (QoS property is throughput)

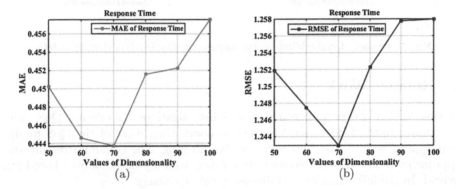

Fig. 6. Impact of embedding vector dimensionality (matrix density = 10%)

4.5   Impact of Dimensionality

Dimensionality determines how many embedding features are extracted from user id and service id, e.g. the dimensionality of embedding vectors in the EFM-Pred model. In order to study impact of the embedding vector dimensionality, we set the embedding vector dimensionality varying from 50 to 100 with a step value of 10 for response time. With regard to throughput, the embedding vector dimensionality is set from 100 to 1000 with a step value of 100. In this experiment, we set the matrix density as 10%. Figures 6 and 7 show the experimental results of response time and throughput respectively. Figure 6 demonstrates that when increasing the embedding vector dimensionality from 50 to 70, the MAE value and RMSE value show a downward trend. While the embedding vector dimensionality is from 70 to 100, the MAE value and RMSE value show an upward tendency. This observation shows that relatively large dimensionality (e.g., 70) can enhance the QoS prediction accuracy. However, if the dimensionality is set too large will cause the overfitting problem, which will potentially hurt the prediction quality. Figure 7 shows the same trend as Fig. 6. But we can obtain the lowest MAE value and RMSE value under the condition of the embedding vector dimensionality is equal to 400, because the range of throughput is wider than response time.

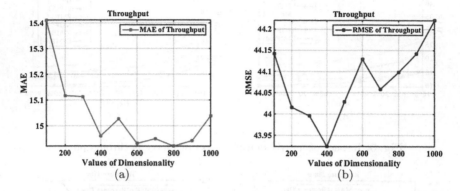

Fig. 7. Impact of embedding vector dimensionality (matrix density = 10%)

5   Related Work

In this section, we present some related investigations on missing QoS value prediction. In the field of service oriented computing, most of the QoS prediction approaches are based on collaborative filtering. The collaborative filtering approaches can be categorized into three types: memory-based, model-based and hybrid. In the following, we will discuss them separately.

The memory-based collaborative filtering approach employs users' historical records to compute the similarity between users or items. This approach includes user-based approach, item-based approach, and the hybrid of them. User-based approaches predict the missing QoS values by measuring the similarity between users. Item-based approaches predict the missing QoS values for the current user by measuring the similarity between services. Examples of memory-based approaches are as follows. Sun et al. [10] present a new similarity measure for Web service similarity computation and propose a novel normal recovery collaborative filtering approach. Xiong et al. [14] propose a collaborative approach to QoS prediction of Web services on unbalanced data distribution. Ma et al. [4] propose an unknown QoS values prediction algorithm to realize some important characteristics of objective QoS datasets.

The model-based collaborative filtering approach tend to apply machine learning algorithms to predict users' rating of unrated items. Examples of model-based approaches are as follows. Wu et al. [13] propose a novel two-phase K-means clustering based credibility-aware QoS prediction method to address the problem of unreliable data offered by untrustworthy users. Yu et al. [15] propose a novel neighbor factor model by taking the latent physical location and network status information into consideration. Zheng et al. [19] propose a neighborhood integrated matrix factorization approach for Web services QoS prediction by taking advantages of the past Web service usage experiences of service users.

The hybrid collaborative filtering approach integrates the memory-based and the model-based collaborative filtering approaches. Examples of hybrid approaches are as follows. Chen et al. [1] propose a neighborhood regularized matrix factorization method by properly incorporating both user and Web service neighborhood relationships. Su et al. [9] present a novel hybrid Web service QoS prediction approach by integrating the direct similarity and transitive indirect similarity of services. Lo et al. [3] propose an extended matrix factorization framework with relational regularization terms inside a neighborhood.

The above memory-based, model-based and hybrid methods can solve the problem of missing QoS prediction to some extent. However, the drawbacks of these approaches are huge sparsity, high time complexity and expensive to implement. But our EFMPred model employs the embedding features extracting techniques to represent the vectors of user id and service id. The embedding vectors can model the interactions between users and Web services. In addition, our embedding based factorization machine model can solve the problem of data sparsity and can be calculated in linear time.

6 Conclusion

This paper proposes an embedding based factorization machine approach to predict missing QoS values for Web service in order to improve the prediction accuracy and avoid time-consuming and expensive Web services invocation. By employing embedding technique and factorization machine model, we can reduce the dimensionality of vectors, learn features with large data sparsity and our EFMPred can be computed in linear time. Therefore, our EFMPred model can be easily extended to large data sets. Comprehensive experiments demonstrate that our approach outperforms other state-of-the-art baseline approaches.

At present, we mainly focus on response time and throughput value prediction. In future, we'd like to apply our model to other QoS properties of the real-world Web services (i.e., failure tolerance, reliability, availability, etc.). Other characteristics of service users and Web services can also be taken into consideration to integrate them into our model.

Acknowledgment. The authors would like to thank the anonymous reviewers for their valuable feedback and comments. The work described in this paper was supported by the National Key Research and Development Program (2016YFB1000101), the National Natural Science Foundation of China (61472338), the Pearl River S&T Nova Program of Guangzhou (201710010046) and the Fundamental Research Funds for the Central Universities under Grant (17lgpy117).

References

1. Chen, Z., Shen, L., You, D., Li, F.: A user dependent web service QoS collaborative prediction approach using neighborhood regularized matrix factorization. In: 2016 IEEE 20th International Conference on Computer Supported Cooperative Work in Design (CSCWD), pp. 316–321. IEEE (2016)

2. Lee, D.D., Seung, H.S.: Learning the parts of objects by non-negative matrix factorization. Nature **401**(6755), 788–791 (1999)
3. Lo, W., Yin, J., Deng, S., Li, Y., Wu, Z.: An extended matrix factorization approach for QoS prediction in service selection. In: 2012 IEEE Ninth International Conference on Services Computing (SCC), pp. 162–169. IEEE (2012)
4. Ma, Y., Wang, S., Hung, P.C., Hsu, C.H., Sun, Q., Yang, F.: A highly accurate prediction algorithm for unknown web service QoS values. IEEE Trans. Serv. Comput. **9**(4), 511–523 (2016)
5. Rendle, S.: Factorization machines. In: 2010 IEEE 10th International Conference on Data Mining (ICDM), pp. 995–1000. IEEE (2010)
6. Resnick, P., Iacovou, N., Suchak, M., Bergstrom, P., Riedl, J.: Grouplens: an open architecture for collaborative filtering of netnews. In: Proceedings of the 1994 ACM Conference on Computer Supported Cooperative Work, pp. 175–186. ACM (1994)
7. Salakhutdinov, R., Mnih, A.: Probabilistic matrix factorization. In: NIPS, vol. 1, pp. 2–1 (2007)
8. Shao, L., Zhang, J., Wei, Y., Zhao, J., Xie, B., Mei, H.: Personalized QoS prediction forWeb services via collaborative filtering. In: 2007 IEEE International Conference on Web Services, ICWS 2007, pp. 439–446. IEEE (2007)
9. Su, K., Ma, L., Xiao, B., Zhang, H.: Web service QoS prediction by neighbor information combined non-negative matrix factorization. J. Intell. Fuzzy Syst. **30**(6), 3593–3604 (2016)
10. Sun, H., Zheng, Z., Chen, J., Lyu, M.R.: Personalized web service recommendation via normal recovery collaborative filtering. IEEE Trans. Serv. Comput. **6**(4), 573–579 (2013)
11. Van Ooyen, A., Nienhuis, B.: Improving the convergence of the back-propagation algorithm. Neural Netw. **5**(3), 465–471 (1992)
12. Willmott, C.J., Matsuura, K.: Advantages of the mean absolute error (MAE) over the root mean square error (RMSE) in assessing average model performance. Climate Res. **30**(1), 79–82 (2005)
13. Wu, C., Qiu, W., Zheng, Z., Wang, X., Yang, X.: QoS prediction of web services based on two-phase k-means clustering. In: 2015 IEEE International Conference on Web Services (ICWS), pp. 161–168. IEEE (2015)
14. Xiong, W., Li, B., He, L., Chen, M., Chen, J.: Collaborative web service QoS prediction on unbalanced data distribution. In: 2014 IEEE International Conference on Web Services (ICWS), pp. 377–384. IEEE (2014)
15. Yu, D., Liu, Y., Xu, Y., Yin, Y.: Personalized QoS prediction for web services using latent factor models. In: 2014 IEEE International Conference on Services Computing (SCC), pp. 107–114. IEEE (2014)
16. Zeng, L., Benatallah, B., Ngu, A.H., Dumas, M., Kalagnanam, J., Chang, H.: QoS-aware middleware for web services composition. IEEE Trans. Softw. Eng. **30**(5), 311–327 (2004)
17. Zhang, L.J., Cai, H., Zhang, J.: Services Computing. Springer, Heidelberg (2007)
18. Zheng, Z., Ma, H., Lyu, M.R., King, I.: Qos-aware web service recommendation by collaborative filtering. IEEE Trans. Serv. Comput. **4**(2), 140–152 (2011)
19. Zheng, Z., Ma, H., Lyu, M.R., King, I.: Collaborative web service qos prediction via neighborhood integrated matrix factorization. IEEE Trans. Serv. Comput. **6**(3), 289–299 (2013)

A Deep Learning Approach for Long Term QoS-Compliant Service Composition

Hamza Labbaci[1,2], Brahim Medjahed[2(✉)], and Youcef Aklouf[1]

[1] USTHB University, Algiers, Algeria
hlabbaci@umich.edu, yaklouf@usthb.dz
[2] University of Michigan - Dearborn, Dearborn, USA
brahim@umich.edu

Abstract. In this paper, we propose a deep learning approach for long-term Quality of Service (QoS)-based service composition. Existing techniques for quality-aware service composition mostly focus on static QoS values observed during composition time. They do not consider potential QoS fluctuations in the long run when selecting services for composition or substitution. Our approach uses deep recurrent Long Short Term Memories (LSTMs) to forecast future QoS. The predicted QoS values are used to accurately recommend components and substitutes in long-term service compositions. Experiments show promising results compared to existing QoS prediction techniques.

Keywords: Service composition · Substitution · Quality of Service (QoS) · Deep learning · LSTMs

1 Introduction

During the last decade, many organizations embraced service-oriented computing technologies, seeking better visibility and more market opportunities. Web services (APIs) with complementary functionalities (called *components*) collaborate as part of the same *service composition* to provide value-added services [5, 7]. The success and longevity of collaborations in a service composition strongly depend on the ability of the different components to maintain *long-term* Quality of Service (QoS) requirements [4]. Developing long-term compositions raises the challenge of selecting components that satisfy QoS requirements over long time periods. Such selection implies predicting long-term QoS trends (i.e., QoS during a long period). The main challenge related to forecasting long-term QoS is that QoS values may fluctuate in the future.

We identify three advantages for leveraging long-term QoS trends during composition. First, developers rely on predicted QoS to accurately select the best services that are likely to fulfill composition requirements over a long time period. This caters for durable partnerships among component services. Second, component services undergo several changes during their lifespan (e.g., a service going out of business) that may lead to breaking contracts between composite and component services. Developers will then be able to substitute components by services with comparable long-term QoS. Third, service providers

© Springer International Publishing AG 2017
M. Maximilien et al. (Eds.): ICSOC 2017, LNCS 10601, pp. 287–294, 2017.
https://doi.org/10.1007/978-3-319-69035-3_20

(e.g., cloud providers) may rely on QoS prediction for better resources management and workload balancing. For instance, they may harness more server resources (processor and memory) during peak periods. Accurate QoS prediction allows service providers to adjust their cloud resources to satisfy users' demands as accurately as possible in the future. This reduces contract disruption between long-term composite services and their components because of QoS violations.

Several techniques for QoS-based service composition have been proposed in the literature [9,11,12]. However, they mostly focus on static QoS values observed during composition time. In practice, QoS varies over time; such future variations need to be taken into consideration while designing composite services. Unlike current techniques, we propose a deep learning approach for long-term service compositions. We use deep recurrent Long Short Term Memories (LSTMs) [3] to predict long-term QoS trends. Such predictions cater for selecting best Web services that satisfy QoS-related composition requirements in the long run. To the best of our knowledge, this is the first work that uses deep learning and particularly deep recurrent LSTMs for long-term QoS-aware service composition and substitution.

The rest of the paper is organized as follows. Section 2 describes our deep learning approach for QoS prediction. Section 3 presents our technique for leveraging the predicted QoS during composition and substitution times. Section 4 discusses the experimental study. Section 5 reviews related work. Section 6 concludes the paper.

2   Using Deep Learning for QoS Prediction

The aim of the proposed approach is to assist developers in designing composite services and substituting components while considering long-term QoS trends. The composition middleware implements techniques to identify, orchestrate, and substitute component services. The way component and substitute services are selected by the middleware is out of the scope of this paper. Our approach augments any existing composition and substitution technique such as the ones proposed in [5] with long-term QoS prediction and compliance capabilities.

2.1   QoS Composition Requirements

Developers provide two kinds of composition requirements to the composition middleware: middleware-specific requirements such as functional and semantic features (out of the scope of this paper) and *QoS requirements*. For each QoS metric, developers specify *preferred* and *acceptable* intervals. Figure 1 shows an example of QoS requirements for processing speed between $[T_0, T_1]$ (e.g., this year's summer season), $[T_1, T_2]$ (e.g. this year's fall season), ..., $[T_7, T_8]$. Gray and dark rectangles refer to acceptable and preferred QoS intervals, respectively. Figure 1 also shows the predicted computation speed $Q_1(t)$, $Q_2(t)$, and $Q_3(t)$ that three services S_1, S_2, and S_3 are likely to guarantee the next two years. Our approach compares the areas under the predicted curves with the area under the required QoS that are either bounded by the acceptable or preferred rectangles.

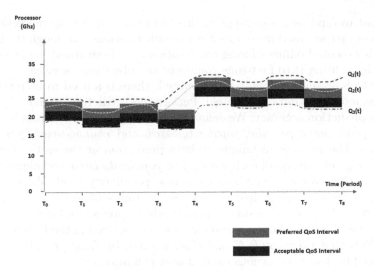

Fig. 1. Examples of QoS Prediction Trends

2.2 Predicting Long-Term QoS Trends

The *QoS Predictor (QP)* handles QoS prediction for all services and stores the predicted QoS curves in a *QoS Repository*. It has access to log files that contain QoS data observed over time for the different Web services in the system. The way QoS is monitored and obtained is out of the scope of this paper. [4] and [2] give details about QoS monitoring techniques.

QP learns from the history of observed QoS values to forecast long-term QoS trend. For that purpose, we train deep recurrent Long Short Term Memories (LSTMs) [3] with sequences of QoS values observed at different periods of time. LSTM is a particular type recurrent nets with the ability to avoid the long-term dependency problem. They can remember information for long periods of time. Unlike classic recurrent nets, LSTMs overcome very well the problem of vanishing gradient and can learn from size variable sequences of data. LSTM is trained with n raw data X_j. Each X_j is composed by an input Q_i and an output Q_{i+1} where Q_i and Q_{i+1} denote observed service QoS at times T_i and T_{i+1} respectively. The goal behind training the LSTM with sequences of QoS is to predict services future QoS values for a given period of time.

Predicting QoS trends is time consuming. To minimize the incurred overhead on the overall composition development (during component selection) and execution (during component substitution) times, we define two techniques for bootstrapping QoS prediction: *random* and *first-hit*. The *random* technique arbitrarily selects a service in the system during off-peak hours, and executes prediction algorithms for that service. This technique has the advantage of calculating predictions offline, with little or no impact on composition/substitution times. However, it may perform prediction for services that are never used in compositions/substitutions. The *first-hit* bootstrapping technique runs prediction algorithms for a service when it first participates in a composition/substitution.

In contrast to random bootstrapping, this technique carries out prediction only for services that are used in compositions or substitutions. Although the first-hit method is executed online (during composition or substitution), its overhead is reduced by limiting it to first-time composed or substituted services.

Once QoS prediction trends are generated, there is a need to keep them up-to-date as more QoS data is gathered. Performing prediction on more QoS data improves prediction accuracy. We define three event-based techniques for updating QoS predictions: *periodic*, *popularity-based*, and *change-based* QoS update techniques. The *periodic* technique updates prediction at the end of each time period T (e.g., at the end of each week). The *popularity-based* technique updates prediction whenever a service reaches a new popularity level. We say that a service is *popular* if it participated in N composition and substitution since the latest update. The *change-based* technique updates prediction for a given service whenever big changes, above a certain level C, are noticed in the QoS log of that service. Note that values of T, N, and C are selected by cloud providers and may be adjusted to deal with various environment conditions.

3   Long-Term QoS Compliance Checking

The composition middleware sends two types of recommendation requests to the *Long-Term QoS Compliance Checker (LQCC)*: composition and substitution requests. A composition recommendation request includes the ID of a potential component along with QoS requirements to LQCC. LQCC requests the QoS prediction trend for the component from the *QoS Predictor*. Then, it checks compatibility between the QoS prediction and QoS requirement intervals, and returns a composition recommendation to the middleware. A substitution recommendation request includes IDs of the services to substitute and potential substitutes to LQCC. LQCC obtains the QoS prediction trends for the component to substitute and potential substitute from the QoS Predictor. Then, it checks whether the two trends are close enough to each other and returns a substitution recommendation to LQCC.

3.1   Checking Compliance for Service Composition

We introduce two heuristics to check long-term QoS compliance for composition: *Conservative* and *Soft* heuristics. The *conservative* heuristic states that a service S is long-term QoS compliant with the developer's QoS requirement iff for each time interval $[T_i, T_{i+1}]$ in the prediction time interval $[\alpha, \beta]$, the area under the predicted QoS curve of S is greater than the area under the lower bound of the *preferred* QoS requirement curve, and is less than or equal the area under the higher bound of the *preferred* QoS requirement curve. The rational behind this heuristic is to make sure the component's QoS prediction curve remains within the preferred interval throughout the various time periods.

$$\int_{t_i}^{t_{i+1}} (q(t) - p_{lower}(t)) > \epsilon \text{ and } \int_{t_i}^{t_{i+1}} (p_{higher}(t) - q(t)) > \epsilon$$

where ϵ ($\epsilon \geq 0$) is a composition compliance threshold, $q(t)$, $p_{higher}(t)$, and $p_{lower}(t)$ stand for the component's predicted QoS, the *preferred* higher bound QoS, and the preferred lower bound QoS respectively.

The *soft* composition compliance heuristic states that a component is long-term QoS compliant with the developer's QoS requirements iff the sum of the areas under the component's predicted QoS curves is superior to the sum of the areas under the lower bound of the *acceptable* QoS curves, and is less than or equals to the sum of the areas under the higher bound of the *preferred* QoS curves. The rationale behind this heuristic is to make sure that the overall component's QoS prediction curve is within any of the preferred or acceptable QoS intervals. The component's curve may fall outside the QoS requirement boundaries within a certain time period $[T_i, T_{i+1}]$ as long as there are other time periods that make up for the QoS loss in $[T_i, T_{i+1}]$.

$$(\sum_{i=\alpha}^{i=\beta-1} \int_{t_i}^{t_{i+1}} (q(t) - a_{lower}(t))) > \epsilon \text{ and } (\sum_{i=\alpha}^{i=\beta-1} \int_{t_i}^{t_{i+1}} (p_{higher}(t) - q(t))) > \epsilon$$

where ϵ is a composition compliance threshold ($\epsilon \geq 0$), $q(t)$, $p_{higer}(t)$, and $a_{lower}(t)$ stand for the predicted QoS, the *preferred* QoS requirement upper bound, and the *acceptable* QoS requirement lower bound.

3.2   Checking Compliance for Service Substitution

Similarly to composition, we introduce two heuristics to check long-term QoS compliance for substitution: *Conservative* and *Soft* substitution heuristics. The *conservative* heuristic states that a service S is long-term QoS compliant with a potential candidate substitute C iff for each time interval $[T_i, T_{i+1}]$ in the prediction time interval $[\alpha, \beta]$, the difference between the two areas under the predicted QoS curves of S and C is less than or equal a threshold value ϵ ($\epsilon \geq 0$).

$$\int_{t_i}^{t_{i+1}} |(q_S(t) - q_C(t))| \leq \epsilon$$

where $q_S(t)$ and $q_C(t)$ stand for the predicted QoS of S and C respectively.

The *soft* heuristic states that a service S is long-term QoS compliant with a potential candidate substitute C iff the sum of the differences between the areas under the predicted QoS curves of S and C is less than or equal to the sum of the areas under the required QoS curves.

$$(\sum_{i=\alpha}^{i=\beta-1} \int_{t_i}^{t_{i+1}} |(q_S(t) - q_C(t))|) \leq \epsilon$$

where ϵ is a threshold such that $\epsilon \geq 0$, $q_S(t)$ and $q_C(t)$ stand for the predicted QoS of S and C, respectively.

4 Experimental Study

The goal of our experiments is to assess the ability of the proposed approach to correctly recommend services for composition and substitution. The accuracy of such recommendation strongly depends on the accuracy of forecasting long-term QoS. We ran our experiments on a 64-bit Windows 10 environment, in a machine equipped with an intel i7 and 12 GO RAM. We used Keras[1] with Google's Tensorflow[2] as back-end for implementing and training the LSTM model. As it is difficult to get the history of real QoS values, we generated synthetic QoS values (disk storage usage) over different periods of time. Generated values are used to train our QoS prediction models.

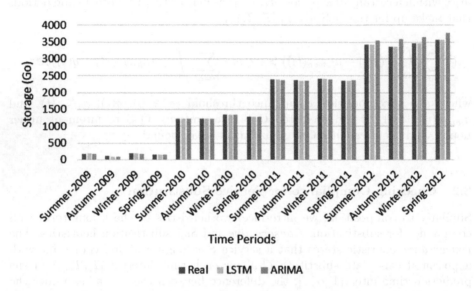

Fig. 2. Comparison of Predicted Storage with LSTMs and ARIMA Models

We compare the accuracy of the proposed prediction with the one that uses ARIMA model [9]. ARIMA (AutoRegressive Integrated Moving Averages) has been successfully used for time series forecasting. Auto regressive means the prediction of $x(t)$ depends on $p = k, p, k \in N$ previous terms. For instance, for $p = 3$, the prediction of $x(t)$ depends on $x(t-1), x(t-2)$, and $x(t-3)$. Moving averages means the prediction depends on the $q = k, q, k \in N$ previous errors.

Figure 2 shows a comparison of the prediction accuracy of our approach (LSTM) and ARIMA. Both models are trained with service storage data from Summer-2009 until Spring-2011 and tested with service storage data from Summer-2012 until Spring-2012. Figure 2 shows that both LSTM and ARIMA achieves comparable accuracy on the training data. However, LSTM outperforms

---

[1] https://keras.io/.
[2] http://www.tensorflow.com/.

ARIMA on test data. The justification is that LSTM uses many deep hidden layers with non linear transformations among the layers such as *sigmoid* and *tanh* functions. LSTM also saves information longer by using the forget and update gates, hence the bigger the training set, the better LSTM learns and the more accurate is the prediction. On the other hand, ARIMA bases the prediction on p lags which means that the prediction depends on p previous terms.

5   Related Work

In this section, we review the main techniques related to QoS-aware composition of Web services. [9] used the Autoregressive Integrated Moving Average (ARIMA) model to predict future behaviours of the service requests. However, it is not suitable for designing long-term composition as it does not gather stochastic request arrivals. [13] used matrix factorization of a user-service matrix to predict future QoS that can be used for designing compositions. Singular Value Decomposition SVD decomposes the user-service matrix into the product of a user matrix and a service matrix. The reconstructed matrix from the previous product contains the predicted QoS values. Previous approaches rely on instantaneous service QoS values for predicting future QoS that can be used for designing compositions. Our approach uses deep recurrent LSTMs to foresee how QoS values are expected to evolve in time. Such prediction allows providers to better allocate resources to services and developers to better select services for designing long-term compositions. Our approach achieves a more accurate QoS forecasting than the linear methods such as ARIMA [9]. Deep recurrent LSTMs use many hidden layers and non linear transformations between the layers such as *tanh* function. [10] proposed a model for cloud service providers that predicts consumer's service usage behavior (i.e., next requests) and computes the costs of these requests with the goal to maximize cloud service providers incomes. [8] proposes an approach to compose customer requests using the provider long-term qualitative model. Long-term qualitative model is represented as a temporal CP-net. IaaS composition is transformed as a preference maximization optimization problem. [6] defines an approach for long-term QoS-aware cloud service composition. It introduces three meta-heuristic namely Genetic Algorithm, Simulated annealing, and Tabu search to select only services with the best averaged long-term QoS. Our approach relies on deep learning for service QoS prediction. Additionally, we use QoS prediction for both long-term service composition and substitution. LSTMs have been successfully used to solve different prediction problems such as predicting human trajectory in crowded spaces [1]. To the best of our knowledge, this is the first work that uses deep learning for designing long-term QoS aware service composition and substitution techniques.

6   Conclusion

In this paper, we proposed a deep learning approach for service composition using long-term predicted QoS trends. We used deep recurrent Long Short Term Memories (LSTMs) to predict QoS trends over future time periods. The predicted

QoS is used during (i) composition time to ascertain that selected components statisfy developers' QoS requirements in the long run and (ii) substitution to verify that a component and its potential substitute have similar QoS trends. Experiments conducted over synthetic data show that the use of LSTMs for QoS prediction outperforms other techniques such as ARIMA.

References

1. Alahi, A., Goel, K., Ramanathan, V., Robicquet, A., Fei-Fei, L., Savarese, S.: Social lstm: Human trajectory prediction in crowded spaces. In: Proceedings of the IEEE Conference on Computer Vision and Pattern Recognition, pp. 961–971 (2016)
2. Ardagna, D., Casale, G., Ciavotta, M., Pérez, J.F., Wang, W.: Quality-of-service in cloud computing: modeling techniques and their applications. J. Internet Serv. Appl. 5(1), 11:1–11:17 (2014)
3. Hochreiter, S., Schmidhuber, J.: Long short-term memory. Neural Comput. 9(8), 1735–1780 (1997)
4. Kritikos, K., Pernici, B., Plebani, P., Cappiello, C., Comuzzi, M., Benbernou, S.: I, B., Kertész, A., Parkin, M., Carro, M.: A survey on service quality description. ACM Comput. Surv. 46(1), 1:1–1:58 (2013)
5. Lemos, A.L., Daniel, F., Benatallah, B.: Web service composition: a survey of techniques and tools. ACM Comput. Surv. 48(3), 33:1–33:41 (2016)
6. Liu, S., Wei, Y., Tang, K., Qin, A.K., Yao, X.: Qos-aware long-term based service composition in cloud computing. In: IEEE Congress on Evolutionary Computation (CEC) 2015, pp. 3362–3369 (2015)
7. Medjahed, B., Benatallah, B., Bouguettaya, A., Ngu, A.H.H., Elmagarmid, A.K.: Business-to-business interactions: issues and enabling technologies. VLDB J. 12(1), 59–85 (2003)
8. Mistry, S., Bouguettaya, A., Dong, H., Erradi, A.: Qualitative economic model for long-term iaas composition. In: International Conference on Service-Oriented Computing, pp. 317–332 (2016)
9. Mistry, S., Bouguettaya, A., Dong, H., Qin, A.K.: Predicting dynamic requests behavior in long-term iaas service composition. In: IEEE International Conference on Web Services (ICWS) 2015, pp. 49–56. IEEE (2015)
10. Mistry, S., Bouguettaya, A., Dong, H., Qin, A.: Metaheuristic optimization for long-term iaas service composition. IEEE Trans. Serv. Comput. (2017)
11. Wang, S., Zhu, X., Yang, F.: Efficient qos management for qos-aware web service composition. Int. J. Web Grid Serv. 10(1), 1–23 (2014)
12. Zeng, L., Benatallah, B., Ngu, A.H., Dumas, M., Kalagnanam, J., Chang, H.: Qos-aware middleware for web services composition. IEEE Trans. Softw. Eng. 30(5), 311–327 (2004)
13. Zhu, J., He, P., Zheng, Z., Lyu, M.R.: Towards online, accurate, and scalable qos prediction for runtime service adaptation. In: IEEE 34th International Conference on Distributed Computing Systems (ICDCS) 2014, pp. 318–327 (2014)

Run-time Service Operation and Management

An Artifact-Driven Approach to Monitor Business Processes Through Real-World Objects

Giovanni Meroni[1]([✉]), Claudio Di Ciccio[2], and Jan Mendling[2]

[1] Dipartimento di Elettronica, Informazione e Bioingegneria,
Politecnico di Milano, Milan, Italy
giovanni.meroni@polimi.it
[2] Institute for Information Business,
Vienna University of Economics and Business, Vienna, Austria
{claudio.di.ciccio,jan.mendling}@wu.ac.at

Abstract. Nowadays, many business processes once intra-organizational are becoming inter-organizational. Thus, being able to monitor how such processes are performed, including portions carried out by service providers, is paramount. Yet, traditional process monitoring techniques present some shortcomings when dealing with inter-organizational processes. In particular, they require human operators to notify when business activities are performed, and to stop the process when it is not executed as expected. In this paper, we address these issues by proposing an artifact-driven monitoring service, capable of autonomously and continuously monitor inter-organizational processes. To do so, this service relies on the state of the artifacts (i.e., physical entities) participating to the process, represented using the E-GSM notation. A working prototype of this service is presented and validated using real-world processes and data from the logistics domain.

Keywords: Artifact-driven process monitoring · Physical artifacts · E-GSM · Inter-organizational monitoring service · Autonomous process monitoring

1 Introduction

In recent years, a large number of organizations opted to outsource some of their business services to external service providers, either partially or entirely [12]. By doing so, many traditionally intra-organizational business processes have become inter-organizational. The adoption of this strategy has brought several advantages. For example, organizations can now focus on their core business, rather than having to deal with support processes, e.g., logistics. Furthermore, specialized service providers usually deal with the externalized processes more efficiently and effectively than internal divisions of organizations operating on different markets. However, outsourcing has also brought some issues, one of which is the inability for an organization to directly control how the outsourced processes are executed. It is up to the service provider to execute these processes as agreed with

M. Maximilien et al. (Eds.): ICSOC 2017, LNCS 10601, pp. 297–313, 2017.
https://doi.org/10.1007/978-3-319-69035-3_21

the organization. In such a case, a service capable to constantly monitor the execution of inter-organizational processes becomes crucial. A process monitoring service allows an organization to know a.o. *(i)* when business activities composing the process are executed, and *(ii)* if their execution order complies with the process model, namely the formal specification of how the process should be performed. This way, countermeasures can be taken in case violations in the execution occur, and a better coordination among the organization and the service providers can be achieved.

Traditionally, monitoring services are included in Business Process Management Systems (BPMSs), namely the software components responsible for automating the execution of business processes [10]. However, a BPMS presents shortcomings when monitoring inter-organizational processes. Firstly, unless an activity is completely automated and fully executed by the BPMS, human operators have to manually notify the BPMS that an activity starts or ends. Such a task disrupts the operator's work, and can be easily forgotten or postponed, thus negatively affecting the reliability of the monitoring. Secondly, whenever the process is not executed as agreed, BPMS usually halt the execution of the process until the violation is manually solved by a human operator. Consequently, the process execution is not tracked until the violation is solved. This is undesirable: In an inter-organizational process, service providers could continue running their processes even though the BPMS halted. Such an issue can be partially mitigated by instructing the BPMS not to halt in case of violations, so as to successively resort to mining techniques to detect the disruptions in the recorded execution log. However, such an approach impedes an organization to promptly react to violations.

To overcome these issues, we propose a novel monitoring service which can autonomously *(i)* monitor the execution of non-automated activities, as long as they interact with machine-tracked real-world objects, and *(ii)* identify incorrectly executed activities yet continue monitoring the process after a violation occurs. The approach we present is built upon the usage of the Extended-GSM (E-GSM) artifact-centric language [20] for the automated monitoring of processes. Our approach is implemented with a software prototype. We demonstrate the efficacy of our approach with an application on a real-world use case from the logistics domain.

The remainder of this paper is structured as follows. Section 2 introduces a motivating example used to describe, in Sect. 3, our approach. The architecture of a monitoring service based on our approach is discussed in Sect. 4. Section 5 validates our work against real processes and data. Finally, Sect. 6 surveys related work and Sect. 7 concludes the paper outlining the future research plans.

2   Motivating Example

To better understand the need for an inter-organizational monitoring service, we focus on a real scenario taken from the logistics domain, which will be used throughout this paper. However, logistics is only one of the possible case studies.

In fact, our solution is beneficial to every inter-organizational business process interacting with real-world objects.

A manufacturer located in the United Kingdom, M, has a long-term provisioning contract with customer C, located in Germany. To send its goods to C, M relies on logistics company L, headquartered in Amsterdam, which owns several inland terminals located nearby the principal airports of Europe. Instead of performing the actual shipments, L outsources them to several truck shippers S, each one responsible for one or more legs (i.e., for all the shipments from the headquarters to a specific terminal and vice-versa). The shipment process from M to C is organized as follows. At first, a container is shipped from the plant of M to a terminal located near London Heathrow Airport, which serves the UK market. We call this leg M-TU. Then, the container is shipped to the headquarters of L (TU-HQ leg). After that, the container is shipped to a terminal located near Frankfurt, which serves the German market (HQ-TG leg). Finally, the container is delivered to C (TG-C leg).

The TU-HQ leg is organized as follows. Firstly, the container is loaded onto a truck of S (Load container), which subsequently starts traveling in the UK (Travel in UK) until either a break is taken (Take break in UK), or the entrance to the Channel tunnel is reached. The alternation of traveling hours with breaks forms a loop which we name UK Loop. In the first case, once the break ends, the truck continues traveling in the UK. In the second case, the truck takes the Channel tunnel (Take Channel tunnel), then continues traveling on continental Europe (Travel in EU) until either it reaches the headquarters, or it takes a break (Take break in EU). We name this loop of travel and breaks within continental Europe as EU Loop. In the first case, the container is unloaded (Unload container) and the process ends. In the last case, the truck continues traveling in Europe once the break ends. The other legs are organized similarly. Once the container is loaded, the truck starts traveling (either in the UK or in continental Europe, depending on the location of the leg) until either the destination is reached, or a break is taken. Similarly to the TU-HQ leg, once the break ends, the truck starts traveling again.

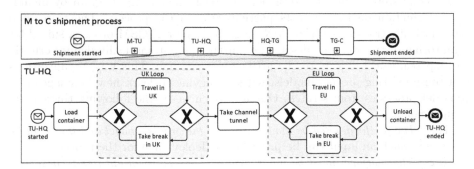

Fig. 1. BPMN diagram of the running example: High-level process model (top), and expanded subprocess TU-HQ (bottom).

The upper part of Fig. 1 depicts the whole shipment process using the Business Process Model and Notation (BPMN) language. The lower part of Fig. 1, on the other hand, depicts the TU-HQ leg. It is worth noting that none of the involved organizations has full control of the execution of the whole process. Since each leg is outsourced to a different truck shipping company S, S controls only those activities inside its own leg, and cannot alter the execution of the other ones. P, C, and L, who are the only organizations interested in the whole process, have no direct control on it. Therefore, to allow each organization to know how the whole process is being run, a monitoring service is needed.

3   Approach

The underlying idea of our approach is that the execution of an activity involving real-world objects is reflected in the modification of their status. In the example of Fig. 1, e.g., the loaded truck updating its position from the European end of the Channel tunnel towards Frankfurt in the physical world indicates the enactment of activity Travel in EU in the sub-process TU-HQ. Updates on the status of trucks are typically provided by AIS/GPS on-board units to the systems of the logistic control rooms. The transmitted information is elaborated and can lead in the process environment to a change of state of the related artifacts. The platform can thus observe the real-world objects involved in the process execution, and compare the evolution of their status with the expected enactment of the process. This allows for a monitoring that does not require a human intervention to signal the progress of process instances. When the process instances' execution differs from the prescribed one, a violation is detected. The platform becomes aware of such a discrepancy when the observed artifacts' state changes do not match with the model of the running process. It can identify which activities are affected, flag them as non compliant, and alert the involved stakeholders.

We propose a four-steps procedure to provide the necessary information. The first step is taking as input a BPMN process diagram, one of the most used formalisms for process modeling, representing the process to be monitored. The second step requires the designer to enrich the BPMN diagram by including information on the artifacts participating in the process. The third step automatically translates the BPMN diagram into an E-GSM process, suited for monitoring distributed processes. The fourth step automatically defines criteria to map real-world objects to the artifacts at runtime. This way, organizations can reuse existing process models, without having to learn new languages and remodel processes from scratch. Our approach poses the following three main requirements.

R1. *The platform must be made aware of the process model and the involved artifacts.* Such an input can be provided at deploy time for the process.

R2. *The platform must be made aware of the physical entities to observe.* The second requirement pertains to the run-time link between real-world objects and artifacts. Not the same truck will be used for all deliveries: Different real-world objects may embody the same process artifact. However, it may not be possible to know at design-time which real-world objects will be involved in the carry-out of every process instance. Oftentimes such an information is available only after the process instance started.

Such a binding should be definable at runtime. By the same line of reasoning, the information on the previously involved artifacts may be no longer relevant to the ongoing process at some stage, as in the case of the truck moving away from the logistics company headquarters once activity TU-HQ is concluded. Hence the following requirement.

R3. *The binding and unbinding of physical entities to process instances has to be made declarable.*

In the following, we explain how our solution meets those requirements.

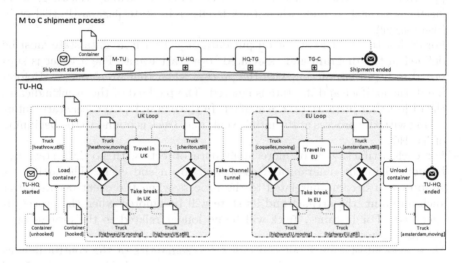

Fig. 2. BPMN process model enriched with information on the participating artifacts.

3.1 Enrichment of the BPMN Process Model with Artifacts

A BPMN process diagram specifies which activities are executed in a process and their control flow relationships. However, to be able to infer when activities start or end based on the state of the artifacts, the diagram must capture this information (requirement R1). Furthermore, the following binding and unbinding mechanisms among artifacts and real-world objects must be specified in the diagram: *(i)* When an artifact starts interacting with the process (R3); *(ii)* How the object impersonating the artifact is notified to the process (R2); *(iii)* When an artifact is no longer related to the process (R3).

To this extent, we resort on the standard BPMN *data objects*, rather than introducing yet another extension of BPMN. Data objects traditionally serve for documentation purposes, yet we use them to model the artifacts and their interactions with the process. Moreover, we establish the following set of rules to guarantee at design-time that the process model contains enough information to completely and unambiguously automate the monitoring of the process at run-time. The explanatory examples provided for the rules are shown in Fig. 2.

- An artifact must be modeled with data objects. The name of the data object identifies the artifact (e.g., Truck), whereas the data state identifies in which condition the artifact is supposed to be (e.g., [highwayUK,moving]).
- Each monitored activity must have at least one input and one output data object. The activity is supposed to start (resp., finish) only when all input (output) data objects exist and have the specified data state. If an activity has two input (output) data objects referring to the same artifact in different data states, the artifact must assume one of the specified states. For example, Travel in UK starts when Truck is either in state [highwayUK,moving], or in [heathrow,moving]. It ends when Truck is either in state [highwayUK,still] or in [cheriton,still].
- For each artifact, at least one output data object with no data state must be defined in the diagram and associated to a start event. The artifact is supposed to begin interacting with the process when that event occurs. Beforehand, the artifact and its state is ignored. The payload of the event indicates the object that instantiates the artifact. In the example, Container starts interacting with the process at its initial event, and Truck is bound to the beginning of TU-HQ.
- For each artifact, zero or more input data objects with no data state can be defined in the diagram and associated to an end event. The artifact is supposed to become unrelated to the process when the event occurs (after such an event, the artifact and its state will be ignored when the process is executed). For instance, Truck will be no longer related to the process once TU-HQ finishes.
- Data associations must not contradict the semantics of the control flow as they are used to identify when activities start or end. For example, Travel in UK cannot be declared to start only when Truck is in [heathrow,moving], otherwise it could not start again after a break along the journey through UK, far from the airport (despite the loop in the process model). Therefore Truck[highwayUK,moving] is set as another input for Travel in UK and as an output of Take break in UK.

Example. Figure 2 shows the process model obtained by extending the one presented in Sect. 2 according to the previously mentioned rules. The input and output data objects of Unload container indicate the preconditions and postconditions for that activity to be executed. To execute Unload container, the container must be hooked to the truck, and the truck must already be parked in the headquarters of L. When Unload container finishes, the container will be unhooked from the truck, and the truck will leave the headquarters of L. As the container participates in the whole process, its data object is associated to the start and end events of the process. On the other hand, a specific truck may only participate to a single subprocess. As such, the data object representing the truck is associated to the start and end events of each subprocess.

3.2   Generation of the E-GSM Process Model

Due to its imperative nature, BPMN treats control flow information in a prescriptive way: The only possible executions of the process are the ones that
comply with the control flow. Therefore, no other way of enacting the process
can take place than the prescribed ones. This assumption is suitable for intra-
organization execution scenarios. However, when it comes to inter-organization
monitoring scenarios, a different paradigm is needed in order to deal with deviations that may arise from the different parties involved. To overcome this limitation, we make use of the E-GSM language [3], an extension of the Guard-Stage-
Milestone (GSM) notation [15] especially devised for monitoring: E-GSM treats
control flow in a descriptive way, and as such it can monitor any possible execution of a process. When a deviation from the control flow is detected, an E-GSM
engine flags the part of the process causing such a deviation as non compliant,
without halting the monitoring.

In E-GSM the units of work that can be performed when the process is executed are represented by *stages*. Stages can be atomic, thus representing a single
task, or can nest other stages, thus representing a process fragment. The conditions that determine when stages become *opened* (the unit of work is being
performed) are represented by *data flow guards*, which we will indicate as "DFG".
The conditions that determine when stages are *closed* (the unit of work is completed) are represented by *milestones*, indicated as "M". Each stage must have at
least one data flow guard and one milestone attached. Control-flow dependencies among stages are represented by *process-flow guards*, henceforth identified
by the acronym "PFG". They are assessed before a stage becomes opened. If
they are evaluated as false, the stage is flagged either as *out of order* (executed
although it should not) or *skipped* (not executed when it should). Starting from
the enriched BPMN process model obtained in the previous step, an E-GSM
model of that process can be automatically produced. To do so, we apply the
following translation rules. They are based upon [4], which we extend to detect
when activities are executed based on the state of the artifacts. The effect of the
application of such rules on the model of Fig. 2 is shown in Fig. 3.

- Given a BPMN atomic activity (e.g., Unload container), a corresponding E-
  GSM stage is produced (e.g., UnloadContainer).
- For each artifact Ar, if a change in its state occurs, events are raised to
  signal that it leaves the previous state (henceforth denoted as Ar^l) and
  enters the current one (Ar^e). For instance, when Truck transitions from
  [heathrow,still] to [heathrow,moving], events $Truck^l$ and $Truck^e$ are produced.
  $Truck^l$ is raised when Truck leaves [heathrow,still], and $Truck^e$ is raised when
  it enters [heathrow,moving].
- The data flow guard (milestone) of a stage is evaluated on Ar^e (Ar^l) for
  each artifact Ar associated with each input (output) data objects of Ar. The
  stage is *opened* (*closed*) if the state assumed by all Ar's is the one indicated by the input (output) data objects of the associated activity. For
  example, LoadContainer.DFG1 is evaluated when $Container^e$ or $Truck^e$ occur.
  LoadContainer is opened if Container is [unhooked], and Truck is in [heathrow,still].

304   G. Meroni et al.

- Given a BPMN event *E* (e.g., *TU-HQ started*), a stage is produced (e.g., `TU-HQStarted`). One data flow guard and one milestone, both requiring *E* to be raised, are attached to the stage. This way, `TU-HQStarted` is opened and immediately closed when *TU-HQ started* occurs.
- As discussed in detail in [4], the BPMN model is decomposed into nested process blocks identified by *(i)* control-flow patterns (e.g., the loop blocks UK Loop and EU Loop, containing the fragments of the process with a structured loop), *(ii)* subprocess activities (e.g., TU-HQ). Each block *B* is translated into a stage *B*s that encloses the inner stages derived from activities, events or process blocks therein. The data flow guard of the block-stage *B*s is the union of the data flow guards of the inner stages, whereas the milestone of *B*s and the process flow guard of the inner stages reflect the control flow pattern expressed by *B*. For instance, TU-HQ is translated into a stage `TU-HQSeq` containing `TU-HQStarted`, `LoadContainer`, `UKLoop`, `TakeChnTunnel`, `EULoop`, `UnloadContainer` and `TU-HQEnded`. `TU-HQEnded.DFG1` is fulfilled only if the control flow is respected, i.e., `TU-HQEnded` is executed only once and immediately after `UnloadContainer` ends.

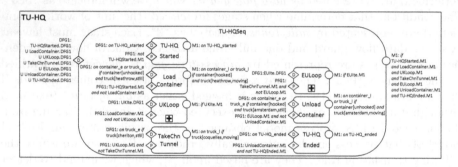

Fig. 3. E-GSM process model derived from the TU-HQ subprocess. For the sake of clarity, stages inside UK Loop and EU Loop are omitted.

Example. Figure 3 shows the E-GSM process model derived from the BPMN process model of Fig. 2. Here, `UnloadContainer.DFG1` is evaluated whenever the artifacts Truck or Container change their state, thus generating events *Truck^l* or *Truck^e*. To mark `UnloadContainer` as opened (i.e., to represent the fact that the container is currently being unloaded from the truck), `UnloadContainer.DFG1` requires that Truck is in [amsterdam,still], and Container is [hooked]. `UnloadContainer.M1` is evaluated when Truck or Container change their state, thus generating events *Truck^l* or *Container^l* respectively. To mark `UnloadContainer` as closed (i.e., to signal that the unloading of the container finished), `UnloadContainer.M1` requires that Truck is in [amsterdam,moving], and Container is [unhooked]. Finally, to ensure that `UnloadContainer` is executed at the right time, `UnloadContainer.PFG1` requires that `UnloadContainer` has not already been executed (thus requiring `UnloadContainer.M1` not to be achieved). Also, `UnloadContainer.PFG1` needs that `EULoop` (directly preceding `UnloadContainer`) has already been executed, hence that `EULoop.M1` was achieved.

3.3   Generation of the Artifact-to-object Mapping Criteria

The E-GSM model generated in the previous step allows us to detect when activities are executed based on the state of the artifacts participating to the process. However, the E-GSM model does not indicate which real-world object will impersonate each artifact (e.g., the artifact Truck is impersonated by the physical truck having license plate "AB123XY"). We capture the mapping criteria among artifacts and objects in a separate document. Such a choice allows us to decouple the process logic from the artifact instantiation logic, which significantly improves the scalability of the platform. Starting from the enriched BPMN process model obtained in the first step, the criteria to map real-world objects to the artifacts can be applied in an automated way. To do so, the following rules are applied:

– Each data association between a BPMN start event and a data object is translated to a mapping criterion. The criterion states that, whenever the event is detected, the artifact represented by the data object is bound to the object identified in the payload of the event. Should the artifact be already bound to a different object, the new binding would replace the existing one. For instance, when the event *TU-HQ started* occurs, Truck is bound to the physical truck whose license plate is specified in the payload of *TU-HQ started*.
– Each data association between a data object and a BPMN end event is translated into mapping criterion. The criterion states that, whenever the event is detected and the artifact represented by the data object is bound to an object, it becomes unbound. If the artifact is already unbound, no action is taken. For instance, when the event *TU-HQ ended* occurs, no truck is bound to Truck.

Example. Figure 4 shows the artifact-to-object mapping criteria derived from the BPMN process model of Fig. 2. Because the Container artifact interacts with the whole process, the binding is expected to occur when the process starts, and the unbinding to occur once the process finishes. Therefore, to bind a physical container to Container, event *Shipment started* should occur. Once *Shipment started*

```
<Mapping>
  <Artifact name="Container">
    <BindingEvent id="shipment_started"/><UnbindingEvent id="shipment_ended"/>
  </Artifact>
  <Artifact name="Truck">
    <BindingEvent id="M-TU_started"/><UnbindingEvent id="M-TU_ended"/>
    <BindingEvent id="TU-HQ_started"/><UnbindingEvent id="TU-HQ_ended"/>
    <BindingEvent id="HQ-TG_started"/><UnbindingEvent id="HQ-TG_ended"/>
    <BindingEvent id="TG-C_started"/><UnbindingEvent id="TG-C_ended"/>
  </Artifact>
</Mapping>
```

Fig. 4. Artifact-to-object mapping criteria.

is detected, Container is bound to the container whose unique identifier (e.g., its serial number) is equal to the one specified in the payload of *Shipment started*. To unbind Container, *shipment ended* should occur. The Truck artifact, on the other hand, interacts when each subprocess is running. Therefore, to bind a physical truck to Truck, any of the events *M-TU started*, *TU-HQ started*, *HQ-TG started*, or *TG-C started* should occur. Similarly, to unbind Truck, *M-TU ended*, *TU-HQ ended*, *HQ-TG ended*, or *TG-C ended* should occur.

4   Architecture and Implementation

Figure 5 shows the architecture of the monitoring service we developed to support inter-organizational processes. To completely automate the monitoring, we assume that the real-world objects embodying the artifacts can autonomously infer their state and submit such an information to the service. This is a feasible assumption in the context of a Wireless Sensor Network (WSN) [1] or the Internet of Things (IoT) [2], where environmental data can be collected by the objects, which can then infer their own state.

To allow the objects to communicate with the service, a *Message Queue Telemetry Transport (MQTT) Broker* is used. MQTT[1] is a queue-based publish/subscribe protocol, which is especially suited for applications where computing power and bandwidth are constrained. The MQTT Broker contains as many topics (i.e., queues) as the objects that can participate to the process. Each of these topics adheres to the following naming convention: /{artifact_type}/{object_id}, where artifact_type is the artifact represented by the object (e.g., a truck), and object_id is the unique identifier of the object (e.g., the license plate of the truck). Whenever the object changes its state, it publishes the updated state on its own topic. The MQTT Broker also contains as many topics as the process instances that are currently being carried out. Each of these topics adheres to the following naming convention:

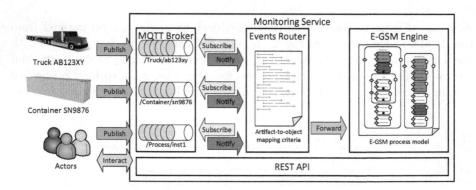

Fig. 5. Architecture of the monitoring service.

---

[1] http://mqtt.org/.

/{*process_name*}/{*instance_id*}, where *process_name* is the name of process model to be monitored (i.e., the shipment from M to C, henceforth MtoCProcess), and *instance_id* is the unique identifier of the process instance (i.e., the actual execution of the process) that is being run. These topics are used by the organizations to send events related to the running processes, but not related to the state of the artifacts (i.e., when a subprocess starts or ends).

The *E-GSM Engine*[2] is the component responsible for monitoring the execution of each process instance. This component takes as input the E-GSM models produced according to Sect. 3.2. Whenever a new execution of the process starts, the E-GSM Engine creates a new model instance, whose identifier *instance_id* is the same as the one of the running process instance. For each model instance, the E-GSM Engine *(i)* keeps track of which activities are ongoing, *(ii)* detects whether they follow the execution flow defined in the model and, if not, *(iii)* marks them as not compliant.

To support late binding and unbinding among objects and artifacts referenced by the process, the *Events Router* component is introduced.[3] By receiving as input the artifact-to-object mapping criteria produced according to Sect. 3.3, the Events Router forwards to each E-GSM model instance only the events produced by the objects that effectively take part in that process execution. Note that, by keeping the binding logic separate from the process logic, the E-GSM instance receives only events coming from those objects that are bound to the running processes. This way, the scalability of the E-GSM engine is affected only by *(i)* the number of processes being run, and *(ii)* the number of objects interacting with those processes, which is way lower than the total number of objects under observation. To do so, the Events Router subscribes to all the /{*process_name*}/{*instance_id*} topics (e.g., /MtoCProcess/inst1). Whenever a new event is published (e.g., process_started), the Events Router checks if a mapping criterion is defined for that event. If no mapping criterion exists, the Events Router forwards the event to the E-GSM instance whose identifier is *instance_id* (e.g., inst1). If a binding criterion exists, the Events Router subscribes to topic /{*artifact_type*}/{*object_id*}, where *object_id* is the object specified in the payload of the event (e.g., /Container/sn9876), and associates to that topic the *instance_id* (e.g., inst1). From that point on, whenever a new change of state is published in /{*artifact_type*}/{*object_id*}, the Events Router forwards it to the E-GSM model instance whose identifier is *instance_id*. For example, if the truck having license plate AB123XY publishes on /Truck/AB123XY that its state changed to [heathrow,moving], the Events Router will notify that Truck is in [heathrow,moving], together with the raising of $Truck^l$ and $Truck^e$ events, to the E-GSM instance inst1. If an unbinding criterion exists, the Events Router unsubscribes to topic /{*artifact_type*}/{*object_id*}, where *object_id* is the object specified in the payload of the event.

Finally, the *Representational State Transfer (REST)* [22] *API* offers an interface for the organizations and the service providers to interact with the

---

[2] Source code at https://bitbucket.org/polimiisgroup/egsmengine.
[3] Source code at https://bitbucket.org/polimiisgroup/eventsrouter.

monitoring service. It allows *(i)* the E-GSM Engine to be provided with the E-GSM model, *(ii)* the Events Router to be instructed with the artifact-to-object mapping criteria, and *(iii)* the organizations and the service providers to determine if the processes are correctly executed. In addition to that, it is responsible for the management of the communication channels between the organizations and service providers, and the monitoring instances: Whenever a new process execution takes place, the REST API instructs the MQTT Broker to create a new /{process_name}/{instance_id} topic. Then, the REST API instructs *(i)* the Events Router to listen to that topic for evaluating the mapping criteria, and *(ii)* the E-GSM Engine to create a new model instance whose identifier is the same as instance_id. Finally, it forwards the instance_id to the involved service providers, to specify the topic on which they should publish the events related to the running process. For instance, when a new shipment from M to C takes place, a new instance id (e.g., inst1) is defined, the MQTT topic /MtoCProcess/inst1 is created, a new E-GSM instance is run, and the notification that inst1 is up is sent to all involved parties. The organizations can then use /MtoCProcess/inst1 to send events concerning that shipment.

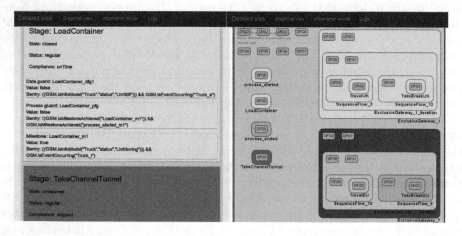

Fig. 6. Screenshot of our service showing a non compliant execution of the TU-HQ leg.

Figure 6 shows a screenshot of the monitoring service displaying a non-compliant execution of the TU-HQ leg. In this case, the truck took a ferry instead of the Channel tunnel. Therefore, our service marks stage TakeChannelTunnel as *skipped* (dark gray). Since TU-HQStarted, LoadContainer, TravelInUK and TakeBreakInUK were executed in compliance with the control flow, they are marked as *on track* (green). Since the truck has not yet taken a break in the European continent, and the end event has not yet been received, TakeBreakInEU and TU-HQEnded are not executed yet (light gray). As the truck is traveling in the European continent, stage TravelInEU is still being executed (yellow). Note that, although a compliance violation occurred, the monitoring is still running.

5   Validation

To demonstrate the applicability and efficacy of our approach on a real-world case, we have conducted an experiment with truck shipments data provided by a European logistics company. [4] This provided material consisted of *(i)* a dataset with the registered positions and speed of trucks involved in the shipments, captured by on-board AIS/GPS systems and henceforth indicated as *GPS log*, and *(ii)* a dataset indicating the shipments' activities start and completion times, manually triggered by the truck drivers and hereinafter denoted as *activity log*. We replayed the GPS log within our platform and checked whether the start and completion events detected by our platform matched with the manually inserted information in the activity log. This way, we could compare our fully-automated approach with a traditional one relying on human intervention. We focused on routes connecting the premises in Amsterdam (AMS) to four other major European airports, namely the London Heathrow airport (LHR), Brussels (BRU), Paris Charles de Gaulle (CDG), and Frankfurt (FRA). For every route, we considered both inbound and outbound routes from/to Amsterdam.

The GPS log and the activity log contained 19966 and 815 entries, respectively, distributed over 77 shipments. The reported shipments took on average 533 min, ranging from less than 3 to more than 27 hours. By analyzing the activity log, we built a BPMN process for the routes, structured similarly to the legs described in Sect. 2. We identified the possible discrete states that each truck can assume through the inspection of the GPS log. Then, we followed the approach described in Sect. 3: First, we enriched each BPMN model with artifacts representing the truck and its states. Then, we generated the E-GSM models and the artifact-to-object mapping criteria. This output was then used to instruct the monitoring platform on which processes to monitor. After that, we used the WSO2 Complex Event Processing platform[5] to replay the GPS log, let our system detect when the truck changed state, and forward such changes to the monitoring service. Finally, we compared the results of the monitoring platform with the activity log. Table 1 shows the results of our experiment.

The monitoring service was able to correctly determine the actual execution of a process for 93.13% of the total instances. For the remaining 6.87%, the issues lay in the determination of when activity Load container was executed. For example, during one shipment of the BRU-AMS route, Load container was not identified as completed, even though it was. This has to be imputed to the limited information available to determine the state of trucks: Our system had only access to their speed and position, thus anomalous slow progressions due to congestions at the logistic platform and along the road caused the misinterpretation of their state.

Moreover, the monitoring service detected activities to be started or ended more often than what had been notified by the truck drivers. The matching

---

[4] The (anonymized) dataset is available at http://purl.org/polimi/martifact/logisticsds-anon (password: GM-CDC-JM-dataset).

[5] See http://wso2.com/products/complex-event-processor/.

Table 1. Results of the validation.

Shipment	AMS-LHR	LHR-AMS	AMS-BRU	BRU-AMS	AMS-CDG	CDG-AMS	AMS-FRA	FRA-AMS	Global
Instances	12	15	9	11	8	10	4	8	77
Median duration [min]	806.28	720.05	306.67	256.30	813.48	483.69	481.32	396.30	533.01
Min. duration [min]	338.47	138.02	153.00	159.62	387.57	353.00	396.10	279.32	138.02
Max. duration [min]	1328.56	1622.03	519.12	388.30	1583.52	723.25	567.47	357.32	1622.03
Correctness [%]	91.67%	100.00%	100.00%	90.91%	100.00%	100.00%	75.00%	87.50%	93.13%
Completeness [%]	58.33%	53.33%	77.78%	90.91%	87.50%	60.00%	100.00%	62.50%	73.79%
Median detection delay [min]	2.73	−0.50	5.33	1.09	14.79	0.80	7.10	2.44	4.22
Median absolute d. delay [min]	12.53	4.57	7.10	5.17	16.57	4.18	8.87	4.88	7.98

cases amounted to 73.79%. Whether the missing entries in the activity log were due to an omission of the driver, or rather due to a wrong detection of the system, is debatable and needs further investigation. However, e.g., whenever the monitoring service notified that activity Travel in EU was ended, and no notification was sent by the truck driver, we inspected the GPS log and noticed that the truck had reached Europe and its speed had amounted to zero for more than a quarter of an hour, which suggests the first hypothesis to be more likely.

To assess the time gain for the detection of the status changes in the process, we computed the delay between when each activity was started or ended, as reported by the manual entries of the activity log, and when the monitoring platform detected it, based on the GPS log. We will henceforth name such time difference as *detection delay*. On average, the median of the detection delays amounted to 4.22 min (7.98 considering the absolute values of the delays), which is negligible for processes that last on average 533 min.

6   Related Work

In this section we briefly report on related work about (*i*) the monitoring of business processes by their interaction with physical objects, and (*ii*) techniques to coordinate inter-organizational processes.

In [14], BPMN data objects are adopted to model information on the artifacts manipulated by the activities composing a process. With respect to our work, [14] expects information on the artifacts to be stored in a relational database. Also, binding mechanisms are implemented as an extension of the BPMN syntax, while our work relies solely on BPMN 2.0 OMG standard constructs. [18] proposes a platform to monitor a process based on its interactions with real-world objects and human operators. Additionally, binding relationships are automatically inferred by observing the execution of the process. However, information on when activities are performed must be explicitly sent to the platform. Also, only the occupation of objects and operators (i.e., if the operator is busy or idle) is taken into consideration. [7] focuses on the process execution monitoring based on physical objects' data. To do so, BPMN constructs are extended to define which events produced by a Complex Event Processing (CEP) determine their activation and termination. Similarly, [5, 8] propose to annotate activities with constraints on attributes that are monitored when the process is executed. This way, it is possible to report if an activity is not executed as expected as soon as a violation occurs. [9] applies that approach to detect anomalies and diversions in the context of air-freight cargo transportation. [17], on the other hand, relies on artifacts and their lifecycle to monitor all the parameters relevant for the execution of a process. This way, Key Performance Indicators (KPIs) on the overall execution of the process and each single activities are derived. None of these solutions deal with the detection of deviations in the process execution flow. Concerning the generation of GSM models from activity-centric languages, different approaches have been proposed by [11, 16]. However, these approaches treat the execution flow in a prescriptive way. Our solution, which extends [4], treats instead execution flow in a descriptive way, thus allowing more flexibility, and uses information on the artifacts to derive guards and milestones.

Traditionally, to monitor process portions carried out by service providers, commitments have been used. Commitments are formal contracts that specify how the interactions between the organization and the service provider should be performed [23]. However, they are mainly focused on the outcome of the outsourced process portion carried out by the service provider, rather than on the activities composing the process. Our work, on the other hand, is better suited whenever the process must strictly adhere to the model, or when a detailed log on how the process was performed is needed. [19], on the other hand, proposes a GSM-based collaboration hub to coordinate logistics processes at the activity level. The hub also adopts GSM to keep track of the execution of the process. However, it relies on explicit notifications to determine when activities are executed. [13] overcomes this limitation by adopting the IoT paradigm: they take advantage of Guards and Milestones to identify when Stages are being executed by predicating on sensor data coming from smart objects. However, the GSM model is expected to be modeled from scratch. Also, both solutions lack mechanisms to detect deviations in the execution of the process with respect to its model.

7 Conclusions and Future Work

This paper presented a monitoring service based on E-GSM to monitor the execution of inter-organizational processes based on the status of the artifacts being manipulated. The paper has also shown how a standard BPMN process model can be used to automatically produce all the information to drive the monitoring service. Finally, mechanisms to dynamically bind and unbind real-world objects to a process execution were presented.

A limitation of this service is the support for only one-to-one mappings among real-world objects and artifacts. Therefore, we plan to also support one-to-many and many-to-many mappings to support batch processes [21]. Furthermore, we will introduce tool support to check the soundness of the annotated BPMN process model (i.e., if changes in the states of the artifacts during a compliant execution do not contradict the control flow). To improve the accuracy of the automatic artifact state-change determination, it is in our plans to integrate machine-learning techniques such as automated discriminative classifiers, as proposed in [6,8,9]. Additionally, we are going to distribute the monitoring service onto the real-world objects impersonating the artifacts, so as to completely take advantage of the IoT paradigm. An extension of this service to monitor processes involving non-tangible objects (e.g., invoices or purchase orders) is also planned.

Acknowledgments. This work has been partially funded by the Italian Project ITS Italy 2020 under the Technological National Clusters program.

References

1. Akyildiz, I., Su, W., Sankarasubramaniam, Y., Cayirci, E.: Wireless sensor networks: a survey. Comput. Netw. **38**(4), 393–422 (2002)
2. Atzori, L., Iera, A., Morabito, G.: The internet of things: a survey. Comput. Netw. **54**(15), 2787–2805 (2010)
3. Baresi, L., Meroni, G., Plebani, P.: A GSM-based approach for monitoring cross-organization business processes using smart objects. In: Reichert, M., Reijers, H.A. (eds.) BPM 2015. LNBIP, vol. 256, pp. 389–400. Springer, Cham (2016). doi:10.1007/978-3-319-42887-1_32
4. Baresi, L., Meroni, G., Plebani, P.: Using the guard-stage-milestone notation for monitoring BPMN-based processes. In: Schmidt, R., Guédria, W., Bider, I., Guerreiro, S. (eds.) BPMDS/EMMSAD-2016. LNBIP, vol. 248, pp. 18–33. Springer, Cham (2016). doi:10.1007/978-3-319-39429-9_2
5. Baumgraß, A., Botezatu, M., Di Ciccio, C., Dijkman, R., Grefen, P., Hewelt, M., Mendling, J., Meyer, A., Pourmirza, S., Völzer, H.: Towards a methodology for the engineering of event-driven process applications. In: Reichert, M., Reijers, H.A. (eds.) BPM 2015. LNBIP, vol. 256, pp. 501–514. Springer, Cham (2016). doi:10.1007/978-3-319-42887-1_40
6. Baumgrass, A., Cabanillas, C., Di Ciccio, C.: A conceptual architecture for an event-based information aggregation engine in smart logistics. In: EMISA, pp. 109–123. GI (2015)
7. Baumgrass, A., Herzberg, N., Meyer, A., Weske, M.: BPMN extension for business process monitoring. In: EMISA 2014, pp. 85–98. GI (2014)
8. Cabanillas, C., Di Ciccio, C., Mendling, J., Baumgrass, A.: Predictive task monitoring for business processes. In: Sadiq, S., Soffer, P., Völzer, H. (eds.) BPM 2014. LNCS, vol. 8659, pp. 424–432. Springer, Cham (2014). doi:10.1007/978-3-319-10172-9_31
9. Di Ciccio, C., van der Aa, H., Cabanillas, C., Mendling, J., Prescher, J.: Detecting flight trajectory anomalies and predicting diversions in freight transportation. Decis. Support Syst. **88**, 1–17 (2016)

10. Dumas, M., La Rosa, M., Mendling, J., Reijers, H.A.: Fundamentals of Business Process Management. Springer, Heidelberg (2013)
11. Eshuis, R., Van Gorp, P.: Synthesizing data-centric models from business process models. Computing **98**(4), 1–29 (2015)
12. Gilley, K.M., Rasheed, A.: Making more by doing less: an analysis of outsourcing and its effects on firm performance. J. Manage. **26**(4), 763–790 (2000)
13. Gnimpieba, Z.D.R., Nait-Sidi-Moh, A., Durand, D., Fortin, J.: Using internet of things technologies for a collaborative supply chain: application to tracking of pallets and containers. Procedia Comput. Sci. **56**, 550–557 (2015)
14. Herzberg, N., Meyer, A., Weske, M.: Improving business process intelligence by observing object state transitions. Data Knowl. Eng. **98**, 144–164 (2015)
15. Hull, R., Damaggio, E., Fournier, F., Gupta, M., Heath, F.T., Hobson, S., Linehan, M., Maradugu, S., Nigam, A., Sukaviriya, P., Vaculin, R.: Introducing the guard-stage-milestone approach for specifying business entity lifecycles. In: Bravetti, M., Bultan, T. (eds.) WS-FM 2010. LNCS, vol. 6551, pp. 1–24. Springer, Heidelberg (2011). doi:10.1007/978-3-642-19589-1_1
16. Köpke, J., Su, J.: Towards quality-aware translations of activity-centric processes to guard stage milestone. In: La Rosa, M., Loos, P., Pastor, O. (eds.) BPM 2016. LNCS, vol. 9850, pp. 308–325. Springer, Cham (2016). doi:10.1007/978-3-319-45348-4_18
17. Liu, R., Vaculín, R., Shan, Z., Nigam, A., Wu, F.: Business artifact-centric modeling for real-time performance monitoring. In: Rinderle-Ma, S., Toumani, F., Wolf, K. (eds.) BPM 2011. LNCS, vol. 6896, pp. 265–280. Springer, Heidelberg (2011). doi:10.1007/978-3-642-23059-2_21
18. Maamar, Z., Faci, N., Sellami, M., Boukadi, K., Yahya, F., Barnawi, A., Sakr, S.: On business process monitoring using cross-flow coordination. Serv. Oriented Comput. Appl. **11**(2), 203–215 (2017)
19. Meijler, T.D., Stollberg, M., Winkler, M., Erler, K.: Coordinating variable collaboration processes in logistics. In: MITIP 2011 (2011)
20. Meroni, G., Di Ciccio, C., Mendling, J.: Artifact-driven process monitoring: dynamically binding real-world objects to running processes. In: CAiSE 2017 Forum, pp. 105–112 (2017). CEUR-WS.org
21. Pufahl, L., Weske, M.: Batch processing across multiple business processes based on object life cycles. In: Abramowicz, W., Alt, R., Franczyk, B. (eds.) BIS 2016. LNBIP, vol. 255, pp. 195–208. Springer, Cham (2016). doi:10.1007/978-3-319-39426-8_16
22. Richardson, L., Ruby, S.: RESTful Web Services - Web Services for the Real World. O'Reilly, Sebastopol (2007)
23. Telang, P.R., Singh, M.P.: Specifying and verifying cross-organizational business models: an agent-oriented approach. IEEE Trans. Serv. Comput. **5**(3), 305–318 (2012)

BenchFoundry: A Benchmarking Framework for Cloud Storage Services

David Bermbach[1]([✉]), Jörn Kuhlenkamp[1], Akon Dey[2,4],
Arunmoezhi Ramachandran[3], Alan Fekete[4], and Stefan Tai[1]

[1] Information Systems Engineering Research Group,
Technische Universität Berlin, Berlin, Germany
{db,jk,st}@ise.tu-berlin.de
[2] Awake Security Inc., Mountain View, CA, USA
akon@awakesecurity.com
[3] Tableau Software Inc., Palo Alto, CA, USA
arunmoezhi@gmail.com
[4] University of Sydney, Sydney, Australia
{akon.dey,alan.fekete}@sydney.edu.au

Abstract. Understanding quality of services in general, and of cloud
storage services in particular, is often crucial. Previous proposals to
benchmark storage services are too restricted to cover the full variety
of NoSQL stores, or else too simplistic to capture properties of use by
realistic applications; they also typically measure only one facet of the
complex tradeoffs between different qualities of service. In this paper, we
present BenchFoundry which is not a benchmark itself but rather is a
benchmarking framework that can execute arbitrary application-driven
benchmark workloads in a distributed deployment while measuring multiple qualities at the same time. BenchFoundry can be used or extended
for every kind of storage service. Specifically, BenchFoundry is the first
system where workload specifications become mere configuration files
instead of code. In our design, we have put special emphasis on ease-of-
use and deterministic repeatability of benchmark runs which is achieved
through a trace-based workload model.

Keywords: Cloud storage services · Benchmarking · Quality of service

1 Introduction

The ability to assess the quality of a service is of great importance in any service-
oriented application architecture. Naturally, a variety of techniques have been
proposed to this end. Many collect basic monitoring data for a specific quality
like performance while some may also include user ratings. Others focus on a
specific objective such as formalization in SLAs or service composition in business processes. Surprisingly, little attention has been paid to assessing services
by running arbitrary application-driven workloads in a distributed deployment
(which is in some cases required by measurement approaches, e.g., [4], but also

© Springer International Publishing AG 2017
M. Maximilien et al. (Eds.): ICSOC 2017, LNCS 10601, pp. 314–330, 2017.
https://doi.org/10.1007/978-3-319-69035-3_22

a prerequisite for benchmark scalability) while measuring multiple qualities at the same time. For this, different application-driven workloads are necessary to impose different kinds of stress to the service under consideration. Distribution-aware quality assessments are needed to reveal otherwise undiscoverable insights. Additionally, each single quality should also be seen in the context of other, potentially conflicting qualities and their particular trade-offs.

In this paper, we will focus on cloud storage services. Today, the sheer number of available cloud storage services and database systems is staggering – in May 2017, nosql-databases.org lists more than 225 NoSQL database projects, a number that does not even include traditional relational database systems and services (RDBMS). Selecting a service from this extensive set for an application scenario requires an understanding of at least two main criteria: (a) functionality, i.e., implemented features, data model, etc., and (b) non-functional properties, i.e., the system qualities provided by the storage service. In this paper, we will focus on the comparability of cloud storage services in terms of quality. We suggest a novel benchmarking approach and middleware to provide the necessary insights into this: For our purposes, a benchmark is a standard workload that is applied to the system or service under test (SUT) while a standard set of measurements are collected in a standard way. For example, the Transaction Processing Council (TPC) has defined TPC-E representing the workload of a brokerage firm, to evaluate on-line transaction processing performance by metrics such as transactions-per-second in relational database systems. The term micro-benchmark is used when the workload does not have the entire range of features of a realistic application, but is limited to exploring the sensitivity to key variables in the workload characteristics [6].

There is a plethora of previous work, not only in general service quality assessment but especially on database benchmarking. However, existing database benchmarking approaches have severe disadvantages: Some approaches, e.g., TPC benchmarks or OLTPBench [9], have strict functional and non-functional requirements on supported database systems which are currently only fulfilled by RDBMS, e.g., Amazon RDS[1]. As such, these benchmarks cannot be used to study NoSQL systems such as Amazon's DynamoDB[2] or S3[3] services. Other approaches, e.g., YCSB [8] or YCSB++ [14] are essentially micro-benchmarks [6]. While these are useful for understanding how tiny changes in workloads affect system quality, they rarely mimic realistic application workloads. Existing approaches are also lacking in regards to extensibility of workloads, multi-quality measurements, (geo-)distribution support of the benchmark out of the box, fine-grained result collection, or ease-of-use. Finally, database benchmarking typically focuses on the database system rather than the service(s) that the database system provides – an important detail when it comes to assessing quality also from a service consumer perspective.

---

[1] aws.amazon.com/rds.

[2] aws.amazon.com/dynamodb.

[3] aws.amazon.com/S3.

Today, application developers often face a significant challenge: to implement the benchmark for all storage services of interest from scratch. Addressing this real-world concern, we present in this paper the result of designing and actually implementing ideas from our previous vision paper [3]: BenchFoundry is not a benchmark itself, rather it is a benchmarking framework which can execute arbitrary application-driven benchmark workloads in a distributed deployment, measure multiple qualities at the same time, and can be used or extended for every kind of storage service. Specifically, BenchFoundry is the first system in this domain where workload specifications become mere configuration files instead of code. In our design, we have put special emphasis on ease-of-use and deterministic repeatability of benchmark runs which is achieved through a trace-based workload model.

One contribution of this paper is to capture detailed requirements or desirable features of benchmarks for cloud services such as storage services; this is in Sect. 2 along with related work. Another contribution is the BenchFoundry proposal as a way to meet these requirements; Sect. 3 gives the high-level overview and Sect. 4 some implementation details. Our final contribution is to evaluate BenchFoundry (Sect. 5) by showing how some requirements are met during case-study experiments. We also discuss limitations and effects of design choices in our approach (Sect. 6).

2   Modern Storage Service Benchmarking

In this section, we use our extensive experience in cloud service benchmarking, e.g., [6], to identify requirements for modern benchmarks in general (and for benchmarking cloud storage services in particular) including their implementations. We also discuss existing work in this field.

> **(R1) Multi-Quality:** *Benchmarks should measure all sides of a particular tradeoff. Exceptions are only permissible where the respective other qualities are comparable; this should be verified by another benchmark.*

Traditionally, database benchmarking has mainly been done for performance evaluation, e.g., through TPC[4] benchmarks or with YCSB [8]. Over the last few years, some approaches have been developed for consistency benchmarking with varying degrees of meaningfulness[5], e.g., [2,4,14,17], security impacts on performance, e.g., [13], as well as an open source project for testing ACID isolation guarantees[6]. However, these are all more or less single quality benchmarks. Still, measuring more than one quality at the same time is crucial since modern distributed database systems and services are inherently affected by tradeoffs [1,4] – being top ranked for one quality is trivial when disregarding the

---

[4] tpc.org.

[5] One of the core requirements for benchmarks is to use meaningful and understandable metrics as well as to offer relevant results to a broad target audience [3,10–12].

[6] github.com/ept/hermitage.

respective other qualities. To make such tradeoff decisions transparent, modern benchmarking should always imply multi-quality benchmarking.

(R2) No Assumptions: *Benchmarks should make as little assumptions on the service under test (SUT) as possible. Instead an ideal case should be identified, deviations tolerated and measured as additional quality metrics for broad applicability and benchmark portability.*

Existing benchmark tools often have strict functional and non-functional requirements on supported storage services, e.g., requiring transactional features with strict ACID guarantees [9]. However, it would be preferable to reach a broader applicability and stronger portability [10, 12] by transforming such strict requirements into measured qualities instead. For instance, transactions could also be executed in a best-effort way while tracking ACID violations as an additional quality metric.

(R3) Realistic Workloads: *Benchmarks should use realistic application-driven workload that mimick the target application as closely as possible.*

Micro-benchmarks certainly have their benefits for some use cases: they are a perfect fit for studying how a system reacts to small workload changes or to test isolated features. They are also easier to implement. However, the relevance of benchmarking results for a given application depends on the similarity of application workload and benchmarking workload – the greater the difference the less relevant are results. Therefore, application-driven benchmarking with realistic workloads that emulate the given use case as close as possible is typically preferable over synthetic micro-benchmarks like YCSB.

(R4) Extensibility: *Benchmarks should be extensible and configurable to account for future application scenarios and new storage services.*

Modern applications evolve at an as yet unheard of pace. As such, modern benchmarking tools need to be extensible and configurable: They must be able to support changes in benchmark workloads which reflect new application developments as well as new storage services which do not exist at the time of designing the benchmark. Typically, this is achieved through adapter mechanisms and suitable abstractions, e.g., in [8]. However, these abstractions should be carefully chosen, e.g., the data model of YCSB is obviously focused on column stores, which makes it a less than perfect fit for other kinds of storage services. We believe that a modern benchmark should distinguish a logical and physical data model in its adapter layer.

(R5) Distribution: *Benchmarks should always be distribution-aware and implementations should come with the necessary coordination logic for running multiple instances in parallel.*

Modern applications as well as underlying storage services are inherently distributed or even geo-distributed. Consequently, a modern benchmark should also be designed for distribution and its implementation should build on measurement clients that can be distributed. Parallelization through distribution is also important when measuring the scalability of storage services or simply for benchmarking a service that is already at scale (scalability of the benchmark tool). Also, some benchmarking approaches heavily rely on distributed execution, e.g., [4]. However, distributing workloads is a challenging problem, e.g., asserting that inserts precede updates to the same database key.

(R6) Fine-Grained Results: *Benchmarks should always log fine-grained results, they should never voluntarily delete information.*

Often, benchmarking tools only report aggregated results, e.g., [8]. While this is convenient for reporting purposes, this effectively loses a wealth of information: results such as the saw pattern or the night/day pattern from [4] would never have been found if the available information were only aggregates or even a CDF. Therefore, benchmarking tools should log detailed results at operation level, i.e., for each operation the outcome, start and end timestamp, retrieved results of read requests, etc.

(R7) Deterministic Execution: *Benchmarks should be able to deterministically re-execute the exact same workload.*

A key aspect of benchmarking is repeatability, i.e., repeating a benchmark run several times should yield identical or comparable results. In this regard, all benchmarking approaches known to the authors have a fundamental problem: they randomly select database keys and generate data at benchmark runtime. While such an approach has obvious benefits, it also means that repeated executions may not always yield comparable results or that seemingly comparable results may in fact have been produced by fundamentally different workloads. When using such implementations, the only way to counter this effect to a certain degree is to use long-running experiments, up to several hours or even days, or to carefully inspect the generated data afterwards (which, however, due to the unavailability of detailed results (R6) is typically not possible). We believe, therefore, that modern benchmarks should be trace-based, i.e., should be able to replay a given workload in a fully deterministic way. In a distributed workload generator, fixing the seed for randomization is not sufficient for producing a deterministic workload, due to the non-deterministic speeds of execution across multiple machines.

(R8) Ease-of-use: *Benchmarks should have ease-of-use as a core focus.*

A benchmark should focus on ease-of-use to foster adoption and use. Often, it is not possible to benchmark all services – relying on results of third parties may be an option. However, this is only possible in case of widespread use of the specific benchmark and also depends on the willingness of people to share their results. Setting up open source systems is often a tedious exercise; we, therefore, believe that a core design focus of benchmark tools should be on ease-of-use. Obviously, this requires benchmarks to also come with an implementation as done for the more recent TPC benchmarks. Ease-of-use is also emphasised by Seybold and Domaschka [16].

3 BenchFoundry Design and Architecture

In BenchFoundry, we address each of the requirements from Sect. 2 through a combination of mechanisms. We will now give an overview of these mechanisms, see also Fig. 1 for a high-level overview of the BenchFoundry architecture.

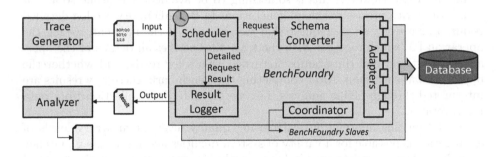

Fig. 1. High-level architecture

3.1 Trace-Based Workload Generation

The first novelty is that we break down the workload generator component into two components: a trace generator and a scheduler. The trace generator produces a workload trace which precisely specifies the order of operations and the time when each operation shall be executed relative to the experiment start. This trace is generated independently of a specific benchmark run, in fact, it may be based on real application traces and is supposed to be reused frequently. At runtime of the experiment, the scheduler retrieves entries from the trace and submits them as independent tasks to a variable-sized thread pool. This happens at the time specified in the trace – BenchFoundry also tracks scheduling precision.

Following this trace-based approach enables us to have fully deterministic executions where all elements of chance are captured within the trace generator (R7). Beyond repeatability, this trace-based approach also means that Bench-Foundry is the first benchmarking toolkit where workloads become mere configuration files: Instead of writing a new workload generator, which typically includes aspects like thread management but also coordination in case of a distributed deployment, we can add new workloads to BenchFoundry by creating a static configuration file – manually, based on an existing real application trace, or programmatically through an existing or new trace generator. While one could argue that writing a trace generator instead of a workload generator only shifts the problem, a workload generator has to be rewritten for every benchmark implementation while a trace generator has to be written just once. Hence, Bench-Foundry is also extensible for new workloads (parts of R4).

3.2 Runtime Measurements and Offline Analysis

The second novelty is that we separate data collection from data interpretation: To our knowledge, existing general purpose database benchmarking tools all calculate metrics at runtime – obviously, this is not very extensible for new metrics. Furthermore, some measurement approaches require data from various measurement clients (e.g., [4]), i.e., calculating metrics creates a significant amount of communication. However, this is something to be avoided at runtime so as not to interfere with precise workload generation. In BenchFoundry, we log detailed results about every single request that we execute. At the moment, we log the operation ID (which together with the trace file specifies all details of the operation), start and end timestamps, returned values for reads, and whether the operation was successful. After completing the benchmark, these raw results are interpreted through offline analysis, i.e., we separate data collection from data interpretation.

Based on this information, calculating quality levels at arbitrary levels of aggregation is possible for a variety of system qualities and metrics, e.g., latency and throughput, consistency (staleness, ordering guarantees), or violations of ACID guarantees.

BenchFoundry logs results as detailed as possible (R6) and, thus, provides information for a variety of qualities and quality metrics (R1). It also aims to transform non-functional requirements into quality metrics (parts of R2).

3.3 Application-Focused Workload Abstraction

Existing benchmarking tools like YCSB typically use independent operations that are generated synthetically as a basis of their workload model; TPC benchmarks usually use transactions comprising multiple operations as their base unit but also describe the notion of emulated clients. In this regard, TPC benchmarks resemble real applications more closely: real database-application interactions typically happen within the scope of a session during which a sequence of transactions is executed by the storage service.

In BenchFoundry, we make this session explicit in our workload abstraction: The basic unit of execution is the *business process*[7]. A business process describes a sequence of database-application interactions, i.e., all interactions that would happen within the scope of a client session for real world applications. All entries of a business process are executed strictly sequentially, there is never parallelism.

---

[7] Which should not be confused with the process understanding of the BPM community.

The subunit of a business process is called *business transaction*. A business transaction is a logical sequence of *business operations* that should ideally, if supported by the storage service, be executed as ACID transactions. However, in the absence of transactional features, BenchFoundry simply executes these on a best effort base and tracks ACID violations. This allows us to compare transactional and non-transactional storage services fairly.

On a logical data schema level, a business operation is an atomic unit that corresponds to a database query. However, only RDBMS use a normalized data schema as their physical schema. Other database classes, e.g., column stores, rely on denormalization where data is kept redundantly to avoid costly queries. Logical updates may, hence, require several service calls. In BenchFoundry, we reflect this through the use of database class-specific *requests*, e.g., a column store request. In the case of RDBMS, each business operation has exactly one request; in the case of other database classes, one or more depending on the physical schema design.

All input files of BenchFoundry are specified on the logical schema level, i.e., BenchFoundry does not make assumptions on the physical schema of the storage service. Instead, it reads the logical schema, automatically creates a physical schema recommendation from this, and then creates the requests based on the physical schema and the original query. In case of column stores and key-values stores, we plan to use one of the approaches from [5,7] for this, for RDBMS we can simply use the normalized data schema, for other datastore classes schema mappings need to be determined and imported manually.

Using a workload abstraction that focuses on the behavior of client applications instead of taking the perspective of the storage service, is a very natural way of modeling workloads. Therefore, using the concepts of business processes, transactions, and operations easily allows developers to model application behavior which then results in the workload that the database experiences. The alternative of using independent operations as a base unit may also lead to very realistic workloads – however, we believe that this is much harder to "get right". As such, BenchFoundry (which is not a benchmark itself) does not guarantee R3 but certainly helps developers achieve it through an easy-to-use workload abstraction. By differentiating logical and physical schema levels, BenchFoundry also gets rid of functional requirements on the SUT which helps for a broad applicability (R2).

3.4   Managed Distribution and Benchmark Phases

BenchFoundry has been designed to be regularly deployed on multiple machines that together form a BenchFoundry cluster. As basic unit of distribution, we use business process instances, i.e., when we run BenchFoundry in a distributed setting, a trace splitter will assign each business process in the trace to a different BenchFoundry instance. As business processes are by definition independent (each process includes all interactions within the scope of a client session), these instances can be executed independently without requiring coordination.

For other aspects which require coordination, BenchFoundry follows a master-slave approach – however, the master cannot become a bottleneck for the system as all coordination happens before the actual benchmark run (see also Fig. 2):

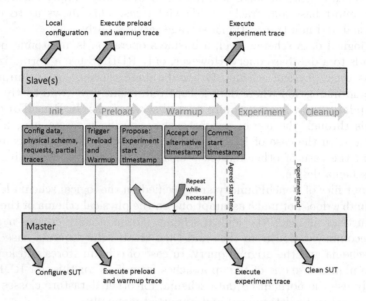

Fig. 2. Execution Phases and Distributed Coordination

During the init phase, the master parses all input files, splits the preload and experiment traces, and configures the SUT (e.g., by creating tables in an RDBMS). Afterwards, the master forwards the partial traces, the warmup trace, and configuration details (including physical schema and requests) to all slaves. When all BenchFoundry instances have been configured, the master signals all slaves to proceed to the preload phase during which the initial data set is loaded into the SUT. This is immediately followed by the warmup phase which serves to warm up database caches.

Once the warmup phase is started, the master proposes a start timestamp for the experiment phase to all slaves. For this, it uses a Two-Phase Commit variant: Instead of denying or accepting the proposal, slaves simply respond with an alternative (later) start timestamp or the proposed timestamp if it is accepted. The master then broadcasts a "commit" with the latest returned timestamp. At the agreed start time, all business processes of the warmup phase are forcibly terminated and the scheduler for the experiment phase is started. Instances that have completed their (partial) experiment trace, terminate autonomously and assert that all results have been logged. The master then proceeds to clean up the SUT, i.e., deletes all data that was written during the benchmark, etc.

All in all, BenchFoundry instances only communicate (a) for distribution of input data, (b) for starting the preload phase, and (c) for agreeing on the start timestamp of the experiment phase. The trace and the business process-based workload abstraction already capture all dependencies in the workload which is why we use them as unit of distribution. Based on this, all other decisions can be made entirely locally without requiring communication. However, it is, therefore, necessary to synchronize the clocks of all BenchFoundry machines.

Since the BenchFoundry design avoids coordination where possible and keeps it outside of the experiment phase when unavoidable, we believe BenchFoundry to be highly scalable. As such, the system is also a natural fit for distributed or even geo-distributed deployments (R5). At the same time, using the master-slave approach together with the phase concept allows us to focus on ease-of-use: All slaves are only started with a port parameter, the master parses all input files and forwards it to slaves which self-configure upon receipt. The master also configures and cleans up the SUT.

4   BenchFoundry Implementation

In this section, we will give an overview of select implementation aspects of our proof-of-concept prototype[8]. We begin by discussing the input formats, before describing already implemented trace generators.

4.1   Input Formats

In BenchFoundry, we decided to split the input trace into several files: Especially long-running benchmarks will have many repetitive entries in the trace, e.g., when issuing an operation repeatedly with different parameters. We, hence, use deduplication both in the input files but also for the in-memory data structures which follow the same format. Figure 3 gives an overview of the trace input files.

Operation List: This file contains all queries that are used in a given workload along with a unique ID. In the queries, we use wildcards for the actual parameter values, e.g., the actual ID value in "SELECT * FROM customer WHERE id=?". All operations are kept in memory where queries are accessible by their ID. In the input file, we use SQL to specify the queries.

Parameter List: This file contains parameter sets along with a unique ID and is also kept in-memory. Using both a parameter ID and an operation ID, an executable query can be assembled at runtime.

Trace: This file contains information on business processes, their composition, and their respective start time. As the file will typically be very large, it contains all entries ordered by time and can, therefore, be read in a streaming mode with a lookahead buffer. Typically, a scheduler will read at least two seconds ahead in the trace to have sufficient time for parameter and operation lookups and, thus, to guarantee on time scheduling. The file format itself demarcates business processes with BOP/EOP (begin/end of process) and business transactions

---

[8] https://github.com/dbermbach/BenchFoundry.

within those with BOT/EOT (begin/end of transaction). The BOP entry also includes the (relative) start timestamp of the process whereas the BOT entry may include an optional delay before starting the respective transaction to model think time of emulated users. Operations in the main trace file are specified as a combination of operation ID, parameter ID, and custom parameter ID (see below). In a BenchFoundry deployment, we will typically have one trace each for preload, warmup, and experiment phase.

Custom Parameter List: This file uses the same format as the parameter list. However, these entries are not used by BenchFoundry directly. Essentially, custom parameters are parameters that are uninterpretedly passed to the actual storage service connectors which may (but do not have to) use them. Example use cases could be consistency levels or the IP address of a specific replica.

Other Files: Beyond the trace files, we also have an input file for the logical data schema which uses SQL DDL statements and a general properties file.

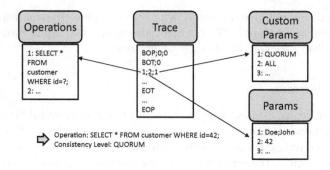

Fig. 3. File and In-Memory Representation of Workloads

When creating an experiment trace, only the experiment trace and the operation list are mandatory. Preload and warmup traces as well as custom parameters are optional and parameters may already be included in the queries.

4.2 Implemented Workloads

Currently, we have implemented two trace generators for BenchFoundry: The first generates traces based on the consistency benchmarking approach from [4] (consbench), i.e., it creates a workload that is designed to provoke upper bounds for staleness. The consbench trace generator is interactively configured with, e.g., the estimated number of replicas, the desired benchmark duration, and the number of tests. It then automatically decides on an appropriate number of BenchFoundry machines based on probability analysis as described in [4] and builds the corresponding input files. The second trace generator is based on

TPC-C[9], TPC's current order and inventory management benchmark. The original TPC-C benchmark describes four transactions; in our BenchFoundry trace generator, users can configure how they want to assemble these into processes.

To ease the implementation of additional trace generators, we have implemented an easy-to-use builder class where trace generators can simply create new business processes through method chaining. This builder class then automatically handles parameter and query deduplication while creating the correct input formats.

5 Evaluation

In this section, we present the results of our evaluation beyond the already presented proof-of-concept implementation; specifically, we present two things: First, we discuss how BenchFoundry fulfills the requirements described in Sect. 2. Second, we take a "systems perspective" and present the results of two experiments which show that BenchFoundry offers precise scheduling for normal load levels but is able to sustain a higher throughput level at the cost of accuracy as well as results showing that BenchFoundry can easily be scaled through distribution.

5.1 Discussion of Requirements in BenchFoundry

In this section, we will briefly discuss how BenchFoundry addresses each of the requirements for modern storage service benchmarks from Sect. 2.

(R1) Multi-Quality: R1 demands that benchmarks should measure all sides of a particular tradeoff. In BenchFoundry, we log detailed results about each operation including start and end timestamp as well as the values actually written. This allows to determine consistency behavior, performance, availability, and other qualities. Scalability and elasticity can be measured by varying the workload intensity (i.e., the "density" of business process starts in the workload trace).

(R2) No Assumptions: R2 demands that benchmarks should make as little assumptions on the SUT as possible, instead they should measure deviations from an ideal state. BenchFoundry only assumes that an SUT should expose a service interface with operations for data manipulation. The mapping to a concrete storage service is handled through adapter mechanisms.

(R3) Realistic Workloads: R3 demands that benchmarks should use realistic application-driven workload that mimick the target application as close as possible. BenchFoundry itself is not a benchmark but rather an execution environment for arbitrary application-driven benchmarks. For this purpose, Bench-Foundry offers a partly-open workload model [15] based on business operations, business transactions, and business processes (which is the most realistic one for

---

[9] tpc.org/tpcc

most scenarios) to benchmark designers. It also comes with a scheduler for closed workload models as used in YCSB [8] and an open workload model is obviously a special case of the partly-open one for which the respective scheduler in Bench-Foundry can be "misused". Therefore, we believe that BenchFoundry offers as much support for R3 as possible without actually designing a benchmark.

(R4) Extensibility: R4 demands that benchmarks should be extensible and configurable to account for both future application scenarios as well as new storage services. BenchFoundry executes arbitrary workload traces and is based on an adapter architecture for storage systems as presented in Fig. 1; it is also extensible with regards to quality metrics measured as it separates the benchmark run from data analysis and logs raw measurement results. We, hence, believe that it is safe to conclude that it fulfills R4.

(R5) Distribution: R5 demands that benchmarks should be designed for distribution. BenchFoundry uses a workload model that can easily be distributed and shifts all necessary coordination logic to a pre-benchmark phase.

(R6) Fine-Grained Results: R6 demands that benchmarks should always log fine-grained results. We could not think of any further measurement results that could possibly be logged in BenchFoundry. However, extending this would be straightforward.

(R7) Deterministic Execution: R7 demands that benchmarks should be able to deterministically re-execute the exact same workload. We address this by using a trace-based workload model which is fully deterministic.

(R8) Ease-of-use: R8 demands that benchmarks should have ease-of-use as a core focus. We tried to reach this goal as much as possible, e.g., by automatically configuring slave machines; if we managed to be successful is to be decided by BenchFoundry users.

5.2   Experiments

While we believe that BenchFoundry fulfills all the requirements initially identified, we also wanted to take a "systems perspective" and experimentally verify whether BenchFoundry is able to scale through distribution (the *DISTRIBUTION* experiment) and also to analyze how scheduling precision of workloads, i.e., the repeatability and determinism of workload execution, is affected by overloading the machines (the *LOAD* experiment).

Experiment Setup. For our experiment setup, we chose a setup that stresses BenchFoundry while keeping our SUT lightly loaded. In a regular benchmarking experiment, this would of course be exactly the other way around. We, therefore, deployed up to five BenchFoundry instances on Amazon EC2[10] t2.small instances and a single MariaDB node as SUT on an m4.xlarge instance.

---

[10] aws.amazon.com/ec2.

We preloaded the database with a small data set of 4211 rows in 9 tables based on the TPC-C specification. For our workload, we also used TPC-C as a basis and designed 4 different business processes with one of the TPC-C transactions each as business transaction; transactions always contained several business operations. We configured our trace generator so that it created a trace with a base unit of 2 business processes per second (constant target throughput) that could be scaled through a load factor. In the following, we will refer to throughput based on the load factor, e.g., a load factor of 10 means that we ran a workload that scheduled 20 business processes per second, each containing a single business transaction with several business operations. In each test run, we sustained the respective throughput for 120 s.

As a metric for the scheduling precision and, thus, the ability to precisely re-execute a given workload, we used the scheduling latency which is defined as the absolute difference in time between the planned start timestamp of a business process and its actual start timestamp. We would also like to point out that collecting data for this metric along with debug-level logging, of course, negatively affects the scheduling latency, i.e., users can expect values at least as good in real benchmark runs.

As already mentioned, we ran two experiments: the *LOAD* experiment and the *DISTRIBUTION* experiment. In the *LOAD* experiment, we used a single BenchFoundry instance and measured the scheduling latency for different target throughputs to (a) analyse scheduling precision for normal load levels and (b) to measure maximum sustainable throughputs on a single instance. We, therefore, tried to use the load factors 1, 5, 25, 125, 250 and 625. In the *DISTRIBUTION* experiment, we used a constant load factor of 50 (a level that was no longer sustainable on a single small instance with reasonable scheduling precision) and ran that workload distributed over two to five BenchFoundry instances.

Results. For each experiment, we show a single chart with a single boxplot for each run. Each boxplot represents a total of 6,000 measurements and shows 5, 25, 50, 75, and 95 percentiles (of scheduling latency in ms) for the corresponding test run.

In the *LOAD* experiment (see Fig. 4a, note the logarithmic scale), we were not able to reach load factors of 250 or 625. In both cases, we encountered an out of memory error so that we recommend to always pay special attention to heap size configuration. In all other experiment runs, we saw the expected behavior: low scheduling latencies for normal load levels that increased with higher sustained throughputs. At a load level of 125, the (small) instance was effectively overloaded resulting in unacceptably high scheduling latencies.

In the *DISTRIBUTION* experiment (see Fig. 4b), we also saw the expected results: BenchFoundry scales almost linearly with the number of nodes, i.e., increasing the number of nodes improves scheduling precision for constant workloads. Since BenchFoundry instances are completely independent during benchmark runs, doubling the load while using twice the number of machines should

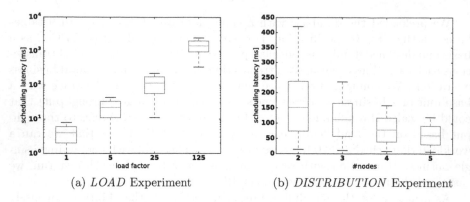

(a) *LOAD* Experiment   (b) *DISTRIBUTION* Experiment

Fig. 4. Experiment Results

not affect scheduling precision negatively, thus, also guaranteeing linear scalability in this regard.

All in all, BenchFoundry is – as expected – able to offer a high scheduling precision (<5–10 ms) and, thus, repeatability for workloads at "normal" load levels, i.e., when the machine is not fully loaded, and experiments indicate that it scales well.

6   Limitations and Effects of Design Choices

In a distributed trace, there may be situations where a faster database service or more powerful compute instances running BenchFoundry may allow some clients to complete a process more quickly than others. This can, of course, result in out-of-order execution of operations from different processes that have implicit dependencies. However, such implicit dependencies should be avoided in a workload design following our process abstraction. Furthermore, faster or slower execution of businesses processes may endanger precise repeatability for very long process instances. Future extensions of BenchFoundry could replace fixed delays between transactions with dynamic delays that depend on execution speed, e.g., execute at $t = 100$ or after 50 ms whatever happens first.

BenchFoundry needs to log fine-grained results to satisfy (R6) which leads to a certain overhead. In our design, we aimed to mitigate any potential impacts. First, we decoupled logging from execution and measurements by using two separate modules for this which communicate asynchronously. Second, we avoid network contention and minimize CPU overheads by having BenchFoundry instances only log raw data locally: Costly correlation of measurements and interpretation of raw results is done after completion of the benchmark run. Third, BenchFoundry was designed to scale well so that the overhead of writing fine-grained results instead of coarse aggregation can be mitigated by adding additional virtual machines to the benchmarking cluster. We believe that this keeps any impact on measurement and workload execution within reasonable bounds. The cost for additional machines is the price we have to pay for getting more meaningful results – in today's inexpensive compute services, this should be negligible in most cases.

7 Conclusion

In this paper, we have presented BenchFoundry, a benchmarking framework that can execute arbitrary application-driven workloads in a distributed deployment while measuring multiple system qualities of a cloud storage service. To our knowledge, BenchFoundry is the first framework that uses trace-based workloads where workloads become mere configuration files for this purpose. Beyond this convenience aspect, trace-based workloads also guarantee precise repeatability of benchmark runs.

We started by identifying requirements for modern storage benchmarks. Based on this, we presented the design and architecture of BenchFoundry before covering implementation details and evaluating our approach. In future work, we plan to implement additional trace generators and database connectors.

Acknowledgements. We would like to thank Sherif Sakr for his contributions during the early stages of the project, Daniel Wenzel for his support during some of our experiments, and Amazon Web Services for providing free access to their services.

References

1. Abadi, D.: Consistency tradeoffs in modern distributed database system design: cap is only part of the story. IEEE Comput. **45**(2), 37–42 (2012)
2. Anderson, E., Li, X., Shah, M.A., Tucek, J., Wylie, J.J.: What consistency does your key-value store actually provide? In: Proceedings of HOTDEP. USENIX (2010)
3. Bermbach, D., Kuhlenkamp, J., Dey, A., Sakr, S., Nambiar, R.: Towards an extensible middleware for database benchmarking. In: Nambiar, R., Poess, M. (eds.) TPCTC 2014. LNCS, vol. 8904, pp. 82–96. Springer, Cham (2015). doi:10.1007/978-3-319-15350-6_6
4. Bermbach, D.: Benchmarking Eventually Consistent Distributed Storage Systems. Ph.D. thesis, Karlsruhe Institute of Technology (2014)
5. Bermbach, D., Mueller, S., Eberhardt, J., Tai, S.: Informed schema design for column store-based database services. In: Proceedings of SOCA. IEEE (2015)
6. Bermbach, D., Wittern, E., Tai, S.: Cloud Service Benchmarking: Measuring Quality of Cloud Services from a Client Perspective. Springer, Cham (2017)
7. Chebotko, A., Kashlev, A., Lu, S.: A big data modeling methodology for apache cassandra. In: Proceedings of BigData. IEEE (2015)
8. Cooper, B.F., Silberstein, A., Tam, E., Ramakrishnan, R., Sears, R.: Benchmarking cloud serving systems with YCSB. In: Proceedings of SOCC. ACM (2010)
9. Difallah, D.E., Pavlo, A., Curino, C., Cudre-Mauroux, P.: OLTP-bench: An extensible testbed for benchmarking relational databases. Proceedings of VLDB **7**(4), 277–288 (2013)

10. Folkerts, E., Alexandrov, A., Sachs, K., Iosup, A., Markl, V., Tosun, C.: Benchmarking in the cloud: what it should, can, and cannot be. In: Nambiar, R., Poess, M. (eds.) TPCTC 2012. LNCS, vol. 7755, pp. 173–188. Springer, Heidelberg (2013). doi:10.1007/978-3-642-36727-4_12

11. Huppler, K.: The art of building a good benchmark. In: Nambiar, R., Poess, M. (eds.) TPCTC 2009. LNCS, vol. 5895, pp. 18–30. Springer, Heidelberg (2009). doi:10.1007/978-3-642-10424-4_3

12. von Kistowski, J., Arnold, J.A., Huppler, K., Lange, K.D., Henning, J.L., Cao, P.: How to build a benchmark. In: Proceedings of ICPE (2015)

13. Müller, S., Bermbach, D., Tai, S., Pallas, F.: Benchmarking the performance impact of transport layer security in cloud database systems. In: Proceedings of IC2E. IEEE (2014)

14. Patil, S., Polte, M., Ren, K., Tantisiriroj, W., Xiao, L., López, J., Gibson, G., Fuchs, A., Rinaldi, B.: Ycsb++: benchmarking and performance debugging advanced features in scalable table stores. In: Proceedings of SOCC. ACM (2011)

15. Schroeder, B., Wierman, A., Harchol-Balter, M.: Open versus closed: a cautionary tale. In: Proceedings of NSDI, vol. 6, p. 18 (2006)

16. Seybold, D., Domaschka, J.: A cloud-centric survey on distributed database evaluation. In: Proceedings of ADBIS (2017)

17. Wada, H., Fekete, A., Zhao, L., Lee, K., Liu, A.: Data consistency properties and the trade-offs in commercial cloud storages: the consumers' perspective. In: Proceedings of CIDR (2011)

Automated Analysis of Cloud Offerings
for Optimal Service Provisioning

José María García$^{(\boxtimes)}$, Octavio Martín-Díaz, Pablo Fernandez,
Antonio Ruiz-Cortés, and Miguel Toro

Universidad de Sevilla, Seville, Spain
{josemgarcia,omartindiaz,pablofm,aruiz,migueltoro}@us.es

Abstract. Cloud computing paradigm has brought an overwhelming variety of cloud services from different providers, each one offering a plethora of configuration and purchasing options for them. Users may have certain requirements and preferences not only concerning service configuration, but also with respect to their usage schedule. In this situation, an appropriate provisioning plan considering all restrictions would help users to achieve their goals while taking into account the different available providers, their pricing and even the usage discounts they provide. In this work, we describe an automated solution that analyzes user needs that include scheduling restrictions to obtain optimized provisioning plans for different cloud providers, which allow users to compare several offerings that possibly consider volume or usage discounts. We validate this solution against a realistic use case, while also providing a prototype implementation in the form of publicly available microservices.

Keywords: Cloud services · Pricing · Provisioning · Analysis

1 Introduction

The emergence of cloud computing have brought a significant shift in the IT industry economics for service providers and consumers alike [1,2]. Cloud services such as Amazon Elastic Computing Cloud (EC2) or Google Compute Engine offer virtual processing and storage resources (commonly referred to as Infrastructure as a Service, or IaaS in short), so that customers can purchase them as a way to reduce operational costs if compared with the procurement of on-premise, private computing infrastructures. However, the myriad of cloud service providers, as well as their overwhelming variety of configuration and purchasing options [3], result in a highly complex provisioning scenario for service consumers.

In this setting, there are major heterogeneity issues that make the comparison among providers rather difficult, e.g. different variables for configurations, additional purchasing variants apart from the usual pay-as-you-go option, billing and charge processes, and particular discount rules, to name a few. Furthermore,

© Springer International Publishing AG 2017
M. Maximilien et al. (Eds.): ICSOC 2017, LNCS 10601, pp. 331–339, 2017.
https://doi.org/10.1007/978-3-319-69035-3_23

users may also find convenient to specify their needs for cloud services provisioning including specific scheduling restrictions. These restrictions provide additional beforehand information concerning not only the number of instances of particular configurations that are needed at a certain time, but also the amount of time they are going to be used.

There are some on-line tools that allow consumers to search for an optimal configuration, such as Cloudorado.com and CloudScreener.com, according to their particular needs. However, these tools do not take into account scheduling. In this work, we present an automatic analysis framework that analyzes and compares cloud service offerings from multiple providers to obtain an optimal provisioning plan according to user needs. This plan specifies the amount and type of instances that have to be purchased and when they have to be initiated and terminated in order to fulfill user needs. We have developed a prototype implementation that has been validated in a particular scenario with two different providers.

The rest of the paper is structured as follows. Section 2 introduces a case study that further motivates our work. Next, Sect. 3 describes the conceptual model of the provisioning process and our solution to obtain optimal plans. Then, Sect. 4 presents the architecture of our solution, and Sect. 5 showcases our validation results. Section 6 discusses the related work. Finally, Sect. 7 concludes the paper and outlines our future work.

2   Motivation

There are several service provisioning scenarios where the usage schedule is known *a priori*. Thus, users can specify their needs including scheduling information so that a corresponding provisioning plan can be derived from it. We can characterize these service scenarios depending on the complexity of the usage scheduling and the configuration of services needed. On the one hand, the usage scheduling may consist on a simple interval when the service will be needed, or rather a complex schedule that includes several intertwined temporal slots. On the other hand, needed services complexity may range from a single service with a particular configuration, to a number of highly configurable services [4].

In the following we focus on a case study on the *virtualization of laboratory classes* in the context of our Software Engineering courses, which falls on the most complex scenario since there may be several different software needs for each course with varying scheduling needs. Furthermore, laboratory classes may have a dynamic evolution from two viewpoints: (1) the software being used on those classes may evolve, usually requiring increasing computing resources, and thus possibly rendering the corresponding hardware obsolete at short notice; and (2) the demand, due to the number of students, may vary along the academic year. In order to increase flexibility and save costs, these classes can be virtualized by purchasing cloud infrastructure to support their dynamic environment.

As an example, let us consider that we need to provide infrastructure for the laboratory classes of a year course beginning on Monday 19th September

2016, which requires a very simple hardware configuration of a two-core CPU with 4 GB RAM. The usage scheduling contemplates weekly, 2-hour sessions for several groups of varying number of students during each semester, which comprises 15 weeks, in addition to open classrooms and specific examination days.

In order to actually provision the infrastructural needs for these laboratory classes, we need to carry out corresponding provisioning actions against a cloud infrastructure service provider. Thus, our solution analyzes user needs, derives their associated provisioning plans aggregating the necessary provisioning actions according to the scheduling restrictions, and searches for suitable service offerings to obtain a corresponding charge plan that sums up the total cost, hence allowing the user to choose the best option in each case. Note that we are not considering additional costs, such as communication expenses, due to the difficulty to estimate *a priori* these aspects.

3   From User Needs to Cloud Services Provisioning Plans

In order to automatically generate a plan that specifies the provisioning events that fulfill certain user needs, we first need to model the relevant descriptions so that our solution can analyze and transform them into the resulting plan. User needs specifies the client's requirements on particular services (in our case study cloud infrastructure services, or IaaS in short). These requirements mainly state (1) the configurations which are needed to execute the client's software, and (2) the expected usage schedule.

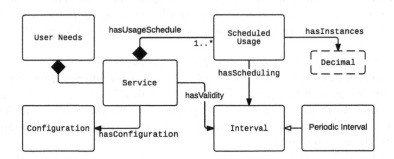

Fig. 1. Conceptual model for user needs

Figure 1 shows our conceptual model representing user needs. User needs are composed of a series of services that represent the different software components that the client needs to deploy to the cloud. In our example, each course is interpreted as a different service, which consists in a virtual machine containing all the relevant software for that course. According to this, each service is associated with its required configuration, which describes the hardware requirements for the requested cloud service instance. Thus, a configuration in case of an IaaS may contain requirements about CPU, memory, IO performance, and storage, among others [3].

Regarding the expected usage schedule, each service enumerated in the user needs is associated with one or more scheduled usage items, which are *temporal composites* that detail the number of instances of the same configuration and the time interval when they are needed. Additionally, a global validity interval can be also specified. Unlike the latter, usage intervals may be periodic and disjoint or overlapped with others. In our motivating example, each course is given in several groups possibly with different timetables. Therefore, each group corresponds to a scheduled usage that specifies both the time interval when the course is given and the number of service instances that are needed, which depends on the group size.

Starting from the user needs, a provisioning plan that contains the actions to fulfill them is generated. It is optimal since (1) each chosen service is the best fit for the configuration expressed in the user needs, and (2) it minimizes the number of instances for each configuration for the whole validity period according to the usage schedule, favoring reserved instances, and hence decreasing the operational costs of cloud infrastructure.

The first step involved in the optimal plan generation is the optimization of usage scheduling. We analyze each service to be deployed separately, since we aim at minimizing the total number of instances needed for each configuration. Our solution takes the scheduling of every service and removes overlaps between time intervals. This is achieved by normalizing and coalescing the time sequence of the scheduling, which are well-known operations in the context of temporal databases [5]. Note that overlapping intervals leads to a higher number of instances to be run simultaneously, while disjoint intervals enables reusing of instances from one interval to the next, increasing their usage percentage so that reservation becomes a better purchasing option, hence diminishing the overall operational costs.

Once the optimal usage scheduling for each service is computed, the second step searches for the optimal service configuration from different providers. Different approaches can be applied to discover a suitable configuration from the pricing lists advertised by various IaaS providers. Our approach looks for the instance configuration from each available provider whose parameters are the closest to those stated in the user needs as in [3].

From the usage scheduling, our solution finally generates a particular provisioning plan for each cloud service provider, describing the minimum number of deployment actions that fulfills the usage schedule. Furthermore, purchasing options are also optimized so that the best purchasing type is chosen for each service instance in order to minimize the total cost of the cloud infrastructure to provision. As explained above, if the expected usage for an instance is long enough then it will be better to make a reservation as long as the provider offers such option. Otherwise, the instance will be used on-demand or pay-as-you-go basis. Thus, our approach enables the comparison of several offerings from different providers, taking into account their available configurations and pricing options.

4   Solution Architecture

In order to realize our approach, we developed a prototype solution that is based on the models described in Sect. 3 and implemented within a microservice architecture integrated in the Governify service management platform[1]. Currently, the prototype implementation supports two widely used cloud providers: Amazon EC2 and Google Compute Engine, but the architecture is designed to provide a systematic extension mechanism by means of adding new RESTful services that share a common interface.

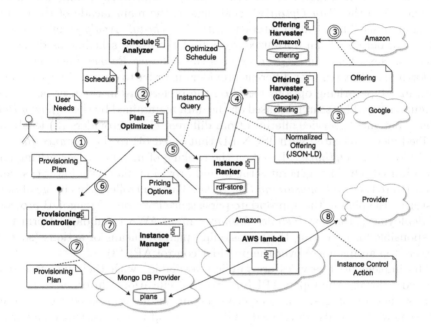

Fig. 2. Microservice architecture of the prototype.

On the one hand, pricing listings are automatically imported and standardized in our system using a JSON-LD [6] parser that takes JSON files published by service providers, such as Amazon[2] or Google[3], and annotate some properties to identify common properties (such as base price, CPU, or memory) using JSON-LD facilities. We use some cloud computing ontologies previously developed [7] as the fundamental schema to annotate configuration and pricing information from these providers, enabling interoperability of their original JSON schemas.

---

[1] https://governify.io.

[2] https://pricing.us-east-1.amazonaws.com/offers/v1.0/aws/AmazonEC2/current/index.json.

[3] https://cloudpricingcalculator.appspot.com/static/data/pricelist.json.

Then, annotated JSON pricing listings are parsed in order to populate the catalog of service offerings from different providers.

On the other hand, user needs are instantiated according to the model discussed in Sect. 3. First, the scheduling items are analyzed to optimize the usage schedule, and then the provisioning plan optimizer component analyzes user needs with its scheduling restrictions in order to obtain a specific provisioning plan that optimize costs for each provider.

From a deployment standpoint, Fig. 2 depicts the microservices architecture of the prototype describing the responsibility distribution and data interaction among services. As a high level overview, the flow starts when some user needs are sent (1) to the *Plan Optimizer* that acts as the main façade of the overall pricing analysis. This element interacts with the *Schedule Analyzer* microservice in order to obtain (2) an optimized version of the usage schedule as described in Sect. 3. Next, the *Plan Optimizer* uses the *Instance Ranker* microservice to develop a global search over different providers in order to obtain (5) a sorted set of instance type pricing options based on the preferences in the user needs (i.e. configurations). This search is based on the data maintained by the *Offering Harvesters* that gather service offerings from different cloud providers (3) to obtain a unified view annotated with JSON-LD that is fed (4) to the *Instance Ranker*. Finally, the *Plan Optimizer*, based on the ranking of instance types pricing and the optimized schedule, generates the actual provision plan with lower cost and send it (6) to the the *Provisioning Controller*. This controller is in charge of both (7) storing the plan in the appropriate persistence layer on a MongoDB provider and deploying (7) a new *Instance Manager* in an AWS Lambda platform that is responsible for executing the provisioning plan by means of actions (such as start or stop an instance) over the provider control API (8).

The implemented services are publicly available[4] with their interface documented following the Open API Initiative Specification[5]; in order to test the services, they all integrate an interactive testing on-line tool based on the Swagger[6] framework. We also developed a GUI for an end-user consisting on a wizard prototype[7]. This tool provides a user-friendly interface for defining needs and launch the appropriate microservices in a user-friendly way.

5   Case Study Validation Results

In order to validate our solution, we carried out the case study described in Sect. 2 using the implemented prototype. We considered service offerings from Amazon and Google. As stated by our user needs, our tool searched for the closer configuration to "`Cpu:2 Mem:4`" in their catalogs, using the approach presented in [3]. According to the *on-demand* purchasing type, the results of the search return a `t2.medium` configuration for Amazon (with a base price of 0.052\$/h),

---

[4] https://pricing.governify.io/.
[5] https://openapis.org/.
[6] https://swagger.io/.
[7] https://designer.governify.io/demo/PlanOptimizer/wizard.

while in case of Google the most suited configurtion corresponds to `n1-std-2-pr` machine with a base price of 0.020\$/h, as of price listings retrieved on October, 1st 2016.

Based on these configurations, our solution generates a different provisioning plan for each provider. These plans allow a fine grained analysis of operational costs. Concretely, a comparative study of corresponding charge plans can be carried out, including the different expected charges per month along with the total cost for the whole provisioning plan. Table 1 shows the optimal charge plan, including discounts, for each provider derived from the provisioning plan generated by our prototype. It is interesting to note that in the Amazon case the maximum savings are derived from a full upfront (advanced payment of reserved instances) at the beginning which results in a considerable initial charge.

Table 1. Charge plans for our case study, discounts applied.

Amazon			Google		
Date	Type	Cost	Date	Type	Cost
Sep 19 2016	Upfront	12080.0\$	*Sustained-use discounts are being applied.*		
Oct 01 2016	On-demand	20.12\$	Oct 02 2016	On-demand	180.52\$
Nov 01 2016	On-demand	67.08\$	Nov 02 2016	On-demand	601.72\$
Dec 01 2016	On-demand	67.08\$	Dec 02 2016	On-demand	601.72\$
...			...		
Total cost		**12884.96\$**	**Total cost**		**7220.66\$**

As a consequence of our analysis, we can determine that in our case study Google is the best option in terms of costs. Moreover, based on a preliminary analysis we realize that Amazon reserved instances prove to be competitive only if their usage is greater than approximately 75% of daily-usage, for a full year. Alternatively Google provides usage-sustained discounts of 25% of monthly-usage starting at the first month without the need for longer reservation periods as in the Amazon case.

The performed experiment validates that our proposal actually optimizes cloud provisioning, automatically generating plans from user needs while considering pricing models and discount rules of several cloud service providers. Although our use case has been kept deliberately simple for the sake of clarity, we can extend the scenario to include multiple courses in order to reach a higher usage ratio. We have already made some initial experiments on this matter, resulting in different comparative results. In particular, we found that Amazon provides more cost-effective options when the instance usage ratio is significant.

6 Related Work

Optimization of cloud provisioning can be considered from different perspectives. From an economic perspective, pricing models are extensively discussed in [8,9]. In [10] authors present a comprehensive method to calculate the total cost of ownership of a cloud infrastructure. In [11] the search is modeled as a multi-objective optimization problem to minimize the overall cost due to data storage, communication, and execution. In [12] different approaches are presented to compute the pricing in the context of offering REST APIs to multiple customers. Modeling pricing and scheduling aspects for edge devices can also establish sharing economy principles in edge and cloud computing [13].

Regarding scheduling, there are some approaches to the provisioning scenario which takes into account the scheduling restrictions for optimization issues using different techniques [14,15]. In [16] authors present a service management which takes into account the optimal trade-off between cost and QoS in the context of elasticity of highly variable workloads. Ran et al. apply a probabilistic model for determining the amount of the reserved instances to minimize the total cost while keeping QoS [17], as in our approach. Note that over-provisioned instances may lead to a low usage ratio and a greater cost, while a scarce reservation will have a poorer waiting time that leads to QoS degradation. Similarly, in [18] authors also get the optimum number for long-term reservation of resources in order to minimize provisioning costs.

7   Conclusions and Future Work

Provisioning plans are of utmost importance when trying to optimize computational resources required to fulfill some user needs during specific time periods. This article presents a solution to automatically derive provisioning plans from user needs specification including scheduling restrictions. After modeling user needs for a particular scenario, our prototype implementation searches for appropriate service configurations from different providers and generates corresponding provisioning plans, optimized both in terms of scheduling and purchasing options, for each provider. Then, our provisioning controller realizes the chosen plan, which is comprised of events that contain the necessary actions needed to fulfill user requirements. As future work, we plan to automatically crawl pricing and service configuration options from other cloud providers, to support multi-cloud provisioning plans, which may provide better performance and cost minimization in certain scenarios, as well as to analyze log files to improve the optimization and execution of existing provisioning plans.

Acknowledgments. Authors would like to thank Felipe Serafim and Daniel Arteaga for their support on the prototype implementation. This work has been partially supported by the EU Commission (FEDER), Spanish and Andalusian R&D&I programmes under grants TIN2015-70560-R, and P12-TIC-1867.

References

1. Armbrust, M., Fox, A., Griffith, R., Joseph, A.D., Katz, R., Konwinski, A., Lee, G., Patterson, D., Rabkin, A., Stoica, I., Zaharia, M.: A view of cloud computing. Commun. ACM **53**(4), 50–58 (2010)

2. Ma, R.T., Lui, J.C., Misra, V.: On the evolution of the internet economic ecosystem. In: Proceedings of the 22nd International Conference on World Wide Web, WWW 2013, pp. 849–860. ACM (2013)
3. García-Galán, J., Trinidad, P., Rana, O.F., Cortés, A.R.: Automated configuration support for infrastructure migration to the cloud. Future Generat. Comp. Syst. **55**, 200–212 (2016)
4. García-Galán, J., García, J.M., Trinidad, P., Fernandez, P.: Modelling and analysing highly-configurable services. In: Proceedings of the 21st International Systems and Software Product Line Conference, SPLC 2017. vol. A, pp. 114–122. ACM (2017)
5. Jensen, C.S., et al.: The consensus glossary of temporal database concepts — February 1998 version. In: Etzion, O., Jajodia, S., Sripada, S. (eds.) Temporal Databases: Research and Practice. LNCS, vol. 1399, pp. 367–405. Springer, Heidelberg (1998). doi:10.1007/BFb0053710
6. Lanthaler, M., Gütl, C.: On using JSON-LD to create evolvable RESTful services. In: Proceedings of the Third International Workshop on RESTful Design, WS-REST 2012, pp. 25–32. ACM (2012)
7. García, J.M., Fernandez, P., Pedrinaci, C., Resinas, M., Cardoso, J., Ruiz-Cortés, A.: Modeling service level agreements with linked USDL agreement. IEEE Trans. Serv. Comput. **10**(1), 52–65 (2017)
8. Al-Roomi, M., Al-Ebrahim, S., Buqrais, S., Ahmad, I.: Cloud computing pricing models: a survey. Int. J. Grid Distrib. Comput. **6**(5), 93–106 (2013)
9. Gamez-Diaz, A., Fernandez, P., Ruiz-Cortes, A.: An analysis of RESTful APIs offerings in the industry. In: Maximilien, M., et al. (eds.) ICSOC 2017. LNCS, vol. 10601, pp. 589–604. Springer, Cham (2017)
10. Li, X., Li, Y., Liu, T., Qiu, J., Wang, F.: The Method and tool of cost analysis for cloud computing. In: 2009 IEEE International Conference on Cloud Computing, pp. 93–100 (2009)
11. Wen, Z., Cala, J., Watson, P., Romanovsky, A.: Cost effective, reliable and secure workflow deployment over federated clouds. IEEE Trans. Serv. Comput. (2016). In press
12. Vukovic, M., Zeng, L.Z., Rajagopal, S.: Model for service license in API ecosystems. In: Franch, X., Ghose, A.K., Lewis, G.A., Bhiri, S. (eds.) ICSOC 2014. LNCS, vol. 8831, pp. 590–597. Springer, Heidelberg (2014). doi:10.1007/978-3-662-45391-9_51
13. García, J.M., Fernandez, P., Ruiz-Cortés, A., Dustdar, S., Toro, M.: Edge and cloud pricing for the sharing economy. IEEE Internet Comput. **21**(2), 78–84 (2017)
14. van den Bossche, R., Vanmechelen, K., Broeckhove, J.: Cost-optimal scheduling in hybrid IaaS clouds for deadline constrained workloads. In: 2010 IEEE International Conference on Cloud Computing, pp. 228–235 (2010)
15. Netjinda, N., Sirinaovakul, B., Achalakul, T.: Cost optimal scheduling in IaaS for dependent workload with particle swarm optimization. J. Supercomput. **68**(3), 1579–1603 (2014)
16. Björkqvist, M., Spicuglia, S., Chen, L., Binder, W.: QoS-aware service VM provisioning in clouds: experiences, models, and cost analysis. In: Basu, S., Pautasso, C., Zhang, L., Fu, X. (eds.) ICSOC 2013. LNCS, vol. 8274, pp. 69–83. Springer, Heidelberg (2013). doi:10.1007/978-3-642-45005-1_6
17. Ran, Y., Yang, J., Zhang, S., Xi, H.: Dynamic IaaS computing resource provisioning strategy with QoS constraint. IEEE Trans. Serv. Comput. **10**(2), 190–202 (2017)
18. Hwang, R., Lee, C., Chen, Y., Zhang-Jian, D.: Cost optimization of elasticity cloud resource subscription policy. IEEE Trans. Serv. Comput. **7**(4), 561–574 (2014)

Middleware for Dynamic Upgrade Activation and Compensations in Multi-tenant SaaS

Dimitri Van Landuyt$^{(\boxtimes)}$, Fatih Gey, Eddy Truyen, and Wouter Joosen

imec-DistriNet, Department of Computer Science, KU Leuven,
Celestijnenlaan 200A, 3001 Leuven, Belgium
{dimitri.vanlanduyt,fatih.gey,eddy.truyen,wouter.joosen}@cs.kuleuven.be

Abstract. Multi-tenant Software as a Service (SaaS) is the cloud computing delivery model that maximizes resource sharing up to the level
of a single application instance, servicing many customer organizations
(tenants) at once. Due to this scale of delivery, a SaaS offering, once successful, becomes difficult to upgrade and evolve without affecting service
continuity, and this in turn limits its capabilities to respond to the reality
of changing customer requirements.

However, not all tenants are equal, and to some organizations such
disruptions are more costly than to others. Supporting different quality
trade-offs for different tenants is often a manual, error-prone task and
far from trivial.

This short paper outlines our middleware design for fine-grained, gradual and continuous evolution of multi-tenant SaaS applications, providing
automated and systematic support for (i) tenant-aware upgrade enactment, and (ii) compensations that allow recovering from negative side-
effects of the upgrade enactment.

1 Introduction

In the Software as a Service (SaaS) delivery model, Internet services are offered
to customer organizations (tenants) on a subscription basis. The SaaS provider
and tenants typically agree on individual service quality levels that such an
application must reliably provide.

A key advantage of SaaS applications is their *cost-efficiency* which is attained
at large scale due to economies-of-scale effects [2]: Run-time resources (such as
the hardware, platforms and supportive services) are shared among multiple tenants up to the level of application instances (an architectural tactic called multi-
tenancy [7]). To minimize the costs per tenant, configuration and customization
activities are commonly outsourced to tenant administrators, a principle called
self service [25].

Such a multi-tenant SaaS application becomes difficult to change and evolve
without affecting overall service continuity and thereby many tenant businesses.
As a result, its capabilities to respond to the reality of changing customer requirements [21] (for example, through *continuous delivery* [24]) are limited. More
specifically, a SaaS application that is expected to attain high levels of service

M. Maximilien et al. (Eds.): ICSOC 2017, LNCS 10601, pp. 340–348, 2017.
https://doi.org/10.1007/978-3-319-69035-3_24

continuity cannot be taken offline for maintenance, i.e. to enact an upgrade, but must continue servicing tenant requests even during upgrade enactment. In addition, due to the high level of resource sharing among tenants, it must be ensured that changes applied for one tenant do not negatively affect other tenants (tenant isolation). Furthermore, service continuity cannot always be ensured (e.g. during the enactment of an incompatible upgrade [4]), such that either the SaaS application becomes temporarily unavailable, or different service qualities are sacrificed, for example functionality and integrity.

An upgrade enactment that maintains one metric of service continuity at the cost of another provides a specific *quality compromise*. A multi-tenant SaaS application that traditionally evolves in one shot [4,11] has no room for considerations on a per-tenant basis. Moreover, in this context, the large scale of operation of the SaaS application has a multiplying effect, which leads to upgrades that potentially have a profound impact on many tenant businesses. This renders traditional approaches such as waiting for application-wide quiescence [19] unfeasible. As different compromises (in terms of quality or functionality) may be considered acceptable to different tenants (depending for example on the tenant SLA), systematic support is required for compromises on a per-tenant basis, both *during* the upgrade enactment and/or *after* the enactment, i.e. by supporting compensatory measures that are enacted after the fact (e.g. rolling back inconsistent transactions). This short paper presents middleware support for continuous evolution of multi-tenant SaaS applications that provides support for both types of compromises on a fine-grained, per-tenant basis.

The remainder of this paper is structured as follows: Sect. 2 derives and motivates the main requirements, whereas Sect. 3 presents our middleware. Section 4 discusses related work, and Sect. 5 concludes the paper.

2   Motivation and Requirements

The following key observations contribute to our motivation: (i) Incompatible software upgrades demand for different quality compromises with respect to the upgrade enactment process; (ii) related work on dynamic software upgrades and dynamic adaptations provides several alternative strategies [1,19,22,23,28], each involving fundamentally different quality compromises (e.g. consistency over availability or vice versa); (iii) to some tenants, software failures (as a cost of a quality compromise) are only harmful for tenants if their effects remain permanent, and when anticipated, such negative consequences can often be corrected though compensatory measures.

The above observations highlight the potential to perform evolution of multi-tenant on a per-tenant, customized manner, but current solutions either involve enacting upgrades in a single shot operation, or require manual effort and are therefore error-prone and expensive.

As such, we state the following requirements for supporting continuous evolution of multi-tenant SaaS applications in a systematic and maximally automated fashion:

R1 Customization support: The nature of the SaaS service degradation and service quality compromises should be customizable and controllable by tenants. This entails:

> **R1a Tenant-isolated upgrade enactment:** Allowing the activation of an upgrade for one tenant without affecting other tenants (tenant isolation) is a key enabler for fine-grained per-tenant customization, as this allows the activation of an upgrade for one tenant to be timely and functionally decoupled from other tenants [14]. It enables, moreover, approaches such as phased cut-off, i.e. to overlap the phase-out of the current version and the phase-in of the upgraded version of service components.

> **R1b Awareness of the upgrade compatibility:** Alternative upgrade paths that each involve different compromises (in terms of quality and functionality) must exploit the compatibility nature [4] of upgrades. This implies in particular that different upgrade activation mechanisms must be developed and supported by the SaaS developer.

R2 Compensation support: For each quality compromise made during upgrade enactment for which significant service degradations are anticipated, automated compensation facilities should be provided that revert or counter-act these, again on a per-tenant basis, in isolation and tailored to the nature of the upgrade at hand (thus, provided by the SaaS developer and configured by the tenant administrator).

3   Middleware Support

Fig. 1 provides an overview of the proposed middleware solution. The top of the figure represents the SaaS application which is structured as a service-oriented application (SOA). Section 3.1 first introduces the `DSlookup` component, which supports tenant- and context-aware dynamic service composition [14,29]. The `Activation Controller` and `Compensation Controller` components both rely extensively on this component and are discussed in Sects. 3.2 and 3.3 respectively.

3.1   Dynamic Multi-tenant Service Composition

Our middleware relies extensively on the underlying ability to manipulate service compositions at run time, and we leverage this mechanism for tenant-aware customization of service bindings [29].

Dynamic service lookup is accomplished by the `DSlookup` component that implements a lazy service composition approach: it resolves only to a specific service binding of a composition at request time. In addition, `DSlookup` allows manipulating its service lookup logic through changing the transaction context of the triggering service request. Multi-tenant customization is accomplished by defining a set of service compositions that serve specific variants of services specific to a tenant (these are part of the tenant configurations, stored in the `Tenant Configuration Repository`) (step (0) in Fig. 2). Tenant context tokens [18,29]

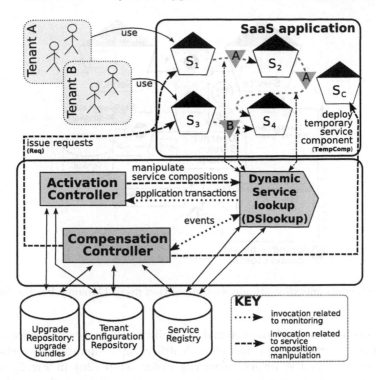

Fig. 1. High-level overview of our middleware, which is comprised of the `DSlookup` component, the `Activation Controller`, and the `Compensation Controller`.

are attached to the call chain when new application transactions are started, and the tenant identity is derived, for example, from authentication data [29].

To allow ensuring version-consistent behavior [23], the dynamic service composition must additionally be aware of the end-to-end application transaction context. This is done with a transaction context token that is attached to all service requests of an application transaction. A service component instance that issues outbound service requests r_O in the course of processing an inbound request r_I must copy the tenant and transaction context of r_I to r_O [18].

Figure 2 illustrates the workings of the `DSlookup` component. A service component instance addresses `DSlookup` to lookup another service component instance that provides a specific interface, attaching the tenant and transaction context token (step (1) in Fig. 2). To fulfill the request, `DSlookup` consults the corresponding tenant configuration from the tenant configuration repository (step (2b)), specifically to find a matching *service binding*. If successful, the reference to an instance[1] of the specified target service is returned to the caller (return arrow for step (1)) who now is able to invoke that service call ((3) in Fig. 2). It is worth noting that service instances are identified by an identifier/type *and* a version.

---

[1] This involves consulting the `Service Registry`, which is omitted here for simplicity.

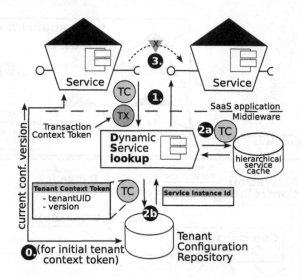

Fig. 2. Dynamic context-aware service composition using **Dynamic Service lookup**.

Service cache. For performance and scalability reasons, each service component instance caches service instance identifiers in a hierarchical cache. The cache is queried in the reverse hierarchy order (step ($2a$) in Fig. 2): only if transaction-specific service instance references cannot be found, generic references are searched.

3.2   Activation Support

Our middleware enables configuration of upgrade activations dynamically and on a per-tenant basis. Upgrade activation is accomplished by dynamically manipulating service compositions, to reroute service lookups to new service versions. As shown in Fig. 1, the key component for coordinating these upgrade activations is the `ActivationController`.

More specifically, the possible upgrade paths for a specific upgrade are encoded in a set of *Activation scripts* (provided by the SaaS developer), and these can be selected or configured by the tenant or SaaS operator. These are code artifacts that are defined in terms of pre-defined service composition manipulation primitives. The following manipulation primitives are currently supported by the middleware:

InitVer Change version for initial tenant context: this primitive provides the capability to change the tenant configuration version used for initial tenant contexts which is stored in the tenant configuration repository. This effectively means that for all tenants that do not refer to a specific version in their service compositions, the newer version will picked as a default.

TokenVer Change version of tenant context token: with this primitive, at DSlookup, the configuration version entry of a tenant context token can be manipulated for specific service-lookup queries *before* the actual lookup. This effectively overrides the selected version.

FailLookup **Deliberately fail service lookup:** using this primitive, DSlookup can be set to fail a specific lookup deliberately, i.e. to return that no service component instances are available.

FlushSC **Flush service reference cache:** the service cache (maintained by every service component instance locally) can be cleared for transaction-specific or generic service instance references, e.g. to immediately effectuate a version upgrade.

As depicted in Fig. 1, the Activation Controller monitors new application transactions (beginning and end), and coordinates the execution of Activation scripts, which in turn entails the invocation of the service composition manipulation primitives discussed above.

3.3 Compensation Support

A compensation is essentially an additional behavior to prevent or recover from a negative side-effect of upgrade enactment. Similarly to the Activation Controller, the Compensation Controller actively monitors the application transactions and perform actions in response to specific events. As with the activation controller scripts, a compensation is put together with *Compensation Primitives*. The following compensation primitives are currently supported:

ManipSC **Manipulate service composition instance:** this primitive is equivalent to the TokenVer primitive discussed earlier.

FailReq **Deliberately fail service requests:** similarly, this primitive is already supported by the FailLookup primitive.

TempComp **Deploy temporary service components:** an upgrade may be shipped with temporary service components that are only deployed during the activation of an upgrade by a compensation artifact (for example, to attain graceful degradation).

Req **Issue service requests:** a compensation may issue additional service requests, for example to start new transactions on behalf of the end user.

A *Compensation script* consists of two key elements: one for specifying events it may have interest in (the **monitor**), and one for defining the appropriate reaction to these events (**action**). Event filters are installed at the DSlookup component at the start of an upgrade. Event filters may refer to service component instances involved, tenant context used at the beginning and the end of the service lookup[2], and the application transaction context.

Relevant events are propagated from DSlookup to the Compensation Controller, which in turn coordinates the execution of the corresponding Compensation script.

---

[2] Note: these two may differ when TokenVer is used.

346   D. Van Landuyt et al.

4   Related Work

We first discuss the broader set of related work on dynamic software updates
(DSU), then we focus on existing support for evolution or customization of cloud
applications and finally, we discuss related work w.r.t. compensation support.

Dynamic Software Updates. Updating an application at run time has been studied for decades [3,15,19], increasingly reducing the impact on its normal operation. There are two dominant and fundamentally different approaches:
(i) *Dynamic software updates* [16] score well on service continuity and focus
on update safety, but are limited to specific types of upgrades; moreover, they
usually depend on memory-invasive operations which are not applicable in a
cloud context.
(ii) *Dynamic Adaptation* techniques [1,17,19,22,23,28] are applied in terms of
components and connectors and are therefore applicable for any type of upgrade
and technology-independent. These techniques can be further divided in two
classes: those that require a safe state (e.g. quiescence) of the application before
performing the upgrade [19,28], and those that support a mixed mode where old
and new versions co-exist [1,17,26].

Although showing this in further detail is part of our future work, using the
manipulation primitives for service composition presented in Sect. 3.2, we can
effectively support these different classes of upgrade strategies simultaneously.
Similar to [17,22,27], our middleware provides an open and versatile platform
for upgrades, specific to the domain of cloud-scale evolution [4].

Middleware Support for Evolution of Cloud Applications. Dumitras et al. [11]
propose a middleware that moves an entire application to a "parallel universe" to
avoid inconsistencies of otherwise incremental upgrades of enterprise-sized cloud
applications. Opposed to theirs, our approach promotes a service component as
the smallest unit for evolution. Others [13,20] support adaptation and evolution of a SaaS application for anticipated upgrades. Ertel et al. [12] present a
framework to support dynamic evolution of dataflow programs. While their support is based on types of applications that are different from multi-tenant SaaS
applications, their work is complementary to ours as it focuses on algorithms
for automated enactment, accounting for state-transfer, referential integrity and
timeliness of dependent upgrades.

Compensations. In relational database transactions [8,9], supporting compensations is a strategy for *forward error recovery* which is an alternative to *backward
error recovery* (i.e. roll-back). *Automatic workaround* [5,6,10] as a related self-
healing tactic on the other hand provides a computed recovery strategy as a
compensation.

Although showing this in further detail is part of our future work, using the
compensation primitives defined in Sect. 3.3, we support the following types of
compensations: (i) inverting or repeating service requests (`Req`), (ii) changing
behavior for specific requests (`ManipSC` and `TempComp`), (iii) deliberately failing
service requests (`FailReq`).

5   Conclusion

We have presented dedicated middleware support for continuous evolution of multi-tenant SaaS applications that essentially implements two measures to reduce the impact of –or at least to increase control over– an upgrade enactment: customization and compensation. Our middleware allows per-tenant, customized and fine-grained service continuity compromises when enacting different types of software upgrades. Compromises that entail a significant sacrifice are complemented by a *compensation* to alleviate their effect in an automated fashion. Our approach allows the SaaS developer to implement upgrade activation and compensation scripts that are based on common manipulation and compensation primitives respectively that are built into the middleware.

The systematic support for both types of measures allow controlling the overall cost of enacting a change (in the course of software evolution) in multi-tenant SaaS applications that are subject to continuous service delivery guarantees, and as such these mechanisms may contribute greatly in reducing the time-to-market of new features.

Acknowledgements. This research is partially funded by the Research Fund KU Leuven, the ADDIS research program funded by KU Leuven GOA, and the DeCoMAdS SBO strategic research project.

References

1. Ajmani, S., Liskov, B., Shrira, L.: Modular Software Upgrades for Distributed Systems. In: Thomas, D. (ed.) ECOOP 2006. LNCS, vol. 4067, pp. 452–476. Springer, Heidelberg (2006). doi:10.1007/11785477_26
2. Armbrust, M., Fox, A., Griffith, R., Joseph, A.D., Katz, R., Konwinski, A., Lee, G., Patterson, D., Rabkin, A., Stoica, I., et al.: A view of cloud computing. Commun. ACM **53**(4), 50–58 (2010)
3. Bloom, T., Day, M.: Reconfiguration and module replacement in argus: theory and practice. Softw. Eng. J. **8**(2), 102–108 (1993)
4. Brewer, E.: Lessons from giant-scale services. IEEE Internet Comput. **5**(4), 46–55 (2001)
5. Carzaniga, A., Gorla, A., Perino, N., Pezzè, M.: Automatic workarounds for web applications. In: FSE 2010, pp. 237–246. ACM, New York (2010)
6. Carzaniga, A., Gorla, A., Pezzè, M.: Self-healing by means of automatic workarounds. In: SEAMS 2008, pp. 17–24. ACM, New York (2008)
7. Chong, F., Carraro, G.: Architectural strategies for catching the long tail (2006). http://msdn.microsoft.com/en-us/library/aa479069.aspx
8. Colombo, C., Pace, G.J.: Recovery within long-running transactions. ACM Comput. Surv. **45**(3), 28:1–28:35 (2013)
9. Davies Jr., C.T.: Recovery semantics for a db/dc system. In: Proceedings of the ACM Annual Conference, pp. 136–141. ACM, New York (1973)
10. de Lemos, R., et al.: Software Engineering for Self-Adaptive Systems: A Second Research Roadmap. In: de Lemos, R., Giese, H., Müller, H.A., Shaw, M. (eds.) Software Engineering for Self-Adaptive Systems II. LNCS, vol. 7475, pp. 1–32. Springer, Heidelberg (2013). doi:10.1007/978-3-642-35813-5_1

11. Dumitraş, T., Narasimhan, P.: Why Do Upgrades Fail and What Can We Do about It? In: Bacon, J.M., Cooper, B.F. (eds.) Middleware 2009. LNCS, vol. 5896, pp. 349–372. Springer, Heidelberg (2009). doi:10.1007/978-3-642-10445-9_18
12. Ertel, S., Felber, P.: A framework for the dynamic evolution of highly-available dataflow programs. In: Middleware (2014)
13. García-Galán, J., Pasquale, L., Trinidad, P., Ruiz-Cortés, A.: User-centric adaptation of multi-tenant services: Preference-based analysis for service reconfiguration. In: SEAMS (2014)
14. Gey, F., Van Landuyt, D., Joosen, W., Jonckers, V.: Continuous evolution of multi-tenant saas applications: a customizable dynamic adaptation approach. In: PESOS, May 2015
15. Gupta, D., Jalote, P., Barua, G.: A formal framework for on-line software version change. Softw. Eng. **22**(2), 120–131 (1996)
16. Hayden, C.M., Magill, S., Hicks, M., Foster, N., Foster, J.S.: Specifying and verifying the correctness of dynamic software updates. In: Verified Software (2012)
17. Hillman, J., Warren, I.: An open framework for dynamic reconfiguration. In: Proceedings of the 26th International Conference on Software Engineering, ICSE 2004, pp. 594–603. IEEE Computer Society, Washington (2004)
18. Jørgensen, B.N., Truyen, E.: Evolution of Collective Object Behavior in Presence of Simultaneous Client-Specific Views. In: Konstantas, D., Léonard, M., Pigneur, Y., Patel, S. (eds.) OOIS 2003. LNCS, vol. 2817, pp. 18–32. Springer, Heidelberg (2003). doi:10.1007/978-3-540-45242-3_4
19. Kramer, J., Magee, J.: The evolving philosophers problem: dynamic change management. Softw. Eng. **16**(11), 1293–1306 (1990)
20. Kumara, I., Han, J., Colman, A., Kapuruge, M.: Runtime Evolution of Service-Based Multi-tenant SaaS Applications. In: Basu, S., Pautasso, C., Zhang, L., Fu, X. (eds.) ICSOC 2013. LNCS, vol. 8274, pp. 192–206. Springer, Heidelberg (2013). doi:10.1007/978-3-642-45005-1_14
21. Lehtonen, T., Suonsyrjä, S., Kilamo, T., Mikkonen, T.: Defining metrics for continuous delivery and deployment pipeline. In: Symposium on Programming Languages and Software Tools (2015)
22. Li, W.: Evaluating the impacts of dynamic reconfiguration on the qos of running systems. JSS **84**(12) (2011). http://www.sciencedirect.com/science/article/pii/S0164121211001439
23. Ma, X., Baresi, L., Ghezzi, C., Panzica La Manna, V., Lu, J.: Version-consistent dynamic reconfiguration of component-based distributed systems. In: FOSE (2011)
24. Neely, S., Stolt, S.: Continuous delivery? easy! just change everything (well, maybe it is not that easy). In: Agile Conference (AGILE), 2013, pp. 121–128 (2013)
25. Sun, W., Zhang, X., Guo, C.J., Sun, P., Su, H.: Software as a service: Configuration and customization perspectives. In: Services (2008)
26. Truyen, E., Vanhaute, B., Joosen, W., Verbaeten, P., Jorgensen, B.: A dynamic customization model for distributed component-based systems. In: Distributed Computing Systems Workshop, pp. 147–152, April 2001
27. Truyen, E., Janssens, N., Sanen, F., Joosen, W.: Support for distributed adaptations in aspect-oriented middleware. In: AOSD (2008)
28. Vandewoude, Y., Ebraert, P., Berbers, Y., D'Hondt, T.: Tranquility: A low disruptive alternative to quiescence for ensuring safe dynamic updates. Softw. Eng. **33**(12), 856–868 (2007)
29. Walraven, S., Truyen, E., Joosen, W.: A Middleware Layer for Flexible and Cost-Efficient Multi-tenant Applications. In: Kon, F., Kermarrec, A.-M. (eds.) Middleware 2011. LNCS, vol. 7049, pp. 370–389. Springer, Heidelberg (2011). doi:10.1007/978-3-642-25821-3_19

Service Adaptation

Risk-Based Proactive Process Adaptation

Andreas Metzger$^{(\boxtimes)}$ and Philipp Bohn

paluno – The Ruhr Institute for Software Technology,
University of Duisburg-Essen, Essen, Germany
{andreas.metzger,philipp.bohn}@paluno.uni-due.de

Abstract. Proactive process adaptation facilitates preventing or mitigating upcoming problems during process execution, such as process delays. Key for proactive process adaptation is that adaptation decisions are based on accurate predictions of problems. Previous research focused on improving aggregate accuracy, such as precision or recall. However, aggregate accuracy provides little information about the error of an individual prediction. In contrast, so called reliability estimates provide such additional information. Previous work has shown that considering reliability estimates can improve decision making during proactive process adaptation and can lead to cost savings. So far, only constant cost functions have been considered. In practice, however, costs may differ depending on the magnitude of the problem; e.g., a longer process delay may result in higher penalties. To capture different cost functions, we exploit numeric predictions computed from ensembles of regression models. We combine reliability estimates and predicted costs to quantify the risk of a problem, i.e., its probability and its severity. Proactive adaptations are triggered if risks are above a pre-defined threshold. A comparative evaluation indicates that cost savings of up to 31%, with 14.8% savings on average, may be achieved by the risk-based approach.

Keywords: Predictive monitoring · Proactive adaptation · Risk · Business process · Machine learning

1 Introduction

Proactive process adaptation allows preventing the occurrence of problems or mitigating the impact of upcoming problems during process execution [29]. Thereby, proactive process adaptation addresses shortcomings of reactive adaptation, such as loss of money (e.g., due to contractual penalties) or time-consuming roll-back and compensation activities [1,20].

Proactive adaptation relies on predictive process monitoring to forecast potential problems [1]. Predictive process monitoring predicts how an ongoing process instance will unfold up to its completion [19,22]. If a potential problem is predicted, this problem is analyzed and adaptation decisions are triggered to prevent or mitigate the predicted problem. As an example, a delay in the expected delivery time for a freight transport process may incur contractual

© The Author(s) 2017
M. Maximilien et al. (Eds.): ICSOC 2017, LNCS 10601, pp. 351–366, 2017.
https://doi.org/10.1007/978-3-319-69035-3_25

penalties [6,14]. If during the execution of such freight transport process a delay is predicted, alternative and thus faster transport services (such as air delivery instead of road delivery) can be scheduled before the delay actually occurs, thereby avoiding contractual penalties.

Problem Statement. A key requirement for proactive adaptation is that the adaptation decisions are based on accurate predictions. Informally, prediction accuracy characterizes the ability of a prediction technique to forecast as many true violations as possible, while – at the same time – generating as few false alarms as possible [29]. Prediction accuracy is important for two main reasons [23]. First, accurate predictions mean more true violations and thus triggering more required adaptations. Each missed required adaptation means one less opportunity for proactively preventing or mitigating a problem. Second, accurate predictions mean less false alarms, and thus triggering less unnecessary adaptations. Unnecessary adaptations incur additional costs for executing the adaptations, while not addressing actual problems.

Previous research on predictive process monitoring and proactive adaptation (see Sect. 5) focused on aggregate accuracy, such as precision or recall. However, aggregate accuracy does not provide direct information about the error of an *individual* prediction. In contrast, so called *reliability estimates* provide such additional information [2]. As an example, an aggregate accuracy of 75% means that, for all predictions, there is the same 75% chance that a prediction is correct. In contrast, the reliability estimate of one prediction may be 60% while for another prediction it may be 90%. Reliability estimates thus facilitate distinguishing between more and less reliable predictions on a case by case basis. In our previous work, we have introduced a predictive monitoring approach that considers such reliability estimates [21]. Experimental results indicate that considering reliability estimates during proactive process adaptation may lead to better decisions in 83% of the cases, entailing cost savings of 14% on average.

Yet, previous work is based on simplistic cost models that only consider constant cost functions. In practice, however, costs may differ depending on the magnitude of the problem (e.g., see [17,24,30]). As an example, a longer delay in the freight transport process may result in higher penalties.

Contributions. We introduce a *risk-based proactive process adaptation* approach that can capture different cost functions. We understand risk as the combination of the severity and the probability of a potential problem (e.g., see ISO 31000 [27]). Risk severity is computed by feeding the predicted magnitude of the problem into the respective cost function. The magnitude of the problem is predicted using ensembles of neural-network regression models. Risk probability is given by the reliability estimate of the prediction. Similar to our previous work, reliability estimates are computed from neural-network ensembles. During run time, an adaptation is triggered if a risk is detected that is greater than a pre-defined risk threshold.

We experimentally analyze the effect of considering risks during proactive adaptation in terms of cost savings. To this end, we perform a comparative evaluation of the risk-based approach with our previous approach, which was based on binary predictions computed from ensembles of classification models.

The remainder of the paper is structured as follows. Section 2 describes the risk-based adaptation approach. Section 3 explains the experimental design, while Sect. 4 presents the experimental results. Section 5 discusses related work, and Sect. 6 concludes with an outlook on future work.

2   Risk-Based Adaptation

This section provides a conceptual overview of our approach for risk-based proactive process adaptation. It explains how we build and combine the prediction models and implement the approach using machine learning technology.

2.1   Conceptual Overview

Figure 1 depicts how our approach computes risk r during process execution, and how this risk is considered for proactive process adaptation.

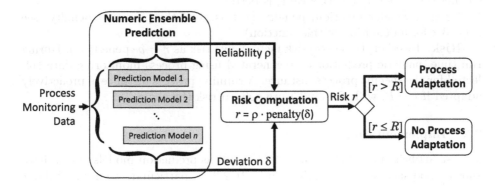

Fig. 1. Overview of risk-based process adaptation (Ensemble size n)

As mentioned above, we quantify risk as a combination of two factors: the probability of the occurrence of a risk event and the severity of that risk event (e.g., such as in ISO 31000 [27]). In our approach, a risk event is the violation of a service level objective; e.g., a delay in a transport process.

Our approach uses an ensemble of regression models to compute the two aforementioned risk factors. Ensemble prediction is a meta-prediction technique that combines the predictions of n prediction models trained to perform the same task [26]. The main aim of ensemble prediction is to increase predictive performance and, in particular, aggregate prediction accuracy. Additionally, ensemble prediction facilitates computing reliability estimates (e.g., see [2, 21]).

In our approach, each prediction model $i \in \{1, \ldots, n\}$ gives a prediction a_i pertaining to the service level objective of interest.

We use these n predictions to compute the two risk factors as follows.

Risk probability. The reliability estimate, ρ, of the prediction gives the risk probability. The intuition here is that a higher reliability of a predicted violation indicates a higher probability for that risk event to actually occur.

The reliability estimate ρ is computed by counting how many models in the ensemble agree on their prediction. Assuming an expected service level objective A for a given process instance, ρ is computed from the predictions a_i as follows:

$$\rho = max_{i=1,\ldots,n}(\frac{|i : a_i \models A|}{n}, \frac{|i : a_i \not\models A|}{n}),$$

with $a_i \models A$ meaning that the *predicted* service level objective fulfills the *expected* service level objective.

Risk severity. For risk severity, first the average predicted deviation, δ, from the expected service level objective A is computed as:

$$\delta = \frac{1}{n} \cdot \sum_{i=1,\ldots,n} (a_i - A)$$

A $\delta > 0$ indicates a violation. Without loss of generality, we assume that a smaller service level objective value is better.

Using a penalty function, penalty(δ), this gives the predicted penalty (see Sect. 3.2 for a definition of this function).

Risk. Together, these two risk factors give risk as $r = \rho \cdot$ penalty(δ). During run time, numeric predictions are generated using process monitoring data collected for the specific process instance. A running process instance is proactively adapted if $r > R$, with R being a pre-defined risk threshold.

2.2   Implementation

We use artificial neural networks (ANNs [15]) as prediction models, which have shown good success in our earlier work [21,22]. In particular, we use multilayer perceptrons as a specific form of ANNs. We use the implementation of multilayer perceptrons (with their standard parameters) of the WEKA open source machine learning toolkit[1]. As attributes for the prediction models, we take the expected and actual times for all services of the process until the point of prediction.

To automatically train the ensembles of ANNs and to compute reliability estimates as well as predicted deviations, we developed a Java tool that exploits the libraries of the WEKA machine learning toolkit.

We use *bagging* (bootstrap aggregating) as a concrete ensemble technique. Bagging uses a single type of prediction technique (ANNs in our case), but uses different training data sets to generate different prediction models. Bagging generates n new training data sets from the whole training set by sampling from the whole training data set uniformly and with replacement. For each of the n new training data sets an individual prediction model is trained. Bagging is generally recommended and used for ANNs [9].

---

[1] http://www.cs.waikato.ac.nz/ml/weka/.

We introduce a normalization factor for deviations in our implementation that ensures that δ lies in the interval $[0, 1]$. This is not a limitation of the approach, but serves to define alternative cost functions in a comparable way. The normalization factor can be computed using the largest observed actual deviation from the training data set, i.e., the data set which is used to train the prediction models. Together with normalizing the cost functions to $[0, 1]$ this gives normalized risks values $r \in [0, 1]$.

3   Comparative Evaluation

This section explains our experimental design and execution, in particular focusing on the cost model with the different considered cost functions.

We aim to experimentally analyze the effect that considering risk has on the overall costs of process execution. We perform a series of experiments, using a real-world process model and data set from the transport and logistics industry. We compare our risk-based approach with the baseline approach introduced previously [21]. This baseline approach uses binary predictions (i.e., "violation"/"non-violation" predictions) computed from ensembles of classification models. The baseline approach only considers constant cost functions.

3.1   Cost Model

We consider two cost factors of proactive process adaptation [21, 23]. On the one hand, one may face penalties in case an adaptation is missed or not effective, as problems remain. On the other hand, an adaptation of the running processes may require effort and resources, and thus incur costs. Figure 2 shows a cost model (in the form of a decision tree) that incorporates these cost factors.

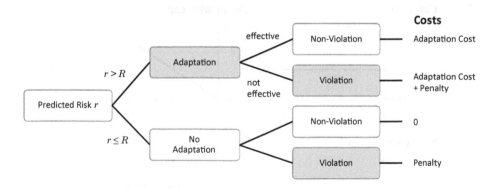

Fig. 2. Costs of proactive process adaptation

In this model, the actual costs of executing a single process instance depend on three main factors: (1) the *predicted risk* and whether it triggers an adaptation; (2) the fulfillment of the service level objective after a triggered *adaptation*; (3) the fulfillment of the service level objective if *no adaptation* is triggered.

3.2   Costs Functions

Penalties and adaptation costs may differ depending on the magnitude of deviation (δ) from expected service level objectives and the extent of adaptation required. As an example, penalties faced in the transport process may be higher if the actual delays in a transport process are longer. Also, using an air transport service for an alternative transport leg may be more expensive compared with using a road transport service.

In particular, this means the cost functions for penalties and adaptation costs may take different shapes. Different types of cost functions have been identified in the literature (e.g., see [18,24,30]). These cost functions share two main characteristics [18]: (1) Cost functions are monotonically increasing; e.g., the penalty for a longer delay is never smaller than the penalty for a shorter delay; (2) Cost functions have a point discontinuity. Before that and including that point, the costs are generally 0, beyond this point costs incur. For our experiments we consider the point discontinuity to be at $\delta = 0$.

To keep the complexity of our experiments manageable, we have chosen three cost functions that represent typical shapes of costs as described in the literature and which may be faced in the transport and logistics domain (the domain of our data set; see Sect. 3.4). The variants of these shapes, as we use them, are shown in Fig. 3. For the step-wise costs, we consider 5 steps, i.e., $s = 5$, for our experiments (the higher s the closer the function will be to the linear function).

To ensure a fair comparison among the resulting costs when using the different cost functions, we choose the parameters for the cost models such that their average costs (across $\delta \in [0,1]$) are the same. This means, $c_{\text{const}} = 1/2 \cdot c_{\text{lin}}$ and $c_{\text{step}} = s/(s+1) \cdot c_{\text{lin}}$.

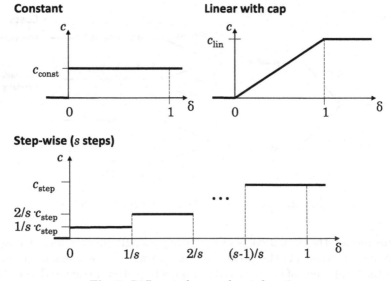

Fig. 3. Different shapes of cost functions

3.3   Experimental Variables

In our experiments, we consider *cost* as a dependent variable. For each process instance, we compute its individual costs according to the cost model defined in Sect. 3.1. The two cost drivers considered are penalties in case of violations and the costs for proactive process adaptation. The total costs are the sum of the individual costs of all process instances.

We consider the following independent variables.

- *Penalty cost function:* We use each of the three cost functions introduced in Sect. 3.2 for determining penalties. Penalty functions serve two purposes: (1) we use the penalty function to compute the *predicted* penalty and thus severity of the risk (see Sect. 2.1); (2) we use the penalty function to compute the *actual* penalty according to the cost model in Sect. 3.1.
- *Adaptation cost function:* We consider different shapes of adaptation costs by using each of the three cost functions from Sect. 3.2. Together with the three cost functions used for penalties, this leads to nine combinations of cost functions considered during our experiments.
- *Adaptation effectiveness* $\alpha \in (0, 1]$: If an adaptation helps achieve the expected service level objectives, we consider such adaptation effective. We use α to represent the fact that not all adaptations might be effective. More concretely, α represents the probability that an adaptation is effective; e.g., $\alpha = 1$ means that all adaptations are effective.
- *Risk threshold* $R \in [0, 1]$: An adaptation is triggered if risk $r > R$. We vary R to reflect difference attitudes towards process risks.

Note that for a concrete problem situation in practice, the concrete values for all of the aforementioned independent variables – with the exception of the risk threshold – are given. The penalty cost function is defined by the respective service level agreement (SLA). The adaptation cost function and the adaptation effectiveness are characteristics of the process execution environment.

3.4   Industry Data Set and Experiment Execution

The data set we use in our experiments stems from operational data of an international freight forwarding company. The data set covers five months of business operations and includes event logs of 3,942 business process instances, comprising a total of 56,082 service executions[2].

The processes and event data comply with IATA's Cargo 2000 standard[3]. Figure 4 shows the BPMN model of the business processes covered by the data set. Up to three smaller shipments from suppliers are consolidated and in turn shipped together to customers to benefit from better freight rates or increased cargo security. The process involves the execution of transport and logistics services, which are labeled using the acronyms of the Cargo 2000 standard.

---

[2] The industry data set is available from http://www.s-cube-network.eu/c2k. The predictions used in our experiments are available from https://uni-duisburg-essen.sciebo.de/index.php/s/oYnNH2PAudkWDfg.

[3] Cargo 2000 (now Cargo iQ: http://cargoiq.org/) is an initiative of IATA.

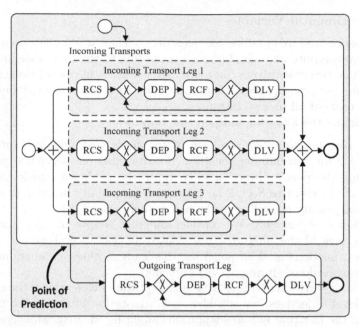

RCS: Receive freight at departure warehouse DEP: Deliver freight to aircraft
RCF: Store freight at arrival warehouse   DLV: Deliver freight from arrival warehouse

Fig. 4. Cargo 2000 transport process and services

In our experiments, we predict, during process execution, whether a transport process instance violates its stipulated delivery deadline. Predictions may be performed at any point in time during process execution, but the point of prediction has an impact on prediction accuracy; e.g., earlier points usually imply lower prediction accuracy [22]. For our experiments, we perform the predictions immediately after the synchronization point of the incoming transport processes as indicated in Fig. 4. Our earlier work indicated reasonably good prediction accuracy (>70%) for this point in process execution, while still leaving time to execute actions required to respond to violations or mitigate their effects [22].

4   Experimental Results

Here, we present and discuss the results of our experimental evaluation.

4.1   Results

Figure 5 gives a first impression of the effect of risk-based proactive adaptation on costs. The figure shows the relative cost savings of our risk-based approach compared with the baseline approach of our previous work for all nine combinations of cost functions. We have chosen $\alpha = 0.9$, which is a relatively high probability of effective process adaptations. Our previous approach has already shown high cost savings for such high α, and thus poses a more challenging baseline for further savings.

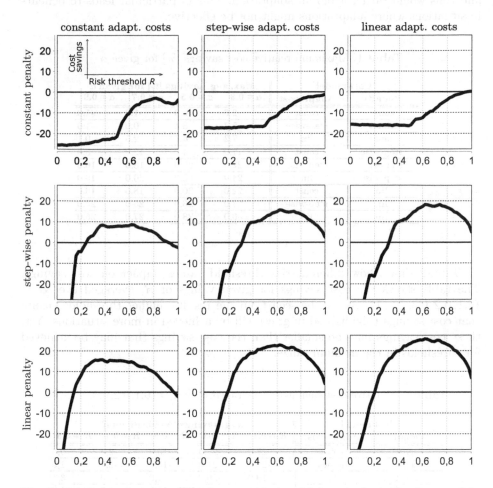

Fig. 5. Relative cost savings [%] when considering risk-based adaptation for $\alpha = 0.9$

As can be seen from Fig. 5, the risk-based approach performs worse than the baseline if we face constant penalties. This is not surprising, as in such case the severity of the risk is constant and thus does not have an effect of risk-based decision making. However, the risk-based approach shows clear cost savings if penalties are non-constant. For the chosen $\alpha = 0.9$, cost savings can be as high as 26%. Cost savings are achieved for all combinations of the non-constant cost functions for risk thresholds that are greater than 0.3.

Table 1 shows the maximum cost savings for different values for α. These results show an interesting trend. The smaller the chance of effective process adaptation, the higher the cost savings of the risk-based approach when compared to the baseline. We attribute this to the fact that the risk-based approach is more conservative and precise when deciding on whether to proactively adapt, and thus would rather avoid an adaptation. This in particular leads to benefits in situations where adaptations might not be effective.

Table 1. Maximum relative cost savings [%] for given α

Cost model		Max. avg. savings [%] for given α			
Penalty	Adapt. cost	$\alpha = 0.3$	$\alpha = 0.5$	$\alpha = 0.7$	$\alpha = 0.9$
const	const	2.6	0.0	-1.0	-1.0
const	step-wise	5.7	3.4	0.9	-1.0
const	lin	7.2	4.9	2.5	0.1
step-wise	const	17.0	14.0	12.0	8.6
step-wise	step-wise	22.0	20.0	18.0	16.0
step-wise	lin	24.0	22.0	20.0	18.0
lin	const	22.0	20.0	18.0	16.0
lin	step-wise	27.0	26.0	25.0	23.0
lin	lin	30.0	28.0	27.0	26.0

Table 2 shows how different risk threshold values impact on cost savings. The table shows the cost savings for given values of R, averaged over $\alpha = \{0.1, 0.2, 0.3, \ldots, 1\}$. As can be seen from the results, higher thresholds ensure that cost savings (highlighted in gray) will be achieved in more situations. Yet, these cost savings may be smaller than the cost savings that may be achieved for thresholds in the medium range.

Table 2. Relative cost savings [%] averaged over $\alpha = \{0.1, 0.2, 0.3, \ldots, 1\}$

Cost model		Avg. savings [%] for given R				
Penalty	Adapt. cost	$R = 0.1$	$R = 0.3$	$R = 0.5$	$R = 0.7$	$R = 0.9$
const	const	-27,0	-27,0	-15,0	-2,2	-0,6
const	step-wise	-20,0	-21,0	-16,0	-2,7	1,9
const	lin	-19,0	-20,0	-17,0	-3,0	3,1
step-wise	const	-3,4	11,0	13,0	10,0	1,7
step-wise	step-wise	-12,0	12,0	18,0	17,0	6,4
step-wise	lin	-14,0	12,0	20,0	20,0	8,6
lin	const	8,6	18,0	19,0	15,0	2,8
lin	step-wise	2,6	21,0	25,0	23,0	8,4
lin	lin	0,6	21,0	27,0	26,0	11,0

Overall, in our experiments the risk-based approach led to cost savings of 14.8% on average. Considering non-constant cost models only, the risk-based approach led to cost savings of 23.4% on average. The maximum savings we measured in our experiments were 31%.

4.2   Discussion

Below we discuss the experimental results with respect to potential threats to validity and limitations in practice.

Internal Validity. To minimize the risk of bias in our results, we performed a 10-fold cross-validation for training and testing the prediction models.

The success of ensemble prediction depends on the accuracy of the individual models, but also on the so called *diversity* among these models [4]. To ensure diversity of the ensemble, we used bagging to generate the individual models (see Sect. 2.2). As bootstrap size (which is the size of the newly generated training data set), we used 80%. Our previous experiments indicated that different bootstrap sizes did not impact the general shape of the experimental results [21].

We used an ensemble of size 100 in our experiments. The size of the ensemble did not lead to different principal findings in our experiments. Yet, by using such a large ensemble, we gain more fine-grained reliability estimates than by using a smaller ensemble. In our case, the ensemble of size 100 delivers reliability estimates with a granularity of 0.01. Training such a large ensemble, however, takes more time than training a smaller ensemble. In our experimental setting, training the ensemble took around one day on a standard desktop PC.

External Validity. Our experimental results are based on a relatively large, industry data set. We have specifically chosen different risk thresholds (R), different probabilities of effective process adaptations (α), as well as different shapes of penalties and adaptation costs to cover different possible situations that may be faced in practice. The process model covers many relevant workflow patterns [31]: sequence; exclusive choice and simple merge; cycles; parallel split and synchronization. Still, our data set is from a single application domain which thus may limit generalizability.

Construct Validity. We took great care to ensure we measure the right things. In particular, we used normalized costs as a common reference to perform the comparative evaluation between the risk-based approach and the baseline approach. Yet, so far, we have not considered aggregate or frame SLAs. In these kinds of SLAs, the presence of multiple service level objective violations incurs penalties; e.g., if more than 5% of the process instances are delayed (e.g., see [6, 14]). To address these kinds of SLAs, we plan to explore approaches for predicting aggregate process outcomes (e.g., see [25]).

5   Related Work

We discuss related work from three angles: reliability, cost and risk.

Reliability-based Prediction and Adaptation. Research on predictive process monitoring (such as [3,5,7,12,13,22,33]) and proactive adaptation (such as [1,20,23]) focused on aggregate prediction accuracy. Only recently, reliability estimates have been considered in the context of predictive process monitoring.

Maggi et al. [19] use decision tree learning for prediction and for computing reliability estimates. They observe that filtering predictions using reliability estimates may improve aggregate accuracy. However, they do not factor in reliability for decision making during process adaptation.

Francescomarino et al. [11] use decision trees and random forests. Only if the reliability of a prediction is above a certain threshold, the prediction is considered. In their experiments, they measure "failure rate" to assess the performance of their predictions. "Failure rate" is defined as the percentage of process instances for which no reliable prediction could be given. Yet, they do not further analyze the effectiveness of their approach in case a process adaptation is made.

In our previous work [21], we employed ensembles of classification models to compute reliability estimates. We have analyzed the effect of using these reliability estimates for process adaptation and have measured an increase of non-violation rates, i.e., the rates of successful process executions.

Cost-based Adaptation. Different ways of factoring in costs during predictive monitoring and proactive adaptation have been presented in the literature. On the one hand, costs may be considered by the prediction technique itself. A prominent class of approaches is cost-sensitive learning [10]. Cost-sensitive learning incorporates asymmetric costs into the learning of prediction models to minimize costs due to prediction errors [34,35]. However, existing cost-sensitive learning techniques do not consider reliability estimates.

On the other hand, costs may be considered when deciding on proactive process adaptations. Cost-based adaptation attempts to minimize the overall costs of process execution and adaptation. Leitner et al. [17] consider the costs of adaptation when deciding on the adaptation of service-oriented workflows. They formalize an optimization problem taking into account costs of violations and costs of applying adaptations. Their experimental results indicate that cost reductions of up to 56% may be achieved. Aschoff and Zisman [1] consider response time and cost values during the proactive adaptation of service compositions. Their experimental results indicate that the cheapest executions were selected in 85% of the cases. However, both aforementioned cost-aware proactive adaptation approaches do not consider prediction reliability.

In our previous work [21], we analyzed the effect of using reliability estimates on costs. In 82.9% of the situations, considering reliability estimates had a positive effect on costs, leading to cost savings of up to 54%, with 14% savings on average. However, we only used a simple cost model with constant costs and did not consider different shapes of costs.

Risk-aware Process Management. Risk-aware process management aims to (1) minimize risks in business processes by design, and (2) to monitor the emergence of risks and apply risk mitigation actions at run time [32]. While research focused mainly on (1), a few approaches have been presented for (2).

Conforti et al. [8] augment process models with so called risk sensors, which collect information from running process instances and exploit historical process data. Each sensor is associated to a risk condition that combines the probability of a problem with a risk threshold. If the probability is greater than the threshold, process managers are notified. Pika et al. [25] follow an approach similar to risk sensors. They propose defining so called process risk indicators, which are patterns observable in event logs that may indicate risks. While the aforementioned authors focused on risk detection and prediction, Kim et al. [16] propose an integrated risk management approach that facilitates proactively mitigating risks at run time. Risk mitigation strategies are expressed as event-condition-action rules. All three aforementioned approaches, however, only quantify the probability of a risk event, but do not quantify the severity of the risk event. Also, the approaches have not been evaluated with respect to how such risk information may improve overall process adaptation; e.g., in terms of costs.

Rogge-Solti and Weske [28] focus on the risk of missing a process deadline. They consider costs incurred by a deadline violation in addition to the probability of that deadline violation. They use stochastic Petri nets to predict the risk of missing a given process deadline. For each of these deadlines specific costs may be assigned. However, the specific costs for each deadline are always constant and thus independent of the magnitude of the deadline violation. In contrast, our approach takes into account cost functions that depend on the magnitude of deviation from expected service level objectives.

6   Conclusion

We have introduced a risk-based approach for proactive process adaptation, which exploits ensembles of regression models to compute the probability and the severity of service level objective violations. Our comparative evaluation provided empirical evidence that risk-based proactive process adaptation may lead to additional cost savings when compared with proactive adaptation based on probability only. Additional cost savings were 14.8% on average (23.4% if considering non-constant cost models), with maximum savings of 31%.

Building on these promising results, we plan to gather further empirical evidence by replicating our experiments using other process models and data sets, such as from port logistics and e-commerce. Further, to handle aggregate and frame SLAs, we will extend our approach to consider penalties caused by multiple service level objective violations.

Acknowledgments. We cordially thank Christina Bellinghoven, Felix Föcker, and Adrian Neubauer for helpful pointers during earlier drafts of the paper. Research leading to these results received funding from the EU's Horizon 2020 research and innovation programme under grant agreement no. 731932 (TransformingTransport) and from the EFRE co-financed operational program NRW.Ziel2 under grant agreement 005-1010-0012 (LoFIP – Cockpits for Operational Management of Transport Processes).

References

1. Aschoff, R., Zisman, A.: QoS-driven proactive adaptation of service composition. In: Kappel, G., Maamar, Z., Motahari-Nezhad, H.R. (eds.) ICSOC 2011. LNCS, vol. 7084, pp. 421–435. Springer, Heidelberg (2011). doi:10.1007/978-3-642-25535-9_28
2. Bosnic, Z., Kononenko, I.: Automatic selection of reliability estimates for individual regression predictions. Knowl. Eng. Rev. **25**(1), 27–47 (2010)

3. Breuker, D., Delfmann, P., Matzner, M., Becker, J.: Designing and evaluating an interpretable predictive modeling technique for business processes. In: Fournier, F., Mendling, J. (eds.) BPM 2014. LNBIP, vol. 202, pp. 541–553. Springer, Cham (2015). doi:10.1007/978-3-319-15895-2_46
4. Brown, G., Wyatt, J.L., Tiño, P.: Managing diversity in regression ensembles. J. Mach. Learn. Res. **6**, 1621–1650 (2005)
5. Cabanillas, C., Di Ciccio, C., Mendling, J., Baumgrass, A.: Predictive task monitoring for business processes. In: Sadiq, S., Soffer, P., Völzer, H. (eds.) BPM 2014. LNCS, vol. 8659, pp. 424–432. Springer, Cham (2014). doi:10.1007/978-3-319-10172-9_31
6. Marquezan, C.C., Metzger, A., Franklin, R., Pohl, K.: Runtime management of multi-level SLAs for transport and logistics services. In: Franch, X., Ghose, A.K., Lewis, G.A., Bhiri, S. (eds.) ICSOC 2014. LNCS, vol. 8831, pp. 560–574. Springer, Heidelberg (2014). doi:10.1007/978-3-662-45391-9_49. (Industry paper)
7. Castellanos, M., Salazar, N., Casati, F., Dayal, U., Shan, M.C.: Predictive business operations management. Int. J. Comput. Sci. Eng. **2**(5/6), 292–301 (2006)
8. Conforti, R., Rosa, M.L., Fortino, G., ter Hofstede, A.H.M., Recker, J., Adams, M.: Real-time risk monitoring in business processes: a sensor-based approach. J. Syst. Softw. **86**(11), 2939–2965 (2013)
9. Dietterich, T.G.: Ensemble methods in machine learning. In: Kittler, J., Roli, F. (eds.) MCS 2000. LNCS, vol. 1857, pp. 1–15. Springer, Heidelberg (2000). doi:10.1007/3-540-45014-9_1
10. Elkan, C.: The foundations of cost-sensitive learning. In: Nebel, B. (ed.) 7th Intl Joint Conference on Artificial Intelligence (IJCAI 2001), Seattle, Washington, pp. 973–978. Morgan Kaufmann (2001)
11. Di Francescomarino, C., Dumas, M., Federici, M., Ghidini, C., Maggi, F.M., Rizzi, W.: Predictive business process monitoring framework with hyperparameter optimization. In: Nurcan, S., Soffer, P., Bajec, M., Eder, J. (eds.) CAiSE 2016. LNCS, vol. 9694, pp. 361–376. Springer, Cham (2016). doi:10.1007/978-3-319-39696-5_22
12. Ghosh, R., Ghose, A., Hegde, A., Mukherjee, T., Mos, A.: QoS-driven management of business process variants in cloud based execution environments. In: Sheng, Q.Z., Stroulia, E., Tata, S., Bhiri, S. (eds.) ICSOC 2016. LNCS, vol. 9936, pp. 55–69. Springer, Cham (2016). doi:10.1007/978-3-319-46295-0_4
13. Grigori, D., Casati, F., Castellanos, M., Dayal, U., Sayal, M., Shan, M.C.: Business process intelligence. Comput. Ind. **53**(3), 321–343 (2004)
14. Gutiérrez, A.M., Cassales Marquezan, C., Resinas, M., Metzger, A., Ruiz-Cortés, A., Pohl, K.: Extending WS-Agreement to Support Automated Conformity Check on Transport and Logistics Service Agreements. In: Basu, S., Pautasso, C., Zhang, L., Fu, X. (eds.) ICSOC 2013. LNCS, vol. 8274, pp. 567–574. Springer, Heidelberg (2013). doi:10.1007/978-3-642-45005-1_47
15. Haykin, S.: Neural Networks and Learning Machines: A Comprehensive Foundation, 3rd edn. Prentice Hall, Englewood Cliffs (2008)
16. Kim, J., Lee, J., Lee, J., Choi, I.: An integrated process-related risk management approach to proactive threat and opportunity handling: a framework and rule language. Knowl. Process Manag. **24**(1), 23–37 (2017)
17. Leitner, P., Hummer, W., Dustdar, S.: Cost-based optimization of service compositions. IEEE Trans. Serv. Comput. **6**(2), 239–251 (2013)
18. Leitner, P., Michlmayr, A., Rosenberg, F., Dustdar, S.: Monitoring, prediction and prevention of SLA violations in composite services. In: International Conference on Web Services (ICWS 2010), Miami, Florida, pp. 369–376. IEEE Computer Society (2010)

19. Maggi, F.M., Di Francescomarino, C., Dumas, M., Ghidini, C.: Predictive monitoring of business processes. In: Jarke, M., Mylopoulos, J., Quix, C., Rolland, C., Manolopoulos, Y., Mouratidis, H., Horkoff, J. (eds.) CAiSE 2014. LNCS, vol. 8484, pp. 457–472. Springer, Cham (2014). doi:10.1007/978-3-319-07881-6_31
20. Metzger, A., Chi, C.H., Engel, Y., Marconi, A.: Research challenges on online service quality prediction for proactive adaptation. In: ICSE 2012 Workshop on European Software Services and Systems Research (S-Cube), Zurich, Switzerland. IEEE (2012)
21. Metzger, A., Föcker, F.: Predictive business process monitoring considering reliability estimates. In: Dubois, E., Pohl, K. (eds.) CAiSE 2017. LNCS, vol. 10253, pp. 445–460. Springer, Cham (2017). doi:10.1007/978-3-319-59536-8_28
22. Metzger, A., Leitner, P., Ivanović, D., Schmieders, E., Franklin, R., Carro, M., Dustdar, S., Pohl, K.: Comparing and combining predictive business process monitoring techniques. IEEE Trans. Syst. Man Cybern. Syst. **45**(2), 276–290 (2015)
23. Metzger, A., Sammodi, O., Pohl, K.: Accurate proactive adaptation of service-oriented systems. In: Cámara, J., de Lemos, R., Ghezzi, C., Lopes, A. (eds.) Assurances for Self-Adaptive Systems. LNCS, vol. 7740, pp. 240–265. Springer, Heidelberg (2013). doi:10.1007/978-3-642-36249-1_9
24. Pernici, B., Siadat, S.H., Benbernou, S., Ouziri, M.: A penalty-based approach for QoS dissatisfaction using fuzzy rules. In: Kappel, G., Maamar, Z., Motahari-Nezhad, H.R. (eds.) ICSOC 2011. LNCS, vol. 7084, pp. 574–581. Springer, Heidelberg (2011). doi:10.1007/978-3-642-25535-9_43
25. Pika, A., van der Aalst, W.M.P., Wynn, M.T., Fidge, C.J., ter Hofstede, A.H.M.: Evaluating and predicting overall process risk using event logs. Inf. Sci. **352–353**, 98–120 (2016)
26. Polikar, R.: Ensemble based systems in decision making. IEEE Circ. Syst. Mag. **6**(3), 21–45 (2006)
27. Purdy, G.: ISO 31000: 2009 - setting a new standard for risk management. Risk Anal. **30**(6), 881–886 (2010)
28. Rogge-Solti, A., Weske, M.: Prediction of business process durations using non-markovian stochastic petri nets. Inf. Syst. **54**, 1–14 (2015)
29. Salfner, F., Lenk, M., Malek, M.: A survey of online failure prediction methods. ACM Comput. Surv. **42**(3), 10:1–10:42 (2010)
30. Schuller, D., Siebenhaar, M., Hans, R., Wenge, O., Steinmetz, R., Schulte, S.: Towards heuristic optimization of complex service-based workflows for stochastic QoS attributes. In: International Conference on Web Services (ICWS 2014), Anchorage, Alaska, pp. 361–368. IEEE Computer Society (2014)
31. Skouradaki, M., Ferme, V., Pautasso, C., Leymann, F., van Hoorn, A.: Micro-benchmarking BPMN 2.0 workflow management systems with workflow patterns. In: Nurcan, S., Soffer, P., Bajec, M., Eder, J. (eds.) CAiSE 2016. LNCS, vol. 9694, pp. 67–82. Springer, Cham (2016). doi:10.1007/978-3-319-39696-5_5
32. Suriadi, S., et al.: Current research in risk-aware business process management - overview, comparison, and gap analysis. Commun. Assoc. Inf. Syst. (CAIS) **34**, 52 (2014)
33. Verenich, I., Dumas, M., La Rosa, M., Maggi, F.M., Di Francescomarino, C.: Complex symbolic sequence clustering and multiple classifiers for predictive process monitoring. In: Reichert, M., Reijers, H.A. (eds.) BPM 2015. LNBIP, vol. 256, pp. 218–229. Springer, Cham (2016). doi:10.1007/978-3-319-42887-1_18
34. Zadrozny, B., Elkan, C.: Learning and making decisions when costs and probabilities are both unknown. In: Lee, D., Schkolnick, M., Provost, F.J., Srikant,

R. (eds.) 7th International Conference on Knowledge Discovery and Data Mining (KDD 2001), San Francisco, California, pp. 204–213. ACM (2001)

35. Zhao, H., Sinha, A.P., Bansal, G.: An extended tuning method for cost-sensitive regression and forecasting. Decis. Support Syst. **51**(3), 372–383 (2011)

A Debt-Aware Learning Approach for Resource Adaptations in Cloud Elasticity Management

Carlos Mera-Gómez[1,2]([✉]), Francisco Ramírez[1], Rami Bahsoon[1],
and Rajkumar Buyya[3]

[1] School of Computer Science, University of Birmingham, Edgbaston B15 2TT, UK
{cxm523,fmr067,r.bahsoon}@cs.bham.ac.uk
[2] Facultad de Ingeniería en Electricidad y Computación,
ESPOL Polythecnic University, Escuela Superior Politécnica del Litoral, ESPOL,
Campus Gustavo Galindo Km 30.5 Vía Perimetral, P.O. Box 09-01-5863,
Guayaquil, Ecuador
cjmera@espol.edu.ec
[3] Cloud Computing and Distributed Systems (CLOUDS) Lab,
School of Computing and Information Systems, The University of Melbourne,
Melbourne, Australia
rbuyya@unimelb.edu.au

Abstract. Elasticity is a cloud property that enables applications and their execution systems to dynamically acquire and release shared computational resources on demand. Moreover, it unfolds the advantage of economies of scale in the cloud through a drop in the average costs of these shared resources. However, it is still an open challenge to achieve a perfect match between resource demand and provision in autonomous elasticity management. Resource adaptation decisions essentially involve a trade-off between economics and performance, which produces a gap between the ideal and actual resource provisioning. This gap, if not properly managed, can negatively impact the aggregate utility of a cloud customer in the long run. To address this limitation, we propose a technical debt-aware learning approach for autonomous elasticity management based on a reinforcement learning of debts in resource provisioning; the adaptation pursues strategic decisions that values the potential utility produced by the gaps between resource supply and demand. We extend CloudSim and Burlap to evaluate our approach. The evaluation indicates that a debt-aware elasticity management obtains a higher utility for a cloud customer, while conforming expected levels of performance.

1 Introduction

Elasticity is the essential characteristic of cloud computing that supports an on-demand provision and release of shared resources based on environmental changes to meet an expected quality of service [10]. This characteristic is one of the enablers for the cloud *economies of scale*, dropping the average cost of computing resources [2]. Therefore, elasticity decisions on resource adaptation should be driven not only by performance considerations but also by an economics perspective to pursue a long-term utility under uncertainty.

© Springer International Publishing AG 2017
M. Maximilien et al. (Eds.): ICSOC 2017, LNCS 10601, pp. 367–382, 2017.
https://doi.org/10.1007/978-3-319-69035-3_26

Although elasticity management techniques continuously perform dynamic resource adaptations; in practical terms, it is impossible to achieve a perfect match between resource provisioning and demand between consecutive adaptations [11, 26]. Therefore, this gap between the ideal and actual resource provisioning calls for a dynamic valuation that incorporates a strategic trade-off between performance and economics. On one hand, this valuation should consider that effects of elasticity adaptations on performance, for example, are not instantaneous due to the *spin-up time* [16]. On the other hand, the same valuation should consider that the economics of these adaptations depends on billing cycles, pricing schemes and resource bundles granularity [28]; as in the case of a *partial usage waste* [14], which results from the additional time charged for a resource between its release and the end of the billing cycle.

In our previous work [23], we proposed an elasticity conceptual model that identifies *technical debts* that are linked to cloud elasticity adaptations taken under uncertainty, and we defined the term *elasticity debt* as the valuation gap between the ideal and actual resource provisioning in elasticity adaptations.

The novel contribution of this paper is an elasticity management approach that autonomously learns the value of elasticity debts and dynamically trades off performance against economics in adaptation decisions. The adaptation pursues to take decisions that maximise the long-term utility of the elastic system by incurring strategic debts. The approach contributes to the fundamentals of technical debt management, where our work is the first to transit the debt analysis from a static to a dynamic perspective through a *reinforcement learning* approach to make strategic adaptation decisions. Technical debt is a metaphor that supports a trade-off analysis between a quick engineering decision that yields immediate benefits at the expense of compromising long-run objectives [15]. Elasticity adaptation can incur an elasticity debt that renders short-term benefits but compromises performance, economics or both. The debt can accumulate if not properly valued. These debts can be retrospectively analysed in a threshold-based reactive management for elasticity or dynamically learnt with a proactive perspective in a reinforcement learning based elasticity management. Reinforcement learning [29] is an approach that seeks optimality in decision-making through a continuous learning that forgoes short-term rewards to achieve higher long-term gains.

The technical debt metaphor has been applied in software architecture, software maintenance and evolution, cloud service selection among others [17]. Additionally, elasticity management based on reinforcement learning with performance and cost metrics has been already applied [4, 19]. However, to our knowledge, our work is the first to value, as a debt, the potential utility produced by the gap of an imperfect elasticity adaptation. We shared this self-adaptive perspective for technical debt in the recent Dagstuhl Seminar 16162 [3]; the suggestion was well received by the technical debt community. Moreover, the contribution is the first to introduce an online learning approach for technical debt; the approach identifies, tracks, and monitors the debt and payback strategies of adaptation decisions in the context of cloud elasticity. We evaluate the approach through a simulation tool that extends CloudSim [5] and Burlap [20]. The results indicate that a reinforcement learning of technical debts achieves a higher aggregate utility for a service provider.

The rest of the paper is organized as follows. Section 2 presents the problem statement and motivates the need for an online learning of elasticity debts, while Sect. 3 provides a detailed overview of our debt-aware learning approach and explains its components. We report the evaluation of our approach in Sect. 4, followed by a discussion of related works in Sect. 5. Finally, Sect. 6 summarizes our conclusions and directions for future research.

2   Problem Statement

In practice, it is impossible to achieve a perfect elasticity i.e. exactly match resource supply with demand [11, 26] due to several reasons such as the difficulty to predict resource demand, coarse computing resource granularities, spin-up times, restrictions on the number of computing resource that can be acquired at once, pricing schemes granularity and billing cycles among others [12, 28]. Hence, elasticity management decisions should optimize for a dynamic resource provision not only in terms of performance metrics but also from an economics perspective that can maximise the utility of the Software as a Service (SaaS) provider (cloud customer) in the long run.

Currently, elasticity is analysed from a performance [11], cost-aware [9, 27] or economics-driven perspective [7, 24]. However, none of these approaches incorporate a strategic valuation of imperfect elastic adaptations to make explicit trade-offs in the decision-making when adjusting a resource provisioning. Consequently, these myopic adaptations lead to a provision of resources that obtains short-term gains when matching the resource demand but can be suboptimal in the long-term with hidden consequences that waste resources or degrade quality of service attributes (e.g. performance, security, reliability), which diminishes the aggregate utility of the cloud customer over time.

The technical debt metaphor supports a reasoned decision-making about quick engineering decisions taken to obtain short-term benefits at the cost of introducing liabilities that compromise long-term system objectives. In dynamic environments, the utility of these decisions can be systematically learnt through a reinforcement learning approach. Reinforcement learning is a technique where a farsighted agent learns from continuous interactions with an environment how to maximize a long-term reward without any a priori knowledge. We combine this online learning with the technical debt metaphor in the context of cloud elasticity to evaluate dynamic trade-offs carried out by elastic adaptation decisions. The consideration of debt motivates a value-oriented perspective to adaptation that systematically links the consequences of these decisions with environmental uncertainty, such as unexpected workload variations, dynamic changes in quality of service or resource failures.

We advocate that elasticity can benefit from a debt-aware learning perspective by making the elasticity debts visible, revealing the performance and economics consequences of adaptation decisions (e.g. over- or under-provisioning states) that are prone to uncertainty and therefore improving the utility achieved by a cloud stakeholder (e.g. SaaS provider) in terms of reducing penalties that relate to Service Level Agreement (SLA) violations and operating costs minimization.

3   Proposed Approach

3.1   Technical Debt on Elasticity

Technical debt is a metaphor that makes visible the valuation of alternatives in a trade-off between an ideal and an actual decision making [8]; where the debt is determined by the valuation of the gap between these two alternatives [18]. The metaphor has shown to be effective to identify, measure and monitor tradeoffs over time. In our previous work [23], we developed the foundations for introducing the built-in decision support of technical debt analysis into the large scale dynamic and adaptive context of cloud elasticity management. We defined *elasticity technical debt* as the valuation of the gap between an optimal and an actual adaptation decision. This debt trades off the performance to obtain with the provisioning of an elasticity adaptation against the economics of that adaptation.

Like a debt in finance, an elasticity debt can be either *strategic* or *unintentional*. The former refers to adaptations that intend to anticipate changing conditions (e.g. workload variations) or mitigate undesired effects (e.g. spin-up time, partial usage waste); whereas the latter refers to delayed or wrong choice of adaptations (e.g. resource thrashing) as a consequence of poor considerations for uncertainty or elasticity determinants. The value of elasticity debts can be observed *retrospectively* in threshold-based elasticity management approaches, or *proactively* in debt-aware approaches that utilise this valuation to analyse and decide elasticity adaptations.

Different from traditional approaches, that mostly consider avoiding over- and under-provisioning states, we *argue* that an elasticity debt-aware approach recognizes the fact that it is practically impossible to achieve a perfect elasticity; and makes use of this fact to explicitly reveal the potential of using this imperfection in the trade-off between economics and performance to adjust strategically the resource provisioning and preserve the utility of the stakeholder. For example, we may intentionally delay an over-provisioning state if the next billing cycle of the resources to be released is not immediate; or if we consider that the spin-up time of launching new resources may affect the SLA performance compliance during a imminent growth in the load.

Figure 1(a) illustrates three cases of debts using a graph that represents a resource demand and supply over time. The first gap is caused by the spin-up time when new virtual machines are launched; the second gap is a consequence of the available resource granularity that makes impossible to launch one and a half machines; and the third less evident gap is the result of a partial usage waste after one machine is released but still charged until the end of the billing cycle. In any case, the debt is not the gap itself. We highlight that a debt corresponds

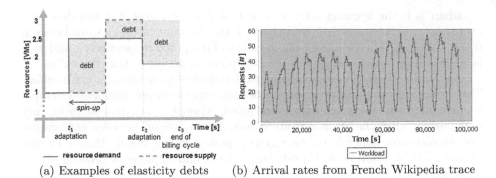

(a) Examples of elasticity debts   (b) Arrival rates from French Wikipedia trace

Fig. 1. Elasticity debts and French Wikipedia trace

to the valuation in terms of the potential utility produced by the gap, where the debt originates.

3.2 Reinforcement Learning

Reinforcement learning [29] is a framework that pursues an optimal decision-making based on the maximization of a cumulative reward in the long-term. The decision-maker or *agent* learns through consecutive interactions with an *environment*, where each *action* modifies the environmental *state* and produces a *reward*, which is the utility that the agent receives from the action. Both, the set of variables that characterizes the new state and the reward are perceived by the agent. This learning technique has already been applied to cloud elasticity management [4,19], where an agent takes resource adaptation decisions based on the current state, which is usually identified by performance thresholds, and achieves a reward, which is given by the new performance monitored after the adaptation takes place.

We follow a model-free reinforcement learning strategy rather a model-based because our learning environment lacks of a predefined transition model that describes the effect of each action a in a given state s by determining the probability of reaching a specific subsequent state s_{t+1}. A model-free strategy uses an *action-utility function*, known as $Q(s, a)$, to estimate the value of performing an action a over a state s. From the available algorithms in this kind of learning strategy, we have adopted *Q-learning* [29] because it is more flexible to explore changes in the environment, making it more convenient for highly dynamic contexts. Furthermore, it is the most common extended algorithm with respect to elasticity management [19].

The Q-learning algorithm learns an optimal decision-making by repeatedly updating the utility of an action a given a state s according to the following update rule:

$$Q(s,a) \leftarrow (1 - \alpha) * Q(s,a) + \alpha * [r + \gamma * max_{a_{t+1}}Q(s_{t+1}, a_{t+1})], \qquad (1)$$

where α is the learning rate (a value that usually starts at 1 and decreases over time), r is the reward of the action, γ is the discount factor (a value between 0 and 1 that adjusts a learner from myopic to far-sighted respectively), and s_{t+1} is the resulting state, and a_{t+1} is the best possible action to take thereafter.

Interactions with the environment are classified as *exploration* or *exploitation*. The former aims to perform random actions to experience environmental changes to preclude from focus on immediate gains; whereas the latter aims to only make use of what the agent already knows. This trade-off between exploration and exploitation depends on an ϵ-greedy policy, which means that a learner exploits the best action with probability $(1-\epsilon)$ and explores a random action with probability ϵ.

3.3   Learning Elasticity Debts

We propose an elasticity management based on a reinforcement learning of technical debts incurred by elasticity adaptations. Our debt-aware learning approach explores and learns elasticity debts over time and then uses this knowledge from previous experiences to incur in strategic adaptations intended to achieve a higher aggregate utility. Making use of the function defined in [24], the utility achieved by a SaaS provider when processes a workload w, composed of jobs or incoming requests denoted by x, is calculated in terms of revenue, penalty and operating costs incurred during the monitored period (i.e. between consecutive elasticity adaptations) by means of Eq. 2:

$$U(w) = R(x) * x_s - P(x) * x_f - \sum_{i=1}^{N} C(vm_i) \int_0^L m_i(t)dt, \qquad (2)$$

where $R(x)$ and $P(x)$ functions return the revenues and penalties per request, respectively; x_s and x_f represent the number of successful and failed requests, respectively, from workload w with respect to defined in the SLA; and $C(vm_i)$ function returns the cost of each of the N virtual machine (VM) types corresponding to their m_i launched instances over the execution time L.

Equation 3 calculates the debt of each adaptation as the utility difference between the actual and the ideal resource provisioning:

$$ElasticityDebt \leftarrow U_{actual} - U_{ideal}, \qquad (3)$$

where U represents the utility obtained by a SaaS provider as cloud customer during a monitoring period. In the best scenario, the elasticity debt would be zero when the actual resource provisioning matched the ideal one required in the period. Otherwise, it will be a negative number.

The approach calculates the debt of an adaptation action (i.e. launch, release or maintain) taken at time t_i when the next one is adopted at t_j, where $t_j > t_i$. For each action, we recreate the circumstances under which this adopted action was serving (from t_i to t_j) and simulate the other two discarded elasticity actions at time t_i to retrospectively determine the ideal action that would have produced

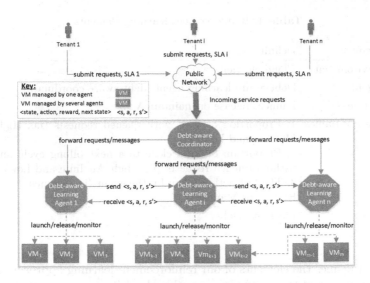

Fig. 2. Reference system model of our debt-aware approach

the highest utility among the three. Then, once we have this ideal utility, we proceed to calculate the incurred debt of the actual adaptation action taken at time t_i by means of Eq. 3.

A reference system model of our approach is shown in Fig. 2, where several tenants subscribe to a multi-tenant SaaS service with a SLA tailored to each individual need. We envision an agent-oriented architecture with hierarchy where agents tend to realise the requirements of multi-tenant users in a decentralised fashion, which promotes a scalable solution and facilitates the collaboration between different agents promising optimization for inter-agents knowledge exchange.

In the model, we grouped running virtual resources in clusters and each of them is managed by a *debt-aware learning agent*, which corresponds to a single tenant. Each debt-aware learning agent is responsible for launching, releasing, and monitoring VMs; it also performs a load balancing and dispatches the incoming requests to be executed in one of the VM in the cluster. Some VMs can be managed simultaneously by more than one learning agent to optimise resource utilization during under-provisioned states.

The incoming requests are received by the *debt-aware coordinator*, which is responsible for creating and destroying learning agents, forwarding incoming service requests from a tenant to the corresponding learning agent, and sending coordination messages such as changes in expected SLAs or refinements in the reinforcement learning process.

The approach can be instantiated with either a single debt-aware learning agent or a multi-agent version. For the latter, we advocate the use of a *parallel reinforcement learning* mechanism [21]; where multiple agents can learn simultaneously elasticity debts and share their learning to speed-up the convergence time.

Table 1. Reinforcement learning elements

Element	Definition
Environment	Cloud elasticity
Agent	Debt-aware learning agent, debt-aware coordinator
Actions	Launch, release or maintain VMs
State variables	1. Proportion of VMs with queued requests (i.e. High, Medium and Low) 2. Proportion of VMs close to a next billing cycle and without queued requests (i.e. High, Medium and Low) 3. The last action taken by the agent (i.e. Launch, Release or Maintain)
Reward	Elasticity Debt

Table 1 defines the elements of our reinforcement learning approach. A debt-aware learning agent takes one of the possible elasticity management actions (i.e. launch, release or maintain), and receives a reward, determined by the elasticity debt that corresponds to the adopted action. Additionally, the learning agent considers the following variables to define a state: (i) a proportion of running VMs with queued request; where the proportion is equally categorized into high, medium or low; (ii) a proportion of running VMs close to a next billing cycle and without queued request; where the proportion is equally categorized into high, medium or low; and (iii) the last action taken by the agent. We avoid unnecessary exploration by including preconditions for two actions: launch and release. For instance, only launch action is available if there is a high number of VMs with queued jobs; or only release action is permitted when a high proportion of VMs are close to a next billing cycle and without queued request.

4 Evaluation

Our experiment intends to compare the aggregate utility that a SaaS provider achieves when adopts a debt-aware reinforcement learning elasticity management against a common threshold-based rule elasticity mechanism and investigate the implication of debt-awareness over time. We are also interested in analysing the results in terms of both performance, through request failure rates, and economics, through deployed VMs and total costs. We instantiated two scenarios from the reference system model in Fig. 2: (i) one with a single debt-aware learning agent; and (ii) another with two agents to illustrate the parallel learning with a minimum inter-agent coordination overhead.

The common threshold-based elasticity management implements the *voting process* offered by *Right Scale* [25]. In this voting mechanism, resource adaptations are taken based on the outcome of a voting process, where each virtual machine votes according to a performance metric (e.g. CPU utilization) decision threshold.

4.1   Experiment Setup

We extended CloudSim [5], a framework for modelling and simulation of cloud infrastructures and services, to support experiments with both the debt-aware learning and the threshold-based approach. For the debt-aware learning, we extended Burlap [20], a framework for implementing reinforcement learning solutions, and integrated this extension with CloudSim. We have made available our implementation for validation and replication in a Git repository[1]. Besides the core functionality, we implemented load balancing and horizontal scaling using a single type of virtual machines, where we considered processing capacity expressed in terms of millions of instructions per second (MIPS). As spin-up times in real infrastructures are variable [22], we make the simulation more realistic with spin-up times that conform to a Gaussian distribution. For the experiments, we extracted 15 days (from day 24 to 38 inclusive) of the French Wikipedia trace available in the Wikipedia page view statistics [30] but scaled to last 27 h to demand a controllable amount of resources, as seen in Fig. 1(b). We parsed the original workload file into the *Standard Workload Format* to ensure compatibility with CloudSim.

We assume that the multi-tenant SaaS service is hosted by an Infrastructure as a Service (IaaS) provider such as *CloudSigma* [6] with its pay-as-you-go pricing scheme and five minute-based billing cycle, a resource granularity in terms of VMs, and a horizontal elasticity method. General simulation parameters are specified in Table 2. Additional specific parameters for the threshold-based and the debt-aware approach, required by Eq. 1, are shown in Tables 3 and 4, respectively.

We performed the experiments on a laptop that runs Windows 10 x64 operating system with 16 GB RAM and Intel Core i7-4500U CPU at 1.8 GHz. We ran the simulation tool 100 times per approach, where average execution times

Table 2. Simulation parameters

Parameter	Value
Spin-up time	a mean of 59.8 s with a standard deviation of 0.03 s
Cool down period	60 s
Billing cycle	Every 5 min
SLA constraint	90% of jobs handled up to 2 s
Price per request	$ 0.0012344
Request's size	4 millions of instructions
Penalty per failed request	$ 0.002
VM processing capacity	14 MIPS
VM cost	$ 0.07 per cycle

---

[1] Link to the repository: https://bitbucket.org/cxm523/kdebtrepo.

Table 3. Threshold-based approach simulation parameters

Parameter	Value
Lower CPU threshold	30%
Upper CPU threshold	95%
Voting agreement threshold	Relative majority among actions

Table 4. Debt-aware approach simulation parameters

Parameter	Value
Learning rate α per state-action pair	Starts at 1, then decays at 0.05 per adaptation up to a minimum of 0.1
Discount factor γ	0.99
ϵ probability	0.05
Proportion of VMs with queued requests	Low (<33%), Medium, High (>66%)
Proportion of VMs close to a next billing cycle and without queued requests	Low (<33%), Medium, High (>66%)
Number of agents for parallel reinforcement learning	2

for the threshold-based approach, the single debt-aware learning and the parallel one are 278, 267 and 222 s, respectively.

4.2 Results

We integrated JFreeChart [13], a chart library, with CloudSim to draw box-and-whisker plots that show the mean, median and quartiles related to failure rates, deployed VMs, total costs and aggregate utilities for the experiments with each approach. Additionally, we draw line charts to depict average failure rates over time and average aggregate utility over time. We start analysing the performance, followed by the economics to end with the overall utility achieved by each mechanism.

Regarding the performance, we compare box-and-whisker plots of failure rates obtained from the management approaches. Figure 3(a) depicts that debt-aware learning experiments achieved a lower number of SLA violations. The average of failures for the threshold-based approach is 7.2%, whereas the single debt-aware approach has a mean of 2.8%. Moreover, the parallel debt-aware approach yields a similar performance with a 2.9% of failed requests. Figure 3(b) illustrates the average failure rates over time for each approach. We observed that both debt-aware learning experiments had a higher failure rate than the threshold-based approach at the beginning of the workload execution. However, after this initial learning period, debt-aware learning experiments drastically improved their performance and the single surpassed the threshold-based management after 22,000 s, whereas the parallel after 35,000 s, approximately.

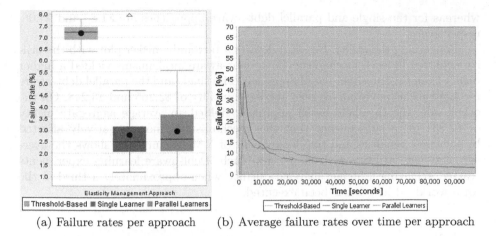

(a) Failure rates per approach   (b) Average failure rates over time per approach

Fig. 3. Performance of the experiments

Considering the economics, Fig. 4(a) presents a box-and-whisker plot with the number of VMs provisioned per approach. The experiment results indicate that debt-aware approaches make a more efficient use of resources. The single and the parallel debt-ware approaches reached an average of 26 and 58 virtual machines, respectively. On the other hand, the threshold-based approach launched more VMs with an average of 133 virtual machines. Consequently, there is a reduction of the total costs incurred by debt-aware elasticity management mechanisms. Figure 4(b) shows a box-and-whisker plot with total costs per approach. Average overall costs for the threshold-based approach are \$9.40,

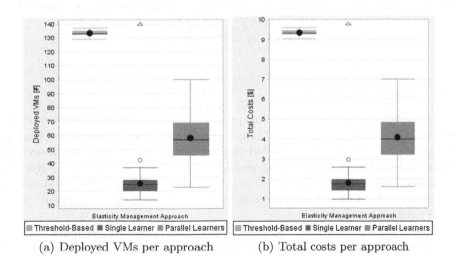

(a) Deployed VMs per approach   (b) Total costs per approach

Fig. 4. Economics of the experiments

whereas for the single and parallel debt-aware approaches are \$1.80 and \$4.08, respectively.

Concerning the utility, Fig. 5(a) depicts a box-and-whisker plot with the utility achieved by each mechanism. Both debt-aware mechanisms yielded a higher utility than the threshold-based approach. The single and the parallel debt-aware mechanisms achieved an average aggregate utility of \$3,265 and \$3,248. On the other side, the threshold-based approach yielded an average aggregate utility of \$2,851, as a consequence that this mechanism is more negatively affected by incurred penalties and the deployment of VMs. Figure 5(b) shows the average aggregate utility over time per approach. Debt-aware learning experiments started achieving a higher aggregate utility when approximately a third of the total workload length has been executed.

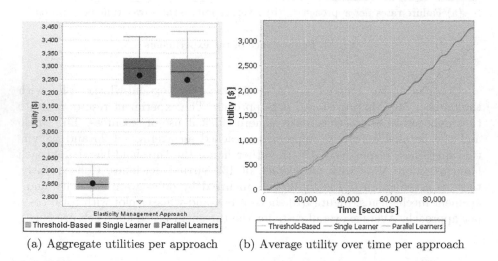

(a) Aggregate utilities per approach   (b) Average utility over time per approach

Fig. 5. Utility of the experiments

4.3   Threats to Validity

We carried out the evaluation of our approach through a simulation that resembles a cloud environment. We built our simulation tool on CloudSim and Burlap, which are the most widely extended frameworks for simulating cloud environments and implementing reinforcement learning experiments, respectively. Our controlled environment facilitates a faster experimentation with diverse scenarios and different IaaS providers. Additionally, we performed the experiments using a real workload trace.

For the sake of simplicity, we considered a SLA with only one quality of service attribute: response time. But, the model is extensible to multiple attributes (e.g. availability, reliability) and multiple SLAs.

5   Related Work

Technical debt community has applied the metaphor in a wide range of decision-making process under uncertainty such as software maintenance and evolution [15], architectural design [18], cloud service selection [1], software testing, sustainability design among others [17]. It has been used as a way to identify, measure and monitor a decision that trades off a quality compliance concern against an economics concern. Furthermore, the metaphor has shown to be effective to raise the visibility of the impact on utility of a suboptimal decision if a change materialises. For example, Li et al. [18] evaluated architectural decisions from a value-oriented perspective and used the debt to monetise the gap between an optimal and suboptimal architecture when a change scenario occurs. Also, Alzaghoul et al. [1] extended the metaphor into cloud service selection to adopt a service substitution that is aware of the potential debt introduced in the composition by each candidate service and makes a decision based on the potential of the selected service to clear the debt when the change scenario materialise. However, none of these works addresses the problem of automating the learning of technical debts. To the best of our knowledge, we are the first to propose an autonomous management of technical debts based on learning and, different from previous works, we are revisiting the metaphor to support run-time management of debts and value creation in self-adaptive and self-management contexts such as cloud elasticity.

Reinforcement learning has already been used as an underlying technique for elasticity management [19]. For instance, Barret et al. [4] designed a parallel Q-learning approach to build an elasticity manager based on a multi-agent system, where each virtual resource is an agent that makes its decisions depending on the load of incoming requests, experienced penalties and deploying costs. However, state variables are purely performance metrics and the reward is based on a minimization of costs and penalties; consequently, the learning ignores the strategic valuation and potential utility of continuous gaps between resource supply and demand as a result of imperfect elasticity adaptations. Jamshidi et al. [12] built a fuzzy control based reinforcement learning approach for autonomous elasticity management that modifies fuzzy elasticity rules for resource provisioning at run-time. However, this work is focused on tuning and improving fuzzy rules to reduce user-dependency in elasticity management. In contrast to prior works, we designed a reinforcement learning approach that considers state variables related to both economics and performance aspects of cloud elasticity and a reward linked to elasticity debts, in order to achieve a management that proactively uses this autonomous learning of technical debts in resource adaptations to estimate the conditions where these debts will potentially pay off.

6   Conclusions and Future Work

We proposed an autonomous elasticity management approach intended to make adaptations that are aware of the unavoidable imperfections of elasticity adaptations in the cloud. Our approach implements a reinforcement learning solution that values the potential utility produced by the dynamic gaps between the ideal and actual resource provisioning over time. We are the first to propose an elasticity decision-making analysis that integrates the strategic decision-making achieved through reinforcement learning techniques, and the value oriented perspective promoted by the technical debt metaphor in changing environments. Simulation results indicate that a reinforcement learning of dynamic technical debts in resource provisioning achieves a higher aggregate utility for the SaaS provider. Moreover, the underlying foundations of our dynamic technical debt approach are generic enough to be applied in other self-adaptive and self-management contexts, where decisions with a trade-off analysis can be strategically taken and aimed at long-term rewards.

In our ongoing research, we are looking at the sensitivity of our approach to attributes of technical debt, including interest, principal, amnesty and leverage. Additionally, we are introducing a technical debt-oriented perspective for multi-tenant applications hosted in inter-clouds architectures.

Acknowledgments. We thank Rommy Márquez and Tao Chen for their helpful comments on the paper.

References

1. Alzaghoul, E., Bahsoon, R.: Economics-driven approach for managing technical debt in cloud-based architectures. In: Proceedings of the 6th IEEE/ACM International Conference on Utility and Cloud Computing (UCC 2013), pp. 239–242. IEEE (2013)
2. Armbrust, M., Fox, A., Griffith, R., Joseph, A.D., Katz, R., Konwinski, A., Lee, G., Patterson, D., Rabkin, A., Stoica, I., et al.: A view of cloud computing. Commun. ACM **53**(4), 50–58 (2010)
3. Bahsoon, R.: Dynamic and adaptive management of technical debt: managing technical debt @runtime. In: Avgeriou, P., Kruchten, P., Ozkaya, I., Seaman, C. (eds.) Managing Technical Debt in Software Engineering (Dagstuhl Seminar 16162), vol. 6, p. 118. Schloss Dagstuhl-Leibniz-Zentrum fuer Informatik (2016)
4. Barrett, E., Howley, E., Duggan, J.: Applying reinforcement learning towards automating resource allocation and application scalability in the cloud. Concurrency Comput. Pract. Exp. **25**(12), 1656–1674 (2013)
5. Calheiros, R.N., Ranjan, R., Beloglazov, A., De Rose, C.A., Buyya, R.: Cloudsim: a toolkit for modeling and simulation of cloud computing environments and evaluation of resource provisioning algorithms. Softw. Pract. Exp. **41**(1), 23–50 (2011)
6. CloudSigma. https://www.cloudsigma.com/ Accessed 1 Oct 2016
7. Fokaefs, M., Barna, C., Litoiu, M.: Economics-driven resource scalability on the cloud. In: Proceedings of the 11th International Workshop on Software Engineering for Adaptive and Self-Managing Systems, pp. 129–139. ACM (2016)
8. Guo, Y., Seaman, C.: A portfolio approach to technical debt management. In: Proceedings of the 2nd Workshop on Managing Technical Debt, pp. 31–34. ACM (2011)

9. Han, R., Ghanem, M.M., Guo, L., Guo, Y., Osmond, M.: Enabling cost-aware and adaptive elasticity of multi-tier cloud applications. Future Gener. Comput. Syst. **32**, 82–98 (2014)
10. Herbst, N.R., Kounev, S., Reussner, R.H.: Elasticity in cloud computing: what it is, and what it is not. In: ICAC, pp. 23–27 (2013)
11. Herbst, N.R., Kounev, S., Weber, A., Groenda, H.: Bungee: an elasticity benchmark for self-adaptive IAAS cloud environments. In: Proceedings of the 10th International Symposium on Software Engineering for Adaptive and Self-Managing Systems, pp. 46–56. IEEE Press (2015)
12. Jamshidi, P., Pahl, C., Mendonça, N.C.: Managing uncertainty in autonomic cloud elasticity controllers. IEEE Cloud Comput. **3**(3), 50–60 (2016)
13. JFree. Jfreechart (2016). https://goo.gl/oi39. Accessed 1 Dec 2016
14. Jin, H., Wang, X., Wu, S., Di, S., Shi, X.: Towards optimized fine-grained pricing of iaas cloud platform. IEEE Trans. Cloud Comput. **3**(4), 436–448 (2015)
15. Kruchten, P., Nord, R.L., Ozkaya, I.: Technical debt: from metaphor to theory and practice. IEEE Softw. **29**(6), 18–21 (2012)
16. Li, A., Yang, X., Kandula, S., Zhang, M.: Cloudcmp: comparing public cloud providers. In: Proceedings of the 10th ACM SIGCOMM Conference on Internet Measurement, pp. 1–14. ACM (2010)
17. Li, Z., Avgeriou, P., Liang, P.: A systematic mapping study on technical debt and its management. J. Syst. Softw. **101**, 193–220 (2015)
18. Li, Z., Liang, P., Avgeriou, P.: Architectural debt management in value-oriented architecting. In: Economics-Driven Software Architecture, pp. 183–204. Elsevier (2014)
19. Lorido-Botran, T., Miguel-Alonso, J., Lozano, J.A.: A review of auto-scaling techniques for elastic applications in cloud environments. J. Grid Comput. **12**(4), 559–592 (2014)
20. MacGlashan, J.: Burlap: The brown-umbc reinforcement learning and planning, June 2016. https://goo.gl/ePrWFA. Accessed 1 Nov 2016
21. Mannion, P., Duggan, J., Howley, E.: Parallel learning using heterogeneous agents. In: Proceedings of the Adaptive and Learning Agents workshop (at AAMAS 2015) (2015)
22. Mao, M., Humphrey, M.: A performance study on the VM startup time in the cloud. In: Proceedings of the 5th IEEE International Conference on Cloud Computing (CLOUD 2012), pp. 423–430. IEEE (2012)
23. Mera-Gómez, C., Bahsoon, R., Buyya, R.: Elasticity debt: a debt-aware approach to reason about elasticity decisions in the cloud. In: Proceedings of the 9th IEEE International Conference on Utility and Cloud Computing (UCC 2016). IEEE (2016)
24. Pandey, A., Moreno, G.A., Cámara, J., Garlan, D.: Hybrid planning for decision making in self-adaptive systems. In: Proceedings of the 10th IEEE International Conference on Self-Adaptive and Self-Organizing Systems (SASO 2016). IEEE (2016)
25. RightScale. Understanding the voting process (2016). goo.gl/HahnWB. Accessed 20 July 2016
26. Schulz, F.: Elasticity in service level agreements. In: Proceedings of the 2013 IEEE International Conference on Systems, Man, and Cybernetics, pp. 4092–4097. IEEE (2013)
27. Sharma, U., Shenoy, P., Sahu, S., Shaikh, A.: A cost-aware elasticity provisioning system for the cloud. In: Proceedings of the 31st International Conference on Distributed Computing Systems (ICDCS 2011), pp. 559–570. IEEE (2011)

28. Suleiman, B., Sakr, S., Jeffery, R., Liu, A.: On understanding the economics and elasticity challenges of deploying business applications on public cloud infrastructure. J. Internet Serv. Appl. **3**(2), 173–193 (2012)
29. Sutton, R.S., Barto, A.G.: Reinforcement Learning: An Introduction, vol. 1. MIT Press, Cambridge (1998)
30. Wikimedia (2016). https://goo.gl/yDhTRN. Accessed 1 Feb 2017

Large-Scale and Adaptive Service Composition Using Deep Reinforcement Learning

Hongbing Wang[1]([✉]), Mingzhu Gu[1], Qi Yu[2], Huanhuan Fei[1], Jiajie Li[1], and Yong Tao[1]

[1] Key Laboratory of Computer Network and Information Integration
and School of Computer Science and Engineering, Southeast University,
Nanjing, China
hbw@seu.edu.cn
[2] College of Computing and Information Sciences,
Rochester Institute of Technology, Rochester, USA
qi.yu@rit.edu

Abstract. Service composition provides an effective way to implement a Service-Oriented Architecture (SOA) by combining existing multiple services to meet user requirements. The increasingly complex user requirements and large amount of services pose a significant challenge to service selection and composition. Furthermore, web services are network based, which are inherently dynamic. The environment of service composition may also be complex and unstable. These demand a service composition solution to adapt to the change of environment. In this paper, we propose a new service composition solution based on Deep Reinforcement Learning (DRL) for adaptive and large-scale service composition problems. The experimental results demonstrate the effectiveness, scalability and self-adaptivity of our approach.

1 Introduction

In service computing, web service composition is the most effective technology to implement a Service-Oriented Architecture (SOA) [10]. In recent years a large number of enterprises distribute and release their products through web services that can be accessed by others. This leads to rapid growth of the number of web services. One service usually does not meet complex user requirements, so it's necessary to combine multiple services to form a *service composition*. Given that the number of services with same functional attributes may be quite large, Quality of Service (QoS) has become an important factor to differentiate competing services. QoS-aware service composition has become a key research direction in the service computing community [1,6].

In practical applications, under the condition of meeting user's requirements, the criteria for evaluating whether a service composition solution has applied values are the quality, adaptability and efficiency of composition [11]. Web services rely on the network environment inherently, so the network fluctuation will lead to changes in QoS performance, such as long delay. Therefore, due to the

© Springer International Publishing AG 2017
M. Maximilien et al. (Eds.): ICSOC 2017, LNCS 10601, pp. 383–391, 2017.
https://doi.org/10.1007/978-3-319-69035-3_27

dynamic network environment, a good web service composition solution needs to adapt to the dynamic environment. In addition, the growth of the number of services with similar functionality but different QoS significantly expands the candidate service space. More specifically, if the number of abstract services in composition workflow is m and the candidate service number is n, there exist n^m possible composition solutions, which leads to a "combinatorial explosion problem" [2,9]. Existing works mainly focus on using reinforcement learning (RL) to adapt to the dynamic environment. However, the existing RL methods show a poor efficiency for large-scale problems [11].

In this paper, we develop an adaptive service composition method based on deep reinforcement learning (DRL), which integrates reinforcement learning and deep learning. RL helps achieve adaptivity in service composition, deep learning is to enhance the ability of expression and generalization.

2   Related Work

In this section, we review some related works that deal with large-scale and adaptive problems in service composition, including the planing solution, reinforcement learning (RL), and deep reinforcement learning (DRL).

In recent years, there are many studies to address the adaptability issue, such as integer programming technology, graph planning, artificial intelligence. In [13], the authors develop a method using AI planning to build the service composition workflow. A repairing approach is used to deal with the changes in process of composition. However, building a service composition workflow needs some priori knowledge about the environment. Reinforcement learning provides an effective method to achieve adaptive service composition. RL is more suited to resolve the incomplete scenario using the trial and error exploration to discover the optimal policy [4]. Wang et al. [12] propose a service composition method based on Markov Decision Process (MDP). This method only utilizes RL, so it cannot deal with lager-scale service composition problems.

To address the high-dimensional inputs in RL, the deep learning which can extract features from raw data can be employed. In [5], a multi-layer perceptron is adopted to approximate the Q-value, leading to a Neural Fitted Q Iteration (NFQ) algorithm. Mnih et al. [7] apply the DRL with the Atari 2600 game, which successful learns control policies from the high dimension sensation input and with expert level performance.

3   Preliminaries

3.1   Reinforcement Learning

In a standard RL framework, the agent interacts with environment by executing certain actions, and gets a feedback, and adjusts its behaviors. Q-learning [3] is an widely used RL method. Q-learning approximates value function of the state-action pair by reducing the difference between neighboring condition estimated Q-value at every step of learning. The update rule of Q-function is defined as.

$$Q\left(s,a\right) \leftarrow (1-\alpha)Q\left(s,a\right) + \alpha\left[r + \gamma\mathrm{max}_{a'}Q\left(s',a'\right)\right] \tag{1}$$

where α is learning rate, γ is the discount factor, and $Q(s,a)$ is the state-action value under state s executing action a. And in RL, the discounted cumulative reward is used to evaluate the result which is defined as:

$$V = \sum_{i=0}^{\infty}\gamma^{i}r_{i} \tag{2}$$

where r_i is the $i-th$ step immediate reward.

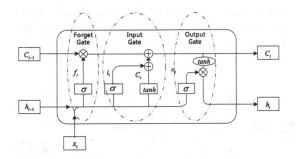

Fig. 1. A simple LSTM block

3.2   Deep Learning

LSTM is a recurrent neural network (RNN) extended with memory. Three other layers are added as hidden memory units compared with the original RNN, including the input gate, output gate, and forget gate. As shown in Fig. 1: The LSTM can be divided into three parts: (1) Forget gate is used to decide what information will be discarded, and the output value will be delivered to cell state C_{t-1}. (2) Determine what information can be put into the cell, which consists of two parts. One part will be updated by the input gate and another part is a new candidate vector created by Tanh layer. (3) Update the old information.

3.3   Deep Reinforcement Learning

Google DeepMind Team combines perception of Deep Learning and decision-making ability of RL to develop Deep Reinforcement Learning (DRL). The learning process is divided into three steps: (1) Through interacting with the environment (achieved by RL), an agent obtains observation and delivers the high dimension results to a neural network, to learn abstract representations; (2) The agent evaluates the action based on repayment value, and maps the current condition to a corresponding action by two kinds of strategy; (3) The environment responds to the action and gets the next observation.

This paper adopts the structure of RNN to remember the continuous state information in a history timeline and uses a Adaptive Deep Q-learning and RNN Composition Network (ADQRCN), which are suitable for service composition.

4   Problem Formulation

Consider someone who wants to arrange his trip schedule after determining departure and return back time. He may consume services, such as weather forecast, flight information search, and hotel reservation. The process of whole trip can be modelled as a transition graph in Fig. 2. It consists of two kinds of nodes. The hollow node represents state node (i.e., abstract service), such as S_0. Another type is a solid node, namely the concrete service. Abstract service refers to a class of services with the same function attributes and different QoS. Every abstract service has multiple concrete services.

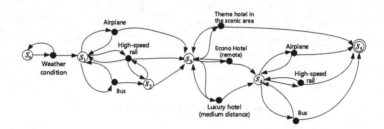

Fig. 2. The MDP-WSC model for vocation planning

Based on the flow chart of vocation planning, we need to construct the model to solve the problem. We model service composition using a Markov Decision Process (MDP) and further exploit how to generate an effective policy.

Definition 1 (MDP-based web service composition (MDP-WSC)). *A MDP-WSC is a 6-tuple MDP-WSC=$< S, S_0, S_\tau, A(.), P, R >$, where*

- *S is a finite set of the world states;*
- *$S_0 \in S$ is the initial state from which an execution of the service composition starts;*
- *$S_\tau \subset S$ is the set of terminal states, indicating an end of composition execution when reaching one state $S_\tau^i \in S_\tau$;*
- *$A(s)$ represents the set of services that can be executed in state $s \in S$;*
- *P is a probability distribution function. When a web service α is invoked, the world makes a transition from its current state s to a succeeding state s'. The probability for this transition is labeled as $P(s'|s, \alpha)$;*

– *R is the immediate reward function. When the current state is s and a service
α is selected, we get an immediate reward $r = R(s, a)$ from the environment
after executing the action.*

The immediate reward from environment can be calculated by the aggregated
QoS value [12]. *Att* represents the attribute of a service, and w is the weighting
factor of *Att*.

$$R(s) = \sum w_i \times \frac{Att_i^s - Att_i^{min}}{Att_i^{max} - Att_i^{min}} \tag{3}$$

5 Service Composition Based on DRL

5.1 RNN in Deep Reinforcement Learning

The purpose of the neural network is mainly to generalize state-action pairs
and the corresponding Q-value. Figure 3 depicts the basic RNN structure in
ADQRCN, where the input layer consists of state and action information collection. The input is passed through a hidden layer composed of 30 Long Short-
Term Memory (LSTM) units and a full connection layer. Finally, the Q value is
generated by the output layer.

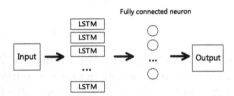

Fig. 3. The structure of ADQRCN

5.2 Learning Strategies

With regard the training of ADQRCN, we adopt a similar method as in [7,8].
The neural network of ADQRCN simulates the Q function, given by formula (4)
which means the neural network $f(s, a; \theta)$ is used to predict the Q-value and
θ are the parameters of neural network. Bellman Equation (5) is used to calculate variance (6). Then, gradient descent (7) is used to update the network
parameters.

$$f(s, a; \theta) \approx Q(s, a; \theta) \tag{4}$$

$$Q(s, a) = r + \gamma max_{a'} Q(s', a'; \theta) \tag{5}$$

$$L = E[(r + \gamma max_{a'} Q(s', a'; \theta) - Q(s, a; \theta))^2] \tag{6}$$

$$\frac{\partial L(\theta)}{\partial \theta} = E[(r + \gamma max_{a'} Q(s', a'; \theta) - Q(s, a; \theta)) \frac{\partial Q(s, a; \theta)}{\partial \theta}] \tag{7}$$

Initialize replay memory D and its capacity N
Initialize action-value function Q with weights θ
Initialize target action-value function $\hat{Q}$ with random weights $\theta^- = \theta$
repeat
  for $t = 1, T$ **do**
    with probability ε select a random action a_t
    otherwise select $a_t = \arg\max_a Q(s_t, a; \theta)$
    Execute action a_t, observe reward r_t and next state s_{t+1}
    $s_{t+1} = s_t$
    Store transition (s_t, a_t, r_t, s_{t+1}) in D
    Sample random minibatch of transitions (s_j, a_j, r_j, s_{j+1}) from D
    if episode terminates at step $j + 1$ **then**
      set $y_j = r_j$
    else
      $y_j = r_j + \gamma\max_{a'} \hat{Q}(s_{j+1}, a'; \theta^-)$
    end if
    Perform a gradient descent step on $(y_j - Q(s_t, a_t; \theta))^2$ w.r.t. θ
    Every C steps reset $\hat{Q} = Q$
  end for
until convergence condition is satisfied, algorithm converges

Algorithm 1. ADQRCN Algorithm

5.3 Algorithm

Algorithm 1 describes the detailed process of training of ADQRCN. At first, the empty dataset of the recurrent neural network is initialized with capacity N. The action-value function Q and the target action-value function $\hat{Q}$ are both implemented by the recurrent neural network with random weights. In the training process, an agent selects an action according to the Q value function and executes the action. After obtaining the reward r_t and next state s_{t+1}, the transition (s_t, a_t, r_t, s_{t+1}) will be stored in the replay memory D. Then, the adjusting process will begin, according to the method in Sect. 5.2, which can improve prediction accuracy of Q value function. The algorithm will repeat the above process until convergence (the service composition result remains the same over two iterations) and output the final service composition result.

6   Experiments and Analysis

We conduct the experiments to assess the proposed Adaptive Deep Reinforcement Learning algorithm (ADQRCN) on three aspects: effectiveness, adaptability and scalability. And the traditional Q-Learning Service Composition Network (QCN) [12] which use the Q-learning and MDP to obtain the optimal service composition is implemented to be compared with our method.

6.1   Experiment Setting

In the experiment, we mainly consider four QoS attributes, including *ResponseTime, Throughput, Availability*, and *Reliability*. The experimental data comes from QWS Dataset[1]. Considering that the scale of QWS Dataset is small, we randomly expand the dataset to simulate a large-scale scenario, which will allow us to verify the advantage of our methods. In the evaluation of result, we use the discounted cumulative reward mentioned in formula (2) to represent the performance of composition scheme.

The experiment environment is based on a Window7 (64bit) system, running on an Intel i7-6700K 4.00GHz CPU with 16GB RAM.

6.2   Result Analysis

6.2.1   Validation of Effectiveness

The experiments are conducted with 100 state nodes (abstract services) and each state node corresponding to 500 candidate services. Therefore, the total number of possible service composition schema is 500^{100}, which qualifies for a large-scale scenario.

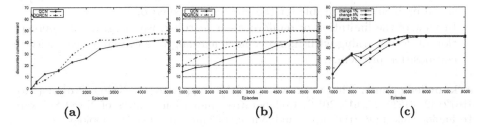

(a)   (b)   (c)

Fig. 4. (a) Validation of effectiveness (b) Validation of Scalability (c)Validation of adaptability

As shown in Fig. 4(a), the ADQRCN is better than the QCN and the ADQRCN converges more rapidly than the QCN. Thus, this experiment also demonstrates the efficiency of ADQRCN. Due to the QCN is based on the table storage with random exploration, its performance is worse than ADQRCN on basis of generalization expression.

6.2.2   Validation of Scalability

In this series of experiments, the number of state nodes are fixed at 100, and candidate services is set as 700 in Fig. 4(b) to compare with the experiment with 500 candidate services in Fig. 4(a). From the figure the convergence rate of ADQRCN significantly outperforms QCN. Because ADQRCN adopts the neural network as the generalization value function, the method maintains strong ability of generalization and the ability to quickly achieve convergence.

---

[1] http://www.uoguelph.ca/~qmahmoud/qws/.

6.2.3 Validation of Adaptability

In the experiment, to simulate a changeable environment, we change 1%, 5% and 10% QoS values of services in period of fixed time (between 2000th episode-2500th episode). The result of three groups of experiments are shown in Fig. 4(c). The fluctuation of services has certain influence on the learning performance, but these effects are temporary. From an overall perspective ADQRCN has stronger adaptability when facing the fluctuations, which may be related to the forecast model.

7   Conclusion

The paper proposes an adaptive deep reinforcement learning framework to ensure the adaptability and efficiency in large-scale service composition. The adaptive deep reinforcement learning framework uses recurrent neural network simulation of reinforcement learning function and effective information storage to improve the ability to scale to a large and dynamic service environment. The main innovation of this paper include the following:

- We propose the MDP-WSC model, which is closer to the real service composition problem and suitable for the large-scale scenario.
- In view of the limitation of reinforcement learning, we integrate the perception of deep learning with reinforcement learning to solve large-scale service composition problem.

Acknowledgments. This work was partially supported by NSFC Projects(Nos. 61672152, 61232007, 61532013), Collaborative Innovation Centers of Novel Software Technology and Industrialization and Wireless Communications Technology.

References

1. Canfora, G., Di Penta, M., Esposito, R., Villani, M.L.: A framework for QOS-aware binding and re-binding of composite web services. J. Syst. Softw. **81**(10), 1754–1769 (2008)
2. Constantinescu, I., Faltings, B., Binder, W.: Large scale, type-compatible service composition. In: Proceedings of the IEEE International Conference on Web Services (ICWS), pp. 506–513. IEEE (2004)
3. Goldberg, D.E., Holland, J.H.: Genetic algorithms and machine learning. Mach. Learn. **3**(2), 95–99 (1988)
4. Kaelbling, L.P., Littman, M.L., Moore, A.W.: Reinforcement learning: a survey. J. Artif. Intell. Res. **4**, 237–285 (1996)
5. Lange, S., Riedmiller, M.: Deep auto-encoder neural networks in reinforcement learning. In: The 2010 International Joint Conference on Neural Networks (IJCNN), pp. 1–8. IEEE (2010)
6. Li, W., Badr, Y., Biennier, F.: Service farming: an ad-hoc and QOS-aware web service composition approach. In: Proceedings of the 28th Annual ACM Symposium on Applied Computing, pp. 750–756. ACM (2013)

7. Mnih, V., Kavukcuoglu, K., Silver, D., Graves, A., Antonoglou, I., Wierstra, D., Riedmiller, M.: Playing Atari with deep reinforcement learning. arXiv preprint (2013). arXiv:1312.5602
8. Mnih, V., Kavukcuoglu, K., Silver, D., Rusu, A.A., Veness, J., Bellemare, M.G., Graves, A., Riedmiller, M., Fidjeland, A.K., Ostrovski, G., et al.: Human-level control through deep reinforcement learning. Nature **518**(7540), 529–533 (2015)
9. Oh, S.C., Lee, D., Kumara, S.R.: Effective web service composition in diverse and large-scale service networks. IEEE Trans. Serv. Comput. (TSC) **1**(1), 15–32 (2008)
10. Trummer, I., Faltings, B.: Optimizing the tradeoff between discovery, composition, and execution cost in service composition. In: Proceedings of the IEEE International Conference on Web Services (ICWS), pp. 476–483. IEEE (2011)
11. Wang, H., Chen, X., Wu, Q., Yu, Q., Zheng, Z., Bouguettaya, A.: Integrating on-policy reinforcement learning with multi-agent techniques for adaptive service composition. In: Franch, X., Ghose, A.K., Lewis, G.A., Bhiri, S. (eds.) ICSOC 2014. LNCS, vol. 8831, pp. 154–168. Springer, Heidelberg (2014). doi:10.1007/978-3-662-45391-9_11
12. Wang, H., Zhou, X., Zhou, X., Liu, W., Li, W., Bouguettaya, A.: Adaptive service composition based on reinforcement learning. In: Maglio, P.P., Weske, M., Yang, J., Fantinato, M. (eds.) ICSOC 2010. LNCS, vol. 6470, pp. 92–107. Springer, Heidelberg (2010). doi:10.1007/978-3-642-17358-5_7
13. Yan, Y., Poizat, P., Zhao, L.: Repairing service compositions in a changing world. In: Lee, R., Ormandjieva, O., Abran, A., Constantinides, C. (eds.) Software Engineering Research, Management and Applications 2010. SCI, vol. 296, pp. 17–36. Springer, Heidelberg (2010)

Service Engineering

ECHO: An Adaptive Orchestration Platform for Hybrid Dataflows across Cloud and Edge

Pushkara Ravindra[✉], Aakash Khochare, Siva Prakash Reddy,
Sarthak Sharma, Prateeksha Varshney, and Yogesh Simmhan

Indian Institute of Science, Bangalore 560012, India
pushkar1593@gmail.com,
{aakhochare,kommareddy,prateeksha}@grads.cds.iisc.ac.in,
sarthakaqua96@gmail.com, simmhan@cds.iisc.ac.in

Abstract. The Internet of Things (IoT) is offering unprecedented observational data that are used for managing Smart City utilities. *Edge* and *Fog* gateway devices are an integral part of IoT deployments to acquire real-time data and enact controls. Recently, *Edge-computing* is emerging as first-class paradigm to complement Cloud-centric analytics. But a key limitation is the lack of a platform-as-a-service for applications spanning Edge and Cloud. Here, we propose ECHO, an orchestration platform for dataflows across distributed resources. ECHO's hybrid dataflow composition can operate on diverse data models – streams, micro-batches and files, and interface with native runtime engines like TensorFlow and Storm to execute them. It manages the application's lifecycle, including container-based deployment and a registry for state management. ECHO can schedule the dataflow on different Edge, Fog and Cloud resources, and also perform dynamic task migration between resources. We validate the ECHO platform for executing video analytics and sensor streams for Smart Traffic and Smart Utility applications on Raspberry Pi, NVidia TX1, ARM64 and Azure Cloud VM resources, and present our results.

1 Introduction

The growth of Internet of Things (IoT) is leading to an unprecedented access to observational data about physical infrastructure such as traffic/surveillance cameras and smart power meters in Smart Cities, as well as social life-style through fitness bands like FitBit and automation assistants like Google Home. Such data streams are integrated with historic data and analytics models to make intelligent decisions, such as managing traffic signaling or power grid optimization in cities [1,2], or controlling devices in your home.

Traditionally, all this decision making and analytics have taken place in the Cloud due to their easy service-oriented access to seemingly infinite resources. Data is streamed from the edge devices and sensors to the data center, and control decisions communicated back from the Cloud analytics to the edge for enactment. This, however, has several down-sides. The *bandwidth* to send high-fidelity video streams to the Cloud can be punitive, and the round-trip *latency* to

© Springer International Publishing AG 2017
M. Maximilien et al. (Eds.): ICSOC 2017, LNCS 10601, pp. 395–410, 2017.
https://doi.org/10.1007/978-3-319-69035-3_28

move data from edge to Cloud, and control signals back can be high. Clouds' pay as you-go-model also *bills* users for data transfers, compute, and storage [3,4].

An integral part of IoT deployments are *Edge and Fog devices* that serve as gateways to interface with sensors and actuators on the field. These are typically collocated or within few network hops of the sensors, and have non-trivial compute capacity. E.g., a Raspberry Pi 2B device, popular on the Edge, has 4 power-efficient ARM cores, each performing at about $\frac{1}{3}^{rd}$ an Intel Xeon E5 core on the Cloud [5]. Devices like the NVIDIA TX1 and Softiron ARM64 servers offer accelerators and energy-efficiency that can be ruggedized for deployment as a Fog layer. Rather than just have them move data and control signals between the field devices and the Cloud, these Edge and Fog resources should be actively considered as first-class computing platforms to complement the Cloud-centric model to reduce the network transfer time and costs [4,6]. There is also the lost opportunity cost of not using their *captive computational* capability.

There have been *ad hoc* or custom applications that indeed leverage Edge, Fog and Cloud resources together. However, a key hurdle to adoption of this distributed paradigm is the lack of a platform ecosystem that simplifies the composition, deployment, and management of applications, micro-services and data seamlessly across these computing layers. In this regard, we are in a situation similar to feature phones before smart phones came along, where middleware has not kept up with hardware and communication advances [3]. In this article, we highlight key requirements for such a distributed orchestration platform to support the novel requirements of IoT applications on diverse resources, reaffirming earlier works [7]. We further propose ECHO, an architecture and platform implementation that addresses these needs, along with a preliminary validation.

Existing commercial and open source solutions partially address this gap. Amazon's Greengrass[1], Microsoft's Azure IoT Edge[2] and IBM Watson IoT provide gateway management SDKs that tightly integrate with their Cloud services. Eclipse Kura and Liota [8,9] are gateway management services which support local applications, while platforms like Edgent, Node.RED, and NiFi support basic dataflow capabilities that are limited to stream or micro-batch data. Our work goes beyond these offerings and examines hybrid data models (stream, micro-batch, batch), generic dataflow composition, pluggability with external platforms (TensorFlow, Storm, Spark), and dynamic migration.

Specifically, we make the following contributions in this paper:

- We highlight the key features and desiderata for a platform to support distributed application composition and execution across Edge, Fog and Cloud devices (Sect. 2).
- We propose ECHO, an architecture and open source platform for computing across Edge and Cloud that meets these requirements, while also leveraging existing open source tools (Sect. 3).
- We validate ECHO for several representative Smart City applications, including video, stream and event analytics (Sect. 4).

---

[1] Amazon AWS Greengrass, https://aws.amazon.com/greengrass/.
[2] Microsoft Azure IoT Edge, http://azure.github.io/iot-edge/.

Besides these contributions, we also review related literature in Sect. 5, and present our conclusions and future work in Sect. 6.

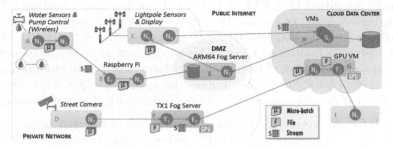

Fig. 1. Motivating Usecase from a Smart Community in a City

2 Requirements and Motivation

Figure 1 illustrates scenarios for a *Smart Community*, where sensors and actuators like water level and quality sensors and pump controls for *smart water management*, environment sensors and digital displays fixed on street light poles for ambient *urban sensing and public notification*, and PTZ cameras for *surveillance and traffic* are present [2]. Edge devices like Raspberry Pi and smart phones, NVidia TX1 and ARM64 Fog servers, along with Cloud VMs, are present in the private (community and Cloud) networks, and the public Internet, for executing analytics and storage. This motivates several key and distinct requirements for an IoT platform that allows composition and execution of decision making applications across Edge, Fog and Cloud resources, as we discuss below.

Dataflow Composition Model. Data-driven IoT applications are well-suited for a dataflow programming model, where user tasks are vertices in a *directed acyclic graph (DAG)* that execute upon data arrival, and edges are channels that route the data between tasks. Many Big Data platforms like *Apache Spark, Storm* and *Google's TensorFlow*, and edge-centric platforms like *Edgent* and *MiNiFi* use a dataflow model. It also allows a library of tasks to be developed and reused by diverse domains, and these tasks form the unit of scheduling on compute resources. E.g., Fig. 1 shows tasks N_1, N_2, E_1 and N_3 tasks operating as a linear dataflow on water events that are processed and stored to a database.

Hybrid Data Sources. IoT applications often operate over thousands of observation streams, performing low-latency event pattern detection, e.g., on water event streams at E_1 in Fig. 1. We also require batch processing on accumulated data for high throughput, say for traffic mining over video segments by T_1. Micro-batches, like from N_1 to N_2, offer a stream of batched tuples, balancing latency and throughput. Hence, *seamlessly allowing hybrid datasets* to pass between tasks in the dataflow is essential, allowing the application composer to select the appropriate data model. Lambda Architecture and platforms like Flink and Spark Streaming affirm the need for such hybrid models. This also affects the *QoS* for the dataflows (e.g., latency, throughput, reliability, price).

Diverse Resource Capabilities. Edge, Fog and Cloud resources have heterogeneous capabilities. Platforms like Pi and Arduino are popular as edge devices (e.g., a Pi 2B with 1 GHz CPU/1 GB RAM running Linux, costing US\$ 35). IoT Fog servers from vendors like Dell and NVIDIA offer energy efficient multicore ARM64 processors and GPGPUs (e.g., NVidia TX1 with a GPU, Softiron ARM64 server). On-demand Cloud VMs at different globally spread-out data centers are also accessible. The software platform must be able to *leverage such Edge, Fog and elastic Cloud VMs* to meet the application QoS, while also being aware of constraints like energy (e.g., if powered by battery or solar) and pricing.

Network Connectivity. IoT compute resources are distributed. So the network connectivity between them is crucial. The resources may be within *local networks* (e.g., Cloud data center, private campus) and *wide-area networks* (e.g., devices across a city), with variability in *bandwidth and latency* ranging from 10–1000 ms and Kbps-Gbps, depending on the medium (3G/WiFi/LoRa). Communication within a *private network*, a *public network*, or between the two with firewalls also impacts the visibility and accessibility of service endpoints. The platform should *transparently resolve this* (e.g., push vs. pull) during dataflow orchestration.

Native Runtime Engines. Numerous Big Data and emerging edge platforms exist for data processing. Some like Spark and Storm are general purpose, allowing custom logic, while others like Edgent and TensorFlow are specialized for event analytics and deep learning, which are popular in IoT. Packages like R may also require command-line execution. These are also optimized for different resources (e.g., VMs, edge, GPU). The execution platform should *leverage the strengths of native runtime engines* while coordinating between them like a "meta-engine" (e.g., data model mapping, public/private networks, scheduling), and also offering basic dataflow orchestration. E.g., in Fig. 1 shows the use of *Edgent* (E_1, E_2) for complex event processing (CEP) on Pis, *TensorFlow* for classifying image batches using deep neural networks on GPUs (T_1, T_2), *Storm* for scalable streaming analysis on Cloud VMs over ambient observations (S_2), with *NiFi* as the baseline dataflow orchestrator ($N_1 - N_9$).

Service-Oriented Architecture. Cloud owes its success to its Service-Oriented Architecture (SOA), at the infrastructure (IaaS), platform (PaaS) and software (SaaS) levels. Edge and Fog platforms can similarly benefit. Infrastructure services at these resource layers can use *containers* like LXC and Dockers for resource sand-boxing. They are more light-weight than hypervisors and offer fast startup, but trade-off strict security with multi-tenancy. *Platform micro-services* are viable on constrained edge and Fog layers for rapid dataflow deployment. A platform service on the edge or Fog resource can perform local task coordination and data transfers across resources, and manage the application lifecycle.

Discovery and Adaptivity. Decentralized IoT resources operate in a dynamic environment where the availability and capacity of edge and Fog resources can vary over time (e.g., network link, mobility, battery level). This is unlike public Clouds that have on-demand and reliable availability. This requires a *scalable registry service* to publish the health metrics of edge and Fog devices, and to track their applications. Maintaining the available data sources, and dataflows is useful when making scheduling decisions, and for provenance and billing. Lastly, the inherent dynamism of the resources, data sources, and applications along with the need to meet QoS for dataflows makes it necessary to support *dynamic migration of dataflows* between different resources as a first class capability.

3   The ECHO Architecture

Here, we propose ECHO, an adaptive orchestration platform for hybrid dataflows across Cloud, Fog and Edge resources[3]. ECHO's design addresses the requirements we identify. Next, we discuss the infrastructure and platform abstractions that ECHO supports, and then delve into its architecture design (Fig. 3).

3.1   Resource Infrastructure

ECHO is designed for resources with diverse capabilities, with a baseline being a Linux device with ≈ 1 GHz CPU/1 GB RAM, and able to run cgroups containers and a Java Runtime. Resources themselves may be devices or servers that are *internally managed* by ECHO (like edge and Fog devices), or *externally managed* IaaS resources, like on-demand VMs from (public/private) Cloud service providers. We have a *Device Service* that acts as an infrastructure fabric to bootstrap and control internally managed resources. It registers the compute, accelerator, memory, disk and network capacity, IP address, visibility of the device from public or private networks, etc. of the device with a *Registry Service* (discussed later) to make it available. It also periodically reports performance statistics of the device (e.g., CPU%, Memory%) for health monitoring.

Internally managed resources use *containers* for application deployment, light-weight resource allocation, sand-boxing applications (and the base device) for limited security, and for billing. We skip this for external resources since the IaaS provider takes these responsibilities. We use LXC containers based on cgroups capability of the Linux kernel, though Docker is also viable but more resource intensive for low-end edge devices. The Device Service starts, stops and manages containers on internal resources, and can deploy the appropriate container image requested for application initiation. The container's lifecycle is also registered with the Registry, along with its periodic performance metrics.

3.2   Programming Model

ECHO adopts a *dataflow programming model* composed as a directed graph allowing cycles, which is similar to but more flexible than DAGs that are widely used in business processes and Big Data applications. Vertices represent tasks (or *processors*) with custom user logic that are executed when an input data item is available, and can generate zero or more output data items. The edges represent the data dependencies and data movement between the tasks.

---

[3] ECHO is available for download at https://github.com/dream-lab/echo.

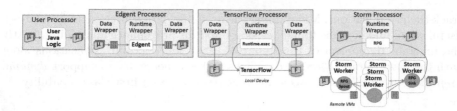

Fig. 2. Wrappers in ECHO for hybrid data models & external engines

Data items consumed and produced by tasks can be of three forms: *streams, files,* or *micro-batches.* Streams have an unbounded sequence of tuples available in-memory, files are a collection of bytes on disk, while micro-batches are a set of tuples or bytes in-memory. User processors are annotated with the data model that they use on their input and output. While we use micro-batch as the default model between processors, ECHO can also map between the stream or files to/from micro-batch. This is done by *data wrappers* around the task logic that accumulate event streams from tasks into windows to form a micro-batch, and similarly replay events from the micro-batch to the task as a stream (Fig. 2). Likewise, micro-batches can be written to and read from the device's file system as files to pass to the task. This eases the development process for the users.

Lastly, the ECHO programming model provides native support for interfacing with external runtime engines using specialized *runtime wrappers* (Fig. 2). These processors take the native dataflow for an external runtime engine, initialize that engine, pass input data to it, and receive the results back, using data wrappers if needed. Such engines may be in-memory Java libraries, command-line executables, or a remote Big Data platform. Specifically, we support *Apache Edgent* [10], an in-memory Java CEP engine for edge devices that consumes and produces event streams, and executes online pattern queries on them. A processor for *Google's TensorFlow* [11] executes classification models as a local Python process, with access to CPU and GPGPU, using file-based input and output. We also support *Apache Storm* and *Spark* platforms on clusters/VMs, using data transfer bindings between a local processor and the remote application.

3.3   Platform Design and Implementation

Figure 3 shows the high level Platform architecture of ECHO. Internally managed devices have the *Device Service* running on them as part of the infrastructure fabric. A *Platform Service* runs on each container or VM and interfaces with a local *Apache NiFi* instance which we use as our default dataflow engine. A *Resource Directory* and *Platform Master* form the core platform services, typically hosted on a public Cloud VM. The devices, their containers and externally managed Cloud VMs available for running user dataflows are registered with the Resource Directory. The master is responsible for managing the lifecycle of a dataflow on behalf of the user by coordinating with the other services. Next, we discuss individual components of ECHO and their interaction pattern.

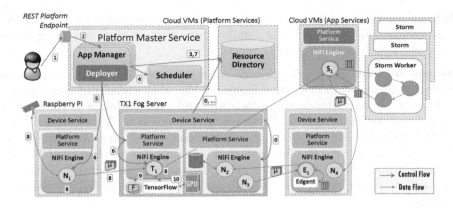

Fig. 3. ECHO Platform Architecture

Resource Directory. The resource directory is a *registry* of all state in the system. We use it to register resources and dataflows but it is naturally suited for data items as well. We use the *Hypercat 3.0* BSI standard [12] that has been developed as a light-weight JSON-based registry for IoT and Smart City assets. Each registered `item` is identified using a unique `href` URI and associated `item-metadata` which is a list of relationship and value pairs. Besides relationships like `description`, geolocation, last updated timestamp and event streams, it also allows user-defined relationships. Hypercat exposes REST-based registration (`POST`) and query (`GET`) of this JSON including geographical and lexicographic search, subscription to event stream updates, and web-based security. We extend an existing Hypercat implementation for our needs[4].

We define a logical hierarchy based on the `href`'s path with the first level having the type of resource, such as *device* or *dataflow*, the next level having the *unique ID* for the item, and subsequently, sub-categories within that item. E.g., for an edge device, we may have *href=http://tempuri.org/device/e97e0195acf4*, while its CPU usage may be at *href=http://tempuri.org/device/e97e0195acf4/CPUUtil*. Since the entire JSON entry for an item is updated when even one relationship changes, having such href-based logical grouping allows fine-grained updates and queries. For devices and containers, we capture information such as the capacity (core, memory, disk, NIC, accelerators), IP address, and the current utilization. For dataflows, we capture the JSON of the actual directed graph of processors, their mapping to specific resources, and their state. This can be further extended to record the data items generated, sensor events streams available, etc. based on user needs for dynamic binding of dataflows to sources.

The entries in the catalog are populated by the Device Service and the Platform Service when resources come online, with a monitoring thread updating the resource usage. The App Manager inserts and updates the state of the dataflow when it is started, updated, rebalanced or stopped. Besides external services

---

[4] https://github.com/HyperCatIoT/node-hypercat.

that can use the catalog, the scheduler queries for information on the available resource capacities to match the dataflow processor requirements using prefix and exact search capabilities of Hypercat.

Device Service. The Device Service is an infrastructure service running on internally managed devices that monitors the device and the containers it spawns. It registers the device on bootup, and each container it spins up or shuts down, with the Resource Directory (step 0 in Fig. 3). The service exposes a REST API that can be used to launch new containers using LXC with specific application images, and turn down unused containers. It also logs the CPU and Memory utilization for each device its containers with the registry. This gives the capacity of the device and also the performance of applications within its containers.

Platform Master and Dataflow Lifecycle. The Platform Master is a REST service responsible for managing a dataflow's lifecycle for the user using other ECHO components. The master itself is registered with the registry for bootstrap. The service exposes three main actions: starting a dataflow, stopping it, and dynamically rebalancing it. These can be easily extended to other variants such as pausing, changing input parameters, or even modifying the structure of the dataflow. Figure 3 illustrates a dataflow starting. Users POST a composed dataflow JSON to the master service, which spawns an *App Manager* thread to handle the request for this dataflow. The master is designed to be stateless, with all state managed in the registry. The manager queries the registry for the available resources – registered containers or VMs and their current capacity, which it passes to the *Scheduler* along with the dataflow. The scheduler is a modular plugin with different possible allocation algorithms that find a suitable mapping from processors in the dataflow to resources, based on the capacity and QoS.

The manager then contacts a *deployer* module that enacts the mapping of processors to resources, connecting them across different resources, and starting the dataflow execution. For this, it invokes a Platform Service running on each resource that in turn interfaces with the local dataflow engine for processor deployment. Once successfully started, the manager assigns a UUID to the dataflow, registers the dataflow JSON and its resource mapping with the registry, and returns the UUID to the user. This UUID can be used to later manage the dataflow, say, to stop it. In this case, the user again contacts the master which spawns a manager that then retrieves the dataflow's state from the Resource Directory. It then works with the deployer to contact the platform services on the resources in which this dataflow's processors are running, stops and undeploys them, and updates the dataflow's state in the registry.

Platform Service and Distributed Orchestration. The container or VM that will host the application runs a *platform service* for managing the dataflow orchestration on it. Depending on the resource availability and sharing allowed between dataflows of the same or different tenants, each container can run all or parts of one or more dataflows. We use *Apache NiFi*, a light-weight engine designed for interactively composing modular processors and executing a dataflow on a single machine, as our base dataflow orchestration engine. NiFi's native data model is a *FlowFile*, which is an in-memory reference to a collection of bytes, which may be persisted to disk as one or more files, along with attributes describing it. We treat a FlowFile as a micro-batch, and provide *data model wrappers* to/from streams and files from FlowFiles.

Processors are user-defined Java logic that can access the attributes of a FlowFile, and its contents as a byte stream, and likewise generate new FlowFiles that are passed to downstream processors in the dataflow by the engine. NiFi offers limited support for distributed devices. Instances on different machines can pass FlowFiles between their processors by manually defining and wiring a *remote process group (RPG)*. RPGs can use HTTP or a binary protocol to push FlowFiles downstream or pull FlowFiles from upstream processors.

We extend NiFi in several ways to meet the listed desiderata. Our platform service uses the NiFi APIs to programmatically deploy and execute fragments of one or more dataflows in a single engine. Since the resource scheduler may map different processors in the dataflow to different resources, each NiFi engine may have only a subset of it. E.g., in Fig. 3, N_1, T_1 and S_1 are part of the same dataflow but placed in a Pi, a TX1 and a VM. We treat NiFi as a local orchestration container for multiple fragments. The deployer coordinates among different NiFi instances by automatically introducing RPGs at the edge-cut of the dataflow graph that span resources. While RPGs currently push FlowFiles downstream, knowledge of network restrictions can be used to decide if an upstream RPG is a client (push) or a server (pull) to the downstream RPG. This ambidirectionality allows the platform to even execute dataflows on resources behind firewalls.

We further introduce specialized *runtime wrapper processors*, as discussed in Sect. 3.2, for native support for external runtime engines. Specifically, we support Edgent for in-memory CEP, TensorFlow for deep learning models using CPU and GPGPU, and Spark and Storm for stream and batch processing of Big Data. While the Edgent processor operates within NiFi, TensorFlow is forked as a process on the local device from the processor. Both these also use data model wrappers, as shown in Fig. 2. The Storm and Spark processors also require support within the native dataflow. Specifically, we have source and sink tasks of the Storm or Spark dataflow interface with the RPGs of NiFi to transfer the FlowFiles between the different engines, with an optional data model wrapper. Users just provide the external engine's dataflow logic to our runtime wrapper processors, which then launches and interacts with it transparently.

Lastly, we provide first-class support for dynamic migration of the dataflows at execution time to adapt to external conditions. Dataflow *rebalancing* refers to the process of migrating running processors from the resources they are present in to different ones. While rebalance is explicitly triggered by the user now, it is possible to have the app manager periodically check the QoS of the application and pro-actively initiate this rebalancing. A user's call to the master to rebalance spawns a manager thread to query the current dataflow and mapping from the registry, and pass it to the scheduler to get an updated resource allocation. The manager then contacts the deployer with the old and the new mappings, which performs a graph "diff" to identify processors that need to be migrated. It then pauses the processors that are being migrated and their adjacent ones, migrates the relevant processors, introduces/removes RPGs at the new/old boundaries, and rewires the processors before resuming them. During this time, unpaused processors continue to execute, though inputs to paused processors will queue.

While rebalancing is an enabling feature, its effective use for meeting the performance requirements of IoT applications requires an intelligent scheduler, which is yet to be integrated [5]. Such a scheduling algorithm can make use of the current resource statistics in the registry and the application QoS to determine the new mapping that is required, while ECHO can transparently enact it.

4   Evaluation and Results

We evaluate the ECHO architecture and implementation for real-world IoT dataflows that support the Smart Community use-case we motivated earlier. We deploy ECHO on an *IoT testbed* at our Indian Institute of Science (IISc) campus in Bangalore with the following setup of local Edge and Fog devices within 2 network hops on the private network, complemented by Microsoft Azure VMs at 2 data centers. The Platform Master and Resource Directory services run on an exclusive DS1 VM each, while the rest are available for deploying applications.

Resource	Count	CPU/GPU	RAM	NIC	Location
Pi 3B Edge	10	900 MHz ARM A53 64 bit, 4 cores	1 GB	100 Mbps	IISc
Pi 2B Edge	2	900 MHz ARM A7 32 bit, 4 cores	1 GB	100 Mbps	IISc
TX1 Fog	1	1.75 GHz ARM A57 64 bit, 4 cores; Nvidia Maxwell, 256 CUDA cores	4 GB	1 Gbps	IISc
Softiron Fog	1	2 GHz AMD A1100 (ARM A57) 64 bit, 8 cores	16 GB	2×10 Gbps	IISc
DS1 v2 VM	4	2.4 GHz Intel Xeon E5 v3, 1 core	3.5 GB	2×1 Gbps	South India
NC6 VM	1	2.6 GHz Intel Xeon E5 v3, 6 cores; Nvidia K80, 4992 CUDA cores	56 GB	1 Gbps	US East

The three IoT application dataflows used in the validation are shown in Fig. 4 and summarized in the table below. These are based on real-world data processing and analytics for smart utility and traffic surveillance scenarios.

Dataflow	Input	Platforms	Data Model	Resources
ETL	NYC Taxi	NiFi, Edgent	μ-batch, Stream	Pi, VM$_{DS1}$, S'iron
YOLO	Pedestrian Video [13]	NiFi, T'Flow, Edgent	μ-batch, Stream, File	Pi, TX1, VM$_{NC6}$
STATS	NYC Taxi	NiFi, Storm	μ-batch, Stream	Pi, VM$_{DS1}$

The Extract Transform Load (*ETL*) dataflow performs data pre-processing and cleaning of sensor observation streams, such as smart grids and environmental sensing, before archiving then to Cloud storage [14]. It parses the input

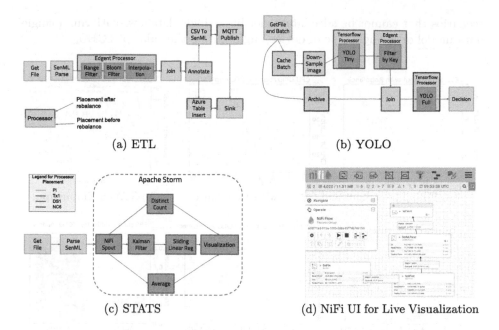

Fig. 4. Smart City dataflows used in evaluation

SenML micro-batch in NiFi, streams each observation to Edgent for filtering, outliers detection, and interpolation using its built-in CEP tasks, annotates it as micro-batches back in a NiFi processor before publishing to an MQTT pub-sub broker and to an Azure NoSQL table concurrently We run it on NY Taxi event streams [14]. The tasks initially run on 4 Pi devices, but are rebalanced and migrated mid-way to also use 2 Cloud VMs.

YOLO [15] is a deep convolutional neural network (CNN) for TensorFlow to classify pedestrians in frames of traffic videos. We use it for both pre and post processing, on edge with low latency and on Cloud with high accuracy. In our dataflow, video segments are in parallel archived on a Pi, and also downsampled to 416×416 px for efficient detection using a YOLO Tiny model on the TX1. YOLO returns a text label and bounding box, which are streamed as tuples to an Edgent processor to detect patterns of interest, say more than 5 people in a frame. Upon a match, we push the corresponding video frames at original resolution ($2.1 \times$ larger) to a Cloud GPU VM for accurate classification by a YOLO Full TensorFlow model. A match triggers an alert for further action.

Lastly, a statistical analytics dataflow (*STATS*) is an IoT application [14] that performs streaming analysis over events with high velocity. It concurrently does a Kalman filter smoothing and linear regression, windowed aggregation, and distinct count of sensors, which are then plotted and the images zipped for publishing online. These tasks are designed as a Storm topology that run on Cloud VMs, with a NiFi processor passing it event batches from the edge, and receiving the response. As we can see, these three dataflows capture real

406   P. Ravindra et al.

scenarios that cannot be adequately met by a single dataflow platform, a single
data model or a single type of device, highlighting the value of ECHO.

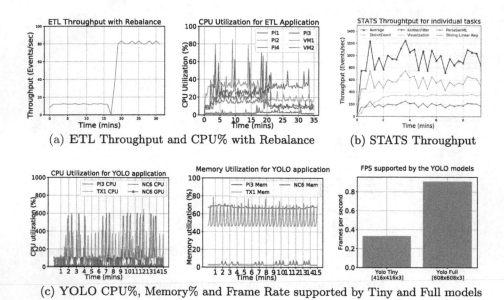

(a) ETL Throughput and CPU% with Rebalance   (b) STATS Throughput

(c) YOLO CPU%, Memory% and Frame Rate supported by Tiny and Full models

Fig. 5. Results for ETL, YOLO and STATS dataflows

Results. We deploy the dataflows on the IoT testbed devices and the VMs
using a custom scheduler, and offer representative samples of the performance
results upon running them continuously. Figure 5a shows the output event rate,
and CPU% on each active device for ETL across time. In the first half, we
schedule the processors only on Pi's but initiate a dynamic rebalance at the
mid-point to additionally use 2 VMs. As we see, the supported event rate jumps
from 15 events/sec to 80 events/sec, with a brief dip while the migration occurs.
We see a corresponding change in the CPU% as well, with the usage on Pi1
increasing as it is retained after rebalance while other Pi's dropping low, and
the VM usage marginally increasing. Despite having more cores, the Pi's have
3x slower clockspeeds, and hence offer limited throughput.

The batch behavior of YOLO clearly shows in its CPU% and Memory%
plots over time in Fig. 5c, with the spikes coinciding with a micro-batch or file
being processed by NiFi or TensorFlow. This happens across CPU, GPU, Pi,
TX1 and VM, but is more prominent on TX1 since it is the most stressed
resource when running the YOLO Tiny model. The frame-rate supported by
YOLO Tiny on TX1 is $\frac{1}{3}^{rd}$ that of Yolo Full on NC6, despite having $\frac{1}{2}$ the
image size. The NC6 VM has a much faster GPU and spare capacity, indicating
that a single GPU VM can service multiple video streams to complement the
Fog servers.

We report the throughput at each NiFi or Storm task in the STATS dataflow in Fig. 5b. We can see that the use of Storm helps support high input rates of over 1000 events/sec. The variation in rates is due to the selectivity of different tasks, that can produce more or fewer events than what they consume. The rates are also smoother than YOLO, reflecting the streaming data model used.

5   Related Work

The lack of middleware for IoT and edge-computing is well recognized [3,4,6,16], even as the growing deployment of such devices and applications use bespoke solutions. [7] offers a gap analysis of IoT platforms, several of which ECHO addresses including the use of Edge, Fog and Cloud resources, easing development of distributed dataflow applications, and automating the environment setup.

Open source projects like *Eclipse Kura* [8] offer a Java-based gateway management project for Linux edge devices that allows application deployment using OSGi containers. But it does not support dataflow composability within or across devices. *VMWare's Liota* [9] is a similar Python-based management stack with sensor, pub-sub and Cloud service bindings that can run local applications on a device. These complement ECHO's PaaS layer and can form the IaaS layer.

Cloud providers like Amazon AWS and Microsoft Azure have extended some of their Cloud features to tightly integrate with edge devices as well. *Amazon's GreenGrass* is an IoT SDK that allows users to deploy AWS Lambda functions on edge devices, and use MQTT for coordination. They also offer bindings with AWS Cloud services like S3 and DynamoDB. *Azure IoT Edge* has a similar goal. In both cases, the SDK offer some programming and management capabilities on the edge but push analytics to their Cloud services. Composability, support for external Edge runtimes, hybrid data model, etc. are non-goals.

Apache Edgent as we saw offers a CEP platform for Edge devices. This is designed as a stand-alone embedded library rather than for composable dataflows. *Node.RED* is similar to NiFi in providing interactive dataflow composition across devices using a Node.js server. But its features are restricted, supporting only JavaScript tasks, although it is more light-weight. *MiNiFi* is a light flavor of NiFi that supports C++ and embedded platforms, but trims many of NiFi's features like online deployment and dynamic migration ability.

IoT Middleware is an active research area as well. The *MiMove project* [16] has proposed an SOA architecture for mobile IoT, with a focus on the functional scalability. A novel probablistic registry allow low-latency approximate queries for registered sensing and actuation services. It does static scheduling of streaming service dataflows using the Dioptase middleware [17], and interfacing across heterogeneous IoT protocols using an Enterprise Service Bus (ESB). ECHO in contrast supports hybrid data models – a higher level abstraction than protocols, richer composition including delegating to external engines, and point-to-point push/pull task communication rather than a central ESB. Advanced scheduling algorithms [5] or device mobility is not a focus in our paper, but future work.

[18] has proposed a programming model for composing IoT applications across mobile, Fog and Cloud layers. They consider a multi-way 3-level dataflow model with computation starting in the Cloud, elastic resources acquired in the Cloud and Fog, and communication possible between all 3 layers. Each edge has one Fog parent based on spatial proximity, that may be reassigned. While a useful abstraction, their strictly hierarchical resource and dataflow model are much more restrictive that our use of any network topology and a directed graph as dataflow. Theirs effectively degenerates to a client-server model.

Mobile Clouds are precursors to IoT where mobile phones off-load applications to Cloud resources. In [19], mobile data stream applications are dynamically partitioned for computation across mobile devices and Cloud. They propose a genetic algorithm for the partitioning to maximize throughput and adapt to changing devices load. They are limited to mobile data stream applications rather than dataflow or hybrid data models We also support Fog resources, native runtime engines and dynamic migration of tasks among the resources. The Hybrid Mobile Edge Computing (HMEC) architecture [20] uses edge devices for mobile applications. They use a peer-to-peer (P2P) approach of both proximate and distant edge devices, and perform *method-based offloading* to improve performance and reduce energy usage. Similarly, [21] offloads tasks to the Cloud using RPC with static analysis and dynamic profiling of mobile applications. It maintains a complete device clone in the Cloud, which can be costly. These are designed for monolithic existing mobile applications rather than *ad hoc* dataflow composition, and neither consider a service paradigm or Fog servers.

P2P frameworks like Seti@home [22] have targeted the use of idle compute capacity in desktops. However, some of the inherent P2P characteristics are missing in an IoT scenario. Device churn is a major factor in P2P but less so for infrastructure IoT, or even mobile devices that are typically within cell communication. This, coupled with the growth of global Cloud data centers, make it feasible for centralized services for coordination.

6   Conclusions

In this paper, we motivate the gaps and propose the requirements for a middleware platform to compose and orchestrate dataflows across Edge, Fog and Cloud resources for IoT applications. Our ECHO platform addresses these design requirements, including novel features such as *dataflow composition*; use of *hybrid data models* like streams, micro-batch and files; inherent support for *external runtime engines* like Edgent, Tensorflow, Storm and Spark; and dynamic migration of tasks across distributed resources for *adaptivity*. ECHO also offers native dataflow orchestration using NiFi, a standards-compliant registry, and containerization for light-weight resource sharing.

We map three real-world IoT applications to ECHO to exercise these features, and ease the composition of distributed dataflows across Edge, Fog and Cloud. Besides meeting the qualitative requirements we identified, the performance results also illustrate the potential benefits of interfacing with external platforms, and smart rebalancing to adapt to dynamism to meet the application QoS.

This paper addresses the highlighted gaps, but much more remains in this emerging area. Using a more decentralized decision making for deployment and scheduling rather than in a single Master may help scale to millions of devices, and the Fog can play a role here. Scalable federated catalogs will be essential to include dynamic data sources and device state updates in the registry. NiFi's inherent support for provenance collection can also be leveraged for auditing, billing and tracking of data. Adaptive scheduling algorithms, migration of stateful tasks, consistently guarantees and fault tolerance also need careful study.

Acknowledgments. The authors would like to thank Microsoft Azure and NVIDIA for resource access, and VMWare for their technical feedback. We would also like to thank Venkatesh Babu and Avishek from the VAL lab at IISc for their inputs on YOLO.

References

1. Simmhan, Y., Aman, S., Kumbhare, A., Liu, R., Stevens, S., Zhou, Q., Prasanna, V.: Cloud-based software platform for big data analytics in smart grids. IEEE/AIP Comput. Sci. Eng. (2013)
2. Amrutur, B., Rajaraman, V., Acharya, S., Ramesh, R., Joglekar, A., Sharma, A., Simmhan, Y., Lele, A., Mahesh, A., Sankaran, S.: An open smart city IoT test bed: street light poles as smart city spines. In: ACM/IEEE International Conference on Internet of Things Design and Implementation (2017)
3. Simmhan, Y.: IoT analytics across edge and cloud platforms. IEEE IoT Newsl., May 2017
4. Garcia Lopez, P., Montresor, A., Epema, D., Datta, A., Higashino, T., Iamnitchi, A., Barcellos, M., Felber, P., Riviere, E.: Edge-centric computing: vision and challenges. ACM Comput. Comm. Rev. (2015)
5. Ghosh, R., Simmhan, Y.: Distributed scheduling of event analytics across edge and cloud, CoRR, no. 1608.01537 (2016)
6. Varshney, P., Simmhan, Y.: Demystifying fog computing: Characterizing architectures, applications and abstractions. In: IEEE International Conference on Fog and Edge Computing (2017)
7. Mineraud, J., Mazhelis, O., Su, X., Tarkoma, S.: A gap analysis of internet-of-things platforms. Comput. Commun. **89**, 5–16 (2016)
8. Eclipse Kura, http://www.eclipse.org/kura/. Accessed 21 June 2017
9. VMware Liota, https://github.com/vmware/liota. Accessed 21 June 2017
10. Apache Edgent, v1.1.0, http://edgent.apache.org/. Accessed 21 June 2017
11. Abadi, M., et al.: Tensorflow: large-scale machine learning on heterogeneous distributed systems. In: USENIX Symposium on Operating Systems Design and Implementation (2016)
12. Beart, P.: Automatic resource discovery for the internet of things - specification, The British Standards Institution. Tech. Rep. PAS 212:2016 (2016)
13. Ess, A., Leibe, B., Schindler, K., van Gool, L.: A mobile vision system for robust multi-person tracking. In: IEEE Conference on Computer Vision and Pattern Recognition (2008)

14. Shukla, A., Chaturvedi, S., Simmhan, Y.: RIoTBench: a real-time IoT benchmark for distributed stream processing platforms, CoRR, no. 1701.08530 (2017)
15. Redmon, J., Farhadi, A.: YOLO9000: better, faster, stronger, CoRR, no. 1612.08242 (2016)
16. Georgantas, N., Billet, B.: Revisiting service-oriented architecture for the IoT: a middleware perspective. In: International Conference on Service Oriented Computing (2016)
17. Billet, B., Issarny, V.: From task graphs to concrete actions: a new task mapping algorithm for the future internet of things. In: IEEE International Conference on Mobile Ad Hoc Sensor Systems (2014)
18. Hong, K., Lillethun, D., Ramachandran, U., Ottenwälder, B., Koldehofe, B.: Mobile fog: a programming model for large-scale applications on the internet of things. In: ACM SIGCOMM Workshop on Mobile Cloud Computing (2013)
19. Yang, L., Cao, J., Yuan, Y., Li, T., Han, A., Chan, A.: A framework for partitioning and execution of data stream applications in mobile cloud computing. ACM SIGMETRICS Performance Eval. Rev. 40(4) (2013)
20. Reiter, A., Prünster, B., Zefferer, T.: Hybrid mobile edge computing: Unleashing the full potential of edge computing in mobile device use cases. In: IEEE/ACM International Symposium on Cluster, Cloud and Grid Computing (CCGrid) (2017)
21. Chun, B.-G., Ihm, S., Maniatis, P., Naik, M., Patti, A.: Clonecloud: elastic execution between mobile device and cloud. In: Conference on Computer Systems (2011)
22. Anderson, D.P., Cobb, J., Korpela, E., Lebofsky, M., Werthimer, D.: Seti@ home: an experiment in public-resource computing. CACM 45(11) (2002)

Ensuring and Assessing Architecture Conformance to Microservice Decomposition Patterns

Uwe Zdun[1(✉)], Elena Navarro[2], and Frank Leymann[3]

[1] Faculty of Computer Science, Research Group Software Architecture,
University of Vienna, Vienna, Austria
uwe.zdun@univie.ac.at
[2] Computing Systems Department, Laboratory of User Interaction and Software
Engineering, University of Castilla-La Mancha, Albacete, Spain
elena.navarro@uclm.es
[3] Institute of Architecture of Application Systems, University of Stuttgart,
Stuttgart, Germany
frank.leymann@iaas.uni-stuttgart.de

Abstract. Microservice-based software architecture design has been widely discussed, and best practices have been published as architecture design patterns. However, conformance to those patterns is hard to ensure and assess automatically, leading to problems such as architectural drift and erosion, especially in the context of continued software evolution or large-scale microservice systems. In addition, not much in the component and connector architecture models is specific (only) to the microservices approach, whereas other aspects really specific to that approach, such as independent deployment of microservices, are usually modeled in other views or not at all. We suggest a set of constraints to check and metrics to assess architecture conformance to microservice patterns. In comparison to expert judgment derived from the patterns, a subset of these constraints and metrics shows a good relative performance and potential for automation.

1 Introduction

Many approaches have been proposed for service-based architecture decomposition (see e.g. [16,19,21,28]). An approach which evolved from established best practices are *microservices*, as Newman [15] points out: "The microservices approach has emerged from real-world use, taking our better understanding of systems and architecture to do SOA well." Lewis and Fowler [14] describe microservices as "an approach to developing a single application as a suite of small services, each running in its own process and communicating with lightweight mechanisms, often an HTTP resource API. These services are built around business capabilities and independently deployable by fully automated deployment machinery." More detailed discussions can be found in [18,27].

© Springer International Publishing AG 2017
M. Maximilien et al. (Eds.): ICSOC 2017, LNCS 10601, pp. 411–429, 2017.
https://doi.org/10.1007/978-3-319-69035-3_29

This paper focuses on architecture decomposition based on the microservices approach. Many required decisions about how to perform the major architecture decomposition into microservices have already been described in form of architectural design patterns [21]. However, those and related patterns can lead to architecture designs in many different variants and combinations of pattern-based design options, making it hard to automatically or semi-automatically judge questions such as: When designing a microservice architecture, how much did a project deviate from the established best practices? After evolving a microservice architecture, are we still in conformance with the chosen microservice patterns? When moving from a monolithic architecture to a microservice architecture, how big is the gap to a microservice-based design?

For checking or assessing such questions related to pattern conformance of the microservice architecture, a high level of automation would be very useful. While it is possible to judge these questions for a small scale architecture manually, in practice it is rarely done in each architecture evolution step, leading to architectural drift and erosion [20]. For larger scale projects, manual assessment is more difficult. For instance, consider the work of an integration architect judging pattern conformance in hundreds of microservices. Here, manual assessment can only work in a cost-effective way, if every team is very disciplined and assesses their own conformance in each evolution step. Further, without automation, at a larger scale with many different stakeholders, judging pattern conformance objectively and uniformly across teams and stakeholders is difficult. These points have led us to address the following research questions:

RQ1: Which measures can be defined to automatically check or assess pattern conformance in microservice decomposition architectures?

RQ2: How well do such measures perform in relation to expert judgment?

RQ3: Given that many defining aspects of microservices (like independent deployment) are modeled outside of a microservice decomposition architectures, what is a set of minimal elements needed in a microservice decomposition architecture to compute meaningful measures?

Our major contributions are the following. Based on existing microservice patterns [21] we have hypothesized a number of constraints and metrics to make an automated judgment on microservice architecture decomposition. To evaluate those constraints and metrics, we have modeled 13 architecture models taken from the practitioner literature and assessed each of them manually regarding its quality and violations of microservice patterns (following as closely as possible the expert judgment of the pattern authors). We have then compared the results in depth and statistically over the whole evaluation model set. Our results are: A subset of the constraints and metrics are quite close to the pattern-based assessment based on the expert judgment taken from the patterns. We identified only a few necessary modeling elements in microservice decomposition architectures, meaning that they are rather easy to create semi-automatically (e.g. using the approach from [6]). Moreover, in those models not much is (only) specific to microservices so that there is still room for improvement. Such further improvement would require detailed modeling of the microservices and thus more manual effort.

This paper is organized as follows. Section 2 compares to related work. Next, we discuss a minimal formal model for microservice-based architecture decomposition in Sect. 3. Section 4 introduces our suggested microservice design constraints and metrics, and Sect. 5 evaluates them for 13 models from practice. Section 6 discusses the RQs regarding the evaluation results, analyses the threats to validity, and concludes.

2   Related Work

Many studies currently study microservice-based architectures in the context of DevOps or container-technologies like Docker (see e.g. [3,8,9]). In addition, quite a number of studies analyse the application of microservices in various application domains such as data centers [12], digital archives [10], or Web apps [25], to name but a few. A recent mapping study [1] confirms that the major interests in these and other studies are mostly the concrete system architectures often in relation to deployment, cloud, monitoring, performance, APIs, scalability, and container-technologies. That is, these studies are related to ours, so far, as their architectures are potential targets for our approach. The additional aspects that are studied in those approaches (like performance, scalability, or deployment aspects) are potential extensions of our approach, as possible future work.

First engineering approaches, specific to microservices are emerging. We have based our work on the microservice patterns by Richardson [21]. For instance, the *API Gateway* pattern is beneficial in a *Microservice Architecture*, but not a must. This pattern proposes "a single entry point for all clients." A variant of *API Gateway* is the *Backend for Frontend* pattern that "defines a separate *API Gateway* for each kind of client." With regard to data stores, the recommended pattern is *Database per Service*, i.e., "an architecture which keeps each microservice's persistent data private to that service and accessible only via its API." Loosely coupled interaction is usually the only intended way how microservices should communicate with each other. This is typically achieved using event-driven communication or messaging [7], in both cases with focus on an eventually consistent approach for communication of data-related operations.

Another set of microservice patterns has been published by Gupta [5], general best practices are discussed in [14], and other similar approaches are summarized in another recent mapping study [16]. So far, however, no automated software engineering tools have been proposed for microservice decomposition in the literature. Engineering approaches rather focus on aspects like support for modeling and composition [11] or migration from monolithic architectures [13]. Related general service design methods focus e.g. on QoS-aware service composition [22] or the involved architecture decisions [28]. While much of the work on service metrics is focused on runtime properties like QoS, some specific design metrics for Web services have been proposed, e.g. focusing on loose coupling [19].

To the best of our knowledge, no general conformance approach for architecture decomposition of microservices – or services in general – exists so far.

Software architecture conformance checking is often based on automated extraction techniques, which could be used as a basis for our approach as well (here following [6]), e.g. using architecture reconstruction approaches [4,24]. Such approaches often can check conformance to architecture patterns [4,6] or other kinds of architectural rules [24]. Other static architecture conformance checking techniques are: dependency-structure matrices, source code query languages, and reflexion models [17]. In such approaches often general software engineering metrics like complexity metrics play a role [17]. Our approach follows the same general strategy like those approaches, but in contrast we focus on specific constraints (or more generally, architecture rules) and metrics derived from microservices best practices – not applicable in a general context, but at the same time more powerful in our specific microservice (or service) context.

3   Modeling Microservice-Based Architecture Decomposition

Figure 1 shows a simple sample microservice decomposition model, as they are modeled in practice (see e.g. [21]). It uses UML2 component model notation with one extension: a *Directed Connector* is modeled using a directed arrow (not part of UML2). Not much in such a model is (only) specific to microservices, but at the same time many aspects may be modeled in a way which is violating some parts of the microservice patterns. This might lead to severe problems in other views of the architecture or system, such as logical, detailed design or deployment views. For instance, a decomposition that would hinder independent deployment, uses many shared dependencies and is mainly based on strongly coupled connectors, so that it would not be following the microservice best practices well.

From an abstract point of view, a microservice-based architecture decomposition is a decomposition into a directed components and connectors graph with a set of component types for each component and a set of connector types for each connector, formally: An architecture decomposition model M is a tuple $(CP, CN, CPT, CNT, cp\_directtype, cn\_directtype, cp\_supertype, cn\_supertype, cp\_type, cn\_type)$ where:

- CP is a finite set of **component nodes**.
- $CN \subseteq CP \times CP$ is an ordered finite set of **connector edges**.
- CPT is a set of **component types**.
- CNT is a set of **connector types**.
- $cp\_directtype : CP \rightarrow \mathbb{P}(CPT)$ is a function that maps each component node cp to its set of **direct component types**,

– $cp\_supertype : CPT \to \mathbb{P}(CPT)$ is a function called **component type hierarchy**. $cp\_supertype(cpt)$ is the set of direct supertypes of cpt; cpt is called the subtype of those supertypes. The transitive closure[1] $cp\_supertype^*$ defines the inheritance in the hierarchy such that $cp\_supertype^*(cpt)$ contains the **direct and indirect (aka transitive) supertypes** of cpt. The inheritance hierarchy is cycle free, i.e. $\forall cpt \in CPT : cp\_supertype^*(cpt) \cap \{cpt\} = \emptyset$.

– $cp\_type : CP \to \mathbb{P}(CPT)$ is a function that maps each component to its set of **direct and transitive component types**, i.e., $\forall cp \in CP, dt \in CPT : dt = cp\_directtype(cp) \Rightarrow cp\_type(cp) = dt \cup cp\_supertype^*(dt)$.

– $cn\_directtype : CN \to \mathbb{P}(CNT)$ is a function that maps each connector cn to its set of **direct connector types**.

– $cn\_supertype : CNT \to \mathbb{P}(CNT)$ is a function called **connector type hierarchy**. $cn\_supertype(cnt)$ is the set of direct supertypes of cnt; cnt is called the subtype of those supertypes. The transitive closure $cn\_supertype^*$ defines the inheritance in the hierarchy such that $cn\_supertype^*(cnt)$ contains the **direct and indirect (aka transitive) supertypes** of cnt. The inheritance hierarchy is cycle free, i.e. $\forall cnt \in CNT : cn\_supertype^*(cnt) \cap \{cnt\} = \emptyset$.

– $cn\_type : CN \to \mathbb{P}(CNT)$ is a function that maps each connector to its set of **direct and transitive connector types**, i.e., $\forall cn \in CN, dt \in CNT : dt = cn\_directtype(cn) \Rightarrow cn\_type(cn) = dt \cup cn\_supertype^*(dt)$.

With this definition, we can rephrase **RQ3** to the question: Which elements of CPT and CNT and which type hierarchy dependencies of those are actually needed in order to compute meaningful constraints and metrics?

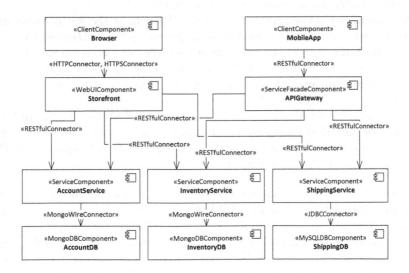

Fig. 1. Sample microservice architecture decomposition model (adapted from [21])

---

[1] All transitive closures in this article are assumed to be calculated with a standard algorithm for transitive closures like Warshall's algorithm.

4   Microservice Design Constraints and Metrics

4.1   Constraints and Metrics Based on Independent Deployment

As microservices are emphasized to be independent units of deployment, one hypothesis we have developed was that a good indicator for microservice-based decomposition could be to check whether *all components are independently deployable or to what degree they are independently deployable*. From the viewpoint of an architecture decomposition model, independently deployable means that no components that are part of a microservice have in-memory connectors (or subclasses thereof or similar strongly coupled connectors) to other components that are part of that microservice. In particular, we do not consider external components, as they are not part of a microservice. Finally, microservice should contain components at the same level of abstraction connected only via loosely coupled interfaces. More formally, we assume there is a supertype of all in-memory connectors (and similar strongly coupled connectors) $InMemoryConnector \in CNT$ and a supertype of all external components $ExternalComponent \in CPT$ (with a subtype $ClientComponent$, i.e. $ExternalComponent \in cp\_supertype^*(ClientComponent)$).

- The function $imc : CP \rightarrow \mathbb{P}(CP)$ maps a component to the set of components that are directly connected to the component via connectors typed as $InMemoryConnector$. We call $imc(cp)$ the **direct in-memory cluster** of a component cp with $\forall cp \in CP : imc(cp) = \{co \in CP \mid \exists cn \in CN : cn = (cp, co) \land InMemoryConnector \in cn\_type(cn)\}$.
- The transitive closure $imc^* : CP \rightarrow \mathbb{P}(CP)$ defines the set of components directly and indirectly connected to a component cp via $InMemoryConnector$ edges. We call $imc^*(cp)$ the **in-memory cluster** of a component cp.
- The function $idcc : CP \rightarrow \mathbb{P}(CP)$ maps a component to its **independently deployable component cluster** such that $\forall cp \in CP : idcc(cp) = \{co \in (\{cp\} \cup imc^*(cp)) \mid ExternalComponent \notin cp\_type(co)\}$.
- The function $idccs : M \rightarrow \mathbb{P}(\mathbb{P}(CP_m))$ maps a model to the set of its **independently deployable component clusters** (i.e., a set of component clusters (CPS) computed with the function $idcc$): $\forall m \in M : idccs(m) = \{CPS \in \mathbb{P}(CP_m) \mid \forall cp \in CP_m : idcc(cp) \in CPS\}^2$.

Based on these definitions we can define the constraint **all components are independently deployable (CAID)**, $CAID : M \rightarrow Boolean$, using the formula below, which computes all independently deployable component clusters CPS in a model m and checks for all CPS that their size is less or equal to 1 using the aggregate function $\mathcal{F}_{count}$. Here, we use the standard aggregate function from relational algebra which counts the number of elements in the collection to compute the size, i.e., it has the same semantics as in SQL. Regarding CAID,

---

[2] We use the notation 'CP_m', 'CN_m' etc. in formulas taking models as input to denote the tuple of elements of the model m; in formulas considering any model, like the previous ones, we omit notation for brevity.

the boolean value 0 means false, i.e. a constraint violation, and 1 means true, i.e. that the constraint is not violated:

$$\forall m \in M : CAID(m) = \begin{cases} 1 \text{ if: } \forall CPS \in idccs(m) : \mathcal{F}_{count}(CPS) \leq 1 \\ 0 \text{ if: } \forall CPS \in idccs(m) : \mathcal{F}_{count}(CPS) > 1 \end{cases}$$

Our implementation of the constraint additionally computes the clusters that have failed to provide precise failure information to the user. Additionally, there is a function for computing the **components violating independent deployability**, $cvid : M \to \mathbb{P}(CP)$, which simply executes the $CAID$ constraint, and returns an empty set if it is not violated, otherwise all components in the violating clusters. We suggest two metrics that can be derived from this constraint and its underlying functions:

- **Ratio of components violating independent deployability to non-external components (RVID)** is based on the constraint CAID. It uses the function $cvid$ to execute the constraint, and returns the number of violating components or an empty set in case of no violation. Then $RVID$ sets their number in ratio to the total number of non-external components. $nec : M \to \mathbb{P}(CP)$ is a helper function returning all components in a model that are not of type *ExternalComponent* (**non-external components**). Here, and in a number of the following metrics counting unique non-external components, we set the component counts in ratio to the model size in terms non-external components, which – compared to the component counts themselves – scales the metric to the interval $[0, 1]$. This, thus, makes metric results for different models more comparable. $RVID : M \to \mathbb{R}$ is defined as follows:

$$\forall m \in M : RVID(m) = \frac{\mathcal{F}_{count}(cvid(m))}{\mathcal{F}_{count}(nec(m))}$$

- **Ratio of independently deployable component clusters to non-external components (RIDC)**, $RIDC : M \to \mathbb{R}$, sets the number of independently deployable component clusters in ratio to the size of the model (in terms of non-external components):

$$\forall m \in M : RIDC(m) = \frac{\mathcal{F}_{count}(idccs(m))}{\mathcal{F}_{count}(nec(m))}$$

4.2 Constraints and Metrics Based on Shared Dependencies

Many of the microservice patterns [21] (for a short summary see Sect. 2) focus on decompositions which *avoid sharing other components or sharing them in a strongly coupled fashion*. Hence, another major idea for constraints and metrics was to base them on the notion of shared components, sharing components, and shared dependencies in the architecture decomposition. With regard to constraints we have envisioned three basic types of constraints: *no shared components* which checks whether there is no shared component; *no sharing components* which checks whether there is no sharing component; *no shared dependencies* which checks whether there is no shared dependency of two components.

As typically different clients can share a microservice, and microservices can themselves share third-party microservices, all external components need to be excluded from these constraints (and metrics). All three constraints are based on the same algorithm for finding the set of shared dependencies of each component in the model, requiring the following functions for this:

- $acd : CP \rightarrow \mathbb{P}(CP)$ is a function which calculates **all direct component dependencies** of a component. That is, $acd(cp)$ is defined formally as: $\forall cp \in CP : acd(cp) = \{cd \in CP \,|\, \exists cn \in CN : cn = (cp, cd)\}$. The transitive closure acd^* defines **all direct and indirect component dependencies** of a component cp.
- $ascd : M \rightarrow \mathbb{P}(CP_m \times (CP_m \times CP_m))$ is a function which maps a model $m \in M$ to a set of tuples containing a component $cp \in CP_m$ and the set of **all shared component dependencies** of that component cp (excluding external components). Each of these shared component dependencies is itself a tuple (oc, sd) being $oc \in CP_m$ the other component with which cp shares a dependency and $sd \in CP_m$ the component which is shared both by oc and cp, expressed formally: $\forall m \in M : ascd(m) = \{(cp, (oc, sd)) \,|\, cp, oc, sd \in CP_m \wedge sd \in acd(cp) \wedge sd \in acd(oc) \wedge ExternalComponent \notin cp\_type(cp) \wedge ExternalComponent \notin cp\_type(oc) \wedge ExternalComponent \notin cp\_type(sd)\}$.
- $sic : M \rightarrow \mathbb{P}(CP_m)$ is a function that provides the set of all **sharing non-external components**, formally defined as: $\forall m \in M : sic(m) = \{cp \in CP_m \,|\, \exists oc, sd CP_m : (cp, (oc, sd)) \in ascd(m)\}$.
- $sdc : M \rightarrow \mathbb{P}(CP_m)$ is a function that provides the set of all **shared non-external components**, formally defined as: $\forall m \in M : sdc(m) = \{sd \in CP_m \,|\, \exists oc, cp CP_m : (cp, (oc, sd)) \in ascd(m)\}$.

The closer study of the three types of constraints revealed that they lead to exactly the same violations: as a shared dependency leads to a sharing and a shared component, either all these constraints are violated or none of them. For this reason, it is enough for us to formally define and study one of those constraints. Here, we define the constraint **no shared non-external component dependencies (NSCD)**, $NSCD : M \rightarrow Boolean$, as ($0$ = false, i.e. a constraint violation, and 1 = true, i.e. no constraint violation):

$$\forall m \in M : NSCD(m) = \begin{cases} 1 \text{ if: } \forall SD \in ascd(m) : \mathcal{F}_{count}(SD) = 0 \\ 0 \text{ if: } \forall SD \in ascd(m) : \mathcal{F}_{count}(SD) > 0 \end{cases}$$

Further for this constraint (and all related metrics) below, we suggest – in addition to the basic constraint – three variants.

- *NSCD-F* excludes *Facade* components from the constraint. Many microservice models (as well as monolithic models) contain *Facades*, such as an *APIGateway* in Fig. 1, as an acceptable way to share microservice components [2]. We thus assume a class $Facade \in CPT$ with classes like *APIGateway* as its subclasses (thus also $\in CPT$ through e.g. $Facade \in cp\_supertype^*(APIGateway)$) and so on. At first we envisioned to automatically compute which components are *Facades*, but unfortunately this design intent is impossible to compute in an unambiguous way. For instance, our evaluation model RB (see Table 1) contains microservices that are directly connected to clients, and, without further information, there is no way to automatically distinguish those from a model in which only *Facades* are modeled. For this reason, all *-F* variants of constraints and metrics require *Facades* to be explicitly modeled. The rationale behind the *-F* variants is: If *Facades* are modeled, we hypothesize that excluding them from the constraints and metrics could lead to a better identification of real issues with regard to shared dependencies. For space reasons, we omit the formal definition here, as it is analogous to the functions/constraints defined above, just excluding *Facades* in the functions.

- *NSCD-C* excludes loosely coupled connectors (event-driven, publish/subscribe style interaction, and message queuing) from further investigation. We assume a class *LooselyCoupledConnector* $\in CNT$ with subclasses such as *EventBased-Connector, PubSubConnector, MessagingConnector* (all also $\in CNT$, using *cn_supertype** relations). That is, only strongly coupled connectors can lead in *-C* variants of constraints and metrics to constraint violations or lower metrics values. As the patterns suggest to use only loosely coupled interaction in event-driven, publish/subscribe style between microservices, we hypothesize that excluding them from the constraints and metrics could lead to a better identification of a real issue with regard to shared dependencies. We expect that the exclusion of loosely coupled connectors makes the results more comparable for different models in the sense that in this way the same model, modeled at different levels of detail, leads to the same metric values and constraint violations. For space reasons, we omit the formal definition here, as it is analogous to the functions/constraints defined above, just excluding *LooselyCoupledConnectors* in the functions.
- *NSCD-FC* is the combination of *NSCD-F* and *NSCD-C*.

All metrics below are defined analogously in a basic version plus three variants. Here, however, the differences between shared components, sharing components, and shared dependencies play a major role, and it is interesting to study which of those basic counts is better suited as a foundation for a shared dependency metric. Firstly, we define the **ratio of sharing non-external components to non-external components (RSIC)**, $RSIC : M \to \mathbb{R}$, based on the count of components returned by the functions *sic* (defined above) set in relation to the non-external components count (based on *nec*) as:

$$\forall m \in M : RSIC(m) = \frac{\mathcal{F}_{count}(sic(m))}{\mathcal{F}_{count}(nec(m))}$$

Secondly, we define the **ratio of shared non-external components to non-external components (RSCC)**, $RSCC : M \to \mathbb{R}$, based on functions *sdc* and *nec*:

$$\forall m \in M : RSCC(m) = \frac{\mathcal{F}_{count}(sdc(m))}{\mathcal{F}_{count}(nec(m))}$$

Finally, we suggest a metric **ratio of shared dependencies of non-external components to possible dependencies (RSDP)**, $RSDP : M \rightarrow \mathbb{R}$ based directly on the number of shared dependencies returned by the function *ascd*. Here we scale the metric using the number of all possible dependencies (i.e., the number of counted components squared). As this value has no specific meaning in the context of our model, we have also compared other scalings in our evaluation like no scaling, the model size in terms components, and all component dependencies. We have chosen only the scaling based on all possible dependencies here, as all other metrics perform weaker in our evaluation, and at the same time none of the other options scales the metric to the normed interval $[0, 1]$. As a result, we suggest the metric:

$$\forall m \in M : RSDP(m) = \frac{\mathcal{F}_{count}(ascd(m))}{(\mathcal{F}_{count}(nec(m)))^2}$$

All metrics, defined in this section, also have *-F, *-C, and *-FC variants, with analogous reasoning to the discussion for *NSCD*. The differences in formal definition to the base variants are the following: The metrics must use adapted versions of the functions, analogously to the *NSCD* variants, and the function *nec* in the divisor of the metrics should be adapted to not consider *Facades* for the two *-F and *-FC variants, as scaling should be done according to the considered components.

5   Evaluation

For performing our evaluation, we have fully implemented our formal model, constraints, metrics, and related algorithms using the Frag Modeling Framework (FMF), a runtime modeling, domain-specific language and generator framework implemented on top of Java/Eclipse which enables us to easier change design decisions made and perform experimentation than in comparable frameworks like the Eclipse Modeling Framework (EMF) (see [26] for more details). Besides extensive test cases, a code generator to generate R scripts has been implemented, used to perform statistical comparison of achieved and expected results for the different constraints and metrics. In addition, we have fully modeled and implemented 13 models in an evaluation model set, summarized in Table 1. Each of the models is either taken directly from a model published by practitioners or adapted according to discussions on the respective referenced Web sites. While the models taken from 4 independent sources[3] are still examples, they all

---

[3] We have adapted Models EC1-8 from [21]. Model RB is adapted from: http://eventuate.io/exampleapps.html. The Models TH1-TH3 are adapted from: https://www.nginx.com/blog/introduction-to-microservices/. Model SA is adapted from: https://www.slideshare.net/smancke/fros-con2014-microservicesarchitecture. For all models, we aimed to stay close to the original model; adaptation mainly means modeling them using our approach to architecture decomposition modeling and in the model variants introducing the described variations.

Table 1. Summary of models used for evaluation and manual assessment of pattern compliance

ID	Size	Short description	Major violations of patterns	VMP	MQ
EC1	10 comp., 11 conn.	E-Commerce model with 3 independent microservices, an API gateway, a Web UI, databases per service, inter-service communication not modeled	None	0	1.0
EC2	13 comp., 19 conn.	Similar to EC1; additionally 1 service consists of 4 components which are realizing different business capabilities	A service contains different subdomains/capabilities or is not modeled at the same abstraction level	1	0.6
EC3	11 comp., 17 conn.	Similar to EC1; additionally models inter-service communication using the Event Sourcing pattern	None	0	1.0
EC4	11 comp., 17 conn.	Similar to EC1; additionally models inter-service communication using the Transaction Log Trailing (or Database Trigger) pattern	None	0	1.0
EC5	8 comp., 11 conn.	Similar to EC1; with only one database, which is shared among the microservices	Shared database	1	0.6
EC6	8 comp., 11 conn.	Same components as in EC1 but all in one shared address space, shared database, API gateway, Web UI	No decomposition into multiple services (all other violations are secondary)	1	0.0
EC7	8 comp., 14 conn.	Similar to EC6; with all in-memory component dependencies explicitly modeled	No decomposition into multiple services (all other violations are secondary)	1	0.0
EC8	11 comp., 19 conn.	Similar to EC2; with only one database, which is shared among the microservices	A service contains different subdomains/capabilities or is not modeled at the same abstraction level; shared database	1	0.4
RB	4 comp., 3 conn.	Single service for restaurant booking, no clients modeled, follows CQRS pattern, uses REDIS for fast denormalized querying	None	0	1.0
TH1	18 comp., 17 conn.	Taxi hailing application: 3 microservices with a layer of 3 backend services in addition to 3 databases per service, shared payment component	Shared, strongly coupled component	1	0.6
TH2	18 comp., 17 conn.	Same as TH1, avoids shared component using loosely coupled connectors	None	0	1.0
TH3	15 comp., 19 conn.	Same components as in TH1 but all in one shared address space, 1 shared database, 1 API gateway, 1 Web UI	No decomposition into multiple services (all other violations are secondary)	1	0.0
SA	15 comp., 19 conn.	Web shop app with 7 services, 5 different data stores, 2 modular Web UIs	None	0	1.0

originate from models developed by practitioners with microservice and monolith implementation experience. Hence, we assume that our evaluation models are close to models used in practice and real practical needs for microservice decomposition (compared e.g. to models created solely by ourselves).

The table also shows our manual, pattern-based assessment of the architecture conformance of each of the models. There are two assessments: *Does the model violate at least one of the microservice patterns (from* [21])*?* We carefully assessed each model for major violations of the patterns. If at least one occurs, we marked it in column Violations of Microservice Patterns (*VMP*) of Table 1 as *true* = 1, otherwise as *false* = 0. In addition, we tried to objectively measure the quality of the model with regard to conformance to the microservice patterns [21]. For this, we use the following rules to compute the Microservice Architecture Quality (Column *MQ* in Table 1) based on a detailed manual inspection of the compliance of the models to the architecture patterns:

- If the *Microservice Architecture* pattern cannot be found at all, that is, the architecture clearly follows a *Monolithic Architecture*, we set *MQ = 0*.
- Otherwise we set *MQ = 1*, and then if one of the violations listed below (each one can occur multiple times) is found, we reduce *MQ* by 0.4 on the first occurrence, by another 0.2 on the second occurrence (of the same or another pattern), another 0.1 on the third occurrence, and so on. Thus, the violation penalty is divided by factor 2 from one violation occurrence to the next because if such a minor violation occurs, the model should not be better rated than 0.6. But even if multiple minor violations happen, the rating should still stay better than the monolithic score of 0. The violations analyzed are the following: (1) A minor violation of the *Microservice Architecture* pattern occurs, such as some microservices contain components corresponding to multiple different capabilities or subdomains, or not all microservices are modeled at the same abstraction level. (2) Internal components share other internal components not using loosely coupled connectors, e.g. realized using *Event-driven Architecture* (or the realization of an *Event-driven Architecture* violates established patterns for event-based communication among microservices such as *Event Sourcing, Transaction Log Tailing, Database Triggers, Application Publishes Events, Command Query Responsibility Segregation*, see [21]). (3) The *Database per Service* pattern is not used, but a *Shared Database*.
- The use of the two API Gateway patterns is beneficial, but does not change the quality assessment. The reason is that API Gateways are also commonly used in monolithic architectures, and a microservice architecture that does not use them is not less well decomposed w.r.t. the microservice patterns. Note that although the API Gateway patterns are still important for our approach, their use is important for calculating some of our constraints and metrics (see discussion on *Facades* below).

We have chosen this scoring scheme because it is close to the suggestions in the patterns and introduces no major subjective bias. In the course of our evaluations, we have compared it to other reasonable scorings, including subjective expert judgment by the authors, and a number of similar mechanical scorings.

The sensitivity to those scorings was generally low, as long as we followed the suggestions from the patterns closely. The evaluation of the constraints leads to binary vectors indicating for each model whether the constraint is violated or not. Below we discuss the results of each of these vectors in detail. In addition, we calculated the Jaccard similarity [23] to the vector built from *VMP* values in Table 1 (*JS_VMP* in Table 2) to get a quick estimate of how well the respective constraint performs in relation to the manual, pattern-based assessment for our evaluation model set. The Jaccard similarity is a common index for binary samples, which is defined as the quotient between the intersection and the union of the pairwise compared variables among two vectors.

Metrics evaluation leads to vectors with positive values which should indicate the quality of the microservice decomposition. Again, we discuss them in detail below. In addition, we compute the Cosine similarity with the vector *MQ* from Table 1 (*CS_MQ* in Table 3) to get a quick estimate of how well the respective metric performs in relation to the pattern-based assessment for our evaluation model set. Cosine similarity is a common measure of similarity between two vectors based on the cosine of the angle between them [23]. Some of the metrics below are reversed compared to *MQ* in the sense that their best value is 0.0, with higher values indicating better quality. Consequently, we compared those metrics to the reversed *MQ*, which is defined as $MQR = 1 - MQ$ (below

Table 2. Evaluation results: constraints (1 - constraint is violated, and 0 - it is not violated)

Constraint	EC1	EC2	EC3	EC4	EC5	EC6	EC7	EC8	RB	TH1	TH2	TH3	RSA	*JS_VMP*
CAID	0	1	0	0	0	1	1	1	0	0	0	1	0	*0.71*
NSCD	1	1	1	1	1	1	1	1	1	1	1	1	1	*0.54*
NSCD-F	0	1	1	1	1	1	1	1	1	1	1	1	1	*0.58*
NSCD-C	1	1	1	1	1	1	1	1	0	1	1	1	0	*0.64*
NSCD-FC	0	1	0	0	1	1	1	1	0	1	0	1	0	*1.0*

Table 3. Evaluation results: metrics

Metric	EC1	EC2	EC3	EC4	EC5	EC6	EC7	EC8	RB	TH1	TH2	TH3	SA	*CS_MQ*	*CS_MQR*
RVID	0.0	0.36	0.0	0.0	0.0	0.83	0.83	0.44	0.0	0.0	0.0	0.89	0.0		*0.96*
RIDC	1.0	0.73	1.0	1.0	1.0	0.33	0.33	0.67	1.0	1.0	1.0	0.22	1.0	*0.97*	
RSIC	0.63	0.73	0.56	0.89	0.83	0.83	0.83	0.89	0.5	0.33	0.33	0.56	0.64		*0.73*
RSIC-F	0.0	0.44	0.43	0.86	0.75	0.75	0.75	0.86	0.5	0.22	0.22	0.43	0.5		*0.74*
RSIC-C	0.63	0.73	0.56	0.56	0.83	0.83	0.83	0.89	0.0	0.33	0.33	0.56	0.0		*0.81*
RSIC-FC	0.0	0.44	0.0	0.0	0.75	0.75	0.75	0.86	0.0	0.22	0.0	0.43	0.0		*0.91*
RSCC	0.75	0.82	0.78	0.78	0.67	0.67	0.67	0.78	0.25	0.5	0.5	0.78	0.64		*0.70*
RSCC-F	0.0	0.44	0.14	0.14	0.25	0.25	1.0	0.57	0.25	0.11	0.11	0.29	0.33		*0.80*
RSCC-C	0.75	0.82	0.67	0.67	0.67	0.67	0.67	0.78	0.0	0.5	0.42	0.78	0.0		*0.76*
RSCC-FC	0.0	0.44	0.0	0.0	0.25	0.25	1.0	0.57	0.0	0.11	0.0	0.29	0.0		*0.85*
RSDP	0.38	0.89	0.54	0.99	0.72	0.72	1.56	1.51	0.13	0.11	0.11	0.62	0.35		*0.79*
RSDP-F	0.0	0.37	0.12	0.61	0.38	0.38	0.75	0.98	0.13	0.02	0.02	0.16	0.08		*0.72*
RSDP-C	0.38	0.89	0.3	0.3	0.72	0.72	1.56	1.51	0.0	0.11	0.07	0.62	0.0		*0.85*
RSDP-FC	0.0	0.37	0.0	0.0	0.38	0.38	0.75	0.98	0.0	0.02	0.0	0.16	0.0		*0.79*

indicated as *CS_MQR*). Alternatively, we could calculate the associated distance metrics, where the distance d is also defined in relation to its associated similarity metric as $d = 1 - s$.

5.1 Evaluation for Constraints and Metrics Based on Independent Deployment

Table 2 shows the results for the constraint **all components are independently deployable (CAID)**[4]. We can see an acceptable Jaccard similarity (0.71) of the constraint violation vector to the pattern-based assessment *VMP*. Inspecting the violations closer, we can see that two violations are not found (false negatives): the violations in Models *EC5* and *TH1*. That is, the constraint does not work well for non-monolithic structures that share a database as in *EC5* or a component as in *TH1*. The constraint works, however, if this issue is combined with other violations as in Model *EC8*.

We have suggested two metrics based on independent deployment: **Ratio of components violating independent deployability to non-external components (RVID)** and **ratio of independently deployable component clusters to non-external components (RIDC)**. RVID sets the unique components in the violations in ratio; that is, 0 indicates the highest possible quality, and higher values indicate lesser quality. Thus, the metric must be compared to the reversed microservice quality vector *MQR*. The cosine similarity *CS_MQR* shows a very high similarity of 0.96. *RIDC*, in contrast, has values ranging from 0 to 1, with 1 indicating the best possible quality, meaning it must be compared to the microservice quality vector *MQ*. Here, we see an even slightly higher cosine similarity *CS_MQ* of 0.97. As both metrics are based on the functions used in *CAID*, they also have the same weakness of not identifying the shared database/component issues in Models *EC5/TH1*, but the high similarity measures show that the indication of quality with regard to the other microservice patterns is rather good for both metrics, with *RIDC* performing slightly better for our evaluation model set.

5.2 Evaluation for Constraints and Metrics Based on Shared Dependencies

No shared non-external component dependencies (NSCD) is violated by all models (6 false positives) and has only a Jaccard similarity of 0.54; it is not a good match. Its variant *NSCD-F*, which excludes sharing by *Facade* components, is slightly better suited, but still has 5 false positives and a Jaccard similarity of only 0.58; the variant *NSCD-C*, which considers only strongly coupled connectors as leading to shared components, is slightly better with 4 false positives and a Jaccard similarity of 0.64. The combination *NSCD-FC* considering no *Facades* and no loosely coupled connectors produces exactly the same vector as the pattern-based assessment *VMP* (and thus the Jaccard similarity is 1.0).

---

[4] In Table 2, 1 means that the constraint is violated, and 0 that it is not violated.

This very good result might be surprising, as the uncombined constraints *NSCD-F* and *NSCD-C* produce rather weak results alone. A closer inspection revealed that in our models there was indeed in each false positive in *NSCD-F* a loosely coupled connector and *NSCD-C* a sharing *Facade* that caused the violation.

For all shared dependencies metrics, the value 0.0 is the best possible value, and higher values indicate lower quality. Thus, the metrics must be compared to the reversed microservice quality vector *MQR*. The **ratio of sharing non-external components to non-external components (RSIC)** shows a moderate cosine similarity *CS_MQR* of 0.73, which is gradually improved by its two variants *RSIC-F* and *RSIC-C* with cosine similarities 0.74 and 0.81, respectively. The combined variant *RSIC-FC* shows the best results with a high cosine similarities of 0.91.

For **ratio of shared non-external components to non-external components (RSCC)** the cosine similarity *CS_MQR* has a moderate value of 0.70. Its variants *RSCC-F* and *RSCC-C* perform better with cosine similarities of 0.80 and 0.76, respectively. Again, the combined variant *RSCC-FC* shows the best results with a high cosine similarities of 0.85, but it is less similar for our evaluation model set than *RSIC-FC*.

Finally, **ratio of shared dependencies of non-external components to possible dependencies (RSDP)** has a good cosine similarity of 0.79 already in its basic variant, but interestingly *RSDP-F* performs weaker with a cosine similarity of only 0.72. Close inspection of the dependencies revealed that this effect is due to the fact that, on the one hand, the *Facade* dependencies make the values for high quality microservice architectures worse, but, on the other hand, they make them much more worse for monolithic architecture, as for them *Facades* have many more dependencies. Thus, monolithic architectures gain in the variant *RSDP-F* comparatively too much. This can, in our numbers for instance, be easily retraced using the values for Models EC1 and EC6. While *RSDP-F* leads to a comparatively better result for EC1 (0.0 instead of 0.38 for *RSDP*), the monolith EC6 improves from 0.72 (which was close to the expected reversed quality of 1.0) to 0.38 (which is much more distant from 1.0). *RSDP-C* leads to the expected improvement with a cosine similarity of 0.85. *RSDP-FC* suffers from the same effect for *Facade* dependencies, and thus has only a moderate cosine similarity of 0.79.

6 Discussion, Threats to Validity and Future Work

Discussion of RQs. With regard to **RQ1** and **RQ2**, we have suggested a number of constraints for checking the quality of microservice decomposition in software architecture models. The variant *NSCD-FC* of the shared dependency based constraints performs best, correctly identifying all constraint violations. The constraint *CAID* based on independent deployment performs worse than *NSCD-FC* (but better than all other *NSCD* variants), as it has issues with correctly identifying violations related to shared databases or components. Nonetheless, both constraints are useful and should be combined in their use. As both identify different lists of violations, inspecting the results of both constraints can help developers to more easily find the root cause of a violation. In addition, our evaluation revealed that CAID has only false negatives; that is, in our evaluation model set, all violations identified are actually violations. Hence, it can be used in addition to *NSCD-FC* with no danger of suggesting non-issues to be fixed. This is not the case for any of the other *NSCD* variants, which yield false positives.

We have also suggested a number of metrics for measuring the quality of microservice decomposition in software architecture models. For both of the metrics based on independent deployment, *RDIC* and *RVID*, we can assess a very high similarity to our pattern-based assessments, and hence they seem to be both good candidates for measuring the quality of microservice decomposition. *RDIC* performs slightly better than *RVID*, but given that the values and interpretations used in the pattern-based quality assessment contain a certain level of subjectivity, our empirical evaluation does not really identify a clear favorite. As they are based on *CAID*, we should be aware that the base function suffers from some false negatives which are part of the metrics' values. Further research would be needed to improve the metrics in this regard.

For the metrics related to shared dependencies, we can assess that none of the metrics is a perfect match for our pattern-based quality assessment, but considering that the values and interpretations used in the pattern-based quality assessment contain a certain level of subjectivity, the achieved similarities of the two metric *RSIC-FC* and *RSCC-FC*, with values of 0.91 and 0.85 are actually quite good matches, with *RSIC-FC* performing a bit better for our evaluation model set. It is interesting that all three *-FC* metrics yield the correct value of 0.0 for well-designed microservice models, and never assign the perfect value for a model with a violation. Unfortunately, the strength of the effect of violations on metrics values is not optimal yet in any of the metrics. For instance, in the best matching metric *RSIC-FC*, EC8 is the worst model; however, in our pattern-based assessment we see its violations as less severe than those e.g. in EC6. *RSSC-FC* is more correct in this regard, but assigns a very strong effect to the violation in EC7, which is actually the same model as EC6, but just models the violation in more detail. It is unfortunate that the metric *RSDP* suffers from the issues related to the strong effect on removing *Facade* dependencies, but its variant *RSDP-C* performs for our evaluation model set just as well as *RSCC-FC*. Therefore, an interesting direction of further research could be to investigate other ways to mitigate the effects of the shared dependencies of the *Facades* instead of excluding them.

Overall, based on our empirical results using one of the metrics *RDIC* or *RVID* seems advisable. The results show that the shared dependency metrics in their current form are inferior. However, our results also indicate that shared dependency constraints and metrics can be improved by modeling more details. Here, we have studied *Facades* and loosely coupled connectors, as they are important structures in the microservice patterns and rather easy to model. Please note that modeling additional details is less needed for constraints and metrics based on independent deployment.

In the context of **RQ3**, we can assess that our decomposition model needs rather minimal extensions (the few component and connector types named above) and is easy to map to existing modeling practices. In particular, in order to fully model our evaluation model set, we needed to introduce 20 component types and 42 connector types, ranging from general notions like *ExternalComponent* and its sub-class *ClientComponent*, to very technology-specific classes like *MongoWireConnector* (a subclass of *DatabaseConnector* connecting to a *MongoDBComponent*, a subclass of *DatabaseComponent*). These would not always be easy to map automatically, but our study has shown that for the suggested constraints and metrics, only a small subset is needed: The constraints on independent deployment require at least that *ExternalComponents* (and its subclass *ClientComponent*) and the connector type *InMemoryConnectors* are modeled. The shared dependencies based constraints require two additional abstractions to be modeled: loosely coupled connectors (as subclasses of *LooselyCoupledConnector*) and *Facade* components. All except *Facade* components are relatively easy to compute automatically, e.g. by inspecting the used technology for a connection. We can claim that our approach can easily be mapped using an automated mapping from the source code to an architecture model, assuming standard component model abstractions, such as those in UML2, e.g. with approaches like our architecture abstraction approach [6].

Future Work. In our approach, we have focused only on modeling additionally details with no to low effort, to enable a high potential for automation and less extra effort compared to existing modeling practices. An interesting direction for future research could be to study how modeling more details could lead to better results in the metrics. For instance, modeling capabilities or subdomains of the microservices, or the detailed domain model, are promising directions to further improve the metrics.

Major Threats to Validity. A threat to validity is that potentially the patterns or our models are not well chosen as study objects and do not represent the domain of microservices well. However, as related practices and similar models have been proposed by many other authors, we judge this threat to be rather low. However, many authors also model other architectural views, and they might have an influence on architecture decomposition – which we want to study as future work. Potentially the authors could have been biased in their judgment, but as we have followed a quite mechanical scoring scheme (based on the patterns, not our own judgment), this threat is mostly limited to our evaluations based on the pattern-based quality assessments (see Sect. 5). Even though we have aimed to follow the argumentations in the microservice patterns [21] as closely as possible, a major threat remains that at least the evaluation scores introduced are subjective to a certain degree. Note that we have tested in the course of our evaluations some other kinds of reasonable scoring scheme, leading to comparable but slightly different results. The sensitivity to those scores was generally low, as long as we followed the suggestions from the patterns closely. In addition, this potential threat to validity is not necessarily a problem, in the sense that a project aiming to apply the constraints and metrics could easily re-run our evaluations with different values that introduce scores according to the project's needs. As we have used pretty basic and standard statistics, we see no major threats to statistical conclusion validity.

Concluding Remarks. In summary, our results show that a subset of the constraints or metrics are quite close to the pattern-based assessment based on the expert judgment taken from the patterns, and we have also shown where the metrics and constraints could be substantially improved. Our results indicate that the best way to reach this goal seems to be more detailed modeling of the microservices (e.g. based on capabilities, subdomains, domain-specific models, and/or modeling at different abstraction levels). However, each of these possible future works would also mean more manual effort, and less potential for automation, but this might not be an issue in all those application cases where designing a well-defined architecture is the goal. With modest effort our results are applicable to other service decomposition schemes than microservices as well.

Acknowledgment. This work was partially supported by Austrian Science Fund (FWF) project ADDCompliance: I 2885-N33; DFG ADDCompliance project: LE 2275/13-1; Spanish Ministry of Economy, Industry and Competitiveness, State Research Agency/European Regional Development Fund, grant Vi-SMARt (TIN2016-79100-R).

References

1. Alshuqayran, N., Ali, N., Evans, R.: A systematic mapping study in microservice architecture. In: IEEE 9th International Conference on Service-Oriented Computing and Applications (SOCA), pp. 44–51. IEEE (2016)
2. De, B.: API patterns. In: API Management, pp. 81–104. Apress, Berkeley, CA (2017). doi:10.1007/978-1-4842-1305-6_5
3. Guo, D., Wang, W., Zeng, G., Wei, Z.: Microservices architecture based cloudware deployment platform for service computing. In: 2016 IEEE Symposium on Service-Oriented System Engineering (SOSE), pp. 358–363. IEEE (2016)
4. Guo, G.Y., Atlee, J.M., Kazman, R.: A software architecture reconstruction method. In: Donohoe, P. (ed.) Software Architecture. ITIFIP, vol. 12, pp. 15–33. Springer, Boston, MA (1999). doi:10.1007/978-0-387-35563-4_2
5. Gupta, A.: Microservice design patterns (2017). http://blog.arungupta.me/microservice-design-patterns/
6. Haitzer, T., Zdun, U.: Semi-automated architectural abstraction specifications for supporting software evolution. Sci. Comput. Program. **90**, 135–160 (2014)
7. Hohpe, G., Woolf, B.: Enterprise Integration Patterns. Addison-Wesley, Boston (2003)
8. Kang, H., Le, M., Tao, S.: Container and microservice driven design for cloud infrastructure DevOps. In: 2016 IEEE International Conference on Cloud Engineering (IC2E), pp. 202–211. IEEE (2016)
9. Kratzke, N.: About microservices, containers and their underestimated impact on network performance. In: Proceedings of Cloud Computing, pp. 165–169 (2015)
10. Kurhinen, H., Lampi, M.: Micro-services based distributable workflow for digital archives. In: Archiving Conference, vol. 1, pp. 47–51. Society for Imaging Science and Tech. (2014)

11. de Lange, P., Nicolaescu, P., Derntl, M., Jarke, M., Klamma, R.: Community application editor: collaborative near real-time modeling and composition of microservice-based web applications. In: Modellierung (Workshops), pp. 123–128 (2016)
12. Le, V.D., Neff, M.M., Stewart, R.V., Kelley, R., Fritzinger, E., Dascalu, S.M., Harris, F.C.: Microservice-based architecture for the NRDC. In: 2015 IEEE 13th International Conference on Industrial Informatics (INDIN), pp. 1659–1664. IEEE (2015)
13. Levcovitz, A., Terra, R., Valente, M.T.: Towards a technique for extracting microservices from monolithic enterprise systems. arXiv preprint arXiv:1605.03175 (2016)
14. Lewis, J., Fowler, M.: Microservices: a definition of this new architectural term, March 2004. http://martinfowler.com/articles/microservices.html
15. Newman, S.: Building Microservices: Designing Fine-Grained Systems. O'Reilly, New York (2015)
16. Pahl, C., Jamshidi, P.: Microservices: a systematic mapping study. In: 6th International Conference on Cloud Computing and Services Science, pp. 137–146 (2016)
17. Passos, L., Terra, R., Valente, M.T., Diniz, R., das ChagasMendonca, N.: Static architecture-conformance checking: an illustrative overview. IEEE Softw. **27**(5), 82–89 (2010)
18. Pautasso, C., Zimmermann, O., Amundsen, M., Lewis, J., Josuttis, N.: Microservices in practice, part 1: reality check and service design. IEEE Softw. **34**(1), 91–98 (2017)
19. Pautasso, C., Wilde, E.: Why is the web loosely coupled?: a multi-faceted metric for service design. In: 18th International Conference on World wide web, pp. 911–920. ACM (2009)
20. Perry, D.E., Wolf, A.L.: Foundations for the study of software architecture. ACM SIGSOFT Softw. Eng. Notes **17**(4), 40–52 (1992)
21. Richardson, C.: A pattern language for microservices (2017). http://microservices.io/patterns/index.html
22. Rosenberg, F., Celikovic, P., Michlmayr, A., Leitner, P., Dustdar, S.: An end-to-end approach for QoS-aware service composition. In: IEEE International Conference on Enterprise Distributed Object Computing Conference (EDOC 2009), pp. 151–160. IEEE (2009)
23. Bramer, M.: Introduction to data mining. Principles of Data Mining. UTCS, pp. 1–8. Springer, London (2016). doi:10.1007/978-1-4471-7307-6_1
24. Van Deursen, A., Hofmeister, C., Koschke, R., Moonen, L., Riva, C.: Symphony: view-driven software architecture reconstruction. In: 4th Working IEEE/IFIP Conference on Software Architecturen (WICSA 2004), pp. 122–132. IEEE (2004)
25. Viennot, N., Lécuyer, M., Bell, J., Geambasu, R., Nieh, J.: Synapse: a microservices architecture for heterogeneous-database web applications. In: 10th European Conference on Computer Systems, p. 21. ACM (2015)
26. Zdun, U.: A DSL toolkit for deferring architectural decisions in DSL-based software design. Inf. Softw. Technol. **52**(7), 733–748 (2010)
27. Zimmermann, O.: Microservices tenets. Comput. Sci. Res. Dev. **32**(3), 301–310 (2017)
28. Zimmermann, O., Gschwind, T., Küster, J., Leymann, F., Schuster, N.: Reusable architectural decision models for enterprise application development. In: Overhage, S., Szyperski, C.A., Reussner, R., Stafford, J.A. (eds.) QoSA 2007. LNCS, vol. 4880, pp. 15–32. Springer, Heidelberg (2007). doi:10.1007/978-3-540-77619-2_2

Polly: A Language-Based Approach for Custom Change Detection of Web Service Data

Elyas Ben Hadj Yahia[1,3]($\boxtimes$), Jean-Rémy Falleri[2], and Laurent Réveillère[2]

[1] University Bordeaux - LaBRI - UMR CNRS 5800, Talence, France
`elyas.bhy@labri.fr`
[2] University Bordeaux - ENSEIRB-MATMECA Bordeaux INP - LaBRI - UMR CNRS 5800, Talence, France
[3] CProDirect, 33700 Mérignac, France

Abstract. An ever-growing number of web service providers expose data that is continuously changing. Use cases arise where being notified about changes made to the data is essential to the client, for instance to know when a user has a new follower on Twitter. Monitoring changes on web services data consists in polling services for the required data, detecting any changes in the targeted data subset, and notifying the user only about the relevant changes. However, each step of this process can be relatively complex, leading to a tedious and challenging implementation for developers. In this paper we introduce POLLY, a domain-specific language for describing change detection strategies in JSON data fetched from REST web APIs. By leveraging the domain knowledge of the user, our domain-specific language offers declarative, concise yet highly-expressive constructs for specifying change detection strategies. We validate our approach using several user-driven scenarios provided by our industrial partner and show that it outperforms the state-of-the-art solutions.

Keywords: DSL · Change detection · API · REST · JSON

1 Introduction

Integration platforms such as IFTTT[1] and Zapier[2] have recently emerged with the aim of orchestrating interactions between a multitude of web services such as Facebook and Twitter [11,13]. They enable end users to describe which actions to trigger when a custom event occurs [16]. For instance, one may want to automatically tweet a message when a specific subway line becomes unavailable. However, most of existing web services do not provide a way to specify custom event notifications. To overcome this limitation, platform owners have developed their own notification system by performing a recurrent polling of monitored services. For each service, the current state is periodically fetched and compared against the previous one to identify specific values that vary over time.

---

[1] https://ifttt.com.
[2] https://zapier.com.

© Springer International Publishing AG 2017
M. Maximilien et al. (Eds.): ICSOC 2017, LNCS 10601, pp. 430–444, 2017.
https://doi.org/10.1007/978-3-319-69035-3_30

When a change is detected, the corresponding event is raised. Because specific code needs to be developed for each event of a service, the set of supported services and events is limited and does not necessarily meet user expectations.

Each step of the monitoring process can be relatively complex. As an example, consider the use of the Facebook service to detect new photos with a given tagged user in a given album. To implement this scenario, one needs first to periodically poll several Facebook API endpoints (the one for the photos and the one for the tags) and navigate through the paginated responses. The resulting aggregated state is then compared against the previous one. However, this comparison requires focusing only on new photos (identified by their unique IDs) while ignoring other irrelevant changes such as the last update time. Even such a simple use case underlines the complexities of this process, which are declined in two different challenges: state computation and change detection.

Although the computation of a state sometimes requires fetching a unique resource from a single API endpoint, it is often necessary to implement more complicated policies. For instance, the construction of a state may require navigating through a set of API endpoints, where several requests must be chained in a particular order to correctly fetch the relevant data. In addition, responses returned by a service can be paginated and thus necessitate several subsequent requests to accumulate all the data. Thus, constructing a state can quickly become laborious.

Once a state has been computed, it is necessary to detect changes with the previous one. However, off-the-shelf techniques can produce unexpected or irrelevant results as in the previous Facebook example in which photos with only a modified last update time should not be reported as different. Developing a generic differencing tool is a well-known complex problem, and can be NP-hard depending both on the change operations that are considered, and on the guarantees about the output size [6].

Our industrial partner, CPRODIRECT, wishes to compete with traditional platforms by enabling fast integration of new service providers and events in its own platform [2]. To reduce time to market, we investigate the challenges of detecting changes in web service data. We focus on modern web services that follow the REST architectural style and exchange data with their consumers in JSON. We introduce a generative language-based approach, POLLY, to simplify change detector construction.

Our contributions are the following:

- We introduce a new approach to change detector construction. Our approach relies on the use of a domain-specific language, POLLY, for describing change detection strategies in JSON data fetched from REST web APIs.
- Our language provides declarative, simple yet highly-expressive constructs for describing how to construct a state from one or multiple API endpoints, how to identify changes in states, and how to produce a custom output.
- We have implemented a compiler that automatically produces an efficient JavaScript implementation which runs on top of a runtime system and hides low-level requirements such as HTTP authentication and pagination.

```
 1  {
 2    "data": [
 3      {
 4        "created_time":
               ↪ "2016-05-20T12:28:57+0000",
 5        "updated_time":
               ↪ "2016-05-20T12:26:57+0000",
 6        "id": "1106290499393017"
 7      }
 8    ],
 9    "paging": {
10      "next": "https://graph.facebook.com/..."
11    }
12  }
```

(a) Excerpt of a list of photos of a Facebook album.

```
 1  {
 2    "data": [
 3      {
 4        "id": "10203528656797589",
 5        "name": "Bob",
 6        "created_time":
               ↪ "2016-05-20T12:39:01+0000",
 7        "x": 73.684210526316,
 8        "y": 74.865350089767
 9      }
10    ],
11    "paging": {
12      "next": "https://graph.facebook.com/..."
13    }
14  }
```

(b) Excerpt of a list of tags of a Facebook photo.

Fig. 1. Excerpt of photos and tags from the Facebook service.

- We show the applicability of POLLY by using it to automatically generate a number of change detectors for widely used web services such as Twitter, Facebook, and GitHub. We demonstrate that POLLY's code is more concise that a manual implementation, and that it outperforms a state-of-the-art, off-the-shelf differencing technique.

The rest of this paper is organized as follows. Section 2 presents the range of issues that arise in detecting changes in web service data, as illustrated by a use case based on Facebook. Section 3 describes the POLLY architecture and introduces a DSL for describing state construction, change detection and custom output construction. Section 4 demonstrates the efficiency and scalability of the POLLY change detector. Section 5 discusses related work. Finally, Sect. 6 concludes and presents future work.

2   Challenges in Service Data Change Detection

To outline the multiple challenges involved when trying to detect changes in service data, we explain in details the scenario described in the introduction: *detecting new photos of a given Facebook album where Alice is tagged.*

In order to detect the new photos, one first needs to gather the complete list of photos of the Facebook album. This can be done by issuing a request on the https://graph.facebook.com/v2.9/:albumId/photos URL, where :albumId is the identifier of the photo album of interest. The Facebook service returns a response as a JSON document as illustrated in Fig. 1a. However, additional processing is needed to bridge the gap between the expected information and what is available in the returned document.

Firstly, the whole list of photos is not received at once, because the response is paginated (i.e. split in several lists of a fixed size). The paging.next attribute gives the URL to query to receive the next batch of photos. Additionally, the tags present on the photos are not part of this response. An additional request per photo is required to gather this information. This request can be made on

```
 1  [
 2    {
 3      "created_time":
              ↪ "2016-05-20T12:26:57+0000",
 4      "updated_time":
              ↪ "2016-05-20T12:28:57+0000",
 5      "id": "1106290499393017",
 6      "data": [
 7        {
 8          "id": "10203528656797589",
 9          "name": "Bob",
10          "created_time":
                  ↪ "2016-05-20T12:39:01+0000",
11          "x": 73.684210526316,
12          "y": 74.865350089767
13        }
14      ]
15    }
16  ]
```

(a) Initial version.

```
 1  [
 2    {
 3      "created_time":
              ↪ "2016-05-20T12:26:57+0000",
 4      "updated_time":
              ↪ "2016-05-20T12:29:57+0000",
 5      "id": "1106290499393017",
 6      "data": [
 7        {
 8          "id": "10203528656797589",
 9          "name": "Bob",
10          "created_time":
                  ↪ "2016-05-20T12:39:01+0000",
11          "x": 76.684210526316,
12          "y": 74.865350089767
13        }
14      ]
15    },
16    {
17      "created_time":
              ↪ "2016-05-20T12:35:57+0000",
18      "id": "2206280499393006",
19      "data": [
20        {
21          "id": "20406528656797578",
22          "name": "Alice",
23          "created_time":
                  ↪ "2016-05-20T12:45:57+0000",
24          "x": 63.684210526316,
25          "y": 62.865350089767
26        }
27      ]
28    }
29  ]
```

(b) Updated version.

Fig. 2. Initial and updated version.

the endpoint https://graph.facebook.com/v2.9/:photoId/tags where :photoId is the identifier of the photo of interest (received in response of the previous request). A request on the tags endpoint yields the result shown in Fig. 1b.

As we can see, this response is paginated as well. One can notice that the requests to gather the tags of each photo can be performed in an asynchronous manner, to improve performance. Finally, the tagged person names are available in these responses. To gather all the required information, the developer has then to manually construct a list that combines the photos and the tags data, as shown in Fig. 2a.

Performing a new polling operation using the same process would produce a new list of photos, as shown in Fig. 2b. By using an off-the-shelf differencing tool, the developer can compute the patch shown in Fig. 3. As it can be noticed, this patch contains two irrelevant changes: the x coordinate of the tag of the first photo and the last update time of the first photo. The only relevant change is the third one, where we can see a newly created photo containing a tag referring to user Alice. Therefore, the developer needs to post-process the patch produced by the differencing tool in order to construct the notification relevant to the scenario.

In this example we clearly show that detecting changes in service data is a tedious operation. It requires navigating across several endpoints, possibly

```
1   [                                           17        "id": "2206280499393006",
2   {                                           18        "data": [
3       "op": "replace",                        19        {
4       "path": "/0/data/0/x",                  20            "id": "0406528656797578",
5       "value": 76.684210526316                21            "name": "Alice",
6   },                                          22            "created_time":
7   {                                                   ↪ "2016-05-20T12:45:57+0000",
8       "op": "replace",                        23            "x": 63.684210526316,
9       "path": "/0/updated_time",              24            "y": 62.865350089767
10      "value": "2016-05-20T12:29:57+0000"     25        }
11  },                                          26        ]
12  {                                           27    },
13      "op": "add",                            28    "path": "/1"
14      "value":                                29  }
15      {                                       30  ]
16          "created_time": "2016-05-20T12:35:57+0000",
```

Fig. 3. JSON diff between the two versions of Fig. 2.

chaining response elements into query parameters, and handling the problem of pagination at each step. When the data is gathered, an off-the-shelf differencing tool may produce irrelevant changes thus requiring either post-processing of the output or developing an ad-hoc differencing algorithm.

3 Approach

As illustrated in Sect. 2, implementing custom change detectors of service data can be challenging for many developers. In this section, we introduce POLLY, a declarative language-based approach that raises the level of abstraction by providing dedicated operators to express state construction, change detection, and output construction within a pipeline of operations. In the remainder of this section, we describe how our approach enables one to simply design efficient custom change detectors.

3.1 Overview of the Polly Language

The POLLY language is based on the YAML [18] syntax and is implemented as a Node.js module. Inspired by dataflow architectures, it is based on processing pipelines for defining custom change detectors. A pipeline is expressed as a series of transformation operations on successive sets of data, where data and operations on it are independent from each other. Each operation performs a specific task, and produces a JSON document that is passed as input for the following operation. POLLY allows the user to specify how to compute a state by fetching a set of API resources, how to detect custom changes that are relevant to his requirements, and how to build a custom output to match the expected outcome. The provided language operators and constructs are described at greater length in the remainder of this section.

Language constructs. By design, each operation processes an input value (represented by the "_" symbol), and produces an output value (represented by the "&" symbol). These default values can be overridden using the *input* and *output*

```
1  - operation: fetch
2    definition:
3      request:
4        url: https://graph.facebook.com
            ↪ /v2.9/:albumId/photos
5        params:
6          albumId: 465607303461343
7        query:
8          access_token: XXXX
9        headers:
10         Accept: application/json
11       template: ~.data
12       pagination:
13         next: ~.paging.next
14  # Or, instead of using template:
15  # output: &:$..data
```

```
1  - operation: fetch
2    definition:
3      repeat:
4        forEach: _
5        placeholders:
6          photoId: ^.id
7      request:
8        url: https://graph.facebook.com
            ↪ /v2.9/:photoId/tags
9        query:
10         access_token: XXXX
11       headers:
12         Accept: application/json
13       pagination:
14         next: ~.paging.next
15       template:
16         photoId: ^.id
17         tags: ~.data
```

(a) POLLY specification for fetching a list of photos for a given album.

(b) POLLY specification for fetching a list of tags for each album photo.

Fig. 4. A minimal example showcasing how to retrieve all photo tags of a Facebook album using POLLY.

keywords at the operation level. Furthermore, POLLY introduces two additional notations. The "~" symbol refers to the response body of a request (Fig. 4a, lines 11 and 13), while the "%" symbol refers to the response headers. The "^" symbol represents the loop iteration cursor (Fig. 4b, lines 6 and 16). This cursor represents the current element being iterated on. All five notations presented in this paragraph support the dot notation for accessing child properties. For example, ~.data references the data attribute at the root of the response document.

Evaluating JSONPath expressions. POLLY relies on the JSONPath [10] specification to describe the selection of a sub-document, as illustrated in line 15 of Fig. 4a. This enables users to easily extract the sub-documents of interest. Thus, a JSONPath expression[3] can be applied on any of the previous symbols, using the following notation: [symbol]:[jsonpath_expr]. For instance, the evaluation of the expression &:$..id is equivalent to evaluating $..id on the output document (&), thus producing all the id fields present in the output document.

3.2   State Construction

The *fetch* operator enables the user to specify how to collect data from a set of API endpoints. These details are specified within the *request* block (Fig. 4a, line 3). Here, the user defines the resource URL using the *url* keyword (line 4). The URL can have parameter placeholders (prefixed by a colon), which are substituted with the matching key from the *params* block (line 5). Furthermore, the DSL offers the ability to specify query parameters (*query*, line 7) as well as HTTP headers (*headers*, line 9) as key-value pairs.

---

[3] The $ symbol represents the root of the current document in JSONPath.

Templating. In the majority of use cases, the user only requires gathering a subset of the collected data. Furthermore, he might also need to include extra information along with the response. The *template* keyword allows specifying a transformation template. This can be expressed directly as an expression, or as a new set of keys where each corresponding value is an expression. For example, line 11 of Fig. 4a shows how to extract the `data` object from the API response (Fig. 1a, line 2). Another example occurs in line 15 of Fig. 4b where we fetch photo tags. Here, we define a new template containing the original photo ID and its tags. This transformation is necessary in order to manually include the photo ID (which is not part of the API response) in the final state.

Pagination. The *pagination* keyword enables the user to indicate how to fetch subsequent pages when the response is paginated (Fig. 4a, line 12). Information about pagination is typically present in an HTTP header or in the body of the response. For example, GitHub returns the full URL of the next page in the `Link` header, while Twitter provides just a cursor for the next page in the body of the response. Other APIs such as Stack Exchange require the user to manually specify the page number as a query parameter when requesting a resource, but do not provide any information about the current or next page number in the body of the response. Instead, they just indicate if there are subsequent pages using a boolean value in the body of the response. To support all these pagination methods, POLLY enables the user to specify how to navigate to the following page using the *next* keyword (line 13). This keyword accepts either an expression containing the full URL of the next page, or key-value pairs specifying the name and value of the query parameter used for pagination (*queryParam*, defaults to the value `page` and auto-incremented by default). After collecting all subsequent pages, the results are flattened in a single array and returned as the output of the operation.

Parallel fetch. In the Facebook example presented in Sect. 2, the user has to first retrieve a list of photo IDs for a given album, then retrieve the tags for each photo. To enable this scenario, POLLY provides the *repeat* keyword (Fig. 4b, line 3). This keyword allows specifying an iteration set from the output of the previous operation (*forEach*, line 4), and corresponding placeholder labels (*placeholders*, line 5). These placeholders are substituted in the URL by their value, thus executing a *request* for each constructed URL. In the Facebook example, this corresponds to fetching the tags for each album photo. By default, all requests are asynchronous and performed in parallel. The output of this operation contains a list of templated objects (line 15), where each object includes the current photo ID and the list of tags for a given photo (e.g. Fig. 1b).

3.3   Change Detection

After computing the state in the previous step, the user can now proceed to specifying a change detection strategy. Our preliminary case studies showed that changes to a JSON document can occur on objects or arrays, and range from additions and suppressions, to value modifications and order changes. In light

```
                                          1    - operation: filterCustom
                                          2      definition:
                                          3        function: !!js/function >
1   - operation: filterArray              4        function (existing, input) {
2     definition:                         5          const result = [];
3       input: _                          6          input.forEach((item) => {
4       identifiers:                       7            const isTagged = item.tags.some((value) => {
5         - ^.photoId                      8              return value.name === 'Alice';
6       find:                              9            });
7         - addedItems                    10            if (isTagged) { result.push(item.photoId); }
8       output: &.addedItems              11          });
                                         12          return { type: "addedTags", items: result };
                                         13        }
```

(a) Specification for detecting new photos.

(b) Custom change detection specification.

Fig. 5. Detecting new photos where Alice is tagged using POLLY.

of these results, the POLLY DSL provides several filtering operators for change detection: *filterObject*, *filterArray* and *filterCustom*. The *filterObject* (resp. *filter-Array*) operator accepts an expression of object (resp. array) type as an input. The *filterCustom* operator enables the user to define custom filtering logic.

Change types. The *find* keyword enables defining a list of change types to detect in the input of the operation (Fig. 5a, line 6). The list of supported change types is presented in Table 1. For each change type listed in the *find* block, a matching object is included in the output of the operation, containing the corresponding data. For instance, listing *addedItems* and *removedItems* in the *find* block would produce as output an array of two objects, each having *addedItems* (resp. *removedItems*) as types, and each having a list of the items that have been detected as recently-added (resp. recently-removed).

Per-change type templating. Although the *template* keyword presented in Sect. 3.2 is also supported in this operation, one might need to specify different templates for different change types. To meet this requirement, POLLY supports an additional keyword *templates* (mutually exclusive with *template*). This keyword allows specifying the change type (e.g. *addedItems*) as key, and the associated template as value.

Targeted monitoring. By default, all keys of the input document are watched for modifications, and any change would mark the document as modified. The optional keyword *watch* can be used to restrict the set of keys to watch for modifications. This enables the user to define what actually constitutes a relevant change. Note that for objects, a key is marked as modified (resp. unmodified) if the value corresponding to the key specified in the *watch* block is modified (resp. unmodified). For arrays, an item is marked as modified (resp. unmodified) if **any** (resp. **all**) of the values corresponding to the keys specified in the *watch* block are modified (resp. unmodified).

Custom item identification. Additionally, when dealing with array items, it is necessary to uniquely identify the items throughout subsequent polls. This allows us to know for example if a given item has been added or removed during the polling interval. However, not all APIs provide unique identifiers on all of their

Table 1. List of supported change types.

	filterObject	filterArray
Change types	*addedKeys*	*addedItems*
	removedKeys	*removedItems*
	modifiedKeys	*modifiedItems*
	unmodifiedKeys	*unmodifiedItems*
		movedItems

resources. Moreover, these identifiers can be present under different key labels. For this reason, we provide an additional keyword called *identifiers*, which allows the user to specify how to uniquely identify an item within a collection (line 4). This can be as simple as providing the path to the id field of an item, a list of fields (e.g. first and last names of a user), or a wildcard to hash the entire item and use it as its own identifier.

Custom filtering. When none of the previous operators are adequate, the *filterCustom* operator can be used to implement one's own custom filtering logic. Figure 5b shows an example of how to filter a list of photos by only selecting those where Alice is tagged. This operator provides a hook function with the previous and current states as parameters (line 4). The user can implement this hook in JavaScript, returning a custom output. In this example, the user iterates on the input array of photos (line 6) and checks whether if Alice is tagged on the current photo (lines 7–9), in which case he retrieves the photo ID (line 10). To avoid any security issues when running user-provided code, this function is executed within an isolated sandbox at runtime.

4   Evaluation

We evaluate our approach using six scenarios provided by our industrial partner CPRODIRECT. We first compare the level of abstractions provided by POLLY (in terms of verbosity) compared to its handwritten counterpart. We then assess the differencing time and the output size of our solution compared to a state-of-the-art differencing tool.

4.1   Scenarios

Our industrial partner CPRODIRECT has defined the six following scenarios to be used in our evaluation. They illustrate the diversity of possible use cases ranging from being notified about new objects to changes of attributes values or order in a ranking.

– **ElasticSearch (ES):** Developer Alice uses an instance of ElasticSearch as a search engine for her e-commerce platform, and wants to be notified when the top 5 best-selling products change in ranking order.

- **Facebook (FB):** Developer Alice wants to monitor a Facebook album where her friends Dan and Dave are participating. Alice would like to be notified only about pictures where Dan and Dave are tagged together.
- **GitHub (GH):** Developer Alice is interested in monitoring GitHub for new projects written in the Go language with over 2,000 stars.
- **Stack Overflow (SO):** Developer Alice wants to monitor StackOverflow for new JavaScript questions where there is an active bounty of over 100 reputation points.
- **Transport for London (TL):** Developer Alice wants to be notified whenever the status of the Victoria subway line changes (e.g. from healthy to faulty).
- **Twitter (TW):** Developer Alice wants to be notified whenever the official *Bordeaux* account has new followers on Twitter.

4.2   Language Verbosity Evaluation

All scenarios described in Sect. 4.1 have been implemented twice by the first author of the paper: once using the JavaScript language on top of the Node.js platform, and once using our domain-specific language POLLY. Note that the JavaScript version was implemented before any research work was done on POLLY, in order to avoid any bias, and to serve as a reference point.

Figure 6 shows the number of lexical tokens used in the Node.js version versus the POLLY version. One can notice that POLLY results in a much smaller program, ranging from 5.5 to 8 times smaller. Furthermore, the figure shows the distribution of tokens across different categories (*fetch*, *diff* and *output*). Other tokens that are not directly related to these (such as module imports and configuration) are assigned to the *other* category. First, we notice that the Node.js implementation requires a lot more boilerplate code than POLLY, with around

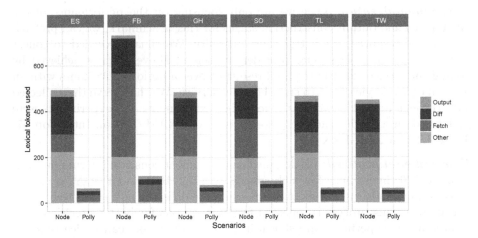

Fig. 6. Lexical tokens used to specify each scenario, using Node.js code *vs.* POLLY.

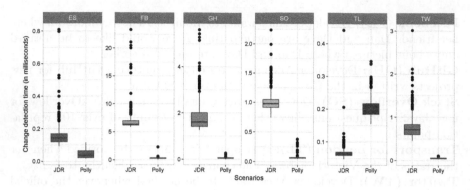

Fig. 7. Change detection time.

200 tokens in the *other* category, compared to 5 for POLLY. Second, we notice that the *output* construction requires more or less the same number of tokens for both approaches, while it requires significantly less tokens for the *fetch* and *diff* categories using the POLLY approach.

4.3   Diff Performance Experiment

Since one of the main benefits of using our approach is to be able to perform a custom differencing based upon domain knowledge of the data returned by the REST APIs, we wanted to evaluate in greater details the advantages of using such a strategy. We compare in this experiment the performance of POLLY against a state-of-the-art generic differencing technique for JSON documents (JDR). We selected JDR as a candidate since prior benchmarks show it outperforms all other JavaScript differencing libraries [7].

Experimental setup. Since we are only focusing on the performance of the differencing and output construction stages for this benchmark, we can prefetch all required resources for better reproducibility. We thus proceeded to collect real data from the six service providers presented above. This is achieved by polling the services for the required resources over a period of 48 hours with an interval of 5 min, yielding 576 snapshots per service. We then serve this collected data through a mock server in the following experiments. All experiments were performed on a single machine powered by 8 GB RAM, and an Intel Core i7-6500U CPU @ 2.50GHz x 4.

Experimental protocol. We designed an experiment consisting in running each scenario 576 times (once for each snapshot) using JDR and POLLY as change detection methods. At each step, we measure the differencing time as well as the output size. This process is repeated for 10 iterations for better precision. The results of this experiment are shown in Figs. 7 and 8. One can notice that the POLLY approach produces lower differencing times and output sizes compared to the JDR approach, apart from the output size for the Facebook (FB) scenario,

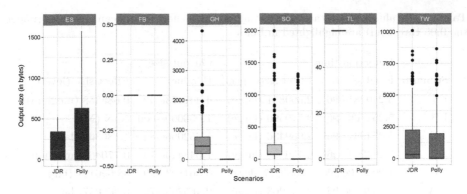

Fig. 8. Output sizes using JDR *vs.* POLLY.

where the output size is equal to 0 for every polling step for both approaches. This is because no modifications occurred during the monitoring period. The difference in output sizes is explained by the fact that JDR produces a JSON Patch [5] (an intermediary document expressing a sequence of operations to apply to a JSON document in order to obtain the final outcome), whereas POLLY directly produces the minimal set of required data as specified in the DSL, which generally tends to be much smaller in size.

Statistical testing. To have a finer-grained analysis of these results, we subject our results to a statistical testing. Our two null hypotheses are that H_0^1 output size is the same for POLLY and JDR and H_0^2 differencing time is the same for POLLY and JDR. Our two alternative hypotheses are H_a^1 output size is lesser for POLLY than JDR and H_a^2 differencing time is lesser for POLLY than JDR. To test these two hypotheses, we used a one-tailed paired Wilcoxon rank test, since it bears no assumptions on the underlying distribution of the differencing time or output size values. To assess the magnitude of the difference between differencing time and output size between the two approaches, we use Cohen's d and report its corresponding level on Cohen's standard scale. The results of this statistical testing are shown in Table 2.

One can notice that most tests are significant under the 0.05 threshold, meaning that POLLY produces significantly smaller outputs in a significantly reduced time compared to the JDR generic differencing approach. The only non-significant test is for the output size of the FB scenario. This is because in this scenario the output size is equal to 0 for every polling step for both approaches.

For the magnitude of the difference, the values range from medium to large, large being by far the most common value (9 times out of 11 values), followed by medium (2 times). This means that POLLY results in a highly improved outcome in terms of output size and differencing time compared to the JDR approach.

Table 2. P-values of our statistical testing and size effect. Significant p-values (under the 0.05 threshold) are highlighted in bold.

Scenario	Detection time		Output size	
	P-value	Effect size (level)	P-value	Effect size (level)
ES	5.240281e-96	2.090851 (large)	4.447673e-42	0.685358 (medium)
FB	5.254766e-96	3.770390 (large)	1.000000e+00	NaN (NA)
GH	5.254964e-96	2.989436 (large)	1.362006e-84	1.186302 (large)
SO	5.254264e-96	6.150168 (large)	1.048446e-74	0.770466 (medium)
TL	1.000000e+00	-4.885277 (large)	6.361893e-99	88.626161 (large)
TW	5.254659e-96	2.846963 (large)	2.465265e-72	0.808057 (large)

5   Related Work

Following the expansion of service-oriented computing, most service providers use the flexible REST architectural style to expose their data [8]. With web applications getting more and more complex, developers often need to navigate through multiple endpoints to retrieve the required resources. Existing efforts focused on a hypermedia-centric approach for describing REST services, using the Resource Linking Language (ReLL) and Petri Nets [1]. However, very few REST APIs provide hyperlinks along their responses in practice, making it harder for developers to gather all resources to compute a given state. To enable this case, our domain-specific language provides the necessary constructs to easily express sequential and parallel request chains of API endpoints, while also supporting pagination.

Due to the rapid growth of the number of web services in the recent decade, composition platforms are gaining more and more traction [12]. These platforms typically allow users to monitor third-party services in order to trigger a composition when a particular event occurs [16]. Thus, it is important to support a wide range of trigger events in order to meet the client's needs, scaling accordingly for all the services supported by the platform. Although previous works focused on providing a framework for automatic detection of relevant changes on websites [4], these do not directly address change detection in REST APIs data, nor do they allow clients to specify what constitutes a relevant change. In contrast, POLLY offers a simple and concise language to rapidly specify custom change detectors, tailored to the user's expectations.

In today's fast-paced web, data is continuously churning to reflect the latest state. Change detection consists in computing a diff between two documents, and identifying any relevant changes. Several existing contributions focus on improving the differencing process. They represent documents as ordered or unordered labeled trees, and aim for optimizing the tree edit distance [3,6,19]. Nonetheless, the problem of finding a minimal patch is $O(n^3)$ to NP-hard for ordered trees (depending on the set of operations considered), and NP-hard for unordered trees [9,14,20]. This leads to the use of practical heuristics that rely on the syntactical properties of the documents in order to provide reasonably good results. As such, additional algorithms have been designed specifically for detecting changes in XML documents [17]. More recently, other algorithms have been designed for JSON documents, which are a combination of unordered and ordered labeled trees [7]. However, POLLY relies on the client's business domain knowledge to finely tune the change detector. This improves the change detection process by enabling the selection of the most adequate strategy, thus discarding any irrelevant data.

With today's growing use of mobile devices, a particular focus is given to energy efficiency. Producing minimal diffs becomes particularly important when dealing with mobile clients, as it helps reducing the bandwidth usage [15]. Our approach addresses this concern by enabling the developer to specify the output resulting from the change detection process. This enables sending only the useful bits of information to the client, discarding all other irrelevant changes, thus reducing the payload size to the bare minimum.

6   Conclusion

Detecting custom changes in service data is a repetitive and tedious task. In this paper, we have presented POLLY, a declarative domain-specific language for this task. POLLY raises the level of abstraction by leveraging the business domain knowledge of users. It enables users to design custom change detectors by providing the necessary constructs to express state computation, change detection and output construction. We have used POLLY to automatically generate custom change detectors for six use cases provided by our industrial partner CPRODIRECT. Our evaluation shows that POLLY outperforms a handwritten implementation in terms of code verbosity, and that POLLY outperforms a state-of-the-art off-the-shelf differencing tool in terms of running time and output size. To showcase our solution, an online demonstration of POLLY is freely available at the following address[4]. As future work, we plan on performing a large-scale developer study, where we assess the benefits of using POLLY in terms of productivity, code quality and maintenance cost.

Acknowledgment. This work was partially supported by CPRODIRECT and the French funding agency ANRT under contract CIFRE-2013/0891.

References

1. Alarcon, R., Wilde, E., Bellido, J.: Hypermedia-Driven RESTful Service Composition. In: Maximilien, E.M., Rossi, G., Yuan, S.-T., Ludwig, H., Fantinato, M. (eds.) ICSOC 2010. LNCS, vol. 6568, pp. 111–120. Springer, Heidelberg (2011). doi:10.1007/978-3-642-19394-1_12

---

[4] https://demo.pollyapp.ml.

2. Ben Hadj Yahia, E., Réveillère, L., Bromberg, Y.-D., Chevalier, R., Cadot, A.: Medley: An Event-Driven Lightweight Platform for Service Composition. In: Bozzon, A., Cudre-Maroux, P., Pautasso, C. (eds.) ICWE 2016. LNCS, vol. 9671, pp. 3–20. Springer, Cham (2016). doi:10.1007/978-3-319-38791-8_1

3. Bille, P.: A survey on tree edit distance and related problems. Theoret. Comput. Sci. **337**(1), 217–239 (2005)

4. Borgolte, K., Kruegel, C., Vigna, G.: Relevant change detection: a framework for the precise extraction of modified and novel web-based content as a filtering technique for analysis engines. In: 23rd International Conference on World Wide Web (2014)

5. Bryan, P., Nottingham, M.: JavaScript Object Notation (JSON) Patch. Technical report (2013). http://www.rfc-editor.org/info/rfc6902

6. Buttler, D.: A short survey of document structure similarity algorithms. In: International Conference on Internet Computing (2004)

7. Cao, H., Falleri, J.-R., Blanc, X., Zhang, L.: JSON Patch for Turning a Pull REST API into a Push. In: Sheng, Q.Z., Stroulia, E., Tata, S., Bhiri, S. (eds.) ICSOC 2016. LNCS, vol. 9936, pp. 435–449. Springer, Cham (2016). doi:10.1007/978-3-319-46295-0_27

8. Fielding, R.T.: Architectural styles and the design of network-based software architectures. Ph.D. thesis, University of California, Irvine (2000)

9. Higuchi, S., Kan, T., Yamamoto, Y., Hirata, K.: An A* algorithm for computing edit distance between rooted labeled unordered trees. In: JSAI International Symposium on Artificial Intelligence (2011)

10. JSONPath: http://goessner.net/articles/JsonPath. Accessed: 02 June 2017

11. Liu, L., Pu, C., Tang, W.: WebCQ-detecting and delivering information changes on the web. In: 9th International Conference on Information and Knowledge Management (2000)

12. Ovadia, S.: Automate the internet with "if this then that" (IFTTT). Behav. Soc. Sci. Librarian **33**(4), 208–211 (2014)

13. Pandey, S., Dhamdhere, K., Olston, C.: WIC: A general-purpose algorithm for monitoring web information sources. In: 30th International Conference on Very Large Data Bases (2004)

14. Pawlik, M., Augsten, N.: RTED: a robust algorithm for the tree edit distance. VLDB Endow. **5**(4), 334–345 (2011)

15. Simon, J., Schmidt, P., Pammer, V.: An energy efficient implementation of differential synchronization on mobile devices. In: 11th International Conference on Mobile and Ubiquitous Systems: Computing, Networking and Services (2014)

16. Ur, B., Pak Yong Ho, M., Brawner, S., Lee, J., Mennicken, S., Picard, N., Schulze, D., Littman, M.L.: Trigger-action programming in the wild: an analysis of 200,000 IFTTT recipes. In: CHI Conference on Human Factors in Computing Systems (2016)

17. Wang, Y., DeWitt, D.J., Cai, J.Y.: X-Diff: An effective change detection algorithm for xml documents. In: 19th International Conference on Data Engineering (2003)

18. YAML: http://www.yaml.org/spec/1.2/spec.html. Accessed: 02 June 2017

19. Zhang, K., Shasha, D.: Simple fast algorithms for the editing distance between trees and related problems. SIAM J. Comput. **18**(6), 1245–1262 (1989)

20. Zhang, K., Statman, R., Shasha, D.: On the editing distance between unordered labeled trees. Inf. Process. Lett. **42**(3), 133–139 (1992)

Design and Evaluation of a Self-Service Delivery Framework

Constantin Adam$^{(\boxtimes)}$, Nikos Anerousis, Muhammed Fatih Bulut,
Robert Filepp, Anup Kalia, Brian Peterson, John Rofrano,
Maja Vukovic, and Jin Xiao

IBM T.J. Watson Research Center, Yorktown Heights, USA
{cmadam,nikos,mfbulut,filepp,anup.kalia,blpeters,rofrano,
maja,jinoaix}@us.ibm.com

Abstract. We present a framework for automating change and service
request management, a process that has remained almost entirely human-
centric, despite the fact that it involves complex workflows, takes a significant amount of time, and is prone to errors. We extend previous work on
modeling process complexity to evaluate the impact of automating business constraints (such as policy approvals and entitlements). Our results
indicate that automation eliminates a significant amount of operational
complexity, reducing it by 68% compared to the Information Technology
Infrastructure Library (ITIL) guidelines, and by 80% compared to actual
client processes. Automation also reduces, between 55% and 82% for different client accounts, the average time that elapses from the moment
that a change request is received until it starts executing.

1   Introduction

IT management has evolved from a human-centric and labor-intensive activity
to a process driven by automation with a few notable exceptions, such as change
and service request management. Traditionally performed via ticketing systems,
the current process involves several humans coordinating its execution: forming,
submitting and analyzing requests, obtaining approvals where needed, assigning
work to a subject matter expert, performing the work, updating records, and
notifying the original requester upon completion. Although an underlying service
management platform enables it, the process is merely facilitating the exchange
of messages between human performers. As a result, it still takes a lot of time
and involves many people, each with their own and distinct role in the process.

In this article, we present our work on automating change management in a
large managed service provider environment. Our work was motivated by the dif-
ficulties inherent to the largely manual change management workflow described
in the Information Technology Infrastructure Library (ITIL) - a set of detailed
best practices for IT Service Management. Not only a multitude of human errors
are possible because of the manual nature of the process (choosing the wrong
endpoint, misinterpreting the request, getting the wrong approval, miscommu-
nicating), but change requests wait for a long time in a queue to be analyzed,

© Springer International Publishing AG 2017
M. Maximilien et al. (Eds.): ICSOC 2017, LNCS 10601, pp. 445–452, 2017.
https://doi.org/10.1007/978-3-319-69035-3_31

approved, or reviewed by a subject matter expert. So, aside from process automation, we have also aimed to automate various business functions, like approvals, or determining entitlements. We have found out that automation benefits change management in several ways: not only the process is faster, as it bypasses several manual steps and the need for coordination, but it also reduces process complexity (and implicitly risk), and offers predictable outcomes.

2 System Architecture

We have built an automated change management workflow starting from the ITIL specification, aiming to keep ITIL functionality intact, while automating as much of the process as possible. This workflow has a reduced number of personas, and an automation role does all the work in most cases. Humans are only needed to initiate changes, approve changes that are not pre-approved automatically, or perform manual pre- and post-execution where needed. Below, in Sect. 2.1 we describe the building blocks of our automated implementation, and in Sect. 2.2 we illustrate the automated functionality using the AIX memory management use case.

2.1 Automated Functionality

We have identified a set of key components that must be automated to streamline the ITIL change management workflow. These building blocks, and the mapping graph between the ITIL and our Self-Service Delivery (SSD) workflows are presented in Fig. 1, and described in more detail below.

1. *Defining User Entitlements* - users are added to groups that give them specific rights to initiate or approve different types of change requests, perform capacity approvals, or manually execute specific operations on the endpoints.
2. *Providing an Interface that Validates User Requests* - users specify change requests through interfaces, or chat bots that provide structure to the received requests and eliminate ambiguity or request misinterpretation.
3. *Retrieving Up-to-date Server State* - real-time access to endpoint state provides accurate input for building change requests, and allows to automatically validate the change request outcomes. Scripts discover on each managed node the state of its resources (file systems, memory, CPU, cron jobs, etc.), and store it in a repository. Discovery runs before (to check the current state) and after (to validate the execution result) a change is made to an endpoint.
4. *Developing Resource Models and Validators* - each managed resource is associated with a software model and a set of validators that check the correctness and the technical feasibility of the change requests for that resource.
5. *Defining Business Policies for Pre-approved Requests* - business policies allow pre-approving change requests with parameters within acceptable ranges, and limit manual approvals to a handful of special cases. They also eliminate the need to monitor a system after a pre-approved change was made, as the successful execution of such a change guarantees its correctness.

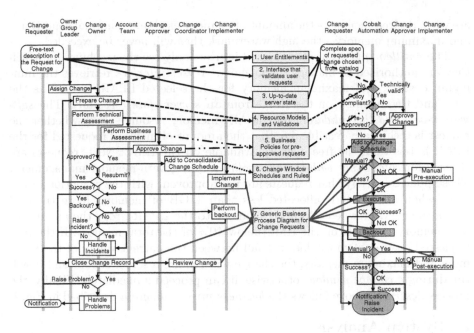

Fig. 1. ITIL (left) vs. SSD (right) automated change management process.

6. *Providing Change Window Schedules and Rules* - each request type has (in the business policies) a flag that specifies whether it needs a change window, or can be executed immediately. If a change window is needed, the requester can choose one from a list computed using change window schedules and rules, or let the change execute during the next available change window.

7. *Generic Business Process Diagram for Change Requests* - all change requests, regardless of their type, follow the same business cycle illustrated in Fig. 2. After initiation, requests undergo syntactic, technical feasibility and business policy compliance checks. Requests that pass all the checks are automatically approved. Requests that fail the business policy checks are approved manually. Approved requests are checked for any pre-requisites, and scheduled for execution immediately, or in a change window. After execution, the system takes any post-execution steps, discovers the new endpoint state, and determines whether the change was successful, or needs to be backed out.

2.2 Case Study: Memory Allocation for AIX LPARs

To illustrate how the building blocks described above automate change management, consider memory allocation on AIX Logical Partitions (LPARs) managed by Hardware Management Consoles (HMC). The LPARs and HMCs are the equivalents of Virtual Machines and Hypervisors. LPAR memory specification includes: minimum memory - the smallest amount acceptable to boot and operate with, desired memory - the amount of memory used under normal conditions, and maximum memory - the high watermark that will never be exceeded.

The *entitlements* ensure that logged in users only see the machines on which they are authorized to manage the memory. *A user interface* retrieves the minimum, desired, and maximum memory for the selected LPAR, as well as the total and free memory on the HMC from an *server state repository*. The *software model and the validators* for the AIX memory resource check whether the request is technically feasible, i.e. that the amount of memory requested for the LPAR is less than the free memory available on the HMC. Next, requests are checked for *compliance with business policies* that govern memory management. These policies specify that requests are pre-approved, with the exception of the cases when an LPAR is allocated less than 1 GB of memory, more than 12 GB of memory, or when allocating memory to the LPAR drops the amount of free memory available on the HMC below 10% of the total memory. If the new requested desired memory does not fall between the current values of the minimum and maximum memory, the change will require a server reboot and it will run during *a change window*; otherwise, it can proceed immediately. Finally, the process described above follows the *business process diagram* described in Fig. 2.

3 System Analysis

We enhance a prior model ([1,2]) to analyze and quantify the complexity of the change management process. We keep the construction of the overall complexity metric based on execution, coordination, and business object complexity, and retain the coordination complexity model. We refine the base model to better reflect three key factors of complexity in IT change management: execution, coordination (link) and business object outcome. Figure 2 shows the T tasks evaluated for complexity. Complexity analysis is performed on a per task basis (C_exe, C_link and C_bo are respectively the execution, coordination, and business object complexity of a task), and it also includes inter-task (between tasks i and $i+1$) coordination ($C\_link_{i,i+1}$) and business object complexity ($C\_bo_{i,i+1}$):

$$C_{total} = \sum_{i=1}^{T}(C\_exe_i + C\_link_i + C\_bo_i) + \sum_{i=1}^{T-1}(C\_link_{i,i+1} + C\_bo_{i,i+1}) \quad (1)$$

Each task t consists of a set of execution blocks T_t, and a set of decision blocks D_t, and its execution complexity is the sum of the complexities of each component in sets T_t and D_t. The complexity of an execution block is the product of its baseline execution complexity C_base_i and the number of roles involved in the execution R_i. C_base_i takes the values 0 for automated, $\{1,2\}$ for tool assisted, and $\{2,3\}$ for manual execution. The complexity of a decision block is the product of three factors: $g_i = \{1,2\}$, which accounts for how well the decision is guided, $c_i = \{1,2,3\}$, which factors the risk/impact if wrong decision is made, and R_i, the number of roles participating in the decision block:

$$C\_exe_t = \sum_{i=1}^{T_t}(C\_base_i R_i) + \sum_{i=1}^{D_t} g_i c_i R_i \quad (2)$$

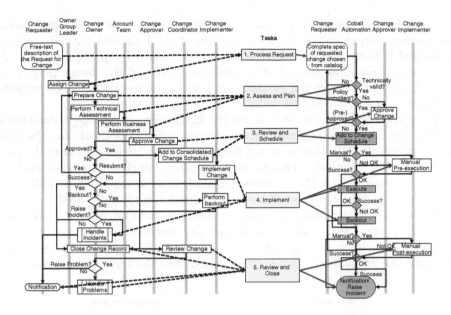

Fig. 2. Task breakdown of ITIL reference model and SSD process

The coordination complexity of a task t is the sum of the complexities of the links that connect its execution blocks. We define the complexity of a link l as the product between its coordination complexity $LinkType_l$, and the number of roles involved in that link (R_l) minus one. $LinkType_l$ takes integer values that account for the communication complexity between two execution blocks: 1 for a straight pass, 2 when one back-forth communication is needed, and 3 when multiple back-forth communication is needed.

$$C\_link_t = \sum_{l=1}^{L_t} LinkType_l(R_l - 1) \tag{3}$$

The business object complexity captures the difficulty of sending, acquiring, and understanding the information communicated between two execution blocks. We denote by BO_t the set of all the business objects that are passed between the execution blocks of a task t. The complexity of a business object o is the product between its ambiguity factor $ambi_o$, and the number of roles involved in the object exchange R_o. The ambiguity factor $ambi_o$ takes the following values: 1 when data can be readily looked up (e.g., ID, Category, etc.); $\{2,3\}$: when data represents system or state information that needs to be discovered (e.g., filesystem path, runstate of a server, etc.); $\{4,5\}$ when data is complex and may need further user input and entitlement verification (e.g., sudo right for a user, system fold access permissions, etc.).

$$C\_bo_t = \sum_{o=1}^{BO_t} ambi_o R_o \tag{4}$$

Note that we can use Eqs. 3 and 4 to compute the inter-task coordination and business object complexities, by looking at the links and business objects exchanged between tasks, instead of execution blocks. By plugging in Eqs. 2, 3, and 4 into Eq. 1, we compute the total complexity of the change process to account for all the execution blocks, coordination efforts and business objects produced.

We carried out the computation for the ITIL reference change management process, the change management process implemented by a client, and the SSD change process for DB, Hardware and Network change categories. Figure 3 shows the results. We can observe that for each category, the client's process tends to be more complex than ITIL reference model. This is expected as ITIL is a reference and additional process and coordination are typically needed when a client implements the change process according to the ITIL reference. Overall, we see SSD significantly reduces the complexity across all the change categories evaluated, showing a reducing of $66\% - 70\%$ compared to the ITIL reference process and a reduction of $79\% - 80\%$ compared to the client change process.

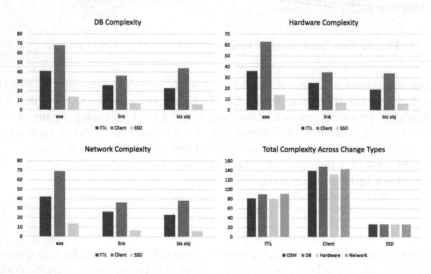

Fig. 3. ITIL, Client and SSD complexity scores for DB, Hardware and Network changes.

4   System Evaluation

To provide a quantitative estimate of the time savings introduced by our automation process, we have analyzed data from the ticketing system repository for three accounts (A for an IT services, B for a logistics, and C for a financial services customer) served by IBM. The change request records contain a text description of the change, the date and time when the request was received ($t_{received}$), when its execution started ($t_{exec-start}$), and ended ($t_{exec-end}$), and when it was closed (t_{closed}). We analyze change requests in the database, hardware, networking and OS management categories. The total time taken by a change request is the sum of pre-execution, execution and post-execution times, calculated using these formulas: $t_{pre-execution} = t_{exec-start} - t_{received}$, $t_{execution} = t_{exec-end} - t_{exec-start}$, and $t_{post-execution} = t_{closed} - t_{exec-end}$

Table 1. Pre-execution times (automated and current) and post-execution times (current)

	Account A	Account B	Account C
Pre-execution time for automation (days)	1.30	1.92	1.85
Current pre-execution time (days)	7.48	4.19	5.60
Current post-execution time (days)	7.61	0.88	0.37
Number of change requests	12385	2357	11050

Table 1 shows the pre- and post-execution times for the three accounts. The pre-execution time for the automation represents a conservative upper-bound, where we assumed that each automated change request will wait for the next available change window, calculated using the schedule for each account (account A has three change windows a week, while accounts B and C have two change windows a week). We calculated this upper bound, as we could not determine from the available data whether a given request would execute immediately, or in a change window. Even under these conservative assumptions, the automation reduces significantly the pre-execution time, between 55% and 82% for different client accounts. The pre-execution times vary between accounts, depending on the complexity of the implementation of the ITIL processes currently in place. We did not see significant improvements in the change execution time; this is not surprising, as considerable research and effort has been put in the execution of the changes. The post-execution time is larger for the accounts where it is customary to monitor the systems where a change took place for several days prior to closing that change. As the monitoring becomes unnecessary for the automated pre-approved changes, we expect our system to considerably cut down the post-execution time, by a percentage proportional to the percentage of pre-approved requests.

5   Related Work

ServiceNow [3], is a commercially available IT Service Management framework that includes both service catalog creation and self-service capabilities, but requires a high degree of customization ([4]). Configuration management software (like Chef [5], or Ansible [6]) allows discovering state and making changes to the endpoints, but does not support the business aspects of the change management process, including entitlements, validation, change windows, compliance with business policies. From the analysis of the complexity of IT service management perspective, [7] analyzes key performance indicators and their inter-relationships, to reason and schedule the transformation of the service delivery systems, while [8] proposes a framework for minimizing human errors in change management from the point of view of change preparation and execution. An infrastructure for evaluating change risk is proposed in [9], by looking at the history of similar changes, performed on endpoints with similar configuration. A model to quantify the complexity of the IT service management process, and the business value of introducing new IT processes is introduced in [1] and [2].

6   Conclusion and Future Work

We have presented a change management system that automates the ITIL workflow, while preserving its functionality, and a model to measure the reduction in complexity brought by the automation. Going forward, we are going to investigate using Terraform [10] for orchestration, and OpenWhisk [11] for implementing the actions in the workflows. By gathering data as our solution is deployed in new accounts, we will prove there is a correlation between the complexity analysis model and the time it takes to process various change requests.

References

1. Diao, Y., Keller, A.: Quantifying the complexity of IT service management processes. In: State, R., Meer, S., O'Sullivan, D., Pfeifer, T. (eds.) DSOM 2006. LNCS, vol. 4269, pp. 61–73. Springer, Heidelberg (2006). doi:10.1007/11907466_6
2. Diao, Y., Bhattacharya, K.: Estimating business value of IT services through process complexity analysis. In: Proceedings of IEEE/IFIP NOMS, pp. 208–215. IEEE, Salvador (2008)
3. Servicenow product documentation. https://docs.servicenow.com/. Accessed 04 Jun 2017
4. Toteva, Z., Alonso, R.A., Granda, E.A., Cheimariou, M.-E., Fedorko, I., Hefferman, J., Lemaitre, S., Clavo, D.M., Pedreira, P.M., Mira, O.P.: Service management at CERN with service-now. J. Phys. **396**, 1–7 (2012)
5. Chef: Deploy new code faster and more frequently. automate infrastructure and applications — chef. https://www.chef.io/. Accessed 04 Jun 2017
6. Ansible is simple it automation. https://www.ansible.com/. Accessed 04 Jun 2017
7. Dasgupta, G.B., Shrinivasan, Y., Nayak, T.K., Nallacherry, J.: Optimal strategy for proactive service delivery management using inter-KPI influence relationships. In: Basu, S., Pautasso, C., Zhang, L., Fu, X. (eds.) ICSOC 2013. LNCS, vol. 8274, pp. 131–145. Springer, Heidelberg (2013). doi:10.1007/978-3-642-45005-1_10
8. Madduri, V.R., Gupta, M., De, P., Anand, V.: Towards mitigating human errors in IT change management process. In: Maglio, P.P., Weske, M., Yang, J., Fantinato, M. (eds.) ICSOC 2010. LNCS, vol. 6470, pp. 657–662. Springer, Heidelberg (2010). doi:10.1007/978-3-642-17358-5_52
9. Güven, S., Murthy, K.: Understanding the role of change in incident prevention. In: Proceedings of CNSM, pp. 268–271. IEEE (2016)
10. Terraform by HashiCorp. https://www.terraform.io/. Accessed 04 Jun 2017
11. Apache openwhisk - serverless, open source cloud platform. https://openwhisk.org/. Accessed 04 Jun 2017

Automated Generation of REST API Specification from Plain HTML Documentation

Hanyang Cao$^{(\boxtimes)}$, Jean-Rémy Falleri, and Xavier Blanc

University of Bordeaux, LaBRI, UMR 5800, 33400 Talence, France
{cao.hanyang,falleri,xblanc}@labri.fr

Abstract. REST is nowadays highly popular and widely adopted by Web services providers. However, most of the Web services providers only provide the documentation of their REST API in plain HTML pages, even if many specification formats exist such as WADL or OpenAPI for example. This prevents the Web Services users to benefit from all the advantages of having a machine-readable specification, such as generating client or server code, generating web services composition, checking formal properties, testing, etc. To face this issue, we provide a fully automated approach that builds a REST API specification from its corresponding plain HTML documentation. By given the root URL of the plain HTML API documentation, our approach automatically extracts the four mandatory parts that compose a specification: the base URL, the path templates, the HTTP verbs and the associated formal parameters. Our approach has been validated with topmost commercial REST based Web Services, and the validation shows that our approach achieves good precision and recall for popular Web Services.

Keywords: REST · APIs · Service description · Specification · OpenAPI

1 Introduction

REST, the architecture style defined by Fielding [5], is nowadays highly popular and widely adopted by most of the Web services providers. All the studies done by researchers [4] or by commercial sites such as ProgrammableWeb[1] state that more than 75% of Web services are now REST oriented.

However, Renzal et al. pinpoint that building REST services is still highly challenging [12]. They further highlight that the first REST best practice is to provide a rigorous specification of the REST API. Such a specification accelerates the development process by automatically generating client-side or server-side stubs [6], or even service composition [14]. Additionally, a rigorous specification can be used to reach a better quality by inferring parameters dependency constraints [16] or performing automating tests production [10] for example.

---

[1] https://www.programmableweb.com/api-research.

© Springer International Publishing AG 2017
M. Maximilien et al. (Eds.): ICSOC 2017, LNCS 10601, pp. 453–461, 2017.
https://doi.org/10.1007/978-3-319-69035-3_32

Several formats have been introduced for defining REST API specifications. One of them is the XML-based language WADL (Web Application Description Language), which is a *de jure* W3C standard [7]. Others, such as OpenAPI specification[2], RAML[3], and Blueprint[4] are JSON-based formats, and are *de facto* standards provided by the industry. However, even if many formats exist and if ones are more popular than the other (OpenAPI turns out to be the most popular one, with over 350,000 downloads per month), no format is widely adopted [11].

More precisely, as identified by Danielsen et al., most of the REST APIs providers only provide their documentation in plain HTML pages [4]. Further, according to an in-depth analysis of the most 20 popular REST Services [12], only 20% of them provide WSDL [2] specifications whereas 75% provide no rigorous specification and only plain HTML pages!

Such a situation then calls for an automatic transformation of plain HTML documentations into rigorous specifications. This will drastically help developers and make them benefit from all the advantages of having a rigorous specification: code and composition generation, test, type checking, etc.

In this paper, we face this problem and provide a fully automated approach that builds an OpenAPI specification from a corresponding plain HTML documentation. We choose OpenAPI because it is currently the most popular. Furthermore, once an OpenAPI specification exists, translating it into another format such as WADL for instance is very easy.

Our approach comes with a prototype implementation that inputs the root URL of the plain HTML API documentation, and that extracts the four mandatory parts that compose an OpenAPI specification: the base URL, the path templates, the HTTP verbs and the associated formal parameters. Our prototype has been validated with topmost commercial REST based Web Services as well as with Web Services selected at random into ProgrammableWeb. The validation shows that our approach achieves good precision and recall especially for popular Web Services.

As a main result, we provide:

- An automated approach that automatically generates an OpenAPI specification from the plain HTML documentation of an existing REST Web Service.
- A validation of our prototype and the OpenAPI specifications it yielded from topmost popular Web Services.

2 AutoREST: An Automatic Generator of REST API Specifications

This section first provides basic and simple definitions for the main concepts of REST API documentation and specification. It then presents an overview of our generator, called AutoREST, and finally presents its three main components.

---

[2] https://www.openapis.org/.
[3] http://raml.org/.
[4] https://apiblueprint.org/.

Definition 1 (REST API HTML Documentation). *A REST API HTML Documentation describes the resources provided by a REST service in plain HTML. It is composed of a set of web pages. Among the set of pages, one page is called the Root Page, and is linked directly or indirectly to all the pages of the set. Finally, all the pages belong to a same domain (the one of the Root Page) and each page may or may not contain useful information to access the service.*

As an example, the Root Page of the Instagram API HTML Documentation is https://www.instagram.com/developer/. From this Root Page, a set of 24 pages that belong to the same "www.instagram.com/developer" domain can be visited following the links between them. Finally some of these pages can be considered to be useful as they describe how to access the service. Other ones can be considered to be useless regarding this purpose as they don't describe how to access the service (e.g., service changelog information).

Definition 2 (REST API Specification). *A REST API Specification rigorously defines how to access the resources provided by a REST service. It is written in a de jure or de facto standard format such as WADL or OpenAPI. At least, it has to describe the following information:*

- *Base URL: The Base URL is the common prefix of all URLs that give access to the resources.*
- *Path Templates: The templates describes how the* Base URL *must be completed to make an URL that does give access to a resource. A template can include variables that are used to identify different but similar resources.*
- *Verbs: The verbs list, for each* Path Template, *the HTTP verbs that are supported by the Web service (GET, PUT, POST, etc.).*
- *Parameters: The parameters, for each couple of* Path Template *and* Verb, *define the list of formal parameters that are supported by the request.*

The objective of our approach (named AutoREST) is to automatically generate a REST API Specification from a REST API HTML Documentation. The Fig. 1 presents the global architecture of our approach. It shows that AutoREST inputs the Root Page of the REST API Documentation of a given Web service and then returns a generated OpenAPI Specification. More precisely, AutoREST performs the following three steps:

Step 1: Identifying all the HTML documentation pages. It gathers all the pages that are directly or indirectly linked by the Root Page and that belong to its domain. The purpose of this step is to identify all the web pages that may describe the REST API. We built a simple crawler that identifies all the web pages that are directly or indirectly linked by the Root Page of the REST API HTML Documentation. Furthermore, our crawler never goes outside of the domain of the Root Page.

Step 2: Classify useful or useless documentation pages. The goal of this step is to select only web pages that do contain useful information for building a REST API specification. As this step preforms a classification, we decided to use machine learning techniques [9].

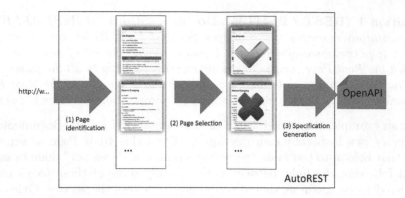

Fig. 1. Global process of our AutoREST

We therefore built a so-called *training set* that contains HTML pages that have been manually classified as being useful (Yes) or useless (No) regarding the purpose of generating a REST API specification. A page was said to be useful if it contains at least one information that can be used to generate a part of a REST API specification. We built that set by getting all the pages of the 15 topmost popular Web Services listed in ProgrammableWeb where popularity is expressed by the number of followers (see full list[5]). We chose to consider 15 Web Services because they gather 90% of all the followers.

Once the training set was built, we then extracted the features it contains. To that extent, each file of the training set has been treated as a plain text (one string) and transformed into a numerical feature vector by tokenizing it, counting tokens occurrences and normalizing tokens. For instance, the string "*Get a list of users who have liked this media ...*" is tokenized by using white spaces as token separators. Then, each token is assigned an integer id, such as {Get: 1, a: 2, list: 3}. Then the tokens are counted ad normalized by using the TF-IDF weighting to build the feature vector [15].

Finally, we computed and evaluated the classifier. We choose Random Forest [8] as the Machine-learning algorithm since it outperforms others on the supervised classification problem [9]. Regarding the size of the training set we tried various sets of different sizes. Result shows performance tends to be stable (96%) when size exceeds 200. Hence we chose to build a *training set* containing 200 HTML files. Our Classifier thus can select web pages that do contain useful information with a high precision (96%) and recall (96%).

Step 3: Extract Information and Generate REST API Specification.
Since each Web service provider might have its own different patterns for displaying API documentation within HTML page, we made a simple comparative study on the same topmost 15 popular Web Services to better understand such patterns. The Table 1 lists the different patterns used by Web service providers

---

[5] https://github.com/caohanyang/REST_OPENAPI/blob/master/APIList.

Table 1. Patterns used by Web server providers to display REST API Specification in HTML pages.

Specification part	Patterns
Base URL	either in a dedicated part of the page or with each *Path Template*
Path Template	either with a partial URL starting with '/' or with a full URL including the *Base URL*
Verbs	Just before or after the path template
Parameters	In a list or in a array, just after the template

to display in an HTML page the four mandatory parts that compose a REST API specification.

Our component embeds different strategies (Regular Expressions, GATE configurations [3], etc.) that corresponds to the different patterns of displaying the informations within the HTML pages. As it cannot have any prior knowledge on how the information is displayed when it analyses a page, it then loop the analysis for each possible configuration and returns the Specification that contains the more *Path Templates*, *Verbs* and *Parameters*.

3 Evaluation

The objective of our evaluation is to measure the quality of the specifications generated by AutoREST. This quality can be measured according to the four mandatory parts of the specification (Base URL, Path Templates, Verbs and Parameters). Furthermore, it has to reflect what the documentation describes. More precisely, we measure the quality of a generated specification according to the following criteria. All criteria are measured manually by comparing the generated specification with its corresponding documentation:

- The quality of the *Base URL* is measured by a boolean. True means that the specification exactly reflects what is written in the documentation.
- The quality of the *Path Templates* is measured by counting the number of Paths templates in the specification and in the documentation, and by checking how much of them match. The quality is then expressed with precision (No. Match/No. in Spec.) and recall (No. Match/No. in Doc.).
- The quality of the *Verbs* is measured by counting the number of Verbs in the specification and in the documentation, and by checking how much of them match. Two verbs match if they have the same Path Template and if they are the same.
- The quality of the *Parameters* is measured by counting the number of Parameters in the specification and in the documentation, and by checking how much of them match. Two parameters match if they have the same Path Template, the same verb, the same name and the same type.

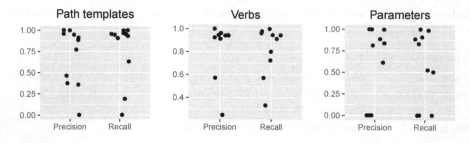

Fig. 2. Results of the topmost popular Web Services

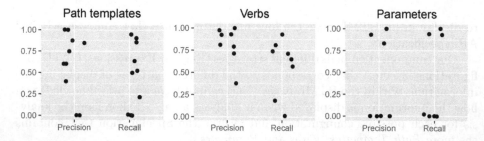

Fig. 3. Results of the random Web Services

Our AutoREST has been developed in Python and Java, and is available on-line as an Open Source Project[6]. We evaluate AutoREST on two sets of Web Services. The first set is composed of the 15 topmost popular Web Services. The second set is composed of 15 Web Services selected at random from ProgrammableWeb. The evaluation done with the first set expresses how AutoREST performs on popular Web Service knowing that it has been trained with a small subset of them for selecting interesting pages, and that its information retrieval rules have been defined by analyzing them (see Sect. 2). The evaluation done with the second set expresses the capacity of AutoREST to generated OpenAPI specifications without any prior knowledge.

As a main result, AutoREST has quite good results for finding the *Base URL*: 11/15 for the topmost popular Web Services, and 10/15 for random Web services. The Figs. 2 and 3 then present the precision and recall for the *Path Templates*, *Verbs* and *Parameters*. It should be noted that when AutoREST fails in finding the *Base URL*, it also fails for all of the other parts. As a consequence, we choose not to show these cases in the Figures.

As we just presented it, AutoREST is quite good for generating a *Base URL*. It fails when the *Base URL* is not documented neither in a dedicated place nor with the *Path Templates*. For example, it fails with Twilio that contains a variable in the base URL. More precisely the *Base URL*

---

[6] https://github.com/caohanyang/REST_OPENAPI.

of Twilio is "https://api.twilio.com/2010-04-01/Accounts/{AccountSid}" where AccountSid is used to authenticate the user.

For *Path templates* the results are good but more debatable. First of all, it is clear that AutoREST performs better for popular Web Services, as it has been trained on it. After the manually investigation, we found AutoREST fails mainly for two reasons. First it uses regular expression to detect URLs but as there are many URLs in web pages it sometimes fails to distinguish the ones that correspond to REST services. Second, it sometimes fails to infer the Path templates which contains path templating. Indeed, some API providers present the Path templates by providing examples. AutoREST then fails in extracting these generic cases. For instance, Twitter lists an example request https://api.twitter.com/1.1/geo/id/df51dec6f4ee2b2c.json in its documentation page. AutoREST then considers it as a Template Path!

For *verbs* the results are quite similar than *Path Templates*. AutoREST performs a little bit better for popular Web Service.

Finally, AutoREST is good to extract the Parameters for popular Web Services but not for the ones that have been randomly selected. The main reason is because the documentation provided by the latter is not structured with tables or lists, as it is expected by our information retrieval component.

4   Related Work

Only three existing works are related to the generation of REST API specifications.

In [13], Sohan et al. provide SpyREST, an approach for generating RESTful API documentation by using an HTTP proxy server. In contrast to our approach that is static, SpyREST is dynamic as it listens to the communications that are performed with the REST Services to generate the documentation. It then requires a client that knows how to call the REST Services and also requires the client to perform all the possible calls.

In [1], Alarcón et al. provides RESTler that crawls a RESTful Service and aims to generate a map that presents all the provided resources and their links. This approach then does not generate a rigorous specification.

5   Conclusion

In this paper we then present AutoREST, an approach for automatically transform an HTML documentation into an OpenAPI specification. It can then be used as a black box tool that only inputs one root URL and that generates an OpenAPI specification. The validation we done shows that AutoREST has quite good results especially with popular Web Services. For randomly selected Web Services it is less successful mainly because the provided HTML documentation is not structured as the one of the topmost popular Web Services.

As a further work, we plan to work on a component that validates the returned OpenAPI specification after its generation by generating and testing calls. Thanks to this component, we then aim at returning an OpenAPI specification that does not contain any faults (100% precision). We also plan to extend machine learning component. Our goal is to strengthen our approach to better identify weak HTML documentation, with the intent to provide error messages indicating that the OpenAPI generation cannot be performed.

References

1. Alarcón, R., Wilde, E.: Restler: crawling restful services. In: Proceedings of the 19th International Conference on World Wide Web, pp. 1051–1052. ACM (2010)
2. Chinnici, R., Moreau, J.J., Ryman, A., Weerawarana, S.: Web services description language (WSDL) version 2.0 part 1: Core language. W3C recommendation 26, 19 (2007)
3. Cunningham, H., Maynard, D., Bontcheva, K., Tablan, V., Aswani, N., Roberts, I., Gorrell, G., Funk, A., Roberts, A., Damljanovic, D., et al.: Developing language processing components with gate version 6 (a user guide). University of Sheffield, UK (2013). http://gate.ac.uk/sale/tao/index.html
4. Danielsen, P.J., Jeffrey, A.: Validation and interactivity of web API documentation. In: 2013 IEEE 20th International Conference on Web Services (ICWS), pp. 523–530. IEEE (2013)
5. Fielding, R.T., Taylor, R.N.: Principled design of the modern web architecture. ACM Trans. Internet Technol. (TOIT) 2(2), 115–150 (2002). http://dl.acm.org/citation.cfm?id=514185
6. Fokaefs, M., Stroulia, E.: Using WADL specifications to develop and maintain rest client applications. In: 2015 IEEE International Conference on Web Services (ICWS), pp. 81–88. IEEE (2015)
7. Hadley, M.J.: Web application description language (WADL) (2006)
8. Ho, T.K.: Random decision forests. In: Proceedings of the Third International Conference on Document Analysis and Recognition, vol. 1, pp. 278–282. IEEE (1995)
9. Koprinska, I., Poon, J., Clark, J., Chan, J.: Learning to classify e-mail. Inf. Sci. 177(10), 2167–2187 (2007)
10. López, M., Ferreiro, H., Francisco, M.A., Castro, L.M.: Automatic generation of test models for web services using WSDL and OCL. In: Basu, S., Pautasso, C., Zhang, L., Fu, X. (eds.) ICSOC 2013. LNCS, vol. 8274, pp. 483–490. Springer, Heidelberg (2013). doi:10.1007/978-3-642-45005-1_37
11. Lucky, M.N., Cremaschi, M., Lodigiani, B., Menolascina, A., De Paoli, F.: Enriching API descriptions by adding API profiles through semantic annotation. In: Sheng, Q.Z., Stroulia, E., Tata, S., Bhiri, S. (eds.) ICSOC 2016. LNCS, vol. 9936, pp. 780–794. Springer, Cham (2016). doi:10.1007/978-3-319-46295-0_55
12. Renzel, D., Schlebusch, P., Klamma, R.: Todays top restful services and why they are not restful. In: Web Information Systems Engineering, WISE 2012, pp. 354–367 (2012)
13. Sohan, S., Anslow, C., Maurer, F.: Spyrest: automated restful API documentation using an HTTP proxy server (n). In: 2015 30th IEEE/ACM International Conference on Automated Software Engineering (ASE), pp. 271–276. IEEE (2015)

14. Wagner, F., Klöpper, B., Ishikawa, F., Honiden, S.: Towards robust service compositions in the context of functionally diverse services. In: Proceedings of the 21st International Conference on World Wide Web, pp. 969–978. ACM (2012)
15. Wu, H.C., Luk, R.W.P., Wong, K.F., Kwok, K.L.: Interpreting TF-IDF term weights as making relevance decisions. ACM Trans. Inf. Syst. **26**(3), 13:1–13:37 (2008). http://doi.acm.org/10.1145/1361684.1361686
16. Wu, Q., Wu, L., Liang, G., Wang, Q., Xie, T., Mei, H.: Inferring dependency constraints on parameters for web services. In: Proceedings of the 22nd International Conference on World Wide Web, pp. 1421–1432. ACM (2013)

Efficient Keyword Search for Building Service-Based Systems Based on Dynamic Programming

Qiang He[1,2]([⊠]), Rui Zhou[2], Xuyun Zhang[3], Yanchun Wang[2], Dayong Ye[2], Feifei Chen[4], Shiping Chen[5], John Grundy[6], and Yun Yang[2]

[1] State Key Laboratory of Software Engineering, Wuhan University, Wuhan, China
[2] Swinburne University of Technology, Hawthorn, Australia
{qhe, rzhou, yanchunwang, dye, yyang}@swin.edu.au
[3] University of Auckland, Auckland, New Zealand
xuyun.zhang@auckland.ac.nz
[4] Federation University, Melbourne, Australia
feifei.chen@federation.edu.au
[5] Data61, CSIRO, Canberra, Australia
shiping.chen@data61.csiro.au
[6] Deakin University, Burwood, Australia
j.grundy@deakin.edu.au

Abstract. The advances in service-oriented architecture (SOA) have fueled the demand for building service-based systems (SBSs) by composing existing services. Finding appropriate component services is a key step during the process for building SBSs. However, existing approaches require that system engineers have detailed knowledge of SOA techniques, which is often too demanding. A recent approach has been proposed to address this issue. However, it suffers from poor efficiency, which is increasingly critical as the service repository continues to grow. To address this issue, this paper proposes KS3+, a new, highly efficient approach that allows a system engineer to query for a system solution with a few keywords that represent the required system tasks. Modeling the problem of answering such a keyword query as a dynamic programming problem, KS3+ can quickly find a system solution composed of services that perform the required system tasks. It offers an efficient paradigm that significantly reduces the time and effort during the process for building SBSs. The results of extensive experiments on a real-world web service dataset demonstrate the high efficiency and effectiveness of KS3+.

Keywords: Service oriented architecture · Service-based systems · Keyword search · Web services

© Springer International Publishing AG 2017
M. Maximilien et al. (Eds.): ICSOC 2017, LNCS 10601, pp. 462–470, 2017.
https://doi.org/10.1007/978-3-319-69035-3_33

1 Introduction

The service-oriented architecture (SOA) has been widely employed by many enterprises to build service-based systems (SBSs) [1, 2]. The component services of an SBS collectively realize the functionality of the SBS, which are often offered as SaaS (Software-as-a-Service) to internal and external users in the cloud environment. The development and popularity of e-business, ecommerce, especially the pay-as-you-go business model promoted by cloud computing, have fueled the rapid growth of services and SBSs, shown by statistics published by programmableweb.com, a web service directory. The process for building an SBS consists of three phases: (1) System Planning: the system engineer empirically identifies and determines the system tasks, e.g., *flight ticket booking, hotel booking*, as well as the execution order of the tasks. (2) Service Discovery: the system engineer, through querying service repositories or service search engines, discovers multiple sets of composable services, each offering one of the required system tasks. (3) Service Selection: the system engineer selects one service from each set of candidate services to compose the target system that fulfills the multi-dimensional constraints and the optimization goal for the system quality, e.g., reliability, response time and cost.

The process above is complicated and requires detailed knowledge of sophisticated SOA techniques in different phases. It has become a major obstacle to broader applications of SOA. There has been a rapid increase in the need for an approach that assists system engineers in quickly finding *system solutions* for their SBSs, including which services to use and in what order they are composed, without going through the above complicated process [3].

We previously presented KS3 to tackle this challenge [4]. KS3 allows system engineers to query for system solutions by entering only a few keywords that represent the required system tasks. Such a *keyword query*, i.e., a query containing keywords that represent the required system tasks, is modeled as a constraint optimization problem and employs the integer programming technique to find system solutions. **However, KS3 suffers from extremely poor efficiency in processing queries on large web service repositories.** According to [4], it takes up to 100 s to answer queries on a repository with 20,000 web services. To address this issue, this paper proposes KS3+, a new, highly efficient approach for building SBSs also based on keyword search techniques.

2 Keyword Search Method

We discuss how KS3+ models keyword queries for system solutions and finds group Steiner trees [4] as answer trees to these keyword queries. We denote the set of keywords in a query Q as $\mathbf{K} = \{k_1, k_2, \ldots, k_l\}$ and use $\mathbf{k}, \mathbf{k_x}$, and $\mathbf{k_y}$ to denote a non-empty set of K where $\mathbf{k}, \mathbf{k_x}, \mathbf{k_y} \subseteq \mathbf{K}$. To represent a group Steiner tree that is rooted at node v and covers a set of keywords $\mathbf{k}$, we use $T(v, \mathbf{k})$. Thus, the group Steiner tree we look for in data graph $G(V, E)$ as answer to Q is $T(v, \mathbf{K})$ where $v \in V$ represents a web service and $e \in E$ represents the composability of two web services. For more details about G, see [4].

2.1   Dynamic Programming Model

In this research, a group Steiner tree $T(v, \mathbf{K})$ of height h (the length of the longest downward path from the root of the group Steiner tree to any leaf) can be found by expanding the group Steiner trees of heights $h = 0, 1, \ldots$, that cover $\mathbf{k} \subseteq \mathbf{k}$. Let $T(v, k)$ be a state in the dynamic programming model, and $w(T(v, \mathbf{k}))$ be the weight of $T(v, \mathbf{k})$, i.e., the total weight of the nodes in $T(v, k)$, the state-transition equation in the dynamic programming model is:

$$w(T(v, \mathbf{k})) = \min\big(w\big(T_g(v, \mathbf{k})\big), w(T_m(v, \mathbf{k}))\big) \tag{1}$$

$$w\big(T_g(v, \mathbf{k})\big) = \min_{u \in N(v)} \{w(T(u, \mathbf{k}) + u)\} \tag{2}$$

$$w(T_m(v, \mathbf{k})) = \min_{\substack{\mathbf{k}=\mathbf{k}_1 \cup \mathbf{k}_2 \\ \wedge \mathbf{k}_1 \cap \mathbf{k}_2 = \emptyset}} \{w(T(v, \mathbf{k}_1) + T(v, \mathbf{k}_2))\} \tag{3}$$

where "+" is an operation to merge a node into a tree or to merge two trees to a new tree, $N(v)$ is the set of node v's neighbors in G, i.e., $v \in G(V, E)$ and $e(u, v) \in E$. Equation (1) indicates that the weight of the a group Steiner tree $T(v, \mathbf{k})$ can be obtained by either of two cases, namely *tree growth*, i.e. Eq. (2), and *tree merging*, i.e. Eq. (3). As indicated by Eq. (2), the tree growth case is that $T_g(v, \mathbf{k})$ can be obtained by growing a node u from the minimum-weight subtree of $T(v, \mathbf{k})$ that is rooted at u (one of v's neighbors) and covers all keywords in $\mathbf{k}$. Equation (3) shows that, in the tree merging case, $T_m(v, \mathbf{k})$ can be obtained by merging two minimum-weight subtrees, both rooted at v, one covering $\mathbf{k}_1$ and the other covering $\mathbf{k}_2$ such that $\mathbf{k} = \mathbf{k}_1 \cup \mathbf{k}_2$ and $\mathbf{k}_1 \cap \mathbf{k}_2 = \emptyset$.

2.2   Answering Keyword Queries

A keyword query Q contains a set of keywords, $\mathbf{K} = \{k_1, \ldots, k_l\}$. Based on Eqs. (1)–(3), KS3+ employs Algorithm 1 to find the minimum group Steiner tree as the answer to query Q_n. In line 1, Algorithm 1 initializes a priority queue of trees Q_T to be empty. The trees in Q_T are always sorted in ascending order by the total number of nodes in the trees, denoted by $|T|$. In lines 2–6, the algorithm locates nodes that contain individual keywords in $\mathbf{K}$. For each node v in G, $v \in V$, if v contains any keywords $\mathbf{k}$ in $\mathbf{K}$, $\mathbf{k} \subseteq \mathbf{k}$, the algorithm enqueues tree $T(v, k)$ into Q_T. At this stage, for each such tree in Q_T, there is $|T(v, k)| = 1$ because there is only one node in each of the trees in Q_T. In lines 7–33, the algorithm iterates to dequeue trees from and enqueue trees into Q_T, and in the meantime grow them with Eq. (2) (lines 12–21) or merge them with Eq. (3) (lines 23–32) to find the minimum group Steiner tree $T(v, \mathbf{k})$, where $v \in V$ and $\mathbf{k} = \mathbf{K}$ (lines 9–11). Equation (2) is implemented by lines 12–21. Given a tree $T(v, \mathbf{k})$ just dequeued from Q_T (line 8), the algorithm considers all v's neighbors, denoted by u, and checks whether there is a tree $T(u, \mathbf{k})$ in Q_T that can be replaced with $T(v, \mathbf{k}) + u$, which contains the same set of keywords $\mathbf{k}$ but with fewer nodes (lines 12–17). If such a $T(u, \mathbf{k})$ does not exist in Q_T, $T(v, \mathbf{k}) + u$ is enqueued into Q_T (lines 18–19). Equation (3) is implemented by lines 23–32. Given a tree $T(v, \mathbf{k_x})$ (line 22), the algorithm attempts to find any existing trees, $T(v, \mathbf{k_y})$, that are also rooted at v and contain keywords $\mathbf{k_x} \cup \mathbf{k_y}$ with more nodes than $T(v, \mathbf{k_x}) + T(v, \mathbf{k_y})$, where $\mathbf{k_x} \neq \mathbf{k_y}$. Any such trees will be replaced with $T(v, \mathbf{k_x}) + T(v, \mathbf{k_y})$ in Q_T (lines 24–28). If there are no such trees, $T(v, \mathbf{k_x}) + T(v, \mathbf{k_y})$ will be enqueued into Q_T (lines 29–30).

We now analyze the worst-case scenario complexity of Algorithm 1 when answering a query Q with a set of keywords $\mathbf{K} = \{k_1, ..., k_l\}$ on a data graph $G = (V, E)$, where $|V| = n$ and $|E| = m$. Let $T(v, \mathbf{k})$ be the tree with the minimum number of nodes of all trees rooted at v containing a subset of keywords $\mathbf{k} \subseteq \mathbf{k}$. There are 3 major components in complexity of Algorithm 1: queue maintenance, tree growth and tree merging.

Algorithm 1: Answer Keyword Query Q

Input: $G(V, E)$, $\mathbf{K} = \{k_1, k_2, ..., k_l\}$
Output: minimum group Steiner tree $T(v, \mathbf{K})$, $v \in V$

```
1:  Q_T ← Ø;
2:  for each v ∈ V do
3:  |   if v contains k ⊆ K
4:  |   |   enqueue T(v, k) into Q_T;
5:  |   end if
6:  end for
7:  while Q_T ≠ Ø do
8:  |   dequeue Q_T to T(v, k);
9:  |   if k = K
10: |   |   return T(v, k);
11: |   end if
12: |   for each u ∈ N(v) do
13: |   |   if ∃ T(u, k) ∈ Q_T
14: |   |   |   if |T(v, k) + u| < |T(u, k)|
15: |   |   |   |   T(u, k) ← T(v, k) + u;
16: |   |   |   |   Q_T ← T(u, k);
17: |   |   |   end if
18: |   |   else
19: |   |   |   T(u, k) ← T(v, k) + u;
20: |   |   end if
21: |   end for
22: |   k_x ← k;
23: |   for each k_y s.t. k_x ∩ k_y = Ø do
24: |   |   if ∃ T(v, k_x ∪ k_y) ∈ Q_T
25: |   |   |   if |T(v, k_x) + T(v, k_y)| < |T(v, k_x ∪ k_y)|
26: |   |   |   |   T(v, k_x ∪ k_y) ← T(v, k_x) + T(v, k_y);
27: |   |   |   |   Q_T ← T(v, k_x ∪ k_y);
28: |   |   |   end if
29: |   |   else
30: |   |   |   Q_T ← T(v, k_x) + T(v, k_y);
31: |   |   end if
32: |   end for
33: end while
```

Lines 12–21: *tree growth* Eq. (2). Lines 23–31: *tree merging* Eq. (3).

Queue maintenance. In total, there are 2^l subsets of $\mathbf{K}$. Thus, the maximum length of Q_T is $2^l n$, i.e., every tree rooted at any $v \in V$ containing any $\mathbf{k} \subseteq \mathbf{k}$ is enqueued into Q_T. The complexity of enqueue/update operations and dequeue operations is dependent on the type of the queue. Here, we employ Fibonacci Heap, which has the complexity of O (1) for the enquene/update operations and $O(\log 2^l n)$ for dequeue operations. Because Algorithm 1 will enqueue or dequeue any $T(v, \mathbf{k})$ into/from Q_T at most once, the complexity of enqueuing and dequeuing all $2^l n$ trees in Q_T is $O(2^l n(l + \log n))$.

Tree growth. Lines 12–21 handle the tree growth operations implementing Eq. (2). The **for** loop iterates for $|N(v)|$ times, trying to find the $T(u, \mathbf{k})$ grown from

$T(v, \mathbf{k}) + u$ with the minimum number of nodes. Here, $|N(v)|$ is the total number of neighbors of v. Thus, the total time for Algorithm 1 to execute the comparison operations in lines 12–21 is $O\left(2^l \sum_{v \in V} |N(v)|\right) = O\left(2^l m\right)$.

Tree merging. Lines 23–32 handle the tree merging operations implementing Eq. (3). For each $T(v, \mathbf{k_x})$ dequeued in line 8, the **for** loop in lines 23–32 enumerates every $\mathbf{k_y}$ that fulfils $\mathbf{k_x} \cap \mathbf{k_y} = \emptyset$, where $\mathbf{k_x}, \mathbf{k_y} \subseteq \mathbf{k}$. Given $|\mathbf{K}| = l$, the total number of possible $\mathbf{k_y}$ is $2^{l - |k_x|}$. Thus, the total time for Algorithm 1 to execute the comparison operations in lines 23–32 is $n \sum_{i=1}^{l-1} C_{l,i} \times 2^{l-i} = O(3^l n)$.

Overall, the complexity of Algorithm 1 is $O(2^l n(l + \log n) + 2^l m + 3^l n)$. This indicates that the efficiency of Algorithm 1 relies exponentially on the number of query keywords. In real world problems where l is a small constant, the complexity of Algorithm 1 becomes $O(n \log n + m)$.

3   Experimental Evaluation

We conducted a series of experiments with a prototype of KS3+ implemented using JDK1.6.0 to compare the efficiency (computational overhead) and effectiveness (success rate) of KS3+ with KS3.

3.1   Experimental Setup

The data graphs and queries used in the experiments are randomly generated using a publicly available and widely used dataset named QWS, which contains the functional information about over 2,500 real-world web services [5]. All experiments were conducted on a machine with Intel i5-4570 CPU 3.20 GHz and 8 GB RAM, running Windows 7 ×64 Enterprise. In the experiments, random data graphs are generated based on the Erdős–Rényi model [6]. The relevance between the query keywords determines whether bridging nodes are needed to identify a system solution. In the data graph, directly relevant keywords are composable and hence belong to adjacent nodes. Bridging services are needed when two keywords are not directly relevant. In the experiments, we used the *keyword distance* to represent the relevance between two query keywords, reflected by the number of hops they are away from each other in the data graph. In the experiments, we fixed the keyword distances at 2 for all queries, which were also randomly generated. To avoid very large solutions, we limited the maximum number of nodes to be included in a solution to twice the number of query keywords.

To comprehensively study the impacts of different parameters on the efficiency and effectiveness of KS3+, we vary four parameters in the experiments, as presented in Table 1. Note that in experiment set #3, the number of edges increases with the number of nodes to maintain the graph density while changing the graph size. For each set of experiments, we average the results obtained from 100 runs.

Table 1. Experiment configuration

Parameter	Set #1	Set #2	Set #3	Set #4
Keyword distance	1 to 10	2	2	2
Number of query keywords (l)	2	2 to 6	2	2
Graph size (number of nodes)	2,000	2,000	2,000 to 20,000	2,000
Graph density (number of edges)	2,000	2,000	2,000 to 20,000	2,000 to 8,000

3.2 Evaluation Results

Efficiency. Figure 1 shows the computation times taken by KS3+ and KS3 to answer keyword queries for systems solutions under different parameter settings. Overall, KS3 + demonstrates a multiple orders of magnitude advantage in efficiency over KS3 under different parameter settings. While KS3 often takes seconds to minutes to answer queries under different parameter settings, KS3+ takes less than 1 ms in most cases. This demonstrates its significant advantage in efficiency over KS3.

Figure 1(a) shows the efficiency of KS3+ in identifying the bridging nodes when the keywords in a query are not directly relevant. When the keyword distance increases from 1 to 10, the average computation time of KS3 increases from 16 ms to 2,899 ms. In the meantime, the average computation time of KS3+ increases from 0.08 ms to 0.40 ms. KS3+ outperforms KS3 significantly, and demonstrates much higher tolerance to the increase in keyword distance. The results shown in Fig. 1(a) demonstrate that KS3+ can efficiently find a system solution even if the keywords entered are only remotely relevant, thanks to its excellent ability to identify bridging nodes.

Figure 1(b) demonstrates the outstanding ability of KS3+ to find a system solution when multiple bridging nodes are needed to connect many keyword nodes. KS3+ demonstrates great performance with an increase from 0.42 ms to 319.69 ms in computation time in response to the increase in the number of query keywords (**referred to as l hereafter**) from 2 to 5. The corresponding increase in the computation time of KS3 is from 1,645 ms to 12,574 ms. Again, KS3+ outperforms KS3 significantly. In particular, when l reaches 6, it takes KS3+ 2,777.92 ms on average to find a system solution, while KS3 cannot even answer the query within a reasonable amount of time. That is why the corresponding data is missing for KS3 in Fig. 1(b). Figure 1(b) shows that KS3+ has a considerably better ability to find bridging nodes than KS3.

Figure 1(c) shows that the increase in the computation time of KS3 increases rapidly with the graph size, while the increase in the computation time KS3+ is almost negligible. On a very large data graph with 20,000 nodes, KS3 takes a significant amount of time (up to 75,000 ms) to answer a query. In the meantime, KS3+ takes only 1.35 ms on average to answer the same query. In a large data graph, the number of group Steiner trees that cover all the keyword nodes is extremely large even when the number of keywords to cover is small. KS3 needs to identify and inspect all those trees. The extremely large search space inevitably leads to long computation time of KS3. KS3+, on the other hand, does not have to inspect all those trees. It prunes invalid trees and grows or merges only the trees that are likely to be part of the final answer tree. Thus, KS3+ can handle queries over large data graphs much more efficiently than KS3.

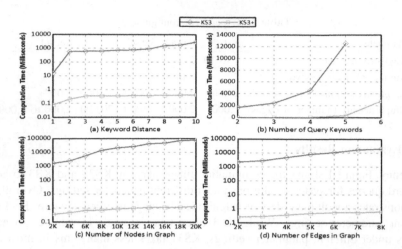

Fig. 1. Computation time under different parameter settings (keyword distance = 2)

Figure 1(d) shows that in a dense data graph, where each service has many neighbors, it takes KS3+ much less time than KS3 to find a system solution. The advantage of KS3+ over KS3 is by multiple orders of magnitudes, similar to the results shown in Fig. 1(a) and (c). As the number of edges increases from 2,000 to 8,000, the average computation time of KS3+ increases accordingly from 0.27 ms to 0.64 ms, versus the increase from 2,256 ms to 20,331 ms for KS3. A higher graph density means more neighbors for each node, leading to more group Steiner trees for KS3 to identify and inspect to answer a query. However, given a tree $T(v, \mathbf{k})$ dequeued in line 8 of Algorithm 1, out of all the neighbors of v, Algorithm 1 would only grow $T(v, \mathbf{k})$ to include those that result in trees containing the same keywords as $T(v, \mathbf{k})$ but with fewer nodes. This prunes most invalid trees and ensures the high efficiency of KS3+.

Effectiveness. We compared the effectiveness of KS3+ and KS3, measured by success rate, i.e., the percentage of cases where an answer to the keyword query can be found. Overall, KS3+ is as effective as KS3, with a consistent success rate of 100% in all experiments under different parameter settings. This indicates that KS3+ can always find a system solution, like KS3. The experimental results demonstrate that KS3+ does not compromise the success rate in finding a solution.

4 Related Work

The process for building an SBS consists of three phases: system planning, service discovery and service selection.

System planning. The system engineer identifies the system tasks required for the target SBS, as well as their execution order. Most system planning techniques are based on artificial intelligence techniques [7]. The general idea is to model the task identification problem as a planning problem. For example, in [7], the authors model the task identification problem as a CSTE planning problem to be solved with an SCP solver.

Service discovery. Through service registries or service portals, the system engineer identifies a set of candidate services for each of the identified system tasks based on the functional and semantic information of candidate services. To improve the accuracy of service matching, several semantic web service languages have been proposed based on ontology techniques, e.g., OWLS-MX [8]. It automates the service matching operation that identifies the services that can perform the required system tasks. Many approaches have been proposed to automate the service discovery process, based on ontology techniques such as logical reasoning and temporal planning [9].

Service selection. The system engineer selects one service from the candidate services for each system task to compose the target SBS. The selected services must collectively fulfil the multi-dimensional quality constraints for the SBS [4], e.g., reliability, response time, cost, etc., which is an NP-complete problem. Integer Programming (IP) is the main technique adopted in this phase. AgFlow [2] is one of the most representative approaches. Following the idea of AgFlow, many researchers have been trying to reduce the computation time for quality-aware service selection [10] or to solve the problem in more complex environments [1, 11].

A planning technique was proposed that explores system solutions by looking up services whose tags match the tags describing the SBS [3]. For each query, the engineer needs to enter a source tag and a destination tag. The proposed technique heuristically identifies the possible service compositions with an entry service according to the source tag and an exit service according to the destination tag. A similar approach is proposed in [12]. A major limitation to these approaches is that each query allows only two tags, i.e., a source tag and a destination tag. Multiple tags can only be entered one by one in different queries that are processed individually until a final solution is found. An error made in an early query can easily make it impossible to find the final solution.

KS3 was proposed in [4]. It overcomes the limitations of the approaches proposed in [3, 12]. However, it suffers from extremely poor efficiency in large-scale scenarios. By modelling keyword queries as dynamic programming problems, KS3+ achieves significantly higher efficiency without sacrificing effectiveness.

5 Conclusions and Future Work

In this paper, we propose KS3+, a novel approach that integrates and automates the system planning, service discovery and service selection operations for building service-based systems (SBSs). It assists system engineers without detailed knowledge of SOA techniques in finding system solutions with only a few keywords that describe the required system tasks. KS3+ offers a new paradigm for building SBSs and can significantly save the time and effort during the process for building SBSs. Making no compromise in effectiveness, KS3+ significantly outperforms KS3 in efficiency.

In our future work, we will enhance KS3+ to answer queries with quality constraints and quality optimization goals.

Acknowledgment. This work is partly supported by Australian Research Council Projects DP170101932, DP150101775 and LP130100324.

References

1. Ardagna, D., Pernici, B.: Adaptive service composition in flexible processes. IEEE Trans. Softw. Eng. **33**(6), 369–384 (2007)
2. Zeng, L., Benatallah, B., Ngu, A.H.H., Dumas, M., Kalagnanam, J., Chang, H.: QoS-aware middleware for web services composition. IEEE Trans. Softw. Eng. **30**(5), 311–327 (2004)
3. Liu, X., Ma, Y., Huang, G., Zhao, J., Mei, H., Liu, Y.: Data-driven composition for service-oriented situational web applications. IEEE Trans. Serv. Comput. **8**(1), 2–16 (2015)
4. He, Q., Zhou, R., Zhang, X., Wang, Y., Ye, D., Chen, F., Grundy, J., Yang, Y.: Keyword search for building service-based systems. IEEE Trans. Softw. Eng. **437**(7), 658–674 (2016)
5. Al-Masri, E., Mahmoud, Q.H.: Investigating web services on the world wide web. In: 17th International Conference on World Wide Web (WWW 2008), pp. 795–804 (2008)
6. Durrett, R.: Random Graph Dynamics. Cambridge University Press, Cambridge (2007)
7. Zou, G., Lu, Q., Chen, Y., Huang, R., Xu, Y., Xiang, Y.: QoS-aware dynamic composition of web services using numerical temporal planning. IEEE Trans. Serv. Comput. **7**(1), 18–31 (2014)
8. Klusch, M., Fries, B., Sycara, K.P.: OWLS-MX: a hybrid semantic web service matchmaker for OWL-S services. J. Web Semant. **7**(2), 915–922 (2009)
9. Cassar, G., Barnaghi, P., Moessner, K.: Probabilistic matchmaking methods for automated service discovery. IEEE Trans. Serv. Comput. **7**(4), 654–666 (2014)
10. Trummer, I., Faltings, B., Binder, W.: Multi-objective quality-driven service selection - a fully polynomial time approximation scheme. IEEE Trans. Softw. Eng. **40**(2), 167–191 (2014)
11. He, Q., Yan, J., Jin, H., Yang, Y.: Quality-aware service selection for service-based systems based on iterative multi-attribute combinatorial auction. IEEE Trans. Softw. Eng. **40**(2), 192–215 (2014)
12. Huang, G., Ma, Y., Liu, X., Luo, Y., Lu, X., Blake, M.B.: Model-based automated navigation and composition of complex service mashups. IEEE Trans. Serv. Comput. **8**(3), 494–506 (2015)

Supporting the Decision of Migrating to Microservices Through Multi-layer Fuzzy Cognitive Maps

Andreas Christoforou[1], Martin Garriga[2(✉)], Andreas S. Andreou[1], and Luciano Baresi[2]

[1] Department of Electrical Engineering, Computer Engineering and Informatics, Cyprus University of Technology, Limassol, Cyprus
[2] Dipartimento di Elettronica, Informazione e Bioingegneria, Politecnico di Milano, Milan, Italy
martin.garriga@polimi.it

Abstract. Microservices architectures are gaining momentum for the development of applications as suites of small, autonomous, and conversational services, which are then easy to understand, deploy and scale. However, one of today's problems is that microservices introduce new complexities to the system and, despite the hype, many factors should be considered when deciding to adopt a microservices architecture. This paper proposes the first Decision Support System (DSS) to migrate to microservices, by identifying the key concepts and drivers regarding through a literature review and feedback from a group of experts from industry and academia. Then, these concepts are organized as a Multi-Layer Fuzzy Cognitive Map (ML-FCM), a graph-based computational intelligence model that captures the behavior of a given problem in nodes that represent knowledge in the domain, and offers the means to study their influence and interrelation. Static and dynamic analysis over the resulting ML-FCM helped us identify the prevailing drivers towards the migration to a microservices architecture.

Keywords: Microservices architectures · Monolith migration · Multi-layer Fuzzy Cognitive Maps

1 Introduction

Microservices architectures are the new weapon-of-choice for the development of cloud-native applications as suites of small, autonomous, and conversational services, which are then easy to understand, deploy, and scale [1]. Migrating to microservices enables optimizing the autonomy, replaceability, and decentralized governance of software architectures [2]. Despite the hype for microservices, both industry and academia still lack consensus on the adequate conditions to embrace and benefit from this new paradigm [3]. Microservices architectures are

© Springer International Publishing AG 2017
M. Maximilien et al. (Eds.): ICSOC 2017, LNCS 10601, pp. 471–480, 2017.
https://doi.org/10.1007/978-3-319-69035-3_34

highly complex, comprising multiple, often conflicting factors. From the industrial perspective, Netflix[1] and SoundCloud[2] are the early adopters of microservices, transitioning from a traditional development model with hundreds of engineers maintaining a monolithic application, to many small teams responsible for the end-to-end development of hundreds of microservices to serve millions of users on a daily basis. The organizational culture shifted from traditional siloed teams to product-oriented teams following a DevOps methodology. The academia is still in an early stage of documenting and analyzing the migration to microservices that is taking place in industry [4], mainly by distilling the key drivers for migrating to microservices (e.g., reusability, decentralized data governance, and scalability) and migration patterns that help structure and generalize the process [5].

Therefore any approach that aims to assist the decision making process must be flexible and dynamically adaptable. In this context, the paper develops a Multi-Layer Fuzzy Cognitive Map (ML-FCM) [6] as the first DSS that captures those key factors towards the migration to a microservices architecture, and offers the means to study their influence and interrelation [7]. Fuzzy Cognitive Maps (FCMs) are computational intelligence, soft computing tools that combine elements of fuzzy logic and neural networks [8]. FCMs capture the behavior of a given problem in nodes that represent knowledge in the application domain [9]. ML-FCMs extend FCMs by the concept of sub-FCMs, that is, smaller structures (maps) of related nodes organized in layers. This grouping offers a way for analyzing parameters at finer levels of granularity [6,10]. This enables tracking the causes for the decision outcome, and offers the ability to study the dependencies between the leading determinants of the decision.

The construction and analysis of the model starts with a literature review to identify an initial set of factors that potentially influence the decision of migrating to microservices. The next step engages a group of experts from industry and academia with related background to the subject. They evaluated and refined the identified factors through questionnaires and interviews. Finally, we performed both static and dynamic analysis [9] over the resulting ML-FCM through graph-analysis and simulation, respectively, which helped us identify the influence that different nodes (concepts) exercise on the decision of migrating to microservices.

To the best of our knowledge, this is the first decision support system (DSS) for migrating to microservices. The suitability of a DSS in this context is suggested in [11], based on reference models for enterprise architectures. Regarding ML-FCMs, they have been used as DSS in the context of novel architectures such as Cloud Adoption [9,12], and extensively applied in sensitive, real-world domains [7].

The rest of the paper is organized as follows. Section 2 details the concepts identification and subsequent construction of the ML-FCM for supporting the

---

[1] https://www.nginx.com/blog/microservices-at-netflix-architectural-best-practices/.
[2] https://developers.soundcloud.com/blog/building-products-at-soundcloud-part-1-dealing-with-the-monolith.

decision of migrating to a microservices architecture. Section 3 discusses the static and dynamic analysis of our model. Finally, Sect. 4 concludes the paper.

2 Decision Support Models

A FCM is a directed graph with nodes representing concepts in a domain and weighted edges describing the various causal relationships that exist among these concepts. A numeric *activation level* per concept denotes the strength of its presence in the problem domain. The map is initialized with a set of activation levels (that represent a particular scenario in the problem domain), and then executed on a series of discrete steps in which the activation levels of the nodes are iteratively updated based on the causation relationship between them, until the map: (1) reaches an equilibrium state, (2) exhibits cyclic behavior, or (3) exhibits chaotic behavior. The former two cases allow one to develop simulation scenarios and perform inferences. The main outcome of the execution is the final activation value of the concept of interest (central node) for that particular scenario. Details about the updating functions for activation levels are given in [9].

The first step to develop a FCM is a Literature Review (LR), for which we followed the key guidelines proposed in [13]. Although a systematic LR is outside the scope of this work, this helped us organize the process of finding and classifying relevant works. We searched for microservices-related articles indexed in different online databases, considered both journal and conference articles, and suppressed duplicated papers, given the overlapping among the search engines and databases.

From this analysis we refined the initial collection up to 46 relevant works[3] to perform concept extraction, that is, identifying and then disambiguating the concepts that are potentially relevant for the decision of migrating to microservices, and are crosscutting through the literature. This process was supported by leveraging our previous experience in analysis frameworks in the context of SOA [14,15].

The initial list of concepts extracted from the literature was delivered to a group of seven experts (researchers and industry practitioners) with a background related to the subject, who evaluated the list and suggested to add, remove, group, or decompose concepts based on their experience. The final list of concepts (summarized in Table 1) is then hierarchically organized, in our case featuring two different layers that focus on specific aspects of the problem, with a total of six sub-FCMs (Table 1).

Based on the identified concepts, the experts completed a questionnaire concerning the causal relationships between nodes (concepts) and their weights, i.e., the degree to which concepts influence each other, fuzzified using seven linguistic values (from *negatively high* to *positively high*) according to a triangular membership function. The activation levels (used to represent different scenarios

---

[3] Due to the space limit, the full list of related work, concept definitions, questionnaires and simulations can be found at: https://goo.gl/JLZPsA.

Table 1. Sub-FCM concept grouping

FCM	Concepts	Central concept	Layer
FCM1	C1 (Governance), C4 (Infrastructure & Management Support), C8 (Maintainability & Evolvability), C9 (Operational Complexity), C10 (Business Complexity), C11 (Reliability), C12 (Security), C13 (Cost), C16 (Design), C22 (DevOps), C28 (Microservices Migration)	C28	1
FCM2	C1 (Governance), C2 (Decentralized Governance), C3 (Data Governance)	C1	2
FCM3	C4 (Infrastructure & Management Support), C5 (Containerization), C6 (Scalability/Elasticity), C7 (Monitoring)	C4	2
FCM4	C13 (Cost), C14 (Migration Cost), C15 (Operations Cost)	C13	2
FCM5	C16 (Design), C17 (Design For Failure), C18 (Granularity and Bounded Context), C19 (Service Contracts), C20 (Communication Model), C21 (Decentralization)	C16	2
FCM6	C22 (DevOps), C23 (Organization Culture), C24 (Infrastructure Automation), C25 (Continuous Deployment and Integration), C26 (Skilled and educated DevOps Teams), C27 (Tool Support)	C22	2

in the problem domain) for the different concepts also consist of five linguistic values, from *very low* to *very high*.

Once all experts defined their causal relationships between concepts as described above, the linguistic values were aggregated and defuzzified, producing a weight matrix (representing the weight of each edge) with numerical values in the interval $[-1, 1]$. The final structure of the model, which consists of the main FCM on the top layer and 5 sub-FCMs on the lower layer, is depicted in Fig. 1.

3 Static and Dynamic Model Analyses

The static and dynamic analyses of the map can help understand and assess the shape and behavior of the model [9]. This will ultimately highlight "hidden" properties and features, as well as points that require particular attention. Static analysis examines the properties of a model prior to its execution, and irrespectively of its behavior over time, by applying notions of Graph Theory. The major categories covered by static analysis are *complexity* of the graph (in terms of *density*, *depth* and *breadth*); *strength* of each node (weight and number of its incoming and outgoing edges); and *tendency* of cycles in the graph (positive cycles amplify any initial activation value and vice-versa). By the end of the static analysis, modelers shall be able to identify the stronger concepts (i.e., those that strongly influence the central concept), reap an indication of how each sub-FCM influences the FCM in the upper layer, and use this information towards setting simulations (i.e., dynamic analysis). Interested readers can refer to [9] for further details on the analysis framework.

Dynamic analysis allows one to assess the behavior of the model in execution through simulations under manually configured scenarios (described through activation values). The main goal is to study the activation levels of the concepts (nodes) and how these levels change over time. The first step is to execute two "extreme" positive and negative scenarios, which should drive the model to the extreme positive/negative outcome (the central concept should get a level close to 1 or 0 respectively). If the model performs as expected, then additional simulations can be run with different configurations and initial activation levels (representing *what-if* scenarios), followed by a study of the correlation of these levels and the final outcome. This should support the significance ranking of the different concepts obtained from the static analysis.

Results of Static Analysis. Table 2 shows that FCM1 (Fig. 1) has high density (number of edges and nodes) and it is above the threshold for medium magnitude (*density* ≥ 0.6). All the second layer sub-FCMs are complete graphs, with density values equal to 1 and high complexity, but mitigated by their fairly small size, between 3 and 6 nodes (6 and 30 edges respectively). Thus, the model can

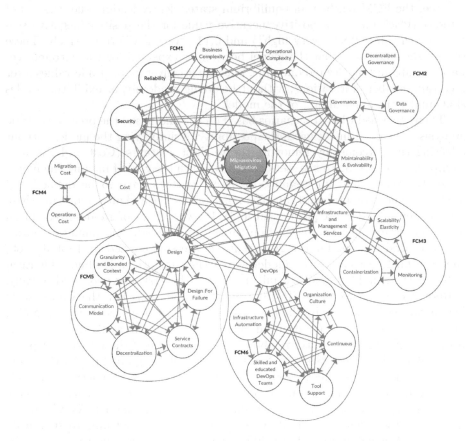

Fig. 1. ML-FCM for the microservices migration problem.

be characterized as a complex two-layer structure [9]. The number of positive feedback cycles is higher than the negative ones for all nodes. This indicates how the model tends to behave: given a slightly positive modification in any activation level, the corresponding level of the central node of interest (Microservices Migration) is promoted, and vice-versa.

Results also suggest that the top three concepts of the main FCM (FCM1) are Infrastructure and Management Services (its activation level is calculated using the concepts in its sub-FCM), Maintainability & Evolvability, and Reliability. This finding calls for further investigation of the behavior of these concepts both individually and as a group, and whether Maintainability& Evolvability and Reliability could be also decomposed so as to understand which factors influence them at a finer granularity. Interestingly, Business Complexity and Cost are the weakest concepts in the ML-FCM. This means that, in the following dynamic analysis, we can simulate whether the model behaves the same when removing these concepts.

Results of Dynamic Analysis. Figure 2 depicts the results for the extreme scenarios (positive and negative) after 100 iterations of the model execution. As we can see, the FCM reached an equilibrium state, clearly leading the concept of interest (black line) to a positive/negative value for the positive/negative scenario, with values 0.89 ("very high") and 0.11 ("very low") respectively. These results show not only that the model behaves as expected for the extreme scenarios, matching the desired outcome, but also it converges to stable values after a certain number of iterations, without behaving randomly, or exhibiting cycles that hinder the applicability of the model.

Then, we posed what-if scenarios based on the findings of the preceding static analysis. Scenario 1 investigates the possibility of simplifying the model without affecting the outcome, by removing the weakest concepts (Cost and Business Complexity, according to the static analysis), with the goal of making the model easier to execute and understand, as fewer concepts have to be defined and analyzed. Thus, we setup and run 20 simulations before and after removing these two concepts (and subsequently sub-FCM4), with a set of randomized initial activation levels. The final activation values (in linguistic and numerical form) of the central concept for the 20 executions are summarized in Table 3. Note that the final outcome of the model across the simulations is almost identical between the simplified and the full model for the first scenario. Additionally, a Root Mean Square Error (RMSE) of 0.016 indicates that the values show low deviation. Conclusively, the first what-if scenario suggests that a simplified model can deliver the same decision outcome without the weakest nodes. This result asks for further discussion about the significance of these two concepts.

Analogously, what-if Scenario 2 defines an overly simplified model that only comprises the three strongest nodes, and the same set of initial activation levels as the previous one. This scenario investigates whether the strongest concepts by themselves can deliver identical results to the original model. As we can see in Table 3, the results show that the simplified model is not able to substitute the original model as it leads to different outcomes, thus fails to capture the

Table 2. Strength and tendency indicators for every sub-FCM.

Sub FCM	Concept	Deg In	Deg Out	Deg Tot	Val Tot	Cycles (+)	Cycles (−)
FCM1 (root)	Governance	8	10	18	6.25	202064	200980
	Infrastructure and management	9	10	19	4.57	207666	206077
	Maintainability and evolvability	9	10	19	7.54	207656	206087
	Operational complexity	8	10	18	5.93	202603	200441
	Business complexity	7	10	17	4.11	198572	196774
	Reliability	9	10	19	5.35	207729	206014
	Security	8	9	17	4.22	202242	199954
	Cost	9	5	14	4.10	180637	178502
	Design	8	10	18	6.24	202590	200454
	DevOps	8	9	17	5.91	199392	197911
FCM2	Governance	2	2	4	1.33	4	0
	Decentralized Governance	2	2	4	1.99	4	0
	Data Governance	2	2	4	2	1.39	0
FCM3	Infrastructure and management services	3	3	6	3	15	0
	Containerization	3	3	6	2.15	15	0
	Scalability/ Elasticity	3	3	6	2.67	15	0
	Monitoring	3	3	6	1.72	15	0
FCM4	Cost	2	2	4	1.63	4	0
	Migration cost	2	2	4	1.14	4	0
	Operations cost	2	2	4	1.08	4	0
FCM5	Design	5	5	10	4.2	325	0
	Design for failure	5	5	10	3.17	325	0
	Granularity and bounded context	5	5	10	4.35	325	0
	Service contracts	5	5	10	3.49	325	0
	Communication model	5	5	10	2.45	325	0
	Decentralization	5	5	10	4.17	325	0
FCM6	DevOps	5	5	10	5.17	325	0
	Organization culture	5	5	10	3.62	325	0
	Infrastructure automation	5	5	10	4.33	325	0
	Continuous Delivery/Deployment	5	5	10	4.85	325	0
	Skilled and educated DevOps teams	5	5	10	3.54	325	0
	Tool support	5	5	10	3.33	325	0

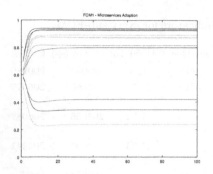 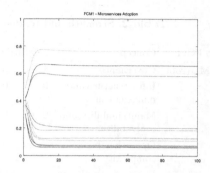

(a) Positive scenario (main concept in black)   (b) Negative scenario (main concept in black)

Fig. 2. Activation values (y-axis) for the concepts in FCM1 throughout 100 iterations (x-axis).

dynamics of the domain under study. Based on this result, one can iteratively add strong nodes to come up with an "optimal" FCM configuration, which only comprises the concepts that truly affect the final outcome.

Table 3. Outcome of what-if scenarios (20 executions, random activation levels).

Run no.	Original model		Sim. Scenario 1		Sim. Scenario 2		Run no.	Original model		Sim. Scenario 1		Sim. Scenario 2	
1	0.48	Med	0.45	Med	0.46	Med	11	0.11	Low	0.13	Low	0.47	Med
2	0.45	Med	0.45	Med	0.46	Med	12	0.51	Med	0.51	Med	0.50	Med
3	0.11	Low	0.13	Low	0.48	Med	13	0.12	Low	0.14	Low	0.51	Med
4	0.12	Low	0.13	Low	0.49	Med	14	0.11	Low	0.13	Low	0.47	Med
5	0.11	Low	0.13	Low	0.46	Med	15	0.48	Med	0.46	Med	0.46	Med
6	0.46	Med	0.46	Med	0.46	Med	16	0.88	High	0.86	High	0.47	Med
7	0.48	Med	0.46	Med	0.46	Med	17	0.54	Med	0.54	Med	0.53	Med
8	0.48	Med	0.49	Med	0.49	Med	18	0.48	Med	0.46	Med	0.46	Med
9	0.48	Med	0.46	Med	0.46	Med	19	0.47	Med	0.47	Med	0.48	Med
10	0.48	Med	0.46	Med	0.46	Med	20	0.51	Med	0.51	Med	0.50	Med
RMSE (20 runs)	0.016		0.22							0.016		0.22	

Finally, a *threat to validity* regarding model construction, refers to domain experts, who may introduce a degree of subjectivity and bias. This is a common weakness in expert-based models, mitigated by the assessment with different scenarios, which show whether the model behaves correctly or not, and allows us to calibrate it accordingly. Furthermore, the group of experts did not include any project manager or executive, whom may lean towards concepts such as Cost and Business Complexity, at the expense of more "technical" concepts. Besides, more experiments are needed, specially by applying the model to real-world scenarios.

4   Conclusions and Future Work

This paper identifies the key concepts and drivers related to the decision of migrating to microservices, by means of a literature review and experts' feedback through questionnaires and interviews. Then, we developed a DSS by organizing these concepts as a ML-FCM, a graph-shaped computational intelligence model that allows one to support decision-makers through automated reasoning.

Our future work comprises fine-tunning the model by considering other concepts, performing simulations with new scenarios, and engaging experts with different background. After that, our goal is to apply the model on real-world cases, and to support the decision-making process of an on-going project.

Acknowledgments. We would like to thank the experts for their valuable feedback. The project leading to this research has received funding from the European Union's Horizon 2020 research and innovation programme under grant agreement No. 692251.

References

1. Lewis, J., Fowler, M.: Microservices: a definition of this new architectural term (2014). http://martinfowler.com/articles/microservices.html
2. Hassan, S., Bahsoon, R.: Microservices and their design trade-offs: a self-adaptive roadmap. In: IEEE International Conference on Services Computing (SCC), pp. 813–818. IEEE (2016)
3. Wootton, B.: Microservices: a definition of this new architectural term (2014). http://highscalability.com/blog/2014/4/8/microservices-not-a-free-lunch.html
4. Richardson, C.: Microservices architectures: who is using microservices? (2014). http://microservices.io/articles/whoisusingmicroservices.html
5. Balalaie, A., Heydarnoori, A., Jamshidi, P.: Migrating to cloud-native architectures using microservices: an experience report. In: Celesti, A., Leitner, P. (eds.) ESOCC Workshops 2015. CCIS, vol. 567, pp. 201–215. Springer, Cham (2016). doi:10.1007/978-3-319-33313-7_15
6. Mateou, N.H., Andreou, A.S.: Tree-structured multi-layer fuzzy cognitive maps for modelling large scale, complex problems. In: International Conference on Intelligent Agents, Web Technologies and Internet Commerce, vol. 2, pp. 131–139. IEEE (2005)
7. Papageorgiou, E.I., Salmeron, J.L.: A review of fuzzy cognitive maps research during the last decade. IEEE Trans. Fuzzy Syst. **21**(1), 66–79 (2013)
8. Jang, J.S.R., Sun, C.T., Mizutani, E.: Neuro-fuzzy and soft computing: a computational approach to learning and machine intelligence (1997)
9. Christoforou, A., Andreou, A.S.: A framework for static and dynamic analysis of multi-layer fuzzy cognitive maps. Neurocomputing **232**, 133–145 (2017)
10. Mateou, N.H., Andreou, A.S.: A framework for developing intelligent decision support systems using evolutionary fuzzy cognitive maps. J. Intell. Fuzzy Syst. **19**(2), 151–170 (2008)

11. Zimmermann, A., Schmidt, R., Sandkuhl, K., Jugel, D., Bogner, J., Möhring, M.: Decision-controlled digitization architecture for internet of things and microservices. In: Czarnowski, I., Howlett, R.J., Jain, L.C. (eds.) IDT 2017. SIST, vol. 73, pp. 82–92. Springer, Cham (2018). doi:10.1007/978-3-319-59424-8_8
12. Christoforou, A., Andreou, A.S.: A multilayer fuzzy cognitive maps approach to the cloud adoption decision support problem. In: 2015 IEEE International Conference on Fuzzy Systems (FUZZ-IEEE), pp. 1–8. IEEE (2015)
13. Kitchenham, B.: Guidelines for performing systematic literature reviews in software engineering. Technical report, Version 2.3 EBSE Technical report. EBSE. sn (2007)
14. Garriga, M., Flores, A., Cechich, A., Zunino, A.: Web services composition mechanisms: a review. IETE Techn. Rev. **32**(5), 376–383 (2015)
15. Garriga, M., Mateos, C., Flores, A., Cechich, A., Zunino, A.: Restful service composition at a glance: a survey. J. Netw. Comput. Appl. **60**, 32–53 (2016)

A Tree-Based Reliability Analysis for Fault-Tolerant Web Services Composition

Yanjun Shu[1]([✉]), Decheng Zuo[1], Hongwei Liu[1], Quan Z. Sheng[2],
Wei Emma Zhang[2], and Jian Yang[2]

[1] School of Computer Science and Technology, Harbin Institute of Technology,
Harbin, China
{yjshu,zuodc,liuhw}@hit.edu.cn
[2] Department of Computing, Macquarie University, Sydney, Australia
{michael.sheng,w.zhang,jian.yang}@mq.edu.au

Abstract. Reliability is critical for choosing, ranking and composing Web services. However, some common situations, such as fault-tolerant strategies and the dynamic operational profile, are not considered in existing reliability analysis. To solve these problems, a tree-based composition structure model is proposed, which is called the Fault-tolerant Composite Web Services Tree (FCWS-T). We separate the nodes in FCWS-T into two types, namely the *control nodes* and the *service nodes*, leading to the representation of various composition structures can be explicitly performed. Then, a reliability simulation method is proposed based on FCWS-T and it can effectively analyze the reliability of a complex Web service. Experiments on a financial management service show the effectiveness of our approach for fault-tolerant Web service compositions.

Keywords: Reliability · Services composition · Fault-tolerant · Simulation

1 Introduction

Nowadays, Service-Oriented Computing (SOC) has emerged as a new way to develop extensible computing systems that evolve from the component-based software engineering. In SOC, the service is a black box to users and it is either an atomic Web service or a complex Web service that is constituted by several smaller, loosely coupled, reusable Web services via the Business Process Execution Language (BPEL) [5]. Reliability is a key issue of Quality of Service (QoS) for choosing and compositing Web services [9], especially for the mission-critical domains such as military or finance. In these domains, systems are complex and built by many component services with different reliabilities, leading to the analysis a very challenging yet crucial task. To perform the reliability analysis of composite Web services, there are two main issues to be resolved:

© Springer International Publishing AG 2017
M. Maximilien et al. (Eds.): ICSOC 2017, LNCS 10601, pp. 481–489, 2017.
https://doi.org/10.1007/978-3-319-69035-3_35

Modeling the composition structure. An appropriate representation of the composition structure is the foundation for reliability analysis. Most existing reliability analysis methods assume that the composite Web service is well-structured by some methodologies such as Service graph [7] and Semi Markov Process (SMP) [9]. However, clear explanation on how the structure model is built from the service composition is either missing or insufficient. In practice, the composition structure is varied in the integration stage and some composite Web services may be black boxes to users. Thus the transition from a composite Web service to the composition structure model requires explicit discussion. As the BPEL process describes the service composition, the problem of modeling the composition structure can be turned into the transition from BPEL to a composition structure model [4]. Moreover, Web services operate in an unstable Internet. Fault tolerance is an effective way to achieve high reliability. Although some existing reliability analysis methods consider the fault-tolerant mechanism in reliability calculation, they do not represent the fault-tolerant strategies in their composition structure models [4,9].

Calculating the composite reliability. *Composite reliability* is the integration of *component reliabilities* with the transition probabilities between every component service. The transition probability can be obtained by statistical analysis of service invocations or empirical study of similar service compositions. All transition probabilities in a composition constitute the service operation profile which is a description of the generated pattern of external service requests expressed in a probabilistic form. Many *composite reliability* calculation methods use various mathematical equations to integrate the *component reliabilities* with the high level composition structure model [1,7,9]. These methods can obtain the *composite reliability* directly and they are applied widely in QoS-based service compositions. However, there are many restrictions on mathematical equations, such as the calculation equations may be very cumbersome and the sensitiveness of components cannot be obtained easily. Moreover, the *composite reliability* is dependent on the operation profile [2]. For a composite Web service, the operation profile may be varied in different time intervals according to users' requests. Although the dynamic operation profile is very important in reliability analysis, it is considered by few composite reliability calculation methods.

Based on above discussions, a tree-based reliability analysis approach is proposed in this paper. We represent the composition structure in a Fault-tolerant Composite Web Services Tree (FCWS-T). There are two types of nodes in FCWS-T: the *control node* and the *service node*. The service node is a leaf of FCWS-T which represents a component service. The control node is the internal node which is used to represent the composition activity of children. By separating the node types of FCWS-T, various structures of the composite Web service can be represented explicitly. Moreover, the FCWS-T can be transformed from the BPEL process or the composition designer's description directly. Considering the limitations of mathematical equations, the discrete-event simulation method [3] is used here for its flexibility in describing the *component reliability* functions. By integrating multiple operation profiles in simulation, the varying operation profile can also be considered in the *composite reliability* analysis.

The remaining paper is organized as follows: Sect. 2 presents the FCWS-T model and the methodology to transform the BPEL to a FCWS-T; Sect. 3 describes the reliability analysis simulation algorithms; Sect. 4 reports the experiments on a finance management service; Sect. 5 provides some conclusions.

2 The FCWS-T Model

2.1 The Definition of a FCWS-T Model

The FCWS-T is defined as a tree in this work. There are two main types of elements in the composition structure: component services and composition activities. Correspondingly, we define two types of nodes, namely *ServiceNodes* and *ControlNodes*, to represent them respectively. The *ControlNodes* represent four basic composition activities which include *Sequence, If, While/Repeat* and *Flow* [5]. The *ServiceNode* describes a component service's reliability and execution time. In reality, the round trip of invoking a component service is more vulnerable than the service execution. In FCWS-T, the link reliability and link time of a component service are considered in the *ServiceNode*. Moreover, only several key component services in a whole composite Web service will be fault-tolerant due to the fault-tolerant strategies application costs significantly in time or resources. Thus in FCWS-T, fault-tolerant strategies are only defined for the *ServiceNodes*. According to the classification in [8], there are three main fault-tolerant strategies: *Retry, Active replication, Passive replication*.

According to the iteration feature of a tree, the following is the definition of FCWS-T model. Every tree node is: *TreeNode* = ⟨*type, parent, childList, weight*⟩.

(1) *type*: The   *ServiceNode* and   *ControlNode*. The   *ServiceNode* is $\{ServiceReli(), ServiceTime(), LinkReli(), LinkTime(), FT\}$, and $FT \in \{None, Retry, Passive, Active\}$. The   *ControlNode* is $\{Sequence, If, Flow, While/Repeat\}$.
(2) *parent*: FCWS-T *TreeNode*, the father of the tree node.
(3) *childList*: $\{child_1, child_2, \cdots, child_n: FCWS - T\,TreeNode\}$.
(4) *weight*: The execution probability p_i relative to the parent node. In the *If* activity, $\{p_i\}$ is the branch execution probability. In the *While/Repeat* activity, p_i represents the probability of executing i times. In both of these two activities, the sum of all branch execution probabilities is 1. In the *Sequence* or *Flow* activity, all children execute in sequence or in parallel and p_i is 1 for the children.

2.2 The Transition from BPEL to FCWS-T

The BPEL process of a composite Web service elucidates the structure activities (i.e., a series of basic composition activities) by nesting and iterations [5]. Here, we build the FCWS-T model directly by parsing BPEL process in two steps.

(1) Extracting the WS-token String from BPEL

We define the WS-token string to represent the lexical analysis results of BPEL. A WS-token string is a set of tuples. Each tuple represents a service sub-composition and it is consisted by four elements: the *left bracket* "(", the *basic composition activity*, the *Web service number*, and the *right bracket* ")". The *left bracket* "(" and the *right bracket* ")" denote the start and the end of a sub-composition activity. The *basic composition activity* can be *Sequence*, *Flow*, *While/Repeat*, *If* and they are denoted as *S*, *F*, *W*, *I*. The *Web service numbers* are the identifiers of component services invoked in the sub-composition of a tuple.

The extraction process includes three parts. First, the BPEL source file is split into strings by lexical analysis. Then, the strings are read in sequence and the corresponding element of a tuple is generated. For example, in a sequence sub-composition, there are two component services which are Service 1 and Service 2. The tuple of this sub-composition is denoted as (*S*12). Finally, by parsing all BPEL strings, a WS-token string is created by constituting the tuples nested.

(2) Mapping the WS-token String to FCWS-T

As an intermediate representation, the WS-token string can be used for transforming BPEL to FCWS-T. Every tuple of the WS-token string represents a Web services sub-composition. Algorithm 1 shows the mapping algorithm from the WS-token string to FCWS-T. The WS-token string is scanned from left to right. A sub-composition starts with the *left bracket* "(" and ends with the *right bracket* ")". The new tree nodes of the *ControlNode* and *ServiceNode* will be created according to the *basic composition activity* and *Web services number* of a tuple. When a sub-composition activity finishes, the corresponding subtree is generated and inserted to FCWS-T as a component service.

Algorithm 1. MapFCWS-T

Input: a WS-token string;
Output: the FCWS-T;
1. $current=0$;
2. **while** ($current$ <WS-token.length)
3.   { $current++$;
4.   **if**(WS-token[$current$]== Composition)
5.   S1.push(WS-token[$current$]); //S1 is a composition activity stack.
6.   **elsif**(WS-token[$current$]== "(")
7.   S2.push(WS-token[$current$]); //S2 is a service stack.
8.   **elsif** (WS-token[$current$]== Number)
9.   S2.push(WS-token[$current$]);
10.   **elsif** (WS-token[$current$]== ")") // A sub-composition activity is ended.
11.   {Con_node=S1.pop(); New_tree=Create_tree(Con_node); //The ControlNode is generated.
12.   Ser_node=S2.pop();
13.   **while**(Ser_node != "(")
14.   {Insert_Node(New_tree, Ser_node); Ser_node=S2.pop(); } // ServiceNodes are inserted.
15.   S2.push(New_tree); } // The subtree is pushed in the service stack as a component service.
16.   **end if**; }

---

3 The Reliability Analysis Simulation Methodology

To calculate the reliability of a service composition, we need a mechanism which can integrate the composition structure model and component reliabilities. The simulation method is an effective way to address these two issues. Moreover, it can explore the "what-if" questions and get more reliability details at the design stage [3]. Here, the discrete-event simulation is adopted to study the failure behavior of each component service in the composition. Then, a simulation algorithm for the whole composite Web service is proposed based on the FCWS-T.

3.1 The Discrete-Event Simulation of Component Reliability

The discrete-event simulation technique [3] has been used to study the failure behavior of Web services which are described by a non-homogeneous continuous time Markov chain (NHCTMC) process. The failures of a Web service are treated as the discrete-events in simulation. The main idea of this technique is to compare a random number x with the probability of a failure occurred (i.e., a event happens) in the infinitesimal interval $(t, t + dt)$. The failure probability is given by $lambda() \times dt$ and $lambda()$ is the failure rate function, which can be provided by service developers or the evaluating third party. If $x > lambda() \times dt$, it means a failure happened in $(t, t + dt)$ and returns 1, otherwise the service executes successfully and returns 0. The Web service reliability can be obtained by the number of failures is divided by the entire simulation times in the period $(0, t)$.

It is costly and not feasible to explore every fault tolerant strategy via testing. The simulation technique can help developers in determining how fault-tolerant Web services will perform when they are employed. In our previous work [6], we have applied the discrete-event simulation method to investigate the reliability problem of fault-tolerant Web services. The reliability simulation algorithms of retry, active replication and passive replication strategies are proposed. Due to space constraints, the details of these simulation algorithms are not discussed.

3.2 The Simulation Algorithm of the Composite Reliability

As the composition structure and component services are distinguished by *ControlNodes* and *ServiceNodes*, the composite reliability simulation just needs to travel FCWS-T according to the type of tree nodes. Algorithm 2 shows the simulation process of composite services. The basic idea of our algorithm is to travel all sub-trees in a preorder. Each sub-tree from the root node is iteratively simulated according to the composition structure of their father node. When the tree node is a *ServiceNode*, the component reliability simulation is executed. The link reliability and service reliability are simulated sequentially for a *ServiceNode*. If a service or link is failed, the simulation stops. The failure times and the execution time are recorded. Otherwise, the simulation will traverse all nodes in FCWS-T and return the execution time.

486 Y. Shu et al.

Algorithm 2. SimulateReli

Input: The FCWS-T, n;
Output: *linkfails[], servicefails[], exetimes[], globatime*;
1. *SimCounting*=0; *globatime*=0;
2. **while** (*SimCounting* <n)
3. {*SimuCounting*++;
4.   TreeNode=FCWS-T.root; *localtime*=*globaltime*;
5.   **while**(TreeNode !=NULL || failureTag==FALSE)
6.   { **if** (Treenode.type is *ControlNode*)
7.   **switch**(TreeNode)
8.   **case** "S": **foreach** *Subtree$_i$* **do** *SimulateReli* (*Subtree$_i$*) in *sequence*; break;
9.   **case** "I": **foreach** *Subtree$_i$* **do** *SimulateReli*(*Subtree$_i$*) in *branch*; break;
10.   **case** "W": **foreach** *Subtree$_i$* **do** *SimulateReli*(*Subtree$_i$*) in *loop*; break;
11.   **case** "F": **foreach** *Subtreei* **do** *SimulateReli*(*Subtreei*) in *parallel*; break;
12.   **elsif** (TreeNode.type is *ServiceNode*)
13.   failureTag=Link_Service_Sim(TreeNode,localtime);
14.   Update *linkfails[], servicefails[], exetimes[], localtime*;
15.   **return** *failureTag*;
16.   **end if**; }
17. *globaltime*+=localtime; }

Table 1. The reliability of component Web services

No.	Service Name	Exeution Time avg (ms)	Reliability
1	Deposit and withdraw	104.4	0.782
2	Intermediate approval	103.17	0.863
3	Primary approval	95.02	0.983
4	Risk assessment	91.47	0.792
5	Loanversion1	88.28	0.804
5	Loanversion2	97.56	0.793
5	Loanversion3	90.46	0.788
6	Advanced approval	127.3	0.887

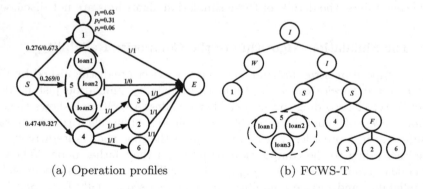

(a) Operation profiles   (b) FCWS-T

Fig. 1. The operation profiles and the FCWS-T model of the financial management composite service

4   Experimental Studies

4.1   The Experiment Setup

A financial management composite service is used to demonstrate the effectiveness of our reliability analysis approach. This composite service provides the deposit and withdrawal service, the investment service and the loan service. The investment service is composed by four component services which are the risk assessment service, the primary approval service, the intermediate approval service and the advanced approval service. Moreover, the passive fault-tolerant strategy is applied for the loan service to ensure its reliability. There are three loan services which are named `loanversion1`, `loanversion2`, `loanversion3`. The reliability of each component service is shown in Table 1. As the loan service is not available in the non-working hours, the working hours operation profile is quite different from the non-working hours. 14,925 test cases are executed during the period of one month. The numbers of test cases in the working hours and non-working hours are 10,031 and 4,894. These two groups of test cases constitute the working hours and non-working hours operation profiles which are shown in Fig. 1(a).

4.2   The Simulation Reliability Analysis Results

This section reports the results of the simulation approach and it is twofold. First, we exhibit the usability of simulation results with multiple operation profiles. Second, we demonstrate how the simulation approach determines the reliability bottleneck and explore the effectiveness of different fault-tolerant strategies.

(1)   The Reliability Simulation Results

The FCWS-T model is generated by transforming the BPEL of the financial management service. First, the WS-token string is extracted from the BPEL and it is $(I(W1)(I(S1)(S4(F326))))$. Then, the FCWS-T is generated. Figure 1(b) shows the FCWS-T of the financial management service. Based on Table 1 and Fig. 1(a), the parameters can be specified for the *ServiceNodes* and *ControlNodes* respectively. In our examples, the *LinkTime*() of services is a random value which ranges from $0ms$ to $200ms$ and the *LinkReli*() of services is set as 0.99 since the financial management service is operating in a small local area network.

As the test cases of working hours and non-working hours are 10,031 and 4,894, the proportion of two operation profiles execution can be assumed as 2:1. We define that every 1,000 simulations of the working hours will follow 500 simulations of the non-working hours. The two operation profiles are alternatively simulated. With 100,000 simulation times, the average reliability and execution time are 0.7383 and 254.84 *ms*. The simulation reliability results of working hours and non-working hours are 0.7541 and 0.6762. As the executions of the working hours profile are twice of the executions of the non-working hours profile, the whole time result is more close to the working hours. Moreover, the reliability of the non-working hours is much lower than the reliability of the working hours. The simulation results suggest that developers need to pay more attention on the reliability of the financial management service in non-working hours.

(2) The Fault-tolerant Strategy of Web Services

Finding the most reliability sensitive component service is essential in applying fault-tolerant strategies. The sensitiveness of every component service can be investigated by changing component reliabilities. When every component reliability is increased by 10% in each composite reliability simulation, Service 1 is found to be the most sensitive component service which has the greatest improvement of the composite reliability. Thus it is an effective way to improve the whole composition reliability by applying fault-tolerant strategies on Service 1.

With the simulation approach, we can further explore the effectiveness of fault-tolerant strategies in improving the reliability of Service 1 and the whole composition. For *Retry* strategy, Service 1 will repeat three times until it succeeds. For *Passive* strategy, three replicas of Service 1 will be executed in order if the prior one is failed. For *Active* strategy, three replicas of Service 1 are executed in parallel. The execution result is the first return of three versions. Each replica is configured with different reliability and execution time. Table 2 shows the simulation results of Service 1 and the whole composition with different fault-tolerant strategies. It can be seen that the reliability of Service 1 is significantly improved by applying fault-tolerant strategies. However, the resources and execution time are also increased. The whole composite reliability can be improved by 14.7%, 16.3% and 16.1%, comparing with no fault-tolerant strategy of Service 1. The composition designer can choose a suitable strategy to improve the reliability of the whole composite Web service based on the simulation results.

Table 2. The Reliability Results of Service 1 with Different Fault-Tolerant Strategies

Attributes		The fault tolerant strategy of Service 1			
		Non_FT	*Retry*	*Passive*	*Active*
Service 1	Resources	1	1	3	3
	Execution Time avg (*ms*)	104.4	235.09	233.88	206.23
	Reliability	0.782	0.9906	0.9927	0.9924
Whole composition	Execution Time avg (*ms*)	254.84	290.66	287.98	277.43
	Reliability	0.7383	0.8464	0.8586	0.8578
	Reliability improved	0%	14.7%	16.3%	16.1%

5 Conclusion

This paper proposes a tree-based reliability analysis approach for fault-tolerant Web services composition. The composition structure is represented by the

FCWS-T model which is a tree. Based on the FCWS-T model and the discrete-event simulation method, the composition structure, the component reliabilities and fault-tolerant strategies can be integrated in the composite reliability analysis. Developers can not only obtain the reliability of the whole composite Web service with multiple operation profiles, but also the sensitiveness of each component Web service and the effectiveness of different fault-tolerant strategies.

Acknowledgement. This work is partially supported by China NSF (No. 6120209 1), the Fundamental Research Funds for Central Universities (No. NSRIF. 2016050) and the State Scholarship Fund of China Scholarship Council (No. 201606125073).

References

1. Ding, Z., Jiang, M., Kandel, A.: Port-based reliability computing for service composition. IEEE Trans. Serv. Comput. **5**(3), 422–436 (2012)
2. Grassi, V., Patella, S.: Reliability prediction for service-oriented computing environments. IEEE Internet Comput. **10**(3), 43–49 (2006)
3. Lin, C.: Analyzing the effect of imperfect debugging on software fault detection and correction processes via a simulation framework. Math. Comput. Model. **54**(11), 3046–3064 (2011)
4. Mukherjee, D., Jalote, P., Gowri Nanda, M.: Determining QoS of WS-BPEL compositions. In: Bouguettaya, A., Krueger, I., Margaria, T. (eds.) ICSOC 2008. LNCS, vol. 5364, pp. 378–393. Springer, Heidelberg (2008). doi:10.1007/978-3-540-89652-4_29
5. OASIS: Web Services Business Process Execution Language (WS-BPEL) v2.0. (2007), http://docs.oasis-open.org/wsbpel/2.0/OS/wsbpel-v2.0-OS.html
6. Shu, Y., Wu, Z., Liu, H., Gao, Y.: A simulation-based reliability analysis approach of the fault-tolerant web services. In: Proceedings of ISMS 2016 (2016)
7. Zheng, H., Yang, J., Zhao, W.: Probabilistic QoS aggregations for service compositions. ACM Trans. Web **10**(2), 1–36 (2016)
8. Zheng, Z., Lyu, M.: A distributed replication strategy evaluation and selection framework for fault tolerant web services. In: Proceedings of ICWS 2008 (2008)
9. Zheng, Z., Trivedi, K., Qiu, K., Xia, R.: Semi-markov models of composite web services for their performance, reliability and bottlenecks. IEEE Trans. Serv. Comput. **6**(1), 1–14 (2015)

Modernization of Information Systems at Red.es: An Approach Based on Gap Analysis and ADM

Marcos López-Sanz[1(✉)], Valeria de Castro[1], Esperanza Marcos[1], and Jorge Moratalla[2]

[1] Kybele Research Group, Rey Juan Carlos University, C/Tulipan s/n, Móstoles, 28933 Madrid, Spain
{marcos.lopez, valeria.decastro, esperanza.marcos}@urjc.es
[2] Red.es. Ministry of Industry, Energy and Tourism, Edificio Bronce, Plaza Manuel Gómez Moreno, s/n, 28020 Madrid, Spain
jorge.moratalla@red.es

Abstract. This paper presents a method for the modernization of information systems that allow organizations to maintain the capabilities of existing information systems. This method defines a horseshoe-like process based on ADM (*Architecture-Driven Modernization*), and applies gap-analysis techniques to detect the possible reuse of current functionalities to build modernized systems. The proposal has been developed, refined and validated at Red.es, one of the Spanish Government's Public Entities. Our proposal includes the definition of a process, the models used in each step, and sets of rules that can be used to progress in this process. The proposed method thus permits systematic progress to be made in a system modernization process: obtaining the business models of the legacy system, comparing them with redefined business models incorporating new business rules, and finally, implementing them by adapting and reusing the existing code.

Keywords: Information system modernization · Domain name management systems · Architecture driven modernization · Gap analysis

1 Introduction

When modernizing public organizations' business processes, the optimization of the services provided, and particularly the Information Systems (IS) supporting them, becomes a key factor [1–3]. The goal is to make them more competitive and efficient in resource use and service delivery, thus improving the State's relationship with its citizens. This is the case of Red.es, a Public Entity linked to the Spanish Ministry of Industry, Energy and Tourism. One of its main duties is to act as the Spanish Authority for the '.es' domain name management. Its current strategy for the promotion of the information society emphasizes the need to adapt its applications IS to aspects of the new legislative framework on interoperability [4] and *eGovernment* [5].

M. Maximilien et al. (Eds.): ICSOC 2017, LNCS 10601, pp. 490–498, 2017.
https://doi.org/10.1007/978-3-319-69035-3_36

This scenario, in which a legacy IS must be upgraded to support new conditions depending on changing business rules [6], represents the main motivation for the proposal presented herein. We have followed the principles of the *Architecture-Driven Modernization* (ADM) initiative issued by the OMG [7] to define a 'horseshoe-like' process based on business analysis [8, 9]. We also propose using *gap analysis* techniques [10] to handle the differences between the current business features and those expected. Gap analysis provides a means to identify how available business services (known as *as-is*) may be assembled within the newly conceived ones (*to-be*) to better meet the organizations' goals [11, 12]. As the paper shows, the synergies of using ADM and gap analysis together can be employed in the definition of a modernization process for legacy IS with changes in the business to support.

The remainder of this article is structured as follows. Section 2 describes the foundations of our proposal. Section 3 presents the IS of Red.es and offers an explanation of our proposal applied to a concrete scenario. Section 4 analyses some related works and, finally Sect. 5 presents some conclusions and future works.

2 Modernization Foundations and Working Scenario

This section briefly shows the two approaches used as foundations for the proposed modernization process: ADM and gap analysis techniques, and introduces the working scenario at Red.es.

2.1 ADM-Based Modernization

ADM [7] defines a set of metamodels at different abstraction levels (mainly positioned in the IT domain) and a series of transformations between them:

- *Abstract Syntax Tree Metamodel* (ASTM): which represents a low-level view of the system, close to the source code.
- *Knowledge Discovery Metamodel* (KDM): that collects aspects from both the technological solution and the logical structure of the system. The KDM metamodel is composed of four layers that represent a conceptual view of the system at different levels: *infrastructure, program elements, runtime resources* and *abstraction*. KDM has been published independently as ISO/IEC 19506:2012 [13].
  We add a third level to these two, corresponding to the business domain, also issued by the OMG for modernization purposes but not as part of ADM:
- *Semantics for Business Vocabulary and Rules* (SBVR): aims to provide a vocabulary for the semantics and business rules associated with the company strategy [14].

2.2 Gap Analysis

Gap analysis is a technique that provides a means to determine how available software assets may be assembled within the newly conceived and redefined business activities that best meet an organization's goals [11, 15]. The inputs of a gap-analysis process are the *as-is* and *to-be* artefacts, while the output includes a set of specifications indicating changes that can be made by incrementally adding more details to existing IS.

In [10], the authors of the current paper presented a framework for gap analysis named GAMBUSE. This proposal adopts a model-engineering approach which includes the identification and manipulation of mappings between *as-is* and *to-be* business models. GAMBUSE compares these two models by using a set of formal definitions of the model elements based on [16].

2.3   Domain Name Management at Red.es

The Public Entity *Red.es* is an organization linked to the Spanish Government's Ministry of Industry, Energy and Tourism which aims to promote the Information Society in our country. Red.es is in charge of performing all the tasks related to managing domain names for the geographical top-level domain for Spain's indicative ('.es'). The number of stakeholders involved in this management and the capabilities demanded have evolved during the last decade [17]. The entity has confronted this situation by changing the IS on demand and applying successive patches to suit the operations required at each moment. This evolution has not been as optimal as expected, resulting in a legacy IS that is hard to evolve and has high maintenance costs.

The increasing need to adapt the system to the new legislation concerning citizens' electronic access to public services [5] and the incorporation of the *National Interoperability Framework Law* [4] to the domain name management system led Red.es to consider modernizing the system via structural and functional changes.

Since the system is too complex for the length of this paper, we shall focus on one of its subsets: '.*es ownership transmission*'. Domain name transmission is a functionality provided by Red.es consisting of the possibility of changing the ownership of a '.es' domain name from one citizen or company to another using the current IS.

3   Modernization of the '.es Ownership Transmission' Scenario

Our proposal for system modernization at Red.es comprises a '*horseshoe*' process [8] based on the ADM approach together with gap analysis (see Fig. 1).

The method proposed starts by defining the IT level models (KDM) and then applies several sets of transformation rules [18] to reach the business level, represented using an SBVR model. This model is used by business analysts who can complete and adapt it with/to new business rules. The gap-analysis technique is then applied in order to obtain the changes that must be made to attain the target (*to-be*) solution.

Step 1: Obtaining the initial KDM logical model. The first step is to obtain a representation of the code of the current system using the concepts defined in the KDM metamodel [13]. In this step, we take advantage of the MoDISCO tool [1] to obtain automatically the KDM model from J2EE implementations. Figure 2 shows an excerpt of the KDM model obtained with MoDISCO. The result is a tree-like representation of the code but using the concepts of the KDM metamodel.

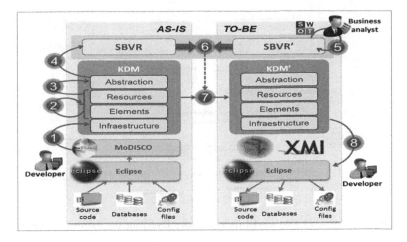

Fig. 1. Steps in our proposal for system modernization.

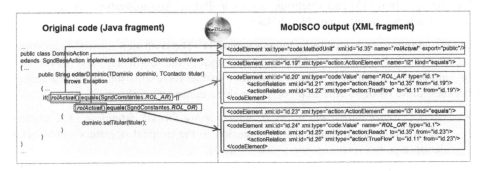

Fig. 2. KDM (XML) model obtained with MoDISCO from original code

Step 2. Refining the KDM logical model. The second step consists of manually manipulating the results obtained with MoDISCO. For example, in Fig. 3 it is possible to observe the creation of an *if* statement but adding the elements representing the corresponding 'true'/'false' branches.

Step 4. Obtaining the as-is business model. The fourth step consists of obtaining the business model corresponding to the current system, i.e. the as-is model. ADM already indicates the existence of transformation rules to obtain the SBVR model from the abstraction layer of the KDM model but does not specify them [7]. One example of these rules is that stating: "each RuleUnit the abstraction layer becomes a Rule element in the SBVR model".

Step 5. Obtaining the to-be business model. After performing a SWOT analysis [20] commissioned by senior managers and conducted by business analysts, Red.es studied various systems in European Registries, which allowed us to obtain the target (to-be) business model. [17]. For instance, the main weakness (which is in turn understood as

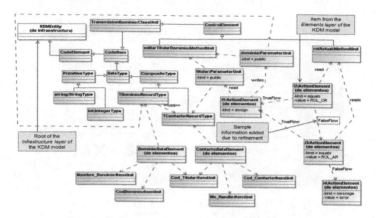

Fig. 3. Refined KDM model (infrastructure layer) for the running scenario.

an opportunity) identified by this analysis was the need to adapt the system to the laws for interoperability [5] and electronic access to Public Administration services [4] in order to achieve an interoperable platform.

Step 6. Mapping as-is and to-be business models. The sixth step consists of applying gap-analysis techniques to the SBVR (*as-is*, output of the fourth step) and SBVR' (*to-be*, output of the fifth step) models to obtain a formal representation of the differences between these models. This step comprises three consecutive phases:

- *Step 6.1: Representing the business models using formal definitions.* The current modernization proposal defines an extension to the original operators to represent relationships between classifiers (see Table 1).

Table 1. New operators added to GAMBUSE notation for classifier relationships.

Item	Description
Contains (C1 ⊆ C2)	Association relationship between 2 classifiers C1 and C2
Inherits (C1 ↓ C2)	'Inherits' relationship between 2 classifiers. *C2 inherits from C1*
Compose (C1 ∈ C2)	'Composition' relationship between 2 classifiers. *C1 is a part of C2*

- *Step 6.2: Applying the operators to analyse both business models.* The next substep consists of identifying the similarities and differences between the elements of both business models. By applying the operators defined by GAMBUSE plus the operators we have added, it is possible to discover which parts of the business are subject to change, and therefore the parts of the system code that will require modification.

- *Step 6.3: Obtaining processing operations.* The output of the previous substep is a set of predicates containing the result of applying the *Intersection* and *Disparity* operators (in both directions). This information is used in the next phase to determine the modifications that should be made to the *as-is* model to attain the *to-be* model.

Step 7. Obtaining the target logical model. The output operations obtained in the previous step are used to define and apply the necessary transformation rules [18] to the *as-is* KDM logical model (*abstraction* layer), obtained in the third step. A *to-be* KDM' model is then obtained in accordance with the new business rules and the *insert/subtract* operations.

Step 8. Obtaining the target implementation. The final step consists of applying the transformation rules defined in the second step in reverse order. This KDM' will be the source used by developers to modify the code that the modernized information system will implement. The transformation rules used for this last step make it possible to code partially the modernized information system [18]. Figure 4 shows an overview of this step in which the source code obtained with the rules and applied to the case scenario are depicted.

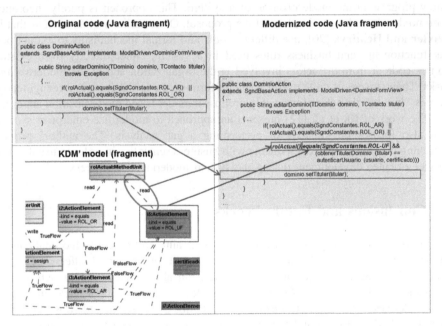

Fig. 4. Overview of the final step of the proposal applied to a fragment of the running scenario.

4   Related Works

In *Model-Driven Engineering* (MDE) the term *modernization* has led to the concept of *Model-Driven Reengineering* (MRE) [21] which has been discussed in several works, some of which are analysed as follows.

Pu et al. [22] propose a set of rules to semi-automatically obtain and update business rules within the scope of Web Engineering using UML diagrams to describe domain-specific operations. This work is one of the earliest proposals to deal with modernizing a legacy system by considering the influence of business rules applied to a concrete domain. However, they restrict their scope of influence to the presentation layer of a Web-based system. Other works [23, 24] similarly propose specific frameworks focused on modelling system behaviour. These works understand the business level from a more flow-oriented viewpoint (business *process*) rather than focusing on the analysis and modelling of the static business *rules* governing the application to be modernized.

Ulrich [9] goes one step further by defining a series of case studies based on different types of ADM-based modernization alternatives, and analysing several real-world case studies. However, although a model-driven approach is used, this work lacks a precise methodology (steps or stages) that could be followed to guide this process. **Van den Heuvel** [26] solves this drawback by providing a set of steps that allow progress in the modernization of a system. This approach is purely theoretical with no details on how to implement the proposal. Other earlier works, such as that by **Baxter and Hendryx** [20], use different tools and formal mechanisms to extract both the functionality and business rules used in a system, either directly from existing source code or from the actors involved in the organization and in the modernization tasks. Their strategy is quite useful when performing the initial steps in a reengineering process, but they do not, unfortunately propose a model-based modernization approach.

The work of **Ilk et al.** [12] presents an approach to modernize enterprise systems that also focuses on the idea of performing a gap analysis. The authors propose enriching the source code components with business semantics in order to use them for service-oriented development during the system modernization process.

5   Conclusions and Future Works

In this paper we have presented a proposal that aims to overcome the challenge of modernizing the current IS at Red.es. To that end, our proposal offers not only a model-driven method based on business rules, but also a practical approach that has been successfully applied at Red.es, covering all the steps of a modernization process. It also defines both a specific *business model* (not explicitly included as part of the original ADM approach) and *transformation rules* with which to semi-automatically obtain the business model from the source logical model. Finally, our proposal also updates a set of mapping operations with which to obtain a logical *to-be* model (KDM' *to-be*) from both the business *to-be* model (SBVR' *to-be*) and the logical *as-is* model (KDM *as-is*), using gap analysis techniques.

This paper has used the case of the ownership transmission of '.es' domain names at Red.es as running scenario to illustrate the proposal. This was chosen since it comprised a representative and complete information flow involving different roles and processes, and also corresponded to a relatively isolated module of the '.es' domain name management IS. Very few of the other proposals studied are able to demonstrate the feasibility and practical application of their proposal, and are in many cases formal and theoretical works that are hard to apply in an actual enterprise environment or even at the Public Administration.

One of the main drawbacks of the proposal, at its current state, relies on the fact that, although model transformation rules have been defined [18], they still need a transformation engine to execute them in order to automate the method as much as possible. In addition, some of the steps still require the designer to manipulate the models manually which is a fact that requires proper training and a precise knowledge of the system under modernization. To that extend, as future work we shall develop a toolkit to permit not only the visual editing and simple validation of models, but also a user-friendly environment for the definition of model transformations and their subsequent execution.

Acknowledgements. This research has been partially funded by the Regional Government of Madrid under the SICOMORo-CM (S2013/ICE-3006) project, by the MASAI (TIN-2011-22617) and ELASTIC (TIN2014-52938-C2-1-R) projects, financed by the Spanish Ministry of Science and Innovation, and by the Service Science, Management and Engineering-GES2ME Research Excellence Group (Ref. 30VCPIGI15) co-funded by Rey Juan Carlos University and Banco Santander.

References

1. Bianchi, A., Caivano, D., Marengo, V., Visaggio, G.: Iterative reengineering of legacy systems. IEEE Trans. Softw. Eng. **29**(3), 225–241 (2003)
2. Comella-Dorda, S., Wallnau, K., Seacord, R., Robert, J.: A Survey of Legacy System Modernization Approaches, Carnegie Mellon University, Tech. Note Cmu/Sei-2000-Tn-003
3. Dedeke, A.: Improving legacy-system sustainability: a systematic approach. IEEE IT Prof. **14**(1), 38–43 (2012)
4. Royal Decree 4/2010 (8 January 2010). Regulates the National Interoperability Framework in the Field of eGovernment
5. Ley 11/2007, de 22 de Junio, de Acceso Electrónico de los Ciudadanos a los Servicios Públicos. BOE 150 (23 de Junio de 2007): 27150–27166 (2007)
6. Seacord, R.C., Plakosh, D., Lewis, G.A.: Modernizing Legacy Systems: Software Technologies, Engineering Processes, and Business Practices. Addison-Wesley, Reading (2003)
7. OMG. Architecture Driven Modernization (ADM) Task Force (2007). http://adm.omg.org/
8. Carnegie Mellon University/SEI. Reengineering: The Horseshoe Model (1999). http://www.sei.cmu.edu/reengineering/horseshoe_model.html
9. Ulrich, W.M., Newcomb, P.H.: Information Systems Transformation: Architecture-Driven Modernization Case Studies. The Morgan Kaufmann/OMG Press (2010)

10. De Castro, V., Marcos, E., Vara, J.M., Van Den Heuvel, W.J., Papazoglou, M.: Applying a Model-Driven Framework for Gap Analysis: Towards Business Service Eng. Uncovering Essential Software Artifacts through Business Process Archeology. IGI Global, Hershey (2013)
11. Bolstorff, P., Rosenbaum, R.: Supply Chain Excellence: A Handbook for Dramatic Improvement Using the SCOR Model, 2nd edn. Amacom, New York (2007)
12. Ilk, N., Zhao, J.L., Goes, P., Hofmann, P.: Semantic enrichment process: an approach to software component reuse in modernizing enterprise systems. Inf. Syst. Front. **13**, 359–370 (2011)
13. OMG. ISO/IEC19506:2012. Architecture Driven Modernization (ADM): Knowledge Discovery Meta Model (KDM), v1.3 (2012). http://www.omg.org/spec/KDM/ISO/19506/pdf
14. OMG. Semantics of Business Vocabulary and Rules (SBVR), OMG Standard, v1.0 (2008)
15. Juan, Y.C., Ou-Yang, C.: Systematic approach for the gap analysis of business processes. Int. J. Prod. Res. **42**, 1325–1364 (2004)
16. Van Den Heuvel, W.J.: Aligning Modern Business Processes and Legacy Systems: A Component-Based Perspective (Cooperative Information Systems). The MIT Press
17. Red.es. Statement of the General Director of Red.es (2 Jan 2010). Procedures for the Assignment Associated with the Registration of Domain Names under ".es" (2010)
18. Moratalla, J.: PREMISA: Un PRoceso para la Evolución y ModernIzación de SistemAs. Rey Juan Carlos University. Ph.D. thesis (2012)
19. Barbier, G., Bruneliere, H., Jouault, F., Lennon, Y., Madiot, F.: MODISCO, a model-driven platform to support real legacy modernization use cases. In: Information Systems Transformation: Architecture-Driven Modernization Case Studies, pp. 365–400 (2010)
20. Humphrey, A.: SWOT Analysis for Management Consulting. Sri Alumni Newsletter (2005)
21. Favre, J.-M.: Foundations of model (Driven) (Reverse) engineering: models - episode I, stories of the Fidus Papyrus and of the Solarus. In: Proceedings of the Dagstuhl Seminar (2004)
22. Pu, J., Yang, H., Xu, B., Xu, L., Cheng-Chung, W.: Combining MDE and UML to reverse engineer web-based legacy systems. In: Proceedings of COMSAC 2008, pp. 718–725. IEEE CS (2008)
23. Pérez-Castillo, R., De Guzmán, I.-R., Piattini, M.: Business process archaeology using marble. Inf. Softw. Technol. **53**, 1023–1044 (2011)
24. Cánovas, J., Garcia-Molina, J.: Extracting models from source code in software modernization. Softw. Syst. Model. **13**(2), 21 (2014). Springer-Verlag
25. Baxter, I., Hendryx, S.: A standards-based approach to extracting business rules. In: Architecture Driven Modernization Workshop, Alexandria, October 2005
26. Van Den Heuvel, W.J., Elgammal, A., Türetken, O., Papazoglou, M.P.: Formalizing and appling compliance patterns for business process compliance. Softw. Syst. Model. **15**(1), 119–146 (2016)

Improving Web Services Design Quality Using Dimensionality Reduction Techniques

Hanzhang Wang and Marouane Kessentini[✉]

Computer and Information Science Department, University of Michigan,
Dearborn, MI, USA
{wanghanz,marouane}@umich.edu

Abstract. In this paper, we propose a dimensionality reduction approach based on PCA-NSGAII to address the Web services modularization problem. Our approach aims at finding the best reduced set of objectives (e.g. quality metrics) that can generate near optimal modularization solutions to fix quality issues in Web services interface. The algorithm starts with a large number of Web service quality metrics as objectives that are reduced based on the correlation between them. This correlation is identified during the execution of the multi-objective algorithm by mining the execution traces of the generated solutions and their evaluations. We evaluated our approach on a set of 22 real world Web services, provided by Amazon and Yahoo. Statistical analysis of our experiments shows that our dimensionality reduction Web services interface modularization approach performed significantly better than the state-of-the-art modularization techniques in terms of generating well-designed Web services interface for users.

1 Introduction

The evolution of Web services may have a negative impact on the design quality of the interface by concatenating many non-cohesive operations that are semantically unrelated, and thus make it unnecessarily complex for users to find relevant operations to be used in their services-based systems. An example of well-known interface design defect is the God object Web service (GOWS) [11] which implements many operations related to different business and technical abstractions in a single service interface leading to low cohesion of its operations and high unavailability to end users because it is over-loaded. Indeed, the choice of how operations should be exposed through a service interface can have an impact on the performance, popularity and reusability of the service and it is not a trivial task [8–10]. On one hand, Web services interface exposing a high number of operations allow their clients to invoke their interfaces many times which significantly deteriorate the service performance. On the other hand, aggregating several operations of an interface into one large operation will reduce the reusability of the service.

In this work, we start from the hypothesis that there may be correlations among any two or more objectives (e.g. quality metrics) that are used to evaluate

© Springer International Publishing AG 2017
M. Maximilien et al. (Eds.): ICSOC 2017, LNCS 10601, pp. 499–507, 2017.
https://doi.org/10.1007/978-3-319-69035-3_37

Web service modularization solutions. Our approach, based on the PCA-NSGA-II methodology [3,13], aims at finding the best and reduced set of objective that represents the quality metrics of interest to the domain expert. A regular multi-objective NSGA-II algorithm [2,4,7] with an initial set of exhaustive metrics is executed for a number of iterations then a PCA component analyzes the correlation between the different objectives using the execution traces. The number of objectives maybe reduced during the next iterations based on the PCA results. The process is repeated several times until a maximum number of iterations is reached to generate a set of non-dominated Web services modularization solutions.

We evaluated our approach on a set of 22 real-world Web services, provided by Amazon and Yahoo. Statistical analysis of our experiments shows that our dimensionality reduction reduced significantly the number of objectives on several case studies to a minimum of 4 objectives. It also generates a smaller number of non-dominated solutions and lower execution time comparing to the use of a regular multi-objective algorithm based on NSGA-II [4]. The obtained results provide also evidence to support the claim that our proposal is more efficient, on average, than existing Web services modularization techniques, not based on heuristic search [1,12]. The paper also evaluates the relevance and usefulness of the suggested interface design improvements for web services user.

2 A Dimensionality Reduction Approach for Web Services Remodularization

The general structure of the proposed approach is described in Fig. 1. The approach takes as inputs a set of quality metrics, several Web services refactoring types, and a Web service to refactor. The first component consists of a regular execution of NSGA-II during a number of iterations. During this phase, NSGA-II [4] will try to find the non-dominated solutions balancing the initial set containing all the objectives such as improving the quality metrics of the service (Table 1) and minimizing the number of refactorings in the proposed solutions.

After a number of iterations, the second component of the algorithm is executed to analyze the execution traces of the first component (solutions and their evaluations), using PCA [6], to check the correlation between the different objectives. When a correlation between two or more objectives is detected, only one of them is selected for future iterations of the first component. Then, the first component is executed again with the new objective set.

The whole process of these two components continue until a maximum number of iterations is reached. A set of non-dominated refacotoring solutions are proposed to the users with the reduced objectives set to select the best Web service refactorings sequence based on his or her preferences.

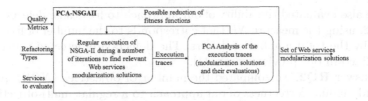

Fig. 1. The proposed approach.

3 Experiments

3.1 Research Questions

We designed our experiments to address the following research questions:

- **RQ1:** To what extent can the proposed dimensionality reduction approach recommends useful Web service refactorings?
- **RQ2:** To what extent does the proposed dimensionality reduction approach reduce the number of objectives while recommending useful refactorings?
- **RQ3:** How does the proposed dimensionality reduction approach perform compared to other existing Web services modularization techniques not based on computational search [1, 12]?

To answer **RQ1**, we considered both automatic and manual validations to evaluate the usefulness of the proposed Web service refactorings. For the automatic validation we compared the proposed Web service refactorings with the expected ones. The expected refactorings are suggested by users (e.g. subjects of our study) to fix existing Web service design defects as detailed later.

$$RE_{recall} = \frac{\mid suggested\ Web\ service\ refactorings \cap expected\ Web\ service\ refactorings \mid}{\mid expected\ Web\ service\ refactorings \mid} \in [0, 1] \tag{1}$$

$$RE_{precision} = \frac{\mid suggested\ Web\ service\ refactorings \cap expected\ Web\ service\ refactorings \mid}{\mid suggested\ refactorings \mid} \in [0, 1] \tag{2}$$

For the manual validation, we asked groups of potential users of our tool to manually evaluate whether the suggested refactorings are feasible and efficient at improving the services quality and achieving their maintainability objectives. We define the metric Manual Correctness (MC) that corresponds to the number of meaningful refactorings divided by the total number of suggested refactorings. MC is given by the following equation:

$$MC_{manualcorrectness} = \frac{\mid relevant\ Web\ service\ refactorings \mid}{\mid suggested\ Web\ service\ refactorings \mid} \in [0, 1] \tag{3}$$

We have also evaluated the ability of our approach to fix design defects, detailed in Sect. 2, using the measure NF that corresponds to the number of fixed defects divided by the total number of defects. The defects are detected using a set of rules defined in our previous work [11].

To answer **RQ2**, we compared the number of objectives (NOB), precision, recall and manual correctness of our approach to a regular multi-objective algorithm (NSGAII) using the same fitness functions adaptation.

To answer **RQ3**, We compared our results with a recent state-of-the art approaches by [1,12]. Athanasopoulos et al. proposed a Web service refactoring approach based on a greedy algorithm to refactor and split Web service interfaces based on different cohesion measures. Ouni et al. proposed a graph decomposition approach for Web services remodularization using coupling and cohesion metrics.

3.2 Experimental Setup

To answer all the above research questions, we conducted our experiment on a benchmark of 22 real-world services provided by Amazon[1] and Yahoo[2]. We selected services with interfaces exposing at least 10 operations. We chose these Web services because their WSDL interfaces are publicly available, and they were previously studied in the literature [1,5]. Table 1 presents our used benchmark.

Our evaluation involved 14 independent volunteer participants including 6 industrial developers and 8 graduate students. In particular, 3 senior developers from *Browser Kings*[3], 3 developers from *Accunet Web Services*[4], 3 MSc and 5 PhD candidates in Software Engineering. We first gathered information about the participant's background. All participants are familiar with service-oriented development and SOAP Web services with an experience ranging from 4 to 9 years. The participants were unaware of the techniques to be evaluated neither the particular research questions, in order to guarantee that there will be no bias in their judgment (Figs. 2 and 3).

3.3 Results

We reported the results of our empirical qualitative evaluation in Fig. 4 (MC). As reported in Fig. 4, most of the Web services modularization solutions recommended by our approach were correct and approved by developers. On average, for the different Web services, 78% of the created port types and applied changes to the initial design are considered as correct, improve the quality, and are found to be useful by the software developers of our experiments. The highest MC score is 84% and was achieved for the Web service GeographicalDictionary, while the lowest score was 67% for AmazonVPCPortType. Thus, this finding indicates

---

[1] http://aws.amazon.com/.
[2] developer.searchmarketing.yahoo.com/docs/V6/reference/.
[3] http://www.browserkings.com.
[4] http://www.accunet.us.

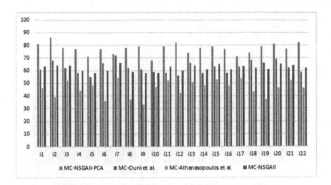

Fig. 2. Median manual correctness value over 30 runs on all the Web services using the different techniques with a 95% confidence level ($\alpha < 5\%$).

Table 1. Amazon and Yahoo benchmark overview.

Service interface	Provider
AutoScalingPortType	Amazon
MechanicalTurkRequesterPortType	Amazon
AmazonFPSPorttype	Amazon
AmazonRDSv2PortType	Amazon
AmazonVPCPortType	Amazon
AmazonFWSInboundPortType	Amazon
AmazonS3	Amazon
AmazonSNSPortType	Amazon
ElasticLoadBalancingPortType	Amazon
MessageQueue	Amazon
AmazonEC2PortType	Amazon
KeywordService	Yahoo
AdGroupService	Yahoo
UserManagementService	Yahoo
TargetingService	Yahoo
AccountService	Yahoo
AdService	Yahoo
CompaignService	Yahoo
BasicReportService	Yahoo
TargetingConverterService	Yahoo
ExcludedWordsService	Yahoo
GeographicalDictionaryService	Yahoo

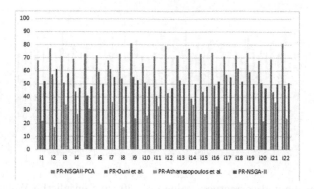

Fig. 3. Median precision value over 30 runs on all the Web services using the different techniques with a 95% confidence level ($\alpha < 5\%$).

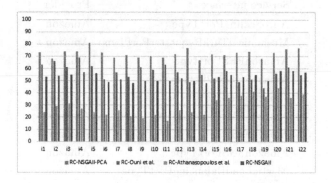

Fig. 4. Median recall value over 30 runs on all the Web services using the different techniques with a 95% confidence level ($\alpha < 5\%$).

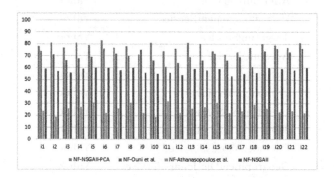

Fig. 5. Median number of fixed design defects value over 30 runs on all the Web services using the different techniques with a 95% confidence level ($\alpha < 5\%$).

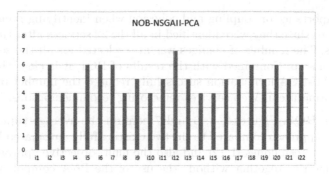

Fig. 6. Median number of objectives value over 30 runs on all the Web services using NSGAII-PCA.

that the results are independent of the size of the Web services and the number of recommended changes to the initial design.

Since the manual correctness MC metric just evaluates the correctness and not the relevance of the recommended solutions, we also compared the proposed modularization changes with some expected ones defined manually by the different groups for the different Web services. Figures 5 and 6 summarize our findings. We found that a considerable number of proposed port types, with an average of more than 76% in terms of precision and recall, were already created by the users manually (expected port types). The recall scores are higher than precision ones since we found that the port types suggested manually by developers could be further decomposed, if necessary. This was confirmed by the qualitative evaluation (MC). In addition, we found that the slight deviation with the expected design is not related to incorrect changes but to the fact that the developers have different scenarios/contexts in using the different operations.

We evaluated also the ability of our approach to fix several types of design defects and to improve the service interface design quality as described in Fig. 7 that depicts the percentage of fixed defects (NF). It is higher than 77% on all the 22 Web services, which is an acceptable score since developers may reject or modify some design changes that fix some defects because they do not consider some of them as very important (their goal is not to fix all design defects in the Web service interface) or because they wanted to focus on improving the cohesion and minimize coupling. Some Web service interfaces, such as Amazon-FWSInboundPortType, have a higher percentage of fixed code smells with an average of more than 83%.

To summarize and answer RQ1, the experimentation results confirm that our approach helps the participants to restructure their Web service interface design efficiently by finding the relevant portTypes and improve the quality of all the 22 Web services.

Results for RQ2. Figure 8 shows that our approach significantly reduced the number of objectives when executed on all the systems. The number of objectives were reduced to only four in several services. The reduced objectives may show the importance of coupling and cohesion when identifying refactoring recommendations since they were identified in all the 22 services after the reduction of objectives. The number of changes was also selected for all the services after the reduction step. Combined with the results of RQ1, it is clear that the proposed NSGAII-PCA formulation successfully reduced the number of objectives while generating useful Web services refactoring recommendations.

Results for RQ3. Figures 4, 5, 6 and 7 confirm the average superior performance of our approach compared to the two existing fully automated Web service modularization techniques [1,12] and also the multi-objective approach combining all the metrics together without the use of the PCA component. Figure 4 shows that our approach provides significantly higher manual correctness results (MC) than all other approaches having MC scores respectively between 48% and 64%, on average as MC scores on the different Web services. The same observation is valid for the precision and recall as described in Figs. 5 and 6. The outperformance of our technique in terms of percentage of fixed defects, as described in Fig. 7, can be explained by the fact that the main goal of existing studies is not to mainly fix these defects. Existing work are mainly limited to the coupling and cohesion metrisc which may not be sufficient to guide the modularization of Web services. In conclusion, our approach provides better results, on average, than all existing fully-automated Web services modularization techniques (answer to RQ3).

4 Conclusion

In this paper, we proposed a dimensionality reduction approach for multi-objective Web services remodularization that adjusts the number of considered objectives during the search for near optimal solutions. The execution traces of the multi-objective algorithm are analyzed using a PCA component to find potential correlation between the objectives (e.g. quality metrics). To evaluate the effectiveness of our tool, we conducted a human study on a set of users who evaluated the tool and compared it with the state-of-the-art Web services modularization techniques. Our evaluation results provide strong evidence that our technique successfully reduced the initial set of large number of objectives/quality metrics. The results also show that our approach outperforms several of existing Web services modularization techniques, not based on heuristic search [1,12].

References

1. Athanasopoulos, D., Zarras, A.V., Miskos, G., Issarny, V.: Cohesion-driven decomposition of service interfaces without access to source code. IEEE Trans. Serv. Comput. 8, 1–18 (2015)
2. Bechikh, S., Kessentini, M., Said, L.B., Ghédira, K.: Chapter four-preference incorporation in evolutionary multiobjective optimization: a survey of the state-of-the-art. Adv. Comput. 98, 141–207 (2015)

3. Deb, K., Saxena, D.: Searching for Pareto-optimal solutions through dimensionality reduction for certain large-dimensional multi-objective optimization problems. In: 2006 IEEE Congress on Evolutionary Computation (CEC 2006), pp. 3353–3360. IEEE, July 2006

4. Deb, K., Jain, H.: An evolutionary many-objective optimization algorithm using reference-point-based nondominated sorting approach, part I: solving problems with box constraints. IEEE Trans. Evol. Comput. **18**(4), 577–601 (2014)

5. Fokaefs, M., Mikhaiel, R., Tsantalis, N., Stroulia, E., Lau, A.: An empirical study on web service evolution. In: IEEE International Conference on Web Services (ICWS), pp. 49–56, July 2011

6. Jackson, J.: A Users Guide to Principal Components. Wiley, New York (1991)

7. Kalboussi, S., Bechikh, S., Kessentini, M., Ben Said, L.: Preference-based many-objective evolutionary testing generates harder test cases for autonomous agents. In: Ruhe, G., Zhang, Y. (eds.) SSBSE 2013. LNCS, vol. 8084, pp. 245–250. Springer, Heidelberg (2013). doi:10.1007/978-3-642-39742-4_19

8. Kessentini, M., Bouchoucha, A., Sahraoui, H., Boukadoum, M.: Example-based sequence diagrams to colored petri nets transformation using heuristic search. In: Kühne, T., Selic, B., Gervais, M.-P., Terrier, F. (eds.) ECMFA 2010. LNCS, vol. 6138, pp. 156–172. Springer, Heidelberg (2010). doi:10.1007/978-3-642-13595-8_14

9. Kessentini, M., Langer, P., Wimmer, M.: Searching models, modeling search: On the synergies of SBSE and MDE. In: Proceedings of the 1st International Workshop on Combining Modelling and Search-Based Software Engineering, pp. 51–54. IEEE Press (2013)

10. Král, J., Zemlicka, M.: Popular SOA antipatterns. In: Computation World: Future Computing, Service Computation, Cognitive, Adaptive, Content, Patterns, pp. 271–276 (2009)

11. Ouni, A., Kessentini, M., Inoue, K., Ó Cinnéide, M.: Search-based web service antipatterns detection. IEEE Trans. Serv. Comput. **10**, 603–617 (2015)

12. Ouni, A., Salem, Z., Inoue, K., Soui, M.: SIM: an automated approach to improve web service interface modularization. In: 2016 IEEE International Conference on Web Services (ICWS), pp. 91–98. IEEE (2016)

13. Saxena, D.K., Duro, J.A., Tiwari, A., Deb, K., Zhang, Q.: Objective reduction in many-objective optimization: linear and nonlinear algorithms. IEEE Trans. Evol. Comput. **17**(1), 77–99 (2013)

Service Recommendation

ARA-Assessor: Application-Aware Runtime Risk Assessment for Cloud-Based Business Continuity

Min Fu[1,2(✉)], Shiping Chen[2,3], Jian Yang[1], Surya Nepal[2,3],
and Liming Zhu[2,3]

[1] Department of Computing, Macquarie University, Sydney, Australia
{min.fu,jian.yang}@mq.edu.au
[2] Data61, CSIRO, Sydney, Australia
{Shiping.Chen,Surya.Nepal,Liming.Zhu}@data61.csiro.au
[3] School of Computer Science and Engineering, UNSW, Sydney, Australia

Abstract. Cloud-based systems are prone to be attacked because they share the same cloud infrastructure, where there may exist hackers and malicious users. As a result, cloud system owners need an on-going security risk assessment mechanism to monitor the risk of their systems so that they can be mitigated in a timely manner to ensure the business continuity. Existing methods of cloud system risk assessment usually do not fully consider the dependencies of the system's cloud resources or the conflicts of the threats on the system. In this paper we propose an application-aware cloud system risk assessment method, called ARA-Assessor, for performing security risk assessment for cloud systems. ARA-Assessor includes a cloud system model used to specify the significance value of each system component and their dependencies. With this application-aware model, the cloud system owners are able to continuously assess the risk of their systems. We evaluate ARA-Assessor with three typical cloud systems on AWS. The experimental results show that our method is capable of continuously assessing the runtime risk for multiple types of cloud systems.

Keywords: Cloud security · Cloud risk · Risk management · Risk assessment

1 Introduction

Cloud computing is widely adopted by businesses and governments, and a large number of them prefer to deploy and run their software applications and enterprise systems on the cloud platform [1, 2]. Since the cloud is a multi-tenancy environment shared by multiple users, a significant concern about cloud systems is their security [2, 3]. A survey from the research firm Gartner in 2015 found that around 95% of the consumers of cloud computing reported cloud security issues [4]. A survey conducted

---

The acronym "ARA" is short for "Application-Aware Risk Assessment".

© Springer International Publishing AG 2017
M. Maximilien et al. (Eds.): ICSOC 2017, LNCS 10601, pp. 511–527, 2017.
https://doi.org/10.1007/978-3-319-69035-3_38

by the Cloud Security Alliance (CSA) in 2016 indicated that at least 35% of the business owners did not trust the security of cloud as much as internal IT systems [5]. Cloud security has become a significant concern for ensuring business continuity [3].

In order to address the security issues of cloud systems and ensure the business continuity despite potential attacks, a useful procedure is to perform security risk assessment for cloud systems at runtime [6, 7]. Existing methods of cloud risk assessment [6, 8–10] largely focus on individual system components. They are concerned with either the application-level attacks that have an impact on service availability [10] or the intrinsic vendor-level risks of the cloud providers themselves [6, 8], and some of them do not fully leverage the risks that result from the on-demand nature of cloud [6, 8, 10]. Another problem with existing cloud risk assessment mechanisms is that they do not consider the complete dependencies of the cloud resources of the cloud system or the full conflictions of the cloud system's threats [9, 10].

As such, in this paper we propose a novel cloud risk assessment framework, called ARA-Assessor, for determining the runtime risk value of the cloud system provided by the system owner. ARA-Assessor is application-aware, which means that the risk assessment leverages the system specification model provided by the system owner. ARA-Assessor relies on the infrastructure-level threats of the cloud system to calculate the risk. We implement ARA-Assessor and evaluate it with three representative types of cloud systems on AWS cloud. The experimental results show that our proposed method is able to continuously and quantitatively assess the runtime risk of cloud systems in an automated way and it is generalizable for multiple cloud systems.

The research contributions of this paper are: (1) we propose a generalizable cloud runtime risk assessment method; (2) we propose a generic cloud system modelling approach and a generic cloud system threats modelling approach; (3) we propose a cloud resource dependencies propagation mechanism and a recursive mechanism for resolving the threats conflictions issue for analyzing cloud system risk.

The remainder of this paper is organized as follows: Sect. 2 describes a motivating example; Sect. 3 discusses cloud system modelling; Sect. 4 discusses cloud system threats modelling; Sect. 5 illustrates our risk assessment method; Sect. 6 presents our experimental evaluation; Sect. 7 discusses the validity and general applicability of our model; Sect. 8 discusses the related work; Sect. 9 provides the conclusion and our future work.

2   A Motivating Example

We use a sample cloud system, as shown in Fig. 1, to discuss the risk management. This cloud system follows the typical 2-tier architecture [11]. The E-Business service and the report generation service run in the web instances. These two services are auto-scaled by the auto-scaling service provided by the Auto Scaling Group (ASG), and the workload requests on these two services are dispatched by the load balancing service provided by the Elastic Load Balancer (ELB). The E-Business service triggers the production database service running inside the production database instance, and the report generation service triggers the report database service running inside the reporting database instance. There is periodical synchronization from the production database store to the reporting database store. A number of potential cloud infrastructure-level threats could occur to this sample cloud system. We categorize these threats into the following categories: (1) threats on the cloud login credentials; (2) threats on the ASG; (3) threats on the LC; (4) threats on web instances; (5) threats on database instances; (6) threats on the ELB; (7) threats on each instance's Amazon Machine Image (AMI); (8) threats on the security group. To study the occurrence frequency of the threats on the cloud system, we analyzed the cloud security report from Alert Logic [12], and obtained the month-to-month attack spread for real-world cloud systems in 2014, as shown in Fig. 2. How to accurately determine the system's risk is a question.

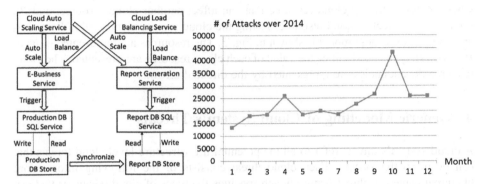

Fig. 1. 2-tier cloud system.   **Fig. 2.** Attacks for real cloud systems in 2014 [12].

3 Generic Modelling of Cloud Systems

A cloud system is deployed on a set of allocated cloud resources. Each cloud resource has a resource id, belongs to a cloud resource type (e.g. ELB), and has a significance value which reflects the importance of the resource. Some cloud resources in the system have dependencies, i.e. the attacks on such a resource can affect its dependent cloud resources. Hence, we can use DAG (Directed Acyclic Graph) to model the cloud system resources. The cloud system model, denoted as S, is represented as:

$$S = (R, E) \tag{1}$$

where R refers to the set of cloud resources, and E refers to the set of cloud resource dependencies. Each element of R, denoted as R_i ($1 \leq i \leq |R|$), is represented as:

$$R_i = (N, V, W) \tag{2}$$

where N denotes resource id, V denotes resource type, and W denotes resource significance value. Each element of E, denoted as E_i ($1 \leq i \leq |E|$), is denoted as:

$$E_i = (R_k, R_m), R_k \in R, R_m \in R \tag{3}$$

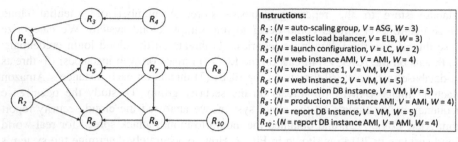

Fig. 3. DAG graph for the sample cloud system.

where R_k refers to any cloud resource that can affect another cloud resource, and R_m refers to R_k's affected cloud resource. Taking the cloud system mentioned in Sect. 2 as an example, its system model is shown in Fig. 3. The resources are represented as R_1 to R_{10}. The id, type and significance value of each cloud resource are presented. The cloud resource dependencies are represented by the directed arrows.

4   Generic Modelling of Cloud System's Threats

A cloud system's threats refer to all the potential infrastructure-level cloud threats that can occur to the system. Each cloud threat consists of the following information: (1) threat name; (2) threat feature which specifies the types of cloud resources that can be directly affected by the threat; (3) threat's directly attacked cloud resources; (4) threat's overall affected cloud resources propagated from the dependencies of the directly attacked resources; (5) threat impact value; (6) threat occurrence probability. Some threats have conflictions with each other, i.e., they are unable to occur at the same time. For example, terminating the database instance and changing database instance type cannot occur simultaneously. Hence, we can model the cloud system's threats as a graph. The cloud system threats model, denoted as T_S, is represented as:

$$T_S = (T, E) \tag{4}$$

where T refers to the set of cloud system threats, and E refers to the set of cloud system threats conflictions. Each element of T, denoted as T_i $(1 \le i \le |T|)$, is represented as:

$$T_i = (N, F, R_D, R_A, I, P) \tag{5}$$

where N denotes each threat's name, F denotes threat's feature, R_D denotes each threat's directly attacked cloud resources set and each element in R_D follows the model defined in Formula (2) in Sect. 3, R_A denotes each threat's overall affected cloud resources set and each element in R_A follows the model defined in Formula (2) in Sect. 3, I denotes each threat's impact value, and P denotes each threat's occurrence probability. Each element of E, denoted as E_i $(1 \le i \le |E|)$, is denoted as:

$$E_i = (T_k, T_m), T_k \in \boldsymbol{T}, T_m \in \boldsymbol{T} \tag{6}$$

where T_k refers to any threat that conflicts with another threat, and T_m refers to T_k's conflicted threat. Taking the sample cloud system mentioned in Sect. 2 as an example, the threats graph of the system is shown in Fig. 4. The threats are T_1 to T_n. The threats conflictions are represented by the undirected edges. T_1 and T_2 cannot occur simultaneously (T_1 conflicts with T_2); T_3 and T_4 cannot occur simultaneously (T_3 conflicts with T_4); T_5 and T_6 cannot occur simultaneously (T_5 conflicts with T_6).

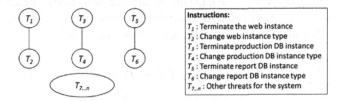

Fig. 4. Threats graph for the sample cloud system.

5 Our Risk Assessment Method

In order for ARA-Assessor to assess the runtime risk for a cloud system, it requires two inputs: (1) the cloud system model S and (2) the cloud full threats model T_F ($T_F = (\boldsymbol{T}, \boldsymbol{E})$). S is manually provided by the cloud system owner who has enough system domain knowledge. The significance value of each cloud resource ranges from 1 to 5. It is determined according to the importance of the internal service. Resource dependencies are determined according to the interactions of the services inside the resources and the dependencies specified in cloud resources documentations [17]. For example, a web instance interacts with a database instance because the web service inside the web instance triggers the database service inside the database instance. For another example, an elastic load balancer (ELB) or an auto-scaling group (ASG) contains multiple web instances. T_F resembles the threats model defined in Sect. 4. We assume T_F is manually prepared by the system owner. The threats set and threats conflictions set of it can be determined by analyzing and understanding the domain knowledge on cloud threats and published dataset [1, 18–21]. The threats in T_F include the threats related to all types of cloud resources, e.g. cloud web instance related threats, cloud database instance related threats, ASG/ELB related threats, etc.

Since attacks on a cloud system are usually unpredictable and can occur at any time, ARA-Assessor periodically assesses the cloud system's risk. We implement ARA-Assessor as a dedicated service, which embodies the concept of "Security as a Service" [16]. Prior to performing a periodical risk assessment, ARA-Assessor first conducts the one-off procedure, which consists of five activities: (1) ARA-Assessor automatically determines the system's threats subset model T_S using the inputs of cloud system model S and full cloud threats model T_F; (2) ARA-Assessor obtains the initial occurrence probability of each threat $T_S \rightarrow T_i$ $(1 \le i \le |T_S \rightarrow T|)$; (3) ARA-Assessor automatically determines the affected cloud resources for each threat $T_S \rightarrow T_i$; (4) the impact value of each threat $T_S \rightarrow T_i$ is calculated; (5) the cloud consumer specifies the frequency of performing risk assessment, e.g. every minute. Then four activities are conducted upon each time tick: (1) ARA-Assessor relies on external attack detection services [13–15] to detect the runtime threats and events that occur to the system, denoted as T_{RT}; (2) we derive a threats sub-model from T_S, denoted as T_S' $(T_S' = (T', E'))$, where T' removes all the conflicted threats of each runtime threat in T_{RT} from $T_S \rightarrow T$, and E' removes all the conflictions with regard to each runtime threat in T_{RT} from $T_S \rightarrow E$); (3) the occurrence probability of each threat in T_S' is updated based on T_{RT}; (4) ARA-Assessor uses the threats sub-model T_S' to calculate the system's risk value for the time tick, denoted as RI_S, as below:

$$RI_S = Max\left(\sum_{j=1}^{|M(T_S')[i] \rightarrow T|} \left(M(T_S')[i] \rightarrow T[j] \rightarrow I\right) \times \left(M(T_S')[i] \rightarrow T[j] \rightarrow P\right)\right) \quad (7)$$

where $M(T_S')$ refers to an array of threats sub-models derived from T_S', each threats sub-model $M(T_S')[i]$ (i ranges from 1 to $|M(T_S')|$) represents a case of threats model that contains all the threats from T_S' which are independent of each other and do not conflict with each other, and this array enumerates complete cases of such threats models for T_S'. For each case, the risk value is calculated, and the maximum of the calculated risk values is the quantified risk of the cloud system for that time tick.

5.1 Determination of Cloud System's Threats Subset Model

The cloud infrastructure-level threats that can occur to the cloud system are a subset of all cloud infrastructure-level threats that can occur to all cloud resources. When we rely on external attack detection tools to detect threats, we should only subscribe the system's threats subset in order to save cost. Hence, we need to determine the cloud system's threats subset. Using the two inputs of cloud system model S and full cloud threats model T_F, the cloud system's threats subset model T_S is determined as below:

$$T_S = (T, E) \quad (8)$$

where T is a subset of $T_F \rightarrow T$, and E is a subset of $T_F \rightarrow E$. Each threat in T_S, denoted as $T_S \rightarrow T_i$, satisfies such a condition: $(T_S \rightarrow T_i \rightarrow F) \cap V(S \rightarrow R) \ne \emptyset$, where V $(S \rightarrow R)$ represents the cloud system's overall resources types set.

Taking the sample cloud system mentioned in Sect. 2 as an illustrating example, the determined threats subset model is the one represented in Fig. 4 in Sect. 4.

5.2 Determination of Threats Initial Occurrence Probabilities

The initial occurrence probabilities of the cloud system's threats can be determined by analyzing cloud attacks historical data such as the security reports from Symantec

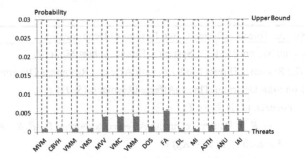

Fig. 5. Threats probabilities for cloud [23].

Corporation [22]. Based on the research on cloud security threats analysis done by the University of Tunis [23], we are able to obtain the threats probabilities as shown in Fig. 5. According to the research, the probability of no cloud threats occurring is 0.97, so the upper bound probability for each cloud threat is 0.03. For simplicity, we assume that the occurrence probabilities of all the threats for the cloud system are 0.03.

5.3 Determination of Cloud Resources Affected by System Threats

The affected cloud resources for a threat refer to the system cloud resources that are affected either directly or indirectly by the threat. The indirectly affected resources are propagated from the directly attacked resources. A challenge with the resource propagation is that the resource dependencies can be multi-layer, which means that a cloud resource's dependent resources can further have dependent resources, and so on. We address this challenge and design the affected resources determination mechanism, as illustrated in Algorithm 1. For each threat, we first determine its directly attacked cloud resources by mapping the feature of the threat with the cloud resources in the system model (DetermineDirectlyAffectedResources($T \rightarrow F$, $S \rightarrow R$)); second, for each directly attacked resource of the threat R, we add it into the threat's affected resources set, and then we use a recursive function to add its overall propagated dependent affected resources into the threat's affected resources set (RecursivelyDetermineAffectedResources(R, $T \rightarrow R_A$)). Inside the recursive function, we first get R's dependent affected cloud resources set (GetAffectedResources(R, $S \rightarrow E$)). If this set is empty, we exit the recursion; otherwise, for each of R's dependent affected resources, R', we add it into the threat's affected resources set, and then we further add its overall propagated dependent resources into the threat's affected resources set.

Algorithm 1: System Threats Affected Cloud Resources Determination

Input:	Cloud System Model S, System's Threats Subset Model T_S
Output:	The System's Threats Model T_S with Affected Resources Determined
1	**Function** DetermineThreatsAffectedResources(S, T_S) {
2	**Foreach** (T in $T_S \rightarrow T$) {
3	$T \rightarrow R_D$ = DetermineDirectlyAffectedResources($T \rightarrow F$, $S \rightarrow R$);
4	**Foreach** (R in $T \rightarrow R_D$) {
5	$T \rightarrow R_A = R \cup (T \rightarrow R_A)$;
6	RecursivelyDetermineAffectedResources(R, $T \rightarrow R_A$); }}
7	**Return** T_S;
8	}
9	
10	**Void Function** RecursivelyDetermineAffectedResources(R, R_A) {
11	**If** (GetAffectedResources(R, $S \rightarrow E$) == Ø) {
12	**Return**; }
13	**Foreach** (R' in GetAffectedResources(R, $S \rightarrow E$)) {
14	$R_A = R' \cup R_A$;
15	RecursivelyDetermineAffectedResources(R', R_A); }
16	}

Taking the sample cloud system mentioned in Sect. 2 as an illustrating example, its system model is represented by Fig. 3 in Sect. 3. One of its threats is "Attack the web instance AMI". This threat's attacking point is R_4. R_4 affects R_3, R_3 further affects R_1, and R_1 further affects R_5 and R_6, and hence the overall affected cloud resources of this threat are R_1, R_3, R_4, R_5 and R_6.

5.4 Calculation of Threats Impact Values

For each threat in the cloud system's infrastructure-level threats set, with its affected cloud resources determined, we are able to compute its impact value based on the significance value of each affected cloud resource. The impact value of each threat in the cloud system's threats subset, denoted as $T_S \rightarrow T_i \rightarrow I$ ($1 \leq i \leq |T_S \rightarrow T|$), is calculated as below:

$$T_S \rightarrow T_i \rightarrow I = \sum_{j=1}^{|T_S \rightarrow T_i \rightarrow R_A|} (T_S \rightarrow T_i \rightarrow R_A[j] \rightarrow W) \tag{9}$$

where $T_S \rightarrow T_i \rightarrow R_A$ denotes the overall affected cloud resources set of each threat, and $T_S \rightarrow T_i \rightarrow R_A[j] \rightarrow W$ denotes the significance value of each affected cloud resource of each threat.

Taking the sample cloud system mentioned in Sect. 2 as an illustrating example, according to Sect. 5.4, the threat of "Attack the web instance AMI" affects the cloud resources of R_1, R_3, R_4, R_5, and R_6, and hence the impact value of this threat is calculated to be 19 $(3 + 2 + 4 + 5 + 5)$.

5.5   Threats Sub-model Derivation

Upon a time tick, the detected the runtime threats and events are denoted as T_{RT}; and the threats sub-model derived from the system's threats set T_S is denoted as T'_S, which removes all the threats in T_{RT} from T_S. If T_{RT} is empty, T'_S is equal to T_S. We define GetConflictedThreats(T, E) as the function to get the conflicted threats set of threat T, and define GetConflictions(T, E) as the function to get the set of conflictions with regard to threat T. Then, T'_S is determined as below:

$$T'_S = (T', E') \tag{10}$$

$$T' = T_S \rightarrow T - \sum_{i=1}^{|T_{RT} \rightarrow T|} \text{GetConflictedThreats}(T_{RT} \rightarrow T_i, T_S \rightarrow E) \tag{11}$$

$$E' = T_S \rightarrow E - \sum_{i=1}^{|T_{RT} \rightarrow T|} \text{GetConflictions}(T_{RT} \rightarrow T_i, T_S \rightarrow E) \tag{12}$$

5.6   Updating of Latest Occurrence Probabilities of Threats

Now, ARA-Assessor needs to perform probability updating for each threat in T'_S based on the detected runtime threats and events, denoted as T_{RT}. The runtime threats detected are those threats that are factually occurring to the cloud system. The runtime events consist of two attacks: (1) CPU-intensive user requests explosion, which means that the attackers send excessive workload requests that significantly affect the CPU utilization of cloud instances to the cloud system; (2) data-intensive user requests explosion, which means that the attackers send excessive workload requests that significantly affect the database to the cloud system. Cloud systems are not necessarily faced with both of the two runtime events. If the cloud system only contains web servers (e.g. web instances running Tomcat service), then it can only have the runtime event of "CPU-intensive user requests explosion"; if the cloud system contains both web servers and database servers, then it can have both runtime events.

For the runtime threats detected upon a time tick, the updated occurrence probability of each detected runtime threat is set to be 1 because it has factually occurred to the cloud system and is causing certain negative consequence on the cloud system.

When either of the two runtime events happens upon a time tick, the probability of the correspondent threat must be updated, and we argue that the updated probability (denoted as P') is relevant to the number of CPU-intensive user requests or data-intensive user requests at that time tick (denoted as W), the threshold number of CPU-intensive user requests or data-intensive user requests for the cloud system (denoted as $W_{threshold}$), and the initial occurrence probability of the correspondent threat (denoted as P). P' must satisfy three requirements: (1) P' is greater than P; (2) P' increases with W; (3) P' converges to 1. Hence, we calculate P' as below:

$$P' = 1 - \frac{1-p}{a^{(W-W_{threshold})}} \tag{13}$$

where a is a constant greater than 1, in order to make P' an increasing function (i.e. P' increases with W). The value of the constant a $(a > 1)$ is determined as below:

$$a = \left(^{\frac{10000 + W_{threshold}}{2} - W_{threshold}}\right)\sqrt{\frac{1-p}{1-\frac{1+p}{2}}} = {}^{\frac{10000-W_{threshold}}{2}}\sqrt{2} \tag{14}$$

5.7   The System Risk Determination Mechanism

The mechanism of calculating the risk based on T'_S is shown in Algorithm 2. We first derive a list of threats models each of which only contains the threats that do not conflict with each other (GetValidThreatsModelsList(T'_S)), then we calculate the risk value for each threats model in the list, and we return the maximum risk value as the final risk for the system. The function of GetValidThreatsModelsList(T'_S) utilizes the recursive mechanism in order to enumerate all the cases where the threats in the threat model of the system are able to occur simultaneously. Inside this function, we first obtain all the threats that do not conflict with any other threats (GetThreatswith-outConflictions(T'_S)). If the number of such threats is equal to the overall threats number, we return such threats as the output of the function; otherwise, if the number of such threats is greater than 0, we first divide the threats model into threats with conflictions (TSubModel) and threats without conflictions (T_W), and then we recursively call the same function (GetValidThreatsModelsList(TSubModel)) using TSubModel as the input; otherwise, if the number of threats without conflictions is 0, we loop through each threat and divide the threats model into each threat and the threats that do not conflict with it, and then we recursively call the same function to obtain the output (GetValidThreatsModelsList(T_C)) and merge it into the final output (TMList).

Algorithm 2: Risk Assessment Algorithm of ARA-Assessor

Input:	Cloud System' Threats Model T_S' upon a Time Tick
Output:	System's Risk R_S for the Time Tick
1	**Function** ComputeSystemRisk (T_S') {
2	**List\<ThreatsModel>** *validTMList* = GetValidThreatsModelsList(T_S');
3	**List\<Double>** *riskValues* = **new List\<Double>**();
4	**Foreach (ThreatsModel** T_M **in** *validTMList*) {
5	$riskValues.\text{Add}(\sum_{i=1}^{\mid(T_M \to T\mid}(T_M \to T[i] \to I) \times (T_M \to T[i] \to P));$ }
6	**Double** R_S = Max(*riskValues*);
8	**Return** R_S; }
9	
10	**List\<ThreatsModel> Function** GetValidThreatsModelsList(**ThreatsModel** T_S') {
11	**ThreatsModel** T_W = GetThreatswithoutConflictions(T_S');
12	**If** ($\mid T_W \to T\mid == \mid T_S' \to T\mid$) {
13	**List\<ThreatsModel>** *TMList* = **new List\<ThreatsModel>**();
14	*TMList*.Add(T_W);
15	**Return** *TMList*; }
16	**Else if** ($\mid T_W \to T\mid > 0$) {
17	**ThreatsModel** *TSubModel* = T_S' - T_W;
18	**List\<ThreatsModel>** *TMList* = GetValidThreatsModelsList(*TSubModel*);
19	**Foreach (ThreatsModel** T_M **in** *TMList*) {
20	T_M += T_W; }
21	**Return** *TMList*; }
22	**Else** {
23	**List\<ThreatsModel>** *TMList* = **new List\<ThreatsModel>**();
24	**Foreach (Threat** T **in** $T_S' \to T$) {
25	**ThreatsModel** T_C = T_S' – GetConflictedThreats(T, $T_S' \to E$);
26	**List\<ThreatsModel>** temp*TMList* = GetValidThreatsModelsList(T_C);
27	*TMList* += temp*TMList*;}
28	**Return** *TMList* ; }}

6 Experimental Evaluation

We implemented the prototype of ARA-Assessor and evaluated it with three typical cloud systems deployed on AWS EC2 [21]. They are: (1) the "all services in one instance" cloud system; (2) the 2-tier cloud system with a production database; (3) the 2-tier cloud system with a production database and a reporting database. Each of them is a simplified version of the real-world cloud system. These three cloud systems are a good representation of all types of cloud systems because they consider a variety of cloud resources composition scenarios of different cloud systems, so they are complete enough to verify the feasibility and generalizability of ARA-Assessor. The experimental environment is shown in Fig. 6. Since we assume we rely on external attack detection services to detect threats and events, we simulate the detection of runtime threats and events. ARA-Assessor triggers the attack detection services by simulation to obtain the simulated detection results, using the generated cloud system model as the input. The output is the cloud system's quantified ongoing runtime risk.

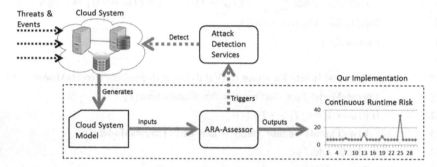

Fig. 6. Experimental environment.

6.1   Experimental Procedure

For each of the three cloud systems, the frequency of performing risk assessment is set to be 1 min. This is in accordance with the monitoring frequency of the CloudWatch function provided by AWS [24]. We simulate the running of each system for 60 min and dynamically inject one or more infrastructure-level threats and events at random time points during each system's running by simulation. The infrastructure-level threats randomly injected are able to occur simultaneously. The events can be injected by using an open source tool named Httperf [25], which is used for generating user workload requests from the client side. Since we use the free-tier cloud resources in our experiments, the allowed maximum number of CPU-intensive workload requests and the allowed maximum number of data-intensive workload requests should follow the requests number threshold of a free-tier instance. Based on our previous empirical study [26], we know that the requests threshold for a free-tier instance is 360 simultaneous requests per machine, including both CPU-intensive requests and data-intensive requests. As such, for the first cloud system, we determine that the CPU-intensive requests threshold is 180 and the data-intensive requests threshold is 180. For the second cloud system, there are initially eight free-tier web instances attached to an ASG and registered with an ELB, and one free-tier database instance shared by the web instances. So, the overall requests number threshold for the system is 2880, so the CPU-intensive requests threshold is 1440 and the data-intensive requests threshold is 1440. For the third cloud system, there are initially six free-tier web instances attached to an ASG and registered with an ELB, six free-tier reporting instances attached to another ASG and registered with another ELB, one free-tier production database instance shared by the web instances, and one free-tier reporting database instance shared by the reporting instances. So, the overall requests number threshold for the system is 4320, and hence the CPU-intensive requests threshold is 2160 and the data-intensive requests threshold is 2160. In the real-world case, the values of the two thresholds of a real industry system should be determined by the system owner. Since we rely on external attack detection tools, we simulate the detection results of threats and events and perform risk assessment. For each of the three cloud systems we run the experiment 50 times and obtain the ongoing risk values and the average execution time of performing risk assessment. The hardware configuration of the ARA-Assessor server is: CPU-Dual Core 2.6 GHz and RAM-8 GB.

6.2   Experimental Results

The assessed risk values and the average execution time for the three cloud systems are shown in Figs. 7, 8 and 9. The results are based on 50 runs.

The risk threshold for each cloud system is determined to be 10.7, 20.5 and 36.3, respectively. Where the risk value is greater than the threshold, it is considered to be

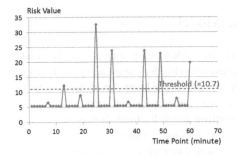
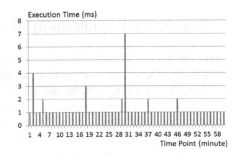

Fig. 7. Risk assessment results for the first cloud system.

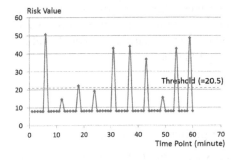
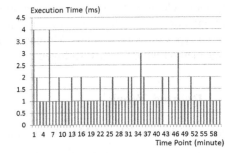

Fig. 8. Risk assessment results for the second cloud system.

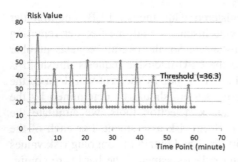 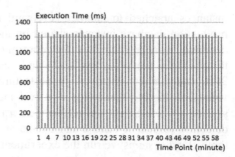

Fig. 9. Risk assessment results for the third cloud system.

high risk and appropriate responses such as performing system recovery should be considered. The average execution time of performing risk assessment for each time point for each cloud system is less than 1300 ms, which is well below the risk assessment time frequency set by the system owner (60000 ms). This also buffers enough time to perform threats and events detection for the systems. The maximum relative standard deviation for the execution time of performing risk assessment for each time point for each cloud system is 1.9%.

7   Validity and Applicability of the Model

First, while the cloud threats concerned by ARA-Assessor are only cloud infrastructure-level, we assume that the business stakeholders and the system owners are capable of figuring out the full set of all infrastructure-level cloud threats. In the implementation of our proposed method, we only consider certain types of infrastructure-level cloud threats when constructing the full cloud threats set, and we argue that by doing this it does not influence our method's validity.

Second, the determination of the initial occurrence probabilities of a cloud system's threats is only based on a limited study of existing research work, and hence the determined probabilities might not be comprehensive enough. We expect the businesses to figure out the probabilities in a more sophisticated manner.

Third, for evaluating the generalizability of ARA-Assessor, we only used three types of cloud systems. Although we argue that these three systems are a good representation of all cloud systems, it is still worthwhile to evaluate our method against more types of cloud systems. Moreover, it would be even better if we could evaluate our method with systems deployed on other cloud platforms.

8   Related Work

8.1   Risks and Threat Models in Cloud Computing

The European Network & Information Systems Agency (ENISA) [18] classifies cloud computing risks into three categories: Organizational, Technical and Legal [1]. The organizational risks refer to "all the risks that may impact the structure of the organization or the business as an entity", e.g. "loss of business reputation due to the tenants sharing the same resources" [1]. The technical risks refer to "problems or failures associated with the provided services or technologies contacted from the cloud service provider" [1], e.g. "malicious insiders/outsiders attacks on cloud" [1]. The legal risks refer to "issues that surround data being exchanged across multiple countries that have different laws and regulations concerning data traversal, protection requirements and privacy laws" [1]. The Cloud Security Alliance (CSA) [19] lists the following threats as the top cloud computing risks: malicious insiders, data loss/leakage, abuse and nefarious use of cloud computing and shared technology vulnerabilities. From the perspective of cloud infrastructure, the cloud threats include attacks on cloud instances (virtual machines), attacks on cloud data storage and attacks on cloud networking facilities such as elastic load balancers or auto scaling groups [20, 27]. From the perspective of SaaS providers or cloud consumers, cloud threats include attacks on different application functions, attacks on the business workflows of cloud systems, and attacks on the service modules of cloud systems [28].

8.2 Existing Risk Assessment Methods for Cloud Computing

Risk is measured in terms of the consequence (or impact) and the likelihood of the attacking event or threat [29]. Researchers from the University of Leeds proposed a cloud risk assessment framework used by cloud service providers and service consumers to assess risk during service deployment and operation [8]. This framework quantitatively assesses the risks in various stages of the service lifecycle, and it considers the risks of both cloud service providers (the cloud consumers) and infrastructure providers (cloud vendors) [8]. The threat impacts are mainly determined by looking at the seven security criteria (e.g. past SLA performance) of cloud providers and the three performance criteria (e.g. past SLA performance) of cloud consumers [8]. This framework calculates risk by computing the cross-product of the threat impacts vector and the threat probabilities vector [8]. However, the main drawback of this risk assessment framework is that it does not consider the threats resulting from the on-demand nature of cloud since it largely focuses on the seven typical security evaluation criteria of various cloud infrastructure providers and the three performance criteria of the cloud consumers. Researchers from Lincoln Laboratory of MIT proposed another risk assessment tool for cloud services, which can be used for evaluating the runtime risk of particular cloud services [9]. This tool assesses system runtime risk based on analyzing a list of possible runtime threats on cloud services. The impact of each threat is determined by investigating how many virtual machines can be affected by the threat, and the probability of each threat is derived from external historical data [9]. However, the major problem with this tool is that its way of calculating threat impacts does not well capture the real natures of the consequences of security failures on cloud, and it does not fully consider the dependencies of cloud resources of the cloud system or the conflictions of cloud system threats. In comparison, our proposed method addresses all of these drawbacks. To the best of our knowledge, it is the first time that such a cloud risk assessment framework is ever proposed.

9   Conclusion and Future Work

Systems deployed on the cloud are prone to security attacks, which is one of the greatest issues with cloud computing. Cloud system risk assessment is helpful for managing and analyzing the security of cloud systems. Since existing methods of cloud system risk assessment usually do not fully consider cloud resources dependencies or cloud system threats conflictions, we proposed ARA-Assessor to continuously perform risk assessment for cloud systems. ARA-Assessor is application-aware and leverages cloud infrastructure-level threats. We implemented the prototype of ARA-Assessor and evaluated it using three typical cloud systems. Based on the experimental results, we can see that our method is able to automatically assess the runtime risk of cloud systems in a continuous manner, and it is generalizable for multiple types of cloud systems. Our future work includes: (1) include the application-level and service-level threats into our risk assessment method; (2) evaluate the feasibility of our method with more types of cloud systems and more cloud platforms.

Acknowledgement. This work is supported by Macquarie University and Data61, CSIRO. The work is partially funded by ARC DP150102966.

References

1. Dahbur, K., et al.: A survey of risks, threats and vulnerabilities in cloud computing. In: Proceedings of the 2011 International Conference on Intelligent Semantic Web-Services and Applications (ISWSA 2011), vol. 12, April 2011
2. NIST: Resource Security. http://csrc.nist.gov/groups/SNS/cloud-computing/
3. Mather, T., et al.: Cloud Security and Privacy: An Enterprise Perspective on Risks and Compliance. O'Reilly Media, Sebastopol (2009). copyright 2009, ISBN: 0596802765, 9780596802769
4. Gartner: Why private clouds fail. Network world official website. http://www.networkworld.com/article/2881794/cloud-computing/gartner-why-private-clouds-fail.html
5. Cloud Security Alliance (CSA): State of Security 2016. CSA Global Enterprise Advisory Board.   https://downloads.cloudsecurityalliance.org/assets/board/CSA-GEAB-State-of-Cloud-Security-2016.pdf
6. Saripalli, P., Walters, B.: QUIRC: a quantitative impact and risk assessment framework for cloud security. In: 3rd IEEE International Conference on Cloud Computing (CLOUD 2010), July 2010
7. Heiser, J., Nicolett, M.: Assessing the security risks of cloud computing. Gartner Research Report 2008, ID no. G00157782, June 2008
8. Djemame, K., et al.: A risk assessment framework for cloud computing. IEEE Trans. Cloud Comput. **4**(3), 265–278 (2016). ISSN: 2168-7161
9. Lippmann, R.P., Riordan, J.F.: Threat-based risk assessment for enterprise networks. Lincoln Lab. J. **22**(1), 33–45 (2016)
10. Kholidy, H.A., et al.: Online risk assessment and prediction models for autonomic cloud intrusion prevention systems. In: AICCSA 2014, November 2014
11. Rahimi, M.R., et al.: MAPCloud: mobile applications on an elastic and scalable 2-tier cloud architecture. In: 5th IEEE International Conference on Utility and Cloud Computing (2012)
12. Alert Logic: The Changing State of Cloud Security. Cloud Security Report 2015 (2015)

13. Nenvani, G., Gupta, H.: A survey on attack detection on cloud using supervised learning techniques. In: IEEE Symposium on Colossal Data Analysis and Networking (CDAN 2016), March 2016
14. Lo, C., Huang, C., Ku, J.: A cooperative intrusion detection system framework for cloud computing networks. In: 39th International Conference on Parallel Processing Workshops (ICPPW 2010), September 2010
15. Zhang, T., et al.: CloudRadar: A Real-time Side-channel Attack Detection System in Clouds. Princeton University publications, Department of Electrical Engineering (2016)
16. Krutz, R.L., Vines, R.D.: Cloud security: a comprehensive guide to secure cloud computing. In: Cloud Security: A Comprehensive Guide to Secure Cloud Computing. Wiley Publishing (2010). ISBN: 0470589876, 9780470589878
17. AWS Cloud Documentation Official Website. http://aws.amazon.com/documentation/. Last access time: 6 Aug 2017, 17:50
18. ENISA: Cloud Computing: Benefits, risks and recommendations for information security (2010)
19. CSA: Top Threats to cloud computing. v1.0 (2010)
20. Chou, T.: Security threats on cloud computing vulnerabilities. Int. J. Comput. Sci. Inf. Technol. (IJCSIT) 5, 79–88 (2013)
21. AWS official Website. http://aws.amazon.com/. Last access time: 6 Aug 2017, 17:55
22. Symantec ISTR: Internet Security Threat Report 2016. Symantec Website, vol. 21, April 2016. https://www.symantec.com/content/dam/symantec/docs/reports/istr-21-2016-en.pdf
23. Jouini, M., Rabai, L.B.A.: Mean failure cost extension model towards security threats assessment: a cloud computing case study. J. Comput. 10, 184–194 (2015). doi:10.17706/jcp.10.3.184-194
24. CloudWatch Website. https://aws.amazon.com/cloudwatch/. Last access time: 6 Aug 2017, 18:40
25. Httpref Website. https://linux.die.net/man/1/httperf. Last access time: 6 Aug 2017, 18:50
26. Fu, M., et al.: Runtime recovery actions selection for sporadic operations on cloud. In: ASWEC 2015, Adelaide, Australia, pp. 185–194, September 2015
27. Sabahi, F.: Cloud computing security threats and responses. In: 3rd IEEE International Conference on Communication Software and Networks (ICCSN 2011), May 2011
28. Subashini, S., Kavitha, V.: A survey on security issues in service delivery models of cloud computing. J. Netw. Comput. Appl. 34(1), 1–11 (2011)
29. Misra, K.: Risk analysis and management: an introduction. In: Misra, K. (ed.) Handbook of Performability Engineering, pp. 667–681. Springer, London (2008)

Personalized Quality Centric Service Recommendation

Yiwen Zhang[1], Xiaofei Ai[1], Qiang He[2(✉)], Xuyun Zhang[3],
Wanchun Dou[4], Feifei Chen[5], Liang Chen[6], and Yun Yang[2]

[1] Anhui University, Hefei, China
zhangyiwen@ahu.edu.cn, aixiaofeiliujiajia@outlook.com
[2] Swinburne University of Technology, Melbourne, Australia
{qhe,yyang}@swin.edu.au
[3] University of Auckland, Auckland, New Zealand
xuyun.zhang@auckland.ac.nz
[4] Nanjing University, Nanjing, China
douwc@nju.edu.cn
[5] Federation University Australia, Ballarat, Australia
feifei.chen@federation.edu.au
[6] Sun Yat-Sen University, Guangzhou, China
chenliang6@mail.sysu.edu.cn

Abstract. The broad application of service-oriented architecture (SOA) has fueled the rapid growth of web and cloud services and service-based systems (SBSs). Tremendous web and cloud services have been deployed all over the world. Finding the right services becomes difficult and critical. Thus, service recommendation has become of paramount research and practical importance. Existing web service recommendation approaches employ utility functions or skyline techniques. However, those approaches have not addressed a critical and fundamental problem: how to recommend services according to a system engineer's quality constraints, e.g., response time, failure rate, etc. To address this issue, we first propose two basic personalized quality centric approaches for service recommendation, which employ the k-nearest neighbors and the dynamic skyline techniques respectively. To overcome the respective limitations of the two basic approaches, we propose two hybrid approaches, namely KNN-DSL and DSL-KNN. Extensive experiments are conducted on a real-world dataset to demonstrate the effectiveness and efficiency of our approaches.

Keywords: Service recommendation · QoS · Dynamic skyline · KNN

1 Introduction

The service-oriented architecture (SOA) allows complex software systems to be built by composing loosely coupled web services [1, 2]. The component services of such a service-based system (SBS) collectively realize the system functionality which is often offered as SaaS (Software-as-a-Service) in the cloud environment.

Figure 1 shows the process for building an example travel booking SBS that requires four services to perform four system tasks. As depicted, the process consists of

M. Maximilien et al. (Eds.): ICSOC 2017, LNCS 10601, pp. 528–544, 2017.
https://doi.org/10.1007/978-3-319-69035-3_39

two phases. The first phase is service recommendation where representative services are identified from the candidate services and recommended to the system engineer [3, 4]. The second phase is service selection where the system engineer selects one service from each set of recommended services to build the target SBS that fulfils the multi-dimensional constraints for the system quality, e.g., response time, failure rate, etc., and in the meantime achieves the optimization goal for the system quality. This is an

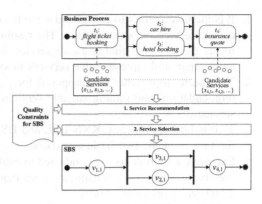

Fig. 1. Process for building an SBS

NP-complete problem often referred to as quality-aware service selection [1, 2, 5, 6].

The development and popularity of e-business, e-commerce, especially the pay-as-you-go business model promoted by cloud computing have fueled the rapid growth of services, indicated by the statistics published by programmableweb.com, an online web service repository. This makes the quality-aware service selection problem intractable. In recent years, a lot of efforts have been devoted to reducing the complexity of the problem of quality-aware service selection through service recommendation [3, 4, 7–9]. Recommending appropriate services reduces the search space of the NP-complete service selection problem. In this way, a system engineer does not have to enumerate all candidate services and their possible combinations. **The key issue here is to identify appropriate candidate services that are most likely to fulfil the system engineer's quality constraints**. Unfortunately, none of the existing web service recommendation approaches has properly addressed this issue. There are three major categories of service recommendation approaches, utility-based, skyline-based [3, 4] and collaborative filtering (CF) based [10, 11]. Utility-based and skyline-based approaches do not properly take into account system engineers' personalized quality constraints. CF-based service recommendation aims to predict the quality of web services. Thus, although labeled as a recommendation approach [10–14], CF-based service recommendation is in fact a prediction approach, not a recommendation approach.

In this paper, we first propose two basic approaches for **personalized quality centric service recommendation**, one based on the KNN (k-nearest neighbors) technique and the other based on the DSL (dynamic skyline) technique. The KNN approach models the service recommendation problem as a nearest neighbor search problem. Given a system engineer's quality constraints, it finds a set of k *suitable services* whose quality values are most similar to the quality constraints. The DSL-based approach models the service recommendation problem as a dynamic skyline query problem. It attempts to find *representative services* that are not dominated by any other services with respect to system engineer's quality constraints.

The main contributions of this research are:

1. It is the first attempt to model and solve the critical problem of personalized quality centric service recommendation. The resolution of this problem naturally complements the existing quality-aware service selection approaches by recommending appropriate and representative services to system engineers.
2. Two basic approaches are proposed for personalized quality centric service recommendation, one finding suitable services while the other finding representative services.
3. Two hybrid approaches, KNN-DSL and DSL-KNN, are proposed to overcome the limitations of the two basic approaches.
4. Extensive experiments are conducted to evaluate the effectiveness and efficiency of the proposed approaches using a dataset that contains the quality information about 2,507 real-world web services.

The rest of this paper is organized as follows. Section 2 analyzes the research problem. Section 3 describes the basic and the hybrid approaches. Section 4 evaluates the proposed approaches. Section 5 reviews the related work. Section 6 concludes the paper and points out future work.

2 Problem Analysis

This section analyzes the research problem with the travel booking SBS presented in Fig. 1. For each of the four system tasks, i.e., t_1, t_2, t_3 and t_4, there is a set of candidate services that can perform the system task but with potentially different quality values, e.g., response time and failure rate. The system engineer needs to select one service from each set of candidate services for building the SBS, i.e., Phase 2. The selected services must collectively fulfil the quality constraints for the system. This problem is commonly known as NP-complete. As the scenario scales up, it becomes intractable. A promising approach for simplifying this problem is, from each set of candidate services, to identify services that are more likely to fulfil the quality constraints for the system, to recommend to the system engineer for selection, i.e., Phase 1. The search space for the problem can be significantly reduced.

To facilitate service recommendation, the global quality constraints for the system must be decomposed into local quality references for individual system tasks. Alrifai et al. proposed an approach in [15] that is widely employed to decompose global quality constraints for a system into local quality references. Given a set of quality constraints for the system, e.g., 800 ms for response time and 1% for failure rate (at least 99 out of 100 service requests must be handled properly), Alrifai et al.'s approach can decompose it into four sets of local quality constraints, one for each of the four tasks, e.g., 120 ms for the response time of performing t_1 and 0.9% for its failure rate.

According to the local quality references for each system task, appropriate services can be identified and recommended to the system engineer. A straightforward approach is to model this problem as a nearest neighbors search problem, as presented in Fig. 2. In Fig. 2, points s_1, ..., s_8 represent the eight candidate services for t_1 and point s_r **represents the** *dummy reference service* with quality references for the response time and failure rate of this task. As indicated in Fig. 2(a), those services that are close

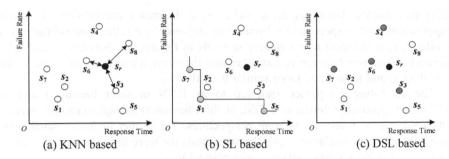

Fig. 2. Approaches for service recommendation

(similar) to s_r in both dimensions, e.g., s_3, s_6 and s_8, are more suitable than those far away from s_r, e.g., s_1, s_2, s_4, s_5 and s_7. Service s_1, in particular, has lower response time and failure rate than most services. Services with such outstanding quality advantages are usually very expensive. The selection of s_1 will most likely violate the cost constraint for the system. In a 3-dimensional space with cost as the third dimension, s_1 might be one of the services most similar to s_r. However, in Fig. 2(a), s_1 is not considered suitable with respect to s_r.

Therefore, we can identify a set of k nearest neighbor services that are most similar to s_r in all quality dimensions. However, there is an inherent limitation to this approach in certain scenarios – the services identified by this approach might not be representative in all quality dimensions. Take Fig. 2(a) for example. Suppose that s_3, s_6 and s_8 are identified as the services most similar to s_r. Services s_6 has the lowest response time and is thus considered the most representative service in terms of low response time among s_3, s_6 and s_8. Service s_3 has the lowest failure rate and is thus considered the most representative in terms of low failure rate among s_3, s_6 and s_8. Now we take a look at s_8. It is not representative in either low response time or low failure rate. Therefore, considering only response time and failure rate, s_3 and s_6, are more appropriate than s_8. According to the definition of skyline [3], s_8 is dominated by s_3 and s_6 because s_8 is no better than s_3 and s_6 in any quality dimensions.

An approach for solving the above non-representativeness problem is to calculate the skyline [3], as presented in Fig. 2(b). Given a set of services, the skyline calculation identifies the set of services that are not dominated by any other services. In the case of Fig. 2(b), the skyline services include s_1, s_5 and s_7, which are superior to the other services in terms of both low response time and low failure rate. They are represented by light grey circles. Hence, they are considered more representative than the other services. However, s_1, s_5 and s_7 are not close to s_r at all. In fact, they are further away from s_r compared to the other services. This is because the skyline calculation uses the origin O as the reference point. As a result, the skyline services are not suitable with respect to s_r. To address this issue, we need to identify the *dynamic skyline services* [16], as presented in Fig. 2(c). The dynamic skyline service calculation uses a given point rather than the origin as the reference point and identifies the dynamic skyline services with respect to the distances to the reference point. In Fig. 2(c), given s_r as the reference point, the dynamic skyline services include s_3, s_4, s_6 and s_7, represented by heavy dark circles. Among s_3, s_4, s_6 and s_7, s_4 is the most representative in terms of response time with respective to s_r because its response time is the most similar to s_r's. Similarly, s_7 is the most representative in terms of failure rate. Services s_3 and s_6 are two tradeoff services between s_4 and s_7 because they have a response time more similar to s_r than s_4 and failure rate more similar to s_r than s_7.

The KNN-based approach (referred to as KNN in short hereafter) and the DSL-based approach (referred to as DSL in short hereafter) attempt to identify services with respect to s_r from two different perspectives. The former identifies suitable services that are most similar to s_r and the latter finds the representative services that are not dominated by any other services with respect to s_r.

In this paper, we use response time and failure rate in the discussion. More quality constraints can be taken into account in a similar manner, which will transform the two-dimensional space into a multi-dimensional one.

3 Recommendation Approaches

3.1 Basic Approaches

In this section, we present the basic KNN and DSL approaches.

KNN Approach. Given a set of candidate services $S = \{s_1, \ldots, s_n\}$, each with p-dimensional quality values, and a reference service s_r with p-dimensional quality references, the candidate services and s_r are first mapped to a p-dimensional space, one dimension for each of the p quality dimensions. For numerical quality dimensions, such as response time, failure rate, reliability, etc., the mapping process is straightforward. To accommodate non-numerical quality dimensions, such as reputation that are expressed by a rating selected from {high, medium, low}, the method discussed in [17] is adopted in this research. Based on a pre-defined hierarchical structure of all possible values, each level of the hierarchy is associated with a numerical value, for example, 3 for high, 2 for medium and 1 for low.

Given a k value, KNN identifies the top k services from S that are most similar to s_r, based on a measure of similarity in the p-dimensional space. To evaluate the similarity between each of the candidate services, $s_i \in S$, $1 \leq i \leq n$, and s_r, we first normalize the quality values of s_i, $1 \leq i \leq n$, as well as s_r, with the min-max normalization technique, which has also been employed by many other researchers [17, 18]:

$$\tilde{q}_p(s_i) = \begin{cases} \frac{q_p^{\max}(S) - q_p(s_i)}{q_p^{\max}(S) - q_p^{\min}(S_i)} & \text{if } q_p^{\max}(S) \neq q_p^{\min}(S) \\ 1 & \text{if } q_p^{\max}(S) = q_p^{\min}(S) \end{cases} \quad (1)$$

where $q_p(s_i)$ is the pth dimensional quality value of s_i, $q_p^{\max}(S)$ and $q_p^{\min}(S)$ are the maximum and minimum values, respectively, for the pth quality dimension among all services in S.

After the normalization, the similarity between a candidate service $s_i \in S$ and the reference service s_r can be evaluated by the Euclidean distance between s_i and s_r:

$$d(s_i, s_r) = \sqrt{\sum_{j=1}^{p} \left(q_j(s_i) - q_j(s_r) \right)^2} \tag{2}$$

Based on Eq. (2), KNN employs Algorithm 1 to identify k services that are most similar to s_r. Algorithm 1 first calculates the Euclidean distance between each service in S and s_r (lines 3–5). It then sorts the services by their distances to s_r in a descending order (line 6). Finally, the algorithm returns the top k services from S as the recommendation results.

KNN requires the k value to be pre-specified, which is a domain-specific parameter. Different applications usually have their own characteristics, and hence inherit different optimal k values. On one hand, an overly small k value cannot ensure that adequate similar services be identified for recommendation. On the other hand, an overly large k value will include dissimilar services in the final recommendation results and will consequently decrease the recommendation accuracy. Therefore, the k value should be set domain-specifically based on experiences and/or experiments. In Sect. 4, we experimentally study the impact of k on recommendation accuracy.

The complexity of Algorithm 1 relies on the employed sorting algorithm. Here, we use the complexity of comparison sort algorithms in the worst-case scenario, i.e., $O(nlogn)$. Thus, Algorithm 1 runs in $O(np + nlogn)$.

DSL Approach. Given a set of points in a p-dimensional space, the skyline calculation is to find the points that are not dominated by any other points. A point s_i dominates another point s_j, if s_i is better than or equal to s_j in all dimensions and strictly better in at least one dimension. In the context of this research, the dominance relations between two services is defined based on their p-dimensional quality values:

Definition 1. Dominance: Given two services, $s_i, s_j \in S$, characterized by p-dimensional quality values, s_i dominates s_j, denoted by $s_i \triangleright s_j$, iff s_i is as good as or better than s_j in all quality dimensions and better in least one quality dimension, i.e., $\forall p \in [1, n]$: $q_p(s_i) \leq q_p(s_j)$ and $\exists p \in [1, n] : q_p(s_i) < q_p(s_j)$.

Based on Definition 1, we formally define the concept of skyline services:

Definition 2. Skyline services: The skyline of S, denoted by S_{SL}, consists of the set of services in S that are not dominated by any other services in S, i.e., $S_{SL} = \{ s_i \in S \mid \neg \exists s_j : s_i \triangleright s_j \}$. The services in S_{SL} are referred to as skyline services.

Generally, the skyline services have the best quality according to their absolute quality values in each quality dimension. However, as discussed in Sect. 2, given a reference service s_r, DSL needs to identify the dynamic skyline services in S. This can be achieved in a new p-dimensional space based on the original space.

Algorithm 1. KNN
Input:
S - Set of candidate services
s_r - Reference service
k - number of services needed
Output:
results - k services most similar to s_r
1   **Begin**
2   *result* ← null;
3   **for** each s in S **do**
4            $\mid$ *s.distance* ← $d(s, s_r)$;
5   **end for**
6   *S.sortByDistance()*;
7   *results* ← *S.takeTop(k)*;
8   **return** *results*;
9   **End**

First, each service $s \in S$ is mapped to a service $s' = (f_1(s), \ldots, f_p(s))$, where $f_i(s) = |q_i(s_r) - q_i(s)|$, $1 \leq i \leq n$. Then, the dynamic skyline of S with respect to functions $f_1, \ldots, f_p$, is obtained by calculating the ordinary skyline in the transformed p-dimensional space with s_r as the origin. Accordingly, dynamic dominance is defined as:

Definition 3. Dynamic dominance: Given two services, $s_i, s_j \in S$, characterized by p-dimensional quality values, and a reference service s_r, s_i dynamically dominates s_j with respect to s_r, denoted by $s_i \succ s_j$, iff $\forall p \in [1, n] : |q_p(s_r) - q_p(s_i)| \leq |q_p(s_r) - q_p(s_j)|$ and $\exists p \in [1, n] : |q_p(s_r) - q_p(s_i)| < |q_p(s_r) - q_p(s_j)|$.

Based on Definition 3, we formally define the concept of dynamic skyline services:

Definition 4. Dynamic skyline services: The dynamic skyline of S, denoted by S_{DSL}, consists the services that are not dynamically dominated by any other services, with respect to a given reference service s_r, i.e., $S_{DSL} = \{s_i \in S \mid \neg \exists s_j : s_j \triangleright s_i\}$. The services in S_{DSL} are referred to as dynamic skyline services.

Figure 3 illustrates the calculation of the dynamic skyline based on Fig. 2(c). First, the original space is transformed into a new one with s_r as the new origin and the absolute distances to s_r as the mapping functions. Then, $s_1, s_2, s_3, s_4, s_5, s_6, s_7$ are mapped into the new space where they are denoted by $s'_1, s'_2, s'_3, s'_4, s'_5, s'_6$ and s'_7. Service s_8 is already in the first quadrant of the new space. After the mapping, the location of s'_8 is exactly the same as s_8 and thus is omitted in Fig. 3. Having mapped all the services into the new space, where they are collectively referred to as S', the calculation of S_{DSL} is equivalent to the calculation of S'_{SL} in the new space. DSL employs Algorithm 2 to calculate the service skyline S_{SL} of a set of candidate services S. It iterates through all services in S (line 4). In each iteration, it selects one service s from S and checks if any other services in S dominate s (lines 5–11). If none, the algorithm includes s in the service skyline S_{SL} (lines 12–14). After processing all the services in S, it returns S_{SL}, i.e., the service skyline that consists of all the skyline services. As presented in Fig. 3, the algorithm returns $S'_{SL} = \{s'_3, s'_4, s'_6, s'_7\}$ as the

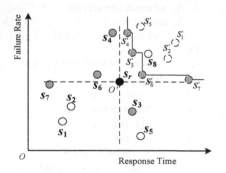

Fig. 3. Identification of dynamic skyline services.

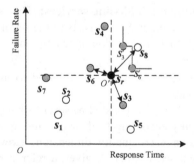

Fig. 4. Recommendation with KNN-DSL

skyline services in the new space. Accordingly, we can determine that $S_{DSL} = \{s_3, s_4, s_6, s_7\}$. As discussed in Sect. 2, s_3 and s_7 are closest to s_r in terms of response time and failure rate respectively. In the meantime, s_4 and s_6 are considered tradeoffs between s_3 and s_7.

Algorithm 2 contains two loops, one nested in the other. Let n be the number of nodes in S. The time complexity of Algorithm 2 is $O(n^2)$.

3.2 Hybrid Approaches

KNN and DSL have respective limitations. This section presents two hybrid approaches, KNN-DSL and DSL-KNN, that overcome those limitations.

KNN-DSL. Given a reference service s_r, DSL identifies representative services. However, it sacrifices the similarity between the identified services and s_r. Take Fig. 3 for example, where $S_{DSL} = \{s_3, s_4, s_6, s_7\}$. In terms of standardized Euclidean distance, s_3 and s_6 are the closest to s_r. In addition, they both belong to the results returned by KNN when $k \geq 2$, as shown in Fig. 2(a). Services s_4 and s_7, on the other hand, are not the next services that are closest to s_r. Compared with s_4 and s_7, s_8 is closer to s_r. In addition, s_2 is closer to s_r than s_4. Thus, some dynamic skyline services should not be recommended as they are dissimilar to s_r.

To address this issue, we propose KNN-DSL, an approach that combines the advantages of KNN and DSL. Given a set of candidate services S and a reference service s_r, it first employs KNN to identify k services most similar to s_r, denoted by S_{KNN}. Then, it calculates the dynamic skyline of S_{KNN}, denoted by $S_{KNN\text{-}DSL}$, using DSL. In this way, KNN-DSL identifies those services that are similar to s_r and, in the meantime, representative with respect to s_r. Figure 4 shows an example based on Fig. 2(a). Suppose $k = 3$ for KNN. First, s_3, s_6 and s_8 are identified as the three services that are most similar to s_r. Then, from s_3, s_6 and s_8, s_3 and s_6 are identified as the dynamic skyline services. The limitation to this approach is that the number of services eventually identified is lower than or equals to k, i.e., $|S_{KNN\text{-}DSL}| \leq k$. Thus, KNN-DSL does not ensure a specific number of services in its recommendation results.

Algorithm 2 . SL
Input:
S - Set of candidate services
Output:
S_{SL} - skyline of S
1   **Begin**
2      $S_{SL} \leftarrow$ null;
3      $skyline \leftarrow$ **true**;
4   **for each** s_i in S **do**
5         $skyline \leftarrow$ **true**;
6   **for each** s_j in S **do**
7   **if** $s_{j \triangleright} s_i$ **then**
8               $skyline \leftarrow$ **false**;
9   **break**;
10   **end if**
11   **end for**
12   **if** $skyline$ = **true**
13           $S_{SL} \leftarrow S_{SL} + s_i$;
14   **end if**
15   **end for**
16   **return** S_{SL}
17 **End**

DSL-KNN Approach. To tackle the limitation of KNN-DSL, we propose DSL-KNN, which combines DSL and KNN to recommend services. Given S and s_r, it first identifies the dynamic skyline services, denoted by S_{DSL}. Then, from S_{DSL}, it identifies k services that are the closest to s_r, denoted by $S_{DSL-KNN}$. If $|S_{DSL-KNN}| < k$, DSL-KNN continues to find $k - |S_{DSL-KNN}|$ more services that are closest to s_r to ensure a total of

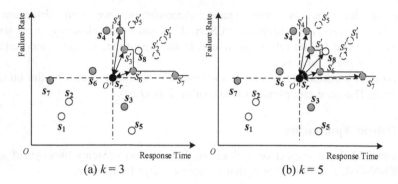

Fig. 5. Recommendation with DSL-KNN

k services in its recommendation results. In this way, the dynamic skylines services are always selected first to ensure the representativeness of some of the recommended services. Figure 5(a) and (b) demonstrate this approach based on Fig. 3 with $k = 3$ and $k = 5$ for KNN respectively. In Fig. 5, DSL-KNN first identifies the dynamic skyline services with respect to s_r, i.e., $S_{DSL} = \{s_3, s_4, s_6, s_7\}$. Then, given $k = 3$, it identifies s_3, s_4 and s_6 from S_{DSL} as the services that are the most similar to s_r. Given $k = 5$, the approach will first select all the services in S_{DSL}, and then select s_8 as the fifth service in addition to S_{DSL} because it is the service that is the closest to s_r among the rest of the services, i.e., s_1, s_2, s_5 and s_8.

Both KNN-DSL and DSL-KNN employ KNN and DSL. Thus, their complexity are both $O(n^2 + np + nlogn) = O(n^2 + np)$.

4 Experimental Evaluation

This section evaluates the proposed approaches through comparison with three existing representative approaches in their effectiveness (measured by recommendation accuracy) and efficiency (measured by computation time).

4.1 Experiment Setup

The experiments were conducted on a publicly available real-world dataset named QWS [19], which has been widely used [6, 9, 17, 20]. We have implemented the four **personalized quality centric approaches** for service recommendation proposed in Sects. 3. For comparison, we have implemented three existing representative **non-personalized quality centric approaches** for service recommendation:

- **RS:** This approach randomly selects k services from the candidate services.
- **UF:** This approach selects k services with the highest utility values, calculated with the widely used utility function [1, 6, 15, 17].
- **SL:** This approach identify skyline services [3, 7, 8].

Metrics for effectiveness. Given a system engineer's quality preferences represented by s_r, personalized quality centric service recommendation aims to find services whose quality is (1) similar to s_r; and (2) representative with respect to s_r. Accordingly, we evaluate the recommendation accuracies of the comparing approaches, which are measured by three metrics, Mean Absolute Error (MAE), Root Mean Squared Error (RMSE) and Non-Dominance Rate (NDR).

MAE is defined as:

$$\text{MAE} = \sum_{i=1}^{|R|} \sqrt{\sum_{j=1}^{p} \left(q_j(s_i) - q_j(s_r)\right)^2} / |R| \tag{3}$$

where R is the set of services returned by the recommendation approach, $q_j(s_i)$ and $q_j(s_r)$ are the jth dimensional quality value of $s_i \in R$ and s_r. An MAE value indicates the average difference between the recommended services and s_r in their p-dimensional quality. **A low MAE value indicates high recommendation accuracy.**

RMSE is defined as:

$$\text{RMSE} = \sqrt{\sum_{i=1}^{|R|} \sum_{j=1}^{p} \left(q_j(s_i) - q_j(s_r)\right)^2 / |R|} \tag{4}$$

During the calculation of RMSE, the individual differences between the recommended services and s_r are each squared and then averaged over R. Similar to MAE, **a low RMSE indicates high recommendation accuracy.**

NDR is defined as:

$$NDR = |R_{DSL}| / |R| \tag{5}$$

where R_{DSL} is the set of dynamic skyline services in R. NDR measures the representativeness of the results. **A high NDR indicates high recommendation accuracy.**

Metric for efficiency. In order to evaluate the efficiency of the proposed approaches, we measure their computational overheads.

To simulate different recommendation scenarios, we have conducted three series of experiments, namely series A, B and C. Table 1 presents the parameter settings. In each experiment, we randomly select n services from the QWS dataset as the candidate services, and another one as s_r. Then, we run the comparing approaches to identify the services to recommend. All approaches are implemented in Java using JDK 1.8. All

Table 1. Experiment parameter settings.

Parameter	Experiment series		
	A	B	C
Number of candidate services (n)	500 to 1000	1000	1000
Number of services to recommend (k)	5	5 to 12	5
Number of quality dimensions (q)	4	4	2 to 9

experiments are conducted on a machine with Intel i7-4790 CPU 3.60 GHz and 16 GB RAM, running Windows 10 x64 Professional.

4.2   Experimental Results

Effectiveness. Figure 6 shows the impact of the number of services in S (denoted by n) on the recommendation accuracies obtained by the approaches. Figure 6(a) and (b) show that KNN-DSL, KNN and DSL-KNN obtain the best recommendation accuracies, measured by their MAE and RMSE values which are much lower than the other four approaches. DSL obtains the fourth best recommendation accuracy overall. This indicates the importance of considering s_r during service recommendation. Interestingly, we observe that UF achieves the worst recommendation accuracy. It finds the services with the best overall quality, which however, are not necessarily preferable to the system engineer, indicated by its extremely high MAE values. Figure 6(a) and (b) also show that the increase in n increases the recommendation accuracies of our approaches, i.e., DSL-KNN, KNN-DSL, KNN and DSL. As n increases, there are more candidate services for the approaches to choose from, increasing the possibility of finding suitable services. Figure 6(c) shows that the services recommended by KNN-DSL and DSL are the most representative, with slight advantages over DSL-KNN. The services recommended by the other four approaches, including KNN, are significantly less representative. It clearly shows the effectiveness of the DSL operator in finding representative services.

Figure 7 demonstrates the impact of the number of services to recommend (denoted by k). Figure 7(a) and (b) show that KNN-DSL, again, achieves the best recommendation results overall in experiment series B, KNN the second, DSL-KNN the third and DSL the fourth. KNN-DSL is the winner because its KNN operator ensures the similarity between the selected k services and s_r with its KNN operator, and then further prunes some of the k services whose quality are relatively dissimilar to s_r with its DSL operator. KNN seconds to KNN-DSL because the non-dynamic-skyline services in its recommendation results lower its recommendation accuracy. Similar to KNN-DSL, DSL-KNN also employs two operators, DSL then KNN. Its DSL operator selects the dynamic skyline services, which are representative however not necessarily very similar to s_r. Thus, its MAE values are not as low as KNN and DSL-KNN. RS, UF and

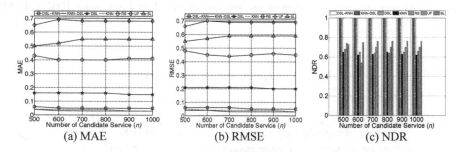

(a) MAE   (b) RMSE   (c) NDR

Fig. 6. Impact of parameter n on accuracy (experiment series A)

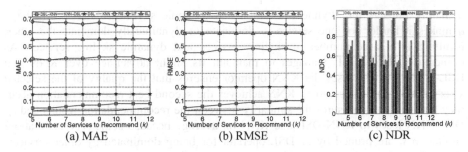

Fig. 7. Impact of parameter k on accuracy (experiment series B)

SL are again no match for our approaches, demonstrated by their significantly higher MAE and RMSE values. Figure 7(a) and (b) also show that the increase in the k value leads to slight increases in the MAE and RMSE values obtained by KNN-DSL, DSL-KNN and SL. As k increases, services that are not quite similar to s_r are also included in the recommendation results, which lowers the recommendation accuracy. The increase in k has no impact on DSL because DSL recommends only the dynamic skyline services which are irrelevant to the k value. Figure 7(c) shows that the recommendation results of KNN-DSL and DSL are all representative. This is because they both employ the DSL operator to ensure the representativeness of the recommendation results. DSL-KNN achieves the third highest representativeness in the recommendation results. Its DSL operator selects only the representative services, i.e., the dynamic skyline services. However, as k increases and exceeds the number of dynamic skyline services identified by its DSL operator, its KNN operator has to include some non-dynamic-skyline services in the recommendation results. These services reduce the overall representativeness of its recommendation results.

Figure 8 shows the impact of the number of quality dimensions (denoted by q). Figure 8(a) and (b) show that KNN-DSL, for the third time, achieves the best recommendation accuracy, outperforming KNN and DSL-KNN, which achieve the second best and third best recommendation accuracy respectively. DSL achieves the fourth highest - however significantly lower - recommendation accuracy. We can also observe that the increase in q decreases the recommendation accuracies achieved by our approaches, indicated by their increasing MAE and RMSE values. The increase in

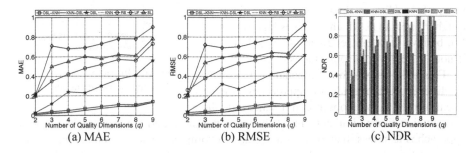

Fig. 8. Impact of number of quality constraints (q) on accuracy (experiment series C)

q mainly impacts the skyline calculation and dynamic skyline calculation. A large q makes it harder for one service to dominate or dynamically dominate the other, resulting in a large number of skyline services and dynamic skyline services. As q increases, KNN-DSL manages to maintain its slight advantage over KNN and DSL-KNN in most cases. Its KNN operator ensures that the quality of the selected k services are the closest to s_r. KNN achieves the second best recommendation accuracy because it also ensures the similarity between the recommendation results and s_r. DSL-KNN loses to KNN-DSL and KNN on average because some services that are similar to s_r are pruned by its DSL operator for being dominated by other services. Figure 8(c) shows that KNN-DSL and DSL consistently obtain highly representative recommendation results. DSL-KNN also obtains representative recommendation results except when $q = 2$. We investigated this interesting phenomenon and found out that when $q = 2$, its DSL identified only a few dynamic skyline services, requiring its KNN operator to find some services that are similar to s_r but are not representative. This lowers the overall representativeness of its recommendation results.

Efficiency. Figure 9 shows the computation times taken by the approaches in experiment series A. As demonstrated, the seven approaches can be categorized into two groups according to their scalability to n, the *slow approaches*, including SL, DSL and DSL-KNN, and the *fast approaches*, including RS, KNN, KNN-DSL and UF. The slow approaches share one thing in common - they have to identify the skyline services or the dynamic skyline services from a large number of candidate services, which is not required for the fast approaches. KNN-DSL, which also employs a DSL operator like DSL and DSL-KNN, takes much less time to complete. It is because its KNN operator selects only k services for its DSL operator to process further. Given that k is usually a small number, its DSL operator does not need take long to finish. The slow approaches take significantly more time than the fast approaches. However, they are in fact not quite slow - they require slightly more than 70 ms to process 1,000 candidate services. In addition, their computation times are roughly linear to n, which indicates high scalability. We believe their efficiency are acceptable in most, if not all, real-world applications.

Figure 10 shows the computation times taken by different recommendation approaches in experiment series C. We observe differences in their

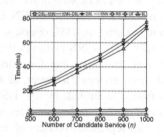

Fig. 9. Impact of parameter n on efficiency (experiment series A)

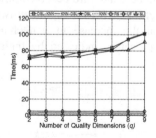

Fig. 10. Impact of parameter q on efficiency (experiment series C)

computation times similar to Fig. 9 between the slow and fast approaches. The fast approaches take less than 10 ms on average to complete. Their computation times are not significantly impacted by the increase in q, which demonstrates their high scalability to q. On the other hand, the slow approaches taking 60 ms to 100 ms to complete, much longer than fast approaches, are still fast enough for most, if not all, real-world applications.

Please note that the computation times of the recommendation approaches in experiment series B, where k varies, are not presented. The k value means to select k services from the processed candidate services. For example, the KNN operator, which employs Algorithm 1 introduced in Sect. 3.1, simply picks the top k services from a set of services sorted by their distance to s_r. UF selects k services in a similar way. Such operations have a complexity of $O(1)$ and do not impact the computation times of the approaches.

4.3   Discussion

Table 2 presents the average MAE, RMSE and NDR values obtained by the recommendation approaches in each experiment series. The lowest and second lowest MAE, RMSE, as well as the highest and the second highest DNR, achieved in each experiment series are highlighted by dark grey and light grey respectively. We can see that on average, KNN-DSL outperforms the other approaches. This indicates that KNN-DSL obtains the most suitable and most representative recommendation results with respect to s_r. In the meantime, KNN-DSL is also highly efficient, as illustrated by Figs. 9 and 10. Thus, KNN-DSL is the best approach for service recommendation in most real-world applications. However, KNN-DSL has a limitation - it does not ensure a certain number of services in its recommendation results. It might eventually finds fewer than k services. Thus, if a number of k services in the recommendation results is mandatory, KNN-DSL is not a proper choice. In those cases, DSL-KNN and KNN are preferable. Table 2 shows that KNN achieves the second lowest MAE and RMSE values, indicating that its recommendation results are close to s_r. However, its advantage over DSL-KNN is only marginal. In addition, its NDR values are much lower than those of DSL-KNN, meaning that its recommendation results are not as representative. Therefore, in most cases, DSL-KNN is a better choice than KNN k services are mandatory. DSL achieves the highest NDR in all three experiment series. However, its MAE and RMSE values are much higher than KNN-DSL, DSL-KNN and KNN. In addition, it does not guarantee the number of services in its recommendation results. As a result, DSL is not the first choice in any envisaged real-world applications.

Table 2. Average performance (MAE/RMSE/NDR)

Experiment series	A			B			C		
KNN-DSL	0.03	0.03	1.00	0.03	0.03	1.00	0.061	0.06	1.00
DSL-KNN	0.05	0.06	0.99	0.07	0.08	0.97	0.08	0.08	0.94
KNN	0.04	0.04	0.06	0.04	0.04	0.50	0.064	0.07	0.65
DSL	0.16	0.21	1.00	0.15	0.20	1.00	0.28	0.33	1.00
RS	0.41	0.46	0.65	0.41	0.47	0.54	0.48	0.52	0.76
UF	0.68	0.69	0.68	0.66	0.67	0.55	0.69	0.69	0.81
SL	0.54	0.58	0.75	0.55	0.59	0.76	0.56	0.58	0.71

5 Related Work

Quality-aware service recommendation is a critical issue in service-oriented computing. Utility-based recommendation [1, 3, 6, 15, 17] and skyline-based recommendation [3] are currently the two most popular approaches for quality-aware service recommendation.

Utility-based recommendation is very straightforward. The utility value of a service indicates how good its overall p-dimensional quality is in comparison with the other candidate services in S - the higher, the better. The utility calculation for a service s_i goes through two phases. First, a utility value is calculated for each of its quality dimensions. Then, the utility of service s_i is calculated by summing its utility values in all p quality dimensions. Given a set of candidate services, utility-based recommendation selects the services with the highest utility values. This approach has been widely employed [1, 3, 6, 15, 17].

The other popular approach for service recommendation is the skyline-based service recommendation. Its process can be found in Sect. 2. It was first employed by Alrifai et al. to select representative services that are not dominated by any other candidate services [3]. Since then, many researchers have attempted to improve the skyline-based service recommendation approach to accommodate more sophisticated environments. To name few, Benouaret et al. propose a concept named alpha-dominant service skyline to address two issues in the approach proposed by Alrifai et al. [7]. First, it treats services with a bad compromise between different quality dimensions in a fairer manner. Second, it improves the efficiency of skyline calculation. Benouaret et al. have also proposed an improved skyline-based approach for service recommendation that handles services' probabilistic quality values [8].

The common and critical limitation of the utility-based and the skyline-based service recommendation is the lack of consideration for system engineers' quality constraints, which have always been a fundamental and critical issue in quality-aware service selection [1, 2, 6, 9, 17, 20], as well as skyline-based service composition [21–23]. This renders the utility-based and skyline-based service recommendation obsolete. As demonstrated in Sect. 4, their recommendation results are neither suitable nor representative.

There is a large body of approaches labeled service recommendation approaches [10–14]. However, aiming to predict the quality values of services, those approaches are not designed for service recommendation.

Our approaches address the limitation of existing recommendation approaches by centering system engineers' quality constraints in the recommendation. By combining the KNN and DSL techniques, our approaches can efficiently recommend suitable and representative services with respect to system engineers' quality preferences.

6 Conclusion and Future Work

In this paper, we first proposed two basic approaches, named KNN and DSL, for personalized quality centric service recommendation, based on k-nearest neighbors and dynamic skyline techniques, respectively. Then, to overcome their limitations, we proposed two hybrid approaches, named KNN-DSL and DSL-KNN. Finally, we presented extensive experiment results to demonstrate their effectiveness and efficiency.

In the future, we will combine the proposed approaches with approaches for service compositions to facilitate an effective and efficient personalized quality centric process for building service-based systems.

Acknowledgment. This work is supported by the National Key Technology R&D Program (No. 2015BAK24B01), the General Research for Humanities and Social Sciences Project of Chinese Ministry of Education (No. 15YJAZH112), the Educational Commission of Anhui Province of China (No. KJ2016A038), and the Australian Research Council Projects DP150101775 and LP130100324. Qiang He is the corresponding author of this paper.

References

1. Ardagna, D., Pernici, B.: Adaptive service composition in flexible processes. IEEE Trans. Softw. Eng. **33**(6), 369–384 (2007)
2. Zeng, L., Benatallah, B., Ngu, A.H.H., Dumas, M., Kalagnanam, J., Chang, H.: QoS-Aware middleware for web services composition. IEEE Trans. Softw. Eng. **30**(5), 311–327 (2004)
3. Alrifai, M., Skoutas, D., Risse, T.: Selecting skyline services for QoS-based web service composition. In: 19th International Conference on World Wide Web, pp. 11–20 (2010)
4. Yu, Q., Bouguettaya, A.: Efficient service skyline computation for composite service selection. IEEE Trans. Knowl. Data Eng. **25**(4), 776–789 (2013)
5. He, Q., Yan, J., Jin, H., Yang, Y.: Quality-aware service selection for service-based systems based on iterative multi-attribute combinatorial auction. IEEE Trans. Softw. Eng. **40**(2), 192–215 (2014)
6. Trummer, I., Faltings, B., Binder, W.: Multi-objective quality-driven service selection - a fully polynomial time approximation scheme. IEEE Trans. Softw. Eng. **40**(2), 167–191 (2014)
7. Benouaret, K., Benslimane, D., Hadjali, A.: On the use of fuzzy dominance for computing service skyline based on QoS. In: 9th IEEE International Conference on Web Services, pp. 540–547 (2011)
8. Benouaret, K., Benslimane, D., Hadjali, A.: Selecting skyline web services from uncertain QoS. In: 9th IEEE International Conference on Services Computing, pp. 523–530 (2012)
9. Tan, T.H., Chen, M., Sun, J., Liu, Y., André, É., Xue, Y., Dong, J.S.: Optimizing selection of competing services with probabilistic hierarchical refinement. In: 38th International Conference on Software Engineering, pp. 85–95 (2016)
10. Zheng, Z., Lyu, M.R.: Collaborative reliability prediction of service-oriented systems. In: 32nd ACM/IEEE International Conference on Software Engineering, pp. 35–44 (2010)
11. Zheng, Z., Lyu, M.R.: Personalized reliability prediction of web services. ACM Trans. Softw. Eng. Methodol. **22**(2), 12 (2013)
12. Zheng, Z., Ma, H., Lyu, M.R., King, I.: Qos-aware web service recommendation by collaborative filtering. IEEE Trans. Serv. Comput. **4**(2), 140–152 (2011)
13. Chen, X., Zheng, Z., Yu, Q., Lyu, M.R.: Web service recommendation via exploiting location and QoS information. IEEE Trans. Parallel Distrib. Syst. **25**(7), 1913–1924 (2014)
14. Yao, L., Sheng, Q.Z., Ngu, A.H., Yu, J., Segev, A.: Unified collaborative and content-based web service recommendation. IEEE Trans. Serv. Comput. **8**(3), 453–466 (2015)

15. Alrifai, M., Risse, T.: Combining global optimization with local selection for efficient QoS-aware service composition. In: 18th International Conference on World Wide Web, pp. 881–890 (2009)
16. Papadias, D., Tao, Y., Fu, G., Seeger, B.: An optimal and progressive algorithm for skyline queries. In: ACM SIGMOD International Conference on Management of Data, pp. 467–478 (2003)
17. He, Q., Yan, J., Jin, H., Yang, Y.: Quality-aware service selection for service-based systems based on iterative multi-attribute combinatorial auction. IEEE Trans. Softw. Eng. 40(2), 192–215 (2014)
18. Zheng, Z., Wu, X., Zhang, Y., Lyu, M.R., Wang, J.: QoS ranking prediction for cloud services. IEEE Trans. Parallel Distrib. Syst. 24(6), 1213–1222 (2013)
19. Al-Masri, E., Mahmoud, Q.H.: Investigating web services on the world wide web. In: 17th International Conference on World Wide Web, pp. 795–804 (2008)
20. He, Q., Zhou, R., Zhang, X., Wang, Y., Ye, D., Chen, F., Grundy, J., Yang, Y.: Keyword search for building service-based systems. IEEE Trans. Softw. Eng. 43(7), 658–674 (2017)
21. Zhao, X., Shen, L.W., Peng, X., Zhao, W.: Finding preferred skyline solutions for SLA-constrained service composition. In: 20th IEEE International Conference on Web Services, pp. 195–202 (2013)
22. Zhang, S., Dou, W., Chen, J.: Selecting Top-k composite web services using preference-aware dominance relationship. In: 20th IEEE International Conference on Web Services, pp. 75–82 (2013)
23. Zhang, F., Hwang, K., Khan, S.U., Malluhi, Q.M.: Skyline discovery and composition of multi-cloud mashup services. IEEE Trans. Serv. Comput. 9(1), 72–83 (2016)

Cataloger: Catalog Recommendation Service for IT Change Requests

Anup K. Kalia$^{(\boxtimes)}$, Jin Xiao, Muhammed F. Bulut, Maja Vukovic,
and Nikos Anerousis

IBM T.J. Watson, Yorktown Heights, NY, USA
anup.kalia@ibm.com, {jinoaix,mfbulut,maja,nikos}@us.ibm.com

Abstract. Service automation improves the efficiency of IT service management processes. Traditionally, IT change management relies on humans to submit a change request ticket or navigate a cumbersome catalog. Today, new systems are created to execute changes based on a service catalog that is linked to back-end application programming interfaces (APIs). Consequently, a user would need to identify the right API among thousands or more items, and fill in all the required parameters. This interaction is fully self-served with little assistance. We present Cataloger a novel recommendation system that enables humans to specify their change requests in natural language sentences and recommends the most appropriate APIs. Cataloger incorporates multi-step process where IT change requests are first classified into categories, tasks and actions (APIs), and then parameters are extracted from the requests. We evaluate a well-known set of machine learning techniques for classification and parameters extraction for Cataloger, and propose a novel feedback method for improved accuracy. We evaluate Cataloger on real-world data from four different clients of IBM. Our evaluation shows that the feedback approach significantly improves the accuracy of identifying categories, tasks, and actions for change requests, thereby, improving the API recommendation to users.

1 Introduction

To improve the efficiency of IT service management processes, a lot of focus has been placed on automation [1] to reduce human error and streamline the operations. Consider IT service change management process that is designed to ensure that codified procedures are followed to handle all changes to control IT infrastructure such as, adding filesystems, recycling database instances, upgrading the memory, and so on. Traditionally, a human expert would submit a ticket to initiate a change request type. These requests would be assigned to another human expert (typically in delivery), who would be executing them. Without standardizations and automation this has often resulted in inconsistent execution (e.g., each administrator executing their own scripts to process the requests) and incomplete and inaccurate requests (e.g., missing parameters, unknown system state, etc.). Compared to earlier days, current user interface based tools have

© Springer International Publishing AG 2017
M. Maximilien et al. (Eds.): ICSOC 2017, LNCS 10601, pp. 545–560, 2017.
https://doi.org/10.1007/978-3-319-69035-3_40

significantly reduced the burden of accessing a specific IT system, checking the availability of IT components and packages on the system, and executing appropriate commands with required parameters. To illustrate it further we show an example of a sample user interface in Fig. 1. The user interface shows a couple of drop-down menus to execute a database specific change requests such as table restore, table backup, Oracle reporting, and so on. IT Change service catalogs are then created to present a common front-end UI for all available IT change service requests. A user is to expected browse and navigate through a catalog service in largely self-service fashion.

Fig. 1. Catalog service for executing database specific change requests.

Through our experience in designing, developing and delivering self-service based change management services for various clients, we have stumbled upon two interesting problems. Firstly, as the number of supported change request types, systems, middlewares, and applications grow, the number of service APIs also grows rapidly. Although a hierarchical organization can be created to assist the user in navigating through the service catalog, the organization may not always conform with a client's IT change organization or fits with its user's IT expertise level. Keyword based search is another popular method of navigating the service catalogs. Unfortunately, it works very poorly on IT service changes due to the large variance in utterances and terminologies used to describe a specific change task and assumes the user know what terminology they should use to search. Secondly, a service API requires a specific set of parameters to be filled, typically presented as a set of list and/or text boxes to a user, who may not perfectly understand what values are expected in what system context, as the API developers intend. To overcome these challenges in an efficient, flexible and user-friendly way, we propose a catalog recommendation service (Cataloger) that takes a natural language based change request as its input and identifies the right service API. It also extracts any parameters as required by the API, from the change request.

Contribution. Cataloger provides the following capabilities: (1) a classification approach to categorize IT change requests into categories, tasks, and actions. The actions can be mapped to APIs, (2) a sequential classification approach to identify parameters in IT change requests that can be mapped to specific parameters in APIs, (3) a feedback based approach that utilizes our parameter classification process to improve the classification of categories, tasks, and action, also to train the change request classifiers for new client data sets. For the evaluation, we consider IT change request types such as database and hardware from multiple clients. We consider that our approach can be generalized to other change categories such as operating system (OS) management, middleware, networking, application, and so on.

Organization. First, we describe the related work. Then, we describe the overall process of associating change requests to a specific catalog service. In the process, we describe the classification techniques to identify categories, tasks, and actions and extract parameters from change requests. Further, we propose a feedback mechanism that improves the classification of categories, tasks, and actions. We provide evaluation for classification and parameter extraction techniques on multi-client change requests using traditional approaches. Further, we provide evaluation of the proposed feedback mechanism. Finally, we summarize our findings and discuss the future work.

2 Related Work

In our contribution, we emphasize on matching the intent of users' change requests to APIs. In terms of identifying intents from change requests, Lucca et al. [13], Kadar et al. [10], Bogojeska et al. [5] propose supervised approaches based on support vector machine, logistic regression and random forests, respectively. The limitations with supervised approach such as support vectors is that they do not consider multi-label or hierarchical multi-label aspect in the intents. There have been several works on minimizing the labeling effort using active learning [21] and hierarchical clustering techniques [14], however, they do not emphasize on matching the intent of users' change requests to the intent of an API or it's parameters. Again, none of the approach emphasize on extracting parameters from change requests that can be mapped to the parameters of an API. Le et al. [12] consider text descriptions to map it to corresponding APIs, however, they do not focus on discovering the intents of text descriptions.

Given the existing approaches, we find the following limitations with the approaches: (1) the approaches to classify change requests are independent of hierarchical intents of APIs. To map change requests to APIs, we need approaches that can extract hierarchical or at least multiple intents from change requests. For example, consider a change request *restore a database xyz* that has labels such as a category: database, a task: database backup, and an action: restore database, (2) existing approaches ignore the parameters of APIs that can be extracted from the change requests using sequential classification techniques. The parameters extracted can be reasoned about for improving the classification of change requests.

3   The Cataloger Approach

We label a IT change requests as a hierarchy of categories, tasks and actions (CTAs): (1) a *category* describes a IT change task based on its broad-stroke technology service areas. For examples, database, hardware, and os management are some of the categories. Categories are long standing and generally technology neutral, (2) a *task* refers to a group of similar change activities under a category. For example, the database category has tasks such as backup, management, user administration, etc. Tasks are technology dependent and distinct from each other, (3) an *action* maps to specific automation APIs which are technology and service provider dependent. For example, the database management task has actions such as create and drop a database (DB), increase and reduce a tablespace size as provided by a service catalog.

CTAs provide us with multiple scopes of increasingly refined coverage of matching APIs to a user's intent. In Table 1, we show examples of change requests and hierarchical labels. Based on CTA, we represent a change request (CR) as the tuple of category (C), task (T), and action (A), and parameters (PR) i.e., CR = ⟨C, T, A, PR⟩. To map a CR to a catalog service, first, we identify ⟨C, T, A⟩ associated to a CR. We adopt different classification techniques to obtain the labels. Second, based on the obtained label A, we extract parameters PR for a user to execute the catalog service. Third, based on parameters PR we evaluate whether a CR has been classified correctly into C, T, and A.

Table 1. Change requests and the hierarchical labels for each request.

Change Requests	Category	Task	Actions
Create new X database on instance Y	database	management	create DB
Enable user X on Y database	database	user admin	grant user
Stop DB2 database on X PROD server: Y	database	run operations	stop DB
Increase CPU for X to 8vcpu	hardware	cpu	increase cpu

Consider the example of a CR i.e., *increase CPU for X to 8vcpu* from Table 1. Based on the classification technique, we first identify C, T, and A as hardware, cpu, and increase cpu, respectively. Then, we extract parameters such as the server name X and the number of cpu i.e., *8vcpu*. Then, we use the parameters to verify if the C, T, and A identified are valid or not. If not we iterate through other values for C, T, and A to match with the appropriate PR. We further describe the feedback approach in Sect. 3.3. Accordingly, our process involves the following four subprocess (Fig. 2): (1) *preprocess CR*: we preprocess users' change requests by removing stop words and stemming them. This helps to reduce the feature space, thereby, reducing the chances of over-fitting, (2) *identify CTA*: we investigate several classification techniques such as the single-label classification (SLC), the multi-label classification (MLC), and the hierarchical multi-label classification (HMLC) to determine which specific technique is most effective in predicting CTAs, (3) *extract Parameters*: We adopt sequential classification techniques such as the conditional random fields (CRF) and the long short-term memory (LSTM) for extracting API-specific parameters from change requests.

In the following subsections, we first present details on the main subprocess: identify CTA and extract parameters. Then, we describe the feedback mechanism.

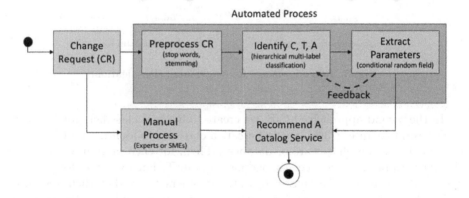

Fig. 2. The process illustrating the identification of a catalog service.

3.1 Classification of Change Requests

As a first step, we extract *n-grams* from the change requests CR. We preprocess the *n-grams* to remove stop words and stemmed them using the Porter stemmer. We remove punctuation such as $\{@, \&, \text{-}, \text{\_}, \#, <, >, (,), [,], \{, \}, *, +, =, :\}$. To vectorize the words, we build a *tf-idf* vectorizer $tf\text{-}idf(tr, d)$ where tr represents the words in the change request d. To normalize $tf\text{-}idf(tr, d)$, we use $L2$-normalization where we convert each *tf-idf* vector to its normal form. We consider a change request CR to have multiple labels in terms of a category C, task T, and an action A, organized into a *hierarchy* based on a specific catalog service, where C is the parent of T which is the parent of A. For classifying the labels, we evaluate a set of well-known techniques. To the best of our knowledge, these techniques have not been applied and evaluated in the context of IT change requests.

Single-Label Classification (SLC) For the single-label classification, we tried two approaches SLC-A and SLC-B. In the first approach SLC-A, we append the labels C, T, and A to create new labels C:T:A. The number of classes generated in this approach is same as number of action labels present in A. To predict the classes, we build a classifier that uses the linear Support Vector Machines (SVM) [7]. For training the model we consider the input data as a set of change requests CR and classes in C:T:A. Figure 3(a) captures the approach at the level of tasks T. For brevity, we omit the action level nodes.

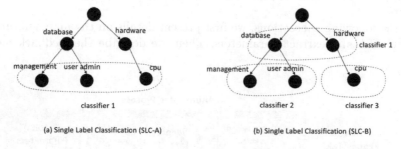

(a) Single Label Classification (SLC-A)   (b) Single Label Classification (SLC-B)

Fig. 3. Two approaches for single-label classification.

In the second approach SLC-B, we create individual classifiers for C, T, and A. For example, in Fig. 3(b), we first create a classifier to identify if a CR belongs to a label in C, i.e., hardware or database. Then, for each label in C, we create classifiers to predict their corresponding tasks in T. For example, for database and hardware labels, we create separate classifiers to predict their respective tasks. We repeat the process for A where we create classifiers with respect to labels in T. For example, we create separate classifiers for database management and user admin. For hardware, we create a classifier for cpu. To create classifiers for C, T, and A, we used the linear SVM [7]. For prediction, we start with prediction of labels in C. Based on the predicted label and the confidence score, we determine the classifier to invoke for labels in T. Figure 3(b) captures the approach as SLC-B at the level of T. The approach is similar to the approach provided by Barutcuoglu et al. [2].

Multi-label Classification (MLC) For multi-label classification, we adopt two approaches. One, RAKEL (RAndom K-labELsets) [19] that considers ensemble of labeled powerset (LP) classifiers [6]. Two, the classifier chain (CC) approach [17] that model correlations between labels while maintaining the acceptable computational complexity.

The RAKEL approach [19] uses the concept of k-labelsets. Consider we have labels $L = 1, \ldots, |L|$ from C, T, and A. A k-labelset refers to a set $Y \subseteq L$ with $k = |Y|$. For simplicity, we use L^k to denote the set of all distinct k-labelsets. The RAKEL approach creates an ensemble of m LP classifiers. For each i in $1, \ldots, m$, RAKEL selects a k-labelset Y_i from L^k without replacement. Then, it learns an LP classifier $h_i \colon X \to P(Y_i)$. For classifying a new instance or a change request, each model h_i provides a binary decision $h_i(x, \lambda_j)$ in the corresponding k-labelsets Y_i. For each label $\lambda_j \in L$ RAKEL computes the average. If the average is greater than 0.5 RAKEL provides a positive result.

The CC approach [17] involves $|L|$ binary classifiers. The classifiers are linked as a chain where each classifier is trained to predict $l_j \in L$. Consider an input domain $x = [x_1, \ldots, x_d]$ with d attributes extracted from CRs and a set of labels $\mathcal{L} = [1, \ldots, L]$ that corresponds to labels in C, T, and A. Each instance of x is mapped with a subset of labels $[y_1, \ldots, y_L]$ represented as an L-vector. In the vector, y_1 is 1 if the label j is associated with an instance x. For training, the approach considers a training data $D = \{x_i, y_i\}$ with N samples. A label is represented as y_j^i where j represents a label in the ith example. During the training phase, the approach forms a classifier chain $h = (h_1, \ldots, h_L)$ where h_j in the chain represents a classifier and is responsible for learning and predicting the binary associations of jth label given the attribute space augmented with prior binary relevance predictions in the chain. The classification approach begins at h_1 and propagates along the chain. For prediction, jth binary classifier predicts the relevance of the jth label.

Hierarchical Multi-label Classification (HMC) Hierarchical label classification considers both labels and the hierarchy constraint among the labels to create a classifier. We examined two approaches. One, the CLUS-HMC approach provided by Vens et al. [20] that learns one tree to predict all the classes. Two, the CSSAG provided by Bi and Kwok [3] that uses the Condensing Sort and Select algorithm (CSSA) to find an optimal approximation of a subtree in a tree.

CLUS-HMC [20] is a decision tree based learner and it considers the following: one, all the labels present in C, T, and A as its classes CL with a partial ordering $\leq_h$ among the classes, i.e., $c_1 \leq_h c_2$; two, it considers a set of T examples (x_i, S_i) where x_i are the features extracted from a change request CR_i and $S_i \in CL$; three, a quality criterion q that rewards models with high predictive accuracy and low complexity. The goal of the approach is to find $f \colon CR \to 2^{CL}$ such that f maximizes q and $c \in f(x) \implies \forall c' \leq_h c : c' \in f(x)$. The approach uses predictive clustering tree (PCT) framework [4] to view a decision tree as a hierarchy of clusters. In the framework, the top node corresponds to a single cluster that is recursively partitioned into smaller clusters.

CSSAG [3] uses kernel dependency estimation (KDE) to reduce large number of labels to manageable single-label learning problems. To preserve the hierarchy information among the labels, CSSAG uses Condensing Short and Select Algorithm that finds an optimal approximation subtree in a tree. The subtree is used to construct a multi-label that is consistent with respect to the tree. For CSSAG, the training data is represented as $\{(x_i, y_i)\}$ where x_i represents features extracted from a change request CR_i and belongs to an input space $\mathcal{X}$, $y_i \in \{0,1\}^d$ is an output vector, and d is the number of labels in C, T, and A. Each y_i can have more than one nonzero entries based on d.

Comparing the Classification Approaches SLC approaches have some limitations. For the SLC-A approach, the classes at the lower levels have less frequencies in the data. In the SLC-B approach, number of classifiers increase based on the number of labels in C, T, and A. The multi-label approach does not suffer from the limitations of SLC, however, it does not consider hierarchy organization of the labels. We evaluated the classifiers on different change requests. The details of our data set and the evaluation methodology is described in Sect. 4. Figure 4 shows the results for the classification of C, T, and A using SLC-A, SLC-B, CC, LP, CLUS-HMC, and CSSAG, respectively. Our evaluations show CC has the best performance. We assume there are multiple reasons contributed to this outcome: one, CTA favors multi-label approaches over single-label; two, CTA has only three hops between the root (C) and leaf (A) and is a complete tree, therefore the organization is too simple for HMLC to be advantageous. However, we are able to leverage the hierarchy of CTA when using the CC approach in our feedback mechanism, as we will describe in Sect. 3.3.

3.2 Extracting Parameters from Change Requests

The classification subprocess associates a change request to a service API. Now, we extract parameters, if present, from the change request. Two methods are considered: Conditional Random Fields (CRF) [8,15] and long short term memory networks (LSTMs) [9]. Some approaches use Hidden Markov Model (HMM) [22] to extract method specification. However, HMM based models consider conditional independence among the observations. Compared to HMM, CRF are agnostic to dependencies between the observations. Apart from CRF and HMM, there are ontology and rule based approaches [12,16,18], however, with the inclusion of data from different clients, they are susceptible to failure.

Conditional Random Fields (CRF) We adopt the named entity recognition technique based on CRF to extract parameters PR from changed requests CR. A change request contains a set of words that can be represented as observations x. Each word can be associated with a label y that represents a state. PR contains a set of parameters that is subset of the labels y. Given x and y, CRF captures the relationship between (x, y) as feature functions. For the classification, CRF employs discriminative modeling where the distribution of $p(y|x)$ is learned directly from the data. A feature function in CRF are of two types: one is based on the state-state pair (y_t, y_{t-1}) and another is based on the state-observation pair (x_t, y_t).

Long Short-Term Memory Network (LSTM) Apart from CRF, we consider LSTM for extracting parameters from change requests. We consider LSTM since it has been recently used for named entity recognition [11]. LSTM is based on recurrent neural networks (RNN) that takes a sequence of inputs $(x_1, x_2, \ldots, x_n)$ as its input and outputs another sequence $(h_1, h_2, \ldots, h_n)$. LSTM captures long range dependencies by incorporating a memory cell. The LSTM using several gates controls the proportion of input to give to the memory cell and the proportion from the previous state to forget. The gates are composed out of a sigmoid neural network layer and a pointwise multiplication operation.

Comparing CRF and LSTM We evaluated the performance of CRF and LSTM against our change requests data set in Sect. 4. Figure 5 shows the performance of the two. We find that LSTM performs much worse than CRF. We believe it is because we do not have sufficient training data. On the contrary, CRF requires the feature set to be specified as input while LSTM does not.

3.3 Feedback Approach

In our automated process, we first classify the change request and then extract parameters from said request. Through our experiments, we came upon the following two observations: one, with CTA, the classification of a CR is more accurate at C and T levels than A. This is not surprising as due to CTA's hierarchical nature, we expect a loss of accuracy further down the hierarchy (hierarchical loss); two, if the classification was wrong, there is no chance parameter extraction would produce a set of valid parameter match (parameter confusion). Hence, it's intuitive to use a failed parameter extraction (for a CR) as a negative API feedback to the classifier, and have a good probability of finding a positive API match by performing parameter extractions on the immediate sibling APIs of the negative one. Our feedback mechanism has the following advantages:

- *improved accuracy of classification*: classification approaches rely on specific words that helps in identifying a relevant C, T, and A. Since change requests have similar words such as action verbs and nouns, confusion increases while narrowing down from categories to actions.
- *a method for onboarding new client* CR *with unsupervised learning*: feedback from parameter extractor on new client's CR with correct labels.
- *decoupled training of catalog classifiers and parameter extractors*: onboarding of new CTA types only requires training of catalog classifiers; onboarding of catalog APIs (to existing CT) only requires training of new parameter extractor of the API.

In Table 2, consider the first two change requests that has been identified with the labels C = database, T = dbbackup, and A = backupdb. Clearly, the first change request does not fall into the database category, however, the keyword such as *backup* lead to the false classification. Similarly, key words such as *add* and *server* lead to the false classification of the fourth change request in Table 2.

Table 2. Examples of change requests with confusion.

Change Request	Category	Task	Action
Backup X database from Y and restore to Z	database	dbbackup	backupdb
Configure LAN backups to LAN-Free backups	database	dbbackup	backupdb
Add 2vCPU to server X	hardware	cpu	increasecpu
Add outbound servers to X for RDP access	hardware	cpu	increasecpu

To avoid the misclassification, we rely on parameters extracted from a change request to identify C, T, and A. Each action A can be associated with some special parameters PR that is relevant to A. For example, backup database has a special parameter such as the backup mode (online, offline), increase tablespace has a special parameter such as the buffer size, increase cpu, or memory has special parameters such as the amount of cpu or memory to be increased, and so on. In our approach, first, based on default parameters for each action, we assign weights to the parameters that indicate the specificity of the action. Based on the weights of parameters in an action we compute expected_weight. Table 3 shows the example of parameters of actions and their weights.

Table 3. Examples of parameters of actions and their weights.

Action	Parameter Weights	Expected Weight
Backup database	action:1, database name:1, destination:1, mode:2, source:1	6
Restore database	action:1, database name:1, destination:1, source:1	6
Increase cpu	action:1, amount:2, server:1,	4
Increase tablespace	action:1, buffer:2, database name:1, server:1, table:2	7
Start db	action:1, database name:1, server:1	3

For any parameter that occurs in more than one action, we consider the weight of the parameter as 1. For example, for parameters such as database and server names, we consider their weight as 1. For parameters, specific to a change request, we consider their weight as 2. For example, we assign the weights for mode for database backup and buffer for tablespace as 2. Based on an incoming change request, we extract their parameters as described in Sect. 3.2. From the parameters, we determine the *actual_weight*. We consider *param_confusion* $= \frac{actual\_weight}{expected\_weight}$ to reason about C, T, and A. Consider the examples of cpu change requests from Table 2. For the change request *Add 2vCPU to server X*, the extracted parameters are the action (add), amount (2vCPU), and the server (X). We compute the actual weight by combining the weights of the action, amount, and the server from Table 3. The *param_confusion* comes to be 1 since we could identify all the parameters from the change request. For the change request *add outbound servers to X for RDP access*, we could identify the action (add) and the server (X). Thus, the *param_confusion* is computed as 0.5. Setting up a high threshold for the *param_confusion* above 0.8 will put the change request to others category.

4   Evaluation Methods

We evaluate our approach shown in Fig. 2 using the real-world data. For the evaluation, we create datasets with change requests from collected from different clients of IBM. Table 4 shows the details of datasets in terms of categories database and hardware. We chose database and hardware categories since they are considered as the most common categories for clients.

Table 4. Datasets prepared from various clients.

Datasets	#Change Requests	Database	Hardware
Client_B	498	296	201
Client_A	5429	3568	1861
Client_M	7213	4254	2959
Client_I	10692	7720	2971

For the database changes, the tasks we consider are (1) *backup, management*, (2) *run operations*, and (3) *user admin*. For the hardware changes, the tasks we consider are (1) *cpu* and (2) *memory*. For the database management task, we consider (1) *create database*, (2) *drop database*, (3) *increase tablespace*, and (3) *reduce tablespace*. For the database backup task, we consider (1) *backup* and (2) *restore* actions. For the database run operations task, we consider (1) *run sql script*, (2) *start database*, and (3) *stop database* actions. For the database user admin, we consider (1) *grant user* and (2) *revoke user* actions. For the hardware cpu task, we consider (1) *increase cpu* and (2) *reduce cpu* actions. For the hardware memory task, we consider the (1) *increase memory* and (2) *reduce memory* actions.

4.1   Evaluation of CTA Classification Approaches

In the first step of the classification, we label the data with respect to C, T, and A. For the labels, we collect the annotations from two annotators and compute their inter-rater agreement score. Then, we resolve the ambiguities to achieve a satisfactory agreement score ($> 80\%$). For the evaluation, we consider six approaches (1) SLC-A, (2) SLC-B, (3) CC, (4) LP, (5) CLUS-HMC, and (5) CSSAG describe in Sect. 3.1. For each approach, we perform the three-fold cross-validation. For each fold, we collect results in terms of macro precision, recall, and f-measure. We provide the results by averaging the results over each fold. Figure 4 shows the results for the classification of C, T, and A using SLC-A, SLC-B, CC, LP, CLUS-HMC, and CSSAG.

From the results, we observe that CC and LP perform better than other approaches across all the datasets. CC and LP perform better than hierarchical approaches such as CLUS-HMC and CSSAG may be due to the following reasons:

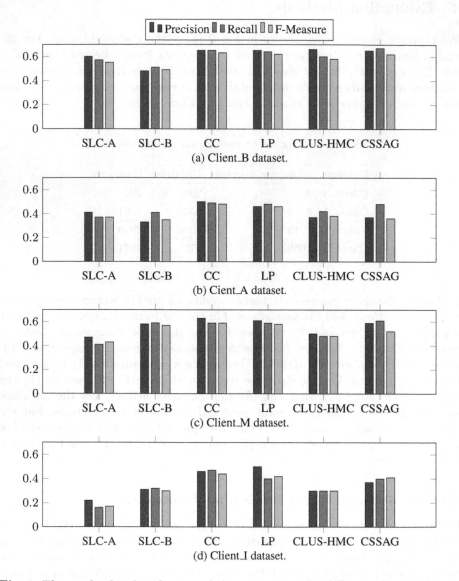

Fig. 4. The results for classification of change requests for different clients in terms macro precision, recall, and f-measure.

one, the depth of the hierarchy we consider is short (i.e., 3) and two, for the classification we consider the abstract for the change requests rather than their descriptions since for most cases descriptions were missing.

4.2   Evaluation of Parameter Extraction Approaches

To evaluate the extraction of parameters we employ CRF and LSTM. For the evaluation, we create separate datasets for each action. Then, we annotate words for each change request. For example, we annotate the change requests *[add, 2GB, RAM, to, server, abc01]* as *[action, amount, , ,server name]*. For empty slots, we extract the postag for each word and replace the empty slots with postags. Thus, for the change request the final set of labels are *[action, amount, ADP, NOUN,server name]*.

Since, CRF needs features to train a model, we extract the following features from a change request: (1) word is numeric, (2) alphanumeric, (3) is in the lower case, (4) is in the upper case, (5) the first letter in the word is upper case, (6) the word is a verb, (7) is a digit, (8) the postag of a word, (9) features related to the previous and (10) the next word in the change request. Compared to CRF, LSTM is agnostic of input features as it learns them directly from the data. Figure 5 shows the results for few actions for CRF and LSTM evaluated across four datasets. For brevity, we omitted results for other actions. The result shows that CRF performs significantly better than LSTM. The result is not surprising considering that LSTM needs a lot more data to train than CRF.

4.3   Evaluation of Feedback Approach

In this approach, we evaluate if the extracted parameters from a change request can be used to improve the classification of the change request. Before we evaluate we create a balanced dataset for each action by oversampling the underrepresented actions. For the evaluation, we consider CC as the baseline approach to identify categories and CRF to extract parameters.

In case of CC, the predicted labels for a database change request can be either [database], [database, management, increase tablespace], or [database, run operations, management, start database, increase tablespace]. Thus, based on the labels, first, we determine the actions to consider. For example, if the label is [database] we consider all the actions under the database category. Then, for each action, we extract parameters from the change request using CRF and compute *param_confusion*. Based on *param_confusion* values for each action, we determine the final label for the change request by choosing the action with maximum value. We compare the label obtained from the feedback approach with the labels obtained from CC. Figure 6 shows the results. Results indicate the feedback approach obtains higher accuracy results than the CC approach.

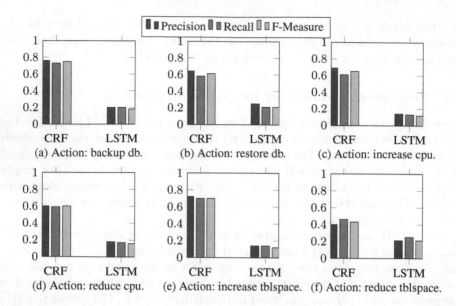

Fig. 5. The results for parameter extraction in terms precision, recall, and f-measure in terms of macro average.

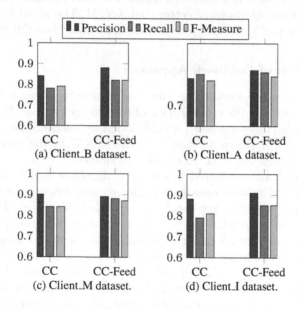

Fig. 6. The results for classification in terms precision, recall, and f-measure in terms of macro average.

5   Conclusion and Discussion

We provide Cataloger that classifies IT change requests into categories, tasks, and actions. For the classification, we employ six approaches: SLC-A, SLC-B, CC, LP, CLUS-HMC, and CSSAG. From the evaluation, we find CC and LP performs better than the other approaches. To extract parameters, we employ sequential classification techniques such as CRF and LSTM. Based on our evaluation, we observe that CRF performs better than LSTM. For the feedback approach, we consider CC and CRF. The feedback based approach based on the parameters improved over CC approach.

Our approach has several limitations. One, the dataset we use is not balanced across all the actions. Thus, we plan to use clustering based approaches [21] to minimize the labeling effort and get more labels. Two, the datasets we create for specific actions to identify parameters are not large. Thus, LSTM performed worse than CRF. We can increase the number of samples for each action to remove the dependency of extracting features using CRF. Third, in the feedback approach, we propose the heuristic approach based on $param\_confusion$ to make decisions. In future, we plan to improve the heuristic approach to improve the accuracy results.

References

1. Ayachitula, N., Buco, M.J., Diao, Y., Surendra, M., Pavuluri, R., Shwartz, L., Ward, C.: IT service management automation - a hybrid methodology to integrate and orchestrate collaborative human centric and automation centric workflows. In: Proceedings of the 4th International Conference on Services Computing, pp. 574–581. IEEE, Salt Lake City (2007)
2. Barutcuoglu, Z., Schapire, R.E., Troyanskaya, O.G.: Hierarchical multi-label prediction of gene function. Bioinformatics **22**(7), 830–836 (2006)
3. Bi, W., Kwok, J.T.: Multi-label classification on tree- and dag-structured hierarchies. In: Proceedings of the 28th International Conference on Machine Learning, pp. 17–24. PMLR, Bellevue (2011)
4. Blockeel, H., Raedt, L.D., Ramon, J.: Top-down induction of clustering trees. In: Proceedings of the 15th International Conference on Machine Learning, pp. 55–63. Morgan Kaufmann Publishers Inc, Madison (1998)
5. Bogojeska, J., Lanyi, D., Giurgiu, I., Stark, G., Wiesmann, D.: Classifying server behavior and predicting impact of modernization actions. In: Proceedings of the 9th International Conference on Network and Service Management, pp. 59–66. IEEE/ACM, Zurich, October 2013
6. Boutell, M.R., Luo, J., Shen, X., Brown, C.M.: Learning multi-label scene classification. Pattern Recogn. **37**, 1757–1771 (2004)
7. Cortes, C., Vapnik, V.: Support-vector networks. Mach. Learn. **20**(3), 273–297 (1995)
8. Finkel, J.R., Grenager, T., Manning, C.: Incorporating non-local information into information extraction systems by gibbs sampling. In: Proceedings of the 43rd Annual Meeting on Association for Computational Linguistics, pp. 363–370. Association for Computational Linguistics, Ann Arbor (2005)

9. Hochreiter, S., Schmidhuber, J.: Long short-term memory. Neural Comput. **9**(8), 1735–1780 (1997)

10. Kadar, C., Wiesmann, D., Iria, J., Husemann, D., Lucic, M.: Automatic classification of change requests for improved it service quality. In: Proceedings of Annual SRII Global Conference, pp. 430–439. IEEE, San Jose, March 2011

11. Lample, G., Ballesteros, M., Subramanian, S., Kawakami, K., Dyer, C.: Neural architectures for named entity recognition. In: Proceedings of Conference of the North American Chapter of the Association for Computational Linguistics: Human Language Technologies, pp. 260–270. ACL, San Diego (2016)

12. Le, V., Gulwani, S., Smartsynth, Z.: Synthesizing smartphone automation scripts from natural language. In: Proceedings of the 11th Annual International Conference on Mobile Systems, Applications, and Services, pp. 193–206. ACM, Taipei (2013)

13. Lucca, G.D.: An approach to classify software maintenance requests. In: Proceedings of the International Conference on Software Maintenance, pp. 93–102. IEEE, Montreal (2002)

14. Maksai, A., Bogojeska, J., Wiesmann, D.: Hierarchical incident ticket classification with minimal supervision. In: Proceedings of IEEE International Conference on Data Mining, pp. 923–928. IEEE, Shenzhen, December 2014

15. McCallum, A., Li, W.: Early results for named entity recognition with conditional random fields, feature induction and web-enhanced lexicons. In: Proceedings of the Seventh Conference on Natural Language Learning, pp. 188–191. Association for Computational Linguistics, Edmonton (2003)

16. Pandita, R., Xiao, X., Zhong, H., Xie, T., Oney, S., Paradkar, A.: Inferring method specifications from natural language api descriptions. In: Proceedings of the 34th International Conference on Software Engineering, pp. 815–825. IEEE, Zurich (2012)

17. Read, J., Pfahringer, B., Holmes, G., Frank, E.: Classifier chains for multi-label classification. Mach. Learn. **85**(3), 333–359 (2011)

18. Saggion, H., Funk, A., Maynard, D., Bontcheva, K.: Ontology-Based Information Extraction for Business Intelligence. In: Aberer, K., Choi, K.-S., Noy, N., Allemang, D., Lee, K.-I., Nixon, L., Golbeck, J., Mika, P., Maynard, D., Mizoguchi, R., Schreiber, G., Cudré-Mauroux, P. (eds.) ASWC/ISWC -2007. LNCS, vol. 4825, pp. 843–856. Springer, Heidelberg (2007). doi:10.1007/978-3-540-76298-0_61

19. Tsoumakas, G., Katakis, I., Vlahavas, I.: Random k-labelsets for multilabel classification. IEEE Trans. Knowl. Data Eng. **23**(7), 1079–1089 (2011)

20. Vens, C., Struyf, J., Schietgat, L., Džeroski, S., Blockeel, H.: Decision trees for hierarchical multi-label classification. Mach. Learn. **73**(2), 185–214 (2008)

21. Wang, F., Sun, J., Li, T., Anerousis, N.: Two heads better than one: Metric+Active learning and its applications for IT service classification. In: Proceedings of 9th International Conference on Data Mining, pp. 1022–1027. IEEE, Miami Beach, December 2009

22. Zhong, H., Zhang, L., Xie, T., Mei, H.: Inferring specifications for resources from natural language api documentation. Autom. Softw. Eng. **18**(3), 227–261 (2011)

ATLAS: A World-Wide Travel Assistant Exploiting Service-Based Adaptive Technologies

Antonio Bucchiarone$^{(\boxtimes)}$, Martina De Sanctis, and Annapaola Marconi

Fondazione Bruno Kessler, Via Sommarive, 18, Trento, Italy
{bucchiarone,msanctis,marconi}@fbk.eu

Abstract. Nowadays, users can count on a large amount of mobility services offering disparate functionalities and providing all needed information. Yet, from a user perspective, properly exploiting the available mobility services to organize journeys meeting personal expectations, is becoming a complex task. Indeed, discover and select the appropriate services in an open and constantly expanding domain, is a challenging and time-consuming task. We claim that a uniform and easy way for exploiting these services while moving around, getting accurate and personalized information is still missing. In this paper we propose a platform for the definition of value-added mobility services by (i) enhancing interoperability among the existing services, (ii) supporting their execution via run-time adaptation, (iii) through the definition of multi-channel front-end applications. On top of the platform, we have implemented and evaluated a world-wide travel assistant.

1 Introduction

Today, a multitude of applications offering flexible, dynamic and personalized mobility services to users are available in the *mobility domain*. These services are designed independently from each other and made available through a large variety of different technologies (e.g., web pages, mobile apps). They provide solutions that are fragmented, limited, and that have a partial coverage (e.g., only planning, only booking) of the overall journey. For instance, *Rome2Rio*[1] is a world-wide multi-modal journey planner, that offers traveling solutions between two given locations, but it is not consistently integrated in the (local) mobility offer of a city (i.e., local bus schedules). *Viaggia Trento*[2], instead, is an accurate local multi-modal planner for the city of Trento. In this context, often the users must interact with different applications to accomplish a journey. This makes the benefits of having multiple and accurate mobility services a drawback instead of an added value for the users. To overcome these limits and to leverage on the potentialities of the available services, we need a systemic and general approach dealing in a uniform way with services of an open and heterogeneous context. In this way, we can facilitate services integration and interoperability.

---

[1] https://www.rome2rio.com/.
[2] http://www.smartcommunitylab.it/apps/viaggia-trento/.

© Springer International Publishing AG 2017
M. Maximilien et al. (Eds.): ICSOC 2017, LNCS 10601, pp. 561–570, 2017.
https://doi.org/10.1007/978-3-319-69035-3_41

In this paper, we present a service delivery platform providing methods and techniques to design and release adaptive service-based applications. The platform capitalizes on the achievements and findings of our research in the last years. In particular, this work represents the combination of the following results: (1) a *design for adaptation* approach supporting the development, deployment and execution of service-based systems operating in dynamic environments [5,6]; (2) a comprehensive framework for *automated service composition* [4] that allows for context-aware service adaptation, and (3) a set of implemented software components and prototypes [1,9]. To show the potentiality offered by the platform, we implemented a world-wide travel assistant (ATLAS) able to provide accurate and context-aware traveling solutions.

In the rest of the paper we discuss the challenges behind this work, we presents all the details of our service delivery platform and its usage, and we report the experimental validation of the platform.

2   Challenges and Application Scenario

Nowadays, users can count on a large amount of mobility services. They may differ depending on the offered functionalities, the targeted users, or the provider. In particular, there are *journey planners* (e.g., Rome2Rio, Google Transit[3]) for finding traveling solutions between two or more given locations. Then, *specific mobility services* are those referring to specific transport modes (e.g., CityBikes[4] focuses exclusively on bike sharing data) or provided by transport companies (e.g., Flixbus[5], Trenitalia[6]). Moreover, an emerging trend is that of *shared mobility services* that are based on the shared use of vehicles, bicycles, or other means (e.g., Bla Bla Car[7]). Mobility services also differ in their *geographic coverage*. For instance, while Google Transit is a *global* planner, since it can be used for planning all around the world, ViaggiaTrento is a *local* planner for the city of Trento. The *transport modes coverage*, instead, measures the number of different transport means handled by mobility services (i.e., *single mode* and *multiple mode*). For instance, Flixbus and Trenitalia refer to a single transport mode, namely bus and train. To the contrary, journey planners usually consider different transport modes. Furthermore, both services dealing with one or a few transport modes and services having a local coverage are characterized by a high accuracy of the provided data. To the contrary, the more global are the services, the more they tend renounce accuracy. Focusing on cities, we can observe that there is a lot of disparate local services, which are specific for a few transport means and very accurate. However, this implies that, while moving around and changing their context, users need to discover and exploit the respective services

---

[3] https://maps.google.com/landing/transit/index.html.
[4] https://www.citybik.es/.
[5] https://www.flixbus.com/.
[6] http://www.trenitalia.com/.
[7] https://www.blablacar.com.

(and applications) in each city. To sum up, besides the huge amount of mobility services available up today, it is still missing for the users the possibility of getting **context-aware**, **accurate** and **personalized** travel solutions while moving around, without using different applications. In this context, there is no need for yet-another-mobility-app. Our goal, instead, is to provide a solution for enhancing mobility services interoperability through their runtime and context-aware discovery and composition, to exploit their potentialities and fill their gaps.

Application Scenario. Sara is living in Trento. She wants to visit Vienna, in Austria. ViaggiaTrento does not give her any results, being Vienna out of region, so she opens the Trenitalia mobile app and she starts planning. Unlikely, the founded solutions implies at least two changes, and she does not like the idea. Sara thinks that a rideshare or a bus solution would be also less expensive, if available. So she checks for both a BlaBlaCar ride and a Flixbus travel. Finally, she founds a cheap and direct solution among the ones given by Flixbus, and she books it. For organizing her travel, Sara has used four different mobility apps, by relying on her knowledge of services, without any support.

3   System Implementation

In this Section, we present our service delivery platform and a world-wide *personAlized TraveL AssiStant – ATLAS* developed on top of it. ATLAS consists in (i) a demonstrator showing the system's models and its execution and evolution through automatic runtime adaptation, and (ii) a Telegram[8] chat-bot, for the interaction with the users. We remark that ATLAS exploits real-world mobility services exposed as open APIs, which are wrapped as domain objects to be effectively part of the system.

3.1   Adaptive Service-Based Systems Through Domain Objects

The *Domain Object Model* [5,6] has been built to satisfy the need for service-based applications adaptable by-design. A domain object represents a uniform way to model independent, heterogeneous, and open services such that they can be easily interconnected thus enhancing *services interoperability*. Each domain object defines the behavior of the service it models–*core process* (e.g., BlaBlaCar ride-sharing), and the functionalities it provides–*fragments* (e.g., offer/require a car ride). Unlike traditional services, domain objects allow the partial specification of the expected behavior of a service by defining *abstract activities*. These activities are defined in terms of the *goal* they need to achieve (e.g., organize a journey). When, at runtime, abstract activities need to be executed, they can be *refined* according to the fragments offered by other domain objects, thus allowing the goal to be reached. Indeed, fragments represent executable processes that can be dynamically discovered, received and executed by a domain object.

---

[8] https://telegram.org/.

While abstract activities goals are defined at design time at a conceptual level, the need for refining them arises at runtime, triggering real services inter-operability. Indeed, only during the execution the system can discover and select the services effectively implementing the functionalities it needs, in the current context (i.e., a specific city). For example, only for users planning journeys starting from Trento, it makes sense to provide them the functionalities of the ViaggiaTrento app. Also fragments can be partially specified. In this way, their execution relies also on fragments provided by other domain objects, thus enabling a *chain of refinements* (as in Fig. 2). The refinement is performed through the application of advanced techniques for dynamic and incremental service composition [3] based on AI planning. We refer to [6] for details on the execution of adaptive systems via dynamic interactions among domain objects.

3.2   Domain Object-Based Platform

The platform is organized in three main layers, as shown in Fig. 1. The **Enablers** leverage on our previous results on the adaptive by-design wrapping of (mobility) services [5,6]. Developers can exploit and wrap up as domain objects the available services in the mobility domain. Besides the design of mobility services, enablers allow also for their runtime operation, as we will see further on. The **Mobility Services** layer exposes the functionalities implemented or facilitated by the Enablers. These services can exploit and/or combine into value-added services the functionalities of the services previously wrapped up and made available by the Enablers (i.e., services for user profiling, planning, booking, monitoring of journeys, etc.). The key idea is that the platform is open to continuous extensions with new services as domain objects. Their functionalities can thus be exploited in a transparent way to provide value-added services. All the platform mobility services can be eventually provided to final users through a range of multi-channels front-end applications that constitute the **Front-end** layer. These can be mobile or desktop applications, and they can be independent or rely on existing services (e.g., chat bots). The runtime operation of the services relies on different enablers.

Domain objects processes are executed by the *Process Engine*. It manages service requests among communicating processes and, when needed, it sends requests for domain objects instantiation to the *Domain Objects Manager*. In this way, correlations among processes are defined. During the normal execution, abstract activities can be met. They need to be refined with one or a composition of fragments modeling services functionalities. To this aim, the process engine sends a request for abstract activity refinement to the *Refinement Handler* component that is in charge of defining the corresponding *adaptation problem*. It defines the *problem domain* by selecting the proper fragments driven by the abstract activity's goal. The adaptation problem is submitted to the *Adaptation Manager* that translates it into a *planning problem* for the *AI Planner* component, which will send back a plan that can be injected into the abstract activity being refined.

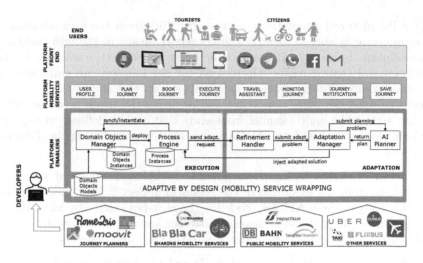

Fig. 1. Domain object-based platform.

3.3 Travel Assistant Implementation

In this Section, with the platform in mind, we detail ATLAS travel assistant[9], and how applications can be realized on top of our platform. To realize a world-wide travel assistant able to provide to the users the proper mobility services in the specific context(s) of their journeys, we selected real-world mobility services exposed as open APIs. We identified their behavior and functionalities and their input and output data. Finally, we wrapped them up as domain objects to be stored in the platform knowledge base. For instance, we wrapped *Rome2Rio* and *Google Transit* as global journey planners and *ViaggiaTrento* as local planner, for the city of Trento. Combining the geographical coverage of global planners with the accuracy of local planners is a concrete example of services interoperability promoted by our platform. Other examples are *Travel for London*[10] as local planner, *BlaBlaCar* as ridesharing service, *CityBikes* as bike sharing services applying to about 400 cities, *Trentino Trasporti*[11] for the public transportation in the Trentino region. Being defined as domain objects, all these services can now be executed, automatically composed and adapted by the Enablers of the platform.

At the Mobility Services platform level, instead, we can find the *Travel Assistant* defined as a value-added service leveraging on the services available in the system. Its main features are the following: (i) given a user planning request, it is able to decide between a *local* or a *global* planning solution; (ii) given the planners responses, it defines the better way to show this responses to the user

---

[9] ATLAS is available here: https://github.com/das-fbk/ATLAS-Personalized-Travel-Assistant.

[10] https://api.tfl.gov.uk/.

[11] http://www.ttesercizio.it/.

(e.g., a list of travel alternatives, a message); (iii) given the user selection, the travel assistant is able to identify the transport means in the legs making the entire solution. In this way, it can incrementally provide to the user specific functionalities and context-aware information for her journey. We emphasize here that the more (mobility) services are wrapped up and stored in the system's knowledge base, the more responsive and accurate the travel assistant will be. Finally, among the multi-channel front-ends that can be defined on top of the platform, we realized ATLAS as a Telegram chat-bot, exploiting the Telegram's open API.

Executing ATLAS. In Fig. 2, we report examples of *chains of incremental refinements*, from the execution of the scenario in Sect. 2. The execution starts from the core process of ATLAS, modeling the chat-bot started by Sara. We focus on the refinement of the `Plan Journey` abstract activity, whose goal consists in finding a travel plan. The refinement generates the following steps.

Step 1. The fragment `PlanJourney` of the Travel Assistant is selected and injected in the process of ATLAS. It allows Sara to insert the source and destination locations and to send a journey plan request. The activities `Plan Request` and `Plan Response` of this fragment model the communication between it and its core process, where the request is handled. In our scenario, being the destination Vienna, the Travel Assistant will go for a global plan, by executing a fragment from the Rome2Rio domain object.

Step 2. To properly show the travel alternatives to the user, an appropriate data visualization pattern must be selected, based on the data format (e.g., a list, a message). This is defined at runtime, by the Data Viewer domain object providing the `DefineDataViewerPattern` fragment for this purpose. Thus, Sara receives the list of the found travel alternatives satisfying her requirements.

Step 3. Sara selects her preferred alternative (suppose the first one, a multi-modal solution made by a train and a bus travels). Based on her choice, the `Define Journey Legs` abstract activity is refined with the `HandleJourneyLegs` fragment, which defines the goal for the `Specialize Journey` abstract activity, whose refinement allows the Travel Assistant to find the proper fragments for each journey leg.

Step 4. The last step shows a *composition* of fragments provided by the transport companies involved in the legs of the user selection (e.g., Sudtirol Alto Adige and Hello). Their execution provides to Sara the proper solutions, from the two companies.

In conclusion, this execution example exhibits the *bottom-up* nature of the approach, from grounding services till the user process. This happens in a completely transparent way for the user that interacts with only one application, ATLAS.

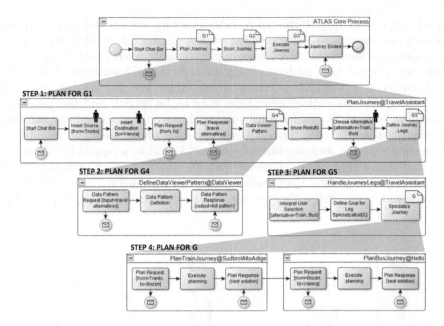

Fig. 2. ATLAS: an example of the system execution via incremental and dynamic refinements. For each fragment, we specify its name and the domain object which it belongs to.

4   Evaluation

To evaluate the *effectiveness* and *efficiency* of our platform, we have run a set of experiments based on real-world problems[12]. We ran ATLAS using a dual-core CPU running at 2.7 GHz, with 8 Gb memory. To show its *feasibility*, we evaluate: (**1**) How long it takes to wrap up real services as domain objects; (**2**) How much automatic refinement (service selection and composition) affects the execution of ATLAS. Based on our experience, we can argue that to wrap a real service as a domain object, the developer needs (i) to master the domain objects modeling notation and (ii) to understand the service behavior, its functionalities, its input/output data format and how to query it. Wrapping time clearly changes between experienced and non-expert developers. From our analysis, it ranges from 4 to 6 h, considering average complex services. Moreover, it is also relevant to claim that this activity is done *una tantum*: after wrapping, the service is seamlessly part of the platform. To evaluate the automatic refinement, we collected both the adaptation and mobility services execution statistics, to understand how long they take, on average, to be executed. We carried out an

---

[12] The specification of ATLAS used for the evaluation contains 14 domain object models, 17 fragment models and 12 types of domain properties. Domain properties are high-level representations of the domain concepts, and they are used to evaluate the conditions under which each fragment can be exploited (for details refer to [5,6]).

experiment considering 10 runs of ATLAS handling various end-users' requests. For each run, more than 150 refinement cases were generated. As shown in Fig. 3, the majority of the problems have a complexity in-between 0 and 19 transitions, while the most complex problems range from 80 to 100 transitions. Notice that the occurrence of complex problems is relatively rare. For all the runs, only 3% of the problems require more than 0.5 s to be solved, and the worst case is anyhow below 1.5 s. To measure how much automatic refinement influences the execution of ATLAS, we compared the data about the time required for adaptation with the response time of real-world services wrapped in ATLAS. As expected, Fig. 4 shows that problems with the most complex planning domain take more planning time than problem with less complexity. In the worst case, the adaptation requires a time close to 1.5 s, while the services response time

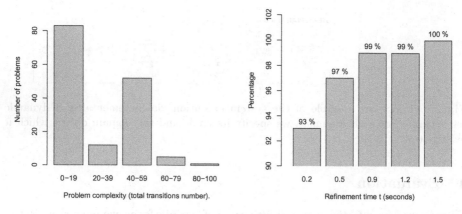

Fig. 3. (Left) **Distribution of Problems Complexity:** it shows the distribution of problem complexity of adaptation problems calculated as the *total amount of transitions* in the state transition systems representations of the domain properties and fragments present in each problem. (Right) **Percentage of refinement problems solved within time t.**

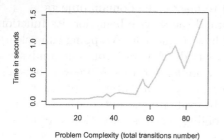

Services Response Time	
Service Name	**Avg. Response Time**
Bla Bla Car	0.78 secs
City Bikes	0.23 secs
Google Transit	0.65 secs
Rome 2Rio	1.20 secs
Travel for London	3.20 secs
Viaggia Trento	0.77 secs

Fig. 4. (Left) **Trend of the Adaptation Time:** it relates the (average) time required to solve a composition problem to the problem complexity. It is computed considering in the 10 runs all the refinement problems having the same complexity. (Right) **Services Response Time:** it refers to (a subset of) ATLAS real mobility services.

ranges from 0.23 to 3.20 s. Moreover, the adaptation takes more time for the most complex problems that are the less frequent to occur. We argue that the automatic refinement responsiveness is equivalent to that of mobility services.

5 Related Work and Conclusion

Open services are easy to understand and to access services and can be exploited to develop applications or new value-added services. Web APIs are the most common way to specify them. To overcome the limitations of semantic web services (i.e., the use of non-standard languages for description) a model for Linked Open Services has been introduced in [7] in which services are viewed as RDF "prosumers". With the rise in popularity of web APIs, platforms for their management and customization, called *API management platform*, have been provided. However, while advances in web services and their composition enable automation and reuse, new challenges have emerged in the case of APIs. The service developer requires sound understanding of the different service types, access-methods, and input/output data formats [8] (e.g., XML, JSON, SOAP, HTTP). ServiceBase [2] proposes a Unified Services Representation Model where common service-related low-level logic can be abstracted and reused by other applications developer. With it a set of APIs have been implemented that expose a common and high-level interface for integrating heterogeneous services in a simplified manner. Organizations like Mashery[13] and Apigee[14] are building on these trends to provide platforms for the management of APIs. For instance, ProgrammableWeb[15] now has more than 10,000 API in its directory. However, despite advances in SOA, complete solutions for open services management are yet required. There is still a need to make services easy to understand and to access. Our service delivery platform is an attempt to solve the previous open issues and to provide a complete solution for open services management and exploitation. The core idea is to factorize the capabilities offered by service providers as a set of building blocks (i.e., domain-objects), which can be easily combined to give place to composite services that can be published and exploited.

In conclusion, we have presented a service delivery platform providing engineering methods and techniques to design and release adaptive service-based applications. We have shown how applications can be realized on top of it exploiting the functionalities provided by real-world services. As stated, our platform requires that services are previously wrapped as domain-objects to be used. Although this may seem a limitation, we can argue that the service wrapping activity can be performed as a collective co-development process, in a crowd-sourcing style. Furthermore, *open data* can help to overcome the limitations imposed by services that are not open. Extensions of our platform refers to the inclusion of functionalities provided by smart things, in the IoT sense, and the support for other forms of run-time adaptation.

---

[13] http://www.mashery.com.
[14] http://apigee.com.
[15] http://www.programmableweb.com.

References

1. DeMOCAS: Domain objects for service-based collective adaptive systems. https://github.com/das-fbk/DeMOCAS/
2. Chai Barukh, M., Benatallah, B.: ServiceBase: a programming knowledge-base for service oriented development. In: Proceedings of 18th International Conference on Database Systems for Advanced Applications, DASFAA 2013, Part II, pp. 123–138 (2013)
3. Bucchiarone, A., Marconi, A., Mezzina, C.A., Pistore, M., Raik, H.: On-the-fly adaptation of dynamic service-based systems: incrementality, reduction and reuse. In: Basu, S., Pautasso, C., Zhang, L., Fu, X. (eds.) ICSOC 2013. LNCS, vol. 8274, pp. 146–161. Springer, Heidelberg (2013). doi:10.1007/978-3-642-45005-1_11
4. Bucchiarone, A., Marconi, A., Pistore, M., Raik, H.: A context-aware framework for dynamic composition of process fragments in the Internet of Services. J. Internet Serv. Appl. **8**(1), 6 (2017)
5. Bucchiarone, A., Sanctis, M., Marconi, A., Pistore, M., Traverso, P.: Design for adaptation of distributed service-based systems. In: Barros, A., Grigori, D., Narendra, N.C., Dam, H.K. (eds.) ICSOC 2015. LNCS, vol. 9435, pp. 383–393. Springer, Heidelberg (2015). doi:10.1007/978-3-662-48616-0_27
6. Bucchiarone, A., De Sanctis, M., Marconi, A., Pistore, M., Traverso, P.: Incremental composition for adaptive by-design service based systems. In: IEEE 23rd International Conference on Web Services (2016)
7. Krummenacher, R., Norton, B., Marte, A.: Towards linked open services and processes. In: Berre, A.J., Gómez-Pérez, A., Tutschku, K., Fensel, D. (eds.) FIS 2010. LNCS, vol. 6369, pp. 68–77. Springer, Heidelberg (2010). doi:10.1007/978-3-642-15877-3_8
8. Lucky, M.N., Cremaschi, M., Lodigiani, B., Menolascina, A., Paoli, F.: Enriching API descriptions by adding API profiles through semantic annotation. In: Sheng, Q.Z., Stroulia, E., Tata, S., Bhiri, S. (eds.) ICSOC 2016. LNCS, vol. 9936, pp. 780–794. Springer, Cham (2016). doi:10.1007/978-3-319-46295-0_55
9. Raik, H., Bucchiarone, A., Khurshid, N., Marconi, A., Pistore, M.: Astro-Captevo: dynamic context-aware adaptation for service-based systems. In: Eighth IEEE World Congress on Services, SERVICES, pp. 385–392 (2012)

Services in Organizations, Business and Society

A Variability Model for Store-Oriented Software Ecosystems: An Enterprise Perspective

Bahar Jazayeri[1]([✉]), Olaf Zimmermann[2], Gregor Engels[1],
and Dennis Kundisch[1]

[1] Paderborn University, Paderborn, Germany
{bahar.jazayeri,gregor.engels,dennis.kundisch}@upb.de
[2] University of Applied Sciences of Eastern Switzerland, Rapperswil, Switzerland
ozimmerm@hsr.ch

Abstract. Pioneers of today's software industry like Salesforce and Apple have established successful ecosystems around their software platforms. Architectural knowledge of the existing ecosystems is implicit and fragmented among online documentation. In protection of intellectual property, existing documentation hardly reveals influential business strategies that affect the ecosystem structure. Thus, other platform providers can hardly learn from the existing ecosystems in order to systematically make reasonable design decisions with respect to their business strategies to create their own ecosystems. In this paper, we identify a variability model for architectural design decisions of a store-oriented software ecosystem product line from an enterprise perspective, comprising business, application, and infrastructure views. We derive the variability model from fragmentary material of existing ecosystems and a rigorous literature review using a research method based on the design science paradigm. To show its validity, we describe real-world ecosystems from diverse domains using the variability model. This knowledge helps platform providers to develop customized ecosystems or to recreate existing designs in a systematic way. This, in turn, contributes to an increase in designer and developer productivity.

Keywords: Software ecosystems · Variabilities · Architectural decisions

1 Introduction

Pioneers of today's software industry like Salesforce and Apple have established successful ecosystems around their software platforms. In literature, software ecosystem is defined as "a software platform, a set of internal and external developers and a community of domain experts in service to a community of users that compose relevant solution elements to satisfy their needs" [1]. Using online stores is known to be a novel way to improve value creation in the market

This work was supported by the German Research Foundation (DFG) within the Collaborative Research Center "On-The-Fly Computing" (CRC 901).

© Springer International Publishing AG 2017
M. Maximilien et al. (Eds.): ICSOC 2017, LNCS 10601, pp. 573–588, 2017.
https://doi.org/10.1007/978-3-319-69035-3_42

by facilitating a fast adoption of request and provision [2,3]. There is a group of ecosystems that use online stores to distribute native and third-party applications. We refer to this group of ecosystems as store-oriented software ecosystems. In recent years, this kind of software ecosystems have diversified in many different ways, e.g., in software type and target group of users [4]. For instance, independent developers of open source communities develop software plug-ins on the basis of development platforms like Eclipse integrated development environment (IDE) and publish them on Eclipse Marketplace[1]. On the contrary, mobile App ecosystems target a completely different user group, i.e., mobile users, by growing around mobile operating systems such as iOS and Android. Whereas, a third group of ecosystems flourishes around cloud computing platforms like Salesforce and Amazon Web Services (AWS).

The architectural knowledge of the existing ecosystems is implicit and available in a fragmentary way among online documentation in form of manuals and "how to" guides as well as entries in questions-and-answers forums. In protection of intellectual property, existing documentation hardly reveals influential business strategies of platform providers that affect the ecosystem structure. Thus, other platform providers can hardly learn from the existing ecosystems to systematically make reasonable design decisions with respect to their business strategies in order to build their own ecosystems. This lack of knowledge hinders novel designs of ecosystems in a variety of domains. For instance, existing Internet-of-Things online stores are still far less mature than their mobile App counterparts [5]. Hence, this question remains open *how to enable systematic development of store-oriented software ecosystems*.

A product line for store-oriented software ecosystems enables the systematic development of these systems and provides a structured knowledge base in this field. According to software product line engineering objectives, such a product line should identify the commonalities and "systematically handles the variation (i.e., the differences)" of the ecosystems that belong to the product line [6]. Some works in literature [7,8] reveal the importance of variability management for various activities of software development, e.g., requirements engineering, design, and testing. Whereas Metzger and Pohl [6] clearly distinguish between variability of a software product line and application variability.

In this paper, we identify variabilities of architectural design decisions for a store-oriented software ecosystem product line. The contribution of this paper is twofold: (a) We derive a variability model from fragmentary material of existing ecosystems and by conducting a rigorous literature review using a research method based on the design science paradigm proposed by Nickerson et al. [9]. The variability model adheres to the well-known enterprise architectural views to support the inclusion of architectural decisions from both business and IT perspectives. (b) We provide insight into a diverse range of real-world software ecosystems in enterprise application, mobile App, cloud computing, open source development, and Internet-of-Things (IoT) by analyzing them based on the variability model. Our in-depth analysis shows that the variability model provides

---

[1] marketplace.eclipse.org, Last Access: May 2017.

a suitable abstraction to describe important technical and business decisions of a diverse range of store-oriented software ecosystems in different domains. This knowledge helps platform providers to create customized ecosystems or to recreate the existing designs in a systematic way. This, in turn, contributes to an increase in designer and developer productivity.

In the following, Sect. 2 describes the research method, which is used to develop the variability model. Section 3 presents the variability model, followed by Sect. 4 that analyzes the existing ecosystems based on the variability model. Section 5 discusses the relation of the variabilities to design artifacts of store-oriented software ecosystems. Section 6 considers related work. Finally, the paper concludes in Sect. 7.

2   Research Method

This section presents a research method that we use to develop a variability model for a store-oriented software ecosystem product line. Nickerson et al. [9] propose a taxonomy development method based on the design science research paradigm [10] to classify objects of study based on their common characteristics. The result is a set of dimensions, while each dimension consists of mutually exclusive and collectively exhaustive characteristics. Initially, meta-characteristics are defined. They are the most comprehensive characteristics that serve as a basis to identify further characteristics for each dimension. The method includes two types of iterations, i.e., empirical-to-conceptual and conceptual-to-empirical iterations. At the end of each iteration, the taxonomy is checked against ending conditions [9].

To derive our variability model, first, we need to identify meta-characteristics. In our case, the meta-characteristics should assist with identifying differentiation points, i.e., initial sources of architectural variabilities, among software ecosystems. We identify three meta-characteristics by referring to the definition of software ecosystem presented in Sect. 1: (a) What a platform consist of, (b) Collaborations upon which a platform supports service provision, and (c) What a platform offers as products/services. Furthermore, we set the ending conditions as follows: The development of variability model is terminated when the last iterations do not result in identification of any new variability or when currently identified variabilities are not further enriched.

In the empirical-to-conceptual iteration, we analyze existing ecosystems with respect to their architectural design decisions and the meta-characteristics, then, we draw the first dimensions of variability model. In our previous work [11], we develop a list of store-oriented software ecosystems in different domains including 18 ecosystems in total (Mobile Apps: Apple App Store, Google Play, Microsoft Store, BlackBerry World, Amazon.com: Apps & Games. Web browser plugins: Mozilla Firefox Marketplace, Google Chrome Store. In-house software: SAP Store. Cloud services: StrikeIron, SalesForce AppExchange, AWS Marketplace, Oracle Cloud Marketplace. Open source software: Eclipse Marketplace, Binpress Marketplace, and Cytoscape App Store. Web services: Mashape. Others: Envato

Market, CTAN: Packages). We take this list as an initial point to examine the existing ecosystems. The ecosystems are chosen from different domains. Afterwards, we analyze the ecosystems by inspecting technical documentation that are available on the Internet. Such documentation usually comes in the form of online manuals in developer portals, "how to" guides and official documentation provided by platform providers as well as samples and demos. In addition, if enrollment in the ecosystems is made possible, we register as developer and experiment the way that the ecosystems work. However, the mentioned activities do not provide us a deep understanding of platform providers' business strategies. Therefore, we additionally explore their annual reports e.g., using AnnualReports.com, and well-reputed business magazines as well as entries in questions-and-answers forums.

In the conceptual-to-empirical iteration, we supplement the variability model with our implication from the literature regarding the meta-characteristics and the differences between the real-world ecosystems and the concepts addressed in the literature. We consider the most influential journal, conference, and workshop publications relevant to software ecosystems (e.g., [1,12–14]) as well as the publications from the International Workshop on Software Ecosystems (IWSECO). The step-wise development of the variabilities is validated by examining ecosystems that are randomly chosen and are not in our initial list. More details on the examination of existing ecosystems, a complete list of sources of the literature review, and the iterations performed during the development of variability model can be found in our technical report [15].

3 Variability Model for Store-Oriented Software Ecosystem Product Line

In this section, first, we present the variabilities of architectural design decisions of a store-oriented software ecosystem product line, i.e., variation points and variants, followed by introducing their dependencies. Then, we discuss the role of business and technical context in realization of variabilities in practice.

3.1 Variation Points and Variants

A variability model that captures alternative design decisions includes variation points and variants. While a variation point refers to the subject of a variability, a variant represents the object of variability [16, p. 62]. Figure 1 shows the variability model. We use the orthogonal variability model (OVM) notation [17] to represent the variabilities as first class architectural knowledge entities. We consider this explicit representation as an advantage for actors of software ecosystems, which usually collaborate from independent development teams and different backgrounds [1]. In Fig. 1, a triangle with solid border line is a mandatory variation point. A triangle with dashed border line is an optional variation point. Each rectangle presents a variant. A variant with solid line variability dependency is

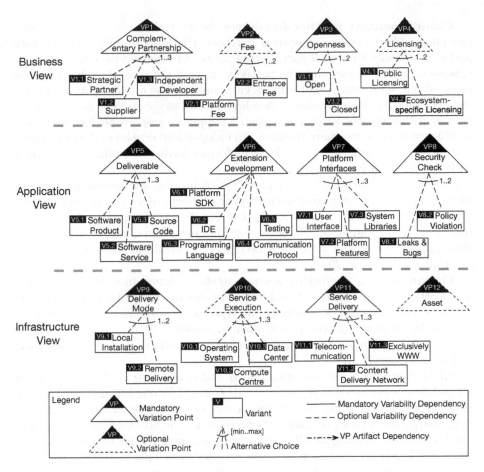

Fig. 1. Excerpt from the variability model for store-oriented software ecosystems [15]

a mandatory design choice whereas a variant with dashed line variability dependency is an optional choice. There can be alternative choices among variants with optional variability dependencies.

The variation points and their variants are organized into three main groups, i.e., business, application, and infrastructure. This clustering is based on well-known architectural views to enterprise architecture [18]. Different enterprise architecture frameworks identify slightly different views. In this paper, we conform to the architectural views provided by TOGAF, which is an enterprise architecture framework standardized by The Open Group[2].

3.1.1 Business view. This view encompasses influential variabilities of business strategies to create an ecosystem environment.

---

[2] www.opengroup.org/subjectareas/enterprise/togaf, Last Access: May 2017.

Complementary partnership defines the strategic decisions that platform providers make to choose ecosystem partners. Platform providers choose such partners in a way that each partner contributes to final service provisioning to ecosystem users. To this end, the partners support the ecosystem by providing value-adding solutions. A platform provider may choose a partner as a strategic partner, supplier, or independent developer. A strategic partner is a long-term partner with deep access to the platform. A supplier is responsible for providing a specific software or hardware resource. An independent developer develops third-party applications on top of the platform despite having an indirect partnership with the platform provider [19].

Fee is a medium for platform providers to protect intellectual property by introducing different degree of payments for platform users and complementary partners. This has a direct relation to different degree of access to the platform that is granted to an actor. Moreover, external developers, who wish to publish their application on the store, may need to pay certain amount of periodic or one-time entrance fee [20].

Openness, as a distinctive business strategy, determines whether content and methods of ecosystems are subject to access or change by complementary partners. Openness has two variants, i.e., open and closed. However, ecosystems can hardly be judged as completely open or closed. The degree of openness in ecosystems depends on the realization of this variation point at management and strategic levels [21].

Licensing is legal rules governing usage and redistribution of software. There are public software licensings such as GNU General Public License (GPL). GPL allows free usage, execute, and altering source code. In general, ecosystems may use such public licenses or may introduce their own licensing system. On one hand, choice of licensing usually conforms to end-user license of agreement. On the other hand, ecosystems may allow external developers to freely decide to make their source code available under a different license [22].

3.1.2 Application view. This view presents architectural decisions concerning the way that software platforms are made extendable. This includes techniques that enable independent developers to develop applications on top of the platforms and security constraints to avoid violating regulation.

Deliverable is the type of software artifact that is delivered to users. This can be software products, software services as well as source code. We distinguish between software products like mobile Apps that are installed on local devices and software services like cloud services that are executed on a remote server. Deliverables accordingly address different target groups of users, e.g., software developers, users of mobile devices, and enterprises.

Extension Development includes techniques that enable independent developers to develop their applications on top of platforms. Integrated development environment (IDE), programming language, communication protocol, and testing functions are the various architectural components that a platform provider may include in the design of an ecosystem. In addition, it is interesting that all ecosystems, which we examined during the development of the variability model, include Software development kits (SDKs) in their architecture. Therefore, we define SDK as a mandatory variant that enable external developers to extend the platforms. Moreover, including Wikis and forums support social communication among developers, who usually work independently [23]. In addition, an ecosystem may enable the composition of external applications. For instance, Intents[3] allows developers to compose Android Apps.

Platform Interfaces are gateways to external developers. The architecture of software platform needs to provide the right modularity and granularity so that the external developers become able to correspond to relevant software components [24]. The variability model recognizes different groups of components as follows: System libraries, graphical user interface components, and platform features. System libraries provide access to core functionalities of platforms, e.g., access to OS kernel, memory management, and resource sharing. Furthermore, there are direct interfaces to built-in capabilities of software platforms. We call such built-in capabilities *platform features*. Platform features are specific to a certain platform or domain that developers often require to work with them, e.g., GPS, camera, and audio control in mobile OS platforms. Essentially, platform providers need to keep the interfaces consistent during ecosystem evolution. This includes suitable change propagation and update management among platform components and third-party applications [25].

Security check includes a wide range of security and policy checking functions to protect ecosystems from malware, unwanted actions, and misuse. A typical way to realize such security checks is to apply a review process when external developers would like to enter the ecosystem. The review process mainly considers security leaks, bugs, and policy violations of externally developed applications before being published on stores.

3.1.3 Infrastructure view. This view comprises the variability of hardware and software infrastructure to realize functions of the application view. This includes deployment and operation of software solutions at the user side.

Delivery mode determines how deliverables are delivered to the users. This can be using local installation of executable files or remote execution of software services. Examples of remote delivery of services are using cloud computing and remote procedure call to web services. A hybrid approach is applied when both variants are chosen.

Service execution implies suitable infrastructure for the execution of deliverables. It is an optional variation point, i.e., in some ecosystems, e.g., where deliverable is source code, no execution of deliverables is needed. While in other ecosystems, e.g., mobile ecosystems, applications require an operating system to be executed. Furthermore, service provision using cloud and web services requires support of distributed compute and data centers.

Service delivery includes the technologies that facilitate delivery of deliverables to the users. This can be exclusively performed on the basis of World

---

[3] developer.android.com/reference/android/content/Intent.html, Last Access: May 2017.

Wide Web or by support of infrastructure suppliers, i.e., providers of telecommunications and content delivery network services. External suppliers may be employed to handle the high performance service delivery in different networks like Intranet, Extranet, and Internet.

Asset is a device or a set of devices provided by platform providers to realize ecosystem deliverable on the user's side. Asset provision is an optional variation point, which can be delegated to complementary partnerships too.

3.2   Variability Constraint Dependencies

The variability model reveals dependencies between the variation points and variants. For readability reasons, the most important dependencies are illustrated in Table 1. Here, a variation point or a variant may require another variation point or variant in order to be realized. Service execution (VP10), telecommunication (V11.1), content delivery network (V11.2) and asset (VP12) require support of suppliers (VP1.2) in order to be realized. This is due to the fact that platform providers are normally software providers, who wish to build an ecosystem around their platforms. Providing all resources, which are required for manufacturing assets and infrastructure to deliver and execute services, if possible for such providers, is very costly.

If a platform provider decides to (partially) close an ecosystem (V3.2), security check at the application view need to be applied (VP8) and source code in SDK needs to be suitably closed (V6.1). Moreover, delivery of software products (V5.1) requires local installation on users' devices (V9.1) whereas delivery of software services (V5.2) requires support of remote servers (V9.2).

Table 1. Variability constraint dependencies

Variation point/Variant	Variation point/Variant	Requires
VP10: Service Execution, V11.1: Telecommunication, V11.2.: Content delivery network, VP12: Asset	V1.2: Supplier	✓
V3.2: Closed	VP8: Security check, V6.1: SDK	✓
V5.1: Software Product	V9.1: Local installation	✓
V5.2: Software Service	V9.2: Cloud delivery	✓

3.3   Business and Technical Context

Business strategy and technical context are the main drivers of architectural decisions in an IT enterprise. This implies the variabilities are subject to different realizations by different platform providers. These differences refer to contextual information, which comes from the context and domain of an enterprise or software project. The contextual information determines why and how a variability is realized in real-world [16, p. 62]. Aggregation of different realizations of the variabilities in Fig. 1 can result in very different ecosystems. For instance, due to certain business strategies, developers in an ecosystem are expected to extend a platform strictly whereas in another ecosystem, developers are free to develop standalone applications for a platform. To consider the role of context, we refer to Kruchten [26] that identifies the most important dimensions of context in software development projects as follows: Size, criticality, age, rate of system change, team distribution, governance model, business model, and presence of a stable architecture. These dimensions are relevant to domain and industry, degree of innovation, corporate and culture, and organizational maturity.

4 Describing Existing Ecosystems by Using the Variability Model

We analyze a diverse range of real-world software ecosystems using the variability model to ensure that the model provides a suitable abstraction to describe ecosystems from different domains. This analysis provides concrete instances for the variations points and variants of Fig. 1. Accordingly we choose five ecosystems from enterprise application, mobile App, cloud computing, open source development, and IoT. The ecosystems are grown on top of different kinds of software platforms and provide different types of software services.

Salesforce.com is a provider of customer relationship management and enterprise services. Salesforce and force.com are its main software platforms. On top of these platforms, a working environment including Salesforce proprietary services and third-party Apps is built. Independent developers publish third-party Apps on the Salesforce's store, namely, AppExchange[4].

Apple Inc. is the provider of mobile and desktop hardware assets (iPhone, MacBook, etc.) and operating systems (iOS and MacOS). iOS acts as a platform for independent developers to develop mobile Apps on top of it. Such Apps can be made available for mobile users on Apple App Store.

Amazon.com is an e-commerce company and the provider of Amazon Web Services (AWS). AWS refer to a wide range of SaaS, PaaS, and IaaS services. Other service providers can customize instances of AWS and trade them on AWS marketplace[5]. AWS marketplace offers such providers licensing and billing services. In addition, Amazon.com is the provider of a smart voice assistant platform, namely Alexa. Alexa is designed to handle tasks like home automation and controlling connected smart devices. Independent developers develop third-party applications, namely Alexa skills, for the Alexa platform. These skills are published on Alexa Skill Store[6].

Eclipse Foundation consists of a hierarchy of leading and contributing projects, which govern the Eclipse ecosystem. Eclipse IDE is the software platform for open source software communities. An organization may officially

---

[4] appexchange.salesforce.com, Last Access: May 2017.
[5] aws.amazon.com/marketplace, Last Access: May 2017.
[6] www.amazon.com/b?node=13727921011, Last Access: May 2017.

Table 2. Describing the ecosystems based on the variabilities of business view

Variation Point	Variant	Provider: salesforce.com Platform: Salesforce and force.com Store: AppExchange	Provider: Apple Inc. Platform: iOS Store: Apple App Store	Provider: Amazon.com Platform: AWS Store: AWS Marketplace	Provider: Eclipse Foundation Platform: Eclipse IDE Store: Eclipse Marketplace	Provider: Amazon.com Platform: Alexa Store: Alexa Skills Store
VP1: Complementary Partnership	V1.1: Strategic Partner	- Deloitte Digital Hub: A customer relationship management web-based App (Deloitte Digital) - Telco Sales-360: A preconfigured telecommunication solution (Tech Mahindra)	- Business and enterprise Apps supported by cloud services optimised for iOS (IBM) - Enterprise Next: A set of consulting services on Apple devices (Deloitte)	- Commercial vendors including IBM, Microsoft, SAP, 10gen, CA, Couchbase, Canonical - Open-source provision from Nginx, Drupal, etc.	- Eclipse Foundation: The core member-based decision makers - Several projects with different degrees of contribution	- Build-in services for several partners, e.g., Spotify, WeMo, Nest, Uber, etc.
	V1.2: Supplier	- Databases, Exadata, and Java platform (Oracle) - Servers with AMD processors (Dell) - Emailing system (MessageSystems). - Security assessment (Symantec) (KPMG) - CDN by a partner	- CDN to deliver App Store contents (Level 3) - Processors (Intel, historically from Samsung and TSMC) - Modems (Intel and Qualcomm depending on local telco provider) - Networking services (AT&T and Verizon)	- AWS Test Drive (Orbitera) - SaaS-based migration and Disaster Recovery solutions (CloudEndure) - Many telco partnerships	Not realized	- Chips (Intel, Conexant) - Voice processing hardware (Conexant)
	V1.3: Independent Developer	- Developers of Apps on Salesforce AppExchange	- Developers of Apps on Apple App Store	- ISVs - Cloud service providers - Consulting partners	- Eclipse committers - Individual projects (e.g., TopCased)	- Developers of Alexa Skills
VP2: Fee	V2.1: Platform Fee	- The platform fee varies with platform licenses	- No fee	- Cost of using AWS (e.g., pay per hour or per day)	- Open-source, non-profit, and free	- No fee for AWS Lambda - Fee for other AWS
	V2.2: Entrance Fee	- Annual fee to list Apps on the store - Different fees for different partnership tiers	- Annual fee to list Apps on the store - Different fees for independent developers and enterprises	- One time fee to list commercial services on the store - No fee for free services	- No fee to list plug-ins on the store	- No fee to list skills on the store - No registration cost
VP3: Openness	V3.1: Open	- force.com IDE - SDKs for iOS and Android - Aura UI Framework	- A few libraries like Open Source Reference Library	- AWS SDKs - Open Source Software projects for AWS	- Eclipse IDE - Eclipse projects (decided by developer)	- Skills Kit SDK for Node.js & Java
	V3.2: Closed	- Most of the platform frameworks	- Most of the platform frameworks	- The platform is mainly closed	- Based on developers' decision	- The platform is mainly closed
VP4: Licensing	V4.1: Public Licensing	- Developers are free to use public licenses for their source code	- Developers are free to use public licenses for their source code	- Externally licensed services (BYOL)	- Developers are free to use other public licenses	Not realized
	V4.2: Ecosystem-specific Licensing	- License Management App (LMA): a tool to enable developers to define licenses for their Apps	- Apple performs the licensing tasks - Developers provide metadata for their App	- Categories of licenses: Commercial software, free, and open Source	- Eclipse Public License (EPL) - Eclipse Distribution License (EDL)	General Amazon Program Materials License Agreement

Table 3. Describing the ecosystems based on the variabilities of application view

Variation Point	Variant	Provider: salesforce.com Platform: Salesforce and force.com Store: AppExchange	Provider: Apple Inc. Platform: iOS Store: Apple App Store	Provider: Amazon.com Platform: AWS Store: AWS Marketplace	Provider: Eclipse Foundation Platform: Eclipse IDE Store: Eclipse Marketplace	Provider: Amazon.com Platform: Alexa Store: Alexa Skills Store
VP5: Deliverable	**V5.1: Software Product**	- CRM Apps	- Mobile Apps	Not realized	- Eclipse plug-ins	Not realized
	V5.2: Software Service	- Cloud services, e.g., work.com	- iCloud services	- AWS-based SaaS, PaaS, and IaaS	- Eclipse Cloud Development - Eclipse Che	- Alexa Skills
	V5.3: Source Code	- Some Apps on AppExchange	- Some Apps (e.g., on GitHub)	- Open source services	- Most of plug.ins & projects	Not realized
VP6: Extension Development	**V6.1: Platform SDK**	- Force.com SDK - Aura UI framework	- iOS SDK: to develop native iOS Apps	- AWS SDKs, e.g., AWS Lambda - Command line and Powershell	- Eclipse SDK: to develop Java applications	- Alexa Skills Kit - Amazon Lex
	V6.2: IDE	- force.com IDE: eclipse plug-in - Point-and-Click App Building	- Xcode IDE	- AWS Tool Kits: Eclipse and Visual Studio plug-ins - AWS web console	- Eclipse IDE (platform)	- Skill Builder to design voice interaction models
	V6.3: Programming Language	- Apex (proprietary) - Visualforce (proprietary)	- Swift (general-purpose programming language)	- General-purpose programming languages - Amazon Simple Queue Service	- Java: The main development language	- Any programming language - JSON to link skills to users' inputs
	V6.4: Communication Protocol	- SOAP API and REST API	- Rest API - XMPP, SIP, etc.	- REST API - SOAP over HTTP	- Internet protocols, e.g., HTTP, TCP	- HTTP(S)
	V6.5: Testing	- Apex testing framework: Basically to create unit tests	- Xcode testing - TestFlight: testing by external testers	- Unit Testing in Eclipse and Visual Studio - AWS Device Farm	- JUnit testing framework	- Service Simulator - Echosim.io
VP7: Platform Interfaces	**V7.1: User Interface**	- VisualEditor Namespace, Canvas Namespace, etc.	- Cocoa Touch Frameworks - Partly Media Frameworks	Not realized	- org.eclipse.ui. perspectives - org.eclipse.s wt - org.eclipse.ui	- Alexa video features
	V7.2: Platform Features	- Search Namespace - ChatterAnswer Namespace - Datacloud Namespace	- Media Frameworks (e.g., audio) - Core Services Frameworks (e.g., iCloud)	- Amazon Simple Email Service - Amazon Elastic MapReduce - Amazon CloudSearch	- Docker APIs - EMF (e.g., org.eclipse.lin uxtools.docke r.feature.*)	- Alexa Voice Service libraries
	V7.3: System Libraries	- System, Messaging, and Database Namespaces	- Core OS Frameworks, e.g., file-system access & memory allocation	- Amazon Elastic Load Balancing - CloudWatch: monitoring of AWS in real-time	- I/O Streams (java.io package) - Memory management (java.nio.Buffer)	- Core voice-enabling technologies
VP8: Security Check	**V8.1: Leaks & Bugs**	- AppExchange Certification	- Store review process: checking broken links, performance, etc.	- Store review process: checking services and their metadata	- Intensive review of Eclipse projects - No checking for plug-ins	- Store certification process
	V8.2: Policy Violation	- Store review process: Apps and their listing data	- Store review process: software & hardware compatibility	- Self-service AMI scanning tool: Checking by providers	- Moderation process: checking plug-ins relevance	- Store submission checklist

Table 4. Describing the ecosystems based on the variabilities of infrastructure view

Variation Point	Variant	Provider: salesforce.com Platform: Salesforce and force.com Store: AppExchange	Provider: Apple Inc. Platform: iOS Store: Apple App Store	Provider: Amazon.com Platform: AWS Store: AWS Marketplace	Provider: Eclipse Foundation Platform: Eclipse IDE Store: Eclipse Marketplace	Provider: Amazon.com Platform: Alexa Store: Alexa Skills Store
VP9: Delivery Mode	V9.1: Local Installation	- Yes (Required by V5.1)	- Yes (Required by V5.1)	Not realized	- Yes (Required by V5.1)	Not realized
	V9.2: Cloud Delivery	- Yes (Required by V5.2)	- Yes (Required by V5.2)	- Yes (Required by V5.2)	- Yes (Required by V5.2)	- Yes (Required by V5.2)
VP10: Service Execution	V10.1: Operating System	- The Salesforce Operating System (SOS)	- iOS (platform)	- Amazon Linux: a Linux-based OS for AWS usage	Not realized	- Amazon Alexa (platform)
	V10.2.: Compute Center	- Requires V1.2 (external supplier)	- Virtual compute centres	- AWS servers - Requires V1.2 (external supplier of TestDrive)	Not realized	- AWS - Third-party web servers
	V10.3: Data Centre	- Requires V1.2 (external supplier)	- Apple data center	- Amazon DynamoDB: NoSQL database	Not realized	- Amazon data centers
VP11: Service Delivery	V11.1: Telecommun -ication	Not realized	- Requires V1.2 (external supplier)	- Requires V1.2 (external supplier)	Not realized	Not realized
	V11.2: Content Delivery Network	- Requires V1.2 (external supplier)	- Requires V1.2 (external supplier)	- Amazon ElastiCache: in-memory caching - Amazon CloudFront	Not realized	Not realized
	V11.3: Exclusively WWW	- Access to the ecosystem, e.g., AppExchange	- iOS Apps providing services over Internet	- Purchase on Marketplace	- Service and product delivery over Internet	- Service delivery over Internet
VP12: Asset		Not realized	- iPhone, iPad (Requires V1.2)	Not realized	Not realized	- Amazon Echo and related assets, e.g., Dot

become a member in the ecosystem. Members have influence on strategic decisions. The degree of influence depends on the level of contribution. Entering the ecosystem as an independent developer is characterized by providing Eclipse-relevant plug-ins. Eclipse marketplace is the online store, where projects and plug-ins are published. In the following, Tables 2, 3 and 4 present the result of analysis of the ecosystems from business, application, and infrastructure views. A cell in the tables presents the way that each ecosystem realizes a variant. We use "Not realized" when an ecosystem does not realize a variant.

5   Relation of Variabilities to Design Artifacts of Store-Oriented Software Ecosystems

An important factor in applicability of variabilities is to understand their relation to design artifacts [16, Chap. 6]. Figure 2 presents the relation of the variation points to design artifacts of store-oriented software ecosystems. In the middle, high-level components and roles are portrayed. Upon two main components, i.e., software platform and store, a trading market between providers and users of software is created. We call these components as a whole an *ecosystem platform*. Moreover, the roles, i.e., platform provider, user, independent developer, strategic partner, and supplier, interact with the ecosystem platform using suitable interfaces. As presented in Sect. 4, the existing ecosystems associate different terminologies to these roles. These differences refer to their different business and technical contexts (cf. Sect. 3.3). For instance, Eclipse Committer and AWS Independent Software Vendors (ISVs) are the terms used for independent developers. While Eclipse Committers are programmers with no revenue expectation, AWS ISVs are the financially motivated providers of AWS-based services.

The complementary partnership variation point is related to the roles in Fig. 2. For readability, the figure excludes these relations. The variation points on the left are applicable to the user side interfaces, which define what to deliver as product/service of an ecosystem and how to deliver it. They include deliverable, delivery model, service execution, and service delivery. Furthermore, the variation points on the right are applicable to the developer side interfaces. Using these variation points, a platform provider decides about platform openness and degree of protecting intellectual property. Such strategies are realized using extension development and platform interfaces. This includes the arrangement of interfaces, code openness, and the features of an extension kit.

Moreover, the licensing, fee, and asset variation points are applicable to both user and developer interfaces. Choices regarding fee defines whether and how users are charged for platform usage, third-party applications, or for publishing on the store. Moreover, introducing ecosystem-specific assets affects platform usage and third-party applications. This highly influences developers work with respect to choices of the extension development. In addition, the security check is related to the store and platform interfaces, which appears in form of a review process to ensure certain quality of third-party applications.

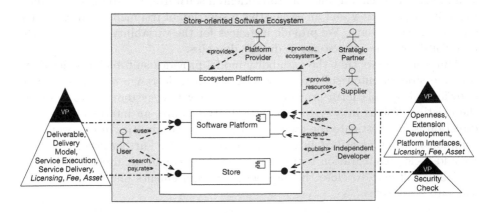

Fig. 2. The OVM artifact dependencies show to which interfaces the VPs apply.

6   Related Work

Until now, little attention is given to architectural variabilities of software ecosystems whereas a large body of literature considers variability mechanisms in the context of software product lines. Berger et al. [27] propose a conceptual framework for variability mechanisms in software ecosystems by analyzing existing ecosystems. The framework is entirely derived from open source projects and provides insights to technical aspects. Our work, however, covers crucial business and technical variabilities by considering both commercial and open source ecosystems. Some other works [20,28] focus on business aspects. Gawer and Cusumano [28] derive practices associated with effective platform leadership. The practices cover strategic decisions regarding platform modularity. Van Angeren et al. [20] draw a conceptual outline for associate models of participation in software ecosystems. The outline covers orchestration aspects including roles, entry barriers, and governance.

On opening software platforms, Jansen et al. [21] consider the spectrum of business model openness from software producers' perspective. The degree of openness is considered from strategic, tactical and operational views, which is completely derived from the business models. Costa et al. [29] consider growth of software ecosystems from single applications, where a group of actors contributes for niche markets. While the authors assume platform providers lose control over the ecosystem growth, our work aims at identifying platform provider's business and technical decisions to create software ecosystems.

7   Conclusion

Software ecosystems have enabled pioneer software providers to develop a successful market on top of their platforms. However, there is still a lack of knowledge for other platform providers to make reasonable design decisions with regards to their own business goals. In this paper, we identify architectural variation points and their variants for store-oriented software ecosystems by conducting a literature review and an exhaustive inspection of fragmentary information on existing ecosystems. We provide instances for the variability model from the real-world software ecosystems in diverse domains.

Our study shows that the variability model provides suitable abstraction to describe store-oriented software ecosystems in a wide range of domains. This knowledge helps platform providers to create novel ecosystems or to re-create the existing designs in a systematic way. In the future, an interesting research direction is to investigate the relation between the variabilities in this work and common features identified in our previous work [11]. Furthermore, traceability and a closer integration between the variabilities and architectural decision modeling will help to close the gap between requirements and architecture of software ecosystems.

References

1. Bosch, J., Bosch-Sijtsema, P.: From integration to composition: on the impact of software product lines, global development and ecosystems. J. Syst. Softw. **83**(1), 67–76 (2010)
2. Jansen, S., Bloemendal, E.: Defining app stores: the role of curated marketplaces in software ecosystems. In: Herzwurm, G., Margaria, T. (eds.) ICSOB 2013. LNBIP, vol. 150, pp. 195–206. Springer, Heidelberg (2013). doi:10.1007/978-3-642-39336-5_19
3. West, J., Mace, M.: Browsing as the killer app: explaining the rapid success of Apple's iPhone. Telecommun. Policy **34**(5), 270–286 (2010)
4. Manikas, K., Hansen, K.M.: Software ecosystems-A systematic literature review. J. Syst. Softw. **86**(5), 1294–1306 (2013)
5. Jazayeri, B., Schwichtenberg, S.: On-the-fly computing meets IoT markets—towards a reference architecture. In: International Conference on Software Architecture Workshops, pp. 120–127. IEEE (2017)
6. Metzger, A., Pohl, K.: Software product line engineering and variability management: achievements and challenges. In: Proceedings of the on Future of Software Engineering, pp. 70–84. ACM (2014)
7. Galster, M., Weyns, D., Tofan, D., Michalik, B., Avgeriou, P.: Variability in software systems-A systematic literature review. IEEE Trans. Softw. Eng. **40**(3), 282–306 (2014)
8. Berger, T., Rublack, R., Nair, D., Atlee, J.M., Becker, M., Czarnecki, K., Wasowski, A.: A survey of variability modeling in industrial practice. In: International Workshop on Variability Modelling of Software-Intensive Systems, p. 7. ACM (2013)
9. Nickerson, R.C., Varshney, U., Muntermann, J.: A method for taxonomy development and its application in information systems. Eur. J. Inf. Syst. **22**(3), 336–359 (2013)
10. Von Alan, R.H., March, S.T., Park, J., Ram, S.: Design science in information systems research. MIS Q. **28**(1), 75–105 (2004)
11. Jazayeri, B., Platenius, M.C., Engels, G., Kundisch, D.: Features of IT service markets: a systematic literature review. In: Sheng, Q.Z., Stroulia, E., Tata, S., Bhiri, S. (eds.) ICSOC 2016. LNCS, vol. 9936, pp. 301–316. Springer, Cham (2016). doi:10.1007/978-3-319-46295-0_19
12. Manikas, K.: Revisiting software ecosystems research: a longitudinal literature study. J. Syst. Softw. **117**, 84–103 (2016)
13. Jansen, S., Finkelstein, A., Brinkkemper, S.: A sense of community: a research agenda for software ecosystems. In: International Conference on Software Engineering Companion Volume, pp. 187–190. IEEE (2009)
14. Bosch, J.: From software product lines to software ecosystems. In: Proceedings of the 13th International Software Product Line Conference, pp. 111–119. Carnegie Mellon University (2009)
15. Jazayeri, B., Zimmermann, O., Engels, G., Kundisch, D.: A variability model for store-oriented software ecosystems: an enterprise perspective - supplementary material, Technical report (2017). https://sfb901.upb.de/uploads/tx_sibibtex/JZEK17.pdf
16. Pohl, K., Böckle, G., van Der Linden, F.J.: Engineering, Software Product Line: Foundations Principles and Techniques. Springer, Heidelberg (2005)

17. Metzger, A., Pohl, K., Heymans, P. Schobbens, P.-Y., Saval, G.: Disambiguating the documentation of variability in software product lines: a separation of concerns, formalization and automated analysis. In: Proceedings of the International Requirements Engineering Conference, pp. 243–253. IEEE (2007)
18. Dietz, J., Proper, E., Tribolet, J., Halpin, T., Hoogervorst, J., Op't Land, M., Ross, R.G., Winter, R.: The Enterprise Engineering Series. Springer, Heidelberg (2009)
19. Eklund, U., Bosch, J.: Using architecture for multiple levels of access to an ecosystem platform. In: Proceedings of the International ACM SIGSOFT Conference on Quality of Software Architectures, pp. 143–148. ACM (2012)
20. Van Angeren, J., Kabbedijk, J., Jansen, S., Popp, K. M.: A survey of associate models used within large software ecosystems. In: Proceedings of the International Workshop on Software Ecosystems, Citeseer, pp. 27–39 (2011)
21. Jansen, S., Brinkkemper, S., Souer, J., Luinenburg, L.: Shades of gray: opening up a software producing organization with the open software enterprise model. J. Syst. Softw. **85**(7), 1495–1510 (2012)
22. Alspaugh, T.A., Asuncion, H.U., Scacchi, W.: The role of software licenses in open architecture ecosystems. In: Proceedings of the International Workshop on Software Ecosystems. CEUR-WS (2009)
23. Schultis, K.-B., Elsner, C., Lohmann, D.: Architecture challenges for internal software ecosystems: a large-scale industry case study. In: Proceedings of the International Symposium on Foundations of Software Engineering, pp. 542–552. ACM (2014)
24. Bosch, J.: Architecture challenges for software ecosystems. In: European Conference on Software Architecture Companion Volume, pp. 93–95. ACM (2010)
25. Cataldo, M., Herbsleb, J.D.: Architecting in software ecosystems: interface translucence as an enabler for scalable collaboration. In: Proceedings of the European Conference on Software Architecture Companion Volume, pp. 65–72. ACM (2010)
26. Kruchten, P.: Contextualizing agile software development. J. Soft. Evol. Process **25**(4), 351–361 (2013)
27. Berger, T., Pfeiffer, R.-H., Tartler, R., Dienst, S., Czarnecki, K., Wasowski, A., She, S.: Variability mechanisms in software ecosystems. Inf. Soft. Technol. **56**(11), 1520–1535 (2014)
28. Gawer, A., Cusumano, M.A.: Industry platforms and ecosystem innovation. J. Prod. Innov. Manag. **31**(3), 417–433 (2014)
29. Costa, G., Silva, F., Santos, R., Werner, C., Oliveira, T.: From applications to a software ecosystem platform: an exploratory study. In: International Conference on Management of Emergent Digital EcoSystems, pp. 9–16. ACM (2013)

An Analysis of RESTful APIs Offerings in the Industry

Antonio Gamez-Diaz(✉), Pablo Fernandez, and Antonio Ruiz-Cortes

Universidad de Sevilla, Seville, Spain
{agamez2,pablofm,aruiz}@us.es

Abstract. As distribution models of information systems are moving to *XaaS* paradigms, microservices architectures are rapidly emerging, having the RESTful principles as the API model of choice. In this context, the term of *API Economy* is being used to describe the increasing movement of the industries in order to take advantage of exposing their APIs as part of their service offering and expand its business model.

Currently, the industry is adopting standard specifications such as OpenAPI to model the APIs in a standard way following the RESTful principles; this shift has supported the proliferation of API execution platforms (*API Gateways*) that allow the XaaS to optimize their costs. However, from a business point of view, modeling offering plans of those APIs is mainly done ad-hoc (or in a platform-dependent way) since no standard model has been proposed. This lack of standardization hinders the creation of API governance tools in order to provide and automate the management of business models in the XaaS industry.

This work presents a systematic analysis of 69 XaaS in the industry that offer RESTful APIs as part of their business model. Specifically, we review in detail the plans that are part of the XaaS offerings that could be used as a first step to identify the requirements for the creation of an expressive governance model of realistic RESTful APIs. Additionally, we provide an open dataset in order to enable further analysis in this research line.

1 Introduction

In the last decade, distribution models of information systems are evolving into *XaaS* [10] paradigms where customers no longer need to buy a perpetual license, host the software or maintain the infrastructure [5]. As part of this trend, the microservices architectures are rapidly emerging as they provide a flexible evolution model [7]. In particular, this architectural model proposes a division of the information system into a set of small services deployed independently which communicate each other using Web APIs that adhere typically to REST principles [6].

This work has been partially supported by the European Commission (FEDER), the Spanish and the Andalusian R&D&I programs (grants TIN2015-70560-R (BELI) and P12–TIC-1867 (COPAS)) and the FPU scholarship program, granted by the Spanish Ministry of Education, Culture and Sports (FPU15/02980).

M. Maximilien et al. (Eds.): ICSOC 2017, LNCS 10601, pp. 589–604, 2017.
https://doi.org/10.1007/978-3-319-69035-3_43

In this context, the term of *API Economy* is being increasingly used to describe the movement of the industries to share their internal business assets as APIs [21] not only across internal organizational units but also to external third parties; in doing so, this trend has the potential of unlocking additional business value through the creation of new assets [3]. In fact, we can find a number of XaaS examples in the industry that are deployed solely as APIs (such as Meaningcloud[1], Flightstats[2] or Twilio[3]).

In order to be competitive in this such a growing market of APIs, at least two key aspects can be identified: (i) *ease of use* for its potential developers; (ii) a flexible usage *plan* that fits their customer's demands.

Regarding the *ease of use* perspective, third party developers need to understand how to use the exposed APIs so it becomes necessary to provide a good training material but, unfortunately, several API providers do not often write a good documentation of their products [8]. Alternatively, in the last year, we found the promising proposal of the *Open API Initiative*[4] (OAI) whose aim is to support the creation, evolution and promotion of a vendor neutral description format for RESTful APIs and that is currently being backed by a growing number of leading industrial stakeholders.

Conversely, from the usage *plans* perspective, to the best of our knowledge, do not exists a widely accepted model to describe usage plans including elements such as cost, functionality restrictions or limits. In this context, we can find some example of API management platforms in the industry (commonly known as *API Gateways*), which have tried to address the problem of usage plans modeling but they are typically constrained by their platform architecture and no interoperable usage plan specification is provided. For instance, Mashape presents a limited governance ecosystem, since it only allows users to define quotas and not rates.

Figure 1 illustrates a real plan extracted from *FullContact*[5], a real-world SaaS offering which includes an API that manages and organizes contacts in a collaborative way, it also matches emails addresses and tries to find as much information as available on the Internet to complete the profiles. Note that in this work, we focus on XaaS offering a RESTful API in order to access either fully or partially to the functionality they offer. In traditional XaaS, these actions are accessed using the graphic user interface.

This example is composed of three plans, one of them is free whereas the remaining are paid. Focusing on paid ones, they have a fixed *price* that is monthly *billed*. Regarding the *limits*, for each resource, a *quota* is being applied; for instance, in the starter plan, only 6000 matches over *Person* are available. Nevertheless, an *overage* is defined, that is, it is possible to overcome the limit by paying a certain amount of money; in this case, $0.006 per each request. Regardless of the accessed resources, a common *rate* of 300 queries per minute is

---

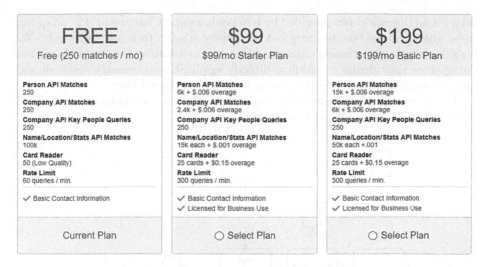

Fig. 1. Example of an API plan.

being applied. In this plan, there are not any *functionality limitation*, even the free plan has the same functionality that paid ones have. In this case, the *free tier* is regulated by *limits* such as *quotas* and *rates*.

The main aim of this paper is to develop the first step towards an expressive, platform neutral, usage plan model that could be used to create open API governance tools. Specifically, this work presents a systematic analysis of the usage plans identified in a wide spectrum of real-world APIs; in doing so, the main contributions of this paper are: (i) present a systematic method to analyze XaaS offerings in the industry including RESTful APIs; (ii) undertake a comparative analysis of 69 industrial APIs selected from two widely used API directories, identifying the common trends related to the modeling of usage plans; (iii) provide an open dataset that can be used to replicate our analysis and to be extended in further researches.

This paper is organized as follows: Sect. 2 shows the methodology that we use in our study as well as the characteristics we analyze. Next, in Sect. 3, we discuss the results of the analysis. In addition, Sect. 4 shows the existing work related to this paper. Finally, Sect. 5 shows some remarks and conclusions.

2   Research Method and Conduct

The study[6] presented herein was entirely conducted during the 2017 first quarter and it is a primary study in which we analyze real-world APIs. Whereas primary research data are collected from, for instance, research subjects or experiments, secondary studies involve the synthesis of existing research. Specifically, our work

---

[6] Data used in this study is publicly available at https://goo.gl/gQPDxz.

is based on the guidelines provided by Kitchenham and Charters in [12], adapting these guides about how to carry out secondary studies to a primary study. We consider that using these guidelines helps to systematize the research we are doing since they define a workflow directly applicable to primary research and give recommendations with the aim of avoiding undesired bias.

In our work, we systematically analyze a set of characteristics in real-world APIs following the steps depicted in Fig. 2.

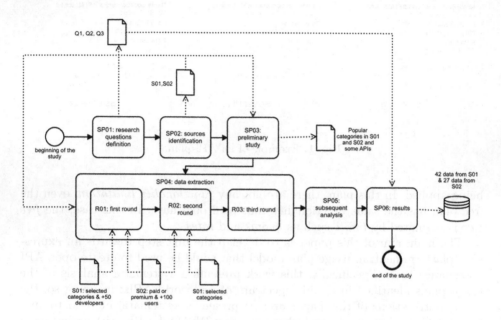

Fig. 2. BPMN representation of the research process.

- **SP01-Research questions definition.** We start our systematic analysis with a series of motivating questions which will drive the investigation. We consider that these questions can pave the way for future research activities. Specifically, we define the following questions:
  - **RQ01.** What are the most common business models in the context of XaaS that offer a RESTful API?
  - **RQ02.** How are the plans, in terms of the characteristics that they have, used in XaaS that provide a RESTful API?
  - **RQ03.** Which regulations do XaaS offerings state over the RESTful APIs?
- **SP02-Sources identification.** Based on the literature and the analysis of the industry that we have conducted, 10 API repositories were collected. Nevertheless, we have considered those ones which *included more than 5000 APIs* and whose *last update date was in the year 2017*, remaining 2 valid sources: **S01-ProgrammableWeb**[7]: with 17511 APIs distributed in 478 categories

---

[7] https://www.programmableweb.com.

and **S02-Mashape**[8] with 7500 APIs distributed in 28 categories. Note that Mashape directory has been recently moved to RapidAPI[9] catalog, so subsequent analysis should be made over RapidAPI rather than Mashape.

- **SP03-Preliminary study.** After a preliminary examination of API directories S01 and S02, the more popular categories in each one were identified. We did a percentile study over the categories and the number of users in each one. Particularly, we fixed P_{97} for S01 and P_{50} for S02. Additionally, we included some handpicked APIs, looking for these ones with complex plans.

- **SP04-Data extraction.** We designed two different forms since the quality criteria have to be used to identify inclusion/exclusion criteria, according to the Kitchenham guidelines [12]. The first one[10] tried to identify basic information about the analyzed API as well as information regarding the plans. The second one[11] went in depth into the overage and both functionality and quota/rate limitations, including the API characteristics showed in Sect. 2.1. 30 students were given S01 and S02 API directories so that they chose two XaaS offerings following the eligibility criteria. They collected manually the required information in a session guided by the authors and they filled out the forms. In order to have a broader vision of the APIs offered in the industry, we defined an incremental process composed of three rounds. We started from defining strict eligibility criteria and the number of developers that the API has. Then we relaxed some criterion so that a new set of APIs was included.

  In the first round (R01) we limited the APIs selected from S01, considering only a certain set of categories[12], according to its popularity (see SP03). In addition, we set a threshold of 50 registered developers in S01 and limited the APIs selected from S02 having, at least, 100 users and being in categories either *paid* or *premium*.

  In the second round (R02) we were informed by some students about they did not found any API according to the established search restrictions. At this moment, we determined to relax the criteria in S01, removing the 50 developers' threshold. After finishing this round, we have collected 62 APIs.

  In the third round (R03) we started the guided session in class to fill out the form. Nevertheless, we noticed that there was a number of APIs without a clear plan, and students found quite difficult to find all the information that we asked for. At this point, we decided to start a new API gathering session with the help of the instructors. After finishing this round, we harvested extra 28 APIs.

---

[8] https://www.mashape.com.

[9] https://rapidapi.com.

[10] Available at https://goo.gl/rqwvH7.

[11] Available at https://goo.gl/sbzXEh.

[12] Mapping, social, e-commerce, mobile, search, tools, messaging, API, video, financial, cloud, payments, enterprise, analytics, data.

– **SP05-Subsequent analysis.** We did a subsequent analysis in two different steps: (i) manual data validation and classification: giving a result a set of 69 analyzed XaaS offerings with more than one plan. We detected some inconsistencies in some points that were manually reviewed and corrected; (ii) ulterior results classification: in which we separated the data gathered regarding the source, obtaining 42 APIs from S01 and 27 from S02.

2.1 Analyzed Attributes

We developed a comparative framework based on 60 attributes grouped in 7 areas illustrating the traceability between the research questions and the gathered characteristics. Following, we describe each group of attributes.

General information (see Table 1). We collected information about the API itself, including the *name* (**GI01**) and the *source* (**GI02**) where these APIs was selected from (i.e. *Mashape* or *ProgrammableWeb*); and the *plans URL* (**GI03**).

API characterization (see Table 1). We distinguished two attributes, *API type* (**AC01**) and *API maturity level* (**AC02**), in terms of giving a more precise classification of APIs. Specifically, we propose a classification of four types for the *API type*: **T01** if the XaaS offering does not provide any API at all; **T02** when the XaaS offering does provide a non-RESTful API; **T03** if the XaaS offering does provide as part of its offer a RESTful API, (e.g., a SaaS which allows customers to access their data in a RESTful way, but the primary access way is a GUI); and **T04** if the XaaS offering is, actually, a RESTful API (e.g., an API to send emails or SMS). For *API type* T03 or T04, we identify a set of three *API maturity levels*: **ML01** if the API does not define any limitations nor explicit Service Level Agreement (SLA); **ML02** when the API defines limitations and/or explicit SLAs but they are not in the plans (i.e., the limitations are applied regardless of the selected plan); and **ML03** if the API defines limitations and/or explicit SLAs depending on the selected plan.

Pricing (see Table 1). We identify economic information of the API pricing including the *currency* (**P01**) in which clients are billed, the *billing cycle* (**P02**) and a set of statistics of the *plan cost* (**P03, P04, P05**).

Business model (see Table 1). We consider the main *primary business model* (**BM05**) in the API, inspired by a number of works in the literature, as shown in Sect. 4. Namely: *free* (**FR**), when no payment is needed; *pay-as-you-go simple* (**PG-S**), when you pay just for the usage you do (e.g., you pay per each request made); *pay-as-you-go with intervals* (**PG-I**), when the payment for each unit depends on the usage volume (e.g., the first 1 K request cost \$0.1 each, but the subsequent \$0.05 each); *tiered with fixed prices* (**TO1**), when each plan has a non-variable price; *tiered with overage* (**TO2**), when existing plans with a certain price and limitations you can overcome the limits by paying an extra amount. We also gathered the *number of plans* (**BM06**) and discover the *existence of discounts per annual upfronts* (**BM01**), the *existence of customs plans* (**BM03**), the *main limitation of the free plan* (**BM04**); or the *existence of a free plan* (**BM02**).

Table 1. First set of API analyzed attributes.

General information	RQ01	RQ02	RQ03
GI01-Name of the API			
GI02-Source	✓	✓	✓
GI03-Plans URL			
API characterization			
AC01-API type	✓	✓	
AC02-API maturity	✓	✓	
Pricing			
P01-Currency used	✓	✓	
P02-Billing cycle	✓	✓	
P03/P04/P05-Plan cost(max/min/avg)	✓	✓	
Business model			
BM01-Existence of discounts per annual upfront	✓	✓	
BM02-Existence of a free plan	✓	✓	
BM03-Existence of custom plans	✓	✓	
BM04-Main limitation of the free plan	✓	✓	
BM05-Main business model	✓	✓	
BM06-Number of plans	✓	✓	

Overage (see Table 2). We define *overage* as the extra cost in which a customer incurs when a certain limitation or set of limitations is exceeded (**O01**). The *overage scope* (**O02**) depends over what item the limitation is made (e.g., requests, the number of resources, etc.). Moreover, we collected data about the *overage cost* (maximum -**O09**-, minimum -**O10**- and average -**O11**- across the different plans) and the *overage limit* (maximum -**O03**-, minimum -**O07**- and average -**O08**- across the different plans), i.e., the amount of scoped data allowed per each overage payment. Furthermore, we consider the *existence of an overage in every paid plan* (**O04**) and we analyze whether in the same paid plan *all the resources have an overage* (**O05**) and *all the resources have the same overage value* (**O06**).

Functionality limitations (see Table 2). We identify the limitations over the API functionality (**FL01**) and study the granularity: *resource access granularity* (**FL02**), if the limitation is applied to the resource endpoint (e.g. it is not possible to access some parts of the resource in some plans); *HTTP method granularity* (**FL03**), if the limitation is applied to a certain HTTP verb (e.g., it is not possible to make a POST in some plans) *request body granularity* (**FL04**), when the limitation is based on the specific payload sent to an endpoint. Furthermore, we identify the *existence of a functionality limitation in every paid plan* (**FL05**) and we analyze whether in the same paid plan *all the resources have a*

Table 2. Second set of API analyzed attributes.

Overage	RQ01	RQ02	RQ03
O01-Existence of an overage	✓	✓	✓
O02-Overage scope		✓	✓
O04-Existence of an overage in every paid plan		✓	✓
O05-In the same paid plan all the res. have an overage		✓	✓
O06-In the same paid plan all the res. have the same overage value		✓	✓
O03/O07/O08-Overage limit value(max/min/avg)		✓	✓
O09/O10/O11-Overage cost (max/min/avg)		✓	✓
Functionality limitations			
FL01-Existence of functionality limitations	✓	✓	✓
FL02-Limitation granularity: resource access			✓
FL03-Limitation granularity: HTTP methods			✓
FL04-Limitation granularity: request body			✓
FL05-Existence of functionality limitations in every paid plan			✓
FL06-In different paid plans each one has the same func. lim.			✓
FL07-In the same paid plan all the resources have a func. lim.			✓

functionality limitation (**FL06**) and *all the resources have the same functionality limitations* (**FL07**).

Quotas/Rates (see Table 3). We analyze two time-based limitations in the API, commonly known as quotas and rates. The main difference is the sliding window that rates have: whereas with quotas it is possible to define limits such as *up to 1000 requests per day*, with rates it is possible to express limits with a relative period of time, such as *up to 100 requests in the last minute*. Specifically, we identify the scope of these limitations: (i) *requests scope* (**Q02/R02**), (ii) *storage scope* (**Q03/R03**); (iii) *resource scope* (**Q04/R04**); (iv) *transaction size scope* (**Q05/R05**) and *other scopes* not explicitly mentioned (**Q06/R06**). Moreover, we collected the value of the limitation (maximum -**Q12/R12**-, minimum -**Q13/R13**- and average -**Q14/R14**- across the plans) and periodicity. Furthermore, we consider the *existence of a functionality limitation in every paid plan* (**Q07/R07**), we analyze if *in different plans each one has the same quotas/rates.* (**Q08/R08**), whether in the same paid plan *all the resources have a quotas/rates* (**Q09/R09**) and, finally, if *all the resources have the same quota/rate value.* (**Q10/R10**).

Table 3. Third set of API analyzed attributes.

Quotas and rates	RQ01	RQ02	RQ03
Q01/R01-Existence of quotas/rates	✓	✓	✓
Q02/R02-Quotas/Rates over requests			✓
Q03/R03-Quotas/Rates over storage			✓
Q04/R04-Quotas/Rates over resources			✓
Q05/R05-Quotas/Rates over transaction size			✓
Q06/R06-Quotas/Rates over another scope			✓
Q07/R07-Quotas/Rates in every paid plan			✓
Q08/R08-Quota/Rates in all resources of different plans			✓
Q09/R09-Quota/Rates in all resources of the same plan			✓
Q10/R10-Same quota/rate value for a given plan & resource			✓
Q11/R11-Quota/rate periodicity			✓
Q12/R12/Q13/R13/Q14/R14-Quota/Rate value (max/min/avg)			✓

3 SP06-Results

In this section, we present the results of the study grouped in three different blocks: (i) attributes regarding the business model and pricing; (ii) aspects related to limitations and overage application; (iii) quotas and rates limitations. Due to the fact that there exist notable differences between the APIs and their governance models, we decided to perform a separate analysis regarding the source of the API: Mashape and ProgrammableWeb.

In Fig. 3 we observe that most of the APIs analyzed are, indeed, the XaaS offering (AC01). In the case of Mashape, all the APIs are T04. Regarding the maturity (AC02), in both cases, we observe that the defined limitations depend on the plan that the client selects. Note we have established a search protocol that picked primarily popular APIs from popular categories, a fact that explains this polarization in AC01 and AC02. A small number of APIs offer a discount per an anticipated payment or upfront (BM01), but the vast majority define a free tier with some specific limitations (B02). In addition, it is frequent to have a way to define custom plans by talking directly to the company (BM03). Regarding the business models (BM05), it is very likely for APIs from Mashape to have a tiered plan with an overage, in contrast to the ones from ProgrammableWeb, in which is common to have a tiered plan with fixed prices. It is remarkable that the more common billing cycle (P02) is *monthly* and the number of plans (BM06) oscillates between two and four.

Figure 4 depicts the most interesting attribute analysis about how limitations are being applied in APIs. First, we observe that a high number limits the operations, rather than functionality or time (BM04). Secondly, from the providers

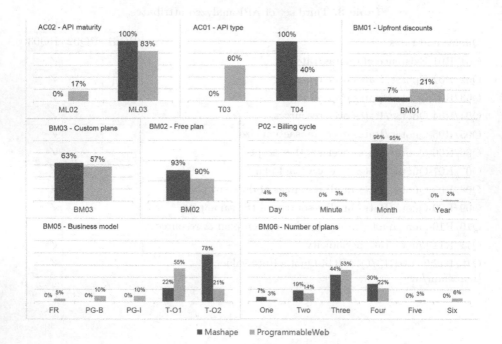

Fig. 3. Business model and pricing analysis.

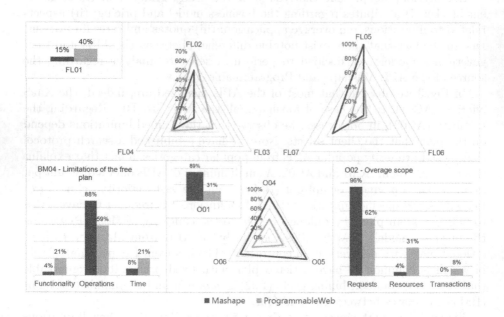

Fig. 4. Limitations and overage analysis.

that apply an overage if a certain limit is reached (O01), it is frequent that all the resources have an overage (O05), but it has not to be the same (O06). The most common scope (O02) is *requests*. On the other hand, some APIs apply limitations over the functionality (FL01), being more frequent in the APIs chosen from ProgrammableWeb. Most of the limitations are applied to the resource itself (FL2). Furthermore, functionality limitations use to be present in every plan (FL05), but they neither are the same across the plans (FL06) nor have the same values (FL07).

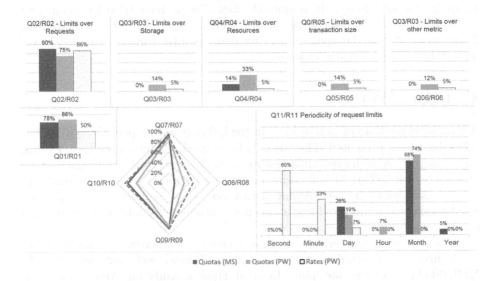

Fig. 5. Quotas and Rates analysis.

In Fig. 5 we observe some charts regarding the limitations using quotas and rates. Whereas both quotas and rates are very frequent (Q01/R01), we have noticed that Mashape does not allow users to define rates. Quotas are usually defined using *monthly* periods, whereas rates are more common to be *secondly* or *minutely* (Q11/R11). Furthermore, most of quotas and rates are defined over requests (Q02/R02), rather than over resources (Q04/R04) or storage (Q03/R03). It is also remarkable that most of quotas and rates have the same values within a plan (Q10/R10), but in different plans they usually have different values (Q08/R08).

Each of these attributes paves the way to give an answer to the stated research questions. Specifically, (i) regarding the most common business models (**RQ01**), as depicted in Fig. 3, BM05 attribute points out that the more common business models are the tiered ones with or without overage; (ii) regarding the plans (**RQ02**), as shown in Fig. 3, most APIs define between two or four plans, with a monthly billing cycle; (iii) regarding the regulations (**RQ03**), as illustrated in Figs. 4 and 5 most XaaS providers apply limitations in somehow. They limit the free tier by restricting the operations allowed and, for paid plans, they define both quotas and rates. These limitations unusually are scoped over the number of requests, and the periodicity intervals range from minutely for quotas, to secondly for rates. This situation may be caused by the lack of versatility and expressivity existent in current modeling tools.

In our analysis, we identify two different threats to the validity of the results herein presented: (i) the size of the sample may not be statistically representative regarding the total population of APIs in the real world. Nevertheless, we have tried to prioritize the more popular categories in each repository so that we can maximize the API usage; (ii) despite the fact that we have tried to do our best when validating data, there may be some errors since the process is manual. Apart from offering the open dataset we plan, as future work, to revisit it and undertake a comprehensive examination.

4 Related Work

A number of analyses of web services in the industry and, especially, of RESTful APIs, have been presented. They usually focus on characteristics inherent to the API design. This work presents a new research direction by developing a systematic study of RESTful APIs focusing on how providers deal with non-functional properties in plans by establishing limitations, such as rates and quotas. We emphasize our work in providing an open and machine-readable dataset to other researchers.

The more relevant literature we have revised is summarized in the following:

A first set of studies is focused on traditional web services (WSDL/ XML/SOAP). On the one hand, Li et al. show a study on Web services [13] in order to get the diversity of the specification of key elements in the industry. Specifically, they focus on statistics based on the number of defined operations, WSDL document size, average words used in the description fields and function diversity. They crawled some web services catalogs and collected information about 570 WSDL documents from active services, nevertheless, they focus only on a single search engine. On the other hand, Al-Masri et al. present a broader study [1] in which the authors have developed a crawler for collecting information about 5077 WSDL references available in different sources, such as Google, Yahoo, Alltheweb and Baidu. They determine statistics about object sizes, technology and function among others. They also point out the disconnection between UDDI registries and the current web, since these registries are incapable of providing Quality of Service (QoS) measurements for registered Web services and they do not clearly define how service providers can advertise business models.

Coinciding with the progressive increase of RESTful APIs, a second set of works are focused on these services. In [14], Maleshkova et al. analyze a set of randomly chosen 222 APIs of ProgrammableWeb, not just RESTful APIs but RPC and hybrid style also. They analyze six API characteristics: general information, types, input parameters, output formats, invocation details and complementary documentation. They found that a lack of a standard format to document APIs. In particular, it shows that APIs suffer from under-specification because some important information (e.g., data type and HTTP methods) are missing. Furthermore, in [18], Renzel et al. show a study over the 20 most popular RESTful Web Services from ProgrammableWeb against 17 RESTful design criteria found in the literature. The point out that hardly any of the services claiming to be RESTful is truly RESTful. This study also offers the full dataset showing the values for each analyzed characteristic. Finally, in [4], Bülthoff et al. analyze a dataset which comprises 45 Web APIs in total, primarily chosen from ProgrammableWeb directory, and provide conclusions about common description forms, output types, usage of API parameters, invocation support, the level of reusability, API granularity and authentication details. In this study, the authors show that an 89% of APIs state and implement rate limitations, either written down as part of the documentation or included with the general terms and conditions.

In a third set of studies in the last years, authors are moving to conducting other analysis to determine how the APIs are evolving and whether best practices are being followed. For instance, in [20], Sohan et al. conduct a case study of 9 evolving APIs to investigate what changes are made between versions and how the changes are documented and communicated to the API users. Furthermore, they extract some recommendations, such as the use of semantic versioning, separate releases for bug fixes and new features, auto-generated API documentation cross-linked with changelogs and providing live API explorers. Next, Palma et al. in [15,16], present a framework to undertake API analysis, specifically, in the first work, they analyze 12 APIs in order to recognize some patterns and anti-patterns for RESTful APIs; in the second work, analogously, they study 15 APIs to detect some linguistic patterns and anti-patterns in URL paths. Furthermore, in [17], Petrillo et al. present a study evaluating and comparing the design of the RESTful APIs of 3 cloud providers in terms of the fulfillment of a catalog of 73 best practices. They show that APIs reach an acceptable level of maturity when they consider best practices related to understandability and reusability. Moreover, in [19], Rodriguez et al. evaluate some good and bad practices in RESTful APIs. In particular, they analyze data logs of HTTP calls collected from the Internet traffic, identify usage patterns from logs and compare these patterns with design best practices.

Furthermore, from an industrial perspective some studies have been carried out; Musser, VP of ProgrammableWeb, highlights in a conference[13] what are the more common business models nowadays. In this sense, Yu et al. carried out a study [25] that analyzes structure and dynamics of ProgrammableWeb, determining that cumulative API use follows a power law distribution: a large number of APIs is used in a few mashups and a small number of APIs is used by many mashups. Furthermore, Haupt et al. present a study [11] of some API properties over 286 Swagger descriptions using a custom framework to analyze these Swagger documents.

---

[13] Available at https://goo.gl/8eZwwv.

In a pricing model perspective, we found initial works such as [2] in which Andrikopoulos et al. present a cost calculator for cloud ecosystems. More specifically, Vukovic et al. have presented some relevant works in the sense API ecosystems analysis and formal representations of service licenses. In [24] they presented a graph-based data model for API ecosystem built on an RDF data store. It stores temporal information about when entities and relationships were created and possibly deleted, allowing insights into the evolution of API ecosystems. On the other hand, in [22] they present a data model for API terms of service that captures a set of non-functional properties of APIs and allows for terms and conditions to be automatically assessed and composed. Later, in [23] they define a formal representation of service license description that facilitates automated license generation and composition. They also care about some QoS parameters and its relationship between the agreed SLA. Nevertheless, they do not identify any limitation that actually exists in real API plans, such as quotas and rates. Moreover, they restrict the concept of Service Level Agreements (SLAs) to two components: condition and action, whereas our approach pretends to go further.

To the best of our knowledge, our work differs from the one presented herein in three specific points: (i) Any of the analyzed works present a study over a number of RESTful APIs in terms of non-functional aspects and limitations (e.g., quotas and rates), plans and business models. (ii) We have carried out our analysis systematically, defining a specific set of objectives and research questions, rules to select the APIs and a specific methodology to analyze the gathered data. (iii) None of the works provides an open dataset in a machine-readable format so that researchers could improve and use the data gathered by authors in further studies. The only one that presents a dataset is [18], nevertheless, they do not offer it in a machine-readable way.

5   Conclusions and Future Work

In this paper, we have systematically studied 69 RESTful APIs of XaaS offerings; after identifying the research questions, we selected two valid sources to extract APIs from: Mashape and ProgrammableWeb. Next, we analyzed a set of characteristics regarding the type of the API, pricing, business models used in the XaaS offering, functionality limitations, overage and quotas and rates. We found that there exists a wider expressibility in terms of API limitations when the API is not explicitly regulated by an API Gateway, such as Mashape.

As an additional value, we believe the results of this study can also be useful for practitioners who plan to design a new plan for an API. Finally, as a future work, we plan to identify: (i) a correlation between the price plan offered and the types of limits; (ii) a specific set of requirements to define a formal governance model that supports a realistic usage plan specification for RESTful APIs, including temporality elements such as scheduling restrictions as defined in [9].

References

1. Al-Masri, E., Mahmoud, Q.H.: Investigating web services on the world wide web. In: WWW 2008, vol. 32(3), pp. 795–804 (2008)
2. Andrikopoulos, V., Song, Z., Leymann, F.: Supporting the migration of applications to the cloud through a decision support system. In: ICSOC 2013, pp. 565–572. IEEE, June 2013
3. Bonardi, M., Brioschi, M., Fuggetta, A.: Fostering collaboration through API economy. In: SER&IP 2016, pp. 32–38 (2016)
4. Bülthoff, F., Maleshkova, M.: RESTful or RESTless – current state of today's top web APIs. In: Presutti, V., Blomqvist, E., Troncy, R., Sack, H., Papadakis, I., Tordai, A. (eds.) ESWC 2014. LNCS, vol. 8798, pp. 64–74. Springer, Cham (2014). doi:10.1007/978-3-319-11955-7_6
5. Fehling, C., Leymann, F., Retter, R., Schupeck, W., Arbitter, P.: Cloud Computing Patterns. Springer, Heidelberg (2014)
6. Fielding, R.T.: Architectural styles and the design of network-based software architectures. Building **54**, 162 (2000)
7. Fowler, M.: Microservices, pp. 1–14 (2014)
8. Forrester. API Management Solutions, Q3 2014. Technical report (2015)
9. García, J.M., Martín-Díaz, O., Fernandez, P., Ruiz-Cortés, A., Toro, M.: Automated analysis of cloud offerings for optimal service provisioning. In: Maximilien, M., Vallecillo, A., Wang, J., Oriol, M. (eds.) ICSOC 2017. LNCS, vol. 10601, pp. 331–339. Springer, Cham (2017)
10. Geelan, J.: Twenty-one experts define cloud computing. Cloud Comput. J. **4**, 5 (2009)
11. Haupt, F., Leymann, F., Scherer, A., Vukojevic-Haupt, K.: A framework for the structural analysis of REST APIs. In: ICSA 2017, p. 4 (2017)
12. Kitchenham, B., Charters, S.: Guidelines for performing systematic literature reviews in software engineering Version 2.3. Engineering **45**(4ve), 1051 (2007)
13. Li, Y., Liu, Y., Zhang, L., Li, G., Xie, B., Sun, J.: An exploratory study of web services on the internet. In: ICWS 2007, pp. 380–387. IEEE (2007)
14. Maleshkova, M., Pedrinaci, C., Domingue, J.: Investigating web APIs on the World Wide Web. In: ECOWS 2010, pp. 107–114. IEEE, December 2010
15. Palma, F., Dubois, J., Moha, N., Guéhéneuc, Y.-G.: Detection of REST patterns and antipatterns: a heuristics-based approach. In: Franch, X., Ghose, A.K., Lewis, G.A., Bhiri, S. (eds.) ICSOC 2014. LNCS, vol. 8831, pp. 230–244. Springer, Heidelberg (2014). doi:10.1007/978-3-662-45391-9_16
16. Palma, F., Gonzalez-Huerta, J., Moha, N., Guéhéneuc, Y.-G., Tremblay, G.: Are RESTful APIs well-designed? Detection of their linguistic (anti)patterns. In: Barros, A., Grigori, D., Narendra, N.C., Dam, H.K. (eds.) ICSOC 2015. LNCS, vol. 9435, pp. 171–187. Springer, Heidelberg (2015). doi:10.1007/978-3-662-48616-0_11
17. Petrillo, F., Merle, P., Moha, N., Guéhéneuc, Y.-G.: Are REST APIs for cloud computing well-designed? An exploratory study. In: Sheng, Q.Z., Stroulia, E., Tata, S., Bhiri, S. (eds.) ICSOC 2016. LNCS, vol. 9936, pp. 157–170. Springer, Cham (2016). doi:10.1007/978-3-319-46295-0_10
18. Renzel, D., Schlebusch, P., Klamma, R.: Today's top "RESTful" services and why they are not RESTful. In: Wang, X.S., Cruz, I., Delis, A., Huang, G. (eds.) WISE 2012. LNCS, vol. 7651, pp. 354–367. Springer, Heidelberg (2012). doi:10.1007/978-3-642-35063-4_26

19. Rodríguez, C., Baez, M., Daniel, F., Casati, F., Trabucco, J.C., Canali, L., Percannella, G.: REST APIs: a large-scale analysis of compliance with principles and best practices. In: Bozzon, A., Cudre-Maroux, P., Pautasso, C. (eds.) ICWE 2016. LNCS, vol. 9671, pp. 21–39. Springer, Cham (2016). doi:10.1007/978-3-319-38791-8_2

20. Sohan, S.M., Anslow, C., Maurer, F.: A case study of web API evolution. In: SERVICES 2015, pp. 245–252. IEEE, June 2015

21. Tan, W., Fan, Y., Ghoneim, A., Hossain, M.A., Dustdar, S.: From the service-oriented architecture to the web API economy. IEEE Internet Comput. **20**(4), 64–68 (2016)

22. Vukovic, M., Laredo, J., Rajagopal, S.: API terms and conditions as a service. In: ISCC 2014, pp. 386–393. IEEE, June 2014

23. Vukovic, M., Zeng, L.Z., Rajagopal, S.: Model for service license in API ecosystems. In: Franch, X., Ghose, A.K., Lewis, G.A., Bhiri, S. (eds.) ICSOC 2014. LNCS, vol. 8831, pp. 590–597. Springer, Heidelberg (2014). doi:10.1007/978-3-662-45391-9_51

24. Wittern, E., Laredo, J., Vukovic, M., Muthusamy, V., Slominski, A.: A graph-based data model for API ecosystem insights. In: ICWS 2014, pp. 41–48. IEEE, June 2014

25. Yu, S., Woodard, C.J.: Innovation in the programmable web: characterizing the mashup ecosystem. In: Feuerlicht, G., Lamersdorf, W. (eds.) ICSOC 2008. LNCS, vol. 5472, pp. 136–147. Springer, Heidelberg (2009). doi:10.1007/978-3-642-01247-1_13

Efficient Influential Individuals Discovery on Service-Oriented Social Networks: A Community-Based Approach

Fanghua Ye[1,3], Jiahao Liu[1,3], Chuan Chen[1,3], Guohui Ling[2], Zibin Zheng[1,3(✉)], and Yuren Zhou[1]

[1] School of Data and Computer Science, Sun Yat-sen University, Guangzhou, China
{yefh5,liujiah9}@mail2.sysu.edu.cn,
{chenchuan,zhzibin,zhouyuren}@mail.sysu.edu.cn
[2] Data Center of WeChat Group, Tencent Technology, Shenzhen, China
randyling@tencent.com
[3] Key Laboratory of Machine Intelligence and Advanced Computing
(Sun Yat-sen University), Ministry of Education, Guangzhou, China

Abstract. With the rapid development of Internet and mobile Internet, service-oriented social networks gain increasing popularity. Discovering a small subset of influential individuals on service-oriented social networks is beneficial for both users and service providers. This issue is formally referred to the influence maximization problem. In this paper, through exploiting the community structures of social networks, we propose two novel community-based approximation algorithms BCAA and ICAA, which have high performance guarantee as well as high efficiency, to address the influence maximization problem. Both BCAA and ICAA discover influential individuals within each individual community rather than the entire network. We further provide performance guarantee analysis of BCAA and ICAA. Finally, extensive experiments are conducted to demonstrate the efficiency and effectiveness of the proposed algorithms.

1 Introduction

With the rapid development of Internet and mobile Internet, social network has become an important platform for people's online life. For example, as one of the most prevalent social network platforms in China, WeChat has more than 800 million monthly active users [1]. Social networks are not only effective tools in connecting individuals, but also powerful platforms for delivering services, which leads to the transformation from traditional social networks to service-oriented social networks. In the service-oriented social networks, to discover a small subset of influential individuals is particularly important. From service providers' perspective, it is cost-effective to target these influential individuals only when they want to promote some services, because these influential individuals are more conductive to propagate services in the form of "word-of-mouth" [2]. From users'

© Springer International Publishing AG 2017
M. Maximilien et al. (Eds.): ICSOC 2017, LNCS 10601, pp. 605–613, 2017.
https://doi.org/10.1007/978-3-319-69035-3_44

perspective, it is trustworthy to follow the recommendations from these influential individuals when they expect to obtain high-quality services. Formally, discovering influential individuals is referred to as *influence maximization*.

During the past few decades, extensive approaches [3–5, 7–11] have been proposed to solve the influence maximization problem. These approaches mainly fall into two categories: (1) greedy algorithms [3, 5, 8, 11], which possess high performance guarantee but are time-consuming; and (2) heuristic algorithms [4, 7, 9, 10], which are time-efficient but lack performance guarantee. Therefore, it is essential to devise new algorithms that have both high efficiency and high performance guarantee.

In this paper, we propose a novel approach with both efficiency and performance guarantee to improve Kempe's greedy algorithm [8]. The basic idea of this approach is to discover influential individuals within communities rather than the entire network, as community structure is a basic and important property of social networks [14] and has prominent effect on the influence spreading process [6, 15]. Intuitively, a community is a set of nodes with dense internal connections and sparse external connections. Individuals within a community tend to have more communications and thus are more likely to influence each other, while individuals across communities tend to have less contacts and thus are less likely to influence each other. Therefore, it is a good approximation to discover influential individuals within communities rather than the entire network. The proposed approach contains two phases: community detection in the first phase and influential individuals discovery in the second phase.

To detect high-quality communities, we first exploit LINE [16], one of the most popular network embedding methods, to extract a d-dimensional vector representation for each node in this network, which preserves the network neighbourhood relationships well. Then the network is partitioned into c communities by utilizing classic k-means algorithm [13] on the basis of the obtained vector representations. After obtaining the communities, we propose two community-based approximation algorithms to discover influential individuals. We first propose the basic community-based approximation algorithm BCAA, which is c times faster than Kempe's greedy algorithm, where c denotes the number of communities. BCAA is a simple improved version of Kempe's greedy algorithm, and the only difference between them is that BCAA estimates the influence spread of a subset of nodes within each individual community instead of the whole network. To further speed up BCAA, we propose the improved community-based approximation algorithm ICAA, which can avoid many wasteful computations by taking advantage of the submodularity property of influence spread (see more details in Sect. 2). We further analyze the performance guarantee of the proposed approach and show that both BCAA and ICAA can obtain a $(1 - e^{-\frac{1}{1+(c-1)\Delta I_c}})$ approximation to the optimal solution, where ΔI_c is the maximal influence spread of a node in the communities that do not contain this node.

In all, our contribution is three-fold: (1) A new community detection method based on network embedding is proposed to detect high-quality communities; (2) Two novel algorithms with high performance guarantee are proposed to discover influential individuals by exploiting the community structures of social networks; (3) Extensive experiments are conducted to demonstrate the effectiveness and efficiency of the proposed algorithms.

2 Problem Statement

A social network can be modeled as a weighted graph $G = (V, E, P)$ with $n = |V|$ nodes and $m = |E|$ edges. Each directed edge $e = (u, v)$ between nodes u and v is associated with a weight $p_{uv} \in [0, 1]$ in P, which represents the probability that node u influences node v.

Let $S \subseteq V$ be the subset of nodes selected as the initial target nodes for influence spreading. We define the *influence spread* of S, denoted by $I(S)$, as the expected number of nodes that are eventually influenced by S under certain spreading model. It is worth noting that $I(S)$ is a *submodular* function, i.e., $I(S \cup \{v\}) - I(S) \geq I(T \cup \{v\}) - I(T)$, for all $v \in V$ and $S \subseteq T \subseteq V$.

To estimate the influence spread $I(S)$, the spreading model should be determined at first. Here, we adopt the independent cascade (IC) model [8]. In IC model, each individual node has two states: active and inactive, and the influence spreading process unfolds in discrete timestamps according to the following rules. When node u becomes active at timestamp t, it can make an attempt to activate each inactive neighbour node v with probability p_{uv} at timestamp $t + 1$. However, u cannot make any further activation attempts at subsequent timestamps. The spreading process runs until no more activations are possible.

Definition 1 (Influence Maximization Problem). *Given a weighted graph $G = (V, E, P)$ and a parameter k, the influence maximization problem aims at discovering a size-k subset of nodes $S \subseteq V$ such that $I(S)$ is maximal.*

3 Proposed Solutions

3.1 Network Embedding Based Community Detection

Network embedding aims at extracting low-dimensional high-quality features for each node in the networks. Definition 2 presents its formal definition.

Definition 2 (Network Embedding). *Given a network $G = (V, E)$, the goal of network embedding is to embed each node $v \in V$ into a low-dimensional space R^d, that is, to learn a mapping function $f_G : V \to R^d$, where $d \ll |V|$. In space R^d, the network neighbourhood of each node is well preserved.*

In this paper, we employ the network embedding model LINE [16], which aims to preserve both the first-order proximity and the second-order proximity of a network. The first-order proximity refers to the local pairwise proximity, while the second-order proximity refers to the similarity of two nodes' neighbourhood network structures. We choose LINE because it preserves the community structures well. Intuitively, two nodes that are directly linked or share many common

---

Algorithm 1. The Basic Community-Based Approximation Algorithm

---
    Input: Graph $G = (V, E, P)$, parameter k
    Output: Seed nodes S_k
1 Partition G into c communities through the NECD procedure;
2 $S_0 \leftarrow \emptyset$;
3 **for** $i = 1$ **to** k **do**
4   **for** each node $v \in V \setminus S_{i-1}$ **do**
5   Let C_v be the community that contains v;
6          $H \leftarrow C_v \cap S_{i-1}$;
7          $M_C(v) \leftarrow I_C(H \cup \{v\}) - I_C(H)$;
8      $S_i \leftarrow S_{i-1} \cup \{\mathrm{argmax}_{v \in V \setminus S_{i-1}} M_C(v)\}$;
9 **return** S_k;

---

neighbours are more inclined to be included in a same community. After obtaining the low-dimensional vector representation of all the nodes, we exploit the classic k-means algorithm [13] to partition the network into c communities. This network embedding based community detection (NECD) procedure can detect high-quality communities with c properly set, and flexibly control the number of communities with reasonable quality guaranteed.

3.2 Basic Community-Based Approximation Algorithm BCAA

In this part, we devise BCAA to improve Kempe's greedy algorithm [8] by taking advantage of network communities. BCAA is outlined in Algorithm 1. Building on the NECD procedure, BCAA first partitions network G into c communities. Then, on the basis of these c communities and under the IC model, BCAA discovers seed nodes one by one iteratively. In each iteration, BCAA selects the node with maximal marginal influence spread as the next seed node (Steps 4-8). However, BCAA computes each node's marginal influence spread within each individual community instead of the entire network, i.e., $M_C(v) \leftarrow I_C(H \cup \{v\}) - I_C(H)$, where $I_C(\cdot)$ and $M_C(\cdot)$ denote community-based influence spread and community-based marginal influence spread respectively, and H denotes the seed nodes contained in the community that contains v (Steps 5-7).

3.3 Improved Community-Based Approximation Algorithm ICAA

In this part, we devise ICAA to improve BCAA by taking advantage of the submodularity of $I(\cdot)$. The key idea of ICAA is that there is no need to immediately recompute the community-based marginal influence spread for all the nodes in $V \setminus S_{i-1}$ in each iteration i. This is because the community-based marginal influence spread of node v computed before is an upper bound of v's current community-based marginal influence spread. What's more, the seed nodes contained in one community cannot affect the community-based marginal influence spread of nodes contained in any other community. Thus, when we are going to

---

Algorithm 2. The Improved Community-Based Approximation Algorithm

---

Input: Graph $G = (V, E, P)$, parameter k
Output: Seed nodes S_k

1 Partition G into c communities through the NECD procedure;
2 $S_0 \leftarrow \emptyset$; Priority Queue $Q \leftarrow \emptyset$;
3 **for** each node $v \in V$ **do**
4 $\quad\quad M_C(v) \leftarrow I_C(\{v\})$;
5 $\quad\quad Q.\text{Push}((v, 0, M_C(v)))$;

6 $(u, f, M_C(u)) \leftarrow Q.\text{Pop}()$;
7 $S_1 \leftarrow S_0 \cup \{u\}$; $i \leftarrow 1$;
8 **while** $i < k$ **do**
9 $\quad\quad (u, f, M_C(u)) \leftarrow Q.\text{Pop}()$;
10 $\quad\quad$ Let C_u be the community that contains u;
11 $\quad\quad H \leftarrow C_u \cap S_i$;
12 $\quad\quad n_u \leftarrow |H|$;
13 $\quad\quad$ **if** $f < n_u$ **then**
14 $\quad\quad\quad\quad$ Recompute u's community-based marginal influence spread, i.e.,
       $\quad\quad\quad\quad \widetilde{M}_C(u) \leftarrow I_C(H \cup \{u\}) - I_C(H)$;
15 $\quad\quad\quad\quad f \leftarrow n_u$;
16 $\quad\quad\quad\quad Q.\text{Push}((u, f, \widetilde{M}_C(u)))$;
17 $\quad\quad$ **else**
18 $\quad\quad\quad\quad S_{i+1} \leftarrow S_i \cup \{u\}$;
19 $\quad\quad\quad\quad i \leftarrow i + 1$;

20 **return** S_k;

---

find a new seed node, we first choose the node with the maximal community-based marginal influence spread as a candidate, then we check if the marginal influence spread of this node should be recomputed. If not, this node is chosen as the next seed node, otherwise we recompute the community-based marginal influence spread of this node. ICAA is outlined in Algorithm 2.

ICAA initially partitions network G into c communities via the NECD procedure. Then, ICAA calculates the community-based influence spread for each node $v \in V$, and pushes a corresponding 3-tuple $(v, 0, M_C(\{v\}))$ into a priority queue Q (Steps 3-5). Here, the second element f of the 3-tuple represents the number of seed nodes that are contained in the community that contains v. Obviously, f should be 0 for each node before the first seed node is determined. Besides, each 3-tuple has a priority associated with the third element, and the 3-tuple whose third element is larger has higher priority. Hence, the node u corresponding to the first 3-tuple in Q has the largest community-based marginal influence spread. Then, ICAA takes u as the first seed node (Steps 6-7). Since u has been selected as a seed node, the community-based marginal influence spread of each node contained in the community that contains u (denoted as C_u) should be recomputed. By the submodularity property of $I(\cdot)$, one can see that the community-based marginal influence spread of each node is non-increasing as more and more seed nodes are determined. That is, the third element of the 3-tuple corresponding to each node is an upper bound of its current community-based marginal influence spread. Building on this observation, the update of the community-based marginal influence spread of each node contained in C_u can be delayed, which will reduce many wasteful computations. Thus, in the while loop, ICAA chooses the node u corresponding to the first 3-tuple in Q as a candidate seed node rather than a new one (Step 9). Assume that the current number of seed nodes contained in C_u is n_u. If $f < n_u$, the community-based marginal influence spread of u is recomputed and f is updated to n_u, then the updated 3-tuple is pushed into Q again (Steps 14-16). If $f = n_u$, node u is selected as the next seed node directly (Steps 18-19). According to this strategy, ICAA discovers the k most influential nodes iteratively.

Let ΔI_c denote the maximal influence spread of a node in the communities that do not contain this node. Now, we analyze the performance guarantee of BCAA and ICAA in Theorem 1.

Theorem 1. *Both BCAA and ICAA obtain a* $(1 - e^{-\frac{1}{1+(c-1)\Delta I_c}})$ *approximation to the optimal solution.*

4   Experiments

4.1   Experimental Settings

In the experiments, we evaluate our proposed approaches on three real-life social networks: WeChat [1] (1 K nodes, 7 K edges and 10 communities), Facebook [12] (4 K nodes, 88 K edges and 10 communities), and Epinions [12] (76 K nodes, 406 K edges and 20 communities). Since the original networks are unweighted, we use the number of common neighbours between two individuals u and v to denote the weight of edge $e = (u, v)$, i.e., $w_{uv} = |nb(u) \cap nb(v)|$, which is used in the NECD procedure. Here we use $nb(u)$ to denote the union of u and its neighbours. The propagation probability of edge $e = (u, v)$ is defined as follows.

$$p_{uv} = 2\frac{|nb(u)| - 1}{|nb(v)| - 1} \cdot \frac{|nb(u) \cap nb(v)|}{|nb(u) \cup nb(v)|}\bar{p} \tag{1}$$

where $\bar{p}$ is the average propagation probability of the whole network. In our experiments, $\bar{p}$ is set to be 0.05.

We employ conventional running time and approximation ratio as evaluation metrics. Running time is used to measure the time efficiency of the proposed algorithms. Approximation ratio is used to measure the approximation degree to the optimal solution $I(S^*)$, which is defined as $I(S)/I(S^*)$.

To evaluate the performance of our proposed algorithms, we select four representative approaches for comparison, which includes two greedy algorithms: GA [8] and CELF++ [5], and two heuristic algorithms: IMRank [4] and Random [3].

4.2 Experimental Results

In the experiments, we fix the dimension number d used in the NECD procedure at 60, and set the number of Monte Carlo simulations t in the IC model as 100.

Exp-1: Running time testing via varying k. In this experiment, we vary the size of seed node set k from 1 to 30 to evaluate the efficiency of different algorithms. Figure 1 depicts the results. Note that we use logarithmic scale for y-axis in this figure. From Fig. 1, we can see that the heuristic algorithms IMRank and Random run very fast, while the greedy algorithms GA and CELF++ run much slower. For our proposed algorithms BCAA and ICAA, we see that both BCAA and ICAA are several orders of magnitude faster than GA and ICAA runs much faster than CELF++ as well. From Fig. 1, we can also see that the running time of ICAA almost does not change when k increases. This is due to the fact that the main time cost of ICAA is to compute the community-based marginal influence spread for every node in the first iteration, and it takes a little time to find the other $(k-1)$ influential individuals in the subsequent iterations.

Exp-2: Approximation ratio testing via varying k. The objective of this experiment is to evaluate the degree of approximation of different algorithms by taking the results of GA as the ground truth. As shown in Fig. 2, CELF++ has the highest approximation ratio, while Random has the lowest one. The approximation ratio of IMRank is unstable and it mainly falls in the range $[0.5, 0.8]$. However, BCAA and ICAA have much more stable and much higher

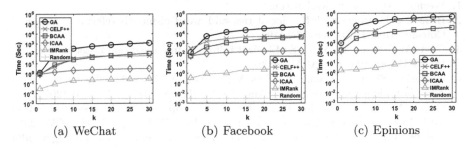

(a) WeChat   (b) Facebook   (c) Epinions

Fig. 1. Running time testing via varying k

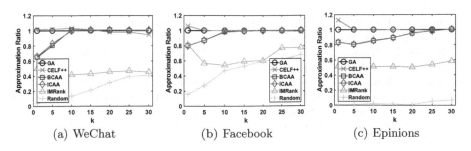

(a) WeChat   (b) Facebook   (c) Epinions

Fig. 2. Approximation ratio testing via varying k

612   F. Ye et al.

approximation ratio. In particular, as k grows larger, the approximation ratio of BCAA and ICAA becomes as close as possible to 1. This result verifies our previous performance guarantee analysis.

5   Conclusion

In this paper, we study the influence maximization problem on service-oriented social networks via taking into account community structures. First, we exploit the classic k-means algorithm based on network embedding to detect communities. Next, we propose the basic community-based approximation algorithm BCAA, which discovers influential individuals within communities instead of the entire network, and then propose the improved community-based approximation algorithm ICAA to further speed up BCAA. We further provide performance guarantee analysis of the proposed algorithms. Finally, we validate our proposed algorithms through experiments.

Acknowledgement. The work described in this paper was supported by the National Key Research and Development Program (2016YFB1000101), the National Natural Science Foundation of China (61472338), and the Pearl River S&T Nova Program of Guangzhou (201710010046). Zibin Zheng is the corresponding author.

References

1. Wechat, http://www.wechat.com/
2. Brown, J.J., Reingen, P.H.: Social ties and word-of-mouth referral behavior. J. Consum. Res. **14**(3), 350–362 (1987)
3. Chen, W., Wang, Y., Yang, S.: Efficient influence maximization in social networks. In: KDD, pp. 199–208. ACM (2009)
4. Cheng, S., Shen, H., Huang, J., Chen, W., Cheng, X.: Imrank: influence maximization via finding self-consistent ranking. In: SIGIR, pp. 475–484. ACM (2014)
5. Goyal, A., Lu, W., Lakshmanan, L.V.: Celf++: optimizing the greedy algorithm for influence maximization in social networks. In: WWW, pp. 47–48. ACM (2011)
6. Halappanavar, M., Sathanur, A.V., Nandi, A.K.: Accelerating the mining of influential nodes in complex networks through community detection. In: Proceedings of the ACM International Conference on Computing Frontiers, pp. 64–71. ACM (2016)
7. Jung, K., Heo, W., Chen, W.: Irie: Scalable and robust influence maximization in social networks. In: ICDM, pp. 918–923. IEEE (2012)
8. Kempe, D., Kleinberg, J., Tardos, É.: Maximizing the spread of influence through a social network. In: KDD, pp. 137–146. ACM (2003)
9. Kim, J., Kim, S.K., Yu, H.: Scalable and parallelizable processing of influence maximization for large-scale social networks? In: ICDE, pp. 266–277. IEEE (2013)
10. Kimura, M., Saito, K., Nakano, R., Motoda, H.: Extracting influential nodes on a social network for information diffusion. Data Min. Knowl. Disc. **20**(1), 70–97 (2010)
11. Leskovec, J., Krause, A., Guestrin, C., Faloutsos, C., VanBriesen, J., Glance, N.: Cost-effective outbreak detection in networks. In: KDD, pp. 420–429. ACM (2007)

12. Leskovec, J., Krevl, A.: SNAP Datasets: Stanford large network dataset collection, http://snap.stanford.edu/data

13. MacQueen, J., et al.: Some methods for classification and analysis of multivariate observations. In: Proceedings of the Fifth Berkeley Symposium on Mathematical Statistics and Probability, Oakland, CA, USA, pp. 281–297 (1967)

14. Newman, M.E.: The structure and function of complex networks. SIAM Rev. **45**(2), 167–256 (2003)

15. Salathé, M., Jones, J.H.: Dynamics and control of diseases in networks with community structure. PLoS Comput. Biol. **6**(4), e1000736 (2010)

16. Tang, J., Qu, M., Wang, M., Zhang, M., Yan, J., Mei, Q.: Line: large-scale information network embedding. In: WWW, pp. 1067–1077. ACM (2015)

Empirical Study on REST APIs Usage in Android Mobile Applications

Mohamed A. Oumaziz[1]([✉]), Abdelkarim Belkhir[2], Tristan Vacher[2], Eric Beaudry[2], Xavier Blanc[1], Jean-Rémy Falleri[1], and Naouel Moha[2]

[1] Univ. Bordeaux - LaBRI - UMR CNRS 5800, Talence, France
{moumaziz,xblanc,falleri}@labri.fr
[2] LATECE, Département d'informatique, Université du Québec à Montréal,
Montreal, Canada
{belkhir.abdelkarim,vacher.tristan}@courrier.uqam.ca,
{beaudry.eric,moha.naouel}@uqam.ca

Abstract. A large set of mobile applications (apps) heavily rely on services accessible through the Web via REST APIs. However, the way mobile apps use services in practice has never been studied. In this paper, we perform an empirical study in the Android ecosystem in which we analyze 500 popular apps and 15 popular services. We also conducted an online survey to identify best practices for Android developers. Our results show that they generally favor invoking services by using official service libraries instead of invoking services with a generic HTTP client. We also present which good practices service libraries should implement.

Keywords: Empirical study · Mobile applications · REST API · Rest services · Android

1 Introduction

Following the REST principles [6], server side applications are nowadays composed of several stateless independent micro-services [11]. They therefore make client side applications consuming more and more REST services [5]. Such evolution brings new challenges especially for the design of Android applications that now have to handle lots of calls to REST services.

However, little is known on how Android apps use REST services in practice. Such knowledge is of high importance for the service providers since it would help them provide facilities to Android developers and hence improve the usability of their REST services. For instance, do the developers prefer to handle JSON documents or Java objects? Do they want dedicated service libraries or do they want to perform the calls by using a HTTP client library?

In this article, we provide answers to these questions by performing an empirical study in the famous Android ecosystem. Our study focuses on two research questions. Our first research question: *"As service users, how*

M. Maximilien et al. (Eds.): ICSOC 2017, LNCS 10601, pp. 614–622, 2017.
https://doi.org/10.1007/978-3-319-69035-3_45

Android developers access popular REST services/APIs in their applications?", aims at identifying the developers' habits for accessing REST services. Our study shows that Android developers prefer to use a dedicated service library developed by the service provider if it exists.

Our second question: *"As service providers, how to design client helper libraries to be popular among mobile applications?"*, aims at identifying which features of service libraries are considered important by developers. For instance, our study shows that the essential features for developers are the existence of a complete documentation, the library's vocabulary consistency with the service's one, the use of raw JSON to exchange data, the handling of authentication, and the ability to fine-tune the HTTP requests issued by the library.

This paper is structured as follows. Sections 2 and 3 respectively describe the study setup and results for the research questions RQ1 and RQ2. Section 4 presents the related work. Section 5 concludes and presents future works.

2   RQ1: *As service users, how Android developers access popular REST services/APIs in their applications?*

In this section, we investigate our first research question. We noticed that there are two main ways to access services from Android apps: directly, by using an HTTP client, or by using a library developed by the provider (official) or by its users (third-party). To assess which method is the most popular, we analyze how 15 popular services are used in a corpus of 500 popular apps. Section 2.1 explains how we build the corpus of services and apps. Section 2.2 explains how apps invoke services. Results and observations are then presented in Sect. 2.3.

2.1   Corpus

Our corpus consists of two sets: a set of popular apps and a set of popular services that are called by the popular apps. Additionally, we also gather the list of libraries that allow Android apps to interact with the services of our corpus.

We started by gathering a set of popular apps. To that extent, we crawled the top 500 most popular apps provided by the Google Play store[1]. We then downloaded the application packages of each app using the AndroZoo dataset maintained by our colleagues from the University of Luxembourg [1]. During this step, we were only able to download 487 app files.

To build the set of popular services, we analyzed the 487 APK files to identify which popular services are called. We then used the AndroGuard tool[2] to extract all the strings contained in the DEX bytecode files of each of our apps. From these strings, we extracted the URLs (i.e. starting with `http[s]://`). We then ranked these URLs by their number of occurrences and filtered out the ones

---

[1] https://play.google.com/store/apps/collection/topselling_free.
[2] https://github.com/androguard/androguard.

that do not correspond to a service (e.g. manual URL browsing). Finally, we manually selected 15 services among the 50 most popular ones.

To identify all the libraries for each service in our corpus, we use Google search with the following query "[service name] android library"; where "[service name]" corresponds to the service's root URL. Then, we manually look at the results to assess whether it describes an official library or a third-party one.

2.2 Experimental Setup

To answer our first research question, we check how apps call services, and in particular if they directly use services by making HTTP requests or if they use a dedicated library. To that extent, we first identify the services used by each app in our corpus. Secondly, we analyze if each app uses a library or not to access the services. Using this data, for each service, we classify the apps into three categories: apps using the service without library, apps using the service with an official library, and apps using a third-party library.

To find out which apps are using a given service we followed these steps. First we manually read the documentation of each service to find their API URL. Secondly, we manually browsed the code of all libraries to find out the list of all the Java packages they contain. Finally, we used the AndroGuard tool again to extract all the strings contained in all apps from our corpus. When we were able to find a service's API URL, we considered that the application used the service. In this case, we also looked for the Java package names of this service's libraries in the strings of the app. When we were able to find a package name in the string list, we assumed that the app is using its corresponding library.

Finally, to analyze how developers access services in practice, we perform the following process. For each service provider, we compute the set of all Android apps from our corpus that use it. Then, we partition this set into three subsets: the set of apps that use the official library, the set of apps that use a third-party library or both the official library and a third-party library, and the set of apps that do not use any library. To discuss the favourite way of developers to access the service, we then compare the size of these subsets, normalized by the size of all apps that use the services. Results are discussed in Sect. 2.3.

2.3 Results

In our results (accessible on our website[3]), we notice that only 5 out of 15 services are accessed with a HTTP client rather than a library. Moreover, 2 out of the 5 services provide no official library (Instagram and OpenStreetMap). Therefore, libraries are favoured to access services. Additionally, for the 10 services where a library is preferred, it is always the official library that is preferred, even if there are only 3 cases where no third-party library is available. In conclusion, **official libraries are the favourite way of developers to access services.**

---

[3] http://se.labri.fr/a/ICSOC17-oumaziz/.

However, although there are many HTTP clients, developers still prefer standard ones that are embedded in the Android Framework. The top four being in order: *HttpUrlConnection*, *HttpsUrlConnection*, *DefaultHttpClient* and *AndroidHttpClient*. We also notice that developers tend to use more than just one HTTP client, this can be related to the features that each client offers depending on developer's needs. For instance, *HttpsUrlConnection* is able to handle HTTPS requests while *HttpUrlConnection* only handles HTTP requests.

2.4 Threats to Validity

We discuss here the threats to validity of our study. The techniques used to detect client libraries and API URLs are not infallible. For instance, if an app is obfuscated, our techniques probably fail to identify URLs and used libraries. Also, there is the construction of URLs by string concatenations. Since we made a static analysis, we cannot catch all possible strings that could be built at runtime. Finally, we had to manually look at all available libraries for each service in our dataset. We may have missed few of them. Our corpus only contains 15 services and about 500 apps. Therefore, our results might not be generalizable to all Android apps. We attempt to provide all the necessary details to replicate our study and analysis, Scripts and datasets are also available online.

3   RQ2: *As service providers, how to design client helper libraries to be popular among mobile applications?*

To answer the second research question, we first studied the steps that apps follow to call a service, and the different kinds of libraries used under the hood. Then, from this process we identified the good and bad practices that should be followed when designing a service library. In the third step, we conducted an online survey to validate these good and bad practices by experts. As a final step, we analyzed official service libraries provided by popular services to verify if the latter are conform to these practices. We now detail each step.

Step 1. Process to consume a service. We study the general process followed by any app to call a service. The process is divided in two sub-processes: Authentication which is optional (where the client asks for access right), and service consumption (where the client interacts with the service). During this process the app uses different libraries for: parsing, OAuth (to ask for permission), and HTTP Clients (to deal with the HTTP protocol).

Step 2. List of good/bad practices when developing a service library. We identify here the good/bad practices that must be followed when designing a service library.

Step 3. Online survey to validate the good and bad practices. The goal of the survey is to confirm the best practices that must be followed by service providers in their libraries to ease consumption by developers. The survey is available online[4]. Based on the good and bad practices identified in *Step 2*, we build a survey on Google Forms and emailed it to 2000 Android developers randomly selected from the top 500 Android apps developers for each Google Play's category. We also submitted the survey as a Reddit Thread on the very active subreddit *Androiddev*, and advertised the survey through social networks. 51 Android developers responded to our survey and 83% of them are familiar with Android development. The survey and its results are available on our website.

Step 4. Analysis of the official REST libraries. Finally, we manually analyzed 11 libraries and 14 services from our corpus. We did not analyze the Open-StreetMap and Instagram services because no libraries are available for these services, and the Google API Client library groups GoogleMaps, GoogleSignIn and YouTube services. All have been analyzed by three experienced Android developers to verify their conformance with the practices identified and validated in the two previous steps. We performed this analysis using their documentation, source code and provided examples.

3.1   Results of Research Question 2

For each identified good/bad practice, we first give a description as follow:

① *JSON vs. XML.* Always choose JSON over XML when both are proposed by the API provider.

② *Typed Response vs. Non-typed Response.* The response returned from the library for a given query should be a Java Object. In contrast, a *Non-typed Response* is a response returned as a JSON or XML format.

③ *Encapsulated HTTP Queries vs. Non-encapsulated HTTP Queries.* The HTTP query should be encapsulated in a method proposed by the interface of your library. A *Non-encapsulated HTTP Query* has to be manually built by the developer with all the needed parameters.

④ *Full vs. Non-exhaustive API support.* The Service Library should cover all the services proposed by the REST API.

⑤ *Consistent vs. Inconsistent vocabulary with documentation.* The vocabulary used in the code when naming classes, methods and attributes should correspond to the one used in the documentation of the REST API.

⑥ *Documented vs. Non-documented Library.* The library should be well documented, the user should be able to understand how to access the REST API endpoints preferably with code samples.

⑦ *Allowing Authentication vs. Third-party Authentication.* When an authentication is required to consume the offered services by the REST API. It is preferable that your Service Library allows authentication.

---

[4] http://bit.ly/clientpractices.

⑧ *Android Specific Functionalities vs. Only General Functionalities.* A good practice is to provide some Android specific functionalities such as widgets, views and fragments instead of providing only general functionalities.

We then chose to further discuss only 5 out of our 8 identified good/bad practices. The survey results are highlighted in bold.

① From our corpus, it seems that APIs favour the JSON format over others. Every library allows to return at least a response in the JSON format and provides sometimes other formats (XML, CSV, etc.). Although JSON is the most popular, it is not by default for all libraries. **In our survey, 92.2% of the developers stated that JSON was preferred.** This could be due to the fact that the JSON format is easier to handle, while also faster to load and to parse compared to XML files [2].

② Over the 11 libraries we studied, 6 return a domain-specific object representing an entity of the API (e.g. a File in the DropBox Library). So users don't need to parse the response. However, some libraries return an object containing data. For example, Facebook returns a GraphResponse object that contains the response, which is either a JSONObject, a JSONArray or a Java String. **In contrast, in our survey more than 70.6% of developers prefer to have responses as Java Strings.**

③ Almost all (10 out of 11) libraries except LinkedIn encapsulate HTTP queries. Users do not have to build their own requests, they can use predefined methods. However, libraries such as Facebook allow to build custom requests while providing encapsulated queries. **In the survey, 37.3% of developers think that modifying encapuslated queries is mandatory, and 47.1% of them think that it is appreciated. Therefore, although the majority of libraries encapsulate queries, developers still prefer to have access and control the queries.**

⑦ All analyzed services require authentication to be used. Authentication is a means to secure which data are reachable to someone, but also to control the request flow for avoiding overloading servers. All libraries implemented the entire service authentication protocol, namely OAuth2. **In the survey, developers confirm the necessity to implement the whole service authentication protocol with 58.8% who appreciate it and 29.4% who request it to be mandatory.**

⑧ Almost half of the libraries (5 out of 11) provide at least one Android specific functionality such as Widgets, Activities, or Views. Providing such functionalities can help developers focus on their own apps instead of trying to integrate logic from a third-party environment. **However, 86.3% of developers consider that providing such functionalities is not important.**

3.2 Threats to Validity

We discuss here the threats to validity of this section. The terminology used in the survey might have been misunderstood by the responders. However we wrote definitions and examples to mitigate these threats. Our survey was answered by only 51 Android developers. Therefore, our findings might not be generalizable.

4 Related Work

In the following, we discuss some relevant research done on assessing bad and good practices in REST APIs as well as research on libraries identification.

Bad and good REST practices. In [12–14], we evaluated the design of several REST APIs based on good and bad REST practices, also called REST patterns and antipatterns. We proposed automatic approaches to detect them. However, we evaluated APIs without considering any interaction with clients, and in particular mobile clients, as we do here. Other works proposed similar (anti-)patterns detection approaches in service applications, but implementing other techniques such as bi-level optimisation problems [17] or ontologies [4].

In [15], Rodriguez et al. evaluated the conformance of design best practices in REST APIs from the perspective of mobile apps. They analyzed these practices on a large dataset of HTTP requests collected from a Mobile Internet traffic. This work is the first that has studied the traffic of HTTP requests from the mobile perspective. However, the best practices analyzed are rather common to any kinds of REST APIs, and they focused on HTTP requests.

In contrast, in this paper, we consider practices that may apply on mobile apps. We take also into account the interaction between clients and REST APIs by analyzing all the process from the authentication to the service consumption, and thus while considering all kinds of message exchanges (requests, responses). We study also how REST APIs are implemented and documented.

Libraries identification. There are several works that have been done for identifying advertisement libraries in Android apps. Book et al. [3] and Grace et al. [7] used a whitelists based method for identification. There are also tools such as AdDetect [10] and PEDAL [9] that applied machine learning techniques (SVM classification) to identify advertising libraries even if apps are obfuscated.

Teyton et al. [16] applied static analysis on the source code on a group of libraries to automatically extract Java package names. They identified 1185 different libraries which they then used to automatically identify Java libraries dependencies. Wang et al. [18] proposed a novel clustering-based technique to automatically identify Android third-party libraries. Their technique identified more than 600 different Android libraries in a corpus of 100,000 apps. Li et al. [8] proposed a novel approach for identifying third-party libraries from Android apps. Rather than using code similarity, they used code dependencies.

In this paper, we used the Java package names as a way to identify libraries. However, we had to identify service libraries, to do so, we used API URLs to determine if an app was using a service and then we applied this library identification technique to look if it was through a service library.

5 Conclusion and Future Work

While nowadays Android apps rely more than ever on REST services, no study has been performed on how Android apps invoke services. We alleviated this situation by performing an empirical study of 15 popular web services on a dataset of almost 500 popular Android apps. We show that developers prefer to use official libraries. We also show that developers prefer to use HTTP clients rather than libraries and prefer default clients provided in the Android Framework.

Second, we propose a list of good/bad practices, identified through an analysis of the practices of popular services and an online survey involving 51 developers. We show that the important features for libraries are: the use of raw JSON, authentication handling and the possibility to fine-tune HTTP requests.

As a future work, we plan to extend our practices' list and to extend the size of our dataset of services and apps in order to have more generalizable results.

Acknowledgement. The authors thank the Android developers for answering the survey. This study is supported by NSERC and FRQNT, Canada and Quebec research grants.

References

1. Allix, K., Bissyandé, T.F., Klein, J., Le Traon, Y.: AndroZoo: collecting millions of android apps for the research community. In: 13th MSR, pp. 468–471 (2016)
2. Betts, T.: Mobile performance testing - JSON vs XML. Blog. https://www.infragistics.com/community/blogs/torrey-betts/archive/2016/04/19/mobile-performance-testing-json-vs-xml.aspx. Accessed 20 June 2017
3. Book, T., Pridgen, A., Wallach, D.S.: Longitudinal analysis of android ad library permissions. arXiv preprint arXiv:1303.0857 (2013)
4. Brabra, H., Mtibaa, A., Sliman, L., Gaaloul, W., Benatallah, B., Gargouri, F.: Detecting cloud (Anti)Patterns: OCCI perspective. In: Sheng, Q.Z., Stroulia, E., Tata, S., Bhiri, S. (eds.) ICSOC 2016. LNCS, vol. 9936, pp. 202–218. Springer, Cham (2016). doi:10.1007/978-3-319-46295-0_13
5. Danielsen, P.J., Jeffrey, A.: Validation and interactivity of web API documentation. In: 20th ICWS, pp. 523–530 (2013)
6. Fielding, R.T.: Architectural Styles and the Design of Network-based Software Architectures. Ph.D. thesis, University of California, Irvine (2000)
7. Grace, M.C., Zhou, W., Jiang, X., Sadeghi, A.R.: Unsafe exposure analysis of mobile in-app. advertisements. In: 5th ACM WiSec, pp. 101–112. ACM (2012)
8. Li, M., Wang, W., Wang, P., Wang, S., Wu, D., Liu, J., Xue, R., Huo, W.: LibD: scalable and precise third-party library detection in android markets. In: 39th ICSE, pp. 335–346. IEEE Press (2017)
9. Liu, B., Liu, B., Jin, H., Govindan, R.: Efficient privilege de-escalation for AD libraries in mobile apps. In: 13th MobiSys, pp. 89–103. ACM (2015)
10. Narayanan, A., Chen, L., Chan, C.K.: Addetect: automated detection of android ad libraries using semantic analysis. In: IEEE ISSNIP 2014, pp. 1–6. IEEE (2014)
11. Newman, S.: Building Microservices - Designing Fine-grained Systems, 1st edn. O'Reilly, New York (2015)

12. Palma, F., Dubois, J., Moha, N., Guéhéneuc, Y.-G.: Detection of REST patterns and antipatterns: a heuristics-based approach. In: Franch, X., Ghose, A.K., Lewis, G.A., Bhiri, S. (eds.) ICSOC 2014. LNCS, vol. 8831, pp. 230–244. Springer, Heidelberg (2014). doi:10.1007/978-3-662-45391-9_16

13. Palma, F., Gonzalez-Huerta, J., Moha, N., Guéhéneuc, Y.-G., Tremblay, G.: Are RESTful APIs well-designed? detection of their linguistic (Anti)Patterns. In: Barros, A., Grigori, D., Narendra, N.C., Dam, H.K. (eds.) ICSOC 2015. LNCS, vol. 9435, pp. 171–187. Springer, Heidelberg (2015). doi:10.1007/978-3-662-48616-0_11

14. Petrillo, F., Merle, P., Moha, N., Guéhéneuc, Y.-G.: Are REST APIs for cloud computing well-designed? an exploratory study. In: Sheng, Q.Z., Stroulia, E., Tata, S., Bhiri, S. (eds.) ICSOC 2016. LNCS, vol. 9936, pp. 157–170. Springer, Cham (2016). doi:10.1007/978-3-319-46295-0_10

15. Rodríguez, C., Baez, M., Daniel, F., Casati, F., Trabucco, J.C., Canali, L., Percannella, G.: REST APIs: a large-scale analysis of compliance with principles and best practices. In: Bozzon, A., Cudre-Maroux, P., Pautasso, C. (eds.) ICWE 2016. LNCS, vol. 9671, pp. 21–39. Springer, Cham (2016). doi:10.1007/978-3-319-38791-8_2

16. Teyton, C., Falleri, J.R., Palyart, M., Blanc, X.: A study of library migrations in java. J. Softw. Evol. Process **26**(11), 1030–1052 (2014)

17. Wang, H., Kessentini, M., Ouni, A.: Bi-level identification of web service defects. In: Sheng, Q.Z., Stroulia, E., Tata, S., Bhiri, S. (eds.) ICSOC 2016. LNCS, vol. 9936, pp. 352–368. Springer, Cham (2016). doi:10.1007/978-3-319-46295-0_22

18. Wang, H., Guo, Y., Ma, Z., Chen, X.: Wukong: a scalable and accurate two-phase approach to android app. clone detection. In: ISSTA 2015, pp. 71–82. ACM (2015)

Services in the Cloud

Revenue-Driven Service Provisioning for Resource Sharing in Mobile Cloud Computing

Hongyue Wu[1,2], Shuiguang Deng[1(✉)], Wei Li[2], Jianwei Yin[1(✉)],
Qiang Yang[3], Zhaohui Wu[1], and Albert Y. Zomaya[2]

[1] College of Computer Science and Technology, Zhejiang University,
Hangzhou, China
{hongyue_wu, dengsg, zjuyjw, wzh}@zju.edu.cn
[2] School of Information Technologies, The University of Sydney,
Sydney, Australia
liwei@it.usyd.edu.au, albert.zomaya@sydney.edu.au
[3] College of Electrical Engineering, Zhejiang University, Hangzhou, China
qyang@zju.edu.cn

Abstract. A new mobile cloud architecture has recently been proposed, where neighbouring mobile devices are brought together as a cohort for resource sharing. Thus, a mobile application can be partitioned into multiple tasks and be performed on different mobile devices, without offloading some tasks to remote cloud services for their processing. In this work, we consider a broker-based architecture, where a proper reward mechanism is used to incentivize users to share their available resources as a service with other mobile devices. Within such a system, each mobile device is rational and justified in maximizing its revenue by using its relatively limited resources to complete the requests allocated by the broker. How to select the appropriate service requests from all incoming requests and complete the selected requests on time so that the revenue can be maximized has become a critical issue for resource sharing. To address this issue, we propose a joint resource sharing and request scheduling approach called RESP (REvenue-driven Service Provision for mobile devices) in a move towards a lightweight one-phase approach for handling request selection, request scheduling and resource allocation for mobile devices. We evaluate the performance of our proposed algorithm through a number of experiments and the experimental results validate the efficacy of our approach.

Keywords: Mobile cloud computing · Scheduling · Service provisioning · Resource sharing

1 Introduction

Mobile devices have been one of the fastest adopted consumer products of all time and highly integrated into our daily life. The manufacturers of mobile devices have also made breakthrough contributions to improve hardware capabilities in terms of computation, communication and storage. The requirements for running applications with

© Springer International Publishing AG 2017
M. Maximilien et al. (Eds.): ICSOC 2017, LNCS 10601, pp. 625–640, 2017.
https://doi.org/10.1007/978-3-319-69035-3_46

high computation requirements, e.g. multimedia processing, social networking and natural language processing on mobile devices become more intense. However, in general, mobile devices are still resource constrained compared to dedicated computers. To enable such applications to run effectively on mobile devices, a natural solution is mobile cloud computing (MCC) [10], so that the mobile devices can offload computationally intensive tasks to the resource-rich cloud service providers, such as Amazon's EC2[1], Microsoft Azure[2] and Rackspace Cloud[3] and complete the applications collaboratively. In most cases, these cloud services are geographically remote from the mobile devices, and a reliable Internet connection is required to transmit the data between the two ends.

By fully utilizing the increasing amount of mobile devices and their ubiquitous presence, a new architecture for MCC has recently been proposed [9], where the neighbouring mobile devices are brought together as a cohort for resource sharing. Using the idle resources of a collection of mobile devices in the vicinity, an application can thus be partitioned into multiple tasks and be performed on different devices collaboratively. With such an approach, the unstable and costly Internet connection of mobile devices is no longer a constraint as it is in the traditional MCC architectures. Also the data exchange among the mobile devices in the local area can benefit from different wireless communication technologies, e.g. WiFi and Bluetooth. To better distinguish the MCC architectures, we refer to the new one that enables device-residing resource sharing as NMCC for the rest of the paper.

One of the key techniques to realize resource sharing in the NMCC is service provisioning, so that the available resources of each mobile device can be provided as on-demand services anytime, anywhere. In contrast to the powerful remote cloud servers, when accommodating excessive service requests, mobile devices may not be able to satisfy all the requests since they have limited computing capabilities and resources. In addition, the remote cloud service providers are equipped with resource-rich devices to allow them to use sophisticated solutions, e.g. machine learning methods for processing incoming requests. As these solutions are normally associated with high computational overhead, they cannot be simply applied to mobile devices. To ensure the quality of service (QoS) on the resource-constrained mobile devices, a lightweight QoS-aware service-based framework needs to be provided to (1) determine whether to accept or reject an incoming service request and (2) perform resource allocation for the selected service requests according to the available resources of a mobile device and the requirements of the tasks to be met. For example, if the remaining energy of a mobile device is high and its available network bandwidth is low, it would be preferable to accept computation intensive service requests rather than communication intensive service requests.

Apart from enabling a lightweight QoS-aware service-based framework in NMCC, it is not hard to see that the service provisioning in such systems strongly depends on the willingness to participate of the owners of mobile devices. To further ensure the

---

[1] http://aws.amazon.com.

[2] http://azure.microsoft.com/en-us/.

[3] http://www.rackspace.com.

quality of services, such NMCC systems need to employ a proper incentive mechanism to motivate the resource sharing of mobile devices [21]. Mobile service requesters can always encourage resource sharing by providing some rewards (e.g. discount, credit points, etc.), so that the mobile device owners can decide the degree of their participation to gain the corresponding revenue. We also assume that all the mobile devices have the same objective to maximize the revenue of their providing services.

In this paper, we study the issue of how to incentivize user participation for addressing the resource sharing in NMCC systems. To tackle the issue, we model it as a service provisioning and resource allocation problem of mobile devices, which is generally a constrained optimization problem. Using the task scheduling technique, we designed a lightweight approach called RESP (REvenue-driven Service Provision for mobile devices) for handling all the incoming requests with the objective of maximizing the revenue of the mobile devices. The approach can achieve efficient service request selection, request scheduling and resource allocation simultaneously. The performed experiments demonstrate that our proposed algorithm outperforms the selected benchmarks and provides the best overall performance for the users.

The rest of the paper is organized as follows. In Sect. 2, we review related works. In Sect. 3, we introduce the models used in this paper and formally define the problem. Then the details of our proposed algorithm are presented and discussed in Sect. 4. In Sect. 5, we show the conducted experiments and analyse the results. Finally, we conclude the paper and outline our future work in Sect. 6.

2 Related Work

The problem of service provision in MCC has been studied extensively, and various approaches have been proposed from different perspectives. Most of them focus on using remote resource-rich cloud services to enhance the capabilities of mobile devices. Liu et al. proposed a novel approach to predict the total workload for facilitating auto scaling resource management [14]. Lee et al. proposed a heuristic algorithm-based auction system to determine when and how the providers should allocate their resources and to which users [13]. Albagli-Kim et al. presented a comparative study of approximation algorithms and heuristics for scheduling jobs with dwindling resource requirements [1]. Maguluri et al. focused on scheduling jobs with unknown duration in clouds, and presented a load balancing and scheduling algorithm [17]. However, these works assume that the services are provided by the remote large-scale cloud servers and stable Internet connections are available, which may not be always true for some mobile users. These approaches cannot be simply applied to the MCC platforms that are formed by a cohort of mobile devices and the required services are provided from these mobile devices.

In recent years, with the rapid development of mobile devices and wireless communication techniques, some works have proposed forming a mobile cloud that avoids a connection being made to a remote cloud by using nearby mobile devices while maintaining the main benefits of resource sharing [7, 8]. Fernando et al. analysed the need for a mobile cloud and highlighted the direction of future work [10]. In [19], the authors discussed the feasibility of mobile service provision on smartphones and presented a performance analysis of mobile devices. Liyanage et al. proposed a lightweight mobile Web service provisioning framework, designed for resource-constrained Internet of Things applications to achieve lightweight mobile Web service provisioning [16]. Moreover, Arslan et al. aimed to develop a distributed computing infrastructure using smartphones, and they implemented a prototype, which employs a novel scheduling algorithm to minimize the makespan of computation tasks [3].

The aforementioned framework for a mobile cloud is promising, and a proper incentive mechanism is the key to motivate users to share their resources within such a system. The incentive mechanisms can generally be divided into two categories, double-sided bidding and single-sided bidding. The Vickrey-Clarke-Groves (VCG) mechanism is a well-known double-sided bidding, however, it induces intensive computational cost [4] in real-world implementations and thus they are difficult to adopt widely in the NMCC systems. For addressing such issues, few researchers have designed several single-side bidding incentive mechanisms for NMCC. In [18], the authors introduced the prototype of mClouds and analysed some incentive strategies that may help mClouds become a viable and effective alternative to the traditional MCC model. In [2], the authors developed the mobile device based cloud system CellCloud and proposed a reputation-based economic incentive model to reward phone owners for sharing the resources of their devices. Besides, an optimal incentive mechanism was developed in [12] to minimize the total payment to all the smartphones.

3   System Models and Problem Formulation

3.1   Mobile Cloud Architecture

Our proposed framework is designed for NMCC systems, which are composed of multiple mobile devices and a trusted broker, as shown in Fig. 1. The broker serves as an intermediary responsible for discovery and communication among the neighbouring mobile devices. The mobile devices are within the coverage of the broker and each one of them could act as two roles within the system simultaneously. One role is service requester who needs to offload tasks to other nearby mobile devices. The other role is service provider who has idle resources and is willing to participate in resource sharing. All mobile devices directly send their service requests and/or service provisioning information to the broker. After receiving such information, the broker performs the matching between service requesters and providers by jointly considering the requirements of the requests and the functionality and QoS of services. Once a service request is received by a mobile device, the device can choose to accept or decline it according to its current status in terms of resource utilization. If a mobile device accepts a service request, it will obtain the corresponding revenue by successfully completing the request. The result of the task will be sent back to the service requester through the broker. If a service request is declined, it will be returned to the broker for reallocation. Eventually, the service requester combines all the received results to obtain the final result.

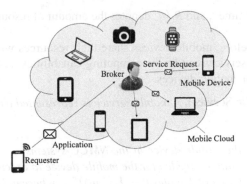

Fig. 1. Mobile cloud architecture

3.2 Mobile Services and Requests

Definition 1 (Mobile Device). *In NMCC systems, a mobile device is represented as a 3-tuple (S, A, I), where:*

- *$S = \{s_1, s_2, \ldots\}$, describing the set of services that a mobile device is able to provide;*
- *A is the function used to describe all the available resources a mobile device can share with other devices. At a given time t, the available resources are denoted as a set of 2-tuples $A_t = \{(r_i, n_i)\}_{i=1}^{m}$, where m is the total number of the types of the available resources that a mobile device can provide, and r_i and n_i denote the type and the amount of the i-th kind of resource, respectively.*
- *I is a function used to describe the current idle resources of a mobile device. Idle resources refer to the resources that are available and not yet occupied by the service requests. At a given time t, it can be represented by $I_t = \{(r_i, n_i)\}_{i=1}^{m}$.*

In our study, we assume that time is slotted and the minimum time slot is a time unit. Similar to a number of existing works in MCC [5, 6, 15, 20] and mobile computing [11], we consider a quasi-static scenario where the mobile devices remain unchanged for a period of time, which may change over consecutive periods in our work. Since most mobile devices are personal devices, the resource sharing should not disturb the predominant usage of the device owners. This hard requirement also means the available resources of mobile devices are varied over time. For example, if the owner of a mobile device wants to download some files, the available bandwidth used to share should be reduced. The amount of idle resources of a mobile device is an important factor for our proposed framework to perform service request selection and scheduling, which will be elaborated later. It can be calculated by

$$I(t, r) = A(t, r) - \sum_{q \in E_t} R_r(q) \tag{1}$$

where $I(t, r)$ denotes the amount of resource r that is idle at time t, $A(t, r)$ denotes the amount of resource r that is available at time t, $q \in E_t$ denotes the request executing on the mobile device at time t, and $R_r(q)$ denotes the amount of resource r that is occupied by the request q.

As mentioned before, mobile devices share their resources with others in the form of services. Mobile services can be the computing capabilities, resources, applications, data, sensors, etc. of mobile devices.

Definition 2 (Mobile Service). *A mobile service is represented as a 5-tuple (d, R, v, F, QoS), where:*

- *d is the index of the mobile device in the NMCC systems;*
- *R describes the resources needed for the mobile device to execute the service, which can be denoted as a set of 2-tuples $R = \{(r_i, n_i)\}_{i=1}^{m}$, where m is the number of types of required resources, and r_i and n_i denote the type and number of the i-th kind of resource, respectively;*
- *v is the revenue the mobile device can obtain by successfully completing the service;*
- *F is the functional description of the service;*
- *QoS is a set of attributes of the requested services, including execution time t^e, which is the makespan needed for a mobile device to execute the service.*

Functional description and QoS parameters are key criteria for the broker to select services for requests in the matching process. In this paper, we mainly consider the execution time of a requested service, since it plays an important role in the scheduling and resource allocation of mobile devices.

Definition 3 (Service Request). *A service request is represented as a 4-tuple (s, d, t^a, t^d), where:*

- *s is the service that is requested;*
- *d is the index of the mobile device, to which the request is delivered;*
- *t^a is the arrival time of the request;*
- *t^d is the deadline for the request to be completed.*

As introduced in Definition 3, a service request consists of information on a required service, service host and time. In the dynamic and versatile mobile environment, service requests are highly likely to express real-time requirements, so we introduce t^d to guarantee that services are completed in time. It is obvious that one request corresponds to one service. In the remaining parts of the paper, we will use the terms request and service interchangeably.

3.3 Problem Statement

Each mobile device manages an execution sequence, by which it conducts service execution, requests insertion, deletion, scheduling, and resource allocation.

Definition 4 (Execution Sequence). *For a mobile device d, its execution sequence describes the services that will be performed on each time unit. It can be formulated as a time function $E_t = \{q_i\}_{i=1}^{n}$, expressing that during time unit t, a mobile device d will process n service requests including q_1, q_2, ..., q_n, simultaneously.*

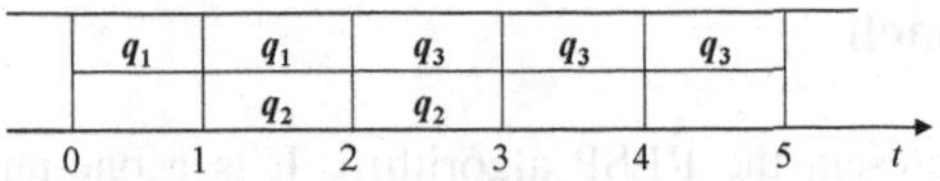

Fig. 2. Execution sequence example

In an execution sequence, each time unit corresponds to a set of service requests that will be processed during that time unit. For example, Fig. 2 shows an example of an execution sequence, which describes the service execution of a mobile device within the time period of 5 time units.

To describe the execution time of a service request, we let $^{\bullet}q$ denote the time when request q starts to be processed and $q^{\bullet}$ denotes the time when q is completed. Corresponding to a given execution sequence, there is a request sequence where the requests involved are sorted by the time when they begin to be executed. We let $E(^{\bullet}q)$ and $E(q^{\bullet})$ denote the request that is right ahead of and right behind q respectively. Specifically, E_l denotes the last request of the execution sequence. For example, according to Fig. 2, we have $E(q_1^{\bullet}) = q_2$, $E(^{\bullet}q_3) = q_2$ and $E_l = q_3$.

Definition 5 (Revenue-Driven Service Provision). *Given a mobile device d, with its available resources $A_t = \{(r_i, n_i)\}_{i=1}^{m}$ and idle resources $I_t = \{(r_j, n_j)\}_{j=1}^{m}$, and the incoming service requests $q_1, q_2, \ldots q_n$, the revenue-driven service provision is to select a set of service requests S from the request sequence and schedule them in the execution sequence E to*

$$\text{Maximize} \sum_{q \in S} v_q,$$

$$\text{s.t.} \quad q^{\bullet} - {}^{\bullet}q = t_q^e, \text{ for each } q \in S \tag{2}$$

$$q^{\bullet} \leq t_q^d, \text{ for each } q \in S \tag{3}$$

$$\forall t, \sum_{q \in E_t \cap S} R_q(r) \leq A_t(r), \text{ for each } r \in A_t \tag{4}$$

It is reasonable to regard maximizing overall revenue of a mobile device as the optimization objective for its service provisioning. Equation 2 implies that the arrangement of each request is in accordance with its execution time. Equation 3 illustrates that each request should be completed before its deadline. Moreover, the allocated resources should not exceed the available resources of the mobile device at any time, as specified in Eq. 4. Therefore, revenue-driven service provision is to select service requests to maximize the revenue of mobile devices, with given dynamic resource constraints and diverse time constraints of requests.

4 RESP Approach

In this section, we present the RESP algorithm. It is a one-phase algorithm, which means that the service request selection, scheduling and resource allocation of a mobile device are made in an integrated manner. The symbols used in this paper are summarized in Table 1.

Table 1. Mathematical Notations

Symbol	Description	Symbol	Description
t_q^a	The arrival time of request q	$E(^*q)$	The request ahead of request q in E
t_q^e	The execution time of request q	$E(q^*)$	The request behind request q in E
t_q^d	The deadline of request q	$E(t^*)$	The request behind the time point t in E
t_q^s	The latest start time of request q	E_l	The last request in the execution sequence E
t_c	The current time	A_t	The available resource set at time t
v_q	The reward for completing request q	$A_t(r)$	The amount of the available resource r at time t
$^\bullet q$	The time slot request q starts to process	$I_t(r)$	The amount of the idle resource r at time t
$q^\bullet$	The time slot request q is completed	R_q	The total required resources of request q
E_t	The requests in E with the same time t	$R_q(r)$	The amount of a required resource r of request q

4.1 RESP Algorithm

Service requests are sent to mobile devices via the broker, so that mobile devices are required to deal with these requests sequentially. For each incoming request, a mobile device needs to make a decision on the following three criteria:

(1) The request can be completed before its deadline;
(2) The request can be allocated with sufficient resources;
(3) The total revenue is increased.

A service request can be accepted by a mobile device for its execution if and only if the above three criteria are all met. We first provide the definition of latest start time, which is a core element of our approach.

Definition 6 (Latest Start Time). *For a given request q, its latest start time is the latest time for a mobile device to start performing it, so that it can be completed before its deadline. The latest start time can be calculated by*

$$t_q^s = t_q^d - t_q^e \tag{5}$$

where t_q^d is the deadline of the request q, and t_q^e is the execution time of the request q.

Figure 3 shows the flowchart of the RESP algorithm. For a given request q_i, we first calculate its latest start time and use it to evaluate whether the request can be completed before its deadline on the device. If the latest start time of the service request is before the current time t_c, the request will not be able to complete in time and it is thus rejected. Otherwise, we schedule it with the accepted but not yet started requests located in the execution sequence E. All the requests are sorted in non-decreasing order according to their deadlines. A reference start time T will be generated for the request q_i. Next, by considering the available resource of a mobile device, we look for the actual start time of q_i. The actual start time can be before, equal to or after the reference start time T.

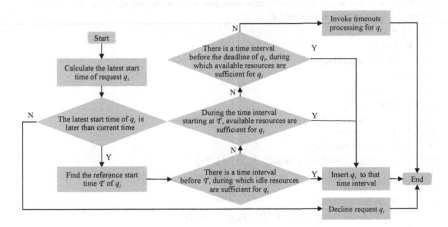

Fig. 3. Flowchart of the RESP algorithm

The pseudo code of the RESP algorithm is shown in Algorithm 1. For an incoming service request q_i, we first calculate its latest start time (line 1) and check whether it can be completed before its deadline (lines 2-3) compared with the current time t_c. If the request is schedulable, we determine its reference start time in the execution sequence according to its deadline (lines 5-7). To do so, we put q_i to the rear of the execution sequence (line 5). If there exists a scheduled request in the execution sequence and its deadline is behind q_i, then the reference start time of q_i should be moved forward (lines 6-7).

Once the reference start time T is determined, we will use the start time minimization technique to check whether q_i can be performed before T (lines 9-12). If there is a time interval where the mobile device has more idle resources than those required (line 10), then q_i can be safely placed into that time interval (line 11) without affecting the execution of the scheduled requests. If no such time interval exists and the latest start time of q_i is not before T (line 13), then we check whether q_i can be started at T. If the mobile device has enough available resources for q_i during its execution period (line 14), then q_i should be started from $\mathcal{T}$ (line 15). If the idle resources during that interval are not enough for q_i, q_i can occupy the resources that have been allocated to other requests with later deadlines (line 15). When this step still does not provide enough resources to perform q_i, the algorithm will continue checking whether there is any time interval between $\mathcal{T}$ and the latest start time of q_i that has sufficient resources (lines 17-21). If one exists, q_i should be inserted to that interval (line 19).

After the above search process, if q_i cannot be inserted into the execution sequence, then the Timeouts algorithm will be invoked (lines 22-23), implying that the mobile device cannot accept all requests. This will lead to either q_i or some other scheduled requests being declined. For the cases that q_i is inserted to the execution sequence and thus causes one or more scheduled requests cannot being started on schedule, the timeouts algorithm needs to be used for these requests.

Algorithm 1. RESP Algorithm

Input: The execution sequence E, the available resources A, and the incoming service request q_i

Output: Updated execution sequence E

1:   $t^s_{q_i} \leftarrow t^d_{q_i} - t^e_{q_i}$
2:   **if** $t^s_{q_i} < t_c$
3:       decline request q_i
4:   **else**
5:       $\mathcal{T} \leftarrow E_l{}^\bullet;\ q \leftarrow E_l$
6:       **while** $t^s_{q_i} < t^s_q$
7:           $\mathcal{T} \leftarrow {}^\bullet q;\ q \leftarrow E({}^*q)$
8:       $Scheduled \leftarrow N$
9:       **for** $t = t_c$ to $\min(\mathcal{T}, t^s_{q_i})$
10:          **if** $\forall t_0 \in (t,\ t + t^e_{q_i})$ and $\forall r \in R_{q_i},\ R_{q_i}(r) < I_{t_0}(r)$
11:              insert q_i to E such that ${}^\bullet q_i = t;\ Scheduled \leftarrow Y$
12:              **break**
13:      **if** not $Scheduled$ && $\mathcal{T} \le t^s_{q_i}$
14:          **if** $\forall t_0 \in (\mathcal{T},\ \mathcal{T} + t^e_{q_i})$ and $\forall r \in R_{q_i},\ R_{q_i}(r) < A_{t_0}(r)$
15:              insert q_i to E s.t. ${}^\bullet q = \mathcal{T};\ Scheduled \leftarrow Y$; postpone the subsequent requests in E
16:          **else**
17:              **while** $t < t^s_{q_0}$
18:                  **if** $\forall t_0 \in (t,\ t + t^e_{q_i})$ and $\forall r \in R_{q_i},\ R_{q_i}(r) < A_{t_0}(r)$
19:                      insert q_i to E s.t. ${}^\bullet q_i = t;\ Scheduled \leftarrow Y$; postpone subsequent requests in E
20:                      **break**
21:                  $t \leftarrow t+1$
22:      **if** not $Scheduled$
23:          Timeouts (E, A, q_i)

4.2   Timeouts Processing Algorithm

In this subsection, we present the timeouts processing algorithm, which is invoked when timeouts occurs. To better describe the algorithm, we first introduce the definition of dominance.

Definition 7 (Dominance). *Given a service request* q_i, *an execution sequence E and a set of scheduled service requests S in E*, q_i *dominates S if and only if*

$$\exists t \text{ s.t. } \forall t_0 \in \left(t, t + t_{q_i}^e\right) \text{ and } \forall r \in R_{q_i},$$

$$R_{q_i}(r) < I_{t_0}(r) + \sum_{q \in S \cap E_{t_0}} R_q(r) \text{ and } v_{q_i} > \sum_{q \in S} v_q \tag{6}$$

In Definition 7, constraint (6) illustrates that there is a time interval, during which the sum of the idle resources and the resources allocated to the requests in S exceeds the required resources of q_i. Meanwhile, the revenue for executing q_i is more than executing all requests in S. Obviously, if q_i dominates S, the requests in S can be safely replaced by q_i, with the revenue for the mobile device increased.

The timeouts process algorithm is shown in Algorithm 2. It is realized by searching for the dominated request set with the minimum price. For each time slot before the reference start time point of an incoming request q_i, the algorithm tries to find a dominated request set with less revenue (lines 2-20). The search is started from the current time to the earlier one of the reference time point and the latest start time (line 2).

Algorithm 2. Timeouts Algorithm
Input: The execution sequence E and available resources A of the mobile device, and service request q_i
Output: Updated execution sequence E

1:   $\mathcal{M} \leftarrow v_{q_i}$
2:   **for** $t = t_c$ to $\min(T, t_{q_i}^s)$
3:   ┌ $q \leftarrow E(t^*)$
4:   │ **if** $\forall t_0 \in (t, t+t_{q_i}^e), \forall r \in R_{q_i}, R_{q_i}(r) < I_{t_0}(r) + R_q(r)$ && $v_q < \mathcal{M}$
5:   │ $Q \leftarrow \{q\}; \mathcal{M} \leftarrow v_q; T \leftarrow t$
6:   │ **else**
7:   │   ┌ $\mathcal{P} \leftarrow \emptyset; V \leftarrow 0$
8:   │   │ **while** $V < \mathcal{M}$ && $\bullet q < t + t_{q_i}^e$
9:   │   │   ┌ **if** $\forall t_0 \in (t, t+t_{q_i}^e), \forall r \in R_{q_i}, R_{q_i}(r) < I_{t_0}(r) + \sum_{q \in \mathcal{P}} R_q(r)$
10: │   │   │   ┌ $Q \leftarrow \mathcal{P}; \mathcal{M} \leftarrow V; T \leftarrow t$
11: │   │   │   └ **break**
12: │   │   │ **else**
13: └   └   └ $\mathcal{P} \leftarrow \mathcal{P} \cup \{q\}; V \leftarrow V + v_q; q \leftarrow E(q^*)$
14: **if** $\mathcal{M} < v_{q_i}$
15:      insert q_i to E such that $\bullet q_i = T$; decline the requests in Q
16: **else**
17:      decline q_i

For each time point, the request starting at it is set as the first request to check (lines 1). If a request is found to be dominated by q_i and with less revenue than the previous minimum revenue, which is represented by $\mathcal{M}$ in the algorithm (line 4), then it will be assigned to the replaced request set, its revenue will be assigned to the minimum revenue, and the time point will be marked (line 5). Otherwise, the algorithm will check whether the following request set can be dominated by q_i and with less revenue (lines 8-13).

If it is, the algorithm will reallocate the minimum revenue, request set and time (line 10). Otherwise, the algorithm will continue expanding the set until we can determine that it is not qualified (line 13).

After the searching process, if the algorithm finds a dominated request with less revenue (line 14), it will replace these requests with q_i and move the subsequent requests accordingly (line 15), otherwise, it means that no request set dominated by q_i is found and q_i should be rejected (line 17).

4.3   Algorithm Analysis

In the following, we prove the effectiveness of the proposed RESP algorithm, by verifying the three conditions mentioned at the beginning of this subsection.

Theorem 1 (Effectiveness of the RESP algorithm). *If service request q_i is inserted to an execution sequence by the RESP algorithm, conditions (1), (2) and (3) hold.*

Proof. If q_i is inserted to the execution sequence by Algorithm 1, we can see the algorithm confirms that q_i can be completed in time before inserting it to any part of the execution sequence (lines 9, 13 and 17), so condition (1) holds. Similarly, the algorithm confirms that the resources are sufficient before inserting q_i (lines 10, 14 and 18), so condition (2) holds. As for condition (3), if the insertion of q_i does not cause timeout of any request, it is obvious that the revenue of the mobile device has increased by v_{q_i}. If the insertion of q_i causes timeout of a request whose revenue is larger than q_i, then the request will be reinserted by Algorithm 2, which also increases the revenue. Therefore, condition (3) holds.

If q_i is inserted to an execution sequence by Algorithm 2, there must be a request set dominated by q_i. Algorithm 2 confirms that the insert time is before $t^s_{q_i}$ (line 2), so if q_i replaces the dominated request set, it can be completed in time, i.e. condition (1) holds. According to Algorithm 2 and Eq. (6), for each time point, the resources allocated to the dominated request set and the idle resources of the mobile device add up to exceed the required resources of q_i, and the revenue of the requests in the dominated request set adds up to exceed the revenue of q_i, therefore conditions (2) and (3) hold.   □

The time complexity of both the RESP Algorithm and Timeouts Algorithm are $O(lt^e n)$, where l denotes the length of the execution sequence, t^e denotes the length of the execution time of the request (the number of time units) and n denotes the number of types of available resources. It implies that the execution time of both algorithms is feasibly low and it would not cause high overhead to mobile devices.

5   Experiments

We have implemented the algorithms in Python and our experiments are conducted on a MacBook Pro (macOS Sierra Version 10.12.5). Since no standard platforms and dataset are available, we generated our experimental data in a synthetic way. Each mobile device is equipped with three kinds of resource. Service requests are randomly generated with the revenue ranging from 1 to 10, execution time is from 1 to 6 and the required number of each resource is from 0 to 5. For each request, the time difference between its deadline and its arrival is from 1 to 10. The number of incoming requests per time unit obeys normal distribution $N(15, 5)$ and is greater than 0. All the following experiments are repeated 200 times and we adopt the average values.

5.1 Effectiveness Evaluation

To evaluate the effectiveness of RESP, we compare it with three well-known scheduling algorithms, namely, First Come First Serve (FCFS), Priority Scheduling (PS), and Genetic Algorithm (GA). FCFS performs service requests according to their arrival time. PS assigns higher priorities to the requests with higher revenue and performs them in a non-increasing order. Both FCFS and PS reject a request if no sufficient resources or time to execute it. GA is a widely used heuristic method in scheduling, and it is realised by successively iterating to generate better solutions. In the following, we vary the mean of the number of incoming requests per time unit from 5 to 40 to compare the effectiveness of the four methods. The result is shown in Fig. 4.

From Fig. 4(a), the RESP approach outperforms FCFS, PS and GA in terms of revenue at all times. FCFS performs worst due to that fact it does not consider the revenue of the requests and only processes them according to their arrival sequence. PS prioritizes the requests by their revenue. To do so, it will cause all the resources to be used to perform the requests with high priorities and the requests with low priorities are ignored. As a result, the total amount of service requests drops and leads to the revenue dropping as well. GA considers both resource and revenue, so its performance is better than FCFS and PS. However, due to its algorithmic complexity, it is hard to generate the optimal solution in an online manner. With the significant performance improvement, our proposed approach does not cause the overuse of mobile devices. As shown in Fig. 4(b), there is no obvious difference in the resource utilization rate of the four methods, which suggests that, by using the RESP approach, mobile devices can create more revenue with same amount of resources.

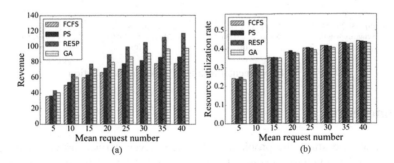

Fig. 4. Experimental results of effectiveness evaluation

5.2   Efficiency Evaluation

To evaluate the efficiency of RESP, we compared the execution time of the four methods. For the GA approach, we set the number of iterations from 20 to 100 with the increment interval of 20. The result is shown in Table 2, from which we can see that the execution time of GA is several orders of magnitude higher than the other three methods. The revenue of GA becomes stable from GA-60, but the overall revenue is still worse than our RESP method.

Table 2. Execution time comparison

	FCFS	PS	RESP	GA-20	GA-40	GA-60	GA-80	GA-100
Revenue	58.4	61.9	76.7	60.6	65.6	69.5	70.0	70.2
Execution time (ms)	0.59	0.62	3.06	386.82	818.80	1145.57	1487.51	1851.06

We further vary the length of the execution sequence, mean requests number, mean execution time and the number of the type of resources respectively to evaluate the scalability of the RESP algorithm. As shown in Fig. 5(a)-(c), with the increasing of the length of execution sequence, mean requests number, mean execution time, the execution time of RESP increases almost linearly, which is in accordance with the analysis given in Subsect. 4.3. Besides, as shown in Fig. 5(d), with the increasing number of the type of resources, the execution time of RESP decreases. This is because the increased resource number makes requests more difficult to be executed and thus decreases the length of the request sequence. Overall, the execution time of RESP is feasibly low and it has good scalability, which demonstrates the applicability of RESP to mobile devices.

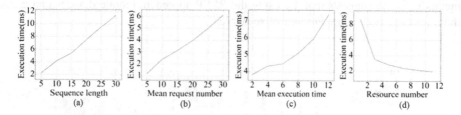

Fig. 5. Experimental results of efficiency evaluation

6   Conclusion

In this paper, we study the problem of revenue-driven service provision for mobile devices. A lightweight service-based approach called RESP (revenue-driven service provision for mobile devices) is proposed to perform service request selection, request scheduling and resource allocation simultaneously, with the objective to maximizing the revenue of the mobile devices. To evaluate the performance of the approach, we have conducted a set of experiments, which demonstrated the efficacy of RESP.

In future, we will focus on elaborating RESP in detail and fine tuning its parameters to improve its performance. Furthermore, we will implement RESP on a real scenario and adjust the algorithm by analysing the feedback.

Acknowledgement. This research was partially supported by Key Research and Development Project of Zhejiang Province (No. 2015C01027, No. 2015C01034, No. 2015C01029, and No. 2017C01013), Natural Science Foundation of Zhejiang Province (No. LY17F020014) and Major Science and Technology Innovation Project of Hangzhou (No. 20152011A03).

References

1. Albagli-Kim, S., Shachnai, H., Tamir, T.: Scheduling jobs with dwindling resource requirements in clouds. In: 2014 International Conference on Computer Communications (INFOCOM), pp. 601–609. IEEE (2014)
2. Al Noor, S., Hasan, R., Haque, M.: Cellcloud: a novel cost effective formation of mobile cloud based on bidding incentives. In: 2014 International Conference on Cloud Computing (CLOUD), pp. 200–207. IEEE (2014)
3. Arslan, M.Y., Singh, I., Singh, S., Madhyastha, H.V., Sundaresan, K., Krishnamurthy, S.V.: CWC: a distributed computing infrastructure using smartphones. IEEE T. Mobile Comput. **14**(8), 1587–1600 (2015)
4. Ausubel, L.M., Milgrom, P.: The lovely but lonely Vickrey auction. Comb. Auct. **17**, 22–26 (2006)
5. Chen, X.: Decentralized computation offloading game for mobile cloud computing. IEEE Trans. Parallel Distrib. Syst. **26**(4), 974–983 (2015)
6. Chen, X., Jiao, L., Li, W., Fu, X.: Efficient multi-user computation offloading for mobile-edge cloud computing. IEEE/ACM Trans. Netw. **24**(5), 2795–2808 (2016)
7. Deng, S., Huang, L., Wu, H., Wu, Z., Zomaya, A.Y.: Constraints-driven service composition in mobile cloud computing. In: 2016 International Conference on Web Services (ICWS), pp. 228–235. IEEE (2016)
8. Deng, S., Huang, L., Wu, H., Tan, W., Taheri, J., Zomaya, A.Y., Wu, Z.: Toward mobile service computing: opportunities and challenges. IEEE Cloud Comput. **3**(4), 32–41 (2016)
9. Dinh, H.T., Lee, C., Niyato, D., Wang, P.: A survey of mobile cloud computing: architecture, applications, and approaches. Wirel. Commun. Mob. Com. **13**(18), 1587–1611 (2013)
10. Fernando, N., Loke, S.W., Rahayu, W.: Mobile cloud computing: a survey. Future Gener. Comput. Syst. **29**(1), 84–106 (2013)
11. Iosifidis, G., Gao, L., Huang, J., Tassiulas, L.: An iterative double auction for mobile data offloading. In: 2013 International Symposium on Modeling & Optimization in Mobile, Ad Hoc & Wireless Networks (WiOpt), pp. 154–161. IEEE (2013)
12. Koutsopoulos, I.: Optimal incentive-driven design of participatory sensing systems. In: 2013 International Conference on Computer Communications (INFOCOM), pp. 1402–1410. IEEE (2013)
13. Lee, C., Wang, P., Niyato, D.: A real-time group auction system for efficient allocation of cloud internet applications. IEEE T. Serv. Comput. **8**(2), 251–268 (2015)
14. Liu, C., Shang, Y., Duan, L., Chen, S., Liu, C., Chen, J.: Optimizing workload category for adaptive workload prediction in service clouds. In: Barros, A., Grigori, D., Narendra, Nanjangud C., Dam, H.K. (eds.) ICSOC 2015. LNCS, vol. 9435, pp. 87–104. Springer, Heidelberg (2015). doi:10.1007/978-3-662-48616-0_6

15. Liu, K., Peng, J., Li, H., Zhang, X., Liu, W.: Multi-device task offloading with time-constraints for energy efficiency in mobile cloud computing. Future Gener. Comput. Syst. **64**, 1–14 (2016)
16. Liyanage, M., Chang, C., Srirama, S. N.: Lightweight mobile web service provisioning for sensor mediation. In: 2015 International Conferences on Mobile Services, pp. 57–64. IEEE (2015)
17. Maguluri, S.T., Srikant, R.: Scheduling jobs with unknown duration in clouds. IEEE ACM T. Netw. **22**(6), 1938–1951 (2014)
18. Miluzzo, E., Cáceres, R. and Chen, Y.F.: Vision: mClouds-computing on clouds of mobile devices. In: 2012 Workshop on Mobile cloud computing and services, pp. 9–14. ACM (2012)
19. Srirama, S.N., Jarke, M., Prinz, W.: Mobile host: a feasibility analysis of mobile web service provisioning. In: UMICS (2006)
20. Wang, C., Yu, F.R., Liang, C., Chen, Q., Tang, L.: Joint computation offloading and interference management in wireless cellular networks with mobile edge computing. IEEE T. Veh. Technol. (2017)
21. Yousafzai, A., Chang, V., Gani, A., Noor, R.M.: Directory-based incentive management services for ad-hoc mobile clouds. Int. J. Inform. Manage. **36**(6), 900–906 (2016)

Continuous Learning as a Service
for Conversational Virtual Agents

Shivali Agarwal$^{(\boxtimes)}$, Shubham Atreja, and Gargi Dasgupta

IBM Research, Bengaluru, India
{shivaaga,shubham.atreja,gaargidasgupta}@in.ibm.com

Abstract. IT support services are moving towards self assist mode by means of cognitive agents. Such cognitive agents are typically being designed as conversational system. It is important that as the agent interacts with users, it should continuously observe, infer and learn as to what is it that it is doing well, what topics is it not able to handle well and what topics it does not seem to know about at all. In this paper, we have proposed a service that enables feedback based learning in cognitive agents. Conversation systems typically support feedback mechanism for example, some of them may ask the users to vote for the answers, or rate the experience/response that they got for their query. We propose a reinforcement learning based model for the agent to continuously learn and improve. To the best of our knowledge, this is a first attempt in modeling the continuous learning problem in conversational systems as a reinforcement learning problem. We also provide the service design for continuous learning as a service in context of conversational agents. We have evaluated the model against real data to show how the learning is helpful in improving agent's performance. The model can also be generalized for any supervised classification problem.

1 Introduction

Cognitive agent can be thought of as a virtual agent which can observe, learn and infer and interact. It has such capabilities as a result of massive training in relevant domains using technologies like machine learning, natural language processing, dialog decision tree flows etc. IT support services are increasingly moving towards self assist mode by means of such cognitive agents. Such an agent is able to act as the first line of contact for customers who would have typically called a human helpdesk. One of the more common manifestation of such agents is in the form of chatbots e.g. 'Spoke' [1]. Many such conversational cognitive agents e.g. 'WSS' [11], have already started making inroads as a frontend for customer support. With the score of services available now [18] for building chat bots/conversational cognitive agent, it has become very easy to design one. The challenge lies in building something which is intelligent and quick learner. Too many of 'I don't know' or wrong answers can make the agents useless. Currently, this problem is handled by designing domain specific agents which hand off to a human agent when it cannot reply satisfactorily [3]. It should be noted that

© Springer International Publishing AG 2017
M. Maximilien et al. (Eds.): ICSOC 2017, LNCS 10601, pp. 641–656, 2017.
https://doi.org/10.1007/978-3-319-69035-3_47

conversational cognitive agents are supposed to understand context and have notions of intents.

Conversation systems(service) in cognitive agents are bootstrapped with basic knowledge through initial training. In order for a conversational agent to be intelligent to identify intents, huge amount of training is needed. There is some work happening around area of active learning [12], semi-supervised [20] learning in order to reduce dependence on labeled data for training. However, none of these techniques leverage feedback from users. The conversational cognitive agents typically support feedback mechanism, for example, some of them may ask the users to vote for the answers, or rate the experience/response that they got for their query. In addition to this, there is a scope of capturing usage logs and gauge implicitly the engagement of users with the system and consider this as a feedback. Such feedback is an extremely important source of self learning and improvement for the cognitive agents. As the agent interacts with users, it should continuously observe, infer and learn from feedback as to what is it that it is doing well, what topics is it not able to handle well and what topics it does not seem to know about at all. These topics are usually the intents of the utterance/query of the user, and a good training data is key to identify intents and have good quality conversations. However, continuous learning to improve training and thereby conversations is a challenging problem and needs utmost care so as to not degrade the existing accuracy. In this paper, we have proposed a service that enables feedback based learning in cognitive agents to continuously improve training data for intent classification in conversation services. More specifically, we propose a reinforcement learning [14] based method to come up with a learning policy for improving the training data for the agent.

The main contributions of this paper are: (i) Modeling the learning problem as a feedback based reinforcement learning one by appropriately defining rewards and state value functions (ii) Deriving the action policies, using this model, that provide improvement suggestions automatically in the form of actionable utterances for continuous learning (iii) Designing automated and manual workflows to act upon the actionable set of utterances and update the training data (iv) Designing the continuous learning framework as a service that uses feedback from user interactions to improve training data by incorporating the policies based workflows mentioned above (v) Implementing the service workflows and evaluate against real data. One of the decisions that was crucial in designing the services was: Should there be a human intervention who vets the automatically generated suggestions before modifying the training data. If there is no human intervention, then it is difficult to address the cases where the feedback adds to the confusion instead of firming up the training data, so we decided to have automated and manual workflows.

To the best of our knowledge, this is a first attempt in modeling the continuous learning problem for intents in conversational systems as a reinforcement learning problem and designing the learning problem as a service. Rest of the paper is outlined as follows. The problem is described in more detail in Sect. 2. Section 3 describes the model, action policies and the workflow algorithm.

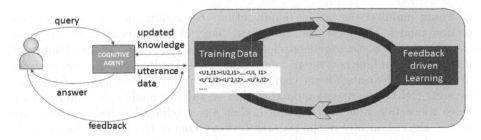

Fig. 1. Overview of Interactions for feedback driven learning

Service components of the continuous learning service are explained in detail in Sect. 4. Section 5 discusses the experiment results, Sect. 6 covers the related work and we conclude with Sect. 7.

2   Problem Overview

Starting with an initial training dataset consisting of utterance and intent pairs used for training conversation service to predict intent from user utterance, the problem objective is to augment it over time using implicit and explicit feedback, and improve the intent classification performance. The problem overview is provided in Fig. 1. The utterance data is a stream of data consisting of user queries/utterances and agent answer/response. The utterances are either the main query or can be supportive dialog to understand the main question. The utterances which capture the main question have to be identified from the dialog flow; we assume that the main utterance identification has been done on the conversation data before passing to learning service. The implicit and explicit feedback associated with the responses are also captured as part of conversation. For example, if the response is in the form of a solution document, then the clicks on the page and time spent in reading the document is an implicit indicator of usefulness while a vote is an explicit feedback. User feedback is an important piece of information to leverage for improvement of a system. Observing and incorporating feedback is however, one of the most challenging aspects of the problem because the feedback interpretation is not always straightforward. For example, we have situations where explicit and implicit feedback convey the opposite sentiment. It can be attributed to an imperfect implicit feedback model, unfriendly user interface even though the content was fine or unmatched user expectations. We do not dwell upon the subjectivity of feedback and model it as per standard notions of implicit feedback in literature [5].

As shown in Fig. 1, the learning cycle needs to be continuous, possibly starting with small training data set. The training data consists of rows of 2-tuples denoted by <utterance(U), intent(I)> pairs such that each intent has at least few training utterances. For example, an intent can be 'CreateSpaceInMailbox' and one of the corresponding utterances can be 'How do I clean my inbox?'.

Learning manifests as making modifications to training data to improve pre-diction model. Modifications are actions like: adding utterances to an intent as examples to boost confidence, identifying utterances that are candidates for new intents, adding new intent labels and more. Feedback is the driving force of continuous learning for the cognitive agent. We propose to use reinforcement learning (RL) to learn action policies, that is, rules to modify the training data. Once the action policies are learned, then the modification logic can be inte-grated algorithmically in the learning service. One of the biggest challenges in using RL method for learning in a conversation system is to model states, value functions and rewards using logs and feedback from conversations.

The advantage of taking feedback based approach to continuously learn is that the intents that are more commonly used improve a lot over time and this information cannot be obtained in a more better way than user interactions. Thus, feedback based learning gives a direction. In many cases, the feedback helps in firming up the confidence automatically as utterances become training examples. The variety in training examples can be obtained with very diverse lin-guistics. The dependence on manual curator reduces a lot. The other advantage of feedback based approach is that the training data can be initialized with a small set of intent and utterance pairs and augmented based on user interactions.

3   Modeling the Continuous Learning Problem Using Reinforcement Learning (RL)

In the following, we give an overview of reinforcement learning and then provide the details of modeling the feedback based learning problem in cognitive agents as an instance of SARSA algorithm [14] for reinforcement learning. The output of reinforcement learning algorithm is optimal action policies for training data improvement which are then modeled as algorithmic workflows. These workflows are used by the continuous learning service as shown in next section.

In reinforcement learning [14], there is an agent, called RL agent, which observes an input state and takes an action determined by a decision policy. Once the action is performed, the agent receives a reward that acts as a reinforcement for the goodness of the action. The information of reward for state/action pair is recorded. By performing actions, and observing the resulting reward, the policy used to determine the best action for a state can be fine-tuned. Eventually, if enough states are observed, an optimal decision policy (referred to as action policy henceforth) will be generated and we will have an agent that performs perfectly in that particular environment. The algorithm used for reinforcement learning here is on-policy algorithm called SARSA [14] which is an iterative one which can be represented as:

$$Q(s_t, a_t) \leftarrow Q(s_t, a_t) + \alpha(r_t + \gamma Q(s_{t+1}, a_{t+1}) - Q(s_t, a_t))$$

where,

α is the learning rate,

γ is the discount factor, a factor of 0 will make the agent "opportunistic" by only considering current rewards,

$Q(s_t, a_t)$: the value of taking action a_t in state s_t under a policy at step t, r_t the reward observed associated with action a_t.

Having provided the background of reinforcement learning, we now explain the setting of SARSA algorithm for reinforcement learning in conversational cognitive agents. The setting is shown in Fig. 2. The conversation system is initialized with a model trained on initial training dataset denoted by Training Data 1. Based on this model, the utterances from the users are analyzed for intents and feedback is collected. To make this system learn and improve over time, we define epochs of learning. The RL agent acts at every epoch and Fig. 2 illustrates the flow for the one complete cycle that happens from epoch to epoch. At each epoch, the agent collects data in terms of conversations that is, user utterances, the output from the model and the user feedback, explicit and implicit. This is shown by the edge labeled 1. Let $\mathcal{A}$ denote the possible action atoms responsible for updating the training data that can be taken by RL agent. These different action atoms are explained below.

- **Add training example**: There are situations where the correct intent is predicted with a low confidence. In such cases, the suggestion provided is to add the utterance as a training data to the low confidence intent.
- **Find correct/alternate intent**: If there is confusion between intents for an utterance, then the correct one should be chosen and the utterance should be added as training example for the correct intent.
- **Add new intent**: This action is suggested when no existing intent in the corpus matches with the intent of the utterance. This is an action type which augments the training data so that the agents knowledge increases.
- **Generate more training data**: The utterances for which more training data is required are taken and then similar utterances from the conversation corpus is found. We use cosine and Jaccard similarity to obtain similar utterances. In addition, paraphrasing is performed using LSTM [9] (out of scope of this paper). We also maintain a dictionary of acronyms in order to find similar utterances. For example, ooo for out of office.
- **Report problem with Solution Quality**: This actionable deals with the cases where intent has been identified correctly, however, the user is not satisfied

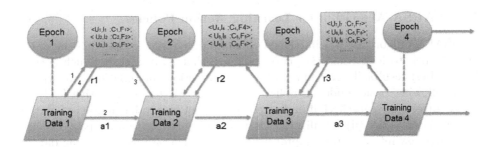

Fig. 2. Reinforcement Learning Model for Intents in Conversation

with the solution provided. In such situations, this is flagged as a potential case of solution quality not being upto the mark.

Let there be $\mathcal{U}$ utterances in an epoch. For each $u \in \mathcal{U}$, it can potentially trigger actions which are of a type in $\mathcal{A}$. The actions taken in an epoch are the augmented set of actions over the utterance set $\mathcal{U}$. Let this action set be denote by A_t. RL agent then takes actions on this data, updates the training data to become Training Data 2 and moves to next epoch of conversations as shown by edge labeled 2. The improvement in intent classification of the utterances in the passed epoch using updated training data is the reward of taking the actions. This is illustrated by edges 3 and 4 in the Fig. 2. The edge 3 shows that newly trained model is used to predict intents for utterances seen in epoch 1 and edge 4 shows the improvement in the prediction accuracy as a result that goes back into the state as a reward for taking the actions. The cycle now repeats for next epoch with the model based on Training Data 2.

We now define the state, Q-function and rewards at epoch t for our learning problem to model SARSA algorithm in order to learn the optimal action policy.

- **State,** s_t: A state at epoch t is defined as- (Training_Data_t, {<Utterance(U_t), Intent(I_t):Confidence(C_t), Feedback(F_t)>})
- **Value** $Q(s_t, A_t)$: Let A_t denote set of actions constituting of atoms from $\mathcal{A}$ taken in state s_t. Then, Q value of taking those actions in the state s_t is defined as the cross-validation accuracy of resultant training data.
- **Reward,** r_t : The improvement in label prediction accuracy for the current epoch t using the updated training data.
- α and γ are fixed at 1.

A state consists of (training model, conversation history) where conversation history is a collection of tuples s.t. a tuple contains <utterances asked, the corresponding predicted intent and the confidence value and the feedback received>. The RL model is now used to learn the action policy. The aim of the policy being learned is: how to combine feedback from users with the model confidence in order to improve overall accuracy and user satisfaction. We now describe the action policy learned using SARSA algorithm for reinforcement learning.

3.1   SARSA Algorithm for Learning Action Policies

The SARSA algorithm was implemented as follows in our setup. The goal of the algorithm is to learn the best action policies, that is, in a state which actions lead to best results. To come up with the state-action combinations, we started with following basic guideline policy for actions: (i) for all negative feedback intent-utterance pair, check if finding correct intent is suitable action or solution quality is an issue. (ii) for all negative feedback intent-utterance pair, check if assigning new intent is most appropriate action. Generate more training data in case of new intent are suggested. (iii) for positive feedback with low confidence threshold, the action is to add the utterance as a training example. The algorithm steps are listed below:

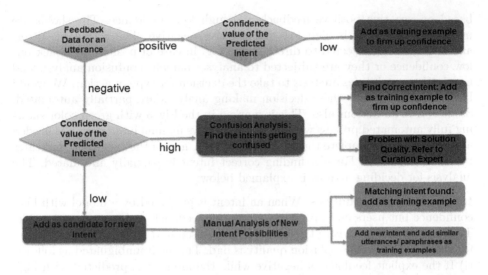

Fig. 3. Action Policy Flow Learned by RL agent

1. Compute training data accuracy in state s_t, denote it by training_acc$_t$. Initially $t = 1$.
2. Run the system for a duration and collect feedback for epoch t. In house teams were used to carry out this step.
3. Manually analyze the utterances that got negative feedback. Take the best possible action for each utterance and note down the details of the tuple <Utterance, Intent_1, Confidence, Feedback, *Action, Intent_2, {Training Examples}*>. Intent_2 is populated in case of find correct intent or new intent actions. Training Examples are also populated in case the actions are to generate more training examples.
4. Analysis of the utterances that got positive feedback is done automatically as there is only one action possible. Update the same tuple structure as in 3.
5. Finalize the updates to training data for next epoch. Determine the training data accuracy with updates denoted training_acc$_{t+1}$.
6. Now, run the training model obtained from training_acc$_{t+1}$ on the utterances of epoch t as test data and get accuracy. Check how many of the utterances that had been taken action on have been predicted correctly as per manual expert judgment. This step is done to compute the rewards for the learnings made in this epoch.
7. Repeat 2 to 6 for each epoch $t+1$, epoch $t+2$ and so on till we gain confidence on state-actions combinations.

The action policies are learned manually by mapping the majority times a type of action was taken for a particular combination of confidence and feedback values across utterance, intent pairs. The action policies, which are effectively state-action possibilities, thus learned are illustrated in the Fig. 3. This figure shows that only a subset of $\mathcal{U}$ is selected as actionable utterances based on negative/positive feedback and high/low confidence. Thresholds are used to decide what is high/low and positive/negative. The actionable utterances are either subjected to direct action e.g. in case of positive feedback but low confidence or they are subjected to analyses namely, confusion analysis and new intent possibilities analysis to take the decision for type of action. We would like to note here that these decision making analyses are partially automated. Same is true for actions also. This is marked in the Fig. 3 with green color showing fully automated process while grey color shows manual intervention is needed at some point to complete the analysis/action. A mix of the two colors indicates partial automation. For e.g. finding correct intent is partially automated. The analysis for deciding actions is explained below.

Intent confusion analysis: When an intent is predicted by a model with high confidence but users end up giving a negative feedback, it becomes actionable. This is either a case where the model got confused and made wrong prediction for the utterance or the solution quality is bad. This is disambiguated as follows: (i) If the explicit feedback is negative while the intent was predicted with high confidence and the user spent some time going through the corresponding solution, then it is considered as a case of bad solution document.
(ii) If above condition does not hold, then the intents getting confused are derived using the automated procedure as: (a) find the similar utterances in the data to the one identified for intent confusion analysis; (b) the intents corresponding to the similar ones form a probable set of confusing intent. Then the action for finding correct intent is triggered explained as follows. If the size of confusing intents set is two, then the other intent is chosen as the correct intent and utterance added as training example automatically. If the size is more or less than two, then the decision of correct intent is made manually. Note: Confusion can arise due to similarity in training utterances for different intents. For manual decision, it is good to check the probable sources of confusion as follows: (a) intents with a very fine level of distinction which is coming out through few keywords in utterances (b) very similar structured utterances have been constructed for different intents for e.g. 'how to set up my printer' and'how to set up my account'.

New Intent analysis:If there is a negative feedback for an utterance and the existing model is also not able to predict an intent with high confidence for any similar utterances, then the utterance becomes an actionable candidate for new intent. When there is a candidate for new intent found, then the analysis for possibility of matching intent from the existing set of intent corpus is done manually. Depending on the findings, there are two possible actions. Either a matching intent is selected by the expert, in which case training example is added or there is no appropriate intent found in the corpus, then a fresh intent is curated by the expert. Note that the manual selection from existing intent corpus is needed to ensure no similar intents get added.

3.2 Implementing the Action Policy

Having learned the policy, we now present the algorithm for implementing the action policies in the conversational agent as follows. This is shown in Algorithm 1.

The algorithm clearly distinguishes the manual and automated workflows. The automated actions are denoted with auto_action and manual actions with manual_action. This is run in each epoch to get the actionable utterances, the ones for which the actions got executed and result of actions on training data. $F(u)$ is the feedback function which is a weighted combination of explicit and implicit feedback normalized to give value in [-1,1]. $C(u)$ is the confidence value of the intent prediction for the utterance u. There are two thresholds defined th_1 and th_2. The threshold th_1 is for confidence value, so any value above this threshold is considered high confidence. We took value of 0.85 for this. The second threshold th_2 is for implicit feedback in terms of timespent. We used 10 sec for this value. The method findSimilarUtterances(u) finds the utterances that

---

Algorithm 1. Algorithm for Applying Actions as per Policy

INPUT: U = unique utterances for epoch n
OUTPUT: updated Training data
 1: compute feedback value $F(u)$ $\forall u \in U$
 2: **for each** $u \in U$ **do**
 3:     **if** $F(u) > 0$ **then**
 4:         **if** $C(u) < th_1$ **then**
 5:             auto_action(u)=add as training example for predicted intent
 6:         **end if**
 7:     **end if**
 8:     **if** $F(u) < 0$ s.t. explicit vote is negative and timespent(u) $< th_2$ **then**
 9:         $S \leftarrow$ findSimilarUtterances(u)
10:         **if** $C(u) > th_1$ **then**
11:             $I \leftarrow$ intentSet(S)
12:             **if** size(I) == 2 **then**
13:                 auto_action(u)=assign_alternate_intent if no explicit negative vote
14:                 auto_action(u)=add u to alternate intent in training data
15:             **else**
16:                 manual_action(u)=choose_correct_intent(u, I) and add_pair_training
17:             **end if**
18:         **else if** $\forall v \in S : C(v) < th_1$ **then**
19:             auto_action(u)= actionable_for_new_intent;
20:             manual_action(u)=find_matching_intent or curate_new_intent;
21:             generate/collect more training examples in case new intent;
22:             add pairs to training data
23:         **end if**
24:     **else if** $F(u) < 0$ s.t. explicit vote is negative and timespent(u) $> th_2$ **then**
25:         auto_action(u)=mark_solution_ document_improvement.
26:     **end if**
27: **end for**

---

are textually similar to u based on Jaccard and cosine similarity. The function intentSet(S) outputs the set of intents that have been predicted for the utterances in the set S. The rest of the action statements follow the logic as explained in the 'intent confusion analysis' and 'new intent analysis' in Sect. 3.1.

4   Service Design for Continuous Learning

The user interacts with Cognitive agent by asking a query. The Conversation Service used by the agent is designed as a classifier that classifies the intent corresponding to the user query, from the existing set of intents. The classifier is trained by providing a few manually annotated example queries for each intent in the system. As the user queries the system, its interactions are stored in a feedback database. The information for similar queries is grouped together. Similar queries are identified based on jaccard similarity index. At each epoch, the learning service reads from the feedback database and generates a set of suggestions based on the encoded action policy by taking into account the user feedback that is captured. The policy module has 3 components: New Intent Candidates, Confusion Analysis and New Intent Analysis. Based on these components, policy based actions are decided and passed on to the action module. The action module then updates the training data using both automated and manual actions. The details of how the learning policy recommendations are used to modify the training data are explained in Algorithm 1. The service can be configured to bypass the manual (Subject Matter Expert (SME)) route. Accuracy analysis is performed on the new training set to ensure that the system has not degraded. Once it is ensured, the training data is updated and the classifier is retrained based on that. There is scope for the training data to be vetted by a human expert (SME) before the classifier is retrained. This functionality may

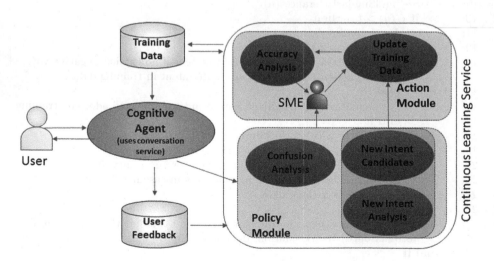

Fig. 4. Continuous Learning Service Design

Table 1. Utterance Analysis

Epoch	Unique Utterances	Actionable	Actioned a:m
0	137	36	3:12
1	137	8	1:3
2	137	29	1:7
3	117	15	3:3

Table 2. Evaluation of Action Policies

Epoch	Intent	Training Size	Acc (%)	Reward
0	127	1417	76.7	8%
1	127	1432	76.6	5. 8%
2	127	1436	75.6	11%
3	128	1444	76.7	5.2%
4	128	1451	76.9	

be required as the user feedback can be non conclusive, and thus it may add confusion to the system. It is possible to use the proposed continuous learning service with any conversation service. We use Watson's Conversation Service [18] as a proof of concept. The service is independent of different notions of feedback as long as the feedback can be cast as explicit and implicit values normalized for a range of [-1,1]. The service should be able to handle different notions of feedback. We have adhered to the standard notions of feedback [5] commonly used for implicit feedback in the design of service and additionally made the implicit feedback value as an input to the system to handle special cases.

5 Experiment Results

Having learned the policy, we implemented the service. We now evaluate the continuous learning that we get with the implementation of the action policies in the conversational agent. While certain policy flows could be automated, others require a manual intervention for which a domain expert was instituted. The data used for the experiments to determine the policy are real user conversations over two months. The service portal that has been trained on initial set of questions and intents was deployed and the conversation logs were collected. The training data had about 127 intents and 1417 utterances. The portal had up/down vote provision which was exercised optionally by users. The implicit feedback was captured through the links clicked on the solutions and the time spent in going through the solution documents. The user logs were sampled after two weeks. The Table 1 shows the number of main utterances asked in each epoch, how many of them were identified as actionable ones by Algorithm 1 and subjected to manual and auto actions. The final column shows the how many were finally acted upon. The ratio a:m shows that 'a' were automated actions and 'm' were analyzed manually. It can be seen from the table that some epochs have higher instances of utterances identified for analysis. This is primarily due to two reasons: users asked questions that could not be predicted with high confidence or were predicted wrong in that epoch. Such epochs provide better opportunity for learning than the ones where the utterances could be answered well by the training data of which epoch 2 is an example. It can also be seen that the actions taken are on a subset of utterances that were analyzed.

This is attributed to manual selection that is a part of the action policy. We had many instances of revise solution quality case and these result in actual actionable utterances being less than the candidate actionable ones. Some of the recommendations do not make it to the training data as the negative feedback was just noise and not the wrong prediction. Then some of the utterances were out of scope or nonsensical (e.g. "What time did you wake up") and hence are rejected for example, if the agent is supposed to answer questions on Websphere issues but some utterances actually ask questions on Oracle DB issues, then these are rejected. There was no pattern observed in terms of ratio of each of these causes for rejected actionable utterances.

We updated the training data, used cross validation to find training data accuracy, then took the next two weeks user utterances as a test data against that and then manually rated it. The accuracy of test data predictions is captured as reward. The Table 2 shows the value of rewards and training data accuracy at each epoch. The last epoch, 4, does not have rewards computed since that is considered as terminal state for the learning agent. The Table 2 shows that the rewards vary from 5% to 11%. An interesting observation was that not all the times adding a training example pushed the confidence of similar utterances above the threshold value of 0.85. This was attributed to structural similarity of the utterance with utterances of other intents. For example, 'how do I setup an X' and 'how do I setup Y' were sometimes confused resulting either low confidence or incorrect prediction. Hence, the percentage improvement is not a numeric function of number of actions taken. The table also shows how the training data got modified with each epoch. It can be seen that there was a new intent added in epoch 3. It can also be observed that the number of utterances is increasing in each epoch in different quantities. The accuracy of training data varies a little in acceptable range. It can be seen that the last epoch ended with an overall improvement in the accuracy. Note that the value of 76.7% in epoch 0 is the cross validation accuracy with initial training data. The accuracy of 76.6% at epoch 1 is the accuracy once the training data got modified based on actions taken after analyzing the utterances in epoch 0. The column called reward on actions captures the improvement in intent predictions as a result of actions taken on the training data. We observe that the rewards are higher when the number of actions taken are higher which is a validation of our action policy. The interesting observation is that training accuracy can decline even with fewer actions taken as observed in epoch 3. The utterances of epoch 2 resulted in very few actionables and yet the impact on resultant training data that was used in epoch 3 was negative. However, this is contrasted in epoch 4 which had minor increase in accuracy inspite of small actionables in epoch 3. Overall, the fact that the accuracy did not drop more than 1% is a validation of robustness of the action policies. This is largely attributed to quality of recommendations and manual decisions. We plan to completely automate the action policy as part of future work.

There is another analysis that was done to see how much of potential improvement is being captured using the feedback based action policies that we have proposed here. It is possible that users do not provide enough feedback due to which the policies are not able to identify the actionable utterances even though there are utterances which could have been worked upon. In this analysis, we had more than 75% cases getting captured across epochs. Thus, we can see that the feedback was very good and we covered most of the important cases for improvement in the training data. There were few cases of new intent possibility that were not captured because there was no feedback provided even though the predictions were with low confidence. To handle such cases, we plan to augment the approach with unsupervised learning in future where the remainder utterances after the ones that have been actioned upon using the policies shall be checked for prediction confidence and then the ones with low confidence will be subjected to clustering. The cluster output will be subjected to manual scrutiny to decide if there is a case for new intent.

Observations: Feedback based reinforcement learning for continuous learning comes with its own challenges in performance. The quality of feedback plays a crucial rule in our model. If the users give random feedback, then the performance of training can deteriorate as we observed in Table 1. In absence of feedback, there will not be much training that can be performed. We observed that the confidence of intent predictions for utterances that were asked repeatedly in more than an epoch and were actioned upon eventually got the intent prediction correct with high confidence. On a positive note, the manual effort in improving training data went down considerably by use of our approach, in some cases from 20 hours to 4 hrs as reported by the experts. This is primarily due to the effort being reduced to just decision making as opposed to first analyzing, evaluating and then deciding.

6   Related Work

We now present the various learning techniques from literature that are relevant to our work. Self training [20] is one such technique. In self training a classifier is first trained with the small amount of labeled data. The classifier is then used to classify the unlabeled data. Typically the most confident unlabeled points, together with their predicted labels, are added to the training set. The classifier is re-trained and the procedure repeated. Note the classifier uses its own predictions to teach itself. The procedure is also called self-teaching or bootstrapping (not to be confused with the statistical procedure with the same name). One can imagine that a classification mistake can reinforce itself. Some algorithms try to avoid this by unlearning unlabeled points if the prediction confidence drops below a threshold. Our approach is more robust and functionally rich compared to this.

Active learning [12] is being increasingly explored and used to come up with training dataset efficiently. Active learning algorithms select examples for labeling in a sequential, data- adaptive fashion, as opposed to passive learning algorithms based on preselected training data. The key to active learning is adaptive data collection. Most experimental work in active learning with real-world data is simulated by letting the algorithm adaptively select a small number of labeled examples from a large labeled dataset. This requires a large, labeled data set to begin with, which limits the scope and scale of such experimental work. The current relabeling based active learning approaches [8] try to relabel based on impact and may end up altering the existing training data a lot more than desired.

Particularly for dialog systems and conversation agents, [16,19] exploited a combination of active and semi-supervised learning approach for better training. As the classifier labels the unlabeled utterances, the ones with high confidence are automatically added to the existing training data and the ones with low confidence are selected for active learning, to be labeled manually and then added to the training data. Understanding the importance of learning from the unlabeled user queries that are logged, [2,4,6,7] exploit them by employing a semi-supervised learning approach to increase their training data. They model click-graphs to infer the labels for the unlabeled user query, using some proximity measures. Our paper differs in two aspects. Firstly, previous works do not take into account the user feedback that is recorded on these queries. Also, the focus is mainly on identifying more examples to expand the training data and improve the classification. We extend our work beyond this through two measures. We perform a confusion analysis to identify misclassified utterances based on the user feedback. We also include a new intent analysis that identifies if a new intent has to be added into the system to address some of the user queries. [13] talks about using reinforced learning for an intent classification task by incorporating user feedback. The task is limited to identifying the correct intent from the set of existing intents and doesn't consider the possibility of adding new intents to the system. For the sake of completeness, we also mention other works [10,17] that talk about using reinforcement learning in a dialog system. Their main aim is to improve the system by identifying the optimal dialog sequence that engages the user and the focus is not on the intent classification task. [15] is another similar work in this domain.

7   Conclusions

As cognitive systems are going to mature in basic functionality, the need for continuous learning service proposed in this work is inevitable. In this paper, we have focused on modeling and implementation of continuous learning for intent classification in conversational agents and showed promising results. Our experiment results for service performance, detailed in Sect. 5 show that (i) training data updates can be made very efficiently (ii) the impact of updates on cross-validation accuracy of training data is gradual which is good (iii) the training data expands with new intents and utterances with time leading to remarkable improvement in intent prediction accuracy (iv) interestingly, accuracy need not be directly proportional to the acted upon utterances (v) noise in feedback or no feedback is a challenge and we shall show in the evaluations how it can impact the actionable vs acted upon ratio. As part of future work, we plan to extend continuous learning (fully/semi automated) to other aspects of conversation systems like dialog flows also and make continuous learning services an integral component of any conversation service.

References

1. AskSpoke. https://doesthathelp.askspoke.com/redefining-the-service-desk-7df61db617c5
2. Celikyilmaz, A., Hakkani-Tür, D., Tur, G.: Leveraging Web Query Logs to Learn User Intent Via Bayesian Latent Variable Model (2011)
3. Dhoolia, P., et al.: A cognitive system for business and technical support: a case study. IBM J. Res. Dev. **61**(1), 7 (2017)
4. Hakkani-Tür, D., Heck, L., Tur, G.: Exploiting query click logs for utterance domain detection in spoken language understanding. In: IEEE International Conference on Acoustics, Speech and Signal Processing (ICASSP), 2011, pp. 5636–5639. IEEE (2011)
5. Joachims, T., Granka, L., Pan, B., Hembrooke, H., Gay, G.: Accurately interpreting clickthrough data as implicit feedback. In: Proceedings of the 28th Annual International ACM SIGIR Conference on Research and Development in Information Retrieval, SIGIR 2005, pp. 154–161 (2005)
6. Li, X., Wang, Y.Y., Acero, A.: Learning query intent from regularized click graphs. In: Proceedings of the 31st Annual International ACM SIGIR Conference on Research and Development in Information Retrieval, pp. 339–346. ACM (2008)
7. Li, X., Wang, Y.Y., Shen, D., Acero, A.: Learning with click graph for query intent classification. ACM Trans. Inf. Syst. (TOIS) **28**(3), 12 (2010)
8. Lin, C.H., Mausam., Weld, D.S.: Re-active learning: active learning with relabeling. In: Proceedings of the Thirtieth AAAI Conference on Artificial Intelligence, AAAI 2016, pp. 1845–1852. AAAI Press (2016)
9. A Beginner's Guide to Recurrent Networks and LSTMs. https://deeplearning4j.org/lstm.html
10. Scheffler, K., Young, S.: Automatic learning of dialogue strategy using dialogue simulation and reinforcement learning. In: Proceedings of the second international conference on Human Language Technology Research, pp. 12–19. Morgan Kaufmann Publishers Inc. (2002)
11. IBM Workplace Support Services with Watson. https://www.ibm.com/in-en/marketplace/end-user-support-services
12. Settles, B.: Active learning literature survey. Technical report (2010)
13. Shibata, T., Egashira, Y., Kurohashi, S.: Chat-Like conversational system based on selection of reply generating module with reinforcement learning. In: Rudnicky, A., Raux, A., Lane, I., Misu, T. (eds.) Situated Dialog in Speech-Based Human-Computer Interaction. SCT, pp. 63–69. Springer, Cham (2016). doi:10.1007/978-3-319-21834-2_6
14. Sutton, R.S., Barto, A.G.: Reinforcement Learning: An Introduction (1998)
15. Thomson, B., Young, S.: Bayesian update of dialogue state: a pomdp framework for spoken dialogue systems. Comput. Speech Lang. **24**(4), 562–588 (2010)
16. Tur, G., Hakkani-Tür, D., Schapire, R.E.: Combining active and semi-supervised learning for spoken language understanding. Speech Commun. **45**(2), 171–186 (2005)

17. Walker, M.A.: An application of reinforcement learning to dialogue strategy selection in a spoken dialogue system for email. J. Artif. Intell. Res. **12**, 387–416 (2000)
18. Watson Developer Cloud-IBM. https://www.ibm.com/watson/developercloud/
19. Wu, W.L., Lu, R.Z., Duan, J.Y., Liu, H., Gao, F., Chen, Y.Q.: Spoken language understanding using weakly supervised learning. Comput. Speech Lang. **24**(2), 358–382 (2010)
20. Zhu, X.: Semi-supervised learning literature survey. Technical report 1530, Computer Sciences, University of Wisconsin-Madison (2005)

Costradamus: A Cost-Tracing System for Cloud-Based Software Services

Jörn Kuhlenkamp[1,2] and Markus Klems[1,2(✉)]

[1] Technische Universität Berlin, Berlin, Germany
`jk@ise.tu-berlin.de`
[2] Information Systems Engineering Research Group, Berlin, Germany
`mk@ise.tu-berlin.de`

Abstract. Cloud providers offer a range of fully managed infrastructure services that enable a "serverless" architecture and development paradigm. Following this paradigm, software services can be built on compositions of cloud infrastructure services that offer fine-granular pay-per-use pricing models. While this development and deployment approach simplifies service development and management, it remains an open challenge to make use of fine-granular pricing models for improving cost transparency and reducing cost of service operations. As a solution, we present Costradamus, a cost-tracing system that implements a generic cost model and three different tracing approaches. With Costradamus, we can derive cost and performance information per API operation. We evaluate our approach and system in a smart grid context and discuss unexpected performance and deployment cost tradeoffs.

Keywords: Tracing · Cloud computing · Deployment costs · Performance

1 Introduction

Serverless computing [14] is an emerging architecture and development paradigm for building cloud-based software services that promises to reduce cost of service development and operations. A serverless service relies entirely on fully managed cloud infrastructure services that offer fine-granular pay-per-use pricing models.

Despite these detailed usage and pricing models, actual capacity usage and billing information is usually presented to users as aggregates, in terms of time (e.g., monthly bills) and resource usage (e.g., per infrastructure service category). This makes it difficult for software service developers to determine the actual capacity usage and associated cost of a single software service and to obtain a cost breakdown per API operation of a single service.

In this paper, we propose an approach and system prototype that solves this problem by enabling **per-request cost-tracing**. Potential applications of our approach are:

1. Cost-debugging tools [7] for developers who thereby gain insight into cost changes that are caused by small source code or deployment changes.

© Springer International Publishing AG 2017
M. Maximilien et al. (Eds.): ICSOC 2017, LNCS 10601, pp. 657–672, 2017.
https://doi.org/10.1007/978-3-319-69035-3_48

2. Systems for improving cost awareness across different teams, in particular, if cross-functional teams work independently on their own microservices. With a cost-tracing system, teams could communicate their service cost to other teams more easily.
3. Software-as-a-Service providers could calculate marginal cost of operations and, based on detailed cost information, design pay-per-use pricing models for their software services that guarantee a stable profit margin.

Our approach enables per-request cost-tracing by using a mix of analytic and experiment-based techniques. We use an analytic cost modeling approach and supply the cost model with input data that is derived through a tracing system which augments each request trace with resource capacity consumption data along its invocation path.

In the following Sect. 2, we give a short overview of serverless computing and distributed tracing. Then, in Sect. 3, we introduce the scenario of a smart grid metering application that is realized with serverless infrastructure. Section 4 shows our first contribution, a generic cost model for serverless infrastructure. In Sect. 5, we present our second contribution, Costradamus, a cost-tracing system that can determine the per-request capacity usage and cost of infrastructure service compositions. In Sect. 6, we present results of our cost measurements and discuss interesting effects that we observed when applying our cost-tracing approach to the smart grid metering application.

2   Background

Serverless computing is a paradigm that introduces a new system architecture approach as well as a new programming, runtime, and deployment model. Serverless architecture is characterized by the extensive use of fully managed cloud services and the absence of self-managed system components, in particular the absence of self-managed servers. Serverless computing is characterized by the use of Serverless Functions (SF), also known as Function-as-a-Service, Cloud Functions, or Serverless Microservices. Examples of SF services include AWS Lambda, Google Cloud Functions, and Azure Functions.

An SF encapsulates business logic and exposes an RPC handler interface for remote procedure calls. Typically, an SF is stateless and can be invoked through events, such as HTTP request events or events by other cloud infrastructure services. The SF lifecycle typically looks like this: a developer bundles the SF business logic source code and uploads it to a storage service. When the SF is invoked, the source code is loaded and executed in a managed, container-based runtime environment. The lifespan of an SF is relatively short, often below one second. For performance-optimization, SF containers are typically re-used for subsequent invocations and only destroyed if no new events have arrived for a prolonged period of time (several minutes), thereby saving infrastructure cost on the provider side.

Although SF deliver on the promise of low operational effort (NoOps), a service that is composed of many small functions creates new management challenges. For this purpose, distributed tracing and debugging solutions are needed, such as Google's Dapper [17]. AWS X-Ray is a similar tracing service that can be used to debug and analyze service compositions that comprise AWS Lambda functions and other AWS infrastructure services. For a sample of requests that clients send to an API Gateway, load balancer, or Lambda function, X-Ray adds a trace id to the request context and then passes the request to the destined service. A trace segment (also known as trace record or span) for the traced service is sent to an X-Ray daemon which buffers segments and uploads batches of segments to the X-Ray API. Downstream service incovactions, such as AWS DynamoDB or AWS Kinesis, can be traced by instrumenting the AWS SDK client that makes the request, e.g., from an EC2 instance or a Lambda function.

3 Application Scenario: Smart Grid Metering

We consider an application scenario in the context of smart grid management. The application scenario is inspired by the PolyEnergyNet project[1]. Continuously, the power grid becomes increasingly dynamic and decentralized in nature. To make timely and knowledgeable decisions for strategic grid expansion and day-to-day grid operation, it becomes increasingly important to meter the state of smart grids with fine granularity. This includes meters in the infrastructure of distributed network operators (DNO) and meters at individual consumers and prosumers.

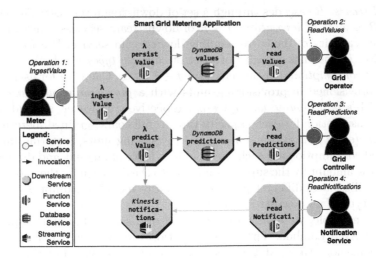

Fig. 1. Application scenario: smart grid metering application.

---

[1] http://www.polyenergynet.de.

A software service provider within the organization of a DNO offers the Smart Grid Metering application (SGMApp) (see Fig. 1). The SGMApp exposes an API comprising four operations that are each backed by cloud services. A request to an API operation triggers a cascade of invocations to downstream services in the back-end. Meters use the `IngestValue` operation to periodically push new metered values. The `ingestValue` service checks parameters and forwards values to `persistValue` and `predictValue`. The `persistValue` service stores values in a database for later analysis. The `predictValue` service uses historical data of the corresponding time series to calculate predictions. Historical data is retrieved from a local cache or from the `values` database service. Predictions are stored in a dedicated database service. If a predicted value significantly deviates from a current value, a notification is sent to a streaming service. Grid operators use the `ReadValues` operation to display the current state of the smart grid. The `readValues` service checks query parameters and retrieves values from `values`. Similarly, automated grid controllers use in addition the `ReadPredictions` operation. The `ReadNotifications` operation allows to consume critical notifications.

4 Software Service Cost Model

In this section, we present a generic cost model for cloud-based software services, and propose metrics to quantify cost and capacity waste per API request.

4.1 Service Model

An *API request* R cascades through a set of downstream services. Therefore, we model R as a set of *invocations* $I \in R$ of downstream services. Each invocation consumes capacity of the corresponding downstream service. Precisely, a single invocation I consumes capacity of a set of *capacity types* $t \in I$. We denote the *measured consumption* of a capacity type $t \in I$ by u_t. Capacity for each capacity type is provisioned in provisioning units with a *provisioning unit size* c_t, and billed with a *provisioning unit price* p_t, respectively. However, a cloud provider meters consumption for each capacity type in full coarse-grained metering units with a *metering unit size* m_t, $m_t \leq c_t$. Provisioning units, metering units, and measured consumption are each specified as a tuple of amount and duration. We refer to the amount by the superscript 0 and to the duration by the superscript 1. Figure 2a illustrates different parameters used to model consumption of a single capacity type of an downstream service.

As an example, we model an invocation of a service function implemented on top of AWS Lambda. The service function uses a single capacity type `mem` denoting memory time. At the creation time of the service function, a service provider configures the service function to use provisioning units of $c_{mem} = (128\,\mathrm{MB}, 100\,\mathrm{ms})$. The provisioning unit price of a single provisioning unit is $p_t = 208\,\mathrm{n\$}$. Provisioning units equal metering units $c_{mem} = m_{mem}$. An example invocation utilizes a constant amount of 60 MB memory over a total runtime of

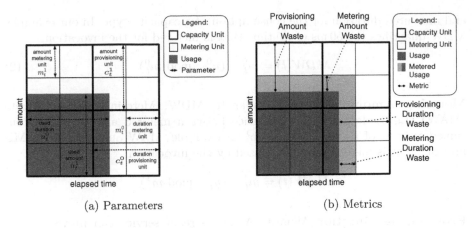

(a) Parameters   (b) Metrics

Fig. 2. Cost model parameters and metrics for a single capacity type.

$600\,\mathrm{ms}$ $u_{mem} = (60\,\mathrm{MB}, 150\,\mathrm{ms})$. Optionally, an invocation that includes data transfer to or from a data center requires modelling of a second capacity type bw denoting network bandwidth.

4.2   Metrics

Based on the service model in Sect. 4.1, we define metrics to quantify per-request cost. On a more fine granular level, waste metrics characterize individual invocations of downstream services. Precisely, waste metrics characterize provisioned and not utilized capacity for invocations. Waste metrics serve the main purpose of supporting a service provider in cost debugging and optimization of software services. Figure 2 illustrates different metrics.

Marginal Request Cost. One of the main motivations behind Costradamus is the quantification of per-request cost. The Marginal Request Cost (MRC) metric (Eq. 1) does exactly that. For a request R, we add costs over all invocations $I \in R$. For each invocation, we add costs over all capacity types $t \in I$. To derive cost per capacity type t, we calculate metered amount and metered duration based on measured amount u_t^0 and measured duration u_t^1 per capacity type. Finally, we obtain MRC by calculating the relative share of provisioning units multiplied by the provisioning unit price p_t.

$$MRC(R) = \sum_{I \in R} \sum_{t \in I} \left\lceil \frac{u_t^0}{m_t^0} \right\rceil * \frac{m_t^0}{c_t^0} * \left\lceil \frac{u_t^1}{m_t^1} \right\rceil * \frac{m_t^1}{c_t^1} * p_t \tag{1}$$

Metering Duration Waste. Cloud providers typically measure how much and for how long a certain capacity is used by an invocation. However, for metering purposes, measured usage is usually rounded up to coarse-grained units. Metering Duration Waste (MDW) (Eq. 2) describes the difference between metered and measured duration for the consumption of a capacity type. In our example, MDW quantifies the 50 ms of runtime that is metered for the invocation.

$$MDW(t) = m_t^0 - (u_t^0 \mod m_t^0) \tag{2}$$

Metering Amount Waste. Similar to MDW, Metering Amount Waste (MAW) (Eq. 3) describes the difference between metered and measured consumed amount of a capacity type. In our example, MAW quantifies the 68MB memory that is metered and never used by the invocation.

$$MAW(t) = m_t^1 - (u_t^1 \mod m_t^1) \tag{3}$$

Provisioning Duration Waste. A downstream service can provision per-invocation capacity or shared capacity for multiple invocations. Provisioning waste metrics characterize provisioned and unused capacity for an invocation in the absence of other invocations. Therefore, Provisioning Duration Waste (PDW) (Eq. 4) describes the difference between provisioned and metered usage duration for a capacity type. In our example, PDW equals 0 ms.

$$PDW(t) = c_t^0 - (u_t^0 \mod c_t^0) \tag{4}$$

Provisioning Amount Waste. Similar to PDW, Metering Amount Waste (PAW) (Eq. 5) describes the difference between provisioned and metered consumed amount of a capacity type.

$$PAW(t) = c_t^1 - (u_t^1 \mod c_t^1) \tag{5}$$

5   Cost-Tracing System

In this section, we present Costradamus, our end-to-end cost-tracing system for software services. In analogy to performance-tracing [15], we define cost-tracing as the activity of collecting detailed cost information of causally-related events in a distributed service-oriented system.

An application consists of multiple services that expose operations through an API. A tracing system collects data that relates to operation calls, including all downstream service invocations. In the next section, we identify design goals for a **cost-tracing** system.

5.1   Design Goals

Costradamus enables users to retrieve performance and cost information. In more detail, we propose and motivate the following design goals for our cost-tracing system.

(D1) **Per-request tracing.** The tracing system should provide fine-granular cost information for individual API operations, such as a single HTTP request.

(D2) **Cost composition.** Operations might invoke complex compositions of services with heterogeneous pricing models. A cost trace should cover the entire service composition and provide measurements in a normalized cost metric.

(D3) **Non-intrusiveness.** Making an application traceable should not have negative side-effects on other non-functional properties, such as availability, reliability, performance, and security.

Our first design goal (D1) is motivated by agile software development methodologies and DevOps best practices which advocate short and continuous cycles in which small software changes are pushed from development to production. With per-request cost traces, small software changes can be evaluated in isolation. Thereby, a developer can inspect performance and cost of a new feature or compare the performance and cost change that accompanies a feature change.

Non-trivial applications consist of many services with heterogeneous pricing models which can be invoked through non-deterministic events, motivating our second design goal (D2). Each trace should contain performance and cost information that allow users to drill down into the cost of all service invocations that are causally related to an API operation.

Our third design goal (D3) relates to general design goals of low performance overhead and application-level transparency [18]. Trace records can either be explicitly or implicitly related to a specific request. An explicit approach adds a reference to a specific entry event, e.g., the entry event id, to each trace record at runtime. An implicit approach assigns trace records to an operation offline and based on statistical correlation. The explicit approach simplifies (D2), however, applications must be instrumented to obtain a trace id reference, with potential negative effects on (D3). We favor (D2) over (D3) and use instrumentation points that can be disabled for production workloads.

5.2   Capacity Usage Tracing Approaches

Costradamus supports three tracing approaches for collecting capacity usage data (T1–T3). We discuss each tracing approach in the context of an example application as illustrated in Fig. 3. The example shows a software service that is composed of four infrastructure services: two function services, a messaging service and a database service. Each function service integrates an instrumentation point for capturing performance and cost data of each infrastructure service invocation. Part of the tracing system is a trace record store (which is a specialized *Message Store* [8]) that persistently stores trace records for later analysis. Whenever an infrastructure service is invoked, an instrumentation point produces a trace record and sends it to the trace record store. In the following, we describe three tracing approaches that take into consideration different types of infrastructure services.

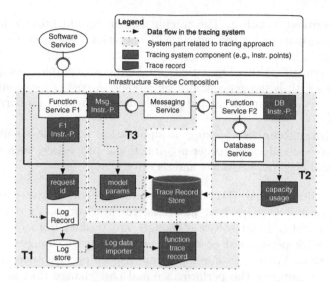

Fig. 3. Example setup of Costradamus showing tracing approaches T1–T3.

T1: Log Import. Tracing approach T1 constructs a capacity usage trace record from data in a (distributed) log store by sending a reference to a log entry to the trace store and later use the reference to query the log store. The example in Fig. 3 shows a function service F1 that writes logs to a log store. A log contains capacity usage and performance information, such as the start and end time of the function invocation, used memory, and billed duration. The log entry for each request in the log store can be identified by a unique request id. The instrumentation point of F1 extracts the request id from the function invocation context and adds it to the meta-data of F1's trace record. Thereby, a log data importer can be used for augmenting function service trace records during the trace collection phase. First, the trace record for F1 is retrieved and the request id is extracted from the trace record. Then, the log store is queried using the request id, and capacity usage information, such as memory and billed duration, are retrieved.

T2: Response Recording. Tracing approach T2 requires capacity usage information from a service invocation response message to construct a trace record. In the example shown in Fig. 3, function service F2 invokes another infrastructure service via a remote procedure call or API request. In the example, F2 invokes a database service. Approach T2 relies on information delivered in the response message of the invoked infrastructure service. For example, the database service AWS DynamoDB returns capacity usage information in provider- and service-specific capacity units. The capacity usage information is extracted from the response and added as meta-data to the trace record that is associated with the database service invocation. For simplifying Fig. 3, we do not show the instrumentation point for tracing function service invoications of F2, which is performed as shown for F1 using the tracing approach T1.

T3: Modeling. Tracing approach T3 creates trace records at runtime with estimated capacity usage values that are modeled by Costradamus based on runtime measurements. This approach can be used if T1 is infeasible because there are no logs or if T2 is infeasible because the service does not send usage data in a response message. Similar to T2, T3 augments a trace record with meta-data. However, instead of capacity usage data from the service response, the trace record meta-data contains service request parameters that can be used for offline capacity usage estimation.

5.3   Prototype

We have implemented Costradamus, a cost-tracing system for AWS cloud infrastructure with Node.js based Lambda functions. The project is available as open source software [1]. For using Costradamus, instrumentation points must be added to the Lambda functions of the software service that should be traced. Furthermore, Amazon's distributed tracing service X-Ray must be activated for these Lambda functions.

Instrumentation Points. Costradamus uses special-purpose instrumentation points to add capacity consumption meta-data to trace records in X-Ray. For adding these instrumentation points, the developer needs to add the costradamus software library as a dependency to the Lambda function source code.

During the execution of a Lambda function and invocation of downstream Lambda, DynamoDB, and Kinesis services from within the function's business logic, we need to capture capacity consumption information that is not included in the plain X-Ray trace records. This is realized by adding a Costradamus subsegment to each parent segment (Lambda, DynamoDB, or Kinesis service invocation). Each Costradamus subsegment contains meta-data that is needed according to the respective tracing approach (T1, T2, or T3).

The instrumentation points require between 1–3 additional lines of code in the Lambda function source code, for each downstream service invocation, and 2 lines for making the Lambda function itself cost-traceable. The code for implementing an instrumentation point is between ca. 10–60 lines of code and should not be much larger for other infrastructure services, besides Lambda, DynamoDB, and Kinesis.

Cost-Tracing Process. After a client invokes a Lambda function that is activated for tracing with X-Ray, the client receives the trace id in the HTTP response header. This trace id is used in a next step to retrieve the corresponding trace record, consisting of segments and subsegments with performance data and some meta-data, from X-Ray (our trace record store). As described in the previous section, for tracing approach T1, in addition to the trace records stored in X-Ray, we retrieve Lambda function logs from CloudWatch. Each Lambda function segment contains a Costradamus meta-data field with the Lambda request id which we extract and use to query the CloudWatch logs within a specific time window, between the start and end times of the Lambda function invocation. Since the logs in CloudWatch materialize with a longer delay than the X-Ray trace records, according to our observations, this operation might need to be repeated several times. The other trace records of DynamoDB and Kinesis invocations already contain all required capacity usage information as Costradamus meta-data.

In the next step, the X-Ray traces are augmented with cost meta-data which is generated on the client by using capacity meta-data as input for the cost modeler. In a further step, the Costradamus consumption subsegments are removed (pruned) from the trace record as they are not needed any more. Each of the three processing steps results in a new file that contains the trace record, so that, after processing, one trace record maps to three trace record files: plain, augmented, and pruned. We use a batch script to process multiple traces with a single command. The pruned files from the last processing step are used as input by a helper tool that creates a CSV file for performance and cost data analysis.

6   Evaluation

We investigate performance/cost tradeoffs of the SGMApp in four experiments.

6.1   Experiment Setup

Implementation. We implement the SGMApp (Sect. 3) with AWS. We use DynamoDB tables for the `values` and `predictions` services and Kinesis streams for the `notifications` service. All other downstream services are implemented as AWS Lambda functions. Operations are published via the Amazon API Gateway service. Invocations of service functions for the `IngestValue` operation are event-based, other invocations are request-response-based. All service functions parallelize invocations of tables and streams. We use a 10 s timeout for all service functions, and exponential backoff as retry strategy.

Workload and Measurements. For each experiment, we run a *Load* phase followed by a *Run* phase. The Load phase writes 600 historical values per meter to the `ValuesTable`. The Run phase issues 100 requests to each of the four API operations with a 1 s wait time between subsequent requests. For brevity, we refer to the operations by O1 (`IngestValue`), O2 (`ReadValues`), O3 (`ReadPredictions`), and O4 (`ReadNotifications`).

Metrics. For each request, we record a trace with segments and subsegments. Figure 4 shows an excerpt of a trace for the `IngestValue` operation. We measure all metrics presented in Sect. 4. In addition, we measure request-execution latency (REL) and invocation-execution latency (IEL) for each invocation of a downstream service. A relation exists between REL and IEL. For a single request, the REL is equal or larger than the sum of all corresponding IELs. We plot traces sorted by MC in ascending order.

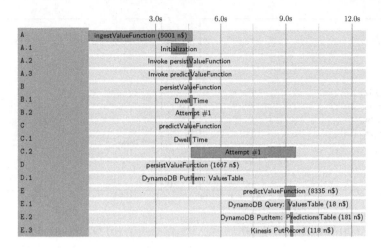

Fig. 4. Excerpt of an ingestValue operation trace with trace segments (for readability named A–E) and subsegments (A.1, A.2, etc.).

Case Study and Experiment Setups. We conduct experiments with four different experiment setups E1–E4 (see Table 1) to quantify performance and costs per API request. E1 serves as a baseline scenario. We compare the other experiments with E1 to investigate the impact of changes to the provisioned infrastructure (E2), business logic (E3), and target data center (E4). Precisely, we use three parameters: provisioned lambda memory in MB [128, 1024], the number of historical meter values and prediction horizon used by the predictValues function [3, 60] and the AWS region [us-east-1, eu-west-1].

6.2   Results and Discussion

E1. Figure 5 illustrates the results for E1. For O2, most traces are subject to a constant cost of 1.8 μ$, this is due to a IEL < 100 ms for readValues and a constant number of meter values that are queried from values. The measurements show increased costs for trace ids >#87 due to an increased 100 < IEL < 400 ms of readValues resulting in a stepwise increase of MRC up to 6.8 μ$. However, the increased IEL should result in a steeper cost increase. Detailed analysis of

Table 1. Summary of parameters for experiment setups E1–E4.

Experiment	Region	Memory [MB]	Interval [s]	Scenario
E1	us-east-1	1024	3	Baseline
E2	us-east-1	128	3	Infrastructure sizing
E3	us-east-1	1024	60	Business logic refinement
E4	eu-west-1	1024	3	Multi-region role-out

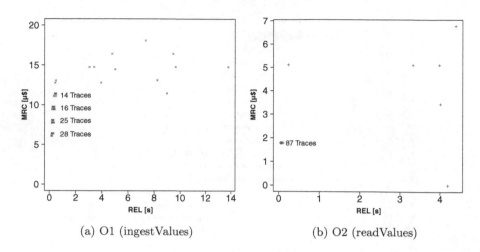

(a) O1 (ingestValues)   (b) O2 (readValues)

Fig. 5. Cost and performance comparison of O1 and O2 for E1 (Baseline).

the corresponding traces reveals that this behavior is caused by failed executions of `readValues` that are not charged by the cloud provider but increase REL. For O1, we observe a higher variation of costs compared to O2. This behavior is caused by a variable runtime of service functions and variable size of data that is queried from `values` and written to `notifications`.

For O1 and O2, around 10% of the traces show a REL > 600 ms and, therefore, can be considered performance outliers. However, compared to O2, we observe that O1 performance outliers show an up to three times higher REL. Detailed analysis shows that the increased REL is caused by failed executions of multiple service functions for the same request. Furthermore, all performance outliers are scheduled in the beginning of a workload. A consistent explanation is a startup time for new containers that back a service function [7].

E2. In comparison to E1, E2 provisions only 128MB memory for containers that back service functions. Therefore, we expect REL to increase and MRC to decrease. We exclude performance outliers and summarize our results in Table 2. For O1, we observe a 200% increase in 95th-percentile REL and a 58% decrease in median MRC. Thus, the results indicate that the REL is bound to the IEL of the three service functions and, therefore, reducing provisioned memory results in a significantly lower performance. For O3, results indicate that REL is not bound to the `readPredictions` and reduced memory does not result in lower performance. Therefore, our experiment suggests that informed decisions on infrastructure sizing can help to identify new deployments that are strictly dominating in terms of performance and deployment costs.

E3. For E3, we change the implementation of `predictValues`. Precisely, the data resolution for the prediction is increased from 3 to 60 m values. Therefore, we expect additional (i) reads on `values` and (ii) writes on `predictions` and `notifications`. Figure 6 compares results for O1. We observe an unexpected

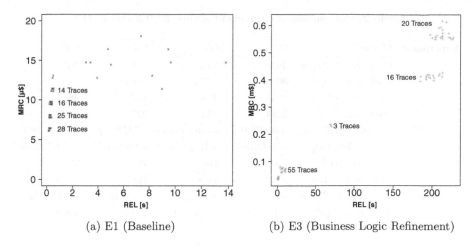

(a) E1 (Baseline)   (b) E3 (Business Logic Refinement)

Fig. 6. Cost and Performance Comparison of O1 (`ingestValue`) for E1 and E3.

significant increase in the 95th-percentile REL by ∼466 times and median MRC by ∼7 times, respectively. We further investigate this behavior, and find that invocations of `predictValues`' require up to three attempts to succeed due to a timeout of 10s. While failed attempts do not increase usage of Lambda, usage increases for invocations of `values`, `predictions` and `notifications` during failed attempts. Therefore, failed executions of service functions can significantly increase MRC. We refer to this effect as *retry cost effect*. Besides the retry cost effect, we observe that `predictValues`' issues more invocations of `values` and `predictions`. Therefore, `predictValues`' results in increases consumption of other downstream services. We refer to this effect as *ripple cost effect*. One implication of the ripple cost effect is that cost testing in an iterative development process should not only rely on isolated tests of single downstream services but also incorporate end-to-end cost testing.

E4. We compare the `us-east-1` and `eu-west-1` regions. Increased prices apply to the `eu-west-1` region for DynamoDB and Kinesis. Thus, we expect an increase MRC under similar REL in comparison to E1. Counterintuitively, we observe lower MRC and REL for the `eu-west-1` region (Table 2). Higher region prices are accompanied by better performance. Therefore, shorter runtimes and lower usage of service functions compensate for higher region prices. One implication of our findings is that cost calculations should not exclusively be based on analytical models but include real measurements.

Design Goals. Costradamus enables us to perform fine-granular per-request tracing (D1), as demonstrated with the experiment results above. We can also measure the cost of complex service compositions (D2), however, each downstream service must be instrumented, requiring the implementation of service-specific instrumentation points. The third design goal of non-intrusiveness (D3) is less prioritized and therefore also not evaluated comprehensively, as we propose

Table 2. Comparison of experiment setups E1/E2 and E1/E4.

Experiment	Metric	O1	O2	O3	O4
E1	95th-prec REL [ms]	452	84	231	303
	Median MC [n$]	8063	1775	1685	5103
E2	95th-prec REL [ms]	1358	424	157	589
	Median MC [n$]	3384	732	226	936
Δ E2, E1	95th-prec REL [ms]	+906(200%)	+340(403%)	−74(32%)	+285(94%)
	Median MC [n$]	−4679(58%)	−1043(59%)	−1459(87%)	−4167(82%)
E4	95th-prec REL [ms]	250	101	78	271
	Median MC [n$]	6242	1790	1687	5110
Δ E4, E1	95th-prec REL [ms]	−202(45%)	+17(21%)	−153(66%)	−33(11%)
	Median MC [n$]	−1821(23%)	+15(1%)	2(0%)	7(0%)

to apply our tracing approach only during development and disable it during production. However, we observed low performance overhead when comparing client-side latency of requests with tracing toggled on/off. This can be explained by the fact that the Costradamus prototype builds on AWS X-Ray which runs as a separate daemon that sends data batches over UDP. A more comprehensive evaluation, in particular of security and availability implications, would be needed to use Costradamus in a production environment, and is a task for future work.

7 Related Work

A large number of tracing frameworks exist to model performance of distributed, server-based applications [3,5,11,18]. We extend this work by providing a cost-tracing system that addresses two unique challenges. First, tracing of consumptions for heterogeneous infrastructure services and capacity types. Second, tracing under highly restricted options to add instrumentation points due to the high abstraction of serverless infrastructure.

Per-request cost is determined by consumed resources in downstream services. Therefore, our work is related to existing research in the area of cloud resource management [9] from the perspective of a cloud user with a focus on application resource demand profiling and application pricing [16]. Existing approaches for resource demand profiling model resource consumption for a given workload to model performance [2,6,12,20], cost [19] or energy consumption [10] as a function of resource consumption. The work by [4] evaluates the tradeoff between profit and customer satisfaction for a traditional virtual machine based infrastructure setup in a compute cloud. In contrast, we do not assume traditional infrastructure services, e.g., virtual machines, but serverless infrastructure services that expose resources on a higher abstraction level, e.g., function, messaging, and database services.

Leitner *et al.* [13] provide closely related work by modeling overall costs of microservice-based cloud applications. In contrast, our work models marginal per-request costs and provides a cost-tracing system. Thereby, we can identify and study performance and cost effects in isolation and greater detail than related experiments on serverless microservice-based applications [7,21].

8   Conclusions

We present Costradamus, a cost-tracing system that enables per-request cost-tracing for cloud-based software services. Costradamus includes a generic cost model and three tracing approaches: log import, response recording, and model-based tracing. We use Costradamus to investigate performance and deployment cost tradeoffs in a smart grid application context. In our experiments, we observe unexpected effects. First, the retry cost effect: In the case of function service invocations that call downstream services, failed attempts to invoke the upstream function, e.g., due to a timeout, can lead to increased cost, even if the failed upstream function invocation itself is not charged. Second, the cost ripple effect: more invocations of an upstream function service can lead to a multiplication of downstream service invocations. These effects illustrate that cost testing should not only rely on isolated tests of single services but consider comprehensive end-to-end cost traces.

Acknowledgement. The work in this paper was performed in the context of the PolyEnergyNet project and partially funded by the Germany Federal Ministry for Economic Affairs and Energy (BMWi) under grant no. "0325737C". The authors assume responsibility for the content.

References

1. Costradamus. https://github.com/markusklems/costradamus. Accessed 15 Jun 2017
2. Björkqvist, M.: Resource management of replicated service systems provisioned in the cloud. Ph.D. thesis, Universita della Svizzera Italiana (2015)
3. Braun, B., Qin, H.: ddtrace: Rich performance monitoring in distributed systems. Technical report, Stanford University (2015)
4. Chen, J., Wang, C., Zhou, B.B., Sun, L., Lee, Y.C., Zomaya, A.Y.: Tradeoffs between profit and customer satisfaction for service provisioning in the cloud. In: Proceedings of the 20th International Symposium on High Performance Distributed Computing, pp. 229–238. ACM (2011)
5. Chen, M., Kiciman, E., Fratkin, E., Fox, A., Brewer, E.: Pinpoint: problem determination in large, dynamic Internet services. In: Proceedings of International Conference on Dependable Systems and Networks, pp. 595–604. IEEE Computer Society (2002)
6. Gandhi, A., Harchol-Balter, M., Raghunathan, R., Kozuch, M.A.: AutoScale: dynamic, robust capacity management for multi-tier data centers. ACM Trans. Comput. Syst. **30**(4), 1–26 (2012)

7. Hendrickson, S., Sturdevant, S., Harter, T., Venkataramani, V., Arpaci-dusseau, A.C., Arpaci-dusseau, R.H.: Serverless computation with OpenLambda. In: USENIX Workshop on Hot Topics in Cloud Computing (2016)
8. Hohpe, G., Woolf, B.: Enterprise Integration Patterns: Designing, Building, and Deploying Messaging Solutions. Addison-Wesley Longman Publishing Co. Inc., Boston (2004)
9. Jennings, B., Stadler, R.: Resource management in clouds: survey and research challenges. J. Netw. Syst. Manag. 23(3), 567–619 (2015)
10. Kansal, A., Zhao, F., Liu, J., Kothari, N., Bhattacharya, A.A.: Virtual machine power metering and provisioning. In Proceedings of the 1st ACM Symposium on Cloud Computing, SoCC 2010, p. 39. ACM Press, New York (2010)
11. Kielmann, T., Hofman, R.F.H., Bal, H.E., Plaat, A., Bhoedjang, R.A.F.: MAGPIE. In: ACM SIGPLAN Notices, number 8, pp. 131–140. ACM, August 1999
12. Kuhlenkamp, J., Rudolph, K., Bermbach, D.: AISLE: assessment of provisioned service levels in public IaaS-based database systems. In: Barros, A., Grigori, D., Narendra, N.C., Dam, H.K. (eds.) ICSOC 2015. LNCS, vol. 9435, pp. 154–168. Springer, Heidelberg (2015). doi:10.1007/978-3-662-48616-0_10
13. Leitner, P., Cito, J., Stöckli, E.: Modelling and managing deployment costs of microservice-based cloud applications. In: Proceedings of of the 9th International Conference on Utility and Cloud Computing, pp. 165–174. ACM Press, New York (2016)
14. Roberts, M.: Serverless Architectures (2016)
15. Sambasivan, R.R., Fonseca, R., Shafer, I., Ganger, G.R.: So, you want to trace your distributed system? Key design insights from years of practical experience. Technical report, Parallel Data Laboratory, Carnegie Mellon University, Pittsburgh, PA 15213-3890 (2014)
16. Sharma, B., Thulasiram, R.K., Thulasiraman, P., Garg, S.K., Buyya, R.: Commodities, pricing cloud compute: a novel financial economic model. In: 12th IEEE/ACM International Symposium on Cluster, Cloud and Grid Computing (CCGRID 2012), pp. 451–457. IEEE, May 2012
17. Sigelman, B.H., Andr, L., Burrows, M., Stephenson, P., Plakal, M., Beaver, D., Jaspan, S., Shanbhag, C.: Dapper, a Large-Scale Distributed Systems Tracing Infrastructure. Google Research, 14 April 2010
18. Sigelman, B.H., Barroso, L.A., Burrows, M., Stephenson, P., Plakal, M., Beaver, D., Jaspan, S., Shanbhag, C.: Dapper, a large-scale distributed systems tracing infrastructure. Technical report, Google (2010)
19. Smith, J.W., Khajeh-Hosseini, A., Ward, J.S., Sommerville, I.: CloudMonitor: profiling power usage. In: 2012 IEEE Fifth International Conference on Cloud Computing, pp. 947–948. IEEE, June 2012
20. Urgaonkar, B., Shenoy, P., Chandra, A., Goyal, P., Wood, T.: Agile dynamic provisioning of multi-tier Internet applications. ACM Trans. Autonom. Adapt. Syst. 3(1), 1–39 (2008)
21. Villamizar, M., Garcés, O., Ochoa, L., Castro, H., Salamanca, L., et al.: Infrastructure cost comparison of running web applications in the cloud using AWS lambda and monolithic and microservice architectures. In: 16th IEEE/ACM International Symposium on Cluster, Cloud and Grid Computing, pp. 179–182. IEEE (2016)

An Automatic Approach for Transforming IoT Applications to RESTful Services on the Cloud

Yu Zhao[1]([⊠]), Ying Zou[1], Joanna Ng[2], and Daniel Alencar da Costa[1]

[1] Queen's University, Kingston, Canada
{yu.zhao,ying.zou,daniel.alencar}@queensu.ca
[2] CAS Research, IBM Canada Software Laboratory, Markham, Canada
jwng@ca.ibm.com

Abstract. Internet of Things (IoT) devices are prevalent in all aspects of our lives, *e.g.*, thermostat and smart lights. Nowadays, IoT devices are controlled by various end-user applications. There is a lack of a standard interface that allows the communication among various IoT devices. In this context, the functionalities of IoT devices may be published as IoT services. IoT services are RESTful services that connect to IoT devices. The uniform interface of IoT services allows them to be integrated with existing applications. We propose an approach that automatically transforms functionalities of IoT devices to IoT services hosted on the cloud. Our approach identifies the code methods from IoT applications that have to be transformed and also extracts service specifications (*e.g.*, input/output parameters) from these methods. Our case study result shows that our approach obtains a precision and a recall above 70%. The identified methods and service specifications are converted to IoT services. Our approach generates IoT services with an accuracy of 96%.

Keywords: IoT · RESTful services · Cloud platform · Code analysis

1 Introduction

The inter-connected physical devices, *i.e.*, the Internet of Things (IoT) devices, are prevalent in several aspects of our lives. For example, IoT devices may sense nearby environments (*e.g.*, obtain the temperature) and react upon an end-user's request to change the physical environment (*e.g.*, turn on the light). IoT applications are designed by application developers to provide functionalities in IoT devices, *e.g.*, to sense the temperature. In the meanwhile, the Internet has turned into a global infrastructure to host heterogeneous web services. End-users may use web services to perform various on-line activities, such as on-line shopping and banking. With web services and IoT devices combined, the possibilities to ease our daily lives increase in magnitude. For instance, an on-line grocery order can be made based on a food consumption alert that is triggered by analyzing the data read from a fridge sensor. However, this combination is not without its limitations. For example, end-users must install a large number

© Springer International Publishing AG 2017
M. Maximilien et al. (Eds.): ICSOC 2017, LNCS 10601, pp. 673–689, 2017.
https://doi.org/10.1007/978-3-319-69035-3_49

of proprietary end-user applications (*e.g.*, mobile applications) on smart phones or computers to access the information of IoT applications in IoT devices. In addition, the diverse end-user applications lack a standard interface to allow the communication among various IoT devices and web services. Therefore, it is not trivial to integrate IoT devices with existing applications [15].

To ease the integration of IoT applications, we are interested in transforming IoT applications to IoT services, using the service-oriented architecture (SOA) to provide the functionalities offered by IoT devices. In particular, SOA based IoT services have two main advantages: (1) interoperability, which allows IoT services to exchange information with web services using a structured data format; (2) easy integration with existing applications due to the uniform interface of IoT services. Research effort has been invested on approaches to provide IoT services for end-users [4,9,15]. Nonetheless, most of these approaches run the IoT services on the IoT devices [4,9,15], which are not optimal, since IoT devices are typically designed with limited resources, *e.g.*, low battery capacity and processing power [15]. In addition, the complexity of SOA standards (*e.g.*, the verbose data format) generates energy and latency overheads in IoT devices that lead developers to spend extra effort when designing IoT services.

To overcome these practical limitations, we focus on automatically transforming the functionalities of IoT devices to IoT services. IoT services are designed using the RESTful paradigm. We use the cloud platform to host IoT services. In contrast to the resource limited IoT devices, the cloud platform has massive storage, high speed network and huge computing power. Furthermore, the cloud platform has the potential to host numerous IoT services and connect IoT devices as well as processing IoT data [16]. Additionally, the functionalities of IoT devices may be managed by standard APIs over the cloud, which may be accessed by end-users from any place.

More specifically, we analyze the source code of IoT applications to identify methods that can be controlled or accessed by end-users. Our approach further extracts the service specifications of the corresponding IoT services. A service specification describes the interface of an IoT service and is composed of three parts: service name, HTTP function and input (or output) parameters. To allow developers to modify the generated service specifications, we also propose a service schema that describes the service specifications of IoT services. The service schema identifies which data of IoT devices that should be stored in the cloud. Moreover, we use the service schema to instantiate IoT services with friendly user interfaces.

We evaluate the effectiveness of our approach through two case studies. Our results reveal that we can identify code methods that should be transformed with a precision of 75% and a recall of 72%. We can also extract service specifications from the source code of IoT applications with a precision of 82% and a recall of 81%. Our approach generates IoT services from IoT applications with an accuracy of 96%. These results show that our approach can accurately transform IoT device functionalities to IoT services.

Paper Organization. In Sect. 2, we present the background of the paper. In Sect. 3, we give an overview of our approach to generate IoT services. In Sect. 4, we describe our case studies. We summarize the related research in Sect. 5. Finally, we conclude our work in Sect. 6.

2   Background

In this section, we provide background material about IoT devices, web services, the programming structure of the source code of IoT applications and IoT services.

2.1   IoT Devices

An IoT device is a physical item that is embedded with a computing system and can be controlled remotely through Bluetooth or Wi-Fi. In our approach, we consider three classes of IoT devices: sensors, actuators and composite devices [11]. A sensor can measure the physical properties of a physical environment at a constant frequency, while an actuator is an IoT device that is controlled by end-users who may change some of its physical properties. For example, a sensor can sense the temperature, while an actuator can receive a command to turn on the light. Finally, a composite device is composed of both sensors and actuators. For example, a thermostat is an IoT device which senses the temperature and may be requested to change the temperature.

2.2   Web Services

A web service is a software component that allows machine-to-machine communication through the world wide web. This communication may be implemented using the Representational State Transfer (REST) [17] architecture style. RESTful services typically use HTTP as the underlying protocol to transfer resources. A resource is located by a Universal Resource Locator (URL). Resources may have various representations, *e.g.*, JSON and XML. To use the resources that are available in the web, clients (*i.e.*, applications) send requests using HTTP functions. The available HTTP functions are GET, POST, PUT and DELETE. The GET function requests a read only access to a resource, while the POST function is used to create a new resource. The PUT function is used to update an existing resource, while the DELETE function is used to remove a resource.

2.3   Programming Structure of the Source Code of IoT Applications

The methods in the source code of IoT applications can be classified into two types: *internal methods* and *external methods*. An *internal method* is related to the set up of an IoT device and is only consumed by methods within the IoT device (*e.g.*, an *init* method to set up an IoT device). An *external method* works as an IoT device interface that can communicate with the cloud. The input variables of an external method may represent the input commands of an actuator (*e.g.*, to turn on the light), while the returned variables may represent the sensed data of a sensor (*e.g.*, the sensed temperature). Since an external method allows end-users to control an IoT device or obtain information from an IoT device, it is possible to transform such a method to an IoT service.

```
def led_control(status):        def getTemperature():
    if status == "ON":              temp ← methods to get
        turn_led_on()                   temperature
    elif status == "OFF":           return temp
        turn_led_off()
```

(a) External method 1   (b) External method 2

Fig. 1. Examples of external methods

Figure 1 shows examples of external methods that are extracted from the hackster.io website.[1] Hackster.io is a website that shares projects on embedded devices (*e.g.*, Raspberry Pi). In Fig. 1, the names of the methods describe the methods' intent (*i.e.*, `led_control` and `getTemperature`). The `led_control` method[2] (Fig. 1a) can receive commands from the cloud (*i.e.*, by using the `status` variable). This method uses an *if-else statement* to identify whether the led has to be turned on or off depending on the `status` variable. The `getTemperature` method[3] (Fig. 1b) retrieves the temperature from a sensor. A developer can define methods within the external method to send the sensed temperature values to the cloud, *e.g.*, `send(temperature, url)`. Table 1 shows the service specification that may be extracted from the two example methods.

Table 1. Service specification that is extracted from the external methods in Fig. 1

Method name	Service name	HTTP function	Input parameters	Output parameters
led_control	led_control	POST	status	
getTemperature	getTemperature	GET		temp

2.4   IoT Services

An IoT device may have multiple functionalities. For instance, an indoor sensor may sense both temperature and humidity. A functionality may be implemented

---

[1] https://www.hackster.io/.

[2] https://www.hackster.io/user3424878278/pool-fill-control-119ab7.

[3] https://www.hackster.io/dexterindustries/add-a-15-display-to-the-raspberry-pi-b8b501.

by one or more external methods. In our approach, each functionality of an IoT device is transformed to an IoT service, which is hosted on the cloud platform. The cloud platform may use various networking protocols to exchange data with IoT devices, such as MQTT [12]. MQTT is a lightweight publish-subscribe messaging protocol designed for exchanging real-time IoT data.

3   Overview of Our Approach

In this section, we present our approach to automatically generate IoT services from IoT applications. Figure 2 shows an overview of our approach. Our approach has four activities. Each activity is explained in a subsection below.

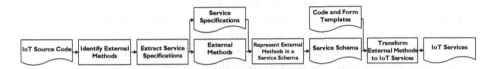

Fig. 2. An overview of our approach

3.1   Identifying External Methods

To save developers' effort on manually finding code methods that should be transformed, we analyze the source code of IoT applications written in Python to investigate whether external methods can be automatically identified. We choose the Python language, since it is suitable for developing IoT applications due to its portability and easy-to-learn syntax [21]. Although our approach is language-independent, we use Python examples to explain our approach implementation. We explain the steps that are involved in this code analysis below.

STEP 1: Parsing Source Code of Methods. To identify external methods, we first analyze the Abstract Syntax Tree (AST) of the source code. An AST is a tree structure that represents the syntax of the source code. Each node in the tree describes a construct (*e.g.*, method name) that is present in the source code. We traverse the tree to identify the following constructs in a method:

- *method name, e.g.*, getTemperature shown in Fig. 1b.
- *input variables, e.g.*, status shown in Fig. 1a.
- *returned variables, e.g.*, temp shown in Fig. 1b.
- *method calls in a method body, e.g.*, turn_led_on() shown in Fig. 1a.
- *if-else statements, e.g.*, if status == "ON" shown in Fig. 1a.

STEP 2: Filtering Internal Methods. An internal method can be identified based on its extracted constructs. Methods with the following *internal features* (IF) are considered as internal methods. Internal methods are filtered out and are not investigated further.

- **IF1:** *method name containing the keywords "init, setup, debug, test".* Method names containing the keywords "init" and "setup" are initialization methods and are used to configure the initial settings, *e.g.*, setting the voltage level of GPIO pins. Method names containing the keywords "debug" and "test" are testing methods, which are used to test the different functionalities of an IoT device. Such testing methods are internal methods in an IoT device.
- **IF2:** *method name starting with "_".* The leading underscore in a method name denotes that the method is for internal use or reserved for the programming language (*e.g.*, an _init_ method) [1].
- **IF3:** *methods that are called within internal methods or defined in internal files.* File names containing the keywords "init, setup, debug, test" or starting with "_" are internal files. Methods that are called within internal methods or defined in internal files are used for initialization and testing.

STEP 3: Processing Method Names. A method name may convey the intent of the method, which can be used to distinguish external methods from internal methods. To identify the semantics of method names, we use the following steps to normalize these names. We split CamelCase words (*e.g.*, *getTemperature* is split into *get* and *temperature*). We remove the punctuation, *e.g.*, "_" and "-". We also remove the suffixes that contain numbers (*e.g.*, *led1* is normalized into *led*). Finally, we remove stop words (*e.g.*, "a", "the" and "is"). We use natural language processing (NLP) techniques to identify the part-of-speech (POS) tag of each word. For example, "get" is tagged as a verb and "temperature" is tagged as a noun. Finally, we perform word stemming to find the root words (*e.g.*, "reduced", "reducing" and "reduces" are normalized to "reduce"). These words are used to extract features for identifying external methods.

STEP 4: Extracting Features for External Methods. We extract the following *external features* (EF) based on the constructs of the methods that are identified in STEP 1.

- **EF1:** *method calls.* If the methods that are called within a method body contain *send* related keywords in their names, *i.e.*, "push, post, publish, send, notify", these methods likely send data to the cloud, *e.g.*, send(temperature, url) and are considered as external methods.
- **EF2:** *if-else statements.* In case a method contains if-else statements that react to the input variables of the method when receiving commands from the cloud, such a method has a high probability of being an external method. For example, the led_control method in Fig. 1a contains if-else statements that react to changes in the status variable.

- **EF3:** *semantic of verbs.* Verbs in method names may represent the action that is performed in a method. For instance, *control* and *get* are the verbs in the examples of Fig. 1. We identify the semantic of verbs to infer external methods. For example, if a verb has keywords that are related to sending and receiving messages (*i.e.*, "push, post, publish, send, notify, subscribe, get, sense, set, receive, control"), we infer that its respective method transmits data to the cloud. These methods are likely external methods.
- **EF4:** *semantic of nouns.* Nouns in method names denote the objects of interest of these methods, *e.g.*, *led* and *temperature* are nouns in the examples of Fig. 1. If these nouns match with IoT service names, their respective method is likely an external method. We identify IoT services by using the iotlist.co[4] website. This website lists various IoT devices, *e.g.*, security cameras and smart lights. For an IoT device, we manually extract their functionalities, each one corresponding to an IoT service name. For example, the Elgato Eve Room Wireless Indoor Sensor[5] will have the *sense air quality, sense temperature* and *sense humidity* IoT service names. In total, we extracted 190 IoT service names. Next, we use the approach described in STEP 3 to extract nouns from the extracted IoT service names. We form a bag of words containing the nouns and match them with the nouns that we find in method names (see STEP 3). For instance, the Wireless Indoor Sensor has a bag containing the *air, quality, temperature* and *humidity* words that we match with the *temperature* word in the `getTemperature` method (see Fig. 1b).

In our approach, we assume that a method is an external method if it has at least two of the features that we identify in STEP 4. For example, the method in Fig. 1a is an external method, since it has the *if-else statements* (*i.e.*, *EF2*) and *semantic of nouns* (*i.e.*, *EF4*) features.

3.2   Extracting Service Specifications

Based on the analyzed external methods, we extract the service specifications for their respective IoT services (see Table 1), *i.e.*, *service name, HTTP function* and *input (or output) parameters.*

We use the method name as the service name. For instance, *led_control* is the service name for the method in Fig. 1a. Then, we use the *external features* described in STEP 4 to distinguish HTTP GET and POST functions. Each HTTP function is associated with two *external features*. Among these *external features*, we split the *semantic of verbs* into *semantic of send* and *semantic of receive* for GET and POST functions, respectively. We explain the details below.

- *HTTP GET:* is associated with the *semantic of send* and *method calls* features. The *semantic of send* denotes that a verb in a method name contains *send* related keywords, *i.e.*, "push, post, publish, send, notify, get, sense". Such methods send data to the cloud, so that GET-based IoT services can identify and retrieve this data.

---

[4] http://iotlist.co/.
[5] https://www.elgato.com/en/eve/eve-room.

- *HTTP POST:* is associated with the *semantic of receive* and *if-else statements* features. The *semantic of receive* denotes that a verb in a method name contains *receive* related keywords, *i.e.*, "set, receive, control, subscribe". An IoT device receives commands from POST-based IoT services.

To determine which HTTP function should be associated with an external method, we count the number of features that belong to an external method. If an external method has a given feature, that feature has a counter of 1 (one). We derive a score for the HTTP GET function (*i.e.*, S_{get}) using Eq. 1 and a score for the HTTP POST function (*i.e.*, S_{post}) using Eq. 2.

$$S_{get} = C_{semantic\ of\ send} + C_{method\ calls} \qquad (1)$$

$$S_{post} = C_{semantic\ of\ receive} + C_{if-else\ statements} \qquad (2)$$

where $C_{semantic\ of\ send}$, $C_{method\ calls}$, $C_{semantic\ of\ receive}$ and $C_{if-else\ statements}$ denote the counters for the respective features.

We use the S_{get} and S_{post} scores to determine whether the HTTP function should be GET or POST, i.e., whichever has the highest value. In case S_{get} is equal to S_{post}, we calculate the fan-in and fan-out of an external method [22]. Fan-in represents the number of input variables of an external method, while fan-out denotes the number of returned variables of an external method. When a fan-in to fan-out ratio is larger than one, the POST function is chosen, since such a ratio indicates that an external method is written to receive data (see `led_control` in Fig. 1a). The GET function is chosen otherwise.

Finally, the parameters of IoT services are extracted based on the identified HTTP functions. For example, the returned variables of a GET-based external method are extracted as the output parameters of the corresponding IoT service. Comparatively, the input variables of a POST-based external method are extracted as the input parameters of the corresponding IoT service. As an example, the `status` variable of the POST-based `led_control` method (shown in Fig. 1a) is extracted as a service input parameter.

3.3   Representing External Methods in a Service Schema

To transform external methods to IoT services, we need a structured data format that describes the extracted service specifications of IoT services. We design a service schema using the Web Ontology Language (OWL) [2]. In the service schema, the identified service name, HTTP function and parameters of a service specification are prefilled. A developer may validate, modify and complete the service schema. Figure 3 shows how we use OWL to define our service schema.

The service schema is composed of four main components: *classes, individuals, relations* and *attributes*. A *class* represents a group of objects with similar properties. For example, an *IoT device* is a class. A *relation* is used to connect the components of our service schema (e.g., an *IoT service hasOperations*). A *class* can be inherited by *sub-classes*. For instance, a *reading* operation, which is used to get the latest value of a sensor, is a sub-class of *operation*. An *individual*

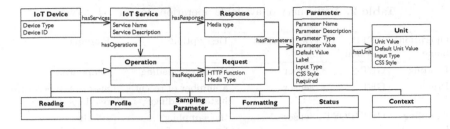

Fig. 3. The service schema

is an instance of a class. Finally, *attributes* declare the properties of a class. For instance, the *IoT device* class has the *device type* and *device id* attributes. The *device type* groups a number of IoT devices that provide similar functionalities. For example, *temperature sensor* may be a device type. The *device id* attribute is unique for each IoT device and is used to distinguish one IoT device from another. The MAC address of an IoT device can be used as a device id.

A functionality of an IoT device publishes a single stream of scalar values (*e.g.*, temperature values) to a channel on the cloud [4]. The stream of scalar values is considered as a resource of an IoT service. This resource is stored in a resource database on the cloud. An IoT service identifies its resources using the *service name, device type* and *device id* attributes. An IoT service provides multiple operations to perform different actions onto a resource. For instance, the IoT service "sense temperature" can obtain the latest reading of the temperature and modify the frequency at which the temperature should be sensed. We identify six operations of IoT services based on the approach proposed by Haggerty *et al.* [4], *i.e.*, *reading, profile, sampling parameter, formatting, status* and *context*. Each external method falls in one of the operations specified in Table 2. The *reading* operation is used to get the latest value of a resource. This operation listens to an IoT service's resource until a new value of that resource is received. Then, the listened value and a timestamp of the value update are returned to end-users. The *status* operation returns the state of a given IoT service (*e.g.*, whether it's on or off). For actuators, an end-user may send a POST request to the *status* operation, which changes the physical state of an IoT device (*e.g.*, to turn on the light). An operation is identified by the URL pattern (see Fig. 4).

IoT devices with the same *device type* value correspond to one unique service schema that is used to describe their respective IoT services. We use the service schema to instantiate IoT services as we describe in Sect. 3.4.

```
<Device Type>/<Device ID>/<Service Name>/<Operation Name>
```

Fig. 4. The URL schema for accessing an operation.

Table 2. A summary of available operations for an IoT service

Operation name	HTTP function	Device class	Description	Example
Reading	GET	sensor	the latest reading	temperature
Profile	GET	sensor	a number of recent history readings	history temperature readings
Sampling Parameter	GET/POST	sensor	the sampling frequency of sensing	100 Hz
Formatting	GET/POST	sensor	the unit of the sensed value	°C, °F
Status	GET/POST	sensor/actuator	the state of the IoT service	turn light on/off
Context	GET/POST	sensor/actuator	the location of the measurement	the location that the temperature is being sensed

3.4   Transforming External Methods to IoT Services

In this section, we describe how our approach automatically transforms external methods to IoT services.

STEP 1: Generating Web Forms. Since end-users may not be familiar with SOA, it is important to provide friendly user interfaces for accessing and controlling IoT services. In this regard, our approach automatically generates web forms by using our proposed service schema and form templates. A template uses the data of a service schema to generate text output, *e.g.*, source code or HTML forms. These generated forms are used to send POST requests to IoT services.

We design our form templates using the FreeMarker template engine.[6] The essential components of a web form are the HTTP function, the operation URL and the parameters to be filled by end-users. We traverse the parameters in our service schema to identify which ones have an *input type* attribute. The *input type* attribute can assume one of the HTML input elements, *i.e.*, *text, radio* and *select*. The *parameter value* attribute (see Fig. 3) defines the available options of a parameter, which end-users can choose, *e.g.*, ON or OFF. A developer may define a CSS style for an input parameter using the *CSS style* attribute. Figure 5 shows an HTML form example for controlling a led. Once an end-user clicks on the "Submit" button, a POST request is submitted to the operation URL.

STEP 2: Instantiating IoT Services. Our approach automatically generates source code to instantiate IoT services using the proposed service schema and code templates. The instantiated IoT services follow the Jersey[7] syntax standard.

---

[6] http://freemarker.org/.
[7] https://jersey.java.net/.

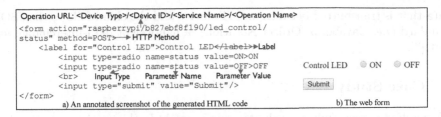

Fig. 5. An annotated screenshot of a web form that is used to control a led. The blue text highlights the data that is extracted from our service schema. (Color figure online)

To instantiate an IoT service, a code template needs to be filled with the information from a service schema. The required information are the HTTP function, an operation URL, a request media type, a response media type and the filled parameters from a web form. We provide code templates for each kind of operation. In a *reading* template, a function is provided to listen to a resource of an IoT service, which then responds end-users with the real-time value. The resources of a given IoT service are located by the *service name*, *device type* and *device id* that are extracted from the URL of the respective service request (see Fig. 4). Once the *profile* operation is requested, the IoT service fetches the last N values of a resource from the database. The N value is specified by end-users as a URL parameter. We also build databases on the cloud for each of the other four operations, *i.e.*, *sampling parameter, formatting, status* and *context*. A GET request of an operation locates the respective database and retrieves the data value. Figure 6 shows an example of an instantiated *profile* operation.

```
@Path("/raspberrypi/b827ebf8f190")──▶ Root URL: <Device Type>/<Device ID>
public class SensingActuatorService{
@GET──▶ HTTP method
@Path("temperature/profile")──▶ Operation URL: <Service Name>/<Operation Name>
@Produces("application/json")──▶ Response Media Type
public Response get_temperature_profile(@DefaultValue("0") @QueryParam("number") int
         number){           The function to access database
    JsonArray response = GetEvent.getEventFromDatabase("temperature",
         "raspberrypi", "b827ebf8f190", number);──▶ Service Name, Device Type and Device ID
    return Response.ok(response.toString()).build();}}
```

Fig. 6. An annotated screenshot of the *profile* operation, which obtains the temperature. The blue text highlights the data that is extracted from our service schema. (Color figure online)

For POST-based operations (*e.g.*, POST status of light), the filled parameters (*e.g.*, ON) must be sent to the respective IoT device. We traverse the parameters of a service schema to identify which parameters end-users should fill. Instantiated POST-based operations use their parameter names (*e.g.*, status) as variables that will retrieve the values that are filled in web forms.

Once end-users invoke an instantiated operation, the generated source code of that operation is accessed by the operation URL and the HTTP function. The data that is transmitted between an IoT device and the cloud follows the JSON standard (*i.e.*, JavaScript Object Notation), a lightweight data-interchange format [3].

4   Case Study

We conduct a case study to evaluate our approach. In this section, we introduce the setup of our case study and we present the obtained results.

4.1   Case Study Setup

To test the effectiveness of our approach on identifying external methods, we analyze IoT applications written in Python. We collect the source code of IoT projects in the "Raspberry Pi" category on the hackster.io website (See Footnote 1). The Raspberry Pi is a credit-card-sized embedded device, which is widely used to develop IoT solutions for home and industrial automation.

Table 3. The distribution of projects and python methods in each domain. *Avg LOC* denotes the average lines of code for each project.

Domain	# Projects	# Methods	Avg LOC	Domain	# Projects	# Methods	Avg LOC
Living	41	7,035	6,349	Environmental sensing	24	763	553
Transportation	10	387	756	Health	21	599	728
Entertainment	41	4,660	1,781	Security	22	1,122	870
Communication	18	2,612	3,891	**Total**	177	17,178	2,520

In total, we collect 1,039 projects, of which 177 contain python methods. We collect a total of 17,178 python methods from these projects. The collected IoT projects have different domains, *e.g.*, living (*e.g.*, light control), communication (*e.g.*, radio receiver) and transportation (*e.g.*, parking system). Table 3 summarizes our collected data. We built a prototype tool as a proof of concept for our approach. Our tool automatically ana-

Fig. 7. A screenshot of our tool that shows the available operations of IoT services to end-users

lyzes IoT applications and generates the corresponding IoT services based on the identified external methods. We use the Raspberry Pi 3 Model B as our IoT device (denoted as *RPi*). The IoT device has a quad-core processor running at 1.2 GHz. We use the IBM cloud platform, which uses the MQTT protocol to communicate with IoT devices. Since we are not allowed to build customized IoT services in such a commercial cloud platform, we use our approach to generate

IoT services in our local server (see Sect. 3.4). Our server transmits data of IoT devices with the IBM cloud platform using the MQTT protocol. Figure 7 shows a screenshot of our prototype tool. An end-user may click on an operation to send a GET request or retrieve a web form to submit a POST request. Our case study answers the following research questions:

RQ1. How effective is our approach to identify external methods and extract service specifications?

RQ2. How accurate is our approach to generate IoT services?

The first author manually evaluates all the results in our case study. Our evaluator has three years' experience on building RESTful services for the service-oriented architecture.

4.2 RQ1: How Effective Is Our Approach to Identify External Methods and Extract Service Specifications?

To measure the effectiveness of our approach, we randomly sample 376 methods from the extracted 17,178 python methods with a 95% confidence level and a 5% confidence interval [25]. We apply our approach (as described in Sect. 3.1) to identify external methods and extract service specifications from the sampled 376 methods. We use precision and recall as shown in Eqs. 3 and 4 to evaluate our approach. *Precision* measures the ratio of correctly retrieved external methods (or service specification parts) from the set of external methods (or service specification parts) that are retrieved by our approach [24]. On the other hand, *recall* measures the ratio of external methods (or service specification parts) from the dataset that our approach could retrieve [24].

$$Precision = \frac{\{relevant\ items\} \cap \{retrieved\ items\}}{\{retrieved\ items\}} \qquad (3)$$

$$Recall = \frac{\{relevant\ items\} \cap \{retrieved\ items\}}{\{relevant\ items\}} \qquad (4)$$

Our results reveal that our approach has an average precision of 75% and a recall of 72% for identifying external methods. As for service specifications, our approach has an average precision of 82% and a recall of 81%. The main reasons for the misidentified external methods and service specifications are the following: (1) We are not able to extract semantic meanings from method names. For instance, the method `getdoorstatus` is an external method to get the door status. However, we could not find the *semantic of nouns* and *semantic of verbs* because this name does not follow the CamelCase pattern. (2) Internal methods that transmit messages within an IoT device may have *external features*. For example, the method `SendParameter` is an internal method that sends parameters using the I2C (Inter-Integrated Circuit) protocol. However, we identify such a method as an external method, since it contains the *semantic of verbs* and *if-else statements* features. (3) The input (or output) parameters are defined in the code method body. For instance, the method `get_ph_reading` has a service parameter *ph_value*. However, the method uses a print function to display the parameter, rather than returning it.

4.3 RQ2. How Accurate Is Our Approach to Generate IoT Services?

Our approach uses a service schema to generate IoT services on the cloud platform. The accuracy of transforming external methods to IoT services is what represents the practical usefulness of our approach. To evaluate the accuracy of generating IoT services, we use the 190 extracted IoT services described in Sect. 3.1. We design external methods on RPi depending on the type of an IoT service. For example, we design four possible external methods for an IoT service that is generated for a sensor. These methods are: *reading, sampling parameter, formatting* and *context*. As for IoT services generated for actuators, we design two external methods: *status* and *context*. We do not design an external method for the *profile* operation, since a *profile* operation is instantiated to fetch a resource from a resource database. We use the approach described in Sect. 3.3 to generate service schemas for the designed external methods. We automatically generate IoT services using our approach (see Sect. 3.4). Equation 5 shows how we measure the accuracy of our approach.

$$Accuracy = \frac{\{\#correctly\ generated\ IoT\ services\}}{\{\#IoT\ services\}} \tag{5}$$

The accuracy is the ratio of the number of correctly generated IoT services to the total number of IoT services. Since an IoT service is composed of several operations, we evaluate whether an operation is correctly instantiated. A GET-based operation is correctly instantiated if, for example, a GET request for the *temperature reading* operation returns the values that match the temperature values sent from RPi. A POST-based operation is correctly instantiated if, for example, the external method on RPi that is used for receiving light status receives the commands from the *light status* operation. An IoT service is correctly generated when all the operations of such an IoT service are correctly instantiated. Our approach achieves an accuracy of 96% (182 out of 190 IoT services) when generating IoT services. Nonetheless, our approach fails to generate IoT services regarding streaming media. A streaming media IoT service constantly delivers and presents multimedia, *e.g.*, video and audio, to end-users. We do not find support in the IBM cloud platform for streaming media of IoT devices.

5 Related Work

We summarize the related work on the service-oriented architecture for IoT devices and code analysis.

5.1 Service-Oriented Architecture for IoT Devices

Service-oriented architecture (SOA) [22] is widely used to represent functionalities of IoT devices [13]. Haggerty *et al.* [4] and Guinard *et al.* [10] design IoT services using the RESTful paradigm. Priyantha *et al.* [15] propose an approach to reduce the resource consumption when running IoT services on IoT devices. The aforementioned approaches build IoT services directly on the resource constrained IoT devices. In contrast to these approaches, we use the cloud platform to run the IoT services. SOCRADES [9,20] describe IoT services using the Device Profile for Web Services (DPWS), a service description language. Other approaches [7,8,27] model IoT services using ontology languages, such as OWL-S. These service models are used to aid the service discovery and selection. Different from the existing approaches, our approach designs the service schema for the automatic service generation to relieve extra effort to build SOA.

5.2 Code Analysis

Code analysis is widely used to aid software understanding and maintenance. For example, Eaddy *et al.* [5] and Robillard *et al.* [18] analyze the dependency and relationship of program elements (*e.g.*, class and method) to identify the source code that is related to a maintenance task. Eisenbarth *et al.* [6] conduct static and dynamic code analysis to focus on the source code that is related to system features. Zhou *et al.* [26] and Wong *et al.* [23] locate source code files that are related to faults in bug reports. Pollock *et al.* [14] use natural language processing techniques to understand the semantic meanings of literals, identifiers and comments to aid the source code searching. Shabtai *et al.* [19] extract features from the source code to classify Android applications. Unlike these approaches, our approach conducts a static code analysis on the method level to identify external methods and extract service specifications for IoT services.

6   Conclusion

To enable the integration of multiple IoT devices in a uniform environment, we provide an approach that automatically transforms functionalities from IoT devices to SOA based IoT services. We also automatically generate web forms for end-users to have a friendly experience when interacting with IoT services. We use the designed service schema and templates to generate IoT services. Our case studies show that we can identify external methods from IoT applications with a precision of 75% and a recall of 72%. We can also extract service specifications from these external methods with a precision of 82% and a recall of 81%. Our approach can generate IoT services with an accuracy of 96%.

In future work, we plan to extend the implementation of our approach to other popular programming languages, such as Java and JavaScript. We also plan to ask developers to use and verify our prototype tool.

References

1. Style guide for python code. https://www.python.org/dev/peps/pep-0008/
2. Bechhofer, S.: Owl: web ontology language. In: Liu, L., Tamer Özsu, M. (eds.) Encyclopedia of Database Systems, pp. 2008–2009. Springer, US (2009)

3. Crockford, D.: The application/json media type for javascript object notation (JSON) (2006)
4. Dawson-Haggerty, S., Jiang, X., Tolle, G., Ortiz, J., Culler, D.: sMAP: a simple measurement and actuation profile for physical information. In: Sensys (2010)
5. Eaddy, M., Aho, A.V., Antoniol, G., Guéhéneuc, Y.G.: Cerberus: tracing requirements to source code using information retrieval, dynamic analysis, and program analysis. In: ICPC, pp. 53–62. IEEE (2008)
6. Eisenbarth, T., Koschke, R., Simon, D.: Locating features in source code. TSE 29(3), 210–224 (2003)
7. Eisenhauer, M., Rosengren, P., Antolin, P.: Hydra: a development platform for integrating wireless devices and sensors into ambient intelligence systems. In: Giusto, D., Iera, A., Morabito, G., Atzori, L. (eds.) The Internet of Things, pp. 367–373. Springer, New York (2010). doi:10.1007/978-1-4419-1674-7_36
8. Escobedo, E.P., Prazeres, C.V., Kofuji, S.T., Teixeira, C.A., da Graça Pimentel, M.: Secoas: an approach to develop semantic and context-aware available services. In: WebMedia, vol. 7, pp. 1–8 (2007)
9. Guinard, D., Trifa, V., Karnouskos, S., Spiess, P., Savio, D.: Interacting with the soa-based internet of things: discovery, query, selection, and on-demand provisioning of web services. TSC 3(3), 223–235 (2010)
10. Guinard, D., Trifa, V., Pham, T., Liechti, O.: Towards physical mashups in the web of things. In: INSS, pp. 1–4. IEEE (2009)
11. Hachem, S., Teixeira, T., Issarny, V.: Ontologies for the internet of things. In: Proceedings of the 8th Middleware Doctoral Symposium, p. 3. ACM (2011)
12. Hunkeler, U., Truong, H.L., Stanford-Clark, A.: Mqtt-s–a publish/subscribe protocol for wireless sensor networks. In: Comsware, pp. 791–798. IEEE (2008)
13. Issarny, V., Bouloukakis, G., Georgantas, N., Billet, B.: Revisiting service-oriented architecture for the IoT: a middleware perspective. In: Sheng, Q.Z., Stroulia, E., Tata, S., Bhiri, S. (eds.) ICSOC 2016. LNCS, vol. 9936, pp. 3–17. Springer, Cham (2016). doi:10.1007/978-3-319-46295-0_1
14. Pollock, L., Vijay-Shanker, K., Hill, E., Sridhara, G., Shepherd, D.: Natural language-based software analyses and tools for software maintenance. In: De Lucia, A., Ferrucci, F. (eds.) ISSSE 2009-2011. LNCS, vol. 7171, pp. 94–125. Springer, Heidelberg (2013). doi:10.1007/978-3-642-36054-1_4
15. Priyantha, N.B., Kansal, A., Goraczko, M., Zhao, F.: Tiny web services: design and implementation of interoperable and evolvable sensor networks (2008)
16. Rao, B.P., Saluia, P., Sharma, N., Mittal, A., Sharma, S.V.: Cloud computing for internet of things & sensing based applications. In: ICST, pp. 374–380 (2012)
17. Richardson, L., Ruby, S.: RESTful Web Services. O'Reilly Media, Inc., Sebastopol (2008)
18. Robillard, M., Murphy, G.C.: Concern graphs: finding and describing concerns using structural program dependencies. In: ICSE, pp. 406–416. IEEE (2002)
19. Shabtai, A., Fledel, Y., Elovici, Y.: Automated static code analysis for classifying android applications using machine learning. In: CIS, pp. 329–333 (2010)
20. de Souza, L.M.S., Spiess, P., Guinard, D., Köhler, M., Karnouskos, S., Savio, D.: SOCRADES: a web service based shop floor integration infrastructure. In: Floerkemeier, C., Langheinrich, M., Fleisch, E., Mattern, F., Sarma, S.E. (eds.) IOT 2008. LNCS, vol. 4952, pp. 50–67. Springer, Heidelberg (2008). doi:10.1007/978-3-540-78731-0_4
21. Tanganelli, G., Vallati, C., Mingozzi, E.: Coapthon: easy development of coap-based IoT applications with python. In: WF-IoT, pp. 63–68. IEEE (2015)

22. Upadhyaya, B., Zou, Y., Xiao, H., Ng, J., Lau, A.: Migration of soap-based services to restful services. In: WSE, pp. 105–114. IEEE (2011)
23. Wong, C.P., Xiong, Y., Zhang, H., Hao, D., Zhang, L., Mei, H.: Boosting bug-report-oriented fault localization with segmentation and stack-trace analysis. In: ICSME, pp. 181–190. IEEE (2014)
24. Zhao, Y., Wang, S., Zou, Y., Ng, J., Ng, T.: Mining user intents to compose services for end-users. In: ICWS, pp. 348–355. IEEE (2016)
25. Zhao, Y., Zhang, F., Shihab, E., Zou, Y., Hassan, A.E.: How are discussions associated with bug reworking?: An empirical study on open source projects. In: ESEM, p. 21. ACM (2016)
26. Zhou, J., Zhang, H., Lo, D.: Where should the bugs be fixed?-more accurate information retrieval-based bug localization based on bug reports. In: ICSE (2012)
27. Zhu, W., Zhou, G., Yen, I.L., Bastani, F.: A PT-SOA model for CPS/IoT services. In: ICWS, pp. 647–654. IEEE (2015)

RobOps: Robust Control for Cloud-Based Services

Cheng Chen[1], Jordi Arjona Aroca[2], and Diego Lugones[2(✉)]

[1] Department of Mechanical Science and Engineering,
University of Illinois at Urbana-Champaign, Champaign, USA
cchen130@illinois.edu
[2] Nokia Bell Labs, Dublin, Ireland
{jordi.arjona_aroca,diego.lugones}@nokia-bell-labs.com

Abstract. Online resource provisioning of applications in cloud is challenging due to the variable nature of workloads and the interference caused by sharing resources. Current on-demand scaling is based on manually configured thresholds that cannot capture the dynamics of applications and virtual infrastructure. This results in slow responses or inaccurate provisioning that lead to unfulfilled service level objectives (SLOs). More automated approaches, in turn, use fixed model structures and feedback loops to control key performance indicators (KPIs). However, workload surges and the non-linear behavior of software (e.g. overload control) make the control mechanisms vulnerable to rapid variations, eventually leading to oscillatory or unstable elasticity. In this paper we introduce RobOps, a robust control system for automated resource provisioning in cloud. RobOps incorporates online system identification (SID) to dynamically model the application and detect variations in the underlying hardware/software. Our framework combines feedforward/feedback control with prompt response to achieve reference performance. The feedforward control allows to compensate for delays in the scaling mechanism and provides robustness to workload surges. We validate RobOps performance using an enterprise communication service. Compared to baseline approaches, RobOps achieves 2X less SLO violations in case of traffic surges, and reduces the impact of interferences at least by 20%.

1 Introduction

Incorporating elasticity to resource management in cloud allows for maximizing the benefits of service providers. Although attractive, provisioning resources on-demand is challenging for applications running in a shared environment and serving varying workloads – particularly for over-the-top applications with stringent service level objectives (SLOs), e.g. video and real-time messaging where over-provisioning is the common practice for resource management [22].

Elasticity in commercial clouds is currently enabled by threshold-based policies that keep track of key performance indicators (KPIs) to instantiate or terminate resources [1,2]. Configuring these thresholds is time consuming, as it

© Springer International Publishing AG 2017
M. Maximilien et al. (Eds.): ICSOC 2017, LNCS 10601, pp. 690–705, 2017.
https://doi.org/10.1007/978-3-319-69035-3_50

involves user expertise and iterative testing. Moreover, thresholds are insufficient to model system dynamics and dependencies. This leads to performance degradation, as variations in traffic rate and elasticity delays across service chains cannot be captured properly [20].

To account for such delays and to better control service dynamics, several proposals combine theoretical models and control theory [19]. In general, these models have static structures (e.g. fix order), with adjustable parameters calibrated using fitting techniques over the available data [6,13]. However, static model structures can fail to represent the cloud stack and the complex characteristics of production software [9]. That is, hardware upgrades and interference of collocated applications can modify model structures significantly. From a software perspective, applications and services can also vary their behavior according to certain system states and workload events, e.g. overload control and traffic prioritization. This variability makes static models inaccurate, causing overshooting in the response of feedback controllers and even instability [21].

We argue that control-based solutions should dynamically update the application model using arbitrary structures that better fit to the current behavior of the cloud environment. Given the constantly changing and shared nature of cloud resources, model updates must be done automatically and performed at runtime. To this end, we extend *System IDentification* (SID) [16] techniques with modifications to allow for detecting model variations online.

In this paper we introduce RobOps, a system that combines online SID with dual feedforward (FF) and feedback (FB) control to operate services in the cloud with robustness to workload surges and infrastructure or software changes. SID enables a data-driven modeling of dynamic systems by leveraging various statistical methods and accuracy criteria. The control mechanism receives model updates at runtime, and adapts the control actions accordingly. The reasons for using a FF compensator are: (1) reducing propagation delays in the FB controller and the impact of scaling latency; (2) changing the elasticity dynamics, i.e. prompt scale-out and conservative scale-in. The FF compensator allows for a fast reaction to traffic changes while the FB controller adapts resource provisioning to track reference KPIs – usually derived from SLOs. This allows RobOps to serve workloads by shifting the control effort between FF and FB controllers according to the workload demand and application state. More specifically, our contributions are the following:

- Online and data-driven system identification that concurrently computes various *multiple input multiple output* (MIMO) models to control elasticity of applications in cloud. Models are calculated automatically and ranked using likelihood criteria which relieves application owners of modeling and profiling tasks, or threshold setting.
- A feedback controller able to adapt the control matrices according to updated models received on the fly. The feedback loop provides stability and ensures that KPIs are close to the desired references.

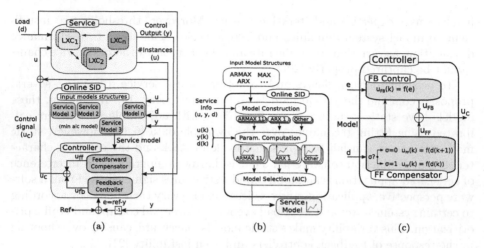

Fig. 1. (a) Overview of RobOps framework for a Linux container (LxC) based service. (b) Online system identification (SID) computes a set of MIMO linear models taking the values of d, u and y as inputs, and returns the model with the minimum Akaike information criteria (AIC) score. (c) Such model, jointly with the variation in d and the error $e = y - ref$ will condition the control input u_c and the final number of instances u in each elastic component of the service.

– A feedforward compensator to drastically reduce the oscillations caused by varying and bursty workload rates that can make the applications to trigger overload control or other similar mechanisms. This compensator performs a switching control that uses short-term predictions to accelerate scale-out in presence of increasing workloads, or scale-in conservatively otherwise.

The paper is organized as follows. An overview of RobOps is given in Sect. 2, while Sects. 3 and 4 describe in detail the online SID modeling and the controllers, respectively. In Sect. 5 we evaluate RobOps against thresholds and other control-based solutions using commercial applications. Section 6 elaborates on related work, while Sect. 7 describes our future work. Finally, we conclude in Sect. 8.

2   RobOps Design

Figure 1a depicts the main components of RobOps. The application or service can run on one or many virtual machines (VM) or Linux containers (LXC) depending on the underlying cloud infrastructure. VMs, as well as LXC, are elastic and can be scaled out. We denote as u the number of instances of each elastic component. The service key performance indicators (KPIs) are the control outputs, denoted as y. KPIs are affected by the execution of workloads, which are denoted as d for consistence with control theory notation. All u, y and d are monitored and sampled at discrete intervals or control periods. Throughout the paper we focus on services that scale horizontally. However, RobOps can also control services that scale vertically using a different set of control inputs u.

The SID module consumes u, y and d to select and configure a model of the service, the selection is based on a best-fit ranking among several models. This model is used to configure the controllers gain, while d and the error $e = ref - y$ are inputs of the controller module. The reference (ref) or setpoint is a set of target values for the control outputs y. We select these values according to the service SLOs. The controller generates a control signal (u_c) that modifies the amount u of instances to maintain the outputs close to their reference values.

Figure 1b gives a closer view of the online SID module. We evaluate several MIMO linear models such as ARX, ARMAX[1] and other finite impulse response (FIR) models [16]. We compute the *Akaike Information Criterion* (AIC) [4] for each model. The model with lowest AIC score has higher likelihood to more accurately represent the service. We describe the online SID in detail in Sect. 3.

Figure 1c illustrates the controller module with a dual FF/FB control. The FB loop aims at reducing the error between references and control outputs, increasing the number of instances when the error is negative and reducing it otherwise. Note that the FB control does not depend directly on the workload. Workload variations affect the control outputs with a certain time lag, which can cause oscillations or overshooting. This can lead to a slow convergence to the desired reference values. To deal with these workload changes we include a FF compensator that varies the provisioned resources to compensate for workload variations. We give a last twist to the FF compensator by switching the control to use either a forecast of the workload or its current value. The forecast is used to act proactively to increasing workloads. Both FB and FF use proportional control and the overall control action is the sum of the FB and FF outputs. We provide details of the controller in Sect. 4.

The robustness of the controller is achieved with both adaptive modeling and disturbance rejection. That is, the online SID module adaptively identifies unseen system dynamics and models the time-varying characteristics of the cloud stack. The FF controller, in turn, compensates for the effect of bursty workloads on the control outputs, rejecting the disturbances to the control system.

RobOps is implemented in Python. We have created a *monitoring* API to aggregate application and system KPIs such as throughput, latency, CPU usage, etc. Similarly, we have developed a *control* API which provides plugin functionality to VM/LXC-based orchestration mechanisms, allowing us to connect to different platforms, currently we support Rancher and OpenStack.

3   Online System Identification

We extend the system identification (SID) framework to enable dynamic and automated modeling. The SID module performs four tasks: (1) analysis of candidate models, (2) model identification, (3) parameters computation and

---

[1] AR stands for AutoRegressive, MA for Moving Average, and X implies the presence of eXogenous inputs.

(4) likelihood evaluation and selection. Differently to other solutions in the field, our framework does not assume a concrete model to represent the service but a pool of model structures. We perform model identification using online monitored data from inputs and outputs (u, y, d) to compute the coefficients of models in the pool. During this fitting, models are classified following the AIC criterion to find the most accurate one and forward it to the controller.

3.1   Selecting the Candidate Models

Considering multiple models helps in capturing the dynamics of heterogeneous clouds, and reduce the limitations of individual models to adapt to hardware changes or interference. We base the RobOps online SID component on the general family of linear models [16], extending it to represent a MIMO system:

$$A(q)y(k) = \frac{B(q)}{J(q)}u(k) + \frac{C(q)}{L(q)}\epsilon(k), \tag{1}$$

where A, B, C, J and L are matrices of rational polynomials with operator q, and $\epsilon(k)$ is noise at the kth control period. As defined in [16], different combinations of these polynomials lead to different model structures. We focus our experiments in the ARX, MAX and ARMAX structures. Each one of these models can have different polynomial order. These structures consider exogenous inputs that capture the effect of the number of instances on the service KPIs. Finally, we select the control period based on the time required to create a new instance. This time depends on the application and virtualization technique (e.g. virtual machines or containers), in this paper we consider values between 20–60 s.

3.2   Model Identification

We now describe how we construct the models. Using control theory notation, we define $u = [u_1, u_2, ..., u_{n_u}]^T$ to denote the number of instances of each service component, while the control outputs $y = [y_1, y_2, ..., y_{n_y}]^T$ represent the KPIs collected from these instances. We denote the incoming workload as d, the disturbance of the service. Service KPIs and workload are measured as discrete time series, i.e. $y(k)$ is the value of y measured at control period k.

In general, cloud services exhibit a near-linear behavior and we can linearize the models in the neighborhood of operating points. If services behave nonlinearly, we can apply linear difference equations with the deviations from an operating point to locally approximate the dynamics of the service. An operating point is defined as a steady state of the service, such that state u, y, and d are stable at this point. At each time k, the parameters u(k), y(k), and d(k) are measured as the deviations from such operating point. Then, the correlation between the deviations of parameters can be approximated linearly, as long as these deviations are small when compared to the operating points.

For generality, we describe the model construction process for ARMAX. We create a set of $n \times n'$ ARMAX models, where n and n' denote the highest order of the AR and MA components, respectively. One of these models will be selected and used as input to our controller. The eXogenous inputs capture the effect of u and d on the control outputs for the FB loop, and the relationship between u and d needed for the FF compensators. Formally, each model is expressed as

$$
\begin{aligned}
\boldsymbol{y}(k+1) =&A_1(k)\boldsymbol{y}(k) + ... + A_n(k)\boldsymbol{y}(k-n+1) + B(k)\boldsymbol{u}(k) \\
&+ C_1(k)\epsilon(k) + ... + C_{n'}(k)\epsilon(k-n'+1) + D(k)d(k).
\end{aligned} \tag{2}
$$

Here, $A_i(k)$ $i = 1, 2, ..., n$ is an $n_y \times n_y$ matrix which captures the correlation among the output time series, being n_y the number of control outputs. $B(k)$ is an $n_y \times n_u$ matrix and captures the correlation between service inputs and control outputs, being n_u the number of service inputs. $C_i(k)$ is an $n_y \times n_y$ matrix capturing the moving average of the control output. Finally, $D(k)$ is an $n_y \times 1$ matrix which captures the correlation between workload and output.

3.3 Model Parameters Computation

After constructing the models we now identify their parameters. Computing static models after a profiling phase has several limitations. First, services running in the cloud usually exhibit a nonlinear behavior when the entire operating range is considered. Second, external interference may alter the model at any time. For these reasons, RobOps computes and updates the model parameters online. Moreover, by updating the model online we avoid a exhaustive profiling phase, also leveraging low order models when few data is available and shifting to higher order models (if more accurate) as the observed data increases.

We use Kalman filters to identify the parameters of the models as proposed in [24]. We rewrite the model (2) in the state space defining the state as $\boldsymbol{x}(k) = [\boldsymbol{y}^T(k), ..., \boldsymbol{y}^T(k-n+1)]^T$, and the state space model becomes:

$$
\begin{aligned}
\boldsymbol{x}(k+1) &= F(k)\boldsymbol{x}(k) + B(k)\boldsymbol{u}(k) + D(k)d(k) + G(k)\epsilon(k) \\
\boldsymbol{y}(k) &= H(k)\boldsymbol{x}(k) + w(k).
\end{aligned} \tag{3}
$$

Here $F(k)$ is the transition matrix which contains the parameters from A_1 to A_n. $H(k)$ represents the map between $\boldsymbol{x}(k)$ and $\boldsymbol{y}(k)$ and it is known for each order of the model, and $w(k)$ is zero-mean Gaussian noise.

At each control period, we measure the control outputs $\boldsymbol{y}(k)$, and observe the number of instance per component $\boldsymbol{u}(k)$ and workload $d(k)$. The state of the system is recursively updated by a Kalman filter. The parameters of the models are identified by maximizing the likelihood function.

3.4 Model Evaluation and Selection

Once we compute the parameters of the models we need to choose the one that better represents the service. Two of the most used criteria for model selection are the Akaike Information Criterion (AIC) and the Bayesian Information Criterion (BIC). Both criteria provide a score for each model that allows to compare their likelihood: $AIC = 2k - 2 \cdot L$, and $BIC = k \cdot ln(s) - 2 \cdot L$, where L is the log-likelihood function, s the number of samples used for the fitting, and k is the number of parameters to be estimated. Both criteria penalize high order models, reducing the risk of overfitting. We use AIC because it usually provides better fits to smaller data windows, while BIC aims at a general model and gets better results as the pool of data increases [4]. Hence, we select the model that results in the lowest AIC score and utilize it for designing the controller. Finally, we define a *minimal switching time* in order to avoid switching models too often.

Computational complexity. The SID module complexity depends on the computation of model parameters and model selection. Model parameters are recursively computed with Kalman filters. Its complexity N_{KL} depends on the size of the data measured in a control period and is bounded by $c_1 \cdot ((n_u + u_y) \times (n + n'))^3 + N_l$ where N_l is the complexity of maximizing the likelihood function, and c_1 is a constant. On the other hand, the complexity of evaluating a model is bounded by $w \cdot c_2 \cdot n_y^2$, where w is the size of the data to compute the AIC score, and c_2 is a constant. The total complexity is bounded by $|\mathcal{M}|(w \cdot c_2 \cdot n_y^2 + \max N_{KL})$, where $\mathcal{M}$ is the set of candidate models.

4 Design of a Feedforward Plus Feedback Controller

This section describes the controller. For a certain workload, the controller adjusts the number of instances u of each component to maintain the value of the service KPIs y around the references r. To achieve this goal, we propose a MIMO adaptive switching control scheme including a FF compensator and a FB controller. Both the FF compensator and FB controller use the model computed by the online SID component described in Sect. 3.

We require a MIMO controller because our service has multiple KPIs to control, and multiple actuators to enforce this control, i.e. the number of instances of each component. The FB controller monitors the control error $e = r - y$ and adjusts u accordingly. However, the effect of abrupt workload variations on KPIs may be inaccurate or delayed, resulting in a slow response of the FB loop. For this reason, the FF compensator complements the FB controller by monitoring the workload and actuating on the service when it varies abruptly. Then, the controller input (or control signal) is the number of instances of each type that have to be scaled out(in) in the current control period. We denote this control signal as u_c. As shown in Fig. 1c, $u_c(k) = u_{FF}(k) + u_{FB}(k)$.

4.1 Design of a Feedforward Controller

The FF compensator is employed to monitor the workload and mitigate the effect of workload surges. To design the controller, we need to quantify online the effect of the workload on the target service. To this purpose, we define the following error function representing the interaction between the FF compensator and the workload on the service $E_1(k) = B(k)u_{FF}(k) + D(k)d(k)$, where matrices $B(k)$ and $D(k)$ come from the model structure presented in Eq. (2). The term $D(k)d(k)$ reflects the effect of the workload on the service KPIs. On the other hand, the term $B(k)u_{FF}(k)$ represents the impact that the FF compensator exerts on the

---

Algorithm 1. Feedforward Controller

1: $u(k), d(k), y(k) \leftarrow Collect\_Metrics()$
2: $B(k), D(k) \leftarrow System\_ID(u(k),\ d(k),\ y(k))$
3: **if** $B(k)$ is invertible **then**
4:     $\boldsymbol{u}_{FF}(k) = -B^{-1}(k)D(k)d(k)$
5: **else if** $dim(y) > dim(u)$ **then**
6:     solve $\boldsymbol{u}_{FF}(k)$ by minimizing $E_1^2(k)$ ($\#E_1(k)$ is overdetermined)
7: **else**
8:     solve $\boldsymbol{u}_{FF}(k)$ by minimizing $E_2^2(k)$ ($\#E_1(k)$ is underdetermined, $E_1(k) = 0$)

---

service KPIs. Hence, $E_1(k)$ represents the amount of KPI variation caused by the workload after being compensated by the FF controller $\boldsymbol{u}_{FF}(k)$.

The computation of $\boldsymbol{u}_{FF}(k)$ depends also on u and y dimensions. If they are equal, and matrix $B(k)$ has full rank, then $\boldsymbol{u}_{FF}(k) = -B^{-1}(k)D(k)d(k)$. If the dimension of u is smaller than the dimension of y (i.e. there are more KPIs to control than components), then E_1 is over-determined. In this case, we minimize the square of main error function $E_1(k)$. If the dimension of u is greater than dimension of y (i.e., more components than KPIs), E_1 is under-determined. In this case, $E_1(k) = 0$ and we need to minimize the square of auxiliary error function $E_2(k) = \hat{\boldsymbol{u}}_{FF}(k) - \boldsymbol{u}_{FF}(k)$. $E_2(k)$ represents the difference between the actual virtual instances $\boldsymbol{u}_{FF}(k)$ and the estimated number of virtual instances $\hat{\boldsymbol{u}}_{FF}(k)$ computed from the model in Eq. (2). Therefore, the control action $\boldsymbol{u}_{FF}(k)$ of the FF controller is the result of minimizing the errors $E_1(k)$ and $E_2(k)$. Algorithm 1 summarizes the different cases to consider when computing $\boldsymbol{u}_{FF}(k)$.

Switching controller. We want our controller to scale out the service fast but scale in more cautiously. For this reason, we propose two different controllers $g_\sigma(u, d)$ for the FF compensator, selected by a switching signal σ that depends on the workload variation $d(k)$. To compute σ we model the time series d as an Auto-Regressive process at each control period k, and use it to predict the future workload $d(k + 1)$. When the forecasted value yields $d(k + 1) > d(k)$, we assign $\sigma = 0$ and $\sigma = 1$ otherwise. The candidate FF controllers are then $\boldsymbol{u}_{FF}(k) = g_0(u(k), d(k + 1))$ and $\boldsymbol{u}_{FF}(k) = g_1(u(k), d(k))$, where g_0, g_1 result from computing $\boldsymbol{u}_{FF}(k)$ as in Algorithm 1 with values $d(k + 1)$ or $d(k)$, respectively. The compensator $g_0(u(k), d(k+1))$ is used with increasing workloads and proactively compensates the workload ahead of time. On the other hand, we use $g_1(u(k), d(k))$ for non increasing workloads, compensating the current workload variation. Finally, to guarantee the stability of the whole control system, the switching controller is restricted to the case of slow switching. A minimal dwell time t_d of 5 to 10 times the control period is used to avoid switching too frequent.

4.2   Design of the Feedback Controller

The FF control by itself is unstable as it calculates the control actions based only on the parameters estimated by open loop models. As system dynamics are not modeled and noise may be aggregated, this can result in large errors.

The FF compensator does not keep track of service KPIs, jeopardizing SLO fulfillment. For this reason, we complement it with a FB loop, which provides stability to the service and ensures that KPIs track the desired references.

The FB loop is based on the model returned by the online SID. This model can be either ARX, MAX or ARMAX of any order. RobOps computes the parameters of a proportional controller adapting to any of these structures. For generality, we show the design of a proportional controller for an ARMAX closed-loop system. This design can be generalized for structures of any order following well establish methods, though. Consider the model from Eq. (2) and substitute the FF control, we obtain: $y(k + 1) = A(k)y(k) + B(k)u_{FB}(k) + E_1(k)$, where the square of the error function $E_1(k)$ is to be minimized by the FF compensator. Note that ϵ is zero-mean system noise and the controller is robust to it. Since the FF controller compensates the majority of the effect of the workload variation $d(k)$, the FB control action will be moderated. The goal of the FB controller is to adjust $u_{FB}(k)$ to maintain $y(k)$ at the reference r. Then, the proportional FB control action is given by: $u_{FB}(k) = K_p(k)e(k) = K_p(k)(r - y)(k)$, where $K_p(k)$ is the proportional FB control gain. We compute $K_p(k)$ using common pole placement strategy which places the closed-loop poles by considering a fast transient response of the system. Since the dynamics of the system is monitored at each time interval, the FB controller can also adapt to the service variations.

5   Evaluation

In this section we evaluate RobOps performance and compare it to different baseline solutions in several scenarios using a commercial communication service. This service runs several containers and supports different types of traffic. We focus on instant messaging traffic and in two specific containerized functions: the *conversation manager* (CM) and *user log manager* (ULM). These functions are elastic and need to be scaled as the number of chats and active users vary. The workload for these functions is measured in number of chats.

Metrics. We assess the performance measuring the time during which SLOs are violated and in what magnitude (a.k.a severity). The KPI to control is component latency, which is the time needed to process a message. According to developers, latency must be below 3 s. Otherwise, the SLO is violated. Severity is measured by comparing the magnitude of latency to the SLO.

Baseline comparison. RobOps(RO) is compared to threshold-based policies (TH) and to a feedback controller (FB) – the same we use in RobOps– with static gains. RobOps and FB control use a reference value of $r = 750$ ms (i.e. $SLO/4$) for both CM and ULM latencies. For TH we set the upper and lower thresholds to r and $0.5 \cdot r$. When these thresholds are exceeded, the number of containers is increased or decreased by one. Reference is fixed to $SLO/4$ to give room to the solutions to scale out containers upon latency increments.

5.1   Evaluating the Dynamic Response

We evaluate the dynamic response of the controllers by injecting workloads with different increasing rates, including steps to simulate traffic surges.

Traffic surges. We study first the case of traffic surges. To do so, we use steps transitioning from 20 to 200, 300, 400 and 500 chats, and monitor the service for 45 control periods, enough for all the controllers to reach a configuration that can handle the injected traffic. Figure 2a shows the results for the 400 chats surge. As the latency reflects the variation on the load with delay, neither FB nor threshold controllers can scale the service in time. RobOps response is faster as the feedforward compensator (FF) scales the service out when the change in the workload is observed, not exceeding the SLO. The FB controller response is faster than thresholds, but still exceeds the SLO. Moreover, the initial provisioning is still tight, leading to more oscillations in the provisioning, exceeding the

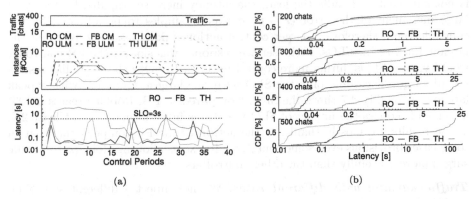

Fig. 2. (a) RobOps's (RO) FF compensator scales out as it observes the surge. FB and TH only react once the latency exceeds the reference, deriving in SLO violations. (b) RobOps can enforce the SLOs for most surges. It shows a faster response than the other controllers with lower impact on the SLOs.

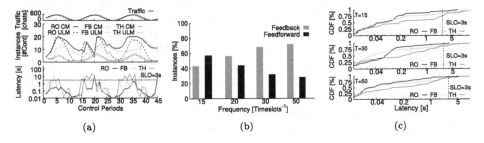

Fig. 3. (a) RobOps is more robust to rapid workload variations than the other approaches, largely reducing or eliminating the impact on performance. (b) This robustness is mostly due to the FF compensator. Its relevance in the aggregated control action increases with the workload variation rate. (c) RobOps rarely exceed the SLOs, even for workloads with high variation rate.

SLOs during 3 control periods. Due to these oscillations, the accumulated action of the FB controller ends up creating more containers than RobOps, but still violating the SLOs. Due to the lack of a model, thresholds increase the number of containers gradually until the latency falls below the reference. This results in violating the SLOs during more than 10 control periods. Finally, the highest latency measured for RobOps is 0.90 times the SLO, while for the FB and thresholds controllers the latency is 2.04 and 8.4 times the SLO, respectively.

Figure 2b shows the latency cumulative distribution function (CDF) for each surge. All three controllers converge to a similar configurations. However, RobOps has some initial overprovisioning due to the FF compensator that allows for faster and less oscillatory convergence, and less SLO violations than the FB controller. Thresholds always have a slower response, more SLO violations and worse latency peaks (up to 45 times the SLO). The FB controller averages a 10% of SLO violations and peaks up to 3.5 times the SLO. However, the FB controller benefits from the characteristics of the service. When the service configuration is not sufficient to handle the load, the latency increases rapidly, leading to a large increment of the error $(r - y)$ between samples to be adjusted by the controller and, therefore, a larger control action, taking less time to bring the latency back below SLOs. If the service response was slower, the FB controller would violate SLOs during more control periods. RobOps shows similar results for all surges, exceeding only the SLO with the largest surge and with a peak latency of roughly 2.7 times the SLO. Compared to FB, RobOps reacts a 10% faster and reduces the impact of SLO violations in performance in at least 2X. These results are mostly thanks to the action of the FF compensator, that in some cases provisions even some containers in excess allowing RobOps to handle surges more gracefully than the other controllers.

Traffic varying with different rates. We now inject 4 different sinusoidal workloads varying between 0 and 560 chats and periods of 15, 20, 30 and 50 control periods. Figure 3a shows the 15 control periods case. Upon workloads with such high variation, RobOps proactively creates a high number of containers due to the action of the FF compensator, exceeding SLOs only 4% of the time. Although the FB controller is the same in RobOps, it exhibits worse results, violating SLOs up to a 14% of the time. This difference is also due to the FF compensator. When the latency is below the reference, the FB controller reduces the number of containers in the service even if the workload is increasing. In these cases, the FF compensator counteracts the negative action of the FB controller. Without the FF, the FB controller reduces the number of containers leading to higher latencies and more SLO violations. Figure 3b shows how FF action is more relevant for low period workloads, having even more weight in the total control action than the FB component for the 15 control periods workload.

Figure 3c shows the latency CDFs for workloads with 15, 30 and 50 control periods. RobOps shows the best results, exceeding SLOs less than 4% of the time, while FB and threshold controllers reach a 14% and 23%, respectively. Similarly, the worst RobOps SLO violation was of 2.4 times the SLO per 4 and 5.3 times for the FB and thresholds. The latency CDFs also show that the results obtained by thresholds and FB get worse as the frequency increases, while RobOps obtains similar results across all experiments, regardless of the variation rate.

5.2   Robustness to Software Changes

We finally evaluate the robustness of the framework by measuring how RobOps adapts to changes in the service. To do so, we inject a sinusoidal workload and then change the number of threads used by the CM and ULM containers. This emulates hardware changes or interferences that reduce the amount of available resources. In particular, we start running the containers with 2 threads, reduce to 1 thread after some time, and finally increase to 4 threads.

Varying container resources leads to changes in the models, and therefore to changes in the gains of the controller. Figure 4a shows the evolution of the 4 coefficients of the inverse of the gain matrix K^{-1}. Matrix K^{-1} reflects the relation between the number of ULMs and CMs and their effect on their latency. We show the coefficient values for each configuration once the model converged.

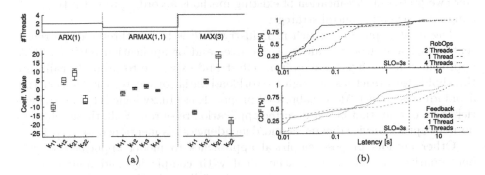

Fig. 4. (a) RobOps adapts to changes in the service. Changes in the available resources are captured by the online SID, adapting the model. This is reflected in the inverse matrix of the gain (K^{-1}), whose coefficients change for each configuration. (b) RobOps has some performance degradation while adapts the model. The feedback controller model is static, failing to provision the service correctly.

Figure 4a shows how the structure and order of the model changed for each configuration. While for the first configuration the service could be represented with an ARX (1), for the remaining configurations it moved to an ARMAX (1,1) and a MAX (3) models. Coefficients k_{11}^{-1} and k_{22}^{-1} decrease when the number of threads increases, as the capability of a container to reduce the service latency is increased. These coefficients are lower for 4 threads than for 2 threads. The behavior of coefficients k_{12}^{-1} and k_{21}^{-1} is the opposite, increasing with the number of threads. Increasing its processing capacity the container is indirectly increasing the latency on the other component, as more workload will arrive at it.

Variations in K affect the number of containers scaled by the FB controller and the FF compensator and, therefore, the capability of the controller to rapidly provision resources. To evaluate the benefits of adapting the model to these changes, we repeat the experiment using a FB controller with static gains. RobOps and the FB controller start knowing the service model for 2 threads. Figure 4b compares their performance for each configuration. RobOps performance falls to approximately a 10% degradation after every configuration change, mostly due to the learning period. On the other hand, the performance of the FB controller degrades severely, increasing from roughly 4% SLO violations when it uses the correct model to a 33.5% and 21.5% once the service moves to 2 and 4 threads, respectively. The performance in the last scenario is better because, with the 2 thread model, the FB controller instantiates containers in excess. The situation is the opposite for the 1 thread configuration, leading to larger SLO violations. Thanks to the online SID module RobOps reduces the impact of interference by up to a 23.5% when compared to the simple FB controller.

6   Related Work

Here we present a classification of existing methods according to both: the modeling approach and control strategy.

The most popular approach in industry [1,2] is to use thresholds to represent high/low utilization values of resources and/or application KPIs [8]. This approach requires significant upfront effort and expertise to properly calibrate thresholds that react fast enough to workload variations at reasonable cost (i.e. avoid idle resources). More elaborated proposals use fuzzy logic [11] to provide a richer set of rules that better describe application resources. Still, these solutions do not capture service dynamics and dependencies, as mentioned in Sect. 1.

Other authors propose empirical approaches to model applications using benchmarks [14]. These approaches deal with complexity and nonlinearities across infrastructure layers by modeling the full stack. Empirical models also require substantial knowledge about the service configuration to benchmark the system properly. Also, benchmarks must be re-executed after hardware upgrades.

Queueing theory has been used as a foundation of several proposals [3,7]. These models have parameters that can be automatically calibrated using Kalman filters [6]. However, queue models are useful to describe stationary states rather than transient, not being suitable for dynamic environments such as cloud.

Another possibility is to use time-series analysis to predict incoming workloads [19] and make scaling decisions in advance. Some examples of these forecasting techniques are exponential smoothing [11], Fourier analysis [10], wavelets [18] or Bayesian classifiers [5]. These predictions need to be combined with empirical or theoretical models to ultimately scale the system resources.

Control theory based solutions are numerous in the literature for both *single input single output* (SISO) and *multiple input multiple output* (MIMO) services. For SISO systems we find solutions using standard PID controllers [12] or fixed gain controllers combined with dynamic thresholding [15]. For MIMO services, feedback control is usually based on state space models combined with adaptive [17,19] or switching control [3]. A limitation of feedback controllers is that delayed responses can lead to oscillatory behaviors or overshooting. Combining feedback and feedforward control can alleviate this limitation. In [23] authors used both controllers empirically obtaining (static) models. Using static models, however, can limit the benefits of the control technique, as shown in Sect. 5.

7   Discussion and Future Work

The evaluation in Sect. 5 shows the applicability and efficiency of RobOps. Still, there are aspects requiring further research and analysis to generalize our results. We have shown that RobOps can identify linear models among different options. When non-linearities are significant we can generalize our method using linear difference equations on the deviations around the operating points. However, we still need to extend our approach to different structures (e.g. non-linear) like Box-Jenkins or NARMAX.

Regarding the control strategy, we tried rather simple proportional controllers as they offer acceptable performance for the service under evaluation. However, we plan to evaluate more scenarios requiring more sophisticated controllers integrated to our SID module and evaluate their impact on modeling aspects (such as accuracy and performance) as well as stability and robustness.

We need to extend our baseline evaluation and compare to other solutions and validate RobOps with more services and applications. One characteristic of the service we used in Sect. 5 is how rapidly latency increases upon underprovisioning. We will evaluate whether RobOps can accurately provision any service with different dynamics and generalize its properties. Finally, we will quantify the cost reduction derived of causing less SLO violations despite of using more resources.

8   Conclusion

In this paper we have introduced RobOps, an automated framework to dynamically control resource provisioning in cloud. RobOps implements online SID to dynamically generate multiple service models eliminating the need for benchmarks and profiling. As the process is automated, user expertise is not required as in today's threshold-based solutions. SID allows to select online the most accurate model from a collection of MIMO models with different structures, enabling RobOps to handle interfering services collocated in the shared infrastructure.

The framework combines FB and FF control, provisioning resources faster than other solutions and reducing SLO violations. Combining FF and FB control with SID results in a framework that adapts to changes in the service and handles rapid workload variations, reaching stable configurations in an agile way.

We evaluate RobOps performance with an enterprise communication service, and compared it to baseline solutions such as FB control or thresholds. RobOps is able to provision resources faster, reducing SLO violations in presence of traffic surges by a more than a 10% and a 19% when compared to FB and thresholds as well as reducing the performance impact by more than 50%. Similarly, RobOps can adapt the service model upon hardware changes, reducing the SLO violations by a 23.5% when compared to FB control.

References

1. Amazon Web Services. https://aws.amazon.com/. Accessed June 2017
2. Google Cloud Platform. https://cloud.google.com/. Accessed June 2017
3. Ali-Eldin, A., Kihl, M., Tordsson, J., Elmroth, E.: Efficient provisioning of bursty scientific workloads on the cloud using adaptive elasticity control. In: Proceedings of the 3rd Workshop on Scientific Cloud Computing Date, pp. 31–40. ACM (2012)
4. Burnham, K., Anderson, D.: Multimodel inference understanding AIC and BIC in model selection. Sociol. Methods Res. **33**(2), 261–304 (2004)
5. Di, S., Kondo, D., Cirne, W.: Google hostload prediction based on Bayesian model with optimized feature combination. J. Parallel Distrib. Comput. **74**(1), 1820–1832 (2014)
6. Gandhi, A., Dube, P., Karve, A., Kochut, A., Zhang, L.: Adaptive, Model-driven Autoscaling for Cloud Applications. In: USENIX 11th International Conference on Autonomic Computing, pp. 57–64 (2014)
7. Han, R., Ghanem, M., Guo, L., Guo, Y., Osmond, M.: Enabling cost-aware and adaptive elasticity of multi-tier cloud applications. Future Gener. Comput. Syst. **32**, 82–98 (2014)
8. Hasan, M., Magana, E., Clemm, A., Tucker, L., Gudreddi, S.: Integrated and autonomic cloud resource scaling. In: Network Operations and Management Symposium, pp. 1327–1334. IEEE, April 2012
9. Hellerstein, J., Diao, Y., Parekh, S., Tilbury, D.: Feedback Control of Computing Systems. Wiley, Hoboken (2004)
10. Jacobson, D., Yuan, D., Scryer, J.N.: Netflix's Predictive Auto Scaling Engine. The Netflix Tech Blog. Accessed April 2016
11. Jamshidi, P., Ahmad, A., Pahl, C.: Autonomic resource provisioning for cloud-based software. In: Proceedings of the 9th International Symposium on Software Engineering for Adaptive and Self-Managing Systems, pp. 95–104 (2014)
12. Janert, P.: Feedback Control for Computer Systems. O'Reilly Media Inc., Sebastopol (2013)
13. Kalyvianaki, E., Charalambous, T., Hand, S.: Self-adaptive and self-configured CPU resource provisioning for virtualized servers using Kalman filters. In: Proceedings of the 6th International Conference on Autonomic Computing. ACM (2009)
14. Lange, S., Nguyen-Ngoc, A., Gebert, S., Zinner, T., Jarschel, M., Kopsel, A., Sune, M., Raumer, D., Gallenmuller, S., Carle, G., Tran-Gia, P.: Performance benchmarking of a software-based LTE SGW. In: Proceedings of the 2015 11th International Conference on Network and Service Management, pp. 378–383. IEEE Computer Society (2015)
15. Lim, H., Babu, S., Chase, J.: Automated control for elastic storage. In: Proceedings of the 7th International Conference on Autonomic Computing. ACM (2010)
16. Ljung, L.: System Identification: Theory for the User. Englewood Cliffs (1987)
17. Nathuji, R., Kansal, A., Ghaffarkhah, A.: Q-clouds: managing performance interference effects for QoS-aware clouds. In: Proceedings of the 5th European Conference on Computer Systems, pp. 237–250. ACM (2010)

18. Nguyen, H., Shen, Z., Gu, X., Subbiah, S., Wilkes, J.: AGILE: elastic distributed resource scaling for infrastructure-as-a-service. In: Proceedings of the 10th International Conference on Autonomic Computing, pp. 69–82. USENIX (2013)

19. Padala, P., Hou, K., Shin, K., Zhu, X., Uysal, M., Wang, Z., Singhal, S., Merchant, A.: Automated control of multiple virtualized resources. In: Proceedings of the 4th ACM European conference on Computer systems, pp. 13–26. ACM (2009)

20. Ranjan, R., Benatallah, B., Dustdar, S., Papazoglou, M.P.: Cloud resource orchestration programming: overview, issues, and directions. IEEE Internet Comput. **19**(5), 46–56 (2015)

21. Reiss, C., Tumanov, A., Ganger, G., Katz, R., Kozuch, M.: Heterogeneity and dynamicity of clouds at scale: Google trace analysis. In: ACM Symposium on Cloud Computing, pp. 7:1–7:13. ACM (2012)

22. Truong, H., Dustdar, S.: Programming elasticity in the cloud. Computer **48**(3), 87–90 (2015)

23. Trushkowsky, B., Bodík, P., Fox, A., Franklin, M., Jordan, M., Patterson, D.: The scads director: scaling a distributed storage system under stringent performance requirements. In: FAST, pp. 163–176 (2011)

24. Wan, E., Van Der Merwe, R.: The unscented Kalman filter for nonlinear estimation. In: Adaptive Systems for Signal Processing, Communications, and Control Symposium, pp. 153–158. IEEE (2000)

Serverless Execution of Scientific Workflows

Qingye Jiang[1]([✉]), Young Choon Lee[2], and Albert Y. Zomaya[1]

[1] The University of Sydney, Sydney, NSW 2008, Australia
qjiang@ieee.org, albert.zomaya@sydney.edu.au
[2] Macquarie University, Sydney, NSW 2109, Australia
young.lee@mq.edu.au

Abstract. In this paper, we present a serverless workflow execution system (DEWE v3[1]) with Function-as-a-Service (FaaS aka serverless computing) as the target execution environment. DEWE v3 is designed to address problems of (1) execution of large-scale scientific workflows and (2) resource underutilization. At its core is our novel *hybrid* (FaaS and dedicated/local clusters) job dispatching approach taking into account resource consumption patterns of different phases of workflow execution. In particular, the hybrid approach deals with the maximum execution duration limit, memory limit, and storage space limit. DEWE v3 significantly reduces the efforts needed to execute large-scale scientific workflow applications on public clouds. We have evaluated DEWE v3 on both AWS Lambda and Google Cloud Functions and demonstrate that FaaS offers an ideal solution for scientific workflows with complex precedence constraints. In our large-scale evaluations, the hybrid execution model surpasses the performance of the traditional cluster execution model with significantly less execution cost.

Keywords: Scientific workflow · Function-as-a-service · Serverless computing

1 Introduction

Scientists in different fields such as high energy physics and astronomy are developing large-scale applications in the form of workflows with many precedence-constrained jobs, e.g., Montage [10], LIGO [1], and CyberShake [9]. Such scientific workflows often become very complex in terms of the number of jobs, the number and size of the input and output data, as well as the precedence constraints between different jobs. Typically, scientists use a workflow management system, such as Pegasus [6], Kepler [3] and Polyphony [18] to manage the execution of their workflows. This requires scientists to setup and configure clusters as the target execution environment, where the smallest unit of computing resource is either a physical server or a virtual machine. As the size of the

---

DEWE v3 is the third *generation* of our Distributed Elastic Workflow Execution system for FaaS in public clouds. DEWE v3 only shares the name with the previous two versions ([11,14]), i.e., it is a complete rewriting.

© Springer International Publishing AG 2017
M. Maximilien et al. (Eds.): ICSOC 2017, LNCS 10601, pp. 706–721, 2017.
https://doi.org/10.1007/978-3-319-69035-3_51

workflow grows, setting up and configuring a large-scale cluster often becomes a challenging task, especially for researchers outside the field of high performance computing (HPC). Also, it is common to observe serious resource underutilization in large-scale clusters, primarily due to the complex precedence constraints among the various jobs in the workflow. Researchers have always been looking for new ways to (a) make it easier for researchers to execute large-scale workflows; and (b) mitigate the resource underutilization issue.

In recent years, Function-as-a-Service (FaaS) such as AWS Lambda [4] and Google Cloud Functions [8] started to gain attention in public clouds. FaaS offers compute services that run code in response to events. The computing resource is automatically managed by the public cloud service provider. The customer pays for the actual amount of computing resource consumed. The dynamic resource allocation mechanism and fine-grained pricing model seem to offer a potential solution for the above-mentioned problems. However, it remains questionable whether such transient execution environment with stringent resource limits is capable of executing large-scale workflows with complex precedence constraints.

In this paper, we present DEWE v3[1], a workflow management and execution system designed with FaaS as the target execution environment. The specific contributions of this paper are:

- We demonstrate that FaaS offers an ideal execution environment for scientific workflows with its dynamic resource allocation mechanism and find-grained pricing model.
- We propose and validate a hybrid execution model that is effective in dealing with the maximum execution duration limit, memory limit, and storage space limit in the FaaS execution environment.
- We demonstrate that DEWE v3 on AWS Lambda is capable of executing large-scale data-intensive scientific workflows. In our large-scale tests, the hybrid execution model achieves shorter execution time with only 70% of the execution cost, as compared with the traditional cluster execution model.
- DEWE v3 significantly simplifies the effort needed to execute large-scale scientific workflows on public clouds.

We evaluate the performance of DEWE v3 on both AWS Lambda and Google Cloud Functions with Montage scientific workflows[2]. The hybrid execution enabled by DEWE v3 takes advantage of fine-grained pricing of FaaS and efficient resource utilization of local clusters. The performance gain from the hybrid execution becomes more apparent as workflows become larger scale.

The rest of this paper is organized as follows. Section 2 describes the motivation of this work. Section 3 describes the design and implementation of DEWE v3. In Sect. 4, we evaluate the performance of DEWE v3 on both AWS Lambda and Google Cloud Functions, using a set of Montage workflows as test cases. Section 5 reviews related work, followed by our conclusions in Sect. 6.

---

[1] The source code is available from https://github.com/qyjohn/DEWE.v3.

[2] Montage (http://montage.ipac.caltech.edu/) is an astronomical image mosaic engine that stitches sky images dealing with hundreds or even thousands of dependent jobs. [10].

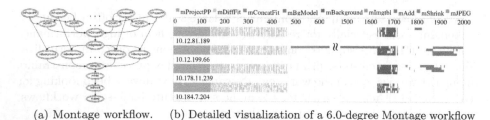

(a) Montage workflow.   (b) Detailed visualization of a 6.0-degree Montage workflow
                         running on 4 m1.xlarge EC2 instances using DEWE v1.

Fig. 1. Execution of Montage Workflow.

2 Motivation

A workflow can be represented by a directed acyclic graph (DAG), where the
vertices represent the tasks and the edges represent the precedence constraints.
Figure 1a describes the structure of a Montage workflow. As the size and complexity of a workflow increases, managing its execution on a cluster with multiple
nodes becomes a complex issue.

Most existing workflow management systems use clusters as the target execution environment. A cluster consists of a set of computing resources called
worker nodes, where a worker node can be either a physical server or a virtual
machine. To execute a workflow, scientists often need to perform a set of administrative tasks including (a) provisioning the computing resources needed; (b)
setting up a cluster with an appropriate shared file system; (c) deploying the
workflow management system on a master node and the job execution agent on
the worker nodes; (d) monitoring the health status of all worker nodes; and (e)
de-provisioning the computing resources when the work is done. These administrative tasks can be quite difficult for scientists without dedicated hardware and
support staff. It is common that people with different levels of expertise come
up with clusters with significant performance differences with the same set of
hardware.

Because of the precedence constraints in a workflow, in certain phases during
the execution only a small number of jobs are eligible to run. The traditional
cluster approach presents a classical dilemma in workflow scheduling and execution – adding more computing resources to the execution environment can speed
up the execution of certain phases of a workflow, but also results in significant
resource underutilization during other phases of the same workflow. In recent
years, researchers have attempted to address the resource underutilization issue
by taking advantage of the elasticity of public clouds. This is achieved by dynamically adding worker nodes to – or removing worker nodes from – the execution
environment base on the actual workload. However, such practice often results in
higher costs because of the one-hour minimum charge pricing model commonly
practiced by most public cloud service providers. Figure 1b visualizes the execution of a 6.0-degree Montage workflow running on a cluster with 4 m1.xlarge
EC2 instances using the DEWE v1 workflow management system. The progress

of the Montage workflow has a four-stage pattern. During the second stage only two single-thread jobs `mConcatFit` and `mBgModel` are running one after another. It took 2025 s to complete the execution of the workflow, with the total cost being 4 instance-hours. If we remove 3 worker nodes after the first phase, then add 3 worker nodes back for the third phase, then the total cost would become 7 instance-hours. As such, dynamically changing the number of worker nodes in the workflow execution environment is not economically feasible without a finer-grained pricing model.

The scientific computing community has long been searching for a workflow management system that is easy to setup and use. Ideally, scientists do not need to know any details about the underlying computing resource such as worker node and file system. The amount of computing resource available in the workflow execution environment can be easily reconfigured. The execution cost should be the actual amount of computing resource consumed, not including the amount of computing resource that is wasted. However, this can not be easily achieved when the smallest unit of computing resource is a physical server or a virtual machine with an hourly pricing model.

The emergence of FaaS in public clouds provides a potential solution to the above-mentioned problem. AWS introduced Lambda in 2014 and Google introduced Cloud Functions in 2016. With FaaS, computing resource is automatically provisioned by the service provider when the function is invoked, and de-provisioned when the function finishes execution. Since the customer does not have access to the execution environment running the code, FaaS is often referred to as "serverless computing". The customer pays for the actual amount of computing resource consumed, which is represented by the size of the function invocation environment times the duration of the invocation.

In light of the recent advancements in FaaS we develop DEWE v3, a workflow management and execution system with FaaS as the target execution environment. With DEWE v3, scientists only need to provision a single server to run the workflow management system. The jobs in the workflow are executed by the FaaS function, whose computing resource is automatically provisioned and de-provisioned by the service provider on demand. DEWE v3 uses object storage service for data staging, including workflow definition, binaries, input and output files. Researchers do not need to setup and configure a shared file system that can be accessed from all worker nodes.

3 Design and Implementation

The DEWE v3 system (Fig. 2) consists of three major components: the workflow management system, the FaaS job handler, and the local job handler. The system utilizes object storage service for binary and data staging. Different components in the system communicate with each other using a set of queues.

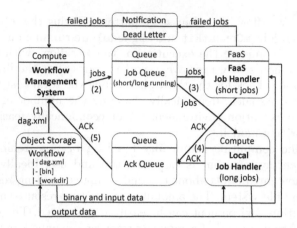

Fig. 2. The architecture of DEWE v3.

3.1 Workflow Management System

The workflow management system runs on a server, which we call the management node. The management node can be an EC2 instance, a GCE instance, or a traditional server or virtual machine. The workflow management system reads (1) the workflow definition (dag.xml) from object storage, parses the workflow definition and stores job dependencies information into a data structure. If a job has no pending dependency precedence requirements, the job is eligible to run and is published to a job queue (2), from which it will be picked up by a job handler for execution (3). When a job is successfully executed by a job handler, the job handler sends an acknowledgement message to an ACK queue (4), indicating the job is now completed. The workflow management system polls the ACK queue for completed jobs (5) and updates the status of all pending jobs that depend on the completed jobs.

The FaaS execution environment usually has a maximum execution duration limit for each invocation. The maximum execution duration limit for AWS Lambda is 300 s. The maximum execution duration limit for Google Cloud Functions is 540 s. In DEWE v3, we can define a set of long-running jobs (long.xml) for the workflow. The execution time of a particular job can be estimated from module testing or previous experiences, or derived based on the time and space complexity of the algorithm. If a job is expected to finish execution within the maximum execution duration limit, it is published into a common job queue, otherwise it is published into a specific job queue for long-running jobs.

3.2 FaaS Job Handler

The FaaS job handler is a function deployed to the respective FaaS service. For both AWS Lambda and Google Cloud Functions, the deployment process includes only three simple steps in the web console: (a) uploading the function package to object storage; (b) specifying the name and method to run; and (c) specifying the memory footprint and default execution timeout for the function. DEWE v3 automatically creates the other components (such as the queues) needed at start up, and terminates these components at shut down.

The FaaS job handler is invoked by incoming messages in the common job queue. Each message represents a job that is eligible to run. By design, an AWS Lambda invocation can contain one or more jobs, while a Google Cloud Functions invocation contains only one job. The FaaS job handler parses the job definitions for the names of the binary and input/output files, as well as the command line arguments. It downloads the binaries and input files from object storage into a temporary folder, then executes the jobs in the temporary folder. When the jobs are successfully executed, the FaaS job handler uploads the output files back to object storage. For both AWS Lambda and Google Cloud Functions, the FaaS execution environment has only 500 MB storage space. Because of this limit, the FaaS job handler deletes all the temporary files when a batch of jobs are successfully executed. A job might fail to execute in the FaaS execution environment for various reasons, including out-of-memory error, out-of-disk-space error, or maximum execution time limit exceeded. The FaaS job handler has a fail over mechanism. If a particular job fails to execute in the FaaS execution environment, it is sent to a dead letter queue for the workflow management system to pick up. The workflow management system resubmits the job to the long-running job queue, from which it is picked up by the local job handler for execution.

Because the FaaS job handler deletes all temporary files, duplicated data transfer between object storage and the FaaS execution environment might occur during the execution, introducing additional communication cost. For example, a 2.00-degree Montage workflow contains 300 mProjectPP jobs, 836 mDiffFit jobs, and 300 mBackground jobs. The sizes of the mProjectPP, mDiffFit and mBackground binaries are 3.2 MB, 0.4 MB and 3.2 MB respectively. If the required binaries have to be transferred once for each and every job, then the binaries alone would create approximately 2 GB inbound data transfer from object storage to the FaaS execution environment. For bigger workflows with a larger number of similar jobs, such duplicated data transfer can become a serious issue.

The FaaS job handler implements two levels of caching for binaries and input/output data. The first level is 'transient' caching, which applies to multiple jobs within the same invocation in AWS Lambda. With transient caching, the FaaS job handler caches the binaries and input/output data within the same invocation, but deletes them at the end of the invocation. If in an invocation the FaaS job handler receives 10 mProjectPP jobs then the mProjectPP binary only needs to be downloaded once, reducing 90% of the repeated data transfer for the mProjectPP binary. The second level is 'persistent' caching, which applies to multiple invocations with the same FaaS execution environment. Both AWS Lambda and Google Cloud Functions reuse the underlying execution environments for performance considerations. If during an invocation a file is created under the /tmp folder, the same file is accessible in other invocations when the execution environment is reused. However, neither AWS nor GCP (Google Cloud Platform) discloses how the FaaS execution environment is reused, so the availability of files created in previous invocations becomes non-deterministic. With persistent caching, the FaaS job handler only caches the binaries for future invocations, because the accumulated size of the input/output data is usually bigger than the amount of storage available. When the FaaS job handler is invoked, it first checks the /tmp folder for previously cached binaries, and transfers only the missing binaries for the invocation. Such persistent caching approach is inconsistent with the stateless design principle. In DEWE v3 this is an optional feature that can be turned on or off.

3.3   Local Job Handler

The local job handler is a multi-thread application running on one or more worker nodes. The level of concurrency equals the number of CPU cores available on the worker node. The local job handler polls the long-running job queue for jobs to execute. When a job is received from the queue, the local job handler parses the job definition for the name of the binary and input/output files, as well as the command line arguments. It downloads the binary and input files from object storage into a temporary folder, then executes the job in the temporary folder. When the job is successfully executed, the job handler uploads the output files back to object storage. Because the worker node usually has sufficient storage space, a caching mechanism is implemented to cache all the binaries and input/output files to avoid duplicated data transfer.

DEWE v3 has an optional switch to enforce local execution. When local execution is enforced, all the jobs in the workflow are submitted to the long-running job queue, from which they are picked up by the local job handler for execution. In this case, DEWE v3 is said to be running in traditional cluster mode.

3.4   Others

DEWE v3 is capable of running in three different modes: (a) traditional cluster mode where all jobs are executed by the local job handler running on a cluster; (b) serverless mode where all jobs are executed by the FaaS job handler running in the FaaS execution environment; and (c) hybrid mode where the short jobs are executed by the FaaS job handler, while the long-running jobs are executed by the local job handler.

On the management node we run an instance of the local job handler by default. With this hybrid approach, DEWE v3 is capable of handling both short and long running jobs, regardless of the maximum execution duration limit imposed by the FaaS execution environment, without the need to provision additional computing resource. To fully utilize the computing resource on

Table 1. The small-scale Montage workflows used in the initial evaluation.

	0.25 Degree	0.50 Degree	1.00 Degree	2.00 Degree
Jobs: mProjectPP	12	32	84	300
Jobs: mDiffFit	21	73	213	836
Jobs: mConcatFit	1	1	1	1
Jobs: mBgModel	1	1	1	1
Jobs: mBackground	12	32	84	300
Jobs: mImgtbl	1	1	1	1
Jobs: mAdd	1	1	1	1
Jobs: mShrink	1	1	1	1
Jobs: mJPEG	1	1	1	1
Input file count	17	37	89	305
Input file size (MB)	25	65	170	630
Output file count	117	353	981	3,713
Output file size (MB)	248	632	1,694	6,069

the management node, DEWE v3 provides the option to route a certain percentage of the short jobs to the long-running job queue, forcing the workflow to be executed in hybrid mode.

4 Evaluation

In this section, we evaluate the performance of DEWE v3 on both AWS Lambda and Google Cloud Functions. The evaluation is divided into three parts – initial evaluation, performance tuning strategy, and large-scale evaluation. For all the experiments described in this section, we perform the same experiment three times, and report the average number as the test result.

While DEWE v3 is applicable to other workflow applications, our evaluation in this study is conducted using Montage workflows due to: (1) the Montage source code and data is publicly available, (2) the project is well maintained and documented so that researchers can easily run the Montage workflow with various tools, and (3) Montage is widely used by the workflow research community as a benchmark tool to compare the performance of different workflow scheduling algorithms and workflow management systems [2,12,13,17].

4.1 Initial Evaluation

In this evaluation, we use four small-scale Montage workflows as test cases – a 0.25-degree Montage workflow, a 0.50-degree Montage workflow, a 1.00-degree Montage workflow, and a 2.00-degree Montage workflow. Table 1 lists the characteristics of these small-scale Montage workflows.

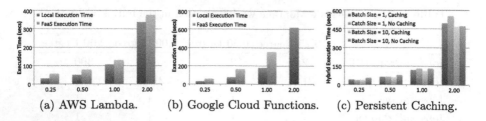

(a) AWS Lambda.   (b) Google Cloud Functions.   (c) Persistent Caching.

Fig. 3. Small-scale Montage workflows running on AWS and GCP with respect to different data sizes, 0.25, 0.50, 1.00 and 2.00, respectively.

With AWS, the management node is a c3.xlarge EC2 instance in the us-east-1 region. The EC2 instance has 4 vCPU, 7.5 GB memory and 100 GB general-purpose SSD EBS volume. The common job queue is a Kinesis stream with 10 shards, and the batch size of the Lambda function trigger is set to 10. The Lambda execution environment has 1536 MB memory. With GCP, the management node is a customized n1-highcpu-4 GCE instance in the us-central1 region. The GCE instance also has 4 vCPU, 7.5 GB memory and 100 GB SSD persistent storage. The Google Cloud Functions execution environment has 2048 MB memory.

In this evaluation, we carry out three sets of experiments. The first set of experiments are run in serverless mode. The only exception is the mImgtbl and mAdd jobs in the 2.00-degree Montage workflow are executed by the local job handler, because the size of the input/output files exceeds the storage space available in the FaaS execution environment. For this particular test, the 2.00-degree Montage workflow is executed in hybrid mode. The second set of experiments are run in traditional cluster mode, where all jobs are executed by the local job handler running on the management node. The third set of experiments are run in hybrid mode to evaluate the effect of persistent caching, with the mConcatFit, mBgModel, mAdd, mShrink and mJPEG jobs being executed by the local job handler running on the management node. In serverless mode, the execution time is noted as FaaS execution time. In cluster mode, the execution time is noted as local execution time. In hybrid mode, the execution time is noted as hybrid execution time. We do not compare the test results obtained from AWS and GCP. Instead, we focus on comparing the execution time observed on the same cloud.

The local and FaaS execution time obtained from AWS is presented in Fig. 3a. In all four test cases, FaaS execution time is slightly longer than local execution time. For the 0.25-degree workflow, FaaS execution time is 80% greater than local execution time. For the 0.50-degree workflow, FaaS execution time is 56% greater than local execution time. For the 1.00-degree workflow, FaaS execution time is 23% greater than local execution time. For the 2.00-degree workflow, FaaS execution time is 11% greater than local execution time. The FaaS execution environment has less vCPU and memory resource than the local execution environment. The local job handler caches all binaries and input/output files throughout the execution, while the FaaS job handler downloads them for each invocation. It is expected that it takes longer for the same job to run by the FaaS job handler. When the workflow is small, the concurrent execution of a small number of jobs by the FaaS job handler is not sufficient to compensate for the above-mentioned performance lost, resulting in relatively longer FaaS execution time. As the size of the workflow grows, the concurrent execution of a larger number of jobs by the FaaS job handler gradually offset the above-mentioned performance lost, reducing the difference between FaaS execution time and local execution time. Considering the small difference between FaaS and local execution times for the 2.00-degree workflow, AWS Lambda seems to be a promising execution environment for workflows with a high level of concurrency.

The local and FaaS execution time obtained from GCP is presented in Fig. 3b. For the 0.25-degree workflow, FaaS execution time is 84% greater than local execution time. For the 0.50-degree workflow, FaaS execution time is 123% greater than local execution time. For the 1.00-degree workflow, FaaS execution time is 99% greater than local execution time. The 2.00-degree workflow fails to execute on Google Cloud Functions within a reasonable time frame due to a large number of "quota exceeded" errors. Google Cloud Functions has a default 1 GB per 100 s quota for inbound and outbound socket data transfer. Montage is a data-intensive workflows, the large amount of data transfer quickly consumes the above-mentioned quota, resulting in the "quota exceeded" errors. When this occurs, Google Cloud Functions waits for the next quota period to execute the jobs waiting in the queue, causing the extra increase in FaaS execution time. In our evaluations we are given a significant quota increase from Google, allowing us to achieve 10 GB inbound and outbound socket data transfer per 100 s. With this new limit, we still frequently encounter the same error for the 2.00-degree Montage workflow. As such, we carry out our subsequent evaluations on AWS only.

The effect of persistent caching is presented in Fig. 3c. When the batch size is 1, the effect of caching is not obvious for smaller workflows (0.25-degree and 0.50-degree), but becomes significant for bigger workflows (1.00-degree and 2.00-degree). This is because the FaaS job handler executes only 1 job during each invocation. The transient caching mechanism is not in effect, and persistent caching becomes the only optimization for binary and data staging. When the batch size is 10, the effect of persistent caching is obvious for smaller workflows (0.25-degree, 0.50-degree and 1.00-degree), but becomes insignificant for bigger workflows (2.00-degree). This is because the FaaS job handler now executes 10 jobs during each invocation. The transient caching mechanism already eliminates 90% of the duplicated transfer for the binaries, with very little space left for further optimization with persistent caching. Therefore, for the subsequent experiments reported in this paper, we turn off the persistent caching option.

4.2 Performance Tuning

In this evaluation, we use a 4.00-degree Montage workflow as the test case. The workflow has 802 `mProjectPP` jobs, 2,316 `mDiffFit` jobs, and 802 `mBackground` jobs, making it an ideal use case for parallel optimization. The workflow has 817 input files with a total size of 2,291 MB, and 10,172 output files with a total size of 17,010 MB. We execute the 4.00-degree Montage workflow in hybrid mode, with the mConcatFit, mBgModel, mAdd, mShrink and mJPEG jobs being executed by the local job handler running on the management node. These jobs are not capable of running in the Lambda execution environment because they run longer than the maximum execution duration limit, or they require more storage or memory resource than what is available. To establish a baseline for performance tuning, we execute the workflow in traditional cluster mode on the management node. The local execution time observed is 950 s.

In hybrid mode, there are three parameters that can affect hybrid execution time, including (a) the number of shards in the Kinesis stream, (b) the batch size for each invocation, and (c) the percentage of short jobs that are handled by the local job handler. In this evaluation, we carry out three sets of experiments, including (a) a fixed number of shards, all short jobs are executed by the FaaS job handler, with the variable being the batch sizes; (b) a fixed batch size, all short jobs are executed by the FaaS job handler, with the variable being the number of shards; and (c) a fixed number of shards and a fixed batch size, with the variable being the percentage of short jobs executed by the local job handler.

In test (a), we used a Kinesis stream with 10 shards as the common job queue, then change the batch size of the Lambda function trigger. As shown in Fig. 4a, the hybrid execution time decreases when the batch size increases. With transient caching, the FaaS job handler caches the binaries and input/output files needed for a particular invocation. Increasing the batch size reduces the number of invocations and the amount of duplicated data transfer, hence the decrease in hybrid execution time. However, the batch size can not be increased indefinitely, because the size of the files to be cached gradually exceeds the storage space limit. For the Montage workflow, We observe that the maximum batch size we can achieve is 30. When the batch size is bigger, we frequently observe jobs fail due to "no space left on device" errors.

In test (b), we set the batch size of the Lambda function trigger to 10, then use Kinesis streams with different number of shards as the common job queue. As shown in Fig. 4b, the hybrid execution time decreases when the number of shards increases. With AWS Lambda, the number of concurrent invocations equals to the number of shards in the Kinesis stream. Increasing the number of shards increases the number of concurrent invocations, hence the decrease in hybrid execution time. As the number of shards continues to increase, the hybrid execution time gradually converges. This is because the workflow has a set of mConcatFit, mBgModel, mAdd, mShrink and mJPEG single-thread jobs that run in a sequential manner. The mBgModel job alone takes approximately 350 s to run, accounting for approximately 45% of the hybrid execution time. These jobs now become the dominating factor in the hybrid execution time.

In test (c), we use a Kinesis stream with 10 shards as the common job queue, the batch size of the Lambda function trigger is set to 30. In addition to the long-running jobs such as mConcatFit, mBgModel, mAdd, mShrink and mJPEG,

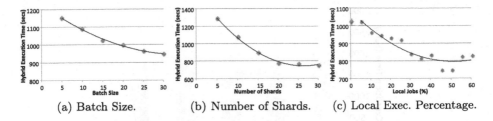

(a) Batch Size.   (b) Number of Shards.   (c) Local Exec. Percentage.

Fig. 4. Execution time of a 4.00-degree Montage workflow on AWS.

Table 2. Large-scale test environments. Hybrid environments differ by the numbers of shards, 28 and 56, respectively; hence Hybrid-28 and Hybrid-56.

	Cluster-1	Cluster-2	Cluster-3	Hybrid-28	Hybrid-56
Instance type	c3.2xlarge	c3.2xlarge	c3.2xlarge	c3.2xlarge	c3.2xlarge
Number of nodes	1	2	3	1	1
Total vCPU cores	8	16	24	8	8
Total memory (GB)	15	30	45	15	15
Total storage (GB)	500	1000	1500	500	500
Job stream shards	0	0	0	28	56
Hourly price (USD)	0.42	0.84	1.26	0.84	1.26
Lambda function (USD)	-	-	-	0.06	0.06
Total cost (USD)	0.42	0.84	1.26	0.90	1.32

we schedule a fraction of the short jobs to the local job handler running on the management node. As shown in Fig. 4c, the hybrid execution model effectively utilize the idling computing resource on the management node, resulting in the decrease in hybrid execution time. However, when the amount of jobs routed to the local job handler exceeds the capacity of the management node, the hybrid execution time starts to increase again.

4.3   Large-Scale Evaluation

In this evaluation, we use a 8.00-degree Montage workflow with a total of 13,274 jobs as the test case. The workflow has 2,655 mProjectPP jobs, 7,911 mDiffFit jobs, and 2,655 mBackground jobs. The workflow has 4,348 input files with a total size of 8,524 MB, and 32,753 output files with a total size of 58,561 MB.

Traditionally, when scientists need to speed up the execution of a workflow, they add worker nodes to the cluster. With the hybrid execution model, we simply use a Kinesis stream with more shards to increase the number of concurrent invocations. To compare the performance between the traditional cluster execution model and the proposed hybrid execution model, we use the local execution time of the workflow on the management node as the baseline. The management node is a c3.2xlarge EC2 instance in the us-east-1 region, with 8 vCPU cores,

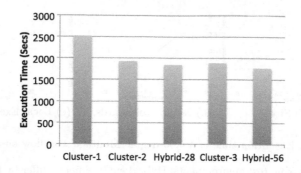

Fig. 5. Execution time of a 8.00-degree Montage workflow on AWS.

15 GB memory and 500 GB general-purpose SSD EBS volume. Then we run two sets of experiments with the same workflow. In the first set of experiments, we compare (a) the cluster execution time on a two-node cluster with 2 × c3.2xlarge EC2 instances with (b) the hybrid execution time on 1 × c3.2xlarge management node with *28 shards* in the Kinesis stream, where 20% of the short jobs are executed by the local job handler. In the second set of experiments, we compare (a) the cluster execution time on a three-node cluster with 3 × c3.2xlarge EC2 instances with (b) the hybrid execution time on 1 × c3.2xlarge management node with *56 shards* in the Kinesis stream, where 15% of the short jobs are executed by the local job handler. For both sets of experiments, the hourly cost of both execution environments is the same. In this test, the execution cost of the Lambda function falls within the AWS Lambda free-tier offering. We estimate the execution cost of the Lambda function based on the number and duration of invocations obtained from CloudWatch and multiply them with the standard pricing. The details of these test environments are listed in Table 2.

Figure 5 presents the test results. In the first set of experiments, the traditional cluster execution model (Cluster-2) achieves 18% speed-up while the new hybrid execution model (Hybrid-28) achieves 22% speed-up, as compared with the baseline obtained on Cluster-1. In the second set of experiments, the traditional cluster execution model (Cluster-3) achieves 20% speed-up while the new hybrid execution model (Hybrid-56) achieves 25% speed-up, as compared with the baseline obtained on Cluster-1. Note that Hybrid-28 achieves more speed-up than Cluster-3, while the total cost of Hybrid-28 is only 70% of Cluster-3.

5 Related Work

There have been an abundance of literature on workflow management systems such as DAGMan [5], Pegasus [6] and Kepler [3]. These frameworks use clusters with multiple worker nodes for as the execution environment. Such approaches tend to be heavy-weight and are inaccessible to scientists who lack dedicated hardware and support staff.

Polyphony [18] was designed and developed with AWS as the target execution environment, but the software is not accessible to the workflow researcher community. The work in [15] deals with scheduling scientific workflows across multiple geographically distributed resource sites; however, the scale of workflows is still limited to small, e.g., 255 tasks per workflow. All of the above-mentioned workflow management systems exhibit inefficiency in scheduling a large number of short-life jobs across multiple worker nodes.

To execute large scale scientific workflows in a cost effective way, the computing resources needed must be carefully planned. Such planning usually involves cost and performance trade-off for scientists. In recent years, researchers spend a significant amount of effort on scheduling and resource allocation algorithms to meet certain deadline and cost constraints [7,11–13,15,17,19]. These works are rather complementary and/or supplementary that can significantly benefit from using DEWE v3.

AWS introduced Lambda [4] in 2014, while Google introduced Cloud Functions [8] in 2016. Malawski [16] reviewed the various options of executing scientific workflows in serverless infrastructures. The author created a prototype workflow executor function using Google Cloud Functions, with Google Cloud Storage for data and binary storage. The author used 0.25-degree and 0.4-degree Montage workflows to evaluate the prototype and found the approach highly promising. Unlike the test cases in our study (up to 8.00-degree Montage workflow), the evaluation in [16] is limited to small-scale workflows. Also, the work in [16] failed to notice the impact of the limited inbound and outbound socket data quota on the execution of data-intensive scientific workflows.

6   Conclusion

In this paper, we present DEWE v3, a workflow management system with FaaS as the target execution environment. We present the design and implementation of DEWE v3, as well as its capability in executing large-scale scientific workflows. We demonstrate that AWS Lambda offers an ideal execution environment for scientific workflow applications with complex precedence constraints. Google Cloud Functions, in its current form, is not suitable for executing scientific workflow applications due to its limited inbound and outbound socket data quota.

We propose and validate a hybrid execution model that is effective in dealing with the various limits imposed by the FaaS execution environment. We take advantage of the hybrid execution model to speed up the workflow execution by fully utilizing the computing resource available on the management node. The largest scale experiment presented in this paper is an 8.00-degree Montage workflow with over 13,000 jobs and more than 65 GB input/output data. The hybrid execution mode achieves shorter execution time with only 70% of the execution cost, as compared to the traditional cluster execution mode. Since each Lambda function invocation can handle up to 30 jobs in one batch, further speed-up can be achieved by scheduling jobs with precedence requirements into a the same invocation. This will be addressed in our future works.

DEWE v3 reduces the effort needed to execute large-scale scientific workflows. It liberates scientist from the tedious administrative tasks involved in the traditional cluster approach, allowing them to focus on their own research work.

References

1. Abramovici, A., Althouse, W.E., et al.: LIGO: the laser interferometer gravitational-wave observatory. Science **256**(5055), 325–333 (1992)
2. Abrishami, S., Naghibzadeh, M., Epema, D.H.: Deadline-constrained workflow scheduling algorithms for infrastructure as a service clouds. Future Gener. Comput. Syst. **29**(1), 158–169 (2013)
3. Altintas, I., Berkley, C., Jaeger, E., Jones, M., Ludascher, B., Mock, S.: Kepler: an extensible system for design and execution of scientific workflows. In: Proceedings of 2004 16th International Conference on Scientific and Statistical Database Management, pp. 423–424 (2004)
4. Amazon Web Services: AWS Lambda (2014), https://aws.amazon.com/lambda/
5. Couvares, P., Kosar, T., Roy, A., Weber, J., Wenger, K.: Workflow management in condor. In: Workflows for e-Science, pp. 357–375 (2007)
6. Deelman, E., Blythe, J., Gil, Y., Kesselman, C., Mehta, G., Patil, S., Su, M.-H., Vahi, K., Livny, M.: Pegasus: mapping scientific workflows onto the grid. In: Dikaiakos, M.D. (ed.) AxGrids 2004. LNCS, vol. 3165, pp. 11–20. Springer, Heidelberg (2004). doi:10.1007/978-3-540-28642-4_2
7. Duan, R., Prodan, R., Fahringer, T.: Performance and cost optimization for multiple large-scale grid workflow applications. In: Proceedings of the 2007 ACM/IEEE Conference on Supercomputing, p. 12. ACM (2007)
8. GCP: Google Cloud Functions (2016), https://cloud.google.com/functions/
9. Graves, R., Jordan, T.H., et al.: Cybershake: a physics-based seismic hazard model for Southern California. Pure. appl. Geophys. **168**(3–4), 367–381 (2010)
10. Jacob, J.C., Katz, D.S., et al.: Montage: a grid portal and software toolkit for science-grade astronomical image mosaicking. Int. J. Comput. Sci. Eng. **4**(2), 73–87 (2009)
11. Jiang, Q., Lee, Y.C., Zomaya, A.Y.: Executing large scale scientific workflow ensembles in public clouds. In: Proceedings of 2015 44th IEEE International Conference on Parallel Processing (ICPP), pp. 520–529. IEEE (2015)
12. Juve, G., Deelman, E.: Resource provisioning options for large-scale scientific workflows. In: Proceedings of 2008 4th IEEE International Conference on eScience, pp. 608–613. IEEE (2008)
13. Lee, Y.C., Zomaya, A.Y.: Stretch out and compact: Workflow scheduling with resource abundance. In: Proceedings of 2013 13th IEEE/ACM International Symposium on Cluster, Cloud and Grid Computing (CCGrid), pp. 219–226. IEEE (2013)
14. Leslie, L.M., Sato, C., Lee, Y.C., Jiang, Q., Zomaya, A.Y.: DEWE: A framework for distributed elastic scientific workflow execution. In: Proceedings of 2015 13th Australasian Symposium on Parallel and Distributed Computing (AusPDC), pp. 3–10 (2015)
15. Maheshwari, K., Jung, E.S., Meng, J., Vishwanath, V., Kettimuthu, R.: Improving multisite workflow performance using model-based scheduling. In: Proceedings of 2014 43rd IEEE International Conference on Parallel Processing (ICPP), pp. 131–140. IEEE (2014)

16. Malawski, M.: Towards serverless execution of scientific workflows-hyperflow case study. In: Proceedings of 2016 11th Workshop on Workflows in Support of Large-Scale Science (WORKS@ SC), pp. 25–33 (2016)

17. Malawski, M., Juve, G., Deelman, E., Nabrzyski, J.: Algorithms for cost-and deadline-constrained provisioning for scientific workflow ensembles in iaas clouds. Future Gener. Comput. Syst. **48**, 1–18 (2015)

18. Shams, K.S., Powell, M.W., et al.: Polyphony: a workflow orchestration framework for cloud computing. In: Proceedings of 2010 10th IEEE/ACM International Conference on Cluster, Cloud and Grid Computing (CCGrid), pp. 606–611 (2010)

19. Tanaka, M., Tatebe, O.: Disk cache-aware task scheduling for data-intensive and many-task workflow. In: Proceedings of 2014 IEEE International Conference on Cluster Computing (CLUSTER), pp. 167–175. IEEE (2014)

A Market-Based Approach for Detecting Malware in the Cloud via Introspection

Nada Alruhaily[1]([⊠]), Carlos Mera-Gómez[1,2], Tom Chothia[1],
and Rami Bahsoon[1]

[1] School of Computer Science, University of Birmingham, Edgbaston B15 2TT, UK
{N.M.Alruhaily,cxm523,T.P.Chothia,R.Bahsoon}@cs.bham.ac.uk
[2] Facultad de Ingeniería en Electricidad y Computación,
Escuela Superior Politécnica del Litoral, ESPOL, ESPOL Polytechnic University,
Campus Gustavo Galindo Km 30.5 Vía Perimetral,
P.O. Box 09-01-5863 Guayaquil, Ecuador
cjmera@espol.edu.ec

Abstract. Traditional anti-virus (AV) solutions are known for their considerable consumption of resources, limiting their usefulness on the cloud. In contrast, cloud-based lightweight malware monitoring approaches consume fewer resources than a full malware scan would normally require, however, they are often prone to false alarms; limiting their effectiveness. In this paper, such a trade-off is addressed by proposing a prioritisation approach, consisting of two protection layers (i.e. lightweight and full malware scanning) to conduct a scalable and effective malware inspection of the cloud Virtual Machines (VMs). The novel contribution of this paper is a market-inspired mechanism that utilises lightweight scanners to prioritise the AV scanning process, by deciding which VM should be thoroughly scanned and when; it will trigger then a full malware scan on a pre-defined percentage of the most critical VMs. The conducted evaluation shows that the framework provides a cost-effective scanning method, while being able to confirm the infection status of the most critical set of VMs; thus maintaining a low rate of false alarms.

1 Introduction

The reliance and popularity of the cloud as an operating and computing environment have witnessed an increase in malicious activities. Using traditional anti-virus (AV) solutions on cloud Virtual Machines (VMs) can lead to a considerable power and memory consumption due to their use of signatures, resulting in an insufficient use of the cloud and VMs resources. A number of security vendors and researchers have endeavoured to address this by proposing cloud-based compatible malware scanning and monitoring techniques to detect abnormal behaviour and malware infections. Garfinkel et al. [6], for example, introduced a technique that allows one VM to monitor and modify the current state of another VM from the outside, while remaining hidden. This technique is referred to as *Virtual Machine Introspection* (VMI); it helps monitoring targeted VMs

© Springer International Publishing AG 2017
M. Maximilien et al. (Eds.): ICSOC 2017, LNCS 10601, pp. 722–730, 2017.
https://doi.org/10.1007/978-3-319-69035-3_52

by checking their memory pages, Windows registry and disk for symptoms of malware infections. VMI can detect malicious behaviour (which can be shared among a number of malware families), as opposed to matching signatures. Moreover, VMI-based malware scanners, that perform external monitoring, are usually shared between a number of VMs. Therefore, such a technique can offer a light monitoring option for the cloud's VMs (e.g. Bitdefender Hypervisor Introspection (HVI) [3], Cloudidea [5], and Forensic Virtual Machines (FVMs) [9]). FVMs is an architecture for using VMI; it make uses of mini-VMs that perform external, live and distributed monitoring of the state of other VMs.

Although the use of lightweight monitoring approaches (e.g. FVMs) can help the cloud provider to reduce the resources consumed [13], and monitor early signs of infection; this could be at the expense of wrongly flagging more VMs as infected. This is because such techniques are based on identifying symptoms that exist in both malicious and normal behaviour, but in different proportions or combinations; where in some cases a clear-cut distinction between the two behaviours is not easy to identify. In contrast, signature-based malware detection systems are known to accurately identify known malware threats with an extremely low rate of false alarms [8], but with the cost of using a relatively high percentage of the VM resources during the scan. Accordingly, the objective of this paper is to provide a way of balancing the trade-off between scanning performance (in terms of the resources used) and accuracy (in terms of the false alarms generated), when detecting malware infections on the cloud.

Towards fulfilling this objective, this paper proposes an early prioritisation system, which consists of two layers of protection (i.e. lightweight and full malware scanning) for a more in-depth scan of customers' VMs. The framework benefits from the fast and light scanning performance of FVMs to identify, at any given time, a pre-defined percentage of VMs that are most likely to contain malware. It will then trigger a full malware scan on this set of VMs. The novelty of this technique is that it utilises a market mechanism to guide the full scanning process based on the criticality of the pieces of information gathered by the distributed monitoring carried out using VMI-based lightweight scanners.

2 Preliminaries

2.1 Virtualisation and Virtual Machine Introspection

Cloud infrastructure relies on virtualisation technology, which allows dividing the resources between multiple instances of VMs that, in turn, results in the efficient use of existing computing resources. Virtual Machine Introspection is a new technique that uses virtualisation to enable one VM on the cloud to scan, monitor and modify the memory pages of another VM from the outside, when granted the required privileges. VMI was first introduced by Garfinkel et al. [6], who suggested that instead of the Intrusion Detection System (IDS) being inherent within the customer's VM, the IDS can be pulled outside the host, which will give it a good overview of the targeted VM. Furthermore, such out-of-the-guest malware monitoring solution decreases the risk of direct attacks on the scanner, in contrast with in-VM malware detection solutions [6].

2.2 Forensic Virtual Machines

Based on the VMI approach, Harrison et al. [9] introduced a framework that makes use of mini-VMs (referred to as Forensic Virtual Machines) to inspect the internal status of other VMs, in order to identify symptoms arising due to a malware infection. FVMs identify symptoms, rather than examining the behaviour itself (similar to diagnosing illness in the human body). Example of symptoms can be appending unexpected values to registry keys, or disabling Windows services, especially those related to updates and security. An FVM is shared among a number of VMs to reduce the creation cost; each FVM is dedicated to identifying the existence of a single symptom. When a symptom is inspected by an FVM, this piece of information is stored on a *blackboard* component, which is shared among the available FVMs.

2.3 Market Mechanism

In markets, sellers and buyers are examples of agents who carry out their trading, based on their own valuation of a good. The decentralised characteristic of the market results from the competitive and self-interested nature of its agents [12].

Auctions constitute one of the most widely studied and applied examples of price-discovery mechanisms. They can offer a dynamic pricing alternative to the traditional posted-pricing mechanism, when there are no fixed prices; or where prices cannot be predetermined for the goods that are offered [4]. Decisions in auctions can be determined based on simultaneous or sequential bidding. In simultaneous bidding, bids are submitted only once, and the prices and allocations are determined immediately; an example is *sealed bid auctions*. This paper is concerned only with sealed bid auctions because decisions are made instantaneously; resulting in an efficient allocation of the scanning resources, without incurring a considerable overhead during the allocation process [7].

3 The Prioritisation System Design

The proposed framework relies on a market-based mechanism to prioritise the VM scanning process. Such a mechanism promotes both a Pareto-efficient equilibrium (i.e. optimal resource allocation) [11], and a highly distributed operation [15], which in our context leads to a scalable prioritisation of limited FVMs to scan a significantly larger number of VMs. It aims to balance the trade-off between scanning performance and the accuracy of detection by achieving the following subgoals: (i) maximising the number of VMs scanned using the lightweight scanners (i.e. FVMs); (ii) minimising false alarms generated, by identifying those most critical VMs and scan them thoroughly. Figure 1 depicts the

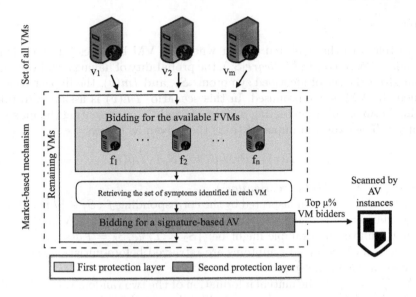

Fig. 1. High-level architecture of the market-based prioritisation approach.

high-level architecture of the proposed market-based prioritisation approach; the framework consists of two protection layers, whereby a bidding process is performed on each.

Consider a set of Virtual Machines $\mathcal{V} = \{v_1, v_2, ..., v_m\}$ and a set of FVMs, $\mathcal{F} = \{f_1, f_2, \cdots, f_n\}$, where $n < m$. At each time step, information gathered previously by the set of FVMs at the *first protection layer* will be used to guide the full malware scan initiated at the *second protection layer*, whereby each VM submits a sealed-bid, to be scanned thoroughly by an AV. To minimise the number of costly scans, only a pre-defined percentage (μ) of the VMs most likely to be infected will be scan using AV instances. In the meantime, the remaining set of VMs, which have not been scanned by AV instances, will submit a sealed-bid, requesting to be inspected further by the FVMs, in order to guide the full malware scan in the next time step. The remainder of this section describes in detail the bidding process at the two protection layers.

First Protection Layer: Scanning VMs with FVMs. The malicious symptoms are subdivided between FVMs, where each FVM scans for a single symptom. It is thus of the utmost importance to identify which symptom should be inspected next on each VM. Therefore, before an FVM moves to a new VM target, it will enter into a deciding state, where every VM submits a sealed bid for each type of FVMs. Given the set of FVMs, $\mathcal{F}$, where each scans for different symptoms (i.e. f_1 scans for S_1, f_2 scans for $S_2 \cdots$, and f_n scans for S_n), the bid submitted by each $v \in \mathcal{V}$ to each f_j is given as follows:

$$Bid(f_j, v) = E(v) + \lambda \cdot I(X; S_j | Z = \mathcal{S}_v) \cdot t(v), \tag{1}$$

where:

- $E(v)$ refers to the expected impact when the VM becomes infected. This is estimated based on $P(Malware|\mathcal{S}_v)$, the probability of having a malware infection given the set of identified symptoms $\mathcal{S}_v$, and $Im(v)$, the impact resulting when the VM is compromised. In this scenario, $Im(v)$ is assumed to take a value between '0', representing no impact, and '5', representing the maximum impact. The expected impact $E(v)$ is then given as follows:

$$E(v) = P(Malware|\mathcal{S}_v) \cdot Im(v). \tag{2}$$

- $x \in X$ (i.e. $X = \{Malware, Benign\}$).
- S_j is the new symptom inspected by the corresponding f_j; $S_j \in \{True, False\}$.
- $\mathcal{S}_v$ is the set of previously scanned symptoms on each $v \in V$ (either found or not found); one example might be: $\{S_2 = True, S_5 = False, S_8 = True\}$. The sets of the scanned symptoms are retrieved before initiating the bidding process at each time step.
- $I(X; S_j|Z = \mathcal{S}_v)$ is the mutual information of the two random values X and S_j, except in this case we are always conditioning on observing the event $Z = \mathcal{S}_v$. We refer to this mathematical expression as '*event-specific conditional mutual information*'; it denotes the amount of information obtained between the two variables X and S_j given the observation of the third random variable $Z = \mathcal{S}_v$. It can be written mathematically as follows:

$$I(X; S_j|Z = \mathcal{S}_v) = \sum_{y \in S_j} \sum_{x \in X} P(x, y|\mathcal{S}_v) \cdot \log \frac{P(x, y|\mathcal{S}_v)}{P(x|\mathcal{S}_v)P(y|\mathcal{S}_v)}. \tag{3}$$

- $t(v)$ is the time elapsed since the VM was visited by any FVM.
- λ is a scaling factor where $\lambda > 0$; it is used to adjust the importance of the information gathered (in terms of its relatedness and recentness) with the impact associated when a VM being compromised.

After the bids are collected at each time step, the price of an FVM type is determined, based on the highest bid submitted; the VMs with the highest bid will then be scanned by that type of FVMs. The symptoms scanned on this layer will help in prioritising the full VM scan initiated at the next step.

Second Protection Layer: Scanning the VMs that Are Most Likely to Be Infected with an AV Instance. On this layer, VMs will bid for a full malware scan, which will confirm whether they are infected. To minimise the costly use of resources, only a predefined percentage μ of the most critical VMs will be scanned. The percentage, μ can be adjusted by the cloud service provider to fulfill two primary goals, (i) maximising the scanning coverage of the available FVMs; and (ii) minimising cases where a costly full malware scan is triggered on a non-critical VM.

At this layer, every $v \in \mathcal{V}$ will submit a sealed bid requesting a thorough scan by a signature-based AV instance, as follows:

$$Bid(AV, v) = P(Malware|\mathcal{S}_v);\tag{4}$$

where, $P(Malware|\mathcal{S}_v)$ is the probability of having a malware infection given the set of identified symptoms, $\mathcal{S}_v$. This probability is calculated according to Baye's Theorem, and is based on the probabilities obtained from over 13.000 malware samples. The remaining set of VMs, which have not been scanned using signature-based AV instances, will then be inspected further by re-entering the bidding process carried out at the *first protection layer*.

4   Experimental Setup and Results

The focus here is on evaluating the performance of this approach in isolation from the cloud's environmental factors, such as data transfer, spin-up times, or placement. Thus, a proof of concept is developed, which extends the simulation tool from our previous work [1] with the proposed mechanism. In addition to the assumptions made on [1] (e.g. the discrete time steps and unchanging status of the infection), we are also assuming that the signature-based AV is up-to-date, and that a signature of the malware exists in the AV database of signatures. This approach was compared to the use of VMI-based lightweight scanners alone under the same settings. In particular, the simulator was initialised with 100 VMs, and 8 FVM types, each type composed of 6 FVM instances. The same set of symptoms were also used, represented on the 8 most informative registry paths (selected based on the *ANOVA F-value*), accessed to modify, add, delete or read a subkey value when infected with a variant of the *W32.Sality* malware family; which have long been ranked as one of the top 20 malware families in [14]. The experiments were also based on a 0.11 probability of malware infection. This was determined based on the most recent report obtained by [2] when conducting the experiments. The value of μ was set to 1, meaning, that only 1% of the VMs most likely to be infected will be scanned by AV instances at each time step[1].

The detection performance of the proposed approach was evaluated here through a comparison of the 95% confidence interval (CI) for the mean of the *True Positive Rate* and *False Positive Rate* derived by simulating the scanning process of the proposed market-based approach, and the lightweight monitoring approach alone. Figure 2 was obtained by recording the results of 15 trials, whereby in each trial, the metrics averaged over 25 completed scans. The fact that there is no overlap in the 95% confidence interval for the mean of both documented rates, demonstrates that with statistical significance, a lower rate of false alarm and a higher detection rate could be achieved using the proposed approach, as shown in Fig. 2(a) and (b), respectively, with as low as 1% usage of the heavyweight scanning resources at each time step. This indicates that the proposed approach managed to guide the full scanning process (represented on

---

[1] Ceil function was used to ensure that at least 1 VM is scanned at each time step.

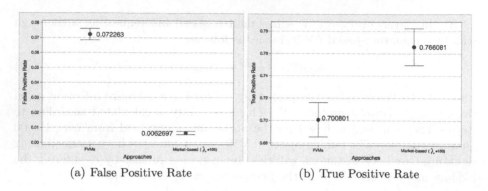

(a) False Positive Rate   (b) True Positive Rate

Fig. 2. 95% CI for the mean.

the 27 AV instances) to confirm the infection status of those VMs that exhibited suspicious behaviour. Consequently, balancing the trade-off appropriately, by accurately identifying malware infections on these suspicious VMs, while promoting lower consumption of the cloud's VMs resources.

5 Related Work

A number of security vendors propose using lightweight in-VM agents to collect information and facilitate the VM scanning process, while the heavy operations will be shifted to a scanning engine deployed on a dedicated VM. Such an approach is susceptible to manipulation by an attacker, due to the lack of isolation [10]. As a result, researchers propose using out-of-the-guest, VMI-based lightweight scanners to inspect the cloud's VMs from the outside [6].

Fischer et al. [5] propose using a system comprising lightweight and heavyweight detection engines which detects abnormal activities on the hosted VMs, using introspection technology and machine learning-based methods. The proposed approach mainly relies on behaviour-based monitoring techniques, which makes it vulnerable to the high rate of false alarms. Furthermore, our work goes one step further by providing a way to allocate the heavyweight scanners efficiently using a market-inspired mechanism.

6 Conclusion and Future Work

This paper has proposed a novel, market-inspired prioritisation approach, which utilises lightweight cloud-based scanners to guide the full VM malware scanning process, thus, promoting lower consumption of cloud resources, while accurately identifying malware infections. As the two layers of protection implement different detection techniques, they are expected to complement each other. The lightweight scanners which perform external monitoring will identify those VMs that need to be thoroughly scanned, without significantly affecting their performance; they will also ensure the integrity of the AV instances installed. Conversely, signature-based AV instances are used to confirm the infection status, due to their ability to accurately identify known malware infections.

The evaluation demonstrates the feasibility of the approach in terms of balancing the trade-off between scanning performance and the accuracy of the detection. As for future work, we are currently working on evaluating the decisions provided by the proposed approach from an economics perspective, and investigating how might such a perspective influence the security decisions.

References

1. Alruhaily, N., Bordbar, B., Chothia, T.: Analysis of mobility algorithms for forensic virtual machine based malware detection. In: 2015 Trustcom/BigDataSE/ISPA, vol. 1, pp. 766–773. IEEE (2015)
2. Barnett, J.: worldwide cloud report, June 2016 (2017). https://resources.netskope. com/h/i/262738806-june-2016-worldwide-cloud-report
3. Bitdefender: Hypervisor introspection, 17 June 2013. https://www.bitdefender. com/business/hypervisor-introspection.html
4. Cassady, R.: Auctions and Auctioneering. Univ of California Press, Berkeley (1967)
5. Fischer, A., et al.: CloudIDEA: a malware defense architecture for cloud data centers. In: Debruyne, C., et al. (eds.) On the Move to Meaningful Internet Systems: OTM 2015 Conferences. LNCS, vol. 9415, pp. 594–611. Springer, Cham (2015). doi:10.1007/978-3-319-26148-5_40
6. Garfinkel, T., Rosenblum, M., et al.: A virtual machine introspection based architecture for intrusion detection. In: NDSS (2003)
7. Gibney, M.A., Jennings, N.R., Vriend, N.J., Griffiths, J.M.: Market-based call routing in telecommunications networks using adaptive pricing and real bidding. In: Albayrak, S. (ed.) IATA 1999. LNCS, vol. 1699, pp. 46–61. Springer, Heidelberg (1999). doi:10.1007/3-540-48165-6_4
8. Griffin, K., Schneider, S., Hu, X., Chiueh, T.: Automatic generation of string signatures for Malware detection. In: Kirda, E., Jha, S., Balzarotti, D. (eds.) RAID 2009. LNCS, vol. 5758, pp. 101–120. Springer, Heidelberg (2009). doi:10.1007/978-3-642-04342-0_6
9. Harrison, K., Bordbar, B., Ali, S.T., Dalton, C.I., Norman, A.: A framework for detecting malware in cloud by identifying symptoms. In: 2012 IEEE 16th International Enterprise Distributed Object Computing Conference (EDOC), pp. 164–172. IEEE (2012)
10. Hongwei, T., Shengzhong, F., Xiaofang, Z., Yan, J.: Virtav: an agentless antivirus system based on in-memory signature scanning for virtual machine. In: 2016 18th International Conference on Advanced Communication Technology (ICACT), pp. 1–2. IEEE (2016)
11. Mas-Colell, A., Whinston, M.D., Green, J.R., et al.: Microeconomic Theory, vol. 1. Oxford University Press, New York (1995)
12. Osborne, M.J., Rubinstein, A.: Bargaining and Markets. Academic press, Cambridge (1990)
13. Shaw, A.L., Bordbar, B., Saxon, J., Harrison, K., Dalton, C., et al.: Forensic virtual machines: dynamic defence in the cloud via introspection. In: 2014 IEEE International Conference on Cloud Engineering (IC2E), pp. 303–310. IEEE (2014)

14. Symantec: Internet security threat report (2017). http://www.symantec.com/security_response/publications/threatreport.jsp
15. Wang, X., Martínez, J.F.: Xchange: a market-based approach to scalable dynamic multi-resource allocation in multicore architectures. In: 2015 IEEE 21st International Symposium on High Performance Computer Architecture (HPCA), pp. 113–125. IEEE (2015)

Trustless Intermediation in Blockchain-Based Decentralized Service Marketplaces

Markus Klems[✉], Jacob Eberhardt, Stefan Tai, Steffen Härtlein,
Simon Buchholz, and Ahmed Tidjani

Information Systems Engineering (ISE), TU Berlin, Berlin, Germany
{mk,je,st}@ise.tu-berlin.de,
{haertlein,simon.buchholz,a.tidjanig}@campus.tu-berlin.de

Abstract. Service marketplaces promise an open platform for sellers and buyers of IT services. The marketplace design usually assumes that market functions, such as match-making, transaction settlement, and dispute resolution are performed by intermediaries in a centralized system. We propose the concept of trustless intermediation to enable new forms of decentralized service marketplaces. By leveraging blockchain-enabled smart contracts we eliminate the need for trust in marketplace intermediaries and reduce barriers of entry, lock-in, and transaction costs, by removing now obsolete trust-establishing mechanisms. **Desema**, our decentralized service marketplace prototype, is a first implementation of this concept that is based on the Ethereum blockchain in combination with IPFS, a peer-to-peer distributed file system.

1 Introduction

A service marketplace enables IT service providers to sell software services and service consumers to discover and use services [15,20]. Despite high hopes, service marketplaces have, so far, not been successful on a larger scale. Systems like the Universal Description, Discovery, and Integration (UDDI) registry have never attracted a critical mass [13]. Deficiencies in current service markets manifest in market barriers, low competition, insufficient service substitutability, insufficient service information, and high transaction costs [16]. A substantial body of work has addressed problems of insufficient service information by offering techniques to improve service descriptions (including service level agreements) and service discovery from a service-oriented computing perspective. Problems related to marketplace pricing strategy and incentive structures for marketplace participation, however, remain. In this paper, we focus on the role of trusted intermediaries in service marketplaces. Centralized marketplaces often lead to deficiencies in the form of lock-in effects and market barriers [8,16]. Dependency on intermediaries can lead to disadvantages for buyers and sellers if their objectives do not align with those of the intermediaries [4,7,9,11].

We propose a concept for a decentralized and trustless service marketplace which is not provided and governed by a single trusted party, but instead by a community of individuals that participate in the marketplace. The design and

© Springer International Publishing AG 2017
M. Maximilien et al. (Eds.): ICSOC 2017, LNCS 10601, pp. 731–739, 2017.
https://doi.org/10.1007/978-3-319-69035-3_53

prototypical implementation of our marketplace system is based on distributed systems technologies that enable decentralization, in particular on a blockchain that can execute smart contracts. We introduce the concept of trustless intermediation in the context of service marketplaces and describe how service discovery, transaction settlement, and dispute resolution can be realized without a trusted third party. This design could potentially overcome fundamental problems, such as lock-in, of traditional centralized service marketplaces. Our system prototype contributes to the development of future blockchain-based decentralized (service) marketplaces and helps to identify technical and non-technical challenges.

2   Background and Related Work

A service marketplace is an online marketplace where suppliers can sell software services [15]. Service consumers can buy and use these software services for composing higher-level services and for building applications [20].

Centralized marketplaces provide mechanisms to facilitate efficient spot trades between large numbers of sellers and buyers by providing match-making and payment transaction processes that are accompanied by trust-building mechanisms, most importantly, reputation and dispute resolution systems. However, relying on reputation as a trust building factor alone can lead to entry barriers for new sellers from whom buyers are less inclined to purchase [8,16]. A main problem of current online dispute resolution systems is enforcement, which is particularly challenging in cross-border e-commerce where no standardized global legal instruments for enforcing contracts exist [12]. Besides a marketplace provider, **trusted intermediaries** might offer additional market functions, in particular match-making (service and price discovery), transaction settlement, and legal/regulatory functions [10]. Reliance on trusted intermediaries can be problematic for buyers and sellers. Trust can be exploited or betrayed, for example, if a match-making intermediary can obtain higher revenues by matching certain buyers with certain sellers [4,9,11], if the marketplace provider forces sellers to vertically integrate with its technology platform [7], or in extreme cases if law enforcement take-down or "exit scams" terminate a marketplace [17].

The development of **decentralized marketplaces** is driven by a desire to establish systems without a central marketplace provider and without trusted intermediaries. Motivations include reducing barriers of entry [8,16], reducing fees [2], increasing resistance to shut-down [14], and improving privacy [18]. There are a few initiatives for building decentralized anonymous marketplaces based on blockchain technologies, such as OpenBazaar, Beaver, and Ties Network. Blockchains are distributed peer-to-peer systems which implement a trustless shared public append-only transaction ledger [19]. Some blockchain systems, such as Ethereum [6,21], support the deployment and execution of smart contracts. A smart contract is a set of automatically enforced digital rules which cannot be manipulated or censored in specification or execution. OpenBazaar [2] is a free and censorship-resistant blockchain-based marketplace for trading goods, using multiple crypto-currencies for payment and settlements. Transactions are performed directly between peers without the involvement of a trusted inter-mediary. Beaver [18] provides a Sybil attack-resistant, anonymous reputation system without relying on a trusted third party. A different blockchain-based marketplace design, described in the Ties Network Whitepaper [3], is to desig-nate special roles to users, e.g., for resolving conflicts, and to make anonymity optional in favor of more traditional reputation-based trust-building approaches.

3   Trustless Intermediation

As a new idea, we introduce the concept of trustless intermediation which replaces traditional trusted intermediaries, such as centralized service registries and payment providers. We define **trustlessness** as a system property which guarantees rules of interaction that are known to and agreed upon by all partici-pants of the system, and which cannot be unilaterally changed. These guarantees are enforced through, what we call **trustless intermediation**, a set of mecha-nisms for *decentralizing the enforcement of rules in a system*, thereby removing the need for and existence of trusted intermediaries.

In the following, we propose two main mechanisms for implementing trustless intermediation in a system: through (1) a set of smart contracts, and (2) sup-porting actors. By using smart contracts, the rules of interaction between sellers and buyers are transparent and self-enforced. If any participant deviates from the rules, the consequential actions, e.g., compensation and punishment, are also known and automatically enforced through smart contracts. Supporting actors provide functions that exceed the capabilities of smart contracts, yet, need to be carefully selected and incentivized, to avoid that they neglect or abuse the marketplace function that they have been assigned.

Based on this concept, we describe functions of a decentralized service mar-ketplace from the perspectives of both service providers (sellers) and service consumers (buyers). We show how service registry, transaction settlement, and service delivery features can be realized with smart contracts and supporting actors in lieu of trusted intermediaries. Figure 1 illustrates the roles and functions in a blockchain-based decentralized service marketplace for a service lifecycle.

Service Registry. A service registry enables basic match-making between ser-vice providers and consumers. Service providers can publish their service descrip-tions to a service registry and service consumers can discover services they need. We realize the service registry with a smart contract that contains references to service providers and service description documents. For this purpose, the ser-vice registry contract needs to maintain state of the provider-to-service mapping, allow providers to publish and update service descriptions, and enable consumers to find services they need. For decentralized service discovery, service descrip-tion documents need to be replicated across multiple nodes in the network. To avoid trust, each consumer should receive and maintain an up-to-date replica of the entire service catalog. In case of updates or shutdowns of services, the impact should be as small as possible for the service consumers. Since providers can remove services from the service catalog and with that prevent purchases, it

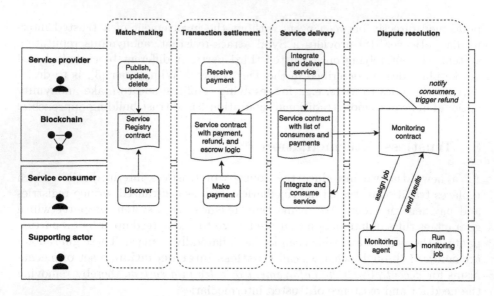

Fig. 1. Roles and functions in a blockchain-based decentralized service marketplace.

is desirable to support a reasonable phase-out process. One approach to incentivize timely announcements of service interface and usage changes is to collect a deposit from service providers on service registration. A smart contract serves as an escrow and only refunds the deposit if a version change was announced by sending a notification to the smart contract with a certain leadtime before service removal. If the announcement has not been made (within the agreed-upon leadtime), the deposit is paid out to the service consumers. A similar approach could be applied to breaking changes during updates.

Transaction Settlement. For each service on the marketplace, a service contract is deployed. This contract contains the business logic for payments and refunds. In order to consume a service, a user invokes the service contract to make a payment in a virtual currency and in the same transaction adds her authentication information to the contract, which is later needed for authenticating the consumer's service requests.

Different payment models can be encoded in a service contract, such as:

- *Time slices:* Once a consumer has selected a service, she subscribes to the service by paying a fee to gain access to the service for a certain time.
- *Utility computing:* A service consumer pays for a certain type of workload, such as the number of requests, the operation types, the payload size, etc.
- *Subscription:* A service consumer pays a subscription fee that gives access to a service up to a certain workload limit.

Service Delivery. The service providers needs to distinguish paid-for service requests from unpaid service requests. We consider two approaches:

- *Proxy Service:* Requests are not sent to the target service directly, but to a proxy verifying the sender's authority before forwarding the request to the designated target.
- *Signature Library:* Sender and receiver both use a library to sign outgoing messages and validate incoming messages.

The Proxy Service approach simplifies service integration for both consumer and provider who do not have to take care of message integrity and caller authorization. On the downside, a provider-side Proxy Service would be a single point of failure for all services using it, and a Proxy Service that is powered by a supporting actor would require trusting a third party.

Using a Signature Library, consumer and provider can directly integrate functions for signing, and signature verification, respectively. Both parties are thereby enabled to freely choose which endpoints require authorization and how to handle errors, such as insufficient funds. On the downside, this solution shifts integration effort to consumer and provider.

Following our main objective of trustless intermediation, we prefer the Signature Library approach, which consists of the following three steps:

1. The consumer signs the payload of service requests. Along with the payload, the signature and public key are sent in the request header.
2. Signature and public key are used by the receiving service to verify that the message body has not been altered.
3. The service verifies that the address belongs to a paying service consumer, processes the request, and sends a success or error response back.

This process requires consumer-side and provider-side service integration. Step 1 requires a signature library that must be used by the consumer to sign all requests that invoke services which have been purchased on the marketplace. Furthermore, a consumer might want to automate the process of making service payments to avoid request errors due to lack of funds. The provider needs to integrate a signature verification library to perform steps 2 and 3.

Dispute Prevention and Resolution. Disputes between provider and consumer can occur, e.g., if a consumer has paid for a service that is frequently unavailable. We identified the following approaches to prevent and resolve disputes: micro-payments, escrows, and escrows with supporting actors.

Micro-payments. One approach to dispute prevention is to allow service consumers to frequently buy short time slices or small units of service access. This limits the consumer's monetary loss in case of a service unavailability. However, there is no direct punishment for the provider's unavailability. As a disadvantage, a service consumer must continuously add deposits to the service contract.

Escrows. A service contract can contain an escrow mechanism. Service providers, for example, could be required to make a deposit to their service contract before offering a service. If a certain share of service consumers report dissatisfaction, the provider would lose that deposit and the escrow contract would use it to compensate consumers. This approach further eliminates trust that consumers would otherwise need when purchasing a provider's service, but needs careful incentive design as sybil and collusion attacks need to be prevented.

Escrows with supporting actors. A supporting actor could serve as a monitoring agent who periodically checks service availability and stores the monitoring results in a smart contract (monitoring contract). These results can then be used to resolve disputes and compensate consumers, e.g., refund a consumer's payment or force the provider to pay a fine in case of service unavailability. Here, the smart contract acts as an escrow and requires a provider deposit so that the fine payment is guaranteed. To incentivize participation in the marketplace, supporting actors need to be rewarded, e.g., by paying them a reasonable fee.

4   Decentralized Marketplace System

In the following, we describe Desema, our decentralized service marketplace prototype, which is available as open source software on Github [1]. Desema is a peer-to-peer system which connects service providers and consumers through a shared public blockchain network, Ethereum, and a distributed data storage system, IPFS. Figure 2 shows the high level system architecture with two Desema clients. The rich client offers marketplace users a web-based graphical user interface. On the left side is a service provider, Bob, who wants to sell API access to his service. For this purpose, Bob uses a local Desema client on his computer to register and publish his service. On the right side of Fig. 2 is a service consumer, Alice, who accesses Desema through her own local client. Alice finds Bob's service in the service catalog, decides to consume the service, and agrees to deposit a payment. Her purchase is facilitated through the service contract. After the purchase, Alice integrates Bob's service into her application. Her application invokes Bob's service with a signed request. For signing a request, the private key of Alice's user account is used. Afterwards, the request body is hashed and the hash is signed. The public key belonging to the private key used is added to the returned signature object, both of which are added to the request header. By calculating Alice's address from her public key and comparing it to his list of paying consumers, Bob's service can identify Alice as a paying consumer and verify request message integrity using a signature library.

Trustless Distributed Data Storage. Business processes in Desema are managed on the blockchain. Storing service metadata and other larger data object on the blockchain would, however, be inefficient and expensive. As a solution to this problem, we introduce an approach for trustless distributed data storage by which only data references are stored on-chain. Instead of using an arbitrary name as an identifier, the identifier is computed from the off-chain stored data itself. Off-chain data changes would immediately change the on-chain identifier and invalidate the reference. Furthermore, data integrity can be checked at any time by computing the identifier from the original data in a smart contract and comparing it to the reference. For off-chaining Desema service metadata, we

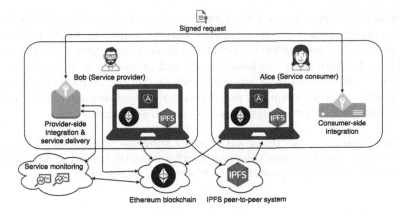

Fig. 2. Desema system architecture.

use the InterPlanetary File System (IPFS) [5], a public peer-to-peer file system which addresses files by their hashes. IPFS peers host their own files as well as copies of other's files to ensure availability. Service metadata is stored off-chain in an IPFS directory structure which contains all service versions in separate sub-folders, and only a file reference address is stored in Ethereum. Using IPNS (InterPlanetary Name Space), we can also support mutable content at a fixed address. As IPNS requires cryptographic authorization by the service owner, trustlessness is not impacted.

Trust-limited Monitoring. Monitoring is performed by supporting actors. We need to ensure that those actors do not compromise the integrity of the marketplace by returning inaccurate monitoring results. Trust in monitoring agents can be limited by randomizing the assignment of monitoring jobs to agents. The assignment is performed by the monitoring contract because otherwise a trusted third-party would be needed. Since the Ethereum Virtual Machine (EVM) cannot generate random numbers, we let the monitoring contract generate pseudo-random numbers that are difficult to predict. As an extension to random assignment, multiple nodes could be assigned monitoring jobs for the same service, whereby monitoring results can be determined through a quorum consensus, thereby further limiting trust in individual monitoring agents.

5   Conclusion

In this paper, we introduce the concept of trustless intermediation in service marketplaces based on blockchain technology and discuss approaches to overcome fundamental problems of traditional marketplace systems, such as barriers of entry, transaction costs and lock-in. We propose a design in which trusted intermediaries that operate a marketplace can be replaced with a set of rules encoded in smart contracts and enforced trustlessly in a blockchain network.

As a proof-of-concept, we present a prototypical implementation of the aforementioned concepts. Based on the experience that we gained by building the prototype, we identify decentralized application engineering challenges. In particular, we address limitations of on-chain storage and propose a solution for trustless and scalable distributed data storage. Open challenges include the design and development of more advanced and incentive-aligned approaches for trustless dispute resolution between service providers and consumers.

Acknowledgements. We thank our students Christian Kniep, Nikola Stavrevski, Ravish Aggarwal, and Xiaonan Qiao who contributed to the prototype development as part of an ISE student lab project in the winter term of 2016/17.

References

1. Desema. https://github.com/markusklems/desema. Accessed 02 June 2017
2. OpenBazaar. https://www.openbazaar.org/. Accessed 15 May 2017
3. Ties Network. https://ties.network/. Accessed 01 Aug 2017
4. Armstrong, M., Zhou, J.: Paying for prominence. Econ. J. **121**, F368–F395 (2011)
5. Benet, J.: IPFS - content addressed, versioned, P2P file system. CoRR abs/1407.3561 (2014). http://arxiv.org/abs/1407.3561
6. Buterin, V.: Ethereum: a next-generation smart contract and decentralized application platform (2014). https://github.com/ethereum/wiki/wiki/%5BEnglish%5D-White-Paper
7. Cornière, A., Taylor, G.: Integration and search engine bias. RAND J. Econ. **45**(3), 576–597 (2014)
8. Einav, L., Farronato, C., Levin, J.: Peer-to-peer markets. Annu. Rev. Econ. **8**, 615–635 (2016)
9. Eliaz, K., Spiegler, R.: A simple model of search engine pricing. Econ. J. **121**(556), F329–F339 (2011)
10. Giaglis, G.M., Klein, S., O'Keefe, R.M.: The role of intermediaries in electronic marketplaces: developing a contingency model. Inf. Syst. J. **12**(3), 231–246 (2002)
11. Hagiu, A., Jullien, B.: Why do intermediaries divert search? Rand J. Econ. **42**(2), 337–362 (2011)
12. Koulu, R.: Blockchains and online dispute resolution: smart contracts as an alternative to enforcement. SCRIPTed **13**, 40 (2016)
13. Legner, C.: Is there a market for web services? In: Di Nitto, E., Ripeanu, M. (eds.) ICSOC 2007. LNCS, vol. 4907, pp. 29–42. Springer, Heidelberg (2009). doi:10.1007/978-3-540-93851-4_4
14. Olsthoorn, M., Winter, J.: Decentral market: self-regulating electronic market (2016)
15. Papazoglou, M.P.: Service-oriented computing: concepts, characteristics and directions. In: Proceedings of the Fourth International Conference on Web Information Systems Engineering (WISE), pp. 3–12. IEEE (2003)
16. Schlauderer, S., Overhage, S.: How perfect are markets for software services? An economic perspective on market deficiencies and desirable market features. In: ECIS (2011)
17. Soska, K., Christin, N.: Measuring the longitudinal evolution of the online anonymous marketplace ecosystem. In: USENIX Security, vol. 15 (2015)

18. Soska, K., Kwon, A., Christin, N., Devadas, S.: Beaver: a decentralized anonymous marketplace with secure reputation. IACR Cryptology ePrint Archive, p. 464 (2016)
19. Tai, S., Eberhardt, J., Klems, M.: Not ACID, not BASE, but SALT - a transaction processing perspective on blockchains. In: Proceedings of the 7th International Conference on Cloud Computing and Services Science, CLOSER, vol. 1, pp. 755–764. INSTICC, ScitePress (2017)
20. Turner, M., Budgen, D., Brereton, P.: Turning software into a service. Computer **36**(10), 38–44 (2003)
21. Wood, G.: Ethereum: a secure decentralised generalised transaction ledger. Ethereum Project Yellow Paper (2014)

Author Index

Printed in the United States
By Bookmasters